Certification and Accreditation Programs Directory

A Descriptive Guide to National Voluntary Certification and Accreditation Programs for Professionals and Institutions

First Edition

ISSN 1084-2128

Certification and Accreditation Programs Directory

A Descriptive Guide to National Voluntary Certification and Accreditation Programs for Professionals and Institutions

First Edition

Michael A. Paré, Editor

 **Gale Research**

An ITP Information/Reference Group Company

Changing the Way the World Learns

NEW YORK • LONDON • BONN • BOSTON • DETROIT
MADRID • MELBOURNE • MEXICO CITY • PARIS
SINGAPORE • TOKYO • TORONTO • WASHINGTON
ALBANY NY • BELMONT CA • CINCINNATI OH

Michael A. Paré, *Editor*

Amanda M. Moran, *Project Coordinator*
Sara T. Bernstein and Linda Thurn, *Contributing Editors*
Amy Hall and Tara E. Sheets, *Contributing Assistant Editors*
Karen Hill, *Managing Editor*

Theresa A. Rocklin, *Manager of Systems and Programming*
Neil S. Yee, *Senior Programmer/Analyst*

Mary Beth Trimper, *Production Director*
Shanna Heilveil, *Production Assistant*

Cynthia D. Baldwin, *Product Design Manager*
Tracey Rowens, *Cover Designer*
Erin Martin, *Desktop Publisher*

Benita L. Spight, *Manager, Data Entry Services*
Gwendolyn S. Tucker, *Data Entry Supervisor*
Constance J. Wells, *Data Entry Associate*

∞' The paper used in this publication meets the minimum requirements of American National Standard for Information Sciences--Permanence Paper for Printed Library Materials, ANSI Z39.48-1984.

⊗ This book is printed on recycled paper that meets Environmental Protection Agency standards.

Copyright © 1996
Gale Research Inc.
835 Penobscot Bldg.
Detroit, MI 48226-4094

ISBN 07876-0463-1
ISSN 1084-2128

Printed in the United States of America

I(T)P™ Gale Research Inc., an International Thomson Publishing Company.
ITP logo is a trademark under license.

10 9 8 7 6 5 4 3 2 1

Contents

Certification Programs

Accreditation Programs

Highlights

Certification and Accreditation Programs Directory (CAPD) brings together, for the first time, detailed information on requirements and procedures for approximately 1600 voluntary certification programs for individuals and over 200 accrediting organizations for educational programs, institutions, businesses, and service providers in one easy-to-use volume.

Detailed entries serve many users

Individuals seeking professional advancement or development; consumers seeking highly qualified professionals to meet their needs; parents or students interested in whether educational institutions meet high standards of excellence; and professionals interested in the certification and accreditation fields.

For each certification program, *CAPD* details:

- Specific certification title awarded
- Number of individuals certified
- Full contact information on the certification granting organization
- Educational, experience, and other requirements
- Exam information, if applicable, including content outlines, frequency and sites for exam administration, and type of exam required.
- Recertification information
- Fees
- Endorsements or accreditation of certification program

For each accreditation program, *CAPD* details:

- Full contact information on the accrediting organization
- Number of institutions accredited
- Application procedures, including list of standards used in accrediting process
- Accreditation procedures, including possible accrediting decisions
- Renewal information
- Fees
- Endorsements or accreditation of accreditation programs

Designed for ease of use

CAPD contains separate occupational chapters for certification programs, with chapter titles based on standard *Occupational Outlook Handbook (OOH)* terms. Within chapters, certification programs are listed according to specific job titles for easy access. Entries in the accreditation section are listed according to specialty area. The Profiles of Certifying Bodies section provides full contact information for each certification granting organization and a listing of titles awarded by each organization. An appendix lists certification title acronyms in alphabetical order for quick reference. The Master Index lists all certification titles, names of certification granting and accrediting organizations, subject headings, and job titles.

What are the Building Blocks of Good Certification and Accreditation Programs?

by

Michael S. Hamm

Certification is defined by the National Organization for Competency Assurance (NOCA) as the process by which a non-governmental agency or association grants recognition of competence to an individual who has met predetermined qualifications specified by that agency or association. The term "certification" is usually applied to an evaluation of an individual's competence, while "accreditation" usually refers to a measurement of a program or organization's performance. Unfortunately, the terms are sometimes used interchangeably and this creates some confusion for the public and employers.

The proliferation of professional and occupational specialties, a highly mobile population, and rapid technological developments have created a demand for nationally recognized methods of identifying competence in a wide range of disciplines. Most certification programs have been developed by national associations, although some have evolved without the benefit of an existing organization base. Other certifications have been created within business and industry. Certification programs usually develop when the leadership in a particular discipline decides there is a need to articulate standards of performance and assure compliance with these standards to protect the public, assist employers, and increase the credibility of the discipline. Sometimes competitive motives come into play in the development of a program, and occasionally the threats of government intervention or legal action have been motivating factors.

Why do employers and the public need to know more about certification programs? Certification programs have experienced tremendous growth in recent years, and each employer needs to know some of the basic principles of certification programs in order to determine the potential benefits of certification for their organization, their own professional development, and their employees. Quality certification programs can help employers and the public determine the competence of individuals who perform a wide range of services. In modern times, the public does not always have the luxury of selecting professionals, tradespeople, and other service providers based on personal contacts or referrals from friends and neighbors. Like it or not, the public and employers are placing greater emphasis on the credentials of people with whom they do business. A proliferation of credentials has arisen out of the public's interest in identifying competent individuals and the obvious economic benefits for the holders of such credentials. Concerns have been expressed by some that the value of quality credentials may be jeopardized by the growing number of credentials that have little meaning to employers or the average citizen.

Characteristics of Good Certification Programs

A sound certification program is developed after a feasibility study has been conducted and a thorough role study or job analysis of the profession/occupation to be certified has been completed. This is an important aspect of the process since the examination questions or performance measurement system should always flow from an objective analysis of job demands rather than a subjective evaluation of competence. Unfortunately, a good role study can be an expensive project for some organizations and there is a temptation to cut costs by developing examinations using only committees of experts. The quality of the examination instrument is one of the most important aspects of the evaluation of a certificate. Anyone seeking a credential or utilizing credentials for hiring purposes should take time to evaluate the characteristics and reputation of the certification program in question. Organizations such as the National Organization for Competency Assurance (NOCA) have developed national accreditation standards to evaluate certification programs. Although accreditation indicates a certification organization has met nationally recognized standards of operation, the absence of national accreditation does not imply a certification has problems or is not valid.

Questions You Should Ask about Certification Programs to Assess Their Value and Reputation

1. Who developed the certification program and why was it developed? Is the sponsoring organization a reputable not-for-profit entity and representative of the highest levels of expertise in the discipline? What factors led to the implementation of the certification program?

2. What is the reputation of the certification organization within the discipline and with related disciplines? Does the board of directors represent certificants of and leadership in the discipline? Does the governing body have a public member? Is the organization sponsoring the certification program independent of a parent organization with potential conflicts of interest?

3. Was the competency assessment instrument developed by a psychometrician (professional test expert) or a nationally recognized testing company? Examinations can be developed by anyone, but a valid and reliable examination requires a formal development process with the assistance of a test expert or psychometrician. How are pass/fail cutoff scores established?

4. Was a role study or job analysis completed before the examination was developed? The quality of the examination and future test questions are dependent upon this important building block of a quality certification program.

5. Is the certification required by or recognized by employers or government agencies? Does possession of the credential assist the certificant in meeting regulatory requirements or licensure standards?

6. Do the benefits of the credential justify the cost?

7. Is the credential offered "for life" or is there a continuing competence requirement? What are the requirements for recertification to ensure continuing competence? Almost no discipline is "static" and there should be some form of continuing competence required in a good certification program. If there are continuing education requirements, can you comply with them at a reasonable cost or expenditure of effort? This question becomes more important for individuals that live in remote or rural areas where travel costs are a compliance factor. Potential applicants in remote areas need to determine whether home study, computer-based training, or other forms of continuing professional development can be used to comply with recertification requirements.

8. Does the organization have a system to remove credentials from incompetent or unethical practitioners? This process increases the credibility of the certification organization and benefits individuals who have obtained the credential.

9. Can anyone sit for the examination, or is it necessary to complete a reasonable set of educational or work experience requirements in order to be eligible to apply for the credential?

10. Is the certification agency accredited or recognized by other national standard-setting organizations such as the National Organization for Competency Assurance (NOCA) and its accrediting body? Accreditation by a nationally recognized organization such as NOCA is an excellent benchmark for determining the overall quality of a certification organization and its examinations.

11. Is the credential national in scope?

12. Is the credential recognized outside of the United States?

Asking these questions will give you a sound basis to judge the value of any credential you are considering for your own professional development or to better understand the credentials of people you interact with or employ in your organization. As an employer, you may wish to verify the attainment of a credential by a prospective employee. Most reputable agencies will confirm the attainment of credentials with employers, but they will not usually provide pass levels, scores, or discipline information to anyone other than the candidate or regulatory agencies. As an employer it is always important to put all credentials in perspective. Certification programs can only measure an individual's knowledge or performance at a particular point in time. Competence in any job is the result of a combination of factors such as knowledge, skill, attitude, and work setting. Even the best certification programs measure only some of these factors.

Characteristics of Good Accreditation Organizations

Accreditation organizations set standards for organizations and measure compliance with these standards. Many people think of accreditation as an activity primarily focused on the academic world, but accreditation organizations measure compliance with standards in many other fields and businesses. As private standard-setting bodies, these organizations have a great deal of freedom in determining the appropriate standards for recognition and procedures for compliance. The ultimate value of an accreditation organization, like a certification organization, is determined by public acceptance of the accreditation standards, the reputation of the accrediting body, and the quality of the organization's leadership. These are not easy details to measure; anyone interested in evaluating an accrediting body should ask the following questions about the organization and its processes.

Questions You Should Ask About Accreditation Organizations to Assess Their Reputation and Credibility

1. How did the accreditation standards evolve and what organizations were responsible for the creation of the accreditation process? Were the standards developed with national input from the field and with appropriate opportunities for discussion and challenges?

2. How long has the accreditation organization been in existence? How many organizations are accredited? Note: Time-tested accreditation processes may not be available in new disciplines, organizations, or businesses.

3. Who runs the accreditation body? Is the accreditation body part of another organization?

4. Is the accreditation recognized and/or endorsed by other organizations, associations, or government entities?

5. Are the accreditation fees reasonable and worth the benefits of recognition?

6. Does the accrediting body have an appeals system and a means of revoking recognition from entities that fail to meet ongoing standards?

7. Are there competing accreditation organizations and, if so, how do their accreditation requirements differ?

8. Do the accreditation standards lead to appropriate outcomes, or do the requirements reflect political considerations and philosophical principles which do not represent a consensus within the industry/discipline?

Developing New Certification or Accreditation Programs

If your organization is considering the development of a certification or accreditation program, be sure to conduct a thorough feasibility study and learn as much about the development process as possible before launching the program. The public expects a high standard of service from certified individuals and accredited organizations. Costs of mistakes or oversights are great in any activity where an individual's professional reputation or potential livelihood is at stake. In the accreditation field, the success or failure of some organizations may be determined by their recognition by accrediting bodies. Due to these circumstances organizations should not consider developing certification or accreditation programs unless they are willing to commit the time and resources to develop credible and well-thought-out programs that can withstand the challenges of public scrutiny and the marketplace. Also, since certification and accreditation standards tend to discriminate among individuals or organizations, the legal consequences of standard-setting activities are of paramount importance.

If you want to learn more about developing certification organizations, contact the National Organization for Competency Assurance (NOCA), a national association of organizations interested in certification and competency assessment issues. NOCA is located at 1200 19th Street, N.W., Suite 300 in Washington, D.C. There are also consultants available who can assist in the development of new accrediting bodies.

————

Michael S. Hamm is the Executive Director of the National Organization for Competency Assurance (NOCA) in Washington, D.C. He is also responsible for the management of the National Commission for Certifying Agencies (NCCA), which is the accrediting body of NOCA.

He is an account executive with Smith, Bucklin and Associates and he has over 16 years experience in association management at state and national levels. Mr. Hamm has a master's degree in health care administration from George Washington University.

Introduction

Certification and Accreditation Programs Directory (CAPD) is the only publication to offer detailed information on national voluntary certification programs for individuals and accreditation programs for educational, business, and service programs and institutions. Previously this information was available only in scattered sources covering specific professions, if at all. Now, a wide range of interested users will benefit from a convenient source of detailed information obtained from approximately 1600 certification granting and over 200 accrediting organizations.

Types of programs covered

CAPD is a comprehensive resource on certification programs that meet these criteria:

- The certification must be voluntary.
- The certification must be for individuals.
- The certification must be available to individuals throughout the U.S.

Certifications that are required in order for an individual to practice or work at a profession or occupation are listed in *Professional and Occupational Licensing Directory (POLD)*. Certification procedures for programs or organizations are listed in *CAPD*'s accreditation section. Certification programs for animals and products are not included in *CAPD*.

Accreditation programs must meet the following criteria:

- Accreditation must be for programs or institutions.
- Accrediting organizations must operate on national, regional, or state level in the U.S.

Continuing education approval programs, except those sponsored by medical organizations, are not included in *CAPD*. Organizations interested in sponsoring continuing education courses for certification programs should contact the certification granting organization directly. Finally, since *CAPD* is intended as a guide to current certification and accreditation practice, discontinued certifications or accrediting organizations are omitted.

Hundreds of occupations represented

CAPD provides comprehensive national certification information on most of the job categories used in the U.S. Department of Labor's *Occupational Outlook Handbook (OOH)*, 1994-95 edition, the most widely held career resource available. *CAPD* also includes occupations not covered in the *OOH*, which were either assigned to existing *OOH* categories or, as necessary, to newly created categories.

Among the new categories that appear as chapter sub-headings are: Acupuncturists; Athletic coaches and referees; Criminalists; Electrologists; Forensic experts and investigators; Secretaries; and Translators. *CAPD* also provides information on athletic and avocational certifications, providing the most comprehensive coverage possible on all types of certification programs.

CAPD provides coverage of a wide range of educational, business, and service accrediting organizations. Educational accrediting organizations include both those that accredit institutions and those that accredit specialized programs within institutions. Business accrediting organizations included in *CAPD* cover fields such as diaper services and real estate. Service accrediting organizations include programs for birthing centers, blind and visually handicapped services, and police departments.

Profiles, Appendix, and Index enhance use

In addition to chapters devoted to specific certification and accreditation programs, *CAPD* also includes a third section, Profiles of Certifying Bodies, an appendix, and a master index. Profiles of Certifying Bodies provides contact information for certifying organizations, along with listings of certifications offered by each organization. The appendix, Certification Acronyms, provides an alphabetical listing of certification acronyms. This allows the user to easily locate a certification when only the acronym is known. The Master Index allows the user to quickly locate certification and accrediting organizations by title, organization name, job category, or subject heading.

Compilation methods

More than 1200 national organizations provided information for the first edition of *Certification and Accreditation Programs Directory*. In addition to mail and telephone contacts with these organizations, the editor researched directories and other publications issued by organizations active in the certification and accreditation fields.

Acknowledgments

The editor would like to thank Meghan O'Meara, who developed the idea for *CAPD*. Special thanks goes to Amanda Moran, in-house editor and contact for this project, without whose advice, input, patience, and hard work this book would not be a reality. Most of all, I would like to thank my wife, Ellen, for her support and understanding, and my new daughter, Chloe, whose arrival helped brighten up the last several months of production on *CAPD*.

David P. Bianco and Robert C. Verkler, Director, Council on Professional Certification, provided valuable input during the planning stages of this edition. Also, thanks goes to Michael S. Hamm, Executive Director, National Organization for Competency Assurance, for advice and for writing the essay *What are the Building Blocks of Good Certification and Accreditation Programs?* at the beginning of this book.

Comments and suggestions are welcome

Users can make important contributions to future editions of *CAPD* by passing along comments and suggestions regarding the format, coverage, and usefulness of this publication. Please address remarks to:

Certification and Accreditation Programs Directory
Gale Research Inc.
835 Penobscot Bldg.
Detroit, MI 48226-4094
Phone: (313)961-2242
Toll Free: (800)877-GALE
Fax: (313)961-6815
Telex: 810 221 7087

User's Guide

Certification and Accreditation Programs Directory (CAPD) is designed for easy consultation. It contains the following sections:

- Certification Programs
- Accreditation Programs
- Profiles of Certifying Bodies
- Appendix: Certification Acronyms
- Master Index

How to find a specific entry

CAPD provides several ways to access information:

Browsing. Open *CAPD* to specific chapter and find all certification or accreditation programs in an occupational or avocational field.

Appendix: Certification Acronyms. This appendix allows access to certification entries when all that is known is the certification title acronym. Acronyms are listed in alphabetical order and citations include full certification title.

Master Index. This index allows the user to quickly locate certification and accrediting organizations by title, organization name, job category, or subject heading.

What's in an entry

Entries provide full contact information and details on the requirements and procedures for initial certification or accreditation and renewal. The fictitious sample entries on the following pages indicate the full range of possible elements; an explanation of each follows.

Certification Sample Entry

① **333**
② **Certified Reference Book Editor (CRBE)**
③ Reference Book Publishers Association (RBPA)
PO Box 9
Metropolis, MI 48000
Phone: (313)555-1111
Fax: (313)555-2222
Toll-Free: (800)555-3333
E-mail: csmith@umich.edu
Chloe Smith, Exec.Dir.
④ **Recipient:** Book publishers. ⑤ **Number of Certified Individuals:** 32. ⑥ **Educational/Experience Requirements:** Must meet the following requirements: (1) Bachelor's degree; and (2) Two years experience.
⑦ **Membership:** Not required. ⑧ **Certification Requirements:** Successful completion of exam. Exam covers: Compilation; Proofreading; and Style. ⑨ **Renewal:** Every five years. Recertification based on successful completion of exam. Renewal fee is $75. ⑩ **Preparatory Materials:** Workshops available. ⑪ **Examination Frequency:** Annual. ⑫ **Examination Sites:** Exam given at sites throughout the U.S. ⑬ **Examination Type:** Multiple-choice. ⑭ **Pass/Fail Rate:** 75 percent pass exam the first time. ⑮ **Waiting Period to Receive Scores:** 30 days. ⑯ **Re-examination:** Must wait six months to retake exam. Fee to retake exam is $50. ⑰ **Accredited By:** National Commission for Certifying Agencies. ⑱ **Endorsed By:** National Association of Book Publishers.

① **Sequential Entry Number.** This number marks the beginning of an entry. References in the index use these entry numbers, not page numbers.

② **Certification Title.** Title, including acronym, awarded to candidate upon successful completion of certification program.

③ **Certification Granting Organization.** Full name, address, telephone number, toll-free number, fax number, e-mail address, if available, and contact person for certification granting organization.

④ **Recipient.** Brief description of individuals for whom certification is designed.

⑤ **Number of Certified Individuals.** Approximate number of certified individuals.

⑥ **Educational/Experience Requirements.** Lists minimum educational and experience prerequisites for certification.

⑦ **Membership.** Lists whether membership in certification granting organization is required.

⑧ **Certification Requirements.** Lists requirements and procedures for certification. Provides course and/or exam outlines when provided by certification granting organization.

⑨ **Renewal.** Length of time before certification must be renewed. Also lists requirements, procedures, and approximate fees for recertification.

⑩ **Materials.** Lists preparatory materials available to aid candidates in the certification process.

⑪ **Examination Frequency.** How often exam is offered.

⑫ **Examination Sites.** Where exam is offered. Certification programs are required to provide accessible testing sites in accordance with the Americans with Disabilities Act (ADA).

⑬ **Examination Type.** What types of questions are used on exam.

⑭ **Pass/Fail Rate.** Pass/fail rates for exam.

⑮ **Waiting Period to Receive Scores.** Length of time candidate should expect to wait for exam scores.

⑯ **Re-examination.** Lists procedures and fees for retaking exams.

⑰ **Fees.** Approximate fees for initial certification. Does not include costs of educational prerequisites.

⑱ **Accredited By.** Identifies groups accredited by the National Commission for Certifying Agencies.

⑲ **Endorsed By.** Lists organizations, other than certification granting organization, that endorse the certification program.

Accreditation Sample Entry

① **750**
② **Commission on Dictionary Accreditation, Reference Book Publishers Association**
③ Reference Book Publishers Association (RBPA)
PO Box 9
Metropolis, MI 48000
Phone: (313)555-1111
Fax: (313)555-2222
Toll-Free: (800)555-3333
E-mail: josmith@umich.edu
Josephine Smith, Exec.Dir.
④ **Recipient:** Publishing companies. ⑤ **Number of Accredited Institutions:** 12. ⑥ **Application Procedures:** Self-assessment, involving administrator and editorial staff, required. Must document compliance with standards in the following areas: Binding; Coverage; and Definitions. ⑦ **Membership:** Required. ⑧ **Accreditation Procedures:** On-site review required. Possible accreditation decisions are: (1) Accreditation; (2) Accreditation Denied, for companies in substantial non-compliance with standards. ⑨ **Renewal:** Every three years. Renewal based on self-assessment and on-site review. Renewal fee is $200, plus actual cost of on-site review. Must also submit annual reports. ⑩ **Restrictions:** Must report changes to editorial staff. ⑪ **State Requirements:** Must hold all applicable local and state licenses. ⑫ **Preparatory Materials:** RBPA Accreditation Manual (reference). ⑬ **Length of Process:** One-two years. ⑭ **Fees:** $300, plus actual cost of on-site review. ⑮ **Accredited By:** U.S. Department of Education. ⑯ **Endorsed By:** National Association of Book Publishers.

① **Sequential Entry Number.** This number marks the beginning of an entry. References in the index use these entry numbers, not page numbers.

② **Title of Accreditation Program.** Full title of accreditation program. This title may be the same as accreditation granting organization in many entries.

③ **Accreditation Granting Organization.** Full name, acronym, address, telephone number, toll-free number, fax number, e-mail address, if available, and contact person for accreditation granting organization.

④ **Recipient.** Brief description of accredited programs or institutions.

⑤ **Number of Accredited Institutions.** Approximate number of accredited institutions and programs.

⑥ **Application Procedures.** Lists application requirements and procedures. Also lists standards used to evaluate institutions and programs, if provided.

⑦ **Membership.** Lists whether membership in accreditation granting organization is required.

⑧ **Accreditation Requirements.** Lists requirements and procedures for initial accreditation. Also lists possible accreditation decisions.

⑨ **Renewal.** Length of time before renewal is necessary. Also lists requirements, procedures, and approximate fees for renewal.

⑩ **Restrictions.** Lists restrictions for accredited programs or institutions.

⑪ **State Requirements.** Lists state or local requirements for accredited programs or institutions.

⑫ **Preparatory Materials.** Lists preparatory materials available to aid programs and institutions in accreditation process.

⑬ **Length of Process.** Approximate length of initial accreditation process.

⑭ **Fees.** Approximate fees for initial accreditation. Also lists required annual fees.

⑮ **Accredited By.** Identifies accrediting organizations accredited by either Commission on Recognition of Postsecondary Accreditation (CORPA) or U.S. Department of Education.

⑯ **Endorsed By.** Lists organizations, other than accrediting organization, that endorse or support the accrediting program.

Profiles of Certifying Bodies

Lists full contact information for certification granting organizations along with titles of certifications offered by each organization. Helpful for organizations that offer certification in several different occupational categories.

Appendix: Certification Acronyms

Lists certification acronyms in alphabetical order, and includes full title of certification. Provides access for users who have only the acronym for a certification title, such as CPCU (Certified Property and Casualty Underwriter).

Master Index

Lists certification and accreditation programs by title and sponsoring organization names. Also includes subject and job title headings listing all related items in one easy-to-find location. Index refers user to sequential entry number, not page number.

Certification Programs

Executive, Administrative, and Managerial Occupations

Accountants and Auditors

1

Accredited in Accountancy
Accreditation Council for
Accountancy and Taxation
(ACAT)
1010 N. Fairfax St.
Alexandria, VA 22314-1574
Phone: (703)549-2228
Fax: (703)549-2984
Marianne M. Anderson, Dir.

Recipient: Professionals providing accounting services to individuals and small to mid-sized businesses. **Educational/Experience Requirements:** none. **Membership:** Not required. **Certification Requirements:** Successful completion of two-part exam. Parts are: (1) Financial Accounting, including: Accounting cycle; Accounting for leases; Accounting for pensions; Accounting principles; Accounts and notes receivable; Adjusting, reversing, and closing enquiries; Cash; Cash vs. accrual processing; Current liabilities; Depreciation, depletion, and amortization; Error correction; Financial statements; Intangible assets; Inventories; Investments; Long term liabilities; Partnerships; Payroll; Property and equipment; Record set-up; Revenue recognition; Stockholder's equity; and Worksheet preparation; and (2) Managerial Accounting, including: Budget; Capital budgeting; Capital investment analysis; Cash flow analysis; Cost-volume-profit analysis; Departmental analysis; Inventory control; Job order costing; Joint costing; Managerial decisions; Process costing; Standard cost and variance analysis; Statement and ratio analysis; Time value of money; Variable vs. absorption costing; and Working capital changes. **Renewal:** Every three years. Recertification based on accumulation of 120 hours of continuing education

(minimum of 20 hours per year). Forty hours must be in accounting related courses other than taxation such as finance, business management, computer science, and business law. **Preparatory Materials:** *Financial and Managerial Accounting* and *Guide to the ACAT Accountancy Exam* (references). Workbook and self-study review course, group review courses, and sample test available. **Examination Frequency:** semiannual - always May and December. **Examination Sites:** Exam given at sites throughout the U.S. **Examination Type:** Multiple-choice. **Waiting Period to Receive Scores:** Eight weeks. **Re-examination:** Must only retake part failed. Must successfully complete exam within three years. There is a fee to retake exam. **Fees:** $50. **Endorsed By:** National Endowment for Financial Education; National Society of Public Accountants.

2

Accredited Tax Advisor
Accreditation Council for
Accountancy and Taxation
(ACAT)
1010 N. Fairfax St.
Alexandria, VA 22314-1574
Phone: (703)549-2228
Fax: (703)549-2984
Marianne M. Anderson, Dir.

Recipient: Professionals providing taxation-related services to individuals and small to mid-sized businesses. **Educational/Experience Requirements:** Must meet one of the following requirements: (1) Master's degree in accounting, law in tax, or tax; (2) Bachelor's degree and one year of experience; or (3) Two years experience. **Membership:** Not required. **Certification Requirements:** Successful completion of six-course self-study program, including exams. Courses

are: (1) Advanced Estate Planning; (2) Case Studies in Tax Planning; (3) Qualified Retirement Plans; (4) Tax Planning for the Highly Compensated; (5) Tax Planning for the Owners of a Closely Held Business; and (6) Tax Practice. **Renewal:** Every three years. Recertification based on accumulation of 90 hours of continuing education. **Preparatory Materials:** Study guides and sample questions and tests available. **Examination Frequency:** Three times per year - always January, May, and September. **Examination Sites:** Exam given at 200 sites throughout the U.S. **Examination Type:** Essay; multiple-choice; short answer. **Endorsed By:** National Endowment for Financial Education; National Society of Public Accountants.

3

Accredited Tax Preparer
Accreditation Council for
Accountancy and Taxation
(ACAT)
1010 N. Fairfax St.
Alexandria, VA 22314-1574
Phone: (703)549-2228
Fax: (703)549-2984
Marianne M. Anderson, Dir.

Recipient: Professionals providing taxation-related services to individuals and small to mid-sized businesses. **Educational/Experience Requirements:** One year of experience. **Membership:** Not required. **Certification Requirements:** Successful completion of two-course self-study program, including exams. Courses are: (1) Tax Preparer I: Individual Tax Returns, covering: Computerized return preparation; Filing; Individual tax returns; and Preparer responsibilities; and (2) Tax Preparer II: Partnership, Corporation, and Fiduciary Tax Returns, covering: Business income tax returns; Corporate tax reporting; Estate and trust tax requirements; Formations and liquidations; Partnership returns and rules; and S corporations. **Renewal:** Every three years. Recertification based on accumulation of 90 hours of continuing education. **Preparatory Materials:** Study guides and sample questions and tests available. **Examination Frequency:** Three times per year - always January, May, and September. **Examination Sites:** Exam given at 200 sites throughout the U.S. **Examination Type:** Multiple-choice. **Fees:** $595. **Endorsed By:** National Endowment for Financial Education; National Society of Public Accountants.

▮4▮

Associate in Insurance Accounting and Finance Life and Health Insurance (AIAF)

Insurance Institute of America
(IIA)
720 Providence Rd.
PO Box 3016
Malvern, PA 19355-0716
Phone: (610)644-2100
Fax: (610)640-9576
Toll Free: (800)644-2101
Dr. Robert J. Gibbons CPCU, VP

Recipient: Professionals in health and life insurance accounting and finance. **Educational/Experience Requirements:** none. **Membership:** Not required. **Certification Requirements:** Successful completion of five courses, including exams. **Renewal:** none. **Examination Type:** Essay. **Endorsed By:** Life Office Management Association.

▮5▮

Associate in Insurance Accounting and Finance Property and Casualty (AIAF)

Insurance Institute of America
(IIA)
720 Providence Rd.
PO Box 3016
Malvern, PA 19355-0716
Phone: (610)644-2100
Fax: (610)640-9576
Toll Free: (800)644-2101
Dr. Robert J. Gibbons CPCU, VP

Recipient: Professionals involved in financial operations of insurance companies. **Educational/Experience Requirements:** None. **Membership:** Not required. **Certification Requirements:** Successful completion of the following courses, in-

cluding exams: (1) Insurance Company Finance; (2) Insurance Information Systems; (3) Insurance Operations, covering internal and external insurance functions; and (4) Statutory Accounting for Property and Liability Insurers. **Renewal:** None. **Examination Type:** Essay. **Endorsed By:** American Council on Education; Insurance Accounting and Systems Association.

▮6▮

Associate in Premium Auditing (APA)

Insurance Institute of America
(IIA)
720 Providence Rd.
PO Box 3016
Malvern, PA 19355-0716
Phone: (610)644-2100
Fax: (610)640-9576
Toll Free: (800)644-2101
Everett D. Randall APA, Asst.VP

Recipient: Insurance professionals involved in premium auditing. **Educational/Experience Requirements:** none. **Membership:** Not required. **Certification Requirements:** Successful completion of the following courses, including exams: (1) Accounting and Finance, including basic accounting and property and casualty insurance company accounting requirements; (2) Ethics, Insurance Perspectives, and Insurance Contract Analysis; (3) Commercial Liability Risk Management and Insurance; (4) Commercial Property Insurance and Risk Management; (5) Premium Auditing Applications; and (6) Principles of Premium Accounting. Courses can be taken through group- or independent-study. **Renewal:** none. **Examination Type:** Essay. **Endorsed By:** American Council on Education; National Society of Insurance Premium Auditors.

▮7▮

Certified Bank Auditor (CBA)

Bank Administration Institute
(BAI)
One Franklin St.
Chicago, IL 60606
Phone: (312)683-2339
Fax: (312)683-2426
Toll Free: (800)323-8552
Dana R. Wertheim, Prog.Mgr.

Recipient: Bank internal auditors. **Number of Certified Individuals:** 4110. **Educational/Experience Requirements:** Bachelor's degree. **Membership:** Not required. **Certification Requirements:** Suc-

cessful completion of four-part exam. Parts are: (1) Accounting, including: Accounting principles; Bank accounting; Financial statements; and Managerial accounting; (2) Auditing Principles and Bank Laws, including: Audit function; Audit techniques; Bank laws and regulations; Internal controls; and Professional standards; (3) Auditing Practices, including: Assets; Audit process; Banking services; Equity; Evaluating internal controls; Income; Liabilities; and Using audit techniques; and (4) General Business, including: Commercial law and the Uniform Commercial Code; Economics; General bank management; and Money markets. The parts can be taken at different times. **Renewal:** Every year. Recertification based on accumulation of 20 hours of continuing education. **Preparatory Materials:** Examination review guides and practice exams available. **Examination Frequency:** semiannual - always June and November. **Examination Sites:** Exam given at sites throughout the U.S. and internationally. **Examination Type:** Multiple-choice. **Pass/Fail Rate:** 75% pass exam. **Waiting Period to Receive Scores:** Eight-ten weeks. **Re-examination:** There is no time limit to retake exam. Must successfully complete exam within three years. **Fees:** $445.

▮8▮

Certified Bank Compliance Officer (CBCO)

Bank Administration Institute
(BAI)
One Franklin St.
Chicago, IL 60606
Phone: (312)553-4600
Fax: (312)683-2426
Joan Vandon, Assoc.Prog.Mgr.

Recipient: Bank compliance officers, auditors, and examiners. **Number of Certified Individuals:** 637. **Educational/Experience Requirements:** Twenty-five hours of acceptable compliance training and one of the following requirements: (1) Three years experience at financial institution or regulatory agency; or (2) One year of experience at financial institution or regulatory agency, and two years experience at bank consulting firm. **Certification Requirements:** Successful completion of exam. Exam consists of following parts: (1) Fair Lending/Non Consumer Compliance Issues; (2) Credit Compliance/Real Estate Compliance; (3) Operations and Deposit Issues Compliance; and (4) Compliance Program Development and Management Issues. Each part may be taken at separate times. **Renewal:** Every year. Recertification based on accumulation of 20 hours of acceptable compliance training. **Preparatory Materials:** Review guides and preparatory courses available. **Examination Frequency:** semiannual. **Examination Sites:** Exam given at sites throughout the U.S. **Pass/Fail Rate:** 75% pass exam. **Fees:** $425.

9

Certified Business Counselor (CBC)
Institute of Certified Business
  Counselors (ICBC)
PO Box 70326
Eugene, OR 97401
Phone: (503)345-8064
Fax: (503)726-2402
Wally Stabbert, Pres.

Recipient: Accountants, appraisers, attorneys, business brokers, consultants, merger and acquisition specialists, estate planners, and others in the financial industry dedicated to the continuing successful operation of privately held businesses, either through change of procedure or ownership. **Number of Certified Individuals:** 150.

10

Certified Hospitality Accountant Executive (CHAE)
International Association of
  Hospitality Accountants (IAHA)
PO Box 203008
Austin, TX 78720-3008
Phone: (512)346-5680
Fax: (512)346-5760

Recipient: Hospitality accounting professionals. **Educational/Experience Requirements:** Must accumulate 100 total points in the following areas: (1) College degrees and courses, seminars, and workshops; (2) Association involvement; (3) Experience; and (4) Contributions to the industry. **Membership:** Not required. **Certification Requirements:** Successful completion of exam.

11

Certified Information Systems Auditor (CISA)
Information Systems Audit and
  Control Association
3701 Algonquin Rd., Ste. 1010
Rolling Meadows, IL 60008
Phone: (708)253-1545
Fax: (708)253-1443
Jon W. Singleton CISA, Exec.V.
  Pres.

Recipient: Professionals involved with information systems auditing, security, and control. **Number of Certified Individuals:** 11,500. **Educational/Experience Requirements:** Five years experience. Associate's degree may be substituted for one year of experience and bachelor's degree for two years experience. University instructor experience will count on a two for one basis. **Membership:** Not required. **Certification Requirements:** Successful completion of exam. Exam consists of following sections: (1) Auditing Standards, Procedures, and Techniques; (2) Organization and Management; (3) Information Processing Facility Operations; (4) Logical Access, Physical Access, and Environmental Controls; (5) Continuity of Operations; (6) Operating Systems Software Development, Acquisition, and Maintenance; (7) Application Software Development, Acquisition, and Maintenance; and (8) Application Systems. **Renewal:** Every three years. Recertification based on accumulation of 120 hours of continuing education. At least 20 hours must be accumulated every year. **Preparatory Materials:** *Candidate's Guide for the CISA Examination* and *CISA Review Manual* (references). Sample test available. **Examination Frequency:** Throughout the year. **Examination Sites:** Exam given at sites throughout the U.S. **Examination Type:** Multiple-choice. **Waiting Period to Receive Scores:** Ten weeks. **Fees:** $300 (members); $375 (nonmembers).

12

Certified Insolvency and Reorganization Accountant (CIRA)
Association of Insolvency
  Accountants (AIA)
31312 Via Colinas, Ste. 101
Westlake Village, CA 91362
Phone: (818)889-8317
Fax: (818)889-5107
Anna M. Szabo, Adm.Dir.

Recipient: Insolvency and bankruptcy accountants. **Number of Certified Individuals:** 212. **Educational/Experience Requirements:** Must meet one of the following requirements: (1) Hold either Certified Public Accountant (CPA), Chartered Accountant, or Certified Management Accountant designation; or (2) Bachelor's degree and four years experience. **Membership:** Required. **Certification Requirements:** Four years experience, 4000 hours of specialized experience in insolvency and reorganization within the previous eight years and successful completion of the following courses, including exams: (1) Account-

ing, Financial Reporting, and Taxes, including: Reorganization accounting; Reorganization and emerging from Chapter 11; Retention and responsibilities of accountants; Statements and accountants' reports; and Taxes; (2) Managing Turnaround and Bankruptcy Cases, including: Business failure causes; Managing bankruptcies; Pre-bankruptcy; Role and services provided by accountants; and Turnarounds and turnaround financing; and (3) Plan Development, including: Chapter 11, 12, and 7; Classes and interests; Disclosures; Financial considerations; Funding; Negotiations; and Taxes. **Renewal:** Every three years. Recertification based on accumulation of 60 hours of related continuing education. **Preparatory Materials:** Course study materials available. **Examination Sites:** Exam given at sites throughout the U.S. **Pass/Fail Rate:** 80% pass exams the first time. **Waiting Period to Receive Scores:** Two weeks. **Re-examination:** There is no time limit to retake exams. **Fees:** $1500.

13

Certified Internal Auditor (CIA)
Institute of Internal Auditors (IIA)
249 Maitland Ave.
Altamonte Springs, FL 32701-4201
Phone: (407)830-7600
Fax: (407)831-5171
Susan Lione, Mgr.

Recipient: Internal auditors involved in the assessment of internal controls, problem solving, management information systems, finance, and accounting. **Number of Certified Individuals:** 21,000. **Educational/Experience Requirements:** Must meet the following requirements: (1) Bachelor's degree; and (2) Two years experience. Either 120 semester hours or 180 quarter hours of college credit or internal auditing experience and 90% of the credits needed for degree may be accepted to fulfill educational requirement. Credentials for candidates from outside the U.S. will be reviewed to assure adequate consideration of cultural and societal differences around the world. Canadian designations such as Chartered Accountant, Certified Management Accountant, and Certified General Accountant are accepted as equivalent to bachelor's degree. Educators may sit for exam after having credentials reviewed by the IIA. Master's degree may be substituted for one year of experience. **Membership:** Not required. **Certification Requirements:** Successful completion of exam. Exam consists of following sections: (1) Internal Audit Process, covering: Internal auditing theory and practice; Investigation; Professionalism and fraud detecting; and Reporting; (2) Internal Audit Skills, covering the following skills: Behavior; Reasoning and problem-solving; Communications; and Statistics and mathematical; (3) Management Control and Information Technology, covering: Accounting; Business disciplines inherent to internal auditing; Information technology; Organization and management; and Quantitative methods; and (4) Audit Environment, covering: Accounting; Economics; Finance; Government regulation; Marketing; and Taxes. **Renewal:** Every two years. Recertification based on either successful completion of exam or accumulation of Continuing Professional Development (CPD) hours. Practicing CIAs must earn 80 CPD hours and non-practicing CIAs must earn 40 CPDs. CPD hours can be earned through association participation, continuing education in related areas, oral presentations, and publication of articles. Lifetime certification available for retired CIAs. **Preparatory Materials:** List of suggested study materials provided. **Examination Frequency:** semiannual - always May and November. **Examination Sites:** Exam given at sites throughout the U.S. and internationally. **Examination Type:** Essay. **Pass/Fail Rate:** 45% pass individual parts of exam on first try; 23% pass all four parts of exam the first time. **Waiting Period to Receive Scores:** Three months. **Re-examination:** Must only retake sections failed. There is a $60 fee to retake each section of exam. **Fees:** $300; $150 (student); free (educators).

█ 14 █

Certified Management Accountant (CMA)

Institute of Certified Management Accountants (ICMA)
Ten Paragon Dr.
Montvale, NJ 07645-1759
Phone: (201)573-9000
Fax: (201)573-8438
Toll Free: (800)638-4427
Dr. Norman E. Hadad CMA, Dir.

Recipient: Management accountants and financial managers. **Educational/Experience Requirements:** Must meet the following requirements: (1) Either bachelor's degree, Certified Public Accountant (CPA) designation, or professional designation comparable to the CMA or CPA issued in foreign country; and (2) Two years experience. Auditors employed by public accounting firms can meet experience requirement with three years experience. Teachers can meet experience requirement if the majority of their course load is in accounting and corporate financial management courses

above the principles level. **Membership:** Required. **Certification Requirements:** Successful completion of four-part exam. Exam parts are: (1) Economics, Finance, and Management, including: Communications; Institutional environment of business; Long-term finance and capital structure; Macroeconomics and international economics; Microeconomics; Organization and management theory; and Working capital management; (2) Financial Accounting and Reporting, including: Analysis of accounts and statement; External auditing; Financial statements; and Reporting requirements; (3) Management Reporting, Analysis, and Behavioral Issues, including: Control and performance evaluation; Cost measurement; and Planning; and (4) Decision Analysis and Information Systems, including: Decision theory and operational decision analysis; Information systems; Internal auditing; Investment decision analysis; and Quantitative methods for decision analysis. CPAs exempt from part two of exam. **Renewal:** Every year. Recertification based on accumulation of 30 hours of continuing education through courses, seminars, workshops, technical meetings, or self-study packages, technical speeches, and published articles. **Preparatory Materials:** Review course, previous exams, and self-study courses available. Reading list provided. **Examination Frequency:** semiannual - always June and December. **Examination Sites:** Exam given at sites throughout the U.S. **Examination Type:** Essay; multiple-choice; problem solving. **Waiting Period to Receive Scores:** 90 days. **Re-examination:** There is a $60 fee per part to retake exam. **Fees:** $240; $120 (student); full-time faculty members are permitted to take exam once at no charge.

█ 15 █

Certified Tax Accountant (CTA)

Institute for Certification of Tax Professionals (ICTP)
1832 Stratford Pl.
Pomona, CA 91768
Phone: (909)629-1460

Recipient: Tax accountants. **Certification Requirements:** Successful completion of exam.

█ 16 █

Certified Tax Consultant (CTC)

Institute for Certification of Tax Professionals (ICTP)
1832 Stratford Pl.
Pomona, CA 91628
Phone: (909)629-1460

Recipient: Tax consultants. **Certification Requirements:** Successful completion of exam.

█ 17 █

Certified Tax Preparer (CTP)

Institute of Tax Consultants (ITC)
7500 212th, SW, No. 205
Edmonds, WA 98026
Phone: (206)774-3521
Fax: (206)672-0461
Carol Kramer, Registrar

Recipient: Tax preparation professionals. **Educational/Experience Requirements:** Must meet one of the following requirements: (1) Degree from post-secondary accounting or income tax program; or (2) Three years experience in last four years. **Membership:** Not required. **Certification Requirements:** Successful completion of exam. Exam covers personal income taxes and is based on IRS publications. Enrolled agents and CPAs may be exempt from exam. **Renewal:** Every two years. Recertification based on accumulation of 60 hours of continuing education. **Preparatory Materials:** List of IRS publications available. **Examination Frequency:** May-December. **Examination Sites:** Exam given through correspondence. **Examination Type:** Multiple-choice; problem solving; true or false. **Pass/Fail Rate:** 80% pass exam the first time. **Waiting Period to Receive Scores:** Six weeks. **Fees:** $100.

█ 18 █

Certified Tax Preparer Master (CTPM)

Institute of Tax Consultants (ITC)
7500 212th, SW, No. 205
Edmonds, WA 98026
Phone: (206)774-3521
Fax: (206)672-0461
Carol Kramer, Registrar

Recipient: Tax preparation professionals. **Educational/Experience Requirements:** Hold Certified Tax Preparer Specialist (CTPS) designation (see separate entry). **Certification Requirements:** Successful completion of research paper and three of five specialty exams. Specialty exams are: C & S Corporations; Estates, Trusts, Gifts, and Fiduciaries; Exempt Organizations; Partnerships; and Tax Planning. **Renewal:** Every two years. Recertification based on continuing education. **Examination Frequency:** Eight times per year - always May-December. **Examination Sites:** Exam given by correspondence. **Examination Type:** Multiple-choice; problem-solving **Fees:** $100.

19

Certified Tax Preparer Specialist (CTPS)
Institute of Tax Consultants (ITC)
7500 212th, SW, No. 205
Edmonds, WA 98026
Phone: (206)774-3521
Fax: (206)672-0461
Carol Kramer, Registrar

Recipient: Tax preparation professionals. **Educational/Experience Requirements:** Hold Certified Tax Preparer (CTP) designation (see separate entry) for one year. **Certification Requirements:** Successful completion of one of five specialty exams. Specialty exams are: C & S Corporations; Estates, Trusts, Gifts, and Fiduciaries; Exempt Organizations; Partnerships; and Tax Planning. **Renewal:** Every two years. Recertification based on continuing education. **Examination Frequency:** May-December. **Examination Sites:** Exam given through correspondence. **Examination Type:** Multiple-choice; problem solving; true or false. **Pass/Fail Rate:** 80% pass exam the first time. **Waiting Period to Receive Scores:** Six weeks. **Fees:** $100

20

Personal Financial Specialist (PFS)
American Institute of Certified
   Public Accountants (AICPA)
1211 Avenue of the Americas
New York, NY 10036
Phone: (212)596-6200
Fax: (201)938-3329
Toll Free: (800)862-4272
Phyllis Bernstein, Dir.

Recipient: Certified Public Accountants (CPAs) specializing in personal financial planning. **Number of Certified Individuals:** 900. **Educational/Experience Requirements:** Three years experience, including at least 250 hours per year. **Membership:** Required. **Certification Requirements:** Successful completion of exam. Exam covers: Estate planning; Investments; Managing risk; Personal financial planning process; Personal income-tax planning; Planning for retire-

ment; and Professional responsibilities and standards. **Renewal:** Every three years. Recertification based on meeting the following requirements: (1) Maintenance of AICPA membership; (2) Maintenance of CPA certificate; (3) Performance of 750 hours of personal financial planning; (4) Accumulation of 72 hours of professional education; and (5) Submission of internal practice review questionnaire. **Preparatory Materials:** Study bibliography provided. **Examination Frequency:** semiannual. **Examination Sites:** Exam given at sites throughout the U.S. **Waiting Period to Receive Scores:** Three months. **Re-examination:** There is no time limit to retake exam. **Fees:** $300.

Administrative Services Managers

21

Certified Forms Consultant (CFC)
National Business Forms
   Association (NBFA)
433 E. Monroe Ave.
Alexandria, VA 22301-1693
Phone: (703)836-6232
Fax: (703)836-2241
Anne Wallace, Prog.Coord.

Recipient: Individuals involved with developing, evaluating, and managing paper and electronic business forms and systems. **Number of Certified Individuals:** 1242. **Educational/Experience Requirements:** Two years experience. **Membership:** Not required. **Certification Requirements:** Successful completion of exam. Exam consists of the following sections: (1) Business Forms Production and Materials, covering: Basic printing processes; Carbon; Carbonless; Composition and preparation; Ink and special materials, including transfer tape, plastic papers, thermal papers, and electrostatic papers; Paper; and Production equipment; (2) Design and Construction, including: Construction; Fastening; Graphics; Machine specifications; Postal regulations; Size; Spacing; Tools and materials; Type selection style; and Use of color; (3) Business Systems and Procedures, including: Basic business functions; Control systems; Forms management; Forms usage and analysis; Systems; Trade customs; and Work simplification; (4) Products and Technology, including: Affixed products; Bar codes; Binders and filing systems; Clean room forms; Continuous forms; Cut sheets; Fine paper; Labels; Mailers; One-write systems (including pegboard); Plastic cards; Promotional printing; Register

forms; Sales books; Stencils; Tags; and Unit sets; and (5) Processing and Handling Equipment, including: Business machines related to forms usage and after-handling; Data output devices; MICR; and OCR. **Renewal:** None. **Preparatory Materials:** Information booklet, including exam content outline, list of suggested reference materials, and sample questions, provided. CFC Study Kit, Product Knowledge Series (reference series), home-study courses, slide set, and study groups available. **Examination Frequency:** semiannual. **Examination Sites:** Exam given at sites throughout the U.S. **Examination Type:** Multiple-choice. **Waiting Period to Receive Scores:** Six weeks. **Re-examination:** Must only retake sections failed. **Fees:** $250. **Endorsed By:** Business Forms Management Association.

22

Certified Mail and Distribution Systems Manager (CMDSM)
Mail Systems Management
   Association (MSMA)
J.A.F. Bldg.
Box 2155
New York, NY 10116
Phone: (607)746-7600
Toll Free: (800)955-MSMA
Lance J. Humphries CMDSM, Pres.

Recipient: Mail services managers and supervisors; distribution, messenger, shipping, receiving, or fulfillment managers or supervisors; administrative, office services, or facilities managers with responsibility for mail and other distribution systems; and vendors and consultants serving the equipment supply or service needs of mail management field. **Number of Certified Individuals:** 43. **Educational/Experience Requirements:** Must meet one of the following requirements: (1) Five years employment in mail/distribution, with at least three in management; or (2) Three years experience as management in mail/distribution, two years membership in MSMA, and letter of recommendation from employer or recognized professional in management. Must also earn 150 total Management Expertise Points in the following areas: (1) Years of Experience (maximum of 80 points); (2) MSMA Association Activities (maximum of 60 points), including attendance at meetings and seminars, making presentations or speeches, and publishing articles; (3) Non-MSMA Association Activities (maximum of 40 points), including magazine subscriptions, attendance at meetings and seminars, and publishing articles; and (4) Education (maximum of 50 points), including degrees and successful completion of approved courses such as: Business Communications; Business Mathematics; Introduction to Information Systems; Organizational Behavior; Principles of Management; Principles of Supervision; Quality and Productivity Management; and Sales Management. **Membership:** Not required. **Certification Requirements:** Successful completion of exam. **Preparatory Materials:** Review course available. **Examination Sites:** Exam given at MAILCOM conference and at sites throughout the U.S. **Examination Type:** Essay; short answer. **Fees:** $175 (members); $225 (nonmembers).

`23`

Certified Transportation Broker (CTB)

Transportation Brokers Conference of America (TBCA)
5845 Richmond Hwy., Ste. 750
Alexandria, VA 22303-1865
Phone: (703)329-1894
Fax: (703)329-1898
Denise Al-Nawasreh, Mgr.

Recipient: Transportation brokers. **Number of Certified Individuals:** 300. **Educational/Experience Requirements:** Experience required. **Membership:** Not required. **Certification Requirements:** Successful completion of three-section exam. Sections are: Basic Business Practices; Broker Operations, Practices, and Services; and Transportation Practices. **Preparatory Materials:** *Business in a Changing World, Transportation,* and *Transportation Brokers: History, Regulations, and Operations* (references). Mentorship program, seminar, and study guide available. **Examination Frequency:** Annual. **Examination Sites:** Exam given at annual convention and at sites throughout the U.S. **Re-examination:** Must only retake section(s) failed. Fees to retake each section are: $25 (members); $75 (nonmembers). **Fees:** $250 (members); $450 (nonmembers).

`24`

Regulatory Affairs Certification

Regulatory Affairs Professionals Society (RAPS)
PO Box 14953
Lenexa, KS 66285-4953
Phone: (913)541-1427
Fax: (913)541-0156

Recipient: Regulatory affairs professionals involved with U.S. laws, regulations, and policies and guidelines in the area of public health and safety, with emphasis on Federal Drug Administration regulated products such as biologics, drugs, and medical devices, along with general regulatory issues. **Educational/Experience Requirements:** Must meet one of the following requirements: (1) Bachelor's degree; or (2) Three years experience. **Certification Requirements:** Successful completion of exam. **Preparatory Materials:** Study guide, including exam content outline and list of suggested study references, provided. Self-assessment exam also available. **Examination Frequency:** Annual. **Examination Sites:** Exam given at sites throughout the U.S. **Examination Type:** Multiple-choice. **Waiting Period to Receive Scores:** Eight weeks. **Re-examination:** There is no limit to how may times exam may be retaken. Fee to retake exam is $150. **Fees:** $250.

Construction and Building Inspectors

`25`

AACE Housing Officer

American Association of Code Enforcement (AACE)
5360 Workman Mill Rd.
Whittier, CA 90601-2298

Recipient: Housing officers employed by municipalities to enforce local housing ordinances providing minimum standards to safeguard life or limb, health, property, and the public welfare. **Certification Requirements:** Successful completion of exam. Exam covers knowledge of relevant codes, standards, and practice necessary for competent inspection of existing housing for code compliance. **Preparatory Materials:** *Candidate Bulletin,* including suggested reference materials, exam content outline, and sample questions, provided. **Examination Frequency:** monthly - except April, August, and December. **Examination Sites:** Exam given at sites throughout the U.S. **Examination Type:** Multiple-choice. **Waiting Period to Receive Scores:** Four-six weeks. **Re-examination:** Must wait four months to retake exam. **Endorsed By:** International Conference of Building Officials.

`26`

AACE Zoning Officer

American Association of Code Enforcement (AACE)
5360 Workman Mill Rd.
Whittier, CA 90601-2298

Recipient: Zoning officers employed by municipalities to enforce local zoning ordinances providing minimum standards to safeguard life and limb, health, property, and the public welfare. **Certification Requirements:** Successful completion of exam. Exam covers knowledge of relevant codes, standards, and practice necessary for competent enforcement of zoning regulations for code compliance. **Preparatory Materials:** *Candidate Bulletin,* including suggested reference materials, exam content outline, and sample questions, provided. **Examination Frequency:** monthly - except April, August, and December. **Examination Sites:** Exam given at sites throughout the U.S. **Examination Type:** Multiple-choice. **Waiting Period to Receive Scores:** Four-six weeks. **Re-examination:** Must wait four months to retake exam. **Endorsed By:** International Conference of Building Officials.

`27`

Aboveground Storage Tank Inspector Certification

American Petroleum Institute (API)
1220 L St., NW
Washington, DC 20005
Phone: (202)682-8000
Fax: (202)962-4776

Recipient: Aboveground storage tank inspectors under API Standard 653. **Educational/Experience Requirements:** Must be employed by inspection agency and meet one of the following requirements: (1) Engineering degree and one year of experience in inspection of tanks, pressure vessels, or piping; (2) Two-year certificate in engineering or technology and two years experience in construction, repair, operation, or inspection of tanks, pressure vessels, or piping, with one year in inspection; (3) High school diploma or equivalent and three years experience in construction, repair, operation, or inspection of tanks, pressure vessels, or piping, with one year in inspection; or (4) Five years experience in inspection of aboveground storage tanks in petroleum or chemical industries. **Certification Requirements:** Successful completion of exam. Exam covers: Administration and record keeping; Corrosion protection; Evaluation of inspection results; Repairs and alterations; Tank dismantling and reconstruction; and Tank inspection, NDE, and testing. **Renewal:** Every three years. Recertification based on continued employment in the field. Renewal fee is $600. **Preparatory Materials:** Application package, including list of suggested references, provided. Body of knowledge provided. **Examination Frequency:** Annual. **Examination Sites:** Exam given at sites throughout the U.S. **Examination Type:** Essay; multiple-choice. **Waiting Period to Receive Scores:** Six-eight weeks. **Fees:** $600.

28

Certified Automatic Door Installation Inspector
American Association of Automatic Door Manufacturers (AAADM)
1300 Sumner Ave.
Cleveland, OH 44115-2851
Phone: (216)241-7333
Fax: (216)241-0105

Recipient: Inspectors of automatic door installation. **Certification Requirements:** Successful completion of training program. Training program covers ANSI/BHMA 156.10, American National Standard for Power Operated Pedestrian Doors.

29

Certified Real Property Inspector (CRPI)
National Association of Property Inspectors (NAPI)
303 W. Cypress St.
PO Box 12528
San Antonio, TX 78212-0528
Phone: (210)225-2897
Fax: (210)225-8450
Toll Free: (800)486-3676

Recipient: Inspectors of all types of residential real property. **Certification Requirements:** Must meet the following requirements: (1) Successfully complete of 150 hour education program in Inspection Management and 75 classroom hours of related education; and (2) Hold state real estate inspector license.

30

Certified Senior Inspector (CSI)
National Association of Property Inspectors (NAPI)
303 W. Cypress St.
PO Box 12528
San Antonio, TX 78212-0528
Phone: (210)225-2897
Fax: (210)225-8450
Toll Free: (800)531-5333

Recipient: Inspectors of all types of commercial and residential real property. **Certification Requirements:** Successful completion of Principles of Property Inspection course. Course covers: Appliances; Electrical systems; Heating and air conditioning; Home construction; Operating an inspection business; Plumbing; and Radon. **Fees:** $525.

31

Company Fire Code Inspector
International Fire Code Institute (IFCI)
5360 Workman Mill Rd.
Whittier, CA 90601-2298
Phone: (310)699-0541

Recipient: Company inspectors involved in in-service inspections of existing buildings. **Certification Requirements:** Successful completion of exam. Exam covers general inspection and provisions for fire safety and special occupancies and processes. **Renewal:** Every three years. **Preparatory Materials:** *Uniform Building Code* and *Uniform Fire Code* (references). *Candidate Bulletin,* including sample questions, provided. **Examination Type:** Multiple-choice. **Waiting Period to Receive Scores:** Four-six weeks. **Reexamination:** Must wait four months to retake exam. There is a fee to retake exam. **Endorsed By:** International Association of Fire Chiefs; International Conference of Building Officials; Western Fire Chiefs Association.

32

Concrete Construction Inspector-in-Training
American Concrete Institute (ACI)
PO Box 19150
Detroit, MI 48219-0150
Phone: (313)532-2600
Fax: (313)538-0655
Richard F. Heitzmann, Dir.

Recipient: Concrete construction inspectors. **Membership:** Not required. **Certification Requirements:** Successful completion of exam. May qualify for Concrete Construction Inspector - Level II designation (see separate entry) with increased education and experience. **Renewal:** Every five years. Recertification based on successful completion of exam. **Preparatory Materials:** List of required reading provided. **Examination Type:** Multiple-choice.

33

Concrete Construction Inspector - Level II
American Concrete Institute (ACI)
PO Box 19150
Detroit, MI 48219-0150
Phone: (313)532-2600
Fax: (313)538-0655
Richard F. Heitzmann, Dir.

Recipient: Concrete construction inspectors. **Educational/Experience Requirements:** Must meet one of the following requirements: (1) Two years of college or technical school and two years experience; (2) High school diploma or equivalent and three years construction testing and/or inspection experience, two years of which must be involved with concrete; or (3) Five years of construction testing and/or inspection experience, two years of which must be with concrete. Experience must include the following: (1) Decision making responsibility and authority; (2) Verification of compliance with plans, specifications, and codes; (3) Evaluation of concrete construction in the field; (4) Documentation and reporting of inspection results; and (5) Proficiency in appropriate areas of concrete construction inspection. **Membership:** Not required. **Certification Requirements:** Successful completion of exam. **Renewal:** Every five years. Recertification based on successful completion of exam. **Preparatory Materials:** List of required reading provided. **Examination Type:** Multiple-choice.

34

Concrete Transportation Construction Inspector
American Concrete Institute (ACI)
PO Box 19150
Detroit, MI 48219-0150
Phone: (313)532-2600
Fax: (313)538-0655
Richard F. Heitzmann, Dir.

Recipient: Concrete transportation construction inspectors. **Educational/Experience Requirements:** Must meet one of the following requirements: (1)

Two years of college or technical school and two years experience; (2) High school diploma or equivalent and three years construction testing and/or inspection experience, two years of which must be involved with concrete; or (3) Five years of construction testing and/or inspection experience, two years of which must be with concrete. Experience must include the following: (1) Decision making responsibility and authority; (2) Verification of compliance with plans, specifications, and codes; (3) Evaluation of concrete construction in the field; (4) Documentation and reporting of inspection results; and (5) Proficiency in appropriate areas of concrete construction inspection. **Membership:** Not required. **Certification Requirements:** Successful completion of exam. **Renewal:** Every five years. Recertification based on successful completion of exam. **Preparatory Materials:** List of required reading provided. Training course available. **Examination Type:** Multiple-choice.

`35`

Concrete Transportation Construction Inspector-in-Training
American Concrete Institute (ACI)
PO Box 19150
Detroit, MI 48219-0150
Phone: (313)532-2600
Fax: (313)538-0655
Richard F. Heitzmann, Dir.

Recipient: Concrete transportation construction inspectors. **Membership:** Not required. **Certification Requirements:** Successful completion of exam. May qualify for Concrete Transportation Construction Inspector designation (see separate entry) with increased education and experience. **Renewal:** Every five years. Recertification based on successful completion of exam. **Preparatory Materials:** List of required reading provided. Training course available. **Examination Type:** Multiple-choice.

`36`

ICBO Building Code Accessibility/Usability Specialist
International Conference of Building Officials (ICBO)
5360 Workman Mill Rd.
Whittier, CA 90601-2298
Phone: (310)699-0541
Fax: (310)692-3853

Recipient: Municipal building code accessibility/usability enforcement in-

spectors. **Educational/Experience Requirements:** none. **Certification Requirements:** Successful completion of exam. **Preparatory Materials:** *Uniform Building Code* and *American National Standard for Accessible and Usable Buildings and Facilities* (references). *Candidate Bulletin,* including suggested references and sample questions, provided. **Examination Frequency:** monthly - except April, August, and December. **Examination Sites:** Exam given at sites throughout the U.S. **Examination Type:** Multiple-choice. **Waiting Period to Receive Scores:** Four-six weeks. **Reexamination:** Must wait four months to retake exam. There is a fee to retake exam.

`37`

ICBO Building Inspector
International Conference of Building Officials (ICBO)
5360 Workman Mill Rd.
Whittier, CA 90601-2298
Phone: (310)699-0541
Fax: (310)692-3853

Recipient: Municipal building code enforcement inspectors. **Educational/Experience Requirements:** none. **Certification Requirements:** Successful completion of exam. Exam covers relevant codes, standards, and practices necessary for competent inspection and evaluation of new and existing buildings for code compliance. **Renewal:** Every three years. **Preparatory Materials:** *Uniform Building Code* (reference). *Candidate Bulletin,* including suggested references and sample questions, provided. **Examination Frequency:** monthly - except April, August, and December. **Examination Sites:** Exam given at sites throughout the U.S. **Examination Type:** Multiple-choice. **Waiting Period to Receive Scores:** Four-six weeks. **Reexamination:** Must wait four months to retake exam. There is a fee to retake exam. **Fees:** $105.

`38`

ICBO CABO One and Two Family Dwelling Inspector
International Conference of Building Officials (ICBO)
5360 Workman Mill Rd.
Whittier, CA 90601-2298
Phone: (310)699-0541
Fax: (310)692-3853

Recipient: Municipal code enforcement inspectors. **Educational/Experience Re-**

quirements: none. **Certification Requirements:** Successful completion of exam. Exam covers relevant codes, standards, and practices necessary for competent inspection and evaluation of new and existing buildings for code compliance. **Renewal:** Every three years. **Preparatory Materials:** *Candidate Bulletin,* including suggested references and sample questions, provided. **Examination Frequency:** monthly - except April, August, and December. **Examination Sites:** Exam given at sites throughout the U.S. **Examination Type:** Multiple-choice. **Waiting Period to Receive Scores:** Four-six weeks. **Reexamination:** Must wait four months to retake exam. There is a fee to retake exam. **Endorsed By:** Council of American Building Officials.

`39`

ICBO Combination Dwelling Inspector
International Conference of Building Officials (ICBO)
5360 Workman Mill Rd.
Whittier, CA 90601-2298
Phone: (310)699-0541
Fax: (310)692-3853

Recipient: Municipal code enforcement inspectors. **Certification Requirements:** Hold ICBO Building Inspector, ICBO Electrical Inspector, ICBO Plumbing Inspector, and ICBO Mechanical Inspector designations (see separate entries).

`40`

ICBO Combination Inspector
International Conference of Building Officials (ICBO)
5360 Workman Mill Rd.
Whittier, CA 90601-2298
Phone: (310)699-0541
Fax: (310)692-3853

Recipient: Municipal code enforcement inspectors. **Educational/Experience Requirements:** none. **Certification Requirements:** Successful completion of exam. Exam covers relevant codes, standards, and practices necessary for competent inspection and evaluation of new and existing buildings for code compliance. **Renewal:** Every three years. **Preparatory Materials:** *Candidate Bulletin,* including suggested references and sample questions, provided. **Examination Frequency:** monthly - except April, August, and December. **Examination Sites:** Exam given at sites throughout the U.S. **Examination Type:** Multiple-choice. **Waiting Period to Receive Scores:** Four-six weeks. **Re-**

examination: Must wait four months to retake exam. There is a fee to retake exam.

41

ICBO Electrical Inspector
International Conference of
　Building Officials (ICBO)
5360 Workman Mill Rd.
Whittier, CA 90601-2298
Phone: (310)699-0541
Fax: (310)692-3853

Recipient: Municipal electrical code enforcement inspectors. **Educational/ Experience Requirements:** none. **Certification Requirements:** Successful completion of exam. Exam covers relevant codes, standards, and practices necessary for competent inspection and evaluation of new and existing buildings for code compliance. **Renewal:** Every three years. **Preparatory Materials:** *National Electrical Code* (reference). *Candidate Bulletin,* including suggested references and sample questions, provided. **Examination Frequency:** monthly - except April, August, and December. **Examination Sites:** Exam given at sites throughout the U.S. **Examination Type:** Multiple-choice. **Waiting Period to Receive Scores:** Four-six weeks. **Re-examination:** Must wait four months to retake exam. There is a fee to retake exam. **Fees:** $105. **Endorsed By:** International Association of Electrical Inspectors.

42

ICBO Elevator Inspector
International Conference of
　Building Officials (ICBO)
5360 Workman Mill Rd.
Whittier, CA 90601-2298
Phone: (310)699-0541
Fax: (310)692-3853

Recipient: Municipal elevator code enforcement inspectors. **Educational/ Experience Requirements:** none. **Certification Requirements:** Successful completion of exam. Exam covers relevant codes, standards, and practices necessary for competent inspection and evaluation of new and existing buildings for code compliance. **Renewal:** Every three years. **Preparatory Materials:** *Candidate Bulletin,* including suggested references and sample questions, provided. **Examination Frequency:** monthly - except April, August, and December. **Examination Sites:** Exam given at sites throughout the U.S. **Examination Type:**

Multiple-choice. **Waiting Period to Receive Scores:** Four-six weeks. **Re-examination:** Must wait four months to retake exam. There is a fee to retake exam.

43

**ICBO Light Commercial
　Combination Inspector**
International Conference of
　Building Officials (ICBO)
5360 Workman Mill Rd.
Whittier, CA 90601-2298
Phone: (310)699-0541
Fax: (310)692-3853

Recipient: Municipal light commercial code enforcement inspectors. **Educational/Experience Requirements:** Hold ICBO Combination Dwelling Inspector designation (see separate entry). **Certification Requirements:** Successful completion of exam. Exam covers relevant codes, standards, and practices necessary for competent inspection and evaluation of new and existing buildings for code compliance. **Renewal:** Every three years. **Preparatory Materials:** *Candidate Bulletin,* including suggested references and sample questions, provided. **Examination Frequency:** monthly - except April, August, and December. **Examination Sites:** Exam given at sites throughout the U.S. **Examination Type:** Multiple-choice. **Waiting Period to Receive Scores:** Four-six weeks. **Re-examination:** Must wait four months to retake exam. There is a fee to retake exam. **Fees:** $105.

44

ICBO Mechanical Inspector
International Conference of
　Building Officials (ICBO)
5360 Workman Mill Rd.
Whittier, CA 90601-2298
Phone: (310)699-0541
Fax: (310)692-3853

Recipient: Municipal mechanical code enforcement inspectors. **Educational/ Experience Requirements:** none. **Certification Requirements:** Successful completion of exam. Exam covers relevant codes, standards, and practices necessary for competent inspection and evaluation of new and existing buildings for code compliance. **Renewal:** Every three years. **Preparatory Materials:** *ICBO Uniform Mechanical Code* (reference). *Candidate Bulletin,* including suggested references and sample questions, provided. **Examination Frequency:**

monthly - except April, August, and December. **Examination Sites:** Exam given at sites throughout the U.S. **Examination Type:** Multiple-choice. **Waiting Period to Receive Scores:** Four-six weeks. **Re-examination:** Must wait four months to retake exam. There is a fee to retake exam. **Fees:** $105. **Endorsed By:** International Association of Plumbing and Mechanical Officials.

45

ICBO Plans Examiner
International Conference of
　Building Officials (ICBO)
5360 Workman Mill Rd.
Whittier, CA 90601-2298
Phone: (310)699-0541
Fax: (310)692-3853

Recipient: Building plans examiners. **Educational/Experience Requirements:** none. **Certification Requirements:** Successful completion of exam. Exam covers relevant codes, standards, and practices necessary for competence in reviewing and checking plans and specifications for compliance with nonstructural aspects of Uniform Building Code (U.B.C.). **Renewal:** Every three years. **Preparatory Materials:** *Uniform Building Code* (reference). *Candidate Bulletin,* including suggested references and sample questions, provided. **Examination Frequency:** monthly - except April, August, and December. **Examination Sites:** Exam given at sites throughout the U.S. **Examination Type:** Multiple-choice. **Waiting Period to Receive Scores:** Four-six weeks. **Re-examination:** Must wait four months to retake exam. There is a fee to retake exam.

46

**ICBO Prestressed Concrete Special
　Inspector**
International Conference of
　Building Officials (ICBO)
5360 Workman Mill Rd.
Whittier, CA 90601-2298
Phone: (310)699-0541
Fax: (310)692-3853

Recipient: Building inspectors of specialized prestressed concrete construction. **Educational/Experience Requirements:** Hold ICBO Reinforced Concrete Special Inspector designation (see separate entry). **Certification Requirements:** Successful completion of exam. Exam covers compliance with design intent according to Section 306 of Uniform Building Code (U.B.C.). **Renewal:** Every three years.

Preparatory Materials: *Candidate Bulletin,* including suggested references and sample questions, provided. **Examination Frequency:** monthly - except April, August, and December. **Examination Sites:** Exam given at sites throughout the U.S. **Examination Type:** Multiple-choice. **Waiting Period to Receive Scores:** Four-six weeks. **Re-examination:** Must wait four months to retake exam. There is a fee to retake exam. **Fees:** $115.

`47`

ICBO Reinforced Concrete Special Inspector
International Conference of
   Building Officials (ICBO)
5360 Workman Mill Rd.
Whittier, CA 90601-2298
Phone: (310)699-0541
Fax: (310)692-3853

Recipient: Building inspectors of specialized reinforced concrete construction. **Educational/Experience Requirements:** none. **Certification Requirements:** Successful completion of exam. Exam covers compliance with design intent according to Section 306 of Uniform Building Code (U.B.C.). **Renewal:** Every three years. **Preparatory Materials:** *Candidate Bulletin,* including suggested references and sample questions, provided. **Examination Frequency:** monthly - except April, August, and December. **Examination Sites:** Exam given at sites throughout the U.S. **Examination Type:** Multiple-choice. **Waiting Period to Receive Scores:** Four-six weeks. **Re-examination:** Must wait four months to retake exam. There is a fee to retake exam. **Fees:** $115.

`48`

ICBO Spray-Applied Fireproofing Special Inspector
International Conference of
   Building Officials (ICBO)
5360 Workman Mill Rd.
Whittier, CA 90601-2298
Phone: (310)699-0541
Fax: (310)692-3853

Recipient: Building inspectors of specialized spray-applied fireproofing. **Educational/Experience Requirements:** none. **Certification Requirements:** Successful completion of exam. Exam covers compliance with design intent according to Section 306 of Uniform Building Code (U.B.C.). **Renewal:** Every three years. **Preparatory Materials:** *Candidate Bulletin,* including suggested references and sample questions, provided. **Examination**

Frequency: monthly - except April, August, and December. **Examination Sites:** Exam given at sites throughout the U.S. **Examination Type:** Multiple-choice. **Waiting Period to Receive Scores:** Four-six weeks. **Re-examination:** Must wait four months to retake exam. There is a fee to retake exam. **Fees:** $85.

`49`

ICBO Structural Masonry Special Inspector
International Conference of
   Building Officials (ICBO)
5360 Workman Mill Rd.
Whittier, CA 90601-2298
Phone: (310)699-0541
Fax: (310)692-3853

Recipient: Building inspectors of specialized structural masonry construction. **Educational/Experience Requirements:** none. **Certification Requirements:** Successful completion of exam. Exam covers compliance with design intent according to Section 306 of Uniform Building Code (U.B.C.). **Renewal:** Every three years. **Preparatory Materials:** *Candidate Bulletin,* including suggested references and sample questions, provided. **Examination Frequency:** monthly - except April, August, and December. **Examination Sites:** Exam given at sites throughout the U.S. **Examination Type:** Multiple-choice. **Waiting Period to Receive Scores:** Four-six weeks. **Re-examination:** Must wait four months to retake exam. There is a fee to retake exam. **Fees:** $115.

`50`

ICBO Structural Steel and Welding Special Inspector
International Conference of
   Building Officials (ICBO)
5360 Workman Mill Rd.
Whittier, CA 90601-2298
Phone: (310)699-0541
Fax: (310)692-3853

Recipient: Building inspectors of specialized structural steel and welding construction. **Educational/Experience Requirements:** none. **Certification Requirements:** Successful completion of exam. Exam covers compliance with design intent according to Section 306 of Uniform Building Code (U.B.C.). **Renewal:** Every three years. **Preparatory Materials:** *Candidate Bulletin,* including suggested references and sample questions, provided. **Examination Frequency:** monthly - except April, August, and December. **Examination Sites:** Exam given

at sites throughout the U.S. **Examination Type:** Multiple-choice. **Waiting Period to Receive Scores:** Four-six weeks. **Re-examination:** Must wait four months to retake exam. There is a fee to retake exam. **Fees:** $115.

`51`

Pressure Vessel Inspector Certification
American Petroleum Institute (API)
1220 L St., NW
Washington, DC 20005
Phone: (202)682-8000
Fax: (202)962-4776

Recipient: Pressure vessel inspectors under API Standard 510. **Educational/Experience Requirements:** Must be employed by inspection agency or owner/user agency and meet one of the following requirements: (1) Engineering degree and one year of experience; (2) Two-year certificate in engineering or technology and two years experience; or (3) High school diploma or equivalent and three years experience. Experience must be in design, construction, repair, operation, or inspection of boilers and pressure vessels. **Certification Requirements:** Must meet one of the following requirements: (1) Hold Jurisdiction Agency certification; (2) Hold certification by National Board of Boiler and Pressure Vessel Inspectors Commission; or (3) Successfully complete exam. Exam covers: Code calculations; Practical knowledge; and Welding procedure and qualification evaluation. **Renewal:** Every three years. Recertification based on continued employment in the field. Renewal fee is $600. **Preparatory Materials:** Application package, including list of suggested references, provided. Body of knowledge provided. **Examination Frequency:** semiannual - always June and December. **Examination Sites:** Exam given at sites throughout the U.S. and Canada. **Examination Type:** Essay; multiple-choice. **Waiting Period to Receive Scores:** Six-eight weeks. **Fees:** $600. **Endorsed By:** National Board of Boiler and Pressure Vessel Inspectors.

`52`

Registered Roof Consultant (RRC)
Roof Consultants Institute (RCI)
7424 Chapel Hill Rd.
Raleigh, NC 27607
Phone: (919)859-0742
Fax: (919)859-1328
Toll Free: (800)828-1902
Sam Huff FRCI, Pres.

Recipient: Roof consultants who inspect and evaluate roof conditions, prepare contracts and specifications, observe construction and quality, and perform laboratory and field tests on existing roofs. **Number of Certified Individuals:** 177. **Educational/Experience Requirements:** Four years experience in roofing with half of the time devoted to roof consulting and meet one of the following requirements: (1) Bachelor's or associate's degree in architecture, engineering, construction, chemistry, or related field; (2) Bachelor's or associate's degree in non-related field and three education points; (3) Seven education points; or (4) Successful completion of approved roofer's apprenticeship program. Education points can be earned through college courses, continuing education, or apprenticeship programs. Experience must include three of the following tasks: Construction observation/quality assurance observations; Laboratory testing: Physical/quantitative analysis; Lectures presented relating to roofing; Legal: Forensic investigations, deposition, and expert testimony; Preparation of contract documents; Publications related to roofing; Research directly related to roofing; Roof condition surveys, audits, or investigations; Roof contracting projects; and Roof moisture surveys (infrared nuclear and/or capacitance). **Membership:** Not required. **Certification Requirements:** Successful completion of two-part exam. Exam covers: Basic design requirements; Design and construction; Evaluation techniques; Low slope and steep roofing; Roof evaluation using visual, nondestructive, and destructive techniques; and Roof systems, including built-up, metal, shingle, single ply, slate, spray applied systems, and tile. Part one covers: Consulting; Latent moisture detection; Loads; Specifications and materials; Uniform and standard codes; and Waterproofing. Part two covers typical roofing problems. **Renewal:** Every year. Recertification based on accumulation of three education points. **Preparatory Materials:** Study guide, including list of reference materials and study questions, provided. Review courses available. **Examination Frequency:** semiannual. **Examination Sites:** Exam given at RCI annual convention and at other sites throughout the U.S. **Examination Type:** Essay; fill-in-the-blank; multiple-choice; problem solving; true or false; word problems. **Re-examination:** Must only retake part failed. Fees to retake exam are: $200 (members); $300 (nonmembers). **Fees:** $200 (members); $300 (nonmembers).

53

Registered Roof Observer (RRO)
Roof Consultants Institute (RCI)
7424 Chapel Hill Rd.
Raleigh, NC 27607
Phone: (919)859-1328
Fax: (919)859-1328
Toll Free: (800)828-1902
Sam Huff FRCI, Pres.

Recipient: Quality assurance observers in roofing. **Number of Certified Individuals:** 21. **Educational/Experience Requirements:** Must have 1.2 Continuing Education Units (CEUs) in roofing, be employed as roofing quality assurance professional, and meet one of the following requirements: (1) Two years experience as quality assurance observer, roofer, roof foreman, or superintendent; or (2) Four years experience in roofing manufacturer sales or as technical representative. **Membership:** Not required. **Certification Requirements:** Successful completion of two-part exam. Exam covers: Drawings; Proper application processes; Roof observations, including construction, design, and methodology; Specifications; Steep and low slope roofing; and Systems, including built-up, metal, shingle, single ply, slate, spray applied systems, and tile. Part one covers: Code requirements; Preconstruction conferences; Procedures; and Common roof system topics. Part two tests specific technical knowledge relating to roofing and waterproofing. May earn certification for all common systems or the following specialties: Asphalt shingles and wood roofing; Built-up roof systems, including modified bitumens; Metal, both structural and architectural, including shingle and sheet systems; Single ply roofs; Slate and tile; Sprayed polyurethane foam systems; and Waterproofing. **Renewal:** Every two years. Recertification based on accumulation of 2.5 continuing education units (CEUs). Renewal fees are: $50 (members); $75 (nonmembers). **Preparatory Materials:** Study guide, including list of reference materials and sample questions, provided. Review courses and seminars available. **Examination Frequency:** semiannual. **Examination Sites:** Exam given at RCI regional meetings, annual convention, and at sites throughout the U.S. **Examination Type:** Fill-in-the-blank; multiple-choice; true or false. **Re-examination:** Must only retake part failed. Must successfully complete exam within two years. **Fees:** $125 (members); $200 (nonmembers).

54

Tank Tightness Testing Certification
International Fire Code Institute (IFCI)
5360 Workman Mill Rd.
Whittier, CA 90601-2298
Phone: (310)699-0541

Recipient: Underground petroleum storage tank (UST) inspectors. **Certification Requirements:** Successful completion of exam. Exam covers: Health and safety for UST workers; Records and reporting; Site preparation/UST system layout; Test variables and leak-detection requirements; and Volumetric and nonvolumetric testing methods and procedures. Alaska, Idaho, and Washington require state specific exams. **Renewal:** Every two years. Recertification based on successful completion of exam. Renewal fee is $50. **Preparatory Materials:** *Candidate Bulletin,* including list of suggested references and sample questions, provided. **Examination Frequency:** By arrangement. **Examination Sites:** Exam given at sites throughout the U.S. **Examination Type:** Multiple-choice. **Waiting Period to Receive Scores:** Immediately. **Re-examination:** Must wait four months to retake exam. **Fees:** $35. State exams require additional fee. **Endorsed By:** International Association of Fire Chiefs; International Conference of Building Officials; Western Fire Chiefs Association.

55

Underground Storage Tank Cathodic Certification
International Fire Code Institute (IFCI)
5360 Workman Mill Rd.
Whittier, CA 90601-2298
Phone: (310)699-0541

Recipient: Underground petroleum storage tank (UST) inspectors. **Certification Requirements:** Successful completion of exam. Exam covers: Cathodic protection design and inspection; Galvanic anode cathodic protection; Health and safety for UST workers; Impressed current cathodic protection; Obtaining site data and measurements; and UST records and certifications. Alaska, Idaho, and Washington require state specific exams. **Renewal:** Every two years. Recertification based on successful completion of exam. Renewal fee is $50. **Preparatory Materials:** *Candidate Bulletin,* including list of suggested references and sample questions, provided. **Examination Frequency:** By arrangement. **Examination Sites:**

Exam given at sites throughout the U.S. **Examination Type:** Multiple-choice. **Waiting Period to Receive Scores:** Immediately. **Re-examination:** Must wait four months to retake exam. **Fees:** $35. State exams require additional fee. **Endorsed By:** International Association of Fire Chiefs; International Conference of Building Officials; Western Fire Chiefs Association.

`56`

Underground Storage Tank Decommissioning Certification
International Fire Code Institute (IFCI)
5360 Workman Mill Rd.
Whittier, CA 90601-2298
Phone: (310)699-0541

Recipient: Underground storage tank (UST) inspectors. **Certification Requirements:** Successful completion of exam. Exam covers: Contaminated soil handling; Health and safety for UST workers; Reporting requirements; Site preparation; Storage and transportation of tanks; and Tank decommissioning and cleaning. Alaska, Idaho, and Washington require state specific exams. **Renewal:** Every two years. Recertification based on successful completion of exam. Renewal fee is $50. **Preparatory Materials:** *Candidate Bulletin,* including list of suggested references and sample questions, provided. **Examination Frequency:** By arrangement. **Examination Sites:** Exam given at sites throughout the U.S. **Examination Type:** Multiple-choice. **Waiting Period to Receive Scores:** Immediately. **Re-examination:** Must wait four months to retake exam. **Fees:** $35. State exams require additional fee. **Endorsed By:** International Association of Fire Chiefs; International Conference of Building Officials; Western Fire Chiefs Association.

`57`

Underground Storage Tank Installation/Retrofitting Certification
International Fire Code Institute (IFCI)
5360 Workman Mill Rd.
Whittier, CA 90601-2298
Phone: (310)699-0541

Recipient: Underground storage tank (UST) inspectors. **Certification Requirements:** Successful completion of exam. Exam covers: Contaminated soil handling; Excavation, bedding, and backfill; Health and safety for UST workers; In-

stalling cathodic protection; Materials; Placement of equipment; Secondary containment; Site preparation; System lining and retrofitting; Tank decommissioning and cleaning; Test methods and testing requirements; and Vapor recovery systems. Alaska, Idaho, and Washington require state specific exams. **Renewal:** Every two years. Recertification based on successful completion of exam. Renewal fee is $50. **Preparatory Materials:** *Candidate Bulletin,* including list of suggested references and sample questions, provided. **Examination Frequency:** By arrangement. **Examination Sites:** Exam given at sites throughout the U.S. **Examination Type:** Multiple-choice. **Waiting Period to Receive Scores:** Immediately. **Re-examination:** Must wait four months to retake exam. **Fees:** $35. State exams require additional fee. **Endorsed By:** International Association of Fire Chiefs; International Conference of Building Officials; Western Fire Chiefs Association.

`58`

Uniform Fire Code Inspector
International Fire Code Institute (IFCI)
5360 Workman Mill Rd.
Whittier, CA 90601-2298
Phone: (310)699-0541

Recipient: General fire prevention and engine company inspectors. **Educational/Experience Requirements:** none. **Certification Requirements:** Successful completion of exam. Exam covers: General provisions for fire safety; Inspections; and Special equipment, occupancies, processes, and subjects. **Renewal:** Every three years. **Preparatory Materials:** *Uniform Building Code* and *Uniform Fire Code* (references). *Candidate Bulletin,* including suggested references and sample questions, provided. **Examination Frequency:** monthly - except April, August, and December. **Examination Sites:** Exam given at sites throughout the U.S. **Examination Type:** Multiple-choice. **Waiting Period to Receive Scores:** Four-six weeks. **Re-examination:** Must wait four months to retake exam. There is a fee to retake exam. **Endorsed By:** International Association of Fire Chiefs; International Conference of Building Officials; Western Fire Chiefs Association.

Construction Contractors and Managers

`59`

Certified Building Official
Council of American Building Officials (CABO)
5203 Leesburg Piike, Ste. 708
Falls Church, VA 22041
Phone: (703)931-4533
Fax: (703)379-1546

Recipient: Building officials. **Certification Requirements:** Successful completion of exam. Exam consists of following modules: (1) Legal, including: Code enforcement; Maintenance; and Prosecution; (2) Management, including: Department financial; Efficiency; Governmental communication; Personnel; Personnel development; Public information/access; and Records; and (3) Technology, including: Architectural, building systems, and structural review; and Field inspection. **Renewal:** Every three years. Recertification based on accumulation of 45 professional development hours through technical education and home study courses, teaching, presentations, publication of related papers, books, or articles, experience, association participation, other certifications, and other related activities. Renewal fee is $30. **Preparatory Materials:** Candidate bulletin, including list of suggested reading and sample questions, provided. **Examination Frequency:** semiannual - always May and November. **Examination Sites:** Exams given at sites throughout the U.S. **Examination Type:** Multiple-choice. **Waiting Period to Receive Scores:** 60 days. **Re-examination:** Must only retake modules failed. There is a $45 fee per module to retake exam. **Fees:** $120. **Endorsed By:** Building Officials and Code Administrators International; International Conference of Building Officials; Southern Building Code Congress International.

`60`

Certified Fence Professional (CFP)
American Fence Association (AFA)
5300 Memorial Dr., Ste. 116
Stone Mountain, GA 30083
Phone: (404)299-5413
Fax: (404)299-8927
Toll Free: (800)822-4342
Richard Fadeley CFP, Chm.

Recipient: Fence professionals. **Number of Certified Individuals:** 400. **Membership:** Not required. **Certification Requirements:** Successful completion of exam. **Preparatory Materials:** *American Standards for Testing and Materials* (reference). Review session available. **Examination Frequency:** Annual. **Examination Sites:** Exam given at ASTM FENCE-TECH trade show. **Examination Type:** Multiple-choice. **Pass/Fail Rate:** 75% pass exam the first time. **Waiting Period to Receive Scores:** Two-three weeks. **Re-examination:** Must wait one year to retake exam. **Fees:** $75 (members); $400 (nonmembers).

61

Certified Graduate Remodeler (CGR)

National Association of Home
  Builders/Remodelers Council
1201 Fifteenth St., NW
Washington, DC 20005-2800
Phone: (202)822-0216
Fax: (202)822-0390
Toll Free: (800)368-5242
Sandy McAdams CGR, Chm.

Recipient: Owners or office, production, or sales managers of remodeling contracting businesses. **Educational/Experience Requirements:** Must meet the following requirements: (1) Five years experience; and (2) Accumulation of 200 points on Professional Profile. **Membership:** Not required. **Certification Requirements:** Successful completion of courses offered by Graduate Builders Institute (GBI), sponsored by Home Builders' Institute, educational arm of National Association of Home Builders. Courses are: (1) Building Codes and Standards, covering: Building permits; Code enforcement and appeal; Codes revision process; Inspections; Organizations that issue and regulate codes and standards; and State and local building departments; (2) Building Technology for Remodelers I, covering: Floor and wall systems; Foundation design, construction, and repair; Hazardous materials handling; Roof structures; and Structural shell systems; (3) Building Technology for Remodelers II, covering: Electrical wiring basics; Exterior finishes; HVAC basics; Interior finishes; Plumbing basics; and Windows and doors; (4) Business Finance for Remodelers, covering: Basic accounting; Bookkeeping; and Financial controls; (5) Business Management, covering: Cost control; Financial record keeping and systems; Handling; Internal staffing and directing; Planning process; Reporting and accounting; Subcontractors; and Supervisory structures; (6) Computer Applications, covering: Accounting; Estimating; Hardware and software; Inventory management; Purchase order control; Scheduling; War-

ranty control; and Word processing; (7) Construction Contracts and Law, covering: Basic elements of construction contract; Builder liability; Contract documents; Contract interpretation; Statutes of limitation; Structures of contract documents; Theories of recovery; and Ways to minimize risk; (8) Customer Service, covering: Customer expectations and behaviors; Delivering products promised; Empowering employees; Motivating satisfied customers; Organizing warranty service; Practical techniques; Repeat and referral sales; Resolving customer conflicts; and Setting service criteria; (9) Design/Build for Remodelers; (10) Energy Efficient Construction, covering: Building techniques; Energy consumption; Energy and glow measurement; Environmental considerations; and Principles of energy transfer and heat flow; (11) Estimating, covering: Basic estimating approaches; Costing categories used in construction estimates; Project costing techniques; and Quantity take-off process; (12) Insurance Reconstruction, covering: Estimating insurance jobs; Management and marketing techniques; Reconstruction methods and technologies; and Working with homeowners and insurance adjusters; (13) Negotiating; (14) Project Management, covering: Building inspections; Customer service programs; Field change requests and discrepancies; Performance standards; Project planning; Quality assurance; Reporting and documenting for recordkeeping and control purposes; Scheduling; and Work-in-progress appraisals; (15) Quality Construction for the Master Builder and Remodeler, covering: Developing quality standards; Improving quality; Judging quality compromises; Quality action plans; and Use methods; (16) Sales and Marketing for Remodelers, covering: Marketing plans; Obtaining and interpreting data; and Sources of market information; and (17) Scheduling, covering: Building schedule; Creating a plan; and Planning and scheduling tools. Number of courses to be successfully completed determined by score on Professional Profile. **Renewal:** Every three years. Recertification based on accumulation of six additional points, including successful completion of at least one additional GBI course or CGR course not taken for original certification. Renewal fees are: $100 (members); $200 (nonmembers). **Examination Frequency:** Courses given throughout the year. **Examination Sites:** Courses given in 37 states in the U.S. and in Canada.

62

Certified Installer (CI)

Water Quality Association (WQA)
4151 Naperville Rd.
Lisle, IL 60532
Phone: (708)505-0160
Fax: (708)505-9637
Dr. Judith A. Grove, Dir.

Recipient: Individuals responsible for planning, installation, and/or servicing of water quality improvement products or systems. **Educational/Experience Requirements:** none. **Membership:** Not required. **Certification Requirements:** Successful completion of exam. **Renewal:** Every three years. Recertification based on accumulation of two Continuing Professional Development credits through: (1) Attendance at Seminars, Workshops, or Convention Sessions (one credit per ten hours); (2) Attendance at WQA-Approved Educational Sessions; (3) Attendance at Educational Sessions Sponsored by Other Organizations; (4) Successful Completion of Measured Learning Sessions, including: Courses taken at colleges or trade schools; Exams successfully completed; or Home study or correspondence courses; and (5) Experiential Learning Experiences, including: Committee service; Individual learning; Presentations; Speeches; and Voluntary service. Renewal fees are: $60 (members); $135 (nonmembers). **Preparatory Materials:** List of suggested study references provided. Seminars and study kit available. **Examination Frequency:** Throughout the year. **Examination Sites:** Exam given at annual convention, mid-year conference, seminars, state and regional conventions, or by arrangement with proctor. **Examination Type:** Multiple-choice; true or false. **Re-examination:** Fees to retake exam are: $60 (members); $90 (nonmembers). **Fees:** $60 (members); $90 (nonmembers).

63

Certified Irrigation Contractor (CIC)

Irrigation Association (IA)
8260 Wilow Oak Corp Dr.
Fairfax, VA 22031
Phone: (703)573-3551
Fax: (703)573-1913
Charles Putnam, Exec.Dir.

Recipient: Professionals who install, repair, and maintain irrigation systems. **Educational/Experience Requirements:** Must meet one of the following requirements: (1) Three years experience; (2) Two years experience and 60 points earned through college courses (five points each), IA Short Course (one point per day), and manufacturer's course (one point per day); or (3) Hold Certified Irrigation Designer (CID) or Certified Irrigation Manager (CIM) designations (see separate entries). **Membership:** Not required. **Certification Requirements:** Successful completion of general, general contractor, and specialty contractor exams. General exam covers: Basic electricity and hydraulics; Irrigation scheduling and terminology; Pumps; and Soil/water/plant relationships. General contractor exam covers: (1) Business and Law, including: Business planning and organization; Contract management; Financial management; Labor laws; License law; Lien law; Project management; Risk management; Safety regulations; and Tax law; (2) Design Fundamentals, including: Electrical; Hydraulics; Plant-water requirements; Scheduling; Sprinkler precipitation rates/infiltration rates; Sprinkler spacing; and Valve sizing; and (3) Equipment - Terminology, Selection, Application, including: Backflow preventers; Control timer; Drip/Micro; Fittings; Pipe; Pumps; Sprinklers; Valves - automatic and manual; and Wire and splice connections. Specialty contractor exam covers: Earthwork; Equipment installation - methods, handling, placement; Reading and interpreting plans and specification; Safety, codes, and permits; Submittals and as-built plans; System and equipment repair and troubleshooting; and Winterization. Candidates who hold CID or CIM designations are exempt from general exam. **Preparatory Materials:** Suggested reading list and study materials available. **Examination Frequency:** Throughout the year. **Examination Sites:** Exam given at annual exposition, IA headquarters, and by arrangement with proctor. **Examination Type:** Multiple-choice. **Reexamination:** Must wait 30 days to retake exams. May retake exams three times. There is a $75 fee to retake each exam. **Fees:** $250 (members); $350 (affiliate society/organization member); $450 (nonmembers).

64

Certified Lighting Management Consultant (CLMC)
International Association of Lighting Management Companies (NALMCO)
34-C Washington Rd.
Princeton Junction, NJ 08550-1028
Phone: (609)799-5501
Jeffrey Barnhart, Exec.Dir.

Recipient: Independent lighting manage- ment contractors that manage, clean, repair, relamp, and retrofit commercial and industrial lighting installations on contract basis. **Educational/Experience Requirements:** Must accumulate points through: (1) Bachelor's degree; (2) Attendance at professional education seminars; (3) Experience; and (4) Membership in professional organizations. **Membership:** Not required. **Certification Requirements:** Successful completion of exam. Exam covers: Ballast, budding and estimating; Cleaning and relamping; Energy management systems; Equipment and safety procedures; Lamps; Lighting controls; Lighting levels; Power reducing devices; and Utility rates. **Renewal:** Every three years. Recertification based on point system similar to initial certification. **Fees:** $500 (member); $1000 (nonmembers).

65

Certified Professional Constructor (CPC)
American Institute of Constructors (AIC)
9887 N. Gandy, Ste. 104
St. Petersburg, FL 33702
Phone: (813)578-0317
Fax: (813)578-9982
Cheryl P. Harris, Exec.Dir.

Recipient: Professionals engaged in construction practice, education, and research. **Membership:** Not required. **Certification Requirements:** Successful completion of exam.

66

Certified Sanitary Supply Professional (CSSP)
Building Service Contractors Association International (BSCAI)
10201 Lee Hwy., Ste. 225
Fairfax, VA 22030
Phone: (703)359-7090
Fax: (703)352-0493
Toll Free: (800)368-3414
Robin Fowler, Sec.

Recipient: Individuals, employees, or owners of firms engaged in the manufacturing, converting, or supplying of products or services used in the building service contracting industry, or individuals or firms whose primary business is the warehousing and distribution of products used in the building service contracting industry. **Educational/Experience Requirements:** One year of experience. **Membership:** Not required. **Certification**

Requirements: Successful completion of exam. Exam covers: Basic math; Chemicals and chemistry; Communications; Customer relations; Employee motivation, relations, retention, and training; First aid; Floor care; General management; Government regulations; Insurance; Labor laws; Metals; Personnel management; Problem solving; Quality control; Restroom cleaning; Retuning jobs; Safety and fire; Security; Technology of the industry; Unions; Warehousing; and Workloading and scheduling. **Renewal:** Every two years. Recertification based on successful completion of exam. Lifetime certification available at age 62. Renewal fee is: $125 (members); $250 (nonmembers). **Preparatory Materials:** Study courses, training modules, and video training programs available. **Examination Frequency:** Throughout the year. **Examination Sites:** Exam given at annual meeting, seminars, trade shows, or by arrangement with proctor. **Reexamination:** Must only retake sections failed. Must successfully complete exam within one year. There is a fee to retake exam. **Fees:** $350 (members); $700 (nonmembers).

67

Certified Tennis Court Builder (CTCB)
United States Tennis Court and Track Builders Association (U.S.T.C.T.B.A.)
720 Light St.
Baltimore, MD 21230-3816
Phone: (410)752-3500
Fax: (410)752-8295
Lee Lowis CTCB, Chm.

Recipient: Tennis court builders. **Membership:** Not required. **Certification Requirements:** Successful completion of exam. Exam covers: Construction data; Court diagrams; and Specifications for tennis courts, dimensions, fencing, and lighting. **Renewal:** Every three years. Recertification based on accumulation of 200 points through: (1) Membership (15 points per year); (2) Attendance at U.S.T.C. & T.B.A. Meetings (20 points per meeting); (3) U.S.T.C. & T.B.A. Committee Activity (15 points); (4) Authorship of Article (25 points); (5) Attendance at Training Courses (five points); (6) Participation in Technical Meeting of Related Association (ten points); and (7) Other Activities (ten points). Renewal fees are: $75 (members); $175 (nonmembers). **Preparatory Materials:** *Tennis Courts '92-'93* (reference). **Examination Frequency:** Throughout the year. **Examination Sites:** Exam given at annual meeting and at association headquarters.

Examination Type: Multiple-choice; true or false. **Re-examination:** May retake exam without additional fee. **Fees:** $75 (members); $175 (nonmembers). **Endorsed By:** Must meet the following requirements: (1) Three years experience; and (2) Successful completion of 50 tennis courts, including at least 20 percent in new construction.

68

Certified Track Builder (CTB)
United States Tennis Court and
Track Builders Association
(U.S.T.C. & T.B.A.)
720 Light St.
Baltimore, MD 21230-3816
Phone: (410)752-3500
Fax: (410)752-8295
Kevin West CTB, Chm.

Recipient: Track builders. **Educational/ Experience Requirements:** Must meet the following requirements: (1) Three years experience; (2) Accumulation of 2000 total construction points in the following categories: Asphalt concrete macadam (30 points); Base preparation (20 points); Layout and engineering (ten points); Simple conversion to 400 meters (ten points); Site preparation (20 points); Surface construction (20 points); Track markings system (20 points); and Underground drainage system (15 points). **Membership:** Not required. **Certification Requirements:** Successful completion of exam. Exam covers: Construction data; Specifications for tracks, dimensions, fencing, and dimensions; and Track diagrams. **Renewal:** Every three years. Re-certification based on accumulation of 200 points through: (1) Membership (15 points per year); (2) Attendance at U.S.T.C. & T.B.A. Meetings (20 points per meeting); (3) U.S.T.C. & T.B.A. Committee Activity (15 points); (4) Authorship of Article (25 points); (5) Attendance at Training Courses (five points); (6) Participation in Technical Meeting of Related Association (ten points); and (7) Other Activities (ten points). Renewal fees are: $75 (members); $175 (nonmembers). **Examination Frequency:** Throughout the year. **Examination Sites:** Exam given at annual meeting and at association headquarters. **Examination Type:** Calculation; fill-in-the-blank; multiple-choice; true or false. **Re-examination:** May retake exam without additional fee. **Fees:** $150 (members); $350 (nonmembers).

69

ICBO Building Contractor
International Conference of
Building Officials (ICBO)
5360 Workman Mill Rd.
Whittier, CA 90601-2298
Phone: (310)699-0541

Recipient: Contractors involved in construction and remodeling of commercial buildings and single or multi-dwelling residential buildings, not exceeding three stories in height. **Certification Requirements:** Successful completion of exam. Exam covers: Building classifications; Concrete; Detailed regulations; Exit requirements; Footings and foundations; Framing; General administrative requirements; Insulation, vents, and access; Masonry; Sheathing and wall coverings; and Type of construction requirements. **Preparatory Materials:** *Uniform Building Code* (reference). Exam content outlines, required competencies, and sample questions provided. **Examination Frequency:** monthly. **Examination Type:** Multiple-choice. **Waiting Period to Receive Scores:** Six weeks. **Re-examination:** Must wait four months to retake exam.

70

ICBO General Contractor
International Conference of
Building Officials (ICBO)
5360 Workman Mill Rd.
Whittier, CA 90601-2298
Phone: (310)699-0541

Recipient: Contractors involved in building, remodeling, or repairing of any structure or addition. **Certification Requirements:** Successful completion of exam. Exam covers: Building classifications; Concrete; Detailed regulations; Exit requirements; Footings and foundations; Framing; General administrative requirements; Insulation, vents, and access; Masonry; Sheathing and wall coverings; and Type of construction requirements. **Preparatory Materials:** *Uniform Building Code* (reference). Exam content outlines, required competencies, and sample questions provided. **Examination Frequency:** monthly. **Examination Type:** Multiple-choice. **Waiting Period to Receive Scores:** Six weeks. **Re-examination:** Must wait four months to retake exam.

71

ICBO Residential Contractor
International Conference of
Building Officials (ICBO)
5360 Workman Mill Rd.
Whittier, CA 90601-2298
Phone: (310)699-0541

Recipient: Contractors involved in construction, remodeling, repair, or wrecking of one- and two-family residences. **Certification Requirements:** Successful completion of exam. Exam covers: Detailed regulations; Exit requirements; Footings, foundations, and slabs; Framing; General administrative requirements; Insulation, vents, and access; Masonry; and Sheathing and wall coverings. **Preparatory Materials:** *Uniform Building Code* (reference). Exam content outlines, required competencies, and sample questions provided. **Examination Frequency:** monthly. **Examination Type:** Multiple-choice. **Waiting Period to Receive Scores:** Six weeks. **Re-examination:** Must wait four months to retake exam.

Cost Estimators

72

Certified Cost Consultant (CCC)
AACE International
209 Prairie Ave., Ste. 100
Morgantown, WV 26507
Phone: (304)296-8444
Fax: (304)291-5728
Toll Free: (800)858-COST
Karyn Conklin, Admin.

Recipient: Cost consultants who apply scientific principles and techniques to problems of cost estimating, cost control, business planning and management science, profitability analysis, project management, and planning and scheduling. **Educational/Experience Requirements:** Must meet one of the following requirements: (1) Eight years experience; or (2) Four years experience and bachelor's degree in either quantity surveying, business, accounting, construction management, computer science, mathematics, or other related field. **Membership:** Not required. **Certification Requirements:** Submission of paper on Total Cost Management and successful completion of exam consisting of the following sections: (1) Supporting Skills and Knowledge, including: Computer operations and operations research; Cost, schedule terminology, and basic applications; and Measurements (metric/English conversion); (2) Cost Estimating and Control, including: Budgeting and cash flow; Chart of accounts and work breakdown structure (WBS); Cost indices and escalation factors; Costing and pricing; Elements of cost; Estimating methods; Operating and manufacturing costs; Risk analysis and contingency; and Types and purpose of estimates; (3) Project Management, including: Contracts and contract administration; Cost and schedule management; Integrated project control; Management theory; Organization and behavioral structures; Quality and materials management; Resource and productivity management; and Social and legal issues in management; and (4) Economic Analysis, including: Comparative economic studies; Constructability analysis and value engineering; Depreciation; Engineering economics, statistics, and probability; Forecasting; Life cycle costs; Profitability; Time value of money; and Value analysis. **Renewal:** Every three years. Recertification based on either successful completion of exam or accumulation of 15 credits through experience, continuing education, authoring and/or presenting papers, serving as industry association official, teaching, and professional development and involvement. **Preparatory Materials:** *Complete Guide to AACE International Certification,* including bibliography of study references, exam content outline, and sample questions, provided. Seminars and workshops available. **Examination Frequency:** semiannual - always June and December. **Examination Sites:** Exam given at annual meeting and at sites throughout the U.S. and internationally. **Re-examination:** There is a $60 fee to retake exam. **Fees:** $200 (members); $300 (nonmembers). **Endorsed By:** Council of Engineering Specialty Boards.

73

Certified Cost Engineer (CCE)
AACE International
209 Prairie Ave., Ste. 100
Morgantown, WV 26507
Phone: (304)296-8444
Fax: (304)291-5728
Toll Free: (800)858-COST
Karyn Conklin, Admin.

Recipient: Cost engineers who apply scientific principles and techniques to problems of cost estimating, cost control, business planning and management science, profitability analysis, project management, and planning and scheduling. **Educational/Experience Requirements:** Must meet the following requirements: (1) Four year degree from accredited engineering program; and (2) Four years experience. **Membership:** Not required.

Certification Requirements: Submission of paper on Total Cost Management and successful completion of exam consisting of the following sections: (1) Supporting Skills and Knowledge, including: Computer operations and operations research; Cost, schedule terminology, and basic applications; and Measurements (metric/English conversion); (2) Cost Estimating and Control, including: Budgeting and cash flow; Chart of accounts and work breakdown structure (WBS); Cost indices and escalation factors; Costing and pricing; Elements of cost; Estimating methods; Operating and manufacturing costs; Risk analysis and contingency; and Types and purpose of estimates; (3) Project Management, including: Contracts and contract administration; Cost and schedule management; Integrated project control; Management theory; Organization and behavioral structures; Quality and materials management; Resource and productivity management; and Social and legal issues in management; and (4) Economic Analysis, including: Comparative economic studies; Constructability analysis and value engineering; Depreciation; Engineering economics, statistics, and probability; Forecasting; Life cycle costs; Profitability; Time value of money; and Value analysis. **Renewal:** Every three years. Recertification based on either successful completion of exam or accumulation of 15 credits through experience, continuing education, authoring and/or presenting papers, serving as industry association official, teaching, and professional development and involvement. **Preparatory Materials:** *Complete Guide to AACE International Certification,* including bibliography of study references, exam content outline, and sample questions, provided. Seminars and workshops available. **Examination Frequency:** semiannual - always June and December. **Examination Sites:** Exam given at annual meeting and at sites throughout the U.S. and internationally. **Examination Type:** Essay; matching; multiple-choice; problem-solving; true or false. **Re-examination:** There is a $60 fee to retake exam. **Fees:** $200 (members); $300 (nonmembers). **Endorsed By:** Council of Engineering Specialty Boards.

74

Certified Cost Estimator/Analyst (CCEA)
Society of Cost Estimating and Analysis (SCEA)
101 S. Whiting St., Ste. 201
Alexandria, VA 22303
Phone: (703)751-8069
Fax: (703)461-7328
Dr. David Lee, Exec. Officer

Recipient: Public and private sector cost estimators and analysts. **Number of Certified Individuals:** 2600. **Educational/Experience Requirements:** Must meet one of the following requirements: (1) Bachelor's degree or higher in related field, including ten SCEA approved courses, and two years experience; (2) Associate's degree and five years experience; or (3) Seven years related experience. **Membership:** Not required. **Certification Requirements:** Successful completion of two-part exam. Part one covers general cost estimating knowledge, including: Contracting; Estimating and analysis; and General management. Part two covers one of the following specialty areas: Cost analysis; Cost estimating; or Economics. **Renewal:** Every five years. Recertification based on either successful completion of exam or accumulation of points through education, experience, and association participation. **Examination Frequency:** Three times per year. **Examination Sites:** Exams given at SCEA local chapter meetings and national conference. **Examination Type:** Multiple-choice. **Pass/Fail Rate:** 67% pass exam the first time. **Re-examination:** There is no time limit to retake exam. **Fees:** $85.

75

Certified Professional Estimator (CPE)
American Society of Professional Estimators (ASPE)
11141 Georgia Ave., Ste. 412
Wheaton, MD 20902
Phone: (301)929-8848
Fax: (301)929-0231
Darnell Lynn Ambrose, Admin.

Recipient: Electrical, general, and mechanical construction estimators; owners, designers, and contracting firms. **Educational/Experience Requirements:** Five years experience and attendance at workshop. **Membership:** Required. **Certification Requirements:** Successful completion of technical paper and exam. Exam covers: Contract terms and conditions; Cost calculations and reporting; Ethics; and Other areas related to the estimating profession. **Renewal:** Every three years. Recertification based on continuing education, teaching educational programs, and involvement in ASPE activities. **Preparatory Materials:** *ASPE Standard Estimating Practice Manual* (reference). Study materials available. **Examination Frequency:** Annual - always November. **Examination Sites:** Exam given by local chapters throughout the U.S. **Waiting Period to Receive Scores:** 60 days. **Re-examination:** Must wait one year to retake exam. May retake exam once.

Education Administrators

76

Certified Athletic Administrator (CAA)

National Interscholastic Athletic Administrators Association (NIAAA)
PO Box 20626
Kansas City, MO 64195-0626
Phone: (816)464-5400
Fax: (816)464-5571

Recipient: Administrators of interscholastic athletics. **Educational/Experience Requirements:** Must meet the following requirements: (1) Bachelor's degree or higher; (2) Home state teaching or administrative certification; (3) Two years experience; and (4) Accumulation of at least 42 of possible 68 points through education and experience. **Membership:** Not required. **Certification Requirements:** Successful completion of exam. Exam covers: Booster clubs; Budget; Communication; Crowd control; Ethics; General administration; Leadership; Legal/legislative; Medical/health and safety; National federation; Office management; Philosophy; and Sportsmanship. Personal or telephone interview may also be requested. **Preparatory Materials:** Study guide provided. **Examination Frequency:** Throughout the year. **Examination Sites:** Exam given at sites throughout the U.S. **Examination Type:** Multiple-choice. **Re-examination:** May retake exam twice. **Fees:** $110 (members); $150 (nonmembers).

Engineering, Science, and Data Processing Managers

77

Associate Insurance Data Manager (AIDM)

Insurance Data Management Association (IDMA)
85 John St.
New York, NY 10038
Phone: (212)669-0496
Fax: (212)669-0535
Richard L. Penberthy, Dir.

Recipient: Insurance data managers.

Educational/Experience Requirements: None. **Certification Requirements:** Successful completion of the following self-study courses, including exams: (1) Insurance Data Collection and Statistical Reporting, including: Automation of insurance information; Cycles of insurance activity; Insurance Services Office; National Association of Independent Insurers; National Association of Independent Insurers statistical plans and data reporting; National Council on Compensation Insurance financial aggregate calls; National Council on Compensation Insurance: Workers Compensation Statistical Plan; Objectives of company automation; Overview of insurance information systems; Ratemaking data and systems; Regulators: data collection and uses; Regulators: reporting requirements and residual markets; Standards and guidelines; Statistical reporting; and Underwriting and claims; (2) Insurance Data Quality, including: Audit guide; Building environment for quality; Change process, methodology, and tools; Controlling environment for quality; Data quality in statistical reporting; History and definition of quality; Insurance data quality in an automated environment; Quality costs; Quality strategies; Sampling; Statistical examinations; and Troubleshooting; (3) Systems Development and Project Management, including: Business process redesign and systems development; Human side of project development; Integrating business and systems issues; Justifying systems projects; Managing for productivity; Managing in a team environment; Managing testing function; Planning; Planning for change; Quality and project management; Systems development process; Systems and project management education; Testing programs; Testing requirements and design; and Testing systems; and (4) Data Administration, including: Approaches to data modeling, data administration implementation, and domain tables; Computer files: storage, organization, and access; Data evolution: reengineering, migration, and ownership; Data integrity/attributes; Data management: control, administration, and the future; Database approach; Database design and data dictionaries; Designing data; Logical data model; Navigational databases; Normalization and domains; Relational design methodology; Relational tools; and Responsibilities.

78

Certified Insurance Data Manager (CIDM)

Insurance Data Management Association (IDMA)
85 John St.
New York, NY 10038
Phone: (212)669-0496
Fax: (212)669-0535
Richard L. Penberthy, Dir.

Recipient: Insurance data managers. **Educational/Experience Requirements:** None. **Certification Requirements:** Successful completion of the following self-study courses, including exams: (1) Insurance Data Collection and Statistical Reporting, including: Automation of insurance information; Cycles of insurance activity; Insurance Services Office; National Association of Independent Insurers; National Association of Independent Insurers statistical plans and data reporting; National Council on Compensation Insurance financial aggregate calls; National Council on Compensation Insurance: Workers Compensation Statistical Plan; Objectives of company automation; Overview of insurance information systems; Ratemaking data and systems; Regulators: data collection and uses; Regulators: reporting requirements and residual markets; Standards and guidelines; Statistical reporting; and Underwriting and claims; (2) Insurance Data Quality, including: Audit guide; Building environment for quality; Change process, methodology, and tools; Controlling environment for quality; Data quality in statistical reporting; History and definition of quality; Insurance data quality in an automated environment; Quality costs; Quality strategies; Sampling; Statistical examinations; and Troubleshooting; (3) Systems Development and Project Management, including: Business process redesign and systems development; Human side of project development; Integrating business and systems issues; Justifying systems projects; Managing for productivity; Managing in a team environment; Managing testing function; Planning; Planning for change; Quality and project management; Systems development process; Systems and project management education; Testing programs; Testing requirements and design; and Testing systems; and (4) Data Administration, including: Approaches to data modeling, data administration implementation, and domain tables; Computer files: storage, organization, and access; Data evolution: reengineering, migration, and ownership; Data integrity/attributes; Data management: control, administration, and the future; Database approach; Database design and data dictionaries; Designing data; Logical data model; Navigational databases; Normalization and domains; Relational design methodology; Relational tools; and Responsibilities. Must also successfully complete four courses from one of the following programs: (1) Chartered Property-Casualty Underwriter (CPCU) Program of the American Institute of Chartered Property-Casualty Underwriters, including: Accounting and Finance; Commercial Liability Risk Management and Insurance; Commercial Property Risk Management and Insurance; Insurance Company Operations; and Property Risk Management and Insurance; (2) Fellow, Life Management Institute (FLMI) Program of Life Office Management Association, including: Accounting in Life and Health Insurance Companies; Life and Health Insurance Company Operations; Mathematics of Life and Health Insurance; and Principles of Life and Health Insurance; or (3) Casualty Actuarial Society.

▮ 79 ▮

Certified Knowledge Engineer (CKE)
International Association of Knowledge Engineers (IAKE)
973D Russell Ave.
Gaithersburg, MD 20879-3276
Phone: (301)948-5390
Fax: (301)926-4243
Toll Free: (800)833-6464

Recipient: Practitioners and professionals in field of knowledge engineering. (Knowledge engineering is concerned with design of reasoning machines and computer systems to receive, organize, and maintain human knowledge.) **Membership:** Not required. **Certification Requirements:** Successful completion of exam. Exams offered in domain oriented knowledge engineering and systems-oriented knowledge engineering. **Fees:** $225 (members); $295 (nonmembers).

Financial Managers

▮ 80 ▮

Accredited Automated Clearing House Professional (AAP)
National Automated Clearing House Association (NACHA)
607 Herndon Pkwy., Ste. 200
Herndon, VA 22070
Phone: (703)742-9190
Fax: (703)787-0996

Recipient: Automated clearing house (ACH) professionals. **Educational/ Experience Requirements:** Two years experience. **Membership:** Not required. **Certification Requirements:** Successful completion of exam. Exam covers: Concepts and fundamentals; Marketing strategies; Payment systems; Professional responsibilities; Risk management; and Rules and regulations. **Renewal:** Every five years. **Preparatory Materials:** *Accredited ACH Professional Handbook,* including glossary and list of suggested study resources, provided. Review sessions available. **Examination Frequency:** Annual. **Examination Sites:** Exam given at sites throughout the U.S. **Examination Type:** Multiple-choice. **Fees:** $195 (members); $345 (nonmembers).

▮ 81 ▮

Accredited Pension Administrator (APA)
National Institute of Pension Administrators (NIPA)
145 W. First St., Ste. A
Tustin, CA 92680-3209
Phone: (714)731-3523
Fax: (714)731-1284

Recipient: Pension administrators; owners, principals, and partners of administration firms; employee benefit consultants; financial personnel responsible for trust assets; insurance executives; and others whose work entails planning, implementation, and/or administration of pension and employee benefit plans. **Membership:** Not required. **Certification Requirements:** Successful completion of six-part independent study program, including exams. Parts are: (1) Fundamentals of Retirement Plans, covering: Retirement income planning; and Retirement plans; (2) Defined Contribution Plans; (3) Defined Benefit and Hybrid Plans; (4) Select Topics in Qualified Plans; (5) Qualified Plan Administration, covering day-to-day practical aspects of plan administration; and (6) Distributions from Qualified Plans, covering taxation of plan distributions. Successful completion of courses for related certifications may be granted equivalency credit. **Renewal:** Every year. Recertification based on accumulation of 15 hours of related continuing education. **Preparatory Materials:** Study guides, including list of reference materials and sample questions, available. **Examination Frequency:** semiannual - always January and June. **Examination Sites:** Exams given at sites throughout the U.S. **Examination Type:** Multiple-choice. **Fees:** $240 (members); $365 (nonmembers).

▮ 82 ▮

Associate Credit Executive (ACE)
Society of Certified Credit Executives (SCCE)
PO Box 419057
St. Louis, MO 63141-1757
Phone: (314)991-3030
Fax: (314)991-3029
Sandra K. Weber, Assoc.Admin.

Recipient: Supervisory professionals in credit services organizations, credit reporting or collection agencies, or consumer credit counseling organizations. **Membership:** Required. **Certification Requirements:** Must meet the following requirements: (1) Attendance at one credit-related meeting, program, or conference with educational focus; and (2) Three years experience. Candidates with less experience may qualify for Credit Associate (CA) designation (see separate entry). May be eligible for Certified Consumer Credit Executive (CCCE), Certified Credit Bureau Executive (CCBE), Certified Collection Agency Executive (CCAE), or Certified Financial Counseling Executive (CFCE) designations (see separate entries) with further experience. **Fees:** $100. **Endorsed By:** International Credit Association.

▮ 83 ▮

Certified Cash Manager (CCM)
Treasury Management Association (TMA)
7315 Wisconsin Ave., Ste. 1250 W.
Bethesda, MD 20814
Phone: (301)907-2862
Fax: (301)907-2864
Paul J. Markovic CCM, Chm.

Recipient: Professionals in corporate cash management, including corporate finance officers, bankers in cash management department, educators, and consultants to cash management industry. **Number of Certified Individuals:** 7000. **Educational/Experience Requirements:** Must meet one of the following requirements: (1) Two years experience; (2) One year of experience and post-baccalaureate business degree; (3) One year of experience and two years teaching experience in related subject full-time at college or university; (4) Two years experience teaching related subject full-time at college or university and advanced business degree; or (5) Four years experience teaching related subject full-time at college or university. Experience must be as banker, in corporate position, or as vendor/consultant. **Membership:** Not required. **Certification Requirements:** Successful completion of exam. Exam covers: Accounts receivable and credit management; Bank relationship management; Banking system; Borrowing; Cash concentration; Collections; Corporate financial function; Disbursements; Forecasting cash flows; Foreign exchange and interest rate management; Information management; International cash management; Investments; and Payment system. **Renewal:** Every six years. Recertification based on accumulation of 72 credits through continuing education, teaching TMA-approved courses at colleges and universities, professional articles published, thesis or dissertation on related topic accepted, and TMA volunteer activity. Lifetime certification awarded after first recertification. **Preparatory Materials:** *Essentials of Cash Management,* Fourth Edition (study guide). Study and review materials, sample questions, and review courses, seminars, study groups, and workshops available. **Examination Frequency:** Annual. **Examination Sites:** Exam given at 60 sites throughout the U.S., Canada, and internationally. **Examination Type:** Multiple-choice. **Waiting Period to Receive Scores:** Six-eight weeks. **Fees:** $296 (members); $486 (non-members). **Re-examination:** Fees to retake exam are: $296 (members); $486 (nonmembers).

84

Certified Collection Agency Executive (CCAE)
Society of Certified Credit Executives (SCCE)
PO Box 419057
St. Louis, MO 63141-1757
Phone: (314)991-3030
Fax: (314)991-3029
Sandra K. Weber, Assoc.Admin.

Recipient: Executives of collection agencies or collection divisions of credit reporting agencies. **Educational/ Experience Requirements:** Must meet the following requirements: (1) Five years experience; (2) Service as association committee or task force member, chairperson, director, or officer; (3) Attendance at three credit-related meetings, programs, or conferences with educational focus; and (4) Contributions to community at large through involvement in educational, civic, political, charitable, religious, or any other activity. **Certification Requirements:** Successful completion of exam. Exam covers: Consumer credit counseling; Credit granting; Credit reporting; and Debt collections. **Renewal:** Every three years. Recertification based on leadership activities, professional development, contributions to

the profession, and recognition within credit industry. There is no renewal fee. **Preparatory Materials:** *Comprehensive Credit Manual,* Fourth Edition (reference). **Examination Type:** Multiple-choice. **Fees:** $200. **Endorsed By:** International Credit Association.

85

Certified Consumer Credit Executive (CCCE)
Society of Certified Credit Executives (SCCE)
PO Box 419057
St. Louis, MO 63141-1757
Phone: (314)991-3030
Fax: (314)991-3029
Sandra K. Weber, Assoc.Admin.

Recipient: Credit-granting or credit services industry managers. **Educational/ Experience Requirements:** Must meet the following requirements: (1) Five years experience; (2) Service as association committee or task force member, chairperson, director, or officer; (3) Attendance at three credit-related meetings, programs, or conferences with educational focus; and (4) Contributions to community at large through involvement in educational, civic, political, charitable, religious, or any other activity. **Membership:** Required. **Certification Requirements:** Successful completion of exam. Exam covers: Consumer credit counseling; Credit granting; Credit reporting; and Debt collections. **Renewal:** Every three years. Recertification based on leadership activities, professional development, contributions to the profession, and recognition within credit industry. There is no renewal fee. **Preparatory Materials:** *Comprehensive Credit Manual,* Fourth Edition (reference). **Examination Type:** Multiple-choice. **Fees:** $200. **Endorsed By:** International Credit Association.

86

Certified Corporate Trust Specialist (CCTS)
Institute for Certified Bankers (ICB)
1120 Connecticut Ave., NW, Ste. 600
Washington, DC 20036
Phone: (202)663-5380
Fax: (202)663-7543
Toll Free: (800)338-0626

Recipient: Professionals in corporate trust field. **Educational/Experience Requirements:** Must meet one of the following requirements: (1) Eight years experi-

ence and 30 hours of recognized professional education; (2) Five years experience and 60 hours of recognized professional education; or (3) Three years experience and 90 hours of recognized professional education. **Membership:** Not required. **Certification Requirements:** Successful completion of exam. Exam consists of the following sections: (1) Core Subjects of Corporate Trust, including: Audit and compliance issues; Credit markets; Registration of securities; and State and federal agencies; (2) Account Administration and Account Management, including: Account acceptance criteria and process; Account closing and preparation process; and Account administration techniques; and (3) Operations and Systems, including: Agency systems; Depository and clearing agencies; Fee billing; Payment functions; Redemption processing; Registered transfer agent roles and functions; Responding to written inquiries; Systems; Tender agent processing; and Transfer of securities. **Renewal:** Every three years. Recertification based on accumulation of 30 continuing education hours through conferences, seminars, or workshops, in-bank training programs, college courses, teaching, video or audio tape review courses, authoring of articles or books, and writing questions for exam. **Preparatory Materials:** Study handbook, including list of recommended study courses, study questions, sample test, and list of suggested reading, available. **Examination Frequency:** semiannual. **Examination Sites:** Exam given at sites throughout the U.S. **Examination Type:** Multiple-choice. **Waiting Period to Receive Scores:** Six-eight weeks. **Re-examination:** Must retake only sections failed. Must successfully complete all sections of exam within three years. There is a $125 fee to retake exam. **Fees:** $600. **Endorsed By:** American Bankers Association.

87

Certified Credit Bureau Executive (CCBE)
Society of Certified Credit Executives (SCCE)
PO Box 419057
St. Louis, MO 63141-1757
Phone: (314)991-3030
Fax: (314)991-3029
Sandra K. Weber, Assoc.Admin.

Recipient: Credit reporting industry managers. **Educational/Experience Requirements:** Must meet the following requirements: (1) Five years experience; (2) Service as association committee or task force member, chairperson, director, or officer; (3) Attendance at three credit-related meetings, programs, or conferences with educational focus; and (4) Contributions to community at large through involvement in educational, civic, political, charitable, religious, or any other activity. **Certification Requirements:** Successful completion of exam. Exam covers: Consumer credit counseling; Credit granting; Credit reporting; and Debt collections. **Renewal:** Every three years. Recertification based on leadership activities, professional development, contributions to the profession, and recognition within credit industry. There is no renewal fee. **Preparatory Materials:** *Comprehensive Credit Manual,* Fourth Edition (reference). **Examination Type:** Multiple-choice. **Fees:** $200. **Endorsed By:** International Credit Association.

▮ 88 ▮

Certified Financial Counseling Executive (CFCE)
Society of Certified Credit Executives (SCCE)
PO Box 419057
St. Louis, MO 63141-1757
Phone: (314)991-3030
Fax: (314)991-3029
Sandra K. Weber, Assoc.Admin.

Recipient: Consumer budgeting and credit counseling industry managers. **Educational/Experience Requirements:** Must meet the following requirements: (1) Five years experience; (2) Service as association committee or task force member, chairperson, director, or officer; (3) Attendance at three credit-related meetings, programs, or conferences with educational focus; and (4) Contributions to community at large through involvement in educational, civic, political, charitable, religious, or any other activity. **Certification Requirements:** Successful completion of exam. Exam covers: Consumer credit counseling; Credit granting; Credit reporting; and Debt collections. **Renewal:** Every three years. Recertification based on leadership activities, professional development, contributions to the profession, and recognition within credit industry. There is no renewal fee. **Preparatory Materials:** *Comprehensive Credit Manual,* Fourth Edition (reference). **Examination Type:** Multiple-choice. **Fees:** $200. **Endorsed By:** International Credit Association.

▮ 89 ▮

Certified Financial Management Executive (CFME)
National Association of Printers and Lithographers (NAPL)
780 Palisade Ave.
Teaneck, NJ 07666
Phone: (201)342-0700
Fax: (201)692-0286
Toll Free: (800)642-NAPL

Recipient: Printing management professionals. **Membership:** Not required. **Certification Requirements:** Successful completion of Financial Management course at NAPL Management Institute at Northwestern University. Course involves using integrated computer models and covers: Asset management; Financial measures of manufacturing and sales performance; Financial statements; Managing purchasing; Measuring performance by operating units; and Sources of profit. Course involves case studies, class participation, group study, and projects. **Examination Frequency:** Annual. **Examination Sites:** Course given at Northwestern University in Evanston, IL. **Fees:** $3200 (members); $4000 (nonmembers).

▮ 90 ▮

Certified Financial Planner (CFP)
Certified Financial Planner Board of Standards
1660 Lincoln St., Ste. 3050
Denver, CO 80264
Phone: (303)830-7543
Fax: (303)860-7388
Edythe McClatchy Pahl, Dir.

Recipient: Professionals who assist individuals and families in determining and reaching financial goals and objectives. **Number of Certified Individuals:** 28,000. **Educational/Experience Requirements:** Must meet the following requirements: (1) Bachelor's degree; (2) Successful completion of approved course work in personal financial planning; and (3) Three years experience. **Membership:** Not required. **Certification Requirements:** Successful completion of exam. **Renewal:** Every two years. Recertification based on accumulation of 30 hours of continuing education. Renewal fee is $75. **Examination Frequency:** semiannual. **Examination Sites:** Exam given at sites throughout the U.S. and internationally. **Examination Type:** Multiple-choice. **Pass/Fail Rate:** 50% pass exam the first time. **Waiting Period to Receive Scores:** Six weeks. **Re-examination:** Must wait six months to retake exam. **Endorsed By:** National Organization for Competency Assurance.

▮ 91 ▮

Certified Municipal Finance Administrator (CMFA)
Municipal Treasurers Association of the United States and Canada (MTA US&C)
1229 19th St., NW
Washington, DC 20036
Phone: (202)833-1017
Fax: (202)833-0375
Stacey Crane, Exec.Dir.

Recipient: Municipal treasurers, deputy or assistant principal officers with public treasury responsibilities, and public treasurers for government entities other than municipalities. **Membership:** Required. **Certification Requirements:** Accumulation of 100 total points in the following categories: (1) Education (maximum of 60 points), including college degrees and courses, educational programs, and other related certifications; and (2) Experience (maximum of 60 points), including work in local, county, state, or federal government, and business and association participation and office holding. **Renewal:** Every five years. Recertification based on accumulation of 50 points through continuing education and experience. Renewal fee is $50. **Fees:** $150.

▮ 92 ▮

Chartered Financial Consultant (CFC)
American College (AC)
270 S. Bryn Mawr Ave.
Bryn Mawr, PA 19010
Phone: (215)526-1490

Recipient: Financial planning professionals who advise in the areas of income tax planning, investments, and wealth accumulation. **Educational/Experience Requirements:** Three years experience. **Membership:** Not required. **Certification Requirements:** Successful completion of the following courses, including exams: (1) Financial Decision Making at Retirement; (2) Financial Planning Applications; (3) Fundamentals of Estate Planning; (4) Fundamentals of Financial Planning; (5) Income Taxation; (6) Individual Life and Health Insurance; (7) Investments; and (8) Wealth Accumulation Planning. Must also successfully complete two electives. Formal classes, study groups, and agency classes may be substituted. **Renewal:** Every two years. Recertification based on accumulation of 60 hours of continuing education. **Examination Type:** Multiple-choice. **Fees:** $3000. **Endorsed By:** American Society of CLU and ChFC.

93

Employee Benefit Certified Trust Professional (EBCTP)
Institute for Certified Bankers (ICB)
1120 Connecticut Ave., NW, Ste. 600
Washington, DC 20036
Phone: (202)663-5380
Fax: (202)663-7543
Toll Free: (800)338-0626

Recipient: Employee benefit trust bankers. **Educational/Experience Requirements:** Must meet one of the following requirements: (1) Bachelor's degree and five years experience, with last two years as officer in employee benefits trust department of bank or trust company; or (2) Eight years experience, with last two years as officer in employee benefits trust department of bank or trust company. Experience must be in employee benefits trust department of bank or trust company, or related experience in law firm, accounting firm, or employee benefits consulting firm. **Membership:** Not required. **Certification Requirements:** Successful completion of exam. Exam consists of the following sections: (1) Plan Type and Design, including: Basic documentation; Legal requirements; Plan management and types; Tax aspects; and Trust agreements; (2) Legal and Regulatory Issues, including: ERISA; Fiduciary liability and trust law; Responsibilities of trustee and plan administrator; and SEC and OCC requirements; (3) Operations and Accounting, including: Accounting functions; Cash statement/accruals/investment reports; Daily valuation; Depositories; Loans; Mutual funds; Participant recordkeeping; and UCC - wire transfers; and (4) Investments, covering investment fundamentals and vehicles, including their associated characteristics, objectives, and risks. **Renewal:** Every three years. Recertification based on accumulation of 30 hours of continuing education. **Endorsed By:** American Bankers Association.

94

Registered Financial Planner (RFP)
Registered Financial Planners Institute (RFPI)
2001 Cooper Foster Park Rd.
Amherst, OH 44001
Phone: (216)282-7176
A.J. Schreiber, Pres.

Recipient: Financial planners for individuals and businesses including insurance agents, attorneys, loan officers, real estate professionals, CPAs, bankers, stock brokers, and securities professionals. **Educational/Experience Requirements:** Two years experience. **Membership:** Required. **Certification Requirements:** Must meet one of the following requirements: (1) Successful completion of RFPI approved classroom or correspondence course. Courses not approved by RFPI may be substituted; or (2) Five years experience. **Renewal:** Every three years. Recertification based on accumulation of 15 hours of continuing education. **Preparatory Materials:** List of approved courses provided. Study programs, correspondence courses, and seminars available. **Fees:** $120.

General Managers and Top Executives

95

Accredited Airport Executive (A.A.E.)
American Association of Airport Executives (AAAE)
4212 King St.
Alexandria, VA 22303
Phone: (703)824-0504
Fax: (703)820-1395
Will James, Exec. Officer

Recipient: Executives of public use airports. **Educational/Experience Requirements:** Bachelor's degree and one year of experience. Additional years of experience can be substituted on a two-for-one basis for years of bachelor's degree. **Membership:** Required. **Certification Requirements:** Must successfully complete the following: (1) Management presentation on issue related to airport management; and (2) Written and oral exams. Candidates with eight years experience qualify for Experience Alternative Program and take different written exam. This exam covers: Dealing with the airport tenants; Dealing with environmental issues both on and off the airport; Fiscal administration of airport budgeting, accounting, financial control, and audit; Interacting with the airport's governing body; Long- and short-term financing of airport improvements; Negotiating airport leases and contracts; Operation and maintenance of public use airport; Representing the airport within the community on aviation matters; Selecting, supervising, and motivating employees; Short- and long-term airport planning process; and Working with local, state, and federal government officials on aviation matters. **Preparatory Materials:** Oral exam study guide available. **Examination Frequency:** Throughout the year. **Examination Sites:** Exam given at National Airport Conference, annual conference, or by arrangement with proctor. **Examination Type:** Essay (Experience Alternative Program exam); multiple-choice. **Waiting Period to Receive Scores:** Four-six weeks for management presentation; immediately for oral exam. **Re-examination:** May not retake exam in the Experience Alternative Program. There is a $75 fee to retake exam. **Fees:** $225.

96

Advanced Certified Fund Raising Executive (ACFRE)
National Society of Fund Raising Executives (NSFRE)
1101 King St., Ste. 700
Alexandria, VA 22314
Phone: (703)684-0410
Fax: (703)684-0540
Toll Free: (800)666-FUWD
Dennis Stefanacci ACFRE, Chair

Recipient: Fund raising professionals and consultants. **Educational/Experience Requirements:** Must meet the following requirements: (1) Hold Certified Fund Raising Executive (CFRE) designation (see separate entry) and successfully renew once; (2) Ten years experience; (3) Bachelor's degree; (4) Active participation in NSSFRE activities and with other fund-raising organizations; (5) Successfully complete of at least one senior-level management course and one senior-level leadership course; (6) Attendance at at least two national fundraising conferences, one of which must be sponsored by NSFRE; and (7) Attendance at or instruction of at least 24 educational contact hours at senior-level development seminars and/or courses. **Membership:** Not required. **Certification Requirements:** Must meet the following requirements: (1) Successful completion of written exam. Exam covers: Fund-raising; General development; Leadership skills; and Management; (2) Submission of portfolio of development materials and written synopsis of use and results, including pertinent planning document relevant to current position. Portfolio will be assessed on amount and kinds of funds raised; and (3) Successful completion of oral peer review by demonstrating competency in two areas, such as: Annual giving; Capital campaigns; Corporate and foundation solicitation; Direct mail; Gift planning; Not-for-profit management; and Special events. **Fees:** $1100.

`97`

Approved Certification Administrator (ACA)

National Certification Commission (NCC)
PO Box 15282
Chevy Chase, MD 20825
Phone: (301)588-1212
Fax: (301)588-1212
Richard C. Jaffeson AICP, Exec. Dir.

Recipient: Professionals who administer certification programs. **Number of Certified Individuals:** 40. **Educational/ Experience Requirements:** Must meet one of the following requirements: (1) Bachelor's degree and five years experience; (2) Master's degree and three years experience; or (3) Ten years experience. **Membership:** Not required. **Certification Requirements:** Submission of the following: (1) Description of certification program; (2) Ethics statement; and (3) Creative project. **Renewal:** Every year. Recertification based on documenting continued work in certification. Renewal fee is $20. **Preparatory Materials:** Certification guide available. **Waiting Period to Receive Scores:** Two weeks. **Fees:** $40.

`98`

Associate Certified Manager (ACM)

Institute of Certified Professional Managers (ICPM)
James Madison Univ.
Harrisonburg, VA 22807
Phone: (703)568-3247
Fax: (703)568-3587
Toll Free: (800)568-4120
Dr. Jackson E. Ramsey, Exec.Dir.

Recipient: Supervisors and managers. **Educational/Experience Requirements:** Must earn points in one of two areas through experience and management training. Candidates who meet requirements in both areas may be eligible for Certified Manager (CM) designation (see separate entry). **Certification Requirements:** Successful completion of the following exams: (1) Personal Skills, covering: Managerial personality; Personal organization; Professionalism; and Self-development; (2) Administrative Skills, covering: Administrative knowledge; Control process; Implementation of the plan; Planning objectives; and Scheduling; and (3) Interpersonal Skills, covering: Employer/employee relationships; Interpersonal relationships and group dynamics; Leadership; Motivation; and Relationships. **Renewal:** Every five years. Recertification based on accumulation of

50 hours of management education through academic coursework, in-house training, teaching management, and self-study. **Preparatory Materials:** Study guides and bibliography available. **Examination Type:** Multiple-choice. **Fees:** $230. **Endorsed By:** National Organization for Competency Assurance.

`99`

Associate in Management (AIM)

Insurance Institute of America (IIA)
720 Providence Rd.
PO Box 3016
Malvern, PA 19355-0716
Phone: (610)644-2100
Fax: (610)640-9576
Toll Free: (800)644-2101
Dr. Kenneth R. Dauscher CPCU, VP

Recipient: Upper- and middle-level insurance management professionals. **Educational/Experience Requirements:** none. **Membership:** Not required. **Certification Requirements:** Successful completion of the following courses, including exams: (1) Human Resource Management; (2) Management, covering basic management concepts and how they apply in insurance organizations; and (3) Organizational Behavior in Insurance. Courses can be taken through group- or independent-study. **Renewal:** none. **Examination Type:** Essay. **Endorsed By:** American Council on Education.

`100`

Associate Service Executive (ASE)

National Association of Service Managers (NASM)
1030 W. Higgins Rd., Ste. 109
Hoffman Estates, IL 60195
Phone: (708)310-9930
Fax: (708)310-9934
Caryn Andersen, Mng.Dir.

Recipient: Experienced managers and executives in the service industry. **Number of Certified Individuals:** 20. **Educational/ Experience Requirements:** Employment history as product support supervisor or manager and earn 36 points through education, experience, industry participation, and NASM membership. **Membership:** Not required. **Certification Requirements:** Successful completion of exam. Must earn Certified Service Executive designation (see separate entry) within seven years. **Renewal:** none. **Examination Frequency:** monthly. **Exami-**

nation Sites: Exams given at local NASM chapter meetings. **Examination Type:** Essay; multiple-choice. **Pass/Fail Rate:** 60-70% pass exam the first time. **Waiting Period to Receive Scores:** 30 days. **Re-examination:** Must wait one year to retake exam. **Fees:** $150.

`101`

Association Management Specialist (AMS)

Community Associations Institute (CAI)
1630 Duke St.
Alexandria, VA 22314
Phone: (703)548-8600
Fax: (703)684-1581
Brad T. Snyder, Coord.

Recipient: Community association managers. **Educational/Experience Requirements:** Two years experience in administrative, facilities, and financial management. **Membership:** Required. **Certification Requirements:** Successful completion of Essentials of Community Association Management course. **Renewal:** Every three years. Recertification based on accumulation of 18 hours of continuing education. **Fees:** $100.

`102`

Certified Administrator of Public Parking

Institutional and Municipal Parking Congress (IMPC)
701 Kenmore Ave., Ste. 200
PO Box 7167
Fredericksburg, VA 22404-7167
Phone: (703)371-7535
Fax: (703)371-8022
Colleen Williamson, Admin.

Recipient: Institutional and government parking managers. **Educational/ Experience Requirements:** Must accumulate points through experience, earning bachelor's degree, and successful completion of IMPC courses and seminars. Must successfully complete five-day IMPC course. **Membership:** Not required. **Certification Requirements:** Successful completion of exam. **Renewal:** Every three years. Recertification based on continuing education and association participation. **Examination Type:** Essay; multiple-choice; short answer. **Waiting Period to Receive Scores:** 30 days.

103

Certified Associate Contracts Manager (CACM)
National Contract Management Association (NCMA)
1912 Woodford Rd.
Vienna, VA 22182
Phone: (703)448-9231
Fax: (703)448-0939
Toll Free: (800)344-8096
James W. Goggins, Exec. VP

Recipient: Individuals concerned with administration, procurement, acquisition, negotiation, and management of government contracts and subcontracts. **Number of Certified Individuals:** 2440. **Educational/Experience Requirements:** Must accumulate seven total points through the following: (1) College Degrees: Associate's degree (two points); Bachelor's degree (four points); Master's/doctorate degree (six points); (2) Nondegree College Course Hours, including: 30-59 hours (one point); 60-89 hours (two points); 90-119 (three points); and More than 120 hours (four points); (3) Contracting Experience (one point per year); and (4) Acquisition Education and Training (one point per course). Each course must be equivalent to 24 or more contact hours. Shorter courses may be combined. Correspondence courses and in-house training may also be evaluated for meeting requirements. **Membership:** Not required. **Certification Requirements:** Successful completion of exam. Exam covers: Competition and acquisition planning; Contract management; Contracting methods and contract types; General contracting management; and Socioeconomic programs. **Renewal:** Every five years. Recertification based on continuing education. Lifetime certification available to CACMs over age of 60. **Preparatory Materials:** Study groups and test-preparation aids available. **Examination Type:** Multiple-choice. **Pass/Fail Rate:** 57 percent pass exam. **Fees:** $90 (members); $120 (nonmembers).

104

Certified Association Executive (CAE)
American Society of Association Executives (ASAE)
1575 Eye St., NW
Washington, DC 20005-1168
Phone: (202)626-2821
Fax: (202)289-4049
Shirley Nycum, Mgr.

Recipient: Association chief executive officers and senior executives. **Number of Certified Individuals:** 2200. **Educational/Experience Requirements:** Must earn points through education and professional activities. **Membership:** Not required. **Certification Requirements:** Successful completion of exam. Exam covers: Association planning, evaluation, and human resources; Association structure, financing, and parent/chapter relations; Credentials and code of ethics; Legislation, regulation, and government relations; Management information systems; Meetings and conventions; Membership, education, marketing, and public relations; and Research and statistics. **Renewal:** Every three years. Recertification based on accumulation of professional credits. Renewal fees are: $110 (members); $150 (nonmembers). **Preparatory Materials:** Study courses and books available. **Examination Type:** Essay; short answer. **Fees:** $385 (members); $480 (nonmembers).

105

Certified Automotive Fleet Manager (CAFM)
National Association of Fleet Administrators (NAFA)
100 Wood Ave., S., Third Fl.
Iselin, NJ 08830-2709
Phone: (908)494-8100
Fax: (908)494-6789
Kevin M. Graham, Dir.

Recipient: Managers of fleets of vehicles for corporations, utilities, and government agencies. **Number of Certified Individuals:** 130. **Educational/Experience Requirements:** Two years experience. **Membership:** Not required. **Certification Requirements:** Successful completion of exam and case study. Exam covers: Accounting and finance; Computerization; Insurance; Law; Management; Safety; Vehicle acquisition and marketing; and Vehicle technology and maintenance. **Renewal:** Every five years. Recertification based on professional activities. **Preparatory Materials:** Study guide, reference readings, videos, textbooks, seminars, and study groups available. **Examination Frequency:** semiannual. **Examination Sites:** Exam given at annual conference or by arrangement with proctor. **Examination Type:** Multiple-choice. **Waiting Period to Receive Scores:** One week. **Fees:** $245 (members); $525 (nonmembers).

106

Certified Business Planning Executive (CBPE)
National Association of Printers and Lithographers (NAPL)
780 Palisade Ave.
Teaneck, NJ 07666
Phone: (201)342-0700
Fax: (201)692-0286
Toll Free: (800)642-NAPL

Recipient: Printing management professionals. **Membership:** Not required. **Certification Requirements:** Successful completion of Business Strategic Planning course at NAPL Management Institute at Northwestern University. Course requires creating and executing business plan and covers: Budgets; Business communication; Financial statements; and Goal setting. Course involves case studies, class participation, group study, and projects. **Examination Frequency:** Annual. **Examination Sites:** Course given at Northwestern University in Evanston, IL. **Fees:** $3200 (members); $4000 (nonmembers).

107

Certified Confidentiality Officer (CCO)
Business Espionage Controls and Countermeasures Association (BECCA)
PO Box 55582
Seattle, WA 98155-0582
Phone: (206)364-4672
Fax: (206)367-3316
Will Johnson, Exec.Dir.

Recipient: Business managers and other professionals concerned with confidentiality issues. **Educational/Experience Requirements:** Must meet one of the following requirements: (1) Ten years experience; (2) Bachelor's degree and five years experience; (3) Master's degree and four years experience; or (4) Doctoral degree and three years experience. Experience in closely related field may be accepted for credit on year-for-year basis with approval of BECCA. **Membership:** Not required. **Certification Requirements:** Successful completion of five self-study courses. Courses are: (1) An Introduction to Business Espionage Controls and Countermeasures; (2) Eavesdropping, Technical Surveillance, and Technical Surveillance Countermeasures; (3) Computer Abuse, Controls, and Countermeasures; (4) Pretext Attacks, Controls, and Countermeasures; and (5) Undercover Attacks, Controls, and Countermeasures. Each course requires the completion of confidentiality survey. Courses can be completed through independent study or at training centers throughout the U.S. **Renewal:** Every year. Recertification based on either successfully completing a confidentiality survey, teaching a confidentiality course, writing an article in the field, or in some other way making a meaningful contribution to the profession. **Preparatory Materials:** Workbooks with study bibliographies provided with self-study courses. **Waiting Period to Receive Scores:** Two weeks. **Fees:** $655 (members); $725 (nonmembers).

`108`

Certified Credit Union Executive (CCUE)

Credit Union National Association (CUNA)
Human Resource Development Division
PO Box 431
Madison, WI 53701-0431
Phone: (608)231-4000
Toll Free: (800)358-5710
Ralph Swoboda, Pres.

Recipient: Credit union employees and volunteers. **Number of Certified Individuals:** 1161. **Educational/Experience Requirements:** Must meet the following requirements: (1) High school diploma or equivalent; and (2) Two years experience. **Certification Requirements:** Successful completion of ten-course training program in credit union management and operation. Required courses are: (1) Business Law, covering: Agencies; Business organization; Consumer protection; Contracts; Creditors rights and debtors' relief; Estates and trusts; Legal systems; Loan and financing transactions; Payments and transfer funds; Personal and real property; Real estate; and Torts and crimes; (2) Credit and Collections, covering: Business and government credit functions; Collection policies, practices, and systems; Control of credit operations; Nature and role of credit decisions; and Numerical scoring systems; (3) Economics and the Monetary System, covering: Basic macroeconomic concepts such as: Elasticity; Gross national product (GNP); Inflation; and Supply and demand; and Issues in money and banking such as: Money supply and its impact on prices and employment, monetary and fiscal policies, and the national debt and international trade; Money's functions; Operations of Federal Reserve System; and Types of financial institutions; (4) Financial Management 1, covering: Cash and investments; Common stock and convertible bonds; Creation of money;

Equity and capitalization; Financial services industry; Forecasting and budgeting; Futures and options; GAP analysis; Long-term debt; Pricing member services and break-even analysis; Supply and cost of credit; Risk and funds management policy; and Time value of money; (5) Introduction to Credit Unions, covering: Basic credit union organization and services; CUNA-affiliated organizations; and Growth of the credit union industry movement; (6) Management, covering: Authority; Communicating; Decision making; Delegating responsibility; Fundamentals of planning; Leadership; Managing conflict and change; Motivation; Organizational process; Problem solving; and Work environment; (7) Personnel Administration, covering: Benefits program; Job evaluation; Hiring employees; Labor relations; Management of personnel; Performance appraisal and training methods; Records management; Salary administration; Supervisory skills; and Systems and procedures; and (8) Risk Management and Insurance, covering: Important aspects of insurance; Property, financial, liability, employee, and member risk exposures; Risk and its identification, measurement, and control; Risk management function; Risk management programs; and Selection of insurance carriers. Must also successfully complete two of the following elective courses: (1) Credit Union Accounting, covering: Accounting for cash, loans, investments, liabilities, member shares, reserves, and undivided earnings; Accounting systems; Adjusting and closing entries; Consumer education; Estate planning; Fixed assets; Internal control procedures and reconciliations; Preparation of cash flow statements; Preparing financial statements; Recording transactions; and Worksheets; (2) Financial Counseling, covering: Consumer credit; Developing financial counseling program; Family resource management; Life insurance and annuities; Savings and investments; and Strategies for financial counseling and evaluation; (3) Financial Management II, covering: Auditing fee income production; CAMEL ratings; Consumer and real estate lending; Cost structure and break-even analysis; Fixed-asset and capital administration; Implementing pricing changes; Investment management; Liquidity management; Managing liabilities and obtaining funds; Pricing strategies; and SLY principle; (4) Marketing, covering: Buyer behavior; Channels of distribution and delivery systems; Developing marketing program; Forecasting and budgeting; Marketing concept; Packaging and branding decisions; Pricing strategy; Product planning; Promotion; Strategic marketing planning process; and Target marketing; (5)

CUNA Management School; and (6) League Management Institute. Candidates may take courses through self-study, group study, credit union league courses, or participating colleges. Each course has exam component. **Preparatory Materials:** Course syllabi, list of required texts, review guides, and study materials available. **Examination Frequency:** Throughout the year. **Examination Sites:** Exams given by arrangement with proctor. **Examination Type:** Multiple-choice. **Fees:** $1150. **Endorsed By:** American Council on Education.

`109`

Certified Fund Raising Executive (CFRE)

National Society of Fund Raising Executives (NSFRE)
1101 King St., Ste. 700
Alexandria, VA 22314
Phone: (703)684-0410
Fax: (703)684-0540
Toll Free: (800)666-FUWD
Dennis Stefanacci ACFRE, Chair

Recipient: Fund raising professionals and consultants. **Number of Certified Individuals:** 3600. **Educational/Experience Requirements:** Five years experience. **Membership:** Not required. **Certification Requirements:** Successful completion of exam. Exam covers: Ethics; Management; Planning; Proposals and solicitations; and Public relations and marketing. **Renewal:** Every three years. Recertification based on continuing education, experience, and professional service. **Examination Frequency:** 12-15 times per year. **Examination Sites:** Exam given at sites throughout North America. **Examination Type:** Multiple-choice. **Pass/Fail Rate:** 70% pass the exam. **Reexamination:** Must wait three months to retake exam. **Fees:** $275 (members); $375 (nonmembers).

`110`

Certified Graphics Arts Executive (CGAE)

National Association of Printers and Lithographers (NAPL)
780 Palisade Ave.
Teaneck, NJ 07666
Phone: (201)342-0700
Fax: (201)692-0286
Toll Free: (800)642-NAPL

Recipient: Printing management professionals. **Membership:** Not required. **Certification Requirements:** Hold three of the following designations: Certified

Business Planning Executive (CBPE); Certified Financial Management Executive (CFME); Certified Production Management Executive (CPME); and Certified Sales and Marketing Executive (CSME) (see separate entries). **Fees:** $9600 (members); 12,000 (nonmembers).

111

Certified Graphics Communications Manager (CGCM)

International Publishing
   Management Association (IPMA)
1205 W. College St.
Liberty, MO 64068-3733
Phone: (816)781-1111
Fax: (816)781-2790
E-mail: CompuServe 71674.1647
Larry E. Aaron CAE, Exec.Dir.

Recipient: In-house graphics arts and printing managers. **Number of Certified Individuals:** 300. **Educational/Experience Requirements:** Five years experience. **Membership:** Required. **Certification Requirements:** Successful completion of seven-part exam. Exam parts are: (1) Computer Skills, including: computer system hardware and software concepts and purchasing; (2) Financial Management, including: Accounting; Budgeting; Financial forecasting; Inventory; and Management reports; (3) General Management, including: Controls; Objectives; Organizations; Planning; and Principles; (4) Personnel Management, including: Current management styles and systems; Development; Employee relations; Hiring; Pay and benefits; and Personnel records; (5) Production Management, including: Engineering; Facilities; Handling and warehousing; Materials management; Organizational planning; Production control; Quality control; and Safety; (6) Skills Application, including: Coordinating production with financial and personnel management; Coordinating technical and computer skills; Computer technology; Decision-making; and General management; and (7) Technical Skills, covering variety of printing and processing techniques. **Renewal:** Every five years. Recertification based on accumulation of 15 professional credits through IPMA or other graphic arts association membership, attendance at IPMA annual conference or other seminars, and writing published articles or lecturing on in-house management. Lifetime certification available for CGCMs age 60 or older after initial renewal. **Preparatory Materials:** *Computers: The Plain English Guide, First Book of Personal Computing, In-Plant Printing Handbook, Photo Offset Fundamentals, Practical Printing Man-*

agement, and *Small Business Management* (references). **Examination Frequency:** Throughout the year. **Examination Sites:** Exam given at IPMA annual conference, regional conferences, and sites throughout the U.S. **Examination Type:** Essay; multiple-choice. **Pass/Fail Rate:** 48% pass exam the first time. **Waiting Period to Receive Scores:** Four weeks. **Re-examination:** There is no fee to retake exam. **Fees:** $225 (members); $450 (nonmembers).

112

Certified International Convention Manager (CICM)

International Institute of
   Convention Management
9200 Bayard Pl.
Fairfax, VA 22032
Phone: (703)978-6287
Fax: (703)978-5524
Dr. Andrea Sigler CICM, Pres.

Recipient: Meeting planners. **Number of Certified Individuals:** 820. **Membership:** Not required. **Certification Requirements:** Must meet the following requirements: (1) Successful completion of seven course self-study program; (2) Participation in at least two international meetings; and (3) Successful completion of written exam. Exam covers: Business and legal aspects; Food and beverage; Intercultural communication; Marketing meetings; On-site coordination; Program planning; Site selection; Thinking and problem solving; and Transportation. Candidates with seven years experience may qualify for certification. **Renewal:** Every three years. Recertification based on accumulation of 20 continuing education units (CEUs) through attendance at seminars, conferences, and roundtables. **Preparatory Materials:** Industry Immersion, providing opportunities to interact with planners and suppliers in the industry, available. Group study, seminars, readings, and checklists also available. **Examination Frequency:** Throughout the year (written); semiannual (oral). **Examination Sites:** Written exam given by correspondence. Oral exam given at annual meeting. **Examination Type:** Case studies; essay; problem-solving. **Waiting Period to Receive Scores:** One week. **Fees:** $1495 (U.S. candidates); $1995 (international candidates).

113

Certified Laundry/Linen Manager (CLLM)

National Association of Institutional
   Linen Management (NAILM)
2130 Lexington Rd., Ste. H
Richmond, KY 40475
Phone: (606)624-0177
Fax: (606)624-3580
Connie Parker, CEO

Recipient: Managers of laundries serving institutions such as hospitals, nursing homes, hotels, schools, and correctional facilities. **Number of Certified Individuals:** 197. **Educational/Experience Requirements:** High school diploma and meet one of the following experience requirements: (1) One year of experience as laundry/linen manager or director; (2) Two years experience as assistant or associate laundry/linen manager or director; or (3) Three years experience as laundry/linen supervisor. **Membership:** Not required. **Certification Requirements:** Successful completion of the following correspondence courses and exams. Courses are: (1) Accounting, covering: Budgeting; Capital equipment; and Laundry expenses and costs; (2) Chemistry, covering: Bacteriology; Equipment; Soil; and Washing mechanics; (3) Equipment, covering: Bid and purchase of laundry equipment; Energy; Hazard control; Maintenance; and Safety; (4) Infection Control, covering: AIDS; Basic control; Disinfectants and antiseptics; Infection control; and Organisms in healthcare; (5) Linen Management, covering: Distribution; Industry-specific purchasing; Inventory; Management subjects; and Review; (6) Management, covering: Basic management and human resources; Ethics; and Federal regulations; (7) Production, covering: Calculations; Schedules; and Time requirements; and (8) Textiles, covering: Specifications on fabric care, construction, fibers, and finishes; and Technical and industry information. **Renewal:** Every three years. Recertification based on accumulation of 45 hours of continuing education. **Examination Sites:** Exams given by arrangement with proctor. **Examination Type:** Multiple-choice; true or false. **Fees:** $318 (members); $530 (nonmembers).

114

Certified Manager (CM)
Institute of Certified Professional
    Managers (ICPM)
James Madison Univ.
Harrisonburg, VA 22807
Phone: (703)568-3247
Fax: (703)568-3587
Toll Free: (800)568-4120
Dr. Jackson E. Ramsey, Exec.Dir.

Recipient: Supervisors and managers. **Educational/Experience Requirements:** Must earn points in two areas through experience and management training. Candidates who meet requirements in only one area may be eligible for Associate Certified Manager (ACM) designation (see separate entry). **Certification Requirements:** Successful completion of the following exams: (1) Personal Skills, covering: Managerial personality; Personal organization; Professionalism; and Self-development; (2) Administrative Skills, covering: Administrative knowledge; Control process; Implementation of the plan; Planning objectives; and Scheduling; and (3) Interpersonal Skills, covering: Employer/employee relationships; Interpersonal relationships and group dynamics; Leadership; Motivation; and Relationships. **Renewal:** Every five years. Recertification based on accumulation of 50 hours of management education through academic coursework, in-house training, teaching management, and self-study. Renewal fee is $30. **Preparatory Materials:** Study guides and bibliography available. **Examination Type:** Multiple-choice. **Fees:** $230. **Endorsed By:** National Organization for Competency Assurance.

115

**Certified Office Automation
    Professional (COAP)**
Office Automation Society
    International (OASI)
5170 Meadow Wood Blvd.
Lyndhurst, OH 44124
Phone: (216)461-4803
Fax: (216)461-4803
E-mail: JBDYKE@aol.com
John Dykeman, Exec.Dir.

Recipient: Office automation professionals responsible for integrating and managing new technologies in office environment. **Number of Certified Individuals:** 1000. **Membership:** Not required. **Certification Requirements:** Must earn 110 points through education, experience, and professional contributions. **Renewal:** Every three years. Recertification

based on accumulation of 90 points through education, experience, and professional contributions. Renewal fee is $90. **Fees:** $135 (members); $185 (nonmembers).

116

**Certified Parking Facility Manager
    (CPFM)**
National Parking Association
    (NPA)
1112 16th St., Ste. 300
Washington, DC 20036
Phone: (202)296-4336
Fax: (202)331-8523
Toll Free: (800)647-PARK
Barbara O'Dell, Exec.Dir.

Recipient: Private and public parking facility supervisors and managers. **Educational/Experience Requirements:** One year of experience. **Membership:** Not required. **Certification Requirements:** Successful completion of exam. Exam covers: (1) Customer Relations, including: Damage claims; Security; and Service safety; (2) Employee Supervision, including: Dealing with skill deficiencies and behavior problems; and Training; and (3) Facility Operations, including: Cash handling; Cleaning; Equipment; and Maintenance. **Renewal:** Every five years. Recertification based on successful completion of exam. **Preparatory Materials:** Study guide available. **Examination Frequency:** quarterly. **Examination Sites:** Exam given at 20 sites throughout the U.S. **Examination Type:** Multiple-choice. **Waiting Period to Receive Scores:** Three-four weeks. **Fees:** $400 (members); $950 (nonmembers).

117

**Certified Production Management
    Executive (CPME)**
National Association of Printers
    and Lithographers (NAPL)
780 Palisade Ave.
Teaneck, NJ 07666
Phone: (201)342-0700
Fax: (201)692-0286
Toll Free: (800)642-NAPL

Recipient: Printing management professionals. **Membership:** Not required. **Certification Requirements:** Successful completion of Production Management course at NAPL Management Institute at Northwestern University. Course covers: Business communications; Capital equipment acquisition; Cost control; Economic impact studies; Efficient plant layouts; Forecasting; Human resource

management; Inventory and production planning; Profit and loss control; Quality assurance procedures; and Scheduling. Course involves case studies, class participation, group study, and projects. **Examination Frequency:** Annual. **Examination Sites:** Course given at Northwestern University in Evanston, IL. **Fees:** $3200 (members); $4000 (nonmembers).

118

**Certified Professional Contracts
    Manager (CPCM)**
National Contract Management
    Association (NCMA)
1912 Woodford Rd.
Vienna, VA 22182
Phone: (703)448-9231
Fax: (703)448-0939
Toll Free: (800)344-8096
James W. Googins, Exec. VP

Recipient: Individuals concerned with administration, procurement, acquisition, negotiation, and management of government contracts and subcontracts. **Number of Certified Individuals:** 4769. **Educational/Experience Requirements:** Must meet the following requirements: (1) Bachelor's degree; (2) Two years experience or Master's degree in procurement or acquisition management; and (3) Successful completion of courses in the following areas: Procurement (two courses); Law (one course); Finance (one course); and Business/procurement-related (four courses). Each course must be equivalent to 24 or more contact hours. Shorter courses may be combined. Correspondence courses, in-house training, teaching of procurement courses, and scholarly works published may also be evaluated for meeting requirement. **Membership:** Not required. **Certification Requirements:** Successful completion of exam. **Renewal:** Every five years. Recertification based on continuing education. Lifetime certification available to CPCMs over the age of 60. Renewal fees are: $60 (members); $80 (nonmembers). **Preparatory Materials:** Workshops, study groups, and workbooks available. **Examination Type:** Essay. **Pass/Fail Rate:** 55 percent pass the exam. **Fees:** $120 (members); $160 (nonmembers).

119

Certified Professional Fleet Manager (CPFM)
National Private Truck Council (NPTC)
66 Canal Center Plaza, Ste. 600
Alexandria, VA 22314
Phone: (703)683-1300
Fax: (703)683-1217

Recipient: Private truck fleet managers. **Educational/Experience Requirements:** Must meet point system requirements. **Certification Requirements:** Successful completion of exam. **Fees:** $150.

120

Certified Professional Services Manager (CPM)
Professional Services Management Institute (PSMI)
4726 Park Rd., Ste. A
Charlotte, NC 28209
Phone: (704)521-8890
Fax: (704)521-8873
Janice B. George, Exec.Adm.Asst.

Recipient: Management professionals in design and related professions. **Membership:** Required. **Certification Requirements:** Must meet point requirements in the following areas: (1) Education (minimum of ten points; maximum of 40 points), including: High school diploma (five points); Years of college or technical school (five points per year; maximum of three points); Bachelor's degree (15 points); Master's degree (ten points); Graduate degree (ten points); Continuing Education Units (CEUs) (two points); and Other certification or registration (five points each; maximum of ten points); (2) Experience (12 points per year; minimum of 30 points; maximum of 80 points); and (3) Service to the Professions (minimum of ten points; maximum of 30 points), including: Membership in professional association or societies (one point per membership per year; maximum of five points for each membership); Office holding in professional society (one-two points per office); and General service to the profession (two points). Certification available in General Management (100 points) or one of the following specialty designations (85 points): (1) Finance/Accounting, including: Accounting basics; Advanced accounting; Business plan preparation; Computer based finance/accounting systems; Financial planning and budgeting; Insurance and risk management; Staff leadership/supervision; and Tax planning; (2) Human Resources, including:

Basic/incentive compensation planning/management; Basic personnel management; Corporate communications; Performance review management/training; Personnel benefit program planning/management; Personnel/corporate policy manual development/management; Professional development program planning and training; Recruiting and interviewing; and Staff leadership/supervision; (3) Marketing Management, including: Client/contract negotiations; Market/client sector/firm services analysis; Marketing plan and strategy development; Marketing/sales staff management; Marketing/sales training of technical staff; Proposal preparation; Sales aids/brochure development; and Staff leadership/supervision; or (4) Operations, including: Branch office management; Library/records management; Multi-discipline/department management; Project planning/management/staffing; Secretarial/clinical/administrative management; Staff leadership/supervision; and Technical specialization functions, including Computer Aided Design/Drafting (CADD), Computer Aided Engineering (CAE), reprographics, and specifications. Points can also be earned through Practice Management, including: Contract administration; Multi-department/discipline management; Office administration; Organization design and development; Ownership transfer; Short- and long-range planning; and Staff leadership/supervision. Specialty designations require majority of qualifying education, experience, and service to the field in the specialty area. **Fees:** $75. **Endorsed By:** Professional Services Management Association.

121

Certified Research Administrator (CRA)
Research Administrators Certification Council (RACC)
c/o Professional Testing Corp.
1211 Avenue of the Americas, 15th Fl.
New York, NY 10036
Phone: (212)852-0404

Recipient: Professionals involved in research and sponsored programs administration for commercial ventures, government, independent research organizations, and universities. **Educational/Experience Requirements:** Must meet one of the following requirements: (1) Master's degree with concentration in research administration; (2) Bachelor's degree and three years experience; or (3) Eight years experience.

Certification Requirements: Successful completion of exam. Exam covers: Financial management; General management: Legal requirements and sponsor interface; and Project development and administration. **Renewal:** Every five years. **Examination Type:** Multiple-choice. **Pass/Fail Rate:** 80% pass exam. **Fees:** $225.

122

Certified Sales Executive (CSE)
Sales and Marketing Executives International (SMEI)
Statler Office Tower
Cleveland, OH 44115
Phone: (216)771-6650
Fax: (216)771-6652
Toll Free: (800)999-1414

Recipient: Sales executives. **Educational/Experience Requirements:** One year of experience as sales manager and earn 35 total points in the following categories: (1) Experience, including: Sales representative (two points per year; maximum of eight points); and Sales/marketing manager (five points per year; maximum of 25 points); (2) Education, including: High school (one point per year; maximum of four points); College (two points per year; maximum of eight points); Masters degree in marketing/business (two points per year; maximum of four points); and Doctorate in marketing/business (two points per year; maximum of six points); (3) Continuing Education, including: SMEI Graduate School of Sales Management and Marketing (eight points per year; maximum of 16 points); SMEI continuing education programs, conventions, or seminars (three points per event; maximum of 12 points); and Other sales/marketing education (three points per event; maximum of 12 points); and (4) Industry Association Participation, including: Membership (one point per year; maximum of two points); Committee membership (two points per year; maximum of four points); Director (four points per year; maximum of eight points); and Officer (six points per year; maximum of 12 points). **Membership:** Not required. **Certification Requirements:** Successful completion of exam. Exam covers: Compensation methods; Evaluation of sales management; Industrial selling; Legal aspects of sales management; Market analysis and forecasting; Performance evaluation or sales representatives; Pricing and pricing policies; Product development and customer service; Recruitment and selection of sales representatives; Sales organization; Sales training; Supervision, control, and motivation; Telemarketing and direct sales; and Wholesaler selling. **Renewal:** Every five years. Recertification based on successful completion of exam and accumulation of 50 points through: (1) Experience (three points per year; maximum of 15 points); (2) Association membership (three points per year; maximum of 15 points); and (3) Continuing education (five points per activity). Renewal fee is $100. **Preparatory Materials:** Study guide provided. **Examination Frequency:** Annual. **Examination Sites:** Exam given at sites throughout the U.S. and Canada. **Examination Type:** Multiple-choice. **Re-examination:** There is no waiting period to retake exam. Must successfully complete exam within two years. There is a $150 fee to retake exam. **Fees:** $500 (members); $600 (nonmembers).

123

Certified Service Executive (CSE)
National Association of Service
　Managers (NASM)
1030 W Higgins Rd., Ste. 109
Hoffman Estates, IL 60195
Phone: (708)310-9930
Fax: (708)310-9934
Caryn Andersen, Mng.Dir.

Recipient: Experienced managers and executives in the service industry. **Number of Certified Individuals:** 100. **Educational/Experience Requirements:** Hold Associate Service Executive designation (see separate entry) and earn 75 points through education, experience, industry participation, and NASM membership. **Certification Requirements:** Successful completion of exam. **Renewal:** Every three years. Recertification based on continuing education, experience, industry participation, and NASM membership. CSEs eligible for Lifetime Certified Service Executive (LCSE) designation (see separate entry) after six years. **Examination Frequency:** monthly. **Examination Sites:** Exam given at local NASM chapter meetings. **Examination Type:** Essay; multiple-choice. **Pass/Fail Rate:** 65% pass exam the first time. **Waiting Period to Receive Scores:** 30 days. **Re-examination:** Must wait one year to retake exam. **Fees:** $150.

124

Lifetime Certified Service Executive (LCSE)
National Association of Service
　Managers (NASM)
1030 W Higgins Rd., Ste. 109
Hoffman Estates, IL 60195
Phone: (708)310-9930
Fax: (708)310-9934
Caryn Andersen, Mng.Dir.

Recipient: Experienced managers and executives in the service industry. **Number of Certified Individuals:** 25. **Membership:** Not required. **Certification Requirements:** Hold and maintain Certified Service Executive designation (see separate entry) for six years and earn 36 points in the previous three years through education, experience, industry participation, and NASM membership. **Renewal:** none. **Fees:** $100.

125

Professional Community Association Manager (PCAM)
Community Associations Institute
　(CAI)
1630 Duke St.
Alexandria, VA 22314
Phone: (703)548-8600
Fax: (703)684-1581
Brad T. Snyder, Coord.

Recipient: Community association managers. **Educational/Experience Requirements:** Three years experience. **Membership:** Required. **Certification Requirements:** Successful completion of Professional Management Development Program and case study. Must also volunteer to assist local chapter, write or review articles for association publications, and work at national conferences. **Renewal:** Every three years. Recertification based on attendance at advanced course, CEO-MC Retreat, or HOA/POA conference. **Fees:** $175.

126

Project Management Professional (PMP)
Project Management Institute
　(PMI)
130 S. State Rd.
Upper Darby, PA 19082
Phone: (610)734-3330
Fax: (610)734-3266

Recipient: Project managers, divisional managers, functional managers, project staff, and administrative staff.

Educational/Experience Requirements: Must accumulate 95 total points in the following areas: (1) Education, including: Continuing education; High school and college degrees; and Professional certifications; (2) Experience, including years supervising, managing, and teaching in the field; and (3) Professional Service, including: Awards; Chapter activities; Industry leadership; Seminars and workshops attended; and Works published. **Membership:** Not required. **Certification Requirements:** Successful completion of exam. Exam based on Project Management Body of Knowledge (PMBOK), which consists of the following eight areas: (1) Project Scope Management, including: Conceptual, scope, and task definition; Scope change management; and Task performance; (2) Project Quality Management, including: Control charts; and Quality control, improvement, and planning; (3) Project Cost Management, including cost budgeting, control, and estimating; (4) Project Contract/Procurement Management, including: Acquisition; and Procurement administration and planning; (5) Project Time Management, including: Duration estimating; Network definition; and Schedule control, definition, and planning; (6) Project Risk Management, including: Risk assessment, control, and identification; and Solution development; (7) Project Human Resources Management, including: Role and responsibility definition; Staffing and organization; and Team building; and (8) Project Communications Management, including: Applications; and Communications environment, planning/process, and skills. **Renewal:** Every seven years. Recertification based on continuing education, experience, and professional activities. **Preparatory Materials:** *PMBOK Glossary* (reference). Handbook, publications, sample exam, and workshops available. **Examination Frequency:** quarterly - always spring, summer, fall, and winter. **Examination Sites:** Exam given at annual seminar/symposium and at sites throughout the U.S. and internationally. **Examination Type:** Multiple-choice. **Fees:** $175 (members); $265 (nonmembers).

127

Registered Laundry/Linen Director (RLLD)
National Association of Institutional
　Linen Management (NAILM)
2130 Lexington Rd., Ste. H
Richmond, KY 40475
Phone: (606)624-0177
Fax: (606)624-3580
Connie Parker, CEO

Recipient: Managers of laundries serving institutions such as hospitals, nursing homes, hotels, schools, and correctional facilities. **Number of Certified Individuals:** 508. **Educational/Experience Requirements:** High school diploma or equivalent. **Membership:** Not required. **Certification Requirements:** Successful completion of three-part program at American Laundry and Linen College, sponsored by NAILM at Eastern Kentucky University. Parts of program are: (1) One-week course, including: Dry cleaning; Infection control; Linen basics; Safety; Team dynamics; and Washroom chemistry; (2) Two-week course, covering: Communication; Equipment; Human resources and training management; Interpersonal relations; and Team dynamics; and (3) Two-week program, covering: Computers; Cost accounting; Human resources; Infection control; and Writing. Each course includes group project and final exam. **Renewal:** Every two years. Recertification based on accumulation of 45 hours of continuing education. **Pass/Fail Rate:** 95% pass each course. **Fees:** $4150 (members); $4595 (nonmembers).

Government Chief Executives and Legislators

128

Certified Public Official (CPO)
National Association of County Recorders, Election Officials, and Clerks (NACRC)
PO Box 1270
Colorado Springs, CO 80901-1270
Phone: (719)520-6216
Fax: (719)520-6212

Recipient: County recorders, clerks, register of deeds, records managers, court clerk/administrators, election officials, or individuals in similar positions. **Membership:** Not required. **Certification Requirements:** Successful completion of 96 credits, including 28 credits through participation in NACRC courses. Other credits may be earned through college or university courses, state association certification programs, and experience. Certification can be earned in one of the following areas: Court administration; Elections administration; Land records administration; and Records management. **Preparatory Materials:** *Certified Public Official Program Workbook* provided. Video tapes of courses also available. **Endorsed By:** National Association of Counties.

Health Services Managers

129

Certification in Central Service Management Concepts (CCSMC)
International Association of Healthcare Central Service Material Management (IAHCSMM)
214 W. Institute Pl., Ste. 307
Chicago, IL 60610
Phone: (312)440-0078
Fax: (312)440-9474
Toll Free: (800)962-8274

Recipient: Central service healthcare material management supervisors. **Educational/Experience Requirements:** Hold Certified Registered Central Service Technician (CRST) designation (see separate entry) and meet one of the following requirements: (1) Successful completion of Principles of Management and Supervision for Central Service Personnel correspondence course. Course covers: Communications; Current issues; Employee and group management; Supervisor's role in recruiting, evaluating, orienting, and retaining staff; and Work analysis and resource control; or (2) Successful completion of general supervisory management course with C or better. **Membership:** Required. **Certification Requirements:** Successful completion of exam. **Renewal:** Every year. **Preparatory Materials:** *Central Service Management Manual, Central Service Technical Manual,* Fourth Edition, and *Material Management and the Healthcare Industry* (references). **Examination Frequency:** By arrangement. **Examination Sites:** Exam given by arrangement with proctor. **Waiting Period to Receive Scores:** Four-six weeks. **Endorsed By:** National Organization for Competency Assurance.

130

Certified Emergency Manager (CEM)
National Coordinating Council on Emergency Management (NCCEM)
7297 Lee Hwy., Ste. N
Falls Church, VA 22042
Phone: (703)533-7672
Fax: (703)241-5603
Elizabeth B. Armstrong, Exec.Dir.

Recipient: Professionals in emergency management, disaster response, and civil defense working for government, industry, and volunteer organizations. **Number of Certified Individuals:** 344.

Educational/Experience Requirements: Must meet the following requirements: (1) Either three years experience or two years experience and bachelor's degree in emergency management; (2) Bachelor's degree or 45 college semester credits in approved areas; and (3) 100 classroom hours in both emergency management and general management. **Certification Requirements:** Successful completion of management essay covering one of the following areas: Local emergency management; Military disaster preparedness; or Private industry. **Renewal:** Every five years. Recertification based on successful completion of exam. **Fees:** $300. **Endorsed By:** Federal Emergency Management Agency; National Emergency Management Association.

131

Certified Health Education Specialist (CHES)
National Commission for Health Education Credentialing (NCHEC)
475 Riverside Dr., Ste. 470
New York, NY 10115
Phone: (212)870-2047
Fax: (212)870-3333

Recipient: Community organizers, health education teachers, health program managers, patient educators, and trainers who design, conduct, and evaluate activities that help improve health of people in businesses, colleges, communities, health care facilities, and schools. **Educational/Experience Requirements:** May qualify through either strictly academic training or combination of academic training, experience, and membership in health education associations. Academic route requires bachelor's degree or higher with either major in community health education, health education, public health education, or school health education, or 25 semester (37 quarter) hours in health education with specific preparation in the following seven areas: (1) Acting as resource person in health education; (2) Assessing individual and community needs for health education; (3) Communicating health and health education needs, concerns, and resources; (4) Coordinating provision of health education services; (5) Evaluating effectiveness of health education programs; (6) Implementing health education programs; and (7) Planning effective health education programs. Combined route requires the following: (1) Bachelor's degree or higher with 15 semester (22 quarter) hours with specific preparation in areas listed above; (2) Ten years experience; and (3) Five years membership in health education related association. **Certification Requirements:** Successful completion of exam. **Renewal:** Every five years. Recertification based on accumulation of 75 hours of continuing education. Renewal fee is $75. **Preparatory Materials:** *Framework for Competency-Based Health Education* (reference). **Examination Frequency:** Annual. **Examination Sites:** Exam given at sites throughout the U.S. **Fees:** $215.

`132`

Certified Health Unit Coordinator (CHUC)

National Association of Health Unit Coordinators (NAHUC)
1311 Brentwood Terrace
Eau Claire, WI 54703
Phone: (715)834-8286
Sandy Ayres, Dir.

Recipient: Individuals involved in non-clinical tasks in nursing unit or physician's office. **Number of Certified Individuals:** 11,000. **Educational/Experience Requirements:** None. **Membership:** Not required. **Certification Requirements:** Successful completion of exam. **Renewal:** Every three years. Recertification based on either successful completion of exam or accumulation of 36 continuing maintenance units (CMUs) through continuing education. Renewal fees are: $95 (exam); $65 (CMUs). **Examination Frequency:** Throughout the year. **Examination Sites:** Exam given at 130 sites throughout the U.S. **Examination Type:** Multiple-choice. **Pass/Fail Rate:** 65% pass exam the first time. **Waiting Period to Receive Scores:** Immediately. **Reexamination:** Must wait three days to retake exam.

`133`

Certified Healthcare Safety Professional, Associate Level (CHSP)

Board of Certified Healthcare Safety (BCHSP)
8009 Carita Ct.
Bethesda, MD 20817

Recipient: Persons working or consulting on medical activity and who are charged with responsibility for hazard control activities. **Certification Requirements:** High school diploma or equivalent, one year of experience, and successful completion of the following courses: (1) Fundamentals of Hospital Safety; (2) Life Safety Code; and (3) Joint Commission on the Accreditation of Healthcare Organizations Requirements. **Fees:** $60.

`134`

Certified Healthcare Safety Professional, Master Level (CHSP)

Board of Certified Healthcare Safety (BCHSP)
8009 Carita Ct.
Bethesda, MD 20817

Recipient: Persons working or consulting on medical activity and who are charged with responsibility for hazard control activities. **Educational/Experience Requirements:** Bachelor's degree and four years experience. An additional year of college may be substituted for one year of experience. Associate or bachelor's degree in safety and health or special achievement may substitute for one year of experience and master's degree for two years. Holding positions of leadership in professional organizations, papers delivered or published, and research may be substituted for one year of experience. Outstanding achievements or extensive experience in safety and health may be substituted for degree requirements with approval of BCHSP. Candidates with less education and/or experience may qualify for Certified Healthcare Safety Professional, Associate Level or Certified Healthcare Safety Professional, Senior Level designations (see separate entries). **Certification Requirements:** Successful completion of six-part exam. Parts of the exam are: (1) Program Management, covering: Efficient management and accident prevention; Line and staff responsibilities; and Management attitudes and motivation; (2) Laws, Regulations, and Standards, covering: Environmental Protection Agency; Joint Commission on Accreditation of Healthcare Organizations Accreditation Factors; National Fire Protection Association; Nuclear Regulatory Commission; and Occupational Safety and Health Administration; (3) Patient Safety, covering: Electrical; Evacuation plans and procedures; Food and sanitation; Radiation; and Slips, trips, and falls; (4) Emergency Management, covering: Essential services and utilities; External disaster; and Internal disaster: fire/bomb; (5) Employee Safety, covering: Anesthetics and infection control; Burns, cuts, and punctures; Chemical and biological exposures; Electrical; Fire prevention, protection, and emergency procedures; Isolation techniques; Lifting and body mechanics; Nursing exposures; and Procedures, dose, and shielding; and (6) Facilities, covering: Electrical safety; Fire protection - construction and extinguishing; Lab safety - flammables and ventilation; Maintenance; Security; and Waste management - storage and disposal. **Fees:** $150.

`135`

Certified Healthcare Safety Professional, Senior Level (CHSP)

Board of Certified Healthcare Safety (BCHSP)
8009 Carita Ct.
Bethesda, MD 20817

Recipient: Persons working or consulting on medical activity and who are charged with responsibility for hazard control activities. **Educational/Experience Requirements:** Must meet one of the following requirements: (1) Bachelor's degree and two years experience; (2) Associate's degree and four years experience; or (3) Eight years experience. Each year of college may be substituted for one year of experience. Candidates with less education and/or experience may qualify for Certified Healthcare Safety Professional, Associate Level designation (see separate entry). Candidates with more education and/or experience may qualify for Certified Healthcare Safety Professional, Master Level designation (see separate entry). **Certification Requirements:** Successful completion of six-part exam. Parts of the exam are: (1) Program Management, covering: Efficient management and accident prevention; Line and staff responsibilities; and Management attitudes and motivation; (2) Laws, Regulations, and Standards, covering: Environmental Protection Agency; Joint Commission on Accreditation of Healthcare Organizations Accreditation Factors; National Fire Protection Association; Nuclear Regulatory Commission; and Occupational Safety and Health Administration; (3) Patient Safety, covering: Electrical; Evacuation plans and procedures; Food and sanitation; Radiation; and Slips, trips, and falls; (4) Emergency Management, covering: Essential services and utilities; External disaster; and Internal disaster: fire/bomb; (5) Employee Safety, covering: Anesthetics and infection control; Burns, cuts, and punctures; Chemical and biological exposures; Electrical; Fire prevention, protection, and emergency procedures; Isolation techniques; Lifting and body mechanics; Nursing exposures; and Procedures, dose, and shielding; and (6) Facilities, covering: Electrical safety; Fire protection - construction and extinguishing; Lab safety - flammables and ventilation; Maintenance; Security; and Waste management - storage and disposal. **Fees:** $150.

136

Certified Managed Care Executives (CMCE)

American Managed Care and
Review Association (AMCRA)
1200 19th St., Ste. 200
Washington, DC 20036-2437
Phone: (202)728-0506
Fax: (202)728-0609

Recipient: Managed care executives and medical directors. **Certification Requirements:** Successful completion of Executive Leadership Program (ELP) or Executive Leadership Program for Medical Directors (ELP-MD). ELP program consists of following components: (1) Academic, including: Health policy; Human resources management; Managed care systems; Marketing and presentation skills; Negotiation skills and conflict management; Organizational development and team building; and Strategic planning and management; and (2) Experiential, including work with professional network and primary mentors who advise candidates. ELP-MD program consists of following components: (1) Academic, including instruction in Administrative and Medical Management. Administrative Management covers: Health policy; Human resources management; Managed care systems and industry trends; Negotiation skills; Organizational development and team building; and Strategic planning and management. Medical Management covers: Capitalization arrangements; Data collection and management systems; Internal and external performance measures; Provider credentialing/contracting; Quality assessment/utilization management; and Technology assessment. **Examination Frequency:** Annual. **Examination Sites:** Courses held at Annual conference and at Northwestern University, Evanston, IL.

137

Certified Manager of Patient Accounts (CMPA)

Healthcare Financial Management
Association (HFMA)
Two Westbrook Corporate Center,
Ste. 700
Westchester, IL 60154
Phone: (708)531-9600
Fax: (708)531-0032
Toll Free: (800)252-HFMA
Richard D. Warmanen FDPHM,
Exec.Dir.

Recipient: Senior healthcare finance professionals, Chief Financial Officers (CFOs), treasurers, administrators, and other individuals specializing in patient account management. **Educational/ Experience Requirements:** Must meet the following requirements: (1) Accumulation of four points for experience. Candidates earn two points for each full year providing financial management services or patient account management services in healthcare institution, related organization, or group or association of such institutions or organizations. Candidates earn one point for each full year providing financial management services or patient account management services to the following: Prepaid healthcare plan or similar insurance organization; Public accounting firm; Educational institution; Federal, state, or local government agency; Consulting firm; or Other organizations involved in healthcare financial management; (2) Two years membership in HFMA; (3) 60 semester hours of college work or HFMA seminar equivalent; and (4) Accumulation of 40 Founder's Points through association membership, educational programs, speeches and public presentations, published articles and other literary contributions, participation in forums or special interest groups, and leadership positions held. Twenty of these points must be earned through HFMA activities and the rest through activities with other organizations. All points must be earned either three years prior to or after successful completion of exam. **Membership:** Required. **Certification Requirements:** Successful completion of two-part exam. Exam covers: Accounting and financial management; Healthcare industry; Information systems and analysis; Management process; and Receivables management. **Renewal:** Every three years. Recertification based on accumulation of 40 Founder's Points. **Preparatory Materials:** Review courses, study guides, manuals, and computerized study guides available. Chapters offer coaching courses, sponsorship programs, and libraries. **Examination Frequency:** semiannual - always February and June. **Examination Sites:** Exam given at CFO Exchange, National Institute, and other sites throughout the U.S. **Examination Type:** Multiple-choice. **Waiting Period to Receive Scores:** 30 days. May retake exam twice. **Endorsed By:** National Organization for Competency Assurance.

138

Certified Medical Manager (CMM)

Professional Association of Health
Care Office Managers
(PAHCOM)
461 E. Ten Mile Rd.
Pensacola, FL 32534-9714
Phone: (904)474-9460
Fax: (904)474-6352
Toll Free: (800)451-9311
Richard Blanchette, Exec.Dir.

Recipient: Small group and solo-practice medical office managers. **Number of Certified Individuals:** 561. **Educational/ Experience Requirements:** Must meet the following requirements: (1) Three years experience; and (2) 12 college credit hours. Each additional year of experience may be substituted for one credit hour. **Membership:** Required. **Certification Requirements:** Successful completion of exam. Exam covers: Billing and collections; Coding analysis; Communication; Conflict management; Employment/ payroll; Financial planning; Health care law; Human resources; Managing and leading; Patient education/practice marketing; Practice accounting; Practice structure; Risk management; Systems analysis and design; Third party reimbursement; and Time management. **Renewal:** Every two years. Recertification based on accumulation of 24 continuing education units (CEUs). Renewal fee is $50. **Preparatory Materials:** *PAHCOM Management Guidebook* (text). Review course available. **Examination Frequency:** Annual. **Examination Sites:** Exam given at annual conference and at sites throughout the U.S. **Examination Type:** Essay; multiple-choice. **Pass/Fail Rate:** 93% pass exam the first time. **Waiting Period to Receive Scores:** Four weeks. **Re-examination:** Must wait one year to retake exam. **Fees:** $250.

139

Certified Medical Staff Coordinator (CMSC)

National Association Medical Staff
Services (NAMSS)
PO Box 23350
Knoxville, TN 37933-1350
Phone: (615)531-3571
Fax: (615)531-9939
Margaret Nicholson, Exec. Officer

Recipient: Medical staff service professionals. **Number of Certified Individuals:** 2100. **Educational/Experience Requirements:** Must meet one of the following requirements: (1) Three years experience and 60 college semester credits; or (2)

Associate's degree from accredited program. **Membership:** Not required. **Certification Requirements:** Successful completion of exam. Exam covers: Administration and management; Medical staff organization; and Medical terminology. **Renewal:** Every three years. Recertification based on accumulation of 30 hours of professional education. **Accredited By:** National Commission for Certifying Agencies. **Endorsed By:** National Organization for Competency Assurance.

❚140❚

Certified Member of the American College of Medical Practice Executives

American College of Medical
 Practice Executives (ACMPE)
104 Inverness Terrace, E.
Englewood, CO 80112-5306
Phone: (303)397-7869
Fax: (303)643-4427
Martha M. Huckaby, Coord.

Recipient: Group medical practice executives involved in ambulatory or other health care management. **Educational/Experience Requirements:** Two years experience or hold full-time faculty position, administrator position, or be student in related college or university program. **Membership:** Required. **Certification Requirements:** Successful completion of three-section exam and accumulation of 50 continuing education hours during each three year period following application. **Renewal:** Every three years. Recertification based on accumulation of 50 hours of continuing eduction. **Preparatory Materials:** Tutorial available. **Examination Frequency:** Annual. **Examination Sites:** Exam given at sites throughout the U.S. **Examination Type:** Essay. **Fees:** $306. **Endorsed By:** Center for Research in Ambulatory Health Care Administration; Medical Group Management Association.

❚141❚

Certified Nursing Home Administrator (CNHA)

American College of Health Care
 Administrators (ACHCA)
325 S. Patrick St.
Alexandria, VA 22314-3571
Phone: (703)549-5822
Fax: (703)739-7901

Recipient: Long-term health care professionals. **Educational/Experience Requirements:** Must meet the following requirements: (1) Two years experience; (2)

Two years licensure as nursing home administrator or as federally qualified nursing home administrator; (3) Bachelor's degree; and (4) 20 hours of continuing education per year for last two years. **Certification Requirements:** Successful completion of two-part exam. Part 1 consists of the following sections: (1) Financial Management, including: Accounting information and control systems; Accounts receivable management; Budgeting; Capital budget decision making; Computer services and systems; Financing capital expenditures; Inventory management and controls; Investment and property management; Legal and regulatory issues; Operating statements; Rate reimbursement negotiations and contracts; and Wage and salary scales and fringe benefits; (2) Laws, Regulations, and Governing Boards, including: Affirmative action/equal employment opportunity laws and regulations; Decision making process of governing body; Governing body's philosophy and goals; Governmental regulations and guidelines; Information needs of governing body; Legislative process; Licensure and certification; Long-term care survey process and procedures; Medicare and Medicaid; Methods for complying with government regulations and guidelines; OBRA, tax, and labor laws; Ombudsman function; Regulations affecting reimbursement, capital expenditure, ownership, disclosure, and reports; and Resident bill of rights; (3) Marketing and Public Relations, including: Advocacy with legislative and regulatory agencies; Assisting families of residents; Informing community about facility/profession; Interpreting and forecasting legislation and regulations; Marketing; Media, peer, and professional relations; Meeting with potential residents and their families; Relations with other health and social care providers; and Relations with relatives of residents and patients; (4) Patient/Resident Care, including: Admissions and discharge planning; Assessment and placement; Diets/nutrition, dental care, and pharmaceutical therapy; Legal and regulatory issues; Medicaid/Medicare conditions of participation; Medical and nursing care and planning; Physical, occupational, recreational, speech and hearing, and social/psychological therapy; Quality assurance; and Resident/patient activities, needs, and grievance procedures; (5) Personnel, including: Consultant/specialist agreements; Dealing with turnover, absenteeism, and tardiness; Ethnic and minority relations; Grievance procedures; Job descriptions; Legal and regulatory issues; Motivation and morale; Orientation programs; Personnel problems/conflicts; Recruiting, hiring, retaining, and dismissing

staff; Staff development and inservice training; Staffing levels; Union relations; and Work procedures; and (6) Physical Resource Management, including: Architectural/environmental design/building codes; Community emergency resources; Employee health, safety, and educational programs; Evaluation procedures for housekeeping and physical plant; Housekeeping procedures; Infection and pest control; Maintenance of building, grounds, and equipment; Materials management; Preventive maintenance; Procedures for designating responsibility in emergency planning; Safety, fire, and disaster procedures; and Training and practice resources and procedures for emergencies. Part 2 covers reasoning skills, ethics, and personality and motivational characteristics. **Renewal:** Every five years. Recertification based on accumulation of 20 hours of continuing education per year and one of the following: (1) Successful completion of exam (no fee); (2) Submission of executive portfolio demonstrating professional activities ($100 fee); (3) Successful completion of executive level course ($100 fee); or (4) Master's degree in management from program accredited by Accrediting Commission on Education for Health Services Administration (see separate entry) ($100 fee). **Preparatory Materials:** Self-study courses and workshops available. **Examination Sites:** Exam given by chapters at sites throughout the U.S. **Examination Type:** Multiple-choice. **Re-examination:** Must wait six months to retake exam.

❚142❚

Certified Professional Bureau Executive (CPBE)

Medical-Dental-Hospital Bureaus of
 America (MDHBA)
1101 17th St., NW., Ste. 1200
Washington, DC 20036
Phone: (202)296-9200
Fax: (202)296-0023

Recipient: Executives of bureaus providing physicians, dentists, hospitals, and clinics with management, bookkeeping, finance, tax, and collection services.

143

Certified Professional in Healthcare Quality (CPHQ)

Healthcare Quality Certification Board (HQCB)
JLM Associates
PO Box 1880
San Gabriel, CA 91778
Phone: (818)286-8074
Fax: (818)286-9415
Toll Free: (800)346-4722

Recipient: Professionals involved in healthcare quality management. **Educational/Experience Requirements:** Must meet the following requirements: (1) Either associate's degree, current licensure as registered nurse (R.N.) or licensed practical nurse (L.P.N.), or certification in medical records technology; and (2) Two years experience in last five years in healthcare quality management/utilization management/risk management activities. Equivalency for education or experience may be granted by HQCB. **Membership:** Not required. **Certification Requirements:** Successful completion of exam. Exam covers: (1) Program Management, including: Organization-wide monitoring and evaluation; Quality assessment; Quality improvement; Risk management; Standards and regulations; and Utilization management; (2) Data Management, including: Computer use; Data analysis and reporting; and Epidemiological methods; and (3) General Administrative, including: Departmental planning; and Human resources. **Renewal:** Every two years. Recertification based on accumulation of 30 hours of continuing education. Renewal fee is $95. **Preparatory Materials:** *Candidate Handbook,* including list of study materials and sample questions, provided. **Examination Frequency:** Annual - always fall. **Examination Sites:** Exam given at sites throughout the U.S. and internationally. **Examination Type:** Multiple-choice. **Waiting Period to Receive Scores:** Six weeks. **Fees:** $250 (members); $285 (nonmembers). **Accredited By:** National Commission for Certifying Agencies. **Endorsed By:** National Association of Healthcare Quality; National Organization for Competency Assurance.

144

Certified Registered Central Service Technician (CRCST)

International Association of Healthcare Central Service Material Management (IAHCSMM)
214 W. Institute Pl., Ste. 307
Chicago, IL 60610
Phone: (312)440-0078
Fax: (312)440-9474
Toll Free: (800)962-8274

Recipient: Central service healthcare material management technicians or infection control personnel. **Educational/Experience Requirements:** Successful completion of Central Service Technical Training correspondence training course. Course covers: Anatomy; Distribution; Equipment management issues; Infection control and sterilization; Instrumentation; Inventory; Microbiology; Packaging; Purchasing; Warehousing; and Working with solutions. **Membership:** Required. **Certification Requirements:** Successful completion of exam. Exam covers: Infection control; Inventory management; Microbiology; Packaging and storage; Safety; and Sterilization. **Renewal:** Every year. Recertification based on accumulation of 12 points. **Preparatory Materials:** *Central Service Management Manual, Central Service Technical Manual,* Fourth Edition, and *Material Management and the Healthcare Industry* (references). **Examination Frequency:** By arrangement. **Examination Sites:** Exam given by arrangement with proctor. **Waiting Period to Receive Scores:** Four-six weeks. **Endorsed By:** National Organization for Competency Assurance.

145

Certified Sterile Processing and Distribution Supervisor (CSPDS)

National Institute for the Certification of Healthcare Sterile Processing and Distribution Personnel (NICHSPDP)
PO Box 558
Annandale, NJ 08801

Recipient: Supervisors in healthcare sterile processing and distribution departments. **Educational/Experience Requirements:** Three years experience. **Certification Requirements:** Successful completion of exam. Exam covers: (1) Fiscal Management, including: Budget monitoring; and Development of department budgets; (2) Personnel Management, including: Arbitrating conflicts; Assisting in development of employee job descriptions; Developing worker time schedule; Evaluating employee performance; Hiring and labor laws; Identifying number of personnel required to carry out department functions; Productivity monitoring of staff; Providing education; and Training personnel; (3) Compliance with Standards, including: Identifying relevant guidelines, recommendations, regulations, and standards; and Maintaining safe working environment; (4) SPD/Central Service Responsibilities, including: Supervising operations of sterile processing; Supervising operations of sterile storage and distribution; and Supervising/performing procedures in decontamination department; (5) Anatomy, Microbiology, and Infection Control, including: Disease transmission and preventative measures; Relationship between human anatomy and physiology and work performed in sterile processing and distribution; and Relationship between microbiology and infection control and work performed in sterile processing and distribution; (6) Administration of Central Service Procedures, including: Assisting in development of policies and procedures; Ethics; Implementing policies and procedures; Monitoring compliance to policies and procedures; Performing facility recall procedures; Preparing emergencies; Responding to emergencies; and Testing procedures; and (7) Inventory and Distribution, including: Assisting in formulation of supply distribution system; Ensuring equipment, instruments, and medical devices are kept in working order; Implementing procedures for storage method; Maintaining sufficient quantities of supplies, equipment, instruments, and medical devices; Monitoring storage methods; Ordering supplies; Receiving supplies; and Using computers. **Renewal:** Every five years. Recertification based on accumulation of 150 points through: (1) Successful completion of exam (75 points); (2) Continuing education (one point per contact hour); (3) Successful completion of college courses in anatomy/physiology, chemistry, communication, computers, English, environmental control, finance, microbiology, psychology, and safety (seven points per credit hour); (4) Experience (five points per year of full-time employment; two-and-one-half points per year of part-time employment); (5) Holding committee chairperson position at local, state, or national level (five points per year); (6) Holding leadership position in local, state, or national chapter related to healthcare (five points per year); (7) Authoring of published papers related to healthcare (10 points per paper); and (8) Making presentations on related subjects (one point per hour; maximum of 10 points per year). **Preparatory Materials:**

Bulletin, including exam content outline, list of suggested references, and sample questions, provided. Study guide available. **Examination Frequency:** semiannual - always April and October. **Examination Sites:** Exam given at sites throughout the U.S. and internationally. **Waiting Period to Receive Scores:** Three-four weeks. **Re-examination:** There is a $130 fee to retake exam. **Fees:** $130. **Accredited By:** National Commission for Certifying Agencies. **Endorsed By:** American Society for Healthcare Central Service Personnel; National Organization for Competency Assurance.

▮ **146**

Distinguished Fellow of the American College of Physician Executives (FACPE)
American College of Physician Executives (ACPE)
4890 W. Kennedy Blvd., Ste. 200
Tampa, FL 33609-2575
Phone: (813)287-2000
Fax: (813)287-8993
Toll Free: (800)562-8088
Roger Schenke, Exec.V.Pres.

Recipient: Physician executives with management or administrative responsibilities in hospitals, group practices, managed care, government, universities, the military, and industry. **Certification Requirements:** Documentation of service to profession. **Endorsed By:** American Medical Association.

▮ **147**

Fellow of the American College of Health Care Administrators (FACHCA)
American College of Health Care Administrators (ACHCA)
325 S. Patrick St.
Alexandria, VA 22314-3571
Phone: (703)549-5822
Fax: (703)739-7901

Recipient: Long-term health care professionals. **Membership:** Required. **Certification Requirements:** Must meet the following requirements: (1) Four years of college or equivalent; (2) Two years experience in administration or related field; (3) 160 hours of continuing education or 11 college semester credits; (4) Involvement in professional activities, including association membership, professional meetings, publications, and teaching; and (5) Participation in civic activities or memberships.

▮ **148**

Fellow of the American College of Medical Practice Executives
American College of Medical Practice Executives (ACMPE)
104 Inverness Terrace, E.
Englewood, CO 80112-5306
Phone: (303)397-7869
Fax: (303)643-4427
Martha M. Huckaby, Coord.

Recipient: Group medical practice executives involved in ambulatory or other health care management. **Educational/Experience Requirements:** Hold Certified Member of the American College of Medical Practice Executives designation (see separate entry). **Membership:** Required. **Certification Requirements:** Submission of professional paper or three case studies and accumulation of 50 continuing education hours during each three year period following application. **Renewal:** Every three years. Recertification based on accumulation of 50 hours of continuing eduction. **Preparatory Materials:** Tutorial available. **Endorsed By:** Center for Research in Ambulatory Health Care Administration; Medical Group Management Association.

▮ **149**

Fellow of the American College of Physician Executives (FACPE)
American College of Physician Executives (ACPE)
4890 W. Kennedy Blvd., Ste. 200
Tampa, FL 33609-2575
Phone: (813)287-2000
Fax: (813)287-8993
Toll Free: (800)562-8088
Roger Schenke, Exec.V.Pres.

Recipient: Physician executives with management or administrative responsibilities in hospitals, group practices, managed care, government, universities, the military, and industry. **Certification Requirements:** Documentation of service to profession. **Endorsed By:** American Medical Association.

▮ **150**

Fellow, Healthcare Financial Management Association (FHFMA)
Healthcare Financial Management Association (HFMA)
Two Westbrook Corporate Center, Ste. 700
Westchester, IL 60154
Phone: (708)531-9600
Fax: (708)531-0032
Toll Free: (800)252-HFMA
Richard D. Warmanen FDPHM, Exec.Dir.

Recipient: Senior healthcare finance professionals, Chief Financial Officers (CFOs), treasurers, administrators, and other individuals who specialize in patient account management. **Educational/Experience Requirements:** Must meet the following requirements: (1) Hold Certified Professional in Healthcare Material Management (CPHM) designation for five years; (2) Be employed in field at supervisory level or above; (3) Submit resume, organizational chart, and written description of at least two recent on-the-job activities; and (4) Submit paper advancing theory/and or practice in the field or give an oral presentation or seminar lecture. **Membership:** Required. **Certification Requirements:** Successful completion of oral review. **Renewal:** Every three years. Recertification based on accumulation of 40 Founders Points. **Preparatory Materials:** Review course, study guides, manuals, and computerized study guides available. Chapters offer coaching courses, sponsorship programs, and libraries. **Examination Frequency:** semiannual - always February and June. **Examination Sites:** Exam given at CFO Exchange, National Institute, and other sites throughout the U.S. **Examination Type:** Multiple-choice. **Waiting Period to Receive Scores:** 30 days. **Endorsed By:** National Organization for Competency Assurance.

▮ **151**

Fellowship in Central Service (FCS)
International Association of Healthcare Central Service Material Management (IAHCSMM)
214 W. Institute Pl., Ste. 307
Chicago, IL 60610
Phone: (312)440-0078
Fax: (312)440-9474
Toll Free: (800)962-8274

Recipient: Central service healthcare material management professionals.

Certification Requirements: Must meet the following requirements: (1) Hold Certification in Central Service Management Concepts (CCSMC) designation (see separate entry); (2) Submit paper in the field; and (3) Successfully complete of interview. **Renewal:** Every five years. Recertification based on accumulation of six continuing education units (CEUs), at least three of which must be from IAH-CSMM sponsored programs and seminars. **Endorsed By:** National Organization for Competency Assurance.

Hotel Managers and Assistants

152

Certified Engineering Operations Executive (CEOE)
Educational Institute of the
American Hotel and Motel
Association
1407 S. Harrison Rd.
PO Box 1240
East Lansing, MI 48826-1240
Phone: (517)353-5500
Fax: (517)353-5527

Recipient: Hotel and motel engineering operations managers. **Educational/ Experience Requirements:** Must meet one of the following requirements: (1) Five years experience; (2) Building operations-related technical license such as: License from military; Stationary engineer, firefighter, or refrigeration license, any class; Steamfitter or plumber; or designation as journeyman, electrician, or carpenter; or (3) Successful completion of postsecondary technical certificate or diploma in area related to building operations, such as air conditioning, heating and refrigeration, construction, or plumbing. Must also meet one of the following requirements: (1) Two years experience and either two-year degree in engineering or hospitality from accredited institution or successful completion of the following Institute courses: Facilities Management; Hospitality Energy and Water Management; Hospitality Industry Engineering Systems; Hospitality Supervision; and Hotel/Motel Security Management; (2) Three years experience; or (3) Two years experience teaching hospitality management courses and two years experience in operations engineering management. All experience must be as director or chief of engineering/ property operations in lodging hospitality company. **Membership:** Not required. **Certification Requirements:** Successful completion of exam. **Preparatory Mate-**

rials: Study guide, including glossary of terms and sample questions, and review classes available. **Examination Frequency:** Throughout the year. **Examination Sites:** Exam given at sites throughout the U.S. or by arrangement with proctor. **Re-examination:** May retake exam once. **Fees:** $200 (members); $250 (nonmembers). **Endorsed By:** American Hotel and Motel Association.

153

Certified Food and Beverage Executive (CFBE)
Educational Institute of the
American Hotel and Motel
Association
1407 S. Harrison Rd.
PO Box 1240
East Lansing, MI 48826-1240
Phone: (517)353-5500
Fax: (517)353-5527

Recipient: Hotel or motel food and beverage managers and directors. **Educational/Experience Requirements:** Must meet one of the following requirements: (1) Two years experience and either two-year degree in hospitality from accredited institution or successful completion of the Food and Beverage Management Specialization program consisting of the following courses: Basic Sanitation; Food and Beverage Service; Food and Beverage Controls; Bar and Beverage Management, Hospitality Purchasing Management, or Food Production Principles; and Hospitality Supervision; (2) Three years experience; or (3) Two years experience teaching hospitality management courses and two years experience in food and beverage management. All experience must be as executive-level manager in hotel food and beverage administration, director/ general manager of restaurant food and beverage facility, or executive chef. **Membership:** Not required. **Certification Requirements:** Successful completion of exam. **Preparatory Materials:** Study guide, including glossary of terms and sample questions, and review classes available. **Examination Frequency:** Throughout the year. **Examination Sites:** Exam given at sites throughout the U.S. or by arrangement with proctor. **Re-examination:** May retake exam once. **Fees:** $275 (members); $325 (nonmembers). **Endorsed By:** American Hotel and Motel Association.

154

Certified Hospitality Educator (CHE)
Educational Institute of the
American Hotel and Motel
Association
1407 S. Harrison Rd.
PO Box 1240
East Lansing, MI 48826-1240
Phone: (517)353-5500
Fax: (517)353-5527
Toll Free: (800)344-3320

Recipient: Post-secondary hospitality educators. **Educational/Experience Requirements:** Must meet one of the following requirements: (1) Two years experience, with minimum of one year in managerial or supervisory position, and bachelor's degree or international diploma; or (2) Five years experience, with minimum of two years experience in managerial or supervisory position. **Certification Requirements:** Must meet the following requirements: (1) Successful completion of course and exam. Course covers: Adding variety to your presentations; Designing effective evaluation systems in less time; Enhancing students' learning with interactive teaching methods; Improving classroom communication; Keeping students' attention with support media; Making course planning more efficient; and Planning productive class sessions; and (2) Submission of demonstration videotape of classroom presentation. **Renewal:** Every five years. Recertification based on experience, continuing education, professional involvement, and educational service. Renewal fee is $100. **Preparatory Materials:** Self-study units and manual provided. **Examination Frequency:** Throughout the year. **Examination Sites:** Exam given at sites throughout the U.S. **Examination Type:** Multiple-choice. **Re-examination:** May retake exam once. Must successfully complete exam within six months. **Fees:** $550.

155

Certified Hospitality Housekeeping Executive (CHHE)
Educational Institute of the
American Hotel and Motel
Association
1407 S. Harrison Rd.
PO Box 1240
East Lansing, MI 48826-1240
Phone: (517)353-5500
Fax: (517)353-5527

Recipient: Hotel and motel hospitality housekeeping managers. **Educational/**

Experience Requirements: Must meet one of the following requirements: (1) Two years experience and either two-year degree in hospitality from accredited institution or successful completion of the following Institute courses: Housekeeping Management; Hotel/Motel Security Management; Front Office Procedures; Hospitality Supervision; and elective; (2) Three years experience; or (3) Two years experience teaching hospitality management courses and two years experience in housekeeping management position within lodging property or with hotel corporate system. All experience must be as executive housekeeper or director of housekeeping operations within lodging hospitality company. **Membership:** Not required. **Certification Requirements:** Successful completion of exam. **Preparatory Materials:** Study guide, including glossary of terms and sample questions, and review classes available. **Examination Frequency:** Throughout the year. **Examination Sites:** Exam given at sites throughout the U.S. or by arrangement with proctor. **Re-examination:** May retake exam once. **Fees:** $275 (members); $325 (nonmembers). **Endorsed By:** American Hotel and Motel Association.

`156`

Certified Hospitality Sales Professional (CHSP)
Educational Institute of the
American Hotel and Motel
Association
1407 S. Harrison Rd.
PO Box 1240
East Lansing, MI 48826-1240
Phone: (517)353-5500
Fax: (517)353-5527

Recipient: Hotel and motel sales professionals. **Educational/Experience Requirements:** Must meet one of the following requirements: (1) One year of experience and either two-year degree in hospitality or sales/marketing from accredited institution or successful completion of the Institute's Marketing and Sales Management Specialization program consisting of the following courses: Convention Management and Service; Hospitality Sales and Marketing; Hospitality Supervision; Marketing of Hospitality Services; and Tourism and the Hospitality Industry; or (2) Two years experience. At least 50 percent of experience must be in positions with hospitality sales responsibility. **Membership:** Not required. **Certification Requirements:** Successful completion of exam. **Renewal:** Every five years. Recertification based on successful completion of professional development activities. Renewal fee is $100.

Preparatory Materials: Study guide, including glossary of terms and sample questions, and review classes available. **Examination Frequency:** Throughout the year. **Examination Sites:** Exam given at sites throughout the U.S. or by arrangement with proctor. **Re-examination:** May retake exam once. **Fees:** $225 (members); $300 (nonmembers). **Endorsed By:** American Hotel and Motel Association.

`157`

Certified Hospitality Supervisor (CHS)
Educational Institute of the
American Hotel and Motel
Association
1407 S. Harrison Rd.
PO Box 1240
East Lansing, MI 48826-1240
Phone: (517)353-5500
Fax: (517)353-5527

Recipient: Supervisors working for hospitality organizations. **Educational/Experience Requirements:** Must meet one of the following educational requirements: (1) Successful completion of nine-workbook series, *Supervisory Skill Builders;* or (2) Successful completion of Institute's Hospitality Supervision or Hospitality Human Resources Management courses. Must also meet the following experience requirements: (1) Three months experience; or (2) Accumulation of three months experience within one year of successful completion of exam. Candidates with nine months experience as supervisor including such tasks as scheduling, training, interviewing, disciplining, inspecting, conducting performance reviews, making decisions and judgement calls while performing daily duties, and having input on hiring and firing decisions within a department meet educational and experience requirements. **Membership:** Not required. **Certification Requirements:** Successful completion of exam. **Examination Frequency:** Throughout the year. **Examination Sites:** Exam given at sites throughout the U.S. or by arrangement with proctor. **Re-examination:** May retake exam once. **Fees:** $75 (members); $85 (nonmembers). **Endorsed By:** American Hotel and Motel Association.

`158`

Certified Hotel Administrator (CHA)
Educational Institute of the
American Hotel and Motel
Association
1407 S. Harrison Rd.
PO Box 1240
East Lansing, MI 48826-1240
Phone: (517)353-5500
Fax: (517)353-5527

Recipient: Hotel and motel administrators. **Educational/Experience Requirements:** Must meet one of the following requirements: (1) Two years experience and either two-year degree in hospitality or successful completion of the Institute's Hospitality Management Diploma program; (2) Three years experience; or (3) Two years experience teaching hospitality management courses and three years experience. All experience must be in position employed by firm responsible for operation of three or more properties, in service as regional or corporate director of operations, or in position with ultimate corporate responsibility for rooms, marketing, accounting and finance, food and beverage, human resources, or engineering. **Membership:** Not required. **Certification Requirements:** Successful completion of exam. **Renewal:** Every five years. Recertification based on accumulation of 60 points through experience, continuing education, professional involvement, and educational service. Lifetime certification available to retired CHAs 65 or older who have completed 25 years in the industry and have renewed at least once. Renewal fee is $75. **Preparatory Materials:** Study guide, including glossary of terms and sample questions, and review classes available. **Examination Frequency:** Throughout the year. **Examination Sites:** Exam given at sites throughout the U.S. or by arrangement with proctor. **Re-examination:** May retake exam once. **Fees:** $375 (members); $425 (nonmembers). **Endorsed By:** American Hotel and Motel Association.

`159`

Certified Human Resources Executive (CHRE)
Educational Institute of the
American Hotel and Motel
Association
1407 S. Harrison Rd.
PO Box 1240
East Lansing, MI 48826-1240
Phone: (517)353-5500
Fax: (517)353-5527

Recipient: Hotel and motel hospitality

human resources managers. **Educational/Experience Requirements:** Must meet one of the following requirements: (1) Two years experience and either two-year degree in human resources management from accredited institution or successful completion of the following Institute courses: Hospitality Industry Training; Hospitality Law; Hospitality Supervision; Human Resources Management; and Organization and Administration; (2) Three years experience; or (3) Two years experience teaching hospitality management courses and two years experience in human resources management position within lodging property or with hotel corporate system. All experience must be as manager/director of personnel, training, or human resources in hospitality property or with hospitality corporate system. **Membership:** Not required. **Certification Requirements:** Successful completion of exam. **Preparatory Materials:** Study guide, including glossary of terms and sample questions, and review classes available. **Examination Frequency:** Throughout the year. **Examination Sites:** Exam given at sites throughout the U.S. or by arrangement with proctor. **Re-examination:** May retake exam once. **Fees:** $275 (members); $325 (nonmembers). **Endorsed By:** American Hotel and Motel Association.

160

Certified Rooms Division Executive (CRDE)

Educational Institute of the
    American Hotel and Motel
    Association
1407 S. Harrison Rd.
PO Box 1240
East Lansing, MI 48826-1240
Phone: (517)353-5500
Fax: (517)353-5527

Recipient: Hotel and motel rooms division managers. **Educational/Experience Requirements:** Must meet one of the following requirements: (1) Two years experience and either two-year degree in hospitality management from accredited institution or successful completion of the Rooms Division Management Specialization program consisting of the following Institute courses: Front Office Procedures; Hospitality Industry Computer Systems; Hospitality Supervision; Housekeeping Management; and Hospitality Law or Hotel/Motel Security Management; (2) Three years experience; or (3) Two years experience teaching hospitality management courses and two years experience in rooms division management. All experience must be as rooms division manager, resident manager,

front office manager, senior assistant manager, or executive assistant manager within lodging hospitality company. **Membership:** Not required. **Certification Requirements:** Successful completion of exam. **Preparatory Materials:** Study guide, including glossary of terms and sample questions, and review classes available. **Examination Frequency:** Throughout the year. **Examination Sites:** Exam given at sites throughout the U.S. or by arrangement with proctor. **Re-examination:** May retake exam once. **Fees:** $275 (members); $325 (nonmembers). **Endorsed By:** American Hotel and Motel Association.

161

Master Hotel Supplier (MHS)

Educational Institute of the
    American Hotel and Motel
    Association
1407 S. Harrison Rd.
PO Box 1240
East Lansing, MI 48826-1240
Phone: (517)353-5500
Fax: (517)353-5527

Recipient: Hotel and motel suppliers. **Educational/Experience Requirements:** Three years experience. **Membership:** Not required. **Certification Requirements:** Successful completion of exam. **Renewal:** Every five years. Recertification based on accumulation of 60 points through experience, continuing education, professional involvement, and educational service. Renewal fee is $75. **Preparatory Materials:** Study guide, including sample questions, and review classes available. **Examination Frequency:** Throughout the year. **Examination Sites:** Exam given at sites throughout the U.S. or by arrangement with proctor. **Re-examination:** May retake exam once. **Fees:** $350 (members); $425 (nonmembers). **Endorsed By:** American Hotel and Motel Association.

Inspectors and Compliance Officers, Except Construction

162

Certified Landfill Enforcement Officer

Solid Waste Association of North
    America (SWANA)
PO Box 7219
Silver Spring, MD 20907-7219
Phone: (301)585-2898
Fax: (301)589-7068

Recipient: Enforcement officers for public and private solid waste landfills. **Membership:** Not required. **Certification Requirements:** Successful completion of course and exam. Course consists of the following lessons: (1) Role of Sanitary Landfills in Integrated Municipal Solid Waste Management; (2) Basics of Site Selection, covering selection of site of landfill and how selection affects design and operation; (3) Complying with Design Requirements, covering: Field interpretation of design; Plan review, reading, and interpretation; and Principles of landfill design; (4) Waste Acceptance and Screening, covering maintenance of control of wastes being delivered to landfill including: Asbestos; Biomedical waste; Hazardous waste; Recyclables; Toxics; and Other materials; (5) Leachate, Landfill Gas, and Settlement, covering: Decomposition process within landfill; Generation of decomposition products; and How various wastes affect decomposition process; (6) Control Processes for LFG and Leachate, covering various control and treatment technologies for: Landfill gas and groundwater monitoring; Landfill gas and leachate; Remedial actions; and Storm water management; (7) Operational Techniques, covering: Cell construction; Equipment utilization; Optimum utilization of site capacity; Procedures to determine compliance with design and permit conditions; Staffing of operations; and Waste control; (8) Compliance and Inspection, covering techniques of inspection of landfills; (9) Closure and Long Term Care, covering requirements for closure and post-closure of a landfill, including: Final cover; Final cover maintenance; Groundwater and landfill gas monitoring; and Settlement control; (10) Landfill Economics, covering costs of equipment, staffing, operations, and compliance monitoring; (11) State/Provincial Regulations; (12) Landfill Safety, including controlling and preventing site access; and (13) Training On-Site Personnel, covering training needs for: Equipment operators; Gate attendants; and Spotters. Course also contains field exercise which covers: Evaluation of landfill against design and permit conditions of facility; Groundwater sampling; Landfill gas sampling; Operations; and Soils. **Renewal:** Every three years. Recertification based on either successful completion of course and exam or accumulation of 30 contact hours of training. Renewal fee is $100. **Examination Type:** Multiple-choice; problem solving; true or false. **Waiting Period to Receive Scores:** Two months. **Re-examination:** May retake exam twice. Must successfully complete exam within one year. **Fees:** $595 (members); $795 (nonmembers).

163

Certified Manager of Landfill Operations
Solid Waste Association of North America (SWANA)
PO Box 7219
Silver Spring, MD 20907-7219
Phone: (301)585-2898
Fax: (301)589-7068

Recipient: Foremen, mangers, and site supervisors of public and private solid waste landfills. **Membership:** Not required. **Certification Requirements:** Successful completion of course and exam. Course consists of the following lessons: (1) Role of Sanitary Landfills in Integrated Municipal Solid Waste Management; (2) Basics of Site Selection, covering selection of site of landfill and how selection affects design and operation; (3) Complying with Design Requirements, covering: Field interpretation of design; Plan review, reading, and interpretation; and Principles of landfill design; (4) Waste Acceptance and Screening, covering maintenance of control of wastes being delivered to landfill including: Asbestos; Biomedical waste; Hazardous waste; Recyclables; Toxics; and Other materials; (5) Leachate, Landfill Gas, and Settlement, covering: Decomposition process within landfill; Generation of decomposition products; and How various wastes affect decomposition process; (6) Control Processes for LFG and Leachate, covering various control and treatment technologies for: Landfill gas and groundwater monitoring; Landfill gas and leachate; Remedial actions; and Storm water management; (7) Operational Techniques, covering: Cell construction; Equipment utilization; Optimum utilization of site capacity; Procedures to determine compliance with design and permit conditions; Staffing of operations; and Waste control; (8) Compliance and Inspection, covering techniques of inspection of landfills; (9) Closure and Long Term Care, covering requirements for closure and post-closure of a landfill, including: Final cover; Final cover maintenance; Groundwater and landfill gas monitoring; and Settlement control; (10) Landfill Economics, covering costs of equipment, staffing, operations, and compliance monitoring; (11) State/Provincial Regulations; (12) Landfill Safety, including controlling and preventing site access; and (13) Training On-Site Personnel, covering training needs for: Equipment operators; Gate attendants; and Spotters. Course also contains field exercise which covers: Evaluation of landfill against design and permit conditions of facility; Groundwater sampling; Landfill gas sampling; Operations; and Soils. **Renewal:** Every three years. Recertification based on either successful completion of course and exam or accumulation of 30 contact hours of training. Renewal fee is $100. **Examination Type:** Multiple-choice; problem solving; true or false. **Waiting Period to Receive Scores:** Two months. **Re-examination:** May retake exam twice. Must successfully complete exam within one year. **Fees:** $595 (members); $795 (nonmembers).

164

Certified Playground Safety Inspector
National Park and Recreation Association (NPRA)
2775 S. Quincy St., Ste. 300
Arlington, VA 22206
Phone: (703)578-5549
Fax: (703)671-6772

Recipient: Playground safety inspectors. **Certification Requirements:** Successful completion of course and exam. Course covers: Developing risk management tools; Identifying hazards on playgrounds; Importance of comprehensive playground safety program from legal perspective; Protrusions and entanglement; and Test methods for entrapment. **Fees:** $270. **Endorsed By:** National Playground Safety Institute.

165

Certified Regulatory Compliance Manager (CRCM)
Institute for Certified Bankers (ICB)
1120 Connecticut Ave., NW, Ste. 600
Washington, DC 20036
Phone: (202)663-5380
Fax: (202)663-7543
Toll Free: (800)338-0626

Recipient: Financial institution regulatory compliance managers. **Educational/Experience Requirements:** Must meet the following requirements: (1) Three years experience; and (2) 80 hours of professional education in regulatory compliance field during previous five years. **Membership:** Not required. **Certification Requirements:** Successful completion of exam. Exam covers: (1) Compliance Enforcement, Penalties, and Administrative Practices, including: Administrative remedies; Civil and criminal penalties; Liability defenses; Litigation; Recordkeeping requirements; and Risk management; (2) Management Skills, including: Analyzing and determining potential impacts; and Developing and implementing action plans; and (3) Regulatory Requirements, including: Corporate or social responsibility; Deposits; Information reporting; Lending; and Safety and soundness of the institution. **Renewal:** Every three years. Recertification based on accumulation of 60 continuing education hours through conferences, seminars, and workshops, in-bank training programs, college courses, teaching, audio- and video-tape programs, authoring of books or articles, or writing exam questions. **Preparatory Materials:** Handbook, including study questions, suggested additional readings, and sample test, available. List of recommended study materials and programs provided. **Examination Frequency:** quarterly. **Examination Sites:** Exams given at sites throughout the U.S. **Examination Type:** Multiple-choice. **Waiting Period to Receive Scores:** Six-eight weeks. **Re-examination:** There is a $125 fee to retake exam. **Fees:** $550. **Endorsed By:** American Bankers Association.

Loan Officers and Counselors

166

Certification in Residential Mortgage Lending (CRML)
National Association of Mortgage Brokers (NAMB)
706 E. Bell Rd., Ste. 101
Phoenix, AZ 85022
Phone: (602)992-6181
Fax: (602)493-8711

Recipient: Entry-level loan processors, loan brokers, and loan officers. **Educational/Experience Requirements:** Must be NAMB member or be sponsored by NAMB member and successfully complete the following independent study courses: (1) Residential Mortgage Lending, covering: Differences between FHA/VA requirements and procedures and conventional loans; Mortgage (deed of trust) and note; Mortgage loan applications; Reducing risks incurred by delinquencies, foreclosures, and REO; Regulations governing residential lending procedures; Secondary mortgage markets; and Servicing and escrow procedures; (2) Residential Mortgage Lending Documentation, covering: Accurate and complete documentation; Collecting and preparing documents required to close loan on schedule; Making credit decisions; Preparing documents that meet regulatory requirements; Preparing loan files; and Underwriting documents; and (3) Residential Mortgage Lending Origination, covering: Federal laws and regulations; Follow-up procedures following loan interview; Loan interviews; Origination and the loan process; and Uniform Residential Loan Application (Form 1003). May successfully complete exam in place of course. **Membership:** Required. **Certification Requirements:** Successful completion of written and oral exams. **Renewal:** none. **Endorsed By:** Institute of Financial Education.

`167`

Certified Consumer Credit Counselor (NFCC)
National Foundation for Consumer Credit
8611 Second Ave., Ste. 100
Silver Spring, MD 20910
Phone: (301)589-5600
Fax: (301)495-5623

Recipient: Consumer credit counselors.

`168`

Certified Factoring Specialist
National Association of Entrepreneurs (NAE)
255 S. Orange Ave., Ste. 624
Orlando, FL 32802
Phone: (407)843-2032
Fax: (407)422-7425

Recipient: Factoring specialists. **Certification Requirements:** Successful completion of courses and exams offered by Open University's International Factoring Institute. **Endorsed By:** Association of Private Mortgage Professionals; National Association of Factoring Professionals.

`169`

Certified Lender-Business Banking (CLBB)
Institute for Certified Bankers (ICB)
1120 Connecticut Ave., NW, Ste. 600
Washington, DC 20036
Phone: (202)663-5380
Fax: (202)663-7543
Toll Free: (800)338-0626

Recipient: Small business bankers. **Educational/Experience Requirements:** Must meet one of the following requirements: (1) Ten years experience, seven of which must have been involved with making loans or managing business relationships; (2) Associate's degree, AIB Commercial Lending Diploma, and eight years experience, six of which must have been involved in making loans or managing relationships; or (3) Bachelor's degree or successful completion of Graduate Banking School and seven years experience, five of which must have been involved in making loans or managing relationships. **Membership:** Not required. **Certification Requirements:** Successful completion of exam. Exam covers: (1) Banking Products and Services, including: Credit and non-credit products for small business customers; Identifying prospects; and Sales and negotiations; (2) Legal, Regulatory, and Ethical Issues, covering Federal laws and regulation and the Uniform Commercial Code as it pertains to: Bankruptcy; Environmental liability; Ethics; Lender liability; and Small business banking; (3) Credit Analysis, including: Accounting; and Evaluation of repayment ability, using historic and projected financial information and non-financial factors such as management ability, ownership, and organization, and the impact of these factors on repayment ability from cash flow, collateral, and guarantees; (4) Loan Structuring, including: Collateral; Covenants and conditions; Credit enhancements: Documentation; Identifying and selecting loan structures; Pricing; and Repayment sources; and (5) Problem Assets, including: Bankruptcy; Collateral reevaluation; Development of workout strategies; Financial and non-financial early warning symptoms of problem assets; Loan classification; and Reserve allocations. **Renewal:** Every three years. Recertification based on accumulation of 45 hours of continuing education through conferences, seminars, and workshops, in-bank training programs, college courses, teaching, or audio- and video-tape programs. **Preparatory Materials:** Handbook, including study questions, suggested additional readings, and sample test, available. List of recommended study

materials and programs provided. **Fees:** $450. **Endorsed By:** American Bankers Association.

`170`

Certified Mortgage Banker (CMB)
Mortgage Bankers Association of America (MBA)
1125 15th St., NW
Washington, DC 20005
Phone: (202)861-6500
Warren Lasko, Exec. VP

Recipient: Mortgage bankers involved in commercial and residential real estate finance. **Educational/Experience Requirements:** Must meet the following requirements: (1) Employment with MBA member firm for one year; (2) Three years experience; and (3) Accumulation of 150 points through college and professional education, association participation, other real estate related certifications, and experience. **Membership:** Required. **Certification Requirements:** Successful completion of written and oral exams. Written exam contains mandatory Comprehensive Industry Issues section and eight specialty sections, four of which must be successfully completed. Specialty sections are: (1) Residential Loan Origination and Underwriting, including: Origination and processing procedures of FHA, VA, and conventional loans; and Residential appraising and Federal National Mortgage Association (FNMA) and Federal Home Loan Mortgage Corporation (FHLMC) underwriting; (2) Residential Loan Servicing and Administration, including: Escrow, collections, and loan accounting procedures; and FNMA, FHLMC, and Government National Mortgage Association (GNMA) servicing guidelines; (3) Residential Loan Marketing and Investor Relations, including: Analysis of company exposure; Marketing of residential loans and selling to FNMA and FHLMC, and through GNMA pools; Risk management and major hedging vehicles; Selling to private investors; and Use of futures and options markets; (4) Commercial Real Estate Lending, including: Analysis of loan submission; Financial statements; Financing techniques; and Lease analysis; (5) Commercial Real Estate Loan Servicing and Administration, including identifying, reviewing, and recommending corrective action for delinquency and workout situations; (6) Construction Lending and Administration, including: Monitoring and dealing with problem construction loans; and Special needs and risks of construction lending for commercial property; (7) Mortgage Instruments, Law, and Government Regulations, including: Bankruptcy; Foreclosure; Mortgage law; Title insurance; and Operation of Federal Reserve, Department of Housing and Urban Development, and other governmental agencies; and (8) Principles of Corporate Strategy for Residential Lenders, including: Corporate planning and growth analysis; Management responsibilities of real estate financial institution, real estate division, or mortgage banking company; and Managing portfolio of real estate loans. Oral exam covers current industry issues and practices. **Examination Frequency:** Throughout the year. **Examination Sites:** Exams given by arrangement with proctor. **Re-examination:** Must only retake sections failed. Must successfully complete exams within one year. **Fees:** $500.

`171`

Certified Mortgage Consultant (CMC)

National Association of Mortgage
　Brokers (NAMB)
706 E. Bell Rd., Ste. 101
Phoenix, AZ 85022
Phone: (602)992-6181
Fax: (602)493-8711

Recipient: Residential or commercial mortgage brokers and wholesale lending professionals. **Educational/Experience Requirements:** One year of membership in NAMB, five years experience, and successful completion of the following independent study courses: (1) Real Estate Law I, covering: Deeds of bargain and sales; Differences between fixtures, personal property, and real property; Easement agreements and property rights; Ownership rights and obligations of joint tenants, tenants in common, and tenants by the entirety; Recording of real estate ownership; Rights of land owners regarding water, minerals, air, and changing technological conditions; Rights and responsibilities of real estate brokers, sellers, and buyers; Transferring title to real estate; Valid quitclaim deeds; and Warranty deeds; (2) Real Estate Law II, covering: Basic elements of contract and mortgage law; Buyers' and sellers' rights in foreclosure; Condominiums; Differences between escrow closings and in-person real estate closings; Federal and state regulations; Mortgages and rights and responsibilities of buyer and seller; Provisions of valid real estate purchase contracts; and Types of fraud and remedies in real estate transactions; (3) Real Estate Principles, covering: Broker-client relationship; Cost, sales comparison, and income approaches to appraising real estate value; Factors influencing real estate value; Fundamentals of property rights

and ownership interests; Institutions and businesses operating in real estate finance field; Real estate contracts; Real estate financing; Real estate insurance; Reducing mortgage lending risks; and Taxes; and (4) Commercial Real Estate Finance or Real Estate Finance. Commercial Real Estate Finance covers: Accrual loans; Bow-tie loans; Debt service coverage ratio; Equity participations; Factors in making loan decision; Fully and partially amortized loans; Interest-reserve loans; Joint ventures; Loan submission packages; Loan-tovalue ratios; MAI appraisals; Personal financial statements; and Wraparound mortgages. Real Estate Finance covers: Analyzing property for loan risk; Federal government lending programs; Financing commercial property; Government requirements for settlement practices and procedures; Home builder commitments; How interest rates are determined for mortgage loans; Land leases; Legal requirements and techniques for home and corporate loans; Sale and leaseback; Sales of equity interests; Selling loans in secondary mortgage market; and Types of lenders operating in primary loan market. May successfully complete exam in lieu of course. **Membership:** Required. **Certification Requirements:** Successful completion of written and oral exams. **Renewal:** Every year. Recertification based on continuing education. **Endorsed By:** Institute of Financial Education.

`172`

Certified Mortgage Investor

National Association of
　Entrepreneurs (NAE)
255 S. Orange Ave., Ste. 624
Orlando, FL 32802
Phone: (407)843-2032
Fax: (407)422-7425

Recipient: Mortgage investors. **Certification Requirements:** Successful completion of courses and exams offered by Open University's National Mortgage Investor's Institute.

`173`

Certified Trust and Financial Advisor (CTFA)

Institute for Certified Bankers (ICB)
1120 Connecticut Ave., NW, Ste. 600
Washington, DC 20036
Phone: (202)663-5380
Fax: (202)663-7543
Toll Free: (800)338-0626
Susan Porter CTFA, Chair

Recipient: Professionals in the personal trust and financial advisement field. **Educational/Experience Requirements:** Must meet one of the following requirements: (1) Ten years experience; (2) Bachelor's degree and five years experience; or (3) Graduation from acceptable personal trust school program of at least 100 hours and three years experience. **Membership:** Not required. **Certification Requirements:** Successful completion of four exams. Exams are: (1) Fiduciary Law and Trust Activities, including: Nature and characteristics of the account relationship; Formal requisites of established account; Powers and duties of the fiduciary; Investment responsibilities; Receipts and payments; Liabilities from contracts, torts, and property ownership; Accounting and compensation; Alteration or termination of the trust; Liabilities of trustees; and Ethics; (2) Personal Finance, Insurance, and Estate Planning, including: Personal finance; Retirement planning; Insurance; Estate planning; and Ethics; (3) Tax Law, including: Income; Transfer tax; Tax planning at issue recognition level; and Ethics; and (4) Investment Management, including: Economics and markets; Portfolio management theories and concepts; Types of investments; Client objectives and constraints; Performance measurement; and Ethics. Certified Financial Analysts (CFAs) (see separate entry) are exempt from Investment Management exam. Certified Financial Planners (CFPs) (see separate entry) are exempt from Personal Finance exam. **Renewal:** Every three years. Recertification based on accumulation of 45 continuing education hours through conferences, seminars, and workshops, in-bank training programs, college courses, teaching, audio- and video-tape programs, or authoring of books or articles. **Preparatory Materials:** Study guides, including study questions, suggested additional readings, and sample test, available. List of recommended study materials and programs provided. **Examination Frequency:** semi-annual - always May and September. **Examination Sites:** Exam given at sites throughout the U.S. **Examination Type:** Multiple-choice. **Re-examination:** Must successfully complete all four exams within three years. There is a $125 fee to retake exam. **Fees:** $600. **Endorsed By:** American Bankers Association.

174

Senior Mortgage Consultant (SMC)
National Association of Mortgage Brokers (NAMB)
706 E. Bell Rd., Ste. 101
Phoenix, AZ 85022
Phone: (602)992-6181
Fax: (602)493-8711

Recipient: Mortgage brokers, mortgage solicitors, and loan officers. **Educational/Experience Requirements:** Must be member of NAMB and state association, have two years experience, and successfully complete the following independent study courses: (1) Real Estate Principles, covering: Broker-client relationship; Cost, sales comparison, and income approaches to appraising real estate value; Factors influencing real estate value; Fundamentals of property rights and ownership interests; Institutions and businesses operating in real estate finance field; Real estate contracts; Real estate financing; Real estate insurance; Reducing mortgage lending risks; and Taxes; (2) Residential Mortgage Lending Documentation, covering: Accurate and complete documentation; Collecting and preparing documents required to close loan on schedule; Making credit decisions; Preparing documents that meet regulatory requirements; Preparing loan files; and Underwriting documents; and (3) Residential Mortgage Lending Origination, covering: Federal laws and regulations; Follow-up procedures following loan interview; Loan interviews; Origination and the loan process; and Uniform Residential Loan Application (Form 1003). Must also successfully complete courses required by state association. May successfully complete exam in place of course. **Membership:** Required. **Certification Requirements:** Successful completion of written and oral exams. **Renewal:** Every year. Recertification based on continuing education. **Endorsed By:** Institute of Financial Education.

Management Analysts and Consultants

175

Certified Fellow in Production and Inventory Management (CFPIM)
APICS-The Educational Society for Resource Management
500 W. Annandale Rd.
Falls Church, VA 22046
Phone: (703)237-8344
Fax: (703)237-4316

Toll Free: (800)444-2742
Donald E. Ledwig, Exec.Dir.

Recipient: Specialists, team leaders, mid-level managers, and top decision makers involved in production and inventory control, including academicians, consultants, and government professionals. **Number of Certified Individuals:** 2100. **Educational/Experience Requirements:** Hold Certified in Production and Inventory Management (CPIM) designation (see separate entry). **Membership:** Not required. **Certification Requirements:** Must demonstrate contributions to the industry through presentations, published works, teaching, and participating in educational activities.

176

Certified in Integrated Resource Management (CIRM)
APICS-The Educational Society for Resource Management
500 W. Annandale Rd.
Falls Church, VA 22046
Phone: (703)237-8344
Fax: (703)237-1017
Toll Free: (800)444-2742
Donald E. Ledwig, Exec.Dir.

Recipient: Project managers, team leaders, aspiring managers, operations staff members, consultants, and individuals interested in horizontal management and cross-functional operations within a company. **Number of Certified Individuals:** 1000. **Membership:** Not required. **Certification Requirements:** Successful completion of self-study modules and exams. Modules are: (1) Customers and Products, including: Field service; Marketing and sales; and Product design and development; (2) Logistics, including: Distribution; Procurement; and Production and inventory control; (3) Manufacturing Processes, including: Industrial facilities management; Manufacturing (production); and Process design and development; (4) Support Functions, including: Finance and accounting; Human resources; Information systems; and Total quality management; and (5) Integrated Enterprise Management, including personal skills necessary for an individual to succeed in an integrated enterprise and building teamwork. First four exams must be successfully completed before fifth may be attempted. **Preparatory Materials:** *CIRM Study Guide: Exam Content Manual* (reference). Reprints of educational articles on curriculum study areas, correspondence study courses, reference books on specific study topics, materials for conducting in-house review courses, educational pro-

grams, and workshops available. **Examination Frequency:** Three times per year. **Examination Sites:** Exam given at APIC's conference and exhibition and at sites throughout the U.S. and internationally. **Examination Type:** Essay; multiple-choice; short answer. **Waiting Period to Receive Scores:** Immediately for exams 1-4; four-six weeks for fifth exam. **Re-examination:** Must wait 60 days to retake exams.

177

Certified Investment Management Analyst (CIMA)
Investment Management Consultants Association (IMCA)
9101 E. Kenyon Ave., Ste. 300
Denver, CO 80237
Phone: (303)770-3377
Fax: (303)770-1812

Recipient: Investment management consultants. **Educational/Experience Requirements:** Three years experience with at least 50 percent of time spent in consulting in areas such as: Manager selection and due diligence; Performance measurement and monitoring; Structuring asset allocation strategies; and Writing investment policies in conjunction with designing, structuring, and implementing investment portfolios. **Membership:** Not required. **Certification Requirements:** Successful completion of course and exam. Course covers: Asset allocation; Beta coefficients; Due diligence and manager selection; Duration and convexity; Ethics; Historical returns; International financial markets; Investment policy; Legal and regulatory environment; Measuring return on portfolio; Performance measurement and attribution; and Risk management. **Renewal:** Every two years. Recertification based on accumulation of 40 hours of continuing education through attending or teaching relevant courses, writing professional articles and books, and attending IMCA conferences. **Preparatory Materials:** Pre-study materials, textbooks, and course workbook provided. **Examination Frequency:** semi-annual - always January and August. **Examination Sites:** Course given at Wharton School, University of Pennsylvania, Philadelphia, PA. **Fees:** $3850 (members); $4350 (nonmembers).

178

Certified Management Consultant (CMC)
Institute of Management
Consultants (IMC)
521 Fifth Ave., 35th Fl.
New York, NY 10175-3598
Phone: (212)697-8262
Fax: (212)949-6571
Claire Rosenzweig CAE, Exec.Dir.

Recipient: Professionals engaged in management consulting publicly and for a fee, who devote a substantial majority of their working time to management consulting, or administrative or supervisory support of management consulting. **Educational/Experience Requirements:** Must have bachelor's degree and three years experience, or five years experience and 40 total points earned through: (1) Education, including college degrees, successful completion of CMC Candidate Study Program and workshops, or certification by another organization; (2) Experience, including work in business, internal and independent consulting, submission of written summaries of projects completed, and documentation of customer satisfaction; and (3) Professional Activities, including attendance at national and regional meetings, teaching courses, and authoring journal articles. **Membership:** no **Certification Requirements:** Successful completion of ethics exam and interview. **Preparatory Materials:** CMC Candidate Study Program available. **Examination Sites:** Exam given by arrangement with proctor. **Fees:** $250 (members); $600 (nonmembers). **Endorsed By:** Council of Consulting Organizations.

179

Certified in Production and Inventory Management (CPIM)
APICS-The Educational Society for
Resource Management
500 W. Annandale Rd.
Falls Church, VA 22046
Phone: (703)237-8344
Fax: (703)237-1017
Toll Free: (800)444-2742
Donald E. Ledwig, Exec.Dir.

Recipient: Specialists, team leaders, mid-level managers, and top decision-makers involved in production and inventory control including academicians, consultants, and government professionals. **Number of Certified Individuals:** 50,000. **Membership:** Not required. **Certification Requirements:** Successful completion of the following self-study modules, including exams. Modules are: (1) Inventory Management, including: Distribution inventory planning and control; Inventory systems; Objectives and policies; and Techniques; (2) Just-in-Time, including: Concepts; Human resource development and involvement; Total quality management; Techniques; Integration and application; and Implementation considerations unique to Just-in-Time/Total Quality Management; (3) Master Planning, including: Forecasting; Order servicing; Production planning; and Master scheduling; (4) Material and Capacity Requirements Planning, including: Concepts; MRP/CRP data management; Material requirements planning; and Capacity requirements planning; (5) Production Activity Control, including: Scope; Capacity control; Priority control; Lead-time management; Supplier interfaces; and Reporting and measurement; and (6) Systems and Technologies, including: Strategic drivers that affect production and inventory management; Choices affecting production and inventory management; Configuring and integrating production and inventory management; Managing the implementation of systems and technologies; and Measuring organizational performance. **Preparatory Materials:** *CPIM Study Guide: Exam Content Manual* (reference). Reprints of educational articles on curriculum study areas, correspondence study courses, reference books on specific study topics, materials for conducting in-house review courses, educational programs, independent study courses, and workshops available. **Examination Sites:** Exam given at APIC's conference and exhibition and at sites throughout the U.S. and internationally. **Waiting Period to Receive Scores:** Immediately. **Re-examination:** Must wait 60 days to retake exam.

180

Certified Professional Business Consultant (CPBC)
Institute of Certified Professional
Business Consultants (ICPBC)
330 S. Wells St., Ste. 1422
Chicago, IL 60606
Fax: (312)360-0388
Toll Free: (800)447-1684
Barbara Boden, Exec.Dir.

Recipient: Business consultants who are practicing management consultants for dentists, physicians, and other healthcare professionals. **Educational/Experience Requirements:** Three years experience. Membership in industry associations recommended. **Membership:** Not required. **Certification Requirements:** Successful completion of exam. **Renewal:** Every two years. Recertification based on accumulation of 70 hours of continuing education. **Preparatory Materials:** Review course and recommended reading list available. **Examination Frequency:** Annual. **Examination Sites:** Exam given at ICPBC annual meeting. **Examination Type:** Multiple-choice. **Re-examination:** Must wait one year to retake exam. **Fees:** $375.

181

Certified Professional Consultant (CPC)
American Consultants League
(ACL)
1290 Palm Ave.
Sarasota, FL 34236
Phone: (813)952-9290
Fax: (813)925-3670
Hubert Bermont, Dir.

Recipient: Consultants in various fields of expertise. **Number of Certified Individuals:** 743. **Educational/Experience Requirements:** none. **Membership:** Not required. **Certification Requirements:** Must successfully complete training course or the following correspondence classes and exams: (1) Getting Started, which deals with basic elements of running business; (2) How to Protect Yourself Legally, which covers legal aspects of operating consulting business; (3) How to Avoid Malpractice, which provides ten basic guidelines for reducing malpractice liability; (4) How to Do Your Own Bookkeeping and Accounting, which covers proper compliance with Internal Revenue Service regulations and the setting up and keeping of simplified records; (5) How to Set Fees for Client Acceptance, which covers fee-setting and bidding on government contracts and competitive bids; and (6) How to Position Your Consultancy as No. 1, which covers publicity and public relations. **Renewal:** none. **Preparatory Materials:** List of required textbooks provided. **Examination Type:** Multiple-choice; true or false. **Waiting Period to Receive Scores:** One week. **Re-examination:** There is no time limit to retake exam. There is no fee to retake exams. **Fees:** $900. **Endorsed By:** Consultants Institute.

Marketing, Advertising, and Public Relations Managers

182

Accredited Business Communicator (ABC)

International Association of
  Business Communicators (IABC)
One Hallidie Plaza, Ste. 600
San Francisco, CA 94102
Phone: (415)433-3400
Fax: (415)362-8762
David J. Paulus, Pres and CEO

Recipient: Organizational communicators and communications managers. **Educational/Experience Requirements:** Must meet one of the following requirements: (1) Nine years experience; (2) Eight years experience and one year of postsecondary education; (3) Seven years experience and Associate's degree or two years of post-secondary education; (4) Six years experience and three years of post-secondary education; or (5) Five years experience and bachelor's degree or higher. **Membership:** Not required. **Certification Requirements:** Must meet the following requirements: (1) Submission of portfolio of four communications projects that covers professional expertise and understanding of communications planning process; (2) Successful completion of written exam. Exam covers: Audience/constituent research; Budgeting and cost control; Communications ethics; General management skills; Goal setting; Investor/shareholder communication; Managing employee communication programs; Measuring effectiveness; Media contact; Oral presentation; Organizational culture and politics; Problem-solving and consulting skills; Project management; Time management; Writing communication plans and proposals for communication programs; and Written communication. Exam also provides choice of questions on specific areas of expertise, such as: Event and conference planning and support; Feedback systems; Magazine editing; Managing community relations programs; Managing publications; Marketing communication; Member communication; Newsletter editing; Speakers' bureaus; and Writing news and features, speeches, and for audiovisuals and video; and (3) Successful completion of oral exam. Exams must be taken within one year of approval of portfolio. **Renewal:** none. **Preparatory Materials:** *Inside Organizational Communications* (book). Bibliography of study materials and workshops available. **Examination Frequency:** Throughout the year. **Examination Sites:** Exams given at IABC conference, district conferences, and by arrangement with proctor. **Examination Type:** Essay. **Re-examination:** Exams must be retaken within one year. Fees to retake exams are: $75 (one section); $125 (two or more sections). **Fees:** $225 (members); $400 (nonmembers).

183

Certified Business Communicator (CBC)

Business Marketing Association (BMA)
150 N. Wacker Dr., Ste. 1760
Chicago, IL 60606
Phone: (312)409-4262
Rick Kean, Exec.Dir.

Recipient: Business-to-business marketing communications professionals. **Number of Certified Individuals:** 2100. **Educational/Experience Requirements:** Eight years experience. Up to four years of college may be substituted for experience. **Membership:** Not required. **Certification Requirements:** Successful completion of exam. Exam covers: Advertising measurement and accountability; Advertising and public relations agencies; Creative fundamentals, including copy, graphics, printing, and audiovisuals; Legal and ethical considerations; Marketing communications techniques, including catalogs, direct mail, exhibits, inquiry management, interactive media, public relations, presentations, sales literature, and telemarketing; Media selection and evaluation; and Planning and budgeting. **Renewal:** Every five years. Recertification based on either maintainence of continuous membership in BMA, successful completion of exam, or demonstration of continued professional education and development. **Examination Frequency:** Annual. **Examination Sites:** Exam given at sites throughout the U.S. **Examination Type:** Multiple-choice. **Pass/Fail Rate:** 81% pass exam. **Fees:** $200 (members); $325 (nonmembers).

184

Certified Hospitality Sales Executive (CHSE)

Hospitality Sales and Marketing
  Association International
  (HSMAI)
1300 L St., NW, Ste. 800
Washington, DC 20005
Phone: (202)789-0089
Fax: (202)789-1725
Cass Folis, Dir.

Recipient: Sales executives, managers, owners, and other hospitality industry executives. **Educational/Experience Requirements:** Must earn 250 points through academic and industry education and experience. **Membership:** Not required. **Certification Requirements:** Must meet the following requirements: (1) Submission of research paper; and (2) Successful completion of exam covering: Customer organizations; Direct-selling and advertising procedures; Internal sales and servicing; Legal concerns; Market trends; Marketing plan; Sales office management; Sales philosophy; Sales-marketing responsibilities; and Sales-operational relationships. **Examination Type:** Essay; multiple-choice. **Fees:** $75 (members); $150 (nonmembers).

185

Certified Incentive Professional (CIP)

Association of Incentive Marketing (AIM)
1620 Rte. 22 E.
Union, NJ 07083
Phone: (908)687-3090
Fax: (908)687-0977
Howard C. Henry, Exec.Dir.

Recipient: Sales and marketing executives of firms buying and selling merchandise for use as consumer premiums and trade incentives. **Number of Certified Individuals:** 100.

186

Certified Manager of Exhibits (CME)

International Exhibitors Association (IEA)
5501 Backlick Rd., Ste. 105
Springfield, VA 22151
Phone: (703)941-3725
Fax: (703)941-8275

Recipient: Managers of exhibits. **Membership:** Not required. **Certification Requirements:** Must submit description of contributions to the industry and earn 70 total points through: (1) Experience (two point per year; six points minimum; 20 points maximum); (2) Shows (two points per show; ten points minimum; 20 points maximum); (3) Education (one point per year; five points maximum); (4) IEA/Drexel University Exhibit Marketing Program (two points per course); (5) TS2 Participation (three points per year; 15 points maximum); (6) Exhibit Related Conferences (one point per conference; five points maximum); (7) Job Related Continuing Education Units (CEUs) (one-two points per CEU; six points minimum; 20 points maximum); (8) Public Speaking (one point per appearance; five points maximum); (9) Published Articles (one point per article; five points maximum); (10) Professional Affiliations (one point per year of membership; five points maximum); and (11) Service Within IEA (one-two points per year per positions held). Candidates may take written exam if required total points not earned. **Renewal:** Every five years. Recertification based on continued employment in the field. **Fees:** $150.

`187`

Certified Marketing Director (CMD)

International Council of Shopping
  Centers (ICSC)
665 Fifth Ave.
New York, NY 10022
Phone: (212)421-8181
Fax: (212)486-0849

Recipient: Shopping center promotion and marketing professionals. **Number of Certified Individuals:** 1300. **Educational/ Experience Requirements:** Must meet one of the following requirements: (1) Four years experience; (2) Three years experience and successful completion of ICSC Marketing I and II certificate programs; or (3) Three years experience and successful completion of college coursework equivalent to Marketing I Certificate program with C average or better and ICSC Marketing II certificate program. Experience must be as shopping center marketing director or equivalent, including marketing research, marketing plan implementation, record keeping, special events implementation, sales promotion, public and community relations, advertising, and media buying. Courses follow lecture and workshop formats. **Membership:** Not required. **Certification Requirements:** Successful completion of written and practical exams. Written exam consists of the following sections: (1) Administration; (2) Internal and External Communications; (3) The Marketing Plan; (4) Media Planning; (5) Product Development/Center Merchandising; and (6) Retailing/Store Merchandising. **Preparatory Materials:** Review course available. **Examination Frequency:** Annual. **Examination Sites:** Exam given at one U.S. site per year. **Examination Type:** Multiple-choice; problem-solving. **Re-examination:** Must retake only exam failed. May retake exams twice. Fees to retake each exam are: $295 (members); $595 (nonmembers). **Fees:** $495 (members); $990 (nonmembers).

`188`

Certified Marketing Executive (CME)

Sales and Marketing Executives
  International (SMEI)
Statler Office Tower
Cleveland, OH 44115
Phone: (216)771-6650
Fax: (216)771-6652
Toll Free: (800)999-1414

Recipient: Marketing executives. **Educational/Experience Requirements:** One year of experience as sales manager and earn 35 total points in the following categories: (1) Experience, including: Sales representative (two points per year; maximum of eight points); and Sales/ marketing manager (five points per year; maximum of 25 points); (2) Education, including: High school (one point per year; maximum of four points); College (two points per year; maximum of eight points); Masters degree in marketing/ business (two points per year; maximum of four points); and Doctorate in marketing/business (two points per year; maximum of six points); (3) Continuing Education, including: SMEI Graduate School of Sales Management and Marketing (eight points per year; maximum of 16 points); SMEI continuing education programs, conventions, or seminars (three points per event; maximum of 12 points); and Other sales/marketing education (three points per event; maximum of 12 points); and (4) Industry Association Participation, including: Membership (one point per year; maximum of two points); Committee membership (two points per year; maximum of four points); Director (four points per year; maximum of eight points); and Officer (six points per year; maximum of 12 points). **Membership:** Not required. **Certification Requirements:** Successful completion of exam. Exam covers: Brand product management; Buyer and consumer behavior; Developing marketing plan; Government regulation of business and trade law; Industrial marketing; International marketing; Marketing analysis; Marketing audit and cost analysis; Marketing concept; Marketing research; Marketing structure and systems; Organizing and staffing marketing function; Promotion of products, services, and ideas; and Scope of marketing management. **Renewal:** Every five years. Recertification based on successful completion of exam and accumulation of 50 points through: (1) Experience (three points per year; maximum of 15 points); (2) Association membership (three points per year; maximum of 15 points); and (3) Continuing education (five points per activity). Renewal fee is $100. **Preparatory**

Materials: Study guide provided. **Examination Frequency:** Annual. **Examination Sites:** Exam given at sites throughout the U.S. and Canada. **Examination Type:** Multiple-choice. **Re-examination:** There is no waiting period to retake exam. Must successfully complete exam within two years. There is a $150 fee to retake exam. **Fees:** $500 (members); $600 (nonmembers).

`189`

Certified Meeting Professional (CMP)

Convention Liaison Council (CLC)
1575 Eye St., NW, Ste. 1190
Washington, DC 20005
Phone: (202)626-2764
Fax: (202)408-9652

Recipient: Meeting industry professionals. **Educational/Experience Requirements:** Three years experience and 75 total points from the following categories: (1) Education and continuing education (15 points maximum); (2) Experience in meeting management (32 points maximum); (3) Management of meetings and people (32 points maximum); (4) Membership in professional organizations (five points maximum); and (5) Professional contributions in meeting management (20 points maximum). **Certification Requirements:** Successful completion of exam. **Renewal:** Every five years. Recertification based on continued involvement in the field and professional development. Renewal fee is $150. **Examination Frequency:** semiannual. **Examination Sites:** Exam given at sites throughout the U.S. and Canada. **Examination Type:** Multiple-choice. **Fees:** $365.

`190`

Certified Printing Service Specialist

Society for Service Professionals in
  Printing
433 Monroe Ave.
Alexandria, VA 22301-1693
Phone: (703)684-0044
Fax: (703)548-9137
Debbie Ayres, Dir.

Recipient: Individuals involved with customer service in printing industry. **Educational/Experience Requirements:** Two years experience. **Membership:** Not required. **Certification Requirements:** Successful completion of exam. Exam covers: Business practices; Communication skills; Materials; Printing process; Printing products; and Work flow organization skills. **Renewal:** none. **Preparatory Materials:** *Printing Service Specialist's Handbook and Reference Guide* (reference). **Examination Frequency:** semiannual - always May and November. **Examination Sites:** Exam given at sites throughout the U.S. **Fees:** $190 (members); $240 (nonmembers).

■ 191

Certified Radio Marketing Consultant (CRMC)
Radio Advertising Bureau (RAB)
1320 Greenway Dr., Ste. 500
Irving, TX 75038
Phone: (214)753-6750
Fax: (214)753-6727
Toll Free: (800)232-3131

Recipient: General or sales managers, account executives, and co/op/vendor, sales promotion, and research directors at stations, rep firms, networks, industry vendors and service providers, and state/local radio associations. **Number of Certified Individuals:** 4000. **Educational/Experience Requirements:** Three years experience as advertising/marketing professional, with at least two years in radio. Part-time, educational, and internship work is credited on two-for-one basis. Graduates of RAB's Radio Sales University receive six months' credit and graduates of RAB correspondence courses receive two years credit toward experience requirement. Account executives, salespeople, and other non-management personnel may qualify if approved by management. **Membership:** Not required. **Certification Requirements:** Must meet the following requirements: (1) Submission of case history dealing with a typical client's marketing needs; and (2) Successful completion of exam. Exam covers: Answering advertiser objections to radio; Competitive media; Marketing, advertising, and business principles; and Radio's dimensions. **Preparatory Materials:** Study materials provided. **Examination Sites:** Exam given at RAB's offices and meetings or by arrangement with proctor. **Fees:** $150 (members); $300 (nonmembers).

■ 192

Certified Rural Electric Communicator (CREC)
National Rural Electric Cooperative Association (NRECA)
1800 Massachusetts Ave., NW
Washington, DC 20036
Phone: (202)857-9513
Fax: (202)857-9791
Marina Johnson, Admin.

Recipient: Communications professionals working for rural electric distribution systems, generation and transmission systems, and statewide, regional, or other rural electric organizations. **Educational/Experience Requirements:** Must meet one of the following requirements: (1) Three years experience; or (2) Bachelor's degree and one year of experience. **Certification Requirements:** Must meet the following requirements: (1) Submission of portfolio consisting of work samples; and (2) Successful completion of exam. **Preparatory Materials:** Certification kit, including exam content outline and suggested study materials, provided. **Examination Frequency:** Annual. **Examination Sites:** Exam given at two sites in the U.S.

■ 193

Certified Sales and Marketing Executive (CSME)
National Association of Printers and Lithographers (NAPL)
780 Palisade Ave.
Teaneck, NJ 07666
Phone: (201)342-0700
Fax: (201)692-0286
Toll Free: (800)642-NAPL

Recipient: Printing management professionals. **Membership:** Not required. **Certification Requirements:** Successful completion of Sales and Marketing Management course at NAPL Management Institute at Northwestern University. Course involves developing sales and marketing plan and covers: Advertising; Budgeting; Buyer and end user characteristics; Customer service; Demand analysis; Forecasting; Market segmentation; Motivation; Pricing and competitive bidding strategies; Product positioning; Promotion; Short- and long-term strategic planning; and Situational/financial analysis. Course involves case studies, class participation, group study, and projects. **Examination Frequency:** Annual. **Examination Sites:** Course given at Northwestern University in Evanston, IL. **Fees:** $3200 (members); $4000 (nonmembers).

■ 194

Marketing Professional (MP)
Society for Marketing Professional Services (SMPS)
99 Canal Center Plaza, Ste. 250
Alexandria, VA 22314
Phone: (703)549-6117
Fax: (703)549-2498
Toll Free: (800)292-7677

Recipient: Marketing professionals providing services in built environment. **Educational/Experience Requirements:** One year of experience. **Membership:** Not required. **Certification Requirements:** Successful completion of exam. **Exam covers:** Business development; Management; Marketing intelligence; Planning; and Promotion. **Preparatory Materials:** *How to Market Professional Design Services* and *Marketing Architectural and Engineering Services* (references). List of suggested study references provided. **Examination Frequency:** semiannual. **Fees:** $185 (members); $500 (nonmembers).

■ 195

Senior Housing Marketing Specialist (SHMS)
National Council on Seniors' Housing (NCOSH)
1201 Fifteenth St., NW
Washington, DC 20005-2800
Toll Free: (800)368-5242

Recipient: Individuals specializing in marketing housing for seniors. **Membership:** Not required. **Certification Requirements:** Must accumulate 100 total points through: (1) Achievement and Awards; (2) Education; (3) Employment History; (4) Marketing Experience; and (5) SHMS Courses. Courses are: (1) Active and Older, including: Active retirement market segment; and Needs of older market living independently and benefiting from services such as dining, housekeeping, and transportation; and (2) Assisted Living, including: Advertising and promotional materials; Developing marketing plan and budget; Developing sales team; Maintenance marketing; and Overview of assisted housing. Fifty points must be earned through experience in senior's housing. **Endorsed By:** National Association of Home Builders.

■ 196

Senior Level Certified Marketing Director
International Council of Shopping Centers (ICSC)
665 Fifth Ave.
New York, NY 10022
Phone: (212)421-8181
Fax: (212)486-0849

Recipient: Shopping center promotion and marketing professionals. **Educational/Experience Requirements:** Hold Certified Marketing Director (CMD) designation (see separate entry).

Certification Requirements: Must earn ten credits every three years through attendance at ICSC conventions, conferences, and meetings, successful completion of industry or college courses, association participation and service, authoring publications, and earning awards and other professional certifications. **Fees:** $90.

Personnel, Training, and Labor Relations Specialists

◼ 197 ◼

Certification in Ergonomics
MTM Association for Standards
   and Research (MTM)
1411 Peterson Ave.
Park Ridge, IL 60068
Phone: (708)823-7120
Fax: (708)823-2319

Recipient: Persons interested in fields of industrial engineering, industrial psychology, and human engineering and Methods Time Measurement (MTM) and MTM-based work measurement systems. **Educational/Experience Requirements:** none. **Membership:** Not required. **Certification Requirements:** Successful completion of course covering ergonomic factors affecting productivity and employee well-being. **Examination Frequency:** Three times per year. **Examination Sites:** Course given in Park Ridge, IL. **Fees:** $750 (members); $900 (nonmembers).

◼ 198 ◼

Certification in MTM-1
MTM Association for Standards
   and Research (MTM)
1411 Peterson Ave.
Park Ridge, IL 60068
Phone: (708)823-7120
Fax: (708)823-2319

Recipient: Persons interested in fields of industrial engineering, industrial psychology, and human engineering and Methods Time Measurement (MTM) and MTM-based work measurement systems. **Membership:** Not required. **Certification Requirements:** Successful completion of course. Course covers: Laboratory problems illustrating principles and use; Practice in analysis of industrial and business operations; and Theory and principles of MTM-1. **Preparatory Materials:** Student manual avail-

able. **Examination Frequency:** Five times per year. **Examination Sites:** Course given in Los Angeles, CA, Park Ridge, IL, and northern New Jersey. **Fees:** $950 (members); $1140 (nonmembers).

◼ 199 ◼

Certification in MTM-1(120)
MTM Association for Standards
   and Research (MTM)
1411 Peterson Ave.
Park Ridge, IL 60068
Phone: (708)823-7120
Fax: (708)823-2319

Recipient: Persons interested in fields of industrial engineering, industrial psychology, and human engineering and Methods Time Measurement (MTM) and MTM-based work measurement systems. **Educational/Experience Requirements:** Hold Certification in MTM-1 designation (see separate entry). **Certification Requirements:** Successful completion of course. Course covers: Ergonomics; Generic, functional, and specific systems; Method improvement; System selection; and Standard data construction.

◼ 200 ◼

Certification in MTM-UAS-A
MTM Association for Standards
   and Research (MTM)
1411 Peterson Ave.
Park Ridge, IL 60068
Phone: (708)823-7120
Fax: (708)823-2319

Recipient: Persons interested in fields of industrial engineering, industrial psychology, and human engineering and Methods Time Measurement (MTM) and MTM-based work measurement systems. **Educational/Experience Requirements:** Hold Certification in MTM-1 or MTM-1(120) designations (see separate entries). **Membership:** Not required. **Certification Requirements:** Successful completion of course covering theory and application of MTM-UAS-A system. **Preparatory Materials:** Student manual available. **Examination Frequency:** Four times per year. **Examination Sites:** Course given in Park Ridge, IL, and northern New Jersey. **Fees:** $650 (members); $780 (nonmembers).

◼ 201 ◼

Certification in MTM-UAS-B
MTM Association for Standards
   and Research (MTM)
1411 Peterson Ave.
Park Ridge, IL 60068
Phone: (708)823-7120
Fax: (708)823-2319

Recipient: Persons interested in fields of industrial engineering, industrial psychology, and human engineering and Methods Time Measurement (MTM) and MTM-based work measurement systems. **Educational/Experience Requirements:** none. **Membership:** Not required. **Certification Requirements:** Successful completion of course. Course covers: Methods improvement; MTM-1 appreciation; and Work simplification training. **Preparatory Materials:** Student manual available. **Examination Frequency:** Four times per year. **Examination Sites:** Course given in Park Ridge, IL, and northern New Jersey. **Fees:** $850 (members); $1000 (nonmembers).

◼ 202 ◼

Certified Benefits Professional (CBP)
American Compensation
   Association (ACA)
14040 N. Northsight Blvd.
Scottsdale, AZ 85260
Phone: (602)951-9191
Fax: (602)483-8352
Jesse M. Smith Jr., Exec.Dir.

Recipient: Human resources professionals in employee benefits field. **Membership:** Not required. **Certification Requirements:** Successful completion of six required exams and three elective exams. Required exams are: (1) Fundamentals of Employee Benefit Programs; (2) Health Care and Insurance Plans; (3) Principles of Accounting and Finance; (4) Quantitative Methods; (5) Retirement Plans; and (6) Total Compensation Management. **Renewal:** Every three years. Recertification based on accumulation of 12 currency credits through continuing education. **Preparatory Materials:** Preparatory courses available.

203

Certified Compensation Professional (CCP)

American Compensation
Association (ACA)
14040 N. Northsight Blvd.
Scottsdale, AZ 85260
Phone: (602)951-9191
Fax: (602)483-8352
Jesse M. Smith Jr., Exec.Dir.

Recipient: Human resource professionals in compensation field. **Membership:** Not required. **Certification Requirements:** Successful completion of six required exams and three elective exams. Required exams are: (1) Job Analysis, Job Documentation, and Job Evaluation; (2) Pay Structures, Pay Rate Determination, and Program Administration; (3) Principles of Accounting and Finance; (4) Quantitative Methods; (5) Regulatory Environments for Compensation Programs; and (6) Total Compensation Management. **Renewal:** Every three years. Recertification based on accumulation of 12 currency credits through continuing education. **Preparatory Materials:** Preparatory courses available.

204

Certified Disability Examiner (CDE)

Commission on Disability Examiner
Certification (CDEC)
9101 Midlothian Tpke., Ste. 200
PO Box 35407
Richmond, VA 23235-0407
Phone: (804)378-8809
Virgil R. May III, Exec.Dir.

Recipient: Physicians, allied health care providers, vocational case managers and evaluators, and rehabilitation counselors and nurses involved in measuring impairment and disability. **Certification Requirements:** Successful completion of three required courses and exam. Courses cover: Functional/work capacity evaluation protocol; Medical correlates of disability; Psychological issues and assessment techniques; and Vocational evaluation techniques. Exam consists of written and practical components. Written component covers: Examination tools, instruments, and worksample selection and utilization; Legislation impacting evaluation protocol; Medical diagnoses/correlates to disability; Practice theory and concepts; Psychological disorders and correlates to disability; and Report writing and results/performance interpretation. Practical component requires evaluation of two patients nor-

mally seen in candidate's daily practice. Courses given at University of Florida Gainesville. **Renewal:** Recertification required. **Preparatory Materials:** *Handbook of Practice Standards and Guidelines* (reference). **Examination Frequency:** Throughout the year. **Examination Sites:** Exam given by correspondence. **Waiting Period to Receive Scores:** Six weeks. **Endorsed By:** National Association of Disability Evaluating Professionals.

205

Certified Employee Assistance Professional (CEAP)

Employee Assistance Professionals
Association (EAPA)
2101 Wilson Blvd., Ste. 500
Arlington, VA 22201
Phone: (703)522-6272
Fax: (703)522-4585
Phillip Flench CEAP, Dir.

Recipient: Individuals working in an employee assistance program. **Educational/Experience Requirements:** Three years experience and 3000 hours in employee assistance programming. **Membership:** Not required. **Certification Requirements:** Successful completion of exam. Exam covers: (1) Work Organizations, including: Employee and labor relations; Organizational dynamics; Policies towards troubled employees; and Types of organizations; (2) Human Resources, including: Benefits; Collective bargaining; Employment legislation and law; Health, safety, and wellness; and Performance appraisals; (3) Employee Assistance Program Management and Practice; (4) Employee Assistance Program Services; (5) Addictions and Chemical Dependencies, including: Concepts; Intervention; rehabilitation; and treatment; and (6) Personal and Psychological Problems, including: Assessments; Crisis management; Interviewing; and Referrals. **Renewal:** Every three years. Recertification based on accumulation of 60 hours of related training, with 36 of those hours in program management, practice, and services. **Examination Frequency:** semiannual - always May and December. **Examination Sites:** Exam given at 30 centers throughout the U.S. and Canada. **Examination Type:** Multiple-choice. **Waiting Period to Receive Scores:** Six weeks. **Re-examination:** There is no time limit to retake exam. **Fees:** $250 (members); $350 (nonmembers). **Endorsed By:** National Organization for Competency Assurance.

206

Certified Employee Benefits Specialist (CEBS)

International Foundation of
Employee Benefit Plans
18700 W Bluemound Rd.
PO Box 1270
Brookfield, WI 53008-1270
Phone: (414)786-6700
Fax: (414)786-2990
Daniel W. Graham, Senior Dir.

Recipient: Professionals involved in employee benefits. **Number of Certified Individuals:** 5500. **Educational/Experience Requirements:** Ten study courses required to successfully complete certification exams. Courses are: (1) Accounting and Finance; (2) Asset Management; (3) Contemporary Benefit Issues and Administration; (4) Contemporary Legal Environment of Employee Benefit Plans; (5) Employee Benefit Concepts and Medical Care Benefits; (6) Employee Benefit Plans and the Economy; (7) Human Resources and Compensation Management; (8) Life, Disability Income, and Other Welfare Benefit Plans; (9) Retirement Plans: Basic Features and Defined Contribution Approaches; and (10) Retirement Plans: Defined Benefit Approaches and Plan Administration. Courses are offered at over 100 institutions and may also be completed through independent- or group-study. **Membership:** Not required. **Certification Requirements:** Successful completion of ten exams. **Renewal:** none. **Examination Frequency:** semiannual - always January and June. **Examination Sites:** Exam given at 180 sites throughout the U.S. **Examination Type:** Multiple-choice. **Waiting Period to Receive Scores:** Four-six weeks. **Re-examination:** There is no time limit to retake exams. **Fees:** $1600.

207

Certified Employee Services and Recreation Administrator (CESRA)

National Employee Services and
Recreation Association (NESRA)
2211 York Rd., Ste. 207
Oak Brook, IL 60521-2371
Phone: (708)368-1280
Fax: (708)368-1286

Recipient: Employee services and recreation professionals. **Educational/Experience Requirements:** Five years experience, with at least three years as chief administrator of programs, and accumulation of 250 total points through education, professional achievements, and experience and activities. Education points may be earned through: (1) College degrees, including: Associate's (50 points maximum); Bachelor's (100 points maximum); Master's (150 points maximum); and Doctorate (200 points maximum); (2) Related Continuing Education (125 points maximum); (3) NESRA Annual Conferences and Exhibits Attended (50 points maximum); and (4) NESRA Regional Conferences Attended (50 points maximum). Professional achievement points may be earned through: (1) NESRA Local, Regional, or National Leadership Positions Held, including: Board member (20 points per year); Committee chairman (15 points per year); and Committee member (ten points per year); (2) Non-NESRA Leadership Positions Held, including: Officer (25 points per year; 75 points maximum); Board member (20 points per year; 60 points maximum); Committee chairman (15 points per year; 45 points maximum); and Committee member (ten points per year; 30 points maximum); (3) Providing Advisory Service to Local, State, or Federal Government Agencies (ten points per engagement; 30 points maximum); (4) Speaking Engagements (five points per engagement; 30 points maximum); (5) Contributions to Publications, including: Articles (ten points maximum); and Other contributions (ten points maximum); (6) Speaker or Instructor at NESRA National or Regional Conference or Guest Lecturer at College or University (ten points per hour; 100 points maximum); and (7) Consultation on Employment Services Management (ten points per organization; 50 points maximum). Experience and activities points may be earned through: (1) Experience in the Field, including: Administrator (ten points per year; 100 points maximum); and Staff (five points per year; 50 points maximum); (2) Experience Outside the Field (five points per year; 30 points maximum); (3) Leadership Positions in Community, Social Services, or Local and State Government Organizations (five points per experience; 30 points maximum); and (4) Honors Received Through NESRA Awards Program (ten points per award; 50 points maximum). **Certification Requirements:** Successful completion of exam. **Fees:** $50.

`208`

Certified Personnel Consultant (CPC)

National Association of Personnel Services (NAPS)
3133 Mt. Vernon Ave.
Alexandria, VA 22305
Phone: (703)684-0180
Fax: (703)684-0071

Recipient: Personnel in permanent placement and recruiting industry. **Educational/Experience Requirements:** Two years experience as owner, manager, partner, or consultant with private placement firm. **Membership:** Not required. **Certification Requirements:** Successful completion of exam. Exam covers: Business situations; Legal knowledge; Program rules; and Standards of business practices. **Renewal:** Every three years. Recertification based on accumulation of continuing education. **Preparatory Materials:** *Certified Personnel Consultants Legal Manual,* Second Edition (reference). **Examination Frequency:** semiannual - usually May and November. **Examination Sites:** Exam given at sites throughout the U.S. **Waiting Period to Receive Scores:** Eight weeks. **Re-examination:** Fees to retake exam are: $149 (members); $279 (nonmembers). **Fees:** $279 (members); $605 (nonmembers).

`209`

Certified Relocation Professional (CRP)

Employee Relocation Council (ERC)
1720 N St., NW
Washington, DC 20036
Phone: (202)857-0857
Fax: (202)467-4012
Karen Ann Reid, Dir.

Recipient: Employee relocation professionals involved in corporate human relations and relocation policy-making. **Educational/Experience Requirements:** Must meet one of the following requirements: (1) Attendance at ERC sponsored meeting in two of last three years; or (2) Employment at ERC member company with two years experience. **Membership:** Required. **Certification Requirements:** Successful completion of exam. Exam covers: Corporate relocation policies and issues; Family relocation issues; Relocation appraising; Relocation tax and legal issues; and Residential real estate (relocation related). **Renewal:** Every three years. Recertification based on accumulation of 30 continuing education credits. Renewal fee is $75. **Preparatory Materials:** Infor-

mation booklet, including list of study materials, provided. **Examination Frequency:** Annual. **Examination Sites:** Exam given at ERC conference and four other sites in the U.S. **Waiting Period to Receive Scores:** Six weeks. **Fees:** $150.

`210`

Certified Temporary-Staffing Specialist (CTS)

National Association of Personnel Services (NAPS)
3133 Mt. Vernon Ave.
Alexandria, VA 22305
Phone: (703)684-0180
Fax: (703)684-0071

Recipient: Staffing professionals in temporary service industry. **Educational/Experience Requirements:** Two years experience as owner, manager, partner, or consultant in temporary service business. **Membership:** Not required. **Certification Requirements:** Successful completion of exam. Exam covers: ADA; Contract issues; Discrimination law; Drug testing; Family leave; Joint employer; Program rules; and Standards of business practice. **Renewal:** Every three years. Recertification based on accumulation of continuing education. **Preparatory Materials:** *Temporary Help Services Operations: A Legal Manual* (reference). **Examination Frequency:** semiannual - usually May and November. **Examination Sites:** Exam given at sites throughout the U.S. **Waiting Period to Receive Scores:** Eight weeks. **Re-examination:** Fees to retake exam are: $149 (members); $279 (nonmembers). **Fees:** $279 (members); $605 (non-members).

`211`

Employment Services Specialist (ESS)

International Association of Personnel in Employment Security (IAPES)
1801 Louisville Rd.
Frankfort, KY 40601
Phone: (502)223-4459
Fax: (502)223-4127
Toll Free: (800)662-2255
Gail Butler-Hiley, Deputy Dir.

Recipient: Officials and others engaged in employment services through municipal, state, provincial, and federal government employment agencies and unemployment compensation agencies. **Educational/Experience Requirements:** Hold Employment and Training Generalist (ETG) designation (see separate entry). **Membership: Not required. **Certification Requirements:** Successful completion of exam. **Renewal:** none. **Preparatory Materials:** Study guide available. **Examination Frequency:** quarterly - always January, April, June, and October. **Examination Sites:** Exam given by local chapters and at annual convention. **Examination Type:** Multiple-choice. **Re-examination:** Fees to retake exam are: $15 (members); $25 (nonmembers). **Fees:** $50 (members); $75 (nonmembers).

▐212▐

Employment and Training Generalist (ETG)
International Association of Personnel in Employment Security (IAPES)
1801 Louisville Rd.
Frankfort, KY 40601
Phone: (502)223-4459
Fax: (502)223-4127
Toll Free: (800)662-2255
Gail Butler-Hiley, Deputy Dir.

Recipient: Officials and others engaged in job placement, unemployment compensation, and labor market information administration through municipal, state, provincial, and federal government employment agencies and unemployment compensation agencies. **Membership:** Not required. **Certification Requirements:** Successful completion of exam. **Renewal:** none. **Preparatory Materials:** Study guide available. **Examination Frequency:** quarterly - always January, April, June, and October. **Examination Sites:** Exam given by local chapters and at annual convention. **Examination Type:** Multiple-choice. **Re-examination:** Fees to retake exam are: $15 (members); $25 (nonmembers). **Fees:** $50 (members); $75 (nonmembers).

▐213▐

Employment and Training Master (ETM)
International Association of Personnel in Employment Security (IAPES)
1801 Louisville Rd.
Frankfort, KY 40601
Phone: (502)223-4459
Fax: (502)223-4127
Toll Free: (800)662-2255
Gail Butler-Hiley, Deputy Dir.

Recipient: Officials and others involved with unemployment insurance through municipal, state, provincial, and federal government employment agencies and

unemployment compensation agencies. **Membership:** Not required. **Certification Requirements:** Successful completion of requirements for following designations: Employment and Training Generalist (ETS); Employment Services Specialist (ESS); Unemployment Insurance Specialist (UIS); Labor Market Information Specialist (LMIS); and Job Training Specialist (JTS) (see separate entries). **Renewal:** none. **Fees:** $250 (members); $375 (nonmembers).

▐214▐

Job Training Specialist (JTS)
International Association of Personnel in Employment Security (IAPES)
1801 Louisville Rd.
Frankfort, KY 40601
Phone: (502)223-4459
Fax: (502)223-4127
Toll Free: (800)662-2255
Gail Butler-Hiley, Deputy Dir.

Recipient: Officials and others engaged in job training through municipal, state, provincial, and federal government employment agencies and unemployment compensation agencies. **Educational/ Experience Requirements:** Hold Employment and Training Generalist (ETG) designation (see separate entry). **Membership:** Not required. **Certification Requirements:** Successful completion of exam. **Renewal:** none. **Preparatory Materials:** Study guide available. **Examination Frequency:** quarterly - always January, April, June, and October. **Examination Sites:** Exam given by local chapters and at annual convention. **Examination Type:** Multiple-choice. **Re-examination:** Fees to retake exam are: $15 (members); $25 (nonmembers). **Fees:** $50 (members); $75 (nonmembers).

▐215▐

Labor Market Information Specialist (LMIS)
International Association of Personnel in Employment Security (IAPES)
1801 Louisville Rd.
Frankfort, KY 40601
Phone: (502)223-4459
Fax: (502)223-4127
Toll Free: (800)662-2255
Gail Butler-Hiley, Deputy Dir.

Recipient: Officials and others engaged in labor market information administration through municipal, state, provincial, and federal government employment agencies

and unemployment compensation agencies. **Educational/Experience Requirements:** Hold Employment and Training Generalist (ETG) designation (see separate entry). **Membership:** Not required. **Certification Requirements:** Successful completion of exam. **Renewal:** none. **Preparatory Materials:** Study guide available. **Examination Frequency:** quarterly - always January, April, June, and October. **Examination Sites:** Exam given by local chapters and at annual convention. **Examination Type:** Multiple-choice. **Re-examination:** Fees to retake exam are: $15 (members); $25 (nonmembers). **Fees:** $50 (members); $75 (nonmembers).

▐216▐

Professional in Human Resources (PHR)
Human Resource Certification Institute (HRCI)
606 N. Washington St.
Alexandria, VA 22314
Phone: (703)548-3440
Fax: (703)836-0367
Cornelia Cont, Mgr.

Recipient: Human resource consultants, educators, practitioners, and researchers. **Educational/Experience Requirements:** Must meet one of the following requirements: (1) Four years experience; (2) Bachelor's degree and two years experience; or (3) Graduate degree and one year of experience. Experience must be in exempt-level position working primarily in human resources field. **Membership:** Not required. **Certification Requirements:** Successful completion of exam. Exam covers: Business and human resources management practices; Compensation and benefits; Employee selection and placement; Employee training and development; Labor and employee relations; and Worker health and safety and organizational security. **Renewal:** Every three years. Recertification based on either successful completion of exam or accumulation of 60 hours of professional education. Renewal fee is $75. **Preparatory Materials:** Study materials available. **Examination Frequency:** Every four-six weeks. **Examination Sites:** Exam given at sites throughout the U.S. **Examination Type:** Multiple-choice. **Fees:** $155 (member); $195 (nonmember). **Endorsed By:** Society for Human Resource Management.

217

Registered Organization Development Consultant (RODC)
Organization Development Institute
11234 Walnut Ridge Rd.
Chesterland, OH 44026
Phone: (216)461-4333
Fax: (216)729-9319
Dr. Donald W. Cole RODC, Pres.

Recipient: Organization development professionals. **Number of Certified Individuals:** 100. **Certification Requirements:** Must meet one of the following educational and experience requirements: (1) Doctorate degree in psychology or allied field and two years experience; (2) Master's degree in psychology, business administration, or allied field, and four years experience; or (3) Bachelor's degree and six years experience. Candidates who are not graduates of program approved by Institute must successfully complete exam. **Renewal:** Every year. Renewal fee is $150. **Preparatory Materials:** none. **Examination Frequency:** Throughout the year. **Examination Type:** Multiple-choice. **Pass/Fail Rate:** 70% pass exam the first time. **Waiting Period to Receive Scores:** Two weeks. **Re-examination:** Must wait one year to retake exam. **Fees:** $150.

218

Registered Organization Development Professional (RODP)
Organization Development Institute
11234 Walnut Ridge Rd.
Chesterland, OH 44026
Phone: (216)461-4333
Fax: (216)729-9319
Dr. Donald W. Cole RODC, Pres.

Recipient: Organization development professionals. **Number of Certified Individuals:** 300. **Membership:** Required. **Certification Requirements:** Professional education and experience. Candidates who are not graduates of program approved by Institute must successfully complete exam. **Renewal:** Every year. Renewal fee is $110. **Fees:** $110.

219

Senior Certified Relocation Professional (SCRP)
Employee Relocation Council (ERC)
1720 N St., NW
Washington, DC 20036
Phone: (202)857-0857
Fax: (202)467-4012
Karen Ann Reid, Dir.

Recipient: Employee relocation professionals involved in corporate human relations and relocation policy-making. **Educational/Experience Requirements:** Hold Certified Relocation Professional (CRP) designation (see separate entry). **Certification Requirements:** Documentation of leadership contributions to the ERC including meeting program participation as speaker or panelist, published articles in association magazine, and special or standing committee service. **Renewal:** Every three years. Recertification based on accumulation of 30 continuing education credits. Renewal fee is $75.

220

Senior Professional in Human Resources (SPHR)
Human Resource Certification Institute (HRCI)
606 N. Washington St.
Alexandria, VA 22314
Phone: (703)548-3440
Fax: (703)836-0367
Cornelia Cont, Mgr.

Recipient: Human resource consultants, educators, practitioners, and researchers. **Educational/Experience Requirements:** Must meet one of the following requirements: (1) Eight years experience; (2) Bachelor's degree and six years experience; or (3) Graduate degree and five years experience. Experience must be in exempt-level position working primarily in human resources field. **Membership:** Not required. **Certification Requirements:** Successful completion of exam. Exam covers: Business and human resources management practices; Compensation and benefits; Employee selection and placement; Employee training and development; Labor and employee relations; and Worker health and safety and organizational security. **Renewal:** Every three years. Recertification based on either successful completion of exam or accumulation of 60 hours of professional education. Renewal fee is $75. **Preparatory Materials:** Study materials available. **Examination Sites:** Exam given at sites throughout the U.S. **Examination**

Type: Multiple-choice. **Waiting Period to Receive Scores:** Every four-six weeks. **Fees:** $285 (members); $325 (nonmembers). **Endorsed By:** Society for Human Resource Management.

221

Unemployment Insurance Specialist (UIS)
International Association of Personnel in Employment Security (IAPES)
1801 Louisville Rd.
Frankfort, KY 40601
Phone: (502)223-4459
Fax: (502)223-4127
Toll Free: (800)662-2255
Gail Butler-Hiley, Deputy Dir.

Recipient: Officials and others involved with unemployment insurance through municipal, state, provincial, and federal government employment agencies and unemployment compensation agencies. **Educational/Experience Requirements:** Hold Employment and Training Generalist (ETG) designation (see separate entry). **Membership:** Not required. **Certification Requirements:** Successful completion of exam. **Renewal:** none. **Preparatory Materials:** Study guide available. **Examination Frequency:** quarterly - always January, April, June, and October. **Examination Sites:** Exam given by local chapters and at annual convention. **Examination Type:** Multiple-choice. **Re-examination:** Fees to retake exam are: $15 (members); $25 (nonmembers). **Fees:** $50 (members); $75 (nonmembers).

Property and Real Estate Managers

222

Accredited Farm Manager (AFM)
American Society of Farm Managers and Rural Appraisers (ASFMRA)
950 S. Cherry St., Ste. 508
Denver, CO 80222
Phone: (303)758-3513
Fax: (303)758-0190
Cheryl L. Cooley, Coord.

Recipient: Professionals trained to assist farm owners, banks, attorneys, farm purchasers, and rural property managers. **Educational/Experience Requirements:** Must meet the following requirements: (1) Three years experience; (2) Bachelor's degree or equivalent; and (3) Submission of farm management report. **Membership:** Not required. **Certification Requirements:** Successful completion of the following courses, including exams, and written and oral exams. Courses are: (1) Advanced Farm Management, covering: Budgeting; Commodity marketing; Conservation planning; Environmental risk management; and Tax law; (2) Agricultural Management, covering ethical standards; (3) Principles of Farm Management, covering: Budgeting; Building valuation; Communications; Insurance; Leasing; Marketing; Operator selections; and Soils and soil fertility; (4) Report Writing School, covering: Grammar; Letter writing; Persuasion and argumentation; Reader's goals; Report content; and Writing styles; and (5) Standards and Ethics. Courses may be challenged by exam with ASFMRA approval. **Renewal:** Every three years. Recertification based on accumulation of 60 continuing education credits. **Preparatory Materials:** Study guides and reference publications available. **Re-examination:** May retake exams once. **Fees:** $2080 (members); $2485 (nonmembers).

223

Accredited Residential Manager (ARM)
Institute of Real Estate
  Management (IREM)
430 N. Michigan Ave.
PO Box 109025
Chicago, IL 60610-9025
Phone: (312)661-0004
Fax: (312)661-1936

Recipient: Residential multi-family real estate managers. **Educational/Experience Requirements:** Spend 50 percent of work time in residential property management and meet the following requirements: (1) High school diploma or equivalent; (2) Documentation of performance or supervision of ten of 22 real estate management functions; and (3) 24 to 48 months experience in one type of residential multi-family real estate management. **Membership:** Required. **Certification Requirements:** Successful completion of one of the following courses, including exam: (1) Course 101: Successful Site Management, covering: Communication; Employment requirements; Ethics; Eviction and collection policies; Fair housing requirements; Hiring and supervising employees; Inspections; Interviewing and orienting new residents; Lease terms; Leasing available apartments; Legal concepts; Maintenance programs; Managing risk; Motivation; Marketing strategy; Property analysis reports; Rent and delinquency require-

ments; Resident retention programs; Screening and choosing new residents; Service contractors; Target markets; and Time management; or (2) Course 102: Successful Management of Public Housing, covering: Communication; Eligibility, rent collection, delinquency, and eviction policies and procedures; Employment requirements and civil service regulations; Fair housing requirements; Hiring and supervising employees; History of government assisted and public housing; Lease terms; Legal concepts; Motivation; Screening, leasing to, interviewing, and orienting new residents; and Time management. **Renewal:** Every two years. Recertification based on experience, continuing education, and association participation. **Preparatory Materials:** *Successful Residential Management* (text). **Examination Frequency:** Throughout the year. **Examination Sites:** Courses given at sites throughout the U.S. **Endorsed By:** National Association of Realtors.

224

Advanced Registered Apartment Manager
National Council of the Multifamily
  Housing Industry
1201 Fifteenth St., NW
Washington, DC 20005-2800
Phone: (202)822-0215
Fax: (202)861-2120
Toll Free: (800)368-5242
Kim Duty, Mgr.

Recipient: Apartment multifamily housing managers. **Educational/Experience Requirements:** Must meet the following requirements: (1) Hold Registered Apartment Management (RAM) designation (see separate entry); (2) Five years general property experience or three years on-site experience; (3) Submit article for publication in *RAM Digest;* and (4) Submit Advanced Registered in Apartment Management Profile. **Certification Requirements:** Successful completion of seven-module training program, including exams. Modules are: Administrative Operations and Management Skills; Advanced Financial Management; Advanced Maintenance; Advanced Marketing and Leasing; Advanced Personnel; Fair Housing for Property Managers; and Legal Issues for Property Managers. May challenge exams without attendance at modules. **Examination Frequency:** Throughout the year. **Examination Sites:** Modules given at sites throughout the U.S. **Fees:** $100. **Endorsed By:** National Association of Home Builders.

225

Certified Apartment Manager (CAM)
National Apartment Association
  (NAA)
1111 Fourteenth St., NW, Ste. 900
Washington, DC 20005
Phone: (202)842-4050
Fax: (202)842-4056

Recipient: On-site apartment managers. **Educational/Experience Requirements:** Must meet the following requirements: (1) Two years experience; and (2) 40 elective credits of academic/professional education. **Certification Requirements:** Must meet the following requirements: (1) Successful completion of Advanced Apartment Management program and Survey of Apartment Management course, including exams; (2) Submission of Apartment Community Analysis; and (3) Successful completion of exam. **Renewal:** Every year. Recertification based on accumulation of five continuing credits. There is a renewal fee. **Endorsed By:** United States Department of Housing and Urban Development.

226

Certified Apartment Property Supervisor (CAPS)
National Apartment Association
  (NAA)
1111 Fourteenth St., NW, Ste. 900
Washington, DC 20005
Phone: (202)842-4050
Fax: (202)842-4056

Recipient: Supervisors responsible for multiple properties and large staffs. **Educational/Experience Requirements:** Two years experience. **Certification Requirements:** Accumulation of 500 points and successful completion of 156-hour program consisting of the following courses, including exams: (1) An Overview of Mid Management, including: Budgets; Decision making; Directing; Handling stress; Job descriptions; Management styles; Negotiating; Office policies and procedures; Organizing; Personnel selection; Problem solving; and Qualities of a supervisor; (2) Property Evaluation and Take Over, including preparation of regional analysis and property fiscal review, development of management strategy, compilation of written information, and preparation of final acquisition report; (3) Financial and Economic Consideration, including: Budget needs in conservation, construction, maintenance, marketing, personnel management, accounting, and acquisitions; and Legal and financial aspects of apartment management; (4) Personnel Policies and Procedures, including: Determining payroll periods; Documenting personnel records and employment agreements; Establishing compensation ranges; Establishing and monitoring policies and procedures; Property inspection checklists; Property visit scheduling; and Reports for directing and monitoring on-site management; (5) Marketing Procedures, including: Analyzing organizational goals; Avoiding crisis management; Developing marketing plan; and Long-term planning; (6) Maintenance Procedures, covering maintenance activities and requirements for landscape, common areas, swimming pools, interiors, and exteriors; and (7) Administrative Control Systems, covering personnel, finance, marketing, and audit control systems. Candidates holding Certified Apartment Manager (CAM) designation (see separate entry) and two additional years of experience may be exempt from coursework. Candidates may challenge up to three courses by successful completion of exams. **Renewal:** Every year. There is a renewal fee.

`227`

Certified Building Service Executives (CBSE)

Building Service Contractors
Association International
(BSCAI)
10201 Lee Hwy., Ste. 225
Fairfax, VA 22030
Phone: (703)359-7090
Fax: (703)352-0493
Toll Free: (800)368-3414
Robin Fowler, Sec.

Recipient: Building service contractors who provide cleaning, facility maintenance, and janitorial services to building owners and managers. **Number of Certified Individuals:** 230. **Educational/ Experience Requirements:** Five years experience, including three years as manager. **Membership:** Not required. **Certification Requirements:** Successful completion of four-section exam. **Examination Frequency:** Throughout the year. **Examination Sites:** Exam given at annual meeting, seminars, trade shows, or by arrangement with proctor. **Waiting Period to Receive Scores:** 30 days. **Re-examination:** Must only retake sections failed. Must successfully complete exam within one year. **Fees:** $350 (members); $700 (nonmembers).

`228`

Certified Club Manager (CCM)

Club Managers Association of
America (CMAA)
1733 King St.
Alexandria, VA 22314
Phone: (703)739-9500
Fax: (703)739-0124
Donald J. Bartell, Coord.

Recipient: Club managers. **Educational/ Experience Requirements:** Must meet one of the following requirements: (1) Bachelor's degree in hospitality, attendance at one CMAA annual conference (with attendance at minimum of four education sessions), CMAA membership for three years, and successful completion of two CMAA workshops or equivalent and the BMI III course; (2) Bachelor's degree in non-related field, attendance at one CMAA annual conference (with attendance at minimum of four education sessions), CMAA membership for four years, and successful completion of four CMAA workshops or equivalent and BMI II and BMI III courses; (3) Bachelor's degree in non-related field, associate's degree in hospitality, attendance at one CMAA annual conference (with attendance at minimum of four education sessions), CMAA membership for three years, and successful completion of two CMAA workshops or equivalent and the BMI III course; or (4) Attendance at one CMAA annual conference (with attendance at minimum of four education sessions), CMAA membership for five years, and successful completion of six CMAA workshops or equivalent and BMI I, BMI II, and BMI III courses. BMI I requirement waived for candidates with associate's degree in hospitality. Attendance at annual conferences above required number can be substituted for one workshop. **Membership:** Required. **Certification Requirements:** Successful completion of exam. **Renewal:** Recertification based on accumulation of 200 credits through continuing education, experience, and association activities. **Preparatory Materials:** Review course available. **Examination Frequency:** quarterly. **Examination Sites:** Exam given at CMMA annual conference and by arrangement with proctor. **Examination Type:** Multiple-choice; true or false. **Re-examination:** Must wait one year to retake exam. **Fees:** $175.

`229`

Certified Facility Manager (CFM)

International Facility Management
Association (IFMA)
One E. Greenway Plaza, Ste. 1100
Houston, TX 77046
Phone: (713)623-4363
Fax: (713)623-6124
Toll Free: (800)359-4362
Lee Kovalchuk, Mgr.

Recipient: Facility managers. **Number of Certified Individuals:** 1200. **Educational/ Experience Requirements:** Must meet one of the following requirements: (1) Four years experience, related degree, and continuing education; (2) Five years experience, unrelated degree, and continuing education; or (3) Eight years experience and post-secondary and continuing education. **Membership:** Not required. **Certification Requirements:** Successful completion of exam. Exam covers: Communication; Facility function; Finance; Human and environmental factors; Operations and maintenance; Planning and project management; Quality assessment and innovation; and Real estate. **Renewal:** Every three years. Renewal fee is $200. **Examination Frequency:** quarterly. **Examination Sites:** Exam given by arrangement with proctor. **Examination Type:** Multiple-choice. **Pass/Fail Rate:** 70% pass exam the first time. **Waiting Period to Receive Scores:** Four-six weeks. **Re-examination:** There is no waiting period to retake exam. **Fees:** $350.

`230`

Certified Financial Manager (CFM)

National Center for Housing
Management (NCHM)
1010 Massachusetts Ave., NW
Washington, DC 20001-5402
Phone: (202)872-1717
Toll Free: (800)368-5625
Roger G. Stevens Jr., Pres.

Recipient: Financial managers of U.S. Department of Housing and Urban Development (HUD) assisted housing communities. **Certification Requirements:** Successful completion of program. Program covers: Accounting systems; Annual audit; Bank accounts; Changes in addition to rent; Credit reports; Default; Distributions; Excess income reports; Financial reporting - monthly; Flexible subsidies - impact; Insurance; Interest; Liquidity; Management reviews - preparation; 92410 - Statement of profit/loss; Owner advances; Payables; Pet deposits; Receivables; Rent; Replacement reserve;

Residential receipts; Security deposits; Special escrows; Subsidy billing; Undo financial burdens; and Utility allowances. **Preparatory Materials:** List of reference materials provided. **Examination Sites:** Program offered at sites throughout the U.S.

231

Certified Leasing Professional (CLP)
National Council of the Multifamily Housing Industry
1201 Fifteenth St., NW
Washington, DC 20005-2800
Phone: (202)822-0215
Fax: (202)861-2120
Toll Free: (800)368-5242
Kim Duty, Mgr.

Recipient: On-site leasing professionals. **Certification Requirements:** Successful completion of training program. **Examination Sites:** Program given at sites throughout the U.S. or through home-study. **Endorsed By:** National Association of Home Builders.

232

Certified Leasing Specialist (CLS)
International Council of Shopping Centers (ICSC)
665 Fifth Ave.
New York, NY 10022
Phone: (212)421-8181
Fax: (212)486-0849

Recipient: Shopping center leasing specialists. **Educational/Experience Requirements:** Must meet one of the following requirements: (1) Four years experience; (2) Three years experience and successful completion of Leasing I and Advanced Leasing certificate programs; (3) Three years experience and successful completion of Advance Leasing certificate program and 30 hours of college-level courses or real estate continuing education courses that are equivalent to Leasing I certificate program; or (4) Three years experience and current real estate sales licensure. Courses follow lecture and workshop formats. **Certification Requirements:** Successful completion of exam. Exam consists of the following sections: (1) Construction; (2) Financing; (3) Leasing Fundamentals; (4) Legal; (5) Operations/Marketing/Promotion; (6) Retailing; and (7) Trade Area Analysis. **Examination Frequency:** Annual. **Examination Sites:** Exam given at one U.S. site per year.

233

Certified Manager of Housing (CMH)
National Center for Housing Management (NCHM)
1010 Massachusetts Ave., NW
Washington, DC 20001-5402
Phone: (202)872-1717
Toll Free: (800)368-5625
Roger G. Stevens Jr., Pres.

Recipient: On-site management personnel of U.S. federal government assisted housing. **Certification Requirements:** Successful completion of course and exam. Course covers community, maintenance, and occupancy management. **Examination Sites:** Course offered at sites throughout the U.S.

234

Certified Manager of Maintenance (CMM)
National Center for Housing Management (NCHM)
1010 Massachusetts Ave., NW
Washington, DC 20001-5402
Phone: (202)872-1717
Toll Free: (800)368-5625
Roger G. Stevens Jr., Pres.

Recipient: Maintenance managers of U.S. federal government assisted housing. **Certification Requirements:** Successful completion of course. Course includes developing maintenance program. **Preparatory Materials:** *Manager of Maintenance Resource Manual* (reference). **Examination Sites:** Course offered at sites throughout the U.S.

235

Certified Occupancy Specialist (COS)
National Center for Housing Management (NCHM)
1010 Massachusetts Ave., NW
Washington, DC 20001-5402
Phone: (202)872-1717
Toll Free: (800)368-5625
Roger G. Stevens Jr., Pres.

Recipient: Professionals involved in U.S. federal government assisted housing. **Certification Requirements:** Successful completion of program, including exam. Program covers: Allowances and adjustments; Annual income; Assets; Billings and vouchers; Eligibility determination; Marketing and outreach; Occupancy standards; Preferences; Recertification procedures; Rent computation; Tenant selection/waiting list; and Verification requirements and procedures. **Preparatory Materials:** *Work and Reference Book* (reference).

236

Certified Park Operator (CPO)
National Association of RV Parks and Campgrounds (NARVC)
8605 Westwood Center Dr., Ste. 201
Vienna, VA 22182-2231
Phone: (703)734-3000
Fax: (703)734-3004

Recipient: Recreational vehicle park and campground operators. **Number of Certified Individuals:** 400. **Educational/Experience Requirements:** One year of experience. **Membership:** not required. **Certification Requirements:** Must earn 75 total credits through the following: (1) Experience; (2) Attendance at national, state, and multi-state meetings/conventions; (3) Association service; (4) Writing of articles or service as course instructor; (5) Education; and (6) Accumulation of continuing Education Credits (CEUs) for attending educational courses. Fifty credits must come from continuing education. **Renewal:** Every three years. Recertification based on accumulation of 25 credits. Lifetime certification available after five renewals. Renewal fees are: $45 (members); $75 (nonmembers). **Fees:** $65 (members); $90 (nonmembers).

237

Certified Pool Spa Operator (CPO)
National Swimming Pool Foundation (NSPF)
10803 Gulfdale, Ste. 300
San Antonio, TX 78216
Phone: (210)525-1227
Fax: (210)344-3713

Recipient: Operators, owners, managers, service companies, and public health officers involved with pools and spas for hotels and motels, municipal pools, public facilities, natatoriums, water parks, competitive facilities, swim clubs, golf, tennis, and fitness clubs that have pool or spa facilities, and high schools, colleges, and universities. **Number of Certified Individuals:** 37,000. **Certification Requirements:** Successful completion of course and exam. Course covers: Automatic feeding equipment; Energy use and conservation; Filtration; Government requirements; Maintenance; Pool equipment; Pool and spa chemistry; Preventive maintenance; Recirculation; Safety; Seasonal care; Storage and handling; Testing; and Treatment. **Renewal:** Every five years. Recertification based on successful completion of course and/or exam. **Preparatory Materials:** *Pool/Spa Operators Handbook* (text).

`238`

Certified Professional Property Administrator (CPPA)

National Property Management
Association (NPMA)
380 Main St., Ste. 290
Dunedin, FL 34698
Phone: (813)736-3788
Fax: (813)736-6707
Bonnie Schlag, Exec.Dir.

Recipient: Individuals interested in professional asset management, primarily working with assets provided by government entities to contractors. **Educational/Experience Requirements:** Three years experience. **Membership:** Required. **Certification Requirements:** Successful completion of the following exams: Acquisition; Consumption; Contract Completion; Disposition; Maintenance; Physical Inventory; Property; Property Audits; Real Property; Receiving and Identification; Records; Reporting; Storage and Movement; Subcontract Administration; and Utilization. Candidates who successfully complete three exams earn Certified Professional Property Specialist (CPPS) designation (see separate entry). **Renewal:** Every five years. Recertification based on accumulation of credit in three of the following activities: (1) Participation in training programs and seminars as planner or speaker; (2) Attendance at NPMA seminars or other related conferences; (3) Accumulation of 15 credits or continuing education units (CEUs); (4) Authoring published papers, thesis, or articles, and participation in community or state oriented activities; (5) Attendance at at least four or more chapter meetings per year; (6) Service as NPMA officer; (7) Service as NPMA committee member; and (8) Experience. Lifetime certification available for retired CPPAs. **Preparatory Materials:** *NPMA Property Manual* (reference). **Fees:** $90.

`239`

Certified Professional Property Manager (CPPM)

National Property Management
Association (NPMA)
380 Main St., Ste. 290
Dunedin, FL 34698
Phone: (813)736-3788
Fax: (813)736-6707
Bonnie Schlag, Exec.Dir.

Recipient: Individuals interested in professional asset management, primarily working with assets provided by government entities to contractors. **Educational/Experience Requirements:** Must meet the following requirements: (1) Hold Certified Professional Property Administrator (CPPA) designation (see separate entry); and (2) Six years experience as property manager, division chief, agency head, warranted property administrator, or other comparable managerial position. **Membership:** Required. **Certification Requirements:** Successful completion of exam. **Renewal:** Every five years. Recertification based on accumulation of credit in three of the following activities: (1) Participation in training programs and seminars as planner or speaker; (2) Attendance at NPMA seminars or other related conferences; (3) Accumulation of 15 credits or continuing education units (CEUs); (4) Authoring published papers, thesis, or articles, and participation in community or state oriented activities; (5) Attendance at at least four or more chapter meetings per year; (6) Serving as NPMA officer; (7) Serving as NPMA committee member; and (8) Experience. Lifetime certification available for retired CPPMs. **Preparatory Materials:** *NPMA Property Manual* (reference). **Examination Type:** Essay. **Fees:** $90.

`240`

Certified Professional Property Specialist (CPPS)

National Property Management
Association (NPMA)
380 Main St., Ste. 290
Dunedin, FL 34698
Phone: (813)736-3788
Fax: (813)736-6707
Bonnie Schlag, Exec.Dir.

Recipient: Individuals interested in professional asset management, primarily working with assets provided by government entities to subcontractors. **Number of Certified Individuals:** 1000. **Membership:** Required. **Certification Requirements:** Successful completion of three of the following exams: Acquisition; Consumption; Contract Completion; Disposition; Maintenance; Physical Inventory; Property; Property Audits; Real Property; Receiving and Identification; Records; Reporting; Storage and Movement; Subcontract Administration; and Utilization. **Renewal:** none. **Preparatory Materials:** *NPMA Property Manual* (reference). **Examination Frequency:** Throughout the year. **Examination Sites:** Exams given by arrangement with proctor. **Examination Type:** Multiple-choice. **Waiting Period to Receive Scores:** One month. **Re-examination:** There is no time limit to retake exams. **Fees:** $90.

`241`

Certified Property Manager (CPM)

Institute of Real Estate
Management (IREM)
430 N. Michigan Ave.
PO Box 109025
Chicago, IL 60610-9025
Phone: (312)661-0004
Fax: (312)661-1936

Recipient: Managers of apartments, office buildings, shopping centers, federally-assisted housing, condominiums, cooperatives, retail strip stores, and industrial properties. **Number of Certified Individuals:** 9500. **Educational/Experience Requirements:** Five years experience and successful completion of three course series, including exams. 300 Series courses (minimum of one course) are: (1) Marketing and Management of Residential Property, including: Analyzing regional and neighborhood trends; Economic alternatives; Emergencies; Enhancing value; Financial analysis techniques; Financing; Goal setting; Inspecting and maintaining a property; Insurance; Management agreements and policies; Managing budgets and budget analysis; Marketing and advertising techniques; Marketing plans; Setting rents; and Tenant profiles; (2) Leasing and Management of Office Buildings, including: Budgeting and understanding financial statements; Communication; Demographics; Economics of alternatives; Emergency procedures; Enhancing property values; Financing; Goal setting; Inspecting properties; Insurance; Maintenance programs; Management agreements; Marketing plans; Motivation; Negotiating leases; Rents; and Target markets; (3) Management and Leasing of Shopping Centers and Retail Space, including: Analyzing trade area; Budgeting; Communication; Economics of alternatives; Emergency procedures; Enhancing property value; Financial statements; Financing; Goal setting; Inspecting properties; Insurance; Leases; Maintenance programs; Management agreements; Managing risk; Marketing plans; Merchants' associations and marketing funds; Motivation; Optimizing tenant mix; Rents; and Target markets; and (4) Professional Management of Government Assisted Housing, which includes case study involving management of government-assisted, multifamily housing. Course 400: Managing Real Estate as an Investment, covers: Cash flow and after-tax analysis; Commercial leases; Cost recovery; Economic indicators; Finance; Financial analysis; Forecasting; Goal setting; Income tax; Inflation and interest rates; Investment alternative tests; Loan packages; Long-range planning; Present value and internal rates of return; Time value of money; and Valuation. Course 500: Problem Solving and Decision-Making for Property Managers, covers the skills necessary to successfully complete a management plan. Course 800: Ethics in Real Estate Management, covers ethical challenges that property managers face. Courses in the 300 and 400 series may be taken in classroom or through home-study. **Membership:** Required. **Certification Requirements:** Successful completion of management plan. **Renewal:** Every two years. Recertification based on accumulation of 12 hours of continuing education. **Preparatory Materials:** Candidate handbook available. **Examination Frequency:** Throughout the year. **Examination Sites:** Courses given at sites throughout the U.S. **Waiting Period to Receive Scores:** 45 days. **Endorsed By:** National Association of Realtors.

242

Certified Public Housing Managers (PHM)

National Association of Housing and Redevelopment Officials (NAHRO)
1320 18th St., NW, 5th Fl.
Washington, DC 20036
Phone: (202)429-2960
Fax: (202)429-9684
Richard Y. Nelson, Exec.Dir.

Recipient: Public housing managers. **Number of Certified Individuals:** 12,000. **Educational/Experience Requirements:** none. **Membership:** Not required. **Certification Requirements:** Successful completion of the following: (1) Exam, which covers: Administration; Maintenance and security; Management; Occupancy cycle; and Tenant services and relations; and (2) Review exercise, requiring candidate to take the role of public housing authority manager and

respond to simulated work conditions. **Renewal:** none. **Examination Type:** Multiple-choice; work-simulation. **Fees:** $350. **Endorsed By:** United States Department of Housing and Urban Development.

243

Certified Shopping Center Manager (CSM)

International Council of Shopping Centers (ICSC)
665 Fifth Ave.
New York, NY 10022
Phone: (212)421-8181
Fax: (212)486-0849

Recipient: Shopping center managers. **Number of Certified Individuals:** 2200. **Educational/Experience Requirements:** Must meet one of the following requirements: (1) Four years experience; (2) Three years experience and successful completion of Management I and II certificate programs; or (3) Three years experience, college coursework equivalent to Management I Certificate program with C average or better, and successful completion of Management II certificate program. Experience must include maintenance, leasing, marketing, and promotion, and shopping center income and expense accounting. Courses follow lecture and workshop formats. **Membership:** Not required. **Certification Requirements:** Successful completion of written and practical exams. Written exam consists of the following sections: (1) Center Accounting, Finance, and Record Keeping; (2) Center Retailing and Merchandising; (3) Insurance and Law; (4) Leasing and Development; (5) Marketing, Promotions, and Community Relations; and (5) Operations and Construction. **Preparatory Materials:** Review course available. **Examination Frequency:** Annual. **Examination Sites:** Exam given at one U.S. site every year. **Examination Type:** Multiple-choice; problem-solving. **Re-examination:** Must retake only exam failed. May retake exams two times. Fees to retake each exam are: $295 (members); $595 (nonmembers). **Fees:** $495 (members); $990 (nonmembers).

244

Consulting Fellow of the National Property Management Association (CF)

National Property Management Association (NPMA)
380 Main St., Ste. 290
Dunedin, FL 34698
Phone: (813)736-3788
Fax: (813)736-6707
Bonnie Schlag, Exec.Dir.

Recipient: Individuals interested in professional asset management, primarily working with assets provided by government entities to contractors. **Educational/Experience Requirements:** Must hold Certified Professional Property Manager (CPPM) designation (see separate entry). **Membership:** Required. **Certification Requirements:** Accumulation of 16 points through: (1) Education; (2) Experience; (3) NPMA leadership positions held; (4) Leadership and achievements in the field; (5) NPMA membership and attendance at events; (6) Participation in seminars and workshops; (7) Authorship of articles; (8) Presentation of programs; and (9) Teaching. **Renewal:** none. **Fees:** $75.

245

Facilities Management Administrator (FMA)

Building Owners and Managers Institute (BOMI)
1521 Ritchie Hwy.
Arnold, MD 21012
Phone: (410)974-1410
Fax: (410)974-1935
Toll Free: (800)235-2664

Recipient: Facilities management administrators. **Certification Requirements:** Successful completion of the following courses and exams: (1) Design, Operation, and Maintenance of Building Systems (Part I), covering: Air-circulating systems; Basic construction materials; Building design and construction; Building envelope; Cooling systems; Fundamentals of heating, ventilating, and air conditioning; Heating systems; HVAC control systems, operation and maintenance, and system components; Interior walls, ceilings, and flooring; Paints, coatings, and wall coverings; Plumbing systems; Roofing systems; and Structural systems; (2) Design, Operation, and Maintenance of Building Systems (Part II), covering: Building security; Cleaning equipment and supplies; Cleaning management and procedures; Electricity and electrical systems; Electrical systems operation and management; Energy management; Fire protection systems; Landscaping and parking; Lighting principles; Maintenance and modernization of elevators; Pest control and solid waste management; Vertical transportation systems; and Window cleaning and architectural metal maintenance; (3) Facilities Management and the Work Environment, covering: Basic physical asset management; Communication; Corporate culture; Corporate finance and capital investment; Decision making methods and information analysis; Facilities management plan; Facilities planning; Global business; Management information systems; Organization; Presentations; and Strategic management and planning; (4) Facilities Planning and Project Management, including: Classifying facility projects; Design development and design review; Facility annual report (space inventory and asset profile); Identifying user needs; Implementation; Organization; Owned vs. leased vs. developed; Planning model; Planning occupancy; Project close-out, evaluation, and post-occupancy evaluation; Rating user needs and buildings; and Specifications for facility performance; (5) Managing Facilities as Assets, covering: Acquisition and disposition; Budgeting costs; Budgeting staff; Capital vs. expense; Cost justification; Estimating; Financial strategies; Finance in procurement; Master plan; Operating plan; Reporting costs; ROA vs. ROI; Tracking performance; and Using spreadsheets; (6) Managing Facilities Technology, covering: Communications; Contract writing for telecommunications services; Costs of technological enhancement; Distributing information; Evaluating new technology; Facilities department information; Managing added technology; Storing and distributing data; and Video teleconferencing and trading rooms; and (7) Managing Real Estate and General Services Activities, covering: Acquisition and disposition; Auxiliary support services; Contract development, negotiation, and administration; Employee and guest services; Facilities management process; Facilities services; Lease documents; Negotiating with agents and brokers; Procurement; Purchase document; Risk management; Site selection; and Transportation services. Comparable experience or education related to a course subject may receive credit for up to three courses. Courses may be taken in instructor-led local classes, accelerated courses, and self-study courses. **Examination Frequency:** Three times per year (self-study) - January, May, and September. **Examination Sites:** Exams given at courses or at local sites throughout the U.S. for self-study courses. **Endorsed By:** Building

Owners and Managers Association International; Society of Property Professionals.

Master Club Manager (MCM)
Club Managers Association of
    America (CMAA)
1733 King St.
Alexandria, VA 22314
Phone: (703)739-9500
Fax: (703)739-0124
Donald J. Bartell, Coord.

Recipient: Club managers. **Educational/ Experience Requirements:** Hold Certified Club Manager (CCM) designation (see separate entry). **Membership:** Required. **Certification Requirements:** Must meet the following requirements: (1) Accumulation of 600 credits, with 250 coming from CMAA approved education programs; (2) Eleven years CMAA membership; (3) Successful completion of BMI V course; and (4) Successful completion Professional Data Form and Monograph.

Real Property Administrator (RPA)
Building Owners and Managers
    Institute (BOMI)
1521 Ritchie Hwy.
Arnold, MD 21012
Phone: (410)974-1410
Fax: (410)974-1935
Toll Free: (800)235-2664

Recipient: Real estate property administrators. **Educational/Experience Requirements:** Three years property management experience in 15 of 24 categories. **Certification Requirements:** Successful completion of six required courses and one elective course, including exams. Required courses are: (1) Design, Operation, and Maintenance of Building Systems (Part I), covering: Air-circulating systems; Basic construction materials; Building design and construction; Building envelope; Cooling systems; Fundamentals of heating, ventilating, and air conditioning; Heating systems; HVAC control systems, operation and maintenance, and system components; Interior walls, ceilings, and flooring; Paints, coatings, and wall coverings; Plumbing systems; Roofing systems; and Structural systems; (2) Design, Operation, and Maintenance of Building Systems (Part II), covering: Building security; Cleaning equipment and supplies; Cleaning management and procedures;

Electricity and electrical systems; Electrical systems operation and management; Energy management; Fire protection systems; Landscaping and parking; Lighting principles; Maintenance and modernization of elevators; Pest control and solid waste management; Vertical transportation systems; and Window cleaning and architectural metal maintenance; (3) Real Property Accounting, covering: Analyzing real estate financial statements; Assuming management of a building; Cash flow statement; Cost controls; Expenditure cycle; Expense budgeting; Financial statements; Income budgeting; Interpreting financial statements; Lease administration: abstraction and additional rent; and Revenue cycle; (4) Law for Property Managers, covering: Agency: creation and responsibilities and authority and termination; Contract law; Contracts: consideration, capacity of parties, and legal objectives; Crimes and intentional torts; Management agreement; Negligence and strict liability; Personal property; Premises liability; Statute of frauds, performance, and legal remedies; and Real property, including conveyances, environmental law, fair housing laws, land use controls, landlord and tenant, lease transactions, secured transactions, and transfer of rights and interests; (5) Real Estate Investment and Finance, covering: Basic approaches to value; Basics of lending; Computers; Current lending practice; Discounted cash flow measurement; Enhancing value; Introduction to value; Investment objectives; Market environment; Ownership vehicles; Present value and internal rate of return; Site and building analysis; and Taxation; and (6) Environmental Health and Safety Issues, covering: Air emissions and pollution control; Asbestos; Compliance with EPA regulations; Emergency response; Guidelines for OSHA compliance; Hazard communication; Hazardous waste/stormwater/wastewater; Indoor air quality; Lead hazards; Legal issues; Office ergonomics; Recordkeeping; Site assessments and audits; and Underground and aboveground storage tanks. Elective courses are: (1) Asset Management, covering: Analyzing property financial information; Building effective property management team; Creating value by directing asset performance; and Developing and executing strategic plan; (2) Fundamentals of Real Property Administration, covering: Asset management; Contracting for services; Economics of real estate; Environmental issues; Ethics; History of the buildings industry; Leadership and management techniques; Life safety and security; Marketing and lease administration; Organization; Reporting and control systems; Role of the property manager in operations; and Tenant improvement, relations, and retention; (3) Leasing and Marketing for Property Managers, covering: Analyzing the market; Lease document; Leasing plan; Marketing plan; Over-built market conditions; Prospecting for tenants and negotiating leases; Public relations and advertising; Renewals and tenant satisfaction; and Tenant finish; and (4) Risk Management and Insurance, covering: Basic insurance policies; Claim adjustment process; Employee benefit plans; Environmental concerns; Insurance companies and their distribution systems; Insurance company operations; Legal environment; Liability insurance policies; Managing real estate loss exposures; Miscellaneous coverage plans; Property and income loss policies; and Risk control and funding mechanisms. Comparable experience or education related to a course subject may receive credit for up to three courses. Courses may be taken in instructor-led local classes, accelerated courses, and self-study courses. **Examination Frequency:** Three times per year (self-study) - January, May, and September. **Examination Sites:** Exams given at courses or at sites throughout the U.S. for self-study courses. **Endorsed By:** Building Owners and Managers Association International; Society of Property Professionals.

248

Registered Apartment Manager (RAM)

National Council of the Multifamily
  Housing Industry
1201 Fifteenth St., NW
Washington, DC 20005-2800
Phone: (202)822-0215
Fax: (202)861-2120
Toll Free: (800)368-5242
Kim Duty, Mgr.

Recipient: Apartment multifamily housing managers. **Educational/Experience Requirements:** Two years experience and 300 total points through: (1) Education (250 maximum points), including: High school; Higher education; RAM School; Continuing education; and Industry related trade shows; (2) Employment Experience (250 maximum points); (3) Professional Involvement (125 maximum points), including: Awards and honors; Community and professional contributions; Involvement in business, civic, professional, or technical associations; Published articles and books; and Speaking/ training engagements; and (4) Professional References (25 maximum points). RAM School covers: Central office management; Leasing; Legal and fair housing issues; Maintenance; Managing

federally assisted housing programs; and Marketing. **Certification Requirements:** Successful completion of exam. Exam covers: Application and move-out; Fair housing and Americans With Disabilities Act (ADA) regulations; Federally assisted and insured housing; Financial management; Maintenance; Marketing; Occupancy files; Office management; Personnel; and Safety and security. **Renewal:** Every three years. Recertification based on accumulation of 75 points through continuing education, attendance at conventions or trade/home shows, seminars, authoring of articles, speaking engagements, and other industry leadership activities. **Preparatory Materials:** *Multihousing Management 1,* Fourth Edition (reference). **Examination Frequency:** Throughout the year. **Examination Sites:** Exam given at annual Multi-Housing World Conference and at sites throughout the U.S. **Examination Type:** Multiple-choice. **Fees:** $195. **Endorsed By:** National Association of Home Builders.

249

Registered Building Service Manager (RBSM)

Building Service Contractors
  Association International
  (BSCAI)
10201 Lee Hwy., Ste. 225
Fairfax, VA 22030
Phone: (703)359-7090
Fax: (703)352-0493
Toll Free: (800)368-3414
Robin Fowler, Sec.

Recipient: Building service managers who supervise cleaning, facility maintenance, and janitorial services for building owners and managers. **Number of Certified Individuals:** 284. **Educational/ Experience Requirements:** One year of experience. **Membership:** Not required. **Certification Requirements:** Successful completion of four-section exam. Exam covers: Basic math; Carpet care; Chemicals and chemistry; Communications; Customer Relations; Employee motivation, relations, retention, and training; First aid; Floor care; General management; Government Regulations; Insurance; Labor laws; Metals; Personnel management; Problem solving; Quality control; Restroom cleaning; Retuning jobs; Safety and fire; Security; Technology of the industry; Unions; Warehousing; and Workloading and scheduling. **Renewal:** Every two years. Recertification based on successful completion of exam. Lifetime certification available at age 62. Renewal fee is $50. **Preparatory Materials:** Building Service Management

Course, training modules, and video training available. **Examination Frequency:** Throughout the year. **Examination Sites:** Exam given at annual meeting, seminars, trade shows, or by arrangement with proctor. **Waiting Period to Receive Scores:** 30 days. **Reexamination:** Must only retake sections failed. There is a fee to retake exam. Must successfully complete exam within one year. **Fees:** $175 (members); $350 (nonmembers).

250

Registered Cooperative Manager (RCM)

National Association of Housing
  Cooperatives (NAHC)
1614 King St.
Alexandria, VA 22314
Phone: (703)549-5201
Fax: (703)549-5204

Recipient: Cooperative housing managers. **Certification Requirements:** Successful completion of the following modules, including exams: (1) History, Organization, and Characteristics of Housing Cooperatives, including: Characteristics and types of housing cooperatives; and Economic, social, and physical advantages of cooperative housing; (2) Duties, Responsibilities, and Skills of Successful Managers of Housing Cooperatives, including: Chain of command; Management skills; Relationships with board, members, and management company; Site manager's role and responsibilities; and Types of managers; (3) Marketing and Sale of Cooperative Memberships, including: Advocating for cooperative living; Introducing prospective members; Marketing plans; Marketing strategies; Providing continuing education on benefits and merits of cooperative living; and Sales procedures in accordance with bylaws and federal regulations; and (4) Quality Control and Maintenance Systems for Effective Cooperative Management, including: Materials; Quality of services; Repairs; and Workmanship. **Renewal:** Recertification based on continuing education.

251

Senior Asset Manager (SAM)

American Society of Asset
  Managers (ASAM)
303 W. Cypress
Box 12528
San Antonio, TX 78212
Phone: (210)225-2897
Fax: (210)225-8450
Toll Free: (800)486-3676
Deborah Deane, Exec.Dir.

Recipient: Real estate asset managers. **Number of Certified Individuals:** 150. **Membership:** Required. **Certification Requirements:** Successful completion of Advanced Commercial Asset Management course and exam. **Renewal:** none. **Examination Type:** Multiple-choice. **Waiting Period to Receive Scores:** Ten days. **Fees:** $100.

■ **252** ■

Senior Certified Shopping Center Manager (SCSM)

International Council of Shopping
   Centers (ICSC)
665 Fifth Ave.
New York, NY 10022
Phone: (212)421-8181
Fax: (212)486-0849

Recipient: Shopping center managers. **Educational/Experience Requirements:** Hold Certified Shopping Center Manager (CSM) designation (see separate entry) for three years. **Certification Requirements:** Must earn ten credits every three years through attendance at ICSC conventions, conferences, and meetings, successful completion of industry or college courses, association participation and service, authoring publications, and earning awards and other professional certifications. **Fees:** $90.

■ **253** ■

Senior Housing Management Specialist

National Council on Seniors'
   Housing (NCOSH)
1201 Fifteenth St., NW
Washington, DC 20005-2800
Toll Free: (800)368-5242

Recipient: Managers of housing for seniors. **Certification Requirements:** Successful completion of seminar. Seminar covers: Americans with Disabilities Act; Assessing government programs; Developing resident services; Fair housing concerns; Managing the aging-inplace; Mastering financial management; and Understanding aging process. **Endorsed By:** National Association of Home Builders.

■ **254** ■

Systems Maintenance Administrator (SMA)

Building Owners and Managers
   Institute (BOMI)
1521 Ritchie Hwy.
Arnold, MD 21012
Phone: (410)974-1410
Fax: (410)974-1935
Toll Free: (800)235-2664

Recipient: Building maintenance administrators. **Educational/Experience Requirements:** Hold Systems Maintenance Technician (SMT) designation (see separate entry). **Certification Requirements:** Successful completion of the following courses: (1) Building Design and Maintenance, covering: Building codes and materials; Cleaning equipment, materials, and procedures; Elevator and escalators; Floors, interior walls, and ceilings; Foundations and structural framing systems; Paints, wall coverings, and doors; Parking facilities and landscape maintenance; Preventive maintenance systems; Roofing systems; and Windows and curtain walls; (2) Energy Management, covering: Air handling systems; Building envelope; Cooling systems; Electrical systems; Fans, pumps, and energy management control systems; Heat reclaim systems and solar energy systems; Heating systems; Lighting systems; Operating conditions; Planning on energy management program; and Plumbing and piping systems; (3) Environmental Issues for the Building Engineer; and (4) Supervision, including: Decision making and leadership; Delegating work; Employee communication and development; Employee counseling and evaluation; Ethics and politics; Handling conflict and applying discipline; Labor contracts, cost reduction, and methods improvement; Motivation; Planning and controlling work; and Safety. Comparable experience or education related to a course subject may receive credit for up to three courses. Courses may be taken in instructor-led local classes, accelerated courses, and self-study courses. **Preparatory Materials:** Telephone hotline. **Examination Frequency:** Three times per year (self-study) - April, July, and December. **Examination Sites:** Exams given at courses or at local sites throughout the U.S. for self-study courses. **Endorsed By:** Building Owners and Managers Association International; Society of Property Professionals.

Purchasing Agents and Managers

■ **255** ■

Certified Professional Public Buyer (CPPB)

Universal Public Purchasing
   Certification Council
Reston International Center
11800 Sunrise Valley Dr., Ste. 1050
Reston, VA 22091
Phone: (703)715-9400
Fax: (703)715-9897
Toll Free: (800)FOR-NIGP
Donald D. Smart CPPB, Coord.

Recipient: Purchasing, procurement, contract administration, and logistics professionals in public sector. **Educational/Experience Requirements:** Must meet one of the following requirements: (1) High school diploma or equivalent, attendance at two NIGP seminars or equivalent, and four years purchasing experience, with at least two years in public sector; (2) Associate's degree in purchasing or related field and three years purchasing experience, with at least two years in public sector; (3) Bachelor's degree in non-related field, attendance at two NIGP seminars, and three years purchasing experience, with at least two years in public sector; (4) Bachelor's degree in purchasing or related field and two years public purchasing experience; or (5) Advanced degree and two years public purchasing experience. Related degrees are: Acquisition management; Contracting; Logistics; Materials management; or Purchasing. Degrees in business management or public administration must include 12 credit hours in at least two of the following disciplines: Contracts; Law; Purchasing/materials management; or Transportation. **Membership:** Not required. **Certification Requirements:** Successful completion of two-part exam. Parts are: (1) Purchasing Related Technical and Operational Functions, covering purchasing related functions; and (2) Organization and Coordination, covering purchasing related aspects of organization and coordination. **Renewal:** Every five years. Recertification based on continuing education and professional development. Lifetime certification available for CPPBs aged 62 or older with 15 years experience. **Preparatory Materials:** List of suggested reference materials, seminars, and texts available. **Examination Frequency:** Throughout the year. **Examination Sites:** Exam given by arrangement with proctor. **Examination Type:** Multiple-choice. **Fees:** $100 (members); $130 (nonmembers). **Endorsed By:** National Institute of Governmental Purchasing.

256

Certified Public Purchasing Officer (CPPO)

Universal Public Purchasing
  Certification Council
Reston International Center
11800 Sunrise Valley Dr., Ste. 1050
Reston, VA 22091
Phone: (703)715-9400
Fax: (703)715-9897
Toll Free: (800)FOR-NIGP
Donald D. Smart CPPP, Coord.

Recipient: Public sector managers of purchasing, procurement, contract administration, and logistics. **Educational/Experience Requirements:** Must meet one of the following requirements: (1) High school diploma or equivalent, attendance at two NIGP seminars, and five years purchasing experience, with at least four years in public sector and two years in supervisory position; (2) Associate's degree in purchasing or related field and four years purchasing experience, with at least three years in public sector and two years in supervisory position; (3) Bachelor's degree in non-related field, attendance at two NIGP seminars, and four years purchasing experience, with at least three years in public sector and two years in supervisory position; (4) Bachelor's degree in purchasing or related field and three years purchasing experience, with at least two years in public sector and two years in supervisory position; and (5) Advanced degree and three years purchasing experience, with at least two years in public sector and two years in supervisory position. Related degrees are: Acquisition management; Contracting; Logistics; Materials management; or Purchasing. Degrees in business management or public administration must include 12 credit hours in at least two of the following disciplines: Contracts; Law; Purchasing/materials management; or Transportation. **Membership:** Not required. **Certification Requirements:** Successful completion of three-part written exam and oral assessment interview. Parts of written exam are: (1) Purchasing Management, covering: Evaluation of purchasing and materials management systems; Model codes; and Planning, organizing, staffing, coordinating, directing, and controlling acquisition systems; (2) Business Management/Public Administration, covering: Budgeting; Government relations; International trade; Management concepts; Professionalism; Quantitative analysis; and World economics; and (3) Purchasing Related Technical and Operational Functions, covering purchasing related functions. Candidates who hold Certified Professional Public Buyer (CPPB) designation

(see separate entry) are exempt from part three of exam. Holders of P.P. designation in Canada are exempt from exam. **Renewal:** Every five years. Recertification based on continuing education and professional development. Lifetime certification available for CPPOs aged 62 or older with 15 years experience. **Preparatory Materials:** List of suggested reference materials, seminars, and texts available. **Examination Frequency:** Throughout the year. **Examination Sites:** Exam given by local chapters or by arrangement with proctor. **Examination Type:** Case studies; multiple-choice. **Fees:** $150 (members); $195 (nonmembers). **Endorsed By:** National Institute of Governmental Purchasing.

257

Certified Purchasing Executive (CPE)

American Purchasing Society (APS)
11910 Oak Trail Way
Port Richey, FL 34668
Phone: (813)862-7998
Fax: (813)862-8199
Harry E. Hough, Pres.

Recipient: Managers of purchasing departments and buyers for businesses. **Number of Certified Individuals:** 1000. **Educational/Experience Requirements:** Provide proof of financial responsibility (including personal credit references) and submit to APS investigation of background. **Membership:** Not required. **Certification Requirements:** Must accumulate 135 total points from the following categories: (1) College degrees: Associate degree, business-related (25-40 points); Bachelor's degree (30-50 points); Law degree (35-50 points); Master's of Business Administration (15-20 points); other Master's (five-ten points); and Doctorate in related field (five-ten points); (2) Individual coursework: Purchasing related (one-ten points); Related courses (one-five points); and Unrelated courses (one point); (3) Experience: General management (one-four points per year); Purchasing positions (four-six points per year); Purchasing management (six-nine points per year); and Director or V.P. of Purchasing (seven-12 points per year); (4) Professional contributions: Articles on purchasing or business (two-ten points); Teaching course on purchasing or business (two-eight points); and Speeches on purchasing and committee work in purchasing management organizations; and (5) Successful completion of exam (0-20 points). Exam covers: Accounting; Economics; General purchasing; Negotiating; and Technical and legal aspects of purchasing. **Renewal:** Every

five years. Recertification based on accumulation 25 points from the categories listed above. Renewal fee is $85. **Preparatory Materials:** Study materials and seminars available. **Examination Frequency:** Throughout the year. **Examination Sites:** Exam given at APS headquarters. **Examination Type:** Essay; multiple-choice; and true or false. **Pass/Fail Rate:** 90% pass exam. **Waiting Period to Receive Scores:** Three-four weeks. **Reexamination:** There is no time limit to retake exam. **Fees:** $189 (members); $225 (nonmembers).

258

Certified Purchasing Manager (C.P.M.)

National Association of Purchasing
  Management (NAPM)
2055 E. Centennial Cir.
PO Box 22160
Tempe, AZ 85285-2160
Phone: (602)752-6276
Fax: (602)752-7890
Toll Free: (800)888-6276
Scott R. Sturzl C.P.M., Dir.

Recipient: Individuals involved in purchasing and materials management. **Number of Certified Individuals:** 25,000. **Educational/Experience Requirements:** Must meet one of the following requirements: (1) Five years experience working in or teaching purchasing management; or (2) Three years experience and four-year college degree. **Membership:** Not required. **Certification Requirements:** Must earn 70 total points from the following areas: (1) Academic Education (maximum of 25 points), including: Associate's degree (eight points); Bachelor's degree (15 points); Master's degree (20 points); and Doctorate degree (25 points). Add five points if major is in business, purchasing, or materials management; (2) College Courses (maximum of four points for those with no degree and six points for those with degree), including: Related classes (three points); and Unrelated classes (one point); (3) Professional Education (maximum of 20 points), including: Two-week program (five points); One-week program (four points); One- to three-day courses of at least seven hours of education each day (one point); Journal articles published (two points each); Allied association certifications (one point each); and Conferences (points vary); (4) Professional Contributions (maximum of 10 points), including service as officer or committee member (one point); (5) Experience (maximum of 20 points; one-three points per year depending on level of responsibility. Ten years maximum experience);

and (6) Successful Completion of Exam (35 points). Exam consists of the following modules: (1) Purchasing, covering: Contract execution, implementation, and administration; Negotiation process; Procurement requests; Solicitation/ evaluation of proposals; and Supplier analysis; (2) Administration, covering: Administrative aspects of purchasing department; and Personnel issues; (3) Supply, covering: Ancillary supply functions; Inventory management; and Material flow; and (4) Current Issues, covering: Computerization; Environmental issues; External/internal relationships; and Forecasting and strategies. **Renewal:** Every five years. Recertification based on either successful completion of exam or accumulation of 12 points through college coursework, seminars, contributions to the profession, and professional education. Lifetime certification available for CPMs age 55 or over. Renewal fees are: $25 (members); $75 (nonmembers). **Preparatory Materials:** Study guide, practice exam, review course, seminars, videos, and other study materials available. **Examination Frequency:** Throughout the year. **Examination Sites:** Exams given at sites throughout the U.S. and internationally. **Examination Type:** Multiple-choice. **Pass/Fail Rate:** 55% pass each exam module. **Waiting Period to Receive Scores:** Immediately. **Re-examination:** Must wait 30 days to retake exam. Must only retake modules failed. **Fees:** $270 (members); $480 (nonmembers). Computer exam option: $390 (members); $560 (nonmembers).

259

Certified Purchasing Professional (CPP)
American Purchasing Society (APS)
11910 Oak Trail Way
Port Richey, FL 34668
Phone: (813)862-7998
Fax: (813)862-8199
Harry E. Hough Ph.D., Pres.

Recipient: Directors or vice-presidents of purchasing function for major corporations who manage significant dollar expenditures and usually have more than a dozen buyers. **Number of Certified Individuals:** 100. **Educational/Experience Requirements:** Provide proof of financial responsibility (including personal credit references) and submit to APS investigation of background. **Membership:** Not required. **Certification Requirements:** Must accumulate 100 total points from the following categories: (1) College degrees: Associate degree, business-related (25-40 points); Bachelor's degree (30-50 points); Law degree (35-50 points); Mas-

ter's of Business Administration (15-20 points); other Master's (five-ten points); and Doctorate in related field (five-ten points); (2) Individual coursework: Purchasing related (one-ten points); Related courses (one-five points); and unrelated courses (one point); (3) Experience: General management (one-four points per year); Purchasing positions (four-six points per year); Purchasing management (six-nine points per year); and Director or V.P. of Purchasing (seven-12 points per year); (4) Professional contributions: Articles on purchasing or business (two-ten points); Teaching course on purchasing or business (two-eight points); and Speeches on purchasing and committee work in purchasing management organizations; and (5) Successful completion of exam (0-20 points). Exam covers: Accounting; Economics; General purchasing; Negotiating; and Technical and legal aspects of purchasing. **Renewal:** Every five years. Recertification based on accumulation of 15 points through categories listed above. Renewal fee is $85. **Preparatory Materials:** Study materials and seminars available. **Examination Frequency:** Throughout the year. **Examination Sites:** Exam given at APS headquarters. **Examination Type:** Essay; multiple-choice; true or false. **Pass/Fail Rate:** 90% pass exam. **Waiting Period to Receive Scores:** Three-four weeks. **Re-examination:** There is no time limit to retake exam. **Fees:** $264 (members); $300 (nonmembers).

Underwriters

260

Accredited Residential Underwriter (ARU)
Mortgage Bankers Association of America (MBA)
1125 15th St., NW
Washington, DC 20005
Phone: (202)861-6500
Warren Lasko, Exec. VP

Recipient: Residential underwriters competent in FHA, VA, and conventional home loans. **Educational/Experience Requirements:** Must meet the following requirements: (1) One year of employment with MBA member firm; (2) Three years experience in processing and/or underwriting one-to-four-unit single-family residential properties, with minimum of one year of experience in underwriting and reviewing credit and property applications associated with one-to-four-unit single-family residential properties; (3) Successful completion of three of the fol-

lowing correspondence courses: Introduction to Mortgage Banking; Loans with a Twist; Mortgage Loan Underwriting; Quality Control in Mortgage Lending; Regulatory Compliance; Residential Secondary Mortgage Market; Understanding Real Estate Appraisal; and Underwriting the Self-Employed Borrower. This requirement waived for candidates who are HUD-approved Direct Endorsement Underwriters or VA-approved Automatic Underwriters; and (4) Successful completion of MBA's Seminar on Appraisal Techniques and Seminar on Underwriting Techniques in Residential Mortgages, including exams. Candidates with ten years experience in processing and underwriting with at least five years experience in single-family residential underwriting are exempt from correspondence course and seminar requirements. **Certification Requirements:** Successful completion of exam. **Renewal:** Every three years. Recertification based on accumulation of 40 hours of continuing education. Renewal fee is $50. **Fees:** $250.

261

Associate, Academy of Life Underwriting (AALU)
Academy of Life Underwriting
c/o Karl Friedman, AALU
Allstate Insurance Company
1411 Lake Cook Rd.
Deerfield, IL 60015
Phone: (708)948-6702
Karl Friedman AALU, Sec.

Recipient: Life insurance underwriters. **Educational/Experience Requirements:** Hold Certificate in Life Underwriting designation (see separate entry). **Certification Requirements:** Successful completion of exam and courses offered by Life Office Management Association (LOMA) and other underwriting organizations. Exam covers: Financial underwriting; Medical topics; Reinsurance; and Underwriting of large amount cases. Courses are: (1) Management of Organizations and Human Resources, covering management theory and practice; (2) Mathematics of Life and Health Insurance, covering the use of compound interest and probability to produce sound premiums, reserves, and policy values for life and health insurance policies; (3) Income Taxation, including: Corporations; Estates; Individuals; Partnerships; Sole proprietorships; Taxation of life insurance and annuities; and Trusts; and (4) Planning for Business Owners and Professionals, including: Inheritance; Insured buy-sell agreement; Key employee life, health, and disability plans; Retirement and estate planning; and Tax and legal aspects of organizing a business. Separate option available for Canadian candidates. **Preparatory Materials:** Handbook, including list of suggested study references, provided. Sample questions available. **Examination Frequency:** Annual. **Examination Sites:** Exam given at sites throughout the U.S., Canada, and Caribbean. **Examination Type:** Multiple-choice; short answer. **Waiting Period to Receive Scores:** Two months. **Endorsed By:** Canadian Institute of Underwriters; Home Office Life Underwriters Association; Institute of Home Office Underwriters.

262

Associate in Underwriting (AU)
Insurance Institute of America (IIA)
720 Providence Rd.
PO Box 3016
Malvern, PA 19355-0716
Phone: (610)644-2100
Fax: (610)640-9576
Toll Free: (800)644-2101
Connor M. Harrison AU, Dir.

Recipient: Insurance professionals involved in commercial lines underwriting. **Educational/Experience Requirements:** none. **Membership:** Not required. **Certification Requirements:** Successful completion of the following courses, including exams: (1) Commercial Liability Underwriting; (2) Commercial Property and Multiple-Lines Underwriting; (3) Commercial Property Insurance and Risk Management; and (4) Commercial Liability Risk Management and Insurance. Courses can be taken through group- or independent-study. **Renewal:** none. **Examination Type:** Essay. **Endorsed By:** American Council on Education.

263

Certificate in Life Underwriting
Academy of Life Underwriting
c/o Karl Friedman, AALU
Allstate Insurance Company
1411 Lake Cook Rd.
Deerfield, IL 60015
Phone: (708)948-6702
Karl Friedman AALU, Sec.

Recipient: Life insurance underwriters. **Certification Requirements:** Successful completion of exam and courses offered by Life Office Management Association (LOMA). Exam covers basic theory and fundamentals of life insurance underwrit-

ing. Courses are: (1) Principles of Life and Health Insurance, including: Basic features of life insurance, health insurance, and annuity products; Policyowner's contractual rights; Principles of insurance; and Process of becoming insured; (2) Life and Health Insurance Company Operations, including: Business organization of insurance industry; and Marketing, actuarial, underwriting, and financial activities of life and health insurance companies; and (3) Legal Aspects of Life and Health Insurance, including: Agency law; Contract law; Corporate law; and Property law. **Preparatory Materials:** Handbook, including list of suggested study references, provided. Sample questions available. **Examination Frequency:** Annual. **Examination Sites:** Exam given at sites throughout the U.S., Canada, and Caribbean. **Examination Type:** Multiple-choice; short answer. **Waiting Period to Receive Scores:** Two months. **Endorsed By:** Canadian Institute of Underwriters; Home Office Life Underwriters Association; Institute of Home Office Underwriters.

264

Chartered Life Underwriter (CLU)
American College (AC)
270 S. Bryn Mawr Ave.
Bryn Mawr, PA 19010
Phone: (215)526-1490

Recipient: Insurance and financial planning professionals who advise in estate, financial, and retirement planning, employee benefit planning, and business/tax planning. **Educational/Experience Requirements:** Three years experience. **Membership:** Not required. **Certification Requirements:** Successful completion of the following self-study courses, including exams: (1) Fundamentals of Estate Planning; (2) Fundamentals of Financial Planning; (3) Group Benefits; (4) Income Taxation; (5) Individual Life and Health Insurance; (6) Investments; (7) Life Insurance Law; and (8) Planning for Retirement Needs. Must also successfully complete two electives. Formal classes, study groups, and agency classes may be substituted. **Renewal:** Every two years. Recertification based on accumulation of 60 hours of continuing education. **Examination Type:** Multiple-choice. **Fees:** $3000. **Endorsed By:** American Society of CLU and ChFC.

265

Chartered Property Casualty Underwriter (CPCU)
American Institute for CPCU (AICPCU)
720 Providence Rd.
PO Box 3016
Malvern, PA 19355-0716
Phone: (610)644-2100
Fax: (610)640-9576
Toll Free: (800)644-2101
Michael W. Elliot CPCU, Asst.VP & Dir.

Recipient: Experienced insurance personnel whose jobs require an understanding of property and liability insurance contracts and functions. **Educational/Experience Requirements:** 36 months experience in last five years. **Membership:** Not required. **Certification Requirements:** Must successfully complete the following courses, including exams: (1) Accounting and Finance; (2) Commercial Liability Risk Management and Insurance; (3) Commercial Property Risk Management and Insurance; (4) Economics; (5) Ethics, Insurance Perspectives, and Insurance Contract Analysis; (6) Insurance Operations; (7) Management; (8) Personal Insurance and Risk Management; (9) The Legal Environment of Insurance; and (10) Insurance Issues and Professional Ethics. Must also successfully complete one elective. Courses may be taken in group study or independently. **Renewal:** none. **Endorsed By:** American Council on Education.

266

Fellow, Academy of Life Underwriting (FALU)
Academy of Life Underwriting
c/o Karl Friedman, AALU
Allstate Insurance Company
1411 Lake Cook Rd.
Deerfield, IL 60015
Phone: (708)948-6702
Karl Friedman AALU, Sec.

Recipient: Life insurance underwriters. **Educational/Experience Requirements:** Must meet the following requirements: (1) Hold Associate, Academy of Life Underwriting (AALU) designation (see separate entry); and (2) Five years experience. **Certification Requirements:** Successful completion of either project paper or exam and courses offered by Life Office Management Association (LOMA). Project paper must be on subject related to underwriting. Exam covers: Basic electrocardiographic patterns and their significance; Commonly encountered diseases and impairments; General anatomy and physiology; Medical abbreviations and terminology; Normal values for commonly encountered laboratory tests; and Underwriting and general management knowledge. Courses are: (1) Marketing Life and Health Insurance; and (2) Fundamentals of Estate Planning I, including: Nature, valuation, disposition, administration, and taxation of property; and Unified estate and gift tax system. Separate option available for Canadian candidates. **Preparatory Materials:** Handbook, including list of suggested study references, provided. Sample questions available. **Examination Frequency:** Annual. **Examination Sites:** Exam given at sites throughout the U.S., Canada, and Caribbean. **Examination Type:** Multiple-choice; short answer. **Waiting Period to Receive Scores:** Two months. **Endorsed By:** Canadian Institute of Underwriters; Home Office Life Underwriters Association; Institute of Home Office Underwriters.

`267`

Life Underwriter Training Council Fellow (LUTCF)

Life Underwriter Training Council (LUTC)
7625 Wisconsin Ave.
Bethesda, MD 20814
Phone: (301)913-5882
Fax: (301)913-0123

Recipient: Life insurance underwriters. **Membership:** Required. **Certification Requirements:** Successful completion of four courses, including exams.

`268`

Registered Employee Benefits Consultant (REBC)

National Association of Health Underwriters (NAHU)
1000 Connecticut Ave., NW, Ste. 810
Washington, DC 20036
Phone: (202)223-5533
Fax: (202)785-2274
Joy F. Pierce, Dir. of Educ.

Recipient: Individuals engaged in promotion, sale, and administration of disability income and health insurance. **Educational/Experience Requirements:** Must meet one of the following requirements: (1) Hold Registered Health Underwriter (RHU) designation (see separate entry); or (2) Three years experience. **Membership:** Not required. **Certification Requirements:** Successful completion of

the following self-study courses, including exams: (1) Employee Welfare Plans, including: Benefits concepts; Expenses; Major medical; Risk management; and Types of benefits; and (2) Retirement and Additional Benefit Plans, including: Benefit plan design/evaluation; Pensions and pension funding; and Other plan programs. Candidates who do not hold RHU designation must also successfully complete the RHU II - Health Insurance course, including exam. Course covers: Different products and programs; Government regulations; Group insurance; and Underwriting. **Renewal:** Recertification based on continuing education and professional development. **Preparatory Materials:** *Employee Benefit Planning* and *Employee Benefits* (texts). Study guides provided. **Examination Frequency:** Throughout the year. **Examination Sites:** Exams given at sites throughout the U.S. **Examination Type:** Multiple-choice. **Re-examination:** There is a $175 fee to retake each exam. **Fees:** $380 (members); $530 (nonmembers).

`269`

Registered Health Underwriter (RHU)

National Association of Health Underwriters (NAHU)
1000 Connecticut Ave., NW, Ste. 810
Washington, DC 20036
Phone: (202)223-5533
Fax: (202)785-2274
Joy F. Pierce, Dir. of Educ.

Recipient: Health and disability insurance underwriters. **Educational/Experience Requirements:** none. **Membership:** Not required. **Certification Requirements:** Successful completion of the following self-study courses, including exams: (1) Advanced Applications of Disability and Health Insurance, including: Business expenses; Cafeteria plans; Cost controls; HMOs; Long- and short-term disability; Long-term care insurance; Major medical; PPOs; and Salary continuation; (2) Disability Income, including: Actuarial functions; Claims and legal functions; Different products and programs; Marketing; Rates; and Taxation; and (3) Health Insurance, including: Different products and programs; Government regulations; Group insurance; Marketing; and Underwriting. **Renewal:** Recertification based on continuing education and professional development. **Preparatory Materials:** *Disability Income Insurance: The Unique Risk, Disability Income: The Sale, the Product, the Market, Fundamentals of Disability Income Insurance, Group Ben-*

efits: Basic Concepts and Alternatives, and *1994 Tax Facts 1 - Life* (texts). Study guides provided. **Examination Frequency:** Throughout the year. **Examination Sites:** Exams given at sites throughout the U.S. **Examination Type:** Multiple-choice. **Re-examination:** There is a $175 fee to retake each exam. **Fees:** $555 (members); $780 (nonmembers).

`270`

Registered Mortgage Underwriter (RMU)

National Association of Review Appraisers and Mortgage Underwriters (NARA/MU)
8383 E. Evans Rd.
Scottsdale, AZ 85260
Phone: (602)998-3000
Fax: (602)998-8022
Robert G. Johnson, Exec.Dir.

Recipient: Real estate professionals and mortgage underwriters who aid in determining value of property. **Membership:** Required. **Certification Requirements:** Two years experience. **Renewal:** none. **Fees:** $265.

Professional Specialty Occupations

Engineers

Chemical Engineers

271

Certified Professional Chemical Engineer (CPChE)
National Certification Commission in Chemistry and Chemical Engineering (NCCCCE)
American Institute of Chemists
7315 Wisconsin Ave., Ste. 502E
Bethesda, MD 20814-3209
Phone: (301)652-2447
Fax: (301)657-3549
Dr. Connie M. Hendrickson CPC, Chair

Recipient: Chemical engineers. **Educational/Experience Requirements:** Bachelor's degree in chemistry, chemical engineering, or closely related field. **Membership:** Not required. **Certification Requirements:** Must earn 300 Certification Units (CUs) in the following areas: (1) Continuing Education (150 CUs maximum), including: College courses taken and taught (ten CUs per semester hour); Seminars (five CUs per seminar); Short courses and workshops (20 CUs per course); and Symposia (15 CUs per symposium); (2) Publications, Reports, and Presentations (120 CUs maximum), including: Books or monographs (50 CUs per book or monograph); Nonrefereed publications (ten CUs per publication); Patents (30 CUs per patent); Presentations (15 CUs per item); Publications (variable number of CUs); Refereed publications (20 CUs per publication); Reports (ten CUs per report; maximum of 50 CUs per year); and Reviewer or referee (ten CUs per item; maximum of 50 CUs per year); (3) Professional Society Participation (50 CUs maximum), including: Office holding (ten CUs per office per year); Scientific meetings (15 CUs per national meeting; seven CUs per regional meeting; and three CUs per local

meeting); and Society participation (15 CUs per activity); and (4) Other Professional Activity (50 CUs maximum), including: Awards (15 CUs per award); Community activities (maximum of 15 CUs per year); Individual activities (ten CUs per year); and Non-specified activities (maximum of 15 CUs per year). **Renewal:** Every three years. Recertification based on accumulation of 300 CUs from same categories as initial certification. Retired CPChEs who have been certified for five years may be granted retired status. **Fees:** $75 (members); $105 (non-members). **Endorsed By:** American Institute of Chemists.

Civil Engineers

272

Certified Ground Water Professional (CGWP)
Association of Ground Water Scientists and Engineers (AGWSE)
6375 Riverside Dr.
Dublin, OH 43017
Phone: (614)761-1711
Fax: (614)761-3446
Toll Free: (800)551-7379
Jacqueline Mack, Liaison

Recipient: Engineers, geologists, hydrologists, and other professionals who use scientific and engineering methods to process and evaluate ground water safety and quality. **Number of Certified Individuals:** 350. **Educational/Experience Requirements:** Bachelor's degree in related field and seven years of progressively more responsible experience. Up to three years of post-baccalaureate academic work may be substituted for experience. **Membership:** Not required.

Certification Requirements: Successful completion of peer review. **Renewal:** Every three years. Recertification based on accumulation of 36 professional development credits through attendance at professional meetings, continuing education, and publishing articles in industry journals. Renewal fee is $75. **Fees:** $125. **Endorsed By:** National Ground Water Association.

Corrosion Engineers and Technicians

273

Cathodic Protection Specialist
NACE International
1440 S. Creek Dr.
PO Box 218340
Houston, TX 77218-8340
Phone: (713)492-0535
Fax: (713)492-8254

Recipient: Corrosion control professionals specializing in cathodic protection. **Educational/Experience Requirements:** Must either hold Senior Corrosion Technologist designation (see separate entry) or have four years experience in responsible position and one of the following: (1) Engineer-in-Training (EIT) registration or equivalent; (2) Professional engineer (PE or P.Eng.) or equivalent registration; or (3) Bachelor's degree in engineering or one of the physical sciences and Ph.D. in engineering or one of the physical sciences that required qualification exam. Experience may include: (1) Investigation of corrosion causes and mechanisms; (2) Investigation, design, and implementation of corrosion control procedures; or (3) Teaching of corrosion related science. **Membership:** Not required. **Certification Requirements:** Successful completion of exam. **Renewal:** Every five years. Recertification based on experience and professional development. **Preparatory Materials:** Handbook, including list of reference materials and sample questions, provided. Courses, conferences, and symposia available. **Examination Sites:** Exam given at national headquarters, regional sites, or by arrangement with proctor. **Examination Type:** Multiple-choice; true and false. **Re-examination:** Must wait six months to retake exam. There is a $150 fee to retake exam. **Fees:** $250 (members); $400 (nonmembers). **Endorsed By:** Council of Engineering Specialty Boards.

274

Chemical Treatments Specialist
NACE International
1440 S. Creek Dr.
PO Box 218340
Houston, TX 77218-8340
Phone: (713)492-0535
Fax: (713)492-8254

Recipient: Corrosion control professionals specializing in chemical treatments. **Educational/Experience Requirements:** Must either hold Senior Corrosion Technologist designation (see separate entry) or have four years experience in responsible position and one of the following: (1) Engineer-in-Training (EIT) registration or equivalent; (2) Professional engineer (PE or P.Eng.) or equivalent registration; or (3) Bachelor's degree in engineering or one of the physical sciences and Ph.D. in engineering or one of the physical sciences that required qualification exam. Experience may include: (1) Investigation of corrosion causes and mechanisms; (2) Investigation, design, and implementation of corrosion control procedures; or (3) Teaching of corrosion related science. **Membership:** Not required. **Certification Requirements:** Successful completion of exam. **Renewal:** Every five years. Recertification based on experience and professional development. **Preparatory Materials:** Handbook, including list of reference materials and sample questions, provided. Courses, conferences, and symposia available. **Examination Sites:** Exam given at national headquarters, regional sites, or by arrangement with proctor. **Examination Type:** Multiple-choice; true and false. **Re-examination:** Must wait six months to retake exam. There is a $150 fee to retake exam. **Fees:** $250 (members); $400 (nonmembers). **Endorsed By:** Council of Engineering Specialty Boards.

275

Corrosion Specialist
NACE International
1440 S. Creek Dr.
PO Box 218340
Houston, TX 77218-8340
Phone: (713)492-0535
Fax: (713)492-8254

Recipient: Corrosion control specialists. **Educational/Experience Requirements:** Must hold either Cathodic Protection Specialist, Chemical Treatments Specialist, Materials Selection/Design Specialist, or Protective Coatings Specialist designation (see separate entries). **Membership:** Not required. **Certification Requirements:** Successful completion of exam. Exam covers: Cathodic protection; Corrosion causes and mechanisms; General corrosion topics; Inhibitors/environmental treatment; Materials and designs; and Protective coatings and linings. **Renewal:** Every five years. Recertification based on experience and professional development. **Preparatory Materials:** Handbook, including list of reference materials and sample questions, provided. Courses, conferences, and symposia available. **Examination Sites:** Exam given at national headquarters, regional sites, or by arrangement with proctor. **Examination Type:** Multiple-choice. **Re-examination:** Must wait six months to retake exam. There is a $150 fee to retake exam. **Fees:** $250 (members); $400 (nonmembers). **Endorsed By:** Council of Engineering Specialty Boards.

276

Corrosion Specialist, G
NACE International
1440 S. Creek Dr.
PO Box 218340
Houston, TX 77218-8340
Phone: (713)492-0535
Fax: (713)492-8254

Recipient: Corrosion control specialists. **Educational/Experience Requirements:** Must meet the following requirements: (1) Hold either Cathodic Protection Specialist, Chemical Treatments Specialist, Materials Selection/Design Specialist, or Protective Coatings Specialist designation (see separate entries); and (2) Graduate with engineering degree from program accredited by Engineering Accreditation Commission of Accreditation Board for Engineering and Technology (see separate entry) or equivalent. **Membership:** Not required. **Certification Requirements:** Successful completion of exam. **Renewal:** Every five years. Recertification based on experience and profes-

sional development. **Preparatory Materials:** Handbook, including list of reference materials and sample questions, provided. Courses, conferences, and symposia available. **Examination Sites:** Exam given at national headquarters, regional sites, or by arrangement with proctor. **Examination Type:** Multiple-choice. **Re-examination:** Must wait six months to retake exam. **Fees:** $150 (members); $300 (nonmembers). **Endorsed By:** Council of Engineering Specialty Boards.

277

Corrosion Specialist, P
NACE International
1440 S. Creek Dr.
PO Box 218340
Houston, TX 77218-8340
Phone: (713)492-0535
Fax: (713)492-8254

Recipient: Corrosion control specialists. **Educational/Experience Requirements:** Must hold both of the following: (1) Either Cathodic Protection Specialist, Chemical Treatments Specialist, Materials Selection/Design Specialist, or Protective Coatings Specialist designation (see separate entries); and (2) Professional engineer (PE) registration or equivalent. **Membership:** Not required. **Certification Requirements:** Successful completion of exam. **Renewal:** Every five years. Recertification based on experience and professional development. **Preparatory Materials:** Handbook, including list of reference materials and sample questions, provided. Courses, conferences, and symposia available. **Examination Sites:** Exam given at national headquarters, regional sites, or by arrangement with proctor. **Examination Type:** Multiple-choice. **Re-examination:** Must wait six months to retake exam. **Fees:** $150 (members); $300 (nonmembers). **Endorsed By:** Council of Engineering Specialty Boards.

278

Corrosion Technician
NACE International
1440 S. Creek Dr.
PO Box 218340
Houston, TX 77218-8340
Phone: (713)492-0535
Fax: (713)492-8254

Recipient: Corrosion technicians capable of performing routine, but well-defined work under close direction. **Educational/Experience Requirements:** Two years experience. Experience may include: (1) Investigation of corrosion causes and mechanisms; (2) Investigation, design, and implementation of corrosion control procedures; or (3) Teaching of corrosion related science. **Membership:** Not required. **Certification Requirements:** Successful completion of exam. **Renewal:** Every three years. Recertification based on experience and professional development. **Preparatory Materials:** Handbook, including list of reference materials and sample questions, provided. Courses, conferences, and symposia available. **Examination Sites:** Exam given at national headquarters, regional sites, or by arrangement with proctor. **Examination Type:** Multiple-choice. **Re-examination:** Must wait three months to retake exam. There is a $75 fee to retake exam. **Fees:** $175 (members); $325 (nonmembers). **Endorsed By:** Council of Engineering Specialty Boards.

279

Corrosion Technologist
NACE International
1440 S. Creek Dr.
PO Box 218340
Houston, TX 77218-8340
Phone: (713)492-0535
Fax: (713)492-8254

Recipient: Corrosion technologists capable of performing some responsible work under close direction. **Educational/ Experience Requirements:** Four years experience. Experience may include: (1) Investigation of corrosion causes and mechanisms; (2) Investigation, design, and implementation of corrosion control procedures; or (3) Teaching of corrosion related science. **Membership:** Not required. **Certification Requirements:** Successful completion of exam. **Renewal:** Every five years. Recertification based on experience and professional development. **Preparatory Materials:** Handbook, including list of reference materials and sample questions, provided. Courses, conferences, and symposia available. **Examination Sites:** Exam given at national headquarters, regional sites, or by arrangement with proctor. **Examination Type:** Multiple-choice. **Re-examination:** Must wait three months to retake exam. There is a $75 fee to retake exam. **Fees:** $175 (members); $325 (nonmembers). **Endorsed By:** Council of Engineering Specialty Boards.

280

Materials Selection/Design Specialist
NACE International
1440 S. Creek Dr.
PO Box 218340
Houston, TX 77218-8340
Phone: (713)492-0535
Fax: (713)492-8254

Recipient: Corrosion control professionals specializing in materials selection and design. **Educational/Experience Requirements:** Must either hold Senior Corrosion Technologist designation (see separate entry) or have four years experience in responsible position and one of the following: (1) Engineer-in-Training (EIT) registration or equivalent; (2) Professional engineer (PE or P.Eng.) or equivalent registration; or (3) Bachelor's degree in engineering or one of the physical sciences and Ph.D. in engineering or one of the physical sciences that required qualification exam. Experience may include: (1) Investigation of corrosion causes and mechanisms; (2) Investigation, design, and implementation of corrosion control procedures; or (3) Teaching of corrosion related science. **Membership:** Not required. **Certification Requirements:** Successful completion of exam. **Renewal:** Every five years. Recertification based on experience and professional development. **Preparatory Materials:** Handbook, including list of reference materials and sample questions, provided. Courses, conferences, and symposia available. **Examination Sites:** Exam given at national headquarters, regional sites, or by arrangement with proctor. **Examination Type:** Multiple-choice; true and false. **Re-examination:** Must wait six months to retake exam. There is a $150 fee to retake exam. **Fees:** $250 (members); $400 (nonmembers). **Endorsed By:** Council of Engineering Specialty Boards.

281

Protective Coatings Specialist
NACE International
1440 S. Creek Dr.
PO Box 218340
Houston, TX 77218-8340
Phone: (713)492-0535
Fax: (713)492-8254

Recipient: Corrosion control professionals specializing in protective coatings. **Educational/Experience Requirements:** Must either hold Senior Corrosion Technologist designation (see separate entry) or have four years experience in responsible position and one of the following:

---

(1) Engineer-in-Training (EIT) registration or equivalent; (2) Professional engineer (PE or P.Eng.) or equivalent registration; or (3) Bachelor's degree in engineering or one of the physical sciences and Ph.D. in engineering or one of the physical sciences that required qualification exam. Experience may include: (1) Investigation of corrosion causes and mechanisms; (2) Investigation, design, and implementation of corrosion control procedures; or (3) Teaching of corrosion related science. **Membership:** Not required. **Certification Requirements:** Successful completion of exam. **Renewal:** Every five years. Recertification based on experience and professional development. **Preparatory Materials:** Handbook, including list of reference materials and sample questions, provided. Courses, conferences, and symposia available. **Examination Sites:** Exam given at national headquarters, regional sites, or by arrangement with proctor. **Examination Type:** Multiple-choice; true and false. **Re-examination:** Must wait six months to retake exam. **Fees:** $250 (members); $400 (nonmembers). **Endorsed By:** Council of Engineering Specialty Boards.

282

Senior Corrosion Technologist
NACE International
1440 S. Creek Dr.
PO Box 218340
Houston, TX 77218-8340
Phone: (713)492-0535
Fax: (713)492-8254

Recipient: Corrosion technologists capable of performing responsible work with minimal supervision. **Educational/ Experience Requirements:** Must meet one of the following requirements: (1) Eight years experience, including four years in responsible position; or (2) Bachelor's degree in one of the physical sciences or engineering and four years experience in responsible position. Experience may include: (1) Investigation of corrosion causes and mechanisms; (2) Investigation, design, and implementation of corrosion control procedures; or (3) Teaching of corrosion related science. **Membership:** Not required. **Certification Requirements:** Successful completion of exam. Exam covers: Cathodic protection; Corrosion causes and mechanisms; General corrosion topics; Inhibitors/ environmental treatment; Materials and designs; and Protective coatings and linings. **Renewal:** Every five years. Recertification based on experience and professional development. **Preparatory Materials:** Handbook, including list of reference materials and sample questions, provided. Courses, conferences, and symposia available. **Examination Sites:** Exam given at national headquarters, regional sites, or by arrangement with proctor. **Examination Type:** Multiple-choice. **Re-examination:** Must wait six months to retake exam. There is a $125 fee to retake exam. **Fees:** $225 (members); $375 (nonmembers). **Endorsed By:** Council of Engineering Specialty Boards.

Electrical and Electronics Engineers

283

Broadband Communications Engineer (BCE)
Society of Cable Television Engineers (SCTE)
669 Exton Commons
Exton, PA 19341
Phone: (215)363-6888
Fax: (215)363-5898
Toll Free: (800)542-5040
E-mail: MarvinSCTE@AOL.com
Marvin Nelson, Dir.

Recipient: Cable television technical professionals. **Number of Certified Individuals:** 100. **Educational/Experience Requirements:** Must meet the following requirements: (1) Five years experience; and (2) Successful completion of formal electronic training in military, at vocational or technical schools, or college. **Membership:** Required. **Certification Requirements:** Successful completion of seven exams. Exams consist of the following sections: Data Networking and Architecture; Distribution Systems; Engineering Management and Professionalism; Signal Processing Centers; Terminal Devices; Transportation Systems; and Video and Audio Signals and Systems. **Renewal:** Every three years. Recertification based on either successful completion of exam or accumulation of 21 recertification units through: (1) SCTE national and local chapter membership (one unit per year); (2) Seminars and meetings (one unit per day); (3) Successful completion of approved courses (one unit per credit hour); (4) Speaking engagements or presenting papers (four units at national level; two units at local level); (5) Publication of articles (four units per article); and (6) Service as officer or on committee (one unit per year). Renewal fee is $15. **Preparatory Materials:** Bibliography available. **Examination Frequency:** Three-six times per year. **Examination Sites:** Exams given at SCTE chapter meetings and regional shows. **Examination Type:** Multiple choice.

Pass/Fail Rate: 55% pass exams the first time. **Waiting Period to Receive Scores:** Two weeks. **Re-examination:** There is no waiting period to retake exams. **Fees:** $70.

284

Certified Broadcast Radio Engineer (CBRE)
Society of Broadcast Engineers (SBE)
8455 Keystone Crossing, Ste. 140
Indianapolis, IN 46240
Phone: (317)253-1640
Fax: (317)253-0418
Linda L. Godby, Exec. Officer

Recipient: Broadcast engineers involved in design, operation, maintenance, or administration of radio broadcast facility or related technology. **Educational/Experience Requirements:** Five years experience. Each year of college can be substituted for one year of experience, up to four years. Professional Engineer (P.E.) license may be substituted for four years experience. **Membership:** Not required. **Certification Requirements:** Successful completion of exam. Exam covers: Operating practice; Problems; Safety; and Theory. **Renewal:** Every five years. Recertification based on either successful completion of exam or accumulation of 20 professional credits through experience, continuing education, publication of articles or papers, presentations or teaching, and association participation. **Preparatory Materials:** Study guide, including sample questions, and study course available. **Examination Frequency:** quarterly. **Examination Sites:** Exams given at National Association of Broadcasters annual convention, SBE annual conference, and by chapters throughout the U.S. **Examination Type:** Multiple-choice. **Fees:** $50 (members); $105 (nonmembers).

285

Certified Broadcast Television Engineer (CBTE)
Society of Broadcast Engineers (SBE)
8455 Keystone Crossing, Ste. 140
Indianapolis, IN 46240
Phone: (317)253-1640
Fax: (317)253-0418
Linda L. Godby, Exec. Officer

Recipient: Broadcast engineers involved in design, operation, maintenance, or administration of television broadcast facility or related technology. **Educational/**

Experience Requirements: Five years experience. Each year of college can be substituted for one year of experience, up to four years. Professional Engineer (P.E.) license may be substituted for four years experience. **Membership:** Not required. **Certification Requirements:** Successful completion of exam. Exam covers: Operating practice; Problems; Safety; and Theory. **Renewal:** Every five years. Recertification based on either successful completion of exam or accumulation of 20 professional credits through experience, continuing education, publication of articles or papers, presentations or teaching, and association participation. **Preparatory Materials:** Study guide, including sample questions, available. **Examination Sites:** Exams given at National Association of Broadcasters annual convention, SBE annual conference, and by chapters throughout the U.S. **Examination Type:** Multiple-choice. **Fees:** $50 (members); $105 (nonmembers).

286

Certified Cogeneration Professional (CCP)
Association of Energy Engineers (AEE)
4025 Pleasantdale Rd., Ste. 420
Atlanta, GA 30340
Phone: (404)447-6415
Fax: (404)446-3969
Tamara K. Parker, Dir.

Recipient: Power generation/cogeneration professionals. **Educational/Experience Requirements:** Must meet one of the following requirements: (1) Bachelor's degree in engineering and/or Professional Engineer (P.E.) registration, and three years experience; (2) Bachelor's degree in business or related degree and five years experience; (3) Two-year technical degree and eight years experience; or (4) Ten years experience. **Membership:** Not required. **Certification Requirements:** Must earn 1400 total points from following areas: (1) Education/registration (700 points maximum); (2) Experience and activities in cogeneration (700 points maximum); and (3) Successful completion of exam (1050 points maximum; 700 points minimum). Exam consists of following sections: Absorption Cooling; Cogeneration Application; Contractural Consideration; Electrical Interconnection; Energy Analysis Feasibility Studies; Environmental Regulations; Financial and Economic Considerations; Fuels; General; Legal; Prime Movers and Boilers; Project Financing and Development; PURPA; Small Scale Cogeneration Systems; and Technology Assessment. **Renewal:** Every three years. Recertification based on accumulation of eight credits. Lifetime certification available after retirement at age 62. Renewal fee is $90. **Preparatory Materials:** Study guide with list of suggested study references provided. Review course available. **Examination Frequency:** Throughout the year. **Examination Sites:** Exams given at sites throughout the U.S. **Examination Type:** Multiple-choice; short-answer; true or false. **Fees:** $150.

287

Certified Demand-Side Management Professional (CDSM)
Association of Energy Engineers
(AEE)
4025 Pleasantdale Rd., Ste. 420
Atlanta, GA 30340
Phone: (404)447-6415
Fax: (404)446-3969
Tamara K. Parker, Dir.

Recipient: Demand-side management energy engineering professionals. **Educational/Experience Requirements:** Must meet the following requirements: (1) Bachelor's degree in business, economics, engineering, or related field, or hold Certified Energy Manager (CEM) designation (see separate entry); and (2) Four years experience. **Certification Requirements:** Must earn 1400 total points in the following areas: (1) Education (350 points maximum); (2) Professional registration (350 points maximum); (3) Experience and activities in demand-side management (350 points maximum); and (4) Successful completion of exam (1040 points maximum; 700 points minimum). Exam consists of following sections: DSM Contracts, Financial, Procurement, and Regulations; Electric Thermal Storage; Energy Service Companies; Integrated Resource Planning; Lighting Efficiency; Monitoring and Evaluation; Rate Design and DSM; and Technologies to Reduce Demand. **Renewal:** Every three years. Recertification based on accumulation of eight professional credits through: (1) Experience (four credits for three years); (2) Association membership (three credits); (3) Continuing education and professional activities (two credits per continuing education unit (CEU), college credit hour, or ten contact hours for seminars); (4) Awards received (two credits each); (5) Articles published (two credits each), and (6) Offices held in professional societies (one credit per year). Lifetime certification available upon retiring and reaching age 62. Renewal fee is $150. **Preparatory Materials:** Study guide, sample questions, and bibliography of suggested reference materials provided. Review seminar available. **Ex-**

amination **Frequency:** Throughout the year. **Examination Sites:** Exam given at sites throughout the U.S. **Examination Type:** Multiple-choice; true or false. **Re-examination:** There is a $50 fee to retake exam. **Fees:** $175.

288

Certified Energy Manager (CEM)
Association of Energy Engineers
(AEE)
4025 Pleasantdale Rd., Ste. 420
Atlanta, GA 30340
Phone: (404)447-6415
Fax: (404)446-3969
Tamara K. Parker, Dir.

Recipient: Energy engineering and management professionals. **Educational/Experience Requirements:** Must meet one of the following requirements: (1) Bachelor's degree in engineering and/or registration as Professional Engineer (P.E.), and three years experience; (2) Bachelor's degree in business or related field and five years experience; (3) Two-year technical degree and eight years experience; or (4) Ten years experience. **Membership:** Not required. **Certification Requirements:** Must earn 1400 total points from following areas: (1) Education (350 points maximum); (2) Professional registration (350 points maximum); (3) Experience and activities in energy management (700 points maximum); and (4) Successful completion of exam (1040 points maximum; 700 points minimum). Exam covers: Boiler and incineration plants; Building envelope; Codes and standards; Cogeneration; Controls; Electrical system utilization; Energy accounting and economics; Energy audits/instrumentation; Energy management systems; Lighting; Maintenance program; Mechanical system (HVAC) utilization; Procurement of fuel; Thermal energy storage; and Utility and process system utilization. **Renewal:** Every three years. Recertification based on accumulation of eight credits through: (1) Experience (four credits per three years); (2) Association membership (three credits); (3) Continuing education and professional activities (two credits per continuing education unit (CEU), college credit hour, or ten contract hours for seminars); (4) Awards received (two credits each); (5) Papers published (two credits each); and (6) Offices held in professional engineering society (one credit per year). Lifetime certification available after retirement at age 62. Renewal fee is $90. **Preparatory Materials:** Study guide, including list of suggested references and sample questions, provided. Exam review course available. **Ex-**

amination **Frequency:** Throughout the year. **Examination Sites:** Exam given at sites throughout the U.S. **Examination Type:** Multiple-choice; true or false. **Re-examination:** There is a $50 fee to retake the exam. **Fees:** $150.

289

Certified Indoor Air Quality Professional (CIAQP)
Association of Energy Engineers
(AEE)
4025 Pleasantdale Rd., Ste. 420
Atlanta, GA 30340
Phone: (404)447-6415
Fax: (404)446-3969
Tamara K. Parker, Dir.

Recipient: Indoor air quality professionals. **Educational/Experience Requirements:** Must meet one of the following requirements: (1) Degree in engineering, science, architecture, business, industrial hygiene, or related field and three years experience; or (2) Technical or Associate degree and four years experience. **Membership:** Not required. **Certification Requirements:** Must earn 1400 total points from following areas: (1) Education (350 points maximum); (2) Professional registration (350 points maximum); (3) Experience and activities in lighting (700 points maximum); and (4) Successful completion of exam (1050 points maximum; 700 points minimum). Exam covers: Building IAQ management; Codes and standards; Diagnosing IAQ problems; Energy and IAQ; Health risks associated with IAQ pollutants; HVAC systems and IAQ; IAQ measurements; Mitigating IAQ problems; Preventing IAQ problems; and Sources of indoor air pollutants. **Renewal:** Every three years. Recertification based on accumulation of eight credits through: (1) Experience (four credits per three years); (2) Association membership (three credits); (3) Continuing education and professional activities (two credits per continuing education unit (CEU), college credit hour, and ten contract hours for seminars); (4) Awards received (two credits each); (5) Papers published (two credits each); and (6) Offices held in professional engineering society (one credit per year). Lifetime certification available after retirement at age 62. Renewal fee is $90. **Preparatory Materials:** Study guide, including list of reference materials and sample questions, provided. Exam preparation course available. **Examination Frequency:** Throughout the year. **Examination Sites:** Exam given at sites throughout the U.S. **Re-examination:** There is a $50 fee to retake exam. **Fees:** $150.

| 290 |

Certified Lighting Efficiency Professional (CLEP)

Association of Energy Engineers (AEE)
4025 Pleasantdale Rd., Ste. 420
Atlanta, GA 30340
Phone: (404)447-6415
Fax: (404)446-3969
Tamara K. Parker, Dir.

Recipient: Lighting management professionals. **Educational/Experience Requirements:** Must meet one of the following requirements: (1) Bachelor's degree in engineering, registration as Professional Engineer (P.E.), or certification as Certified Energy Manager (CEM) (see separate entry), and three years experience; (2) Bachelor's degree in business or related field and five years experience; (3) Two-year technical degree and eight years experience; or (4) Ten years experience. **Membership:** Not required. **Certification Requirements:** Must earn 1400 total points from following areas: (1) Professional registration (350 points maximum); (2) Education (350 points maximum); (3) Experience and activities in lighting (700 points maximum); and (4) Successful completion of exam (1040 points maximum; 700 points minimum). Exam covers: Codes and standards; Design basics; DSM and lighting efficiency; Environmental safety; Lamps and ballasts; Lighting controls, evaluation and economics, fundamentals, and system maintenance; and Quantity and quality of illumination. **Renewal:** Every three years. Recertification based on accumulation of eight credits through: (1) Experience (four credits per three years); (2) Association membership (three credits); (3) Continuing education and professional activities (two credits per continuing education unit (CEU), college credit hour, and ten contract hours for seminars); (4) Awards received (two credits each); (5) Papers published (two credits each); and (6) Offices held in professional engineering society (one credit per year). Lifetime certification available after retirement at age 62. Renewal fee is $90. **Preparatory Materials:** Study guide, including list of reference materials and sample questions, provided. Exam preparation course available. **Examination Frequency:** Throughout the year. **Examination Sites:** Exam given at sites throughout the U.S. **Examination Type:** Multiple-choice; true or false. **Fees:** $150.

| 291 |

Certified Professional Broadcast Engineer (CPBE)

Society of Broadcast Engineers (SBE)
8455 Keystone Crossing, Ste. 140
Indianapolis, IN 46240
Phone: (317)253-1640
Fax: (317)253-0418
Linda L. Godby, Exec. Officer

Recipient: Broadcast engineers involved in design, operation, maintenance, or administration of broadcast facility or related technology. **Membership:** Not required. **Certification Requirements:** Must meet the following requirements: (1) Twenty years experience in AM/FM radio or television; (2) Hold Senior Broadcast Engineer designation (see separate entry); and (3) Submit statement that describes professional experience, educational background, and training in the following areas: Continuing education; Maintenance; Management or supervision; and Systems design. Professional Engineer (P.E.) license may be substituted for four years experience. **Renewal:** Every five years. Recertification based on either successful completion of exam or accumulation of 30 professional credits through experience, continuing education, publication of articles or papers, presentations or teaching, and association participation. Lifetime certification available after 20 years of continuous certification. **Fees:** $100 (members); $155 (nonmembers).

| 292 |

Certified Senior Radio Engineer (CSRE)

Society of Broadcast Engineers (SBE)
8455 Keystone Crossing, Ste. 140
Indianapolis, IN 46240
Phone: (317)253-1640
Fax: (317)253-0418
Linda L. Godby, Exec. Officer

Recipient: Broadcast engineers involved in design, operation, maintenance, or administration of radio broadcast facility or related technology. **Educational/Experience Requirements:** Ten years experience. Each year of college can be substituted for one year of experience, up to four years. Professional Engineer (P.E.) license may be substituted for four years experience. **Membership:** Not required. **Certification Requirements:** Successful completion of exam. Exam covers: Operating practices; Problems; Safety; Supervision and management;

and Theory. **Renewal:** Every five years. Recertification based on either successful completion of exam or accumulation of 25 professional credits through experience, continuing education, publication of articles or papers, presentations or teaching, and association participation. Lifetime certification available after 20 years of continuous certification. **Preparatory Materials:** Study guide, including sample questions, and study course available. **Examination Sites:** Exam given at National Association of Broadcasters annual convention, SBE annual conference, and by chapters throughout the U.S. **Examination Type:** Essay; multiple-choice. **Fees:** $75 (members); $130 (nonmembers).

| 293 |

Certified Senior Television Engineer (CSTE)

Society of Broadcast Engineers (SBE)
8455 Keystone Crossing, Ste. 140
Indianapolis, IN 46240
Phone: (317)253-1640
Fax: (317)253-0418
Linda L. Godby, Exec. Officer

Recipient: Broadcast engineers involved in design, operation, maintenance, or administration of television broadcast facility or related technology. **Educational/Experience Requirements:** Ten years experience. Each year of college can be substituted for one year of experience, up to four years. Professional Engineer (P.E.) license may be substituted for four years experience. **Membership:** Not required. **Certification Requirements:** Successful completion of exam. Exam covers: Operating practices; Problems; Safety; Supervision and management; and Theory. **Renewal:** Every five years. Recertification based on either successful completion of exam or accumulation of 25 professional credits through experience, continuing education, publication of articles or papers, presentations or teaching, and association participation. Lifetime certification available after 20 years of continuous certification. **Preparatory Materials:** Study guide, including sample questions, available. **Examination Sites:** Exam given at National Association of Broadcasters annual convention, SBE annual conference, and by chapters throughout the U.S. **Examination Type:** Essay; multiple-choice. **Fees:** $75 (members); $130 (nonmembers).

`294`

Electromagnetic Compatibility Engineer

National Association of Radio and Telecommunications Engineers (NARTE)
PO Box 678
Medway, MA 02053
Phone: (508)533-8333
Fax: (508)533-3815
Toll Free: (800)89N-ARTE

Recipient: Electromagnetic compatibility (EMC) engineers. **Educational/ Experience Requirements:** Nine years experience. Bachelor's degree in engineering, engineering technology, or one of the physical sciences may be substituted for four years of experience. Each year of study in non-completed engineering program may be substituted for one year of experience. Bachelor's degree in non-related field may be substituted for two years of experience. May substitute up to one year of postgraduate study in engineering for experience. Teaching in engineering may be substituted for up to two years of experience. **Certification Requirements:** Successful completion of exam. Exam covers: Antennas; Bonding; Conducted interference; Electromagnetic pulse; Electrostatic discharge; EMC test plans; EMI analysis; EMI prediction; Equipment design; Field theory; Filter theory; Filtering; Grounding; Interface control; Intersystem and intra-system design; Lightning protection; Materials and special devices; Mathematics/spectrum analysis; Military specification standards and handbooks; Radiated interference; Safety; Shielding; Terminology; Test equipment; and Test facilities. Each year of additional experience may add one percent to exam score. **Renewal:** Every year. Recertification based on continuing education. Renewal fee is $40. **Preparatory Materials:** Study guide, including list of suggested study references, available. **Examination Frequency:** quarterly - always March, May, September, and December. **Examination Sites:** Exam given at sites throughout the U.S. **Examination Type:** Multiple-choice. **Waiting Period to Receive Scores:** Four weeks. **Reexamination:** Must wait 90 days to retake exam. There is a $20 fee to retake exam. **Fees:** $40.

`295`

Electrostatic Discharge Control Engineer

National Association of Radio and Telecommunications Engineers (NARTE)
PO Box 678
Medway, MA 02053
Phone: (508)533-8333
Fax: (508)533-3815
Toll Free: (800)89N-ARTE

Recipient: Electrostatic discharge control (ESDC) engineers. **Educational/ Experience Requirements:** Nine years experience. Bachelor's degree in engineering, engineering technology, or one of the physical sciences may be substituted for four years of experience. Each year of study in non-completed engineering program may be substituted for one year of experience. Bachelor's degree in non-related field may be substituted for two years of experience. May substitute up to one year of postgraduate study in engineering for experience. Teaching in engineering may be substituted for up to two years of experience. **Certification Requirements:** Successful completion of exam. Exam covers: Body charge evaluation and control; Clean room equipment and material control; Device sensitivity test and measurement; Equipment design; ESD analysis (devices and systems); ESD control material in-field testing; ESD loss analysis; ESD prediction (devices and systems); ESD program design and management; ESD shielding analysis; ESD theory; Flooring; Garment control and evaluation; Grounding technology; In field ESD controls; Intersystem and intrasystem design; Ionization devices and systems; Laboratory test and analysis of ESDC packaging materials; Manufacturing plant handling procedures; Manufacturing/repair facility evaluation, survey, and auditing; Materials tests and measurement; Math/ physics; Plant equipment ESD control and evaluation; Production aids and tool evaluation; Safety; Standards/ specifications; System test and measurement; Terminology; and Workstations. Each year of additional experience may add one percent to exam score. **Renewal:** Every year. Recertification based on continuing education. Renewal fee is $40. **Examination Frequency:** quarterly - always March, May, September, and December. **Examination Sites:** Exam given at sites throughout the U.S. **Examination Type:** Multiple-choice. **Waiting Period to Receive Scores:** Four weeks. **Reexamination:** Must wait 90 days to retake exam. There is a $20 fee to retake exam. **Fees:** $40.

`296`

Radio and Telecommunications Engineer, Class I

National Association of Radio and Telecommunications Engineers (NARTE)
PO Box 678
Medway, MA 02053
Phone: (508)533-8333
Fax: (508)533-3815
Toll Free: (800)89N-ARTE

Recipient: Radio and telecommunications engineers working with either non RF radiating or RF radiating systems and equipment. **Educational/Experience Requirements:** Eight years experience. Bachelor's degree in electrical engineering, electrical engineering technology, or physical science may be substituted for four years of experience. Credit may be granted for each year of study in non-completed program. May substitute professional engineer (PE) designation or designation from country other than the U.S. for four years of experience. Candidates with less experience may quality for Radio and Telecommunications Engineer, Class II or III designations (see separate entries). **Certification Requirements:** Successful completion of exam. Must also earn one endorsement in either RF radiating or non-RF radiating systems and equipment through either successful completion of exam or credential review. RF endorsements are: Administrative/Regulatory; Aeronautical/Marine; Antenna Systems; Broadcast AM; Broadcast FM; Broadcast TV; Cellular Radio Systems; Control Systems (including SCADA); Education; Frequency Coordination (Class I and II Engineer only); Interference Analysis/ Suppression; International Broadcast; International Public Fixed; Landmobile Systems; LF, MF, and HF Radio (Non Broadcast); Microwave Systems; Millimeter Wave Systems; Power Line Carrier; Radar Systems; Satellite Systems; Scatter Systems; Special Field Test; and Telegraphy. Non-RF endorsements are: Administrative/Regulatory; Cable Transmission Systems; Circuit Design; Common Channel Signaling (CCS); Computer Telecommunications; Control Systems; Education; Encryption, Voice, and Data; Equipment Appraiser; Fiber Optic Splicing; Lightwave Systems; Multiplex Systems; Operations; Power Systems; Station Equipment; Switching Systems; Telephone Inside Plant; Telephone Local Outside Plant; Telephone Toll Outside Plant; Test Equipment Calibration; Traffic Engineering; and Wire Transmission Systems. May also earn Master endorsements with proof of proficiency in six endorsements. **Renewal:**

Every year. Renewal fee is $60. **Preparatory Materials:** Reference guides and study materials available. **Examination Frequency:** quarterly - always March, May, September, and December. **Examination Sites:** Exam given at sites throughout the U.S. **Fees:** $60; $5 (per endorsement).

297

Radio and Telecommunications Engineer, Class II

National Association of Radio and Telecommunications Engineers (NARTE)
PO Box 678
Medway, MA 02053
Phone: (508)533-8333
Fax: (508)533-3815
Toll Free: (800)89N-ARTE

Recipient: Radio and telecommunications engineers working with either non RF radiating or RF radiating systems and equipment. **Educational/Experience Requirements:** Six years experience. Bachelor's degree in electrical engineering, electrical engineering technology, or physical science may be substituted for four years of experience. Credit may be granted for each year of study in non-completed program. May substitute professional engineer (PE) designation or designation from country other than the U.S. for four years of experience. May qualify for Radio and Telecommunications Engineer, Class I designation (see separate entry) with increased experience. Candidates with less experience may qualify for Radio and Telecommunications Engineer, Class III designation (see separate entry). **Certification Requirements:** Successful completion of exam. Must also earn one endorsement in either RF radiating or non-RF radiating systems and equipment through either successful completion of exam or credential review. RF endorsements are: Administrative/Regulatory; Aeronautical/Marine; Antenna Systems; Broadcast AM; Broadcast FM; Broadcast TV; Cellular Radio Systems; Control Systems (including SCADA); Education; Frequency Coordination (Class I and II Engineer only); Interference Analysis/ Suppression; International Broadcast; International Public Fixed; Landmobile Systems; LF, MF, and HF Radio (Non Broadcast); Microwave Systems; Millimeter Wave Systems; Power Line Carrier; Radar Systems; Satellite Systems; Scatter Systems; Special Field Test; and Telegraphy. Non-RF endorsements are: Administrative/Regulatory; Cable Transmission Systems; Circuit Design; Common Channel Signaling (CCS);

Computer Telecommunications; Control Systems; Education; Encryption, Voice, and Data; Equipment Appraiser; Fiber Optic Splicing; Lightwave Systems; Multiplex Systems; Operations; Power Systems; Station Equipment; Switching Systems; Telephone Inside Plant; Telephone Local Outside Plant; Telephone Toll Outside Plant; Test Equipment Calibration; Traffic Engineering; and Wire Transmission Systems. May also earn Master endorsements with proof of proficiency in six endorsements. **Renewal:** Every year. Renewal fee is $50. **Preparatory Materials:** Reference guides and study materials available. **Examination Frequency:** quarterly - always March, May, September, and December. **Examination Sites:** Exam given at sites throughout the U.S. **Fees:** $50; $5 (per endorsement).

298

Radio and Telecommunications Engineer, Class III

National Association of Radio and Telecommunications Engineers (NARTE)
PO Box 678
Medway, MA 02053
Phone: (508)533-8333
Fax: (508)533-3815
Toll Free: (800)89N-ARTE

Recipient: Radio and telecommunications engineers working with either non RF radiating or RF radiating systems and equipment. **Educational/Experience Requirements:** Four years experience. Bachelor's degree in electrical engineering, electrical engineering technology, or physical science may be substituted for experience requirement. May qualify for Radio and Telecommunications Engineer, Class I or II designations (see separate entries) with increased experience. **Certification Requirements:** Successful completion of exam. **Renewal:** Every year. Renewal fee is $40. **Preparatory Materials:** Reference guides and study materials available. **Examination Frequency:** quarterly - always March, May, September, and December. **Examination Sites:** Exam given at sites throughout the U.S. **Fees:** $40; $5 (per endorsement).

Industrial Engineers

299

Certified Manufacturing Engineer (CMfgE)

Manufacturing Engineering Certification Institute (MECI)
Society of Manufacturing Engineers
One SME Dr.
PO Box 930
Dearborn, MI 48121-0930
Phone: (313)271-1500
Fax: (313)271-2861
Toll Free: (800)733-4763
John Covalchuck CMfgE, Chair

Recipient: Manufacturing engineers. **Educational/Experience Requirements:** Ten years combined education and experience, with maximum of five years of education. **Membership:** Not required. **Certification Requirements:** Successful completion of two-part exam. Part one covers: Applied sciences; Computer applications and engineering design; and Mathematics. Part two covers: Facility operations; Floor operations; Manufacturing processes and practices; Material handling; and Product and tool design. May chose from following specialties for part two of exam: (1) Integration and Control, including: Automation; CAM; CIM; Common networks; Computer systems; Machine vision; and Robotics; (2) Processes, including: Assembly; Casting; Electronics manufacturing; Fabrication; Finishing; Material forming; Material removal; and Molding; and (3) Support Operations, including: Design; Maintenance; Management; Material handling; Planning; and Scheduling. Professional Engineers (P.E.s) may be exempt from part one of exam. **Renewal:** Every three years. Recertification based on either successful completion of exam or accumulation of 36 credits through continuing education, patents earned, technical papers published and presented, teaching, and other significant accomplishments in the field. Renewal fees are: Credit option: $40 (members); $50 (nonmembers); Exam option: $90 (members); $150 (nonmembers). **Preparatory Materials:** *Fundamentals of Manufacturing* (reference). Study guide, including list of references and sample questions, provided. Review courses and practice exams available. **Examination Frequency:** semiannual - always May and December. **Examination Sites:** Exams given at chapters and universities throughout the U.S. **Examination Type:** Multiple-choice. **Waiting Period to Receive Scores:** 60 days. **Fees:** $90 (members); $150 (nonmembers). **Endorsed By:** Society of Manufacturing Engineers.

Logisticians

300

Certification in Transportation and Logistics (CTL)
American Society of Transportation and Logistics (AST&L)
216 E. Church St.
Lock Haven, PA 17745
Phone: (717)748-8515
Fax: (717)748-9118

Recipient: Professionals in logistics and transportation. **Educational/Experience Requirements:** Must meet one of the following requirements: (1) Two years education at accredited college or university; or (2) Five years experience. **Membership:** Required. **Certification Requirements:** Successful completion of research paper and four of the following exams: (1) Transportation Economics, including: Basic economic principles that affect decisions related to transportation; Carrier management; Overview of modes of transportation and their effect on the economy; and Role of government in regulating and providing transportation services; (2) Logistics, covering concepts, analytical techniques, human behavioral conditions, and operating procedures of logistics systems management; (3) General Management Principles, including: Accounting and finance; Marketing; and Production; (4) Legal Realm of Transportation and Logistics, including: Antitrust and pricing laws; Commercial contract laws governing transportation in the U.S.; and Economic laws and regulations; (5) International Transportation and Logistics, including: Exporting and importing; International transportation; Ocean carrier management; Port administration; Regulation and policy issues; and Sourcing; and (6) Transport Systems, including: Carrier management; General characteristics of transport system; Traffic management; and Transportation policy issues. Exams 1, 2, and 3 are required. Candidates may substitute coursework or experience for successful completion of each exam with approval of AST&L. **Preparatory Materials:** Correspondence courses, study guides, past exam outlines, and study groups available. **Examination Frequency:** semiannual - always given in April and November. **Examination Sites:** Exam given at sites throughout the U.S. **Examination Type:** Essay; multiple-choice; problem solving.

301

Certified Professional Logistician (C.P.L.)
Society of Logistics Engineers (SOLE)
8100 Professional Pl., Ste. 211
New Carrollton, MD 20785
Phone: (301)459-8446
Fax: (301)459-1522

Recipient: Logisticians within commerce, industry, defense, federal and local government agencies, and both academic and private institutions. **Educational/Experience Requirements:** Must meet one of the following requirements: (1) Nine years experience; (2) Bachelor's degree and five years experience; (3) Master's degree and four years experience; or (4) Doctoral degree and three years experience. Each year of undergraduate coursework in logistics subjects may be substituted for one year of experience. **Membership:** Not required. **Certification Requirements:** Successful completion of exam. Exam consists of following sections: (1) Systems Management, including: Concepts of systems and logistics; Logistic support, its elements, and concepts; Logistics planning and implementation; Organization for logistics; Principles and functions of management; Proposals and contract negotiations; Relationship and integration of systems engineering and logistic support functions; Staffing, directing, and controlling; System evaluation factors and methodology; and System hardware and software; (2) System Design and Development, including: Formal design review; System engineering; and System test and evaluation; (3) Acquisition and Production Support, including: Acquisition of logistic support resources; and Production support; and (4) Distribution and Customer Support, including: Customer support; Equipment phase-out and disposition; and Physical supply and distribution. **Preparatory Materials:** Bibliography of study materials and sample questions provided. Preparatory training course also available. **Examination Frequency:** semiannual - always May and November. **Examination Sites:** Exam given at sites throughout the U.S. and internationally. **Examination Type:** Multiple-choice. **Re-examination:** Must only retake section failed if three sections are successfully completed. Must successfully complete exam within five examination dates. Fee to retake exam is $25. **Fees:** $75 (members); $150 (nonmembers).

Mechanical Engineers

302

Certified Facilities Environmental Professional (CFEP)
American Institute of Plant Engineers (AIPE)
8189 Corporate Park Dr., Ste. 305
Cincinnati, OH 45242
Phone: (513)489-2473
Fax: (513)247-7422

Recipient: Plant engineers involved in environmental compliance. **Educational/Experience Requirements:** Must meet one of the following requirements: (1) Bachelor's of Science degree and three years experience; or (2) Master's degree in environmental engineering and one year of experience. Three years of experience may be substituted for each year of bachelor's degree. **Membership:** Not required. **Certification Requirements:** Successful completion of exam. **Preparatory Materials:** Review course available. **Examination Frequency:** Annual. **Examination Sites:** Exam given at annual conference. **Examination Type:** Multiple-choice. **Fees:** $150 (members); $250 (nonmembers).

Petroleum Engineers

303

Petroleum Operations Engineer (POE)
American Society of Petroleum Operations Engineers (ASPOE)
PO Box 6174
Arlington, VA 22206
Phone: (703)768-4159
Fax: (703)684-7476
Edward Crumpler, Sec.

Recipient: Professionals who design, supervise the construction and maintenance of, and consult on petroleum marketing installations and the storage and handling of distilled petroleum products. **Number of Certified Individuals:** 191. **Educational/Experience Requirements:** Ten years experience. Education may be substituted for portion of the experience requirement. **Membership:** Required. **Certification Requirements:** Successful completion of two exams. Exams cover: Civil engineering; Construction documentation; Corrosion protection; Design and construction of underground storage tanks; Electrical design and construction; Environmental assessment; Facility design, construction, maintenance, and operation; Hydraulics; Permitting, licensing, zoning, and environmental assessment; Petroleum product chemistry; Petroleum storage and distribution; Pumps, meters, loaders; Regulations; and Testing, monitoring, and inventory control. **Renewal:** none. **Preparatory Materials:** List of study materials provided. **Examination Frequency:** semiannual. **Examination Sites:** Exam given at ASPOE headquarters. **Examination Type:** Multiple-choice; problem-solving. **Pass/Fail Rate:** 60% pass exams the first time. **Waiting Period to Receive Scores:** Two weeks. **Re-examination:** Must wait six months to retake exams. **Fees:** $125.

Stationary Engineers

304

Certified Plant Engineer (CPE)
American Institute of Plant
　Engineers (AIPE)
8180 Corporate Park Dr.
Cincinnati, OH 45242
Phone: (513)489-2473
Fax: (513)247-7422
Elizabeth B. Howell, Mgr.

Recipient: Plant engineers and managers of industrial, commercial, or institutional facilities. **Educational/Experience Requirements:** Must meet one of the following requirements: (1) Hold Registered Professional Engineer (PE) designation; (2) Bachelor's degree in engineering, architecture, or engineering technology and either six years plant engineering/facilities management experience or four years management level plant engineering/facilities management experience; or (3) No degree or degree in unrelated field and either eight years experience in plant engineering/facilities management or six years management level plant engineering/facilities management experience. **Membership:** Not required. **Certification Requirements:** Successful completion of exam. Exam covers economics, maintenance, management, and the following engineering disciplines: Civil; Electrical; Environmental; and Mechanical. Candidates may be exempt from exam if they hold PE designation and have four years experience. **Renewal:** Every five years. Recertification based on continuing education and professional activities. **Preparatory Materials:** Self-study guides, review pack, and classroom and video review courses available. **Examination Frequency:** By arrangement. **Examination Sites:** Exam given by arrangement with proctor. **Examination Type:** Multiple-choice. **Re-examination:**

Fees to retake exam are: $45 (members); $75 (nonmembers). **Fees:** $105 (members); $160 (nonmembers).

Architects and Surveyors

Landscape Architects

305

Certified Landscape Irrigation Auditor (CLIA)
Irrigation Association (IA)
8260 Wilow Oak Corp Dr.
Fairfax, VA 22031
Phone: (703)573-3551
Fax: (703)573-1913
Charles Putnam, Exec.Dir.

Recipient: Landscape irrigation auditors. **Membership:** Not required. **Certification Requirements:** Successful completion of training course and exam. Exam covers: Field data collection; Historical irrigation water usage; Irrigation audit terms; Irrigation scheduling; and Site inspection. **Renewal:** Every three years. Recertification based on continuing education. **Preparatory Materials:** *Landscape Irrigation Auditor Handbook* (reference). **Examination Frequency:** Throughout the year. **Examination Type:** Multiple-choice. **Fees:** $100.

Surveyors

306

Certified Hydrographer
American Congress on Surveying and Mapping (ACSM)
5410 Grosvenor Ln.
Bethesda, MD 20814-2122
Phone: (301)493-0200
Fax: (301)493-8245
Denise E. Calvert, Coord.

Recipient: Individuals who perform inshore plane and offshore hydrographic geodetic surveys. **Number of Certified Individuals:** 190. **Educational/**

Experience Requirements: Education and experience assessed by certification board on individual basis. **Membership:** Not required. **Certification Requirements:** Successful completion of exam. Exam covers planning, performing, and completing survey while demonstrating knowledge and techniques in the following areas: Methodology; Quality assurance; Standards; and Tools. **Examination Sites:** Exam given by correspondence. **Examination Type:** Essay. **Fees:** $125.

307

Certified Mapping Scientist - GIS/LIS
American Society for Photogrammetry and Remote Sensing (ASPRS)
5410 Grosvenor Ln., Ste. 210
Bethesda, MD 20814-2160
Phone: (301)493-0290
Fax: (301)493-0208

Recipient: Mapping scientists involved in geographic information or land information (GIS/LIS) systems design and or systems application of data base management and computer programs that allow for utilization of spatially referenced data bases for solving user analysis requirements. **Educational/Experience Requirements:** Must meet the following requirements: (1) Four years experience in mapping sciences or photogrammetry; and (2) Five years experience in GIS/LIS. May substitute one year of credit for each college degree earned in engineering or the natural or physical sciences. May substitute two years of credit for bachelor's degree in surveying. **Membership:** Not required. **Certification Requirements:** Successful completion of written or oral exam, if required. **Renewal:** Every five years. Recertification based on accumulation of 25 points in the following

categories: (1) Professional Employment (20 points maximum); (2) Technical Conference Attendance or Participation (four points maximum); (3) College/Workshop Coursework (eight points maximum); and (4) Peer Reviewed Articles and Service on Panels (eight points maximum). Renewal fees are: $125 (members); $225 (nonmembers). **Fees:** $100 (members); $200 (nonmembers).

308

Certified Mapping Scientist-In-Training
American Society for Photogrammetry and Remote Sensing (ASPRS)
5410 Grosvenor Ln., Ste. 210
Bethesda, MD 20814-2160
Phone: (301)493-0290
Fax: (301)493-0208

Recipient: Entry-level mapping scientists. **Certification Requirements:** Must meet one of the following requirements: (1) Bachelor's degree in engineering or the natural sciences, successful completion of seven required courses either during degree program or during training period, and eight years experience, five in professional position; (2) Associate's degree in photogrammetry, surveying, related mapping technology, or related general science program, successful completion of seven courses either during degree program or during training period, and eight and one-half years experience, five in professional position; or (3) Three years experience as technician in mapping sciences or surveying, successful completion of seven required courses, and nine years experience, five in professional position. Required courses are: Analytical Geometry; Calculus; Computer Aided Cartography; Computer Aided Design; Construction and/or Boundary Surveying; Differential Equations; Elementary Computer Programming; Introduction to Photogrammetry; Introduction to Cartography; Introduction to Geographic Information Systems; Introduction to Remote Sensing; Physics (Introductory Electricity and Waves); and Principles of Chemistry. Must submit annual reports to Trainer/Counselor assigned as mentor.

`309`

Certified Mapping Scientist - Remote Sensing
American Society for
  Photogrammetry and Remote
  Sensing (ASPRS)
5410 Grosvenor Ln., Ste. 210
Bethesda, MD 20814-2160
Phone: (301)493-0290
Fax: (301)493-0208

Recipient: Mapping scientists who analyze images acquired from aircraft, satellites, or ground based platforms using visual or computer assisted technology. **Educational/Experience Requirements:** Must meet the following requirements: (1) Three years experience in photogrammetric applications; and (2) Six years experience in remote sensing and interpretation of data from various imaging systems and/or design of remote sensing systems, either analog or digital. May substitute one year of credit for each college degree earned in engineering or the natural or physical sciences. May substitute two years of credit for bachelor's degree in surveying. **Membership:** Not required. **Certification Requirements:** Successful completion of written or oral exam, if required. **Renewal:** Every five years. Recertification based on accumulation of 25 points in the following categories: (1) Professional Employment (20 points maximum); (2) Technical Conference Attendance or Participation (four points maximum); (3) College/Workshop Coursework (eight points maximum); and (4) Peer Reviewed Articles and Service on Panels (eight points maximum). Renewal fees are: $125 (members); $225 (nonmembers). **Fees:** $100 (members); $200 (nonmembers).

`310`

Certified Marine Surveyor (CMS)
National Association of Marine
  Surveyors (NAMS)
PO Box 9306
Chesapeake, VA 23321-9306
Toll Free: (800)822-NAMS
Evie Hobbs, Office Mgr.

Recipient: Marine surveyors. **Number of Certified Individuals:** 400. **Educational/Experience Requirements:** Must meet one of the following requirements: (1) Five years experience; or (2) Two years experience and sufficient related marine industry experience (credited at two years to one as marine surveyor) adding up to five years credit. **Membership:** Required. **Certification Requirements:** Successful completion of exam. Exams offered in: Cargo; General; Hull and Machinery; and Yachts and Small Craft. **Renewal:** Every five years. Recertification based on accumulation of 30 hours of professional education. **Fees:** $420.

`311`

Certified Photogrammetrist
American Society for
  Photogrammetry and Remote
  Sensing (ASPRS)
5410 Grosvenor Ln., Ste. 210
Bethesda, MD 20814-2160
Phone: (301)493-0290
Fax: (301)493-0208

Recipient: Professionals involved with photo and image-based mapping and surveys. **Educational/Experience Requirements:** Nine years experience, with five years in position of professional responsibility. May substitute one year of credit for each college degree earned in engineering or the natural or physical sciences. May substitute two years of credit for bachelor's degree in surveying. **Membership:** Not required. **Certification Requirements:** Successful completion of oral or written exam, if required. **Renewal:** Every five years. Recertification based on accumulation of 25 points in the following categories: (1) Professional Employment (20 points maximum); (2) Technical Conference Attendance or Participation (four points maximum); (3) College/Workshop Coursework (eight points maximum); and (4) Peer Reviewed Articles and Service on Panels (eight points maximum). Renewal fees are: $125 (members); $225 (nonmembers). **Fees:** $100 (members); $200 (nonmembers).

`312`

Certified Photogrammetrist-In-Training
American Society for
  Photogrammetry and Remote
  Sensing (ASPRS)
5410 Grosvenor Ln., Ste. 210
Bethesda, MD 20814-2160
Phone: (301)493-0290
Fax: (301)493-0208

Recipient: Entry-level photogrammetrists. **Certification Requirements:** Must meet one of the following requirements: (1) Bachelor's degree in engineering or the natural sciences, successful completion of seven required courses either during degree program or during training period, and eight years experience, five in professional position; (2) Associate's degree in photogrammetry, surveying, related mapping technology, or related general science program, successful completion of seven courses either during degree program or during training period, and eight and one-half years experience, five in professional position; or (3) Three years experience as technician in mapping sciences or surveying, successful completion of seven required courses, and nine years experience, five in professional position. Required courses are: Analytical Geometry; Calculus; Computer Aided Cartography; Computer Aided Design; Construction and/or Boundary Surveying; Differential Equations; Elementary Computer Programming; Introduction to Photogrammetry; Introduction to Cartography; Introduction to Geographic Information Systems; Introduction to Remote Sensing; Physics (Introductory Electricity and Waves); and Principles of Chemistry. Must submit annual reports to Trainer/Counselor assigned as mentor.

`313`

Certified Survey Technician, Level I (CST)
Survey Technician Certification
  Board (STCB)
c/o American Congress on
  Surveying and Mapping
5410 Grosvenor Ln.
Bethesda, MD 20814-2122
Phone: (301)493-0200
Fax: (301)493-8245

Recipient: Survey technicians. **Educational/Experience Requirements:** None. May qualify for Certified Survey Technician, Level II or III designations (see separate entries) with increased experience. **Membership:** Not required.

Certification Requirements: Successful completion of exam. Exam covers the following work elements: (1) First Aid and Safety, including: Safety procedures for surveying and construction companies; Traffic control; and Treatment practices for medical emergencies; (2) Field Equipment and Instruments, including: Care, cleaning, and use of surveying tools and equipment, including field radios; and Names, purpose and parts, setup, transport, and calibration of various surveying field instruments; (3) Survey Computations, including mathematics and measurements relating to surveying (including linear, angular, elevations, and unit systems conversion); (4) Types of Surveys; (5) Survey Control Points; (6) Electronic Instruments, including handling, setup, and care of electronic instruments and their accessories; (7) Field Operations, including: Compass reading; Establishing points; Leveling; Line clearing; and Taping; (8) Survey Notes; (9) Surveying History; (10) Plan and Map Reading; and (11) Drafting/CAD, including drafting skills, tools, and procedures. **Preparatory Materials:** List of contents of work elements, sample questions, and list of suggested study references provided. **Examination Frequency:** quarterly. **Examination Type:** Multiple-choice. **Re-examination:** Must retake exam within one year. There is a $75 fee to retake exam. **Fees:** $105. **Endorsed By:** American Congress on Surveying and Mapping; National Society of Professional Surveyors.

314

Certified Survey Technician, Level II (CST)
Survey Technician Certification
  Board (STCB)
c/o American Congress on
  Surveying and Mapping
5410 Grosvenor Ln.
Bethesda, MD 20814-2122
Phone: (301)493-0200
Fax: (301)493-8245

Recipient: Survey technicians. **Educational/Experience Requirements:** One and one-half years (3000 hours) of experience. Seven hundred and fifty hours may be earned through education. Candidates with less experience may qualify for Certified Survey Technician, Level I designation (see separate entry). May qualify for Certified Survey Technician, Level III designation (see separate entry) with increased experience. **Membership:** Not required. **Certification Requirements:** Successful completion of one of the following specialty exams: (1) Boundary Instrument Person; (2) Com-

puter Operator; (3) Construction Instrument Person; and (4) Drafter. Exams cover the following work elements: (1) Types of Surveys, including: Construction surveys; Leveling; Metes and bounds surveys; Photo control surveys; Public land surveys; Traversing; Triangulation; and Trilateration; (2) Field Equipment and Instruments, including: Care, cleaning, and use of surveying tools and equipment, including field radios; and Operation, checking, and basic field adjustments on transits, total stations, total electronic stations, data collectors, levels, compass, tribachs, and tripods; (3) Survey Computations, including: Algebra; Basic surveying computations; Computer operating system; Coordinate geometry; Geometry; Reduction checking of field notes for determination of positions and elevations; Trigonometry; and Using hand-held calculator or microcomputer; (4) Benchmarks and Horizontal Control Points, including: Interpreting control point records and data sheets; and Locating points in the field; (5) Field Operations, including: Basic sources of measurement errors; Coordinating field work for variety of standard types of surveys; Observing the Sun and Polaris for true North determination; and Principles of staking and stake markings; (6) Field Notes, including: As-build surveys; Boundary surveys; Cross-section surveys; Layout; Leveling; Profile; Topographic mapping; and Traversing; (7) Plan Reading and Preparation, including: Boundary plans; Computer-aided drafting (CAD); Developing existing and finished contours; Foundation plans; Highway plans; Horizontal and vertical curves; Pipeline plans; Profile and cross sections; and Site plans; (8) Principles of the Profession, including: Ethics; Professional associations; Responsibility; and Technical standards; and (9) First Aid and Safety, including: Safety procedures for variety of surveying and construction operations; Traffic control; and Treatment practices for medical emergencies. Candidates must document experience in each specialty area for which exam is attempted. **Preparatory Materials:** Candidate booklet, including list of suggested study references and sample questions, provided. **Examination Frequency:** quarterly. **Examination Type:** Multiple-choice. **Re-examination:** Must retake exam within one year. There is a $75 fee to retake exam. **Fees:** $105; $35 (second specialty exam). **Endorsed By:** American Congress on Surveying and Mapping; National Society of Professional Surveyors.

315

Certified Survey Technician, Level III (CST)
Survey Technician Certification
  Board (STCB)
c/o American Congress on
  Surveying and Mapping
5410 Grosvenor Ln.
Bethesda, MD 20814-2122
Phone: (301)493-0200
Fax: (301)493-8245

Recipient: Survey technicians. **Educational/Experience Requirements:** Three and one-half years (7000 hours) experience. One thousand seven hundred and fifty hours can be earned through education. Candidates with less experience may qualify for Certified Survey Technician, Level I or II designations (see separate entries). **Membership:** Not required. **Certification Requirements:** Successful completion of exam in one of the following specialty areas: (1) Chief Computer Operator; (2) Chief Draftsperson; (3) Party Chief - Construction; and (4) Party Chief Boundary. Exams cover the following work elements: (1) First Aid and Safety, including: Occupational Safety and Health Administration (OSHA) standards; Safety procedures for surveying and construction operations; Traffic control; and Treatment practices for variety of medical emergencies; (2) Field Equipment and Instruments, including: Care, cleaning, and use of variety of surveying tools and equipment, including field radios; and Operating, checking, and performing basic field adjustments on rods, compass, transits, levels, tribrachs, theodolites, EDMI, total stations, data collectors, and tripods; (3) Mathematics and Computations, including: Algebra; Area and quantities computations; Basic surveying mathematics; Geometry; Intersection computations including closure and adjustments; Inverse; Level loop computations and adjustments; Traverse; Trigonometry; and Vertical and horizontal curves computations; (4) Types of Surveys, including: As-built; Construction; Metes and bounds; Photo control; Public land; and State plane coordinate; (5) Field Operations, including: Construction layout methods and procedures; Observation of the Sun and Polaris for true North determination; Repeating observations and precision measurements using steel tapes and theodolites; Traversing; and Triangulation; (6) Field Notes, including: As-built surveys; Boundary surveys; Construction layout; Leveling; Profile and cross-section surveys; Topographic mapping; and Traversing; (7) Office Operations, including: Computer aided drafting (CAD); Microcomputer operating systems and hardware peripherals; and Using hand calculations or micro-computer software; (8) Benchmarks and Horizontal Control Points, including: Control point records and data sheets; and Locating points in the field; (9) Plan Reading and Preparation, including: Boundary plans; Developing existing and finished contours; Foundation plans; Highway plans; Horizontal and vertical curves; Pipeline plans; Profiles and cross sections; and Site plans; (10) Principles of the Profession, including: Ethics; Professional associations; Professional responsibility; and Technical standards; and (11) Supervisory Skills, including: Client contacts; Coordinating and supervising field work and staking and stake marking for variety of standard types of surveys; Dealing with public and governmental agencies; Equipment; Field crew management; Field and office operations; Job charges; Local and state land use regulations relating to lot site development; Office work flow procedures; Problem solving techniques; Record keeping; Scheduling; Supplies management; and Time keeping. Candidates must document one additional year of experience in specialty for each additional specialty exam attempted. **Preparatory Materials:** Candidate booklet, including list of suggested study references and sample questions, provided. **Examination Frequency:** quarterly. **Examination Type:** Multiple-choice. **Re-examination:** Must retake exam within one year. There is a $75 fee to retake exam. **Fees:** $105; $35 (second specialty exam). **Endorsed By:** American Congress on Surveying and Mapping; National Society of Professional Surveyors.

316

Certified Survey Technician, Level IV (CST)
Survey Technician Certification
  Board (STCB)
c/o American Congress on
  Surveying and Mapping
5410 Grosvenor Ln.
Bethesda, MD 20814-2122
Phone: (301)493-0200
Fax: (301)493-8245

Recipient: Survey technicians. **Educational/Experience Requirements:** Must meet the following requirements: (1) Hold Certified Survey Technician, Level III designation (see separate entry); and (2) Five and one-half years (11,000 hours) experience. Two thousand and fifty hours may be earned through education. Hours of experience are cumulative from previous level designations earned. Candidates with less experience may

qualify for Certified Survey Technician, Level I, II, or III designations (see separate entries). **Membership:** Not required. **Certification Requirements:** Successful completion of one of the following specialty exams: (1) Chief Computer Operator; (2) Chief Draftsperson; (3) Party Chief - Boundary; and (4) Party Chief - Construction. Exam covers the following work elements: (1) First Aid and Safety, including: Safety procedures for variety of surveying and construction operations; Traffic control; and Treatment practices for medical emergencies; (2) Field Equipment and Instruments, including: Care, cleaning, and use of variety of surveying tools and equipment, including field radios; Compass; Data collectors; EDMI; Equipping personnel; Levels; Purchase and maintenance of field equipment and instruments; Repeating observations; Steel taping; Theodolites; Total electronic stations; Total stations; Transits; Tribrachs; and Tripods; (3) Mathematics and Computations, including: Adjustment computations; Algebra; Astronomic azimuth determination; Basic principles of measurement; Basic surveying computations; Closure; Coordinate geometry; EDM baseline comparison computations; Error propagation; Geometry; Land use regulations relating to lot and site development; Lot, area, and intersection computations; Precision determination; Taping corrections; Traverse and level loop computations; and Trigonometry; (4) Types of Surveys, including: As-built; Construction; Global positioning (GPS) and geographic/land information (G/LIS) systems; Horizontal control; Hydrographic surveying; Leveling; Metes and bounds; Mining surveying; Photogrammetric surveying; Public land; State Plane Coordinate; and Traversing; (5) Field Operations, including: Coordinating and supervising field work; Job expenses; Record timing; and Timekeeping; (6) Field Notes and Note Reduction, including: As-built surveys; Boundary surveys; Layout; Leveling; Profile and cross section surveys; Topographic mapping; and Traversing; (7) Survey Computer Operations, including: Field data and resulting positional information; Hand calculations or microcomputer software; Microcomputer operating systems; and Peripheral computer equipment and supplies; (8) Benchmarks and Horizontal Control Points, including: Data sheets; and Control point records; (9) Plan Reading and Preparation, including: Computer aided drafting (CAD); and Coordinating design elements into final drawings; (10) Principles of the Profession, including: Ethics; Professional responsibility; and Technical standards; and (11) Supervisory Skills, including: Basic budgeting; Client con-

tacts; Cost control techniques; Dealing with public and governmental agencies; Equipment; Evaluating personnel performance; Field crew management; Office work flow procedures; On-site officer operation; Problem solving techniques; Scheduling; Supplies management; and Training personnel. Candidates must document one additional year of experience in specialty for each additional specialty exam attempted. **Preparatory Materials:** Candidate booklet, including list of suggested study references and sample questions, provided. **Examination Frequency:** semiannual. **Examination Sites:** Exam given by correspondence. **Examination Type:** Essay. **Fees:** $105; $75 (second specialty exam). **Endorsed By:** American Congress on Surveying and Mapping; National Society of Professional Surveyors.

Computer, Mathematical, and Operations Research Occupations

Actuaries

317

Associate, Casualty Actuarial Society (ACAS)
Casualty Actuarial Society (CAS)
1110 N. Glebe Rd., Ste. 600
Arlington, VA 22201
Phone: (703)276-3100
Fax: (703)276-3108

Recipient: Actuaries involved in casualty and property insurance. **Number of Certified Individuals:** 992. **Educational/Experience Requirements:** Successful completion of Course on Professionalism. **Certification Requirements:** Successful completion of the following exams: (1) Calculus and Linear Algebra, covering differential and integral calculus and linear algebra and including: Analytic geometry of two and three dimensions; Applications of derivatives and integrals, including multiple integrals; Bases; Derivatives, integrals, and partial derivatives; Determinants; Dimension; Eigenvectors and eigenvalues; Elementary set theory, including unions, intersections, and complements; Finite and infinite sequences and series, including Taylor series expansion; Fundamental theorem of integral calculus; Kernel and image space; Limits, continuity, differentiability, and integrability; Linear equations, vector spaces, and generating sets; Linear transformations; Matrices; Mean value theorem; Real and complex numbers; Scalar products; Standard algebraic and transcendental functions, including polynomial, rational, trigonometric, logarithmic, and exponential functions; and Subspaces; (2) Probability and Statistics, including: Applications of sampling distributions to confidence intervals and to tests for means and variances; Axioms and elementary theorems of probability; Bayesian estimation; Binomial, poisson,

normal, chi-square, T, F, and other probability distributions; Central limit theorem; Conditional and marginal distribution; Expectation, mean, variance, and moment generating functions of probability distributions; Independence, conditional probability, and Bayes' theorem; Interpretation of experimental results; Method of Least Squares; Multivariate distribution; Permutations and combinations; Point estimation, including maximum likelihood estimation and application of criteria such as consistency, unbiasedness, and minimum variance; Random variables; Regression and correlation; Sample spaces; Tests of statistical hypotheses, including power functions, Type I and Type II errors, Neyman-Pearson lemma, and likelihood ratio tests; and Transformations of random variables; (3) Applied Statistical Methods, including: Forecasting; Regression analysis; and Time Series analysis; (4) Introduction to Property and Casualty Insurance, including: Marketing; Policies; Product design and modification; Ratemaking; Settlement of claims; and Underwriting; (5) Numerical Methods, including: Iteration and interpolation; Linear systems; and Numerical integration; (6) Interest and Life Contingencies, including: Actuarial mathematics; Amortization; Annuities; Life annuities; Life insurance; Life insurance products and their characteristics; Multiple decrement models; Multiple life functions; Net premiums and net premium reserves; Sinking funds; Stationary populations; Survival functions and mortality tables; and Theory of interest and interest functions; (7) Credibility Theory and Loss Distributions, including: Bayes' Theory; Making inferences from insurance data; Statistical concepts of location and dispersion; and Statistical distributions useful to insurance; (8) Principles of Economics, including: Macroeconomic theory; and Microeconomic theory; (9) Theory of Risk and Insurance, including: Handling risk;

and Identifying risk; (10) Principles of Ratemaking and Data for Ratemaking, including: Calendar year versus accident year versus policy year; Claim cost projection versus current cost index approach; Classification; Compilation and presentation of insurance statistics for statistical and ratemaking purposes; Credibility theory; Impact of deductibles, coinsurance, and insurance-to-value programs; Individual risk ratemaking; Internal versus external indices; Liability increased limits ratemaking; Planning and use of internal statistical material; Pure premium versus loss ratio; Ratemaking techniques; Relation to loss development; Sources and uses of external statistics; Territorial and classification relatives; Trend and loss development factors; and Trending and projecting losses and premiums; (11) Premium, Loss, and Expense Reserves, including: Allocated loss expense reserves; Loss and loss expense reserve levels; Loss reserving methods; Principles and standards; Statutory Annual Statement reserves; Unallocated loss expense reserves; and Unearned premium reserve; and (12) Insurance Accounting, Expense Analysis, and Published Financial Information, including: Annual Statement Blank; Generally Accepted Accounting Principles (GAAP); Insurance Expense Exhibit; and Statutory accounting principles. Successful completion of exams given by other actuarial organizations may be substituted for ACAS exams. Some exams have separate components for Canadian candidates. **Preparatory Materials:** *Foundations of Casualty Actuarial Science* (reference). *Syllabus of Examinations,* including list of suggested study references, provided. Sample questions provided. Study kits available. **Examination Frequency:** semiannual - always May and November. **Examination Sites:** Exams given at sites throughout the U.S., Canada, and internationally. **Examination Type:** Essay; multiple-choice; true or false. **Waiting**

Period to Receive Scores: Eight weeks. **Endorsed By:** American Academy of Actuaries; Canadian Institute of Actuaries; Society of Actuaries.

`318`

Associate of the Society of Actuaries (ASA)

Society of Actuaries (SoA)
475 N. Martingdale Rd., Ste. 800
Schaumburg, IL 60173-2226
Phone: (708)706-3500
Fax: (708)706-3599

Recipient: Actuaries. **Educational/ Experience Requirements:** none. **Membership:** Required. **Certification Requirements:** Accumulation of 300 credits through successful completion of courses, including exams. Required courses (255 total credits) are: (1) Calculus and Linear Algebra (30 credits), including: Analytical geometry of two and three dimensions; Derivatives, integrals, and their applications; Functions, equations, and inequalities; Fundamental theorem of calculus; Limits, continuity, differentiability, and integrability; Linear equations, vector spaces, and bases (spanning sets), dimension, and subspaces; Matrices, determinants, eigenvectors, and eigenvalues; Partial derivatives, multiple integrals, and their applications; Polar coordinates and parametric equations; Scalar products, linear transformations, and kernal and image space; Sequence and series, including Taylor series expansion; and Standard algebraic and transcendental functions, including exponential, logarithmic, polynomial, rational, and trigonometric functions; (2) Probability and Statistics (30 credits), including: Applications of sampling distributions to confidence intervals and to tests for means and variance; Axioms and elementary theorems of probability; Bayesian estimation; Binomial, Poisson, normal, chi-square, t, F, and other probability distributions; Central limit theorem; Conditional and marginal distributions; Independence, conditional probability, and Bayes' theorem; Interpretation of experimental results; Method of least squares; Multivariate distributions; Permutations and combinations; Point estimation, including maximum likelihood estimation, method of moments, and application of criteria such as consistency, unbiasedness, and minimum variance; Random variables; Regression and correlation; Sample spaces; Tests of statistical hypotheses, including power functions, Type I and Type II errors, Neyman-Pearson lemma, and likelihood ratio tests; and Transformations of random variables; (3) Applied

Statistical Methods (15 credits), including: Forecasting; Regression analysis; and Time series analysis; (4) Mathematics of Compound Interest (ten credits), including: Amortization schedules and sinking funds; Annuities certain; Bonds and related securities; Measurement of interest, including accumulated and present value factors; and Yield rates; (5) Actuarial Mathematics (40 credits), including: General rules for symbols of actuarial functions; Illustrative life table; Illustrative service table; Insurance models, including expenses; Life annuities; Life insurance; Mathematical formulas useful in actuarial mathematics; Multiple decrement models; Multiple life functions; Net premium reserves; Net premiums; Nonforfeiture benefits and dividends; Normal distribution table; Survival distributions and life tables; and Valuation theory for pension plans; (6) Risk Theory (15 credits), including: Applications of risk theory; Collective risk models over an extended period; Collective risk models for single period; Economics of insurance; and Individual risk models for short term; (7) Survival Models and Construction of Tables (15 credits), including: Evaluation of estimators from sample data; Methods of estimating parametric models from both complete and incomplete data samples, including parametric models with concomitant variables; Methods of estimating tabular models from both complete and incomplete data samples, including actuarial, moment, and maximum likelihood estimation techniques; Nature and properties of survival models, including both parametric and tabular models; Practical issues in survival model estimation; and Valuation schedule exposure formulas; (8) Introduction to Financial Security Programs (30 credits), including: Design, administration, marketing, and underwriting of private individual financial security programs; Design and underwriting of employee benefit plans; Regulation and taxation of financial security programs and insurance companies; and Social insurance programs; (9) Introduction to Actuarial Practice (25 credits), including: Introduction to pension funding; Pricing of life insurance and annuities; and Valuation of liabilities and financial reporting for life insurance companies; (10) Introduction to Asset Management and Corporate Finance (30 credits), including: Asset management; Corporate finance; Financial markets and asset definition; Macroeconomics; and Portfolio management and investment strategy; and (11) Principles of Asset/Liability Management (15 credits), including: Asset management issues; General product design; Pricing and valuation issues; and Tools and techniques of asset and liabil-

ity management. Elective courses (45 credits required) are: (1) Operations Research (15 credits), including: Dynamic programming; Integer programming; Linear programming; Project scheduling; Queuing theory; and Simulation; (2) Numerical Methods (ten credits), including: Interpolation; Iteration; Linear systems; and Numerical integration; (3) Credibility Theory and Loss Distributions (20 credits); (4) Intensive Seminar on Applied Statistical Methods (ten credits), including: Dynamic programming; Integer programming; Linear programming; Project scheduling; Queuing theory; and Simulation; (5) Intensive Seminar on Risk Theory (ten credits); (6) Mathematics of Demography (ten credits), including: Conventional and adjusted measures of mortality; Demographic characteristics and trends in Canada and the U.S.; Evaluation of demographic data; Introduction to applications of demographic characteristics and trends to actuarial work; Mathematics of stable and stationary populations; and Measures of fertility; (7) Mathematics of Graduation (ten credits), including: Analysis and critique of various models; Graduation by moving-weighted average, graphic, Whittaker, Bayesian, parametric, and smooth-junction interpolation methods; Problems involved in making and testing graduations of mortality tables or other series that are likely to be encountered in course of actuary's work; Statistical considerations; and Two dimensional graduation; (8) Financial Management (20 credits), including: Financial management; Taxation; and Valuation of liabilities; (9) Design of Distribution of Group Benefits (30 credits), including including: Basic concepts and environment; Group insurance coverages and plan design; and Underwriting, marketing, and administration; (10) Survey of Actuarial Practice Individual Life Insurance and Annuities (30 credits), including: Marketing; Pricing; Product design; and Valuation and financial statements; (11) Life Insurance Law and Taxation - U.S. (ten credits), including: Effective tax communication and inapplicable federal rate; Federal income taxation; State and local taxation of life insurance companies; and Summary of life insurance company taxation; (12) Principles of Pension Valuation I - U.S. (15 credits); (13) Pension Funding Vehicles (15 credits), including: Investment management; and Pension funding arrangements; (14) Regulatory Requirements for Pension Plans - U.S. (25 credits), including: Actuarial cost methods; ERISA requirements; Excise taxes; Maximum deductible contributions for federal income tax purposes; Minimum funding requirements; Prohibited transactions and fiduciary responsibilities; Standards of performance for enrolled actuaries; and Valuation of plan assets; (15) Introduction to Property and Casualty Insurance (ten credits); (16) Principles of Ratemaking and Data for Ratemaking (20 credits); and (17) Premium, Loss, and Expense Reserves, Insurance Accounting, Expense Analysis, and Published Financial Information (20 credits). Separate courses available for Canadian candidates. Credit may be granted for exams successfully completed for other organizations. May earn up to 30 credits for successful completion of research paper. **Preparatory Materials:** Study guides, including list of suggested reading and sample questions, available. Seminars and workshops also available. **Examination Frequency:** Annual - always October or November. **Examination Sites:** Exams given at sites throughout the U.S. and Canada. **Examination Type:** Multiple-choice; short answer. **Waiting Period to Receive Scores:** Eight-ten weeks. **Endorsed By:** American Academy of Actuaries; American Society of Pension Actuaries; Canadian Institute of Actuaries; Casualty Actuarial Society; Conference of Consulting Actuaries; Joint Board for the Enrollment of Actuaries; National Organization for Competency Assurance.

319

Associated Professional Member, American Society of Pension Actuaries (APM)
American Society of Pension
Actuaries (ASPA)
4350 N. Fairfax Dr., Ste. 820
Arlington, VA 22203
Phone: (703)516-9300
Fax: (703)516-9308
Chester Salkind, Exec.Dir.

Recipient: Attorneys, licensed certified public accountants (CPAs), and enrolled agents involved with pensions or pension-related services. **Membership:** Required. **Certification Requirements:** Three years experience. **Renewal:** Every two years. Recertification based on accumulation of points through continuing education.

320

Certified Pension Consultant (CPC)
American Society of Pension
Actuaries (ASPA)
4350 N. Fairfax Dr., Ste. 820
Arlington, VA 22203
Phone: (703)516-9300
Fax: (703)516-9308
Chester Salkind, Exec.Dir.

Recipient: Consultants in various areas of qualified benefit and retirement plans. **Educational/Experience Requirements:** Three years experience. **Membership:** Required. **Certification Requirements:** Successful completion of the following exams: (1) Administrative and Consulting Aspects of Defined Benefit Plans, covering: Benefit calculations; Rules, terminations, and changes; Funding and accounting; and Traditional plan variations; (2) Administrative and Consulting Aspects of Defined Contribution Plans, covering: Employee stock ownerships (ESOP); 401(k); Profit sharing; and Simplified employee pensions (SEP); (3) Advanced Retirement Plan Consulting, which tests depth of knowledge and ability to apply this knowledge to comprehensive pensions problems; (4) Financial and Fiduciary Aspects of Qualified Plans, which covers: Accounting and financial reporting; Distribution; Estate planning; Fiduciary standards; Plan assets; Protection and terminations; and Taxation; and (5) Qualification and Operation of Retirement Plans, covering: Fiduciary responsibilities; Investment vehicles and performance; Participation and distribution requirements; Qualifications; Reporting and disclosure; Taxes; and Types of plans. **Renewal:** Every two years. Recertification based on accumulation of points through continuing education. **Preparatory Materials:** Study courses available. **Examination Type:** Essay; multiple-choice; short answer. **Fees:** $1000.

321

Fellow, Casualty Actuarial Society (FCAS)
Casualty Actuarial Society (CAS)
1110 N. Glebe Rd., Ste. 600
Arlington, VA 22201
Phone: (703)276-3100
Fax: (703)276-3108

Recipient: Actuaries involved in casualty and property insurance. **Number of Certified Individuals:** 1309. **Educational/Experience Requirements:** Hold Associate, Casualty Actuarial Society designation (see separate entry). **Certification Requirements:** Successful completion of the following exams: (1) Tort Law and Statuary Insurance, including: Automobile no-fault; "First Party" compensation systems; Insurance coverages mandated by statute; Legal foundations; Social insurance; and Workers' compensation; (2) Regulation and Regulatory Issues, including: Availability of insurance; Classification; Conduct of insurance business; Government agencies; Guaranty funds; Insurance con-

tracts; Insurance groups; Insurer profitability; Judicial decisions; Monitoring for solvency; Policy language; Rate regulation; Ratemaking; Shared markets; and Unfair competition; (3) Advanced Ratemaking, including: Classification ratemaking topics; and Excess and deductible rating; (4) Individual Rate Rating, including: Credibility; Excess loss charge concepts; Insurance charge; Loss distribution; Loss limitation; Prospective rating or experience rating; Rate modification concepts; Rating plans; and Retrospective rating; (5) Financial Operations of Insurance Companies, including: Cost of capital; Federal income taxes; Inflation rates; Interest rates; Investment income; Premium-to-surplus ratios; Risk premiums; and Underwriting profits; and (6) Reinsurance, Assets, Valuation, Solvency, and Capital, including: Asset and investment risk; Asset liability management; Dynamic solvency testing; Effects of reinsurance transactions on company operating results and other financial information; Methods employed to analyze costs; Reinsurance programs; Reinsurer underwriting; Risk based capital requirements; Risk sharer; and Valuation and solvency. **Preparatory Materials:** *Foundations of Casualty Actuarial Science* (reference). *Syllabus of Examinations,* including list of suggested study references, provided. Sample questions provided. Study kits available. **Examination Frequency:** semiannual - always May and November. **Examination Sites:** Exams given at sites throughout the U.S., Canada, and internationally. **Examination Type:** Essay; multiple-choice; true or false. **Waiting Period to Receive Scores:** Eight weeks. **Endorsed By:** Society of Actuaries.

322

Fellow of the Society of Actuaries
Society of Actuaries (SOA)
475 N. Martingdale Rd., Ste. 800
Schaumburg, IL 60173-2226
Phone: (708)706-3500
Fax: (708)706-3599

Recipient: Actuaries. **Educational/Experience Requirements:** Must hold Associate of the Society of Actuaries (ASA) designation (see separate entry). **Membership:** Required. **Certification Requirements:** Accumulation of 300 credits through successful completion of courses, including exams, and Fellowship Admissions Course. Required courses are: (1) Calculus and Linear Algebra (30 credits), including: Analytical geometry of two and three dimensions; Derivatives, integrals, and their applications; Functions, equations, and inequalities; Fundamental theorem of calculus; Limits, continuity, differentiability, and integrability; Linear equations, vector spaces, and bases (spanning sets), dimension, and subspaces; Matrices, determinants, eigenvectors, and eigenvalues; Partial derivatives, multiple integrals, and their applications; Polar coordinates and parametric equations; Scalar products, linear transformations, and kernal and image space; Sequence and series, including Taylor series expansion; and Standard algebraic and transcendental functions, including exponential, logarithmic, polynomial, rational, and trigonometric functions; (2) Probability and Statistics (30 credits), including: Applications of sampling distributions to confidence intervals and to tests for means and variance; Axioms and elementary theorems of probability; Bayesian estimation; Binomial, Poisson, normal, chi-square, T, F, and other probability distributions; Central limit theorem; Conditional and marginal distributions; Independence, conditional probability, and Bayes' theorem; Interpretation of experimental results; Method of least squares; Multivariate distributions; Permutations and combinations; Point estimation, including maximum likelihood estimation, method of moments, and application of criteria such as consistency, unbiasedness, and minimum variance; Random variables; Regression and correlation; Sample spaces; Tests of statistical hypotheses, including power functions, Type I and Type II errors, Neyman-Pearson lemma, and likelihood ratio tests; and Transformations of random variables; (3) Applied Statistical Methods (15 credits), including: Forecasting; Regression analysis; and Time series analysis; (4) Mathematics of Compound Interest (ten credits), including: Amortization schedules and sinking funds; Annuities certain; Bonds and related securities; Measurement of interest, including accumulated and present value factors; and Yield rates; (5) EA-1, Segment A (ten credits); (6) Actuarial Mathematics (40 credits), including: General rules for symbols of actuarial functions; Illustrative life table; Illustrative service table; Insurance models, including expenses; Life annuities; Life insurance; Mathematical formulas useful in actuarial mathematics; Multiple decrement models; Multiple life functions; Net premium reserves; Net premiums; Nonforfeiture benefits and dividends; Normal distribution table; Survival distributions and life tables; and Valuation theory for pension plans; (7) Risk Theory (15 credits), including: Applications of risk theory; Collective risk models over an extended period; Collective risk models for single period; Economics of insurance; and Individual risk

models for short term; (8) Survival Models and Construction of Tables (15 credits), including: Evaluation of estimators from sample data; Methods of estimating parametric models from both complete and incomplete data samples, including parametric models with concomitant variables; Methods of estimating tabular models from both complete and incomplete data samples, including actuarial, moment, and maximum likelihood estimation techniques; Nature and properties of survival models, including both parametric and tabular models; Practical issues in survival model estimation; and Valuation schedule exposure formulas; (9) Introduction to Financial Security Programs (30 credits), including: Design, administration, marketing, and underwriting of private individual financial security programs; Design and underwriting of employee benefit plans; Regulation and taxation of financial security programs and insurance companies; and Social insurance programs; (10) Introduction to Actuarial Practice (25 credits), including: Introduction to pension funding; Pricing of life insurance and annuities; and Valuation of liabilities and financial reporting for life insurance companies; (11) Introduction to Asset Management and Corporate Finance (30 credits), including: Asset management; Corporate finance; Financial markets and asset definition; Macroeconomics; and Portfolio management and investment strategy; and (12) Principles of Asset and Liability Management (15 credits), including: Asset management issues; General product design; Pricing and valuation issues; and Tools and techniques of asset and liability management. Must also accumulate 90 credits through successful completion of courses in one of the following specialties: Finance; Group and health benefits; Individual life and annuity; Investment; and Pension. Required finance courses are: (1) Financial Management (20 credits), including: Financial management; Taxation; and Valuation of liabilities; (2) Advanced Topics in Valuation and Financial Reporting (25 credits), including: Actuarial reserve determination; Financial management and solvency of life insurance companies; and Financial reporting for U.S. life insurance companies; (3) Corporate Finance (15 credits), including: Agency theory; Capital structure; Corporate structure and holding companies; Cost of capital; GAAP/STAT/TAX issues; Mergers and acquisitions; and Risk adjusted surplus; (4) Applied Corporate Finance (20 credits), including: Financial management and risk exposures of financial institutions; Investment banking; and Raising of capital; and (5) Corporate Strategy and Solvency Management (ten

credits), including: Rating agencies; Solvency; and Strategy management. Elective finance courses are: (1) Derivative Securities: Theory and Application (15 credits), including: Option theory and non-parallel yield curve shifts; Practical applications of theory; and Stochastic calculus; (2) Advanced Portfolio Management (15 credits), including: Asset management; and Portfolio theory; and (3) Applied Asset and Liability Management (20 credits), including: General asset and liability management; Pension; and Swaps. Required group and health benefits courses are: (1) Design and Distribution of Group Benefits (30 credits), including: Basic concepts and environment; Group insurance coverages and plan design; and Underwriting, marketing, and administration; (2) Life Insurance Law and Taxation (ten credits), including: Common life insurance policy provisions; Laws relative to individual and group life and health insurance contracts; Making, continuation, contest, and settlement of insurance contracts; and System of taxation of life insurance companies; (3) Group Financial Management and Regulation (20 credits); and (4) Group and Individual Insurance Pricing (20 credits), including: Alternate methods of funding; Expense analysis; Impact of marketplace considerations; Loss ratio analysis; Methods of collecting and using data; Pricing deductibles and coinsurance; Principles and techniques of pricing; Significance of underwriting; Sources of data; Time series projection; and Utilization studies. Elective group and health benefits courses are: (1) Cost Containment and Managed Care for Health Benefits (ten credits); (2) Continuing Care Retirement Communities and Long-Term Care Insurance (ten credits), including: Continuing care retirement communities; and Long term care insurance; (3) Non-Pension Post-retirement and Post-employment Benefits (ten credits), including: Funding methods; Plan design; Regulatory environment; Tax aspects; and Techniques of periodic actuarial valuations; (4) Flexible Benefit Plans (ten credits), including: Design; Experience; Implementation; Option selection considerations; Pricing of new and existing plans; and Regulation; and (5) Health Policy (ten credits), including: Cost projections; Current health care environment; Principles for establishing health policy; and Proposed changes to U.S. system. Required individual life and annuity courses are: (1) Survey of Actuarial Practice - Individual Life Insurance and Annuities (30 credits), including: Marketing; Pricing; Product design; and Valuation and financial statements; (2) Life Insurance Law and Taxation (ten credits), including: Effective tax communication and inapplicable federal rate; Federal income taxation; State and local taxation of life insurance companies; and Summary of life insurance company taxation; (3) Advanced Design and Pricing (25 credits), including: Policyholder taxation; Product development; Product-specific issues; and Regulatory environment; and (4) Advanced Topics in Valuation and Financial Reporting (25 credits), including: Actuarial reserve determination; Financial management and solvency of life insurance companies; and Financial reporting for U.S. life insurance companies. Elective individual life and annuity courses are: (1) Individual Health Insurance (25 credits), including: Actuarial reserves and financial reporting; Plan design and administrative aspects; and Pricing and profitability; (2) Marketing Individual Life Insurance and Annuities (ten credits), including: Managing marketing effort; Market research; Marketing process; Product selection; and Target marketing; (3) Selection of Risks (ten credits), including: Financial implications of underwriting; Medically impaired risk; Nonphysical underwriting factors; Older insurance population; Preferred risk underwriting; Report on protective value of laboratory testing; Testing for cause; Tobacco risk; Underwriting dread disease benefits; and Underwriting and reinsurance; and (4) Reinsurance Topics (15 credits), including: Financial reinsurance; Regulation of reinsurance; Reinsurance administration; Reinsurance coverages and pricing; Risk transfer reinsurance; and Valuation and financial reporting for reinsurance. Required investment courses are: (1) Financial Management (20 credits), including: Financial management; Taxation; and Valuation of liabilities; (2) Derivative Securities: Theory and Application (15 credits), including: Option theory and non-parallel yield curve shifts; Practical applications of theory; and Stochastic calculus; (3) Advanced Portfolio Management (15 credits), including: Asset management; and Portfolio theory; (4) Applied Corporate Finance (20 credits), including: Financial management and risk exposures of financial institutions; Investment banking; and Raising of capital; and (5) Applied Asset and Liability Management (20 credits), including: General asset and liability management; Pension; and Swaps. Elective investment courses are: (1) Advanced Topics in Valuation and Financial Reporting (25 credits), including: Actuarial reserve determination; Financial management and solvency of life insurance companies; and Financial reporting for U.S. life insurance companies; (2) Corporate Finance (15 credits), including: Agency theory; Capital structure; Corporate structure

and holding companies; Cost of capital; GAAP/STAT/TAX issues; Mergers and acquisitions; and Risk adjusted surplus; and (3) Corporate Strategy and Solvency Management (ten credits), including: Rating agencies; Solvency; and Strategy management. Required pension courses are: (1) Principles of Pension Valuation I (15 credits); (2) Design of Retirement Programs (15 credits), including: Age-weighted defined contribution plans; Cash balance plans; Cost of living allowances; Defined benefit safe harbors; Non-qualified plans; $150,000 limit within qualified plans; Open window retirement programs; Section 401(I) permitted disparity; Tax-sheltered annuities after tax reform; and Tax-sheltered annuity programs for employees of public schools and certain tax-exempt organizations; (3) Pension Funding Vehicles (15 credits), including: Investment management; and Pension funding arrangements; (4) Regulatory Requirements for Pension Plans (25 credits), including: Actuarial cost methods; ERISA requirements; Excise taxes; Maximum deductible contributions for federal income tax purposes; Minimum funding requirements; Prohibited transactions and fiduciary responsibilities; Standards of performance for enrolled actuaries; and Valuation of plan assets; and (5) Principles of Pension Valuation II, and Accounting Standards for Pension Plans (20 credits), including: Accounting for pension costs and obligations; Pension valuation principles; and Regulatory and professional considerations in valuing pension obligations. Elective pension courses are: (1) International Pension Issues (20 credits), including: Accounting and taxation issues; and Fundamentals of overseas retirement plans; (2) OASDI Program in the U.S. (ten credits); (3) Actuary as Expert Witness (ten credits), including: Actuarial testimony; Preparation of actuarial reports; Role of cases and precedents; Structured settlements; Valuation of future loss in wrongful death cases; Valuation of lost wages and benefits in accidental injury and wrongful dismissal cases; and Valuation of pension benefits in marital dissolution cases; and (4) Executive Compensation (ten credits). General elective courses are: (1) Intensive Seminar on Applied Statistical Methods (ten credits), including: Dynamic programming; Integer programming; Linear programming; Project scheduling; Queuing theory; and Simulation; (2) Operations Research (15 credits), including: Dynamic programming; Integer programming; Linear programming; Project scheduling; Queuing theory; and Simulation; (3) Numerical Methods (ten credits), including: Interpolation; Iteration; Linear systems; and Numerical integration; (4) Intensive

Seminar on Risk Theory (ten credits); (5) Mathematics of Demography (ten credits), including: Conventional and adjusted measures of mortality; Demographic characteristics and trends in Canada and the U.S.; Evaluation of demographic data; Introduction to applications of demographic characteristics and trends to actuarial work; Mathematics of stable and stationary populations; and Measures of fertility; and (6) Mathematics of Graduation (ten credits), including: Analysis and critique of various models; Graduation by moving-weighted average, graphic, Whittaker, Bayesian, parametric, and smooth-junction interpolation methods; Problems involved in making and testing graduations of mortality tables or other series that are likely to be encountered in course of actuary's work; Statistical considerations; and Two-dimensional graduation. Separate courses available for Canadian candidates. Credit may be granted for exams successfully completed for other organizations. May earn up to 30 credits for successful completion of research paper. **Preparatory Materials:** Study guides, including list of suggested reading and sample questions, available. Seminars and workshops also available. **Examination Frequency:** Annual - always October or November. **Examination Sites:** Exams given at sites throughout the U.S. and Canada. **Examination Type:** Multiple-choice; short answer. **Waiting Period to Receive Scores:** Eight-ten weeks. **Endorsed By:** American Academy of Actuaries; American Society of Pension Actuaries; Canadian Institute of Actuaries; Casualty Actuarial Society; Conference of Consulting Actuaries; Joint Board for the Enrollment of Actuaries; National Organization for Competency Assurance.

323

Fellow, Society of Pension Actuaries (FSPA)
American Society of Pension Actuaries (ASPA)
4350 N. Fairfax Dr., Ste. 820
Arlington, VA 22203
Phone: (703)516-9300
Fax: (703)516-9308
Chester Salkind, Exec.Dir.

Recipient: Enrolled actuaries. **Educational/Experience Requirements:** Hold Member, Society of Pension Actuaries (MSPA) designation (see separate entry). **Membership:** Required. **Certification Requirements:** Successful completion of the following exams: (1) Advanced Actuarial Practice, which covers: Civil litigation; Consulting; Federal regulations and acts; Financial accounting: Inflation impact on benefits; IRS rulings and notices; and Pension asset valuation and performance measurement; (2) Advanced Retirement Plan Consulting, which tests depth of knowledge and ability to apply this knowledge to comprehensive pension problems; and (3) Financial and Fiduciary Aspects of Qualified Plans, covering: Accounting and financial reporting; Distribution; Estate planning; Fiduciary standards; Plan assets; Protection; Termination; and Taxation. **Renewal:** Every two years. Recertification based on accumulation of points through continuing education. **Examination Type:** Essay; multiple-choice; problem-solving; short answer. **Fees:** $1050.

324

Member, Society of Pension Actuaries (MSPA)
American Society of Pension
Actuaries (ASPA)
4350 N. Fairfax Dr., Ste. 820
Arlington, VA 22203
Phone: (703)516-9300
Fax: (703)516-9308
Chester Salkind, Exec.Dir.

Recipient: Enrolled actuaries. **Educational/Experience Requirements:** Three years experience. **Membership:** Required. **Certification Requirements:** Successful completion of three examinations necessary for enrolled actuary certification. **Renewal:** Every two years. Recertification based on accumulation of points through continuing education. **Fees:** $530.

325

Qualified Pension Administrator (QPA)
American Society of Pension
Actuaries (ASPA)
4350 N. Fairfax Dr., Ste. 820
Arlington, VA 22203
Phone: (703)516-9300
Fax: (703)516-9308
Chester Salkind, Exec.Dir.

Recipient: Qualified plan administrators. **Educational/Experience Requirements:** Two years experience. **Membership:** Required. **Certification Requirements:** Successful completion of the following exams: (1) Administrative and Consulting Aspects of Defined Benefit Plans, covering: Benefit calculations, rules, terminations, and changes; Funding and accounting; and Traditional plan variations; (2) Administrative and Con-

sulting Aspects of Defined Contribution Plans, covering: Employee stock ownerships (ESOP); 401(k); Profit sharing; and Simplified employee pensions (SEP); and (3) Qualification and Operation of Retirement Plans, covering: Fiduciary responsibilities; Investment vehicles and performance; Participation and distribution requirements; Qualifications; Reporting and disclosure; Taxes; and Types of plans. Must also successfully complete Pension Administrator's Course, a self-study course and exam. Course covers: Basics of plan administration; IRD requirements; Plan documents; Reporting and disclosure requirements; Roles and responsibilities; Trust accounting; and Types of plans. **Renewal:** Every two years. Recertification based on accumulation of points through continuing education. **Preparatory Materials:** Study course available. **Examination Type:** Case study; multiple-choice; short answer. **Fees:** $650.

Computer Systems Analysts

326

Associate Computing Professional (ACP)
Institute for Certification of
Computing Professionals (ICCP)
2200 E. Devon Ave., Ste. 268
Des Plaines, IL 60018-4503
Phone: (708)299-4227
Fax: (708)299-4280
E-mail: Compuserve 74040,3722

Recipient: Computer professionals. **Educational/Experience Requirements:** Basic knowledge of information processing and one of the programming languages. **Certification Requirements:** Successful completion of core exam and one programming exam. Core exam covers: Associated disciplines; Data and information; Human and organization framework; Systems concepts; Systems development; and Technology. Programming exams are: (1) BASIC, including: Arrays; Characteristics of BASIC program; Control statements; Data; Expressions and assignments; Functions; Input and output; and String manipulation; (2) C, including: Control flow; Data types; Functions; Library functions and environment; Operators and expressions; Pointers and arrays; Preprocessor; Standard I/O library; and Structure and unions; (3) COBOL, including: Compiler commands; Debugging; Divisions and sections; and General; (4) Pascal, including: Arrays; Control structures; Defined

data types; Elementary topics; General files; Pointers; Procedures and functions; Records; Recursion; and Test files; and (5) RPG/400, including: Arrays and tables; Calculation operations; Data; Debugging; File processing; General topics; and Program control. **Preparatory Materials:** Review courses, audio cassette instruction, and exam review outlines, including sample questions, available. **Examination Frequency:** By arrangement. **Examination Sites:** Exam given at 230 sites throughout the U.S., Canada, and internationally. **Re-examination:** Must successfully complete exams within three years. **Fees:** $210.

327

Certified Computing Professional (CCP)
Institute for Certification of
Computing Professionals (ICCP)
2200 E. Devon Ave., Ste. 268
Des Plaines, IL 60018-4503
Phone: (708)299-4227
Fax: (708)299-4280
E-mail: Compuserve 74040,3722

Recipient: Computer professionals. **Educational/Experience Requirements:** Forty-eight months experience in data processing systems, programming, management, and teaching computer-based information systems. Education can be substituted for experience in the following ways: (1) Bachelor's or graduate degree in information systems or computer science (24 months); (2) Associate Computing Professional (ACP) designation (see separate entry) (24 months); (3) Bachelor's or graduate degree in related area including accounting, business, engineering, mathematics, sciences, or statistics (18 months); (4) Bachelor's or graduate degree in unrelated area (12 months); and (5) Associate's degree or diploma (two year program) in information systems or computer science (12 months). **Certification Requirements:** Successful completion of core exam and two specialty exams. Core exam covers: Data and information; Human and organization framework; Systems concepts; System development; Technology; and Related disciplines. Specialty exams are: (1) Business Information Systems, including: BIS applications; BIS consideration; and BIS environment; (2) Communications, including: Data communications theory; Established communications systems; Hardware; ISO OSI reference model; Networking theory; and Usage and design; (3) Data Resource Management, including: Data analysis; Data base design; and Data resource management functions; (4) Management, including:

General management and organizational concepts; Information systems management; and Project management; (5) Procedural Programming, including: Data and file organization; Integration with hardware and software; Procedural program structure; Procedural programming consideration; and Program design; (6) Software Engineering, including: Computer system engineering; Configuration management; Programming languages and coding; Software design; Software maintenance; Software project planning; Software quality assurance; Software requirements; and Software testing; (7) Systems Development, including: System analysis; Systems analyst as professional; and system design and implementation; (8) Systems Programming, including: Computer architecture and implementation; Concurrent and distributed processing; Data management systems; Language processing; Languages; Operating systems; Performance evaluation; Software Tools; and Systems management; and (9) Systems Security, including: Information and system security; Recovery from information service interruptions; Risk assessment; Security management; and Security in system design. Programming track requires successful completion of core exam, one specialty exam, and two of the following programming language exams: (1) BASIC, including: Arrays; Characteristics of BASIC program; Control statements; Data; Expressions and assignments; Functions; Input and output; and String manipulation; (2) C, including: Control flow; Data types; Functions; Library functions and environment; Operators and expressions; Pointers and arrays; Preprocessor; Standard I/O library; and Structure and unions; (3) COBOL, including: Compiler commands; Debugging; Divisions and sections; and General; (4) Pascal, including: Arrays; Control structures; Defined data types; Elementary topics; General files; Pointers; Procedures and functions; Records; Recursion; and Test files; and (5) RPG/400, including: Arrays and tables; Calculation operations; Data; Debugging; File processing; General topics; and Program control. **Renewal:** Every three years. Recertification based on successful completion of exam or accumulation of 120 contact hours of continuing education. **Preparatory Materials:** *DPMA SIG-CP ICCP Certification Review Manual* (reference). Review courses, audio cassette instruction, and exam review outlines, including sample questions, available. **Examination Frequency:** Throughout the year. **Examination Sites:** Exam given at 230 sites throughout the U.S., Canada, and internationally. **Examination Type:** Multiple-choice. **Reexamination:** Must wait 30 days to retake

exams. Must successfully complete exams within three years. **Fees:** $140 (per exam).

328

Certified NetWare 2 Administrator
Novell
122 East 1700 South
Provo, UT 84606-6194
Phone: (801)429-5508
Toll Free: (800)233-EDUC

Recipient: NetWare 2 computer network administrators. **Educational/Experience Requirements:** Knowledge of DOS and microcomputer concepts. **Certification Requirements:** Successful completion of exam. **Preparatory Materials:** List of test objectives provided. Course, video, and self-study programs available. **Examination Frequency:** Throughout the year. **Examination Sites:** Exam given at sites throughout the U.S.

329

Certified NetWare 3 Administrator
Novell
122 East 1700 South
Provo, UT 84606-6194
Phone: (801)429-5508
Toll Free: (800)233-EDUC

Recipient: NetWare 3 computer network administrators. **Educational/Experience Requirements:** Knowledge of DOS and microcomputer concepts. **Certification Requirements:** Successful completion of exam. **Preparatory Materials:** List of test objectives provided. Course, video, and self-study programs available. **Examination Frequency:** Throughout the year. **Examination Sites:** Exam given at sites throughout the U.S.

330

Certified NetWare 4 Administrator
Novell
122 East 1700 South
Provo, UT 84606-6194
Phone: (801)429-5508
Toll Free: (800)233-EDUC

Recipient: NetWare 4 computer network administrators. **Educational/Experience Requirements:** Knowledge of DOS and microcomputer concepts. **Certification Requirements:** Successful completion of exam. **Preparatory Materials:** List of test objectives provided. Course, video, and self-study programs available. **Examination Frequency:** Throughout the year.

Examination Sites: Exam given at sites throughout the U.S.

331

Certified NetWare Engineer (CNE)
Novell
122 East 1700 South
Provo, UT 84606-6194
Phone: (801)429-5508
Toll Free: (800)233-EDUC

Recipient: Computer network engineers specializing in Novell products. **Educational/Experience Requirements:** Knowledge of DOS and microcomputer or Unix OS Fundamental concepts. **Certification Requirements:** Accumulation of credit through successful completion of courses, including exams. Prerequisite requirement is five credits earned through the following courses: DOS/Microcomputer Concepts (two credits); Networking Technologies (three credits); and Unix OS Fundamentals for Netware Users (two credits). Operating System requirement is seven credits earned through one of the following tracks: (1) NetWare 3.1x Track, including: NetWare 3.1x Administration (three credits); NetWare 3.1x Advanced Administration (two credits); and NetWare 3.1x Installation and Configuration Workshop (two credits); (2) NetWare 3.1x/4 Track, including: NetWare 3.1x Administration (three credits); NetWare 3.1x Advanced Administration (two credits); NetWare 3.11 to 4 Update (two credits); and NetWare 4 Installation and Configuration Workshop (two credits); (3) NetWare 4 Track, including: NetWare 4x Administration (three credits); NetWare 4 Administration (three credits); NetWare 4 Advanced Administration (two credits); and NetWare 4 Installation and Configuration Workshop (two credits); or (4) UnixWare Track, including: UnixWare Installation and Configuration (two credits); UnixWare System Administration (three credits); and UnixWare Advanced System Administration (two credits). Core requirement is five credits earned through successful completion of NetWare Service and Support course. Elective requirement is two credits earned through the following courses: Administering NetWare for Macintosh (one credit); Administering NetWare for Macintosh 4.01 (one credit); AppWare Programming: Visual AppBuilder (two credits); Fundamentals of Internetwork and Management Design (two credits); LAN WorkPlace for DOS 4.1 (two credits); LANalyzer for Windows (one credit); NetWare Connect (two credits); NetWare 4 Directory Services Design (two credits); NetWare Global MHS (two credits); NetWare Internetworking Products (two credits); NetWare/IP (one credit); NetWare for LAT (two credits); NetWare Expert for NMS (two credits); NetWare NFS Gateway (two credits); NetWare for SAA 1.3b: Installation and Troubleshooting (three credits); NetWare 3.11 to 4 Update (two credits); NetWare Navigator (two credits); NetWare NFS (two credits); NetWare TCP/IP Transport (two credits); NetWare 2.2 Advanced System Manager (two credits); NetWare 2.2 System Manager (three credits); Printing with NetWare (two credits); and Product Information (one credit). **Renewal:** Recertification based on continuing education. **Preparatory Materials:** Catalog of courses provided. Self-study programs and self-assessment tests available. **Examination Frequency:** Throughout the year. **Examination Sites:** Exams given at sites throughout the U.S. **Reexamination:** May retake exams one time. **Endorsed By:** CNE Professional Association.

332

Certified NetWare Instructor (CNI)
Novell
122 East 1700 South
Provo, UT 84606-6194
Phone: (801)429-5508
Fax: (801)429-5363
Toll Free: (800)233-EDUC

Recipient: Instructors for Novell computer software courses. **Certification Requirements:** Must meet the following requirements: (1) Attendance at course candidate wants to teach; (2) Successful completion of proficiency tests; and (3) Successful completion of Instructor Performance Evaluation (IPE). **Preparatory Materials:** Catalog of courses provided.

333

Certified System Engineer (CSE)
Wordperfect
c/o Novell
122 East 1700 South
Provo, UT 84606-6194
Phone: (801)429-5508
Fax: (801)429-5363
Toll Free: (800)233-EDUC

Recipient: Professionals who assist, consult with, or train WordPerfect InForms 1.0 software users. **Certification Requirements:** Successful completion of exam. **Preparatory Materials:** List of test objectives, study guides and kits, and practice exams available. **Examination Fre-**

quency: Throughout the year. **Examination Sites:** Exam given at sites throughout the U.S. **Examination Type:** Multiple-choice. **Fees:** $120.

334

Certified UnixWare Administrator
Novell
122 East 1700 South
Provo, UT 84606-6194
Phone: (801)429-5508
Toll Free: (800)233-EDUC

Recipient: UnixWare computer network administrators. **Educational/Experience Requirements:** Knowledge of DOS and microcomputer concepts. **Certification Requirements:** Successful completion of exam. **Preparatory Materials:** List of test objectives provided. Course, video, and self-study programs available. **Examination Frequency:** Throughout the year. **Examination Sites:** Exam given at sites throughout the U.S.

335

Enterprise Certified NetWare Engineer (CNE)
Novell
122 East 1700 South
Provo, UT 84606-6194
Phone: (801)429-5508
Fax: (801)429-5363
Toll Free: (800)233-EDUC

Recipient: Computer network engineers specializing in Novell products. **Educational/Experience Requirements:** Must hold Certified Network Engineer (CNE) designation (see separate entry). **Certification Requirements:** Accumulation of 19 credits through successful completion of courses, including exams. Must accumulate seven-ten credits through successful completion one of the following paths: (1) NetWare 4.x Administration; NetWare 4 Administration; NetWare 4 Advanced Administration; NetWare 3.1x Administration; and NetWare 3.1x Advanced Administration (ten total credits); (2) Netware 4.x Administration; NetWare 4 Administration; NetWare 4 Advanced Administration; UnixWare System Administration; and UnixWare Advanced System Administration (ten total credits); (3) NetWare 4.x Administration; NetWare 4 Administration; and NetWare 4 Advanced Administration (seven total credits); and (4) NetWare 3.1x Administration; NetWare 3.1x Advanced Administration; and NetWare 3.11 to 4 Update (seven total credits). Must accumulate nine-12 credits

through successful completion of combination of the following elective courses: Administering NetWare for Macintosh 4.01 (one credit); Administering NetWare for Macintosh 3.12 (one credit); AppWare Programming: Visual AppBuilder (two credits); Fundamentals of Internetwork and Management Design (two credits); LANalyzer for Windows (one credit); LAN WorkPlace for DOS 4.1 Administration (two credits); NetWare Connect (two credits); NetWare Expert for NMS (two credits); NetWare 4 Directory Services Design (two credits); NetWare 4 Installation and Configuration Workshop (two credits); NetWare Global MHS (two credits); NetWare Internetworking Products (two credits); NetWare/IP (one credit); NetWare for LAT (two credits); NetWare Navigator (two credits); NetWare NFS (two credits); NetWare NFS Gateway (one credit); NetWare for SAA 1.3b: Installation and Troubleshooting (three credits); NetWare TCP/IP (two credits); NetWare 3.1x Installation and Configuration Workshop (two credits); NetWare 2.2 Advanced System Manager (two credits); NetWare 2.2 System Manager (three credits); Printing with NetWare (two credits); Product Information (one credit); and UnixWare Installation and Configuration (two credits). **Renewal:** Recertification based on continuing education. **Preparatory Materials:** Catalog of courses provided. Self-study program and self-assessment test available. **Examination Frequency:** Throughout the year. **Examination Sites:** Exams given at sites throughout the U.S. **Re-examination:** May retake exams one time.

Ergonomics Professionals

336

Certified Human Factors Professional (CHFP)
Board of Certification in Professional Ergonomics (BCPE)
PO Box 2811
Bellingham, WA 98227
Phone: (206)671-7601
Fax: (206)671-7681
Dieter W. Johns CPE, Exec.Dir.

Recipient: Ergonomics/human factors practitioners. Ergonomics is a body of knowledge about human abilities, limitations, and characteristics that are relevant to design. **Educational/Experience Requirements:** Must meet the following requirements: (1) Master's degree in the field. Educational equivalent within engineering or life and natural sciences will be considered; (2) Four years experience, primarily in ergonomic design; or (3) Presentation of example of professional work on technical product, process, or environment incorporating applied ergonomic data, methods, or principles. **Certification Requirements:** Successful completion of exam. Exam covers: Design of human machine interface; Humans as systems components (capabilities/limitations); Methods and techniques; Professional practice; and Systems design and organization. **Renewal:** Every three years. Recertification based on continuing education. **Preparatory Materials:** List of suggested study references available. **Examination Frequency:** semiannual - always spring and fall. **Examination Sites:** Exam given at universities in the spring and annual meeting in the fall. **Examination Type:** Essay; multiple-choice; short answer. **Waiting Period to Receive Scores:** 90 days. **Re-examination:** Must wait six months to retake exam. There is a fee to retake exam. **Fees:** $200. **Endorsed By:** Center for Registration of European Ergonomics; Human Factors and Ergonomics Society.

337

Certified Professional Ergonomist (CPE)
Board of Certification in
   Professional Ergonomics (BCPE)
PO Box 2811
Bellingham, WA 98227
Phone: (206)671-7601
Fax: (206)671-7681

Recipient: Ergonomics/human factors practitioners. Ergonomics is a body of knowledge about human abilities, limitations, and characteristics that are relevant to design. **Number of Certified Individuals:** 570. **Educational/Experience Requirements:** Must meet the following requirements: (1) Master's degree in ergonomics. Educational equivalent within engineering or life and natural sciences will be considered; (2) Four years experience, primarily in ergonomic design; and (3) Presentation of example of professional work on technical product, process, or environment incorporating applied ergonomic data, methods, or principles. **Membership:** Not required. **Certification Requirements:** Successful completion of exam. Exam covers: Design of human machine interface; Humans as systems components (capabilities/limitations); Methods and techniques; Professional practice; and Systems design and organization. **Renewal:** Every three years. Recertification based on continuing education. **Prepara-**

tory **Materials:** List of suggested study references available. **Examination Frequency:** semiannual - always spring and fall. **Examination Sites:** Exam given at universities in the spring and annual meeting in the fall. **Examination Type:** Essay; multiple-choice; short answer. **Waiting Period to Receive Scores:** 90 days. **Re-examination:** Must wait six months to retake exam. There is a fee to retake exam. **Fees:** $200. **Endorsed By:** Center for Registration of European Ergonomics; Human Factors and Ergonomics Society.

Operations Research Analysts

338

Certified Specialist in Analytical Technology (CSAT)
ISA, The International Society for
   Measurement and Control
67 Alexander Dr.
PO Box 12277
Research Triangle Park, NC 27709
Phone: (919)549-8411
Fax: (919)549-8288
E-mail: INFO@ISA.ORG
Quentin S. Clark, Dir.

Recipient: Professionals involved in analytical technology. **Number of Certified Individuals:** 78. **Educational/Experience Requirements:** Must meet one of the following requirements: (1) Eight years combined education, with minimum of associate's degree or successful completion of two years education in engineering, engineering technology, or related science, and minimum of three years experience; or (2) Ten years experience. **Membership:** Not required. **Certification Requirements:** Successful completion of exam. Exam covers the following domains: (1) Basic Principles of Process Analyzer Systems, including: Detecting the components of interest; Extracting representative sample; Meeting health, safety, and environmental requirements; Preparing sample; Transmitting data to device or system; and Transporting sample to analyzer; (2) Selection and Application of Process Analyzer Systems, including: Establishing requirements for process analyzer system; Examining system parameters; Performing project analysis; Researching equipment that meets requirements; and Selecting process analyzer system; (3) Integration, Design, and Implementation of Process Analyzer Systems, including: Determining location of process analyzer system; Determining necessary field components; Developing

basis for design and project scope; Generating specifications and drawings; and Installing and commissioning specified process analyzer system; and (4) Maintenance and Operation of Process Analyzer Systems, including: Applying systematic troubleshooting principles to repair process analyzer system; Checking calibration and verifying data integrity; Checking physical parameters and data validity in order to determine need for repair; Developing and implementing preventive maintenance schedule; Ensuring process analyzer system operates properly and meets customer needs; and Keeping and implementing preventive maintenance schedule. **Preparatory Materials:** Training course and study guide, including bibliography and sample questions, available. **Examination Frequency:** quarterly. **Examination Sites:** Exam given at ISA conferences and exhibitions and at sites throughout the U.S. and Canada. **Examination Type:** Multiple-choice. **Waiting Period to Receive Scores:** Two weeks. **Re-examination:** Must wait 30 days to retake exam. May retake exam three times. There is a fee to retake exam. **Fees:** $140 (members); $190 (nonmembers).

339

Certified Specialist in Measurement Technology (CSMT)
ISA, The International Society for
   Measurement and Control
67 Alexander Dr.
PO Box 12277
Research Triangle Park, NC 27709
Phone: (919)549-8411
Fax: (919)549-8288
E-mail: INFO@ISA.ORG
Quentin S. Clark, Dir.

Recipient: Professionals involved in measurement technology. **Educational/ Experience Requirements:** Must meet one of the following requirements: (1) Eight years combined education, with minimum of associate's degree or successful completion of two years education in engineering, engineering technology, or related science, and minimum of three years experience; or (2) Ten years experience. **Membership:** Not required. **Certification Requirements:** Successful completion of exam. **Preparatory Materials:** Training course and exam preparation guide, including bibliography and sample questions, available. **Examination Frequency:** quarterly. **Examination Sites:** Exam given at ISA conferences and exhibitions and at sites throughout the U.S. **Re-examination:** May retake exam three times. **Fees:** $160 (members); $210 (nonmembers).

Statisticians

340

Certification in Statistical Process Control, Facilitator (CSPCF)

Statistical Process Control Society (SPCS)
PO Box 1203
Avon, CT 06001
Phone: (203)676-8890
Fax: (203)676-2238
Eugene A. Fitzgerald, Chair

Recipient: Statistical process control (SPC) facilitators qualified to plan and implement an SPC system. **Membership:** Not required. **Certification Requirements:** Successful completion of exam. **Examination Frequency:** semiannual - always January and June. **Examination Sites:** Exam given at sites throughout the U.S. **Fees:** $75 (members); $125 (nonmembers).

341

Certification in Statistical Process Control, Operational (CSPCO)

Statistical Process Control Society (SPCS)
PO Box 1203
Avon, CT 06001
Phone: (203)676-8890
Fax: (203)676-2238
Eugene A. Fitzgerald, Chair

Recipient: Statistical process control production operators. **Membership:** Not required. **Certification Requirements:** Successful completion of exam. **Examination Frequency:** semiannual - always January and June. **Examination Sites:** Exam given at sites throughout the U.S. **Fees:** $50 (members); $100 (nonmembers).

342

Certification in Statistical Process Control, Technical (CSPCT)

Statistical Process Control Society (SPCS)
PO Box 1203
Avon, CT 06001
Phone: (203)676-8890
Fax: (203)676-2238
Eugene A. Fitzgerald, Chair

Recipient: Statistical process control technicians. **Membership:** Not required. **Certification Requirements:** Successful completion of exam. **Examination Frequency:** semiannual - always January and June. **Examination Sites:** Exam given at sites throughout the U.S. **Fees:** $75 (members); $125 (nonmembers).

Life Scientists

Agricultural Scientists

343

Associate Professional Agronomist (APA)
American Society of Agronomy (ASA)
677 S. Segoe Rd.
Madison, WI 53711
Phone: (608)273-8080
Fax: (608)273-2021
Cleo C. Tindall, Registrar

Recipient: Professionals involved in agronomy. **Membership:** Not required. **Certification Requirements:** Bachelor's, master's, or doctorate degree in agronomy or related field. May qualify for Certified Professional Agronomist (CPA) designation (see separate entry) with further experience. **Fees:** $20 (members); $25 (nonmembers).

344

Associate Professional Crop Scientist (APCS)
American Society of Agronomy (ASA)
677 S. Segoe Rd.
Madison, WI 53711
Phone: (608)273-8080
Fax: (608)273-2021
Cleo C. Tindall, Registrar

Recipient: Professionals involved in crop science. **Membership:** Not required. **Certification Requirements:** Bachelor's, master's, or doctorate degree in crop science or related field. May qualify for Certified Professional Crop Scientist (CPCS) designation (see separate entry) with further experience. **Fees:** $20 (members); $25 (nonmembers). **Endorsed By:** Crop Science Society of America.

345

Associate Professional Crop Specialist (APCS)
American Society of Agronomy (ASA)
677 S. Segoe Rd.
Madison, WI 53711
Phone: (608)273-8080
Fax: (608)273-2021
Cleo C. Tindall, Registrar

Recipient: Professionals involved in crop science. **Membership:** Not required. **Certification Requirements:** Bachelor's, master's, or doctorate degree in crop science or related field. May qualify for Certified Professional Crop Specialist (CPCS) designation (see separate entry) with further experience. **Fees:** $20 (members); $25 (nonmembers). **Endorsed By:** Crop Science Society of America.

346

Associate Professional in Horticulture (APH)
American Society of Agronomy (ASA)
677 S. Segoe Rd.
Madison, WI 53711
Phone: (608)273-8080
Fax: (608)273-2021
Cleo C. Tindall, Registrar

Recipient: Professionals involved in horticulture. **Membership:** Not required. **Certification Requirements:** Bachelor's, master's, or doctorate degree in horticulture or related field. May qualify for Certified Professional Horticulturist (CPH) designation (see separate entry) with further experience. **Fees:** $20 (members); $25 (nonmembers).

347

Associate Professional Plant Pathologist (APPP)
American Society of Agronomy (ASA)
677 S. Segoe Rd.
Madison, WI 53711
Phone: (608)273-8080
Fax: (608)273-2021
Cleo C. Tindall, Registrar

Recipient: Professionals involved in plant pathology. **Membership:** Not required. **Certification Requirements:** Bachelor's, master's, or doctorate degree in weed science or related field. May qualify for Certified Professional Plant Pathologist (CPPP) designation (see separate entry) with further experience. **Fees:** $20 (members); $25 (nonmembers).

348

Associate Professional Soil Classifier (APSC)
American Society of Agronomy (ASA)
677 S. Segoe Rd.
Madison, WI 53711
Phone: (608)273-8080
Fax: (608)273-2021
Cleo C. Tindall, Registrar

Recipient: Professional soil classifiers. **Membership:** Not required. **Certification Requirements:** Bachelor's, master's, or doctorate degree in soil science or related field. May qualify for Certified Professional Soil Classifier (CPSC) designation (see separate entry) with further experience. **Fees:** $20 (members); $25 (nonmembers). **Endorsed By:** Soil Science Society of America

■ **349**

Associate Professional Soil Scientist (APSS)
American Society of Agronomy (ASA)
677 S. Segoe Rd.
Madison, WI 53711
Phone: (608)273-8080
Fax: (608)273-2021
Cleo C. Tindall, Registrar

Recipient: Professionals involved in soil science. **Membership:** Not required. **Certification Requirements:** Bachelor's, master's, or doctorate degree in soil science or related field. May qualify for Certified Professional Soil Scientist (CPSS) designation (see separate entry) with further experience. **Fees:** $20 (members); $25 (nonmembers). **Endorsed By:** Soil Science Society of America.

■ **350**

Associate Professional Soil Specialist (APSS)
American Society of Agronomy (ASA)
677 S. Segoe Rd.
Madison, WI 53711
Phone: (608)273-8080
Fax: (608)273-2021
Cleo C. Tindall, Registrar

Recipient: Professionals involved in soil science. **Membership:** Not required. **Certification Requirements:** Bachelor's, master's, or doctorate degree in soil science or related field. May qualify for Certified Professional Soil Specialist (CPSS) designation (see separate entry) with further experience. **Fees:** $20 (members); $25 (nonmembers). **Endorsed By:** Soil Science Society of America.

■ **351**

Associate Professional in Weed Science (APWS)
American Society of Agronomy (ASA)
677 S. Segoe Rd.
Madison, WI 53711
Phone: (608)273-8080
Fax: (608)273-2021
Cleo C. Tindall, Registrar

Recipient: Professionals involved in weed science. **Membership:** Not required. **Certification Requirements:** Must hold bachelor's, master's, or doctorate degree in weed science or related field. May qualify for Certified Professional in Weed Science (CPWS) designation (see separate entry) with increased experience. **Fees:** $20 (members); $25 (nonmembers).

■ **352**

Certified Crop Adviser (CCA)
American Society of Agronomy (ASA)
677 S. Segoe Rd.
Madison, WI 53711
Phone: (608)273-8080
Fax: (608)273-2021
Cleo C. Tindall, Registrar

Recipient: Professionals who provide crop management recommendations to farmers. **Educational/Experience Requirements:** Must meet one of the following requirements: (1) High school diploma and four years experience; (2) Associate's degree with 15 semester hours in agricultural sciences and three years experience; (3) Bachelor's degree with 15 semester hours of agricultural sciences and two years experience; or (4) Hold ASA Certified Professional designation (see separate entry). Supervised work experience or internship may be substituted for up to one year of experience. May qualify for Associate Crop Advisor (ACA) designation (see separate entry) with less experience. **Membership:** Not required. **Certification Requirements:** Successful completion of state/regional and national exams. **Renewal:** Every two years. Recertification based on accumulation of 40 hours of continuing education, 20 of which must be in approved areas. **Endorsed By:** Crop Science Society of America.

■ **353**

Certified Professional Agronomist (CPA)
American Society of Agronomy (ASA)
677 S. Segoe Rd.
Madison, WI 53711
Phone: (608)273-8080
Fax: (608)273-2021
Cleo C. Tindall, Registrar

Recipient: Professional agronomists. **Membership:** Not required. **Certification Requirements:** Must meet one of the following requirements: (1) Bachelor's degree in agronomy or related field, meet minimum core requirements, and five years experience; (2) Master's degree in agronomy or related field, meet minimum core requirements, and three years experience; (3) Doctorate degree in agronomy or related field, meet mini-

mum core requirements, and one year of experience; (4) Meet degree and experience requirements, but not core requirements, and successful completion of exam. Oral exam may also be required; (5) Meet experience requirement with degree in unrelated field and successful completion of exam; and (6) Meet experience requirements and degree in agronomy or related field from non-U.S. or Canadian college or university and successful completion of exam. Oral exam may also be required. May qualify for Associate Professional Agronomist (APA) designation (see separate entry) with less experience. **Renewal:** Every three years. Recertification based on continuing education. **Re-examination:** Must wait six months to retake exam. May retake exam one time. There is no fee to retake exam. **Fees:** $40 (members); $50 (nonmembers).

■ **354**

Certified Professional Crop Scientist (CPCS)
American Society of Agronomy (ASA)
677 S. Segoe Rd.
Madison, WI 53711
Phone: (608)273-8080
Fax: (608)273-2021
Cleo C. Tindall, Registrar

Recipient: Professional crop scientists. **Membership:** Not required. **Certification Requirements:** Must meet one of the following requirements: (1) Bachelor's degree in crop science or related field, meet minimum core requirements, and five years experience; (2) Master's degree in crop science or related field, meet minimum core requirements, and three years experience; (3) Doctorate degree in crop science or related field, meet minimum core requirements, and one year of experience; (4) Meet degree and experience requirements, but not core requirements, and successful completion of exam. Oral exam may also be required; (5) Meet experience requirement with degree in nonrelated field and successful completion of exam; and (6) Meet experience requirements and degree in crop science or related field from non-U.S. or Canadian college or university and successful completion of exam. Oral exam may also be required. May qualify for Associate Professional Crop Scientist (APCS) designation (see separate entry) with less experience. **Renewal:** Every three years. Recertification based on continuing education. **Re-examination:** Must wait six months to retake exam. May retake exam one time. There is no fee to retake exam. **Fees:** $40 (members); $50 (nonmembers);

$100 (exam option). **Endorsed By:** Crop Science Society of America.

355

Certified Professional Horticulturist (CPH)

American Society of Agronomy (ASA)
677 S. Segoe Rd.
Madison, WI 53711
Phone: (608)273-8080
Fax: (608)273-2021
Cleo C. Tindall, Registrar

Recipient: Professionals involved in horticulture. **Membership:** Not required. **Certification Requirements:** Must meet one of the following requirements: (1) Bachelor's degree in horticulture or related field, meet minimum core requirements, and five years experience; (2) Master's degree in horticulture or related field, meet minimum core requirements, and three years experience; (3) Doctorate degree in horticulture or related field, meet minimum core requirements, and one year of experience; (4) Meet degree and experience requirements, but not core requirements, and successful completion of exam. Oral exam may also be required; (5) Meet experience requirement with degree in non-related field and successful completion of exam; and (6) Meet experience requirements and degree in horticulture or related field from non-U.S. or Canadian college or university and successful completion of exam. Oral exam may also be required. May qualify for Associate Professional in Horticulture (APH) designation (see separate entry) with less experience. **Renewal:** Every three years. Recertification based on continuing education. **Re-examination:** Must wait six months to retake exam. May retake exam one time. There is no fee to retake exam. **Fees:** $40 (members); $50 (nonmembers); $100 (exam option).

356

Certified Professional Plant Pathologist (CPPP)

American Society of Agronomy (ASA)
677 S. Segoe Rd.
Madison, WI 53711
Phone: (608)273-8080
Fax: (608)273-2021
Cleo C. Tindall, Registrar

Recipient: Professionals involved in plant pathology. **Membership:** Not required. **Certification Requirements:** Must meet one of the following requirements: (1) Bachelor's degree in plant pathology or related field, meet minimum core requirements, and five years experience; (2) Master's degree in plant pathology or related field, meet minimum core requirements, and three years experience; or (3) Doctorate degree in plant pathology or related field, meet minimum core requirements, and one year of experience. May qualify for Associate Professional Plant Pathologist (APPP) designation (see separate entry) with less experience. **Renewal:** Every three years. Recertification based on continuing education. **Fees:** $40 (members); $50 (nonmembers).

357

Certified Professional Soil Classifier (CPSC)

American Society of Agronomy (ASA)
677 S. Segoe Rd.
Madison, WI 53711
Phone: (608)273-8080
Fax: (608)273-2021
Cleo C. Tindall, Registrar

Recipient: Soil classifiers. **Membership:** Not required. **Certification Requirements:** Must have five years experience and meet one of the following requirements: (1) Bachelor's, master's, or doctorate degree in soil science or related field and meet minimum core requirements; (2) Meet degree and experience requirements, but not core requirements, and successful completion of exam. Oral exam may also be required; (3) Meet experience requirement with degree in non-related field and successful completion of exam; and (4) Meet experience requirements and degree in soil science or related field from nonU.S. or Canadian college or university and successful completion of exam. Oral exam may also be required. May qualify for Associate Professional Soil Classifier (APSC) designation (see separate entry) with less experience. **Renewal:** Every three years. Recertification based on continuing education. **Re-examination:** Must wait six months to retake exam. May retake exam one time. There is no fee to retake exam. **Fees:** $40 (members); $50 (nonmembers); $100 (exam option). **Endorsed By:** Soil Science Society of America.

358

Certified Professional Soil Scientist (CPSS)

American Society of Agronomy (ASA)
677 S. Segoe Rd.
Madison, WI 53711
Phone: (608)273-8080
Fax: (608)273-2021
Cleo C. Tindall, Registrar

Recipient: Professional soil scientists. **Membership:** Not required. **Certification Requirements:** Must meet one of the following requirements: (1) Bachelor's degree in soil science or related field, meet minimum core requirements, and five years experience; (2) Master's degree in soil science or related field, meet minimum core requirements, and three years experience; (3) Doctorate degree in soil science or related field, meet minimum core requirements, and three years experience; (4) Meet degree and experience requirements, but not core requirements, and successful completion of exam. Oral exam may also be required; (5) Meet experience requirement with degree in non-related field and successful completion of exam; and (6) Meet experience requirements and degree in soil science or related field from non-U.S. or Canadian college or university and successful completion of exam. Oral exam may also be required. May qualify for Associate Professional Soil Scientist (APSS) designation (see separate entry) with less experience. **Renewal:** Every three years. Recertification based on continuing education. **Re-examination:** Must wait six months to retake exam. May retake exam one time. There is no fee to retake exam. **Fees:** $40 (members); $50 (nonmembers); $100 (exam option). **Endorsed By:** Soil Science Society of America.

359

Certified Professional Soil Specialist (CPSS)

American Society of Agronomy (ASA)
677 S. Segoe Rd.
Madison, WI 53711
Phone: (608)273-8080
Fax: (608)273-2021
Cleo C. Tindall, Registrar

Recipient: Soil specialists. **Membership:** Not required. **Certification Requirements:** Must meet one of the following requirements: (1) Bachelor's degree in soil science or related field, meet minimum core requirements, and five years experience; (2) Master's degree in soil science or related field, meet minimum core requirements, and three years experience; (3) Doctorate degree in soil science or related field, meet minimum core requirements, and one year of experience; (4) Meet degree and experience requirements, but not core requirements, and successful completion of exam. Oral exam may also be required; (5) Meet experience requirement with degree in non-related field and successful completion of exam; and (6) Meet experience requirements and degree in soil science or related field from non-U.S. or Canadian college or university and successful completion of exam. Oral exam may also be required. May qualify for Associate Professional Soil Scientist (APSS) designation (see separate entry) with less experience. **Renewal:** Every three years. Recertification based on continuing education. **Re-examination:** Must wait six months to retake exam. May retake exam one time. There is no fee to retake exam. **Fees:** $40 (members); $50 (nonmembers); $100 (exam option). **Endorsed By:** Soil Science Society of America.

360

Certified Professional in Weed Science (CPWS)
American Society of Agronomy (ASA)
677 S. Segoe Rd.
Madison, WI 53711
Phone: (608)273-8080
Fax: (608)273-2021
Cleo C. Tindall, Registrar

Recipient: Professionals involved in weed science. **Membership:** Not required. **Certification Requirements:** Must meet one of the following requirements: (1) Bachelor's degree in weed science or related field, meet minimum core requirements, and five years experience; (2) Master's degree in weed science or related field, meet minimum core requirements, and three years experience; or (3) Doctorate degree in weed science or related field, meet minimum core requirements, and one year of experience. May qualify for Associate Professional in Weed Science (APWS) designation (see separate entry) with less experience. **Renewal:** Every three years. Recertification based on continuing education. **Fees:** $40 (members); $50 (nonmembers).

Biological Scientists

361

Associate Fisheries Scientist (AFS)
American Fisheries Society (AFS)
5410 Grosvenor Ln., Ste. 110
Bethesda, MD 20814
Phone: (301)897-8616
Fax: (301)897-8096
Paul Brouha, Exec.Dir.

Recipient: Fisheries professionals engaged in or directing fisheries programs, projects, and research. **Membership:** Not required. **Certification Requirements:** Bachelor's degree, including 30 semester credits in biology, four courses in fisheries and aquatic sciences, 15 credits in physical sciences, six credits in mathematics, and six credits in communications. AFSs must earn Certified Fisheries Scientist (CFS) designation (see separate entry) within ten years. **Renewal:** none. **Fees:** $50 (members); $100 (nonmembers).

362

Board Certified Entomologist (BCE)
Entomological Society of America (ESA)
9301 Annapolis Rd.
Lanham, MD 20706-3115
Phone: (301)731-4535
Fax: (301)731-4538
Harry A. Bradley, Exec.Dir.

Recipient: Professionals interested in insect phenomena and pest management and control. **Number of Certified Individuals:** 660. **Educational/Experience Requirements:** Must meet one of the following requirements: (1) Bachelor's degree in related field and three years experience; (2) Master's degree in related field and two years experience; or (3) Doctoral degree in related field and one year of experience. **Membership:** Not required. **Certification Requirements:** Successful completion of both general and specialty exams. Specialty exams are: General Entomology; Medical/Veterinary Entomology; Pesticide Development Analysis and Toxicology; Plant Related Entomology; Regulatory; and Urban and Industrial Entomology. BCEs may take specialty exams in more than one specialty. **Renewal:** Every three years. Recertification based on accumulation of 72 continuing education units through educational activities, conferences, workshops, licensing and credentialing, writing, and association participation. **Pass/Fail Rate:** 70% pass exams.

363

Certified Clinical Biochemical Geneticist
American Board of Medical Genetics (ABMG)
9650 Rockville Pike
Bethesda, MD 20814-3998
Phone: (301)571-1825
Fax: (301)571-1895
Sharon Robinson, Admin.

Recipient: Medical doctors, doctors of osteopathy, and Ph.D.s competent to perform and interpret biochemical analyses relevant to diagnosis and management of human genetic diseases and act as consultants regarding laboratory diagnosis for broad range of disorders. **Educational/Experience Requirements:** Must meet the following requirements: (1) Doctoral degree in related discipline; (2) Successful completion of two year clinical biochemical genetics training program; (3) Submission of logbook of 150 cases; and (4) Submission of Clinical Biochemical Genetics Analyst and Method Competency List. ABMG maintains reciprocal agreement with Canadian College of Medical Genetics. **Certification Requirements:** Successful completion of general and specialty exams. **Renewal:** Every ten years. **Examination Frequency:** triennial. **Re-examination:** Must wait three years to retake exams. Must retake both exams. May retake exams two times. Fees to retake exams are: $400 (general); $200 (specialty). **Fees:** $1350. **Endorsed By:** American Board of Medical Specialties; American Medical Association; Council on Medical Education.

364

Certified Clinical Cytogeneticist
American Board of Medical Genetics (ABMG)
9650 Rockville Pike
Bethesda, MD 20814-3998
Phone: (301)571-1825
Fax: (301)571-1895
Sharon Robinson, Admin.

Recipient: Medical doctors, doctors of osteopathy, and Ph.D.s competent to perform and interpret cytogenetic analyses relevant to diagnosis and management of human genetic diseases and act as consultants regarding laboratory diagnosis for broad range of disorders. **Educational/Experience Requirements:** Must meet the following requirements: (1) Doctoral degree in related discipline; (2) Successful completion of two year cytogenetics training program; (3) Submission of logbook of 150 cases; and (4) Submission of Clinical Cytogenetics Method Competency List. ABMG maintains reciprocal agreement with Canadian College of Medical Genetics. **Certification Requirements:** Successful completion of general and specialty exams. **Renewal:** Every ten years. **Examination Frequency:** triennial. **Reexamination:** Must wait three years to retake exams. Must retake both exams. May retake exams two times. Fees to retake exams are: $400 (general); $200 (specialty). **Fees:** $1350. **Endorsed By:** American Board of Medical Specialties; American Medical Association; Council on Medical Education.

365

Certified Clinical Geneticist
American Board of Medical
  Genetics (ABMG)
9650 Rockville Pike
Bethesda, MD 20814-3998
Phone: (301)571-1825
Fax: (301)571-1895
Sharon Robinson, Admin.

Recipient: Clinical geneticist. **Educational/Experience Requirements:** Must meet the following requirements: (1) Hold medical or osteopathic medical degree; (2) Successfully complete two years of clinical residency program; and (3) Submit logbook of 150 cases. ABMG maintains reciprocal agreement with Canadian College of Medical Genetics. **Certification Requirements:** Successful completion of general and specialty exams. **Renewal:** Every ten years. **Examination Frequency:** triennial. **Reexamination:** Must wait three years to retake exams. Must retake both exams. May retake exams two times. Fees to retake exams are: $400 (general); $200 (specialty). **Fees:** $1350. **Endorsed By:** American Board of Medical Specialties; American Medical Association; Council on Medical Education.

366

**Certified Clinical Molecular
  Geneticist**
American Board of Medical
  Genetics (ABMG)
9650 Rockville Pike
Bethesda, MD 20814-3998
Phone: (301)571-1825
Fax: (301)571-1895
Sharon Robinson, Admin.

Recipient: Medical doctors, doctors of osteopathy, and Ph.D.s competent to perform and interpret molecular analyses relevant to diagnosis and management of human genetic diseases and act as consultants regarding laboratory diagnosis for broad range of disorders. **Educational/Experience Requirements:** Must meet the following requirements: (1) Doctoral degree in related discipline; (2) Successful completion of two year molecular genetics training program; (3) Submission of logbook of 150 cases; and (4) Submission of Clinical Molecular Genetics Tests and Method Competency List. ABMG maintains reciprocal agreement with Canadian College of Medical Genetics. **Certification Requirements:** Successful completion of general and specialty exams. **Renewal:** Every ten years. **Examination Frequency:** triennial. **Reexamination:** Must wait three years to retake exams. Must retake both exams. May retake exams two times. Fees to retake exams are: $400 (general); $200 (specialty). **Fees:** $1350. **Endorsed By:** American Board of Medical Specialties; American Medical Association; Council on Medical Education.

367

Certified Fisheries Scientist (CFS)
American Fisheries Society (AFS)
5410 Grosvenor Ln., Ste. 110
Bethesda, MD 20814
Phone: (301)897-8616
Fax: (301)897-8096
Paul Brouha, Exec.Dir.

Recipient: Fisheries professionals engaged in or directing fisheries programs, projects, and research. **Membership:** Not required. **Certification Requirements:** Must meet one of the following requirements: (1) Bachelor's degree and five years experience; (2) Master's degree and four years experience; or (3) Doctoral degree and two years experience. Must have 30 semester credits in biology, four courses in fisheries and aquatic sciences, 15 credits in physical sciences, six credits in mathematics, and six credits in communications. May qualify for Associate Fisheries Scientist (AFS) designation with less education and experience. **Renewal:** none. **Fees:** $100 (members); $200 (nonmembers).

368

Certified Ph.D. Medical Geneticist
American Board of Medical
  Genetics (ABMG)
9650 Rockville Pike
Bethesda, MD 20814-3998
Phone: (301)571-1825
Fax: (301)571-1895
Sharon Robinson, Admin.

Recipient: Ph.D.'s working in association with medical specialist, affiliated with clinical genetics program, serving as consultant to medical and dental specialists, and/or serving in supervisory capacity in medical genetics program. **Educational/Experience Requirements:** Must meet the following requirements: (1) Ph.D. in genetics, human genetics, or related field; (2) Successful completion of two year medical genetics training program; and (3) Submission of logbook of 150 cases. ABMG maintains reciprocal agreement with Canadian College of Medical Genetics. **Certification Requirements:** Successful completion of general and specialty exams. **Renewal:** Every ten years. **Examination Frequency:** triennial. **Reexamination:** Must wait three years to retake exams. Must retake both exams. May retake exams two times. Fees to retake exams are: $400 (general); $200 (specialty). **Fees:** $1350. **Endorsed By:** American Board of Medical Specialties; American Medical Association; Council on Medical Education.

369

Registered Microbiologist (RM)
American Society for Microbiology
  (ASM)
1325 Massachusetts Ave., NW
Washington, DC 20005
Phone: (202)737-3600
Rori B. Ferensic, Coord.

Recipient: Entry-level qualified microbiologists in clinical and nonclinical settings. **Educational/Experience Requirements:** Bachelor's degree with acceptable coursework and one year of experience. **Certification Requirements:** Successful completion of exam. Exam covers: Applied microbiology; Laboratory instruments and equipment; Operations; Preparation; Procedures; and Sample collection and handling. Certification available in the following specialty areas: Clinical and Public Health Microbiology; and Consumer Products and Quality Assurance Microbiology. **Renewal:** Every five years. **Examination Type:** Multiple-choice.

370

Specialist Microbiologist (SM)
American Society for Microbiology
  (ASM)
1325 Massachusetts Ave., NW
Washington, DC 20005
Phone: (202)737-3600
Rori B. Ferensic, Coord.

Recipient: Microbiologists in clinical and

non-clinical settings. **Educational/ Experience Requirements:** Must meet one of the following requirements: (1) Master's degree or higher and four years experience; (2) Medical degree and successful completion of residency in clinical microbiology; or (3) Seven years post-baccalaureate lab experience. **Certification Requirements:** Successful completion of exam. Exam covers: Applied microbiology; Laboratory instruments and equipment: Operations; Preparation; Procedures: and Sample collection and handling. Certification available in the following specialty areas: Public Health and Medical Laboratory Microbiology; and Consumer and Industrial Microbiology. **Renewal:** Every five years. **Examination Type:** Multiple-choice.

Foresters and Conservation Scientists and Workers

▮371▮

Certified Arborist
International Society of
   Arboriculture (ISA)
PO Box GG
Savoy, IL 61874-9902
Phone: (217)355-9411
Fax: (217)355-9516

Recipient: Arborists. **Educational/ Experience Requirements:** Must meet one of the following requirements: (1) Three years experience; or (2) Two years experience and associate's or bachelor's degree in related field. Experience should include diagnosis, establishment, fertilization, installation, pruning, and treatment of tree problems, cabling and bracing, climbing, or other services that directly relate to arboriculture. **Membership:** Not required. **Certification Requirements:** Successful completion of exam. Exam consists of the following domains: (1) Tree Nutrition and Fertilization; (2) Installation and Establishment; (3) Tree Biology; (4) Tree, Soil, and Water Relations; (5) Identification and Selection; (6) Safety and Climbing; (7) Pruning; (8) Diagnosis and Treatment; (9) Cabling, Bracing, and Lightning Protection; and (10) Trees, People, and Ecology (Construction Damage and Hazard Trees). **Renewal:** Every three years. Recertification based on either successful completion of exam or accumulation of 30 continuing education units (CEUs) through successful completion of courses, home study programs, seminars, and workshops. Renewal fees are: $75

(members); $125 (nonmembers). **Preparatory Materials:** Study guide, including list of suggested study references, available. **Examination Frequency:** Throughout the year. **Examination Sites:** Exam given by local chapters, at seminars, or by arrangement with proctor. **Examination Type:** Multiple-choice. **Waiting Period to Receive Scores:** Four-six weeks. **Re-examination:** Must only retake domains failed. **Fees:** $100 (member); $150 (nonmembers).

▮372▮

**Certified Ground Water
   Professional (CGWP)**
National Ground Water Association
   (NGWA)
6375 Riverside Dr.
PO Box 9050
Dublin, OH 43017-0950
Phone: (614)761-1711
Fax: (614)761-3446
Toll Free: (800)551-7379

Recipient: Scientists, engineers, and regulatory officials in ground water field. **Certification Requirements:** Must meet the following requirements: (1) Bachelor's degree; (2) Seven years of progressively more responsible professional experience; and (3) Submission of five publications, reports, or other documents. Experience must involve application of scientific or engineering principles and methods to execution of work including: (1) Understanding of occurrence, movement, and composition of ground water; (2) Development, management, or regulation of ground water; and (3) Teaching and research of ground water subjects at university level. Master's degree may be substituted for two years of experience and doctorate degree in ground water related field may be substituted for three years of experience. **Renewal:** Every three years. Recertification based on accumulation of 36 credits through: (1) Attendance at technical meetings (three credits per day); (2) Participating in or teaching short courses and workshops (four credits per day); (3) Publications in refereed journals (eight credits per article); (4) Teaching at universities, colleges, or junior colleges where not normally employed (two credits per one semester or quarter hour); (5) Oral presentations of papers at technical society meetings (four credits per paper presented); and (6) Successful completion of college courses in related subjects (seven credits per semester credit unit/ five credits per quarter credit unit). Renewal fee is $85. **Fees:** $150. **Endorsed By:** Association of Ground Water Scientists and Engineers.

▮373▮

Certified Lake Manager (CLM)
North American Lake Management
   Society (NALMS)
PO Box 5443
Madison, WI 53705-5443
Phone: (608)233-2836
Fax: (608)233-3186

Recipient: Professionals involved in the management of a pond, lake, or reservoir, or other body of water and its watershed. **Certification Requirements:** Successful completion of Professional Data Matrix, a point system based on personal and professional background.

▮374▮

**Certified Professional Soil Erosion
   and Sediment Control Specialist
   (CPESC)**
Soil and Water Conservation
   Society (SWCS)
7515 NE Ankeny Rd.
Ankeny, IA 50021-9764
Phone: (515)289-2331
Fax: (515)289-1227
Toll Free: (800)843-7645

Recipient: Erosion and sediment control specialists. **Number of Certified Individuals:** 700. **Educational/Experience Requirements:** Must meet one of the following requirements: (1) Ten years experience; (2) Bachelor's degree in related field and six years experience; (3) Master's degree in related field and four years experience; or (4) Ph.D. degree in related field and two years experience. Degrees must be in engineering (agricultural, civil, or environmental), geology, soil science, natural resources science or management, or other related fields. Candidates from outside the U.S. or Canada must meet additional requirements. **Membership:** Not required. **Certification Requirements:** Successful completion of written and/or oral exam. Exams cover principles, practices, and legislation of soil erosion and sediment control. **Preparatory Materials:** Tutoring available at annual meeting. **Examination Frequency:** Throughout the year. **Examination Sites:** Exam given at annual meeting, chapter meetings, or by arrangement with proctor. **Fees:** $75 (members); $100 (nonmembers). **Re-examination:** May retake exam once without fee. **Endorsed By:** American Society of Agronomy; International Erosion Control Association.

375

Certified Range Management Consultant (CRMC)

Society for Range Management (SRM)
1839 York St.
Denver, CO 80206
Phone: (303)355-7070
Fax: (303)355-5059
H.D. Galt, Chair

Recipient: Consultants in rangeland resources management who specialize in applying conservation principles to grazing and impact grazing has on rangeland ecology. **Number of Certified Individuals:** 50. **Membership:** Not required. **Certification Requirements:** Five years experience and one of the following requirements: (1) Bachelor's degree in range management; (2) Master's degree in range management or science; or (3) Doctorate degree in range management or science. Experience must include solving minimum of three distinct problems in rangeland management. Must also be able to demonstrate ability to collect and analyze ecological information, proficiency in applying ecological principles, and skill in writing reports. Candidates with bachelor's degree or higher in field related to range management may qualify. Candidates with ten years experience in field may qualify. **Renewal:** Every five years. Recertification based on continued professional activity. Renewal fee is $25. **Preparatory Materials:** none. **Fees:** $250.

376

Certified Water Specialist, Level I (CWS I)

Water Quality Association (WQA)
4151 Naperville Rd.
Lisle, IL 60532
Phone: (708)505-0160
Fax: (708)505-9637
Dr. Judith A. Grove, Dir.

Recipient: Owners or managers of businesses involved in sale, installation, and/or manufacturing of water quality improvement products and services; and individuals in related fields. **Educational/Experience Requirements:** none. **Membership:** Not required. **Certification Requirements:** Successful completion of exam. **Renewal:** Every three years. Recertification based on accumulation of three Continuing Professional Development credits through: (1) Attendance at Seminars, Workshops, or Convention Sessions (one credit per ten hours); (2) Attendance at WQA-Approved Educa-tional Sessions; (3) Attendance at Educational Sessions Sponsored by Other Organizations; (4) Successful Completion of Measured Learning Sessions, including: Courses taken at colleges or trade schools; Exams successfully completed; or Home study or correspondence courses; and (5) Experiential Learning Experiences, including: Committee service; Individual learning; Presentations; Speeches; and Voluntary service. Renewal fees are: $60 (members); $135 (nonmembers). **Preparatory Materials:** List of suggested study references provided. Seminars and study kit available. **Examination Frequency:** Throughout the year. **Examination Sites:** Exam given at annual convention, mid-year conference, seminars, state and regional conventions, or by arrangement with proctor. **Examination Type:** Multiple-choice; true or false. **Re-examination:** Fees to retake exam are: $60 (members); $90 (nonmembers). **Fees:** $60 (members); $90 (nonmembers).

377

Certified Water Specialist, Level II (CWS II)

Water Quality Association (WQA)
4151 Naperville Rd.
Lisle, IL 60532
Phone: (708)505-0160
Fax: (708)505-9637
Dr. Judith A. Grove, Dir.

Recipient: Owners or managers of businesses involved in sale, installation, and/or manufacturing of water quality improvement products and services; and individuals in related fields. **Educational/Experience Requirements:** Hold Certified Water Specialist, Level I designation (see separate entry). **Membership:** Not required. **Certification Requirements:** Successful completion of one of the following exams: Demineralization by Ion Exchange; Disinfection; Filtration; and Reverse Osmosis. **Renewal:** Every three years. Recertification based on accumulation of three Continuing Professional Development credits through: (1) Attendance at Seminars, Workshops, or Convention Sessions (one credit per ten hours); (2) Attendance at WQA-Approved Educational Sessions; (3) Attendance at Educational Sessions Sponsored by Other Organizations; (4) Successful Completion of Measured Learning Sessions, including: Courses taken at colleges or trade schools; Exams successfully completed; or Home study or correspondence courses; and (5) Experiential Learning Experiences, including: Committee service; Individual learning; Presentations; Speeches; and Voluntary service. Renewal fees are: $60 (members); $135 (nonmembers). **Preparatory Materials:** List of suggested study references provided. Seminars and study kit available. **Examination Frequency:** Throughout the year. **Examination Sites:** Exams given at annual convention, mid-year conference, seminars, state and regional conventions, or by arrangement with proctor. **Examination Type:** Multiple-choice; true or false. **Re-examination:** Fees to retake each exam are: $35 (members); $55 (nonmembers). **Fees:** $35 (members); $55 (nonmembers).

378

Certified Water Specialist, Level III (CWS III)

Water Quality Association (WQA)
4151 Naperville Rd.
Lisle, IL 60532
Phone: (708)505-0160
Fax: (708)505-9637
Dr. Judith A. Grove, Dir.

Recipient: Owners or managers of businesses involved in sale, installation, and/or manufacturing of water quality improvement products and services; and individuals in related fields. **Educational/Experience Requirements:** Hold Certified Water Specialist, Level I designation (see separate entry). **Membership:** Not required. **Certification Requirements:** Successful completion of two of the following exams: Demineralization by Ion Exchange; Disinfection; Filtration; and Reverse Osmosis. **Renewal:** Every three years. Recertification based on accumulation of three Continuing Professional Development credits through: (1) Attendance at Seminars, Workshops, or Convention Sessions (one credit per ten hours); (2) Attendance at WQA-Approved Educational Sessions; (3) Attendance at Educational Sessions Sponsored by Other Organizations; (4) Successful Completion of Measured Learning Sessions, including: Courses taken at colleges or trade schools; Exams successfully completed; or Home study or correspondence courses; and (5) Experiential Learning Experiences, including: Committee service; Individual learning; Presentations; Speeches; and Voluntary service. Renewal fees are: $60 (members); $135 (nonmembers). **Preparatory Materials:** List of suggested study references provided. Seminar and study kit available. **Examination Frequency:** Throughout the year. **Examination Sites:** Exams given at annual convention, mid-year conference, seminars, state and regional conventions, or by arrangement with proctor. **Examination Type:** Multiple-choice; true or false. **Re-examination:**

Fees to retake each exam are: $35 (members); $55 (nonmembers). **Fees:** $70 (members); $110 (nonmembers).

■ 379 ■

Certified Water Specialist, Level IV (CWS IV)
Water Quality Association (WQA)
4151 Naperville Rd.
Lisle, IL 60532
Phone: (708)505-0160
Fax: (708)505-9637
Dr. Judith A. Grove, Dir.

Recipient: Owners or managers of businesses involved in sale, installation, and/or manufacturing of water quality improvement products and services; and individuals in related fields. **Educational/ Experience Requirements:** Hold Certified Water Specialist, Level I designation (see separate entry). **Membership:** Not required. **Certification Requirements:** Successful completion of three of the following exams: Demineralization by Ion Exchange; Disinfection; Filtration; and Reverse Osmosis. **Renewal:** Every three years. Recertification based on accumulation of three Continuing Professional Development credits through: (1) Attendance at Seminars, Workshops, or Convention Sessions (one credit per ten hours); (2) Attendance at WQA-Approved Educational Sessions; (3) Attendance at Educational Sessions Sponsored by Other Organizations; (4) Successful Completion of Measured Learning Sessions, including: Courses taken at colleges or trade schools; Exams successfully completed; or Home study or correspondence courses; and (5) Experiential Learning Experiences, including: Committee service; Individual learning; Presentations; Speeches; and Voluntary service. Renewal fees are: $60 (members); $135 (nonmembers). **Preparatory Materials:** List of suggested study references provided. Seminars and study kit available. **Examination Frequency:** Throughout the year. **Examination Sites:** Exams given at annual convention, mid-year conference, seminars, state and regional conventions, or by arrangement with proctor. **Examination Type:** Multiple-choice; true or false. **Re-examination:** Fees to retake each exam are: $35 (members); $55 (nonmembers). **Fees:** $105 (members); $165 (nonmembers).

■ 380 ■

Certified Water Specialist, Level V (CWS V)
Water Quality Association (WQA)
4151 Naperville Rd.
Lisle, IL 60532
Phone: (708)505-0160
Fax: (708)505-9637
Dr. Judith A. Grove, Dir.

Recipient: Owners or managers of businesses involved in sale, installation, and/or manufacturing of water quality improvement products and services; and individuals in related fields. **Educational/ Experience Requirements:** Hold Certified Water Specialist, Level I designation (see separate entry). **Membership:** Not required. **Certification Requirements:** Successful completion of the following exams: Demineralization by Ion Exchange; Disinfection; Filtration; and Reverse osmosis. **Renewal:** Every three years. Recertification based on accumulation of three Continuing Professional Development credits through: (1) Attendance at Seminars, Workshops, or Convention Sessions (one credit per ten hours); (2) Attendance at WQA-Approved Educational Sessions; (3) Attendance at Educational Sessions Sponsored by Other Organizations; (4) Successful Completion of Measured Learning Sessions, including: Courses taken at colleges or trade schools; Exams successfully completed; or Home study or correspondence courses; and (5) Experiential Learning Experiences, including: Committee service; Individual learning; Presentations; Speeches; and Voluntary service. Renewal fees are: $60 (members); $135 (nonmembers). **Preparatory Materials:** List of suggested study references provided. Seminars and study kit available. **Examination Frequency:** Throughout the year. **Examination Sites:** Exams given at annual convention, mid-year conference, seminars, state and regional conventions, or by arrangement with proctor. **Examination Type:** Multiple-choice; true or false. **Re-examination:** Fees to retake each exam are: $35 (members); $55 (nonmembers). **Fees:** $140 (members); $220 (nonmembers).

■ 381 ■

Professional Hydrogeologist (PHG)
American Institute of Hydrology (AIH)
3416 University Ave., SE
Minneapolis, MN 55414-3328
Phone: (612)379-1030
Fax: (612)379-0169

Recipient: Hydrogeologists involved in design, water resources management, or land use planning. **Educational/ Experience Requirements:** Must meet the following requirements: (1) Degree in hydrology, hydrogeology, engineering, or physical or natural sciences including five semester or eight quarter hours each in chemistry, physics, and calculus and 25 semester or 37 quarter hours in hydrology/hydrogeology related courses; (2) Five years experience; and (3) Published research in professional, institute, or consulting firm publications or agency reports. Educational requirement may be waived for candidate's whose received last degree prior to 1970 and have proven professional ability through experience and publications in the field. Credit is given for academic or teaching experience for one-half of each year after graduation. Full-time work at research institute may be substituted for professional experience and part-time consulting work may be considered if done for an established consulting firm. Publication requirement may be waived for candidates who have provided outstanding service to the field through teaching and/or administrative and technical work. **Membership:** Not required. **Certification Requirements:** Successful completion of two-part exam. Part I covers basic principles of surface and ground water hydrology, including: Chemistry; Engineering; Geology; Mathematics; Meteorology; Physics; Soil science; and Other related disciplines. Part II covers: Engineering design; Municipal or land use planning; Regional or on-site investigations; Research formulation; Water resource management; and Other issues in hydrogeology. Must pass Part I before attempting Part II. Candidates with extensive experience or who hold professional registrations may be exempt from all or part of exam. **Renewal:** Every five years. **Preparatory Materials:** List of recommended reading provided. **Examination Type:** Short-answer. **Re-examination:** Must only retake part failed. May retake exam twice. **Fees:** $365.

■ 382 ■

Professional Hydrologist (PH)
American Institute of Hydrology (AIH)
3416 University Ave., SE
Minneapolis, MN 55414-3328
Phone: (612)379-1030
Fax: (612)379-0169

Recipient: Hydrologists involved in design, water resources management, or land use planning. **Educational/ Experience Requirements:** Must meet the following requirements: (1) Degree in hydrology, hydrogeology, engineering, or physical or natural sciences, including five semester or eight quarter hours each in chemistry, physics, and calculus and 25 semester or 37 quarter hours in hydrology/hydrogeology related courses; (2) Five years experience; and (3) Publication of research in professional, institute, or consulting firm publications or agency reports. Educational requirement may be waived for candidates who received last degree prior to 1970 and have proven professional ability through experience and publications in the field. Credit is given for academic or teaching experience for one-half of each year after graduation. Full-time work at research institute may be substituted for professional experience and part-time consulting work may be considered if done for an established consulting firm. Publication requirement may be waived for candidates who have provided outstanding service to the field through teaching and/or administrative and technical work. **Membership:** Not required. **Certification Requirements:** Successful completion of two-part exam. Part I covers basic principles of surface and ground water hydrology, including: Chemistry; Engineering; Geology; Mathematics; Meteorology; Physics; Soil science; and Other related disciplines. Part II covers: Engineering design; Municipal or land use planning; Regional or on-site investigations; Research formulation; Water resource management; and Other issues in hydrology. Must pass Part I before attempting Part II. Candidates with extensive experience or who hold professional registrations may be exempt from all or part of exam. **Renewal:** Every five years. **Preparatory Materials:** List of recommended reading provided. **Examination Type:** Short-answer. **Re-examination:** Must only retake part failed. May retake exam twice. **Fees:** $365.

383

Professional Hydrologist - Ground Water (PH-GW)
American Institute of Hydrology (AIH)
3416 University Ave., SE
Minneapolis, MN 55414-3328
Phone: (612)379-1030
Fax: (612)379-0169

Recipient: Hydrologists involved in ground water management. **Educational/Experience Requirements:** Must meet the following requirements: (1) Degree in hydrology, hydrogeology, engineering, or physical or natural sciences including five semester or eight quarter hours each

in chemistry, physics, and calculus and 25 semester or 37 quarter hours in hydrology/hydrogeology related courses; (2) Five years experience; and (3) Published research in professional, institute, or consulting firm publications or agency reports. Educational requirement may be waived for candidates who received last degree prior to 1970 and have proven professional ability through experience and publications in the field. Credit is given for academic or teaching experience for one-half of each year after graduation. Full-time work at research institute may be substituted for professional experience and part-time consulting work may be considered if done for an established consulting firm. Publication requirement may be waived for candidates who have provided outstanding service to the field through teaching and/or administrative and technical work. **Membership:** Not required. **Certification Requirements:** Successful completion of two-part exam. Part I covers basic principles of surface and ground water hydrology, including: Chemistry; Engineering; Geology; Mathematics; Meteorology; Physics; Soil science; and Other related disciplines. Part II covers: Engineering design; Municipal or land use planning; Regional or on-site investigations; Research formulation; Water resource management; and Other issues in hydrology. Must pass Part I before attempting Part II. Candidates with extensive experience or who hold professional registrations may be exempt from all or part of exam. **Renewal:** Every five years. **Preparatory Materials:** List of recommended reading provided. **Examination Type:** Short-answer. **Re-examination:** Must only retake part failed. May retake exam twice. **Fees:** $365.

384

Professional Hydrologist - Water Quality (PH-WQ)
American Institute of Hydrology (AIH)
3416 University Ave., SE
Minneapolis, MN 55414-3328
Phone: (612)379-1030
Fax: (612)379-0169

Recipient: Hydrologists involved in water quality. **Educational/Experience Requirements:** Must meet the following requirements: (1) Degree in hydrology, hydrogeology, engineering, or physical or natural sciences including five semester or eight quarter hours each in chemistry, physics, and calculus and 25 semester or 37 quarter hours in hydrology/hydrogeology related courses; (2) Five years experience; and (3) Published re-

search in professional, institute, or consulting firm publications or agency reports. Educational requirement may be waived for candidate's who received last degree prior to 1970 and have proven professional ability through experience and publications in the field. Credit is given for academic or teaching experience for one-half of each year after graduation. Full-time work at research institute may be substituted for professional experience and part-time consulting work may be considered if done for an established consulting firm. Publication requirement may be waived for candidates who have provided outstanding service to the field through teaching and/or administrative and technical work. **Membership:** Not required. **Certification Requirements:** Successful completion of two-part exam. Part I covers basic principles of surface and ground water hydrology, including: Chemistry; Engineering; Geology; Mathematics; Meteorology; Physics; Soil science; and Other related disciplines. Part II covers: Engineering design; Municipal or land use planning; Regional or on-site investigations; Research formulation; Water resource management; and Other issues in hydrogeology. Must pass Part I before attempting Part II. Candidates with extensive experience or who hold professional registrations may be exempt from all or part of exam. **Renewal:** Every five years. **Preparatory Materials:** List of recommended reading provided. **Examination Type:** Short-answer. **Pass/Fail Rate:** Must only retake part failed. May retake exam twice. **Fees:** $365.

Mineralogists

385

Certified Professional Landman (CPL)
American Association of Professional Landmen
4100 Fossil Creek Blvd.
Ft. Worth, TX 76137-2791
Phone: (817)847-7700
Fax: (817)847-7704
Jack E. Deeter, Exec. Officer

Recipient: Land management professionals in mineral, mining, and petroleum industries. **Educational/Experience Requirements:** Must meet one of the following requirements: (1) Ten years experience; (2) Bachelor's degree and seven years experience; (3) Bachelor's degree or equivalent, with emphasis in natural resources or venture management, and six years experience; or (4) Advanced degree in related area and six years experience. Must have five years experience in land-work and two years experience supervising negotiations for acquisition or divestiture of mineral rights or of business agreements that provide for exploration for, and/or development of, minerals. One hundred credits of AAPL-approved continuing education may be substituted for one year of experience. **Membership:** Not required. **Certification Requirements:** Successful completion of exam. Exam sections are: Contracts, Titles, and Real Property Law; Ethics; Federal and Indian Lands; Oil, Gas, and Mineral Lease and Lease Administration; and Well Trades, Energy Economics, and Pooling and Unitization of Fee Lands. **Renewal:** Every five years. Recertification based on either successful completion of exam or accumulation of 100 credits through: (1) Experience (maximum of 70); and (2) Attendance at AAPL annual meeting and educational seminars, college courses, other continuing education programs, and authoring technical articles. Must also accumulate two ethics recertification credits. Lifetime certification available for retired CPLs. **Examination Type:** Case study; multiple-choice. **Re-examination:** Must only retake sections failed. Each section may be retaken two times. Exam must be successfully completed within two years. **Fees:** $80 (members); $525 (nonmembers).

Physical Scientists

Chemists

386

Approved Chemist
American Oil Chemists' Society
  (AOCS)
PO Box 3489
Champaign, IL 61826-3489
Phone: (217)359-2344
Fax: (217)351-8091

Recipient: Chemists and technicians proficient in use of methodologies utilized in Smalley Sample Program used at AOCS accredited independent and industrial laboratories. **Certification Requirements:** Successful completion of evaluation. Must demonstrate ability to perform analysis using Smalley Check Sample Program. **Renewal:** Every year. Recertification based on successful completion of evaluation.

387

Certified Marine Chemist
National Fire Protection
  Association International (NFPA)
One Batterymarch Park
PO Box 9101
Quincy, MA 02269-9101
Phone: (617)770-3000
Fax: (617)770-0700
Toll Free: (800)344-3555

Recipient: Marine chemists who implement safety practices concerning space entry and hot work during construction, alteration, repair, and scrapping of marine vessels. **Certification Requirements:** Successful completion of the following: (1) 20 module correspondence course; (2) Exam, which covers NFPA standards, Coast Guard and OSHA regulations, and shipyard industrial hygiene; and (3) Per-

sonal interview. **Renewal:** Every five years.

388

Certified Professional Chemist (CPC)
National Certification Commission
  in Chemistry and Chemical
  Engineering (NCCCCE)
American Institute of Chemists
7315 Wisconsin Ave., Ste. 502E
Bethesda, MD 20814-3209
Phone: (301)652-2447
Fax: (301)657-3549
Dr. Connie M. Hendrickson CPC,
  Chair

Recipient: Chemists. **Educational/Experience Requirements:** Bachelor's degree in chemistry, chemical engineering, or closely related field. **Membership:** Not required. **Certification Requirements:** Must earn 300 Certification Units (CUs) in the following areas: (1) Continuing Education (150 CUs maximum), including: College courses taken and taught (ten CUs per semester hour); Seminars (Five CUs per seminar); Short courses and workshops (20 CUs per course); and Symposia (15 CUs per symposium); (2) Publications, Reports, and Presentations (120 CUs maximum), including: Books or monographs (50 CUs per book or monograph); Nonrefereed publications (ten CUs per publication); Patents (30 CUs per patent); Presentations (15 CUs per item); Publications (variable number of CUs); Refereed publications (20 CUs per publication); Reports (ten CUs per report; maximum of 50 CUs per year); and Reviewer or referee (ten CUs per item; maximum of 50 CUs per year); (3) Professional Society Participation (50 CUs maximum), including: Office holding (ten CUs per office per year); Scientific meetings (15 CUs per national meet-

ing; seven CUs per regional meeting; and three CUs per local meeting); and Society participation (15 CUs per activity); and (4) Other Professional Activity (50 CUs maximum), including: Awards (15 CUs per award); Community activities (maximum of 15 CUs per year); Individual activities (ten CUs per year); and Non-specified activities (maximum of 15 CUs per year). **Renewal:** Every three years. Recertification based on accumulation of 300 CUs from same categories as initial certification. Retired CPCs who have been certified for five years may be granted retired status. **Fees:** $75 (members); $105 (nonmembers). **Endorsed By:** American Institute of Chemists.

389

Clinical Chemist (CCT)
National Registry in Clinical
  Chemistry (NRCC)
1155 16th St., NW
Washington, DC 20036
Phone: (202)745-1698
Fax: (202)872-4615
Gilbert E. Smith Ph.D., Exec.Dir.

Recipient: Clinical chemists. **Educational/Experience Requirements:** Must meet the following requirements: (1) Bachelor's degree in one of the biological, chemical, or physical sciences, including 24 semester or 36 quarter hours in chemistry and eight semester or 12 quarter hours total from the following: Chemistry; Computer science; General biology; Genetics; Molecular biology; Pharmaceutical science; Pharmacology; Physics; and Physiology; and (2) Six years of post-bachelor's clinical laboratory experience, with two years experience dealing with human specimens for diagnostic and/or therapeutic purposes within last six years. Candidates with experience in narrow aspect of clinical chemistry may be granted limited certification in one of the following areas: Animal clinical chemistry; Clinical chemistry research; Endocrinology; Environmental safety; and Metabolic diseases. Master's degree may be substituted for two years of experience and doctoral degree may be substituted for four years of experience. Candidates whose education was earned outside of the U.S. must have credentials evaluated. **Certification Requirements:** Successful completion of exam. Exam covers: Basic science; Laboratory practice; Management and administration; Methodology; Patient preparation; and Specimen collection and handling. **Renewal:** Every year. **Examination Frequency:** Annual - always June. **Examination Sites:** Exam given at sites throughout the U.S. **Examination Type:** Multiple-choice. **Re-examination:** May retake exam twice. Fee to retake exam is $100. **Fees:** $150. **Endorsed By:** American Association for Clinical Chemistry; American Board of Clinical Chemistry; American Board of Forensic Toxicology; American Chemical Society; American Institute of Chemists; American Society of Clinical Pathologists; National Academy of Clinical Biochemistry.

390

Clinical Chemistry Technologist (CCT)
National Registry in Clinical
Chemistry (NRCC)
1155 16th St., NW
Washington, DC 20036
Phone: (202)745-1698
Fax: (202)872-4615
Gilbert E. Smith Ph.D., Exec.Dir.

Recipient: Clinical chemistry technologists. **Educational/Experience Requirements:** Must meet the following requirements: (1) Bachelor's degree in one of the biological, chemical, or physical sciences, including 12 semester or 18 quarter hours in chemistry and four semester or six quarter hours total from the following: Chemistry; Computer science; General biology; Genetics; Molecular biology; Pharmaceutical science; Pharmacology; Physics; and Physiology; and (2) One year of post-bachelor's broad clinical laboratory experience dealing with human specimens for diagnostic and/or therapeutic purposes within last five years. Candidates with experience in narrow aspect of clinical chemistry may be granted limited certification in one of the following areas: Animal clinical chemistry; Clinical chemistry research; Endocrinology; Environmental safety; and Metabolic diseases. Candidates whose education was earned outside of

the U.S. must have credentials evaluated. **Certification Requirements:** Successful completion of exam. Exam covers: Basic science; Laboratory practice; Management and administration; Methodology; Patient preparation; and Specimen collection and handling. **Renewal:** Every year. **Examination Frequency:** Annual - always June. **Examination Sites:** Exam given at sites throughout the U.S. **Examination Type:** Multiple-choice. **Re-examination:** May retake exam twice. Fee to retake exam is $100. **Fees:** $150. **Endorsed By:** American Association for Clinical Chemistry; American Board of Clinical Chemistry; American Board of Forensic Toxicology; American Chemical Society; American Institute of Chemists; American Society of Clinical Pathologists; National Academy of Clinical Biochemistry.

391

Diplomate of the American Board of Clinical Chemistry (DABCC)
American Board of Clinical
Chemistry (ABCC)
2101 L St., NW, Ste. 202
Washington, DC 20037-1526
Fax: (202)887-5093
Toll Free: (800)892-1400
Dr. Herbert Malkus, Chm.

Recipient: Clinical and toxicological chemists. **Educational/Experience Requirements:** Must meet the following requirements: (1) Either Doctor of Philosophy degree, doctoral degree in chemistry or another of the chemical, physical, or biological sciences, or Doctor of Medicine (M.D.) degree; (2) 24 semester hours or equivalent in undergraduate and/or graduate level chemistry courses, with minimum of four semester hours or equivalent in biochemistry courses at the graduate level; and (3) Five years experience. Candidates with education from outside the U.S. or Canada must have credentials evaluated. **Certification Requirements:** Successful completion of exam. Certification available in clinical and toxicological chemistry. Candidates who hold Clinical Chemist designation (see separate entry) may be exempted from part of clinical chemistry exam. **Preparatory Materials:** Sample questions provided. **Examination Frequency:** semiannual - always February and July. **Examination Sites:** Exam given in February at sites throughout the U.S. and in July at annual meeting. **Re-examination:** May retake all or part of exam one time. All parts of exam must be successfully completed within two years. **Fees:** $400. **Endorsed By:** Academy of Clinical Laboratory Physicians

and Scientists; American Association for Clinical Chemistry; American Chemical Society; American Institute of Chemists; American Society of Biochemistry and Molecular Biology; Association of Clinical Scientists; National Academy of Clinical Biochemistry; National Registry in Clinical Chemistry.

392

Diplomate of the American Board of Toxicology
American Board of Toxicology
(ABA)
PO Box 30054
Raleigh, NC 27622-0054
Phone: (919)782-0036
Fax: (919)782-0036

Recipient: Professionals specializing in toxicology. **Educational/Experience Requirements:** Must meet one of the following requirements: (1) Doctoral degree in related field and three years experience; (2) Master's degree in related field and seven years post-baccalaureate experience; or (3) Bachelor's degree in related field and ten years experience. Must submit description of experience and toxicological activities. **Certification Requirements:** Successful completion of exam. **Examination Type:** Multiple-choice. **Re-examination:** May retake exam three times. Must successfully complete exam within four years. **Fees:** $300.

393

Toxicological Chemist
National Registry in Clinical
Chemistry (NRCC)
1155 16th St., NW
Washington, DC 20036
Phone: (202)745-1698
Fax: (202)872-4615
Gilbert E. Smith Ph.D., Exec.Dir.

Recipient: Toxicological chemists. **Educational/Experience Requirements:** Must meet the following requirements: (1) Bachelor's degree in one of the biological, chemical, or physical sciences, including 32 semester or 48 quarter hours in chemistry; and (2) Four years of post-bachelor's experience in toxicology, with two years experience dealing with human specimens and which may include interpretation of data, within last eight years. Master's degree may be substituted for one year of experience and doctoral degree may be substituted for two years of experience. Candidates whose education was earned outside of the U.S. must have credentials evaluated. **Certification**

Requirements: Successful completion of exam. Exam covers: Basic science; Drugs of abuse; Laboratory practice; Management and administration; Methodology; Patient preparation; Poisons; Specimen collection and handling; and Therapeutic drugs. **Renewal:** Every year. **Examination Frequency:** Annual - always June. **Examination Sites:** Exam given at sites throughout the U.S. **Examination Type:** Multiple-choice. **Re-examination:** May retake exam twice. Fee to retake exam is $100. **Fees:** $150. **Endorsed By:** American Academy of Forensic Sciences; American Association for Clinical Chemistry; American Board of Clinical Chemistry; American Board of Forensic Toxicology; American Chemical Society; American Institute of Chemists; American Society of Clinical Pathologists; National Academy of Clinical Biochemistry.

Environmental Professionals

394

Associate Environmental Professional (AEP)
National Registry of Environmental Professionals (NREP)
PO Box 2068
Glenview, IL 60025
Phone: (708)724-6631
Fax: (708)724-4223
Richard A. Young, Exec.Dir.

Recipient: Individuals involved in environmental, health, and safety project coordination and management. **Educational/Experience Requirements:** Bachelor's degree, including two years in related discipline such as environmental engineering, health/science, environmental management, or hazardous materials management. Three years of experience may be substituted for each year of academic degree program. **Membership:** Not required. **Certification Requirements:** Successful completion of exam. Exam covers: Emergency conditions - spills and injuries; Federal environmental regulations; Global issues, ecosystems, and endangered species; Hazardous materials, chemistry, and safety; Noise and occupational health; Project management/coordination theory; Project planning; Public relations; and Treatment technologies for air, surface, process, and ground water. **Renewal:** Every year. Renewal fee is $90. **Preparatory Materials:** Lists of approved review workshops and recommended reading provided. **Examination Frequency:** Throughout the year. **Examination Sites:** Exam given at sites

throughout the U.S. or by arrangement with proctor. **Examination Type:** Multiple-choice. **Pass/Fail Rate:** 70 percent pass exam the first time. **Waiting Period to Receive Scores:** Two-four weeks. **Re-examination:** There is no time limit to retake exam. There is a $50 fee to retake exam. **Fees:** $50.

395

Associate Environmental Property Assessor (AEPA)
National Registry of Environmental Professionals (NREP)
PO Box 2068
Glenview, IL 60025
Phone: (708)724-6631
Fax: (708)724-4223
Richard A. Young, Exec.Dir.

Recipient: Individuals involved in inspection and evaluation of environmental risk in real property. **Membership:** Not required. **Certification Requirements:** Successful completion of exam. Exam covers: Basic concepts of federal environmental laws and health effects; Document analysis; Pollutant control and transport mechanisms and development of auditable environmental risk inventory; Sampling theory and techniques; and Site history analysis. May qualify for Registered Environmental Property Assessor (REPA) designation (see separate entry) with increased education or experience. **Renewal:** Every year. Renewal fee is $90. **Preparatory Materials:** Lists of approved review workshops and recommended reading provided. **Examination Frequency:** Throughout the year. **Examination Sites:** Exam given at sites throughout the U.S. or by arrangement with proctor. **Examination Type:** Multiple-choice. **Pass/Fail Rate:** 70 percent pass exam the first time. **Waiting Period to Receive Scores:** Two-four weeks. **Re-examination:** There is no time limit to retake exam. There is a $90 fee to retake exam. **Fees:** $90.

396

Associate Environmental Trainer (AET)
National Environmental Training Association (NETA)
2930 E. Camelback Rd., Ste. 185
Phoenix, AZ 85016-4412
Phone: (602)956-6099
Fax: (602)956-6399
Charles L. Richardson, Exec.Dir.

Recipient: Trainers for industry, government, educational institutions, and orga-

nizations who instruct personnel in environmental or safety and health regulations and procedures. **Educational/Experience Requirements:** One year of experience, 45 hours of training, and accumulation of three total eligibility units through: (1) College Degrees: Associate's (one point); Bachelor's (two points); and Master's or Doctorate (three points); and (2) Experience (one point per year). Candidates with more education and experience may qualify for Certified Environmental Trainer (CET) designation (see separate entry). **Membership:** Not required. **Certification Requirements:** Successful completion of Instructional Technology exam and one specialty exam. Instructional Technology exam covers: Administrative and management issues; Communication; Design and evaluation instruments for training; Design and preparation of training programs; Evaluation of training and application results; Needs assessment; and Training delivery. Specialty exams are: (1) Management and Transportation of Hazardous Materials and Waste, including: CERCLA/SARA; Hazardous Materials Transportation Act; Occupational Safety and Health Administration (OSHA) regulations; and Resource Conservation and Recovery Act (RCRA); (2) Occupational Safety and Health, including: Accident prevention and hazard awareness; Emergency response; Fire prevention/protection; Industrial hygiene; Personal protective equipment; and Regulatory standards; (3) Wastewater Treatment, including: Equipment operations and maintenance; Plant management and operation; and Treatment processes; (4) Water Treatment, including: Equipment operations and maintenance; Plant management and operation; and Treatment processes; and (5) Air Quality Management, including: Asbestos; Lead; and Other indoor air hazards. Candidates who pass state exam equivalent to Association of Boards of Certification (ABC) class III certification, or higher, have certification at highest level offered by state, or are listed in ABC's *National Reciprocity Register* are exempt from Water Treatment and Wastewater Treatment exams. Holders of Certified Industrial Hygienist (CIH), Certified Safety Professional (CSP), or Occupational Safety and Health Technologist (OSHT) designations (see separate entries) may be exempt from Occupational Safety and Health exam. **Preparatory Materials:** Exam guide, including sample questions and suggested study references, provided. Workshops and exam review available. **Examination Frequency:** Throughout the year. **Examination Sites:** Exam given at annual conference, other conferences and expositions, or by arrangement with proctor. **Waiting Period to Receive Scores:** Six weeks. **Re-examination:** Must wait 90 days to retake exams. Must retake only exam failed. May retake exams two times. Must successfully complete exams within two years. **Fees:** $380 (members); $570 (non-members).

`397`

Certified Environmental Auditor (CEA)

National Registry of Environmental Professionals (NREP)
PO Box 2068
Glenview, IL 60025
Phone: (708)724-6631
Fax: (708)724-4223
Richard A. Young, Exec.Dir.

Recipient: Environmental professionals who conduct compliance and risk audits of operating facilities, related equipment, and on-going procedures. **Educational/Experience Requirements:** Must meet the following requirements: (1) Bachelor's degree in environmentally-related discipline; and (2) Two years experience. Associate Environmental Professional (AEP) registration (see separate entry) may be substituted for bachelor's degree. **Membership:** Not required. **Certification Requirements:** Successful completion of exam. Exam covers: Corrective actions; Elements of environmental audits; Inspection techniques; Permits and licenses; Presentation of findings; Record keeping; Regulatory requirements; Safety and personnel training; and Treatment processes and equipment. **Renewal:** Every year. Renewal fee is $90. **Preparatory Materials:** Lists of approved review workshops and recommended reading provided. **Examination Frequency:** Throughout the year. **Examination Sites:** Exam given at sites throughout the U.S. or by arrangement with proctor. **Examination Type:** Multiple-choice. **Pass/Fail Rate:** 70 percent pass exam the first time. **Waiting Period to Receive Scores:** Two-four weeks. **Re-examination:** There is no time limit to retake exam. There is a $90 fee to retake exam. **Fees:** $90.

`398`

Certified Environmental Health Technician (CEHT)

National Environmental Health Association (NEHA)
720 S. Colorado Blvd, South Tower, 970
Denver, CO 80222-1925
Phone: (303)756-9090
Fax: (303)691-9490
Kip Lytle MBA, Admin.

Recipient: Environmental health technicians involved in identifying, preventing, and eliminating environmental health hazards. **Educational/Experience Requirements:** High school diploma or equivalent, two years experience, and successful completion of one of the following: (1) Two-year program in environmental health field, including air pollution, community noise, housing hygiene, milk and food sanitation, occupational health, radiation health, solid wastes, vector control, and water and wastewater; or (2) Military technical school, including environmental health, preventive medicine, and veterinary medicine. **Membership:** Not required. **Certification Requirements:** Successful completion of exam. Exam covers: Air; Food; Housing; Occupational health and hazardous exposure; Public health; Solid waste; Vector and pest control; Wastewater; and Water. **Renewal:** Every two years. Recertification based on accumulation of 12 hours of continuing education through self-study courses, seminars, workshops, and attendance at conferences. Renewal fees are: $35 (members); $60 (nonmembers). **Preparatory Materials:** List of suggested study references provided. Self-study modules available. **Examination Sites:** Exam given by arrangement with proctor. **Examination Type:** Multiple-choice. **Fees:** $55 (member); $105 (nonmembers).

`399`

Certified Environmental Professional (CEP)

Academy of Board Certified Environmental Professionals (ABCEP)
5165 MacArthur Blvd., NW
Washington, DC 20016-3315
Phone: (202)966-8974
Fax: (202)966-1977
Karen Greenwood, Prog. Executor

Recipient: Environmental specialists. **Number of Certified Individuals:** 400. **Educational/Experience Requirements:** Nine years experience, with five years in position of responsible charge or supervision. One year of experience will be credited for candidates holding master's degree, and two years will be credited for doctorate degree. Personal interview usually required. **Membership:** Not required. **Certification Requirements:** Successful completion of exam. **Examination Type:** Essay. **Fees:** $250 (members); $325 (nonmembers). **Endorsed By:** National Association of Environmental Professionals.

`400`

Certified Environmental Trainer (CET)

National Environmental Training Association (NETA)
2930 E. Camelback Rd., Ste. 185
Phoenix, AZ 85016-4412
Phone: (602)956-6099
Fax: (602)956-6399
Charles L. Richardson, Exec.Dir.

Recipient: Trainers for industry, government, educational institutions, and organizations who instruct personnel in environmental or safety and health regulations and procedures. **Educational/Experience Requirements:** Three years experience, 270 hours of training, and accumulation of six total eligibility units through: (1) College Degrees: Associate's (one point); Bachelor's (two points); and Master's or Doctorate (three points); and (2) Experience (one point per year). May qualify for Associate Environmental Trainer (AET) designation (see separate entry) with less education and experience. **Membership:** Not required. **Certification Requirements:** Successful completion of Instructional Technology exam and one specialty exam. Instructional Technology exam covers: Administrative and management issues; Communication; Design and evaluation instruments for training; Design and preparation of training programs; Evaluation of training and application results; Needs assessment; and Training delivery. Specialty exams are: (1) Management and Transportation of Hazardous Materials and Waste, including: CERCLA/SARA; Hazardous Materials Transportation Act; Occupational Safety and Health Administration (OSHA) regulations; and Resource Conservation and Recovery Act (RCRA); (2) Occupational Safety and Health, including: Accident prevention and hazard awareness; Emergency response; Fire prevention/protection; Industrial hygiene; Personal protective equipment; and Regulatory standards; (3) Wastewater Treatment, including: Equipment operations and maintenance; Plant management and operation; and Treatment processes; (4) Water Treatment, including: Equipment operations and maintenance; Plant management and operation; and Treatment processes; and (5) Air Quality Management, including: Asbestos; Lead; and Other indoor air hazards. Candidates who pass state exam equivalent to Association of Boards of Certification (ABC) class III certification, or higher, have certification at highest level offered by state, or are listed in ABC's *National Reciprocity Register* are exempt from Water Treatment and Wastewater Treatment exams. Holders of Certified Industrial Hygienist (CIH), Certified Safety Professional (CSP), or Occupational Safety and Health Technologist (OSHT) designations (see separate entries) may be exempt from Occupational Safety and Health exam. **Renewal:** Every three years. Recertification based on association participation, continuing education, and experience. There is a renewal fee. **Preparatory Materials:** Exam guide, including sample questions and suggested references, provided. Workshops and exam review available. **Examination Frequency:** Throughout the year. **Examination Sites:** Exam given at annual conference, other conferences and expositions, or by arrangement with proctor. **Waiting Period to Receive Scores:** Six weeks. **Re-examination:** Must wait 90 days to retake exams. Must retake only exam failed. May retake exams two times. Must successfully complete exams within two years. **Fees:** $380 (members); $570 (nonmembers).

401

Certified Health and Safety, Portable Sanitation Worker
Portable Sanitation Association
  International (PSA)
7800 Metro Pkwy., Ste. 104
Bloomington, MN 55425
Phone: (612)854-8300
Fax: (612)854-7560
Toll Free: (800)822-3020
Ron Inman, Chm.

Recipient: Contractors engaged in renting and servicing portable sanitation equipment for construction sites, recreational activities, emergencies, and other uses. **Number of Certified Individuals:** 281. **Educational/Experience Requirements:** One year of experience. **Membership:** Not required. **Certification Requirements:** Successful completion of instruction course and exam. **Renewal:** Every three years. **Preparatory Materials:** Workbook available. **Examination Frequency:** Six times per year. **Examination Sites:** Exam given at sites throughout the U.S. **Examination Type:**

Multiple-choice. **Pass/Fail Rate:** 90% pass exam the first time. **Waiting Period to Receive Scores:** Two weeks. **Re-examination:** There is no time limit to retake exam. **Fees:** $50 (members); $100 (nonmembers).

402

Diplomate of the American Academy of Sanitarians (DAAS)
American Academy of Sanitarians
  (AAS)
829 Brookside Dr.
Miami, OK 74354
Phone: (918)540-2025
James W. Pees DAAS, Exec. Sec.-Treas.

Recipient: Sanitarians and environmental health professionals. **Certification Requirements:** Must meet the following requirements: (1) Master's or higher degree in public health, environmental health sciences, or area of scientific or administrative specialization bearing upon environmental management; (2) Current registration as sanitarian or environmental health specialist; (3) Seven years experience, including two years at supervisory level; and (4) Submission of paper acceptable for publication in national journal of environmental health. **Fees:** $40.

403

Diplomate, Environmental Engineer
American Academy of
  Environmental Engineers
  (AAEE)
130 Holiday Ct., Ste. 100
Annapolis, MD 21401
Phone: (410)266-3311
Fax: (410)266-7653
Elizabeth W. Andrews, Mgr.

Recipient: Environmental engineers. **Number of Certified Individuals:** 2500. **Educational/Experience Requirements:** Must meet the following requirements: (1) Bachelor's degree in engineering or related field; (2) Current licensure as professional engineer (P.E.); and (3) Eight years experience. **Membership:** Required. **Certification Requirements:** Successful completion of written and oral exams. Certification available in the following areas: Air pollution control; General environmental engineering; Hazardous waste management; Industrial hygiene; Radiation protection; Solid waste management; and Water supply and wastewater. **Renewal:** Every year. Recertification based on continuing professional development. Renewal fee is $125. **Prepara-**

tory Materials: Study guides available. **Examination Frequency:** Throughout the year. **Examination Sites:** Exams given at sites throughout the U.S. **Examination Type:** Multiple-choice. **Pass/Fail Rate:** 90% pass exams the first time. **Waiting Period to Receive Scores:** 60-90 days. **Re-examination:** There is no waiting period to retake exams. **Fees:** $150.

404

Environmental Assessment Consultant (EAC)
National Society of Environmental
  Consultants (NSEC)
PO Box 12528
303 W. Cypress
San Antonio, TX 78212
Phone: (210)225-2897
Fax: (210)225-8450
Toll Free: (800)486-3676
Dr. Gary T. Deane, Exec.Dir.

Recipient: Professionals involved in real estate environmental screening and site assessment. **Number of Certified Individuals:** 1000. **Membership:** Required. **Certification Requirements:** Submission of Phase I Environmental Site Assessment report and successful completion of the following courses, including exams: (1) Environmental Site Assessment, covering: Air pollution; Asbestos; Drinking water; Ethical and legal considerations; Inspections; Lead paint; Poly chlorinated biphenyls; Radon; Soil contaminants; UREA formaldehyde; and Wetlands/flood plains; (2) Real Estate Environmental Screening (Commercial); and (3) Residential Environmental Screening, covering: Environmental hazards, laws, and risks; Non-scope considerations; Records review; and Site description, interviews, and reconnaissance. **Renewal:** none. **Examination Type:** Multiple-choice. **Waiting Period to Receive Scores:** Ten days. **Fees:** $610.

405

Environmental Screening Consultant (ESC)
National Society of Environmental
  Consultants (NSEC)
PO Box 12528
303 W. Cypress
San Antonio, TX 78212
Phone: (210)225-2897
Fax: (210)225-8450
Toll Free: (800)486-3676
Dr. Gary T. Deane, Exec.Dir.

Recipient: Environmental real estate screening consultants. **Membership:** Not required. **Certification Requirements:** Successful completion of the following courses: (1) Environmental Site Assessment; (2) Real Estate Environmental Screening (Commercial); and (3) Residential Environmental Screening. **Fees:** $560.

406

Qualified Environmental Professional (QEP)

Institute of Professional Environmental Practice (IPEP)
One Gateway Center, Third Fl.
Pittsburgh, PA 15222
Phone: (412)232-0901
Fax: (412)232-0181
Stephanie Walsh, Exec.Dir.

Recipient: Environmental professionals. **Number of Certified Individuals:** 229. **Educational/Experience Requirements:** Must meet one of the following requirements: (1) Bachelor's degree in science-related field and five years experience; or (2) Bachelor's degree in non-science-related field and eight years experience. **Membership:** Not required. **Certification Requirements:** Successful completion of written exam. Candidates with bachelor's degree in science and 15 years experience or bachelor's degree in non-science-related field and 20 years experience are eligible to take oral exam. **Renewal:** Every five years. Recertification based on continuing education and professional activities. **Preparatory Materials:** Study guide available. **Examination Frequency:** semiannual. **Examination Sites:** Exam given at sites throughout the U.S. and Canada. **Examination Type:** Multiple-choice. **Pass/Fail Rate:** 85% pass exam the first time. **Waiting Period to Receive Scores:** One-two months (written exam); immediately (oral exam). **Re-examination:** Must wait ten months to retake written exam. There is no time limit to retake oral exam. **Fees:** $225 (members); $300 (nonmembers). **Endorsed By:** Air and Waste Management Association; American Academy of Environmental Engineers; National Association of Environmental Professionals; Water Environment Federation.

407

Registered Environmental Health Specialist/Registered Sanitarian (REHS/RS)

National Environmental Health Association (NEHA)
720 S. Colorado Blvd, South Tower, 970
Denver, CO 80222-1925
Phone: (303)756-9090
Fax: (303)691-9490
Kip Lytle MBA, Admin.

Recipient: Environmental health specialists and sanitarians. **Educational/Experience Requirements:** Must meet one of the following requirements: (1) Bachelor's degree or higher in environmental health from program whose curriculum is accredited by National Environmental Health Science and Protection Accreditation Council (see separate entry) or from accredited college or university; or (2) Bachelor's degree in unrelated field including algebra or higher level math course and 30 semester hours (45 quarter hours) in biology, chemistry, physics, other physical sciences, or sanitary engineering, and two years experience. **Membership:** Not required. **Certification Requirements:** Successful completion of exam. Exam covers: (1) Food, including: Epidemiology; Legal aspects; Microbiology, physics, and chemical agents; Plan review; Protection/sanitation; Risk assessment/management/communication; Sampling and testing; and Toxicology; (2) Water and Waste Water, including: Drinking water; Epidemiology; Ground water; Land use; Legal aspects; Microbiology, physics, and chemical agents; Plan review; Risk assessment/management/communication; Sampling and testing; Surface water; Toxicology; and Waste water; (3) Air, including: Ambient air; Epidemiology; Indoor air; Legal aspects; Microbiology, physics, and chemical agents; Pollution control technology; Risk assessment/management/communication; Sampling and testing; and Toxicology; (4) Vector and Pest Control, including: Epidemiology; Legal aspects; Microbiology, physics, and chemical agents; Pesticides; Risk assessment/management/communication; Sampling and testing; Sanitation and control; and Toxicology; (5) Hazardous Materials Management, including: Emergency response; Epidemiology; Handling and storage; Legal aspects; Processing; Risk assessment/management/communication; Sampling and testing; Toxicology; and Transportation; (6) Waste Management, including: Biomedical waste; Epidemiology; Hazardous waste; Legal aspects; Mixed waste; Reduction; Resource recovery; Risk assessment/management/communication; Sampling and testing; Soil and land use; Solid waste; Toxicology; and Transportation; (7) Radiation, including: Electromagnetic field radiation; Epidemiology; Ionizing radiation; Legal aspects; Non-ionizing radiation; Risk assessment/management/communication; Safety and protection; Sampling and testing; and Toxicology; (8) Recreation, including: Camping areas; Epidemiology; Injury prevention and control; Land use; Legal aspects; Microbiology, physics, and chemical agents; Natural bathing areas; Plan review; Playgrounds; Pools, spas, and hottubs; Risk assessment/management/communication; Sampling and testing; and Toxicology; (9) Housing and Institutions, including: Epidemiology; Infection control; Injury prevention and control; Legal aspects; Plan review; Risk assessment/management/communication; Sanitation; and Toxicology; (10) Occupational Health and Safety, including: Epidemiology; Injury prevention and control; Legal aspects; Physical agents; Risk assessment/management/communication; Sampling and testing; and Toxicology; (11) General Environmental Health and Scientific Concepts, including: Basic sciences; Epidemiology; Injury prevention and control; Microbiological; Statistics; and Toxicology; and (12) Program Planning and Legal Aspects, including: Data management; Enforcement/investigative techniques; Government organization; and Risk assessment/management/communication. Candidates who hold current state registration and have successfully completed national registered sanitarian exam are exempt from exam. **Renewal:** Every two years. Recertification based on accumulation of 24 hours of continuing education through self-study courses, seminars, workshops, and attendance at conferences. Renewal fees are: $45 (members); $95 (nonmembers). **Preparatory Materials:** List of suggested study references provided. Self-study modules available. **Examination Sites:** Exam given by arrangement with proctor. **Fees:** Exam option: $95 (members); $160 (nonmembers). Exam exempt option: $55 (members); $100 (nonmembers).

408

Registered Environmental Manager (REM)

National Registry of Environmental
   Professionals (NREP)
PO Box 2068
Glenview, IL 60025
Phone: (708)724-6631
Fax: (708)724-4223
Richard A. Young, Exec.Dir.

Recipient: Individuals involved in environmental, health, and safety project coordination and management. **Educational/Experience Requirements:** Must meet the following requirements: (1) Bachelor's degree in related disciplines such as physical, biological, or health sciences, engineering, or environmental majors; and (2) Three years experience. Three years of additional experience may be substituted for each year of academic degree program. **Membership:** Not required. **Certification Requirements:** Successful completion of exam. Exam covers: Emergency conditions - spills and injuries; Federal environmental regulations; Global issues, ecosystems, and endangered species; Hazardous materials, chemistry, and safety; Noise and occupational health; Project management/coordination theory; Project planning; Public relations; and Treatment technologies for air, surface, process, and ground water. **Renewal:** Every year. Renewal fee is $90. **Preparatory Materials:** Lists of approved review workshops and recommended reading provided. **Examination Frequency:** Throughout the year. **Examination Sites:** Exam given at sites throughout the U.S. or by arrangement with proctor. **Examination Type:** Multiple-choice. **Pass/Fail Rate:** 70 percent pass exam first time. **Waiting Period to Receive Scores:** Two-four weeks. **Re-examination:** There is no time limit to retake exam. There is a $150 fee to retake exam. **Fees:** $150.

409

Registered Environmental Professional (REP)

National Registry of Environmental
   Professionals (NREP)
PO Box 2068
Glenview, IL 60025
Phone: (708)724-6631
Fax: (708)724-4223
Richard A. Young, Exec.Dir.

Recipient: Environmental professionals. **Membership:** Not required. **Certification Requirements:** Must meet the following requirements: (1) Advanced college de-gree in field of science or technology directly related to environmental work; and (2) Hold certification from another approved organization for which successful completion of exam was necessary. **Renewal:** Every year. Renewal fee is $90. **Fees:** $90.

410

Registered Environmental Property Assessor (REPA)

National Registry of Environmental
   Professionals (NREP)
PO Box 2068
Glenview, IL 60025
Phone: (708)724-6631
Fax: (708)724-4223
Richard A. Young, Exec.Dir.

Recipient: Individuals involved in inspection and evaluation of environmental risk in real property. **Educational/Experience Requirements:** Must meet the following requirements: (1) Bachelor's degree in environmentally-related discipline; and (2) Three years experience. Associate Environmental Professional (AEP) registration (see separate entry) may be substituted for bachelor's degree. **Membership:** Not required. **Certification Requirements:** Successful completion of exam. Exam covers: Basic concepts of federal environmental laws and health effects; Document analysis; Pollutant control and transport mechanisms and development of auditable environmental risk inventory; Sampling theory and techniques; and Site history analysis. **Renewal:** Every year. Renewal fee is $90. **Preparatory Materials:** Lists of approved review workshops and recommended reading provided. **Examination Frequency:** Throughout the year. **Examination Sites:** Exam given at sites throughout the U.S. or by arrangement with proctor. **Examination Type:** Multiple-choice. **Pass/Fail Rate:** 70 percent pass exam the first time. **Waiting Period to Receive Scores:** Two-four weeks. **Re-examination:** There is no time limit to retake exam. There is a $90 fee to retake exam. **Fees:** $90.

411

Registered Environmental Scientist (RES)

National Registry of Environmental
   Professionals (NREP)
PO Box 2068
Glenview, IL 60025
Phone: (708)724-6631
Fax: (708)724-4223
Richard A. Young, Exec.Dir.

Recipient: Environmental scientists.

Educational/Experience Requirements: Must meet the following requirements: (1) Bachelor's degree program in related discipline such as environmental engineering, health/science, environmental management, or hazardous materials management; and (2) Two years experience. Three years of additional experience may be substituted for each year of academic degree program. **Membership:** Not required. **Certification Requirements:** Successful completion of exam. Exam covers basic knowledge of: Biology; Chemistry; Earth science; Environmental health; Physics; and Zoology. **Renewal:** Every year. Renewal fees are: $50 (governmental employee); $90 (non-governmental employee). **Preparatory Materials:** Lists of approved review workshops and recommended reading provided. **Examination Frequency:** Throughout the year. **Examination Sites:** Exam given at sites throughout the U.S. or by arrangement with proctor. **Examination Type:** Multiple-choice. **Pass/Fail Rate:** 70 percent pass exam the first time. **Waiting Period to Receive Scores:** Two-four weeks. **Re-examination:** There is no time limit to retake exam. Fees to retake exam are: $50 (governmental employees); $90 (non-governmental personnel). **Fees:** $50 (governmental employees); $90 (non-governmental personnel).

412

Registered Hazardous Substances Professional (RHSP)

National Environmental Health
   Association (NEHA)
720 S. Colorado Blvd, South Tower, 970
Denver, CO 80222-1925
Phone: (303)756-9090
Fax: (303)691-9490
Kip Lytle MBA, Admin.

Recipient: Individuals involved in hazardous materials/waste management field. **Educational/Experience Requirements:** Must meet one of the following requirements: (1) Bachelor's degree in hazardous materials/waste management or bachelor's degree in unrelated field and associate's degree or certificate in hazardous materials/waste management, and 30 months experience; (2) Bachelor's degree in environmental health from university program accredited by National Environmental Health Science and Protection Accreditation Council (see separate entry) or recognized accreditation body and three years experience; (3) Graduate degree in environmental science or related environmental program and three years experience; (4) Bachelor's degree with major course work (30 semester or 45 quarter hours) in the physical sciences and four years experience; or (5) Bachelor's degree in unrelated field, 50 hours of related continuing education over last three years, and five years experience. **Membership:** Not required. **Certification Requirements:** Successful completion of exam. Exam covers: (1) Federal Regulations, including: Enforcement/due process; Intent; and Standards; (2) Public/Industry Participation, including: Communications network and plan (mediation, pitfalls, and right-to-know); and Public media communications (risk notification); (3) Risk Assessment/Risk Management, including: Definitions; Difference RA/RM; Dose response assessment; Epidemiology; Exposure; Hazard identification; Inference; Interagency coordination; Public perception; and Risk characterization; (4) Sampling/Monitoring, including: Chain of custody; Monitoring equipment; QA/QC; Safety/person protection; and Techniques; (5) Toxicology, including: Categories of toxins; Definitions; Dose response; Effects; and Routes of exposure; and (6) Treatment/Disposal, including: BAT; Criteria/standards; Emergency measures; Facilities; Siting; and Types/procedures. **Renewal:** Every two years. Recertification based on either successful completion of exam or accumulation of 24 hours of continuing education through self-study courses, seminars, workshops, and attendance at conferences. Renewal fees are: $55 (members); $105 (nonmembers). **Preparatory Materials:** List of suggested study references provided. Review manual and workshop available. **Examination Sites:** Exam given by arrangement with proctor. **Examination Type:** Multiple-choice. **Fees:** $135 (member); $210 (nonmembers).

▎413▎

Registered Hazardous Substances Specialist (RHSS)
National Environmental Health Association (NEHA)
720 S. Colorado Blvd, South Tower, 970
Denver, CO 80222-1925
Phone: (303)756-9090
Fax: (303)691-9490
Kip Lytle MBA, Admin.

Recipient: Individuals involved in hazardous materials/waste management field. **Educational/Experience Requirements:** Must meet one of the following requirements: (1) Associate's degree or certificate in hazardous materials/waste management; or (2) High school diploma or equivalent and two years experience. **Membership:** Not required. **Certification**

Requirements: Successful completion of exam. Exam covers: Determination and characterization of hazardous wastes; Disposal options and restrictions; Federal laws and regulations; Mixed wastes; Permitting and record keeping requirements; Personal protection; Proper handling, packaging, and storage; Sampling and analysis procedures and interpretations; Short/long term hazardous waste management responsibilities; Transportation and manifesting; Waste reduction and recycling; and Waste treatment technologies. **Renewal:** Every two years. Recertification based on either successful completion of exam or accumulation of 24 hours of continuing education through self-study courses, seminars, workshops, and attendance at conferences. Renewal fees are: $45 (members); $95 (nonmembers). **Preparatory Materials:** List of suggested study references provided. Review manual available. **Examination Type:** Multiple-choice. **Fees:** $95 (member); $155 (nonmembers).

Geologists and Geophysicists

▎414▎

Certified Professional Geologist (CPG)
American Institute of Professional Geologists (AIPG)
7828 Vance Dr., Ste. 103
Arvada, CO 80003-2125
Phone: (303)431-0831
Fax: (303)431-1332

Recipient: Geologists. **Certification Requirements:** Successful completion of peer review process, including evaluation of education, experience, technical competence, and ethical conduct.

Meteorologists

▎415▎

Certified Consulting Meteorologist (CCM)
American Meteorological Society (AMS)
45 Beacon St.
Boston, MA 02108
Phone: (617)227-2425
Fax: (617)742-8718
E-mail: hallgren@aip.org
Richard E. Hallgren, Exec. Dir.

Recipient: Professional meteorologists who consult or provide meteorological

services. **Number of Certified Individuals:** 500. **Educational/Experience Requirements:** Five years experience and meet one of the following requirements: (1) Bachelor's degree or higher in atmospheric or related oceanic or hydrological sciences; (2) Bachelor's degree or higher in science or engineering and currently utilizing degree in employment in atmospheric or related oceanic or hydrological sciences; or (3) Successful completion of 20 college semester hours in atmospheric or related oceanic or hydrological sciences and three years experience in last five years. Master's degree may be substituted for one year of experience and doctoral degree may be substituted for two years. **Membership:** Not required. **Certification Requirements:** Must meet the following requirements: (1) Successful completion of written exam; (2) Submission of published paper or report; and (3) Successful completion of oral exam. Exam includes hypothetical problems that a CCM may face in consulting situation. **Fees:** $250 (members); $560 (nonmembers).

Physicists and Astronomers

▎416▎

Certified Health Physicist (CHP)
American Board of Health Physics (ABHP)
1313 Dolley Madison Blvd., Ste. 402
McLean, VA 22101
Phone: (703)790-1745
Fax: (703)790-9063

Recipient: Health physicists. **Educational/Experience Requirements:** Six years experience, with three years in applied health physics, and meet one of the following requirements: (1) Bachelor's degree in physical science or engineering, or a biological science with minor in physical science or engineering; (2) Bachelor's degree in physical science or engineering, or a biological science without a minor in physical science or engineering and 20 semester hours of college or university course work in physical sciences, engineering, or mathematics; or (3) Sixty semester hours of college or university course work in physical or biological science, engineering, or mathematics, of which 20 hours must be in physical sciences, engineering, or mathematics. Experience must be in at least one of the following areas: (1) Establishment and/or evaluation of radiation protection program; (2) Design and/or evaluation of design of radiation protection aspects of facility; (3) Design and implementation of radiation protection training course or program; (4) Development of experimental and/or measurement program designed to answer questions related to radiation protection; (5) Evaluation of measurement data; (6) Analysis and solution of radiation protection problems; and (7) Preparation, interpretation, and implementation of recommendations and regulations. Advanced degrees in health physics or closely related area of study may be substituted for up to two years of experience. **Certification Requirements:** Must meet the following requirements: (1) Submission of written report. Report may be facility evaluation, protection guidance document, major monitoring program, or another type of complex or comprehensive effort; and (2) Successful completion of two-part exam. **Renewal:** Every four years. Recertification based on accumulation of continuing education credits through approved courses, meetings, and other activities. **Examination Frequency:** Annual - always June or July. **Examination Sites:** Exam given at annual meeting and at sites throughout the U.S. **Reexamination:** May retake exam once. Must successfully complete both parts of exam within seven years. **Fees:** $300. **Endorsed By:** American Academy of Health Physics; American Association of Physicists in Medicine; Conference of Radiation Control Program Directors; Health Physics Society.

Lawyers, Judges, and Legal Specialists

Lawyers and Judges

417

Civil Trial Advocate
National Board of Trial Advocacy
  (NBTA)
18 Tremont St., Fourth Fl., Ste. 403
Boston, MA 02108
Phone: (617)720-2032
Fax: (617)720-2038
E-mail: rhugus@word.std.com
Roberta A. Hugus, Exec.Dir.

Recipient: Civil trial specialists. **Educational/Experience Requirements:** Must meet the following requirements: (1) Be member of bar in good standing; (2) Five years experience with 30% concentration in civil law; (3) Submission of trial court brief or memorandum filed in trial court within last three years; (4) 45 hours of continuing legal education in last three years, including: Teaching courses or seminars in trial law; Participation as panelist, speaker, or workshop leader at educational or professional conferences; and Authorship of books or articles published in professional journals on trial law; (5) Participation as lead counsel in 40 contested matters involving the taking of evidence such as hearings, motions, and depositions; and (6) Participation as lead counsel in at least 15 trials of civil matters to verdict or judgment, including not less than 45 trial days with at least five of these trials being presented to a jury. **Certification Requirements:** Successful completion of exam. **Renewal:** Every five years. Recertification based on accumulation of 45 hours of continuing legal education. Renewal fee is $300. **Preparatory Materials:** Manual available. **Examination Frequency:** semiannual - always January and July. **Examination Sites:** Exam given at 20-30 sites throughout the U.S. **Examination Type:** Essay. **Pass/Fail Rate:** 85%

pass exam the first time. **Waiting Period to Receive Scores:** Three months. **Re-examination:** May retake exam once. **Fees:** $600. **Endorsed By:** American Bar Association.

418

Criminal Trial Advocate
National Board of Trial Advocacy
  (NBTA)
18 Tremont St., Fourth Fl., Ste. 403
Boston, MA 02108
Phone: (617)720-2032
Fax: (617)720-2038
E-mail: rhugus@word.std.com
Roberta A. Hugus, Exec.Dir.

Recipient: Criminal trial specialists. **Educational/Experience Requirements:** Must meet the following requirements: (1) Be member of bar in good standing; (2) Five years experience with 30 percent concentration in civil law; (3) Submission of trial court brief or memorandum filed in trial court within last three years; (4) 45 hours of continuing legal education in last three years; (5) Participation as lead counsel in 40 contested matters involving taking of evidence such as hearings, motions, and depositions; and (6) Participation as lead counsel in at least 15 trials of criminal matters, to verdict or judgment, in which offense might have had maximum penalty of five years or more, including not less than 45 days of trial with at least five of these trials presented to jury. Continuing education may include: Authorship of books or articles published in professional journals on trial law; Participation as panelist, speaker, or workshop leader at educational or professional conferences; and Teaching courses or seminars in trial law. **Certification Requirements:** Successful completion of exam. **Renewal:** Every five years. Recertification based on accumulation of 45

hours of continuing legal education. Renewal fee is $300. **Preparatory Materials:** Examination manual available. **Examination Frequency:** semiannual - always January and July. **Examination Sites:** Exam given at 20-30 sites throughout the U.S. **Examination Type:** Essay. **Pass/Fail Rate:** 85 percent pass exam the first time. **Waiting Period to Receive Scores:** Three months. **Re-examination:** May retake exam once. **Fees:** $600. **Endorsed By:** American Bar Association.

419

Diplomate of the American Board of Professional Liability Attorneys
American Board of Professional
  Liability Attorneys (ABPLA)
175 E. Shore Rd.
Great Neck, NY 11023
Phone: (516)487-1990
Fax: (516)487-4304
Toll Free: (800)633-6255
Harvey F. Wachsman, Pres.

Recipient: Attorneys involved in accounting, legal, and medical liability. **Educational/Experience Requirements:** Must meet the following requirements: (1) Current bar membership; (2) Five years experience, with at least 25 percent of practice in specialty area in each of last three years; (3) Experience as lead counsel in at least 15 trials of civil matters to verdict or judgment, including not less than 45 days of trial. At least five trials must be to jury or federal judge; (4) Submission of trial court memorandum/brief prepared and filed within last three years; and (5) 36 hours of related continuing legal education in last three years. **Certification Requirements:** Successful completion of exam. Certification available in the following professional liability areas: Accounting; Legal; and

Medical. **Renewal:** Every five years. **Fees:** $350. **Endorsed By:** American Bar Association.

Legal Specialists

▮420▮

Casualty Claim Law Associate (CCLA)

American Educational Institute (AEI)
179 Mt. Airy Rd.
PO Box 356
Basking Ridge, NJ 07920-0356
Phone: (908)766-0909
Fax: (908)766-9710
Toll Free: (800)631-8183

Recipient: Insurance claim law associates. **Certification Requirements:** Successful completion of Legal Principles and Liability programs. Legal Principles program consists of following courses: (1) Law of Contracts, covering: Acceptance; Basic concepts; Consideration; Contract defenses; Offer; and Specific types of contracts; (2) Tort Concepts, covering: Absolute liability; Fundamentals; Intentional torts; Negligence; and Parties liable; (3) Tort Theories and Defenses, covering: Defenses; Emotional distress; Employment relationships; Governmental liability; Premises liability; and Prenatal injuries; (4) Law of Agency, covering: Authority of the agent; Creation of the agency relationship; Liability of the parties; Ratification of agent's acts; Termination of agency; and Types of agency relationships; (5) Law of Bailments, covering: Bailments; Common carriers; and Innkeepers, hotels, and motels; (6) Law of Damages, covering: Bodily injury; Breach of contract; Fundamentals; Liens; Permanent disability; Property damage; Rules affecting damages; Survival actions; and Wrongful death; (7) Law of Subrogation, covering: Arbitration; Common law subrogation; Defenses; Indemnity and contribution; and Types of subrogation actions. Liability program requires successful completion of required courses and three elective courses. Required courses are: (1) Liability Insurance Principles, covering: Insurer's duties; Liability contract conditions; and Liability policy contract; (2) Comparative Negligence, Contribution, and Settlements, covering: Comparative negligence; Counterclaims and setoff; Effect of comparative negligence on other legal rules; Joint tortfeasors; Negligence and contributory negligence; Special verdicts; and Survey; (3) Law of Evidence, covering: Examination of witnesses; Fun-

damental principles; Hearsay evidence; Hearsay exceptions; and Methods of proof; and (4) Pleadings and Practice, covering: Alternative dispute resolution; Appeals; Discovery; Judgements; Judicial system; Jurisdictional requirements; Motions; Parties; Pleadings; Post-trial motions; Pre-trial conference; Process; Process to compel attendance at trial or for discovery; Settlement of claims before or after judgment; Third party practice; and Trial. Elective courses are: (1) Law of Automobiles, covering: Contributory negligence - imputed negligence; Duties of motorists; Duties to particular parties; Law applicable to automobile accidents; Motorists defined; and Parties liable; (2) Law of Automobile Insurance: First Party Coverages and No-Fault, covering: First party coverages; Medical payments; and No-fault automobile insurance; (3) Law of Automobile Insurance: Liability and Uninsured Motorists, covering: Exclusions; Liability coverage; Other liability provisions; and Uninsured motorist coverage; (4) Law of Insurance: General Liability, covering: Bodily injury and property damages; Claims made CGL; Compensatory and punitive damages; General liability exclusion; Legal liability; and Liability accident or occurrence; (5) Medical Malpractice, covering: Defenses; Duties and liability of the hospital; Duties and liabilities of the nurse; Duties and liabilities of the nursing home; Duties and liability of the pharmacist; Medical malpractice recovery limitations; Physicians and surgeons; and Theories of liability; (6) Professional Liability, covering the following duties and liabilities: Attorney; Directors and officers; Insurance professional; and Public accountant; (7) Products Liability, covering: Contribution and indemnity; Defenses; Negligence; Strict liability in tort; and Warranty liability; (8) Law of Environmental Claims, covering: Coverage issues under CERCLA; Environmental statutes; Insurance and environmental claims; Liability coverage issues; Pollutant and contaminant; Property coverage issues; and Theories of liability; (9) Alternative Dispute Resolution, covering: Arbitration; Arbitration and the insurance policy; Hybrid dispute resolution; Intercompany arbitration; Mediation; and Negotiation; and (10) Homeowners: Liability Coverages, covering: Additional coverages; Conditions; Coverage E - personal liability; Coverage F - medical payments to others; and Section II Exclusions. Each course has exam component. Courses are self-study. May challenge Legal Principles program by exam. **Examination Type:** Essay; multiple-choice. **Fees:** $1630; $965 (exam challenge option). **Endorsed By:** Society of Claim Law Associates.

▮421▮

Casualty Claim Law Specialist (CCLS)

American Educational Institute (AEI)
179 Mt. Airy Rd.
PO Box 356
Basking Ridge, NJ 07920-0356
Phone: (908)766-0909
Fax: (908)766-9710
Toll Free: (800)631-8183

Recipient: Insurance casualty claim law specialists. **Certification Requirements:** Successful completion of liability program. Liability program requires successful completion of required courses and three elective courses. Required courses are: (1) Liability Insurance Principles, covering: Insurer's duties; Liability contract conditions; and Liability policy contract; (2) Comparative Negligence, Contribution, and Settlements, covering: Comparative negligence; Counterclaims and setoff; Effect of comparative negligence on other legal rules; Joint tortfeasors; Negligence and contributory negligence; Special verdicts; and Survey; (3) Law of Evidence, covering: Examination of witnesses; Fundamental principles; Hearsay evidence; Hearsay exceptions; and Methods of proof; and (4) Pleadings and Practice, covering: Alternative dispute resolution; Appeals; Discovery; Judgements; Judicial system; Jurisdictional requirements; Motions; Parties; Pleadings; Post-trial motions; Pre-trial conference; Process; Process to compel attendance at trial or for discovery; Settlement of claims before or after judgment; Third party practice; and Trial. Elective courses are: (1) Law of Automobiles, covering: Contributory negligence - imputed negligence; Duties of motorists; Duties to particular parties; Law applicable to automobile accidents; Motorists defined; and Parties liable; (2) Law of Automobile Insurance: First Party Coverages and No-Fault, covering: First party coverages; Medical payments; and No-fault automobile insurance; (3) Law of Automobile Insurance: Liability and Uninsured Motorists, covering: Exclusions; Liability coverage; Other liability provisions; and Uninsured motorist coverage; (4) Law of Insurance: General Liability, covering: Bodily injury and property damages; Claims made CGL; Compensatory and punitive damages; General liability exclusion; Legal liability; and Liability accident or occurrence; (5) Medical Malpractice, covering: Defenses; Duties and liability of the hospital; Duties and liabilities of the nurse; Duties and liabilities of the nursing home; Duties and liability of the pharmacist; Medical malpractice recovery limitations; Physicians and surgeons; and Theories of liability; (6) Professional Liability, covering the following duties and liabilities: Attorney; Directors and officers; Insurance professional; and Public accountant; (7) Products Liability, covering: Contribution and indemnity; Defenses; Negligence; Strict liability in tort; and Warranty liability; (8) Law of Environmental Claims, covering: Coverage issues under CERCLA; Environmental statutes; Insurance and environmental claims; Liability coverage issues; Pollutant and contaminant; Property coverage issues; and Theories of liability; and Alternative Dispute Resolution, covering: Arbitration; Arbitration and the insurance policy; Hybrid dispute resolution; Inter-company arbitration; Mediation; and Negotiation; and (10) Homeowners: Liability Coverages, covering: Additional coverages; Conditions; Coverage E - personal liability; Coverage F - medical payments to others; and Section II Exclusions. Each course has exam component. Courses are self-study. **Preparatory Materials:** Tutoring service available. **Examination Type:** Essay; multiple-choice. **Fees:** $815. **Endorsed By:** Society of Claim Law Associates.

422

Casualty-Fraud Claim Law Associate (CCLA/FCLA)
American Educational Institute (AEI)
179 Mt. Airy Rd.
PO Box 356
Basking Ridge, NJ 07920-0356
Phone: (908)766-0909
Fax: (908)766-9710
Toll Free: (800)631-8183

Recipient: Insurance casualty and fraud claim law specialists. **Certification Requirements:** Hold Casualty Claim Law Associate (CCLA) and Fraud Claim Law Associate (FCLA) designations (see separate entries). **Endorsed By:** Society of Claim Law Associates.

423

Casualty-Property Claim Law Associate (CCLA/PCLA)
American Educational Institute (AEI)
179 Mt. Airy Rd.
PO Box 356
Basking Ridge, NJ 07920-0356
Phone: (908)766-0909
Fax: (908)766-9710
Toll Free: (800)631-8183

Recipient: Insurance casualty and property claim law specialists. **Certification Requirements:** Hold Casualty Claim Law Associate (CCLA) and Property Claim Law Associate (PCLA) designations (see separate entries). **Endorsed By:** Society of Claim Law Associates.

424

Casualty-Workers' Compensation Claim Law Associate (CCLA/WCLA)
American Educational Institute (AEI)
179 Mt. Airy Rd.
PO Box 356
Basking Ridge, NJ 07920-0356
Phone: (908)766-0909
Fax: (908)766-9710
Toll Free: (800)631-8183

Recipient: Insurance casualty and workers' compensation claim law specialists. **Certification Requirements:** Hold Casualty Claim Law Associate (CCLA) and Workers' Compensation Claim Law Associate (WCLA) designations (see separate entries). **Endorsed By:** Society of Claim Law Associates.

425

Fraud Claim Law Associate (FCLA)
American Educational Institute (AEI)
179 Mt. Airy Rd.
PO Box 356
Basking Ridge, NJ 07920-0356
Phone: (908)766-0909
Fax: (908)766-9710
Toll Free: (800)631-8183

Recipient: Insurance fraud claim specialists. **Certification Requirements:** Successful completion of Legal Principles and Fraud programs. Legal Principles program consists of following courses, including exams: (1) Law of Contracts, covering: Acceptance; Basic concepts; Consideration; Contract defenses; Offer; and Specific types of contracts; (2) Tort Concepts, covering: Absolute liability; Fundamentals; Intentional torts; Negligence; and Parties liable; (3) Tort Theories and Defenses, covering: Defenses; Emotional distress; Employment relationships; Governmental liability; Premises liability; and Prenatal injuries; (4) Law of Agency, covering: Authority of agent; Creation of agency relationship; Liability of parties; Ratification of agent's acts; Termination of agency; and Types of agency relationships; (5) Law of Bailments, covering: Bailments; Common

carriers; and Innkeepers, hotels, and motels; (6) Law of Damages, covering: Bodily injury; Breach of contract; Fundamentals; Liens; Permanent disability; Property damage; Rules affecting damages; Survival actions; and Wrongful death; and (7) Law of Subrogation, covering: Arbitration; Common law subrogation; Defenses; Indemnity and contribution; and Types of subrogation actions. Claims Fraud Investigation and Defense Program consists of the following courses, including exams: (1) Recognizing Fraud, covering: Legal definitions; Recognizing fraud potential; and Types of fraud; (2) Special Investigation, covering: Reporting; and Special investigation techniques; (3) Proving Fraud, covering: Constitutional issues; Criminal proceedings; Discovery and privilege; Evidence of other incidents; Hearsay; and Using experts in fraud cases; (4) Handling Suspicious Claims: The Policy and Its Requirements, covering: Criminal actions; Insurer's duties; Parties to insurance contract; Policy conditions; Policy as contract; and Remedies; and (5) Avoiding Bad Faith and Civil Liability in Handling Suspicious Claims, covering: Exposure; Good faith and other defenses; and Other theories. Courses are self-study. May challenge Legal Principles program by exam. **Examination Type:** Essay; multiple-choice. **Fees:** $1490; $825 (exam challenge option). **Endorsed By:** Society of Claim Law Associates.

426

Fraud Claim Law Specialist (FCLS)
American Educational Institute (AEI)
179 Mt. Airy Rd.
PO Box 356
Basking Ridge, NJ 07920-0356
Phone: (908)766-0909
Fax: (908)766-9710
Toll Free: (800)631-8183

Recipient: Insurance fraud claim law specialists. **Certification Requirements:** Successful completion of the following Claims Fraud Investigation and Defense Program courses, including exams: (1) Recognizing Fraud, covering: Legal definitions; Recognizing fraud potential; and Types of fraud; (2) Special Investigation, covering: Reporting; and Special investigation techniques; (3) Proving Fraud, covering: Constitutional issues; Criminal proceedings; Discovery and privilege; Evidence of other incidents; Hearsay; and Using experts in fraud cases; (4) Handling Suspicious Claims: The Policy and Its Requirements, covering: Criminal actions; Insurer's duties; Parties to insurance contract; Policy conditions; Policy as contract; and Remedies; and (5) Avoiding Bad Faith and Civil Liability in Handling Suspicious Claims, covering: Exposure; Good faith and other defenses; and Other theories. Courses are self-study. **Examination Type:** Essay; multiple-choice. **Fees:** $675. **Endorsed By:** Society of Claim Law Associates.

427

Property Claim Law Associate (PCLA)
American Educational Institute (AEI)
179 Mt. Airy Rd.
PO Box 356
Basking Ridge, NJ 07920-0356
Phone: (908)766-0909
Fax: (908)766-9710
Toll Free: (800)631-8183

Recipient: Insurance property claim law specialists. **Certification Requirements:** Successful completion of Legal Principles and Property programs. Legal Principles program consists of following courses: (1) Law of Contracts, covering: Acceptance; Basic concepts; Consideration; Contract defenses; Offer; and Specific types of contracts; (2) Tort Concepts, covering: Absolute liability; Fundamentals; Intentional torts; Negligence; and Parties liable; (3) Tort Theories and Defenses, covering: Defenses; Emotional distress; Employment relationships; Governmental liability; Premises liability; and Prenatal injuries; (4) Law of Agency, covering: Authority of agent; Creation of agency relationship; Liability of parties; Ratification of agent's acts; Termination of agency; and Types of agency relationships; (5) Law of Bailments, covering: Bailments; Common carriers; and Innkeepers, hotels, and motels; (6) Law of Damages, covering: Bodily injury; Breach of contract; Fundamentals; Liens; Permanent disability; Property damage; Rules affecting damages; Survival actions; and Wrongful death; and (7) Law of Subrogation, covering: Arbitration; Common law subrogation; Defenses; Indemnity and contribution; and Types of subrogation actions. Property program requires successful completion of required courses and three elective courses: Required courses are: (1) Property Insurance Principles, covering: Insurance contract; Property insurance adjuster; and Property insurance agent and broker; (2) Fire and Extended Coverage Perils, covering: Common provisions; Extended coverage; and Fire insurance; (3) Loss Adjustment and Subrogation, covering: Other interests; Rights and responsibilities of insured; Rights and responsibilities of insurer; and Subrogation; and (4) Arson and Fraud, covering: Actions against insurer; Arson; and Fraud. Elective courses are: (1) Homeowners: Property Coverages, covering: Farm property and mobile homeowners policies; Homeowners policies; and Property coverages; (2) Homeowners: Liability Coverages, covering: Additional coverages; Conditions; Coverage E - personal liability; Coverage F - medical payments to others; and Section II Exclusions; (3) Commercial Property Coverage, covering: Boiler and machinery insurance; Burglary, larceny, robbery, and theft insurance; General provisions; Reporting form insurance; and Time element insurance; (4) Inland Marine Coverage, covering: Bailments; Transportation coverages; and Warehouses; and (5) Yacht and Boatowners Insurance, covering: Admiralty law; First party insurance; Medical payments; Third party insurance; and Workers' compensation insurance. Each course has exam component. Courses are self-study. May challenge Legal Principles program by exam. **Examination Type:** Essay; multiple-choice. **Fees:** $1630; $965 (exam challenge option). **Endorsed By:** Society of Claim Law Associates.

428

Property Claim Law Specialist (PCLS)
American Educational Institute (AEI)
179 Mt. Airy Rd.
PO Box 356
Basking Ridge, NJ 07920-0356
Phone: (908)766-0909
Fax: (908)766-9710
Toll Free: (800)631-8183

Recipient: Insurance property claim law specialists. **Certification Requirements:** Successful completion of Property program. Property program requires successful completion of required courses and three elective courses: Required courses are: (1) Property Insurance Principles, covering: Insurance contract; Property insurance adjuster; and Property insurance agent and broker; (2) Fire and Extended Coverage Perils, covering: Common provisions; Extended coverage; and Fire insurance; (3) Loss Adjustment and Subrogation, covering: Other interests; Rights and responsibilities of the insured; Rights and responsibilities of the insurer; and Subrogation; and (4) Arson and Fraud, covering: Actions against the insurer; Arson; and Fraud. Elective courses are: (1) Homeowners: Property Coverages, covering: Farm property and mobile homeowners policies; Homeowners policies; and Property coverages; (2) Homeowners: Liability Coverages, cover-

ing: Additional coverages; Conditions; Coverage E - personal liability; Coverage F - medical payments to others; and Section II - Exclusions; (3) Commercial Property Coverage, covering: Boiler and machinery insurance; Burglary, larceny, robbery, and theft insurance; General provisions; Reporting form insurance; and Time element insurance; (4) Inland Marine Coverage, covering: Bailments; Transportation coverages; and Warehouses; and (5) Yacht and Boatowners Insurance, covering: Admiralty law; First party insurance; Medical payments; Third party insurance; and Workers' compensation insurance. Each course has exam component. Courses are self-study. **Examination Type:** Essay; multiple-choice. **Fees:** $815. **Endorsed By:** Society of Claim Law Associates.

429

Property-Fraud Claim Law Associate (PCLA/FCLA)
American Educational Institute (AEI)
179 Mt. Airy Rd.
PO Box 356
Basking Ridge, NJ 07920-0356
Phone: (908)766-0909
Fax: (908)766-9710
Toll Free: (800)631-8183

Recipient: Insurance property and fraud claim law specialists. **Certification Requirements:** Hold Property Claim Law Associate (PCLA) and Fraud Claim Law Associate (FCLA) designations (see separate entries). **Endorsed By:** Society of Claim Law Associates.

430

Property-Workers' Compensation Claim Law Associate (PCLA/WCLA)
American Educational Institute (AEI)
179 Mt. Airy Rd.
PO Box 356
Basking Ridge, NJ 07920-0356
Phone: (908)766-0909
Fax: (908)766-9710
Toll Free: (800)631-8183

Recipient: Insurance property and workers' compensation claim law specialists. **Certification Requirements:** Hold Property Claim Law Associate (PCLA) and Worker's Compensation Claim Law Associate (WCLA) designations (see separate entries). **Endorsed By:** Society of Claim Law Associates.

431

Senior Claim Law Associate (SCLA)

American Educational Institute (AEI)
179 Mt. Airy Rd.
PO Box 356
Basking Ridge, NJ 07920-0356
Phone: (908)766-0909
Fax: (908)766-9710
Toll Free: (800)631-8183

Recipient: Insurance claim law specialists. **Certification Requirements:** Hold three of the following designations: Casualty Claim Law Associate (CCLA); Fraud Claim Law Associate (FCLA); Property Claim Law Associate (PCLA); and Workers' Compensation Claim Law Associate (WCLA) (see separate entries). **Endorsed By:** Society of Claim Law Associates.

432

Workers' Compensation Claim Law Associate (WCLA)

American Educational Institute (AEI)
179 Mt. Airy Rd.
PO Box 356
Basking Ridge, NJ 07920-0356
Phone: (908)766-0909
Fax: (908)766-9710
Toll Free: (800)631-8183

Recipient: Insurance workers' compensation claim law specialists. **Certification Requirements:** Successful completion of Legal Principles and Workers' Compensation programs. Legal Principles program consists of the following courses: (1) Law of Contracts, covering: Acceptance; Basic concepts; Consideration; Contract defenses; Offer; and Specific types of contracts; (2) Tort Concepts, covering: Absolute liability; Fundamentals; Intentional torts; Negligence; and Parties liable; (3) Tort Theories and Defenses, covering: Defenses; Emotional distress; Employment relationships; Governmental liability; Premises liability; and Prenatal injuries; (4) Law of Agency, covering: Authority of agent; Creation of agency relationship; Liability of parties; Ratification of agent's acts; Termination of agency; and Types of agency relationships; (5) Law of Bailments, covering: Bailments; Common carriers; and Innkeepers, hotels, and motels; (6) Law of Damages, covering: Bodily injury; Breach of contract; Fundamentals; Liens; Permanent disability; Property damage; Rules affecting damages; Survival actions; and Wrongful death; and (7) Law of Subrogation, covering: Arbitration; Common law subrogation; Defenses; Indemnity and contribution; and Types of subrogation actions. Workers' Compensation program consists of the following courses: (1) Introduction to Workers' Compensation Origin and Development, covering: Employers' liability at common law; Employers' liability statutes; Exclusive remedy; Extraterritorial effect; Introduction to workers' compensation statutes; and Types of acts and security; (2) Employment Relationship in Workers' Compensation, covering: Company executives as employees; Employer and employee; Multiple employers; and Special types of employment; (3) Course and Scope of Employment in Workers' Compensation, covering: Injuries; and Work relation; (4) Workers' Compensation Benefits, covering: Death benefits; Disability benefits; Medical benefits; Rehabilitation; and Second injury funds; (5) Federal Workers' Compensation Law, covering: Extension of LHWCA; Longshore and harbor workers; and Other federal employees compensation statutes; (6) Workers' Compensation and Employers' Liability Policy, covering: Employer liability insurance; Endorsements; General section; Information page; and Insuring agreements; and (7) Practice and Procedures in Workers' Compensation, covering: Defenses; Hearings and appeals; Investigation; Reserves; Settlement; and Third party actions. Each course has exam component. Courses are self-study. May challenge Legal Principles program by exam. **Examination Type:** Essay; multiple-choice. **Fees:** $1630; $965 (exam challenge option). **Endorsed By:** Society of Claim Law Associates.

433

Workers' Compensation Claim Law Specialist (WCLS)

American Educational Institute (AEI)
179 Mt. Airy Rd.
PO Box 356
Basking Ridge, NJ 07920-0356
Phone: (908)766-0909
Fax: (908)766-9710
Toll Free: (800)631-8183

Recipient: Insurance workers' compensation claim law specialists. **Certification Requirements:** Successful completion of Workers' Compensation program courses, including exams. Courses are: (1) Introduction to Workers' Compensation Origin and Development, covering: Employers' liability at common law; Employers' liability statutes; Exclusive remedy; Extraterritorial effect; Introduction to workers' compensation statutes; and Types of acts and security; (2) Employment Relationship in Workers' Compensation, covering: Company executives as employees; Employer and employee; Multiple employers; and Special types of employment; (3) Course and Scope of Employment in Workers' Compensation, covering: Injuries; and Work relation; (4) Workers' Compensation Benefits, covering: Death benefits; Disability benefits; Medical benefits; Rehabilitation; and Second injury funds; (5) Federal Workers' Compensation Law, covering: Extension of LHWCA; Longshore and harbor workers; and Other federal employees compensation statutes; (6) Workers' Compensation and Employers' Liability Policy, covering: Employer' liability insurance; Endorsements; General section; Information page; and Insuring agreements; and (7) Practice and Procedures in Workers' Compensation, covering: Defenses; Hearings and appeals; Investigation; Reserves; Settlement; and Third party actions. Courses are self-study. **Examination Type:** Essay; multiple-choice. **Fees:** $815. **Endorsed By:** Society of Claim Law Associates.

434

Workers' Compensation-Fraud Claim Law Associate (WCLA/FCLA)

American Educational Institute (AEI)
179 Mt. Airy Rd.
PO Box 356
Basking Ridge, NJ 07920-0356
Phone: (908)766-0909
Fax: (908)766-9710
Toll Free: (800)631-8183

Recipient: Insurance workers' compensation and fraud claim law specialists. **Certification Requirements:** Hold Workers' Compensation Claim Law Associate (WCLA) and Fraud Claim Law Associate (FCLA) designations (see separate entries). **Endorsed By:** Society of Claim Law Associates.

Social Scientists and Urban Planners

Economists and Marketing Research Analysts

435

Associate in Research and Planning (ARP)
Insurance Institute of America (IIA)
720 Providence Rd.
PO Box 3016
Malvern, PA 19355-0716
Phone: (610)644-2100
Fax: (610)640-9576
Toll Free: (800)644-2101
Karen K. Porter J.D., Asst.Dir.

Recipient: Professionals in the insurance or related businesses who work in research or planning. **Educational/Experience Requirements:** none. **Membership:** Not required. **Certification Requirements:** Successful completion of the following courses, including exams: (1) Business Research Methods; (2) Strategic Management for Insurers; (3) Ethics, Insurance Perspectives, and Insurance Contract Analysis; (4) Insurance Operations; (5) Economics; and (6) Related Studies. Courses can be taken through group- or independent-study. **Renewal:** none. **Examination Type:** Essay. **Endorsed By:** American Council on Education; Society of Insurance Research.

436

Associate in Research and Planning (Life Insurance Option) (ARP)
Insurance Institute of America (IIA)
720 Providence Rd.
PO Box 3016
Malvern, PA 19355-0716
Phone: (610)644-2100
Fax: (610)640-9576
Toll Free: (800)644-2101
Karen K. Porter J.D., Asst.Dir.

Recipient: Professionals in the life insurance industry working in research or planning. **Educational/Experience Requirements:** none. **Membership:** Not required. **Certification Requirements:** Successful completion of the following courses, including exams: (1) Business Research Methods; (2) Strategic Management for Insurers; and (3) FLMI courses 1, 2, 4, 8, and 10-MS offered by the Life Office Management Association's Life Management Institute. Courses can be taken through group- or independent-study. **Renewal:** none. **Examination Type:** Essay. **Endorsed By:** American Council on Education; Life Office Management Association; Society of Insurance Research.

437

Certified Economic Developer (CED)
American Economic Development Council (AEDC)
9801 W. Higgins Rd., Ste. 540
Rosemont, IL 60018-4726
Phone: (708)692-9944
Fax: (708)696-2990
Valerie M. Johnson, Sec.

Recipient: Industrial, economic, and area development managers. **Number of Certified Individuals:** 630. **Educational/Experience Requirements:** Must have five years experience (five points) and earn additional three points through the following: (1) AEDC Membership (one point per year); (2) Professional Experience (one point per year over five years); (3) College Degrees (1-3 points based on degree); (4) Attendance at AEDC Economic Development Course (one point) and AEDC Economic Development Institute (two points); (5) Successful Completion of Economic Development Program at University of Waterloo, Canada; and (6) Successful completion of U.S. Chamber of Commerce Institute for Organizational Management. **Membership:** Not required. **Certification Requirements:** Successful completion of written and oral exams. **Renewal:** Every three years. Recertification based on continuing education. Renewal fees are: $165 (members); $275 (nonmembers). **Preparatory Materials:** *Candidate's Guide* provided. **Examination Frequency:** Six times per year. **Examination Sites:** Exams given at annual conference and other sites throughout the U.S. **Examination Type:** Essay; multiple-choice. **Pass/Fail Rate:** 34% pass exam the first time. **Waiting Period to Receive Scores:** Immediately. **Re-examination:** There is no time limit to retake exam. Must only retake exam failed. Must successfully complete both exams within three years. Fees to retake exams are: $80 (members); $130 (nonmembers). **Fees:** $240 (members); $400 (nonmembers).

Psychologists

438

Diplomate in Behavioral Psychology

American Board of Behavioral Psychology
2100 E. Broadway, Ste. 313
Columbia, MO 65201-6082
Phone: (314)875-1267
Fax: (314)443-1199
Toll Free: (800)255-7792
Nicholas Palo, Exec. Officer

Recipient: Psychologists involved in applied behavior analysis, cognitive behavior therapy, and cognitive therapy. **Educational/Experience Requirements:** Must meet the following requirements: (1) Doctoral degree in psychology or equivalent; (2) Two-three years postdoctoral experience and training; and (3) Current licensure to practice. **Membership:** Not required. **Certification Requirements:** Must meet the following requirements: (1) Submission of two written work samples; and (2) Successful completion of oral exam. **Examination Frequency:** semiannual. **Examination Sites:** Exam given at sites throughout the U.S. **Pass/Fail Rate:** 72% pass exam the first time. **Waiting Period to Receive Scores:** 30 days. **Re-examination:** There is no time limit to retake exam. **Fees:** $700. **Endorsed By:** American Board of Professional Psychology; American Psychological Association.

439

Diplomate in Clinical Neuropsychology

American Board of Clinical Neuropsychology
2100 E. Broadway, Ste. 313
Columbia, MO 65201-6082
Phone: (314)875-1267
Fax: (314)443-1199
Toll Free: (800)255-7792
Nicholas Palo, Exec. Officer

Recipient: Psychologists involved in evaluation of brain-behavior relationships and treatment of cognitive, attentional, learning, and memory disorders. **Educational/Experience Requirements:** Must meet the following requirements: (1) Doctoral degree in psychology or equivalent; (2) Two-three years postdoctoral experience and training; and (3) Current licensure to practice. **Membership:** Not required. **Certification Requirements:** Must meet the following requirements: (1) Submission of two

written work samples; and (2) Successful completion of oral exam. **Examination Frequency:** semiannual. **Examination Sites:** Exam given at sites throughout the U.S. **Pass/Fail Rate:** 72% pass exam the first time. **Waiting Period to Receive Scores:** 30 days. **Re-examination:** There is no time limit to retake exam. **Fees:** $700. **Endorsed By:** American Board of Professional Psychology; American Psychological Association.

440

Diplomate in Clinical Psychology

American Board of Clinical Psychology
2100 E. Broadway, Ste. 313
Columbia, MO 65201-6082
Phone: (314)875-1267
Fax: (314)443-1199
Toll Free: (800)255-7792
Nicholas Palo, Exec. Officer

Recipient: Psychologists involved in assessment and treatment of mental, physical, emotional, and behavioral disorders. **Educational/Experience Requirements:** Must meet the following requirements: (1) Doctoral degree in psychology or equivalent; (2) Two-three years postdoctoral experience and training; and (3) Current licensure to practice. **Membership:** Not required. **Certification Requirements:** Must meet the following requirements: (1) Submission of two written work samples; and (2) Successful completion of oral exam. **Examination Frequency:** semiannual. **Examination Sites:** Exam given at sites throughout the U.S. **Pass/Fail Rate:** 72% pass exam the first time. **Waiting Period to Receive Scores:** 30 days. **Re-examination:** There is no time limit to retake exam. **Fees:** $700. **Endorsed By:** American Board of Professional Psychology; American Psychological Association.

441

Diplomate in Counseling Psychology

American Board of Counseling Psychology
2100 E. Broadway, Ste. 313
Columbia, MO 65201-6082
Phone: (314)875-1267
Fax: (314)443-1199
Toll Free: (800)255-7792
Nicholas Palo, Exec. Officer

Recipient: Psychologists involved in use of client-centered and educationally focused counseling techniques intended to enhance functioning of normal individu-

als. **Educational/Experience Requirements:** Must meet the following requirements: (1) Doctoral degree in psychology or equivalent; (2) Two-three years postdoctoral experience and training; and (3) Current licensure to practice. **Membership:** Not required. **Certification Requirements:** Must meet the following requirements: (1) Submission of two written work samples; and (2) Successful completion of oral exam. **Examination Frequency:** semiannual. **Examination Sites:** Exam given at sites throughout the U.S. **Pass/Fail Rate:** 72% pass exam the first time. **Waiting Period to Receive Scores:** 30 days. **Re-examination:** There is no time limit to retake exam. **Fees:** $700. **Endorsed By:** American Board of Professional Psychology; American Psychological Association.

442

Diplomate in Family Psychology

American Board of Family Psychology
2100 E. Broadway, Ste. 313
Columbia, MO 65201-6082
Phone: (314)875-1267
Fax: (314)443-1199
Toll Free: (800)255-7792
Nicholas Palo, Exec. Officer

Recipient: Psychologists involved in assessment and treatment of individuals, couples, and families from family systems perspective. **Educational/Experience Requirements:** Must meet the following requirements: (1) Doctoral degree in psychology or equivalent; (2) Two-three years postdoctoral experience and training; and (3) Current licensure to practice. **Membership:** Not required. **Certification Requirements:** Must meet the following requirements: (1) Submission of two written work samples; and (2) Successful completion of oral exam. **Examination Frequency:** semiannual. **Examination Sites:** Exam given at sites throughout the U.S. **Pass/Fail Rate:** 72% pass exam the first time. **Waiting Period to Receive Scores:** 30 days. **Re-examination:** There is no time limit to retake exam. **Fees:** $700. **Endorsed By:** American Board of Professional Psychology; American Psychological Association.

443

Diplomate in Forensic Psychology
American Board of Forensic
  Psychology
2100 E. Broadway, Ste. 313
Columbia, MO 65201-6082
Phone: (314)875-1267
Fax: (314)443-1199
Toll Free: (800)255-7792
Nicholas Palo, Exec. Officer

Recipient: Psychologists involved in practice of psychology as related to law and the legal system. **Educational/ Experience Requirements:** Must meet the following requirements: (1) Doctoral degree in psychology or equivalent; (2) Two-three years postdoctoral experience and training; and (3) Current licensure to practice. **Membership:** Not required. **Certification Requirements:** Must meet the following requirements: (1) Submission of two written work samples; and (2) Successful completion of oral exam. **Examination Frequency:** semiannual. **Examination Sites:** Exam given at sites throughout the U.S. **Pass/Fail Rate:** 72% pass exam the first time. **Waiting Period to Receive Scores:** 30 days. **Re-examination:** There is no time limit to retake exam. **Fees:** $700. **Endorsed By:** American Board of Professional Psychology; American Psychological Association.

444

Diplomate in Health Psychology
American Board of Health
  Psychology
2100 E. Broadway, Ste. 313
Columbia, MO 65201-6082
Phone: (314)875-1267
Fax: (314)443-1199
Toll Free: (800)255-7792
Nicholas Palo, Exec. Officer

Recipient: Psychologists involved in science and practice of psychology related to health, including prevention, treatment, and rehabilitation process of illness. **Educational/Experience Requirements:** Must meet the following requirements: (1) Doctoral degree in psychology or equivalent; (2) Two-three years postdoctoral experience and training; and (3) Current licensure to practice. **Membership:** Not required. **Certification Requirements:** Must meet the following requirements: (1) Submission of two written work samples; and (2) Successful completion of oral exam. **Examination Frequency:** semiannual. **Examination Sites:** Exam given at sites throughout the U.S. **Pass/Fail Rate:** 72% pass exam the

first time. **Waiting Period to Receive Scores:** 30 days. **Re-examination:** There is no time limit to retake exam. **Fees:** $700. **Endorsed By:** American Board of Professional Psychology; American Psychological Association.

445

Diplomate in Industrial/Organizational Psychology
American Board of
  Industrial/Organizational
  Psychology
2100 E. Broadway, Ste. 313
Columbia, MO 65201-6082
Phone: (314)875-1267
Fax: (314)443-1199
Toll Free: (800)255-7792
Nicholas Palo, Exec. Officer

Recipient: Psychologists involved in applying psychology to problems of organizations and individuals and groups in organizational settings. **Educational/ Experience Requirements:** Must meet the following requirements: (1) Doctoral degree in psychology or equivalent; (2) Two-three years postdoctoral experience and training; and (3) Current licensure to practice. **Membership:** Not required. **Certification Requirements:** Must meet the following requirements: (1) Submission of two written work samples; and (2) Successful completion of oral exam. **Examination Frequency:** semiannual. **Examination Sites:** Exam given at sites throughout the U.S. **Pass/Fail Rate:** 72% pass exam the first time. **Waiting Period to Receive Scores:** 30 days. **Re-examination:** There is no time limit to retake exam. **Fees:** $700. **Endorsed By:** American Board of Professional Psychology; American Psychological Association.

446

Diplomate in School Psychology
American Board of School
  Psychology
2100 E. Broadway, Ste. 313
Columbia, MO 65201-6082
Phone: (314)875-1267
Fax: (314)443-1199
Toll Free: (800)255-7792
Nicholas Palo, Exec. Officer

Recipient: Psychologists involved in practice of psychology related to facilitation of learning and promotion of mental health in schools and educational settings. **Educational/Experience Requirements:** Must meet the following require-

ments: (1) Doctoral degree in psychology or equivalent; (2) Two-three years postdoctoral experience and training; and (3) Current licensure to practice. **Membership:** Not required. **Certification Requirements:** Must meet the following requirements: (1) Submission of two written work samples; and (2) Successful completion of oral exam. **Examination Frequency:** semiannual. **Examination Sites:** Exam given at sites throughout the U.S. **Pass/Fail Rate:** 72% pass exam the first time. **Waiting Period to Receive Scores:** 30 days. **Re-examination:** There is no time limit to retake exam. **Fees:** $700. **Endorsed By:** American Board of Professional Psychology; American Psychological Association.

447

Health Service Provider in Psychology
National Register for Health Service
  Providers in Psychology
1120 G St., NW, Ste. 330
Washington, DC 20005
Phone: (202)783-7663
Fax: (202)347-0550
Judy E. Hall Ph.D., Exec. Officer

Recipient: Individuals providing health services in psychology. **Number of Certified Individuals:** 16,000. **Educational/ Experience Requirements:** Must meet the following requirements: (1) Doctoral degree in psychology; (2) Two years experience; and (3) Current licensure at independent practice level. **Membership:** Not required. **Certification Requirements:** Must meet ethical standards. **Renewal:** Every year. Renewal fee is $75. **Fees:** $250.

448

Nationally Certified School Psychologist (NCSP)
National Association of School
  Psychologists (NASP)
8455 Colesville Rd., Ste. 1000
Silver Spring, MD 20910
Phone: (301)608-0500
Fax: (301)608-2514
Anne R. Rood, Dir.

Recipient: School psychologists. **Number of Certified Individuals:** 15,000. **Educational/Experience Requirements:** Successful completion of sixth year specialist (master's degree plus thirty graduate semester hours) or higher degree in school psychology. Must include sixty graduate semester hours of course work, practica, and 1200 hour supervised internship, with 600 hours in school setting. Credentials of graduates of nonapproved programs must be accepted by NASP. **Membership:** Not required. **Certification Requirements:** Successful completion of exam. **Renewal:** Every three years. Recertification based on accumulation of 75 hours of continuing professional development. Renewal fees are: $65 (members); $100 (nonmembers). **Preparatory Materials:** none. **Examination Frequency:** Three times per year. **Examination Sites:** Exam given at sites throughout the U.S. **Examination Type:** Multiple-choice. **Waiting Period to Receive Scores:** Six weeks. **Re-examination:** There is no time limit to retake exam. **Fees:** $80 (members); $120 (nonmembers).

Psychotherapists

449

Clinical Associate of the American Board of Medical Psychotherapists
American Board of Medical Psychotherapists (ABMP)
Physicians' Park B, Ste. 11
345 24th Ave., N.
Nashville, TN 37203-1519
Phone: (615)327-2978
Fax: (615)327-9235

Recipient: Psychiatrists, psychologists, clinical social workers, nurses, professional counselors, and clinical faculty practicing psychotherapy with medical and psychiatric populations. **Educational/Experience Requirements:** Must meet the following requirements: (1) Terminal degree; (2) Three years supervised experience; and (3) Submission of work sample. May qualify for Fellow and Diplomate of the American Board of Medical Psychotherapists designation (see separate entry) with increased experience. **Certification Requirements:** Successful completion of written and oral exams. **Renewal:** Every year. Recertification based on accumulation of 14 hours of continuing education. **Fees:** $400.

450

Fellow and Diplomate of the American Board of Medical Psychotherapists
American Board of Medical Psychotherapists (ABMP)
345 24th Ave., N.
Nashville, TN 37203-1519
Phone: (615)327-2978
Fax: (615)327-9235

Recipient: Psychiatrists, psychologists, clinical social workers, nurses, professional counselors, and clinical faculty practicing psychotherapy with medical and psychiatric populations. **Educational/Experience Requirements:** Must meet the following requirements: (1) Terminal degree; (2) Five or six years supervised experience; and (3) Submission of work sample. Candidates with less experience may qualify for Clinical Associate of the American Board of Medical Psychotherapists designation (see separate entry). **Certification Requirements:** Successful completion of written and oral exams. **Renewal:** Every year. Recertification based on accumulation of 14 hours of continuing education. **Fees:** $400.

Sociologists

451

Certified Clinical Sociologist (CCS)
Sociological Practice Association (SPA)
c/o Dr. Linda R. Webber
Dept. of Sociology and Anthropology
SUNY Institute of Technology
PO Box 3050
Utica, NY 13504-3050
Dr. Linda R. Webber, Chair

Recipient: Clinical sociologists. **Educational/Experience Requirements:** Must meet the following requirements: (1) Master's degree or higher; and (2) Demonstrated knowledge of sociological principles, experience in sociology, and description of clinical methods used in practice. **Membership:** Required. **Certification Requirements:** Successful completion of Certification Demonstration, requiring understanding of sociology, skills in applying this understanding with interventionist focus, and ethical practice. **Renewal:** none. **Examination Frequency:** Annual. **Examination Sites:** Demonstrations held during Annual meeting.

Urban and Regional Planners

452

Certified Planner
American Institute of Certified Planners (AICP)
1776 Massachusetts Ave., NW
Washington, DC 20036
Phone: (202)872-0611
Fax: (202)872-0643

Recipient: City, regional, rural, and urban planners. **Educational/Experience Requirements:** Must meet one of the following requirements: (1) Eight years experience; (2) Bachelor's degree in planning and three years experience; (3) Graduate degree in planning and two years experience; or (4) Bachelor's or graduate degree in non-related field and four years experience. Experience positions must meet the following requirements: (1) Influenced public decision-making in the public interest; (2) Employed appropriately comprehensive point of view; (3) Applied planning process appropriate to the situation; and (4) Involved professional level of responsibility and resourcefulness. Full members of the Canadian Institute of Planners are eligible to take exam. **Membership:** Required. **Certification Requirements:** Successful completion of exam. **Renewal:** None. **Preparatory Materials:** Chapters provide educational programs. **Examination Frequency:** Annual. **Examination Sites:** Exam given at sites throughout the U.S. and Canada. **Examination Type:** Multiple-choice. **Waiting Period to Receive Scores:** Ten weeks. **Re-examination:** There is a $225 fee to retake exam. **Fees:** $265. **Endorsed By:** American Planning Association.

Social and Religious Workers and Counselors

Counselors

453

Certified Clinical Mental Health Counselor (CCMHC)
National Board for Certified
   Counselors (NBCC)
3-D Terrace Way
Greensboro, NC 27403
Phone: (910)547-0607
Fax: (910)547-0017
Toll Free: (800)398-5389
Thomas W. Clawson, Exec.Dir.

Recipient: Counselors who specialize in mental health counseling. **Number of Certified Individuals:** 1750. **Educational/ Experience Requirements:** Must meet the following requirements: (1) Hold National Certified Counselor (NCC) designation (see separate entry); (2) 60 semester hours of graduate level courses; and (3) Supervised post-master's experience. **Membership:** Not required. **Certification Requirements:** Successful completion of exam and work sample evaluation. **Renewal:** Every five years. Recertification based on either successful completion of exam or continuing education. Renewal fee is $25. **Preparatory Materials:** Preparatory guide available. **Examination Frequency:** semiannual - always spring and fall. **Examination Sites:** Exam given at sites throughout the U.S. and internationally. **Examination Type:** Case study; multiple-choice. **Pass/Fail Rate:** 85% pass exam the first time. **Re-examination:** Must wait six months to retake exam. **Fees:** $340. **Accredited By:** National Commission for Certifying Agencies. **Endorsed By:** National Organization for Competency Assurance.

454

Certified Eating Disorders Associate (CEDA)
International Association of Eating
   Disorders Professionals (IAEDP)
123 NW 13th St., Ste. 206
Boca Raton, FL 33432
Phone: (407)338-6494
Fax: (407)338-9913
Toll Free: (800)800-8126

Recipient: Eating disorder professionals. **Educational/Experience Requirements:** Successful completion of IAEDP-approved Certificate Program. **Membership:** Not required. **Certification Requirements:** Successful completion of exam. **Renewal:** Every two years. Recertification based on accumulation of 20 related continuing education units (CEUs). Renewal fees are: $80 (members); $305 (nonmembers). **Preparatory Materials:** List of suggested reading provided. **Examination Frequency:** Throughout the year. **Examination Sites:** Exam given at IADEP office and at regional sites throughout the U.S. and internationally. **Examination Type:** Multiple-choice. **Waiting Period to Receive Scores:** 30 days. **Fees:** $225 (members); $450 (nonmembers).

455

Certified Eating Disorders Specialist (CEDS)
International Association of Eating
   Disorders Professionals (IAEDP)
123 NW 13th St., Ste. 206
Boca Raton, FL 33432
Phone: (407)338-6494
Fax: (407)338-9913
Toll Free: (800)800-8126

Recipient: Eating disorder professionals. **Educational/Experience Requirements:** Bachelor's degree in related field, professional licensure, and one of the following: (1) 4000 hours of experience; or (2) 2000 hours of experience and successful completion of core curriculum of IAEDP-approved Certificate Program. **Certification Requirements:** Successful completion of exam. **Renewal:** Every two years. Recertification based on accumulation of 20 related continuing education units (CEUs). Renewal fees are: $80 (members); $305 (nonmembers). **Preparatory Materials:** List of suggested reading provided. **Examination Frequency:** Throughout the year. **Examination Sites:** Exam given at IADEP office and at regional sites throughout the U.S. and internationally. **Examination Type:** Multiple-choice. **Waiting Period to Receive Scores:** 30 days. **Fees:** $225 (members); $450 (nonmembers).

456

Certified Educational Planner
Independent Educational
   Consultants Association (IECA)
4085 Chain Bridge Rd.
Fairfax, VA 22030
Phone: (703)591-4850

Recipient: Educational planners **Educational/Experience Requirements:** Must accumulate points through education and experience. **Certification Requirements:** Successful completion of exam.

457

Certified Poetry Therapist (CPT)
National Association for Poetry
  Therapy (NAPT)
PO Box 551
Port Washington, NY 11050
Phone: (516)944-9791
Fax: (516)944-5818

Recipient: Poetry therapy and bibliotherapy practitioners. Poetry therapy and bibliotherapy are terms used to describe intentional use of written word to further therapeutic goals with individuals and groups. **Membership:** Required. **Certification Requirements:** Must meet training requirements in the following areas: (1) Experience (120 hours); (2) Supervision (60 hours); (3) Didactic study of poetry therapy (200 hours); and (4) Peer experience in poetry therapy (60 hours). Must also demonstrate knowledge in the following areas: Abnormal psychology; Creative writing; Human development; Literature of various genres; Methods of psychotherapy and group process; Personality; and Poetic devices. Candidates with more extensive training may qualify for Registered Poetry Therapist (RPT) designation (see separate entry). **Preparatory Materials:** *Guide to Training Requirements for Credentialing as a Poetry Therapist* (reference). **Fees:** $70.

458

Certified Practitioner (CP)
American Board of Examiners in
  Psychodrama, Sociometry, and
  Group Psychotherapy
  (ABEPSGP)
PO Box 15572
Washington, DC 20003-0572
Phone: (202)483-0514
Dale Richard Buchanan Ph.D.,
  Exec.Dir.

Recipient: Psychodrama, sociometry, and group psychotherapy practitioners. **Educational/Experience Requirements:** Must meet the following requirements: (1) 780 hours of training in the field, including minimum of 620 hours from individuals who hold Trainer, Educator, Practitioner (TEP) designation (see separate entry) and maximum of 160 hours from candidates for the TEP designation; (2) Master's degree in related field; (3) Postgraduate training/education in human growth and development, theories of personality, abnormal behavior (psychopathology), methods of psychotherapy, and social systems; (4) One year of supervised experience, including 80 psycho-

drama sessions, 40 of which must be supervised; and (5) Participation in the field, demonstrated through professional memberships, activities, and written materials published. **Certification Requirements:** Successful completion of: (1) Written exam, covering: Ethics; History; Methodology; Philosophy; Related fields; Research; and Sociometry; and (2) Direct observation of clinical session which tests the candidate's ability to direct psychodrama session and includes warm-up, action structure, and closure. **Preparatory Materials:** Study guide, including previous exams, available. **Examination Frequency:** Annual - always third Saturday in October. **Examination Sites:** Exams given by arrangement with proctor. **Examination Type:** Essay. **Endorsed By:** American Society of Group Psychotherapy and Psycodrama.

459

Certified Rehabilitation Counselor (CRC)
Commission on Rehabilitation
  Counselor Certification (CRCC)
1835 Rohlwing Rd., Ste. E
Rolling Meadows, IL 60008
Phone: (708)394-2104

Recipient: Rehabilitation counselors providing services to persons with physical, mental, developmental, cognitive, and emotional disabilities. **Educational/Experience Requirements:** Must meet one of the following requirements: (1) Master's degree in rehabilitation counseling from program accredited by Council on Rehabilitation Education (see separate entry) and 600 semester or 480 quarter hour internship under supervision of CRC; (2) Master's degree in rehabilitation counseling from non-accredited program, 600 semester or 480 quarter hour internship under supervision of CRC, and twelve months experience under the supervision of CRC; or (3) Master's degree in rehabilitation counseling from non-accredited program and 24 months experience, including twelve months under the supervision of CRC. Candidates with master's degree in field other than rehabilitation counseling must meet one of the following requirements: (1) One graduate course each in the following areas: Theories and Techniques of Counseling; Assessment; Occupational Information or Job Placement; Medical or Psychosocial Aspects of Disabilities; and Community Resources or Delivery of Rehabilitation Services; and 36 months of experience, with 12 months under the supervision of CRC; (2) Two graduate courses each in the following areas: Theories and Techniques of Counseling; As-

sessment; Occupational Information or Job Placement; Medical or Psychosocial Aspects of Disabilities; and Community Resources or Delivery of Rehabilitation Services; and 48 months of experience, with 12 months under the supervision of CRC; or (3) One graduate course in Theories and Techniques of Counseling and 60 months of experience, with 12 months under the supervision of CRC. Candidates with doctorate degree with an emphasis on rehabilitation must have one graduate course in Theories and Techniques of Counseling, 600 hours of internship at the doctoral level under the supervision of CRC, and 12 months experience under the supervision of CRC. Candidates with doctorate degree in unrelated discipline must have one graduate course in Theories and Techniques of Counseling, 36 months of post-doctoral experience in rehabilitation counseling education program, and supervision of student and/or direct clinical work with population of persons with disabilities. Students in rehabilitation master's degree program may apply for certification prior to graduation after completion of 600 semester or 480 quarter hours of internship supervised by CRC. Candidates without 12 months experience supervised by CRC may qualify for provisional certification by completing accelerated program of continuing education and work supervised by CRC. Graduates of universities outside of the U.S. and Canada may qualify if they meet educational and experience requirements. **Certification Requirements:** Successful completion of exam. Exam covers: (1) Foundations of Rehabilitation in the U.S., including: Basic principles of rehabilitation; Disability conditions; History of rehabilitation philosophy and legislation; and Rehabilitation counseling ethics; (2) Client Assessment, including: Client information; Interpreting assessment results; Principles, types, and techniques of assessment; and Resources for assessment; (3) Planning and Service Delivery, including: Identification of community resources and case management; Knowledge of service delivery; Rehabilitation plan development; and Synthesis of client information; (4) Counseling and Interviewing, including: Behavior change modalities; Foundations of interviewing; Principles of human behavior; and Theories and techniques in vocational and affective counseling; and (5) Job Development and Placement, including: Job development; Job seeking skills; Occupational and labor market information; and Placement and follow-up. **Renewal:** Every five years. Recertification based on either successful completion of exam or accumulation of 100 hours of continuing education. Lifetime certification available for retired

CRCs. Renewal fee is $125. **Preparatory Materials:** Certification guide, including reading list and sample questions, provided. **Examination Frequency:** semiannual - usually April and October. **Examination Sites:** Exam given at sites throughout the U.S. and Canada. **Examination Type:** Multiple-choice. **Waiting Period to Receive Scores:** Ten weeks. **Re-examination:** May retake exam once. Must successfully complete exam within one year. There is a $125 fee to retake exam. **Fees:** $225. **Accredited By:** National Commission for Certifying Agencies. **Endorsed By:** American Rehabilitation Counseling Association; National Organization for Competency Assurance; National Rehabilitation Counseling Association.

⬛ **460**

Counselor, American Board of Examiners in Pastoral Counseling

American Board of Examiners in
  Pastoral Counseling (ABEPC)
261 Spring St.
Cheshire, CT 06410
Phone: (203)271-3733
Toll Free: (800)358-9966
E-mail: CompuServe 72163,2447
Fred A. Clark, Dir.

Recipient: Pastoral counselors. **Educational/Experience Requirements:** Must meet the following requirements: (1) Bachelor's degree, training institute certificate, or equivalent; (2) 100 hours of supervised counseling; and (3) 50 hours of personal psychotherapy. Must work to achieve Fellow, American Board of Examiners in Pastoral Counseling designation (see separate entry). **Membership:** Not required. **Certification Requirements:** Must meet one of the following requirements: (1) Successful completion of written and oral exams; or (2) Submission of taped, unedited counseling sessions. **Renewal:** Every year. Recertification based on personal counseling, training counselors, and accumulation of continuing education units (CEUs). **Preparatory Materials:** List of recommended books and test guide available. **Examination Frequency:** Throughout the year. **Examination Sites:** Exams given at several sites throughout the U.S. **Examination Type:** Essay; multiple-choice. **Pass/Fail Rate:** 65% pass exams the first time. **Waiting Period to Receive Scores:** Three-four weeks. **Re-examination:** Must wait four months to retake exams. There is a $60 fee to retake exams. **Fees:** $60.

⬛ **461**

Diplomate, American Board of Examiners in Pastoral Counseling

American Board of Examiners in
  Pastoral Counseling (ABEPC)
261 Spring St.
Cheshire, CT 06410
Phone: (203)271-3733
Toll Free: (800)358-9966
E-mail: CompuServe 72163,2447
Fred A. Clark, Dir.

Recipient: Pastoral counselors. **Educational/Experience Requirements:** Must meet the following requirements: (1) Doctoral degree or successful completion of equivalent professional training and internship; (2) 350 hours of supervised counseling; (3) 200 hours providing supervised training to intern counselors or teaching in subject area; and (4) 100 hours of personal psychotherapy. Candidates who do not meet these requirements may be eligible for Fellow, American Board of Examiners in Pastoral Counseling or Counselor, American Board of Examiners in Pastoral Counseling designations (see separate entries). **Membership:** Not required. **Certification Requirements:** Must meet one of the following requirements: (1) Successful completion of written and oral exams; or (2) Submission of taped, unedited counseling sessions. **Renewal:** Every year. Recertification based on personal counseling, training counselors, and accumulation of continuing education units (CEUs). **Preparatory Materials:** List of recommended books and test guide available. **Examination Frequency:** Throughout the year. **Examination Sites:** Exams given at sites throughout the U.S. **Examination Type:** Essay; multiple-choice. **Pass/Fail Rate:** 65% pass exams the first time. **Waiting Period to Receive Scores:** Three-four weeks. **Re-examination:** Must wait four months to retake exams. There is a $60 fee to retake exams. **Fees:** $60.

⬛ **462**

Diplomate of the American Board of Vocational Experts

American Board of Vocational
  Experts (ABVE)
5700 Old Orchard Rd., 1st Fl.
Skokie, IL 60077-1057
Phone: (708)966-0074
Fax: (708)966-9418

Recipient: Vocational experts involved in counseling, psychology, and rehabilitation in both private and public sectors. **Educational/Experience Requirements:**

Must meet the following requirements: (1) Master's or doctorate degree in human services or related field; and (2) Seven years experience in vocational expert forensics in assessment of vocational capacity with training in the following: Functional capacity measures; Job analysis, placement, and surveys; Psychological testing and measurement; and Work sample assessment. **Certification Requirements:** Must meet following requirements: (1) Successful completion of exam; and (2) Documented distinguished performance in the field, including: Association leadership positions held; Presentations; Published works; and (4) Serving in study groups or on legislative committees. **Renewal:** Every three years. Recertification based on either successful completion of exam or accumulation of 42 hours of professional education. **Preparatory Materials:** Review course available. **Examination Frequency:** semiannual - always spring and fall. **Examination Sites:** Exam given at ABVE conferences.

⬛ **463**

Fellow, American Board of Examiners in Pastoral Counseling

American Board of Examiners in
  Pastoral Counseling (ABEPC)
261 Spring St.
Cheshire, CT 06410
Phone: (203)271-3733
Toll Free: (800)358-9966
E-mail: CompuServe 72163,2447
Fred A. Clark, Dir.

Recipient: Pastoral counselors. **Educational/Experience Requirements:** Must meet the following requirements: (1) Master's degree or equivalent; (2) 200 hours of supervised counseling; (3) 100 hours supervising intern counseling students or teaching; and (4) 80 hours of personal psychotherapy. Candidates who do not meet these requirements may be eligible for Counselor, American Board of Examiners in Pastoral Counseling designation (see separate entry). **Membership:** Not required. **Certification Requirements:** Must meet one of the following requirements: (1) Successful completion of written and oral exams; or (2) Submission of taped, unedited counseling sessions. **Renewal:** Every year. Recertification based on personal counseling, training counselors, and accumulation of continuing education units (CEUs). **Preparatory Materials:** List of recommended books and test guide available. **Examination Frequency:** Throughout the year. **Examination Sites:** Exams given at several sites throughout the U.S. **Examination Type:** Essay;

multiple-choice. **Pass/Fail Rate:** 65% pass exams the first time. **Waiting Period to Receive Scores:** Three-four weeks. **Reexamination:** Must wait four months to retake exams. There is a $60 fee to retake exams. **Fees:** $60.

464

Fellow of the American Board of Vocational Experts

American Board of Vocational
  Experts (ABVE)
5700 Old Orchard Rd., 1st Fl.
Skokie, IL 60077-1057
Phone: (708)966-0074
Fax: (708)966-9418

Recipient: Vocational experts involved in counseling, psychology, and rehabilitation in both private and public sectors. **Educational/Experience Requirements:** Must meet the following requirements: (1) Master's or doctorate degree in human services or related field; and (2) Three years experience in vocational expert forensics in assessment of vocational capacity with training in the following: Functional capacity measures; Job analysis, placement, and surveys; Psychological testing and measurement; and Work sample assessment. May qualify for Diplomate of the American Board of Vocational Experts designation (see separate entry) with increased experience. **Certification Requirements:** Successful completion of exam. **Renewal:** Every three years. Recertification based on either successful completion of exam or accumulation of 42 hours of professional education. **Preparatory Materials:** Review course available. **Examination Frequency:** semiannual - always spring and fall. **Examination Sites:** Exam given at ABVE conferences.

465

Humanist Counselor

Humanist Society of Friends (HSA)
Seven Harwood Dr.
PO Box 1188
Amherst, NY 14226-7188
Phone: (716)839-5080
Toll Free: (800)743-6646
Mary Murchison-Edwards, Admin.

Recipient: Humanist counselors legally authorized to act as clergy. **Number of Certified Individuals:** 150. **Educational/Experience Requirements:** Must meet the following requirements: (1) One year of membership; and (2) Qualifications in medical or professional helping or healing field. **Membership:** Required.

Certification Requirements: Successful completion of application and interview. **Renewal:** Every two-five years. **Fees:** $40. **Endorsed By:** American Humanist Association.

466

Humanist Officiant

Humanist Society of Friends (HSA)
Seven Harwood Dr.
PO Box 1188
Amherst, NY 14226-7188
Phone: (716)839-5080
Toll Free: (800)743-6646
Mary Murchison-Edwards, Admin.

Recipient: Humanist officiants legally authorized to act as clergy. **Number of Certified Individuals:** 150. **Educational/Experience Requirements:** One year of membership. **Membership:** Required. **Certification Requirements:** Successful completion of application and interview. **Renewal:** Every two-five years. **Fees:** $40. **Endorsed By:** American Humanist Association.

467

Master Addictions Counselor (MAC)

National Board for Certified
  Counselors (NBCC)
3-D Terrace Way
Greensboro, NC 27403
Phone: (910)547-0607
Fax: (910)547-0017
Toll Free: (800)398-5389
Thomas W. Clawson, Exec.Dir.

Recipient: Counselors who specialize in addictions counseling. **Membership:** Not required. **Certification Requirements:** Hold National Certified Counselor (NCC) designation (see separate entry) and have additional education and experience in addictions counseling. **Renewal:** Every five years. Recertification based on continuing education. Renewal fee is $25. **Fees:** $190. **Accredited By:** National Commission for Certifying Agencies. **Endorsed By:** National Organization for Competency Assurance.

468

National Certified Addiction Counselor Level I (NCAC I)

National Association of Alcoholism
  and Drug Abuse Counselors
  Certification Commission (NCC)
3717 Columbia Pike, Ste. 300
Arlington, VA 22204-4254
Phone: (703)920-4644
Fax: (800)377-1136
Toll Free: (800)548-0497

Recipient: Alcoholism and drug abuse counselors working for employers, labor unions, health care providers, educators, and other practitioners. **Educational/Experience Requirements:** Must meet the following requirements: (1) Current state certification or licensure; (2) Three years or 6000 hours supervised experience; and (3) 270 contact hours of education and training, including six hours each of AIDS/HIV and ethics training. Experience may include: EAP, ACOA, and codependency counseling; Internships; Prevention, intervention, and DUI experience provided there was substantial client counseling; and Teaching, training, and clinical supervision; and Unpaid employment. Candidates with more education and experience may qualify for National Certified Addiction Counselor II (NCAC II) designation (see separate entry). **Membership:** Not required. **Certification Requirements:** Successful completion of exam. Exam covers: (1) Pharmacology of Psychoactive Substances, including: Addiction process; Definitions of pharmacology; and Drug classification; (2) Counseling Service, including: Client evaluations; Continuing care; Counseling; Education; Patient care/management; Special issues/populations; and Treatment planning; (3) Theoretical Base of Counseling, including: Addiction; Behavioral/cognitive/analytical/theories; Family; and Human growth and development; and (4) Professional Issues, including: Ethics; Law and regulation; and Professional behavior. **Renewal:** Every two years. **Preparatory Materials:** Handbook, including bibliography, exam content outline, and sample questions, provided. **Examination Frequency:** semiannual - always April and October. **Examination Sites:** Exam given at sites throughout the U.S. **Waiting Period to Receive Scores:** Six weeks. **Reexamination:** Fees to retake exam are: $95 (members); $175 (nonmembers). **Fees:** $95 (members); $175 (nonmembers).

469

National Certified Addiction Counselor Level II (NCAC II)
National Association of Alcoholism and Drug Abuse Counselors Certification Commission (NCC)
3717 Columbia Pike, Ste. 300
Arlington, VA 22204-4254
Phone: (703)920-4644
Fax: (800)377-1136
Toll Free: (800)548-0497

Recipient: Alcoholism and drug abuse counselors working for employers, labor unions, health care providers, educators, and other practitioners. **Educational/ Experience Requirements:** Must meet the following requirements: (1) Current state certification or licensure; (2) Five years or 10,000 hours supervised experience; and (3) 450 contact hours of education and training, including six hours each of AIDS/HIV and ethics training. Experience may include: EAP, ACOA, and codependency counseling; Internships; Prevention, intervention, and DUI experience provided there was substantial client counseling; Teaching, training, and clinical supervision; and Unpaid employment. Candidates with less education and experience may qualify for National Certified Addiction Counselor I (NCAC I) designation (see separate entry). **Membership:** Not required. **Certification Requirements:** Successful completion of exam. Exam covers: (1) Pharmacology of Psychoactive Substances, including: Addiction process; Definitions of pharmacology; and Drug classification; (2) Counseling Service, including: Client evaluations; Continuing care; Counseling; Education; Patient care/ management; Special issues/populations; and Treatment planning; (3) Theoretical Base of Counseling, including: Addiction; Behavioral/cognitive/analytical/ theories; Family; and Human growth and development; and (4) Professional Issues, including: Ethics; Law and regulation; and Professional behavior. **Renewal:** Every two years. **Preparatory Materials:** Handbook, including bibliography, exam content outline, and sample questions, provided. **Examination Frequency:** semi-annual - always April and October. **Examination Sites:** Exam given at sites throughout the U.S. **Waiting Period to Receive Scores:** Six weeks. **Re-examination:** Fees to retake exam are: $95 (members); $175 (nonmembers). **Fees:** $95 (members); $175 (nonmembers).

470

National Certified Career Counselor (NCCC)
National Board for Certified Counselors (NBCC)
3-D Terrace Way
Greensboro, NC 27403
Phone: (910)547-0607
Fax: (910)547-0017
Toll Free: (800)398-5389
Thomas W. Clawson, Exec.Dir.

Recipient: Counselors who aid in developing individualized career plans. **Number of Certified Individuals:** 875. **Educational/Experience Requirements:** Hold National Certified Counselor (NCC) designation (see separate entry) and have additional education and experience in career counseling. **Membership:** Not required. **Certification Requirements:** Successful completion of exam. **Renewal:** Every five years. Recertification based on either successful completion of exam or continuing education. Renewal fee is $25. **Preparatory Materials:** Preparatory material available. **Examination Frequency:** semiannual - always spring and fall. **Examination Sites:** Exam given at sites throughout the U.S. and internationally. **Examination Type:** Multiple-choice. **Pass/Fail Rate:** 85% pass exam the first time. **Re-examination:** Must wait six months to retake exam. **Fees:** $340. **Accredited By:** National Commission for Certifying Agencies. **Endorsed By:** National Organization for Competency Assurance.

471

National Certified Counselor (NCC)
National Board for Certified Counselors (NBCC)
3-D Terrace Way
Greensboro, NC 27403
Phone: (910)547-0607
Fax: (910)547-0017
Toll Free: (800)398-5389
Thomas W. Clawson, Exec.Dir.

Recipient: Counselors who assist persons with aging, vocational development, adolescence, family, and marital concerns. **Number of Certified Individuals:** 21,000. **Educational/Experience Requirements:** Must meet the following requirements: (1) Graduate degree in counseling with 48 semester or 72 quarter hours in specified courses; and (2) Two years post-master's degree supervised experience. **Membership:** Not required. **Certification Requirements:** Successful completion of exam. **Renewal:** Every five years. Recertification based on either successful

completion of exam or continuing education. Renewal fee is $25. **Preparatory Materials:** Preparatory guide available. **Examination Frequency:** semiannual - always spring and fall. **Examination Sites:** Exam given at sites throughout the U.S. and internationally. **Examination Type:** Multiple-choice. **Pass/Fail Rate:** 85% pass exam the first time. **Waiting Period to Receive Scores:** Six-eight weeks. **Re-examination:** Must wait six months to retake exam. **Fees:** $350. **Accredited By:** National Commission for Certifying Agencies. **Endorsed By:** National Organization for Competency Assurance.

472

National Certified Gerontological Counselor (NCGC)
National Board for Certified Counselors (NBCC)
3-D Terrace Way
Greensboro, NC 27403
Phone: (910)547-0607
Fax: (910)547-0017
Toll Free: (800)398-5389
Thomas W. Clawson, Exec.Dir.

Recipient: Counselors specializing in meeting counseling needs of older people. **Number of Certified Individuals:** 200. **Membership:** Not required. **Certification Requirements:** Hold National Certified Counselor (NCC) designation (see separate entry) and have additional education and experience in gerontological counseling. **Renewal:** Every five years. Recertification based on continuing education. Renewal fee is $25. **Fees:** $50. **Accredited By:** National Commission for Certifying Agencies. **Endorsed By:** National Organization for Competency Assurance.

473

National Certified School Counselor (NCSC)
National Board for Certified Counselors (NBCC)
3-D Terrace Way
Greensboro, NC 27403
Phone: (910)547-0607
Fax: (910)547-0017
Toll Free: (800)398-5389
Thomas W. Clawson, Exec.Dir.

Recipient: Counselors specializing in school counseling. **Number of Certified Individuals:** 650. **Membership:** Not required. **Certification Requirements:** Hold National Certified Counselor (NCC) designation (see separate entry) and have additional education and experience in school counseling. **Renewal:** Every five years. Recertification based on continuing education. Renewal fee is $25. **Fees:** $50. **Accredited By:** National Commission for Certifying Agencies. **Endorsed By:** National Organization for Competency Assurance.

474

Registered Poetry Therapist (RPT)
National Association for Poetry
    Therapy (NAPT)
PO Box 551
Port Washington, NY 11050
Phone: (516)944-9791
Fax: (516)944-5818

Recipient: Poetry therapy and bibliotherapy practitioners. Poetry therapy and bibliotherapy are terms used to describe intentional use of written word to further therapeutic goals with individuals and groups. **Membership:** Required. **Certification Requirements:** Must meet training requirements in the following areas: (1) Experience (300 hours); (2) Supervision (100 hours); (3) Didactic study of poetry therapy (250 hours); (4) Institutional experience (165 hours); (5) Peer experience in poetry therapy (60 hours); and (6) Other meritorious learning (100 hours). Must also demonstrate knowledge in the following areas: Abnormal psychology; Creative writing; Human development; Literature of various genres; Methods of psychotherapy and group process; Personality; and Poetic devices. Candidates with less training may qualify for Certified Poetry Therapist (CPT) designation (see separate entry). Training in preparation for CPT designation may be applied to RPT requirements. **Preparatory Materials:** *Guide to Training Requirements for Credentialing as a Poetry Therapist* (reference). **Fees:** $75.

475

Trainer, Educator, Practitioner (TEP)
American Board of Examiners in
    Psychodrama, Sociometry, and
    Group Psychotherapy
    (ABEPSGP)
PO Box 15572
Washington, DC 20003-0572
Phone: (202)483-0514
Dale Richard Buchanan Ph.D.,
    Exec.Dir.

Recipient: Psychodrama, sociometry, and group psychotherapy practitioners. **Educational/Experience Requirements:** Must meet the following requirements: (1) Hold Certified Practitioner (CP) des-

ignation (see separate entry); (2) Three years experience; (3) Document participation in 144 hours of supervised training workshops, including 48 hours of supervision from a TEP; (4) 100 hours of professional development in the field; and (5) Participate in professional activities and attendance at conferences. **Certification Requirements:** Successful completion of: (1) Written exam, which covers: Ethics; History; Methodology; Philosophy; Related fields; Research; and Sociometry; and (2) Direct observation of clinical session which tests candidate's ability to teach and train the philosophy, techniques, and process of psychodrama, sociometry, and group psychotherapy. **Preparatory Materials:** Study guide, including previous exams, available. **Examination Frequency:** Annual - always third Saturday in October. **Examination Sites:** Exam given by arrangement with proctor. **Examination Type:** Essay. **Endorsed By:** American Society of Group Psychotherapy and Psychodrama.

Human Services Workers

476

Certified Case Manager (CCM)
Certification of Insurance
    Rehabilitation Specialists
    Commission (CIRSC)
1835 Rohlwing Rd., Ste. D
Rolling Meadows, IL 60008
Phone: (708)818-0292

Recipient: Health and human services professionals with specialized knowledge and experience in identifying health and wellness service providers. Case managers work with individuals requiring health services and ensures timely and cost-effective use of resources for clients and reimbursement sources. **Educational/Experience Requirements:** Must meet the following requirements: (1) Either current licensure as registered nurse (R.N.) or professional licensure or certification as health and human services professional in program that requires successful completion of exam and bachelor's degree in field that promotes physical, psychosocial, and vocational well-being of persons being served; and (2) 24 to 56 months of case management and clinical experience. Experience may be in the following areas: Benefit systems and cost benefit analysis; Case management concepts; Community resources; Coordination and service delivery; and Medical, physical, and psychological aspects of case management. **Certification Requirements:** Successful completion of

exam. Exam covers: (1) Coordination and Service Delivery, including: Assessing clinical information to develop treatment plans; Available treatment modalities; Average duration of treatment associated with disabilities; Communicating case objectives to those who need to know them; Data gathering procedures; Disease process of medical illnesses; Establishing treatment goals that meet client's health care needs and referral sources' requirements; Establishing working relationships with referral sources; Facilitating implementation of medical directives; Integrating clinical information; Legal and ethical issues pertaining to confidentiality; Levels of care in acute phase and chronic phase; Making referrals for assessments; Medical terminology; Obtaining accurate history; Obtaining needed medical supplies; Principles of informed consent; Resource assessment; Restrictions on release of confidential information; and Usual and customary treatments for specific diagnoses; (2) Medical, Physical, and Psychological Aspects of Case Management, including: Acting as advocate for individuals health care needs; Assessing variables affecting health and functioning; Assisting individuals with development of short- and long-term health goals; Characteristics of functional and dysfunctional coping and their implications for health care; Identifying cases with potential for high-risk complications; Individual's use of and response to medication; Interaction of biological and social factors pertaining to wellness and independence; Interactions of psychological and social factors pertaining to wellness and independence; Methods for assessing individual's present level of physical/mental impairment; Psychological characteristics of disabling conditions; Psychological and physical characteristics of illnesses; Psychological and physical characteristics of wellness; and Scope of practice of health care providers; (3) Benefit Systems and Cost Benefit Analysis, including: Analyzing health care plans for appropriateness; Acquiring data necessary to determine cost of care; Competitive costs for medical/health care services; Cost containment strategies that maximize individual's access to funding; Coverage, exclusions, and conditions of insurance policy; Evaluating necessary medical services for cost containment; Evaluating quality of necessary medical services; Health care delivery systems; Home health resources; Identifying cases that would benefit from alternative care; Methods to determine cost effectiveness; Negotiating rates to maximize available funding for individual's health care needs; and Requirement for prior approval by payor; (4) Case Management Concepts, including: Applying problem-solving techniques to case management process; Case management philosophy and principles; Determining benefits individual derives from case management services; Developing case management plans addressing individual's needs; Documenting case management services; Evaluating effectiveness of case management; Identifying predictors of outcomes of case management services; Legislation affecting case management process; Liability issues for case management activities; Planning and goal development techniques; Role of case manager; and Strategies used to access medical records; and (5) Community Resources, including: Adaptive equipment needed for individuals with disabilities; Americans with Disabilities Act; Assistive devices needed by individuals with disabilities; Client's need for vocational services; Establishing client's support system; Explaining services and available resources to individuals with disabilities; Federal legislation affecting individuals with disabilities; and Interviewing techniques. **Renewal:** Every five years. Recertification based on either successful completion of exam or accumulation of 80 hours of continuing education. Renewal fee is $125. **Preparatory Materials:** Certification guide, including exam content outline, glossary of terms, list of suggested study references, and sample questions, provided. **Examination Frequency:** semiannual - always May and November. **Examination Sites:** Exam given throughout the U.S. **Examination Type:** Multiple-choice. **Waiting Period to Receive Scores:** Ten weeks. **Re-examination:** May retake exam once. Must successfully complete exam within one year. Fee to retake exam is $150. **Fees:** $275. **Endorsed By:** Association of Rehabilitation Nurses; Case Management Society of America; Insurance Rehabilitation Study Group; National Association of Rehabilitation Professionals in the Private Sector; National Council on Rehabilitation Education; National Council of Self-Insurers; National Rehabilitation Counseling Association; Vocational Evaluation and Work Adjustment Association.

477

Certified Claims Assistance Professional (CCAP)
National Association of Claims Assistance Professionals (NACAP)
4724 Florence Ave.
Downers Grove, IL 60515
Phone: (708)963-3500
Fax: (708)803-6334
E-mail: Compuserve 70400.705
Kathryn Dokes, Exec.Dir.

Recipient: Claims assistance professionals who assist consumers in resolving health insurance claims filing problems. **Number of Certified Individuals:** 25. **Educational/Experience Requirements:** Must meet either minimum educational or experience requirements. Minimum educational requirement can be met through one of the following: (1) Degree in approved related field; (2) Current, approved certification; or (3) Current insurance agent or broker's license. Minimum experience requirement can be me through one of the following: (1) Two years experience in claims assisting; or (2) Three years experience in one of the following areas: Ambulance service; Health care consulting; Health claims insuring; Independent medical billing facility; Medical facility; Medical practice; Medical reimbursement; Medical supplying; Parenteral/enteral nutrition; or Prosthetics or orthotics. **Membership:** Not required. **Certification Requirements:** Successful completion of two-section exam. Section one covers: Claims processing management; Client rights and entitlement concepts; Health care provider responsibilities; Math; Reimbursement methods; Terminology; and Third party payer systems. Section two covers: Administrative appeals process; Basic insurance concepts; Obtaining additional information; Organizing and maintaining client data; and Reconciling payment to claims. **Renewal:** Every five years. Recertification based on either successful completion of exam or continuing education. **Preparatory Materials:** *Candidate Handbook,* including list of recommended reading and sample questions, available. **Examination Frequency:** semiannual. **Examination Sites:** Exam given at sites throughout the U.S. **Examination Type:** Multiple-choice. **Pass/Fail Rate:** 80% pass exam the first time. **Waiting Period to Receive Scores:** Six-eight weeks. **Re-examination:** Must wait six months to retake exam. May retake exam two times. **Fees:** $250.

478

Certified Disability Consultant
American Board of Professional Disability Consultants (ABPDC)
1350 Beverly Rd., Ste. 115-327
McClean, VA 22101
Phone: (703)790-8644

Recipient: Professionals involved in treatment, assessment, or representation of people with disabilities or personal injuries. **Educational/Experience Requirements:** Must meet the following requirements: (1) Master's degree in counseling, education, law, medicine, nursing,

occupational therapy, osteopathy, physical therapy, podiatry, psychology, social work, or speech-language-hearing; (2) Current licensure; and (3) Five years experience. **Certification Requirements:** Submission of two work samples. **Fees:** $225.

479

Certified Electronic Claims Professional (CECP)
National Association of Claims Assistance Professionals (NACAP)
4724 Florence Ave.
Downers Grove, IL 60515
Phone: (708)963-3500
Fax: (708)803-6334
E-mail: Compuserve 70400.705
Kathryn Dokes, Exec.Dir.

Recipient: Professionals providing electronic claims filing services to physicians and health providers. **Number of Certified Individuals:** 25. **Educational/Experience Requirements:** Must meet either minimum educational or experience requirements. Minimum educational requirement can be met through one of the following: (1) Degree in approved related field; (2) Current, approved certification; or (3) Current insurance agent or broker's license. Minimum experience requirement can be met through one of the following: (1) Two years experience as electronic claims professional; or (2) Three years experience in data processing, software development, service bureau employment, management of information systems, systems consulting, health care consulting, or medical reimbursement. **Membership:** Not required. **Certification Requirements:** Successful completion of two-part exam. Section one covers: Claims processing management; Client rights and entitlement concepts; Health care provider responsibilities; Math; Reimbursement methods; Terminology; and Third party payer systems. Section two covers: Claims submission methods; Computer knowledge; Data security; Editing, auditing, and reporting; and Transmission methods. **Renewal:** Every five years. Recertification based on either successful completion of exam or continuing education. **Preparatory Materials:** *Candidate Handbook,* including list of recommended reading and sample questions, available. **Examination Frequency:** semiannual. **Examination Sites:** Exam given at sites throughout the U.S. **Examination Type:** Multiple-choice. **Pass/Fail Rate:** 80% pass exam the first time. **Waiting Period to Receive Scores:** Six-eight weeks. **Re-examination:** Must wait six months to retake exam. May retake exam two times. **Fees:** $250.

▮480▮

Certified Human Service Provider (CHSP)
American Association of Direct
   Human Service Personnel
   (AADHSP)
1832 Little Rd.
Parma, MI 49269
Phone: (517)531-5820
Toll Free: (800)333-6894

Recipient: Direct service personnel for non-profit organizations who have direct contact with population identified by organization's mission statement objectives. **Educational/Experience Requirements:** none. **Membership:** Not required. **Certification Requirements:** Must successfully complete the following: (1) Home study of college level text books covering required curriculum; (2) Class and exam. Exam covers: Communication skills; General psychology; General sociology; Marketing and public relations of services; Personal growth curriculum; Stress and time management; and Values effecting job; and (3) On the job assignment in area that is not currently part of job description, including written summary of assignment. **Renewal:** Every three years. Recertification based on accumulation of continuing education units (CEUs). **Examination Type:** Multiple-choice. **Endorsed By:** American Council on Education.

▮481▮

Certified Insurance Rehabilitation Specialist (CIRS)
Certification of Insurance
   Rehabilitation Specialists
   Commission (CIRSC)
1835 Rohlwing Rd., Ste. D
Rolling Meadows, IL 60008
Phone: (708)818-0292

Recipient: Professionals involved with insurance rehabilitation services. **Educational/Experience Requirements:** Must meet one of the following requirements: (1) Current licensure as registered nurse (R.N) or certification as Certified Rehabilitation Counselor (CRC) (see separate entry) and 24 months experience; (2) Master's or Doctoral degree, including required coursework, and 24-36 months experience; (3) Bachelor's degree with major in rehabilitation and 36 months experience; or (4) Bachelor's, master's, or doctoral degree in any field and 60 months experience. Experience must be in insurance rehabilitation case management in four of the following five areas: Carrying out case work/case man-

agement activities; Developing and monitoring rehabilitation services/care; Performing job placements and/or vocational assessments; Providing forensic rehabilitation services; and Understanding and using provisions of disability legislation and/or labor union policies/procedures. **Certification Requirements:** Successful completion of exam. Exam covers: (1) Job Placement and Vocational Assessment, including: Community's academic/vocational training resources; Conducting job, labor market, and transferable-skills and job-readiness analyses; Disabling conditions and how they relate to functional requirements of jobs; Implementing job-readiness, training, and job development activities; Job modifications; Labor market information; and Vocational/psychometric evaluations; (2) Case Management and Human Disabilities, including: Goals and objectives; Identifying problems and making decisions; Implementing plans; Intervention strategies; Interviewing clients; Managing caseloads and casework process; Monitoring progress; and Writing effective reports; (3) Rehabilitation Services and Care, including: Analyzing home environments and accessibility needs; Arranging for post-hospital care; Cost containment strategies; Obtaining appropriate durable goods; and Purchasing policies and procedures; (4) Disability Legislation, including: Americans with Disabilities Act; Equal Employment Opportunity Act; Fair Labor Standards Act; Federal accessibility standards; Federal affirmative action requirements; Labor union practices; and Occupational Health and Safety Act; and (5) Forensic Rehabilitation, including: Expert testimony; Legal issues related to client consent and confidentiality; and Written reports for use in legal proceedings. **Renewal:** Every five years. Recertification based on either successful completion of exam or accumulation of 80 hours of continuing education. Renewal fee is $125. **Preparatory Materials:** Certification guide, including exam content outline, glossary of terms, list of suggested study references, and sample questions, provided. **Examination Frequency:** semi-annual - always April and October. **Examination Sites:** Exam given throughout the U.S. **Examination Type:** Multiple-choice. **Waiting Period to Receive Scores:** Ten weeks. **Re-examination:** May retake exam once. Must successfully complete exam within one year. Fee to retake exam is $125. **Fees:** $225. **Endorsed By:** Association of Rehabilitation Nurses; Case Management Society of America; Insurance Rehabilitation Study Group; National Association of Rehabilitation Professionals in the Private Sec-

tor; National Council on Rehabilitation Education; National Council of Self-Insurers; National Rehabilitation Counseling Association; Vocational Evaluation and Work Adjustment Association.

▮482▮

Certified Service Facilitator (CSF)
American Association of Direct
   Human Service Personnel
   (AADHSP)
1832 Little Rd.
Parma, MI 49269
Phone: (517)531-5820
Toll Free: (800)333-6894

Recipient: Direct service personnel in human service organizations responsible for case management. **Educational/Experience Requirements:** none. **Membership:** Not required. **Certification Requirements:** Must successfully complete the following: (1) Home study of college level text books covering required curriculum; (2) Class and exam covering all aspects of case management; and (3) Homework assignment. **Renewal:** Every three years. Recertification based on accumulation 12 continuing education units (CEUs). **Examination Type:** Multiple-choice. **Endorsed By:** American Council on Education.

▮483▮

Certified in Volunteer Administration (CVA)
Association for Volunteer
   Administration (AVA)
PO Box 4584
Boulder, CO 80306
Phone: (303)541-0238
Fax: (303)541-0277
Lois Milne CVA, Mgr.

Recipient: Individuals working in multidisciplinary settings responsible for the management or administration of volunteer resources. **Number of Certified Individuals:** 100. **Educational/Experience Requirements:** Two years experience or equivalent. **Membership:** Not required. **Certification Requirements:** Submission of the following: (1) Formal application, including self-assessment and narrative documenting experience; and (2) Portfolio, including career development plan and seven narratives documenting performance, professionalism, and attitudes. Must submit portfolio within three years of formal application. **Renewal:** Every five years. Recertification based on submission of essays on continuing contributions to the profession, continued professional self-development, and professional philosophy. **Preparatory Materials:** Workshops available. **Fees:** $215 (members); $415 (nonmembers).

484

Diplomate, American Board of Professional Disability Consultants
American Board of Professional Disability Consultants (ABPDC)
1350 Beverly Rd., Ste. 115-327
McClean, VA 22101
Phone: (703)790-8644

Recipient: Professionals involved in treatment, assessment, or representation of people with disabilities or personal injuries. **Educational/Experience Requirements:** Must meet the following requirements: (1) Doctoral degree in counseling, education, law, medicine, nursing, occupational therapy, osteopathy, physical therapy, podiatry, psychology, social work, or speech-language-hearing; (2) Current licensure; and (3) Three years experience. **Certification Requirements:** Submission of two work samples. **Fees:** $285.

Roman Catholic Priests

485

Certified Airport Chaplain (CAC)
National Catholic Conference of Airport Chaplains (NCCAC)
Chicago O'Hare Airport
PO Box 66353
Chicago, IL 60666
Phone: (312)686-2636
Fax: (312)686-0130
Rev. John A. Jamnicky, Pres.

Recipient: Roman Catholic priests, deacons, and lay persons engaged in ministry at major airports. **Number of Certified Individuals:** 10. **Educational/Experience Requirements:** One year of full-time, or three years of part-time, experience. **Membership:** Required. **Certification Requirements:** Successful completion of exam. **Renewal:** Every five years. **Examination Frequency:** Annual. **Examination Sites:** Exam given at NCCAC annual meeting. **Pass/Fail Rate:** 90 percent pass exam the first time. **Waiting Period to Receive Scores:** Two days. **Reexamination:** Must wait one year to retake exam.

486

Certified Chaplain
National Association of Catholic Chaplains (NACC)
3501 S. Lake Dr.
PO Box 07473
Milwaukee, WI 53207-0473
Phone: (414)483-4898
Fax: (414)483-6712
Rev. Robert A. Rochon, Chair

Recipient: Chaplains involved in ministry of pastoral care. **Number of Certified Individuals:** 2522. **Membership:** Required. **Certification Requirements:** Successful completion of four units of clinical pastoral education and interview. Must also submit written materials. **Renewal:** Every five years. Recertification based on continuing education and peer review. **Examination Frequency:** Three times per year. **Examination Sites:** Interview given at regional sites throughout the U.S. **Pass/Fail Rate:** 90% pass exam the first time. **Fees:** $105.

Social Workers

487

Diplomate in Clinical Social Work (DCSW)
National Association of Social Workers (NASW)
750 First St., NE, Ste. 700
Washington, DC 20002
Phone: (202)408-8600
Fax: (202)336-8327
Toll Free: (800)638-8799
Isadora Hare, Dir.

Recipient: Clinical social workers. **Number of Certified Individuals:** 23,000. **Educational/Experience Requirements:** Must meet the following requirements: (1) Master's or doctoral degree in social work from program accredited by Council on Social Work Education (see separate entry); (2) Five years clinical experience; and (3) Successful completion of state exam. **Membership:** Not required. **Certification Requirements:** Successful completion of exam. **Renewal:** none. **Preparatory Materials:** Information on exam content and format provided. **Examination Sites:** Exam given at 70 sites throughout the U.S. **Examination Type:** Essay. **Waiting Period to Receive Scores:** 60 days. **Fees:** $270 (members); $370 (nonmembers).

488

Member, Academy of Certified Baccalaureate Social Workers
Academy of Certified Baccalaureate Social Workers (ACBSW)
National Association of Social Workers
750 First St., NE
Washington, DC 20002
Phone: (202)336-8232
Fax: (202)336-8327
Toll Free: (800)638-8799
Marianne Josem ACSW, Credentials Assoc.

Recipient: Social workers. **Number of Certified Individuals:** 2300. **Educational/Experience Requirements:** Must meet the following requirements: (1) Bachelor's degree in social work from program accredited by Council on Social Work Education (see separate entry); and (2) Two years experience. **Membership:** Not required. **Certification Requirements:** Successful completion of exam. **Renewal:** none. **Preparatory Materials:** Application, including sample questions and list of recommended reference books, provided. **Examination Frequency:** Annual. **Examination Sites:** Exam given at sites throughout the U.S. **Examination Type:** Multiple-choice. **Waiting Period to Receive Scores:** Four-six weeks. **Reexamination:** Must wait one year to retake exam. **Fees:** $95 (members); $210 (nonmembers).

489

Member of the Academy of Certified Social Workers
Academy of Certified Social Workers (ACSW)
c/o National Association of Social Workers
750 First St., NE, Ste. 700
Washington, DC 20002
Phone: (202)336-8222
Fax: (202)336-8313
Toll Free: (800)638-8799
Isadora Hare, Exec. Officer

Recipient: Social workers. **Number of Certified Individuals:** 61,000. **Educational/Experience Requirements:** Must meet the following requirements: (1) Master's in Social Work (MSW) degree from program accredited by Council on Social Work Education (see separate entry); and (2) Two years post-masters supervised experience. **Membership:** Required. **Certification Requirements:** Successful completion of exam. **Preparatory Materials:** *ACSW Study Guide,* Third

Edition (reference). **Examination Frequency:** semiannual. **Examination Sites:** Exam given at 70 sites throughout the U.S. **Examination Type:** Multiple-choice. **Pass/Fail Rate:** 92% pass exam the first time. **Waiting Period to Receive Scores:** Five-six weeks. **Re-examination:** Must wait six months to retake exam. **Fees:** $165.

490

School Social Work Specialist
National Association of Social
 Workers (NASW)
750 First St., NE, Ste. 700
Washington, DC 20002-4241
Phone: (202)336-8232
Fax: (202)336-8327
Toll Free: (800)638-8799
Marianne Josem ACSW,
 Credentials Assoc.

Recipient: Social workers practicing in public and private schools, preschools, special education programs, and residential school settings. **Number of Certified Individuals:** 3000. **Educational/ Experience Requirements:** Must meet the following requirements: (1) Master's degree in social work from program accredited by Council on Social Work Education (see separate entry); and (2) Two years experience. One year of school social work practicum as part of graduate training may be substituted for one year of experience. **Membership:** Not required. **Certification Requirements:** Successful completion of school social work portion of National Teachers Examination. **Renewal:** Every three years. Recertification based on successful completion of exam and accumulation of 30 contact hours of continuing education. Renewal fees are: $45 (members); $100 (nonmembers). **Preparatory Materials:** Application bulletin, including sample questions, provided. **Examination Frequency:** Three times per year - always March, July, and November. **Examination Sites:** Exam given at sites throughout the U.S. **Examination Type:** Multiple-choice. **Re-examination:** Must wait four months to retake exam. **Fees:** $95 (members); $210 (nonmembers).

Recreation Workers

Athletic Coaches and Referees

491

Advanced Instructor, United States Professional Racquetball Organization
United States Professional Racquetball Organization
1615 W. Uintah
Colorado Springs, CO 80904-2921
Phone: (719)635-5396

Recipient: Racquetball instructors. **Membership:** Required. **Certification Requirements:** Successful completion of clinic and practical, set up, skills, and written exams. Clinic covers: Budgeting; Club programming; Drills; Group lessons; Juniors; Lesson plans; Parts of the game; Pay/compensation; Private lessons; Promotions; Teaching programs; and Techniques. Must earn Professional, United States Professional Racquetball Organization designation (see separate entry) within 18 months. **Renewal:** Every year. Recertification based on accumulation of 100 hours of teaching experience. **Examination Frequency:** Throughout the year. **Examination Sites:** Exam given at sites throughout the U.S. **Fees:** $198.

492

Advanced Level Coach, United States Amateur Confederation of Roller Skating
United States Amateur Confederation of Roller Skating (USAC/RS)
4730 South St.
PO Box 6579
Lincoln, NE 68506
Phone: (402)483-7551
Fax: (402)483-1465
Dwain Hebda, Dir.

Recipient: Competitive roller skating coaches in art, speed, and roller hockey roller skating. **Educational/Experience Requirements:** none. **Membership:** Required. **Certification Requirements:** Successful completion of exam. **Renewal:** Every three years. **Preparatory Materials:** Textbooks available. **Examination Frequency:** Throughout the year. **Examination Sites:** Exam given at sites throughout the U.S. **Examination Type:** Multiple-choice; true or false. **Pass/Fail Rate:** 40% pass exam the first time. **Waiting Period to Receive Scores:** Two-three weeks. **Re-examination:** There is no time limit to retake exam. **Endorsed By:** Federation Internationale de Roller Skating; Pan American Sports Organization; U.S. Olympic Committee.

493

Advanced Programmer, United States Professional Racquetball Organization
United States Professional Racquetball Organization
1615 W. Uintah
Colorado Springs, CO 80904-2921
Phone: (719)635-5396

Recipient: Racquetball programmers. **Membership:** Required. **Certification Requirements:** Successful completion of clinic and exam. **Examination Frequency:** Throughout the year. **Examination Sites:** Exam given at sites throughout the U.S. **Fees:** $150.

494

Associate Instructor, United States Professional Tennis Registry
United States Professional Tennis Registry (USPTR)
PO Box 4739
Hilton Head Island, SC 29938
Phone: (803)785-7244
Fax: (800)421-6289
Toll Free: (800)421-6289

Recipient: Tennis instructors. **Educational/Experience Requirements:** U.S. candidates must be members of U.S. Tennis Association. **Membership:** Required. **Certification Requirements:** Successful completion of written, skills, teaching, error detection, and ball handling exams. **Preparatory Materials:** *USPTR Instructor's Guide* (reference). Courses, manuals, videos, and workshops available. **Fees:** $95. **Endorsed By:** U.S. Tennis Association.

495

Certified Interscholastic Coach (CIC)
National High School Athletic Coaches Association
One Purlieu Pl., Ste. 128
Winter Park, FL 32792
Phone: (407)679-1414
Fax: (407)679-6621
Donald Prokes, Exec.Dir.

Recipient: High school athletic coaches. **Educational/Experience Requirements:** None. **Certification Requirements:** Successful completion of exam. **Renewal:** None. **Preparatory Materials:** Preparatory course and study guide available. **Examination Frequency:** Annual. **Examination Sites:** Exam given at annual convention. **Examination Type:** Multiple-choice. **Fees:** $40.

▐ 496 ▐

Certified Level Coach, United States Amateur Confederation of Roller Skating
United States Amateur Confederation of Roller Skating (USAC/RS)
4730 South St.
PO Box 6579
Lincoln, NE 68506
Phone: (402)483-7551
Fax: (402)483-1465
Dwain Hebda, Dir.

Recipient: Competitive roller skating coaches in art, speed, and roller hockey roller skating. **Educational/Experience Requirements:** none. **Membership:** Required. **Certification Requirements:** Successful completion of exam. **Renewal:** Every three years. **Preparatory Materials:** Textbooks available. **Examination Frequency:** Throughout the year. **Examination Sites:** Exam given by correspondence. **Examination Type:** Multiple-choice; true or false. **Pass/Fail Rate:** 40% pass exam the first time. **Waiting Period to Receive Scores:** Two-three weeks. **Re-examination:** There is no time limit to retake exam. **Fees:** $25. **Endorsed By:** Federation Internationale de Roller Skating; Pan American Sports Organization; U.S. Olympic Committee.

▐ 497 ▐

Certified Professional Tennis Instructor (CPTI)
United States National Tennis Academy
1014 Ferris Ave., Ste. 1042-E
Waxahachie, TX 75165
Phone: (214)937-0311
Fax: (214)937-0450
Toll Free: (800)452-8519
Joe Cockerham, Dir.

Recipient: Tennis teachers. **Number of Certified Individuals:** 1302. **Educational/Experience Requirements:** Tennis playing ability at or above intermediate level. **Membership:** Required. **Certification Requirements:** Successful completion of 20-lesson self-study program, including exams. **Renewal:** none. **Examination Frequency:** Throughout the year. **Examination Sites:** Courses and exams given at the Academy. **Examination Type:** Multiple-choice. **Pass/Fail Rate:** 75% pass exams the first time. **Waiting Period to Receive Scores:** One week. **Re-examination:** Must wait six months to retake exams. **Fees:** $349.

▐ 498 ▐

Certified Riding Instructor
Association for Horsemanship Safety and Education
5318 Old Bullard Rd.
Tyler, TX 75703
Phone: (903)509-2473
Fax: (903)509-2474
Toll Free: (800)399-0138
Dan Arnold, Dir.

Recipient: Instructors and coaches of horseback riding in various riding styles. **Number of Certified Individuals:** 3500. **Educational/Experience Requirements:** Must demonstrate group dynamics, horse riding, management, pedagogy, and risk management skills. **Membership:** Required. **Certification Requirements:** Must meet the following requirements: (1) Forty hours of evaluated teaching; (2) Successful completion of evaluation of riding skills; and (3) Successful completion of exams. **Renewal:** Every three years. **Preparatory Materials:** Manuals of horsemanship, instructor's manual, and standards for group riding available. **Examination Frequency:** Exams given 70 times per year. **Examination Sites:** Exams given at 55 sites throughout the U.S., Canada, and Australia. **Examination Type:** Fill-in-the-blank; multiple-choice; problem-solving; short essay. **Waiting Period to Receive Scores:** One-four days. **Re-examination:** Must wait six months to retake exams. **Fees:** $300.

▐ 499 ▐

Certified Sidesaddle Instructor and Judge (CSI/J)
World Sidesaddle Federation
Box 1104
Bucyrus, OH 44820
Phone: (419)284-3176
Fax: (419)284-3176
E-mail: LBowlby@aol.com
Linda A. Bowlby, Pres.

Recipient: Individuals capable of instructing individuals or groups in art of riding sidesaddle or of judging sidesaddle classes. **Number of Certified Individuals:** 19. **Educational/Experience Requirements:** Experience recommended. **Membership:** Required. **Certification Requirements:** Successful completion of exam and oral presentation. **Renewal:** none. **Preparatory Materials:** Manual, equipment and attire guidelines, and other current books and publications available. **Examination Frequency:** Annual. **Examination Sites:** Exam given at annual convention. **Examination Type:** Essay. **Pass/Fail Rate:** 96% pass exam the first time.

Waiting Period to Receive Scores: One week. **Re-examination:** Must wait one year before retaking exam. **Fees:** $150.

▐ 500 ▐

Coach, United States Judo Association
United States Judo Association
19 N. Union Blvd.
Colorado Springs, CO 80909
Phone: (309)647-1179
George R. Weers Jr., Exec. Officer

Recipient: Judo coaches. **Number of Certified Individuals:** 400. **Membership:** Required. **Certification Requirements:** Must meet the following requirements: (1) Successful completion of course and exam; and (2) Conducting of demonstration course. **Renewal:** Every four years. Recertification based on successful completion of course. **Preparatory Materials:** Manuals available. **Examination Frequency:** Throughout the year. **Examination Sites:** Course given at sites throughout the U.S. **Examination Type:** Essay; multiple-choice; problem solving. **Pass/Fail Rate:** 100% pass exam the first time. **Waiting Period to Receive Scores:** Immediately. **Fees:** $25.

▐ 501 ▐

Examiner Certification, United States Judo Association
United States Judo Association
19 N. Union Blvd.
Colorado Springs, CO 80909
Phone: (916)673-8244
Fax: (916)674-7182
Dr. Charles R. Robinson, Exec. Officer

Recipient: Judo examiners. **Number of Certified Individuals:** 350. **Membership:** Required. **Certification Requirements:** Successful completion of course requiring demonstration of judo techniques. **Renewal:** Every four years. Recertification based on successful completion of course. **Preparatory Materials:** Manuals, videos, and other materials available. **Examination Frequency:** Throughout the year. **Examination Sites:** Course given at sites throughout the U.S. **Pass/Fail Rate:** 100% pass exam the first time. **Waiting Period to Receive Scores:** Immediately. **Fees:** $25.

502

Gymnastics Coach/Instructor
United States Association of
 Independent Gymnastic Clubs
 (USAIGC)
235 Pinehurst Rd.
Wilmington, DE 19803
Phone: (302)656-3706

Recipient: Gymnastics coaches at independent gymnastic clubs. **Membership:** Required. **Certification Requirements:** Successful completion of correspondence course. Course covers: Coaching philosophy; Red Cross first aid; Sports medicine; Sports pedagogy; Sports physiology; Sports psychology; and Sport safety. **Preparatory Materials:** Instructors guide, reference book, and study guide available.

503

**High School/Collegiate Coach,
 United States Professional
 Racquetball Organization**
United States Professional
 Racquetball Organization
1615 W. Uintah
Colorado Springs, CO 80904-2921
Phone: (719)635-5396

Recipient: Racquetball coaches. **Membership:** Required.

504

**Instructor of Beginner Through
 Advanced (IBA)**
American Riding Instructor
 Certification Program (ARICP)
PO Box 282
Alton Bay, NH 03810
Phone: (603)875-4000
Fax: (603)875-7771

Recipient: Horse riding instructors. **Educational/Experience Requirements:** Must be 21 years old, have six years experience, and ride at advanced intermediate level or better. **Membership:** Not required. **Certification Requirements:** Successful completion of general exams and one specialty exam. General exams are: (1) General Horsemanship; (2) General Instructor; and (3) The Horse, including: Basic care of the horse; Conformation defects; Points of horse; and Proper care. Specialty exams are: (1) Combined Training, including concepts and exercises of dressage, cross country, and stadium jumping; (2) Distance Riding: Endurance and Competitive, including: Pleasure trail and organized

group trail rides; and Knowledge of training, horsemanship, safety, and good conditioning practices; (3) Dressage, including: Concepts; Exercises; and Movements; (4) Driving, including: Correct and safe harnessing procedures; Knowledge of pleasure driving; and Training of horse and whip; (5) Hunt Seat, including: Knowledge of equitation and exercises in flat work; and Jumping through three feet, six inches; (6) Mounted Patrol Training Officer, including: Concepts; Equitation and exercises in flat work; Jumping concepts and related exercises; Mounted police procedures; Movement and exercises; Patrol procedures; Reschooling and re-claiming mounts; and Unit objectives; (7) Open Jumper, including: Flat and fence work; and Jumper rules; (8) Recreational Riding, including basic horsemanship for those who ride for pleasure and recreation; (9) Saddle Seat; (10) Side-Saddle, including: Basic work over fencing; Competitive sidesaddle riding; Correct equitation and dress; and Knowledge of various styles of riding sidesaddle; and (11) Stock Seat, including: Barrel racing; Pole bending; Reining; Trail; and Western riding. Must also successfully complete oral exam and submit video demonstrating teaching techniques. Must hold General Police Instructor designation from Department of Criminal Justice Standards to take Mounted Patrol Training Officer specialty exam. **Preparatory Materials:** Sample test questions and list of suggested reading material provided. **Examination Frequency:** Throughout the year. **Examination Sites:** Exam given at annual program and at sites throughout the U.S. **Fees:** $395. **Endorsed By:** American Riding Instructors Association.

505

**Instructor of Beginner Through
 Intermediate (IBI)**
American Riding Instructor
 Certification Program (ARICP)
PO Box 282
Alton Bay, NH 03810
Phone: (603)875-4000
Fax: (603)875-7771

Recipient: Horse riding instructors. **Educational/Experience Requirements:** Must be 21 years old, have three years experience, and ride at intermediate level or better. **Membership:** Not required. **Certification Requirements:** Successful completion of general exams and one specialty exam. General exams are: (1) General Horsemanship; (2) General Instructor; and (3) The Horse, including: Basic care of the horse; Conformation defects; Points of horse; and Proper care.

Specialty exams are: (1) Combined Training, including concepts and exercises of dressage, cross country, and stadium jumping; (2) Distance Riding: Endurance and Competitive, including: Pleasure trail and organized group trail rides; and Knowledge of training, horsemanship, safety, and good conditioning practices; (3) Dressage, including: Concepts; Exercises; and Movements; (4) Driving, including: Correct and safe harnessing procedures; Knowledge of pleasure driving; and Training of horse and whip; (5) Hunt Seat, including: Knowledge of equitation and exercises in flat work; and Jumping through three feet; (6) Mounted Patrol Training Officer, including: Basic concepts and exercises of dressage through training level; Beginner jumping concepts; Horsemanship, safety, and conditioning; Knowledge of equitation and exercises in flat work; Related cavaletti exercises; and Training and reschooling mounts; (7) Open Jumper, including: Flat and fence work; and Jumper rules; (8) Recreational Riding, including basic horsemanship for those who ride for pleasure and recreation; (9) Saddle Seat; (10) Side-Saddle, including: Correct fitting of tack and equipment; Correct turnout of horse and rider for both formal and informal showing; Proper position at all gaits; and Training of horse to sidesaddle; and (11) Stock Seat. Must submit curriculum for a complete Mounted Police Academy or Department of Criminal Justice Standards in-service to take Mounted Patrol Training Officer exam. Must also successfully complete oral exam and submit video demonstrating teaching techniques. **Preparatory Materials:** Sample test questions and list of suggested reading material provided. **Examination Frequency:** Throughout the year. **Examination Sites:** Exam given at sites throughout the U.S. **Fees:** $395. **Endorsed By:** American Riding Instructors Association.

506

Instructor in Training (IT)
American Riding Instructor
 Certification Program (ARICP)
PO Box 282
Alton Bay, NH 03810
Phone: (603)875-4000
Fax: (603)875-7771

Recipient: Horse riding instructors. **Educational/Experience Requirements:** Must be 18 years old and submit written description of personal philosophy of riding. **Membership:** Not required. **Certification Requirements:** Successful completion of general exams and one specialty exam. General exams are: (1)

General Horsemanship; (2) General Instructor; and (3) The Horse, including: Basic care of the horse; Conformation defects; Points of horse; and Proper care. Specialty exams are: (1) Combined Training, including concepts and exercises of dressage, cross country, and stadium jumping; (2) Distance Riding: Endurance and Competitive, including: Pleasure trail and organized group trail rides; and Knowledge of training, horsemanship, safety, and good conditioning practices; (3) Dressage, including: Concept; Exercises; and Movements; (4) Driving, including: Correct and safe harnessing procedures; Knowledge of pleasure driving; and Training of horse and whip; (5) Hunt Seat, including: Knowledge of equitation and exercises in flat work; and Jumping through three feet; (6) Mounted Patrol Training Officer, including: Basic concepts and exercises of dressage through training level; Beginner jumping concepts; Horsemanship, safety, and conditioning; Knowledge of equitation and exercises in flat work; Related cavaletti exercises; and Training and reschooling mounts; (7) Open Jumper, including: Flat and fence work; and Jumper rules; (8) Recreational Riding, including basic horsemanship for those who ride for pleasure and recreation; (9) Saddle Seat; (10) Side-Saddle, including: Correct fitting of tack and equipment; Correct turnout of horse and rider for both formal and informal showing; Proper position at all gaits; and Training of horse to sidesaddle; and (11) Stock Seat. Must also successfully complete oral exam. **Preparatory Materials:** Sample test questions and list of suggested reading material provided. **Examination Frequency:** Throughout the year. **Examination Sites:** Exam given at sites throughout the U.S. **Fees:** $395. **Endorsed By:** American Riding Instructors Association.

507

Instructor, United States Professional Racquetball Organization

United States Professional
   Racquetball Organization
1615 W. Uintah
Colorado Springs, CO 80904-2921
Phone: (719)635-5396

Recipient: Racquetball instructors. **Membership:** Required. **Certification Requirements:** Successful completion of clinic and practical, set up, skills, and written exams. Clinic covers: Budgeting; Club programming; Drills; Group lessons; Juniors; Lesson plans; Parts of the game; Pay/compensation; Private lessons; Promotions; Teaching programs;

and Techniques. Must earn Advanced Instructor, United States Professional Racquetball Organization designation (see separate entry) within 18 months. **Renewal:** Every year. Recertification based on accumulation of 75 hours of teaching experience. **Examination Frequency:** Throughout the year. **Examination Sites:** Exam given at sites throughout the U.S. **Waiting Period to Receive Scores:** Six weeks. **Fees:** $198.

508

Instructor, United States Professional Tennis Registry

United States Professional Tennis
   Registry (USPTR)
PO Box 4739
Hilton Head Island, SC 29938
Phone: (803)785-7244
Fax: (800)421-6289
Toll Free: (800)421-6289

Recipient: Tennis instructors. **Educational/Experience Requirements:** U.S. candidates must be members of U.S. Tennis Association. **Membership:** Required. **Certification Requirements:** Successful completion of written, skills, teaching, error detection, and ball handling exams. **Preparatory Materials:** *USPTR Instructor's Guide* (reference). Courses, manuals, videos, and workshops available. **Fees:** $95. **Endorsed By:** U.S. Tennis Association.

509

Ju Jitsu Certification, United States Judo Association

United States Judo Association
19 N. Union Blvd.
Colorado Springs, CO 80909
Phone: (708)564-4333
Ben Bergwerf, Exec. Officer

Recipient: Ju jitsu instructors. **Number of Certified Individuals:** 2000. **Membership:** Required. **Certification Requirements:** Successful completion of course and exam. Course requires demonstrating ju jitsu techniques. **Preparatory Materials:** Study manuals provided. **Examination Frequency:** Throughout the year. **Examination Sites:** Exam given at camps and seminars. **Examination Type:** Multiple-choice. **Pass/Fail Rate:** 100% pass exam the first time. **Waiting Period to Receive Scores:** Immediately.

510

Kata Certification, United States Judo Association

United States Judo Association
19 N. Union Blvd.
Colorado Springs, CO 80909
Phone: (310)941-1306
Gregory L. Fernandez, Exec. Officer

Recipient: Judo kata instructors. There are nine kata, or formal prearranged techniques, in judo. **Number of Certified Individuals:** 280. **Membership:** Required. **Certification Requirements:** Successful completion of course for each kata requiring the demonstration of judo techniques. **Renewal:** Every three years. Recertification based on successful completion of course. **Preparatory Materials:** *Student of Judo, Study Born for the Mat, Kodokan Illustrated,* and *Judo Formal Techniques* (references). **Examination Frequency:** Throughout the year. **Examination Sites:** Courses given throughout the U.S. **Pass/Fail Rate:** 100% pass course first time. **Waiting Period to Receive Scores:** Immediately. **Fees:** $25.

511

Kata Judge Certification, United States Judo Association

United States Judo Association
19 N. Union Blvd.
Colorado Springs, CO 80909
Phone: (405)321-5022
Dr. Joel E. Holloway, Exec. Officer

Recipient: Judo kata judges. There are nine kata, or formal prearranged techniques, in judo. **Number of Certified Individuals:** 50. **Educational/Experience Requirements:** Hold Kata Certification, United States Judo Association (see separate entry). **Membership:** Required. **Certification Requirements:** Successful completion of course and exam. **Renewal:** Every three years. Recertification based on successful completion of course. **Examination Frequency:** Throughout the year. **Examination Sites:** Exam given at tournament sites. **Examination Type:** Multiple-choice. **Pass/Fail Rate:** 100% pass exam the first time. **Waiting Period to Receive Scores:** Immediately. **Fees:** $25.

512

Master Professional, United States Professional Racquetball Organization

United States Professional
Racquetball Organization
1615 W. Uintah
Colorado Springs, CO 80904-2921
Phone: (719)635-5396

Recipient: Racquetball instructors. **Membership:** Required. **Certification Requirements:** Successful completion of clinic and practical, set up, skills, and written exams. Clinic covers: Budgeting; Club programming; Drills; Group lessons; Juniors; Lesson plans; Parts of the game; Pay/compensation; Private lessons; Promotions; Teaching programs; and Techniques. **Examination Frequency:** Throughout the year. **Examination Sites:** Exam given at sites throughout the U.S. **Fees:** $198.

513

Master Professional, United States Professional Tennis Registry

United States Professional Tennis
Registry (USPTR)
PO Box 4739
Hilton Head Island, SC 29938
Phone: (803)785-7244
Fax: (800)421-6289
Toll Free: (800)421-6289

Recipient: Tennis instructors. **Educational/Experience Requirements:** U.S. candidates must be members of U.S. Tennis Association. **Membership:** Required. **Certification Requirements:** Successful completion of written, skills, teaching, error detection, and ball handling exams. **Preparatory Materials:** *USPTR Instructor's Guide* (reference). Courses, manuals, videos, and workshops available. **Fees:** $95. **Endorsed By:** U.S. Tennis Association.

514

National Referee (Level III)

American Amateur Racquetball
Association (AARA)
1685 W. Uintah
Colorado Springs, CO 80904-2921
Phone: (719)635-5396
Fax: (719)635-0685
Jim Hiser, Assoc.Exec.Dir.

Recipient: Racquetball referees. **Educational/Experience Requirements:** Must meet the following requirements: (1) Be member of AARA or AARA-recognized state association for two years; (2) Referee at least 15 matches as Regional Referee (Level II) (see separate entry) at AARA-sanctioned tournaments at level four or higher, including at least two semi-finals matches and two finals matches in an open division; and (3) Attend rules and refereeing clinic since becoming Regional Referee (Level II) and in last year. Must have been Regional Referee (Level II) for one year. **Membership:** Required. **Certification Requirements:** Must meet the following requirements: (1) Successful completion of exams; and (2) Successful rating in last year from National Referee (Level III) while refereeing semi-finals and finals matches in an open division at AARA-sanctioned tournament at level six or higher. **Preparatory Materials:** *AARA Rulebook* and *Officiating Racquetball* (references). **Re-examination:** There is no fee to retake exam.

515

National Team Coach, United States Professional Racquetball Organization

United States Professional
Racquetball Organization
1615 W. Uintah
Colorado Springs, CO 80904-2921
Phone: (719)635-5396

Recipient: U.S. national team racquetball coaches. **Membership:** Required.

516

Professional, United States Professional Racquetball Organization

United States Professional
Racquetball Organization
1615 W. Uintah
Colorado Springs, CO 80904-2921
Phone: (719)635-5396

Recipient: Racquetball instructors. **Membership:** Required. **Certification Requirements:** Successful completion of clinic and practical, set up, skills, and written exams. Clinic covers: Budgeting; Club programming; Drills; Group lessons; Juniors; Lesson plans; Parts of the game; Pay/compensation; Private lessons; Promotions; Teaching programs; and Techniques. Must earn Master Professional, United States Professional Racquetball Organization designation (see separate entry) within 18 months. **Renewal:** Every year. Recertification based on accumulation of 100 hours of teaching experience. **Examination Frequency:** Throughout the year. **Examination Sites:** Exam given at sites throughout the U.S. **Fees:** $198.

517

Professional, United States Professional Tennis Registry

United States Professional Tennis
Registry (USPTR)
PO Box 4739
Hilton Head Island, SC 29938
Phone: (803)785-7244
Fax: (800)421-6289
Toll Free: (800)421-6289

Recipient: Tennis instructors. **Educational/Experience Requirements:** U.S. candidates must be members of U.S. Tennis Association. **Membership:** Required. **Certification Requirements:** Successful completion of written, skills, teaching, error detection, and ball handling exams. **Preparatory Materials:** *USPTR Instructor's Guide* (reference). Courses, manuals, videos, and workshops available. **Fees:** $95. **Endorsed By:** U.S. Tennis Association.

518

Programmer, United States Professional Racquetball Organization

United States Professional
Racquetball Organization
1615 W. Uintah
Colorado Springs, CO 80904-2921
Phone: (719)635-5396

Recipient: Racquetball programmers. **Membership:** Required. **Certification Requirements:** Successful completion of clinic and exam. **Examination Frequency:** Throughout the year. **Examination Sites:** Exam given at sites throughout the U.S. **Fees:** $150.

519

Referee Certification, United States Judo Association

United States Judo Association
19 N. Union Blvd.
Colorado Springs, CO 80909
Phone: (203)348-6553
Richard J. Celotto, Exec. Officer

Recipient: Judo referees. **Number of Certified Individuals:** 320. **Educational/Experience Requirements:** Must hold black belt in judo. **Membership:** Required. **Certification Requirements:** Must meet the following requirements: (1) Attendance at seminar; (2) Successful completion of exam; and (3) Successful completion of review at regional or national tournament. **Renewal:** Every three years. **Preparatory Materials:** *International Judo Federation Referee Rules* (manual). **Examination Frequency:** Throughout the year. **Examination Sites:** Exam given at tournament sites. **Examination Type:** Multiple-choice; true or false. **Pass/Fail Rate:** 30% pass exam the first time. **Waiting Period to Receive Scores:** Immediately. **Fees:** $25.

| 520 |

Regional Referee (Level II)
American Amateur Racquetball
    Association (AARA)
1685 W. Uintah
Colorado Springs, CO 80904-2921
Phone: (719)635-5396
Fax: (719)635-0685
Jim Hiser, Assoc.Exec.Dir.

Recipient: Racquetball referees. **Educational/Experience Requirements:** Must be member of AARA or AARA-recognized state association for one year and have done each of the following within last year: (1) Refereed at least ten matches as State Referee (Level I) (see separate entry) at AARA-sanctioned tournaments at level three or higher, including at least two finals matches in an open division; and (2) Attended rules and refereeing clinic since becoming State Referee (Level I). Must have been State Referee (Level I) for one year. **Membership:** Required. **Certification Requirements:** Must meet the following requirements: (1) Successful completion of exam within last year; and (2) Successful rating in last year from Regional Referee (Level II) or National Referee (Level III) (see separate entry) while refereeing semi-finals or finals match in an open division at AARA-sanctioned tournament at level three or higher. **Renewal:** Every three years. **Preparatory Materials:** *AARA Rulebook* and *Officiating Racquetball* (references). **Re-examination:** There is no fee to retake exam.

| 521 |

**State/Individual Coach, United
    States Professional Racquetball
    Organization**
United States Professional
    Racquetball Organization
1615 W. Uintah
Colorado Springs, CO 80904-2921
Phone: (719)635-5396

Recipient: Racquetball coaches. **Membership:** Required.

| 522 |

State Referee (Level I)
American Amateur Racquetball
    Association (AARA)
1685 W. Uintah
Colorado Springs, CO 80904-2921
Phone: (719)635-5396
Fax: (719)635-0685
Jim Hiser, Prog.Dir.

Recipient: Racquetball referees. **Educational/Experience Requirements:** Must have done each of the following within last year: (1) Refereed at least ten matches at AARA-sanctioned tournaments at level two or higher, including at least one match that was a final in an open division; and (2) Attended rules and refereeing clinic. **Membership:** Required. **Certification Requirements:** Must meet the following requirements: (1) Successful completion of exam; and (2) Successful rating in last year from Regional Referee (Level II) or National Referee (Level III) (see separate entries) while refereeing finals match in an open division at AARA-sanctioned tournament at level two or higher. **Renewal:** Every three years. **Preparatory Materials:** *AARA Rulebook* and *Officiating Racquetball* (references). **Re-examination:** There is no fee to retake exam.

Athletic Trainers

| 523 |

Active Sports Medicine Trainer
American Sports Medicine
    Association Board of Certification
    (ASMABOC)
660 Duarte Rd.
Arcadia, CA 91007
Phone: (818)445-1978
Joe S. Borland CSMT, Chm.

Recipient: Sports medicine trainers. **Certification Requirements:** Must meet the following requirements: (1) High school diploma; (2) Be 18 years old or older; and (3) Five years experience as head athletic trainer or sports medicine trainer and be under direct supervision of Certified Sports Medicine Trainer (CSMT) (see separate entry), certified athletic trainer, or registered sports medicine trainer or therapist.

| 524 |

Athletic Trainer Certified (ATC)
National Athletic Trainers
    Association (NATA)
c/o Columbia Assessment Services
3725 National Dr., Ste. 213
Raleigh, NC 27612
Phone: (919)787-2721

Recipient: Athletic trainers. **Educational/Experience Requirements:** Bachelor's degree, current certification in first aid and CPR, and experience in actual practice and/or game coverage in one of the following high-risk sports: Basketball; Football; Gymnastics; Hockey; Lacrosse; Rugby; Soccer; Volleyball; and Wrestling. Must also successfully complete one of the following: (1) NATA-approved athletic training education program of no less than two years that includes 800 hours of athletic training experience under the supervision of Certified Athletic Trainer (C.A.T.) (see separate entry); or (2) 1500 hours of experience under C.A.T. in no less than two calendar years and not more than five years and at least one formal course in each of the following areas: Advanced athletic training (or one course each in therapeutic modalities and rehabilitative exercise); Basic athletic training; Health; Human anatomy; Human physiology; Kinesiology/biomechanics; and Physiology of exercise. At least 1000 hours must be attained in traditional athletic setting at interscholastic, intercollegiate, or professional sports level. Students in their last college semester or quarter may apply to take exam. **Membership:** Not required. **Certification Requirements:** Successful completion of three-part exam. Exam covers: Health care administration; Prevention of athletic injuries; Professional development and responsibility; Recognition, evaluation, and immediate care of athletic injuries; and Rehabilitation and reconditioning of athletic injuries. **Renewal:** Every three years. Recertification based on current CPR certification and continuing education. **Examination Frequency:** Five times per year. **Examination Sites:** Exam given at sites throughout the U.S. **Re-examination:** Must only retake parts failed. Must successfully complete exam within one year. There is a fee to retake exam. **Fees:** $275 (members); $325 (non-members). **Accredited By:** National Commission for Certifying Agencies. **Endorsed By:** National Organization for Competency Assurance.

525

Certified Athletic Trainer (C.A.T.)
National Athletic Trainers
 Association (NATA)
c/o Columbia Assessment Services
3725 National Dr., Ste. 213
Raleigh, NC 27612
Phone: (919)787-2721

Recipient: Athletic trainers working under direction of licensed physician. **Educational/Experience Requirements:** Bachelor's degree, current certification in first aid and CPR, and experience in actual practice and/or game coverage with one of the following high-risk sports: Basketball; Football; Gymnastics; Hockey; Lacrosse; Rugby; Soccer; Volleyball; and Wrestling. Must also successfully complete one of the following: (1) NATA-approved athletic training education program of no less than two years that includes 800 hours of athletic training experience under supervision of Certified Athletic Trainer (C.A.T.); or (2) 1500 hours of experience under C.A.T. in no less than two calendar years and not more than five years and at least one formal course in each of the following areas: Advanced athletic training (or one course each in therapeutic modalities and rehabilitative exercise); Basic athletic training; Health; Human anatomy; Human physiology; Kinesiology/biomechanics; and Physiology of exercise. At least 1000 hours must be attained in traditional athletic setting at interscholastic, intercollegiate, or professional sports level. Students in last college semester or quarter may apply to take exam. **Membership:** Not required. **Certification Requirements:** Successful completion of three-part exam. Exam covers: Health care administration; Prevention of athletic injuries; Professional development and responsibility; Recognition, evaluation, and immediate care of athletic injuries; and Rehabilitation and reconditioning of athletic injuries. **Renewal:** Every three years. Recertification based on current CPR certification and continuing education. **Examination Frequency:** Five times per year. **Examination Sites:** Exam given at sites throughout the U.S. **Re-examination:** Must only retake parts failed. Must successfully complete exam within one year. There is a fee to retake exam. **Fees:** $275 (members); $325 (nonmembers). **Accredited By:** National Commission for Certifying Agencies. **Endorsed By:** National Organization for Competency Assurance.

526

Certified Sports Medicine Trainer (CSMT)
American Sports Medicine
 Association Board of Certification
 (ASMABOC)
660 Duarte Rd.
Arcadia, CA 91007
Phone: (818)445-1978
Joe S. Borland CSMT, Chm.

Recipient: Sports medicine trainers. **Educational/Experience Requirements:** Current CPR certification, successful completion of EMT1 course or current EMT or health professions medical licensure, and one of the following: (1) Certification as athletic trainer or sports medicine trainer from another association; (2) Successful completion of 1000 hour internship; (3) Successful completion of college courses or equivalent in athletic training and 500 hour internship; (4) Successful completion of course in physical therapy and 200 hour internship; (5) Successful completion of course of study and qualifications as paramedic, registered nurse (R.N.), or licensed vocational nurse (L.V.N.) and 300 hour internship; or (6) Five years experience as athletic trainer or sports medicine trainer. Internships must be under direct supervision of CSMT, certified athletic trainer, or registered sports medicine trainer or therapist. **Certification Requirements:** Successful completion of written, oral, and practical exams.

527

Certified Student Trainer
American Sports Medicine
 Association Board of Certification
 (ASMABOC)
660 Duarte Rd.
Arcadia, CA 91007
Phone: (818)445-1978
Joe S. Borland CSMT, Chm.

Recipient: Students actively assisting athletic training program or sports medicine program at school. **Educational/Experience Requirements:** Must meet the following requirements: (1) Be 18 years of age or under; (2) Accumulate 600 hours working as Student Trainer (see separate entry); and (3) Demonstrate competence in the following areas: First aid and emergency procedures; Strapping; Taping; and Use of heat, massage, ice, and whirlpool. **Certification Requirements:** Successful completion of written, oral, and practical exams.

528

Pre-Active Sports Medicine Trainer
American Sports Medicine
 Association Board of Certification
 (ASMABOC)
660 Duarte Rd.
Arcadia, CA 91007
Phone: (818)445-1978
Joe S. Borland CSMT, Chm.

Recipient: Students actively assisting athletic training program or sports medicine program at school. **Certification Requirements:** Must meet the following requirements: (1) High school diploma; (2) Be 18 years old or older; and (3) Have experience under direct supervision of Certified Sports Medicine Trainer (CSMT) (see separate entry), certified athletic trainer, or registered sports medicine trainer or therapist.

529

Student Trainer
American Sports Medicine
 Association Board of Certification
 (ASMABOC)
660 Duarte Rd.
Arcadia, CA 91007
Phone: (818)445-1978
Joe S. Borland CSMT, Chm.

Recipient: Students actively assisting athletic training program or sports medicine program at school. **Certification Requirements:** Must be 18 years old or under and work under direct supervision of Certified Sports Medicine Trainer (CSMT) or Certified Athletic Trainer (C.A.T.) (see separate entry).

Fitness Instructors

530

ACSM Exercise Leader
American College of Sports
 Medicine (ACSM)
PO Box 1440
Indianapolis, IN 46206-1440
Phone: (317)637-9200
Fax: (317)634-7817

Recipient: Individuals involved in "on-the-floor" exercise leadership, either for groups or individuals, based on valid exercise prescriptions developed by others and/or based on field results. **Educational/Experience Requirements:** Current CPR certification. **Membership:** Not required. **Certification Require-**

ments: Successful completion of written and practical exams. Written exam covers: Communication; Counseling; Exercise science, including kinesiology, functional anatomy, exercise physiology, nutrition, health-appraisal techniques, and injury prevention; Motivational techniques; Population-general health and fitness information; and Safe and effective methods of exercise. Practical exam consists of the following sections: (1) Heart Rate/Cycle Ergometer; (2) Exercise Modification; and (3) Group Leadership. **Renewal:** Recertification based on current CPR certification and accumulation of continuing education or medical education credits. **Preparatory Materials:** *Guidelines for Exercise Testing and Prescription,* Fourth Edition and *Resource Manual for Guidelines for Exercise Testing and Prescription,* Second Edition (references). Study guide, including list of reference materials and sample questions, provided. Workshop available. **Examination Frequency:** Throughout the year. **Examination Sites:** Exams given at sites throughout the U.S. **Examination Type:** Multiple-choice. **Waiting Period to Receive Scores:** Four-six weeks. **Reexamination:** There is no time limit to retake exams. May retake exams as many times as needed. Must successfully complete both exams within one year. **Fees:** $125 (members); $150 (nonmembers).

531

ACSM Exercise Program Director

American College of Sports
 Medicine (ACSM)
PO Box 1440
Indianapolis, IN 46206-1440
Phone: (317)637-9200
Fax: (317)634-7817
Gordon Blackburn Ph.D., Chair

Recipient: Professionals administering clinical exercise programs. **Educational/ Experience Requirements:** The following are recommended: (1) Graduate degree in allied health field; and (2) One year experience in cardiac rehabilitation program or in which at least part of participants are cardiac patients. **Membership:** Not required. **Certification Requirements:** Successful completion of written and practical exams. Written exam covers: Electrocardiography; Exercise physiology and testing; Medical management; Prescription; and Program administration. **Renewal:** Recertification based on current CPR certification and accumulation of continuing education or medical education credits. **Preparatory Materials:** *Guidelines for Exercise Testing and Prescription,* Fourth Edition and *Resource Manual for Guidelines for Exercise*

Testing and Prescription, Second Edition (references). Study guide, including list of reference materials and sample questions, provided. Workshop available. **Examination Frequency:** Throughout the year. **Examination Sites:** Exams given at sites throughout the U.S. **Examination Type:** Multiple-choice. **Waiting Period to Receive Scores:** Four-six weeks. **Fees:** $375 (members); $425 (nonmembers).

532

ACSM Exercise Specialist

American College of Sports
 Medicine (ACSM)
PO Box 1440
Indianapolis, IN 46206-1440
Phone: (317)637-9200
Fax: (317)634-7817
Gordon Blackburn Ph.D., Chair

Recipient: Individuals involved in graded exercise testing, prescription, and leadership, patient counseling, and education in clinical exercise programs for individuals with cardiovascular, pulmonary, and metabolic diseases. **Educational/ Experience Requirements:** The following are recommended: (1) Four months (600 hours) experience; (2) Bachelor's degree in allied health field; (3) CPR in Basic Life Support, Level C (two-man) certification; and (4) Hold ACSM Exercise Test Technologist and ACSM Health/ Fitness Instructor designations (see separate entries). **Membership:** Not required. **Certification Requirements:** Successful completion of written and practical exams. Written exam covers: ECG; Emergency/safety; Exercise physiology; Exercise programming; Health appraisal/fitness; Human behavior/ psychology; Metabolic calculations; and Pathophysiology/Risk factors. Practical exam covers: Arrythmia identification and interpretation; Emergency action; Exercise leadership; Graded exercise testing; Inpatient counseling; Metabolism; Musculoskeletal assessment; and Pulmonary. **Renewal:** Recertification based on current CPR certification and accumulation of continuing education or medical education credits. **Preparatory Materials:** *Guidelines for Exercise Testing and Prescription,* Fourth Edition and *Resource Manual for Guidelines for Exercise Testing and Prescription,* Second Edition (references). Study guide, including list of reference materials and sample questions, provided. Workshop available. **Examination Frequency:** Throughout the year. **Examination Sites:** Exams given at sites throughout the U.S. **Examination Type:** Multiple-choice. **Waiting Period to Receive Scores:** Four-six weeks. **Reexamination:** Must wait six months to

retake written exam and nine months to retake practical exam. May retake written exam two times. Must successfully complete both exams within two years. **Fees:** $570 (members); $670 (nonmembers).

533

ACSM Exercise Test Technologist

American College of Sports
 Medicine (ACSM)
PO Box 1440
Indianapolis, IN 46206-1440
Phone: (317)637-9200
Fax: (317)634-7817
Gordon Blackburn Ph.D., Chair

Recipient: Individuals involved with many aspects of graded exercise testing in clinical health care environment employing variety of activity modes. **Educational/Experience Requirements:** Current CPR certification. Recommended that candidate participate in 250 symptom limited graded exercise tests for clinical population. **Membership:** Not required. **Certification Requirements:** Successful completion of written and practical exams. Written exam covers: Electrocardiography; Emergency procedures/safety; Exercise physiology; Functional anatomy and biomechanics; Health appraisal and fitness testing; Human behavior/psychology; Human development/aging; and Pathophysiology/risk factors. Practical exam covers: Assessing patient's health/ medical status; Assisting with administration of exercise tests; Checking equipment calibration; Communication/ patient interaction; Emergency/subacute responses; History/assessment/ evaluation; Organizational skills; Professional interactions with patients and peers; Recognizing arrhythmias or ECG changes; Responding to emergency and subacute scenarios; and Testing skills. **Renewal:** Recertification based on current CPR certification and accumulation of continuing education or medical education credits. **Preparatory Materials:** *Guidelines for Exercise Testing and Prescription,* Fourth Edition and *Resource Manual for Guidelines for Exercise Testing and Prescription,* Second Edition (references). Study guide, including list of reference materials and sample questions, provided. Workshop available. **Examination Frequency:** Throughout the year. **Examination Sites:** Exams given at sites throughout the U.S. **Examination Type:** Multiple-choice. **Waiting Period to Receive Scores:** Four-six weeks. **Reexamination:** Must successfully complete both exams within one year. **Fees:** $200 (members); $250 (nonmembers).

534

ACSM Health/Fitness Director
American College of Sports
  Medicine (ACSM)
PO Box 1440
Indianapolis, IN 46206-1440
Phone: (317)637-9200
Fax: (317)634-7817
Bill Grantham, Chair

Recipient: Administrative leaders of health fitness programs in corporate, clinical, commercial, or community settings in which apparently healthy individuals participate in health promotion and fitness related activities. **Educational/Experience Requirements:** Current CPR certification. The following are recommended: (1) Undergraduate or graduate degree or equivalent in health and fitness or related field; and (2) Three years experience. **Membership:** Not required. **Certification Requirements:** Successful completion of written and practical exams. Exams cover: Applied exercise physiology; Business planning; Exercise science, including kinesiology, functional anatomy, exercise physiology, nutrition, risk factor identification, lifestyle modification techniques, and injury prevention; Facility and program management; Health related issues; Program business administration; Situational management; and Staff training and administration. **Renewal:** Recertification based on current CPR certification and accumulation of continuing education or medical education credits. **Preparatory Materials:** *Guidelines for Exercise Testing and Prescription,* Fourth Edition and *Resource Manual for Guidelines for Exercise Testing and Prescription,* Second Edition (references). Study guide, including list of reference materials and sample questions, provided. **Examination Frequency:** Throughout the year. **Examination Sites:** Exams given at sites throughout the U.S. **Examination Type:** Multiple-choice. **Waiting Period to Receive Scores:** Four-six weeks. **Fees:** $740 (members); $840 (nonmembers).

535

ACSM Health/Fitness Instructor
American College of Sports
  Medicine (ACSM)
PO Box 1440
Indianapolis, IN 46206-1440
Phone: (317)637-9200
Fax: (317)634-7817
Dr. Richard B. Kreider FACSM,
  Coord.

Recipient: Individuals who conduct exercise programs for people who are apparently healthy or who have a controlled disease. **Educational/Experience Requirements:** Current CPR certification. The following are recommended: (1) Undergraduate degree or equivalent in health and fitness or related field; and (2) Experience in lifestyle behavior modification counseling skills and hands-on experience with exercise leadership. **Membership:** Not required. **Certification Requirements:** Successful completion of written and practical exams. Written exam covers: Counseling; Educational and behavior modification techniques; Exercise science, including kinesiology, functional anatomy, exercise physiology, nutrition, and injury prevention; Health status identification; Long-range goals; Motivational techniques; Physiological and psychological aspects of exercise; Risk factors; and Scientific principles of conditioning. Practical exam consists of the following sections: (1) Anthropometric Measurement; (2) Body Composition Assessment; (3) Exercise Demonstration and Modification; (4) Flexibility Assessment; (5) Muscular Endurance Assessment; (6) Selected Skills or Preparing to Conduct a Physical Work Capacity Test; and (7) Selected Skills of Conducting a Physical Work Capacity Test. **Renewal:** Recertification based on current CPR certification and accumulation of continuing education or medical education credits. **Preparatory Materials:** *Guidelines for Exercise Testing and Prescription,* Fourth Edition and *Health/Fitness Instructor's Handbook,* Second Edition (references). Study guide, including list of reference materials and sample questions, provided. Workshop available. **Examination Frequency:** Throughout the year. **Examination Sites:** Exams given at sites throughout the U.S. **Examination Type:** Multiple-choice. **Waiting Period to Receive Scores:** Four-six weeks. **Re-examination:** There is no time limit to retake exams. May retake exams as many times as needed. Must successfully complete both exams within one year. **Fees:** $170 (members); $220 (nonmembers).

536

Adapted Group Exercise Leader
National Handicapped Sports
  (NHS)
451 Hungerford Dr., Ste. 100
Rockville, MD 20850
Phone: (301)217-0960
Fax: (301)217-0968
Toll Free: (800)996-4NHS
Trudy Orgel, Coord.

Recipient: Rehabilitation and fitness professionals, exercise instructors, personal trainers, program directors, and physical, occupational, and recreational therapists. **Number of Certified Individuals:** 200. **Educational/Experience Requirements:** Basic exercise/fitness instructor certification and/or working knowledge of major muscle groups, basic exercise science, and principles of conditioning. **Membership:** Not required. **Certification Requirements:** Successful completion of workshop and exam. Workshop covers: Adapting aerobic dance exercise; Applied anatomy and kinesiology; Equipment modifications; Flexibility training; Group aerobic dance workout; Modifications of aerobic conditioning principles; Physical disabilities: characteristics and exercise considerations; Practical application of strengthening and flexibility principles; Principles of aerobic conditioning; Principles of anaerobic conditioning with modifications; and Teaching aerobic dance exercise. **Renewal:** Every two years. Recertification based on submission of demonstration video. Renewal fee is $60. **Preparatory Materials:** *Fitness Programming and Physical Disability* (manual). **Examination Frequency:** Four-six times per year. **Examination Sites:** Workshops given at sites throughout the U.S. **Examination Type:** Multiple-choice; true or false. **Pass/Fail Rate:** 75 percent pass exam the first time. **Waiting Period to Receive Scores:** Two weeks. **Re-examination:** There is no time limit to retake exam. **Fees:** $295.

537

**Adaptive Fitness Instructor
  Certification**
Aerobics and Fitness Association of
  America (AFAA)
15250 Ventura Blvd., Ste. 200
Sherman Oaks, CA 91403-3297
Phone: (818)905-0040
Fax: (818)990-5468
Linda Pfeffer, Pres.

Recipient: Fitness instructors involved with mainstreaming individuals with variety of physical disabilities into regularly scheduled fitness classes. **Educational/Experience Requirements:** Must hold AFAA Primary Certification (see separate entry). **Membership:** Not required. **Certification Requirements:** Successful completion of workshop. Workshop covers: Dependent handling; Fitness assessment and disability awareness; Management of injuries; Modifications to exercise routines; and Risk factors. **Examination Frequency:** Throughout the year. **Examination Sites:** Workshop given at sites throughout the U.S. **Endorsed By:** National Handicapped Sports.

`538`

Advanced Fitness Certification

National Dance-Exercise
 Instructor's Training Association
 (NDEITA)
1503 S. Washington Ave., Ste. 208
Minneapolis, MN 55454-1037
Phone: (612)340-1306
Fax: (612)340-1619
Toll Free: (800)237-6242
Michael Wollman, Exec.Dir.

Recipient: Fitness instructors.
Educational/Experience Requirements:
Current CPR certification and experience
in fitness education. **Membership:** Not
required. **Certification Requirements:**
Successful completion of workshop and
exam. Workshop includes demonstrations and lectures. Exam covers: Anatomy; Exercise physiology; Posture
screening; and Safety in exercise. **Renewal:** Every year. Recertification based
on successful completion of workshop
and exam. Renewal fee is $109. **Prepara-
tory Materials:** Manual and study guide
provided. **Examination Frequency:**
Weekly. **Examination Sites:** Workshops
given at sites throughout the U.S. **Examination Type:** Fill-in-the-blank; matching; multiple-choice; true or false. **Pass/
Fail Rate:** 90 percent pass exam the first
time. **Waiting Period to Receive Scores:**
Immediately. **Re-examination:** There is
no time limit to retake exam. There is a
$129 fee to retake exam. **Fees:** $129.
Endorsed By: American College of
Sports Medicine; American Council on
Exercise.

`539`

Advanced Physical Fitness Specialist (Adv. PFS)

Cooper Institute for Aerobics
 Research
12330 Preston Rd.
Dallas, TX 75230
Phone: (214)386-0306
Toll Free: (800)635-7050
Kenneth H. Cooper, Exec. Officer

Recipient: Personal trainers and fitness
and health professionals. **Educational/
Experience Requirements:** Hold one of
the following: Group Exercise Leadership (GEL); Physical Fitness Specialist
(PFS); or Program Director Specialist
(PDS) designations (see separate entries);
or another basic exercise certification.
Certification Requirements: Successful
completion of course. **Preparatory Materials:** Resource manuals. **Fees:** $550.

`540`

AFAA Primary Certification

Aerobics and Fitness Association of
 America (AFAA)
15250 Ventura Blvd., Ste. 200
Sherman Oaks, CA 91403-3297
Phone: (818)905-0040
Fax: (818)990-5468
Linda Pfeffer, Pres.

Recipient: Fitness instructors.
Educational/Experience Requirements:
Current CPR certification, group exercise teaching experience, and understanding of exercise theory. **Membership:** Not
required. **Certification Requirements:**
Successful completion of workshop and
exam. Workshop covers: Basic kinesiology and injury prevention; Body alignment; Exercise physiology; Nutrition and
body composition; Selection and modification; and Sequencing. **Renewal:** Every
two years. Recertification based on accumulation of 15 credit units of continuing
education. **Preparatory Materials:** *Aerobics: Theory and Practice* and *AFAA Basic Exercise Standards and Guidelines*
(texts). Self-study workbook available.
Examination Frequency: Throughout the
year. **Examination Sites:** Exam given at
sites throughout the U.S. **Re-
examination:** There is a fee to retake
exam.

`541`

Aquatic Fitness Instructor Certification

Aquatic Exercise Association
 (AEA)
PO Box 1609
Nokomis, FL 34274
Phone: (813)486-8600
Fax: (813)486-8820

Recipient: Aquatic exercise professionals.
Educational/Experience Requirements:
Current CPR certification, group exercise experience, and working knowledge
of the aquatic environment. **Certification
Requirements:** Successful completion of
workshop, including written and practical exams. Written exam covers: Aquatic
principles; Basic anatomy; Class programming; Exercise physiology; Injury
prevention; Legal consideration; Programming; and Special populations.
Practical exam tests ability to assemble
and lead a simple exercise sequence. **Renewal:** Every two years. Recertification
based on accumulation of 15 hours of
continuing education. **Preparatory Materials:** Objectives, study manual, and list
of reference materials provided. Preparation workshop also available. **Examina-**

tion **Frequency:** Throughout the year.
Examination Sites: Exams given at sites
throughout the U.S. **Waiting Period to
Receive Scores:** Four-six weeks.

`542`

Certification for Personal Trainers and Fitness Counselors

Aerobics and Fitness Association of
 America (AFAA)
15250 Ventura Blvd., Ste. 200
Sherman Oaks, CA 91403-3297
Phone: (818)905-0040
Fax: (818)990-5468
Linda Pfeffer, Pres.

Recipient: Personal trainers and fitness
counselors who work on one-to-one basis
with exercise clients. **Educational/
Experience Requirements:** Must meet
one of the following requirements: (1)
Hold AFAA Primary Certification (see
separate entry); or (2) Successfully complete Introduction to Exercise Science
course. **Membership:** Not required.
Certification Requirements: Successful
completion of workshop. Workshop covers: Behavior modification strategies;
Counseling procedures and leadership
skills; Designing resistance training programs; Fitness assessment and testing;
Introduction to special populations; Obesity, nutrition, and recommendations for
fat loss; Principles of fitness counseling;
Role and responsibilities of personal
trainer/counselor; and Wellness and individual responsibility. **Examination Frequency:** Throughout the year. **Examination Sites:** Workshop given at sites
throughout the U.S.

`543`

Certified Aerobics Instructor

American Council on Exercise
 (ACE)
5820 Oberlin Dr., Ste. 102
San Diego, CA 92121
Toll Free: (800)825-3636

Recipient: Group exercise instructors.
Educational/Experience Requirements:
Must be 18 years old and hold current
CPR certification. **Membership:** Not required. **Certification Requirements:** Successful completion of exam. Exam covers: (1) Exercise Science, including:
Anatomy; Kinesiology; Psychological;
and Physiology; (2) Exercise Programming, including: Choreography; Equipment; Music selection; and Safety; (3)
Instructional Techniques, including:
Emergency procedures; Injury prevention; and Teaching methodologies and

strategies; and (4) Professional Responsibility, including: Ethics; Insurance; Legal principles and issues; and Professional growth. **Renewal:** Every two years. Recertification based on accumulation of 1.5 continuing education credits. **Preparatory Materials:** *Aerobics Instructor* (manual). Sample exam and review and training courses available. **Examination Frequency:** quarterly - always January, April, July, and October. **Examination Sites:** Exam given at sites throughout the U.S. and internationally. **Examination Type:** Multiple-choice. **Waiting Period to Receive Scores:** Four weeks. **Re-examination:** There is a $50 fee to retake exam. **Fees:** $145. **Endorsed By:** National Organization for Competency Assurance.

544

Certified Instructor of the National Swimming Pool Foundation
National Swimming Pool
   Foundation (NSPF)
10803 Gulfdale, Ste. 300
San Antonio, TX 78216
Phone: (210)525-1227
Fax: (210)344-3713

Recipient: Instructors certified to teach Certified Pool Spa Operator (CPSO) (see separate entry) course. **Educational/Experience Requirements:** Must hold CPSO designation. **Certification Requirements:** Successful completion of course and communications, practical, and technical exams.

545

Certified Personal Trainer
American Council on Exercise
   (ACE)
5820 Oberlin Dr., Ste. 102
San Diego, CA 92121
Toll Free: (800)825-3636

Recipient: Group exercise instructors. **Educational/Experience Requirements:** Must be 18 years old and hold current CPR certification. **Membership:** Not required. **Certification Requirements:** Successful completion of exam. Exam covers: (1) Health Screening, including: Identification of health problems; and Understanding client's goals and lifestyles; (2) Evaluation and Reevaluation, including: Analysis of fitness data; Emergency procedures; Fitness tests; and Re-evaluation procedures; (3) Individual Program Design, including: Core sciences (anatomy, applied kinesiology, exercise physiology, and nutrition); Equipment and training methods; and Program

design; (4) Program Implementation, including: Basic first aid and CPR; Equipment maintenance; Motivational techniques; and Exercise techniques; and (5) Professional/Legal/Ethical, including: Ethics; Laws; Professional limitations; and Scope of practice. **Renewal:** Every two years. Recertification based on accumulation of 1.5 continuing education credits. **Preparatory Materials:** *Personal Trainer* (manual). Sample exam and review and training courses available. **Examination Frequency:** quarterly - always January, April, July, and October. **Examination Sites:** Exam given at sites throughout the U.S. and internationally. **Examination Type:** Multiple-choice. **Waiting Period to Receive Scores:** Four weeks. **Re-examination:** There is a $50 fee to retake exam. **Fees:** $145. **Endorsed By:** National Organization for Competency Assurance.

546

Certified Personal Trainer (CPT)
Certified Strength and Conditioning
   Specialist Agency
PO Box 83469
Lincoln, NE 68501
Phone: (402)476-6669
Fax: (403)476-7141
Thomas R. Baechle CSCS, Exec.
   Dir.

Recipient: Fitness professionals. **Educational/Experience Requirements:** Current CPR certification. **Membership:** Not required. **Certification Requirements:** Successful completion of exam. Exam covers: Client consultation/assessment; Emergency procedures; Legal issues; Program planning; Safety; and Techniques of exercise. **Renewal:** Every three years. Recertification based on accumulation of six continuing education units (CEUs). Renewal fee is $21. **Preparatory Materials:** List of suggested articles, audiotapes, videotape, and workbook available. **Examination Frequency:** Six times per year. **Examination Sites:** Exams given at sites throughout the U.S., Canada, and Japan. **Examination Type:** Multiple-choice. **Pass/Fail Rate:** 74% pass exam the first time. **Waiting Period to Receive Scores:** Four weeks. **Re-examination:** Must wait two months to retake exam. **Fees:** $150. **Accredited By:** National Commission for Certifying Agencies. **Endorsed By:** National Organization for Competency Assurance; National Strength and Conditioning Association.

547

Certified Strength and Conditioning Specialist (CSCS)
Certified Strength and Conditioning
   Specialist Agency
PO Box 83469
Lincoln, NE 68501
Phone: (402)476-6669
Fax: (403)476-7141
Thomas R. Baechle CSCS, Exec.
   Dir.

Recipient: Fitness professionals. **Number of Certified Individuals:** 3061. **Educational/Experience Requirements:** Bachelor's degree and current CPR certification. **Membership:** Not required. **Certification Requirements:** Successful completion of two-part exam. Parts are: (1) Scientific Foundations, covering exercise science and nutrition; and (2) Practical/Applied, covering: Exercise techniques; Organization and administration; Program design; and Testing and evaluation. **Renewal:** Every three years. Recertification based on accumulation of six continuing education units (CEUs). Renewal fee is $21. **Preparatory Materials:** List of suggested articles, audiotapes, videotape, and workbook available. **Examination Frequency:** Six times per year. **Examination Sites:** Exams given at sites in the U.S., Canada, and Japan. **Examination Type:** Multiple-choice. **Pass/Fail Rate:** 58% pass exam the first time. **Re-examination:** Must wait two months to retake exam. **Fees:** $150. **Accredited By:** National Commission for Certifying Agencies. **Endorsed By:** National Organization for Competency Assurance; National Strength and Conditioning Association.

548

Coordinator of Water Fitness Programs
United States Water Fitness
   Association (USWFA)
PO Box 3279
Boynton Beach, FL 33424
Phone: (407)732-9908
Fax: (407)732-0950
John R. Spannuth, Pres. and CEO

Recipient: Water fitness program coordinators. **Number of Certified Individuals:** 200. **Educational/Experience Requirements:** None. **Membership:** Not required. **Certification Requirements:** Successful completion of course, including exam. **Renewal:** Every two years. Recertification based on successful completion of course and exam. **Preparatory Materials:** Manual available. **Examination Fre-**

quency: Throughout the year. **Examination Sites:** Exam given by correspondence. **Examination Type:** Fill-in-the-blank; multiple-choice; true or false. **Pass/Fail Rate:** 98% pass exam the first time. **Waiting Period to Receive Scores:** Two weeks. **Re-examination:** There is no time limit to retake exam. **Fees:** $178.

549

First-Aid and Emergency Response Certification

Aerobics and Fitness Association of America (AFAA)
15250 Ventura Blvd., Ste. 200
Sherman Oaks, CA 91403-3297
Phone: (818)905-0040
Fax: (818)990-5468
Linda Pfeffer, Pres.

Recipient: Fitness instructors specializing in emergency and first-aid situations in exercise or fitness setting. **Certification Requirements:** Successful completion of workshop, including written and practical exams. Workshop covers: Allergic reactions; Bandaging; Burns; Controlling bleeding; Dislocations; Electrical emergencies; Fractures; Head injuries; Heart attacks; Heat cramps; Heat exhaustion; Heat stroke; Hypoglycemic attacks; Hypothermia; Nosebleeds; Open wounds; Pregnancy emergencies; Seizures; Shock; Splinting techniques; Sprains; Strains; and Stroke. Must develop emergency-action plan and exposure-control plan.

550

Group Exercise Leadership (GEL)

Cooper Institute for Aerobics Research
12330 Preston Rd.
Dallas, TX 75230
Phone: (214)386-0306
Toll Free: (800)635-7050
Kenneth H. Cooper, Exec. Officer

Recipient: Health and fitness professionals, exercise instructors, aerobic dancers, owners and managers of fitness clubs and centers, teacher trainers, dieticians who prescribe exercise programs, physical therapists, military and law enforcement physical trainers, personal trainers, and students entering the fitness industry. **Educational/Experience Requirements:** Must be 18 years old, have current CPR certification, and hold one of the following: Advanced Physical Fitness Specialist (Adv. PFS); Physical Fitness Specialist (PFS); or Program Director Specialist (PDS) designations (see separate entries); or another basic exercise certification.

Certification Requirements: Successful completion of workshop. Workshop covers: Exercise choreography; Group assessment methods; Leadership/teaching techniques; Motivation strategies; Program planning; Proper body alignment; Rhythmical skills and techniques; Safety programming; Scientific foundations; Scripting classes; and Supervision techniques. Workshop includes exam, lesson and music plan, and presentation of exercise routine. **Preparatory Materials:** Resource manuals available. **Examination Type:** Multiple-choice.

551

Low Impact/Weighted Workout Certification

Aerobics and Fitness Association of America (AFAA)
15250 Ventura Blvd., Ste. 200
Sherman Oaks, CA 91403-3297
Phone: (818)905-0040
Fax: (818)990-5468
Linda Pfeffer, Pres.

Recipient: Fitness instructors. **Membership:** Not required. **Certification Requirements:** Successful completion of workshop and exam. Workshop covers: Anatomy and kinesiology; Instructional techniques; Physiology of strength; and Principles of weight training. **Preparatory Materials:** *AFAA Standards and Guidelines for Low Impact* and *AFAA Standards and Guidelines for Weighted Workouts* (references). **Examination Frequency:** Throughout the year. **Examination Sites:** Exam given at sites throughout the U.S. **Re-examination:** There is a fee to retake exam.

552

Master Water Fitness Instructor

United States Water Fitness Association (USWFA)
PO Box 3279
Boynton Beach, FL 33424
Phone: (407)732-9908
Fax: (407)732-0950
John R. Spannuth, Pres. and CEO

Recipient: Water exercise instructors. **Number of Certified Individuals:** 100. **Educational/Experience Requirements:** Must meet the following requirements: (1) Hold Water Fitness Instructor designation (see separate entry); (2) Two years experience; and (3) 100 hours of water exercise teaching. **Membership:** Not required. **Certification Requirements:** Successful completion of Advanced Water Exercise Instructors course, including

exam. **Renewal:** Every two years. **Preparatory Materials:** Manuals and study materials available. **Examination Frequency:** Throughout the year. **Examination Sites:** Exam given at sites throughout the U.S. **Examination Type:** Fill-in-the-blank; multiple-choice; true or false. **Pass/Fail Rate:** 90% pass exam the first time. **Waiting Period to Receive Scores:** Immediately. **Re-examination:** There is no time limit to retake exam. **Fees:** $150.

553

National Certified Aerobics Instructor

National Dance-Exercise Instructor's Training Association (NDEITA)
1503 S. Washington Ave., Ste. 208
Minneapolis, MN 55454-1037
Phone: (612)340-1306
Fax: (612)340-1619
Toll Free: (800)237-6242
Michael Wollman, Exec.Dir.

Recipient: Aerobics instructors. **Membership:** Not required. **Certification Requirements:** Successful completion of workshop and exam. Workshop includes demonstrations and lectures. Exam covers: Anatomy; Exercise physiology; Posture screening; and Safety in exercise. **Renewal:** Every year. Recertification based on successful completion of workshop and exam. Renewal fee is $109. **Preparatory Materials:** Manual and study guide provided. **Examination Frequency:** Weekly. **Examination Sites:** Workshops given at sites throughout the U.S. **Examination Type:** Fill-in-the-blank; matching; multiple-choice; true or false. **Pass/Fail Rate:** 90 percent pass exam the first time. **Waiting Period to Receive Scores:** Immediately. **Re-examination:** There is no time limit to retake exam. There is $129 fee to retake exam. **Fees:** $129. **Endorsed By:** American College of Sports Medicine; American Council on Exercise.

554

National Certified Aerobics Instructor - Step

National Dance-Exercise Instructor's Training Association (NDEITA)
1503 S. Washington Ave., Ste. 208
Minneapolis, MN 55454-1037
Phone: (612)340-1306
Fax: (612)340-1619
Toll Free: (800)237-6242
Michael Wollman, Exec.Dir.

Recipient: Aerobics instructors with training in step aerobics. **Educational/Experience Requirements:** Current CPR certification. **Membership:** Not required. **Certification Requirements:** Successful completion of workshop and exam. Workshop includes demonstrations and lectures. Exam covers: Anatomy; Exercise physiology; Posture screening; and Safety in exercise. **Renewal:** Every year. Recertification based on successful completion of workshop and exam. Renewal fee is $109. **Preparatory Materials:** Manual and study guide provided. **Examination Frequency:** Weekly. **Examination Sites:** Workshops given at sites throughout the U.S. **Examination Type:** Fill-in-the-blank; matching; multiple-choice; true or false. **Pass/Fail Rate:** 90 percent pass exam the first time. **Waiting Period to Receive Scores:** Immediately. **Re-examination:** There is no time limit to retake exam. There is a $129 fee to retake exam. **Fees:** $129. **Endorsed By:** American College of Sports Medicine; American Council on Exercise.

555

Personal Pool Specialty Certification
Aquatic Exercise Association (AEA)
PO Box 1609
Nokomis, FL 34274
Phone: (813)486-8600
Fax: (813)486-8820

Recipient: Aquatic exercise professionals and personal trainers. **Educational/Experience Requirements:** Must meet the following requirements: (1) Current CPR certification; and (2) Either undergraduate degree in related field or certification from another exercise related association. **Certification Requirements:** Successful completion of workshop. Workshop covers: Exercise principles; Marketing; Programming; Session format; Setting up your own business; and Other related topics.

556

Physical Fitness Specialist (PFS)
Cooper Institute for Aerobics Research
12330 Preston Rd.
Dallas, TX 75230
Phone: (214)386-0306
Toll Free: (800)635-7050
Kenneth H. Cooper, Exec. Officer

Recipient: Personal trainers and health and fitness professionals in wellness cen-

ters, fitness clubs, fire safety, governmental, and law enforcement agencies, sports medicine organizations, dietetic clinics, rehabilitation programs, and corporate organizations. **Educational/Experience Requirements:** Current CPR certification. **Certification Requirements:** Successful completion of workshop. Workshop covers: Anatomy; Exercise physiology; Exercise prescriptions; Feedback methods; Fitness assessment and goal setting; Kinesiology; Motivational techniques; Nutritional programs; Safety programming; Screening options; and Wellness and coronary risk. Workshop includes exam, development of program packet for a partner, and assessment practicum. **Preparatory Materials:** Resource manuals available. **Examination Type:** Multiple-choice. **Fees:** $550.

557

Professional Fitness Trainer
National Health Club Association (NHCA)
12596 W. Bayaud Ave.
Denver, CO 80228
Phone: (303)753-6422
Fax: (303)986-6813
Toll Free: (800)765-6422
Dr. Marc Rabinoff, Coord.

Recipient: Fitness trainers. **Certification Requirements:** Successful completion of exam. Exam covers: Anatomy; Biomechanics; Care and prevention of injuries; Conditioning programs; Designing training; Exercise motivation; First aid; Kinesiology; Nutrition; Physiology; Risk management; Selection and application of fitness tests; Special populations; and Weight management. **Preparatory Materials:** Manual and study guide available. **Fees:** $69.95.

558

Program Director Specialist (PDS)
Cooper Institute for Aerobics Research
12330 Preston Rd.
Dallas, TX 75230
Phone: (214)386-0306
Toll Free: (800)635-7050
Kenneth H. Cooper, Exec. Officer

Recipient: Fitness and health professionals. **Educational/Experience Requirements:** Hold one of the following: Advanced Physical Fitness Specialist (Adv. PFS); Groups Exercise Leadership (GEL); or Physical Fitness Specialist (PFA) (see separate entries); or another basic exercise certification. **Certification**

Requirements: Successful completion of course. Course covers exercise programming, leadership, supervision, and administrative skills. **Preparatory Materials:** Resource manuals. **Fees:** $550.

559

Step Reebok Certification
Aerobics and Fitness Association of America (AFAA)
15250 Ventura Blvd., Ste. 200
Sherman Oaks, CA 91403-3297
Phone: (818)905-0040
Fax: (818)990-5468
Linda Pfeffer, Pres.

Recipient: Fitness instructors. **Educational/Experience Requirements:** Suggested prerequisites are: (1) AFAA Primary Certification (see separate entry); and (2) Successful completion of Step Reebok and Step Reebok Combinations and Variations 1 home-study courses. **Membership:** Not required. **Certification Requirements:** Successful completion of workshop and written and practical exams. Workshop covers: Biomechanics and injury prevention; Instruction skills and techniques; Physiology; Professional responsibility; and Research and scientific background in physiology and biomechanics. **Preparatory Materials:** Step Reebok manual available. **Examination Frequency:** Throughout the year. **Examination Sites:** Exam given at sites throughout the U.S. **Re-examination:** There is a fee to retake exams.

560

Teaching the Overweight Certification
Aerobics and Fitness Association of America (AFAA)
15250 Ventura Blvd., Ste. 200
Sherman Oaks, CA 91403-3297
Phone: (818)905-0040
Fax: (818)990-5468
Linda Pfeffer, Pres.

Recipient: Fitness instructors working with overweight students. **Educational/Experience Requirements:** Must hold AFAA Primary Certification (see separate entry). **Membership:** Not required. **Certification Requirements:** Successful completion of workshop. Workshop covers: Anatomy and physiology; Cardiovascular/medical considerations; Exercise programming; Health appraisal; Nutrition and diet management; and Psychology and motivation. **Preparatory Materials:** *AFAA Standards and Guide-*

lines for Teaching the Overweight (reference).

561

Water Fitness Instructor
United States Water Fitness
　Association (USWFA)
PO Box 3279
Boynton Beach, FL 33424
Phone: (407)732-9908
Fax: (407)732-0950
John R. Spannuth, Pres. and CEO

Recipient: Water exercise instructors. **Number of Certified Individuals:** 2000. **Educational/Experience Requirements:** None. **Membership:** Not required. **Certification Requirements:** Successful completion of course and exam. **Renewal:** Every two years. Recertification based on successful completion of home study and test materials. **Preparatory Materials:** Course materials and other study items available. **Examination Frequency:** Throughout the year. **Examination Sites:** Exam given at 50 sites throughout the U.S. **Examination Type:** Fill-in-the-blank; multiple-choice; true and false. **Pass/Fail Rate:** 85-90 percent pass exam the first time. **Waiting Period to Receive Scores:** Immediately. **Re-examination:** There is no time limit to retake exam. **Fees:** $178.

562

**Weightroom/Resistance Training
　Certification**
Aerobics and Fitness Association of
　America (AFAA)
15250 Ventura Blvd., Ste. 200
Sherman Oaks, CA 91403-3297
Phone: (818)905-0040
Fax: (818)990-5468
Linda Pfeffer, Pres.

Recipient: Fitness instructors who work one-on-one with clients in weightrooms. **Educational/Experience Requirements:** Current CPR certification and meet one of the following requirements: (1) Hold either AFAA Primary Certification or Personal Trainer/Fitness Counselor Certification designations (see separate entries); (2) Successfully complete of either Exercise Science Fundamentals or Introduction to Exercise Science courses; or (3) College degree in exercise science. **Membership:** Not required. **Certification Requirements:** Successful completion of workshop. Workshop covers: Anatomy and kinesiology; Lifting and spotting techniques conducted in weightroom; Muscular strength and endurance; Pro-

gram design and implementation for various populations; and Safety issues and industry guidelines for weightroom. **Preparatory Materials:** Study guide provided. **Examination Frequency:** Throughout the year. **Examination Sites:** Workshop given at sites throughout the U.S. **Fees:** $251 (members); $279 (non-members).

Movement Teachers

563

**American Center for the Alexander
　Technique Teacher Certification**
American Center for the Alexander
　Technique (ACAT)
129 W. 67th St.
New York, NY 10023
Phone: (212)799-0468

Recipient: Individuals trained in Alexander Technique, an educational technique developed by Frederick Matthias Alexander that enables individuals to use their bodies with ease, grace, flexibility, and freedom from strain in any physical activity. **Educational/Experience Requirements:** Must be 21 years of age and meet the following requirements: (1) Documentation of 30 Alexander lessons successfully completed; and (2) Bachelor's degree or at least three years of undergraduate study. **Certification Requirements:** Successful completion of three-year program consisting of three ten-week terms per year. Program includes lectures, demonstrations, readings and discussions, independent study, and practical hands-on work. **Endorsed By:** Accrediting Council for Continuing Education and Training; North American Society of Teachers of the Alexander Technique.

564

Certified Rolfer
Rolf Institute
PO Box 1868
Boulder, CO 80306
Phone: (303)449-5903
Fax: (303)449-5978
Toll Free: (800)530-8875
Liesel Orend, Educ.Dir.

Recipient: Rolfers and movement teachers. (Rolfing is technique devised by Dr. Ida P. Rolf, an American biochemist, for reordering the body to bring its major segments toward vertical alignment.) **Number of Certified Individuals:** 870. **Membership:** Required. **Certification Re-**

quirements: Successful completion of training at Rolf Institute and exam. **Renewal:** Every year. Renewal fee is $450. **Examination Frequency:** Four times per year. **Examination Sites:** Exam given at Rolf Institute. **Examination Type:** Multiple-choice; short answer. **Pass/Fail Rate:** 93% pass exam the first time. **Waiting Period to Receive Scores:** Immediately. **Re-examination:** May retake exam two times.

Recreation Workers

565

Advanced Rider
Horsemanship Safety Association
　(HSA)
Drawer 39
Fentress, TX 78622-0039
Toll Free: (800)798-8106

Recipient: Horseback riders. **Educational/Experience Requirements:** Meet requirements for Intermediate Rider designation (see separate entry). **Certification Requirements:** Must meet requirements in horse management, jumping, and skills. **Preparatory Materials:** *Horse Science Instructor's Handbook, Horsemanship Safety Instructor's Manual,* and *Mounted Games Manual* (references). *Instructor's Handbook of Horsemanship Safety,* including list of requirements, provided. **Endorsed By:** American Medical Equestrian Association.

566

Advanced Scuba Diver
National Association of Underwater
　Instructors (NAUI)
PO Box 14650
Montclair, CA 91763-1150
Phone: (909)621-5801
Fax: (909)621-6405
Toll Free: (800)553-6284

Recipient: Scuba divers. **Certification Requirements:** Successful completion of the following: (1) Course. Course covers: Air consumption; Buoyancy control; Dive planning; Emergency procedures; In-water diving skills; and Lifesaving; and (2) Eight open-water dives. Dives cover: Deep and simulated decompression diving; Light salvage; Navigation; Night diving; and Search and recovery.

567

Assistant Instructor of Yang Short Form T'ai Chi
Patience T'ai Chi Association (PTCA)
PO Box 350532
Brooklyn, NY 11235
Phone: (718)332-3477
William C. Phelps, Pres.

Recipient: Instructors of yang short form T'ai Chi. **Membership:** Required. **Certification Requirements:** Successful completion of training program. Must complete program with no major errors and less than ten minor errors. Candidates who complete program with no errors qualify for Instructor of Yang Short Form T'ai Chi designation (see separate entry). Candidates who have studied with Instructor for two years will be considered for certification. **Renewal:** none. **Preparatory Materials:** Bibliography available. Instruction video and written material available. **Examination Frequency:** By arrangement. **Examination Sites:** Exam given at national headquarters or by arrangement. **Waiting Period to Receive Scores:** Immediately. **Fees:** $50 per hour (testing fee); $25 (certification fee).

568

Beginning Rider
Horsemanship Safety Association (HSA)
Drawer 39
Fentress, TX 78622-0039
Toll Free: (800)798-8106

Recipient: Horseback riders ready to learn canter or lope. **Certification Requirements:** Must meet requirements in horse management and skills. **Preparatory Materials:** *Horse Science Instructor's Handbook, Horsemanship Safety Instructor's Manual,* and *Mounted Games Manual* (references). *Instructor's Handbook of Horsemanship Safety,* including list of requirements, provided. **Endorsed By:** American Medical Equestrian Association.

569

Certified Instructor
North American Riding for the Handicapped Association (NARHA)
PO Box 33150
Denver, CO 80233
Toll Free: (800)369-RIDE

Recipient: Horseback riding instructors for handicapped students. **Educational/Experience Requirements:** Must meet the following requirements: (1) Be 21 years of age or older; (2) Document 120 hours instructing riders with disabilities in mounted activities; and (3) Hold current CPR and first aid certification. **Membership:** Required. **Certification Requirements:** Successful completion of exam and evaluation of videotaped lesson. Exam covers: Appropriate use of horses and equipment to facilitate desired results; Basic first-aid for horses; Basic horse psychology and training; Disabilities and their relationships to therapeutic riding; Stable management; Suitability of horses for therapeutic riding programs; and Terminology relating to disabilities. Videotaped lesson must cover: (1) Instruction of Riders with Physical and/or Cognitive Disabilities, including: Appropriate equipment; Appropriate exercises; Appropriate games; Appropriate safety; Effective use of horse; Effective use of volunteers; Mounting and dismounting of each student; Teaching techniques; Transitions in gaits, including halt; and Walk, trot, and canter; (2) Instruction of Riders Without Disabilities, including: Backing of horse; Change of impulsion at walk and trot; Diagonals; Figure-eight at canter demonstrating simple lead changes; and Half-seat position; and (3) Applicant's Riding Demonstration, including: Ability to adjust pace within gait; Correct position while mounted; Figure-eight at a trot (posting) and canter demonstrating simple lead changes; Grooming and tacking; Half-seat at trot over ground poles; Halt and back; Mounting; Suitability of horse for therapeutic riding program, including conformation and gait; Walk, trot (sitting and posting), and canter; and Warm-up and cool-down of horse. Must also submit lesson plans and class and rider lists. Certification available in the following disabilities: Cognitive; Physical. **Renewal:** Every year. Recertification based on accumulation of 20 hours of approved continuing education. **Preparatory Materials:** List of suggested study references provided. **Examination Frequency:** Throughout the year. **Examination Sites:** Exam given at annual conference and at sites throughout the U.S. **Reexamination:** Fee to retake exam is $150. **Fees:** $150.

570

Certified Leisure Associate (CLA)
National Recreation and Park Association (NRPA)
2775 S. Quincy St., Ste. 300
Arlington, VA 22206
Phone: (703)820-4940
Fax: (703)671-6772
Toll Free: (800)626-6772

Recipient: Recreation and leisure professionals. **Membership:** Not required. **Certification Requirements:** Must meet one of the following requirements: (1) Associate's degree in recreation, park resources, or leisure services; (2) Associate's degree in non-recreation related subject and two years experience; or (3) High school diploma or equivalent and four years experience. **Renewal:** Every two years. Recertification based on accumulation of two continuing education units (CEUs). Renewal fees are: $20 (members); $30 (nonmembers). **Fees:** $30 (members); $40 (nonmembers).

571

Certified Leisure Professional (CLP)
National Recreation and Park Association (NRPA)
2775 S. Quincy St., Ste. 300
Arlington, VA 22206
Phone: (703)820-4940
Fax: (703)671-6772
Toll Free: (800)626-6772

Recipient: Recreation and leisure professionals. **Educational/Experience Requirements:** Must meet one of the following requirements: (1) Bachelor's degree or higher from program accredited by Council on Accreditation, National Recreation and Park Association (see separate entry); (2) Bachelor's degree or higher in recreation, park resources, and leisure services from non-accredited institution and two years experience; or (3) Bachelor's degree in non-recreation related subject and five years experience. **Membership:** Not required. **Certification Requirements:** Successful completion of exam. Exam covers: (1) Leisure Services Management, including: Budget and finance; Marketing; Policy Formulation and Interpretation; Public Relations; and Staff development and supervision; (2) Leisure/Recreation Program Delivery, including: Assessment; Evaluation; Implementation; and Planning; (3) Natural Resource and Facilities Management, including: Development; Maintenance and planning; and Management; and (4) Therapeutic Recreation. **Renewal:** Every two years. Recertification based on accumulation of two continuing education units (CEUs). Renewal fees are: $30 (members); $40 (nonmembers). **Preparatory Materials:** *Candidate Handbook,* including list of suggested references and sample questions, provided. **Examination Sites:** Exam given at sites throughout the U.S. **Examination Type:** Multiple-choice. **Waiting Period to Receive Scores:** Several weeks. **Re-examination:** Fees to retake exams are: $40 (members); $50 (nonmembers). **Fees:** $40 (members); $50 (nonmembers).

`572`

Certified Recreational Sports Specialist (CRSS)
National Intramural-Recreational Sports Association (NIRSA)
850 SW 15th St.
Corvallis, OR 97333
Phone: (503)737-2088
Fax: (503)737-2026
Joell L. Fitch, Asst.Dir for Educ.

Recipient: Entry-level professionals in recreational sports. **Educational/Experience Requirements:** Must meet one of the following requirements: (1) Bachelor's degree in recreational sports or related field; (2) Bachelor's degree in unrelated field and 1200 hours experience in recreational sports; or (3) Six years experience. **Membership:** Required. **Certification Requirements:** Successful completion of exam. **Renewal:** none. **Preparatory Materials:** Study guide available. **Examination Frequency:** 12-15 times per year. **Examination Sites:** Exam given at sites throughout the U.S. **Examination Type:** Multiple-choice. **Waiting Period to Receive Scores:** 10-14 days. **Re-examination:** There is no time limit to retake exam. **Fees:** $25.

`573`

Certified Rider Candidate
Horsemanship Safety Association (HSA)
Drawer 39
Fentress, TX 78622-0039
Toll Free: (800)798-8106

Recipient: Horseback riders. **Certification Requirements:** Must meet requirements in horse management and skills in round pen or small ring. **Preparatory Materials:** *Horse Science Instructor's Handbook, Horsemanship Safety Instructor's Manual,* and *Mounted Games Manual* (references). *Instructor's Handbook of Horsemanship Safety,* including

list of requirements, provided. **Endorsed By:** American Medical Equestrian Association.

`574`

Community Water Safety Certification
American Red Cross (ARC)
431 18th St., NW
Washington, DC 20006
Phone: (202)737-8300

Recipient: Individuals trained in water safety. **Certification Requirements:** Successful completion of course. Course covers: Boating; Buckets and bathtubs; Camps and group trips; Fishing and hunting; Ice activities; Lakes, ponds, and rivers; Oceans; Pools and spas; Sailboarding; Snorkeling and scuba; Surfing; Tubing and rafting; Water skiing; and Waterparks. **Preparatory Materials:** Posters and videos available. **Examination Sites:** Courses given by local and state chapters.

`575`

Early Intermediate Rider
Horsemanship Safety Association (HSA)
Drawer 39
Fentress, TX 78622-0039
Toll Free: (800)798-8106

Recipient: Horseback riders who have begun to canter. **Certification Requirements:** Must meet requirements in horse management, jumping, and skills. **Preparatory Materials:** *Horse Science Instructor's Handbook, Horsemanship Safety Instructor's Manual,* and *Mounted Games Manual* (references). *Instructor's Handbook of Horsemanship Safety,* including list of requirements, provided. **Endorsed By:** American Medical Equestrian Association.

`576`

Head Lifeguard
American Red Cross (ARC)
431 18th St., NW
Washington, DC 20006
Phone: (202)737-8300

Recipient: Supervisory lifeguards responsible for lifeguard staff, patrons, and facility. **Certification Requirements:** Successful completion of course. Course covers: Emergency response; Injury prevention; Interacting with public; Lifeguard selection; Minimizing risks; Roles and responsibilities of head lifeguard;

Teambuilding; and Training. **Preparatory Materials:** *Head Lifeguard* (text). **Examination Sites:** Courses given by local and state chapters.

`577`

Horse Safety Assistant Instructor (HSAI)
Horsemanship Safety Association (HSA)
Drawer 39
Fentress, TX 78622-0039
Toll Free: (800)798-8106

Recipient: Horse safety instructors. **Educational/Experience Requirements:** Must be 18 years of age and hold current first aid and CPR certifications. May qualify for Horse Safety Instructor (HSI) designation (see separate entry) with increased experience. **Certification Requirements:** Successful completion of clinic, including exam. Clinic covers: Basic safety principles; Emergency procedures; Equine related games; General horse care; Horse and rider psychology; Personal skill improvement; Safety methods; and Teaching methods as core curriculum. **Renewal:** Every three years. **Preparatory Materials:** *Horse Science Instructor's Handbook, Horsemanship Safety Instructor's Manual, HSA Handbook,* and *Mounted Games Manual* (references). *Instructor's Handbook of Horsemanship Safety,* including list of requirements, provided. **Fees:** $400. **Endorsed By:** American Medical Equestrian Association.

`578`

Horse Safety Assistant Trail Guide (HSGA)
Horsemanship Safety Association (HSA)
Drawer 39
Fentress, TX 78622-0039
Toll Free: (800)798-8106

Recipient: Horse safety trail guides. **Educational/Experience Requirements:** Must be 18 years of age and hold current first aid and CPR certifications. May qualify for Horse Safety Trail Guide (HSG) designation (see separate entry) with increased experience. **Certification Requirements:** Successful completion of clinic or course, including exam. Must be able to demonstrate ability to make good judgments in hypothetical emergency situations. **Renewal:** Every three years. **Preparatory Materials:** *Horse Science Instructor's Handbook, Horsemanship Safety Instructor's Manual, HSA Hand-*

book, and *Mounted Games Manual* (references). *Instructor's Handbook of Horsemanship Safety,* including list of requirements, provided. **Fees:** $400. **Endorsed By:** American Medical Equestrian Association.

579

Horse Safety Clinician (HSC)
Horsemanship Safety Association
    (HSA)
Drawer 39
Fentress, TX 78622-0039
Toll Free: (800)798-8106

Recipient: Horse safety clinicians. **Educational/Experience Requirements:** Must meet the following requirements: (1) Hold either Horse Safety Instructor (HSI) or Horse Safety Instructor/Trainer (HSI/T) designations (see separate entries); (2) Submit plan for proposed clinic, including videos; and (3) Hold current first aid and CPR certifications. **Certification Requirements:** Must meet the following requirements: (1) Participation as assistant to HSC in at least two clinics and submission of written evaluation for each; and (2) Successful completion of exam. **Renewal:** Every five years. **Preparatory Materials:** *Horse Science Instructor's Handbook, Horsemanship Safety Instructor's Manual,* and *Mounted Games Manual* (references). *Instructor's Handbook of Horsemanship Safety,* including list of requirements, provided. **Fees:** $300. **Endorsed By:** American Medical Equestrian Association.

580

Horse Safety Instructor (HSI)
Horsemanship Safety Association
    (HSA)
Drawer 39
Fentress, TX 78622-0039
Toll Free: (800)798-8106

Recipient: Horse safety instructors. **Educational/Experience Requirements:** Must be 21 years of age and meet the following requirements: (1) Hold current first aid and CPR certifications; and (2) Five years experience. Candidates with less experience may qualify for Horse Safety Assistant Instructor (HSAI) designation (see separate entry). **Certification Requirements:** Successful completion of clinic, including exam. Clinic covers: Basic safety principles; Emergency procedures; Equine related games; General horse care; Horse and rider psychology; Personal skill improvement; Safety methods; and Teaching methods as core curriculum. **Renewal:** Every three years.

Preparatory Materials: *Horse Science Instructor's Handbook, Horsemanship Safety Instructor's Manual, HSA Handbook,* and *Mounted Games Manual* (references). *Instructor's Handbook of Horsemanship Safety,* including list of requirements, provided. **Fees:** $400. **Endorsed By:** American Medical Equestrian Association.

581

Horse Safety Instructor/Trainer (HSI/T)
Horsemanship Safety Association
    (HSA)
Drawer 39
Fentress, TX 78622-0039
Toll Free: (800)798-8106

Recipient: Horse safety instructors and trainers. **Educational/Experience Requirements:** Must be 21 years of age and meet the following requirements: (1) Hold Horse Safety Instructor (HSI) designation (see separate entry); (2) Hold current first aid and CPR certifications; and (3) Ten years experience in teaching, training, or showing, averaging five shows per year. **Certification Requirements:** Successful completion of training program, including exam. Program covers: Basic safety principles; Emergency procedures; Equine related games; General horse care; Horse and rider psychology; Personal skill improvement; Safety methods; and Teaching methods as core curriculum. **Renewal:** Every three years. **Preparatory Materials:** *Horse Science Instructor's Handbook, Horsemanship Safety Instructor's Manual,* and *Mounted Games Manual* (references). *Instructor's Handbook of Horsemanship Safety,* including list of requirements, provided. **Fees:** $500. **Endorsed By:** American Medical Equestrian Association.

582

Horse Safety Riding Instructor Basic (HSRIB)
Horsemanship Safety Association
    (HSA)
Drawer 39
Fentress, TX 78622-0039
Toll Free: (800)798-8106

Recipient: Horse safety instructors for camp or summer camp-like programs. **Educational/Experience Requirements:** Must be 21 years of age and hold current first aid and CPR certifications. **Certification Requirements:** Successful completion of clinic, including exam. Clinic covers: Basic safety principles;

Emergency procedures; Equine related games; General horse care; Horse and rider psychology; Personal skill improvement; Safety methods; and Teaching methods as core curriculum. **Renewal:** Every three years. **Preparatory Materials:** *Horse Science Instructor's Handbook, Horsemanship Safety Instructor's Manual, HSA Handbook,* and *Mounted Games Manual* (references). *Instructor's Handbook of Horsemanship Safety,* including list of requirements, provided. **Fees:** $400. **Endorsed By:** American Medical Equestrian Association.

583

Horse Safety Trail Guide (HSG)
Horsemanship Safety Association
    (HSA)
Drawer 39
Fentress, TX 78622-0039
Toll Free: (800)798-8106

Recipient: Horse safety trail guides. **Educational/Experience Requirements:** Must be 21 years of age and meet the following requirements: (1) Hold current first aid and CPR certifications; and (2) Two years experience. Candidates with less experience may qualify for Horse Safety Assistant Trail Guide (HSGA) designation (see separate entry). **Certification Requirements:** Successful completion of clinic or course, including exam. Must be able to demonstrate ability to make good judgments in hypothetical emergency situations. **Renewal:** Every three years. **Preparatory Materials:** *Horse Science Instructor's Handbook, Horsemanship Safety Instructor's Manual, HSA Handbook,* and *Mounted Games Manual* (references). *Instructor's Handbook of Horsemanship Safety,* including list of requirements, provided. **Fees:** $400. **Endorsed By:** American Medical Equestrian Association.

584

Instructor of Yang Short Form T'ai Chi
Patience T'ai Chi Association
    (PTCA)
PO Box 350532
Brooklyn, NY 11235
Phone: (718)332-3477
William C. Phelps, Pres.

Recipient: Instructors of yang short form T'ai Chi. **Membership:** Required. **Certification Requirements:** Successful completion of training program. Must complete program without mistakes to be certified. Candidates with no major er-

145

rors and less than ten minor errors may qualify for Assistant Instructor of Yang Short Form T'ai Chi designation (see separate entry). **Renewal:** none. **Preparatory Materials:** Bibliography available. Instruction video and written material available. **Examination Frequency:** By arrangement. **Examination Sites:** Exam given at national headquarters or by arrangement. **Waiting Period to Receive Scores:** Immediately. **Fees:** $50 per hour (testing fee); $25 (certification fee).

| 585 |

Intermediate Rider
Horsemanship Safety Association (HSA)
Drawer 39
Fentress, TX 78622-0039
Toll Free: (800)798-8106

Recipient: Horseback riders. **Educational/Experience Requirements:** Meet requirements for Early Intermediate Rider designation (see separate entry). **Certification Requirements:** Must meet requirements in horse management, jumping, and skills. **Preparatory Materials:** *Horse Science Instructor's Handbook, Horsemanship Safety Instructor's Manual,* and *Mounted Games Manual* (references). *Instructor's Handbook of Horsemanship Safety,* including list of requirements, provided. **Endorsed By:** American Medical Equestrian Association.

| 586 |

Lifeguard
American Red Cross (ARC)
431 18th St., NW
Washington, DC 20006
Phone: (202)737-8300

Recipient: Lifeguards. **Certification Requirements:** Successful completion of course. Course covers: CPR; Emergency preparation; Facility operations; Facility surveillance; First aid for injuries; First aid for sudden illness;Interacting with public; Patron surveillance; Preventing aquatic injuries; Rescue skills; and Spinal injury management. Additional training available in the following: Waterfront lifeguarding; and Waterpark lifeguarding. **Preparatory Materials:** *Lifeguarding Today* (text). **Examination Sites:** Courses given by local and state chapters.

| 587 |

Lifeguarding Instructor
American Red Cross (ARC)
431 18th St., NW
Washington, DC 20006
Phone: (202)737-8300

Recipient: Instructors qualified to teach American Red Cross lifeguarding and water safety courses. **Certification Requirements:** Successful completion of course. Course covers: Course administration and planning; Providing corrective feedback; Recognizing skill errors; and Teaching progressions for lifeguarding and water safety skills. **Examination Sites:** Courses given by local and state chapters.

| 588 |

Master Scuba Diver
National Association of Underwater Instructors (NAUI)
PO Box 14650
Montclair, CA 91763-1150
Phone: (909)621-5801
Fax: (909)621-6405
Toll Free: (800)553-6284

Recipient: Scuba divers. **Certification Requirements:** Successful completion of course. Course covers: Diving theory; Equipment familiarization; In-depth dive planning for multi-day and high altitude dives; Physical fitness; Practice skills; and Scuba lifesaving.

| 589 |

NAUI Assistant Instructor
National Association of Underwater Instructors (NAUI)
PO Box 14650
Montclair, CA 91763-1150
Phone: (909)621-5801
Fax: (909)621-6405
Toll Free: (800)553-6284

Recipient: Skin diving and snorkeling instructors. **Educational/Experience Requirements:** Must be 18 years of age and meet the following requirements: (1) Physician's approval for diving within past twelve months; (2) Hold Advanced Scuba Diver designation (see separate entry) or equivalent; (3) Six months diving experience; (4) 20 logged open-water dives; (5) Ten hours of bottom time; and (6) Hold Diving Rescue Techniques Certification (see separate entry) or equivalent. **Certification Requirements:** Successful completion of program. Program covers: Course coordination; Dive orga-

nization and control; Diver escorting techniques; Diving knowledge and skills; Equipment and buoyancy checks; Legal aspects of diving instruction; Rescue and emergency procedures; and Teaching methods and presentations. Candidates must provide own equipment and meet minimum water skills requirements. **Preparatory Materials:** *Advanced Diving Technology and Techniques, Mastering NAUI Leadership, NAUI Textbook II, Openwater I Instructor Guide, Openwater I Student Training Kit,* and *Standards and Procedures Manual* (references). Guide, including bibliography of suggested reference materials and lists of required knowledge and water skills and equipment, provided.

| 590 |

NAUI Divemaster
National Association of Underwater Instructors (NAUI)
PO Box 14650
Montclair, CA 91763-1150
Phone: (909)621-5801
Fax: (909)621-6405
Toll Free: (800)553-6284

Recipient: Skin diving and snorkeling dive leaders. **Educational/Experience Requirements:** Must be 18 years of age and meet the following requirements: (1) Physician's approval for diving within past twelve months; (2) Hold Advanced Scuba Diver designation (see separate entry) or equivalent; (3) One year of diving experience; (4) 25 logged open-water dives; (5) 20 hours of bottom time within last two years; and (6) Hold Diving Rescue Techniques Certification (see separate entry) or equivalent. **Certification Requirements:** Successful completion of program, including ten open-water dives. Program covers: Assisting with instruction; Conducting of specialized activities including shore, boat, night, and deep dives; Group dive organization; Legal aspects of divemastering; Planning, briefing, and debriefing techniques; Problem recognition and resolution; and Rescue and emergency procedures. Candidates must provide own equipment and meet minimum water skills requirements. **Preparatory Materials:** *Advanced Diving Technology and Techniques, Mastering NAUI Leadership, NAUI Textbook II, Openwater I Instructor Guide, Openwater I Student Training Kit,* and *Standards and Procedures Manual* (references). Guide, including bibliography of suggested reference materials and lists of required knowledge and water skills and equipment, provided.

| 591 |

NAUI Diving Rescue Techniques Certification
National Association of Underwater
    Instructors (NAUI)
PO Box 14650
Montclair, CA 91763-1150
Phone: (909)621-5801
Fax: (909)621-6405
Toll Free: (800)553-6284

Recipient: Scuba divers specializing in dive rescue techniques. **Certification Requirements:** Successful completion of course.

| 592 |

NAUI Instructor
National Association of Underwater
    Instructors (NAUI)
PO Box 14650
Montclair, CA 91763-1150
Phone: (909)621-5801
Fax: (909)621-6405
Toll Free: (800)553-6284

Recipient: Skin diving and snorkeling instructors in classroom and confined and open-water environments. **Educational/Experience Requirements:** Must be 18 years of age and meet the following requirements: (1) Hold either NAUI Divemaster or NAUI Assistant Instructor designations (see separate entries); (2) Successfully complete NAUI Instructor Preparatory Course (PREP) within last two years; and (3) Log 50 dives with minimum of 25 hours bottom time. **Certification Requirements:** Successful completion of program. Program covers: Decompression and dive tables; Diving physics; Effective oral communication; Environment; Equipment; Lesson objectives; Medical aspects; Methods and student evaluation criteria for confined and open-water training; Organizing, scheduling, and marketing scuba program; Physiology; Preparing lesson guides and training aids; and Teaching theory and methods. Program evaluation consists of exam, diving rescue, classroom and in-water training, and skills demonstrations. Candidates must provide own equipment and meet minimum academic knowledge and water skills requirements. **Preparatory Materials:** *Advanced Diving Technology and Techniques, Mastering NAUI Leadership, NAUI Textbook II, Openwater I Instructor Guide, Openwater I Student Training Kit,* and *Standards and Procedures Manual* (references). Guide, including bibliography of suggested reference materials and lists of required knowledge and water skills and equip-

ment, provided. **Examination Sites:** Courses given at sites throughout the world.

| 593 |

NAUI Skin Diving Leader
National Association of Underwater
    Instructors (NAUI)
PO Box 14650
Montclair, CA 91763-1150
Phone: (909)621-5801
Fax: (909)621-6405
Toll Free: (800)553-6284

Recipient: Skin diving and snorkeling instructors. **Educational/Experience Requirements:** Must be 18 years of age and meet the following requirements: (1) Physician's approval for diving within past twelve months; (2) Certification as skin or scuba diver; (3) Eight hours of logged open-water skin diving or scuba experience; (4) Hold Diving Rescue Techniques Certification (see separate entry) or equivalent; and (5) Current certification in two-person CPR and first aid. **Certification Requirements:** Successful completion of program. Program covers: Budgeting; Course development; Diving safety; Group management; Legal aspects; Physiology; Practical methods of skin diving and snorkeling instruction in the water; Promotion; Rescue and emergency procedures; Skin diving fitness; Skin diving physics; and Teaching techniques. **Preparatory Materials:** *Openwater I Instructor Guide* and *Standards and Procedures Manual* (references).

| 594 |

Openwater I Scuba Diver
National Association of Underwater
    Instructors (NAUI)
PO Box 14650
Montclair, CA 91763-1150
Phone: (909)621-5801
Fax: (909)621-6405
Toll Free: (800)553-6284

Recipient: Entry-level scuba divers. **Certification Requirements:** Successful completion of the following: (1) Minimum of 11 hours of academic study covering: Dive safety; Diving physics; Environment; Medicine; and Physiology; (2) 12 in-pool training hours; and (3) Five open water dives.

| 595 |

Openwater II Scuba Diver
National Association of Underwater
    Instructors (NAUI)
PO Box 14650
Montclair, CA 91763-1150
Phone: (909)621-5801
Fax: (909)621-6405
Toll Free: (800)553-6284

Recipient: Scuba divers. **Educational/Experience Requirements:** Hold Openwater I Scuba Diver designation (see separate entry). **Certification Requirements:** Successful completion of course, including six open-water dives. Course covers: Navigation; Night diving; and Search and recovery.

| 596 |

PSIA Certified Level I Instructor
Professional Ski Instructors of
    America (PSIA)
133 S. Van Gordon, Ste. 101
Lakewood, CO 80228
Phone: (303)987-9390
Fax: (303)988-3005

Recipient: Ski instructors. **Educational/Experience Requirements:** Successful completion of teacher preparation training program. **Membership:** Required. **Certification Requirements:** Successful completion of exam. Exam covers skiing, teaching, and technical skills. Skiing skills are: (1) Free Skiing, including: General; and Versatility; and (2) Demonstrations, including: Wedge christy turns; and Wedge turns. Teaching skills are: (1) Knowledge, including: American Teaching System (ATS); Common behavior patterns of children; Learning styles; Responsibility Code; Student needs of specific groups; and Task styles; and (2) Application, including: Handling of class; Skier services and activities; and Teaching techniques. Technical skills are: (1) Terminology; (2) Equipment; (3) Skiing Model/Skill Development, including: Center line reference maneuvers; Fundamental skiing skills; and Phases of a turn; and (4) Movement Analysis, including: Basic movement patterns; Cause-and-effect relationships; Lesson plans; and Prioritizing skill. **Examination Sites:** Exam given at regional sites throughout the U.S.

`597`

PSIA Certified Level II Instructor
Professional Ski Instructors of
   America (PSIA)
133 S. Van Gordon, Ste. 101
Lakewood, CO 80228
Phone: (303)987-9390
Fax: (303)988-3005

Recipient: Ski instructors. **Educational/ Experience Requirements:** Successful completion of teacher preparation training program. **Membership:** Required. **Certification Requirements:** Successful completion of exam. Exam covers skiing, teaching, and technical skills. Skiing skills are: (1) Free Skiing, including: Bumps; General; and Versatility; and (2) Demonstrations, including: Open parallel turns; Wedge christy turns; and Wedge turns. Teaching skills are: (1) Knowledge, including: Cognitive, affective, and physical development of students; Command, task, reciprocal, and small group teaching styles; Responsibility Code; and Teaching model; and (2) Application, including: Lateral learning; Learning partnership; Lesson content; Skier services and activities; Student performance; Teaching model; and Teaching styles. Technical skills are: (1) Terminology; (2) Equipment; (3) Skiing Model/Skill Development, including: Center line reference goals; Forces acting on skier during turn; and Situational variations of skill application; and (4) Movement Analysis, including: Basic movement patterns; Cause-and-effect relationships; Exercises and tasks; Lesson plans; and Prioritizing skill. **Examination Sites:** Exam given at regional sites throughout the U.S.

`598`

PSIA Certified Level III Instructor
Professional Ski Instructors of
   America (PSIA)
133 S. Van Gordon, Ste. 101
Lakewood, CO 80228
Phone: (303)987-9390
Fax: (303)988-3005

Recipient: Ski instructors. **Educational/ Experience Requirements:** Successful completion of teacher preparation training program. **Membership:** Required. **Certification Requirements:** Successful completion of exam. Exam covers skiing, teaching, and technical skills. Skiing skills are: (1) Free Skiing, including: Bumps; General; and Versatility; and (2) Demonstrations, including: Dynamic parallel turns; Open parallel turns; Wedge christy turns; and Wedge turns. Teaching skills are: (1) Knowledge, including: Responsibility Code; Teaching

and learning styles; and Teaching and learning theory; and (2) Application, including: Cognitive, affective, and physical development needs; Individualizing group and semi-private lessons; Learning theory; Outcomes and strategies; Skier services and activities; Teaching model; and Teaching styles. Technical skills are: (1) Terminology; (2) Equipment; (3) Skiing Model/Skill Development, including: External and internal forces; Populations of skiers; and Skill blending; and (4) Movement Analysis, including: Balance; Basic movement patterns; Cause-and-effect relationships; Exercises and tasks; Phases of turn; Prioritizing skills; Skill blending; Skill deficiencies and proficiencies; and Tactics. **Examination Sites:** Exam given at regional sites throughout the U.S.

`599`

PSIA Registered Instructor
Professional Ski Instructors of
   America (PSIA)
133 S. Van Gordon, Ste. 101
Lakewood, CO 80228
Phone: (303)987-9390
Fax: (303)988-3005

Recipient: Ski instructors. **Educational/ Experience Requirements:** Successful completion of teacher preparation training program. **Membership:** Required. **Certification Requirements:** Successful completion of exam. Exam covers PSIA education and the American Teaching System (ATS). PSIA education covers: (1) Introduction to PSIA, including: History; Organization; Philosophy; and Purpose; (2) Ski Industry, including: Organization of ski area; Role of ski instruction; and Teamwork; and (3) Professionalism, including: Basic principles and philosophies; Behaviors; and Demonstrating professionalism. American Teaching System covers: (1) Introduction to ATS, including: Ski center line reference maneuvers; and Ski variations of reference maneuvers in different on-hill situations; (2) Class Organization and Handling, including: Lesson format; Providing individual attention; and Safety and responsibility; (3) Risk Management, including: Decision-making; and Instructor's Responsibility Code; and (4) Customer Service, including: Customer-oriented behavior; and Philosophy. **Examination Sites:** Exam given at regional sites throughout the U.S.

`600`

Registered Instructor
North American Riding for the
   Handicapped Association
   (NARHA)
PO Box 33150
Denver, CO 80233
Toll Free: (800)369-RIDE

Recipient: Horseback riding instructors for handicapped students. **Educational/ Experience Requirements:** Must meet the following requirements: (1) Be 18 years of age or older; (2) Document 25 hours of riding instruction; and (3) Hold current CPR and first aid certification. **Membership:** Required. **Certification Requirements:** Successful completion of exam and evaluation of videotaped lesson. Exam covers: Disabilities; Horsemanship; and Safety. Lesson should include: (1) Instruction of Riders with Physical and/or Cognitive Disabilities, including: Appropriate equipment; Appropriate exercises; Appropriate games; Appropriate safety; Effective use of horse; Effective use of volunteers; Mounting and dismounting of one student; Teaching techniques; Transitions in gaits, including halt; and Walk, trot, and canter; and (2) Applicant's Riding Demonstration, including: Diagonals and leads; and Walk, trot (sitting and posting), canter, and halt, both directions. Must also submit lesson plans and class and rider lists. **Renewal:** Every year. Recertification based on accumulation of ten hours of approved continuing education. **Preparatory Materials:** List of suggested study references provided. **Examination Sites:** Exam given by correspondence. **Waiting Period to Receive Scores:** Four-six months. **Re-examination:** Fee to retake exam is $40. **Fees:** $40.

`601`

Specialty Scuba Diver
National Association of Underwater
   Instructors (NAUI)
PO Box 14650
Montclair, CA 91763-1150
Phone: (909)621-5801
Fax: (909)621-6405
Toll Free: (800)553-6284

Recipient: Scuba divers specializing in specific area. **Educational/Experience Requirements:** Hold Openwater I Scuba Diver designation (see separate entry) or equivalent training. **Certification Requirements:** Successful completion of 12 to 24 hours of combined classroom and in-water training. Specialties are: Cave and cavern diving; Computer assisted diving; Deep diving; Diving rescue; Dry suit; Ice diving; Industrial orientation; Introduction to underwater archaeology; Night diving; River diving; Search and recovery; Underwater environment; Underwater hunting; Underwater photography; and Wreck diving.

602

Water Safety Instructor
American Red Cross (ARC)
431 18th St., NW
Washington, DC 20006
Phone: (202)737-8300

Recipient: Instructors qualified to teach American Red Cross swimming and water safety courses. **Educational/ Experience Requirements:** Successful completion of precourse session. **Certification Requirements:** Successful completion of course. Course covers: Course and lesson planning; Cultural diversity training; Disabilities and other conditions; Fitness and training; Motor learning and hydrodynamic principles; Providing corrective feedback; Recognizing skill errors; and Teaching progressions.

Teachers and Librarians

Adult and Vocational Education Teachers

603

LLA Certified Supervising Trainer
Laubach Literacy Action (LLA)
1320 Jamesville Ave.
Box 131
Syracuse, NY 13210
Phone: (315)422-9121
Fax: (315)422-6369

Recipient: Literacy trainers. **Educational/Experience Requirements:** Must meet the following requirements: (1) Hold LLA Certified Trainer designation (see separate entry); and (2) Successfully complete Supervising Trainer workshop. **Membership:** Required. **Certification Requirements:** Successful completion of training and evaluation of apprentice trainer. Must teach apprentice how to conduct tutor workshop and develop training techniques and skills. Workshop must include: (1) Background, including: Extent, causes, and effects of illiteracy; and Needs and problems facing speakers of languages other than English; (2) Roles and Responsibilities, including: Appropriate state or national organizations, including LLA; Learners and tutors; and Local program; (3) Adult Learners, including: Acquiring a second language; Learning styles; Needs; Problem solving; and Similarities and differences; (4) Planning/Assessment, including: Evaluation of progress; Goal setting; Initial assessment; and Lesson planning; (5) Instruction, including: Primary instructional approach; and Selection and use of appropriate materials and teaching techniques; (6) Schedule and Format, including: Individualized activities; Length of instructional time; and Training techniques; (7) Presentation of Workshop, including: Delivery; Group interaction; Knowledge of content; Management; and

Methods; and (8) Evaluation. **Renewal:** Every three years. Recertification based on continued involvement in tutoring adult learners and training tutors and trainers. **Preparatory Materials:** *LLA Certification Team Handbook* and *LLA Guidelines for Effective Tutor Workshops* (references). Manual, including glossary of terms, provided. Workshops also available.

604

LLA Certified Trainer
Laubach Literacy Action (LLA)
1320 Jamesville Ave.
Box 131
Syracuse, NY 13210
Phone: (315)422-9121
Fax: (315)422-6369

Recipient: Individuals who train literacy or English as a Second Language (ESL) volunteer tutors. **Educational/Experience Requirements:** Successful completion of the following: (1) Training as tutor to teach literacy or ESL skills to adults; and (2) Trainer workshop. **Membership:** Required. **Certification Requirements:** Plan, organize, and manage tutor workshop. Workshop must include: (1) Background, including: Extent, causes, and effects of illiteracy; and Needs and problems facing speakers of languages other than English; (2) Roles and Responsibilities, including: Appropriate state or national organizations, including LLA; Learners and tutors; and Local program; (3) Adult Learners, including: Acquiring a second language; Learning styles; Needs; Problem solving; and Similarities and differences; (4) Planning/Assessment, including: Evaluation of progress; Goal setting; Initial assessment; and Lesson planning; (5) Instruction, including: Primary instructional approach; and Selection and use of appropriate materials and teaching techniques; (6)

Schedule and Format, including: Individualized activities; Length of instructional time; and Training techniques; (7) Presentation of Workshop, including: Delivery; Group interaction; Knowledge of content; Management; and Methods; and (8) Evaluation. **Renewal:** Every three years. Recertification based on continued involvement in tutoring adult learners and training tutors and/or trainers. **Preparatory Materials:** *LLA Certification Team Handbook* and *LLA Guidelines for Effective Tutor Workshops* (references). Manual, including glossary of terms, provided. **Examination Sites:** Trainer Workshop available at state and national meetings and conferences.

Archivists and Curators

605

Certified Archivist (CA)
Academy of Certified Archivists (ACA)
600 S. Federal St., Ste. 504
Chicago, IL 60605
Phone: (312)922-0140
Fax: (312)347-1452
Frank B. Evans, Pres.

Recipient: Individuals involved in management of current records, archival administration, and custody of historical manuscripts for government agencies, colleges and universities, historical societies, museums, libraries, businesses, and religious institutions. **Number of Certified Individuals:** 917. **Educational/Experience Requirements:** Must meet one of the following requirements: (1) Master's degree, including or supplemented by nine semester hours (12 quarter hours) of approved graduate archives administration study, and one year of experience; (2) Master's degree and two years experience; or (3) Bachelor's degree and three years experience. Qualifying experience must be as professional archivist actively exercising responsibility in acquisition, preservation, management, reference, and control of archival materials. **Membership:** Required. **Certification Requirements:** Successful completion of exam. Exam covers all areas of archival practice, including: Government archives; Manuscripts; Organizational and institutional records (current and noncurrent); and Personal papers. Exam consists of the following sections: (1) Selection; (2) Arrangement and Description; (3) Reference Services and Access; (4) Preservation and Protection; (5) Outreach and Promotion; (6) Program Planning and Assessment; and (7) Professional, Ethical, and Legal Responsibilities. **Renewal:** Every five years. Recertification based on either successful completion of exam or continuing education, experience, and professional volunteer activities. There is no fee to renew. **Preparatory Materials:** Handbook available. **Examination Frequency:** Annual. **Examination Sites:** Exam given at annual meeting. **Examination Type:** Multiple-choice. **Pass/Fail Rate:** 75% pass exam the first time. **Waiting Period to Receive Scores:** Four-six weeks. **Reexamination:** Must wait one year to retake exam. There is no limit to how many times exam may be retaken. There is a $50 fee to retake exam. **Fees:** $200. **Endorsed By:** Society of American Archivists.

Genealogists

`606`

Certified American Indian Lineage Specialist
Board for Certification of
   Genealogists (BCG)
PO Box 5816
Falmouth, VA 22403-5816

Recipient: Genealogists specializing in American Indian genealogy.

`607`

Certified American Lineage Specialist
Board for Certification of
   Genealogists (BCG)
PO Box 5816
Falmouth, VA 22403-5816

Recipient: Genealogists specializing in American genealogy.

`608`

Certified Genealogical Instructor
Board for Certification of
   Genealogists (BCG)
PO Box 5816
Falmouth, VA 22403-5816

Recipient: Individuals teaching genealogy.

`609`

Certified Genealogical Lecturer
Board for Certification of
   Genealogists (BCG)
PO Box 5816
Falmouth, VA 22403-5816

Recipient: Genealogical lecturers.

`610`

Certified Genealogical Record Searcher
Board for Certification of
   Genealogists (BCG)
PO Box 5816
Falmouth, VA 22403-5816

Recipient: Individuals involved in genealogical research.

`611`

Certified Genealogist
Board for Certification of
   Genealogists (BCG)
PO Box 5816
Falmouth, VA 22403-5816

Recipient: Genealogists.

Librarians

`612`

Distinguished Member, Academy of Health Information Professionals
Academy of Health Information
   Professionals
c/o Medical Library Association
Six N. Michigan Ave., Ste. 300
Chicago, IL 60602-4805
Phone: (312)419-9094
Fax: (312)419-8950
Dr. Reneta E. Webb CAE, Dir.

Recipient: Health information librarians. **Educational/Experience Requirements:** Ten years experience and meet one of the

following requirements: (1) Master's degree in library or information science accredited by the Committee on Accreditation of the American Library Association (see separate entry); or (2) Master's degree in non-related field and coursework in each of the following essential knowledge areas: Health sciences environment and information policies; Health sciences information services; Health sciences resource management; Information systems and technology; Instructional support systems; Management of information services; and Research, analysis, and interpretation. **Certification Requirements:** Accumulation of 120 total points in last five years through: (1) Educational Activities (maximum of 40 points), including academic courses and continuing education activities; (2) Individual Accomplishments, including: Conference attendance; Continuing education course development; Editing; Exhibits; Professional association activities (minimum of five points; minimum of five points through Medical Library Association activities); Publishing; Software development and media preparations; Teaching; and Other professional activities. **Renewal:** Every five years. Recertification based on accumulation of 50 points through same categories as initial certification. **Endorsed By:** Medical Library Association.

`613`

Member, Academy of Health Information Professionals
Academy of Health Information
   Professionals
c/o Medical Library Association
Six N. Michigan Ave., Ste. 300
Chicago, IL 60602-4805
Phone: (312)419-9094
Fax: (312)419-8950
Dr. Reneta E. Webb CAE, Dir.

Recipient: Health information librarians. **Educational/Experience Requirements:** Five years experience and meet one of the following requirements: (1) Master's degree in library or information science accredited by Committee on Accreditation of the American Library Association (see separate entry); or (2) Master's degree in non-related field and coursework in each of the following essential knowledge areas: Health sciences environment and information policies; Health sciences information services; Health sciences resource management; Information systems and technology; Instructional support systems; Management of information services; and Research, analysis, and interpretation. Candidates with less experience may qualify for Provisional

Member, Academy of Health Information Professionals designation (see separate entry). **Certification Requirements:** Accumulation of 50 total points in last five years through: (1) Educational Activities, including academic courses and continuing education activities; and (2) Individual Accomplishments, including: Conference attendance; Continuing education course development; Editing; Exhibits; Professional association activities; Publishing; Software development and media preparations; Teaching; and Other professional activities. **Renewal:** Every five years. Recertification based on accumulation of 50 points through same categories as initial certification. **Endorsed By:** Medical Library Association.

614

Provisional Member, Academy of Health Information Professionals
Academy of Health Information Professionals
c/o Medical Library Association
Six N. Michigan Ave., Ste. 300
Chicago, IL 60602-4805
Phone: (312)419-9094
Fax: (312)419-8950
Dr. Reneta E. Webb CAE, Dir.

Recipient: Health information librarians. **Certification Requirements:** Less than five years experience and meet one of the following requirements: (1) Master's degree in library or information science accredited by Committee on Accreditation of the American Library Association (see separate entry); or (2) Master's degree in non-related field and coursework in each of the following essential knowledge areas: Health sciences environment and information policies; Health sciences information services; Health sciences resource management; Information systems and technology; Instructional support systems; Management of information services; and Research, analysis, and interpretation. Candidates earn Member, Academy of Health Information Professionals designation (see separate entry) with five years experience. **Renewal:** Every year. Recertification based on accumulation of eight points through: (1) Educational Activities, including academic courses and continuing education activities; and (2) Individual Accomplishments, including: Conference attendance; Continuing education course development; Editing; Exhibits; Professional association activities; Publishing; Software development and media preparations; Teaching; and Other professional activities. **Endorsed By:** Medical Library Association.

615

Senior Member, Academy of Health Information Professionals
Academy of Health Information Professionals
c/o Medical Library Association
Six N. Michigan Ave., Ste. 300
Chicago, IL 60602-4805
Phone: (312)419-9094
Fax: (312)419-8950
Dr. Reneta E. Webb CAE, Dir.

Recipient: Health information librarians. **Educational/Experience Requirements:** Five years experience and meet one of the following requirements: (1) Master's degree in library or information science accredited by Committee on Accreditation of the American Library Association (see separate entry); or (2) Master's degree in non-related field and coursework in each of the following essential knowledge areas: Health sciences environment and information policies; Health sciences information services; Health sciences resource management; Information systems and technology; Instructional support systems; Management of information services; and Research, analysis, and interpretation. **Certification Requirements:** Accumulation of 50 total points in last five years through: (1) Educational Activities (maximum of 40 points), including academic courses and continuing education activities; (2) Individual Accomplishments, including: Conference attendance; Continuing education course development; Editing; Exhibits; Professional association activities (minimum of five points); Publishing; Software development and media preparations; Teaching; and Other professional activities. **Renewal:** Every five years. Recertification based on accumulation of 50 points through same categories as initial certification. **Endorsed By:** Medical Library Association.

Parliamentarians

616

Certified Parliamentarian (CP)
American Institute of Parliamentarians (AIP)
10535 Metropolitan Ave.
Kensington, MD 20895-2627
Phone: (301)946-9220
Fax: (301)949-5255
Joyce C. Parks, Dir.

Recipient: Parliamentarians and others interested in parliamentary procedure.

Number of Certified Individuals: 356. **Educational/Experience Requirements:** Must have knowledge of not less than four different parliamentary authorities. Experience, ability as a parliamentarian, and association participation must be reviewed by AIP. May qualify for Certified Professional Parliamentarian (CPP) designation (see separate entry) with further experience. **Membership:** Required. **Certification Requirements:** Successful completion of oral and written exams. Exams cover parliamentary law and procedures. **Renewal:** none. **Preparatory Materials:** List of study sources available. **Examination Frequency:** semiannual. **Examination Sites:** Exams given by arrangement with proctor. **Examination Type:** Multiple-choice; problem-solving; short-answer; short essay. **Pass/Fail Rate:** 50% pass exams the first time. **Waiting Period to Receive Scores:** Six weeks. **Re-examination:** Must wait one year to retake exams. **Fees:** $60.

617

Certified Professional Parliamentarian (CPP)
American Institute of Parliamentarians (AIP)
10535 Metropolitan Ave.
Kensington, MD 20895-2627
Phone: (301)946-9220
Fax: (301)949-5255
Joyce C. Parks, Dir.

Recipient: Parliamentarians and others interested in parliamentary procedure. **Number of Certified Individuals:** 201. **Educational/Experience Requirements:** Must have knowledge of not less than four different parliamentary authorities. Experience, ability as a parliamentarian, and association participation must be reviewed by AIP. May qualify for Certified Parliamentarian (CP) designation (see separate entry) with less experience. **Membership:** Required. **Certification Requirements:** Successful completion of oral and written exams. Exams cover parliamentary law and procedures. **Renewal:** none. **Preparatory Materials:** List of study sources available. **Examination Frequency:** semiannual. **Examination Sites:** Exams given by arrangement with proctor. **Examination Type:** Multiple-choice; problem-solving; short-answer; short essay. **Pass/Fail Rate:** 50% pass exams the first time. **Waiting Period to Receive Scores:** Six weeks. **Re-examination:** Must wait one year to retake exams. **Fees:** $50.

618

Professional Registered Parliamentarians (PRP)
National Association of
   Parliamentarians (NAP)
6601 Winchester Ave., Ste. 260
Kansas City, MO 64133
Phone: (816)356-5604

Recipient: Individuals interested in parliamentary procedure. **Membership:** Required.

619

Registered Parliamentarian (RP)
National Association of
   Parliamentarians (NAP)
6601 Winchester Ave., Ste. 260
Kansas City, MO 64133-4657
Phone: (816)356-5604

Recipient: Individuals interested in parliamentary procedure. **Membership:** Required.

Teachers

620

National Board Certified Teacher
National Board for Professional
   Teaching Standards (NBPTS)
300 River Pl., Ste. 3600
Detroit, MI 48207
Phone: (313)259-0830
Fax: (313)259-0973
Toll Free: (800)532-1813

Recipient: Teachers. **Number of Certified Individuals:** 81. **Educational/Experience Requirements:** Must meet the following requirements: (1) Bachelor's degree; (2) Three years experience; and (3) Current licensure as teacher or equivalent. **Certification Requirements:** Must meet the following requirements: (1) Submission of school-site portfolio, including student work with teachers' written comments, lesson plans, and videotapes of interaction with a class; and (2) Participation in performance-based assessment center activities, such as simulation, structured interviews, and collegial discussions. Certification planned in all subject areas and the following student developmental levels: Early Childhood (ages 3-8); Middle Childhood (ages 7-12); Early and Middle Childhood (ages 3-12); Early Adolescence (ages 11-15); Adolescence and Young Adulthood (ages 14-18); and Early Adolescence through Young Adulthood (ages 11-18). **Preparatory Materials:** *What Teachers Should Know and Be Able to Do* (reference). List of suggested reference materials provided. **Examination Frequency:** Annual. **Examination Sites:** Assessment held at sites throughout the U.S. **Fees:** $975.

Health Diagnosing Practitioners

Chiropractors

621

Board Certified Thermographer
American Board of Chiropractic
   Thermologists
c/o Phillip L. Smith, DC
318 S. Burnside Ave.
Gonzales, LA 70737
Phone: (504)644-8671
Phillip L. Smith DC, Exec. Officer

Recipient: Thermographers.
Educational/Experience Requirements:
Two years experience, 100 hours of education, and successful completion of 250 studies. Must submit the following types of studies: (1) Cervical with upper extremities (two studies); (2) Lumbar with lower extremities (two studies); and (3) Either cervical or lumbar with extremities (one study). **Certification Requirements:** Successful completion of written and practical exams. Must successfully complete written exam before attempting practical exam. Exams cover: Differential examination; History and physics; Instrumentation; Medicolegal implications; Patient and clinical protocol; Report writing; Theory behind physiology and pathophysiology of human body as related to thermography; and Thermographic evaluation. **Renewal:** Recertification based on attendance at seminar, teaching, or submission of paper. **Endorsed By:** American Chiropractic Association.

622

Board Eligible, American Board of
   Chiropractic Orthopedics
American Board of Chiropractic
   Orthopedics
c/o James Brandt, DC
330 Northdale Blvd.
Coon Rapids, MN 55448
Phone: (612)755-4300
James Brandt DC, Exec. Officer

Recipient: Chiropractors specializing in orthopedics. **Certification Requirements:** Three hundred and sixty hours of education. Must earn Diplomate of the American Board of Chiropractic Orthopedics (DABCO) designation (see separate entry) within four years. **Endorsed By:** American Chiropractic Association.

623

Board Eligible, American
   Chiropractic Board of Nutrition
American Chiropractic Board of
   Nutrition
c/o Donald E. Huml, DC
430 79th St.
Brooklyn, NY 11209
Phone: (718)748-6644
Donald E. Huml DC, Exec. Officer

Recipient: Chiropractors specializing in nutrition. **Certification Requirements:** Three hundred hours of education. Must earn Diplomate of the American Chiropractic Board of Nutrition (DACBN) designation (see separate entry) within three years. **Endorsed By:** American Chiropractic Association.

624

Board Eligible, American
   Chiropractic Board of
   Occupational Health
American Chiropractic Board of
   Occupational Health
c/o David Gilkey, DC
9975 N. Wardsworth Pkwy., Ste. J2
Broomfield, CO 80021
Phone: (303)425-5723
David Gilkey DC, Exec. Officer

Recipient: Chiropractors specializing in occupational health. **Certification Requirements:** Three hundred hours of coursework. Must earn Diplomate of the American Chiropractic Board of Occupational Health (DACBOH) designation (see separate entry). **Endorsed By:** American Chiropractic Association.

625

Board Eligible, American
   Chiropractic Neurology Board
American Chiropractic Neurology
   Board
c/o Stephen Taylor, DC
2720 San Pedro, NE
Albuquerque, NM 87110
Stephen Taylor DC, Exec. Officer

Recipient: Chiropractors specializing in neurology. **Certification Requirements:** Three hundred hours of education. Must earn Diplomate of the American Chiropractic Neurology Board (DACNB) designation (see separate entry). **Endorsed By:** American Chiropractic Association.

`626`

Certified Chiropractic Sports Physician (CCSP)

American Chiropractic Board of Sports Physicians
c/o John G. Scaringe, DC
2740 S. Bristol, Ste. 104
Santa Ana, CA 92704-6232
Phone: (310)947-8755
John G. Scaringe DC, Exec. Officer

Recipient: Chiropractors specializing in sports medicine. **Educational/Experience Requirements:** One hundred hours of education. May qualify for Diplomate of the American Chiropractic Board of Sports Physicians (DACBSP) designation (see separate entry) with more education. **Certification Requirements:** Successful completion of exam. Exam covers: Anatomy; CPR; Evaluation and management; Exercise physiology; Neurology; Pathology; Physiology; and X-ray. **Renewal:** None. **Endorsed By:** American Chiropractic Association.

`627`

Diplomate of the American Board of Chiropractic Internists (DABCI)

American BRD of Chiropractic Internists
c/o Brian K. Wilson, DC
3601 S. Broadway
Englewood, CO 80110
Phone: (303)761-8521
Brian K. Wilson DC, Exec. Officer

Recipient: Chiropractors specializing in internal disorders. **Endorsed By:** American Chiropractic Association

`628`

Diplomate of the American Board of Chiropractic Orthopedics (DABCO)

American Board of Chiropractic Orthopedics
c/o James Brandt, DC
330 Northdale Blvd.
Coon Rapids, MN 55448
Phone: (612)755-4300
James Brandt DC, Exec. Officer

Recipient: Chiropractors specializing in orthopedics. **Educational/Experience Requirements:** Three hundred and sixty hours of education. **Certification Requirements:** Successful completion of exam. **Renewal:** None. **Endorsed By:** American Chiropractic Association.

`629`

Diplomate of the American Chiropractic Board of Nutrition (DACBN)

American Chiropractic Board of Nutrition
c/o Donald E. Huml, DC
430 79th St.
Brooklyn, NY 11209
Phone: (718)748-6644
Donald E. Huml DC, Exec. Officer

Recipient: Chiropractors specializing in nutrition. **Educational/Experience Requirements:** Three hundred hours of education. **Certification Requirements:** Successful completion of exam. Exam covers: Biochemistry and physiology of nutrition; Blood disorders; Cardiovascular-pulmonary disease; Diabetes mellitus and hypoglycemia; Diagnostic evaluation in clinical nutrition; Dietary and nutritional aspects and management of general disease; Dietary and nutritional aspects and management of neuropsychiatric disorders; Disorders of endocrine system and metabolism; Fever and infections; G.I. cavity; Musculoskeletal disorders; Nutrients and their characteristics, functions, and metabolism; Nutrition in infancy, adolescence, pregnancy, and lactation; Nutrition and physiological stress; Nutritional considerations in clinical geriatrics; Oral cavity; Trauma; and Urogenital system. **Renewal:** Recertification required. **Endorsed By:** American Chiropractic Association.

`630`

Diplomate of the American Chiropractic Board of Occupational Health (DACBOH)

American Chiropractic Board of Occupational Health
c/o David Gilkey, DC
9975 N. Wardsworth Pkwy., Ste. J2
Broomfield, CO 80021
Phone: (303)425-5723
David Gilkey DC, Exec. Officer

Recipient: Chiropractors specializing in occupational health. **Educational/Experience Requirements:** Three hundred hours of coursework. **Certification Requirements:** Successful completion of exam. **Renewal:** None. **Endorsed By:** American Chiropractic Association.

`631`

Diplomate of the American Chiropractic Board of Radiology (DACBR)

American Chiropractic Board of Radiology
c/o Gary Casper, DC
6361 Washington Ave.
University City, MO 63130
Phone: (314)726-2939
Gary Casper DC, Exec. Officer

Recipient: Chiropractors specializing in radiology. **Educational/Experience Requirements:** Successful completion of post-graduate program. **Certification Requirements:** Successful completion of written and oral exams. Written exam covers: Abdomen; Head and neck; Menstruation and spinal imaging; Pathology of spine and appendicular skeleton; Physics; Radiation health; and Thorax. Oral exam requires case presentation and film interpretation. **Renewal:** Recertification based on one of the following: (1) Attendance at workshop or CDI symposium; (2) Submission of paper on radiology; or (3) Teaching 12 hours of related education. **Endorsed By:** American Chiropractic Association.

`632`

Diplomate of the American Chiropractic Board of Sports Physicians (DACBSP)

American Chiropractic Board of Sports Physicians
c/o John G. Scaringe, DC
2740 S. Bristol, Ste. 104
Santa Ana, CA 92704-6232
Phone: (310)947-8755
John G. Scaringe DC, Exec. Officer

Recipient: Chiropractors specializing in sports medicine. **Educational/Experience Requirements:** Three hundred hours of education. Candidates with less education may qualify for Certified Chiropractic Sports Physician (CCSP) designation (see separate entry). **Certification Requirements:** Successful completion of exam. Exam covers: Anatomy; CPR; Evaluation and management; Exercise physiology; Neurology; Pathology; Physiology; and X-ray. **Renewal:** Every two years. Recertification based on accumulation of ten continuing education credits. **Endorsed By:** American Chiropractic Association.

633

Diplomate of the American Chiropractic Neurology Board (DACNB)

American Chiropractic Neurology
Board
c/o Stephen Taylor, DC
2720 San Pedro, NE
Albuquerque, NM 87110
Stephen Taylor DC, Exec. Officer

Recipient: Chiropractors specializing in neurology. **Educational/Experience Requirements:** Three hundred hours of education. **Certification Requirements:** Successful completion of exam. **Renewal:** Recertification based on one of the following: (1) 12 hours of coursework in neurology; (2) Publishing of paper; or (3) Successful completion of symposium. **Endorsed By:** American Chiropractic Association.

Dentists

634

Academy of Laser Dentistry, Category I Certification

Academy of Laser Dentistry (ALD)
401 N. Michigan Ave.
Chicago, IL 60611-4267
Phone: (312)644-6610
Fax: (312)321-6869
Nicholas J. Leever, Exec.Dir.

Recipient: Dentists specializing in the use of lasers. **Educational/Experience Requirements:** None. **Certification Requirements:** Successful completion of course. Course covers basic understanding of laser physics and uses of lasers in dentistry.

635

Academy of Laser Dentistry, Category II Certification

Academy of Laser Dentistry (ALD)
401 N. Michigan Ave.
Chicago, IL 60611-4267
Phone: (312)644-6610
Fax: (312)321-6869
Nicholas J. Leever, Exec.Dir.

Recipient: Dentists specializing in the use of lasers. **Educational/Experience Requirements:** Current licensure as dentist. **Certification Requirements:** Successful completion of written and clinical proficiency exams. **Preparatory Materials:** *Curriculum Guidelines and Standards for Dental Laser Education* (reference). List

of suggested references provided. Preparatory courses available. **Examination Frequency:** Throughout the year. **Examination Sites:** Exams given at sites throughout the U.S. **Fees:** $350.

636

Academy of Laser Dentistry, Category III (Master Status) Certification

Academy of Laser Dentistry (ALD)
401 N. Michigan Ave.
Chicago, IL 60611-4267
Phone: (312)644-6610
Fax: (312)321-6869
E-mail: NLEEVER@SBA.COM
Nicholas J. Leever, Exec.Dir.

Recipient: Dentists specializing in the use of lasers. **Number of Certified Individuals:** 43. **Educational/Experience Requirements:** Must meet the following requirements: (1) Hold Academy of Laser Dentistry, Category II Certification (see separate entry); and (2) Current licensure as dentist. **Membership:** Required. **Certification Requirements:** Successful completion of written, clinical proficiency, and oral exams. Written exam covers all wavelengths. Oral exam requires presentation of clinical case studies. **Preparatory Materials:** *Curriculum Guidelines and Standards for Dental Laser Education* and *Essential Elements of Clinical Case Studies* (references). List of suggested references provided. Preparatory courses available. **Examination Frequency:** Annual. **Examination Sites:** Exam given at annual conference. **Pass/Fail Rate:** 97% pass exam. **Waiting Period to Receive Scores:** One week. **Reexamination:** Must wait one year to retake exam. **Fees:** $800.

637

Board Eligible, American Board of Endodontics

American Board of Endodontics (ABE)
211 E. Chicago Ave., Ste. 100
Chicago, IL 60611
Phone: (312)266-7310
Susan Burkhardt, Adm.Sec.

Recipient: Dentists specializing in endodontics. **Certification Requirements:** Must meet the following requirements: (1) Graduation from dental school accredited by Commission on Dental Accreditation (CDA) (see separate entry); (2) Successful completion of two-year training program in endodontics accredited by CDA; and (3) Four years experi-

ence. Must earn Diplomate of the American Board of Endodontics designation (see separate entry) within three years. **Endorsed By:** American Dental Association; Commission on Dental Accreditation; Council on Dental Education.

638

Board Eligible, American Board of Oral and Maxillofacial Surgery

American Board of Oral and
Maxillofacial Surgery (ABOMS)
625 N. Michigan Ave., Ste. 1820
Chicago, IL 60611
Phone: (312)642-0070
Fax: (312)642-8584

Recipient: Dentists specializing in oral and maxillofacial surgery. **Certification Requirements:** Must meet the following requirements: (1) Graduation from U.S. dental school accredited by Commission on Dental Accreditation (CDA) (see separate entry) or foreign dental school providing equivalent educational background; (2) Successful completion of residency in oral and maxillofacial surgery accredited by CDA; (3) Current licensure to practice oral and maxillofacial surgery in the U.S. or documentation of being on active duty with the U.S. Federal Services; (4) Submission of lists of surgical cases performed in last 12 months of residency training program and during last 12 months of practice; (5) Submission of list of 16 surgical cases performed since completion of residency in which candidate actively participated as operating surgeon and had principal responsibility for preoperative, operative, and postoperative care of patient. Cases must be in the following areas: Dentofacial and craniofacial deformities (three cases required); Management of complications (one case required); Management of pathologic conditions (three cases required); Reconstructive surgery (six cases required); and Trauma (three cases required); and (6) One year of post-residency practice, which may be in combination with teaching, research, or advanced education. Foreign applicants who do not practice in U.S. are exempt from this requirement. Must successfully complete written and oral exams to earn Diplomate of the American Board of Oral and Maxillofacial Surgery designation (see separate entry). **Preparatory Materials:** Application booklet provided. **Endorsed By:** American Association of Oral and Maxillofacial Surgeons; American Dental Association.

639

Board Eligible, American Board of Orthodontics

American Board of Orthodontics (ABO)
401 N. Lindbergh Blvd., Ste. 308
St. Louis, MO 63141
Phone: (314)432-6130
Fax: (314)432-8170
Dr. George D. Selfridge DDS, Exec.Dir.

Recipient: Orthodontists. **Educational/ Experience Requirements:** Must meet the following requirements: (1) Doctoral degree from dental school accredited by Council on Dental Education (see separate entry); (2) Successful completion of two-year training program in orthodontics; and (3) Five years restricted practice. **Membership:** Required. **Certification Requirements:** Successful completion of exam. Exam may cover: (1) Histology, including: Applied; General; and Oral; (2) Pathology, including: Applied; General; and Oral; (3) Embryology, Growth, and Development, including: Craniofacial; and Dental; (4) Genetics, including: Applied; Cellular; Chemical; and Descriptive; (5) Anatomy, including: Applied; Comparative; Dental; General; Head and neck; and Oral; (6) Microbiology, including: Antibiotics; Bacteriology; Disinfection; Immunology; Infection; Sterilization; and Virology; (7) Biochemistry, including: Applied; and General; (8) Physiology, including: Applied; and General; (9) Dental Materials, including: Adhesives; Cements; Metals; Polymers; and Other materials; (10) Bio-Mechanics, including: Force systems; Orthodontic appliances; and Physics of tooth movement; (11) Statistics, including: Descriptive; Inferential; and Research methodology; (12) Orthognathic Surgery, including: Anatomy; Orthodontic diagnosis; Orthodontic treatment; and Surgical procedures; (13) Occlusion, Temporomandibular Joint, and Gnathology, including: Applied; Diagnosis; and Theory; (14) Orthodontics, including: Biometrics; Case analysis; Diagnosis; Mechanotherapy; Objectives; Retention; Stability; and Treatment plan; (15) Endodontics, including: Differential diagnosis of facial pain; Emergencies; and Orthodontic application; (16) Speech Pathology, including: Cleft plate; Theory; and Treatment: myofunctional therapy; (17) Psychology and Behavioral Sciences, including: Applied: child, adolescent, and adult; Patient management and cooperation; and Theory; (18) Periodontics, including: Disease; Occlusal trauma; Therapy; and Theory; and (19) Mixed Dentition, including: Early treatment; Functional considerations, cross bite correction; Habit control, open bite correction; Interceptive guidance; and Trauma. Must earn Diplomate of the American Board of Orthodontics designation (see separate entry) within ten years. **Renewal:** None. **Preparatory Materials:** Manual, including exam content outline and case report requirements, provided. **Examination Frequency:** Annual. **Examination Sites:** Exam given at annual session and at sites throughout the U.S. **Examination Type:** Multiple-choice. **Waiting Period to Receive Scores:** Seven-ten working days. **Endorsed By:** American Association of Orthodontists; American Dental Association.

640

Board Eligible, American Board of Pediatric Dentistry

American Board of Pediatric Dentistry (ABPD)
1193 Woodgate Dr.
Carmel, IN 46033-9232
Phone: (317)573-0877
Fax: (317)846-7235
James R. Roche D.D.S., Exec.Sec.-Treas.

Recipient: Dentists specializing in pediatric dentistry. **Educational/Experience Requirements:** Must meet the following requirements: (1) Graduation from dental program accredited by Commission on Dental Accreditation (CDA) (see separate entry); and (2) Successful completion of two-year training program in pediatric dentistry accredited by CDA. **Certification Requirements:** Successful completion of exam. Must earn Diplomate of the American Board of Pediatric Dentistry designation (see separate entry) within eight years. **Preparatory Materials:** List of suggested study references provided. **Examination Frequency:** Annual. **Examination Sites:** Exam given at sites throughout the U.S. **Re-examination:** Must only retake sections failed. Retake fee is $100. **Fees:** $200. **Endorsed By:** American Academy of Pediatric Dentistry; American Dental Association; Commission on Dental Accreditation; Council on Dental Education.

641

Board Eligible, American Board of Periodontology

American Board of Periodontology (ABP)
c/o Gerald M. Bowers, D.D.S.
University of Maryland
Baltimore Coll. of Dental Surgery
666 W. Baltimore St., Rm. 3-C-08
Baltimore, MD 21201
Phone: (410)706-2432
Fax: (410)706-0074
Gerald M. Bowers D.D.S., Exec. Sec.-Treas.

Recipient: Dentists specializing in periodontology. **Educational/Experience Requirements:** Must meet the following requirements: (1) Graduation from dental school accredited by Commission on Dental Accreditation (CDA) (see separate entry); and (2) Successful completion of advanced educational program in periodontics accredited by CDA. **Certification Requirements:** Successful completion of exam. Exam covers: Basic sciences; Clinical practice; Oral medicine; Oral pathology; Periodontal histology and pathology; and Periodontal literature. Must earn Diplomate of the American Board of Periodontology designation (see separate entry) within six years. **Examination Frequency:** Annual. **Examination Sites:** Exam given at annual meeting. **Examination Type:** Multiple-choice. **Re-examination:** Fee to retake exam is $450. **Fees:** $900. **Endorsed By:** American Academy of Periodontology; American Dental Association.

642

Board Eligible, American Board of Prosthodontics

American Board of Prosthodontics
PO Box 8437
Atlanta, GA 30306
Dr. William D. Culpepper, Exec. Dir.

Recipient: Dentists specializing in prosthodontics. **Certification Requirements:** Successful completion of advanced education program of two years or more in length accredited by Commission on Dental Accreditation (see separate entry). Must earn Diplomate of the American Board of Prosthodontics designation (see separate entry) within six years. **Endorsed By:** Academy of Prosthodontics; American Academy of Maxillofacial Prosthetics; American College of Prosthodontics; American Dental Association; American Prosthetics Society; Federation of Prosthodontic Organizations.

| 643 |

Certified Dental Consultant

American Association of Dental
Consultants (AADC)
919 Deer Park Ave.
North Babylon, NY 11703
Phone: (516)587-5049
Fax: (913)749-1140
Toll Free: (800)896-0707
Dr. Alan M. Helerstein MPA, Sec.-Treas.

Recipient: Dental consultants for insurance carriers, self-insured plans, administrators, or commercial consulting entities. **Membership:** Required. **Certification Requirements:** Successful completion of exam. **Endorsed By:** Must meet the following requirements: (1) Ten years experience in clinical practice of dentistry; (2) Retention as consultant for five years; (3) Attendance at two out of three spring workshops held immediately prior to year of taking exam; and (4) Active membership in AADC for two years.

| 644 |

Diplomate of the American Board of Dental Public Health

American Board of Dental Public
Health
1321 NW 47th Terrace
Gainesville, FL 32605
Phone: (904)378-6301
Dr. Stanley Lotzkar D.D.S., Exec. Sec.

Recipient: Dentists involved in public health dentistry. **Educational/Experience Requirements:** Graduate from accredited school of dentistry in U.S. or Canada, four years experience in health or preventive medicine, and two years advanced educational preparation earned through successful completion of one of the following: (1) One year program accredited by Council on Education for Public Health (see separate entry) leading to graduate degree in public health, and residency in dental public health; (2) Two year program accredited by Commission on Dental Accreditation (see separate entry) leading to graduate degree in public health; or (3) Two years of advanced education in dental public health from non-accredited program and residency program. **Membership:** Not required. **Certification Requirements:** Successful completion of two-part exam. First part consists of two project reports. **Examination Frequency:** Annual. **Examination Sites:** Exam given at one site every year. **Re-examination:** May retake exam one time. There is a $100 fee to

retake exam. **Fees:** $350. **Endorsed By:** American Association of Public Health Dentistry; American Dental Association.

| 645 |

Diplomate of the American Board of Endodontics

American Board of Endodontics
(ABE)
211 E. Chicago Ave., Ste. 100
Chicago, IL 60611
Phone: (312)266-7310
Susan Burkhardt, Adm.Sec.

Recipient: Dentists specializing in endodontics. **Educational/Experience Requirements:** Must meet the following requirements: (1) Graduation from dental school accredited by Commission on Dental Accreditation (CDA) (see separate entry); (2) Successful completion of two-year training program in endodontics accredited by CDA; and (3) Four years experience. **Certification Requirements:** Successful completion of written and oral exams and submission of 20 clinical case reports. Written exam covers: Anatomy; Biochemistry; Biostatistics; Clinical endodontics; Dental materials; Embryology; General and oral pathology; Immunology; Inflammation; Microanatomy; Microbiology; Oral medicine; Pharmacology; Pupal and periradicular pathobiology; Radiology; Related dental disciplines; and Vascular and neurophysiology. Lifetime certification available for retired Diplomates. **Preparatory Materials:** *Standards for Advanced Specialty Education Programs in Endodontics* (reference). **Examination Frequency:** Annual - always spring (oral) and fall (written). **Re-examination:** May retake exams and submit case portfolios two times. Must successfully complete all requirements within three years. Retake fees are: $100 (written); $250 (case reports and oral exam). **Fees:** $1000. **Endorsed By:** American Dental Association; Commission on Dental Accreditation; Council on Dental Education.

| 646 |

Diplomate of the American Board of Oral and Maxillofacial Surgery

American Board of Oral and
Maxillofacial Surgery (ABOMS)
625 N. Michigan Ave., Ste. 1820
Chicago, IL 60611
Phone: (312)642-0070
Fax: (312)642-8584

Recipient: Dentists specializing in oral

and maxillofacial surgery. **Educational/Experience Requirements:** Must meet the following requirements: (1) Graduation from U.S. dental school accredited by Commission on Dental Accreditation (CDA) (see separate entry) or foreign dental school providing equivalent educational background; (2) Successful completion of residency in oral and maxillofacial surgery accredited by CDA; (3) Current licensure to practice oral and maxillofacial surgery in the U.S. or documentation of being on active duty with the U.S. Federal Services; (4) Submission of lists of surgical cases performed in last 12 months of residency training program and during last 12 months of practice; (5) Submission of list of 16 surgical cases performed since completion of residency in which candidate actively participated as operating surgeon and had principal responsibility for preoperative, operative, and postoperative care of patient. Cases must be in the following areas: Dentofacial and craniofacial deformities (three cases required); Management of complications (one case required); Management of pathologic conditions (three cases required); Reconstructive surgery (six cases required); and Trauma (three cases required); and (6) One year of post-residency practice, which may be in combination with teaching, research, or advanced education. Foreign applicants who do not practice in U.S. are exempt from this requirement. **Certification Requirements:** Successful completion of written and oral exams. Exams cover biological sciences and clinical practice of oral and maxillofacial surgery. Oral exam consists of two parts: (1) Comprehensive Oral Exam; and (2) Case Defenses, including defense of five cases submitted by candidate. Candidates hold Board Eligible, American Board of Oral and Maxillofacial Surgery designation (see separate entry) prior to successful completion of exams. **Renewal:** Every ten years. Recertification based on successful completion of exam. **Preparatory Materials:** Application booklet provided. **Re-examination:** May retake written exam twice and oral exam three times. Must only retake part of oral exam failed. Must successfully complete written exam within two years and oral exam within three years. **Endorsed By:** American Association of Oral and Maxillofacial Surgeons; American Dental Association.

159

647

Diplomate of the American Board of Oral Pathology

American Board of Oral Pathology (ABOP)
One Urban Centre, Ste. 690
4830 W. Kennedy Blvd.
PO Box 25915
Tampa, FL 33622-5915
Phone: (813)286-2444
Fax: (813)289-5279

Recipient: Oral pathologists. **Educational/Experience Requirements:** Must meet the following requirements: (1) Successful completion of advanced training program in oral pathology approved by Council on Dental Education (see separate entry); and (2) Five years combined education and experience. **Certification Requirements:** Successful completion of exam. Exam covers: Anatomy; Basic biological sciences; Clinical pathology; Cytology; Oncology; Oral diagnosis; Oral pathology; Oral and systemic diseases; Pathology; Surgical pathology; and Radiology. **Renewal:** Recertification required. **Examination Frequency:** Throughout the year. **Reexamination:** Must wait one year to retake exam. May retake exam once. Must successfully complete exam within five years. There is a fee to retake exam. **Endorsed By:** American Academy of Oral Pathologists.

648

Diplomate of the American Board of Orthodontics

American Board of Orthodontics (ABO)
401 N. Lindbergh Blvd., Ste. 308
St. Louis, MO 63141
Phone: (314)432-6130
Fax: (314)432-8170
Dr. George D. Selfridge DDS, Exec.Dir.

Recipient: Orthodontists. **Number of Certified Individuals:** 1799. **Educational/Experience Requirements:** Must meet the following requirements: (1) Doctoral degree from dental school accredited by Council on Dental Education (see separate entry); (2) Successful completion of two-year training program in orthodontics; and (3) Five years restricted practice. **Membership:** Required. **Certification Requirements:** Successful completion of written and clinical/oral exams. Written exam may cover: (1) Histology, including: Applied; General; and Oral; (2) Pathology, including: Applied; General; and Oral; (3) Embryology, Growth, and Development, including: Craniofacial; and Dental; (4) Genetics, including: Applied; Cellular; Chemical; and Descriptive; (5) Anatomy, including: Applied; Comparative; Dental; General; Head and neck; and Oral; (6) Microbiology, including: Antibiotics; Bacteriology; Disinfection; Immunology; Infection; Sterilization; and Virology; (7) Biochemistry, including: Applied; and General; (8) Physiology, including: Applied; and General; (9) Dental Materials, including: Adhesives; Cements; Metals; Polymers; and Other materials; (10) Bio-Mechanics, including: Force systems; Orthodontic appliances; and Physics of tooth movement; (11) Statistics, including: Descriptive; Inferential; and Research methodology; (12) Orthognathic Surgery, including: Anatomy; Orthodontic diagnosis; Orthodontic treatment; and Surgical procedures; (13) Occlusion, Temporomandibular Joint, and Gnathology, including: Applied; Diagnosis; and Theory; (14) Orthodontics, including: Biometrics; Case analysis; Diagnosis; Mechanotherapy; Objectives; Retention; Stability; and Treatment plan; (15) Endodontics, including: Differential diagnosis of facial pain; Emergencies; and Orthodontic application; (16) Speech Pathology, including: Cleft plate; Theory; and Treatment: myofunctional therapy; (17) Psychology and Behavioral Sciences, including: Applied: child, adolescent, and adult; Patient management and cooperation; and Theory; (18) Periodontics, including: Disease; Occlusal trauma; Therapy; and Theory; and (19) Mixed Dentition, including: Early treatment; Functional considerations, cross bite correction; Habit control, open bite correction; Interceptive guidance; and Trauma. Oral exam includes discussion of cases provided by ABO and candidate, including cases in the following areas: Adult malocclusion; Class I malocclusion; Class II Division 1 Malocclusion; Class II Division 2 malocclusion; Early treatment malocclusion; Severe skeletal discrepancy; and Significant transverse discrepancy. Oral exam covers: Alignment of permanent second molars; Complete space closure; Coordinated ideal arciform; Dental health; Excellent occlusion; Facial harmony; Favorable axial inclination of all teeth; Favorable correction of rotations of all teeth; Favorable intercuspation of teeth free of interferences and trauma; Favorable overjet and overbite relationship; Good stability; Good vertical control; Maximum esthetics of teeth and face; Optimal function; and Treatment complementing facial growth. **Renewal:** None. **Preparatory Materials:** Manual, including written exam content outline and case report requirements, provided. **Examination Frequency:** Annual - always February/March (oral exam). **Examination Sites:** Written exam given at annual session and at sites throughout the U.S. Oral exam given at ABO headquarters. **Examination Type:** Multiple-choice. **Waiting Period to Receive Scores:** Seven-ten working days. **Fees:** $930. **Endorsed By:** American Association of Orthodontists; American Dental Association.

649

Diplomate of the American Board of Pediatric Dentistry

American Board of Pediatric Dentistry (ABPD)
1193 Woodgate Dr.
Carmel, IN 46033-9232
Phone: (317)573-0877
Fax: (317)846-7235
James R. Roche D.D.S., Exec.Sec.-Treas.

Recipient: Dentists specializing in pediatric dentistry. **Educational/Experience Requirements:** Must meet the following requirements: (1) Graduation from dental program accredited by Commission on Dental Accreditation (CDA) (see separate entry); and (2) Successful completion of two-year training program in pediatric dentistry accredited by CDA. **Certification Requirements:** Successful completion of qualifying, general and applied knowledge, and clinical exams. Qualifying exam covers current references in the field. General and applied knowledge exam covers recognition and decision-making regarding various clinical conditions, diagnosis, treatment planning, and patient care. Clinical exam can be completed through site visit or review of four cases. Cases chosen for review should be from the following categories: (1) Trauma; (2) Periodontal therapy; (3) Management of a malocclusion; (4) Restorative therapy under sedation or general anesthesia; and (5) Restorative therapy for child with special health care needs. **Renewal:** Every ten years. Recertification based on successful completion of exam. **Preparatory Materials:** List of suggested study references provided. **Examination Frequency:** Annual. **Examination Sites:** Exam given at sites throughout the U.S. **Re-examination:** There is no limit to how many times exam may be retaken. Retake fees are: $100 (general); $500 (general and applied); $500 (case review); $1000 (site visit). **Fees:** $1200 (case review option); $1700 (site visit option). **Endorsed By:** American Academy of Pediatric Dentistry; American Dental Association; Commission on Dental Accreditation; Council on Dental Education.

650

Diplomate of the American Board of Periodontology
American Board of Periodontology (ABP)
c/o Gerald M. Bowers, D.D.S.
University of Maryland
Baltimore Coll. of Dental Surgery
666 W. Baltimore St., Rm. 3-C-08
Baltimore, MD 21201
Phone: (410)706-2432
Fax: (410)706-0074
Gerald M. Bowers D.D.S., Exec. Sec.-Treas.

Recipient: Dentists specializing in periodontology. **Educational/Experience Requirements:** Must meet the following requirements: (1) Graduation from dental school accredited by Commission on Dental Accreditation (CDA) (see separate entry); and (2) Successful completion of advanced educational program in periodontics accredited by CDA. **Certification Requirements:** Successful completion of written and oral exams. Written exam covers: Basic sciences; Clinical practice; Oral medicine; Oral pathology; Periodontal histology and pathology; and Periodontal literature. Oral exam requires defense of two case reports submitted by candidate and covers: Consideration of alternate choices of therapy; Diagnosis of periodontal, other dental, and extra-oral conditions; Documentation and presentation; Establishment of maintenance program; Etiology; Evaluation of results; Intra- and extra-oral findings; Management of hypothetical clinical situations; Medical and dental history; Occlusal and dental assessment; Patient management; Periodontal clinical and radiographic evaluation; Prognosis determination; Therapy provided; and Treatment plan. Candidates hold Board Eligible, American Board of Periodontology designation (see separate entry) prior to successful completion of oral exam. **Renewal:** Every three years. Recertification based on professional development activities. **Examination Frequency:** Annual. **Examination Sites:** Written exam given at annual meeting. Oral exam given at one site in the U.S. **Examination Type:** Multiple-choice. **Re-examination:** Fees to retake exams are: $450 (written); $500 (oral). **Fees:** $1400. **Endorsed By:** American Academy of Periodontology; American Dental Association.

651

Diplomate of the American Board of Prosthodontics
American Board of Prosthodontics
PO Box 8437
Atlanta, GA 30306
Dr. William D. Culpepper, Exec. Dir.

Recipient: Dentists specializing in prosthodontics. **Educational/Experience Requirements:** Must meet the following requirements: (1) Successful completion of advanced education program of two years or more in length accredited by Commission on Dental Accreditation (see separate entry); and (2) Four years experience. **Certification Requirements:** Successful completion of five-part exam. Exam consists of written, patient presentation, and oral sections. Exam covers: Fixed prosthodontics; Implant prosthodontics; Maxillofacial prosthetics; Occlusion; Related arts and sciences; and Removable prosthodontics. **Examination Frequency:** Annual - always February (parts one and two of exam) and June (parts three-five of exam). **Re-examination:** Must only retake parts failed. May retake each part two times. Fee to retake each part of exam is $200. **Fees:** $1150. **Endorsed By:** Academy of Prosthodontics; American Academy of Maxillofacial Prosthetics; American College of Prosthodontics; American Dental Association; American Prosthetics Society; Federation of Prosthodontic Organizations.

Physicians

652

Added Qualifications in Neuroradiology of the American Board of Radiology
American Board of Radiology (ABR)
5255 E. Williams Circle, Ste. 6800
Tucson, AZ 85711
Phone: (520)790-2900
Fax: (520)790-3200
M. Paul Capp M.D., Exec.Dir.

Recipient: Radiologists specializing in neuroradiology. **Educational/Experience Requirements:** Must meet the following requirements: (1) Hold either Diplomate in Radiology or Diagnostic Radiology of the American Board of Radiology (see separate entries); (2) Successfully complete one year of practice or training in neuroradiology; and (3) Either successfully complete one year fellowship in neuroradiology or five years of practice experience, with one-third of time devoted to neuroradiology. Experience must include: Angiograms (selected carotid/vertebral, 150 cases); Myelograms (50 cases); and Computed topography and magnetic resonance imaging of the head, neck, and spine (7500 cases). Experience can include: Actual performance and interpretation of examinations and procedures; Attendance at related conferences; Consultation with referring physicians; and Pre- and post-procedure visits with patients. **Certification Requirements:** Successful completion of oral exam. Exam covers: (1) Brain and Its Coverings, including: Degenerative disease/dementia; Extra-axial; Intra-axial; Trauma; and Vascular; (2) Skull Base and ENT, including: Larynx and thyroid; Oral cavity and oropharynx; Orbit; Pituitary; Sinuses/nasal cavity; and Temporal bone; and (3) Spine, including: Congenital malformations; Degenerative disease; Disc disease; Epidural disease; Intradural disease; Trauma; and Vascular malformations. **Renewal:** Every ten years. **Examination Frequency:** Annual. **Re-examination:** Must wait one year to retake exam. May retake exam twice. **Endorsed By:** American Association of Physicists in Medicine; American Board of Medical Specialties; American College of Radiology; American Medical Association; American Radium Society; American Roentgen Ray Society; American Society for Therapeutic Radiology and Oncology; Association of University Radiologists; Council on Medical Education; Radiological Society of North America.

653

Added Qualifications in Pediatric Radiology of the American Board of Radiology
American Board of Radiology (ABR)
5255 E. Williams Circle, Ste. 6800
Tucson, AZ 85711
Phone: (520)790-2900
Fax: (520)790-3200
M. Paul Capp M.D., Exec.Dir.

Recipient: Radiologists specializing in pediatric radiology. **Educational/Experience Requirements:** Must meet the following requirements: (1) Hold either Diplomate in Radiology or Diagnostic Radiology of the American Board of Radiology (see separate entries); (2) Successfully complete one year of training in pediatric radiology following completion of residency; (3) Successfully complete one year of practice or training in pediatric radiology; and (4) Either successfully complete one year fellowship in pediatric radiology program accredited by Accreditation Council for Graduate Medical Education (see separate entry) or five years of practice experience, with one-third of time devoted to pediatric radiology. **Certification Requirements:** Successful completion of oral exam. Exam covers: (1) Chest, Cardiac, Facial Bones, ENT, and Airway, including: Airway, tongue, and nasopharynx; Cardiovascular (in chest); Facial bones, sinuses, and mastoids; and Lungs and chest wall; (2) Musculoskeletal, Spine, and CNS, including: Brain and skull; Musculoskeletal; and Spine; and (3) GI, GU, and Interventional, including: Colon and general abdominal problems; Duodenum and small bowel; Esophagus and stomach; Kidney; Liver, spleen, and pancreas; Ureter and bladder; Urethra, genital, and adrenal; and Vascular and interventional. **Renewal:** Every ten years. **Examination Frequency:** Annual. **Re-examination:** Must wait one year to retake exam. **Endorsed By:** American Association of Physicists in Medicine; American Board of Medical Specialties; American College of Radiology; American Medical Association; American Radium Society; American Roentgen Ray Society; American Society for Therapeutic Radiology and Oncology; Association of University Radiologists; Council on Medical Education; Radiological Society of North America.

`654`

American Board of Family Practice Certificate of Added Qualification in Geriatric Medicine

American Board of Family Practice (ABFP)
2228 Young Dr.
Lexington, KY 40505-4294
Phone: (606)269-5626
Fax: (606)266-9699
Dr. Paul R. Young, Exec.Dir.

Recipient: Physicians specializing in family practice with expertise in care of the elderly. **Educational/Experience Requirements:** Must meet the following requirements: (1) Hold Diplomate of the American Board of Family Practice designation (see separate entry); (2) Current unrestricted licensure to practice medicine in the U.S. or Canada; and (3) Successfully complete two years of formal training in geriatric medicine accredited by Accreditation Council for Graduate Medical Education (see separate entry). **Certification Requirements:** Successful completion of exam. Exam covers clinical situations involving: Diagnosis; Natural history of diseases; Prognosis and

etiology; and Treatment. Interpretations of physiologic data, electrocardiograms, and imaging studies used in caring for geriatric patients may be required. **Renewal:** Every ten years. **Examination Frequency:** biennial - always even numbered years. **Examination Type:** Multiple-choice; true or false. **Endorsed By:** American Board of Internal Medicine; American Board of Medical Specialties; American Medical Association; Council on Medical Education.

`655`

American Board of Family Practice Certificate of Added Qualification in Sports Medicine

American Board of Family Practice (ABFP)
2228 Young Dr.
Lexington, KY 40505-4294
Phone: (606)269-5626
Fax: (606)266-9699
Dr. Paul R. Young, Exec.Dir.

Recipient: Physicians specializing in family practice with expertise in sports medicine. **Educational/Experience Requirements:** Hold Diplomate of the American Board of Family Practice designation (see separate entry), current unrestricted licensure to practice medicine in the U.S. or Canada, and one of the following: (1) Successfully complete one year sports medicine fellowship program associated with residency in emergency medicine, family practice, internal medicine, or pediatrics accredited by Accreditation Council for Graduate Medical Education (see separate entry); or (2) Thirty hours of approved continuing medical education related to sports medicine in last five years and five years practice experience consisting of at least twenty percent of time devoted to sports medicine in one of the following areas: Diagnosis, treatment, management, and disposition of common sports injuries and illness; Emergency assessment and care of acutely injured athletes; Exercise as treatment; Field supervision of athletes; Management of medical problems in the athlete; and Rehabilitation of ill and injured athletes. **Certification Requirements:** Successful completion of exam. Exam covers: Anatomy related to exercise; Basic and nutritional principles and their application to exercise; Effects of disease on exercise and use of exercise in care of medical problems; Ethical principles as applied to exercise and sports; Functioning as team physician; Growth and development related to exercise; Guidelines of evaluation prior to participation in exercise; Medical-legal aspects of exercise and sports; Pathology and pathophysiology of

illness and injury as it relates to exercise; Physical conditioning requirements for various activities; Physiology and biomechanics of exercise; Prevention, evaluation, management, and rehabilitation of injuries; Promotion of physical fitness and healthy lifestyles; Psychological aspect of exercise, performance, and competition; and Understanding pharmacology and effects of therapeutic, performance-enhancing, and recreational drugs. **Renewal:** Every ten years. **Examination Frequency:** biennial - always even numbered years. **Examination Sites:** Exam given at sites throughout the U.S. **Fees:** $550. **Endorsed By:** American Board of Emergency Medicine; American Board of Internal Medicine; American Board of Medical Specialties; American Board of Pediatrics; American Medical Association; Council on Medical Education.

`656`

Board Eligible, American Board of Anesthesiology

American Board of Anesthesiology (ABA)
100 Constitution Plaza
Hartford, CT 06103-1796
Phone: (203)522-9857
Fax: (203)522-6626
Francis P. Hughes Ph.D., Exec.Sec.

Recipient: Anesthesiologists. **Certification Requirements:** Must meet the following requirements: (1) Graduation from medical school in U.S. or Canada accredited by Liaison Committee for Medical Education (see separate entry) or Committee on Accreditation of Canadian Medical Schools, or school of osteopathic medicine accredited by Bureau of Professional Education, American Osteopathic Association (see separate entry); (2) Current unrestricted license to practice medicine; and (3) Successful completion of residency program accredited by Accreditation Council for Graduate Medical Education (see separate entry). Graduates of medical schools outside the U.S. or Canada must have certificate from Educational Commission for Foreign Medical Graduates or documentation of training for those who entered post-doctoral medical training via Fifth Pathway of the American Medical Association. Must earn Diplomate of the American Board of Anesthesia designation (see separate entry). **Endorsed By:** American Board of Medical Specialties; American Medical Association; American Society of Anesthesiologists; Council on Medical Education.

657

Board Eligible, American Board of Internal Medicine
American Board of Internal
Medicine (ABIM)
3624 Market St.
Philadelphia, PA 19104-2675
Phone: (215)243-1500
Fax: (215)382-4702
Toll Free: (800)441-ABIM

Recipient: Physicians specializing in internal medicine. **Certification Requirements:** Must meet the following requirements: (1) Graduation from medical school accredited by Liaison Committee on Medical Education (see separate entry) or Committee for Accreditation of Canadian Medical Schools, or osteopathic medical school accredited by Bureau of Professional Education, American Osteopathic Association (see separate entry); (2) Current unrestricted licensure to practice medicine in the U.S. or Canada; and (3) Successful completion of three-year residency program accredited by Accreditation Council for Graduate Medical Education (ACGME) (see separate entry). Clinical Investigators may qualify for certification by meeting the following requirements: (1) Successful completion of two-year residency program accredited by ACGME; and (2) Two years of research during which 80 percent of time dedicated to investigative activities. Graduates of foreign medical schools must have credentials evaluated by Educational Commission for Foreign Medical Graduates or successfully complete postdoctoral medical training in the U.S. via the "Fifth Pathway" plan of the American Medical Association. Must successfully complete exam to earn Diplomate of the American Board of Internal Medicine designation (see separate entry) within six years. **Preparatory Materials:** *Policies and Procedures for Certification in Internal Medicine,* including list of suggested study references, provided. **Endorsed By:** American Board of Medical Specialties; American Medical Association; Council on Medical Education.

658

Board Eligible, American Osteopathic Board of Anesthesiology
American Osteopathic Board of
Anesthesiology
17201 E. U.S. Hwy. 40, Ste. 204
Independence, MO 64055
Phone: (816)373-4700
Toll Free: (800)842-2622
Diann Hubbard, Corres.Sec.

Recipient: Osteopathic physicians specializing in anesthesiology. **Membership:** Required. **Certification Requirements:** Must meet the following requirements: (1) Graduation from college of osteopathic medicine accredited by Bureau of Professional Education, American Osteopathic Association (see separate entry); (2) Current licensure to practice medicine; (3) Two years of membership in either American Osteopathic Association or Canadian Osteopathic Association; (4) Successful completion of internship accredited by Council on Postdoctoral Training of the American Osteopathic Association (see separate entry); (5) Successful completion of three-year residency in anesthesiology accredited by Council on Postdoctoral Training of the American Osteopathic Association; (6) Practice in anesthesiology subsequent to successful completion of residency; (7) Submission of list of anesthetic procedures; (8) Submission of case reports of anesthetics administered; and (9) Submission of list and discussion of mortalities. Must earn Diplomate of the American Osteopathic Board of Anesthesiology designation (see separate entry) within six years. **Endorsed By:** American Osteopathic Association; American Osteopathic College of Anesthesiologists; Bureau of Osteopathic Specialists.

659

Board Eligible, American Osteopathic Board of Dermatology
American Osteopathic Board of
Dermatology (AOBD)
25510 Plymouth Rd.
Redford, MI 48239
Phone: (313)937-1200
Thomas H. Bonino D.O., Sec.-
Treas.

Recipient: Osteopathic physicians specializing in dermatology. **Membership:** Required. **Certification Requirements:** Must meet the following requirements: (1) Graduation from college of osteopathic medicine accredited by Bureau of Professional Education, American Osteopathic Association (see separate entry); (2) Current licensure to practice medicine; (3) Two years of membership in either American Osteopathic Association or Canadian Osteopathic Association; (4) Successful completion of internship accredited by Council on Postdoctoral Training of the American Osteopathic Association (see separate entry); and (5) Successful completion of three-year residency in dermatology accredited by Council on Postdoctoral Training of the American Osteopathic Association. Must

earn Diplomate of the American Board of Osteopathic Dermatology designation (see separate entry) within six years. **Endorsed By:** American Osteopathic Association; Bureau of Osteopathic Specialists.

660

Board Eligible, American Osteopathic Board of Emergency Medicine
American Osteopathic Board of
Emergency Medicine (AOBEM)
142 E. Ontario St., Ste. 217
Chicago, IL 60611
Phone: (312)335-1065
Fax: (312)335-5489
Toll Free: (800)847-0057
Josette Fleming, Admin.

Recipient: Osteopathic physicians specializing in emergency medicine. **Membership:** Required. **Certification Requirements:** Must meet the following requirements: (1) Graduation from college of osteopathic medicine accredited by Bureau of Professional Education, American Osteopathic Association (see separate entry); (2) Current licensure to practice medicine; (3) Two years of membership in either American Osteopathic Association or Canadian Osteopathic Association; (4) Successful completion of one year internship accredited by Council on Postdoctoral Training of the American Osteopathic Association (see separate entry); (5) Successful completion of three year residency in emergency medicine accredited by Council on Postdoctoral Training of the American Osteopathic Association; and (6) Seven years practice of emergency medicine, including one year of post-residency practice. Experience may include: Administration; Clinical practice in 24-hour emergency facility; and Teaching. Must earn Diplomate of the American Board of Osteopathic Emergency Medicine designation (see separate entry) within six years. **Endorsed By:** American Osteopathic Association; Bureau of Osteopathic Specialists.

661

Board Eligible, American Osteopathic Board of Family Practice
American Osteopathic Board of
Family Practice (AOBFP)
330 E. Algonquin Rd., Ste 2
Arlington Heights, IL 60005
Phone: (708)640-8477
Carol A. Tomba MBA, Exec.Dir.

Recipient: Osteopathic physicians specializing in family practice. **Membership:** Required. **Certification Requirements:** Must meet the following requirements: (1) Graduation from college of osteopathic medicine accredited by Bureau of Professional Education, American Osteopathic Association (see separate entry); (2) Current licensure to practice medicine; (3) Two years of membership in American Osteopathic Association; (4) Successful completion of one year internship accredited by Council on Postdoctoral Training of the American Osteopathic Association (see separate entry); and (5) Successful completion of two year residency in family practice accredited by Council on Postdoctoral Training of the American Osteopathic Association. Must earn Diplomate of the American Osteopathic Board of Family Practice designation (see separate entry) within six years. **Endorsed By:** American College of Osteopathic Family Physicians; American Osteopathic Association; Bureau of Osteopathic Specialists.

662

Board Eligible, American Osteopathic Board of Internal Medicine
American Osteopathic Board of
   Internal Medicine
5200 S. Ellis Ave.
Chicago, IL 60615
Phone: (312)947-4881
Gary L. Slick D.O., Exec.Dir.

Recipient: Osteopathic physicians specializing in internal medicine. **Membership:** Required. **Certification Requirements:** Must meet the following requirements: (1) Graduation from college of osteopathic medicine accredited by Bureau of Professional Education, American Osteopathic Association (see separate entry); (2) Current licensure to practice medicine; (3) Two years of membership in either American Osteopathic Association or Canadian Osteopathic Association; (4) Successful completion of internship accredited by Council on Postdoctoral Training of the American Osteopathic Association (see separate entry); and (5) Successful completion of residency in internal medicine accredited by Council on Postdoctoral Training of the American Osteopathic Association. Must earn Diplomate of the American Osteopathic Board of Internal Medicine designation (see separate entry) within six years. **Endorsed By:** American Osteopathic Association; Bureau of Osteopathic Specialists.

663

Board Eligible, American Osteopathic Board of Nuclear Medicine
American Osteopathic Board of
   Nuclear Medicine
5200 S. Ellis Ave.
Chicago, IL 60615
Phone: (312)947-4490
George T. Caleel D.O., Sec.-Treas.

Recipient: Osteopathic physicians specializing in nuclear medicine. **Membership:** Required. **Certification Requirements:** Must meet the following requirements: (1) Graduation from college of osteopathic medicine accredited by Bureau of Professional Education, American Osteopathic Association (see separate entry); (2) Current licensure to practice medicine; (3) Two years of membership in either American Osteopathic Association or Canadian Osteopathic Association; (4) Successful completion of one year internship accredited by Council on Postdoctoral Training of the American Osteopathic Association; and (5) Either certification in internal medicine, pathology, or radiology from board affiliated with Bureau of Osteopathic Specialists and successful completion of one year residency in nuclear medicine or successful completion of two year residency in nuclear medicine. Residencies must be accredited by Council on Postdoctoral Training of the American Osteopathic Association (see separate entry). Alternate combinations of education and training may be considered on individual basis. Must earn Diplomate of the American Osteopathic Board of Nuclear Medicine designation (see separate entry) within six years. **Endorsed By:** American College of Osteopathic Internists; American Osteopathic Association; American Osteopathic Board of Internal Medicine; American Osteopathic Board of Pathology; American Osteopathic Board of Radiology; American Osteopathic College of Pathologists; American Osteopathic College of Radiology; Bureau of Osteopathic Specialists.

664

Board Eligible, American Osteopathic Board of Obstetrics and Gynecology
American Osteopathic Board of
   Obstetrics and Gynecology
   (AOBOG)
5200 S. Ellis Ave.
Chicago, IL 60615
Phone: (312)947-4630
Joseph P. Bonanno D.O., Sec.-
Treas.

Recipient: Osteopathic physicians specializing in obstetrics and gynecology. **Membership:** Required. **Certification Requirements:** Must meet the following requirements: (1) Graduation from college of osteopathic medicine accredited by Bureau of Professional Education, American Osteopathic Association (see separate entry); (2) Current licensure to practice medicine; (3) Two years of membership in either American Osteopathic Association or Canadian Osteopathic Association; (4) Successful completion of internship accredited by Council on Postdoctoral Training of the American Osteopathic Association (see separate entry); (5) Successful completion of residency in obstetrics and gynecology accredited by Council on Postdoctoral Training of the American Osteopathic Association; (6) Twenty-four months practice subsequent to successful completion of training; and (7) Submission of case logs. Must earn Diplomate of the American Osteopathic Board of Obstetrics and Gynecology designation (see separate entry) within six years. **Endorsed By:** American Osteopathic Association; Bureau of Osteopathic Specialists.

665

Board Eligible, American Osteopathic Board of Ophthalmology and Otorhinolaryngology
American Osteopathic Board of
   Ophthalmology and
   Otorhinolaryngology
Three Mackoil Ave.
Dayton, OH 45403
Phone: (513)252-0868
Sharon Alexiades, Exec.Sec.

Recipient: Osteopathic physicians specializing in ophthalmology or otorhinolaryngology. **Membership:** Required. **Certification Requirements:** Must meet the following requirements: (1) Graduation from college of osteopathic medicine accredited by Bureau of Professional

Education, American Osteopathic Association (see separate entry); (2) Current licensure to practice medicine; (3) Two years of membership in either American Osteopathic Association or Canadian Osteopathic Association; (4) Successful completion of internship accredited by Council on Postdoctoral Training of the American Osteopathic Association (see separate entry); (5) Successful completion of three year residency accredited by Council on Postdoctoral Training of the American Osteopathic Association; and (6) Submission of case logs. Must earn Diplomate designation in specialty of board within six years. (7) Successful completion of written, oral, and clinical exams. Exams cover: Diagnostic and therapeutic procedures; Familiarity with current advances; and Scientific bases of problems. Must successfully complete written exam before attempting oral and clinical exams. **Examination Frequency:** Annual. **Examination Sites:** Exams given at one site in the U.S. **Endorsed By:** American Osteopathic Association; Bureau of Osteopathic Specialists.

666

Board Eligible, American Osteopathic Board of Orthopaedic Surgery
American Osteopathic Board of Orthopaedic Surgery
450 Powers Ave., Ste. 105
Harrisburg, PA 17109
Phone: (717)561-8560
Kay I. Rittenhouse, Exec.Sec.

Recipient: Osteopathic physicians specializing in orthopaedic surgery. **Membership:** Required. **Certification Requirements:** Must meet the following requirements: (1) Graduation from college of osteopathic medicine accredited by Bureau of Professional Education, American Osteopathic Association (see separate entry); (2) Current licensure to practice medicine; (3) Two years of membership in American Osteopathic Association; (4) Successful completion of internship accredited by Council on Postdoctoral Training of the American Osteopathic Association (see separate entry); (5) Successful completion of four year residency in orthopedic surgery accredited by Council on Postdoctoral Training of the American Osteopathic Association; (6) Documentation of 200 major operative procedures in one calendar year; and (7) One year of practice subsequent to successful completion of training. Must earn Diplomate of the American Board of Osteopathic Orthopaedic Surgery designation (see separate entry) within six years. **Endorsed By:**

American Osteopathic Association; American Osteopathic Academy of Orthopedics; Bureau of Osteopathic Specialists.

667

Board Eligible, American Osteopathic Board of Pathology
American Osteopathic Board of Pathology
450 Powers Ave., Ste. 105
Harrisburg, PA 17109
Phone: (717)561-8560
Kay I. Rittenhouse, Exec.Sec.

Recipient: Osteopathic physicians specializing in pathology. **Membership:** Required. **Certification Requirements:** Must meet the following requirements: (1) Graduation from college of osteopathic medicine accredited by Bureau of Professional Education, American Osteopathic Association (see separate entry); (2) Current licensure to practice medicine; (3) Two years of membership in American Osteopathic Association or Canadian Osteopathic Association; (4) Successful completion of internship accredited by Council on Postdoctoral Training of the American Osteopathic Association (see separate entry); and (5) Successful completion of four year residency accredited by Council on Postdoctoral Training of the American Osteopathic Association. Must earn Diplomate designation in specialty of pathology within six years. **Endorsed By:** American Osteopathic Association; Bureau of Osteopathic Specialists.

668

Board Eligible, American Osteopathic Board of Pediatrics
American Osteopathic Board of Pediatrics (AOBP)
142 E. Ontario St., Sixth Fl.
Chicago, IL 60611
Phone: (312)280-5881
Ida Sorci, Prog.Coord.

Recipient: Osteopathic physicians specializing in pediatrics. **Membership:** Required. **Certification Requirements:** Must meet the following requirements: (1) Graduation from college of osteopathic medicine accredited by Bureau of Professional Education, American Osteopathic Association (see separate entry); (2) Current licensure to practice medicine; (3) Two years of membership in American Osteopathic Association or Canadian Osteopathic Association; (4) Successful completion of internship accredited by

Council on Postdoctoral Training of the American Osteopathic Association (see separate entry); and (5) Successful completion of two year residency in pediatrics accredited by Council on Postdoctoral Training of the American Osteopathic Association. Must earn Diplomate of the American Osteopathic Board of Pediatrics designation (see separate entry) within six years. **Endorsed By:** American Osteopathic Association; Bureau of Osteopathic Specialists.

669

Board Eligible, American Osteopathic Board of Preventive Medicine
American Osteopathic Board of Preventive Medicine
Box 226
U.S. Air Force Academy, CO 80840-2200
Phone: (719)472-3560
George E. Hill D.O., Sec.-Treas.

Recipient: Osteopathic physicians specializing in preventive medicine. **Membership:** Required. **Certification Requirements:** Must meet the following requirements: (1) Graduation from college of osteopathic medicine accredited by Bureau of Professional Education, American Osteopathic Association (see separate entry); (2) Current licensure to practice medicine; (3) Two years of membership in American Osteopathic Association or Canadian Osteopathic Association; (4) Successful completion of internship accredited by Council on Postdoctoral Training of the American Osteopathic Association (see separate entry); (5) Master of Public Health degree; and (6) Successful completion of one year of training accredited by Council on Postdoctoral Training of the American Osteopathic Association. Must earn Diplomate designation in one of the specialties of preventive medicine within six years. **Endorsed By:** American Osteopathic Association; Bureau of Osteopathic Specialists.

670

Board Eligible, American Osteopathic Board of Proctology
American Osteopathic Board of Proctology
104A Kings Way West
Sewell, NJ 08080
Phone: (609)582-7900
Todd Schachter D.O., Sec.-Treas.

Recipient: Osteopathic physicians specializing in proctology. **Membership:** mnr **Certification Requirements:** Must meet the following requirements: (1) Graduation from college of osteopathic medicine accredited by Bureau of Professional Education, American Osteopathic Association (see separate entry); (2) Current licensure to practice medicine; (3) Two years of membership in American Osteopathic Association or Canadian Osteopathic Association; (4) Successful completion of internship accredited by Council on Postdoctoral Training of the American Osteopathic Association (see separate entry); (5) Successful completion of two years of training in proctology accredited by Council on Postdoctoral Training of the American Osteopathic Association; (6) Two years of practice subsequent to successful completion of training; (7) Documentation of 200 operative procedures; (8) Submission of 50 case reports; and (9) Submission of thesis on subject related to proctology. Must earn Diplomate of the American Osteopathic Board of Proctology designation (see separate entry) within six years. **Endorsed By:** American Osteopathic Association; American Osteopathic College of Proctology; Bureau of Osteopathic Specialists.

671

Board Eligible, American Osteopathic Board of Radiology
American Osteopathic Board of Radiology
119 E. Second St.
Milan, MO 63556
Phone: (816)265-4011
Pamela A. Smith, Exec.Dir.

Recipient: Osteopathic physicians specializing in radiology. **Membership:** Required. **Certification Requirements:** Must meet the following requirements: (1) Graduation from college of osteopathic medicine accredited by Bureau of Professional Education, American Osteopathic Association (see separate entry); (2) Current licensure to practice medicine; (3) Two years of membership in American Osteopathic Association or Canadian Osteopathic Association; (4) Successful completion of internship accredited by Council on Postdoctoral Training of the American Osteopathic Association (see separate entry); and (5) Successful completion of three or four years of training in radiology accredited by Council on Postdoctoral Training of the American Osteopathic Association. Must earn Diplomate designation in one of the specialties of radiology within six years. **Endorsed By:** American Osteopathic Association: Bureau of Osteopathic Specialists.

672

Board Eligible, American Osteopathic Board of Rehabilitation Medicine
American Osteopathic Board of Rehabilitation Medicine
9058 W. Church St.
Des Plaines, IL 60016
Phone: (708)699-0048
Julie Pickett-Atae, Exec.Asst.

Recipient: Osteopathic physicians specializing in rehabilitation medicine. **Membership:** Required. **Certification Requirements:** Must meet the following requirements: (1) Graduation from college of osteopathic medicine accredited by Bureau of Professional Education, American Osteopathic Association (see separate entry); (2) Current licensure to practice medicine; (3) Two years of membership in American Osteopathic Association or Canadian Osteopathic Association; (4) Successful completion of internship accredited by Council on Postdoctoral Training of the American Osteopathic Association (see separate entry); (5) Successful completion of three years of training in rehabilitation medicine accredited by Council on Postdoctoral Training of the American Osteopathic Association; (6) Two years practice subsequent to successful completion of training; and (7) Submission of 200 case records. Training must include: Anatomy; Biochemistry; Electrotherapy; Hydrotherapy; Kinesitherapy; Occupational therapy; Pathology; Pharmacology; Physics; Physiology; Radiation therapy; Rehabilitation; and Thermotherapy. Must earn Diplomate of the American Osteopathic Board of Rehabilitation Medicine designation (see separate entry) within six years. **Endorsed By:** American Osteopathic Association; Bureau of Osteopathic Specialists.

673

Board Eligible, American Osteopathic Board of Surgery
American Osteopathic Board of Surgery
Three MacKoil Ave.
Dayton, OH 45403
Phone: (513)252-0868
Sharon Alexiades, Corres.Sec.

Recipient: Osteopathic surgeons. **Membership:** Required. **Certification Requirements:** Must meet the following requirements: (1) Graduation from college of osteopathic medicine accredited by Bureau of Professional Education, American Osteopathic Association (see sepa-

rate entry); (2) Current licensure to practice medicine; (3) Two years of membership in American Osteopathic Association or Canadian Osteopathic Association; (4) Successful completion of internship accredited by Council on Postdoctoral Training of the American Osteopathic Association (see separate entry); (5) Successful completion of training accredited by Council on Postdoctoral Training of the American Osteopathic Association; (6) Submission of log of major operative cases performed during previous year; and (7) Submission of list of mortalities. Must earn Diplomate designation in surgical specialty within six years. **Endorsed By:** American College of Osteopathic Surgeons; American Osteopathic Association; Bureau of Osteopathic Specialists.

674

Certificate of Added Qualification in Clinical and Laboratory Immunology
American Board of Allergy and Immunology (ABAI)
3624 Market St.
Philadelphia, PA 19104-2675
Phone: (215)349-9466
Fax: (215)222-8669
Dr. Herbert C. Mansmann Jr., Exec.Sec.

Recipient: Physicians specializing in clinical and laboratory immunology. **Educational/Experience Requirements:** Must meet the following requirements: (1) Hold Diplomate designation with either the ABAI, American Board of Internal Medicine, or American Board of Pediatrics (see separate entries); and (2) One year of formal training in immunologically-based subspecialty. **Certification Requirements:** Successful completion of exam. **Examination Type:** Multiple-choice. **Waiting Period to Receive Scores:** Three months. **Endorsed By:** American Academy of Allergy and Immunology; American Academy of Pediatrics; American Board of Internal Medicine; American Board of Medical Specialties; American Board of Pediatrics; American College of Allergy and Immunology; American Medical Association; Clinical Immunology Society; Council on Medical Education.

675

Certificate of Added Qualifications in Surgical Critical Care

American Osteopathic Board of
  Surgery
Three MacKoil Ave.
Dayton, OH 45403
Phone: (513)252-0868
Sharon Alexiades, Corres.Sec.

Recipient: Osteopathic surgeons specializing in surgical critical care. **Educational/Experience Requirements:** Must meet the following requirements: (1) Hold Diplomate designation in surgical specialty; and (2) Successfully complete one year of training in surgical critical care accredited by Council on Postdoctoral Training of the American Osteopathic Association (see separate entry). **Membership:** Required. **Certification Requirements:** Successful completion of exam. **Endorsed By:** American College of Osteopathic Surgeons; American Osteopathic Association; Bureau of Osteopathic Specialists.

676

Certificate of Added Qualifications in Vascular and Interventional Radiology of the American Board of Radiology

American Board of Radiology
  (ABR)
5255 E. Williams Circle, Ste. 6800
Tucson, AZ 85711
Phone: (520)790-2900
Fax: (520)790-3200
M. Paul Capp M.D., Exec.Dir.

Recipient: Radiologists specializing in vascular and interventional radiology. **Educational/Experience Requirements:** Must meet the following requirements: (1) Hold either Diplomate in Radiology or Diagnostic Radiology of the American Board of Radiology (see separate entries); (2) Successfully complete one year training in vascular and interventional radiology following completion of residency; (3) Submit documentation of 500 invasive cases, including: Angiograms (100 cases); Angioplasties (25 cases); and Nephrostomies (15 cases); (4) Successfully complete one year of practice or training in vascular and interventional radiology; and (5) Five years experience, with one-third of time devoted to vascular and interventional radiology. Experience can include: Actual performance and interpretation of examinations and procedures; Attendance at related conferences; Consultation with referring physicians; and Pre- and post-procedure visits with patients. **Certification Requirements:** Successful completion of oral exam. Exam consists of following parts: (1) Diagnostic Vascular Radiology, including: Angiography; Computerized tomography; Magnetic resonance angiography; Noninvasive vascular studies; and Vascular ultrasound; (2) NonVascular Interventional Procedures; and (3) Therapeutic Vascular Procedures. Exam covers following procedures: (1) Diagnostic Vascular Radiology, including: Angiography (arterial and venous); Disease classification; Magnetic resonance angiography; Noninvasive vascular studies; and Vascular ultrasound; (2) Therapeutic Vascular Procedures, including: Angioplasty; Atherectomy and other endovascular interventions; Embolization; Fibrinolysis; Foreign body retrieval; IVC filter placement; Miscellaneous vascular therapeutic procedures; Pharmacologic therapy; Stent placement; and TIPS; and (3) Non-Vascular Interventional Procedures, including: Abscess drainage - abdomen, pelvis, chest, and extremity; Biliary drainage; Biliary stent placement; Biopsy procedures; Drainage of fluid collections; Enteric dilatations and stent placement; Gastrostomy; Nephrostomy; and Renal stent placement. **Renewal:** Every ten years. **Examination Frequency:** Annual. **Re-examination:** Must wait one year to retake exam. **Endorsed By:** American Association of Physicists in Medicine; American Board of Medical Specialties; American College of Radiology; American Medical Association; American Radium Society; American Roentgen Ray Society; American Society for Therapeutic Radiology and Oncology; Association of University Radiologists; Council on Medical Education; Radiological Society of North America.

677

Certification of Added Qualifications in Occupational Medicine

American Osteopathic Board of
  Preventive Medicine
Box 226
U.S. Air Force Academy, CO
  80840-2200
Phone: (719)472-3560
George E. Hill D.O., Sec.-Treas.

Recipient: Osteopathic physicians specializing in occupational medicine. **Educational/Experience Requirements:** Must meet the following requirements: (1) Certification from board affiliated with Bureau of Osteopathic Specialists; (2) 100 hours of postgraduate training in occupational medicine; and (3) Submission of relevant scientific paper and/or practice documents. **Membership:** Required. **Certification Requirements:** Successful completion of written, oral, and clinical exams. Exams cover: Diagnostic and therapeutic procedures; Familiarity with current advances; and Scientific bases of problems. **Renewal:** Every seven years. Recertification based on successful completion of exam. **Examination Frequency:** Annual. **Examination Sites:** Exams given at one U.S. site. **Endorsed By:** American Osteopathic Association; Bureau of Osteopathic Specialists.

678

Certification of Special Proficiency in Osteopathic Manipulative Medicine

American Osteopathic Board of
  Special Proficiency in Osteopathic
  Manipulative Medicine
3500 DePauw Blvd., Ste. 1080
Indianapolis, IN 46268
Phone: (317)879-1881
Stephen J. Noone CAE, Exec.Dir.

Recipient: Osteopathic physicians specializing in manipulative medicine. **Educational/Experience Requirements:** Must meet the following requirements: (1) Graduation from college of osteopathic medicine accredited by Bureau of Professional Education, American Osteopathic Association (see separate entry); (2) Current licensure to practice medicine; (3) Two years of membership in American Osteopathic Association or Canadian Osteopathic Association; (4) Successful completion of internship accredited by Council on Postdoctoral Training of the American Osteopathic Association (see separate entry); (5) Successful completion of training in manipulative medicine accredited by Council on Postdoctoral Training of the American Osteopathic Association; and (6) Submission of five case histories. **Membership:** Required. **Certification Requirements:** Successful completion of written, oral, and practical exams. Must successfully complete written exam before attempting oral and practical exams. **Renewal:** Every ten years. **Examination Frequency:** Annual. **Examination Sites:** Exams given in Indianapolis, IN. **Endorsed By:** American Osteopathic Association; Bureau of Osteopathic Specialists.

679

Certification in Sports Medicine
American Board of Certification in
   Family Practice
804 Main St., Ste. D
Forest Park, GA 30050
Phone: (404)363-8263
Fax: (404)361-2285
Toll Free: (800)447-9397

Recipient: Physicians specializing in sports medicine. **Educational/Experience Requirements:** Must meet the following requirements: (1) Graduation from school of medicine accredited by Bureau of Professional Education, American Osteopathic Association or Liaison Committee on Medical Education (see separate entries); (2) Current unrestricted licensure to practice medicine; (3) Certification from board recognized by American Association of Physician Specialists, American Board of Medical Specialties, or Bureau for Osteopathic Specialists; (4) Either successful completion of two year fellowship in sports medicine or five years experience as team physician at high school level or higher; and (5) Submission of ten cases. **Membership:** Not required. **Certification Requirements:** Successful completion of oral, written, and clinical exams. **Renewal:** Recertification required. **Fees:** $600. **Endorsed By:** American Association of Physician Specialists; Board of Certification in Emergency Medicine.

680

Certified in Quality Assurance and Utilization Review (CQUAR)
American Board of Quality
   Assurance and Utilization Review
   Physicians (ABQAURP)
4890 W. Kennedy Blvd., Ste. 260
Tampa, FL 33609
Phone: (813)286-4411
Fax: (813)286-4387
Carla T. Murrill CRT, Exec. VP

Recipient: Physicians, registered nurses, and other health and human services professionals involved in quality assurance and utilization review. **Number of Certified Individuals:** 6500. **Educational/Experience Requirements:** Must meet the following requirements; (1) Current unrestricted licensure; (2) Two years experience; and (3) Twenty hours of continuing medical education or attendance at ABQAURP sponsored course. **Membership:** Required. **Certification Requirements:** Successful completion of exam. **Renewal:** Every three years. Recertification based on either attendance at

ABQAURP seminar or successful completion of home-study course. Renewal fees are: $275 (physicians); $175 (non-physicians). **Preparatory Materials:** Audiotapes, books, and videotapes available. **Examination Frequency:** Six times per year. **Examination Sites:** Exam given at sites throughout the U.S. **Examination Type:** Multiple-choice. **Pass/Fail Rate:** 85% pass exam the first time. **Waiting Period to Receive Scores:** Six-eight weeks. **Re-examination:** There is no waiting period to retake exam. **Fees:** $750 (physicians); $375 (non-physicians). **Endorsed By:** National Board of Medical Examiners.

681

Diplomate in Aerospace Medicine of the American Osteopathic Board of Preventive Medicine
American Osteopathic Board of
   Preventive Medicine
Box 226
U.S. Air Force Academy, CO
   80840-2200
Phone: (719)472-3560
George E. Hill D.O., Sec.-Treas.

Recipient: Osteopathic physicians specializing in aerospace medicine. **Educational/Experience Requirements:** Must meet the following requirements: (1) Graduation from college of osteopathic medicine accredited by Bureau of Professional Education, American Osteopathic Association (see separate entry); (2) Current licensure to practice medicine; (3) Two years of membership in American Osteopathic Association or Canadian Osteopathic Association; (4) Successful completion of internship accredited by Council on Postdoctoral Training of the American Osteopathic Association (see separate entry); (5) Master of Public Health degree; and (6) Successful completion of one year of training in aerospace medicine accredited by Council on Postdoctoral Training of the American Osteopathic Association. **Membership:** Required. **Certification Requirements:** Successful completion of written, oral, and clinical exams. Exams cover: Diagnostic and therapeutic procedures; Familiarity with current advances; and Scientific bases of problems. **Renewal:** Every ten years. Recertification based on successful completion of exam. **Examination Frequency:** Annual. **Examination Sites:** Exam given at one U.S. site. **Endorsed By:** American Osteopathic Association; Bureau of Osteopathic Specialists.

682

Diplomate in Allergy and Immunology of the American Osteopathic Board of Internal Medicine
American Osteopathic Board of
   Internal Medicine
5200 S. Ellis Ave.
Chicago, IL 60615
Phone: (312)947-4881
Gary L. Slick D.O., Exec.Dir.

Recipient: Physicians specializing in allergy and immunology. **Educational/Experience Requirements:** Must meet the following requirements: (1) Hold Diplomate of the American Osteopathic Board of Internal Medicine designation (see separate entry); and (2) Successfully complete two year training program in allergy and immunology accredited by Council on Postdoctoral Training of the American Osteopathic Association (see separate entry). **Membership:** Required. **Certification Requirements:** Successful completion of exam. **Renewal:** Every ten years. **Examination Frequency:** Annual - always August. **Examination Sites:** Exam given at one U.S. site. **Endorsed By:** American Osteopathic Association; Bureau of Osteopathic Specialists.

683

Diplomate of the American Board of Abdominal Surgery
American Board of Abdominal
   Surgery
675 Main St.
Melrose, MA 02176
Phone: (617)655-6101

Recipient: Abdominal surgeons. **Educational/Experience Requirements:** Must meet the following requirements: (1) Graduate from approved medical school; (2) Current licensure to practice medicine; (3) Successful completion of internship of not less than 12 months; (4) Successful completion of minimum of two years of general surgical residency; and (5) Successful completion of either two years of abdominal surgical residency or preceptorship. **Certification Requirements:** Successful completion of written and oral exams. Written exam covers: Basic sciences; and Clinical abdominal surgery. Oral exam covers: Anatomy; Pathology; Radiology; and Surgical diagnosis and management. Oral exam may include examination of patients. Candidates who have successfully completed exams of related surgical specialty board may be exempt from written exam. Must successfully complete written exam and three years of surgical practice before attempting oral exam. **Renewal:** Every year. Recertification based on attendance at one surgical course and one surgical meeting. **Re-examination:** Must wait one year to retake exams. Exams may be retaken one time. **Fees:** $625. **Endorsed By:** American Board of Medical Specialties; American Medical Association; Council on Medical Education.

684

Diplomate of the American Board of Allergy and Immunology

American Board of Allergy and
  Immunology (ABAI)
3624 Market St.
Philadelphia, PA 19104-2675
Phone: (215)349-9466
Fax: (215)222-8669
Dr. Herbert C. Mansmann Jr.,
  Exec.Sec.

Recipient: Physicians specializing in allergy and immunology. **Educational/ Experience Requirements:** Must meet the following requirements: (1) Hold Diplomate designation with American Board of Internal Medicine and/or American Board of Pediatrics (see separate entries); (2) Successfully complete two years of residency or fellowship in allergy/ immunology program or equivalent training; and (3) Hold current unrestricted licensure to practice medicine. **Certification Requirements:** Successful completion of exam. **Renewal:** Every ten years. Recertification based on successful completion of exam. **Examination Type:** Multiple-choice. **Waiting Period to Receive Scores:** Three months. **Endorsed By:** American Academy of Allergy and Immunology; American Academy of Pediatrics; American Board of Internal Medicine; American Board of Medical Specialties; American Board of Pediatrics; American College of Allergy and Immunology; American Medical Association; Clinical Immunology Society; Council on Medical Education.

685

Diplomate of the American Board of Anesthesiology

American Board of Anesthesiology
  (ABA)
100 Constitution Plaza
Hartford, CT 06103-1796
Phone: (203)522-9857
Fax: (203)522-6626
Francis P. Hughes Ph.D., Exec.Sec.

Recipient: Anesthesiologists. **Educational/Experience Requirements:** Must meet the following requirements: (1) Graduation from medical school in U.S. or Canada accredited by Liaison Committee for Medical Education (see separate entry) or Committee on Accreditation of Canadian Medical Schools, or school of osteopathic medicine accredited by Bureau of Professional Education, American Osteopathic Association (see separate entry); (2) Current unrestricted license to practice medicine; and (3) Successful completion of residency program accredited by Accreditation Council for Graduate Medical Education (see separate entry). Graduates of medical schools outside the U.S. or Canada must have certificate from Educational Commission for Foreign Medical Graduates or documentation of training for those who entered post-doctoral medical training via Fifth Pathway of the American Medical Association. **Certification Requirements:** Successful completion of written and oral exams. **Renewal:** None. **Examination Frequency:** Annual (written) - always July. semiannual (oral) - always spring and fall. **Examination Sites:** Written exam given at sites throughout the U.S. and Canada. Oral exam given at two sites in the U.S. every year. **Re-examination:** Must wait one year to retake oral exam. May retake exams two times. Fees to retake exams are: $200 (written); $700 (oral). **Fees:** $1100. **Endorsed By:** American Board of Medical Specialties; American Medical Association; American Society of Anesthesiologists; Council on Medical Education.

686

Diplomate of the American Board of Anesthesiology with Special Qualifications in Critical Care Medicine

American Board of Anesthesiology
  (ABA)
100 Constitution Plaza
Hartford, CT 06103-1796
Phone: (203)522-9857
Fax: (203)522-6626
Francis P. Hughes Ph.D., Exec.Sec.

Recipient: Anesthesiologists specializing in critical care medicine. **Educational/ Experience Requirements:** Must meet the following requirements: (1) Hold Diplomate of the American Board of Anesthesiology designation (see separate entry); (2) Current unrestricted license to practice medicine; and (3) Successfully complete 12-month critical care training program accredited by Accreditation Council for Graduate Medical Education

(see separate entry). **Certification Requirements:** Successful completion of exam. **Renewal:** None. **Examination Frequency:** biennial. **Examination Sites:** Exam given at one or more sites in the U.S. **Re-examination:** May retake exam two times. **Fees:** $1000. **Endorsed By:** American Board of Medical Specialties; American Medical Association; American Society of Anesthesiologists; Council on Medical Education.

687

Diplomate of the American Board of Anesthesiology with Special Qualifications in Pain Management

American Board of Anesthesiology
  (ABA)
100 Constitution Plaza
Hartford, CT 06103-1796
Phone: (203)522-9857
Fax: (203)522-6626
Francis P. Hughes Ph.D., Exec.Sec.

Recipient: Anesthesiologists specializing in pain management. **Educational/ Experience Requirements:** Must meet the following requirements: (1) Hold Diplomate of the American Board of Anesthesiology designation (see separate entry); (2) Current unrestricted license to practice medicine; and (3) Successfully complete 12-month pain management training program accredited by Accreditation Council for Graduate Medical Education (see separate entry) or equivalent. **Certification Requirements:** Successful completion of exam. **Renewal:** None. **Examination Frequency:** biennial. **Examination Sites:** Exam given at one or more sites in the U.S. **Re-examination:** May retake exam two times. **Fees:** $1000. **Endorsed By:** American Board of Medical Specialties; American Medical Association; American Society of Anesthesiologists; Council on Medical Education.

688

Diplomate of the American Board of Certification in Anesthesiology

American Board of Certification in
  Anesthesiology
804 Main St., Ste. D
Forest Park, GA 30050
Phone: (404)363-8263
Fax: (404)361-2285
Toll Free: (800)447-9397

Recipient: Physicians specializing in anesthesiology. **Educational/Experience Requirements:** Must meet the following requirements: (1) Graduation from school of medicine accredited by Bureau of Professional Education, American Osteopathic Association or Liaison Committee on Medical Education (see separate entries); (2) Current unrestricted licensure to practice medicine; (3) Successful completion of internship accredited by American Osteopathic Association Division on Postdoctoral Training or Accreditation Council for Graduate Medical Education (ACGME) (see separate entries); (4) Successful completion of osteopathic residency accredited by American Osteopathic Association Division on Postdoctoral Training or residency in anesthesiology accredited by ACGME; (5) Two years practice; (6) Current staff privileges at institution accredited by Committee on Hospital Accreditation or Joint Commission for Accreditation of Healthcare Organizations (see separate entries); (7) 50 hours of continuing medical education in anesthesia during previous two years; and (8) Submission of 25 case reports. **Certification Requirements:** Successful completion of written and oral exams. **Renewal:** Recertification required. **Examination Frequency:** Annual - always June. **Examination Sites:** Exam given at annual meeting. **Fees:** $700. **Endorsed By:** American Association of Physician Specialists.

`689`

Diplomate of American Board of Certification in Anesthesiology with Added Qualifications in Pain Management

American Board of Certification in Anesthesiology
804 Main St., Ste. D
Forest Park, GA 30050
Phone: (404)363-8263
Fax: (404)361-2285
Toll Free: (800)447-9397

Recipient: Physicians specializing in pain management. **Educational/Experience Requirements:** Hold certification in anesthesia from board recognized by either American Association of Physician Specialists, American Board of Medical Specialties, or Bureau of Osteopathic Specialists, and one of the following: (1) Successful completion of six months of training in pain management in program accredited by Accreditation Council on Graduate Medical Education or American Osteopathic Association Division on Postdoctoral Training (see separate entries); or (2) Two years practice and accumulation of 20 hours of continuing education in pain management within last year. May also be required to submit case reports and documentation. **Mem-**

bership: Required. **Certification Requirements:** Successful completion of exams. **Examination Frequency:** Annual - always January. **Examination Sites:** Exam given at annual mid-winter meeting. **Fees:** $550. **Endorsed By:** American Association of Physician Specialists.

`690`

Diplomate of the American Board of Certification in Dermatology

American Board of Certification in Dermatology
804 Main St., Ste. D
Forest Park, GA 30050
Phone: (404)363-8263
Fax: (404)361-2285
Toll Free: (800)447-9397

Recipient: Physicians specializing in dermatology. **Educational/Experience Requirements:** Must meet the following requirements: (1) Graduation from school of medicine accredited by Bureau of Professional Education, American Osteopathic Association or Liaison Committee on Medical Education (see separate entries); (2) Current unrestricted licensure to practice medicine; (3) Successful completion of rotating internship accredited by American Osteopathic Association Division on Postdoctoral Training or Accreditation Council for Graduate Medical Education (see separate entries); (4) Successful completion of approved three-year program in dermatology; (5) Submission of 150 case histories; and (6) Documentation of 50 hours of postgraduate dermatological courses, lectures, seminars, and research conferences attended during each of three previous years. **Membership:** Required. **Certification Requirements:** Successful completion of exam. **Renewal:** Recertification required. **Examination Frequency:** Annual - always June. **Examination Sites:** Exam given at annual meeting. **Fees:** $650. **Endorsed By:** American Association of Physician Specialists.

`691`

Diplomate of the American Board of Certification in Internal Medicine

American Board of Certification in Internal Medicine
804 Main St., Ste. D
Forest Park, GA 30050
Phone: (404)363-8263
Fax: (404)361-2285
Toll Free: (800)447-9397

Recipient: Physicians specializing in internal medicine. **Educational/Experience**

Requirements: Must meet the following requirements: (1) Graduation from school of medicine accredited by Bureau of Professional Education, American Osteopathic Association or Liaison Committee on Medical Education (see separate entries); (2) Current unrestricted licensure to practice medicine; (3) Experience and training requirements established by Board; and (4) Active or pending staff privileges at institution accredited by Committee on Hospital Accreditation or Joint Commission for Accreditation of Healthcare Organizations (see separate entries). **Membership:** Required. **Certification Requirements:** Successful completion of exam. **Renewal:** Recertification required. **Examination Frequency:** Annual - always June. **Examination Sites:** Exam given at annual meeting. **Fees:** $900. **Endorsed By:** American Association of Physician Specialists.

`692`

Diplomate of the American Board of Certification in Neurology/Psychiatry

American Board of Certification in Neurology/Psychiatry
804 Main St., Ste. D
Forest Park, GA 30050
Phone: (404)363-8263
Fax: (404)361-2285
Toll Free: (800)447-9397

Recipient: Physicians specializing in neurology and psychiatry. **Educational/Experience Requirements:** Must meet the following requirements: (1) Graduation from school of medicine accredited by Bureau of Professional Education, American Osteopathic Association or Liaison Committee on Medical Education (see separate entries); (2) Current unrestricted licensure to practice medicine; (3) Successful completion of internship accredited by American Osteopathic Association Division on Postdoctoral Training or Accreditation Council for Graduate Medical Education (ACGME) (see separate entries); (4) Successful completion of osteopathic residency accredited by American Osteopathic Association Division on Postdoctoral Training or residency in either neurology or psychiatry accredited by ACGME; (5) Documentation of minimum of 100 major cases; and (6) Submission of ten case reports. **Certification Requirements:** Successful completion of exams. **Renewal:** Recertification required. **Examination Frequency:** Annual - always June. **Examination Sites:** Exam given at annual meeting. **Fees:** $600. **Endorsed By:** American Association of Physician Specialists.

693

Diplomate of the American Board of Certification in Orthopedic Surgery
American Board of Certification in Orthopedic Surgery
804 Main St., Ste. D
Forest Park, GA 30050
Phone: (404)363-8263
Fax: (404)361-2285
Toll Free: (800)447-9397

Recipient: Physicians specializing in orthopedic surgery. **Educational/ Experience Requirements:** Must meet the following requirements: (1) Graduation from school of medicine accredited by Bureau of Professional Education, American Osteopathic Association or Liaison Committee on Medical Education (see separate entries); (2) Current unrestricted licensure to practice medicine; (3) Successful completion of internship accredited by American Osteopathic Association Division on Postdoctoral Training or Accreditation Council for Graduate Medical Education (ACGME) (see separate entries); (4) Successful completion of osteopathic residency accredited by American Osteopathic Association Division on Postdoctoral Training or residency in orthopedic surgery accredited by ACGME; (5) Documentation of minimum of 200 surgical procedures; (6) Active staff privileges for two years at institution accredited by Committee on Hospital Accreditation or Joint Commission for Accreditation of Healthcare Organizations (see separate entries); (7) Submission of ten case reports; and (8) Submission of log of surgical procedures performed for previous two years, broken down by year and surgical group. **Membership:** Required. **Certification Requirements:** Successful completion of written, oral, and clinical exams. Must successfully complete clinical exam within 24 months of successful completion of written and oral exams. **Renewal:** Recertification required. **Examination Frequency:** Annual (oral and written exams) - always June. **Examination Sites:** Oral and written exams given at annual meeting. **Fees:** $350, plus actual costs of clinical exam. **Endorsed By:** American Association of Physician Specialists.

694

Diplomate of the American Board of Certification in Radiology
American Board of Certification in Radiology
804 Main St., Ste. D
Forest Park, GA 30050
Phone: (404)363-8263
Fax: (404)361-2285
Toll Free: (800)447-9397

Recipient: Physicians specializing in radiology. **Educational/Experience Requirements:** Must meet the following requirements: (1) Graduation from recognized college of medicine; (2) Current licensure to practice medicine; (3) Successful completion of internship accredited by American Osteopathic Association Division on Postdoctoral Training or Accreditation Council for Graduate Medical Education (ACGME) (see separate entries); (4) Successful completion of osteopathic residency accredited by American Osteopathic Association Division on Postdoctoral Training or residency in diagnostic radiology accredited by ACGME; (5) Current staff privileges for three years at institution accredited by Committee on Hospital Accreditation or Joint Commission on Accreditation of Healthcare Organizations (see separate entries); (6) Documentation of reading of minimum of 30,000 X-rays; and (7) Submission of logs of X-rays taken at candidate's institution for prior year. **Membership:** Required. **Certification Requirements:** Successful completion of exams. **Renewal:** Recertification required. **Examination Frequency:** semiannual - always January and June. **Examination Sites:** Exams given at midwinter and annual meetings. **Fees:** $1100. **Endorsed By:** American Association of Physician Specialists.

695

Diplomate of the American Board of Chelation Therapy
American Board of Chelation Therapy (ABCT)
70 W. Huron St.
Chicago, IL 60610
Phone: (312)787-ABCT
Fax: (312)266-7291
Jack Hank, Exec.Dir.

Recipient: Specialists in field of chelation therapy. (Chelation therapy is used in cases of blood poisoning and involves use of metal binding and bio-inorganic agents intravenously infused into bloodstream to "pick up" and remove calcium, lead, or other toxic heavy metals and restore cellular homeostasis. Because of lack of controlled studies for conditions other than calcinosis, digitalis toxicity, and excessive body storage of heavy metals, chelation therapy is not considered standard medical procedure.) **Educational/ Experience Requirements:** Must meet the following requirements: (1) Current licensure as physician; (2) Submission of letter documenting 1000 administered chelations; (3) Submission of six patient charts, each of which must be indexed and summarized; (4) Submission of ten exam questions which must be in form outlined by ABCT and referenced; and (5) Two years continuous membership in American College of Advancement in Medicine, Great Lakes Association of Clinical Medicine, or Nutritional Biomedical Association. **Membership:** Required. **Certification Requirements:** Successful completion of workshop and oral and written exams. **Endorsed By:** American College of Advancement in Medicine; Great Lakes Association of Clinical Medicine; Nutritional Biomedical Association.

696

Diplomate of the American Board of Colon and Rectal Surgery
American Board of Colon and Rectal Surgery (ABCRS)
20600 Eureka Rd., Ste. 713
Taylor, MI 48180
Phone: (313)282-9400
Fax: (313)282-9402
Herand Abcarian M.D., Exec.Dir.

Recipient: Colon and rectal surgeons. **Educational/Experience Requirements:** Must meet the following requirements: (1) Successfully complete five year training program in general surgery; (2) Successfully complete one year of residency; (3) Hold Diplomate of the American Board of Surgery designation (see separate entry); (4) Hold current unrestricted licensure to practice medicine in country of residence; and (5) Devote majority of practice to colon and rectal surgery. May be required to submit case reports and/or bibliography of books and papers published. **Certification Requirements:** Successful completion of written and oral exams. Written exam covers theory and practice of colon and rectal surgery with separate exams on pathology and radiology. Oral exam covers: Clinical experience; Problem-solving ability; and Surgical judgment. **Renewal:** Every eight years. **Preparatory Materials:** List of approved residency training programs. **Examination Frequency:** Annual - always spring (written) and fall (oral). **Examination Sites:** Exams given at one site in the

U.S. **Waiting Period to Receive Scores:** Four-six weeks. **Re-examination:** Must wait one year to retake exams. Each exam may be retaken two times. Fees to retake exams are: $400 (written); $500 (oral). **Fees:** $1200. **Endorsed By:** American Board of Medical Specialties; American Board of Surgery; American College of Surgeons; American Society of Colon and Rectal Surgeons; American Medical Association; Council on Medical Education.

697

Diplomate of the American Board of Dermatology
American Board of Dermatology (ABD)
Henry Ford Hospital
Detroit, MI 48202-2689
Phone: (313)874-1088
Fax: (313)872-3221
Harry J. Hurley M.D., Exec.Dir.

Recipient: Physicians specializing in dermatology. **Educational/Experience Requirements:** Must meet the following requirements: (1) Degree from medical school approved by Liaison Committee on Medical Education or school of osteopathy approved by Bureau of Professional Education, American Osteopathic Association (see separate entries); (2) Current unrestricted licensure to practice medicine; and (3) Successful completion of residency program accredited by Accreditation Council for Graduate Medical Education (see separate entry) or Royal College of Physicians and Surgeons of Canada. Graduates of medical programs from outside the U.S. or Canada must have credentials evaluated by Educational Commission for Foreign Medical Graduates. **Certification Requirements:** Successful completion of two-part exam. Part one covers: Anatomy; Biochemistry; Clinical dermatology; Cutaneous allergy and immunology; Cutaneous oncology; Dermatologic surgery; Dermatopathology; Electron microscopy as related to dermatology; Entomology; Epidemiology; Genetics; Internal medicine as it pertains to dermatology; Medical ethics; Molecular biology; Pediatric dermatology; Pharmacology; Photobiology and cutaneous microbiology; Physical therapy; Physiology; Preventive dermatology; Radiation physics; Radiation therapy; and Sexually transmitted diseases. Part two covers clinical and laboratory dermatology in the following areas: Bacteria; Bacterial cultures; Culture mounts; Dark-field micrographs; Dermatologic surgical procedures; Electron micrographs; Fungal cultures; Histochemical and fluorescent photomicrographs; Histopathologic sections; Organisms; Parasites; Rickettsiae; Roentgenograms; Skin scrapings and smears; Tzanck preparations; and Viruses. Part two also includes practical component on dermatopathology. **Renewal:** Every ten years. **Examination Frequency:** Annual - always fall. **Examination Type:** Multiple-choice. **Re-examination:** May retake exam twice. Must only retake part failed. Fee to retake exam is $1150. **Fees:** $1250. **Endorsed By:** American Academy of Dermatology; American Board of Medical Specialties; American Dermatological Association; American Medical Association; Council on Medical Education.

698

Diplomate of the American Board of Dermatology with Special Qualification in Clinical and Laboratory Dermatological Immunology
American Board of Dermatology (ABD)
Henry Ford Hospital
Detroit, MI 48202-2689
Phone: (313)874-1088
Fax: (313)872-3221
Harry J. Hurley M.D., Exec.Dir.

Recipient: Physicians specializing in clinical and laboratory dermatological immunology. **Educational/Experience Requirements:** Must meet the following requirements: (1) Hold Diplomate of the American Board of Dermatology designation (see separate entry); (2) Successful completion of one year fellowship; and (3) Successful completion of one year of training in accredited program. **Certification Requirements:** Successful completion of exam. **Examination Frequency:** Annual - always fall. **Fees:** $1000. **Endorsed By:** American Academy of Dermatology; American Board of Medical Specialties; American Dermatological Association; American Medical Association; Council on Medical Education.

699

Diplomate of the American Board of Dermatology with Special Qualification in Dermatopathology
American Board of Dermatology (ABD)
Henry Ford Hospital
Detroit, MI 48202-2689
Phone: (313)874-1088
Fax: (313)872-3221
Harry J. Hurley M.D., Exec.Dir.

Recipient: Physicians specializing in dermatopathology. **Educational/Experience Requirements:** Must meet one of the following requirements: (1) Hold either Diplomate of the American Board of Dermatology or American Board of Pathology designations (see separate entries) and one year of training in program accredited by Accreditation Council for Graduate Medical Education (see separate entry); or (2) Hold both Diplomate of the American Board of Dermatology and American Board of Pathology designations. **Certification Requirements:** Successful completion of exam. **Examination Frequency:** Annual - always fall. **Fees:** $1200. **Endorsed By:** American Academy of Dermatology; American Board of Medical Specialties; American Board of Pathology; American Dermatological Association; American Medical Association; Council on Medical Education.

700

Diplomate of the American Board of Emergency Medicine
American Board of Emergency Medicine (ABEM)
3000 Coolidge Rd.
East Lansing, MI 48823-6319
Phone: (517)332-4800
Fax: (517)332-2234
Benson S. Munger Ph.D., Exec.Dir.

Recipient: Physicians specializing in emergency medicine. **Educational/Experience Requirements:** Must meet the following requirements: (1) Graduation from medical school in U.S. or Canada or approved schools of osteopathic medicine that meet credential requirements; (2) Successful completion of 36-month post-doctorate residency program accredited by Residency Review Committee for Emergency Medicine (see separate entry) or Royal College of Physicians and Surgeons; (3) Current licensure to practice medicine in the U.S. or Canada; and (4) Accumulation of 50 hours of continuing education in emergency medicine every year, starting one year from the date of successful completion of residency. Candidates graduating from medical school outside of the U.S. or Canada must provide a verified and translated diploma. **Certification Requirements:** Successful completion of written and oral exams. **Renewal:** Every ten years. **Endorsed By:** American Board of Medical Specialties; American Medical Association; Council on Medical Education.

701

Diplomate of the American Board of Environmental Medicine
American Board of Environmental Medicine (ABEM)
4510 W. 89th St.
Prairie Village, KS 66207
Phone: (913)341-0765
Fax: (913)341-3625
Jill Dietz, Exec.Dir.

Recipient: Physicians specializing in environmental medicine. **Educational/Experience Requirements:** Must meet the following requirements: (1) Current licensure as physician or surgeon; and (2) Either three years experience, successful completion of approved residency or fellowship in environmental or preventive medicine, or equivalent training. **Certification Requirements:** Successful completion of written and oral exams. Oral exam consists of presentation of three cases that demonstrate: Ability to defend work-up and treatment of patient; Ability to record and maintain clear, concise, and legible records; and Required work-up for environmentally ill patient. **Preparatory Materials:** List of suggested references and resources provided. **Examination Type:** Multiple-choice. **Fees:** $1000. **Endorsed By:** American Academy of Environmental Medicine; International Board of Environmental Medicine.

702

Diplomate of the American Board of Family Practice
American Board of Family Practice (ABFP)
2228 Young Dr.
Lexington, KY 40505-4294
Phone: (606)269-5626
Fax: (606)266-9699

Recipient: Medical and osteopathic doctors practicing family medicine. **Educational/Experience Requirements:** Must meet the following requirements: (1) Medical Doctor (M.D.) or Doctor of Osteopathy (D.O.) degree from institutions accredited by either Liaison Committee on Medical Education (see separate entry), Committee for Accreditation of Canadian Medical Schools, or American Osteopathic Association (see separate entry); (2) Current unrestricted license to practice medicine in the U.S. or Canada; and (3) Successful completion of 36-month residency program accredited by Residency Review Committee for Family Practice (see separate entry). Graduates of foreign medical schools must receive Standard Certificate from the Educational Commission for Foreign Medical Graduates. One year of foreign residency training may be transferred with approval of the ABFP. Physicians certified by Royal College of General Practitioners of Great Britain or Royal New Zealand College of General Practitioners may qualify to take exam. Physicians certified by College of Family Physicians of Canada must successfully complete additional requirements. **Certification Requirements:** Successful completion of exam. Exam covers: Community medicine; Diagnosis; Geriatrics; Gynecology; Internal medicine; Management; Obstetrics; Pediatrics; Prevention of disease; Psychiatry and behavioral sciences; and Surgery. **Renewal:** Every seven years. Recertification based on successful completion of exam. **Examination Frequency:** Annual - always second Friday in July. **Examination Sites:** Exam given at sites throughout the U.S. **Endorsed By:** American Board of Medical Specialties; American Medical Association; Council on Medical Education.

703

Diplomate of the American Board of Internal Medicine
American Board of Internal Medicine (ABIM)
3624 Market St.
Philadelphia, PA 19104-2675
Phone: (215)243-1500
Fax: (215)382-4702
Toll Free: (800)441-ABIM

Recipient: Physicians specializing in internal medicine. **Educational/Experience Requirements:** Must meet the following requirements: (1) Graduate from medical school accredited by Liaison Committee on Medical Education (see separate entry) or Committee for Accreditation of Canadian Medical Schools, or osteopathic medical school accredited by Bureau of Professional Education, American Osteopathic Association (see separate entry); (2) Hold current unrestricted licensure to practice medicine in the U.S. or Canada; and (3) Successfully complete three year residency program accredited by Accreditation Council for Graduate Medical Education (ACGME) (see separate entry). Clinical Investigators may qualify for certification by meeting the following requirements: (1) Successful completion of two-year residency program accredited by ACGME; and (2) Two years of research during which 80 percent of time dedicated to investigative activities. Graduates of foreign medical schools must have credentials evaluated by Educational Commission for Foreign Medical Graduates or successfully complete postdoctoral medical training in the U.S. via the "Fifth Pathway" plan of the American Medical Association. **Certification Requirements:** Successful completion of exam. Candidates hold Board Eligible, American Board of Internal Medicine designation (see separate entry) prior to successful completion of exam. **Renewal:** Recertification based on self-evaluation process and successful completion of exam. **Preparatory Materials:** *Policies and Procedures for Certification in Internal Medicine,* including list of suggested study references, provided. **Examination Frequency:** Annual - always August. **Examination Sites:** Exam given at sites throughout the U.S. and Canada. **Re-examination:** May retake exam three times. Must successfully complete exam within six years. **Endorsed By:** American Board of Medical Specialties; American Medical Association; Council on Medical Education.

704

Diplomate of the American Board of Internal Medicine with Added Qualifications in Adolescent Medicine
American Board of Internal Medicine (ABIM)
3624 Market St.
Philadelphia, PA 19104-2675
Phone: (215)243-1500
Fax: (215)382-4702
Toll Free: (800)441-ABIM

Recipient: Physicians specializing in adolescent medicine. **Educational/Experience Requirements:** Hold Diplomate of the American Board of Internal Medicine designation (see separate entry) and meet one of the following requirements: (1) Five years experience with at least 20 hours per week devoted to adolescent medicine; (2) Five years combined training and practice; or (3) Two years of training in adolescent medicine program associated with residency in internal medicine or pediatrics accredited by Accreditation Council for Graduate Medical Education (see separate entry). **Certification Requirements:** Successful completion of exam. Exam covers: Family dynamics and other social and emotional development; Illnesses and disabilities that appear or become worse during adolescence; Juvenile justice; Legal and ethical issues, including advocacy; Mental illnesses of adolescence; Nutrition and eating disorders; Organ-specific conditions of significance during teenage years; Physical and physiologic changes associated with pubertal maturation; Public health issues, including demographics, social epidemiology, and population-based interventions; Reproductive health issues; Sports medicine; and Substance abuse. **Renewal:** Every ten years. **Examination Type:** Multiple-choice. **Fees:** $950. **Endorsed By:** American Board of Medical Specialties; American Board of Pediatrics; American Medical Association; Council on Medical Education.

`705`

Diplomate of the American Board of Internal Medicine with Added Qualifications in Clinical and Laboratory Immunology

American Board of Internal
  Medicine (ABIM)
3624 Market St.
Philadelphia, PA 19104-2675
Phone: (215)243-1500
Fax: (215)382-4702
Toll Free: (800)441-ABIM

Recipient: Physicians specializing in clinical and laboratory immunology. **Certification Requirements:** Successful completion of exam. **Endorsed By:** American Board of Medical Specialties; American Medical Association; Council on Medical Education.

`706`

Diplomate of the American Board of Internal Medicine with Added Qualifications in Critical Care Medicine

American Board of Internal
  Medicine (ABIM)
3624 Market St.
Philadelphia, PA 19104-2675
Phone: (215)243-1500
Fax: (215)382-4702
Toll Free: (800)441-ABIM

Recipient: Physicians specializing in critical care medicine. **Educational/ Experience Requirements:** Hold Diplomate of the American Board of Internal Medicine designation (see separate entry) and successfully complete of one of the following requirements: (1) Two year fellowship in critical care medicine accredited by Accreditation Council for Graduate Medical Education (ACGME) (see separate entry); or (2) Two years of fellowship training in general internal medicine accredited by ACGME, including six months of critical care medicine, and one year of fellowship training in critical care medicine accredited by ACGME. **Certification Requirements:** Successful completion of exam. Exam covers: Ad-

ministrative and management principles and techniques; Cardiovascular, physiology, pathology, pathophysiology, and therapy; CNS physiology, pathology, pathophysiology, and therapy; Ethical and legal aspects of critical care medicine; Gastrointestinal acute disorders; Genitourinary, obstetric, and gynecologic acute disorders; Hematologic disorders related to acute illness; Infectious disease physiology, pathology, pathophysiology, and therapy; Metabolic and endocrinologic aspects of critical illness; Monitoring, bioengineering, and biostatistics; Perioperative problems and anesthetic complications (medical management); Pharmacokinetics and dynamics: drug metabolism, toxicity, and excretion in critical illness; Psychosocial aspects of critical care medicine; Renal physiology, pathology, pathophysiology, and therapy; Respiratory physiology, pathology, pathophysiology, and therapy; Resuscitation; and Trauma and burns (medical management). **Renewal:** Every ten years. Recertification based on successful completion of exam. **Examination Frequency:** Annual. **Examination Sites:** Exam given at sites throughout the U.S. **Examination Type:** Multiple-choice. **Waiting Period to Receive Scores:** Four months. **Fees:** $980. **Endorsed By:** American Board of Medical Specialties; American Medical Association; Council on Medical Education.

`707`

Diplomate of the American Board of Internal Medicine with Added Qualifications in Geriatric Medicine

American Board of Internal
  Medicine (ABIM)
3624 Market St.
Philadelphia, PA 19104-2675
Phone: (215)243-1500
Fax: (215)382-4702
Toll Free: (800)441-ABIM

Recipient: Physicians specializing in geriatric internal medicine. **Educational/ Experience Requirements:** Must meet the following requirements: (1) Hold Diplomate of the American Board of Internal Medicine designation (see separate entry); and (2) Successfully complete two years of training in geriatric medicine accredited by Accreditation Council for Graduate Medical Education (see separate entry) or Royal College of Physicians and Surgeons of Canada. **Certification Requirements:** Successful completion of exam. Exam covers: (1) Clinical Situations, covering diagnosis, treatment, prognosis, and etiology and natural history of disease; (2) Interpreta-

tion of Physiologic Data, Electrocardiograms, and Imaging Studies; (3) Biology of Aging, including: Changes in drug metabolism; Epidemiology; Immunology; Nutritional requirements; and Research methodologies; (4) Geriatric Care Issues, including: Geriatric assessment and rehabilitation; Management of patients in long-term care settings; Preventive medicine; and Psychosocial, ethical, legal, and economic issues; (5) Medical Diseases, including: Dermatology; Diagnosis and treatment of diseases requiring modified approach to management; Falls; Gynecology; Incontinence; Ophthalmology; Otorhinolaryngology; Preoperative assessment and postoperative management; and Relevant organ systems; and (6) Neuropsychiatry, including: Cognitive and affective changes; Dementia; Diagnosis and management of cerebrovascular disease; and Sensory impairment. **Renewal:** Every ten years. Recertification based on successful completion of exam. **Examination Frequency:** Annual. **Examination Type:** Multiple-choice. **Endorsed By:** American Board of Family Practice; American Board of Medical Specialties; American Medical Association; Council on Medical Education.

`708`

Diplomate of the American Board of Internal Medicine with Added Qualifications in Sports Medicine

American Board of Internal
  Medicine (ABIM)
3624 Market St.
Philadelphia, PA 19104-2675
Phone: (215)243-1500
Fax: (215)382-4702
Toll Free: (800)441-ABIM

Recipient: Physicians specializing in sports medicine. **Educational/Experience Requirements:** Hold Diplomate of the American Board of Internal Medicine designation (see separate entry) and meet one of the following requirements: (1) Successful completion of one year sports medicine fellowship accredited by Accreditation Council for Graduate Medical Education (see separate entry); or (2) Five years experience, with 20 percent of time devoted to sports medicine, and 30 hours of related continuing education during last five years. **Certification Requirements:** Successful completion of exam. Exam covers: Anatomy related to exercise; Basic nutritional principles and their application to exercise; Effects of disease on exercise and use of exercise in care of medical problems; Ethical principles as applied to exercise and sports; Functioning as team physician; Growth and development related to exercise;

Guidelines for evaluation prior to participation in exercise; Medical-legal aspects of exercise and sports; Pathology and pathophysiology of illness and injury as it relates to exercise; Physical conditioning requirements for various activities; Physiology and biomechanics of exercise; Prevention, evaluation, management, and rehabilitation of injuries; Promotion of physical fitness and healthy lifestyles; Psychological aspects of exercise, performance, and competition; and Understanding pharmacology and effects of therapeutic, performance-enhancing, and recreational drugs. **Renewal:** Every ten years. **Examination Sites:** Exam given at sites throughout the U.S. **Examination Type:** Multiple-choice. **Endorsed By:** American Board of Emergency Medicine; American Board of Family Practice; American Board of Medical Specialties; American Board of Pediatrics; American Medical Association; Council on Medical Education.

709

Diplomate of the American Board of Medical Management
American Board of Medical
　Management (ABMM)
4890 W. Kennedy Blvd., Ste. 200
Tampa, FL 33609-2815
Phone: (813)287-2815
Fax: (813)287-8993
Leslie A. Thornton, Exec.Dir.

Recipient: Physicians specializing in medical management. **Educational/ Experience Requirements:** Must meet the following requirements: (1) Graduation from medical school accredited by Liaison Committee on Medical Education or osteopathic college of medicine accredited by Bureau of Professional Education, American Osteopathic Association (see separate entries); (2) Current licensure to practice medicine; (3) Three years experience rendering patient care; (4) Certification in specialty recognized by American Board of Medical Specialties or American Osteopathic Association; (5) Two years experience in health care management in last ten years; and (6) 150 hours of management education in last ten years, 50 of which must have been conducted by ACPE or accredited college or university. Advanced degree in management may be substituted for education requirement. Candidates whose medical education was completed outside the U.S or Canada must hold Standard Certificate granted by Educational Council for Foreign Medical Graduates. Candidates who are not certified must document professional activities and achievements. **Certification Require-**

ments: Successful completion of exam. **Renewal:** Every ten years. **Examination Frequency:** Annual. **Fees:** $100.

710

Diplomate of the American Board of Neurological Surgery (DABNS)
American Board of Neurological
　Surgery (ABNS)
6550 Fannin St., Ste. 2139
Houston, TX 77030
Phone: (713)790-6015
Fax: (713)794-0207
Mary Louise Sanderson, Admin.

Recipient: Physicians specializing in neurological surgery. **Number of Certified Individuals:** 4127. **Educational/ Experience Requirements:** Must meet the following requirements: (1) Graduation from approved medical school in state, province, or country of residence; (2) Current unrestricted license to practice medicine; (3) Successful completion of 12 months of training in fundamental clinical skills; (4) Successful completion of 60 months of residency training in the U.S. accredited by Accreditation Council for Graduate Medical Education or Canadian equivalent; and (5) Submission of log of cases for at least 12 months. Training in fundamental skills can be achieved in one of the following ways: (1) Training in approved general surgery program in U.S. or Canada; (2) Training under auspices of accredited neurosurgical program; (3) Holding Diplomate of the American Board of Surgery designation (see separate entry); or (4) Holding fellowship in surgery from Royal College of Surgeons of Australasia, Canada, Edinburgh, England, Glasgow, or Ireland. Up to 12 months of training from institutions outside the U.S. or Canada may be credited towards requirement. **Certification Requirements:** Successful completion of written and oral exams. Written exam covers: Fundamental clinical skills/ critical care; Neuroanatomy; Neurobiology; Neurochemistry; Neurology; Neuropathology; Neuropharmacology; Neurophysiology; Neuroradiology; and Neurosurgery. Oral exam involves case study and covers: Neurosurgery-intracranial disease; Neurosurgery-spinal and peripheral nerve disease; and Neurosurgical neurology. **Renewal:** none. **Preparatory Materials:** none. **Examination Frequency:** Annual (written) - usually last Saturday in March; semiannual (oral)-always spring and fall. **Examination Sites:** Written exam given by accredited residency programs. Oral exam given throughout the U.S. in the spring and in Houston, TX, in the fall. **Examination**

Type: Multiple-choice. **Pass/Fail Rate:** 70 percent (written); 85 percent (oral). **Waiting Period to Receive Scores:** Four-six weeks (written); immediately (oral). **Re-examination:** May retake oral exam one time. Fees to retake exams are: $375 (written); $1175 (oral). **Fees:** $1910. **Endorsed By:** American Academy of Neurological Surgeons; American Association of Neurological Surgeons; American Board of Medical Specialties; American College of Surgeons; American Medical Association; Congress of Neurological Surgeons; Council on Medical Education; Neurosurgical Society of America; Society of Neurological Surgeons.

711

Diplomate of the American Board of Nuclear Medicine
American Board of Nuclear
　Medicine (ABNM)
900 Veteran Ave.
Los Angeles, CA 90024
Phone: (310)825-6787
Fax: (310)825-9433

Recipient: Physicians specializing in nuclear medicine. **Number of Certified Individuals:** 4159. **Educational/Experience Requirements:** Must meet the following requirements: (1) Graduation from medical school accredited by Liaison Committee on Medical Education (see separate entry) or school of osteopathy accredited by Bureau of Professional Education, American Osteopathic Association (see separate entry); (2) Successful completion of one-year preparatory post-doctoral training program accredited by Accreditation Council for Graduate Medical Education (ACGME) (see separate entry), Royal College of Physicians and Surgeons of Canada (RCPSC), or Professional Corporation of Physicians of Quebec (PCPQ); (3) Successful completion of two-year formal residency training program in nuclear medicine accredited by ACGME, RCPSC, or PCPQ within last ten years; and (4) Current unrestricted licensure to practice medicine in U.S. or Canada. Partial credit may be given for residencies successfully completed in clinical disciplines closely related to nuclear medicine. Graduates of medical schools outside the U.S. or Canada must have credentials approved by Educational Commission for Foreign Medical Graduates. **Certification Requirements:** Successful completion of written and oral exams. Written exam covers management of patients in the area of clinical nuclear medicine, including, but not limited to: Computer sciences; *In vitro* and *in vivo* measurements; Instrumentation; Medical effects of exposure to ionizing radiation; Medical management of persons exposed to ionizing radiation; Medical nuclear physics; Nuclear imaging; Pathology; Physiology; Principles of nuclear magnetic resonance imaging; Radiation biology; Radiation protection; Radiation safety; Radioassay/radiobioassay; Radiopharmaceutical chemistry; Safe management and disposal of radioactive substances; Statistics; and Therapy with unsealed radionuclides. **Renewal:** Every ten years. **Preparatory Materials:** Brochure and sample questions provided. **Examination Frequency:** Annual. **Examination Sites:** Exam given at sites throughout the U.S. **Waiting Period to Receive Scores:** Four months. **Re-examination:** There is a $1700 fee to retake exams. **Fees:** $1700. **Endorsed By:** American Board of Internal Medicine; American Board of Medical Specialties; American Board of Pathology; American Board of Radiology; American Medical Association; Council on Medical Education; Society of Nuclear Medicine.

`712`

Diplomate of the American Board of Obstetricians and Gynecologists for Osteopathic Specialists

American Board of Obstetricians and Gynecologists for Osteopathic Specialists
804 Main St., Ste. F
Forest Park, GA 30050
Phone: (404)363-8263
Fax: (404)361-2285
Toll Free: (800)447-9397

Recipient: Osteopathic physicians specializing in obstetrics and gynecology. **Educational/Experience Requirements:** Must meet the following requirements: (1) Graduation from approved osteopathic medical college; (2) Current licensure to practice medicine; (3) Successful completion of approved one year internship; (4) Four years of approved training in obstetrics and gynecology; (5) Submission of list of obstetric and gynecological procedures performed in last year; (6) Submission of list of 200 obstetric and gynecological procedures; (7) and Submission of ten cases. Five years of practice may be substituted for one year of training. **Certification Requirements:** Successful completion of written and oral exams and on-site evaluation. **Examination Frequency:** Annual - always June. **Examination Sites:** Exams given at annual meeting and seminar. **Fees:** $600, plus actual costs of on-site evaluation. **Endorsed By:** American Association of Physician Specialists.

`713`

Diplomate of the American Board of Obstetrics and Gynecology

American Board of Obstetrics and Gynecology (ABOG)
2915 Vine St.
Dallas, TX 75204-1069
Phone: (214)871-1619
Fax: (214)871-1943
Norman F. Gant M.D., Exec.Dir.

Recipient: Physicians specializing in obstetrics and gynecology. **Educational/Experience Requirements:** Must meet the following requirements: (1) Degree from medical school approved by Liaison Committee on Medical Education or school of osteopathy approved by Bureau of Professional Education, American Osteopathic Association (see separate entries); (2) Current unrestricted licensure to practice medicine; and (3) Successful completion of residency program accredited by Accreditation Council for Graduate Medical Education (see separate entry) or Royal College of Physicians and Surgeons of Canada. Graduates of medical programs from outside the U.S. or Canada must have credentials evaluated by Educational Commission for Foreign Medical Graduates. **Certification Requirements:** Successful completion of written and oral exams. Written exam covers: (1) Basic Science, including: Anatomy; Embryology; Epidemiology; Fetal physiology; Genetics; Immunology; Microbiology; Pharmacology; Physiology of gynecology and reproductive endocrinology; and Physiology of pregnancy; (2) Clinical Gynecology, including: Anatomic disorders; Benign neoplasms of the breast and pelvic organs; Diagnostic tests and methods; Geriatric gynecology; Infections of genital tract; Pediatric gynecology; Preand postoperative care; Sexually transmitted diseases; and Surgical principles; (3) Clinical Obstetrics, including: Complications and abnormalities of pregnancy, labor, and delivery; Conduct of pregnancy; Human pregnancy overview; Normal labor and delivery; Operative obstetrics and abnormalities of puerperium; Preconceptual counseling; and Prenatal diagnosis; (4) Endocrinology and Fertility, including: Abnormal reproductive endocrinology; Adenomyosis; Ectopic pregnancy; Endometriosis; Ethical problems in gynecology; Infertility; Menopause; and Normal reproductive endocrinology; (5) Medical, Surgical and Psychiatric Diseases in the Non-Pregnant Woman, and Medical, Surgical, and Psychiatric Diseases in Pregnancy and Complications of Pregnancy, including: Cardiovascular diseases; Connective tissue diseases; Diseases of liver and gallbladder; Diseases of skin; Diseases of urinary tract; Endocrine diseases; Ethical problems in gynecology; Gastrointestinal diseases; Gynecologic conditions complicating pregnancy; Hematologic diseases; Infection during pregnancy; Neoplastic disease; Neurologic diseases; Psychiatric diseases; and Pulmonary diseases; (6) Oncology and Pathology, including: Benign; Carcinoma; Carcinoma of breast; Cervix and vagina; Cytopathology; Endometrial hyperplasia; Gross and microscopic pathology of cervix, cord, corpus, endometrium, fetus, membranes, ovary, oviduct, placenta, trophoblast, vagina, and vulva; Intra-epithelial neoplasm of cervix; Ovarian neoplasms; Premalignant and malignant lesions; Principles of chemotherapy and radiation therapy; Response of genital organs to infection, trauma, therapy, pregnancy, and aging; Trophoblastic disease; Uterine sarcomas; Vulva malignancies; and Vulva and vagina; and (7) Primary/Preventive Medicine, including: Cardiovascular risk factors; Contraception; Crisis intervention; Detection of high risk groups; Diet and exercise; Immunizations; Patient education and counseling; Periodic history; Physical examination and diagnostic studies for various age groups; Prevention of disease; Screening tests; Sexuality; and Substance abuse. Must have two years of practice following successful completion of written exam, hold unrestricted hospital privileges, and submit list of patients to attempt oral exam. Oral exam covers cases submitted by candidate and clinical problems. **Renewal:** Every ten years. Recertification based on successful completion of exam. Renewal fee is $800. **Examination Frequency:** Annual - always June (written) and November (oral). **Examination Type:** Multiple-choice. **Waiting Period to Receive Scores:** Nine weeks (written exam). **Re-examination:** May retake oral exam two times. Fees to retake exams are: $500 (written); $800 (oral). **Fees:** $1300. **Endorsed By:** American Board of Medical Specialties; American College of Obstetricians and Gynecologists; American Gynecological and Obstetrical Society; American Medical Association; Association of Professors of Gynecology-Obstetrics; Council on Medical Education.

714

Diplomate of the American Board of Obstetrics and Gynecology with Added Qualification in Critical Care
American Board of Obstetrics and Gynecology (ABOG)
2915 Vine St.
Dallas, TX 75204-1069
Phone: (214)871-1619
Fax: (214)871-1943
Norman F. Gant M.D., Exec.Dir.

Recipient: Physicians specializing in obstetric and gynecologic critical care. **Educational/Experience Requirements:** Must meet the following requirements: (1) Hold Diplomate of the American Board of Obstetrics and Gynecology designation (see separate entry); and (2) Successfully complete of one year of approved training. **Certification Requirements:** Successful completion of either Surgical Critical Care exam administered by American Board of Surgery or Critical Care Medicine exam administered by American Board of Anesthesiology. **Renewal:** Every ten years. **Endorsed By:** American Board of Anesthesiology; American Board of Medical Specialties; American Board of Surgery; American College of Obstetricians and Gynecologists; American Gynecological and Obstetrical Society; American Medical Association; Association of Professors of Gynecology-Obstetrics; Council on Medical Education.

715

Diplomate of the American Board of Ophthalmology
American Board of Ophthalmology (ABO)
111 Presidential Blvd., Ste. 241
Bala Cynwyd, PA 19004
Phone: (610)664-1175

Recipient: Physicians specializing in ophthalmology. **Certification Requirements:** Successful completion of written and oral exams. Written exam covers: Anticipation and recognition of complications; Ethics; Evaluation of clinical data; External disease and cornea; Glaucoma, cataract, and anterior segment; Neuro-ophthalmology; Ophthalmic pathology; Optics, refraction, and contact lenses; Pediatric ophthalmology; Plastic surgery and orbital diseases; Relation of pathogenesis to disease process; Retina, vitreous, and uvea; and Utilization of diagnostic and therapeutic procedures. Oral exam covers data acquisition, diagnosis,

and treatment in the following areas: (1) Anterior Segment of the Eye, including anatomy, embryology, physiology, and pathology of abnormalities and diseases of the cornea, anterior chamber angle, iris, ciliary body, and lens, conditions affecting these structures, and medical and surgical therapies used to alleviate or cure these conditions; (2) External Eye and Adnexa, including: Anatomy, embryology, and physiology of the structures comprising the lacrimal systems, lids, cornea, conjunctiva, and anterior sclera; Differential diagnosis; Indications for, principles of, and complications of surgical procedures utilized to alleviate abnormalities and diseases affecting these tissues; Medical therapy; and Pathologic substrate; (3) Neuro-Ophthalmology and Orbit, including: Anatomy of orbit and neuro-anatomy of afferent and efferent visual systems; Clinical features, pathology, differential diagnosis, and management of disorders of orbit, visual pathways, oculomotor system, pupillomotor pathways, including indications for, principles of, and complications of orbital surgery; Conventional X-ray imaging; CT scanning and magnetic resonance imaging; Ultrasonography; Visual field testing; and Visually evoked responses; (4) Optics, Refraction, and Visual Physiology, including: Ametropia; Basic principles of physical and geometrical optics; Methods of correction of ametropia, including spectacles, contact lenses, intraocular lenses, and kerato-refractive surgery; Methods for prescribing protective lenses, absorptive lenses, and aids for low vision; Operation of standard optical instruments; Principles of lens design; Principles and techniques of refraction; and Visual physiology, including visual acuity, light and dark adaptation, accommodation, and color vision; (5) Pediatric Ophthalmology and Strabismus, including: Anatomy, pathology, and physiology of neuromuscular mechanisms subserving ocular motility and binocular vision; Clinical features, differential diagnosis, natural course, and management of various types of comitant and noncomitant deviations; Diseases affecting eyes of infants and children and associated systemic abnormalities; Methods of examination for detection and assessment of sensory and ocular motor disorders; and Principles and complications of surgery upon extraocular muscles; and (6) Posterior Segment of the Eye, including anatomy, embryology, physiology, and pathology of abnormalities and diseases of vitreous, retina, choroid, and posterior sclera, conditions affecting these structures, and medical and surgical therapies used to alleviate or cure these conditions. **Renewal:** Every ten years. Recertification based on: (1) Current licensure to prac-

tice medicine in the U.S. or Canada; (2) Accumulation of 50 continuing medical education (CME) credits per year accredited by Accreditation Council for Continuing Medical Education (see separate entry); (3) Successful completion of Knowledge Assessment, accomplished by successful completion of written or oral exams; (4) Successful completion of Review of Practice, accomplished by successful completion of exam or submission of case survey; and (5) Successful completion of Identification of Practice-Type, accomplished by completion of application describing practice and submission of representative patient records. **Examination Frequency:** Annual (written); semiannual (oral). **Examination Type:** Multiple-choice. **Re-examination:** May retake written exam one time and oral exam two times. Must successfully complete written and oral exams within six years. **Fees:** $1470. **Educational/Experience Requirements:** Must meet the following requirements: (1) Graduation from medical school or school of osteopathy; (2) Successful completion of one post-graduate year in program accredited by Accreditation Council for Graduate Medical Education (ACGME) (see separate entry) or Royal College of Physicians and Surgeons of Canada (RCPSC); (3) Successful completion of 36-month formal residency training program accredited by ACGME or RCPSC; and (4) Current licensure to practice medicine in the U.S. or Canada. Candidates who completed medical education outside the U.S. or Canada must have credentials evaluated by Educational Commission for Foreign Medical Graduates. **Endorsed By:** American Academy of Ophthalmology; American Board of Medical Specialties; American Medical Association; American Ophthalmological Society; Council on Medical Education.

716

Diplomate of the American Board of Orthopaedic Surgery
American Board of Orthopaedic Surgery (ABOS)
400 Silver Cedar Ct.
Chapel Hill, NC 27514
Phone: (919)929-7103
Fax: (919)942-8988

Recipient: Physicians specializing in orthopaedic surgery. **Educational/Experience Requirements:** Must meet the following requirements: (1) Graduation from accredited medical school in the U.S. or Canada; (2) Current unrestricted licensure to practice medicine; and (3) Successful completion of residency accredited by Accreditation Council for

Graduate Medical Education (see separate entry). **Certification Requirements:** Successful completion of written and oral exams. Must successfully complete 22 months of practice prior to attempting oral exam. Oral exam covers cases submitted by candidate. Cases should be submitted in the following areas: Amputation; Arthrodesis; Complications; Excision; Fracture and/or dislocation; Incision; Introduction or removal; Manipulation; and Repair, revision, or reconstruction. **Renewal:** Every ten years. **Re-examination:** Must successfully complete oral exam within five years of successful completion of written exam. **Fees:** $2570. **Endorsed By:** American Academy of Orthopaedic Surgeons; American Board of Medical Specialties; American Medical Association; American Orthopaedic Association; Council on Medical Education.

| 717 |

Diplomate of the American Board of Orthopaedic Surgery with Added Qualifications in Surgery of the Hand

American Board of Orthopaedic
  Surgery (ABOS)
400 Silver Cedar Ct.
Chapel Hill, NC 27514
Phone: (919)929-7103

Recipient: Physicians specializing in surgery of the hand. **Educational/ Experience Requirements:** Must meet the following requirements: (1) Hold Diplomate of the American Board of Orthopaedic Surgery designation (see separate entry); (2) Two years practice of surgery of the hand; (3) Hold full operating privileges in hospital accredited by Joint Commission on Accreditation of Healthcare Organizations (see separate entry); (4) Successfully complete one year fellowship accredited by Accreditation Council for Graduate Medical Education (see separate entry); and (5) Submit surgical case list for 12-month period. **Certification Requirements:** Successful completion of exam. **Renewal:** Every ten years. **Re-examination:** May retake exam two times. **Fees:** $1500.

| 718 |

Diplomate of the American Board of Otolaryngology

American Board of Otolaryngology
  (ABO)
5615 Kirby Dr., Ste. 936
Houston, TX 77005-2452
Phone: (713)528-6200
Robert W. Cantrell M.D., Exec.V. Pres.

Recipient: Physicians specializing in otolaryngology. **Educational/Experience Requirements:** Must meet the following requirements: (1) Graduation from approved school of medicine or osteopathy; (2) Current unrestricted licensure to practice medicine; (3) One year of general surgical residency training; (4) Successful completion of three years of otolaryngology residency training accredited by Accreditation Council for Graduate Medical Education (see separate entry) or royal College of Physicians and Surgeons or Canada; (5) One additional year of residency training in otolaryngology, general surgery, or other residencies or internships; and (6) Submission of Operative Experience Report containing log of all surgical procedures. Graduates of otolaryngologic training programs in United Kingdom, Republic of Ireland, New Zealand, and Australia may qualify to take exam by meeting special requirements. **Certification Requirements:** Successful completion of oral and written exams. Exams cover: Chemical senses and allergy, endocrinology, and neurology as they relate to head and neck; Cognitive management of congenital, inflammatory, endocrine, neoplastic, degenerative, and traumatic states; Communication sciences, including knowledge of audiology and speech-language pathology; Diagnosis and diagnostic methods; Habilitation and rehabilitation techniques and procedures; Morphology, physiology, pharmacology, pathology, microbiology, biochemistry, genetics, and immunology relevant to head and neck; Research methodology; Respiratory and upper alimentary systems; and Therapeutic and diagnostic radiology. **Examination Frequency:** Annual - always spring (oral) and fall (written). **Re-examination:** Must wait one year to retake written exam. May retake written exam as many times as necessary and retake oral exam two times. **Fees:** $1600. **Endorsed By:** American Academy of Otolaryngology-Head and Neck Surgery; American Medical Association: Council on Medical Education.

| 719 |

Diplomate of the American Board of Pain Medicine

American Board of Pain Medicine
5700 Old Orchard Rd., First Fl.
Skokie, IL 60077-1057
Phone: (708)966-0459
Fax: (708)966-9418
Jeffrey W. Engle, Contact

Recipient: Physicians specializing in pain medicine. **Number of Certified Individuals:** 240. **Educational/Experience Requirements:** Must meet the following requirements: (1) Current unrestricted licensure to practice medicine; (2) Board certification in specialty recognized by American Board of Medical Specialties (ABMS); and (3) Two years experience practicing pain medicine. Faculty of national college may be exempt from ABMS board certification requirement. **Certification Requirements:** Successful completion of exam. Exam covers: Anatomy and physiology; Compensation/ disability and medical-Legal issues; Medical diagnostics; Medical/surgical techniques of pain management; Pain Assessment; Pharmacology; Psychological/ psychiatric aspects of pain; and Types of pain. **Preparatory Materials:** Bulletin, including list of references and sample questions, provided. **Examination Frequency:** Annual. **Examination Sites:** Exam given at sites throughout the U.S. **Examination Type:** Multiple-choice. **Waiting Period to Receive Scores:** Four-eight weeks. **Re-examination:** May retake exam twice. **Fees:** $1200. **Endorsed By:** Academy of Pain Medicine.

| 720 |

Diplomate of the American Board of Pathology with Added Qualification in Cytopathology

American Board of Pathology
  (ABP)
PO Box 25915
Tampa, FL 33622-5915
Phone: (813)286-2444
Fax: (813)289-5279

Recipient: Pathologists specializing in cytopathology. **Educational/Experience Requirements:** Must meet the following requirements: (1) Hold certification in anatomic and clinical pathology or anatomic pathology from ABP; and (2) Either one year of training in cytopathology in program accredited by Accreditation Council for Graduate Medical Education (ACGME) (see separate entry) or approved by ABP or two years experience approved by ABP.

Combined training in anatomic pathology and cytopathology available. **Certification Requirements:** Successful completion of exam. **Examination Frequency:** biennial - always odd-numbered years. **Examination Sites:** Exam given at one site in the U.S. **Fees:** $1200. **Endorsed By:** American Board of Medical Specialities; American Medical Association; American Society of Clinical Pathologists; Council on Medical Education.

721

Diplomate of the American Board of Pathology with Special Qualification in Blood Banking/Transfusion Medicine
American Board of Pathology (ABP)
PO Box 25915
Tampa, FL 33622-5915
Phone: (813)286-2444
Fax: (813)289-5279

Recipient: Pathologists specializing in blood banking and transfusion medicine. **Educational/Experience Requirements:** Must meet one of the following requirements: (1) Hold certification in anatomical and clinical pathology or clinical pathology from ABP or certification with special qualification in hematology from another board affiliated with American Board of Medical Specialties (ABMS) and either one year of training in blood banking/transfusion medicine or two years of experience; or (2) Certification from board affiliated with ABMS and two years of training. Training must be in program accredited by Accreditation Council for Graduate Medical Education (see separate entry) or approved by ABP. Experience must be approved by ABP. Combined training in clinical pathology and blood banking/transfusion medicine available. **Certification Requirements:** Successful completion of exam. **Examination Frequency:** biennial - always odd-numbered years. **Examination Sites:** Exam given at one site in the U.S. **Fees:** $1200. **Endorsed By:** American Board of Medical Specialities; American Medical Association; American Society of Clinical Pathologists; Council on Medical Education.

722

Diplomate of the American Board of Pathology with Special Qualification in Chemical Pathology
American Board of Pathology (ABP)
PO Box 25915
Tampa, FL 33622-5915
Phone: (813)286-2444
Fax: (813)289-5279

Recipient: Pathologists specializing in chemical pathology. **Educational/Experience Requirements:** Must meet one of the following requirements: (1) Hold certification in anatomical and clinical pathology or clinical pathology from ABP and either one year of training in chemical pathology in program accredited by Accreditation Council for Graduate Medical Education (ACGME) (see separate entry) or approved by ABP or two years experience approved by ABP; or (2) Hold certification from board affiliated with American Board of Medical Specialties and two years of training in clinical pathology in program accredited by ACGME. Combined training in clinical pathology and chemical pathology available. **Certification Requirements:** Successful completion of exam. **Examination Frequency:** biennial - always odd-numbered years. **Examination Sites:** Exam given at one site in the U.S. **Fees:** $1200. **Endorsed By:** American Board of Medical Specialities; American Medical Association; American Society of Clinical Pathologists; Council on Medical Education.

723

Diplomate of the American Board of Pathology with Special Qualification in Dermatopathology
American Board of Pathology (ABP)
PO Box 25915
Tampa, FL 33622-5915
Phone: (813)286-2444
Fax: (813)289-5279

Recipient: Pathologists specializing in dermatopathology. **Educational/Experience Requirements:** Must meet the following requirements: (1) Hold either certification in anatomical or clinical pathology from ABP or Diplomate of the American Board of Dermatology designation (see separate entry); and (2) One year of training in dermatopathology in program accredited by Accreditation Council for Graduate Medical Education

(see separate entry) or approved by ABP. **Certification Requirements:** Successful completion of exam. **Examination Frequency:** biennial - always odd-numbered years. **Examination Sites:** Exam given at one site in the U.S. **Fees:** $1200. **Endorsed By:** American Board of Dermatology; American Board of Medical Specialities; American Medical Association; American Society of Clinical Pathologists; Council on Medical Education.

724

Diplomate of the American Board of Pathology with Special Qualification in Forensic Pathology
American Board of Pathology (ABP)
PO Box 25915
Tampa, FL 33622-5915
Phone: (813)286-2444
Fax: (813)289-5279

Recipient: Pathologists specializing in forensic pathology. **Educational/Experience Requirements:** Must meet the following requirements: (1) Hold certification in anatomical pathology or anatomical and clinical pathology from the ABP; and (2) Successful completion of either one year of training in forensic pathology in program accredited by Accreditation Council for Graduate Medical Education (see separate entry) or approved by ABP or two years experience acceptable to ABP. Combined training in anatomic pathology and forensic pathology available. **Certification Requirements:** Successful completion of exam. **Examination Frequency:** biennial - always odd-numbered years. **Examination Sites:** Exam given at one site in the U.S. **Fees:** $1200. **Endorsed By:** American Board of Medical Specialities; American Medical Association; American Society of Clinical Pathologists; Council on Medical Education.

725

Diplomate of the American Board of Pathology with Special Qualification in Hematology
American Board of Pathology (ABP)
PO Box 25915
Tampa, FL 33622-5915
Phone: (813)286-2444
Fax: (813)289-5279

Recipient: Pathologists specializing in hematology. **Educational/Experience Requirements:** Must meet one of the following requirements: (1) Hold certification in anatomical and clinical pathology or clinical pathology from ABP or certification with special qualification in hematology from another board affiliated with the American Board of Medical Specialties (ABMS) and either one year of training in blood banking/transfusion medicine in program accredited by Accreditation Council for Graduate Medical Education (ACGME) (see separate entry) or approved by ABP or two years of experience acceptable to ABP; or (2) Certification from board affiliated with ABMS and two years training in program accredited by ACGME. Combined training in clinical pathology and hematology available. **Certification Requirements:** Successful completion of exam. **Examination Frequency:** biennial - always odd-numbered years. **Examination Sites:** Exam given at one site in the U.S. **Fees:** $1200. **Endorsed By:** American Board of Medical Specialities; American Medical Association; American Society of Clinical Pathologists; Council on Medical Education.

726

Diplomate of the American Board of Pathology with Special Qualification in Immunopathology
American Board of Pathology
(ABP)
PO Box 25915
Tampa, FL 33622-5915
Phone: (813)286-2444
Fax: (813)289-5279

Recipient: Pathologists specializing in immunopathology. **Educational/Experience Requirements:** Must meet one of the following requirements: (1) Hold Diplomate in Anatomic and Clinical Pathology of the American Board of Pathology designation (see separate entry) and either one year of training in immunopathology in program accredited by Accreditation Council for Graduate Medical Education (ACGME) (see separate entry) or approved by ABP or two years experience acceptable to ABP; (2) Hold certification in either anatomic pathology or clinical pathology from ABP and either two years of training in immunopathology in program accredited by ACGME or approved by ABP or four years experience acceptable to ABP; or (3) Hold certification in either anatomic pathology or clinical pathology from ABP with special qualification in either blood/banking/transfusion medicine, clinical pathology, hematology, or medical microbiology, and either one year of training in program accredited by

ACGME or approved by ABP or two years experience acceptable to ABP. Combined training in anatomic pathology and immunopathology available. **Certification Requirements:** Successful completion of exam. **Examination Frequency:** biennial - always odd-numbered years. **Examination Sites:** Exam given at one site in the U.S. **Fees:** $1200. **Endorsed By:** American Board of Medical Specialities; American Medical Association; American Society of Clinical Pathologists; Council on Medical Education.

727

Diplomate of the American Board of Pathology with Special Qualification in Medical Microbiology
American Board of Pathology
(ABP)
PO Box 25915
Tampa, FL 33622-5915
Phone: (813)286-2444
Fax: (813)289-5279

Recipient: Pathologists specializing in medical microbiology. **Educational/Experience Requirements:** Must meet one of the following requirements: (1) Hold certification in anatomic and clinical pathology or clinical pathology from ABP or Board certification from board affiliated with American Board of Medical Specialties (ABMS) with special qualification in infectious disease, and either one year of training in medical microbiology in program accredited by Accreditation Council for Graduate Medical Education (ACGME) (see separate entry) or approved by ABP or two years experience in clinical laboratory medical microbiology approved by ABP; or (2) Hold certification from board affiliated with ABMS and two years training in program accredited by ACGME. Combined training in clinical pathology and medical microbiology available. **Certification Requirements:** Successful completion of exam. **Examination Frequency:** biennial - always odd-numbered years. **Examination Sites:** Exam given at one site in the U.S. **Fees:** $1200. **Endorsed By:** American Board of Medical Specialities; American Medical Association; American Society of Clinical Pathologists; Council on Medical Education.

728

Diplomate of the American Board of Pathology with Special Qualification in Neuropathology
American Board of Pathology
(ABP)
PO Box 25915
Tampa, FL 33622-5915
Phone: (813)286-2444
Fax: (813)289-5279

Recipient: Pathologists specializing in neuropathology. **Educational/Experience Requirements:** Must meet one of the following requirements: (1) Hold certification in either anatomic and clinical pathology or anatomic pathology from ABP and two years training in neuropathology accredited by Accreditation Council for Graduate Medical Education (ACGME) (see separate entry) or approved by ABP; or (2) Hold certification in clinical pathology or board certification from board affiliated with American Board of Medical Specialties and one year of training in anatomic pathology and two years of training in neuropathology accredited by ACGME or approved by ABP. Combined training in anatomic pathology and neuropathology available. **Certification Requirements:** Successful completion of exam. **Examination Frequency:** biennial - always odd-numbered years. **Examination Sites:** Exam given at one site in the U.S. **Fees:** $1200. **Endorsed By:** American Board of Medical Specialities; American Medical Association; American Society of Clinical Pathologists; Council on Medical Education.

729

Diplomate of the American Board of Pathology with Special Qualification in Pediatric Pathology
American Board of Pathology
(ABP)
PO Box 25915
Tampa, FL 33622-5915
Phone: (813)286-2444
Fax: (813)289-5279

Recipient: Pathologists specializing in pediatric pathology. **Educational/Experience Requirements:** Must meet the following requirements: (1) Hold certification in anatomic and clinical pathology or anatomic pathology from ABP or certification in anatomic pathology or general pathology from Royal College of Physicians and Surgeons of Canada; and (2) Either one year of training in pediatric pathology in program accredited by

Accreditation Council for Graduate Medical Education (ACGME) (see separate entry) or approved by ABP or two years experience approved by ABP. **Certification Requirements:** Successful completion of exam. **Examination Frequency:** biennial - always odd-numbered years. **Examination Sites:** Exam given at one site in the U.S. **Fees:** $1200. **Endorsed By:** American Board of Medical Specialities; American Medical Association; American Society of Clinical Pathologists; Council on Medical Education.

Diplomate of the American Board of Pediatrics
American Board of Pediatrics (ABP)
111 Silver Cedar Ct.
Chapel Hill, NC 27514-1651
Phone: (919)929-0461
Fax: (919)929-9255

Recipient: Physicians specializing in pediatrics. **Educational/Experience Requirements:** Must meet the following requirements: (1) Graduation from medical school accredited by Liaison Committee on Medical Education (see separate entry) or Royal College of Physicians and Surgeons of Canada (RCPSC), or college of osteopathic medicine accredited by Bureau of Professional Education, American Osteopathic Association (see separate entry); (2) Current unrestricted licensure to practice medicine; and (3) Successful completion of residency accredited by Accreditation Council for Graduate Medical Education (see separate entry) or RCPSC. Graduates of medical programs from outside the U.S. or Canada must have credentials evaluated by Educational Commission for Foreign Medical Graduates. **Certification Requirements:** Successful completion of exam. **Renewal:** Every seven years. **Preparatory Materials:** Sample questions provided. **Examination Frequency:** Annual - always fall. **Examination Sites:** Exam given at sites throughout the U.S. **Examination Type:** Multiple-choice. **Fees:** $1135. **Endorsed By:** American Academy of Pediatrics; American Board of Medical Specialties; American Medical Association; Council on Medical Education.

Diplomate of the American Board of Pediatrics with Special Qualifications in Adolescent Medicine
American Board of Pediatrics (ABP)
111 Silver Cedar Ct.
Chapel Hill, NC 27514-1651
Phone: (919)929-0461
Fax: (919)929-9255

Recipient: Pediatricians specializing in adolescent medicine. **Educational/Experience Requirements:** Must meet the following requirements: (1) Hold Diplomate of the American Board of Pediatrics designation (see separate entry); (2) Current unrestricted licensure to practice medicine; and (3) Successful completion of residency accredited by Accreditation Council for Graduate Medical Education (see separate entry). **Certification Requirements:** Successful completion of exam. **Renewal:** Every seven years. **Examination Frequency:** Annual. **Endorsed By:** American Academy of Pediatrics; American Board of Medical Specialties; American Medical Association; Council on Medical Education.

Diplomate of the American Board of Pediatrics with Special Qualifications in Neonatal-Perinatal Medicine
American Board of Pediatrics (ABP)
111 Silver Cedar Ct.
Chapel Hill, NC 27514-1651
Phone: (919)929-0461
Fax: (919)929-9255

Recipient: Pediatricians specializing in neonatal and perinatal medicine. **Educational/Experience Requirements:** Must meet the following requirements: (1) Hold Diplomate of the American Board of Pediatrics designation (see separate entry); (2) Current unrestricted licensure to practice medicine; and (3) Successful completion of residency accredited by Accreditation Council for Graduate Medical Education (see separate entry). **Certification Requirements:** Successful completion of exam. **Renewal:** Every seven years. **Examination Frequency:** Annual. **Endorsed By:** American Academy of Pediatrics; American Board of Medical Specialties; American Medical Association; Council on Medical Education.

Diplomate of the American Board of Pediatrics with Special Qualifications in Pediatric Cardiology
American Board of Pediatrics (ABP)
111 Silver Cedar Ct.
Chapel Hill, NC 27514-1651
Phone: (919)929-0461
Fax: (919)929-9255

Recipient: Pediatricians specializing in pediatric cardiology. **Educational/Experience Requirements:** Must meet the following requirements: (1) Hold Diplomate of the American Board of Pediatrics designation (see separate entry); (2) Current unrestricted licensure to practice medicine; and (3) Successful completion of residency accredited by Accreditation Council for Graduate Medical Education (see separate entry). **Certification Requirements:** Successful completion of exam. **Renewal:** Every seven years. **Examination Frequency:** Annual. **Endorsed By:** American Academy of Pediatrics; American Board of Medical Specialties; American Medical Association; Council on Medical Education.

Diplomate of the American Board of Pediatrics with Special Qualifications in Pediatric Critical Care Medicine
American Board of Pediatrics (ABP)
111 Silver Cedar Ct.
Chapel Hill, NC 27514-1651
Phone: (919)929-0461
Fax: (919)929-9255

Recipient: Pediatricians specializing in pediatric critical care medicine. **Educational/Experience Requirements:** Must meet the following requirements: (1) Hold Diplomate of the American Board of Pediatrics designation (see separate entry); (2) Current unrestricted licensure to practice medicine; and (3) Successful completion of residency accredited by Accreditation Council for Graduate Medical Education (see separate entry). **Certification Requirements:** Successful completion of exam. **Renewal:** Every seven years. **Examination Frequency:** Annual. **Endorsed By:** American Academy of Pediatrics; American Board of Medical Specialties; American Medical Association; Council on Medical Education.

735

Diplomate of the American Board of Pediatrics with Special Qualifications in Pediatric Emergency Medicine

American Board of Pediatrics (ABP)
111 Silver Cedar Ct.
Chapel Hill, NC 27514-1651
Phone: (919)929-0461
Fax: (919)929-9255

Recipient: Pediatricians specializing in pediatric emergency medicine. **Educational/Experience Requirements:** Must meet the following requirements: (1) Hold Diplomate of the American Board of Pediatrics designation (see separate entry); (2) Current unrestricted licensure to practice medicine; and (3) Successful completion of residency accredited by Accreditation Council for Graduate Medical Education (see separate entry). **Certification Requirements:** Successful completion of exam. **Renewal:** Every seven years. **Examination Frequency:** Annual. **Endorsed By:** American Academy of Pediatrics; American Board of Medical Specialties; American Medical Association; Council on Medical Education.

736

Diplomate of the American Board of Pediatrics with Special Qualifications in Pediatric Endocrinology

American Board of Pediatrics (ABP)
111 Silver Cedar Ct.
Chapel Hill, NC 27514-1651
Phone: (919)929-0461
Fax: (919)929-9255

Recipient: Pediatricians specializing in pediatric endocrinology. **Educational/Experience Requirements:** Must meet the following requirements: (1) Hold Diplomate of the American Board of Pediatrics designation (see separate entry); (2) Current unrestricted licensure to practice medicine; and (3) Successful completion of residency accredited by Accreditation Council for Graduate Medical Education (see separate entry). **Certification Requirements:** Successful completion of exam. **Renewal:** Every seven years. **Examination Frequency:** Annual. **Endorsed By:** American Academy of Pediatrics; American Board of Medical Specialties; American Medical Association; Council on Medical Education.

737

Diplomate of the American Board of Pediatrics with Special Qualifications in Pediatric Gastroenterology

American Board of Pediatrics (ABP)
111 Silver Cedar Ct.
Chapel Hill, NC 27514-1651
Phone: (919)929-0461
Fax: (919)929-9255

Recipient: Pediatricians specializing in pediatric gastroenterology. **Educational/Experience Requirements:** Must meet the following requirements: (1) Hold Diplomate of the American Board of Pediatrics designation (see separate entry); (2) Current unrestricted licensure to practice medicine; and (3) Successful completion of residency accredited by Accreditation Council for Graduate Medical Education (see separate entry). **Certification Requirements:** Successful completion of exam. **Renewal:** Every seven years. **Examination Frequency:** Annual. **Endorsed By:** American Academy of Pediatrics; American Board of Medical Specialties; American Medical Association; Council on Medical Education.

738

Diplomate of the American Board of Pediatrics with Special Qualifications in Pediatric Hematology-Oncology

American Board of Pediatrics (ABP)
111 Silver Cedar Ct.
Chapel Hill, NC 27514-1651
Phone: (919)929-0461
Fax: (919)929-9255

Recipient: Pediatricians specializing in pediatric hematology and oncology. **Educational/Experience Requirements:** Must meet the following requirements: (1) Hold Diplomate of the American Board of Pediatrics designation (see separate entry); (2) Current unrestricted licensure to practice medicine; and (3) Successful completion of residency accredited by Accreditation Council for Graduate Medical Education (see separate entry). **Certification Requirements:** Successful completion of exam. **Renewal:** Every seven years. **Examination Frequency:** Annual. **Endorsed By:** American Academy of Pediatrics; American Board of Medical Specialties; American Medical Association; Council on Medical Education.

739

Diplomate of the American Board of Pediatrics with Special Qualifications in Pediatric Infectious Diseases

American Board of Pediatrics (ABP)
111 Silver Cedar Ct.
Chapel Hill, NC 27514-1651
Phone: (919)929-0461
Fax: (919)929-9255

Recipient: Pediatricians specializing in pediatric infectious diseases. **Educational/Experience Requirements:** Must meet the following requirements: (1) Hold Diplomate of the American Board of Pediatrics designation (see separate entry); (2) Current unrestricted licensure to practice medicine; and (3) Successful completion of residency accredited by Accreditation Council for Graduate Medical Education (see separate entry). **Certification Requirements:** Successful completion of exam. **Renewal:** Every seven years. **Examination Frequency:** Annual. **Endorsed By:** American Academy of Pediatrics; American Board of Medical Specialties; American Medical Association; Council on Medical Education.

740

Diplomate of the American Board of Pediatrics with Special Qualifications in Pediatric Nephrology

American Board of Pediatrics (ABP)
111 Silver Cedar Ct.
Chapel Hill, NC 27514-1651
Phone: (919)929-0461
Fax: (919)929-9255

Recipient: Pediatricians specializing in pediatric nephrology. **Educational/Experience Requirements:** Must meet the following requirements: (1) Hold Diplomate of the American Board of Pediatrics designation (see separate entry); (2) Current unrestricted licensure to practice medicine; and (3) Successful completion of residency accredited by Accreditation Council for Graduate Medical Education (see separate entry). **Certification Requirements:** Successful completion of exam. **Renewal:** Every seven years. **Examination Frequency:** Annual. **Endorsed By:** American Academy of Pediatrics; American Board of Medical Specialties; American Medical Association; Council on Medical Education.

741

Diplomate of the American Board of Pediatrics with Special Qualifications in Pediatric Pulmonology

American Board of Pediatrics (ABP)
111 Silver Cedar Ct.
Chapel Hill, NC 27514-1651
Phone: (919)929-0461
Fax: (919)929-9255

Recipient: Pediatricians specializing in pediatric pulmonology. **Educational/ Experience Requirements:** Must meet the following requirements: (1) Hold Diplomate of the American Board of Pediatrics designation (see separate entry); (2) Current unrestricted licensure to practice medicine; and (3) Successful completion of residency accredited by Accreditation Council for Graduate Medical Education (see separate entry). **Certification Requirements:** Successful completion of exam. **Renewal:** Every seven years. **Examination Frequency:** Annual. **Endorsed By:** American Academy of Pediatrics; American Board of Medical Specialties; American Medical Association; Council on Medical Education.

742

Diplomate of the American Board of Pediatrics with Special Qualifications in Pediatric Rheumatology

American Board of Pediatrics (ABP)
111 Silver Cedar Ct.
Chapel Hill, NC 27514-1651
Phone: (919)929-0461
Fax: (919)929-9255

Recipient: Pediatricians specializing in pediatric rheumatology. **Educational/ Experience Requirements:** Must meet the following requirements: (1) Hold Diplomate of the American Board of Pediatrics designation (see separate entry); (2) Current unrestricted licensure to practice medicine; and (3) Successful completion of residency accredited by Accreditation Council for Graduate Medical Education (see separate entry). **Certification Requirements:** Successful completion of exam. **Renewal:** Every seven years. **Examination Frequency:** Annual. **Endorsed By:** American Academy of Pediatrics; American Board of Medical Specialties; American Medical Association; Council on Medical Education.

743

Diplomate of the American Board of Physical Medicine and Rehabilitation (ABPMR)

American Board of Physical Medicine and Rehabilitation
Norwest Center, Ste. 674
21 First St., SW
Rochester, MN 55902-3009
Phone: (507)282-1776
Fax: (507)282-9242
Joachim L. Opitz M.D., Exec.Dir.

Recipient: Physicians specializing in physical medicine and rehabilitation. **Number of Certified Individuals:** 4642. **Educational/Experience Requirements:** Must meet the following requirements: (1) Graduation from medical school accredited by Liaison Committee on Medical Education (see separate entry) or Canadian Medical Association, or graduate from osteopathic medical school accredited by Bureau of Professional Education, American Osteopathic Association (see separate entry); (2) Current unrestricted medical or osteopathic medical license; and (3) Successful completion of 48-month residency accredited by Accreditation Council for Graduate Medical Education (see separate entry). Graduates from medical schools outside the U.S. must meet additional requirements. **Certification Requirements:** Successful completion of exam consisting of written and oral parts. Exam covers: Anatomy; Biomechanics; Biophysics of physical agents; Cerebral and spinal cord injuries and diseases; Electricity; Electrodiagnosis; Electromyography; Histopathology of muscles, nerves, bones, joints, soft tissues, and central nervous system; Kinetics and functional systems; Mechanics; Methods of assessing psychological and vocational needs of patients; Musculoskeletal; Neuroanatomy; Neuromuscular diseases; Pathology; Pharmacology; Physical agents and methods; Physics; Physiology of nerve, muscle, and bone; and Rheumatic diseases. Must successfully complete one year of clinical practice, fellowship, or research experience after residency training to take oral exam. **Renewal:** Every ten years. Recertification based on either accumulation of 500 hours of continuing education or successful completion of exam. **Examination Frequency:** Annual - usually May. **Examination Sites:** Exam given at three sites in the U.S. **Waiting Period to Receive Scores:** Two-three weeks. **Reexamination:** Must only retake part failed. **Fees:** $1300. **Endorsed By:** American Academy of Physical Medicine and Rehabilitation; American Board of Medical Specialties; American Medical Association; Association of Academic Physiatrists; Council on Medical Education.

744

Diplomate of the American Board of Plastic Surgery

American Board of Plastic Surgery (ABPS)
Seven Penn Center, Ste. 400 1635 Market St.
Philadelphia, PA 19103-2204
Phone: (215)587-9322

Recipient: Plastic surgeons. **Educational/ Experience Requirements:** Must meet the following requirements: (1) Graduation from school of medicine accredited by Liaison Council on Medical Education (see separate entry) or school of osteopathic medicine accredited by Bureau of Professional Education, American Osteopathic Association (see separate entry); (2) Current unrestricted licensure to practice medicine; (3) Successful completion of three-year surgical residency accredited by Accreditation Council for Graduate Medical Education (ACGME) (see separate entry) or Royal College of Physicians and Surgeons; (4) Successful completion of two-year plastic surgery residency accredited by ACGME; (5) Two years practice in plastic surgery; (6) Operating privileges at hospital accredited by Joint Commission on Accreditation of Healthcare Organizations (see separate entry); (7) Submission of case list from last 12 months; and (8) Submission of ten case reports. Candidates who attained medical education outside the U.S., Canada, or Puerto Rico must hold certificate from Educational Commission for Foreign Medical Graduates or successfully complete program through Fifth Pathway of the American Medical Association. **Certification Requirements:** Successful completion of written and oral exams. Written exam covers: Aesthetic (cosmetic) surgery, psychiatry, and legal medicine; Basic knowledge of pathology, biologic behavior or neoplasms, inflammation, and repair; Basic techniques, wound healing, microsurgery, and transplantation; Burns, sepsis, metabolism, trauma, resuscitation, nutrition, endocrinology, shock, and hematology; Congenital anomalies, genetics, teratology, facial deformity, speech pathology, gynecology, and genitourinary problems; Gross and functional anatomy and embryology; Hand, peripheral nerves, and rehabilitation; Maxillofacial and craniofacial surgery and microsurgery; Pre- and postoperative care, anesthesia, cardiorespiratory care, complications, and clinical pharmacology; Trunk, lower extremity, musculoskeletal system, pressure ulcers, and rehabilitation; and Tumors of the head and neck, skin, and breast. Oral exam covers theory and practice of plastic surgery and requires defense of case reports submitted by candidate. **Examination Frequency:** Annual - always spring (written). **Examination Sites:** Written exam given at one site in the U.S. and oral exam given at two sites in the U.S. **Examination Type:** Multiple-choice; true or false. **Re-examination:** May retake exams two times. **Fees:** $2400. **Endorsed By:** American Association for Hand Surgery; American Association of Plastic Surgeons; American Board of Medical Specialties; American Board of Surgery; American College of Surgeons; American Medical Association; American Society for Aesthetic Plastic Surgery; American Society of Maxillofacial Surgeons; American Society of Plastic and Reconstructive Surgeons; American Society for Surgery of the Hand; American Surgical Association; Association of Academic Chairmen of Plastic Surgery; Canadian Society of Plastic Surgeons; Council on Medical Education; Council of Regional Societies of Plastic and Reconstructive Surgery; Plastic Surgery Research Council; Society of Head and Neck Surgeons.

745

Diplomate of the American Board of Preventive Medicine
American Board of Preventive Medicine (ABPM)
9950 W. Lawrence Ave., Ste. 106
Schiller Park, IL 60176
Phone: (708)671-1750
Fax: (708)671-1751
Dr. Alice R. Ring M.P.H., Exec. Dir.

Recipient: Physicians specializing in preventive medicine. **Number of Certified Individuals:** 6800. **Educational/Experience Requirements:** Must meet the following requirements: (1) Graduation from either medical school accredited by Liaison Committee on Medical Education (see separate entry), school of osteopathy accredited by Bureau of Professional Education, American Osteopathic Association (see separate entry), or from medical school located outside the U.S. or Canada; (2) Current unrestricted license to practice medicine in U.S. or Canada; (3) Successful completion of one year of supervised postgraduate clinical training provided as part of accredited residency or internship program; (4) Master of Public Health degree or equivalent, including course content in biostatistics, epidemiology, health services management and administration, and environmental health; (5) Successful completion of one year residency practicum in program accredited by Accreditation Council for Graduate Medical Education (see separate entry); (6) One year

of special training, research, or training in the field; and (7) Training in one of the following specialties for two of the preceding five years: Aerospace medicine; Occupational medicine; or Public health and general preventive medicine. Equivalency credit may be granted for practice, research, or teaching in field and for other certifications held. **Certification Requirements:** Successful completion of two-part exam. Part one covers general preventive medicine. Part two covers one of the following specialties: Aerospace medicine; Occupational medicine; and Public health and general preventive medicine. **Preparatory Materials:** Information booklet and study guide provided. **Examination Frequency:** Annual. **Examination Sites:** Exam given in Chicago, IL. **Examination Type:** Multiple-choice. **Pass/Fail Rate:** 72 percent pass exam the first time. **Waiting Period to Receive Scores:** Three months. **Re-examination:** Must wait one year to retake exam. May retake exam once. **Fees:** $1200. **Endorsed By:** Aerospace Medical Association; American Board of Medical Specialties; American College of Preventive Medicine; American Medical Association; American Public Health Association; Association of Schools of Public Health; Association of Teachers of Preventive Medicine; Canadian Public Health Association; Council on Medical Education.

746

Diplomate of the American Board of Psychiatry and Neurology with Added Qualifications in Clinical Neurophysiology
American Board of Psychiatry and Neurology (ABPN)
500 Lake Cook Rd., Ste. 335
Deerfield, IL 60015-5249
Phone: (708)945-7900
Fax: (708)945-1146

Recipient: Physicians specializing in clinical neurophysiology. **Educational/Experience Requirements:** Must meet the following requirements: (1) Hold certification awarded by American Board of Psychiatry and Neurology; and (2) One year of training in clinical neurophysiology or equivalent accredited by Accreditation Council for Graduate Medical Education (see separate entry). **Certification Requirements:** Successful completion of exam. Exam covers: Autonomic testing; Central EEG-EMG; Evoked potentials; Instrumentation; Physiology; Polysomnography; Signal analysis; and Surgery-ICU monitoring. **Renewal:** Every ten years. Recertification based on successful completion of exam.

Examination Frequency: Annual. **Examination Sites:** Exam given at regional sites throughout the U.S., Canada, and internationally. **Examination Type:** Multiple-choice. **Re-examination:** May retake exam one time. There is a $525 fee to retake exam. **Fees:** $875. **Endorsed By:** American Academy of Neurology; American Board of Medical Specialties; American Medical Association; American Neurological Association; American Psychiatric Association; Council on Medical Education.

747

Diplomate of the American Board of Sleep Medicine
American Board of Sleep Medicine
1610 14th St., NW, Ste. 302
Rochester, MN 55901
Phone: (507)287-9819
Fax: (507)287-6008

Recipient: Ph.D.s or physicians specializing in sleep medicine. **Number of Certified Individuals:** 432. **Educational/Experience Requirements:** May qualify as either Ph.D. or physician. Ph.D. candidates must meet the following requirements: (1) Ph.D. degree or equivalent with doctoral specialization in health-related field; (2) Two years supervised clinical training or its equivalent, with one year in broadly-defined clinical training program; (3) One year training in clinical sleep disorders under supervision of Diplomate of the American Board of Sleep Medicine working in sleep disorders center; and (4) Participation in evaluation of 25 patients, under supervision, including both interviewing and polysomnographic testing, interpretation of 50 polysomnograms and 25 multiple sleep latency tests, and carrying out of behavioral treatments for minimum of five patients. Candidates should also be familiar with American Psychological Association's *Ethical Standards of Psychologists*. Physician candidates must meet the following requirements: (1) Medical or osteopathic medical degree; (2) Unrestricted license to practice medicine in U.S. or Canada; (3) Successful completion of residency program accredited by Accreditation Council for Graduate Medical Education (see separate entry); (4) Certification by primary specialty board recognized by American Board of Medical Specialties, Royal College of Physicians and Surgeons of Canada, Certificate College of Family Physicians, or equivalent board for osteopathic medicine; and (5) One year of training in sleep medicine under supervision of Diplomate of the American Board of Sleep Medicine or accredited fellowship training program. May substitute combination of education and experience for this requirement. **Certification Requirements:** Successful completion of two-part exam. Part I covers: Artifact recognition; Basic skills of monitoring, record reading, and interpretation; Biochemistry; Biological rhythms; Clinical disorders of sleep; Clinical polysomnography; Diagnostic procedures; Dreaming and behavior; Endocrinology; Epidemiology; Etiology; Interpretation; Legal/medical issues; Maturational changes; Neuroanatomy; Pattern recognition; Patient safety issues; Pharmacology; Physiology; Psychopathology; Psychophysiology; Sleep medicine; Sleep in other medical, psychiatric, and neurologic disorders; Sleep stage scoring; Sleep/wake cycles and stages; Sleep/wake disorders; Symptomatology; and Treatment. Part II covers: Behavioral treatments; Diagnostic and treatment options; Ethics; Interpretation of PSG's; Outlining clinical diagnostic and treatment options; Polysomnogram reading and interpretation; and Research. **Preparatory Materials:** *The International Classification of Sleep Disorders* (reference). Booklet, including list of suggested reading, provided. **Examination Frequency:** Annual - always April (Part II) and October (Part I). **Examination Sites:** Part I given at sites throughout the U.S. and Part II given at one site in the U.S. **Examination Type:** Essay; multiple-choice. **Waiting Period to Receive Scores:** Two-three months. **Re-examination:** May retake exams one time. Must successfully complete exams within two years. **Fees:** $900. **Endorsed By:** Association of Sleep Disorders Centers.

748

Diplomate of the American Board of Surgery
American Board of Surgery (ABS)
1617 John F. Kennedy Blvd., Ste. 860
Philadelphia, PA 19103-1847
Phone: (215)568-4000
Dr. Wallace P. Ritchie Jr., Exec. Dir.

Recipient: Surgeons. **Educational/Experience Requirements:** Must meet the following requirements: (1) Graduation from accredited college of allopathic or osteopathic medicine in the U.S. or Canada; (2) Current unrestricted licensure to practice medicine; (3) Successful completion of residency accredited by Accreditation Council for Graduate Medical Education (see separate entry) or Royal College of Physicians and Surgeons; and (4) Hold admitting privileges to surgical service in accredited hospital, or be en-

gaged in pursuing additional graduate education in component of surgery or one of the other recognized surgical specialties. Graduates of medical programs from outside the U.S. or Canada must have credentials evaluated by Educational Commission for Foreign Medical Graduates. **Certification Requirements:** Successful completion of written and oral exams. Written exam covers basic sciences applicable to surgery and general surgical principles. Oral exam covers: Anatomy; Bacteriology; Biochemistry; Clinical entities; Level of surgical judgment; Pathology; Physiology; and Problem solving ability. **Examination Frequency:** Annual (written); six times per year (oral). **Examination Sites:** Exams given at sites throughout the U.S. **Examination Type:** Multiple-choice. **Re-examination:** May retake exams two times. Must successfully complete oral exam within five years of successful completion of written exam. Fees to retake exams are: $400 (written); $600 (oral). **Fees:** $1200. **Endorsed By:** American Association for the Surgery of Trauma; American Board of Colon and Rectal Surgery; American Board of Medical Specialties; American Board of Plastic Surgery; American Board of Thoracic Surgery; American College of Surgeons; American Medical Association; American Pediatric Surgical Association; American Surgical Association; Association for Academic Surgery; Association of Program Directors in Surgery; Central Surgical Association; Council on Medical Education; Joint Council of the Vascular Societies; New England Surgical Society; Pacific Coast Surgical Association; Society for Surgery of the Alimentary Tract; Society of Surgical Oncology; Society of University Surgeons; Southern Surgical Association; Western Surgical Association.

749

Diplomate of the American Board of Surgery with Added Qualifications in General Vascular Surgery
American Board of Surgery (ABS)
1617 John F. Kennedy Blvd., Ste. 860
Philadelphia, PA 19103-1847
Phone: (215)568-4000
Dr. Wallace P. Ritchie Jr., Exec. Dir.

Recipient: Surgeons specializing in general vascular surgery. **Educational/Experience Requirements:** Must meet the following requirements: (1) Hold Diplomate of the American Board of Surgery designation (see separate entry); (2) Cur-

rent unrestricted licensure to practice medicine; (3) Successfully complete of program in general vascular surgery accredited by Accreditation Council for Graduate Medical Education (see separate entry) or Royal College of Physicians and Surgeons of Canada; and (4) Submission of list of major vascular reconstructive procedures conducted. **Certification Requirements:** Successful completion of written and oral exams. **Renewal:** Every ten years. Recertification based on successful completion of exam, continuing medical education, and submission of list of cases performed at hospital at which candidate holds privileges for last year. Renewal fee is $600. **Examination Frequency:** Annual - always late spring or early summer (oral) and fall (written). **Examination Sites:** Written exam given at sites throughout the U.S. **Examination Type:** Multiple-choice. **Re-examination:** May retake written exam four times and oral exam two times. Fees to retake exams are: $400 (written); $750 (oral). **Fees:** $1250. **Endorsed By:** American Association for the Surgery of Trauma; American Board of Colon and Rectal Surgery; American Board of Medical Specialties; American Board of Plastic Surgery; American Board of Thoracic Surgery; American College of Surgeons; American Medical Association; American Pediatric Surgical Association; American Surgical Association; Association for Academic Surgery; Association of Program Directors in Surgery; Central Surgical Association; Council on Medical Education; Joint Council of the Vascular Societies; New England Surgical Society; Pacific Coast Surgical Association; Society for Surgery of the Alimentary Tract; Society of Surgical Oncology; Society of University Surgeons; Southern Surgical Association; Western Surgical Association.

750

Diplomate of the American Board of Surgery with Added Qualifications in Surgery of the Hand
American Board of Surgery (ABS)
1617 John F. Kennedy Blvd., Ste. 860
Philadelphia, PA 19103-1847
Phone: (215)568-4000
Dr. Wallace P. Ritchie Jr., Exec. Dir.

Recipient: Surgeons specializing in surgery of the hand. **Educational/Experience Requirements:** Must meet the following requirements: (1) Hold Diplomate of the American Board of Surgery designation (see separate entry); (2) Two years post-training experience; (3) Current unrestricted licensure to practice medicine; (4) Successfully complete one-year fellowship accredited by Accreditation Council for Graduate Medical Education (see separate entry); (5) Hold full operating privileges in accredited hospital; (6) Document contributions to the field through administration, publication, research, and teaching; and (7) Submit list of cases during consecutive 12-month period in last two years including cases in at least six of the following categories: Bone and joint; Congenital; Contracture and joint stiffness; Microvascular; Nerve; Nonoperative; Skin and wound problems; Tendon and muscle; and Tumor. **Certification Requirements:** Successful completion of exam. **Renewal:** Every ten years. **Examination Frequency:** Annual. **Examination Type:** Multiple-choice. **Re-examination:** May retake exam twice. Fee to retake exam is $1000. **Fees:** $500. **Endorsed By:** American Association for the Surgery of Trauma; American Board of Colon and Rectal Surgery; American Board of Medical Specialties; American Board of Plastic Surgery; American Board of Thoracic Surgery; American College of Surgeons; American Medical Association; American Pediatric Surgical Association; American Surgical Association; Association for Academic Surgery; Association of Program Directors in Surgery; Central Surgical Association; Council on Medical Education; Joint Council of the Vascular Societies; New England Surgical Society; Pacific Coast Surgical Association; Society for Surgery of the Alimentary Tract; Society of Surgical Oncology; Society of University Surgeons; Southern Surgical Association; Western Surgical Association.

751

Diplomate of the American Board of Surgery with Added Qualifications in Surgical Critical Care
American Board of Surgery (ABS)
1617 John F. Kennedy Blvd., Ste. 860
Philadelphia, PA 19103-1847
Phone: (215)568-4000
Dr. Wallace P. Ritchie Jr., Exec. Dir.

Recipient: Surgeons specializing in surgical critical care. **Educational/Experience Requirements:** Must meet the following requirements: (1) Hold Diplomate of the American Board of Surgery designation (see separate entry); (2) Current unrestricted licensure to practice medicine; and (3) Successfully complete program in surgical critical care accredited by Ac-

creditation Council for Graduate Medical Education (see separate entry). **Certification Requirements:** Successful completion of exam. **Renewal:** Every ten years. Recertification based on successful completion of exam, continuing medical education, and submission of list of 25 cases performed at hospital at which candidate holds privileges for last year. Renewal fee is $600. **Examination Frequency:** Annual. **Examination Type:** Multiple-choice. **Re-examination:** May retake exam four times. **Fees:** $750. **Endorsed By:** American Association for the Surgery of Trauma; American Board of Colon and Rectal Surgery; American Board of Medical Specialties; American Board of Plastic Surgery; American Board of Thoracic Surgery; American College of Surgeons; American Medical Association; American Pediatric Surgical Association; American Surgical Association; Association for Academic Surgery; Association of Program Directors in Surgery; Central Surgical Association; Council on Medical Education; Joint Council of the Vascular Societies; New England Surgical Society; Pacific Coast Surgical Association; Society for Surgery of the Alimentary Tract; Society of Surgical Oncology; Society of University Surgeons; Southern Surgical Association; Western Surgical Association.

752

Diplomate of the American Board of Surgery with Special Qualifications in Pediatric Surgery
American Board of Surgery (ABS)
1617 John F. Kennedy Blvd., Ste. 860
Philadelphia, PA 19103-1847
Phone: (215)568-4000
Dr. Wallace P. Ritchie Jr., Exec. Dir.

Recipient: Surgeons specializing in pediatric surgery. **Educational/Experience Requirements:** Must meet the following requirements: (1) Hold Diplomate of the American Board of Surgery designation (see separate entry); (2) Current unrestricted licensure to practice medicine; (3) Successfully complete of two-year residency in pediatric surgery accredited by Accreditation Council for Graduate Medical Education (see separate entry) or Royal College of Physicians and Surgeons of Canada; (4) Hold surgical privileges in approved hospitals; and (5) Submit list of pediatric surgical procedures conducted. **Certification Requirements:** Successful completion of written and oral exams. **Renewal:** Every ten years. Recertification based on successful completion

of exam, continuing medical education, and submission of list of cases performed by candidate for last year. Renewal fee is $600. **Examination Frequency:** biennial - always spring, even numbered years (oral), and fall, odd numbered years (written). **Examination Type:** Multiple-choice. **Re-examination:** May retake exams two times. Fees to retake exams are: $400 (written); $750 (oral). **Fees:** $1250. **Endorsed By:** American Association for the Surgery of Trauma; American Board of Colon and Rectal Surgery; American Board of Medical Specialties; American Board of Plastic Surgery; American Board of Thoracic Surgery; American College of Surgeons; American Medical Association; American Pediatric Surgical Association; American Surgical Association; Association for Academic Surgery; Association of Program Directors in Surgery; Central Surgical Association; Council on Medical Education; Joint Council of the Vascular Societies; New England Surgical Society; Pacific Coast Surgical Association; Society for Surgery of the Alimentary Tract; Society of Surgical Oncology; Society of University Surgeons; Southern Surgical Association; Western Surgical Association.

753

Diplomate of the American Board of Thoracic Surgery
American Board of Thoracic Surgery (ABTS)
One Rotary Center, Ste. 803
Evanston, IL 60201
Phone: (708)475-1520
Fax: (708)474-6240
Richard J. Cleveland M.D., Sec.

Recipient: Physicians specializing in thoracic surgery. **Educational/Experience Requirements:** Must meet the following requirements: (1) Hold Diplomate of the American Board of Surgery designation (see separate entry); and (2) Successfully complete 24 month residency accredited by Accreditation Council for Graduate Medical Education (see separate entry). **Certification Requirements:** Successful completion of written and oral exams. **Renewal:** Every ten years. **Preparatory Materials:** Booklet of information provided. **Examination Frequency:** Annual. **Re-examination:** May retake each exam two times. Must successfully complete written exams within four years. Must successfully complete oral exam within four years after successful completion of written exam. Fees to retake exam are: $875 (written); $925 (oral). **Fees:** $2170. **Endorsed By:** American Association for Thoracic Surgery; American Board of Medical Specialties; American Board of

Surgery; American College of Surgeons; American Medical Association; American Surgical Association; Council on Medical Education; Society of Thoracic Surgeons; Thoracic Surgery Director's Association.

754

Diplomate of the American Board of Urology

American Board of Urology (ABU)
31700 Telegraph Rd., Ste. 150
Bingham Farms, MI 48025
Phone: (810)646-9720
Alan D. Perlmutter M.D., Exec.Sec.

Recipient: Physicians specializing in urology. **Educational/Experience Requirements:** Must meet the following requirements: (1) Degree from medical school approved by Liaison Committee on Medical Education or school of osteopathy approved by Bureau of Professional Education, American Osteopathic Association (see separate entries); (2) Current unrestricted licensure to practice medicine; and (3) Successful completion of residency program accredited by Accreditation Council for Graduate Medical Education (see separate entry) or Royal College of Physicians and Surgeons of Canada. Graduates of medical programs from outside the U.S. or Canada must have credentials evaluated by Educational Commission for Foreign Medical Graduates. **Certification Requirements:** Successful completion of qualifying exam and three-section certifying exam. Qualifying exam covers: Adrenal diseases; Andrology (including infertility); Calculous disease (including endourology and shock-wave lithotripsy); Congenital anomalies; Endocrinology; Female urology; Infectious diseases; Neurourology and urodynamics; Obstructive diseases; Pediatric urology; Psychological disorders; Renal transplantation; Renovascular hypertension; Sexuality and impotence; Trauma; and Urologic oncology. Certifying exam includes assessment of clinical competence through review of practice logs and peer review and three practical exams. Candidates must have completed 18 months of practice before attempting certifying exam and submit log of surgical cases. Six months credit may be substituted for fellowship relevant to urology of one year or longer. **Renewal:** Every ten years. Renewal fee is $900. **Examination Frequency:** Annual - always January or February (certifying) and May or June (qualifying). **Examination Sites:** Exams given at sites throughout the U.S. **Reexamination:** Must only retake sections of certifying exam failed. Must success-

fully complete exams within five years. Fees to retake exams are: $825 (qualifying); $300 (per section of certifying exam). **Fees:** $1650. **Endorsed By:** American Association of Clinical Urologists; American Association of Genito-Urinary Surgeons; American Board of Medical Specialties; American College of Surgeons; American Medical Association; American Urological Association; Council on Medical Education; Society of University Urologists; and Urology Section of the American Academy of Pediatrics.

755

Diplomate of the American Osteopathic Board of Anesthesiology

American Osteopathic Board of Anesthesiology
17201 E. U.S. Hwy. 40, Ste. 204
Independence, MO 64055
Phone: (816)373-4700
Toll Free: (800)842-2622
Diann Hubbard, Corres.Sec.

Recipient: Osteopathic physicians specializing in anesthesiology. **Educational/Experience Requirements:** Must meet the following requirements: (1) Graduation from college of osteopathic medicine accredited by Bureau of Professional Education, American Osteopathic Association (see separate entry); (2) Current licensure to practice medicine; (3) Two years of membership in either American Osteopathic Association or Canadian Osteopathic Association; (4) Successful completion of internship accredited by Council on Postdoctoral Training of the American Osteopathic Association; (5) Successful completion of three-year residency in anesthesiology accredited by Council on Postdoctoral Training of the American Osteopathic Association (see separate entry); (6) Practice in anesthesiology subsequent to successful completion of residency; (7) Submission of list of anesthetic procedures; (8) Submission of case reports of anesthetics administered; and (9) Submission of list and discussion of mortalities. **Membership:** Required. **Certification Requirements:** Successful completion of written, oral, and clinical exams. Exams cover: Diagnostic and therapeutic procedures; Familiarity with current advances; and Scientific bases of problems. **Examination Frequency:** Annual. **Examination Sites:** Oral and written exams given at one site each in the U.S. Clinical exam given onsite. **Endorsed By:** American Osteopathic Association; American Osteopathic College of Anesthesiologists; Bureau of Osteopathic Specialists.

756

Diplomate of the American Osteopathic Board of Dermatology

American Osteopathic Board of Dermatology (AOBD)
25510 Plymouth Rd.
Redford, MI 48239
Phone: (313)937-1200
Thomas H. Bonino D.O., Sec.-Treas.

Recipient: Osteopathic physicians specializing in dermatology. **Educational/Experience Requirements:** Must meet the following requirements: (1) Graduation from college of osteopathic medicine accredited by Bureau of Professional Education, American Osteopathic Association (see separate entry); (2) Current licensure to practice medicine; (3) Two years of membership in either American Osteopathic Association or Canadian Osteopathic Association; (4) Successful completion of internship accredited by Council on Postdoctoral Training of the American Osteopathic Association (see separate entry); and (5) Successful completion of three-year residency in dermatology accredited by Council on Postdoctoral Training of the American Osteopathic Association. **Membership:** Required. **Certification Requirements:** Successful completion of written and clinical exams. Exams cover: Diagnostic and therapeutic procedures; Familiarity with current advances; and Scientific bases of problems. **Renewal:** Every ten years. Recertification based on accumulation of 75 hours of approved continuing medical education. **Examination Frequency:** Annual. **Examination Sites:** Exams given at annual meeting. **Endorsed By:** American Osteopathic Association; Bureau of Osteopathic Specialists.

757

Diplomate of the American Osteopathic Board of Dermatology with Added Qualifications in MOHS Micrographic Surgery

American Osteopathic Board of Dermatology (AOBD)
25510 Plymouth Rd.
Redford, MI 48239
Phone: (313)937-1200
Thomas H. Bonino D.O., Sec.-Treas.

Recipient: Osteopathic physicians specializing in MOHS micrographic surgery. **Educational/Experience Requirements:** Must meet the following requirements:

(1) Hold Diplomate of the American Osteopathic Board of Dermatology designation (see separate entry); and (2) Successfully complete twelve-month residency in MOHS micrographic surgery accredited by Council on Postdoctoral Training of the American Osteopathic Association (see separate entry). **Membership:** Required. **Certification Requirements:** Successful completion of written and clinical exams. **Examination Frequency:** Annual. **Examination Sites:** Exams given at annual meeting.

758

Diplomate of the American Osteopathic Board of Emergency Medicine
American Osteopathic Board of Emergency Medicine (AOBEM)
142 E. Ontario St., Ste. 217
Chicago, IL 60611
Phone: (312)335-1065
Fax: (312)335-5489
Toll Free: (800)847-0057
Josette Fleming, Admin.

Recipient: Osteopathic physicians specializing in emergency medicine. **Educational/Experience Requirements:** Must meet the following requirements: (1) Graduation from college of osteopathic medicine accredited by Bureau of Professional Education, American Osteopathic Association (see separate entry); (2) Current licensure to practice medicine; (3) Two years of membership in either American Osteopathic Association or Canadian Osteopathic Association; (4) Successful completion of one year internship accredited by Council on Postdoctoral Training of the American Osteopathic Association (see separate entry); (5) Successful completion of three year residency in emergency medicine accredited by Council on Postdoctoral Training of the American Osteopathic Association; and (6) Seven years practice of emergency medicine, including one year of post-residency practice. Experience may include: Administration; Clinical practice in 24-hour emergency facility; and Teaching. Combined training in internal medicine and emergency medicine available. **Membership:** Required. **Certification Requirements:** Successful completion of written and clinical exams. Exams cover: Diagnostic and therapeutic procedures; Familiarity with current advances; and Scientific bases of problems. Must successfully complete written exam prior to attempting oral exam. **Renewal:** Every ten years. Recertification based on successful completion of exam. **Examination Frequency:** Annual (written); semi-annual (oral). **Examination Sites:** Exams

given at one site in the U.S. **Endorsed By:** American Osteopathic Association; Bureau of Osteopathic Specialists; National Board of Osteopathic Medical Examiners.

759

Diplomate of the American Osteopathic Board of Family Practice
American Osteopathic Board of Family Practice (AOBFP)
330 E. Algonquin Rd., Ste 2
Arlington Heights, IL 60005
Phone: (708)640-8477
Carol A. Tomba MBA, Exec.Dir.

Recipient: Osteopathic physicians specializing in family practice. **Educational/Experience Requirements:** Must meet the following requirements: (1) Graduation from college of osteopathic medicine accredited by Bureau of Professional Education, American Osteopathic Association (see separate entry); (2) Current licensure to practice medicine; (3) Two years of membership in American Osteopathic Association; (4) Successful completion of one year internship accredited by Council on Postdoctoral Training of the American Osteopathic Association (see separate entry); and (5) Successful completion of two year residency in family practice accredited by Council on Postdoctoral Training of the American Osteopathic Association. **Membership:** Required. **Certification Requirements:** Successful completion of written and oral/practical exams. Exams cover: Diagnostic and therapeutic procedures; Familiarity with current advances; and Scientific bases of problems. **Renewal:** Every ten years. Recertification based on successful completion of exam and accumulation of 225 hours of approved continuing medical education every three years. **Examination Frequency:** Annual. **Examination Sites:** Exams given at one site in the U.S. **Endorsed By:** American College of Osteopathic Family Physicians; American Osteopathic Association; Bureau of Osteopathic Specialists.

760

Diplomate of the American Osteopathic Board of Family Practice with Added Qualifications in Adolescent and Young Adult Medicine
American Osteopathic Board of Family Practice (AOBFP)
330 E. Algonquin Rd., Ste 2
Arlington Heights, IL 60005
Phone: (708)640-8477
Carol A. Tomba MBA, Exec.Dir.

Recipient: Osteopathic physicians specializing in adolescent and young adult medicine. **Educational/Experience Requirements:** Must meet the following requirements: (1) Hold Diplomate of the American Osteopathic Board of Family Practice designation (see separate entry); and (2) Successfully complete two year training program in adolescent and young adult medicine accredited by Council on Postdoctoral Training of the American Osteopathic Association (see separate entry) or four years practice experience. **Membership:** Required. **Certification Requirements:** Successful completion of exam. **Endorsed By:** American College of Osteopathic Family Physicians; American Osteopathic Association; Bureau of Osteopathic Specialists.

761

Diplomate of the American Osteopathic Board of Family Practice with Added Qualifications in Geriatric Medicine
American Osteopathic Board of Family Practice (AOBFP)
330 E. Algonquin Rd., Ste 2
Arlington Heights, IL 60005
Phone: (708)640-8477
Carol A. Tomba MBA, Exec.Dir.

Recipient: Osteopathic physicians specializing in geriatric medicine. **Educational/Experience Requirements:** Must meet the following requirements: (1) Hold Diplomate of the American Osteopathic Board of Family Practice designation (see separate entry); and (2) Successfully complete two year training program in geriatric medicine accredited by Council on Postdoctoral Training of the American Osteopathic Association (see separate entry). **Membership:** Required. **Certification Requirements:** Successful completion of exam. **Examination Frequency:** Annual. **Examination Sites:** Exam given at one U.S. site. **Endorsed By:** American College of Osteopathic

Family Physicians; American Osteopathic Association; American Osteopathic Board of Internal Medicine; Bureau of Osteopathic Specialists.

762

Diplomate of the American Osteopathic Board of Family Practice with Added Qualifications in Sports Medicine
American Osteopathic Board of Family Practice (AOBFP)
330 E. Algonquin Rd., Ste 2
Arlington Heights, IL 60005
Phone: (708)640-8477
Carol A. Tomba MBA, Exec.Dir.

Recipient: Osteopathic physicians specializing in sports medicine. **Educational/Experience Requirements:** Must meet the following requirements: (1) Hold Diplomate of the American Osteopathic Board of Family Practice designation (see separate entry); and (2) Successfully complete one year residency program in sports medicine accredited by Council on Postdoctoral Training of the American Osteopathic Association (see separate entry) or four years practice experience. **Membership:** Required. **Certification Requirements:** Successful completion of exam. **Examination Frequency:** Annual. **Examination Sites:** Exam given at one U.S. site. **Endorsed By:** American College of Osteopathic Family Physicians; American Osteopathic Academy of Sports Medicine; American Osteopathic Association; American Osteopathic Board of Emergency Medicine; American Osteopathic Board of Internal Medicine; American Osteopathic Board of Pediatrics; American Osteopathic Board of Preventive Medicine; American Osteopathic Board of Rehabilitation Medicine; Bureau of Osteopathic Specialists.

763

Diplomate of the American Osteopathic Board of Internal Medicine
American Osteopathic Board of Internal Medicine
5200 S. Ellis Ave.
Chicago, IL 60615
Phone: (312)947-4881
Gary L. Slick D.O., Exec.Dir.

Recipient: Osteopathic physicians specializing in internal medicine. **Educational/Experience Requirements:** Must meet the following requirements: (1) Graduation from college of osteo-

pathic medicine accredited by Bureau of Professional Education, American Osteopathic Association (see separate entry); (2) Current licensure to practice medicine; (3) Two years of membership in either American Osteopathic Association or Canadian Osteopathic Association; (4) Successful completion of internship accredited by Council on Postdoctoral Training of the American Osteopathic Association (see separate entry); and (5) Successful completion of residency in internal medicine accredited by Council on Postdoctoral Training of the American Osteopathic Association. Combined training in emergency medicine or pediatrics and internal medicine available. **Membership:** Required. **Certification Requirements:** Successful completion of written/clinical exams and oral interview. Exam covers: Diagnostic and therapeutic procedures; Familiarity with current advances; and Scientific bases of problems. **Renewal:** Every ten years. **Examination Frequency:** Annual. **Examination Sites:** Exams given at one site in the U.S. **Endorsed By:** American Osteopathic Association; Bureau of Osteopathic Specialists.

764

Diplomate of the American Osteopathic Board of Internal Medicine with Added Qualifications in Critical Care Medicine
American Osteopathic Board of Internal Medicine
5200 S. Ellis Ave.
Chicago, IL 60615
Phone: (312)947-4881
Gary L. Slick D.O., Exec.Dir.

Recipient: Osteopathic physicians specializing in critical care medicine. **Educational/Experience Requirements:** Hold Diplomate of the American Osteopathic Board of Internal Medicine designation (see separate entry) and meet one of the following training requirements: (1) Successful completion of three years training in cardiology, two years training in pulmonary diseases, and one year of training in critical care medicine; (2) Fours years combined training in cardiology and critical care medicine; (3) Three years combined training in pulmonary diseases and critical care medicine; or (4) Two years training in critical care medicine. Training must be accredited by Council on Postdoctoral Training of the American Osteopathic Association (see separate entry). **Membership:** Required. **Certification Requirements:** Successful completion of exam. **Renewal:** Every ten years. **Endorsed By:** American Osteo-

pathic Association; Bureau of Osteopathic Specialists.

765

Diplomate of the American Osteopathic Board of Internal Medicine with Added Qualifications in Geriatric Medicine
American Osteopathic Board of Internal Medicine
5200 S. Ellis Ave.
Chicago, IL 60615
Phone: (312)947-4881
Gary L. Slick D.O., Exec.Dir.

Recipient: Osteopathic physicians specializing in geriatric medicine. **Educational/Experience Requirements:** Must meet the following requirements: (1) Hold Diplomate of the American Osteopathic Board of Internal Medicine designation (see separate entry); and (2) Successfully complete two year training program in geriatric medicine accredited by Council on Postdoctoral Training of the American Osteopathic Association (see separate entry). **Membership:** Required. **Certification Requirements:** Successful completion of exam. **Renewal:** Every ten years. **Examination Frequency:** Annual. **Examination Sites:** Exam given at one U.S. site. **Endorsed By:** American Osteopathic Association; Bureau of Osteopathic Specialists.

766

Diplomate of the American Osteopathic Board of Nuclear Medicine
American Osteopathic Board of Nuclear Medicine
5200 S. Ellis Ave.
Chicago, IL 60615
Phone: (312)947-4490
George T. Caleel D.O., Sec.-Treas.

Recipient: Osteopathic physicians specializing in nuclear medicine. **Educational/Experience Requirements:** Must meet the following requirements: (1) Graduation from college of osteopathic medicine accredited by Bureau of Professional Education, American Osteopathic Association (see separate entry); (2) Current licensure to practice medicine; (3) Two years of membership in either American Osteopathic Association or Canadian Osteopathic Association; (4) Successful completion of one year internship accredited by Council on Postdoctoral Training of the American Osteopathic Association (see separate entry);

and (5) Either certification in internal medicine, pathology, or radiology from board affiliated with Bureau of Osteopathic Specialists and successful completion of one year residency in nuclear medicine or successful completion of two year residency in nuclear medicine. Residencies must be accredited by Council on Postdoctoral Training of the American Osteopathic Association. Alternate combinations of education and training may be considered on individual basis. **Membership:** Required. **Certification Requirements:** Successful completion of written, oral, and clinical exams. Exams cover: Diagnostic and therapeutic procedures; Familiarity with current advances; and Scientific bases of problems. Must successfully complete written exam before attempting oral and clinical exams. **Renewal:** Every ten years. **Endorsed By:** American College of Osteopathic Internists; American Osteopathic Association; American Osteopathic Board of Internal Medicine; American Osteopathic Board of Pathology; American Osteopathic Board of Radiology; American Osteopathic College of Pathologists; American Osteopathic College of Radiology; Bureau of Osteopathic Specialists.

`767`

Diplomate of the American Osteopathic Board of Nuclear Medicine with Added Qualifications in *In Vivo* and *In Vitro* Nuclear Medicine

American Osteopathic Board of
  Nuclear Medicine
5200 S. Ellis Ave.
Chicago, IL 60615
Phone: (312)947-4490
George T. Caleel D.O., Sec.-Treas.

Recipient: Osteopathic physicians specializing in *in vivo* and *in vitro* nuclear medicine. **Educational/Experience Requirements:** Must meet the following requirements: (1) Hold Diplomate of the American Osteopathic Board of Nuclear Medicine designation (see separate entry); (2) Hold certification in either internal medicine, pathology, or radiology from board affiliated with Bureau of Osteopathic Specialists; and (3) Successfully complete 500 hours of clinical training and 200 hours of didactic training. Training must include: Basic radiation biology; Instrumentation; Mathematics pertaining to use and measurement of radioactivity; Principles of radiation safety; Radiation physics; Radiation protection; and Radiopharmaceutical chemistry. **Membership:** Required. **Certification Requirements:** Successful completion of written, oral, and clinical exams. Exams cover:

Diagnostic and therapeutic procedures; Familiarity with current advances; and Scientific bases of problems. Must successfully complete written exam before attempting oral and clinical exams. **Renewal:** Every ten years. **Endorsed By:** American College of Osteopathic Internists; American Osteopathic Association; American Osteopathic Board of Internal Medicine; American Osteopathic Board of Pathology; American Osteopathic Board of Radiology; American Osteopathic College of Pathologists; American Osteopathic College of Radiology; Bureau of Osteopathic Specialists.

`768`

Diplomate of the American Osteopathic Board of Nuclear Medicine with Added Qualifications in Nuclear Cardiology

American Osteopathic Board of
  Nuclear Medicine
5200 S. Ellis Ave.
Chicago, IL 60615
Phone: (312)947-4490
George T. Caleel D.O., Sec.-Treas.

Recipient: Osteopathic physicians specializing in nuclear cardiology. **Educational/Experience Requirements:** Must meet the following requirements: (1) Hold Diplomate of the American Osteopathic Board of Nuclear Medicine designation (see separate entry); (2) Hold certification in either internal medicine, pathology, or radiology, or subspecialty certification in cardiology, from board affiliated with Bureau of Osteopathic Specialists; and (3) Successfully complete 500 hours of clinical training and 200 hours of didactic training. **Membership:** Required. **Certification Requirements:** Successful completion of written, oral, and clinical exams. Exams cover: Diagnostic and therapeutic procedures; Familiarity with current advances; and Scientific bases of problems. Must successfully complete written exam before attempting oral and clinical exams. **Renewal:** Every ten years. **Endorsed By:** American College of Osteopathic Internists; American Osteopathic Association; American Osteopathic Board of Internal Medicine; American Osteopathic Board of Pathology; American Osteopathic Board of Radiology; American Osteopathic College of Pathologists; American Osteopathic College of Radiology; Bureau of Osteopathic Specialists.

`769`

Diplomate of the American Osteopathic Board of Nuclear Medicine with Added Qualifications in Nuclear Imaging and Therapy

American Osteopathic Board of
  Nuclear Medicine
5200 S. Ellis Ave.
Chicago, IL 60615
Phone: (312)947-4490
George T. Caleel D.O., Sec.-Treas.

Recipient: Osteopathic physicians specializing in nuclear imaging and therapy. **Educational/Experience Requirements:** Must meet the following requirements: (1) Hold Diplomate of the American Osteopathic Board of Nuclear Medicine designation (see separate entry); (2) Hold certification in either internal medicine, pathology, or radiology from board affiliated with Bureau of Osteopathic Specialists; and (3) Successfully complete 1000 hours of clinical training and 200 hours of didactic training. **Membership:** Required. **Certification Requirements:** Successful completion of written, oral, and clinical exams. Exams cover: Diagnostic and therapeutic procedures; Familiarity with current advances; and Scientific bases of problems. Must successfully complete written exam before attempting oral and clinical exams. **Renewal:** Every ten years. **Endorsed By:** American College of Osteopathic Internists; American Osteopathic Association; American Osteopathic Board of Internal Medicine; American Osteopathic Board of Pathology; American Osteopathic Board of Radiology; American Osteopathic College of Pathologists; American Osteopathic College of Radiology; Bureau of Osteopathic Specialists.

`770`

Diplomate of the American Osteopathic Board of Obstetrics and Gynecology

American Osteopathic Board of
  Obstetrics and Gynecology
  (AOBOG)
5200 S. Ellis Ave.
Chicago, IL 60615
Phone: (312)947-4630
Joseph P. Bonanno D.O., Sec.-
  Treas.

Recipient: Osteopathic physicians specializing in obstetrics and gynecology. **Educational/Experience Requirements:** Must meet the following requirements: (1) Graduation from college of osteopathic medicine accredited by Bureau of

Professional Education, American Osteopathic Association (see separate entry); (2) Current licensure to practice medicine; (3) Two years of membership in either American Osteopathic Association or Canadian Osteopathic Association; (4) Successful completion of internship accredited by Council on Postdoctoral Training of the American Osteopathic Association (see separate entry); (5) Successful completion of residency in obstetrics and gynecology accredited by Council on Postdoctoral Training of the American Osteopathic Association; (6) Twenty-four months practice subsequent to successful completion of training; and (7) Submission of case logs. **Membership:** Required. **Certification Requirements:** Successful completion of written, oral, and clinical exams. Clinical exam includes chart review and exit interview. **Renewal:** Every ten years. **Examination Frequency:** Annual. **Examination Sites:** Exams given in Chicago, IL. **Endorsed By:** American Osteopathic Association; Bureau of Osteopathic Specialists.

|771|

Diplomate of the American Osteopathic Board of Orthopaedic Surgery

American Osteopathic Board of Orthopaedic Surgery
450 Powers Ave., Ste. 105
Harrisburg, PA 17109
Phone: (717)561-8560
Kay I. Rittenhouse, Exec.Sec.

Recipient: Osteopathic physicians specializing in orthopaedic surgery. **Educational/Experience Requirements:** Must meet the following requirements: (1) Graduation from college of osteopathic medicine accredited by Bureau of Professional Education, American Osteopathic Association (see separate entry); (2) Current licensure to practice medicine; (3) Two years of membership in American Osteopathic Association; (4) Successful completion of internship accredited by Council on Postdoctoral Training of the American Osteopathic Association (see separate entry); (5) Successful completion of four year residency in orthopedic surgery accredited by Council on Postdoctoral Training of the American Osteopathic Association; (6) Documentation of 200 major operative procedures in one calendar year; and (7) One year of practice subsequent to successful completion of training. **Membership:** Required. **Certification Requirements:** Successful completion of written, oral, and clinical exams. Exams cover: Diagnostic and therapeutic procedures; Familiarity with current advances; and

Scientific bases of problems. Must successfully complete written exam before attempting oral and clinical exams. Must successfully complete written exam before attempting oral exam. Must successfully complete oral exam and one year of practice before attempting clinical exam. **Renewal:** Every ten years. **Examination Frequency:** Annual. **Examination Sites:** Exams given at one site in the U.S. **Endorsed By:** American Osteopathic Association; American Osteopathic Academy of Orthopedics; Bureau of Osteopathic Specialists.

|772|

Diplomate of the American Osteopathic Board of Pediatrics

American Osteopathic Board of Pediatrics (AOBP)
142 E. Ontario St., Sixth Fl.
Chicago, IL 60611
Phone: (312)280-5881
Ida Sorci, Prog.Coord.

Recipient: Osteopathic physicians specializing in pediatrics. **Educational/Experience Requirements:** Must meet the following requirements: (1) Graduation from college of osteopathic medicine accredited by Bureau of Professional Education, American Osteopathic Association (see separate entry); (2) Current licensure to practice medicine; (3) Two years of membership in American Osteopathic Association or Canadian Osteopathic Association; (4) Successful completion of internship accredited by Council on Postdoctoral Training of the American Osteopathic Association (see separate entry); and (5) Successful completion of two year residency in pediatrics accredited by Council on Postdoctoral Training of the American Osteopathic Association. Combined training available in internal medicine and pediatrics. **Membership:** Required. **Certification Requirements:** Successful completion of written and oral/clinical exams. Exams cover: Diagnostic and therapeutic procedures; Familiarity with current advances; and Scientific bases of problems. **Renewal:** Every seven years. **Examination Frequency:** Annual. **Endorsed By:** American Osteopathic Association; Bureau of Osteopathic Specialists.

|773|

Diplomate of the American Osteopathic Board of Pediatrics with Special Qualifications in Adolescent and Young Adult Medicine

American Osteopathic Board of Pediatrics (AOBP)
142 E. Ontario St., Sixth Fl.
Chicago, IL 60611
Phone: (312)280-5881
Ida Sorci, Prog.Coord.

Recipient: Osteopathic physicians specializing in adolescent and young adult medicine. **Educational/Experience Requirements:** Must meet the following requirements: (1) Hold Diplomate of the American Osteopathic Board of Pediatrics designation (see separate entry); and (2) Successfully complete three year residency in adolescent and young adult medicine accredited by Council on Postdoctoral Training of the American Osteopathic Association (see separate entry). **Membership:** Required. **Certification Requirements:** Successful completion of written and oral/clinical exams. Exams cover: Diagnostic and therapeutic procedures; Familiarity with current advances; and Scientific bases of problems. **Renewal:** Every seven years. **Examination Frequency:** Annual. **Endorsed By:** American Osteopathic Association; Bureau of Osteopathic Specialists.

|774|

Diplomate of the American Osteopathic Board of Pediatrics with Special Qualifications in Neonatology

American Osteopathic Board of Pediatrics (AOBP)
142 E. Ontario St., Sixth Fl.
Chicago, IL 60611
Phone: (312)280-5881
Ida Sorci, Prog.Coord.

Recipient: Osteopathic physicians specializing in neonatology. **Educational/Experience Requirements:** Must meet the following requirements: (1) Hold Diplomate of the American Osteopathic Board of Pediatrics designation (see separate entry); and (2) Successfully complete three year residency in neonatology accredited by Council on Postdoctoral Training of the American Osteopathic Association (see separate entry). **Membership:** Required. **Certification Requirements:** Successful completion of written and oral/clinical exams. Exams cover: Diagnostic and therapeutic procedures;

Familiarity with current advances; and Scientific bases of problems. **Renewal:** Every seven years. **Examination Frequency:** Annual. **Endorsed By:** American Osteopathic Association; Bureau of Osteopathic Specialists.

775

Diplomate of the American Osteopathic Board of Pediatrics with Special Qualifications in Pediatric Allergy/Immunology
American Osteopathic Board of Pediatrics (AOBP)
142 E. Ontario St., Sixth Fl.
Chicago, IL 60611
Phone: (312)280-5881
Ida Sorci, Prog.Coord.

Recipient: Osteopathic physicians specializing in pediatric allergy and immunology. **Educational/Experience Requirements:** Must meet the following requirements: (1) Hold Diplomate of the American Osteopathic Board of Pediatrics designation (see separate entry); and (2) Successfully complete three year residency in pediatric allergy and immunology accredited by Council on Postdoctoral Training of the American Osteopathic Association (see separate entry). **Membership:** Required. **Certification Requirements:** Successful completion of written and oral/clinical exams. Exams cover: Diagnostic and therapeutic procedures; Familiarity with current advances; and Scientific bases of problems. **Renewal:** Every seven years. **Examination Frequency:** Annual. **Endorsed By:** American Osteopathic Association; Bureau of Osteopathic Specialists.

776

Diplomate of the American Osteopathic Board of Pediatrics with Special Qualifications in Pediatric Cardiology
American Osteopathic Board of Pediatrics (AOBP)
142 E. Ontario St., Sixth Fl.
Chicago, IL 60611
Phone: (312)280-5881
Ida Sorci, Prog.Coord.

Recipient: Osteopathic physicians specializing in pediatric cardiology. **Educational/Experience Requirements:** Must meet the following requirements: (1) Hold Diplomate of the American Osteopathic Board of Pediatrics designation (see separate entry); and (2) Successfully complete three year residency in

pediatric cardiology accredited by Council on Postdoctoral Training of the American Osteopathic Association (see separate entry). **Membership:** Required. **Certification Requirements:** Successful completion of written and oral/clinical exams. Exams cover: Diagnostic and therapeutic procedures; Familiarity with current advances; and Scientific bases of problems. **Renewal:** Every seven years. **Examination Frequency:** Annual. **Endorsed By:** American Osteopathic Association; Bureau of Osteopathic Specialists.

777

Diplomate of the American Osteopathic Board of Pediatrics with Special Qualifications in Pediatric Hematology/Oncology
American Osteopathic Board of Pediatrics (AOBP)
142 E. Ontario St., Sixth Fl.
Chicago, IL 60611
Phone: (312)280-5881
Ida Sorci, Prog.Coord.

Recipient: Osteopathic physicians specializing in pediatric hematology and oncology. **Educational/Experience Requirements:** Must meet the following requirements: (1) Hold Diplomate of the American Osteopathic Board of Pediatrics designation (see separate entry); and (2) Successfully complete three year residency in pediatric hematology and oncology accredited by Council on Postdoctoral Training of the American Osteopathic Association (see separate entry). **Membership:** Required. **Certification Requirements:** Successful completion of written and oral/clinical exams. Exams cover: Diagnostic and therapeutic procedures; Familiarity with current advances; and Scientific bases of problems. **Renewal:** Every seven years. **Examination Frequency:** Annual. **Endorsed By:** American Osteopathic Association; Bureau of Osteopathic Specialists.

778

Diplomate of the American Osteopathic Board of Pediatrics with Special Qualifications in Pediatric Infectious Diseases
American Osteopathic Board of Pediatrics (AOBP)
142 E. Ontario St., Sixth Fl.
Chicago, IL 60611
Phone: (312)280-5881
Ida Sorci, Prog.Coord.

Recipient: Osteopathic physicians specializing in pediatric infectious diseases. **Educational/Experience Requirements:** Must meet the following requirements: (1) Hold Diplomate of the American Osteopathic Board of Pediatrics designation (see separate entry); and (2) Successfully complete three year residency in pediatric infectious diseases accredited by Council on Postdoctoral Training of the American Osteopathic Association (see separate entry). **Membership:** Required. **Certification Requirements:** Successful completion of written and oral/clinical exams. Exams cover: Diagnostic and therapeutic procedures; Familiarity with current advances; and Scientific bases of problems. **Renewal:** Every seven years. **Examination Frequency:** Annual. **Endorsed By:** American Osteopathic Association; Bureau of Osteopathic Specialists.

779

Diplomate of the American Osteopathic Board of Pediatrics with Special Qualifications in Pediatric Intensive Care
American Osteopathic Board of Pediatrics (AOBP)
142 E. Ontario St., Sixth Fl.
Chicago, IL 60611
Phone: (312)280-5881
Ida Sorci, Prog.Coord.

Recipient: Osteopathic physicians specializing in pediatric intensive care. **Educational/Experience Requirements:** Must meet the following requirements: (1) Hold Diplomate of the American Osteopathic Board of Pediatrics designation (see separate entry); and (2) Successfully complete three year residency in pediatric intensive care accredited by Council on Postdoctoral Training of the American Osteopathic Association (see separate entry). **Membership:** Required. **Certification Requirements:** Successful completion of written and oral/clinical exams. Exams cover: Diagnostic and therapeutic procedures; Familiarity with current advances; and Scientific bases of problems. **Renewal:** Every seven years. **Examination Frequency:** Annual. **Endorsed By:** American Osteopathic Association; Bureau of Osteopathic Specialists.

780

Diplomate of the American Osteopathic Board of Pediatrics with Special Qualifications in Pediatric Nephrology
American Osteopathic Board of Pediatrics (AOBP)
142 E. Ontario St., Sixth Fl.
Chicago, IL 60611
Phone: (312)280-5881
Ida Sorci, Prog.Coord.

Recipient: Osteopathic physicians specializing in pediatric nephrology. **Educational/Experience Requirements:** Must meet the following requirements: (1) Hold Diplomate of the American Osteopathic Board of Pediatrics designation (see separate entry); and (2) Successfully complete three year residency in pediatric nephrology accredited by Council on Postdoctoral Training of the American Osteopathic Association (see separate entry). **Membership:** Required. **Certification Requirements:** Successful completion of written and oral/clinical exams. Exams cover: Diagnostic and therapeutic procedures; Familiarity with current advances; and Scientific bases of problems. **Renewal:** Every seven years. **Examination Frequency:** Annual. **Endorsed By:** American Osteopathic Association; Bureau of Osteopathic Specialists.

781

Diplomate of the American Osteopathic Board of Pediatrics with Special Qualifications in Pediatric Pulmonary
American Osteopathic Board of Pediatrics (AOBP)
142 E. Ontario St., Sixth Fl.
Chicago, IL 60611
Phone: (312)280-5881
Ida Sorci, Prog.Coord.

Recipient: Osteopathic physicians specializing in pediatric pulmonary medicine. **Educational/Experience Requirements:** Must meet the following requirements: (1) Hold Diplomate of the American Osteopathic Board of Pediatrics designation (see separate entry); and (2) Successfully complete three year residency in pediatric pulmonary medicine accredited by Council on Postdoctoral Training of the American Osteopathic Association (see separate entry). **Membership:** Required. **Certification Requirements:** Successful completion of written and oral/clinical exams. Exams cover: Diagnostic and therapeutic procedures; Familiarity with current advances; and Scientific bases of problems. **Renewal:** Every seven years. **Examination Frequency:** Annual. **Endorsed By:** American Osteopathic Association; Bureau of Osteopathic Specialists.

782

Diplomate of the American Osteopathic Board of Proctology
American Osteopathic Board of Proctology
104A Kings Way West
Sewell, NJ 08080
Phone: (609)582-7900
Todd Schachter D.O., Sec.-Treas.

Recipient: Osteopathic physicians specializing in proctology. **Educational/Experience Requirements:** Must meet the following requirements: (1) Graduation from college of osteopathic medicine accredited by Bureau of Professional Education, American Osteopathic Association (see separate entry); (2) Current licensure to practice medicine; (3) Two years of membership in American Osteopathic Association or Canadian Osteopathic Association; (4) Successful completion of internship accredited by Council on Postdoctoral Training of the American Osteopathic Association (see separate entry); (5) Successful completion of two years of training in proctology accredited by Council on Postdoctoral Training of the American Osteopathic Association; (6) Two years of practice subsequent to successful completion of training; (7) Documentation of 200 operative procedures; (8) Submission of 50 case reports; and (9) Submission of thesis on subject related to proctology. **Membership:** Required. **Certification Requirements:** Successful completion of written, oral, and clinical exams. Exams cover: Diagnostic and therapeutic procedures; Familiarity with current advances; and Scientific bases of problems. **Examination Frequency:** Annual. **Examination Sites:** Exams given at one U.S. site. **Endorsed By:** American Osteopathic Association; American Osteopathic College of Proctology; Bureau of Osteopathic Specialists.

783

Diplomate of the American Osteopathic Board of Radiology with Added Qualifications in Angiography and Interventional Radiology
American Osteopathic Board of Radiology
119 E. Second St.
Milan, MO 63556
Phone: (816)265-4011
Pamela A. Smith, Exec.Dir.

Recipient: Osteopathic physicians specializing in angiography and interventional radiology. **Educational/Experience Requirements:** Must meet the following requirements: (1) Hold Diplomate certification from Board in either diagnostic radiology or radiation oncology (see separate entries); and (2) One year of training in angiography and interventional radiology. **Membership:** Required. **Certification Requirements:** Successful completion of exam. Exam covers: Diagnostic and therapeutic procedures; Familiarity with current advances; and Scientific bases of problems. May be required to successfully complete clinical evaluation. **Examination Frequency:** Annual. **Endorsed By:** American Osteopathic Association; Bureau of Osteopathic Specialists.

784

Diplomate of the American Osteopathic Board of Radiology with Added Qualifications in Body Imaging
American Osteopathic Board of Radiology
119 E. Second St.
Milan, MO 63556
Phone: (816)265-4011
Pamela A. Smith, Exec.Dir.

Recipient: Osteopathic physicians specializing in body imaging. **Educational/Experience Requirements:** Must meet the following requirements: (1) Hold Diplomate certification from Board in either diagnostic radiology or radiation oncology (see separate entries); and (2) One year of training in body imaging. **Membership:** Required. **Certification Requirements:** Successful completion of exam. Exam covers: Diagnostic and therapeutic procedures; Familiarity with current advances; and Scientific bases of problems. May be required to successfully complete clinical evaluation. **Examination Frequency:** Annual. **Endorsed By:** American Osteopathic Association; Bureau of Osteopathic Specialists.

785

Diplomate of the American Osteopathic Board of Radiology with Added Qualifications in Diagnostic Ultrasound

American Osteopathic Board of Radiology
119 E. Second St.
Milan, MO 63556
Phone: (816)265-4011
Pamela A. Smith, Exec.Dir.

Recipient: Osteopathic physicians specializing in diagnostic ultrasound. **Educational/Experience Requirements:** Must meet the following requirements: (1) Hold Diplomate certification from Board in either diagnostic radiology or radiation oncology (see separate entries); and (2) One year of training in diagnostic ultrasound. **Membership:** Required. **Certification Requirements:** Successful completion of exam. Exam covers: Diagnostic and therapeutic procedures; Familiarity with current advances; and Scientific bases of problems. May be required to successfully complete clinical evaluation. **Examination Frequency:** Annual. **Endorsed By:** American Osteopathic Association; Bureau of Osteopathic Specialists.

786

Diplomate of the American Osteopathic Board of Radiology with Added Qualifications in Neuroradiology

American Osteopathic Board of Radiology
119 E. Second St.
Milan, MO 63556
Phone: (816)265-4011
Pamela A. Smith, Exec.Dir.

Recipient: Osteopathic physicians specializing in neuroradiology. **Educational/Experience Requirements:** Must meet the following requirements: (1) Hold Diplomate certification from Board in either diagnostic radiology or radiation oncology (see separate entries); and (2) One year of training in neuroradiology. **Membership:** Required. **Certification Requirements:** Successful completion of exam. Exam covers: Diagnostic and therapeutic procedures; Familiarity with current advances; and Scientific bases of problems. May be required to successfully complete clinical evaluation. **Examination Frequency:** Annual. **Endorsed By:** American Osteopathic Association; Bureau of Osteopathic Specialists.

787

Diplomate of the American Osteopathic Board of Radiology with Added Qualifications in Nuclear Radiology

American Osteopathic Board of Radiology
119 E. Second St.
Milan, MO 63556
Phone: (816)265-4011
Pamela A. Smith, Exec.Dir.

Recipient: Osteopathic physicians specializing in nuclear radiology. **Educational/Experience Requirements:** Must meet the following requirements: (1) Hold Diplomate certification from Board in either diagnostic radiology or radiation oncology (see separate entries); and (2) One year of training in nuclear radiology. **Membership:** Required. **Certification Requirements:** Successful completion of exam. Exam covers: Diagnostic and therapeutic procedures; Familiarity with current advances; and Scientific bases of problems. May be required to successfully complete clinical evaluation. **Examination Frequency:** Annual. **Endorsed By:** American Osteopathic Association; Bureau of Osteopathic Specialists.

788

Diplomate of the American Osteopathic Board of Radiology with Added Qualifications in Pediatric Radiology

American Osteopathic Board of Radiology
119 E. Second St.
Milan, MO 63556
Phone: (816)265-4011
Pamela A. Smith, Exec.Dir.

Recipient: Osteopathic physicians specializing in pediatric radiology. **Educational/Experience Requirements:** Must meet the following requirements: (1) Hold Diplomate certification from Board in either diagnostic radiology or radiation oncology (see separate entries); and (2) One year of training in pediatric radiology. **Membership:** Required. **Certification Requirements:** Successful completion of exam. Exam covers: Diagnostic and therapeutic procedures; Familiarity with current advances; and Scientific bases of problems. May be required to successfully complete clinical evaluation. **Examination Frequency:** Annual. **Endorsed By:** American Osteopathic Association; Bureau of Osteopathic Specialists.

789

Diplomate of the American Osteopathic Board of Rehabilitation Medicine

American Osteopathic Board of Rehabilitation Medicine
9058 W. Church St.
Des Plaines, IL 60016
Phone: (708)699-0048
Julie Pickett-Atae, Exec.Asst.

Recipient: Osteopathic physicians specializing in rehabilitation medicine. **Educational/Experience Requirements:** Must meet the following requirements: (1) Graduation from college of osteopathic medicine accredited by Bureau of Professional Education, American Osteopathic Association (see separate entry); (2) Current licensure to practice medicine; (3) Two years of membership in American Osteopathic Association or Canadian Osteopathic Association; (4) Successful completion of internship accredited by Council on Postdoctoral Training of the American Osteopathic Association (see separate entry); (5) Successful completion of three years of training in rehabilitation medicine accredited by Council on Postdoctoral Training of the American Osteopathic Association; (6) Two years practice subsequent to successful completion of training; and (7) Submission of 200 case records. Training must include: Anatomy; Biochemistry; Electrotherapy; Hydrotherapy; Kinesitherapy; Occupational therapy; Pathology; Pharmacology; Physics; Physiology; Radiation therapy; Rehabilitation; and Thermotherapy. **Membership:** Required. **Certification Requirements:** Successful completion of written, oral, and clinical exams. **Renewal:** Every seven years. **Examination Frequency:** Annual. **Endorsed By:** American Osteopathic Association; Bureau of Osteopathic Specialists.

790

Diplomate of the American Osteopathic Board of Surgery

American Osteopathic Board of Surgery
Three MacKoil Ave.
Dayton, OH 45403
Phone: (513)252-0868
Sharon Alexiades, Corres.Sec.

Recipient: Osteopathic surgeons. **Educational/Experience Requirements:** Must meet the following requirements: (1) Graduation from college of osteopathic medicine accredited by Bureau of Professional Education, American Osteopathic Association (see separate entry);

(2) Current licensure to practice medicine; (3) Two years of membership in American Osteopathic Association or Canadian Osteopathic Association; (4) Successful completion of internship accredited by Council on Postdoctoral Training of the American Osteopathic Association (see separate entry); (5) Successful completion of four year residency in surgery accredited by Council on Postdoctoral Training of the American Osteopathic Association; (6) Submission of log of major operative cases performed during previous year; and (7) Submission of list of mortalities. **Membership:** Required. **Certification Requirements:** Successful completion of written, oral, and clinical exams. Exams cover: Basic sciences; Current advances in surgical philosophy and techniques; Diagnostic, operative, and therapeutic procedures; Osteopathic philosophy of surgery applied to diagnosis and management of surgical diseases; Surgical judgment; and Surgical principles. **Examination Frequency:** Annual. **Examination Sites:** Exams given at one U.S. site. **Endorsed By:** American College of Osteopathic Surgeons; American Osteopathic Association; Bureau of Osteopathic Specialists.

791

Diplomate in Anatomic Pathology of the American Board of Pathology
American Board of Pathology (ABP)
PO Box 25915
Tampa, FL 33622-5915
Phone: (813)286-2444
Fax: (813)289-5279

Recipient: Pathologists specializing in anatomic pathology. **Educational/ Experience Requirements:** Must meet the following requirements: (1) Graduate from medical school accredited by Liaison Committee for Medical Education (see separate entry), osteopathic college of medicine accredited by Bureau of Professional Education, American Osteopathic Association (see separate entry), or foreign medical school acceptable to ABP; (2) Hold current unrestricted license to practice medicine; (3) Either successfully complete three years of training accredited by Accreditation Council for Graduate Medical Education (ACGME) (see separate entry) or hold Diplomate in Clinical Pathology of the American Board of Pathology and successfully complete two years of training in anatomic pathology accredited by ACGME; and (4) Successfully complete approved credentialing year involving additional research or training in pathol-

ogy. Experience, fellowships, graduate degrees, or research activities may be substituted for training with approval of ABP. **Certification Requirements:** Successful completion of written and oral exams. **Examination Frequency:** semiannual - always May and November. **Fees:** $1000. **Endorsed By:** American Board of Medical Specialists; American Medical Association; American Society of Clinical Pathologists; Council on Medical Education.

792

Diplomate in Anatomic Pathology of the American Osteopathic Board of Pathology
American Osteopathic Board of Pathology
450 Powers Ave., Ste. 105
Harrisburg, PA 17109
Phone: (717)561-8560
Kay I. Rittenhouse, Exec.Sec.

Recipient: Osteopathic physicians specializing in anatomic pathology. **Educational/Experience Requirements:** Must meet the following requirements: (1) Graduation from college of osteopathic medicine accredited by Bureau of Professional Education, American Osteopathic Association (see separate entry); (2) Current licensure to practice medicine; (3) Two years of membership in American Osteopathic Association or Canadian Osteopathic Association; (4) Successful completion of internship accredited by Council on Postdoctoral Training of the American Osteopathic Association (see separate entry); and (5) Successful completion of three year residency in anatomic pathology accredited by Council on Postdoctoral Training of the American Osteopathic Association. **Membership:** Required. **Certification Requirements:** Successful completion of written, oral, and practical exams. **Renewal:** Every ten years. **Examination Frequency:** Annual. **Examination Sites:** Exams given at one site in the U.S. **Endorsed By:** American Osteopathic Association; Bureau of Osteopathic Specialists.

793

Diplomate in Anatomic Pathology and Laboratory Medicine of the American Osteopathic Board of Pathology
American Osteopathic Board of Pathology
450 Powers Ave., Ste. 105
Harrisburg, PA 17109
Phone: (717)561-8560
Kay I. Rittenhouse, Exec.Sec.

Recipient: Osteopathic physicians specializing in anatomic pathology and laboratory medicine. **Educational/ Experience Requirements:** Must meet the following requirements: (1) Graduation from college of osteopathic medicine accredited by Bureau of Professional Education, American Osteopathic Association (see separate entry); (2) Current licensure to practice medicine; (3) Two years of membership in American Osteopathic Association or Canadian Osteopathic Association; (4) Successful completion of internship accredited by Council on Postdoctoral Training of the American Osteopathic Association (see separate entry); and (5) Successful completion of four year residency in anatomic pathology and laboratory medicine accredited by Council on Postdoctoral Training of the American Osteopathic Association. **Membership:** Required. **Certification Requirements:** Successful completion of written, oral, and practical exams. **Renewal:** Every ten years. **Examination Frequency:** Annual. **Examination Sites:** Exams given at one site in the U.S. **Endorsed By:** American Osteopathic Association; Bureau of Osteopathic Specialists.

794

Diplomate of the Board of Certification in Emergency Medicine
Board of Certification in Emergency Medicine
804 Main St., Ste. D
Forest Park, GA 30050
Phone: (404)363-8263
Fax: (404)361-2285
Toll Free: (800)447-9397

Recipient: Physicians specializing in emergency medicine. **Educational/ Experience Requirements:** Must meet the following requirements: (1) Graduation from school of medicine accredited by Bureau of Professional Education, American Osteopathic Association or Liaison Committee on Medical Education (see separate entries); (2) Current unrestricted licensure to practice medicine; (3) Current certification at "Provider" level in American Heart Association's Advanced Cardiac Life Support program and American College of Surgeons Advanced Trauma Life Support program; (4) Submission of ten cases; and (5) Either successful completion of emergency medicine residency accredited by American Osteopathic Association Division on Postdoctoral Training or Accreditation Commission for Graduate Medical Education (see separate entry), accredited primary care residency, or certification program in primary care specialty recognized by American Association of Physician Specialists, American Board of Medical Specialties, Bureau for Osteopathic Specialists, and five years (7000 hours) experience. Candidates with six years (10,000 hours) experience may qualify for certification. **Membership:** Not required. **Certification Requirements:** Successful completion of written and oral exams. Written exam covers: Abdominal and gastrointestinal disorders; Administrative aspects of emergency medicine; Cardiovascular disorders; Cutaneous disorders; Emergency medical services and systems; Endocrine, metabolic, and nutritional disorders; Environmental disorders; Head and neck disorders; Hematologic and oncologic disorders; Immune systems disorders and AIDS; Musculoskeletal disorders; Nervous system disorders; Obstetrical and gynecological disorders; Pediatric disorders; Procedures and skills of emergency medicine; Psychological and behavioral disorders; Systemic and cutaneous infectious disorders; Thoracic and respiratory disorders; Toxicology and clinical pharmacology; Traumatic disorders; and Urological and renal disorders. **Renewal:** Every five years. Recertification based on: (1) Successful completion of exam; (2) Current certification at "Provider" level in American Heart Association's Advanced Cardiac Life Support program and American College of Surgeons Advanced Trauma Life Support program; (3) Submission of 10 case reports; and (4) Accumulation of 250 hours of continuing medical education in family practice, with 50 hours under auspices of AAPS. Renewal fee is $500. **Preparatory Materials:** List of suggested study references provided. Review courses available. **Examination Frequency:** semiannual - always January and June. **Examination Type:** Multiple-choice. **Waiting Period to Receive Scores:** 30 days. **Re-examination:** May retake exams two times. There is a $950 fee to retake exams. **Fees:** $1050. **Endorsed By:** American Academy of Emergency Physicians; American Association of Physician Specialists.

795

Diplomate of the Board of Certification in Family Practice

Board of Certification in Family
Practice
804 Main St., Ste. D
Forest Park, GA 30050
Phone: (404)363-8263
Fax: (404)361-2285
Toll Free: (800)447-9397

Recipient: Physicians specializing in family practice. **Educational/Experience Requirements:** Must meet the following requirements: (1) Graduation from school of medicine accredited by Bureau of Professional Education, American Osteopathic Association or Liaison Committee on Medical Education (see separate entries); (2) Current unrestricted licensure to practice medicine; (3) Successful completion of internship accredited by American Osteopathic Association Division on Postdoctoral Training or Accreditation Council for Graduate Medical Education (ACGME) (see separate entries); (4) Submission of ten cases; and (5) Successful completion of osteopathic residency accredited by American Osteopathic Association Division on Postdoctoral Training or residency accredited by ACGME. Candidates with six years experience and 600 hours of continuing medical education within last six years may also qualify. **Membership:** Not required. **Certification Requirements:** Successful completion of written, oral, and practical exams. Written exam covers general medical knowledge and two of the following specialty fields: Emergency medicine; General surgery; Geriatric medicine; Internal medicine; Obstetrics and gynecology; and Pediatrics. Allopathic physicians are exempt from practical exam. **Renewal:** Every five years. Recertification based on submission of 25 case reports and accumulation of 250 continuing medical education hours in family practice, with 75 hours under auspices of AAPS. May be required to successfully complete oral exam. Renewal fee is $300. **Preparatory Materials:** List of suggested study references provided. Review courses available. **Examination Frequency:** Annual - always June. **Examination Type:** Multiple-choice. **Waiting Period to Receive Scores:** 60 days. **Re-examination:** May retake exams two times. There is a $750 fee to retake exams. **Fees:** $750. **Endorsed By:** American Academy of Osteopathic Family Practitioners; American Association of Physician Specialists.

796

Diplomate of the Board of Certification in Geriatric Medicine

Board of Certification in Geriatric
Medicine
804 Main St., Ste. D
Forest Park, GA 30050
Phone: (404)363-8263
Fax: (404)361-2285
Toll Free: (800)447-9397

Recipient: Physicians specializing in geriatric medicine. **Educational/Experience Requirements:** Must meet the following requirements: (1) Graduation from school of medicine accredited by Bureau of Professional Education, American Osteopathic Association or Liaison Committee on Medical Education (see separate entries); (2) Current unrestricted licensure to practice medicine; (3) Submission of six case reports; (4) Either current board certification in family practice, general practice, or internal medicine, or successful completion of osteopathic residency accredited by American Osteopathic Association Division on Postdoctoral Training or residency accredited by Accreditation Council for Graduate Medical Education (see separate entries); and (5) Documentation that 65 percent of practice is spent in geriatrics. Graduates of fellowship programs, instructors in geriatric medicine, or candidates with equivalent experience may be considered for certification. **Certification Requirements:** Successful completion of exams. **Renewal:** Recertification required. **Examination Frequency:** semiannual - always January and June. **Examination Sites:** Exam given at midwinter and annual meetings. **Fees:** $600. **Endorsed By:** American Association of Physician Specialists.

797

Diplomate of the Board of Certification in Surgery

Board of Certification in Surgery
804 Main St., Ste. D
Forest Park, GA 30050
Phone: (404)363-8263
Fax: (404)361-2285
Toll Free: (800)447-9397

Recipient: Physicians specializing in surgery. **Educational/Experience Requirements:** Must meet the following requirements: (1) Graduation from school of medicine accredited by Bureau of Professional Education, American Osteopathic Association or Liaison Committee on Medical Education (see separate entries);

(2) Current unrestricted licensure to practice medicine; (3) Successful completion of internship accredited by American Osteopathic Association Division on Postdoctoral Training or Accreditation Council for Graduate Medical Education (ACGME) (see separate entries); (4) Successful completion of osteopathic residency accredited by American Osteopathic Association Division on Postdoctoral Training or residency in general surgery accredited by ACGME; (5) Documentation of minimum of 200 surgical procedures; (6) Active staff privileges for two years at institution accredited by Committee on Hospital Accreditation or Joint Commission for Accreditation of Healthcare Organizations (see separate entries); (7) Submission of ten case reports; and (8) Submission of log of surgical procedures performed for previous two years, broken down by year and surgical group. **Membership:** Required. **Certification Requirements:** Successful completion of written and clinical exams. May also be required to successfully complete oral exam. Must successfully complete clinical exam before March 1 of year following successful completion of written exam. **Renewal:** Recertification required. **Examination Frequency:** Annual - always June. **Examination Sites:** Exams given at annual meeting. **Fees:** $500. **Endorsed By:** American Association of Physician Specialists.

798

Diplomate in Cardiology of the American Osteopathic Board of Internal Medicine
American Osteopathic Board of Internal Medicine
5200 S. Ellis Ave.
Chicago, IL 60615
Phone: (312)947-4881
Gary L. Slick D.O., Exec.Dir.

Recipient: Physicians specializing in cardiology. **Educational/Experience Requirements:** Must meet the following requirements: (1) Hold Diplomate of the American Osteopathic Board of Internal Medicine designation (see separate entry); and (2) Successfully complete three year training program in cardiology accredited by Council on Postdoctoral Training of the American Osteopathic Association (see separate entry). **Membership:** Required. **Certification Requirements:** Successful completion of exam. **Renewal:** Every ten years. **Examination Frequency:** Annual - always August. **Examination Sites:** Exam given at one U.S. site. **Endorsed By:** American Osteopathic Association; Bureau of Osteopathic Specialists.

799

Diplomate in Cardiovascular Disease of the American Board of Internal Medicine
American Board of Internal Medicine (ABIM)
3624 Market St.
Philadelphia, PA 19104-2675
Phone: (215)243-1500
Fax: (215)382-4702
Toll Free: (800)441-ABIM

Recipient: Physicians specializing in cardiovascular disease. **Educational/Experience Requirements:** Must meet the following requirements: (1) Hold Diplomate of the American Board of Internal Medicine designation (see separate entry); and (2) Successful completion of training program accredited by Accreditation Council for Graduate Medical Education (see separate entry), Royal College of Physicians and Surgeons of Canada, or Professional Corporation of Physicians of Quebec. **Certification Requirements:** Successful completion of exam. **Renewal:** Every ten years. Recertification based on self-evaluation process, evaluation of credentials, and successful completion of exam. **Examination Frequency:** biennial. **Examination Sites:** Exam given at sites throughout the U.S., Puerto Rico, and Canada. **Fees:** $980. **Endorsed By:** American Board of Medical Specialties; American Medical Association; Council on Medical Education.

800

Diplomate in Cardiovascular Disease of the American Board of Internal Medicine with Added Qualifications in Clinical Cardiac Electrophysiology
American Board of Internal Medicine (ABIM)
3624 Market St.
Philadelphia, PA 19104-2675
Phone: (215)243-1500
Fax: (215)382-4702
Toll Free: (800)441-ABIM

Recipient: Physicians specializing in clinical cardiac electrophysiology. **Educational/Experience Requirements:** Must meet the following requirements: (1) Hold Diplomate in Cardiovascular Disease of the American Board of Internal Medicine designation (see separate entry); (2) Successfully complete three years of training in cardiovascular disease accredited by Accreditation Council for Graduate Medical Education (see separate entry); (3) Successfully complete one year of training in clinical cardiac electrophysiology; and (4) Spend 50 percent of time involved in clinical cardiac electrophysiology. **Certification Requirements:** Successful completion of exam. Exam covers: (1) Basic Electrophysiology, including: Autonomic nervous control of cardiac electrical activity; Formation and propagation of normal and abnormal impulses; and Mechanisms of clinically significant arrhythmias and conduction disturbances; (2) Evaluation and Management of Patients (Ambulatory and Hospitalized), covering clinical syndromes resulting from bradyarrhythmias or tachyarrhythmias; (3) Indications for and Interpretation of Noninvasive Diagnostic Studies, including: Ambulatory electrocardiography; Continuous in-hospital cardiac monitoring; Esophageal, scalar, and signal-averaged electrocardiography; Exercise testing; Relevant imaging studies; and Tilt testing; (4) Indications for and Interpretation of Diagnostic Intracardiac Electrophysiologic Studies; (5) Indication for and Effects of Noninvasive Therapeutic Techniques, including: Cardiopulmonary resuscitation; Cardioversion; Defibrillation; and Esophageal and transcutaneous pacing; (6) Indications for and Effects of Invasive Therapeutic Techniques, including: Catheter and surgical ablation of/for arrhythmias; and Pacemaker and cardioverter-defibrillator implantation; and (7) Pharmacology, Pharmacokinetics, and Use of Antiarrhythmic Agents and Other Drugs that Affect Cardiac Electrical Activity. **Renewal:** Every ten years. Recertification based on successful completion of exam. **Examination Frequency:** biennial - always even-numbered years. **Examination Type:** Multiple-choice; true or false. **Endorsed By:** American Board of Medical Specialties; American Medical Association; Council on Medical Education.

801

Diplomate in Child and Adolescent Psychiatry of the American Board of Psychiatry and Neurology
American Board of Psychiatry and Neurology (ABPN)
500 Lake Cook Rd., Ste. 335
Deerfield, IL 60015-5249
Phone: (708)945-7900
Fax: (708)945-1146

Recipient: Psychiatrists specializing in child and adolescent psychiatry. **Educational/Experience Requirements:** Must meet the following requirements: (1) Hold Diplomate in Psychiatry of the American Board of Psychiatry and Neurology designation (see separate entry);

and (2) Two years of training in child and adolescent psychiatry accredited by Accreditation Council for Graduate Medical Education (see separate entry). **Certification Requirements:** Successful completion of written exam and three-section oral exam. Exams cover: Collaborative personnel; Developmental disturbance; Etiological mechanisms; Normal personality development; Pathological deviations from infancy through adolescence; Psychological testing; Psychopathology; Therapeutic measures and planning; and Types of social planning. Sections of oral exam are: Adolescence; Consultation; and Preschool/grade school. **Renewal:** Every ten years. **Reexamination:** May retake exams one time. Must only retake oral exam section failed if two sections successfully completed. Fees to retake exams are: $675 (written); $1075 (oral). **Fees:** $1400. **Endorsed By:** American Academy of Neurology; American Board of Medical Specialties; American Medical Association; American Neurological Association; American Psychiatric Association; Council on Medical Education.

`802`

Diplomate in Child Neurology of the American Osteopathic Board of Neurology and Psychiatry
American Osteopathic Board of Neurology and Psychiatry
2250 Chapel Ave., W., Ste. 100
Cherry Hill, NJ 08002-2000
Phone: (609)482-9000
William F. Ranieri D.O., Sec.-Treas.

Recipient: Osteopathic physicians specializing in child neurology. **Educational/Experience Requirements:** Hold Diplomate in Neurology of the American Osteopathic Board of Neurology and Psychiatry designation (see separate entry), successfully complete one year internship, and successfully complete one of the following: (1) Two year residency in child neurology and two year residency in neurology; or (2) One year residency in neurology and one year residency in pediatrics. Training must be accredited by Council on Postdoctoral Training of the American Osteopathic Association (see separate entry). **Membership:** Required. **Certification Requirements:** Successful completion of exam. **Renewal:** Every ten years. **Endorsed By:** American Osteopathic Association; Bureau of Osteopathic Specialists.

`803`

Diplomate in Child Psychiatry of the American Osteopathic Board of Neurology and Psychiatry
American Osteopathic Board of Neurology and Psychiatry
2250 Chapel Ave., W., Ste. 100
Cherry Hill, NJ 08002-2000
Phone: (609)482-9000
William F. Ranieri D.O., Sec.-Treas.

Recipient: Osteopathic physicians specializing in child psychiatry. **Educational/Experience Requirements:** Must meet the following requirements: (1) Hold Diplomate in Psychiatry of the American Osteopathic Board of Neurology and Psychiatry designation (see separate entry); (2) Successfully complete one year internship; (3) Successfully complete two years of training in psychiatry; and (4) Successfully complete two years of training in child psychiatry. Training must be accredited by Council on Postdoctoral Training of the American Osteopathic Association (see separate entry). **Membership:** Required. **Certification Requirements:** Successful completion of exam. **Renewal:** Every ten years. **Endorsed By:** American Osteopathic Association; Bureau of Osteopathic Specialists.

`804`

Diplomate in Clinical Pathology of the American Board of Pathology
American Board of Pathology (ABP)
PO Box 25915
Tampa, FL 33622-5915
Phone: (813)286-2444
Fax: (813)289-5279

Recipient: Pathologists specializing in clinical pathology. **Educational/Experience Requirements:** Must meet the following requirements: (1) Graduate from medical school accredited by Liaison Committee for Medical Education (see separate entry), osteopathic college of medicine accredited by Bureau of Professional Education, American Osteopathic Association (see separate entry), or foreign medical school acceptable to ABP; (2) Hold current unrestricted license to practice medicine; (3) Either successfully complete three years of training accredited by Accreditation Council for Graduate Medical Education (ACGME) (separate entry) or hold Diplomate in Anatomic Pathology of the American Board of Pathology and designation (see separate entry) successfully

complete two years training in clinical pathology accredited by ACGME; and (4) Successfully complete approved credentialing year involving additional research or training in pathology. Experience, fellowships, graduate degrees, or research activities may be substituted for training with approval of ABP. **Certification Requirements:** Successful completion of written and oral exams. **Examination Frequency:** semiannual - always May and November. **Fees:** $1000. **Endorsed By:** American Board of Medical Specialists; American Medical Association; American Society of Clinical Pathologists; Council on Medical Education.

`805`

Diplomate in Clinical Tropical Medicine
American Society of Tropical Medicine and Hygiene (ASTMH)
60 Revere Dr., Ste. 500
Northbrook, IL 60062
Phone: (708)480-9592
Fax: (708)480-9282

Recipient: Physicians specializing in clinical tropical medicine. **Educational/Experience Requirements:** Must hold current unrestricted license to practice medicine in the U.S. or Canada and meet education and experience requirements. **Certification Requirements:** Successful completion of exam. **Examination Frequency:** biennial - next 1996. **Endorsed By:** American College of Preventive Medicine.

`806`

Diplomate in Combined Anatomic and Clinical Pathology of the American Board of Pathology
American Board of Pathology (ABP)
PO Box 25915
Tampa, FL 33622-5915
Phone: (813)286-2444
Fax: (813)289-5279

Recipient: Pathologists specializing in anatomic and clinical pathology. **Educational/Experience Requirements:** Must meet the following requirements: (1) Graduate from medical school accredited by Liaison Committee for Medical Education (see separate entry), osteopathic college of medicine accredited by Bureau of Professional Education, American Osteopathic Association (see separate entry), or foreign medical school acceptable to ABP; (2) Hold current unrestricted license to practice medicine; (3) Successfully complete four years of training accredited by Accreditation Council for Graduate Medical Education (see separate entry); and (4) Successfully complete of approved credentialing year involving additional research or training in pathology. Experience, fellowships, graduate degrees, or research activities may be substituted for training with approval of ABP. **Certification Requirements:** Successful completion of written and oral exams. **Examination Frequency:** semiannual - always May and November. **Fees:** $1200. **Endorsed By:** American Board of Medical Specialities; American Medical Association; American Society of Clinical Pathologists; Council on Medical Education.

807

Diplomate in Critical Care Medicine of the Board of Certification in Surgery
Board of Certification in Surgery
804 Main St., Ste. D
Forest Park, GA 30050
Phone: (404)363-8263
Fax: (404)361-2285
Toll Free: (800)447-9397

Recipient: Physicians specializing in critical care medicine. **Educational/Experience Requirements:** Must meet the following requirements: (1) Graduation from school of medicine accredited by Bureau of Professional Education, American Osteopathic Association or Liaison Committee on Medical Education (see separate entries); (2) Current unrestricted licensure to practice medicine; (3) Successful completion of internship accredited by American Osteopathic Association Division on Postdoctoral Training or Accreditation Council for Graduate Medical Education (ACGME) (see separate entries); (4) Successful completion of osteopathic residency accredited by American Osteopathic Association Division on Postdoctoral Training or residency accredited by ACGME; (5) Active staff privileges for two years at institution accredited by Committee on Hospital Accreditation or Joint Commission for Accreditation of Healthcare Organizations (see separate entries); and (6) Submission of ten case reports. **Membership:** Required. **Certification Requirements:** Successful completion of written and clinical exams. May also be required to successfully complete oral exam. Must successfully complete clinical exam before March 1 of year following successful completion of written exam. **Renewal:** Recertification required. **Examination Frequency:** Annual - always June. **Exam-**ination Sites:** Exams given at annual meeting. **Fees:** $500. **Endorsed By:** American Association of Physician Specialists.

808

Diplomate in Diagnostic Radiology of the American Board of Radiology
American Board of Radiology (ABR)
5255 E. Williams Circle, Ste. 6800
Tucson, AZ 85711
Phone: (520)790-2900
Fax: (520)790-3200
M. Paul Capp M.D., Exec.Dir.

Recipient: Specialists in radiological physics. **Educational/Experience Requirements:** Must meet the following requirements: (1) Graduation from medical school in U.S. or Canada accredited by Liaison Committee on Medical Education (see separate entry) or college of osteopathic medicine accredited by Bureau of Professional Education, American Osteopathic Association (see separate entry); and (2) Successful completion of four-year residency accredited by Accreditation Council for Graduate Medical Education or American Osteopathic Association Division on Postdoctoral Training (see separate entries). Graduates of foreign medical schools must have credentials evaluated. **Certification Requirements:** Successful completion of written and oral exams. Written exam covers: (1) Diagnostic Physics and Equipment, including: Basic physics; Contrast media; Factors affecting image quality and radiation exposure; Image intensifiers; Magnetic resonance; Radiation safety; Recording systems; Television and cine systems; Tomography and computerized tomography; Ultrasonography; and X-ray tubes; (2) Physics of Nuclear Radiology, including: Basic physics; Dosimetry; Equipment; Measurements; and Statistics; (3) Radiation Biology, including: Cellular effects and cell kinetics; Factors modifying response; Fractionation and irradiation of cancer; Histopathologic responses; Response of organs; Subcellular effects; Tissue kinetics and tissue effects; and Total body effects; and (4) Diagnostic Radiology, including: Breast radiology; Cardiovascular system; Central nervous system, including facial bones, mastoids, neck, and para-nasal sinuses; Chest; Gastrointestinal tract; Genitourinary tract; Nuclear radiology; Pediatric radiology; Skeletal system; and Ultrasonography. Oral exam covers plain film diagnosis, contrast studies, and special diagnostic procedures in the following anatomical ar-eas: (1) Bones and Joints; (2) Chest, including: Heart and great vessels; Lungs; Mediastinum; Pleura; and Thoracic structures; (3) Gastrointestinal Tract, including: Esophagus; Gallbladder; Intestines; Liver; Pancreas; Spleen; and Stomach; (4) Genitourinary Tract; (5) Neuroradiology, including: Hypopharynx; Larynx; Lymphatic and other soft tissues; Mastoids; Oropharynx; Sinuses; Skull; Spine; and Vascular; (6) Cardiovascular Radiology; (7) Nuclear Radiology; (8) Ultrasonography; (9) Pediatric Radiology; and (10) Breast Radiology. **Preparatory Materials:** Booklet, including sample questions, provided. **Examination Frequency:** Annual (oral) - always May or June. **Examination Sites:** Written exam given at sites throughout the U.S. **Examination Type:** Multiple-choice. **Re-examination:** May retake exams two times. **Endorsed By:** American Association of Physicists in Medicine; American Board of Medical Specialties; American College of Radiology; American Medical Association; American Radium Society; American Roentgen Ray Society; American Society for Therapeutic Radiology and Oncology; Association of University Radiologists; Radiological Society of North America.

809

Diplomate in Diagnostic Radiology of the American Osteopathic Board of Radiology
American Osteopathic Board of Radiology
119 E. Second St.
Milan, MO 63556
Phone: (816)265-4011
Pamela A. Smith, Exec.Dir.

Recipient: Osteopathic physicians specializing in diagnostic radiology. **Educational/Experience Requirements:** Must meet the following requirements: (1) Graduation from college of osteopathic medicine accredited by Bureau of Professional Education, American Osteopathic Association (see separate entry); (2) Current licensure to practice medicine; (3) Two years of membership in American Osteopathic Association or Canadian Osteopathic Association; (4) Successful completion of internship accredited by Council on Postdoctoral Training of the American Osteopathic Association (see separate entry); and (5) Successful completion of four years of training in diagnostic radiology accredited by Council on Postdoctoral Training of the American Osteopathic Association. **Membership:** Required. **Certification Requirements:** Successful completion of written, oral, and clinical exams. Exams cover: Diagnostic and therapeutic procedures; Familiarity with current advances; and Scientific bases of problems. **Examination Frequency:** Annual. **Examination Sites:** Exams given at one U.S. site each. **Endorsed By:** American Osteopathic Association; Bureau of Osteopathic Specialists.

▐ 810 ▐

Diplomate in Diagnostic Radiology with Special Competence in Nuclear Radiology of the American Board of Radiology
American Board of Radiology (ABR)
5255 E. Williams Circle, Ste. 6800
Tucson, AZ 85711
Phone: (520)790-2900
Fax: (520)790-3200
M. Paul Capp M.D., Exec.Dir.

Recipient: Radiologists specializing in nuclear radiation. **Educational/ Experience Requirements:** Must meet the following requirements: (1) Hold either Diplomate in Radiology or Diagnostic Radiology of the American Board of Radiology (see separate entries); and (2) Successfully complete residency in nuclear radiology accredited by Accreditation Council for Graduate Medical Education. **Certification Requirements:** Successful completion of oral exam. Exam covers following anatomical areas: Bone, bone marrow, genitourinary tract, tumor, and abscess localization; Central nervous system, endocrinology, gastrointestinal tract, hepatobiliary tract, and spleen; and Cardiopulmonary systems and quality assurance. Exam also covers following subjects: (1) Clinical Nuclear Radiology, including: Cardiovascular system; Central nervous system; Endocrine system; Gastrointestinal system; Genitourinary system; Hepatobiliary system and spleen; Musculoskeletal system; Neoplasm and abscess localization; and Respiratory system; (2) Physics of Nuclear Radiology, including: Basic medical nuclear physics; Dosage and dosimetry; Measurements and statistics of counting; Nuclear instrumentation; Protection and safety; and Radioactivity; (3) Radiation Biology, including: Carcinogenesis; Cell structure in biology; Cellular radiation injury and repair; Genetics; and Organ radiobiology; and (4) Basic Science, including: Physiology of organ systems; Principles of imaging and image analysis; Radiochemistry; Radiopharmacology; and Tracer theory. **Examination Frequency:** Annual. **Re-examination:** Must wait one year to retake exam. **Endorsed By:** American Association of Physicists in Medicine; American Board of Medical

Specialties; American College of Radiology; American Medical Association; American Radium Society; American Roentgen Ray Society; American Society for Therapeutic Radiology and Oncology; Association of University Radiologists; Council on Medical Education; Radiological Society of North America.

▐ 811 ▐

Diplomate in Endocrinology of the American Osteopathic Board of Internal Medicine
American Osteopathic Board of Internal Medicine
5200 S. Ellis Ave.
Chicago, IL 60615
Phone: (312)947-4881
Gary L. Slick D.O., Exec.Dir.

Recipient: Physicians specializing in endocrinology. **Educational/Experience Requirements:** Must meet the following requirements: (1) Hold Diplomate of the American Osteopathic Board of Internal Medicine designation (see separate entry); and (2) Successfully complete two year training program in endocrinology accredited by Council on Postdoctoral Training of the American Osteopathic Association (see separate entry). **Membership:** Required. **Certification Requirements:** Successful completion of exam. **Renewal:** Every ten years. **Examination Frequency:** Annual - always August. **Examination Sites:** Exam given at one U.S. site. **Endorsed By:** American Osteopathic Association; Bureau of Osteopathic Specialists.

▐ 812 ▐

Diplomate in Endocrinology, Diabetes, and Metabolism of the American Board of Internal Medicine
American Board of Internal Medicine (ABIM)
3624 Market St.
Philadelphia, PA 19104-2675
Phone: (215)243-1500
Fax: (215)382-4702
Toll Free: (800)441-ABIM

Recipient: Physicians specializing in endocrinology, diabetes, and metabolism. **Educational/Experience Requirements:** Must meet the following requirements: (1) Hold Diplomate of the American Board of Internal Medicine designation (see separate entry); and (2) Successful completion of training program accredited by Accreditation Council for Graduate Medical Education (see separate en-

try), Royal College of Physicians and Surgeons of Canada, or Professional Corporation of Physicians of Quebec. **Certification Requirements:** Successful completion of exam. **Renewal:** Every ten years. Recertification based on self-evaluation process, evaluation of credentials, and successful completion of exam. **Examination Frequency:** biennial. **Examination Sites:** Exam given at sites throughout the U.S., Puerto Rico, and Canada. **Fees:** $980. **Endorsed By:** American Board of Medical Specialties; American Medical Association; Council on Medical Education.

▐ 813 ▐

Diplomate in Facial Plastic Surgery of the American Osteopathic Board of Ophthalmology and Otorhinolaryngology
American Osteopathic Board of Ophthalmology and Otorhinolaryngology
Three Mackoil Ave.
Dayton, OH 45403
Phone: (513)252-0868
Sharon Alexiades, Exec.Sec.

Recipient: Osteopathic physicians specializing in facial plastic surgery. **Educational/Experience Requirements:** Must meet the following requirements: (1) Graduation from college of osteopathic medicine accredited by Bureau of Professional Education, American Osteopathic Association (see separate entry); (2) Current licensure to practice medicine; (3) Two years of membership in either American Osteopathic Association or Canadian Osteopathic Association; (4) Successful completion of internship accredited by Council on Postdoctoral Training of the American Osteopathic Association (see separate entry); (5) Successful completion of four year residency in ophthalmology or otorhinolaryngology accredited by Council on Postdoctoral Training of the American Osteopathic Association; and (6) Submission of case logs. **Membership:** Required. **Certification Requirements:** Successful completion of written, oral, and clinical exams. Exams cover: Diagnostic and therapeutic procedures; Familiarity with current advances; and Scientific bases of problems. Must successfully complete written exam before attempting oral and clinical exams. **Examination Frequency:** Annual. **Examination Sites:** Exams given at one site in the U.S. **Endorsed By:** American Osteopathic Association; Bureau of Osteopathic Specialists.

814

Diplomate in Forensic Pathology of the American Osteopathic Board of Pathology

American Osteopathic Board of
Pathology
450 Powers Ave., Ste. 105
Harrisburg, PA 17109
Phone: (717)561-8560
Kay I. Rittenhouse, Exec.Sec.

Recipient: Osteopathic physicians specializing in forensic pathology. **Educational/Experience Requirements:** Must meet the following requirements: (1) Hold Diplomate in Anatomic Pathology and Laboratory Medicine of the American Osteopathic Board of Pathology designation (see separate entry); and (2) Successfully complete one year of training accredited by Council on Postdoctoral Training of the American Osteopathic Association (see separate entry). **Membership:** Required. **Certification Requirements:** Successful completion of written, oral, and practical exams. **Renewal:** Every ten years. **Examination Frequency:** Annual. **Examination Sites:** Exams given at one site in the U.S. **Endorsed By:** American Osteopathic Association; Bureau of Osteopathic Specialists.

815

Diplomate in Gastroenterology of the American Board of Internal Medicine

American Board of Internal
Medicine (ABIM)
3624 Market St.
Philadelphia, PA 19104-2675
Phone: (215)243-1500
Fax: (215)382-4702
Toll Free: (800)441-ABIM

Recipient: Physicians specializing in gastroenterology. **Educational/Experience Requirements:** Must meet the following requirements: (1) Hold Diplomate of the American Board of Internal Medicine designation (see separate entry); and (2) Successful completion of training program accredited by Accreditation Council for Graduate Medical Education (see separate entry), Royal College of Physicians and Surgeons of Canada, or Professional Corporation of Physicians of Quebec. **Certification Requirements:** Successful completion of exam. **Renewal:** Every ten years. Recertification based on self-evaluation process, evaluation of credentials, and successful completion of exam. **Examination Frequency:** biennial. **Examination Sites:** Exam given at sites throughout the U.S., Puerto Rico, and Canada. **Fees:** $980. **Endorsed By:** American Board of Medical Specialties; American Medical Association; Council on Medical Education.

816

Diplomate in Gastroenterology of the American Osteopathic Board of Internal Medicine

American Osteopathic Board of
Internal Medicine
5200 S. Ellis Ave.
Chicago, IL 60615
Phone: (312)947-4881
Gary L. Slick D.O., Exec.Dir.

Recipient: Physicians specializing in gastroenterology. **Educational/Experience Requirements:** Must meet the following requirements: (1) Hold Diplomate of the American Osteopathic Board of Internal Medicine designation (see separate entry); and (2) Successfully complete two year training program in gastroenterology accredited by Council on Postdoctoral Training of the American Osteopathic Association (see separate entry). **Membership:** Required. **Certification Requirements:** Successful completion of exam. **Renewal:** Every ten years. **Examination Frequency:** Annual - always August. **Examination Sites:** Exam given at one U.S. site. **Endorsed By:** American Osteopathic Association; Bureau of Osteopathic Specialists.

817

Diplomate in General Vascular Surgery of the American Osteopathic Board of Surgery

American Osteopathic Board of
Surgery
Three MacKoil Ave.
Dayton, OH 45403
Phone: (513)252-0868
Sharon Alexiades, Corres.Sec.

Recipient: Osteopathic surgeons specializing in general vascular surgery. **Educational/Experience Requirements:** Must meet the following requirements: (1) Graduation from college of osteopathic medicine accredited by Bureau of Professional Education, American Osteopathic Association (see separate entry); (2) Current licensure to practice medicine; (3) Two years of membership in American Osteopathic Association or Canadian Osteopathic Association; (4) Successful completion of internship accredited by Council on Postdoctoral Training of the American Osteopathic Association (see separate entry); (5) Successful completion of five years of training accredited by Council on Postdoctoral Training of the American Osteopathic Association; (6) Submission of log of major operative cases performed; (7) Submission of list of mortalities; and (8) Successful completion of qualifying exam. **Membership:** Required. **Certification Requirements:** Successful completion of written, oral, and clinical exams. Exams cover: Basic sciences; Current advances in surgical philosophy and techniques; Diagnostic, operative, and therapeutic procedures; Osteopathic philosophy of surgery applied to diagnosis and management of surgical diseases; Surgical judgment; and Surgical principles. **Examination Frequency:** Annual. **Examination Sites:** Exams given at one U.S. site. **Endorsed By:** American College of Osteopathic Surgeons; American Osteopathic Association; Bureau of Osteopathic Specialists.

818

Diplomate in Gynecologic Oncology of the American Osteopathic Board of Obstetrics and Gynecology

American Osteopathic Board of
Obstetrics and Gynecology
(AOBOG)
5200 S. Ellis Ave.
Chicago, IL 60615
Phone: (312)947-4630
Joseph P. Bonanno D.O., Sec.-
Treas.

Recipient: Osteopathic physicians specializing in gynecologic oncology. **Educational/Experience Requirements:** Must meet the following requirements: (1) Hold Diplomate of the American Osteopathic Board of Obstetrics and Gynecology designation (see separate entry); and (2) Successfully complete residency in gynecologic oncology accredited by Council on Postdoctoral Training of the American Osteopathic Association (see separate entry). **Membership:** Required. **Certification Requirements:** Successful completion of exam. **Renewal:** Every ten years. **Examination Frequency:** Annual. **Endorsed By:** American Osteopathic Association; Bureau of Osteopathic Specialists.

819

Diplomate in Hematology of the American Board of Internal Medicine

American Board of Internal
  Medicine (ABIM)
3624 Market St.
Philadelphia, PA 19104-2675
Phone: (215)243-1500
Fax: (215)382-4702
Toll Free: (800)441-ABIM

Recipient: Physicians specializing in hematology. **Educational/Experience Requirements:** Must meet the following requirements: (1) Hold Diplomate of the American Board of Internal Medicine designation (see separate entry); and (2) Successful completion of training program accredited by Accreditation Council for Graduate Medical Education (see separate entry), Royal College of Physicians and Surgeons of Canada, or Professional Corporation of Physicians of Quebec. **Certification Requirements:** Successful completion of exam. **Renewal:** Every ten years. Recertification based on self-evaluation process, evaluation of credentials, and successful completion of exam. **Examination Frequency:** biennial. **Examination Sites:** Exam given at sites throughout the U.S., Puerto Rico, and Canada. **Fees:** $980. **Endorsed By:** American Board of Medical Specialties; American Medical Association; Council on Medical Education.

820

Diplomate in Hematology of the American Osteopathic Board of Internal Medicine

American Osteopathic Board of
  Internal Medicine
5200 S. Ellis Ave.
Chicago, IL 60615
Phone: (312)947-4881
Gary L. Slick D.O., Exec.Dir.

Recipient: Physicians specializing in hematology. **Educational/Experience Requirements:** Must meet the following requirements: (1) Hold Diplomate of the American Osteopathic Board of Internal Medicine designation (see separate entry); and (2) Successfully complete two year training program in hematology accredited by Council on Postdoctoral Training of the American Osteopathic Association (see separate entry). **Membership:** Required. **Certification Requirements:** Successful completion of exam. **Renewal:** Every ten years. **Examination Frequency:** Annual - always August. **Examination Sites:** Exam given at one U.S.

site. **Endorsed By:** American Osteopathic Association; Bureau of Osteopathic Specialists.

821

Diplomate in Hematology and Medical Oncology of the American Board of Internal Medicine

American Board of Internal
  Medicine (ABIM)
3624 Market St.
Philadelphia, PA 19104-2675
Phone: (215)243-1500
Fax: (215)382-4702
Toll Free: (800)441-ABIM

Recipient: Physicians specializing in hematology and medical oncology. **Educational/Experience Requirements:** Must meet the following requirements: (1) Hold Diplomate of the American Board of Internal Medicine designation (see separate entry); and (2) Successful completion of training program accredited by Accreditation Council for Graduate Medical Education (see separate entry), Royal College of Physicians and Surgeons of Canada, or Professional Corporation of Physicians of Quebec. **Certification Requirements:** Successful completion of exam. **Renewal:** Every ten years. Recertification based on self-evaluation process, evaluation of credentials, and successful completion of exam. **Examination Frequency:** biennial. **Examination Sites:** Exam given at sites throughout the U.S., Puerto Rico, and Canada. **Fees:** $980. **Endorsed By:** American Board of Medical Specialties; American Medical Association; Council on Medical Education.

822

Diplomate in Hematology and Oncology of the American Osteopathic Board of Internal Medicine

American Osteopathic Board of
  Internal Medicine
5200 S. Ellis Ave.
Chicago, IL 60615
Phone: (312)947-4881
Gary L. Slick D.O., Exec.Dir.

Recipient: Physicians specializing in hematology and oncology. **Educational/Experience Requirements:** Must meet the following requirements: (1) Hold Diplomate of the American Osteopathic Board of Internal Medicine designation (see separate entry); and (2) Successfully complete three year training program in

hematology and oncology accredited by Council on Postdoctoral Training of the American Osteopathic Association (see separate entry). **Membership:** Required. **Certification Requirements:** Successful completion of exam. **Renewal:** Every ten years. **Examination Frequency:** Annual - always August. **Examination Sites:** Exam given at one U.S. site. **Endorsed By:** American Osteopathic Association; Bureau of Osteopathic Specialists.

823

Diplomate in Infectious Disease of the American Board of Internal Medicine

American Board of Internal
  Medicine (ABIM)
3624 Market St.
Philadelphia, PA 19104-2675
Phone: (215)243-1500
Fax: (215)382-4702
Toll Free: (800)441-ABIM

Recipient: Physicians specializing in infectious diseases. **Educational/Experience Requirements:** Must meet the following requirements: (1) Hold Diplomate of the American Board of Internal Medicine designation (see separate entry); and (2) Successful completion of training program accredited by Accreditation Council for Graduate Medical Education (see separate entry), Royal College of Physicians and Surgeons of Canada, or Professional Corporation of Physicians of Quebec. **Certification Requirements:** Successful completion of exam. **Renewal:** Every ten years. Recertification based on self-evaluation process, evaluation of credentials, and successful completion of exam. **Examination Frequency:** biennial. **Examination Sites:** Exam given at sites throughout the U.S., Puerto Rico, and Canada. **Fees:** $980. **Endorsed By:** American Board of Medical Specialties; American Medical Association; Council on Medical Education.

824

Diplomate in Infectious Disease of the American Osteopathic Board of Internal Medicine

American Osteopathic Board of
  Internal Medicine
5200 S. Ellis Ave.
Chicago, IL 60615
Phone: (312)947-4881
Gary L. Slick D.O., Exec.Dir.

Recipient: Physicians specializing in infectious diseases. **Educational/Experience Requirements:** Must meet the following requirements: (1) Hold Diplomate of the American Osteopathic Board of Internal Medicine designation (see separate entry); and (2) Successfully complete two year training program in infectious disease accredited by Council on Postdoctoral Training of the American Osteopathic Association (see separate entry). **Membership:** Required. **Certification Requirements:** Successful completion of exam. **Renewal:** Every ten years. **Examination Frequency:** Annual - always August. **Examination Sites:** Exam given at one U.S. site. **Endorsed By:** American Osteopathic Association; Bureau of Osteopathic Specialists.

825

Diplomate in Laboratory Medicine of the American Osteopathic Board of Pathology

American Osteopathic Board of Pathology
450 Powers Ave., Ste. 105
Harrisburg, PA 17109
Phone: (717)561-8560
Kay I. Rittenhouse, Exec.Sec.

Recipient: Osteopathic physicians specializing in laboratory medicine. **Educational/Experience Requirements:** Must meet the following requirements: (1) Graduation from college of osteopathic medicine accredited by Bureau of Professional Education, American Osteopathic Association (see separate entry); (2) Current licensure to practice medicine; (3) Two years of membership in American Osteopathic Association or Canadian Osteopathic Association; (4) Successful completion of internship accredited by Council on Postdoctoral Training of the American Osteopathic Association (see separate entry); and (5) Successful completion of three year residency in laboratory medicine accredited by Council on Postdoctoral Training of the American Osteopathic Association. **Membership:** Required. **Certification Requirements:** Successful completion of written, oral, and practical exams. **Renewal:** Every ten years. **Examination Frequency:** Annual. **Examination Sites:** Exams given at one site in the U.S. **Endorsed By:** American Osteopathic Association; Bureau of Osteopathic Specialists.

826

Diplomate in Maternal-Fetal Medicine of the American Osteopathic Board of Obstetrics and Gynecology

American Osteopathic Board of Obstetrics and Gynecology (AOBOG)
5200 S. Ellis Ave.
Chicago, IL 60615
Phone: (312)947-4630
Joseph P. Bonanno D.O., Sec.-Treas.

Recipient: Osteopathic physicians specializing in maternal and fetal medicine. **Educational/Experience Requirements:** Must meet the following requirements: (1) Hold Diplomate of the American Osteopathic Board of Obstetrics and Gynecology designation (see separate entry); and (2) Successfully complete residency in maternal-fetal medicine accredited by Council on Postdoctoral Training of the American Osteopathic Association (see separate entry). **Membership:** Required. **Certification Requirements:** Successful completion of exam. **Renewal:** Every ten years. **Examination Frequency:** Annual. **Endorsed By:** American Osteopathic Association; Bureau of Osteopathic Specialists.

827

Diplomate in Medical Oncology of the American Board of Internal Medicine

American Board of Internal Medicine (ABIM)
3624 Market St.
Philadelphia, PA 19104-2675
Phone: (215)243-1500
Fax: (215)382-4702
Toll Free: (800)441-ABIM

Recipient: Physicians specializing in medical oncology. **Educational/Experience Requirements:** Must meet the following requirements: (1) Hold Diplomate of the American Board of Internal Medicine designation (see separate entry); and (2) Successful completion of training program accredited by Accreditation Council for Graduate Medical Education (see separate entry), Royal College of Physicians and Surgeons of Canada, or Professional Corporation of Physicians of Quebec. **Certification Requirements:** Successful completion of exam. **Renewal:** Every ten years. Recertification based on self-evaluation process, evaluation of credentials, and successful completion of exam. **Examination Frequency:** biennial. **Examination Sites:**

Exam given at sites throughout the U.S., Puerto Rico, and Canada. **Fees:** $980. **Endorsed By:** American Board of Medical Specialties; American Medical Association; Council on Medical Education.

828

Diplomate in Nephrology of the American Board of Internal Medicine

American Board of Internal Medicine (ABIM)
3624 Market St.
Philadelphia, PA 19104-2675
Phone: (215)243-1500
Fax: (215)382-4702
Toll Free: (800)441-ABIM

Recipient: Physicians specializing in nephrology. **Educational/Experience Requirements:** Must meet the following requirements: (1) Hold Diplomate of the American Board of Internal Medicine designation (see separate entry); and (2) Successful completion of training program accredited by Accreditation Council for Graduate Medical Education (see separate entry), Royal College of Physicians and Surgeons of Canada, or Professional Corporation of Physicians of Quebec. **Certification Requirements:** Successful completion of exam. **Renewal:** Every ten years. Recertification based on self-evaluation process, evaluation of credentials, and successful completion of exam. **Examination Frequency:** biennial. **Examination Sites:** Exam given at sites throughout the U.S., Puerto Rico, and Canada. **Fees:** $980. **Endorsed By:** American Board of Medical Specialties; American Medical Association; Council on Medical Education.

829

Diplomate in Nephrology of the American Osteopathic Board of Internal Medicine

American Osteopathic Board of Internal Medicine
5200 S. Ellis Ave.
Chicago, IL 60615
Phone: (312)947-4881
Gary L. Slick D.O., Exec.Dir.

Recipient: Physicians specializing in nephrology. **Educational/Experience Requirements:** Must meet the following requirements: (1) Hold Diplomate of the American Osteopathic Board of Internal Medicine designation (see separate entry); and (2) Successfully complete two year training program in nephrology accredited by Council on Postdoctoral

Training of the American Osteopathic Association (see separate entry). **Membership:** Required. **Certification Requirements:** Successful completion of exam. **Renewal:** Every ten years. **Examination Frequency:** Annual - always August. **Examination Sites:** Exam given at one U.S. site. **Endorsed By:** American Osteopathic Association; Bureau of Osteopathic Specialists.

830

Diplomate in Neurological Surgery of the American Osteopathic Board of Surgery

American Osteopathic Board of Surgery
Three MacKoil Ave.
Dayton, OH 45403
Phone: (513)252-0868
Sharon Alexiades, Corres.Sec.

Recipient: Osteopathic surgeons specializing in neurological surgery. **Educational/Experience Requirements:** Must meet the following requirements: (1) Graduation from college of osteopathic medicine accredited by Bureau of Professional Education, American Osteopathic Association (see separate entry); (2) Current licensure to practice medicine; (3) Two years of membership in American Osteopathic Association or Canadian Osteopathic Association; (4) Successful completion of internship accredited by Council on Postdoctoral Training of the American Osteopathic Association (see separate entry); (5) Successful completion of five years of training accredited by Council on Postdoctoral Training of the American Osteopathic Association; (6) Submission of log of major operative cases performed during previous year; and (7) Submission of list of mortalities. **Membership:** Required. **Certification Requirements:** Successful completion of written, oral, and clinical exams. Exams cover: Basic sciences; Current advances in surgical philosophy and techniques; Diagnostic, operative, and therapeutic procedures; Osteopathic philosophy of surgery applied to diagnosis and management of surgical diseases; Surgical judgment; and Surgical principles. **Examination Frequency:** Annual. **Examination Sites:** Exams given at one U.S. site. **Endorsed By:** American College of Osteopathic Surgeons; American Osteopathic Association; Bureau of Osteopathic Specialists.

831

Diplomate in Neurology of the American Board of Psychiatry and Neurology

American Board of Psychiatry and Neurology (ABPN)
500 Lake Cook Rd., Ste. 335
Deerfield, IL 60015-5249
Phone: (708)945-7900
Fax: (708)945-1146

Recipient: Physicians specializing in neurology. **Educational/Experience Requirements:** Must meet the following requirements: (1) Graduation from medical school accredited by Liaison Committee for Medical Education (see separate entry); (2) Current unrestricted licensure to practice medicine; (3) Successful completion of internship in internal medicine or neurology accredited by Accreditation Council for Graduate Medical Education (ACGME) (see separate entry); and (4) Successful completion of residency in neurology accredited by ACGME. Candidates whose medical education was earned outside the U.S. must meet additional requirements. **Certification Requirements:** Successful completion of written and oral exams. Written exam covers both neurology and psychiatry in the following areas: Alcoholism and substance abuse; Altered states of consciousness; Basic and clinical neuropharmacology; Behavioral and personality changes associated with structural alterations; Cerebrospinal fluid; Developmental and other disorders of childhood; Diagnostic procedures; Doctor-patient relationship; Genetics; Memory disorders and cortical dysfunction; Neuroanatomy; Neurochemistry; Neuroendocrinology; Neuroimaging; Neuroimmunology/neurovirology; Neuroophthalmology; Neuro-otology; Neuropathology; Neurophysiology; Non-pharmacologic therapeutic modalities; Psychiatric problems associated with medical disease; Psychopathology and diagnostic criteria; and Psychopharmacology. Oral exam requires examination of patient and covers adult and child clinical neurology. **Renewal:** Every ten years. **Examination Frequency:** Annual (written) - always fall. Three-four times per year (oral). **Examination Sites:** Written exam given at regional sites in the U.S. and Canada and oral exam given at selected sites in the U.S. **Re-examination:** May retake written exam one time and oral exam two times. Fees to retake exams are: $675 (written); $1075 (oral). **Fees:** $1400. **Endorsed By:** American Academy of Neurology; American Board of Medical Specialties; American Medical Association; American Neurological Association; American Psychiatric Association; Council on Medical Education.

832

Diplomate in Neurology of the American Board of Psychiatry and Neurology with Special Qualification in Child Neurology

American Board of Psychiatry and Neurology (ABPN)
500 Lake Cook Rd., Ste. 335
Deerfield, IL 60015-5249
Phone: (708)945-7900
Fax: (708)945-1146

Recipient: Physicians specializing in child neurology. **Educational/Experience Requirements:** Must meet the following requirements: (1) Graduation from medical school accredited by Liaison Committee for Medical Education (see separate entry); (2) Current unrestricted licensure to practice medicine; (3) Successful completion of two years of training accredited by Accreditation Council for Graduate Medical Education (ACGME) (see separate entry); and (4) Successful completion of three-year residency in child neurology accredited by ACGME. Candidates whose medical education was earned outside the U.S. must meet additional requirements. **Certification Requirements:** Successful completion of written and oral exams. Written exam covers both neurology and psychiatry in the following areas: Alcoholism and substance abuse; Altered states of consciousness; Basic and clinical neuropharmacology; Behavioral and personality changes associated with structural alterations; Cerebrospinal fluid; Developmental and other disorders of childhood; Diagnostic procedures; Doctor-patient relationship; Genetics; Memory disorders and cortical dysfunction; Neuroanatomy; Neurochemistry; Neuroendocrinology; Neuroimaging; Neuroimmunology/neurovirology; Neuroophthalmology; Neuro-otology; Neuropathology; Neurophysiology; Non-pharmacologic therapeutic modalities; Psychiatric problems associated with medical disease; Psychopathology and diagnostic criteria; and Psychopharmacology. Oral exam requires examination of patient and covers adult and child clinical neurology. **Renewal:** Every ten years. **Examination Frequency:** Annual (written) - always fall. Three-four times per year (oral). **Examination Sites:** Written exam given at regional sites in the U.S. and Canada and oral exam given at selected sites in the U.S. **Re-examination:** May retake written exam one time and oral exam two times. Fees to retake exams are: $675 (written); $1075 (oral). **Fees:** $1400. **Endorsed By:** American Academy of Neurology; American Board of Medical Specialties; American Medical Association; American Neurological Association; American

Psychiatric Association; Council on Medical Education.

833

Diplomate in Neurology of the American Osteopathic Board of Neurology and Psychiatry

American Osteopathic Board of Neurology and Psychiatry
2250 Chapel Ave., W., Ste. 100
Cherry Hill, NJ 08002-2000
Phone: (609)482-9000
William F. Ranieri D.O., Sec.-Treas.

Recipient: Osteopathic physicians specializing in neurology. **Educational/Experience Requirements:** Must meet the following requirements: (1) Graduation from college of osteopathic medicine accredited by Bureau of Professional Education, American Osteopathic Association (see separate entry); (2) Current licensure to practice medicine; (3) Two years of membership in either American Osteopathic Association or Canadian Osteopathic Association; (4) Successful completion of one year internship accredited by Council on Postdoctoral Training of the American Osteopathic Association (see separate entry); and (5) Successful completion of three year residency in neurology accredited by Council on Postdoctoral Training of the American Osteopathic Association. One year of credit given for successful completion of two years in non-neurology residency. **Membership:** Required. **Certification Requirements:** Successful completion of written, oral, and clinical exams. Exams cover: Diagnostic and therapeutic procedures; Familiarity with current advances; and Scientific bases of problems. Must successfully complete written exam before attempting oral and clinical exams. **Renewal:** Every ten years. **Endorsed By:** American Osteopathic Association; Bureau of Osteopathic Specialists.

834

Diplomate in Occupational-Environmental Medicine of the American Osteopathic Board of Preventive Medicine

American Osteopathic Board of Preventive Medicine
Box 226
U.S. Air Force Academy, CO 80840-2200
Phone: (719)472-3560
George E. Hill D.O., Sec.-Treas.

Recipient: Osteopathic physicians specializing in occupational and environmental medicine. **Educational/Experience Requirements:** Must meet the following requirements: (1) Graduation from college of osteopathic medicine accredited by Bureau of Professional Education, American Osteopathic Association (see separate entry); (2) Current licensure to practice medicine; (3) Two years of membership in American Osteopathic Association or Canadian Osteopathic Association; (4) Successful completion of internship accredited by Council on Postdoctoral Training of the American Osteopathic Association (see separate entry); (5) Master's of Public Health degree; and (6) Successful completion of one year of training in occupational and environmental medicine accredited by Council on Postdoctoral Training of the American Osteopathic Association. **Membership:** Required. **Certification Requirements:** Successful completion of written, oral, and clinical exams. Exams cover: Diagnostic and therapeutic procedures; Familiarity with current advances; and Scientific bases of problems. **Renewal:** Every seven years. Recertification based on successful completion of exam. **Examination Frequency:** Annual. **Examination Sites:** Exams given at one U.S. site. **Endorsed By:** American Osteopathic Association; Bureau of Osteopathic Specialists.

835

Diplomate in Oncology of the American Osteopathic Board of Internal Medicine

American Osteopathic Board of Internal Medicine
5200 S. Ellis Ave.
Chicago, IL 60615
Phone: (312)947-4881
Gary L. Slick D.O., Exec.Dir.

Recipient: Physicians specializing in oncology. **Educational/Experience Requirements:** Must meet the following requirements: (1) Hold Diplomate of the American Osteopathic Board of Internal Medicine designation (see separate entry); and (2) Successfully complete two year training program in oncology accredited by Council on Postdoctoral Training of the American Osteopathic Association (see separate entry). **Membership:** Required. **Certification Requirements:** Successful completion of exam. **Renewal:** Every ten years. **Examination Frequency:** Annual - always August. **Examination Sites:** Exam given at one U.S. site. **Endorsed By:** American Osteopathic Association; Bureau of Osteopathic Specialists.

836

Diplomate in Ophthalmology of the American Osteopathic Board of Ophthalmology and Otorhinolaryngology

American Osteopathic Board of Ophthalmology and Otorhinolaryngology
Three Mackoil Ave.
Dayton, OH 45403
Phone: (513)252-0868
Sharon Alexiades, Exec.Sec.

Recipient: Osteopathic physicians specializing in ophthalmology. **Educational/Experience Requirements:** Must meet the following requirements: (1) Graduation from college of osteopathic medicine accredited by Bureau of Professional Education, American Osteopathic Association (see separate entry); (2) Current licensure to practice medicine; (3) Two years of membership in either American Osteopathic Association or Canadian Osteopathic Association; (4) Successful completion of internship accredited by Council on Postdoctoral Training of the American Osteopathic Association (see separate entry); (5) Successful completion of three year residency in ophthalmology accredited by Council on Postdoctoral Training of the American Osteopathic Association; and (6) Submission of case logs. **Membership:** Required. **Certification Requirements:** Successful completion of written, oral, and clinical exams. Exams cover: Diagnostic and therapeutic procedures; Familiarity with current advances; and Scientific bases of problems. Must successfully complete written exam before attempting oral and clinical exams. **Examination Frequency:** Annual. **Examination Sites:** Exams given at one site in the U.S. **Endorsed By:** American Osteopathic Association; Bureau of Osteopathic Specialists.

837

Diplomate in Ophthalmology of the Board of Certification in Surgery

Board of Certification in Surgery
804 Main St., Ste. D
Forest Park, GA 30050
Phone: (404)363-8263
Fax: (404)361-2285
Toll Free: (800)447-9397

Recipient: Physicians specializing in ophthalmology. **Educational/Experience Requirements:** Must meet the following requirements: (1) Graduation from school of medicine accredited by Bureau of Professional Education, American Osteopathic Association or Liaison Committee on Medical Education (see separate entries); (2) Current unrestricted licensure to practice medicine; (3) Successful completion of internship accredited by American Osteopathic Association Division on Postdoctoral Training or Accreditation Council for Graduate Medical Education (ACGME) (see separate entries); (4) Successful completion of osteopathic residency accredited by American Osteopathic Association Division on Postdoctoral Training or residency accredited by ACGME; (5) Active staff privileges for two years at institution accredited by Committee on Hospital Accreditation or Joint Commission for Accreditation of Healthcare Organizations (see separate entries); and (6) Submission of ten case reports. **Membership:** Required. **Certification Requirements:** Successful completion of written and clinical exams. May also be required to successfully complete oral exam. Must successfully complete clinical exam before March 1 of year following successful completion of written exam. **Renewal:** Recertification required. **Examination Frequency:** Annual - always June. **Examination Sites:** Exams given at annual meeting. **Fees:** $500. **Endorsed By:** American Association of Physician Specialists.

838

Diplomate in Otorhinolaryngology of the American Osteopathic Board of Ophthalmology and Otorhinolaryngology

American Osteopathic Board of
   Ophthalmology and
   Otorhinolaryngology
Three Mackoil Ave.
Dayton, OH 45403
Phone: (513)252-0868
Sharon Alexiades, Exec.Sec.

Recipient: Osteopathic physicians specializing in otorhinolaryngology. **Educational/Experience Requirements:** Must meet the following requirements: (1) Graduation from college of osteopathic medicine accredited by Bureau of Professional Education, American Osteopathic Association (see separate entry); (2) Current licensure to practice medicine; (3) Two years of membership in either American Osteopathic Association or Canadian Osteopathic Association; (4) Successful completion of internship accredited by Council on Postdoctoral Training of the American Osteopathic Association (see separate entry); (5) Successful completion of four year residency in otorhinolaryngology accredited by Council on Postdoctoral Training of the American Osteopathic Association; and

(6) Submission of case logs. **Membership:** Required. **Certification Requirements:** Successful completion of written, oral, and clinical exams. Exams cover: Diagnostic and therapeutic procedures; Familiarity with current advances; and Scientific bases of problems. Must successfully complete written exam before attempting oral and clinical exams. **Examination Frequency:** Annual. **Examination Sites:** Exams given at one site in the U.S. **Endorsed By:** American Osteopathic Association; Bureau of Osteopathic Specialists.

839

Diplomate in Otorhinolaryngology of the Board of Certification in Surgery

Board of Certification in Surgery
804 Main St., Ste. D
Forest Park, GA 30050
Phone: (404)363-8263
Fax: (404)361-2285
Toll Free: (800)447-9397

Recipient: Physicians specializing in otorhinolaryngology. **Educational/Experience Requirements:** Must meet the following requirements: (1) Graduation from school of medicine accredited by Bureau of Professional Education, American Osteopathic Association or Liaison Committee on Medical Education (see separate entries); (2) Current unrestricted licensure to practice medicine; (3) Successful completion of internship accredited by American Osteopathic Association Division on Postdoctoral Training or Accreditation Council for Graduate Medical Education (ACGME) (see separate entries); (4) Successful completion of osteopathic residency accredited by American Osteopathic Association Division on Postsecondary Training or residency accredited by ACGME; (5) Active staff privileges for two years at institution accredited by Committee on Hospital Accreditation or Joint Commission for Accreditation of Healthcare Organizations (see separate entries); and (6) Submission of ten case reports. **Membership:** Required. **Certification Requirements:** Successful completion of written and clinical exams. May also be required to successfully complete oral exam. Must successfully complete clinical exam before March 1 of year following successful completion of written exam. **Renewal:** Recertification required. **Examination Frequency:** Annual - always June. **Examination Sites:** Exam given at annual meeting. **Fees:** $500. **Endorsed By:** American Association of Physician Specialists.

840

Diplomate in Otorhinolaryngology and Facial Plastic Surgery of the American Osteopathic Board of Ophthalmology and Otorhinolaryngology

American Osteopathic Board of
   Ophthalmology and
   Otorhinolaryngology
Three Mackoil Ave.
Dayton, OH 45403
Phone: (513)252-0868
Sharon Alexiades, Exec.Sec.

Recipient: Osteopathic physicians specializing in otorhinolaryngology and facial plastic surgery. **Educational/Experience Requirements:** Must meet the following requirements: (1) Graduation from college of osteopathic medicine accredited by Bureau of Professional Education, American Osteopathic Association (see separate entry); (2) Current licensure to practice medicine; (3) Two years of membership in either American Osteopathic Association or Canadian Osteopathic Association; (4) Successful completion of internship accredited by Council on Postdoctoral Training of the American Osteopathic Association (see separate entry); (5) Successful completion of four year residency in otorhinolaryngology and facial plastic surgery accredited by Council on Postdoctoral Training of the American Osteopathic Association; and (6) Submission of case logs. **Membership:** Required. **Certification Requirements:** Successful completion of written, oral, and clinical exams. Exams cover: Diagnostic and therapeutic procedures; Familiarity with current advances; and Scientific bases of problems. Must successfully complete written exam before attempting oral and clinical exams. **Examination Frequency:** Annual. **Examination Sites:** Exams given at one site in the U.S. **Endorsed By:** American Osteopathic Association; Bureau of Osteopathic Specialists.

841

Diplomate in Plastic and Reconstructive Surgery of the American Osteopathic Board of Surgery

American Osteopathic Board of
   Surgery
Three MacKoil Ave.
Dayton, OH 45403
Phone: (513)252-0868
Sharon Alexiades, Corres.Sec.

Recipient: Osteopathic surgeons specializing in plastic and reconstructive surgery. **Educational/Experience Requirements:** Must meet the following requirements: (1) Graduation from college of osteopathic medicine accredited by Bureau of Professional Education, American Osteopathic Association (see separate entry); (2) Current licensure to practice medicine; (3) Two years of membership in American Osteopathic Association or Canadian Osteopathic Association; (4) Successful completion of internship accredited by Council on Postdoctoral Training of the American Osteopathic Association (see separate entry); (5) Successful completion of five years of training accredited by Council on Postdoctoral Training of the American Osteopathic Association; (6) Submission of log of major operative cases performed during previous year; (7) Submission of list of mortalities; and (8) Successful completion of qualifying exam. **Membership:** Required. **Certification Requirements:** Successful completion of written, oral, and clinical exams. Exams cover: Basic sciences; Current advances in surgical philosophy and techniques; Diagnostic, operative, and therapeutic procedures; Osteopathic philosophy of surgery applied to diagnosis and management of surgical diseases; Surgical judgment; and Surgical principles. **Examination Frequency:** Annual. **Examination Sites:** Exams given at one U.S. site. **Endorsed By:** American College of Osteopathic Surgeons; American Osteopathic Association; Bureau of Osteopathic Specialists.

<hr>

842

Diplomate in Psychiatry of the American Board of Psychiatry and Neurology

American Board of Psychiatry and Neurology (ABPN)
500 Lake Cook Rd., Ste. 335
Deerfield, IL 60015-5249
Phone: (708)945-7900
Fax: (708)945-1146

Recipient: Psychiatrists. **Educational/Experience Requirements:** Must meet the following requirements: (1) Graduation from medical school accredited by Liaison Committee for Medical Education (see separate entry); (2) Current unrestricted licensure to practice medicine; (3) Successful completion of internship accredited by Accreditation Council for Graduate Medical Education (ACGME) (see separate entry); and (4) Successful completion of residency accredited by ACGME. Candidates whose medical education was earned outside the U.S. must meet additional requirements. **Certification Requirements:** Successful

completion of written and oral exams. Written exam covers both neurology and psychiatry in the following areas: Biological and psychosocial dimensions of psychiatry; Clinical psychiatry (phenomenology, diagnosis, and treatment); Neuroanatomy; Neuropathology; Neuropharmacology and clinical diagnostic procedures, including cerebrospinal fluid, neuroophthalmology, electroencephalography, and neuro-imaging; Normal and abnormal growth and development through the life cycle; and Therapy and clinical neurology (management of patients with neurologic disorders). Oral exam requires examination of patients and covers clinical psychiatry. **Renewal:** Every ten years. **Examination Frequency:** Annual (written) - always fall. Three-four times per year (oral). **Examination Sites:** Written exam given at regional sites in the U.S. and Canada and oral exam given at selected sites in the U.S. **Re-examination:** May retake written exam one time and oral exam two times. Fees to retake exams are: $675 (written); $1075 (oral). **Fees:** $1400. **Endorsed By:** American Academy of Neurology; American Board of Medical Specialties; American Medical Association; American Neurological Association; American Psychiatric Association; Council on Medical Education.

<hr>

843

Diplomate in Psychiatry of the American Board of Psychiatry and Neurology with Added Qualifications in Addiction Psychiatry

American Board of Psychiatry and Neurology (ABPN)
500 Lake Cook Rd., Ste. 335
Deerfield, IL 60015-5249
Phone: (708)945-7900
Fax: (708)945-1146

Recipient: Psychiatrists specializing in addiction psychiatry. **Educational/Experience Requirements:** Must meet the following requirements: (1) Hold Diplomate in Psychiatry of the American Board of Psychiatry and Neurology designation (see separate entry); and (2) One year of training in addiction psychiatry or equivalent accredited by Accreditation Council for Graduate Medical Education (see separate entry). **Certification Requirements:** Successful completion of exam. Exam covers: Biological and behavioral basis of practice; Evaluation and consultation; Laboratory assessment; Pharmacology of drugs; Pharmacotherapy; and Psychosocial treatment. **Renewal:** Every ten years. Recertification based on successful completion of exam.

Examination Frequency: Annual. **Examination Sites:** Exam given at regional sites throughout the U.S., Canada, and internationally. **Examination Type:** Multiple-choice. **Re-examination:** May retake exam one time. There is a $525 fee to retake exam. **Fees:** $875. **Endorsed By:** American Academy of Neurology; American Board of Medical Specialties; American Medical Association; American Neurological Association; American Psychiatric Association; Council on Medical Education.

<hr>

844

Diplomate in Psychiatry of the American Board of Psychiatry and Neurology with Added Qualifications in Forensic Psychiatry

American Board of Psychiatry and Neurology (ABPN)
500 Lake Cook Rd., Ste. 335
Deerfield, IL 60015-5249
Phone: (708)945-7900
Fax: (708)945-1146

Recipient: Psychiatrists specializing in forensic psychiatry. **Educational/Experience Requirements:** Must meet the following requirements: (1) Hold Diplomate in Psychiatry of the American Board of Psychiatry and Neurology designation (see separate entry); and (2) One year of training in forensic psychiatry or equivalent accredited by Accreditation Council for Graduate Medical Education (see separate entry). **Certification Requirements:** Successful completion of exam. **Renewal:** Every ten years. Recertification based on successful completion of exam. **Examination Frequency:** Annual. **Examination Sites:** Exam given at regional sites throughout the U.S., Canada, and internationally. **Examination Type:** Multiple-choice. **Re-examination:** May retake exam one time. There is a $525 fee to retake exam. **Fees:** $875. **Endorsed By:** American Academy of Neurology; American Board of Medical Specialties; American Medical Association; American Neurological Association; American Psychiatric Association; Council on Medical Education.

845

Diplomate in Psychiatry of the American Board of Psychiatry and Neurology with Added Qualifications in Geriatric Psychiatry

American Board of Psychiatry and
Neurology (ABPN)
500 Lake Cook Rd., Ste. 335
Deerfield, IL 60015-5249
Phone: (708)945-7900
Fax: (708)945-1146

Recipient: Psychiatrists specializing in geriatric psychiatry. **Educational/ Experience Requirements:** Must meet the following requirements: (1) Hold Diplomate in Psychiatry of the American Board of Psychiatry and Neurology designation (see separate entry); and (2) One year of training in geriatric psychiatry or equivalent accredited by Accreditation Council for Graduate Medical Education (see separate entry). **Certification Requirements:** Successful completion of exam. Exam covers: Basic science aspects of aging; Development and psychosocial aspects of aging; Diagnostic methods; General medicine/psychiatry interface; Neurological aspects of aging; Psychopathology and psychiatric diagnosis; and Treatment. **Renewal:** Every ten years. Recertification based on successful completion of exam. **Examination Frequency:** Annual. **Examination Sites:** Exam given at regional sites throughout the U.S., Canada, and internationally. **Examination Type:** Multiple-choice. **Re-examination:** May retake exam one time. There is a $525 fee to retake exam. **Fees:** $875. **Endorsed By:** American Academy of Neurology; American Board of Medical Specialties; American Medical Association; American Neurological Association; American Psychiatric Association; Council on Medical Education.

846

Diplomate in Psychiatry of the American Osteopathic Board of Neurology and Psychiatry

American Osteopathic Board of
Neurology and Psychiatry
2250 Chapel Ave., W., Ste. 100
Cherry Hill, NJ 08002-2000
Phone: (609)482-9000
William F. Ranieri D.O., Sec.-Treas.

Recipient: Osteopathic physicians specializing in psychiatry. **Educational/ Experience Requirements:** Must meet the following requirements: (1) Graduation from college of osteopathic medicine ac-

credited by Bureau of Professional Education, American Osteopathic Association (see separate entry); (2) Current licensure to practice medicine; (3) Two years of membership in either American Osteopathic Association or Canadian Osteopathic Association; (4) Successful completion of one year internship accredited by Council on Postdoctoral Training of the American Osteopathic Association (see separate entry); and (5) Successful completion of three year residency in psychiatry accredited by Council on Postdoctoral Training of the American Osteopathic Association. One year of credit given for successful completion of two years in non-psychiatry residency. **Membership:** Required. **Certification Requirements:** Successful completion of written, oral, and clinical exams. Exams cover: Diagnostic and therapeutic procedures; Familiarity with current advances; and Scientific bases of problems. Must successfully complete written exam before attempting oral and clinical exams. **Renewal:** Every ten years. **Endorsed By:** American Osteopathic Association; Bureau of Osteopathic Specialists.

847

Diplomate in Public Health of the American Osteopathic Board of Preventive Medicine

American Osteopathic Board of
Preventive Medicine
Box 226
U.S. Air Force Academy, CO 80840-2200
Phone: (719)472-3560
George E. Hill D.O., Sec.-Treas.

Recipient: Osteopathic physicians specializing in public health. **Educational/ Experience Requirements:** Must meet the following requirements: (1) Graduation from college of osteopathic medicine accredited by Bureau of Professional Education, American Osteopathic Association (see separate entry); (2) Current licensure to practice medicine; (3) Two years of membership in American Osteopathic Association or Canadian Osteopathic Association; (4) Successful completion of internship accredited by Council on Postdoctoral Training of the American Osteopathic Association (see separate entry); (5) Master's of Public Health degree; and (6) Successful completion of one year of training in public health accredited by Council on Postdoctoral Training of the American Osteopathic Association. **Membership:** Required. **Certification Requirements:** Successful completion of written, oral, and clinical exams. Exams cover: Diagnostic and therapeutic procedures; Fa-

miliarity with current advances; and Scientific bases of problems. **Renewal:** Every seven years. Recertification based on successful completion of exam. **Examination Frequency:** Annual. **Examination Sites:** Exams given at one U.S. site. **Endorsed By:** American Osteopathic Association; Bureau of Osteopathic Specialists.

848

Diplomate in Pulmonary Disease of the American Board of Internal Medicine

American Board of Internal
Medicine (ABIM)
3624 Market St.
Philadelphia, PA 19104-2675
Phone: (215)243-1500
Fax: (215)382-4702
Toll Free: (800)441-ABIM

Recipient: Physicians specializing in pulmonary disease. **Educational/Experience Requirements:** Must meet the following requirements: (1) Hold Diplomate of the American Board of Internal Medicine designation (see separate entry); and (2) Successful completion of training program accredited by Accreditation Council for Graduate Medical Education (see separate entry), Royal College of Physicians and Surgeons of Canada, or Professional Corporation of Physicians of Quebec. **Certification Requirements:** Successful completion of exam. **Renewal:** Every ten years. Recertification based on self-evaluation process, evaluation of credentials, and successful completion of exam. **Examination Frequency:** biennial. **Examination Sites:** Exam given at sites throughout the U.S., Puerto Rico, and Canada. **Fees:** $980. **Endorsed By:** American Board of Medical Specialties; American Medical Association; Council on Medical Education.

849

Diplomate in Pulmonary Disease of the American Osteopathic Board of Internal Medicine

American Osteopathic Board of
Internal Medicine
5200 S. Ellis Ave.
Chicago, IL 60615
Phone: (312)947-4881
Gary L. Slick D.O., Exec.Dir.

Recipient: Physicians specializing in pulmonary disease. **Educational/Experience Requirements:** Must meet the following requirements: (1) Hold Diplomate of the American Osteopathic Board of Internal Medicine designation (see separate entry); and (2) Successfully complete two year training program in pulmonary disease accredited by Council on Postdoctoral Training of the American Osteopathic Association (see separate entry). **Membership:** Required. **Certification Requirements:** Successful completion of exam. **Renewal:** Every ten years. **Examination Frequency:** Annual - always August. **Examination Sites:** Exam given at one U.S. site. **Endorsed By:** American Osteopathic Association; Bureau of Osteopathic Specialists.

850

Diplomate in Radiation Oncology of the American Board of Certification in Radiology

American Board of Certification in
  Radiology
804 Main St., Ste. D
Forest Park, GA 30050
Phone: (404)363-8263
Fax: (404)361-2285
Toll Free: (800)447-9397

Recipient: Physicians specializing in radiation oncology. **Educational/Experience Requirements:** Must meet the following requirements: (1) Graduation from recognized college of medicine; (2) Current licensure to practice medicine; (3) Successful completion of internship accredited by American Osteopathic Association Division on Postdoctoral Training or Accreditation Council for Graduate Medical Education (ACGME) (see separate entries); (4) Successful completion of osteopathic residency accredited by American Osteopathic Association Division on Postdoctoral Training or residency in radiation oncology accredited by ACGME; (5) Current staff privileges at institution accredited by Committee on Hospital Accreditation or Joint Commission on Accreditation of Healthcare Organizations (see separate entries); and (6) Submission of proof of management of minimum of 150 cases in prior year, including consultation and end of treatment summary. **Membership:** Required. **Certification Requirements:** Successful completion of oral and written exams. **Examination Frequency:** Annual - always June. **Examination Sites:** Exams given at annual meeting. **Fees:** $1100. **Endorsed By:** American Association of Physician Specialists.

851

Diplomate in Radiation Oncology of the American Board of Radiology

American Board of Radiology
  (ABR)
5255 E. Williams Circle, Ste. 6800
Tucson, AZ 85711
Phone: (520)790-2900
Fax: (520)790-3200
M. Paul Capp M.D., Exec.Dir.

Recipient: Physicians specializing in radiation oncology. **Educational/Experience Requirements:** Must meet the following requirements: (1) Graduation from medical school in the U.S. or Canada accredited by Liaison Committee on Medical Education (see separate entry) or school of osteopathy accredited by Bureau of Professional Education, American Osteopathic Association (see separate entry); (2) Successful completion of four year residency accredited by Accreditation Council on Graduate Medical Education (see separate entry); and (3) Current basic CPR certification. Candidates whose medical education was earned outside of U.S. or Canada must have credentials evaluated. **Certification Requirements:** Successful completion of written and oral exams. Written exam covers: (1) Physics of Radiation Therapy, including: Basic physics; Dosimetry; Instruments and measurements; Protection and safety; and Radioactivity (radium and physics of therapeutically employed radionuclides); (2) Radiation Biology, including: Factors modifying response; Fractionation and irradiation of cancer; Response of organs; Subcellular and cellular effects in cell kinetics; Tissue kinetics and tissue effects; and Total body effects; (3) Oncology, including general principles and consideration of neoplasms of the following systems: Breast tumors; Central nervous system; Chest; Gynecological and urological neoplasms; Head and neck; Hematopoietic system; Miscellaneous group (thyroid, skin, gastrointestinal tract, and other groups); Pediatric neoplasms; and Skeletal system; and (4) Treatment Planning and Technique, including: Anatomy; Dosage distribution; Dose and fractionation; Optimum beams; Precision and errors in treatment planning; Selection of optimum volume; Sources for various clinical situations; Techniques involving treatment of various anatomic and organ groups; and Tumor localization. Oral exam covers malignancies in the following anatomical sites: Breast; Central nervous system and pediatric malignancies; Gastrointestinal tract; Genitourinary tract; Gynecologic malignancies; Head, neck, and skin; Lung and mediastinum, soft tissue, and bone; and Reticuloendo-

thelial system. Exam covers following topics pertaining to primary malignancies of respective anatomical site: (1) Epidemiology, covering influence of sex, age, occupation, geography, and other factors; (2) Pathologic Classification, including relative incidence of each type and radiation response relative to histology; (3) Site(s) of Primary Occurrence, including: Anatomy of region; Diagnostic procedures to evaluate primary disease; Physical findings; and Relative incidence of such occurrence; (4) Modes of Metastases, covering anatomical considerations and incidence of types of metastases; (5) Sites of Metastases, including: Anatomy of spread; Diagnostic studies to evaluate metastases; and Incidence of spread to various sites; (6) Extent of Disease, including: Clinical staging; Pathologic staging when applicable; Physical findings in the different clinical staging; Studies available to aid in clinical staging; and Systems of clinical staging; (7) Complications of Primary and/or Secondary Disease, including: Anatomical considerations; Methods of evaluating complications; Pathologic considerations; and Physiologic considerations; (8) Discussions of Indicated Treatment - Primary Disease, including: Chemotherapy; Radiation therapy; and Surgery; (9) Indicated Treatment - Metastatic Disease; (10) Radiation Dosimetry and Treatment Planning, including: Methods of use of dosimetry; Optimal beams and/or radionuclides; Systems available for dosimetry; and Techniques of treatment planning; and (11) Clinical Applications of Radiation Biology, including: Complications of radiation; Fractionation, split dose, pre-op radiation, and other related issues; Hyperthermia; Immunology; NSD; OER; Postoperative radiation therapy; Repair and recovery; and Total body irradiation. **Renewal:** Every ten years. **Preparatory Materials:** Booklet of information, including sample questions, provided. **Examination Frequency:** Annual - always May or June (oral). **Examination Type:** Multiple-choice. **Reexamination:** Must wait one year to retake exams. May retake exams two times. **Endorsed By:** American Association of Physicists in Medicine; American Board of Medical Specialties; American College of Radiology; American Medical Association; American Radium Society; American Roentgen Ray Society; American Society for Therapeutic Radiology and Oncology; Association of University Radiologists; Council on Medical Education; Radiological Society of North America.

852

Diplomate in Radiation Oncology of the American Osteopathic Board of Radiology

American Osteopathic Board of
  Radiology
119 E. Second St.
Milan, MO 63556
Phone: (816)265-4011
Pamela A. Smith, Exec.Dir.

Recipient: Osteopathic physicians specializing in radiation oncology. **Educational/Experience Requirements:** Must meet the following requirements: (1) Graduation from college of osteopathic medicine accredited by Bureau of Professional Education, American Osteopathic Association (see separate entry); (2) Current licensure to practice medicine; (3) Two years of membership in American Osteopathic Association or Canadian Osteopathic Association; (4) Successful completion of internship accredited by Council on Postdoctoral Training of the American Osteopathic Association (see separate entry); and (5) Successful completion of three years of training in radiation oncology accredited by Council on Postdoctoral Training of the American Osteopathic Association. **Membership:** Required. **Certification Requirements:** Successful completion of written, oral, and clinical exams. Exams cover: Diagnostic and therapeutic procedures; Familiarity with current advances; and Scientific bases of problems. **Examination Frequency:** Annual. **Examination Sites:** Exams given at one U.S. site each. **Endorsed By:** American Osteopathic Association; Bureau of Osteopathic Specialists.

853

Diplomate in Radiological Physics of the American Board of Radiology

American Board of Radiology
  (ABR)
5255 E. Williams Circle, Ste. 6800
Tucson, AZ 85711
Phone: (520)790-2900
Fax: (520)790-3200
M. Paul Capp M.D., Exec.Dir.

Recipient: Specialists in radiological physics. **Educational/Experience Requirements:** Must meet the following requirements: (1) Bachelor's degree in physics or applied physics or either engineering, chemistry, physical chemistry, or applied mathematics, with minor in physics; (2) Master's or doctoral degree in medical physics or either a physical science, applied mathematics, or engineering field, with minor in physics; (3) Successful completion of formal course work in biological sciences; and (4) Five years experience with departments or divisions of diagnostic radiology, nuclear medicine, and radiation oncology, including three years experience in specialty area of radiological physics. **Certification Requirements:** Successful completion of two-part written exam and oral exam. Part I of written exam covers: Anatomy; Atomic and nuclear physics; Basic physical principles; Basic radiobiology; Basic statistics and biostatistics; Biochemistry; Concepts of dosimetry; Elementary physiology; Instrumentation and measurement techniques; Interactions of radiation with matter; Medical terminology; Medical uses of radiation sources; Nature and sources of radiation; Nuclear magnetic resonance; Radiation protection; Radioactivity; Radiochemistry; Spacial distribution and transmission of radiation; and Ultrasound. Part II of written exam may be taken in one or more of the following sub-fields: (1) Diagnostic Radiological Physics, including: Calibration of diagnostic equipment; Computers; Diagnostic generating equipment and sources; Dosimetry; Geometric considerations; Grids; Image intensifiers; Information transfer theory; Installation design; Magnetic resonance imaging; Magnification techniques; Quality assurance; Radiation protection; Recording media and their application; Sensitometry; Special devices and techniques; Survey techniques; Tomographic devices and techniques; Ultrasound; and Video systems; (2) Medical Radiological Physics, including: Anatomical and physiological considerations; Calibration of nuclear medicine equipment and devices; Computers; Dosimetry; Information transfer theory; Installation design; Quality assurance; Radiation measuring and imaging equipment; Radiation protection; Radioactive sources for diagnosis and therapy; Sensitometry; Specific medical nuclear techniques; Statistics of counting; and Survey techniques; and (3) Therapeutic Radiological Physics, including: Dose calculations; Installation design; Measurements of radiation quantity and quality; Physical principles of radiation therapy; Quality assurance; Radiation protection; Radiation sources and units; Radiobiological principles of therapy; Survey techniques; and Treatment planning and setup. Each specialty exam covers: Applied radiological physics; Protection in radiological physics; Teaching of radiological physics; and Theoretical radiological physics. Oral exam covers: (1) Design of Radiation Installations, including: Air concentrations of radioactivity; Barrier calculation; Departmental design; Distance and shielding; Report preparation; Shielding design for primary, scattered, and leakage radiation; Time; Use and occupancy factors; and Workload; (2) Calibration of Radiation Equipment, including: Calibrations and evaluations of measuring, recording, and imaging devices; Calibrations and evaluations of all types of ionizing and nonionizing radiation sources and installations; Characteristics and use of calibration equipment; and Measurements of radiation quantity and quality; (3) Radiation Hazard Control, including: Characteristics of survey equipment; Evaluation of radiation hazards; Nuclear medicine and radiation therapy; Personnel monitoring; Radiation protection principles; Radiation regulations and requirements; Radiation standards and units; Radiation surveys in diagnostic radiology; and Responsibilities of radiation protection office; (4) Radiation Dosage, including: Calculation of dose from photon and particle beams and radionuclide sources; Computers and their applications; Grids; Infusion techniques; Physical factors affecting dose; Rotational therapy; Special techniques and devices; Tomography; Ultrasound; and Wedge filters; and (5) Equipment, including: Diagnostic radiological equipment; Nuclear magnetic resonance equipment; Nuclear medicine equipment; Principles and properties of radiation generating equipment; Radiation sources; Radiation therapy equipment; and Ultrasound equipment. **Examination Frequency:** Annual. **Examination Sites:** Written exam given at sites throughout the U.S. **Examination Type:** Multiple-choice; true or false. **Re-examination:** May retake exams two times. **Endorsed By:** American Association of Physicists in Medicine; American Board of Medical Specialties; American College of Radiology; American Medical Association; American Radium Society; American Roentgen Ray Society; American Society for Therapeutic Radiology and Oncology; Association of University Radiologists; Radiological Society of North America.

854

Diplomate in Reproductive Endocrinology of the American Osteopathic Board of Obstetrics and Gynecology

American Osteopathic Board of
Obstetrics and Gynecology
(AOBOG)
5200 S. Ellis Ave.
Chicago, IL 60615
Phone: (312)947-4630
Joseph P. Bonanno D.O., Sec.-
Treas.

Recipient: Osteopathic physicians specializing in reproductive endocrinology. **Educational/Experience Requirements:** Must meet the following requirements: (1) Hold Diplomate of the American Osteopathic Board of Obstetrics and Gynecology designation (see separate entry); and (2) Successfully complete residency in reproductive endocrinology accredited by Council on Postdoctoral Training of the American Osteopathic Association (see separate entry). **Membership:** Required. **Certification Requirements:** Successful completion of exam. **Renewal:** Every ten years. **Examination Frequency:** Annual. **Endorsed By:** American Osteopathic Association; Bureau of Osteopathic Specialists.

855

Diplomate in Rheumatology and Allergy and Immunology of the American Board of Internal Medicine

American Board of Internal
Medicine (ABIM)
3624 Market St.
Philadelphia, PA 19104-2675
Phone: (215)243-1500
Fax: (215)382-4702
Toll Free: (800)441-ABIM

Recipient: Physicians specializing in rheumatology and allergy and immunology. **Educational/Experience Requirements:** Must meet the following requirements: (1) Hold Diplomate of the American Board of Internal Medicine designation (see separate entry); and (2) Successful completion of training program accredited by Accreditation Council for Graduate Medical Education (see separate entry), Royal College of Physicians and Surgeons of Canada, or Professional Corporation of Physicians of Quebec. **Certification Requirements:** Successful completion of exam. **Renewal:** Every ten years. Recertification based on self-evaluation process, evaluation of credentials, and successful completion of

exam. **Examination Frequency:** biennial. **Examination Sites:** Exam given at sites throughout the U.S., Puerto Rico, and Canada. **Fees:** $980. **Endorsed By:** American Board of Medical Specialties; American Medical Association; Council on Medical Education.

856

Diplomate in Rheumatology of the American Board of Internal Medicine

American Board of Internal
Medicine (ABIM)
3624 Market St.
Philadelphia, PA 19104-2675
Phone: (215)243-1500
Fax: (215)382-4702
Toll Free: (800)441-ABIM

Recipient: Physicians specializing in rheumatology. **Educational/Experience Requirements:** Must meet the following requirements: (1) Hold Diplomate of the American Board of Internal Medicine designation (see separate entry); and (2) Successful completion of training program accredited by Accreditation Council for Graduate Medical Education (see separate entry), Royal College of Physicians and Surgeons of Canada, or Professional Corporation of Physicians of Quebec. **Certification Requirements:** Successful completion of exam. **Renewal:** Every ten years. Recertification based on self-evaluation process, evaluation of credentials, and successful completion of exam. **Examination Frequency:** biennial. **Examination Sites:** Exam given at sites throughout the U.S., Puerto Rico, and Canada. **Fees:** $980. **Endorsed By:** American Board of Medical Specialties; American Medical Association; Council on Medical Education.

857

Diplomate in Rheumatology of the American Osteopathic Board of Internal Medicine

American Osteopathic Board of
Internal Medicine
5200 S. Ellis Ave.
Chicago, IL 60615
Phone: (312)947-4881
Gary L. Slick D.O., Exec.Dir.

Recipient: Physicians specializing in rheumatology. **Educational/Experience Requirements:** Must meet the following requirements: (1) Hold Diplomate of the American Osteopathic Board of Internal Medicine designation (see separate entry); and (2) Successfully complete two

year training program in rheumatology accredited by Council on Postdoctoral Training of the American Osteopathic Association (see separate entry). **Membership:** Required. **Certification Requirements:** Successful completion of exam. **Renewal:** Every ten years. **Examination Frequency:** Annual - always August. **Examination Sites:** Exam given at one U.S. site. **Endorsed By:** American Osteopathic Association; Bureau of Osteopathic Specialists.

858

Diplomate in Thoracic Cardiovascular Surgery of the American Osteopathic Board of Surgery

American Osteopathic Board of
Surgery
Three MacKoil Ave.
Dayton, OH 45403
Phone: (513)252-0868
Sharon Alexiades, Corres.Sec.

Recipient: Osteopathic surgeons specializing in thoracic cardiovascular surgery. **Educational/Experience Requirements:** Must meet the following requirements: (1) Graduation from college of osteopathic medicine accredited by Bureau of Professional Education, American Osteopathic Association (see separate entry); (2) Current licensure to practice medicine; (3) Two years of membership in American Osteopathic Association or Canadian Osteopathic Association; (4) Successful completion of internship accredited by Council on Postdoctoral Training of the American Osteopathic Association (see separate entry); (5) Successful completion of four years of training in surgery accredited by Council on Postdoctoral Training of the American Osteopathic Association; (6) Successful completion of two years of training in thoracic surgery accredited by Council on Postdoctoral Training of the American Osteopathic Association; (7) Submission of log of major operative cases performed during previous year; (8) Submission of list of mortalities; and (9) Successful completion of qualifying exam. **Membership:** Required. **Certification Requirements:** Successful completion of written, oral, and clinical exams. Exams cover: Basic sciences; Current advances in surgical philosophy and techniques; Diagnostic, operative, and therapeutic procedures; Osteopathic philosophy of surgery applied to diagnosis and management of surgical diseases; Surgical judgment; and Surgical principles. **Examination Frequency:** Annual. **Examination Sites:** Exams given at one U.S. site. **Endorsed By:** American College of Osteopathic Surgeons; American Osteopathic Association; Bureau of Osteopathic Specialists.

859

Diplomate in Urological Surgery of the American Osteopathic Board of Surgery

American Osteopathic Board of
  Surgery
Three MacKoil Ave.
Dayton, OH 45403
Phone: (513)252-0868
Sharon Alexiades, Corres.Sec.

Recipient: Osteopathic surgeons specializing in urological surgery. **Educational/ Experience Requirements:** Must meet the following requirements: (1) Graduation from college of osteopathic medicine accredited by Bureau of Professional Education, American Osteopathic Association (see separate entry); (2) Current licensure to practice medicine; (3) Two years of membership in American Osteopathic Association or Canadian Osteopathic Association; (4) Successful completion of internship accredited by Council on Postdoctoral Training of the American Osteopathic Association (see separate entry); (5) Successful completion of five years of training accredited by Council on Postdoctoral Training of the American Osteopathic Association; (6) Submission of log of major operative cases performed during previous year; (7) Submission of list of mortalities; and (8) Successful completion of qualifying exam. **Membership:** Required. **Certification Requirements:** Successful completion of written, oral, and clinical exams. Exams cover: Basic sciences; Current advances in surgical philosophy and techniques; Diagnostic, operative, and therapeutic procedures; Osteopathic philosophy of surgery applied to diagnosis and management of surgical diseases; Surgical judgment; and Surgical principles. **Examination Frequency:** Annual. **Examination Sites:** Exams given at one U.S. site. **Endorsed By:** American College of Osteopathic Surgeons; American Osteopathic Association; Bureau of Osteopathic Specialists.

860

Fellow of the American Academy of Environmental Medicine (AAEM)

American Academy of
  Environmental Medicine
4510 W. 89th St.
Prairie Village, KS 66207
Phone: (913)341-0765
Fax: (913)341-3625

Recipient: Physicians specializing in environmental medicine, which includes illnesses or health problems caused by adverse, allergic, or toxic reactions to environmental substances. **Certification Requirements:** Successful completion of exam.

Podiatrists

861

Board Qualified, American Board of Podiatric Orthopedics and Primary Medicine

American Board of Podiatric
  Orthopedics and Primary
  Medicine (ABPOPM)
401 N. Michigan Ave., Ste. 2400
Chicago, IL 60611-4267
Phone: (312)321-5139
Fax: (312)644-1815
Jeffrey P. Knezovich, Exec.Dir.

Recipient: Podiatrists specializing in orthopedics and primary medicine. **Membership:** Required. **Certification Requirements:** Successful completion of appropriate exam towards certification and demonstrated capability in diagnosis and medical management of foot and ankle disease. Must earn Diplomate, American Board of Podiatric Orthopedic and Primary Medicine designation (see separate entry) within three years. **Endorsed By:** American Podiatric Medical Association; Council on Podiatric Medical Education.

862

Board Qualified, American Board of Podiatric Surgery

American Board of Podiatric
  Surgery (ABPS)
1601 Dolores St.
San Francisco, CA 94110-4906
Phone: (415)826-3200
Fax: (415)826-4640
John L. Bennett, Exec.Dir.

Recipient: Podiatrists specializing in foot surgery. **Educational/Experience Re-**

---

quirements: Must meet the following requirements: (1) Doctor of Podiatric Medicine degree from college of podiatric medicine accredited by Council on Podiatric Medical Education (CPME) (see separate entry); and (2) Successful completion of residency accredited by CPME. **Certification Requirements:** Successful completion of exam. Must earn Diplomate in Foot Surgery of the American Board of Podiatric Surgery designation (see separate entry) within seven years. **Preparatory Materials:** Study guide, including sample questions, provided. Self-assessment exam available. **Examination Frequency:** Annual. **Examination Sites:** Exam given at one U.S. site. **Examination Type:** Matching; multiple-choice. **Waiting Period to Receive Scores:** Two months. **Reexamination:** Must wait one year to retake exam. Fee to retake exam is $450. **Fees:** $650. **Endorsed By:** American Podiatric Medical Association; Council on Podiatric Medical Education.

863

Diplomate of the American Board of Podiatric Orthopedics and Primary Medicine

American Board of Podiatric
  Orthopedics and Primary
  Medicine (ABPOPPM)
401 N. Michigan Ave., Ste. 2400
Chicago, IL 60611-4267
Phone: (312)321-5139
Fax: (312)644-1815
Jeffrey P. Knezovich, Exec.Dir.

Recipient: Podiatrists involved in orthopedics and primary medicine. **Number of Certified Individuals:** 1666. **Educational/ Experience Requirements:** Must meet the following requirements: (1) Doctor of Podiatric Medicine (DPM) degree; (2) Postdoctoral education; and (3) Four years postdoctoral clinical experience. May also be required to submit cases. **Membership:** Required. **Certification Requirements:** Successful completion of written and oral exams. **Renewal:** Every ten years. Recertification based on successful completion of self-assessment exam. **Preparatory Materials:** Study guide available. **Examination Frequency:** Annual. **Examination Sites:** Exam given in Chicago, IL. **Examination Type:** Multiple-choice. **Pass/Fail Rate:** 71% pass exams the first time. **Waiting Period to Receive Scores:** Six weeks. **Reexamination:** Must wait one year to retake exams. **Fees:** $975. **Endorsed By:** American Podiatric Medical Association; Council on Podiatric Medical Education.

864

Diplomate of the American Board of Podiatric Surgery with Certification in Foot and Ankle Surgery
American Board of Podiatric
    Surgery (ABPS)
1601 Dolores St.
San Francisco, CA 94110-4906
Phone: (415)826-3200
Fax: (415)826-4640
John L. Bennett, Exec.Dir.

Recipient: Podiatrists specializing in foot and ankle surgery. **Educational/Experience Requirements:** Must meet the following requirements: (1) Hold Diplomate of the American Board of Podiatric Surgery with Certification in Foot Surgery designation (see separate entry); (2) Successfully complete residency accredited by CPME; (3) Four years of postdoctoral clinical experience; and (4) Submission of list of 25 cases in reconstructive rearfoot/ankle surgery. **Certification Requirements:** Successful completion of written and oral exams. Exams cover: Diagnosis of general medical problems; Structures which affect the foot, ankle, and leg; and Surgical management of foot diseases, deformities, and/or trauma. **Renewal:** Every ten years. Recertification based on successful completion of exam. **Preparatory Materials:** Study guide, including sample questions, provided. Self-assessment exam available. **Examination Frequency:** Annual. **Examination Sites:** Exam given at one U.S. site. **Examination Type:** Matching; multiple-choice. **Waiting Period to Receive Scores:** Two months. **Reexamination:** Must wait one year to retake exams. Fee to retake exams are $300. **Fees:** $500. **Endorsed By:** American Podiatric Medical Association; Council on Podiatric Medical Education.

865

Diplomate of the American Board of Podiatric Surgery with Certification in Foot Surgery
American Board of Podiatric
    Surgery (ABPS)
1601 Dolores St.
San Francisco, CA 94110-4906
Phone: (415)826-3200
Fax: (415)826-4640
John L. Bennett, Exec.Dir.

Recipient: Podiatrists specializing in foot surgery. **Educational/Experience Requirements:** Must meet the following requirements: (1) Doctor of Podiatric Medicine degree from college of podiat-

ric medicine accredited by Council on Podiatric Medical Education (CPME) (see separate entry); (2) Successful completion of residency accredited by CPME; (3) Four years of postdoctoral clinical experience; and (4) Submission of list of 65 cases performed in last five years. **Certification Requirements:** Successful completion of written and oral exams. Exams cover diagnosis of general medical problems and surgical management of foot diseases, deformities, and/or trauma, and those structures which affect the foot and ankle. Candidates hold Board Qualified, American Board of Podiatric Surgery designation (see separate entry) prior to successful completion of oral exam. **Renewal:** Every ten years. Recertification based on successful completion of exam. **Preparatory Materials:** Study guide, including study questions, provided. Self-assessment exam available. **Examination Frequency:** Annual. **Examination Sites:** Exam given at one U.S. site. **Examination Type:** Matching; multiple-choice. **Waiting Period to Receive Scores:** Two months. **Reexamination:** Must wait one year to retake exams. Must only retake exam failed. Fee to retake each exam is $450. **Fees:** $1100. **Endorsed By:** American Podiatric Medical Association; Council on Podiatric Medical Education.

Veterinarians

866

Certified Member of the International Association of Equine Dental Technicians
International Association of Equine
    Dental Technicians (IAEDT)
PO Box 6095
Wilmington, DE 19804
Phone: (302)892-9215
Toll Free: (800)334-6095
Gail A. Emerson, Pres.

Recipient: Equine dental technicians, veterinary technicians, and veterinarians. **Number of Certified Individuals:** 30. **Educational/Experience Requirements:** Submission of list of case load for previous twelve months. **Membership:** Not required. **Certification Requirements:** Successful completion of written and practical exams. Written exam covers: Aging; Anatomy and physiology of the head and mouth; Biting; Dental abnormalities; Eruption schedule; General horse health; Nutrition; and Tooth structure and function. Practical exam includes performing dental maintenance on two horses. **Renewal:** Every two years.

Recertification based on attendance at IAEDT annual meeting and continuing education. **Preparatory Materials:** Reading and reference list and study guide available. **Examination Frequency:** Annual. **Examination Sites:** Exam given at annual conference. **Examination Type:** Essay; fill-in-the-blank; multiple-choice; true or false. **Pass/Fail Rate:** 85% pass exam the first time. **Waiting Period to Receive Scores:** Immediately. **Reexamination:** Must wait one year to retake exams. **Fees:** $200.

867

Certified Veterinary Acupuncturist
International Veterinary
    Acupuncture Society (IVAS)
c/o Dr. Merideth L. Snader
2140 Conestoga Rd.
Chester Springs, PA 19425
Phone: (215)827-7245
Fax: (215)687-3605
Dr. Merideth L. Snader, Exec.Dir.

Recipient: Veterinary acupuncturists. **Educational/Experience Requirements:** Current licensure as veterinarian. Veterinary students in third year of study may qualify. **Certification Requirements:** Successful completion of Course in Veterinary Acupuncture and written and practical exams. Must also submit case reports. **Fees:** $2100.

868

Diplomate of the American Board of Veterinary Practitioners
American Board of Veterinary
    Practitioners (ABVP)
530 Church St., Ste. 300
Nashville, TN 37219-2394
Phone: (615)254-3687
Fax: (615)254-7047
Dee Ann Walker, Admin.

Recipient: Veterinarians having broad knowledge of many clinical subjects within practice category. **Educational/Experience Requirements:** Must meet the following requirements: (1) Graduation from college of veterinary medicine accredited by Council on Education of the American Veterinary Medical Association (see separate entry); (2) Current licensure; (3) One year of practice or rotating internship; and (4) Successful completion of residency or five years experience. Graduates of colleges of veterinary medicine outside the U.S. must hold certificate from Educational Commission for Foreign Veterinary Graduates. **Membership:** Required. **Certification Require-**

ments: Successful completion of one of the following exams: Avian; Beef cattle; Canine and feline; Dairy; Equine; Feline; Food animal; and Swine health management. **Renewal:** Every ten years. Recertification based on successful completion of exam. **Examination Frequency:** Annual - always December. **Endorsed By:** American Veterinary Medical Association.

╺869╸

Diplomate of the American Board of Veterinary Toxicology

American Board of Veterinary Toxicology (ABVT)
c/o Dr. Robert H. Poppenga, DVM
School of Veterinary Medicine, New Bolton Center
Univ. of Pennsylvania
383 W. Street Rd.
Kennett Square, PA 19348
Phone: (610)444-5800
Dr. Robert H. Poppenga DVM, Sec.-Treas.

Recipient: Veterinarians specializing in toxicology. **Educational/Experience Requirements:** Must meet the following requirements: (1) Either graduate from veterinary school accredited by Council on Education of the American Veterinary Medical Association (see separate entry), earn certificate of accreditation from approved foreign university, or be legally qualified to practice veterinary medicine in the U.S., Canada, or other country; and (2) Document either two accepted peer-reviewed publications, two funded research projects, or equivalent activity. Must also meet one of the following training requirements: (1) Four years training in toxicology, including completion of advanced degree, and experience in teaching of toxicology, toxicological research, or practice of veterinary clinical or diagnostic toxicology. Two years of this requirement must be subsequent to graduation from veterinary school and be under supervision of Diplomate of ABVT; (2) Two years experience in clinical practice of veterinary medicine, which may include practice of clinical and/or diagnostic veterinary toxicology, subsequent to graduation from veterinary school, and successful completion of three year residency or other training program in toxicology, teaching of toxicology, toxicological research, or practice of veterinary clinical and/or diagnostic toxicology; or (3) Documentation of authorship of five research papers or clinical reports and submission of evidence of acceptable experience and training. **Certification Requirements:** Successful

completion of exam. Exam covers: Antidotal procedures; Damage-response relationships; Environmental toxicology - industrial, water, and air contamination; Metabolism and detoxication; Residues and residual effects of chemicals and radiation in foods; Testing for safety, including experimental design and interpretation; Toxicology of inorganic compounds; Toxicology of natural and synthetic organic compounds; Toxicology of plant poisons and biotoxins; Toxicology of radiation and radiomimetic compounds; and Usefulness, definitions, and philosophies of toxicology. **Renewal:** Lifetime certification available for retired Diplomates. **Endorsed By:** American Veterinary Medical Association.

╺870╸

Diplomate of the American College of Laboratory Animal Medicine

American College of Laboratory Animal Medicine (ACLAM)
200 Summerwinds Dr.
Cary, NC 27511
Phone: (919)859-5985
Fax: (919)851-3126
Charles W. McPherson DVM, Exec.Dir.

Recipient: Veterinarians specializing in providing medical care and management to animals used in medical, veterinary medical, and biological research and testing. **Number of Certified Individuals:** 485. **Educational/Experience Requirements:** Must meet the following requirements: (1) Graduation from college or school of veterinary medicine accredited by Council on Education of the American Veterinary Medical Association (see separate entry), or possess Educational Commission for Foreign Veterinary Graduate certificate; (2) Publication of article on laboratory animal medicine in refereed journal; and (3) Successful completion of formal laboratory animal medicine training program and four years of post-degree combined training and experience, or six years experience. Post-degree experience in research that utilized animals may be substituted on a two for one basis. **Certification Requirements:** Successful completion of written and practical exams. Written exam covers: (1) Animal Experimentation, including: Animal models (including induced and spontaneous models, experimental surgical models, and genetic manipulations); Protocol review, experimental design, and biostatistics; Research funding, ethics, and animal welfare issues, including organizations opposing and supporting animal research; and Research methodology, including molecular biology,

gnotobiology and techniques and equipment for sampling, dosing, and monitoring biologic functions; (2) Clinical Laboratory Animal Medicine and Surgery, including: Anesthesia, analgesia, sedation, and euthanasia; Animal disease surveillance and preventive medicine; Laboratory animal clinical diagnosis and therapeutics, including clinical pharmacology, internal medicine, and diagnostic imaging; Laboratory animal clinical pathology, including techniques and interpretation of results in virology, microbiology, hematology, clinical biochemistry, and parasitology; and Surgical management (pre-, intra-, and post-operative); (3) Laboratory Animal Biology, including: Anatomy and taxonomy; Behavior of laboratory animals, including species specific behavior, behavioral models, and environmental enhancement; Genetics and nomenclature; and Physiology and metabolism, including reproductive physiology; (4) Laboratory Animal Pathology, including: Infectious diseases; Neoplastic diseases; Nutritional/metabolic diseases, including aging; and Other diseases, including immunologic and husbandry related; and (5) Laboratory Animal Resources Management, including: Animal facility design and management; Husbandry, including breeding, nutrition, barrier housing, and other housing methods; Laws, regulations, and guidelines affecting animal research; and Safety, including occupational health, zoonosis control and safe handling of biologic agents, radioisotopes, and chemicals. **Renewal:** Every six years. **Examination Frequency:** Annual. **Examination Sites:** Exams given at annual meeting. **Examination Type:** Multiple-choice; short answer. **Re-examination:** Must only retake exam failed. Must successfully complete both exams within 26 months. **Fees:** $325. **Endorsed By:** American Veterinary Medical Association.

╺871╸

Diplomate of the American College of Poultry Veterinarians

American College of Poultry Veterinarians (ACPV)
Box 1227
Fayetteville, AR 72702-1227
Phone: (501)575-4390
Fax: (501)521-1810
J. Kirk Skeeles DVM, Sec.-Treas.

Recipient: Veterinarians specializing in poultry. **Educational/Experience Requirements:** Must meet the following requirements: (1) Either graduate from college of veterinary medicine accredited by Council on Education of the American Veterinary Medical Association (see separate entry), successfully complete National Board Examination in veterinary medicine, or be qualified to practice veterinary medicine; (2) Either hold Doctor of Veterinary Medicine (DVM) or equivalent and master's level degree or equivalent or higher post-graduate degree with major in poultry science, successful completion of approved training program in poultry veterinary medicine, or five years experience; and (3) Either author at least one scientific article or two research or technical case reports in refereed journals, submit three case research reports, or a combination of articles and cases. Graduates of colleges of veterinary medicine outside of the U.S. must hold certificate from Educational Commission for Foreign Veterinary Graduates. **Certification Requirements:** Successful completion of basic and applied exams. Basic exam covers: Biochemistry; Breeding; Economics; Environmental management; Food safety and quality; Laboratory techniques; Modern commercial production; Nutrition; Poultry housing; and Processing. Applied exam covers: Laboratory findings; Production data; and Specimens. **Renewal:** Every ten years. Recertification based on successful completion of exam and continuing education. Lifetime certification available for retired Diplomates. **Examination Frequency:** Annual. **Examination Sites:** Exam given at annual meeting. **Re-examination:** May retake each exam two twice. Must successfully complete both exams within three years. **Endorsed By:** American Veterinary Medical Association.

872

Diplomate of the American College of Theriogenologists
American College of Theriogenologists
2727 W. Second St., Ste. 450
PO Box 2118
Hastings, NE 68902-2118
Phone: (402)463-0392
Fax: (402)463-5683
Don Ellerbee, Exec.Dir.

Recipient: Veterinarians specializing in animal reproduction. **Number of Certified Individuals:** 290. **Educational/ Experience Requirements:** Must meet the following requirements: (1) Hold Doctor of Veterinary Medicine (D.V.M.) degree; and (2) Successfully complete either two years of advanced training or six years post-graduate practice and successfully complete two year training and tutelage program. **Certification Requirements:** Successful completion of written and practical exams. Exams cover all animal

species, with emphasis on domesticated animals. **Renewal:** none. **Examination Type:** Essay; multiple-choice. **Re-examination:** May retake exams three times. **Endorsed By:** American Veterinary Medical Association; Society for Theriogenology.

873

Diplomate of the American College of Veterinary Anesthesiologists
American College of Veterinary Anesthesiologists (ACVA)
c/o Ann E. Wagner, DVM
Coll. of Veterinary Medicine
Colorado State Univ.
Fort Collins, CO 80523-1275
Phone: (303)491-0346
Fax: (303)491-1275
Ann E. Wagner DVM, Exec.Sec.

Recipient: Veterinary anesthesiologists. **Educational/Experience Requirements:** Must meet the following requirements: (1) Graduation from college of veterinary medicine accredited by Council on Education of the American Veterinary Medical Association (see separate entry); (2) Current licensure to practice veterinary medicine; (3) Successful completion of one year internship; (4) Successful completion of two-year residency or equivalent; and (5) Submission of manuscript published in referred journal. Graduates of foreign veterinary medical schools must hold certificate from Educational Commission for Foreign Veterinary Graduates. **Membership:** Required. **Certification Requirements:** Successful completion of written and oral exams. **Examination Frequency:** Annual. **Endorsed By:** American Veterinary Medical Association.

874

Diplomate of the American College of Veterinary Behaviorists
American College of Veterinary Behaviorists (ACVB)
c/o Dr. K. Houpt
Dept. of Physiology
Coll. of Veterinary Medicine
Cornell Univ.
Ithaca, NY 14853-6401
Phone: (607)253-3450
Fax: (607)253-3846
Dr. K. Houpt, Sec.

Recipient: Veterinarians interested in behavioral science. **Number of Certified Individuals:** 8. **Educational/Experience Requirements:** Must meet the following

requirements: (1) Graduate from college of veterinary medicine accredited by Council on Education of the American Veterinary Medical Association (see separate entry) or be qualified to practice veterinary medicine; (2) Successfully complete behavioral residency program or equivalent; (3) Have article published in refereed journal; and (4) Submit three case reports. Graduates of colleges of veterinary medicine outside of the U.S. must hold certificate from Educational Commission for Foreign Veterinary Graduates. **Certification Requirements:** Successful completion of exam. Exam covers: Basics of behavior of various species; Basics of behavioral principles; and Clinical application of behavior in various species. **Examination Frequency:** Annual. **Examination Sites:** Exam given at annual meeting. **Waiting Period to Receive Scores:** 90 days. **Endorsed By:** American Veterinary Medical Association.

875

Diplomate of the American College of Veterinary Clinical Pharmacology
American College of Veterinary Clinical Pharmacology (ACVCP)
c/o Dr. Cyril R. Clarke, MRCVS
Dept. of Physiological Sciences
Coll. of Veterinary Medicine
Oklahoma State Univ.
Stillwater, OK 74078-0353
Phone: (405)744-8093
Fax: (405)744-8263
Dr. Cyril R. Clarke MRCVS, Exec. Officer

Recipient: Veterinarians specializing in clinical pharmacology. **Number of Certified Individuals:** 19. **Educational/ Experience Requirements:** Must meet the following requirements: (1) Graduation from college of veterinary medicine accredited by Council on Education of the American Veterinary Medical Association (see separate entry); (2) Successful completion of two-year residency or equivalent training; and (3) Submission of manuscript published in peer reviewed journal. Graduates of colleges of veterinary medicine outside of the U.S. must hold certificate from Educational Commission for Foreign Veterinary Graduates. **Certification Requirements:** Successful completion of Phase I and Phase II exams. Phase I exam covers: Analytical methods; Biostatistics; Clinical therapeutic trial design; Comparative pharmacology; Mechanisms of disease; Pathophysiologic processes; Pharmacodynamics; and Pharmacokinetics. Phase

II consists of written and oral exams. Must successfully complete one year of training in clinical pharmacology and submit additional manuscript published in peer-reviewed publication subsequent to successful completion of Phase I exam and prior to attempting Phase II exams. **Examination Sites:** Phase I exam given by arrangement with proctor. **Endorsed By:** American Veterinary Medical Association.

876

Diplomate of the American College of Veterinary Dermatology

American College of Veterinary Dermatology (ACVD)
c/o Craig E. Griffin, DVM
Animal Dermatology Clinic
13240 Evening Creek Dr.
San Diego, CA 92128
Phone: (619)486-4600
Fax: (619)486-4681
Craig E. Griffin DVM, Sec.

Recipient: Veterinarians specializing in dermatology. **Educational/Experience Requirements:** Must meet the following requirements: (1) Graduate from veterinary school or college; (2) Be approved to practice veterinary medicine in U.S. or Canada; (3) Successfully complete one year internship; (4) Successfully complete two years of education in dermatology after internship under supervision of Diplomate of the ACVD; (5) Submit article published in or accepted by refereed journal; and (6) Submit three cases. **Certification Requirements:** Successful completion of exam. Exam covers: (1) Types of Skin and Skin Disorders, including: Cellular and subcellular; Clinical; Etiologic; Microscopic and macroscopic; and Physiologic and pathologic; (2) Types of Animals, including: Large, laboratory, and exotic animals; and Small animal, general and comparative; and (3) Subject Content, including: Bacteriology; Endocrinology; Immunology; Internal medicine (dermatology); Miscellaneous (allergy); Mycology; Neoplasia; Parasitology; and Structure and function. **Examination Frequency:** Annual. **Fees:** $250. **Endorsed By:** American Veterinary Medical Association.

877

Diplomate of the American College of Veterinary Emergency and Critical Care

American College of Veterinary Emergency and Critical Care (ACVECC)
c/o James N. Ross, DVM
School of Veterinary Medicine
Tufts Univ.
200 Westboro Rd.
North Grafton, MA 01536
Phone: (508)839-7950
Fax: (508)839-7922
James N. Ross DVM, Exec.Sec.

Recipient: Veterinarians specializing in emergency medicine and critical care. **Educational/Experience Requirements:** Must meet the following requirements: (1) Graduation from college of veterinary medicine accredited by Council on Education of the American Veterinary Medical Association (see separate entry) or be licensed to practice; (2) Successful completion of either one year rotating internship and approved three-year residency program in emergency and critical care medicine or five-year alternative training program; (3) Submission of either four case reports or one refereed article published in peer reviewed veterinary journal; and (4) Six hours teaching experience in emergency and/or critical care topics. Graduates of foreign colleges of veterinary medicine must hold certificate from Educational Commission for Foreign Veterinary Graduates. **Membership:** Required. **Certification Requirements:** Successful completion of three-part exam. Part I covers: Anatomy; Clinical aspects; Immunology; Microbiology; Nutrition; Pathophysiology; Pharmacology; and Physiology. Part II may be written or oral. Part III requires examination of five case reports. **Examination Frequency:** Annual. **Examination Type:** Multiple-choice. **Waiting Period to Receive Scores:** 60 days. **Reexamination:** Must only retake part failed if two parts successfully completed. May retake written exam twice. **Endorsed By:** American Veterinary Medical Association.

878

Diplomate of the American College of Veterinary Internal Medicine

American College of Veterinary Internal Medicine (ACVIM)
7175 W. Jefferson Ave., Ste. 2125
Lakewood, CO 80235
Phone: (303)980-7136
Fax: (303)980-7137
Toll Free: (800)245-9081

Recipient: Veterinarians specializing in internal medicine. **Educational/Experience Requirements:** Must meet the following requirements: (1) Degree in veterinary medicine from veterinary school accredited by Council on Education of the American Veterinary Medical Association (see separate entry); and (2) Successful completion of residency program in veterinary internal medicine. **Membership:** Required. **Certification Requirements:** Successful completion of general and specialty exams. **Renewal:** none. **Preparatory Materials:** General information guide available. **Examination Frequency:** Annual. **Examination Sites:** Exams given at annual forum. **Examination Type:** Essay; multiple-choice. **Pass/Fail Rate:** 70 percent pass exams the first time. **Waiting Period to Receive Scores:** Two-three months. **Fees:** $400. **Endorsed By:** American Veterinary Medical Association.

879

Diplomate of the American College of Veterinary Microbiologists

American College of Veterinary Microbiologists (ACVM)
c/o Dr. H. G. Purchase
Coll. of Veterinary Medicine
Mississippi State Univ.
PO Box 9825
Mississippi State, MS 38762-9825
Phone: (601)325-1205
Fax: (601)325-1066
Dr. H. G. Purchase, Sec.-Treas.

Recipient: Veterinarians specializing in microbiology. **Educational/Experience Requirements:** Either graduate from college of veterinary medicine accredited by Council on Education of the American Veterinary Medical Association (see separate entry) or be qualified to practice veterinary medicine, submit two articles published in refereed journal, and meet one of the following requirements: (1) Ph.D. in microbiology; (2) Master's degree with major emphasis in microbiology and two years experience; or (3) Doctor of Veterinary Medicine (DVM) degree and ten years of increasingly responsible experience in teaching, independent research, or diagnostics. Graduates of colleges of veterinary medicine outside of the U.S. must hold certificate from Educational Commission for Foreign Veterinary Graduates. **Certification Requirements:** Successful completion of written and oral exams. Written exam covers: Bacteriology; Immunology; Infectious diseases; Mycology; and Virology. Oral exams given in the following specialty areas: Bacteriology - Mycology; Immunology; and Virology. **Examination Frequency:** Annual - always September (written) and December (oral). **Examination Sites:** Written exam given by arrangement with proctor. Oral exam given in Chicago, IL. **Examination Type:** Multiple-choice. **Endorsed By:** American Veterinary Medical Association.

880

Diplomate of the American College of Veterinary Nutrition (DACVN)
American College of Veterinary
   Nutrition (ACVN)
c/o Dr. John Bauer, DACVN
College of Veterinary Medicine
Texas A & M Univ.
College Station, TX 77843-4461
Dr. John Bauer DACVN, Sec.-
   Treas.

Recipient: Veterinarians specializing in animal nutrition. **Educational/ Experience Requirements:** Must meet the following requirements: (1) Graduation from college of veterinary medicine; (2) Current licensure to practice veterinary medicine; (3) Membership in organized association of veterinarians, such as the American Veterinary Medical Association, and American Academy of Veterinary Nutrition; (4) One year of general clinical experience; (5) Successful completion of two-year residency in veterinary nutrition; (6) Publication of two scientific reports in refereed journal; (7) Submission of three clinical case or herd problem reports having significant nutritional component and in which candidate has personally supervised nutritional management; and (8) Submission of questions for future exams. Equivalent alternative training may be accepted with approval of ACVN. Graduates of colleges of veterinary medicine from outside the U.S. must possess certificate of accreditation in veterinary medicine from Educational Commission for Foreign Veterinary Graduates or equivalent. **Certification Requirements:** Successful completion of three-section exam. Section one covers: Biochemistry; General medicine; Metabolic aspects of surgery; Pathophysiology; Physiology; and Principles of nutrition. Section two covers: Clinical nutrition; Nutritional pathology; and Practical nutrition (feeding and nutritional management). Section three requires choice of exam from the following: Comparative (large and small animal); Large animal; and Small animal. Section three exams cover: Problem-solving in clinical situations; Ration evaluation; and Ration formulation. **Examination Fre-**

quency: Annual. **Examination Sites:** Exam usually given at annual conference. **Examination Type:** Essay; multiple-choice. **Waiting Period to Receive Scores:** 90 days. **Re-examination:** Must only retake sections failed. May retake each section two times. There is a $75 fee to retake each section. Must successfully complete exam within six years. **Fees:** $300. **Endorsed By:** American Academy of Veterinary Nutrition; American Veterinary Medical Association.

881

Diplomate of the American College of Veterinary Ophthalmologists
American College of Veterinary
   Ophthalmologists (AVMO)
c/o Dr. Mary B. Glaze
Veterinary Clinical Sciences
Louisiana State Univ.
Baton Rouge, LA 70803
Phone: (504)346-3333
Fax: (504)346-3295
Dr. Mary B. Glaze, Sec.-Treas.

Recipient: Veterinary ophthalmologists. **Educational/Experience Requirements:** Must meet the following requirements: (1) Graduate of accredited college of veterinary medicine; (2) Current licensure to practice veterinary medicine; and (3) Successful completion of three years training following graduation, two years of which must be in approved ophthalmology residency program. There may be additional requirements at the discretion of the AVMO. **Certification Requirements:** Successful completion of written, oral, and practical exams. **Endorsed By:** American Veterinary Medical Association.

882

Diplomate of the American College of Veterinary Preventive Medicine
American College of Veterinary
   Preventive Medicine (ACVPM)
c/o Dr. Stanley O. Hewins
3126 Morning Creek
San Antonio, TX 78247
Fax: (210)524-3944
Toll Free: (800)374-4944
Dr. Stanley O. Hewins, Exec.V.
   Pres.

Recipient: Veterinarians specializing in preventive medicine. **Educational/ Experience Requirements:** Must meet the following requirements: (1) Graduate from college of veterinary medicine ac-

credited by Council on Education of the American Veterinary Medical Association (see separate entry) or be qualified to practice veterinary medicine; and (2) Six years experience, three of which may be a formal training program. Graduates of colleges of veterinary medicine outside of the U.S. must hold certificate from Educational Commission for Foreign Veterinary Graduates. **Certification Requirements:** Successful completion of exam. **Endorsed By:** American Veterinary Medical Association.

883

Diplomate of the American College of Veterinary Radiology
American College of Veterinary
   Radiology (ACVR)
PO Box 87
Glencoe, IL 60022
Phone: (708)251-5517
Fax: (708)446-8618
Dr. M. Bernstein, Exec.Dir.

Recipient: Veterinarians specializing in radiology. **Educational/Experience Requirements:** Must meet the following requirements: (1) Graduate from college of veterinary medicine; (2) Be qualified to practice veterinary medicine; and (3) Successfully complete residency program or equivalent. **Certification Requirements:** Successful completion of written and oral exams. Written exam consists of following sections: Alternate Imaging; Anatomy; Physics of Diagnostic Radiology; Physiology/Pathophysiology; Radiation Therapy, Radiation Biology, and Radiation Protection; and Radiographic Contrast Procedures. Oral exam consists of the following required core subjects: Abdomen, primarily small animal; Diagnostic ultrasound; Musculoskeletal, divided between small and large animals; Technical errors and artifacts; and Thorax, primarily small animal. Must also successfully complete one of the following elective subjects: C.T. and M.R.I.; Diagnostic nuclear medicine; Large animal diagnostics; Radiation oncology; and Small animal diagnostics. **Examination Frequency:** Annual. **Re-examination:** May retake exam once. **Endorsed By:** American Veterinary Medical Association.

▇884▇

Diplomate of the American College of Veterinary Surgeons

American College of Veterinary
Surgeons (ACVS)
4330 East-West Hwy., Ste. 1117
Bethesda, MD 20814
Phone: (301)718-6504
Fax: (301)656-0989

Recipient: Veterinary surgeons. **Number of Certified Individuals:** 4642. **Educational/Experience Requirements:** Must meet the following requirements: (1) Graduate of veterinary college accredited by Council on Education of the American Veterinary Medical Association (see separate entry) or meet all requirements for licensure of foreign veterinary graduates as defined by American Veterinary Medical Association; (2) Successful completion of one-year rotating internship; (3) Successful completion of three-year residency; and (4) Submission of at least one research manuscript advancing knowledge in the field. **Certification Requirements:** Successful completion of three-section exam. Written section covers: Anatomy; Diagnosis; Gastrointestinal, cardiovascular, respiratory, musculoskeletal, urogenital, neurologic, and integumentary surgery; Organ systems; Pathology; Pharmacology and anesthesia; Physiology; and Surgical techniques and treatment. Practical section involves evaluation during either large or small animal surgery and may cover: Anatomical specimens; Instruments; Pathologic and histologic specimens; Radiographs; and Surgical diseases. Oral section includes questions on orthopedics and neurology and soft tissue surgery and covers case management prior to, during, and after surgery. **Examination Type:** Multiple-choice; short answer. **Re-examination:** Must only retake sections failed. May retake each section three times. Must successfully complete exam within four years. There is a $350 fee to retake exam. **Fees:** $950. **Endorsed By:** American Veterinary Medical Association.

▇885▇

Diplomate of the American College of Zoological Medicine

American College of Zoological
Medicine (ACZM)
c/o Dr. George Kollias, Jr.
Dept. of Clinical Services
Sec. of Wildlife Medicine
New York State Veterinary Coll.
Cornell, NY 14853
Phone: (607)253-3049
Fax: (607)253-3708
Dr. George Kollias Jr., Sec.

Recipient: Veterinarians specializing in zoological medicine. **Number of Certified Individuals:** 27. **Certification Requirements:** Successful completion of two-part exam. First part covers: Amphibians; Birds; Fish; Mammals; and Reptiles. Second part covers one of the following: Aquatic medicine; Avian; Primary captive zoo animal; Reptile/amphibian; and Wildlife. **Endorsed By:** American Veterinary Medical Association.

▇886▇

Diplomate of the American Veterinary Dental College

American Veterinary Dental College
(AVDC)
c/o Dr. Sandra Manfra Marretta
Coll. of Veterinary Medicine
Univ. of Illinois
1008 W. Hazelwood Dr.
Urbana, IL 61801
Phone: (217)333-5300
Fax: (217)244-1475
Dr. Sandra Manfra Marretta, Sec.

Recipient: Veterinary dentists. **Number of Certified Individuals:** 29. **Educational/Experience Requirements:** Must meet the following requirements: (1) Graduate from college of veterinary medicine; (2) Submit dental log of veterinary oral/dental cases in recent 12-month period; and (3) Successfully complete of residency or equivalent. **Certification Requirements:** Successful completion of written and practical exams. Exams cover: Embryology; Endodontics; Genetics; Oncology; Oral anatomy; Oral/maxillo-facial surgery; Oral radiology; Orthodontics; Periodontics; and Restoratives. **Examination Frequency:** Annual. **Re-examination:** May retake exam two times. **Endorsed By:** American Veterinary Medical Association.

▇887▇

Diplomate in Cardiology of the American College of Veterinary Internal Medicine

American College of Veterinary
Internal Medicine (ACVIM)
7175 W. Jefferson Ave., Ste. 2125
Lakewood, CO 80235
Phone: (303)980-7136
Fax: (303)980-7137
Toll Free: (800)245-9081

Recipient: Veterinarians specializing in cardiology. **Educational/Experience Requirements:** Must meet one of the following requirements: (1) Degree in veterinary medicine from veterinary school accredited by Council on Education of the American Veterinary Medical Association (see separate entry); and (2) Successful completion of residency program in veterinary cardiology. **Membership:** Required. **Certification Requirements:** Successful completion of general and specialty exams. **Renewal:** none. **Preparatory Materials:** General information guide available. **Examination Frequency:** Annual. **Examination Sites:** Exams given at annual forum. **Examination Type:** Essay; multiple-choice. **Pass/Fail Rate:** 70 percent pass exams the first time. **Waiting Period to Receive Scores:** Two-three months. **Fees:** $400. **Endorsed By:** American Veterinary Medical Association.

▇888▇

Diplomate in Epidemiology of the American College of Veterinary Preventive Medicine

American College of Veterinary
Preventive Medicine (ACVPM)
c/o Dr. Stanley O. Hewins
3126 Morning Creek
San Antonio, TX 78247
Fax: (210)524-3944
Toll Free: (800)374-4944
Dr. Stanley O. Hewins, Exec.V.
Pres.

Recipient: Veterinarians specializing in epidemiology. **Educational/Experience Requirements:** Must meet the following requirements: (1) Hold Diplomate of the American College of Veterinary Preventive Medicine designation (see separate entry); (2) Two years experience within last five years, with at least 25 percent of time devoted to epidemiology; and (3) Document competency in teaching, research, or practice that has contributed to development of epidemiology. **Certification Requirements:** Successful completion of exam. **Endorsed By:** American Veterinary Medical Association.

889

Diplomate in Neurology of the American College of Veterinary Internal Medicine

American College of Veterinary
   Internal Medicine (ACVIM)
7175 W. Jefferson Ave., Ste. 2125
Lakewood, CO 80235
Phone: (303)980-7136
Fax: (303)980-7137
Toll Free: (800)245-9081

Recipient: Veterinarians specializing in neurology. **Educational/Experience Requirements:** Must meet one of the following requirements: (1) Degree in veterinary medicine from veterinary school accredited by Council on Education of the American Veterinary Medical Association (see separate entry); and (2) Successful completion of residency program in veterinary neurology. **Membership:** Required. **Certification Requirements:** Successful completion of general and specialty exams. **Renewal:** none. **Preparatory Materials:** General information guide available. **Examination Frequency:** Annual. **Examination Sites:** Exams given at annual forum. **Examination Type:** Essay; multiple-choice. **Pass/Fail Rate:** 70 percent pass exams the first time. **Waiting Period to Receive Scores:** Two-three months. **Fees:** $400. **Endorsed By:** American Veterinary Medical Association.

890

Diplomate in Oncology of the American College of Veterinary Internal Medicine

American College of Veterinary
   Internal Medicine (ACVIM)
7175 W. Jefferson Ave., Ste. 2125
Lakewood, CO 80235
Phone: (303)980-7136
Fax: (303)980-7137
Toll Free: (800)245-9081

Recipient: Veterinarians specializing in oncology. **Educational/Experience Requirements:** Must meet one of the following requirements: (1) Degree in veterinary medicine from veterinary school accredited by Council on Education of the American Veterinary Medical Association (see separate entry); and (2) Successful completion of residency program in veterinary oncology. **Membership:** Required. **Certification Requirements:** Successful completion of general and specialty exams. **Renewal:** none. **Preparatory Materials:** General information guide available. **Examination Frequency:** Annual. **Examination Sites:** Exams given at annual forum. **Examination**

Type: Essay; multiple-choice. **Pass/Fail Rate:** 70 percent pass exams the first time. **Waiting Period to Receive Scores:** Two-three months. **Fees:** $400. **Endorsed By:** American Veterinary Medical Association.

891

Diplomate in Veterinary Clinical Pathology of the American College of Veterinary Pathologists

American College of Veterinary
   Pathologists (ACVP)
875 Kings Hwy., Ste. 200
Woodbury, NJ 08096
Phone: (609)848-7784
Fax: (609)853-0411

Recipient: Veterinary clinical pathologists in private practice, meat inspection, general and special diagnostic laboratories, teaching, research, and Veterinary Corps of the Armed Forces. **Educational/Experience Requirements:** Must meet the following requirements: (1) Graduation from college or school of veterinary medicine accredited by Council on Education of the American Veterinary Medical Association (see separate entry); and (2) Successful completion of three year residency in veterinary clinical pathology in program that trains veterinary pathologists as one of its primary functions. **Certification Requirements:** Successful completion of exam. Exam consists of following sections: (1) Clinical Biochemistry; (2) Cytology-Surgical Pathology; (3) General Pathology; and (4) Hematology. **Renewal:** none. **Examination Type:** Essay; multiple-choice. **Re-examination:** May retake exam twice. Must only retake sections failed if two sections successfully completed. Must successfully complete exam within four years. **Fees:** $450. **Endorsed By:** American Veterinary Medical Association.

892

Diplomate in Veterinary Pathology of the American College of Veterinary Pathologists

American College of Veterinary
   Pathologists (ACVP)
875 Kings Hwy., Ste. 200
Woodbury, NJ 08096
Phone: (609)848-7784
Fax: (609)853-0411

Recipient: Veterinary pathologists working in private practice, meat inspection, general and special diagnostic laboratories, teaching, research, and Veterinary

Corps of the Armed Forces. **Educational/Experience Requirements:** Must meet the following requirements: (1) Graduation from college or school of veterinary medicine accredited by Council on Medical Education of the American Veterinary Medical Association (see separate entry); and (2) Successful completion of three year residency in veterinary pathology in program that trains veterinary pathologists as one of its primary functions. **Certification Requirements:** Successful completion of exam. Exam consists of following sections: (1) General Pathology; (2) Gross Pathology; (3) Microscopic Pathology; and (4) Veterinary Pathology, including the following areas: Clinical; Dog and cat; Laboratory animal, poultry, and wildlife; and Large animal. **Renewal:** none. **Examination Type:** Multiple-choice. **Re-examination:** May retake exam twice. Must only retake sections failed if two sections successfully completed. Must successfully complete exam within four years. **Fees:** $450. **Endorsed By:** American Veterinary Medical Association.

Health Assessment and Treating Occupations

Childbirth and Child Care Assistants

893

ASPO-Certified Childbirth Educators
American Society for Psychoprophylaxis in Obstetrics (ASPO)
1200 19th St., NW, Ste. 300
Washington, DC 20036
Phone: (202)857-1128
Fax: (202)857-1130
Toll Free: (800)368-4404

Recipient: Childbirth educators using Lamaze method. **Number of Certified Individuals:** 10,000. **Educational/Experience Requirements:** Must meet one of the following requirements: (1) Graduation from ASPO/Lamaze Childbirth Educator Program, which includes self-study modules and seminar; or (2) Current licensure as registered nurse (R.N.), Registered Physical Therapist (R.P.T.), Medical Doctor (M.D.), or Certified Nurse Midwife (CNM) (see separate entry), bachelor's degree or higher, three years experience, consisting of at least 144 instructional hours, and 30 contact hours of related continuing education within past three years. **Certification Requirements:** Successful completion of exam. **Renewal:** Every three years. Recertification based on either successful completion of exam or accumulation of 30 contact hours of related continuing education.

894

Certified Nurse-Midwife (CNM)
American College of Nurse-Midwives (ACNM)
8401 Corporate Dr., Ste. 630
Landover, MD 20785
Phone: (301)459-1321
Fax: (301)731-7825

Recipient: Nurse-midwives. **Educational/Experience Requirements:** Must meet the following requirements: (1) Current licensure as registered nurse (R.N.); and (2) Successful completion of program in nurse-wifery (or in master's degree program, including all basic nurse-midwifery theoretical and clinical requirements of nurse-wifery component) accredited by Division of Accreditation of the ACNM (see separate entry). Graduates of foreign universities must successfully complete accredited pre-certification program. **Certification Requirements:** Successful completion of exam.

895

Child Development Associate (CDA)
Council for Early Childhood Professional Recognition (CECPR)
1341 G St., NW, Ste. 400
Washington, DC 20005
Phone: (202)265-9090
Fax: (202)265-9161
Toll Free: (800)424-4310
Carol Brunson Phillips, Exec.Dir.

Recipient: Caregivers and program directors in center-based, home visitor, and family day-care programs. **Number of Certified Individuals:** 61,000. **Certification Requirements:** Must meet one of the following requirements: (1) Direct assessment, consisting of 480 hours of experience, 120 hours of formal child care education or training in eight specific areas, and successful completion of formal observation of performance, written exam, and oral interview; or (2) Successful completion of CDA Professional Preparation Program (P3), a one-year program consisting of 480 hours of field work, 120 hours of course work, and final evaluation interview. **Renewal:** Every three years. **Examination Type:** Multiple-choice. **Fees:** $325 for direct assessment; $1500 for P3.

896

Childbirth Assistant (CA)
National Association of Childbirth Assistants (NACA)
936-B Seventh St., No. 301
Novato, CA 94945
Toll Free: (800)868-NACA
Claudia Lowe, Prog.Dir.

Recipient: Childbirth assistants. **Number of Certified Individuals:** 500. **Educational/Experience Requirements:** Education or training in women's and family care, parenting, or childbirth. **Membership:** Required. **Certification Requirements:** Successful completion of either correspondence course, including exam, or workshop, including study modules. **Renewal:** Every two years. Recertification based on continuing education. Renewal fee is $85. **Preparatory Materials:** *Becoming a Childbirth Assistant* and *Planning for a Positive Birth Experience* (references). **Examination Frequency:** Throughout the year. **Examination Sites:** Exam given by correspondence. **Examination Type:** Essay. **Pass/Fail Rate:** 90% pass exam the first time. **Waiting Period to Receive Scores:** Two-six weeks. **Re-examination:** There is no time limit to retake exam. **Fees:** $275-$425.

897

Childbirth Educator (CE)
National Association of Childbirth
  Assistants (NACA)
936-B Seventh St., No. 301
Novato, CA 94945
Toll Free: (800)868-NACA
Claudia Lowe, Prog.Dir.

Recipient: Childbirth educators. **Number of Certified Individuals:** 100. **Educational/Experience Requirements:** Knowledge or interest in women's and family care and childbirth. **Membership:** Required. **Certification Requirements:** Successful completion of correspondence course, including exam, and in-service training. **Renewal:** Every two years. Recertification based on continuing education. Renewal fee is $45. **Preparatory Materials:** *Becoming a Childbirth Assistant, Confident Childbirth, Guided Self-Hypnosis for Childbirth and Beyond, Labor Support Techniques,* and *Planning for a Positive Birth Experience* (references). **Examination Frequency:** Throughout the year. **Examination Sites:** Exam given by correspondence. **Examination Type:** Essay. **Pass/Fail Rate:** 95% pass exam the first time. **Waiting Period to Receive Scores:** Two-six weeks. **Re-examination:** There is no time limit to retake exam. **Fees:** $695.

898

Childbirth Educator
Certified Perinatal Educators
  Association (CPEA)
Four David Ct.
Novato, CA 94947
Phone: (415)893-0439
Claudia Lowe, Dir.

Recipient: Childbirth educators who assist women and couples prepare for childbirth. **Number of Certified Individuals:** 25. **Educational/Experience Requirements:** Knowledge or interest in women's and family care and childbirth. **Membership:** Required. **Certification Requirements:** Successful completion of correspondence course, including exam, and in-services. **Renewal:** Every two years. Recertification based on continuing education. Renewal fee is $45. **Preparatory Materials:** *Becoming a Childbirth Assistant, Confident Childbirth, Guided Self-Hypnosis for Childbirth and Beyond, Labor Support Techniques,* and *Planning for a Positive Birth Experience* (references). **Examination Frequency:** Throughout the year. **Examination Sites:** Exam given by correspondence. **Examination Type:** Essay. **Pass/Fail Rate:** 95% pass exam the first time. **Waiting Period**

to **Receive Scores:** Two-six weeks. **Re-examination:** There is no waiting period to retake exam. **Fees:** $575.

899

Fellow of the American College of Childbirth Educators (FACCE)
American College of Childbirth
  Educators (ACCE)
c/o   Amer.   Soc.   for
  Psychoprophylaxis in Obstetrics
1101 Connecticut Ave., NW, Ste.
  700
Washington, DC 20036
Phone: (202)857-1128
Fax: (202)857-1130
Toll Free: (800)368-4404

Recipient: Childbirth educators teaching the Lamaze method. **Educational/Experience Requirements:** Hold ASPO/Lamaze Certified Childbirth Educator (ACCE) designation (see separate entry) and membership in American Society for Psychoprophylaxis in Obstetrics/Lamaze (ASPO/Lamaze). **Membership:** Required. **Certification Requirements:** Documentation of significant contributions to childbirth education, family-centered maternity care, and ASPO/Lamaze including community volunteer activities, in-service programs, lectures, publications, and research. **Fees:** $35. **Endorsed By:** American Society for Psychoprophylaxis in Obstetrics/Lamaze.

900

Guided Self-Hypnosis Educator
Birth Support Providers,
  International (BSPI)
Four David Ct.
Novato, CA 94947
Toll Free: (800)818-BSPI
Claudia Lowe, Dir.

Recipient: Childbirth educators specializing in guided self-hypnosis. **Educational/Experience Requirements:** Education or training in childbirth or hypnosis. **Membership:** Required. **Certification Requirements:** Successful completion of either correspondence course, including exam, or workshop, including study modules. **Renewal:** Every two years. Recertification based on continuing education. Renewal fee is $55. **Preparatory Materials:** *Becoming a Childbirth Assistant* and *Guided Self-Hypnosis for Childbirth and Beyond* (references). **Examination Frequency:** Throughout the year. **Examination Sites:** Exam given by correspondence. **Examination Type:** Essay. **Waiting Period to Receive Scores:** Two-

six weeks. **Re-examination:** There is no waiting period to retake exam. **Fees:** $400.

901

International Board Certified Lactation Consultant (IBCLC)
Association for Lactation
  Consultant Certification (ALCC)
PO Box 2348
Falls Church, VA 22042-0348
Phone: (703)560-7330
Fax: (703)560-7332

Recipient: Lactation consultants working in hospitals, clinics, nutrition programs, the community, and private practice. **Educational/Experience Requirements:** Must meet one of the following requirements: (1) Bachelor's degree or higher, 2500 hours experience, and 30 hours of continuing education related to breast-feeding within last three years; or (2) Either associate's degree, diploma registered nurse, or two years academic credit, 4000 hours experience, and 30 hours of continuing education within last three years. Alternate pathways are available for individuals with one of the following: (1) Doctor of medicine degree; (2) Degree with accredited human lactation major; (3) Successful completion of lactation course of at least 150 hours; (4) One hundred hours of supervised clinical experience within lactation education program; or (5) Six-eight thousand hours of experience. **Certification Requirements:** Successful completion of exam. **Renewal:** Every five years. Recertification based on either successful completion of exam or continuing education. **Preparatory Materials:** Candidate's information booklet provided. **Examination Frequency:** Annual - always last Monday in July. **Examination Sites:** Exam given at sites throughout the U.S. and internationally. **Examination Type:** Multiple-choice. **Accredited By:** National Commission for Certifying Agencies. **Endorsed By:** International Board of Lactation Consultant Examiners; National Organization for Competency Assurance.

902

Positive Pregnancy and Parenting Fitness Instructor
Positive Pregnancy and Parenting
  Fitness (PPPF)
RR 1, Box 172
Glen View Rd.
Waitsfield, VT 05673
Phone: (802)496-5222
Fax: (802)496-5222

Toll Free: (800)433-5523
Sylvia Klein Olkin MS, Founder

Recipient: Fitness instructors working with pregnant women or new mothers and babies. **Number of Certified Individuals:** 100. **Educational/Experience Requirements:** College degree and professional experience. **Membership:** Required. **Certification Requirements:** Successful completion of workshop and exam. Must submit the following within two years: (1) Video tape of workshop taught; (2) Report detailing goals and objectives, programs taught, and personal development; (3) Student evaluation forms from classes taught; (4) Audio or video tapes of three book reviews; and (5) Article or book review for newsletter. Must attend exercise session taught by another instructor and regional or national sharing day sponsored by PPPF or another childbirth education organization. **Renewal:** Every three years. Recertification based on attendance at seminars and conferences and submitting book reviews. **Preparatory Materials:** List of study references provided. Manual, text books, and audio cassette tapes available. **Examination Frequency:** By arrangement. **Examination Sites:** Exam given by correspondence. **Examination Type:** Essay; multiple-choice. **Pass/Fail Rate:** 95% pass exam the first time. **Waiting Period to Receive Scores:** Two weeks. **Re-examination:** Must wait three months to retake exam. **Fees:** $684. **Endorsed By:** American College of Nurse-Midwives; American Council on Education; American Society for Psychoprophylaxis in Obstetrics.

903

Postpartum and Breastfeeding Assistant (PBA)
National Association of Childbirth Assistants (NACA)
936-B Seventh St., No. 301
Novato, CA 94945
Toll Free: (800)868-NACA
Claudia Lowe, Prog.Dir.

Recipient: Postpartum and breastfeeding assistants. **Educational/Experience Requirements:** Education or training in women's and family care, parenting, or childbirth. **Membership:** Required. **Certification Requirements:** Successful completion of either correspondence course, including exam, or workshop, including study modules. **Renewal:** Every two years. Recertification based on continuing education. Renewal fee is $85. **Preparatory Materials:** *Becoming a Childbirth Assistant* (reference). **Examination Frequency:** Throughout the year.

Examination Sites: Exam given by correspondence. **Examination Type:** Essay. **Waiting Period to Receive Scores:** Two-six weeks. **Re-examination:** There is no waiting period to retake exam. **Fees:** $475.

Dietitians and Nutritionists

904

Certified Diabetes Educator (CDE)
National Certification Board for Diabetes Educators (NCBDE)
444 N. Michigan Ave., Ste. 1240
Chicago, IL 60611-3901
Phone: (312)644-2233
Fax: (312)644-4411
Toll Free: (800)338-DMED

Recipient: Health care professionals practicing diabetes education. **Educational/Experience Requirements:** Two thousand hours experience and meet one of the following requirements: (1) Master's degree in nutrition, social work, clinical psychology, exercise physiology, or health education; or (2) Hold current license, registration, or certification as registered nurse, dietician, pharmacist, physician, physician assistant, podiatrist, physical therapist, or occupational therapist. Experience must be in planned program providing individuals and their families with training and information designed to develop or improve knowledge and skills for living with diabetes. Planned program contains elements of educational assessment, evaluation, follow-up, and patient education. **Membership:** Not required. **Certification Requirements:** Successful completion of exam. Exam covers: (1) Physiology and Pathophysiology, including: Clinical signs and symptoms; Definitions and classifications; Diagnostic criteria; Epidemiology; Etiology and pathophysiology; and Normal physiology; (2) Nonpharmacologic Therapies, including: Exercise; and Nutrition; (3) Pharmacologic Intervention, including: Drug interactions; Glucagon; Insulin; and Oral hypoglycemic agents; (4) Monitoring and Management, including: Blood glucose monitoring; Life cycle issues affecting management; Management challenges; and Urine monitoring; (5) Complications: Prevention, Symptoms, Course, Treatment, including: Acute; Chronic; and Preventive care; (6) Psychosocial Factors, including: Coping and adapting; Impact of diabetes; Self-care and treatment adherence; Stress; and Support systems; and (7) Principles of Teaching and

Learning, including: Assessment; Documentation; Evaluation; Follow-up; General principles; Goal setting; Interventions; and Program development. **Renewal:** Every five years. Recertification based on successful completion of exam. Renewal fees are: $140 (members); $190 (nonmembers). **Preparatory Materials:** Handbook, including sample questions and study references, provided. **Examination Sites:** Exam given at sites throughout the U.S. and Canada. **Examination Type:** Multiple-choice. **Waiting Period to Receive Scores:** Six weeks. **Re-examination:** Fees to retake exam are: $160 (members); $210 (nonmembers). **Fees:** $160 (members); $210 (nonmembers). **Endorsed By:** American Association of Diabetes Educators.

905

Certified Dietary Manager (CDM)
Certifying Board for Dietary Managers (CBDM)
One Pierce Pl., Ste. 1220W
Itasca, IL 60143
Phone: (708)775-9200
Fax: (708)775-9250
Katherine Church RD, Special Advisor

Recipient: Institutional food service managers and supervisors who work primarily in healthcare facilities. **Number of Certified Individuals:** 9159. **Educational/Experience Requirements:** Must meet one of the following requirements: (1) Active or associate membership in Dietary Managers Association (DMA); (2) Successful completion of DMA-approved training program for dietary managers; (3) Bachelor's degree in food management or related field or successful completion of American Dietetic Association (ADA)-approved dietetic technician associate degree program; or (4) Successful completion of state approved dietary manager training program and two years experience. **Membership:** Not required. **Certification Requirements:** Successful completion of exam. Exam covers: Food/kitchen operation, production, and management; Human resource management within food facilities; and Patient/client nutrition, service, and education. **Renewal:** Every three years. Recertification based on accumulation of 45 hours of approved continuing education. **Examination Frequency:** Annual. **Examination Sites:** Exam given at 50 sites throughout the U.S. **Examination Type:** Multiple-choice. **Pass/Fail Rate:** 72% pass exam the first time. **Waiting Period to Receive Scores:** Six weeks. **Re-examination:** Must wait one year to retake exam. **Fees:** $100 (members); $200 (nonmembers). **Accredited By:** National Commission for Certifying Agencies. **Endorsed By:** Dietary Managers Association; National Organization for Competency Assurance.

906

Certified Nutrition Support Dietician (CNSD)

National Board of Nutrition Support Certification (NBNSC)
8630 Fenton St., Ste. 412
Silver Spring, MD 20910-3805
Phone: (301)587-6315
Janet Gannon, Dir.

Recipient: Registered dieticians specializing in nutrition support. **Number of Certified Individuals:** 2000. **Educational/ Experience Requirements:** Must be registered dietician. Two years experience recommended. **Membership:** Not required. **Certification Requirements:** Successful completion of exam. Exam covers: (1) Nutritional Assessment and Reassessment, including: Anatomy and physiology applied to nutrition support; Nutrient requirements; and Nutritional status; (2) Therapeutic Plan, including: Administration; Diet and product selection; Goals and objectives; Home therapy; and Specialized nutrition support; (3) Implementation, including: Administration procedures; Patient education; and Product preparation; (4) Patient Monitoring and Evaluation, including: Adequacy of intake; Alterations in feeding plan; and Tolerance; and (5) Professional Issues, including: Documenting nutritional care; Ethical and legal issues; Facility and agency accreditation; Health care legislation; Quality issues; Research in clinical settings; and Roles and responsibilities. **Renewal:** Every five years. Recertification based on successful completion of exam. **Preparatory Materials:** *Nutrition Support Dietetics Core Curriculum* (reference). Handbook, including exam content outline, list of suggested study references, and sample questions, provided. Self-assessment program, audio tapes, and review courses available. **Examination Frequency:** Annual - always spring and fall. **Examination Sites:** Exam given at sites throughout the U.S. **Examination Type:** Multiple-choice. **Waiting Period to Receive Scores:** Six weeks. **Re-examination:** There is no limit to the number of times exam may be retaken. Fees to retake exam are: $190 (members); $250 (nonmembers). **Fees:** $190 (members); $250 (nonmembers). **Endorsed By:** American Society for Parenteral and Enteral Nutrition.

907

Certified Nutritional Consultant (CNC)

American Association of Nutritional Consultants (AANC)
880 Canarios Ct., No. 210
Chula Vista, CA 91910
Phone: (619)482-8533

Recipient: Nutritional consultants. **Membership:** Required. **Certification Requirements:** Successful completion of the following (1) Series of exams; and (2) Paper demonstrating proficiency in areas of general and applied nutrition and practice management. **Preparatory Materials:** List of recommended text books provided. **Examination Sites:** Exam given by correspondence. **Re-examination:** Must wait 30 days to retake exam. Must wait 60 days before retaking exam second time. There is a $15 fee to retake exam. **Fees:** $150.

908

Certified Professional Natural Hygienist

International Association of Professional Natural Hygienists (IAPNH)
204 Stambaugh Bldg.
Youngstown, OH 44503
Phone: (216)746-5000
Fax: (216)746-1836
Mark A. Huberman, Sec.-Treas.

Recipient: Primary care doctors specializing in fasting supervision as an integral part of natural hygiene care. **Number of Certified Individuals:** 25. **Educational/ Experience Requirements:** Must meet the following requirements: (1) Graduate degree in medicine, osteopathy, chiropractic, or naturopathy; and (2) Current licensure. **Membership:** Required. **Certification Requirements:** Successful completion of internship residency program with Certified Professional Natural Hygienist. **Renewal:** Every year. **Preparatory Materials:** *Fasting for Renewal of Life, Pristine Way of Life,* and *Science and Fine Art of Fasting* (references).

909

Fellow of the American Council of Applied Clinical Nutrition (FACACN)

American Council of Applied Clinical Nutrition (ACACN)
PO Box 509
Florissant, MO 63032
Phone: (314)921-3997

Recipient: Professionals involved in applied clinical nutrition. **Certification Requirements:** Successful completion of course and exam. Course consists of the following modules: (1) Nutritional Biochemistry I, including: Chemical components of carbohydrates and lipids; and Protoplasm and tissues; (2) Nutritional Biochemistry II, covering proteins and alpha amino acids and their occurrence and function; (3) Nutritional Biochemistry III, covering biochemistry or digestion and production of digestive enzymes; (4) Clinical Endocrinology, covering nutrient components of endocrine hormones; (5) Nutritional Biochemistry IV, including: Metabolic pathways; Nutrients of life; and Oil-soluble vitamins; (6) Nutritional Biochemistry V, including: Metabolic pathways; Nutrients of life; and Water-soluble vitamins; (7) Nutritional Biochemistry VI, including: Macrominerals and micro-minerals; and Water-soluble and water dispersible minerals; (8) Nutritional Laboratory Diagnosis I and II, including: Interpretation of contemporary laboratory tests; Significance of specific laboratory tests as biological barometers for determining presence of clinical and subclinical nutritional deficiency states; and Specific nutritional deficiencies which appear to be intimately related to certain abnormal laboratory values; and (9) Nutritional Laboratory Diagnosis III, covering specific laboratory panels. Course available on-site and on cassette. **Fees:** $995.

910

Horticultural Therapist Registered (HTR)

American Horticultural Therapy Association (AHTA)
362A Christopher Ave.
Gaithersburg, MD 20879-3660
Phone: (301)948-3010
Fax: (301)869-2397
Stephen F. Hubin, Coord.

Recipient: Horticultural therapists. **Membership:** Required. **Certification Requirements:** Must meet one of the following requirements: (1) Degree in horticultural therapy, including 1000 hour internship, and one year of experience; or (2) One year of experience and accumulation of four points through: (A) Education, including: Degreed coursework; Internships; and Non-degreed coursework; (B) Employment; and (C) Professional Activities, including: AHTA service; Authorship of publications; Coordination of workshops; Presentations given; and Supervision of interns. **Renewal:** Every year. Renewal fee is $25. **Fees:** $60.

911

Horticultural Therapist Technician (HTR)
American Horticultural Therapy
    Association (AHTA)
362A Christopher Ave.
Gaithersburg, MD 20879-3660
Phone: (301)948-3010
Fax: (301)869-2397
Stephen F. Hubin, Coord.

Recipient: Horticultural therapy technicians. **Membership:** Required. **Certification Requirements:** Must meet the following requirements: (1) Either one year of employment experience or two years combined employment and volunteer experience; and (2) Accumulation of two points through: (A) Education, including: Degreed coursework; Internships; and Nondegreed coursework; (B) Employment; and (C) Professional Activities, including: AHTA service; Authorship of publications; Coordination of workshops; Presentations given; and Supervision of interns. **Renewal:** Every year. Renewal fee is $25. **Fees:** $60.

912

Master Horticultural Therapist (HTM)
American Horticultural Therapy
    Association (AHTA)
362A Christopher Ave.
Gaithersburg, MD 20879-3660
Phone: (301)948-3010
Fax: (301)869-2397
Stephen F. Hubin, Coord.

Recipient: Horticultural therapists. **Membership:** Required. **Certification Requirements:** Four years experience and one of the following: (1) Master's degree in horticultural therapy; or (2) Accumulation of six points through: (A) Education, including: Degreed coursework; Internships; and Non-degreed coursework; (B) Employment; and (C) Professional Activities, including: AHTA service; Authorship of publications; Coordination of workshops; Presentations given; and Su-

pervision of interns. **Renewal:** Every year. Renewal fee is $25. **Fees:** $60.

913

Registered Dietetic Technician (RDT)
Commission on Dietetic
    Registration (CDR)
216 W. Jackson Blvd., Ste. 800
Chicago, IL 60606-6995
Phone: (312)899-0040
Fax: (312)899-1772

Recipient: Dietetic technicians. **Educational/Experience Requirements:** Must meet one of the following requirements: (1) Successful completion of Dietetic Technician program accredited by Commission on Accreditation/Approval for Dietetics Education (see separate entry); or (2) Bachelor's degree, including American Dietetic Association (ADA) minimum academic requirements, and successful completion of supervised field experience. Graduates of programs outside the U.S. must have their credentials validated for equivalency. Candidates who completed educational requirements more than five years before application must successfully complete additional coursework. **Certification Requirements:** Successful completion of exam. **Preparatory Materials:** Study guide, including exam content outline, list of suggested study references, and practice exam, available. **Examination Sites:** Exam given at sites in the U.S. and internationally. **Accredited By:** National Commission for Certifying Agencies. **Endorsed By:** American Dietetic Association; National Organization for Competency Assurance.

914

Registered Dietician (RD)
Commission on Dietetic
    Registration (CDR)
216 W. Jackson Blvd., Ste. 800
Chicago, IL 60606-6995
Phone: (312)899-0040
Fax: (312)899-1979

Recipient: Dietitians. **Educational/Experience Requirements:** Bachelor's degree, successful completion of Didactic Program in Dietetics, and successful completion of one of the following programs accredited by the Commission on Accreditation/Approval for Dietetics Education (see separate entry): (1) Dietetic internship consisting of at least 900 hours of supervised practice; (2) Coordinated program culminating in bachelor's

degree and including at least 900 hours of supervised practice; or (3) Preprofessional practice program consisting of at least 900 hours of supervised practice. Graduates of programs outside the U.S. must have their credentials validated for equivalency. Candidates who completed educational requirements more than five years before application must successfully complete additional coursework. **Certification Requirements:** Successful completion of exam. **Preparatory Materials:** Study guide, including exam content outline, list of suggested study references, and practice exam, available. **Examination Sites:** Exam given at sites in the U.S. and internationally. **Accredited By:** National Commission for Certifying Agencies. **Endorsed By:** American Dietetic Association; National Organization for Competency Assurance.

915

Specialist in Clinical Nutrition
American Board of Nutrition
    (ABN)
Univ. of Alabama at Birmingham
Dept. of Nutrition Sciences
1675 University Blvd., WEBB 234
Birmingham, AL 35294-3360
Phone: (205)975-8788
Fax: (205)934-7049

Recipient: Physicians involved in clinical nutrition. **Educational/Experience Requirements:** Must meet the following requirements: (1) Graduation from medical school or school of osteopathy; (2) Certification by medical board affiliated with American Board of Medical Specialties (ABMS); and (3) Either one year postgraduate training in clinical nutrition or two years postgraduate training in closely related ABMS approved specialty training program. Training program must include review of nutritional biochemistry and clinical experience with nutritional problems. Participation in nutrition surveys, research, teaching, and patient consultation recommended. **Certification Requirements:** Successful completion of both comprehensive exam and one specialty exam. Comprehensive exam covers: Alcohol and other substance abuse; Body composition, body weight, and energy; Cancer; Carbohydrates and fiber; Chemical additives; Development; Diabetes mellitus; Diet and allergy; Dietary goals and recommended dietary allowance; Drug-nutrient interactions; Eating disorders; Exercise and environmental stress; Fads and vegetarianism; Food contamination; Food processing; Gastrointestinal disease; Gastrointestinal tract; General aspects of nutrition; Geriatrics; Growth and development; Handicap conditions and rehabilitation; Hormones and nutritional regulation; Hunger and satiety; Hyperlipidemia and coronary artery disease; Hypertension; Inborn errors; Lipids; Metabolism; Minerals; Neurological diseases; Nutritional anemias; Nutritional assessment and support; Obesity; Other endocrine disorders; Pregnancy and lactation; Protein; Recommended dietary intake; Renal disease; Skeletal and connective tissue diseases; Stress, immunity, and AIDS; Trace materials; Vitamins; Water and acid-base balance; and World food supply and hunger. Specialty exams are: (1) Childhood Nutrition for the Pediatrician, covering: Anemia; Breastfeeding; Calorie-protein requirements; Failure to thrive; Hyperlipidemia; Long-term TPN/complications; Malabsorption; Neonatal nutrition; Nutritional assessment; and Obesity; (2) Adult Nutrition for the Internist or General Surgeon, covering: Aging; AIDS and immunology; Alcohol and liver disease; Anemias; Cancer; Diabetes; Gastrointestinal disease; Hospital malnutrition/assessment; Hyperlipidemia; Hypertension; Malabsorption; Obesity; and Osteoporosis; and (3) Mixed Pediatric and Adult Nutrition. **Preparatory Materials:** Handbook, including sample questions, provided. **Examination Frequency:** Annual. **Examination Type:** Case study; matching; multiple-choice; true or false. **Waiting Period to Receive Scores:** 60 days. **Fees:** $1000.

`916`

Specialist in Human Nutrition
American Board of Nutrition
  (ABN)
Univ. of Alabama at Birmingham
Dept. of Nutrition Sciences
1675 University Blvd., WEBB 234
Birmingham, AL 35294-3360
Phone: (205)975-8788
Fax: (205)934-7049

Recipient: Health care professionals involved in human nutrition. **Educational/Experience Requirements:** Must meet the following requirements: (1) Ph.D. degree or equivalent, with background in biological sciences and courses in principles of nutrition and supporting sciences, and medical and public applications of nutrition; and (2) Two years postdoctoral training and experience in human nutrition, including one year in clinical nutrition teaching and/or consultation. Participation in nutrition surveys or research are recommended. **Certification Requirements:** Successful completion of comprehensive exam and one specialty exam. Comprehensive exam covers: Alcohol and other substance abuse; Body compo-

sition, body weight and energy; Cancer; Carbohydrates and fiber; Chemical additives; Development; Diabetes mellitus; Diet and allergy; Dietary goals and recommended dietary allowance; Drug-nutrient interactions; Eating disorders; Exercise and environmental stress; Fads and vegetarianism; Food contamination; Food processing; Gastrointestinal disease; Gastrointestinal tract; General aspects of nutrition; Geriatrics; Growth and development; Handicap conditions and rehabilitation; Hormone and nutritional regulation; Hunger and satiety; Hyperlipidemia and coronary artery disease; Hypertension; Inborn errors; Lipids; Metabolism; Minerals; Neurological diseases; Nutritional anemias; Nutritional assessment and support; Obesity; Other endocrine disorders; Pregnancy and lactation; Protein; Recommended dietary intake; Renal disease; Skeletal and connective tissue diseases; Stress and immunity and AIDS; Trace materials; Vitamins; Water and acid-base balance; and World food supply and hunger. Specialty exams are: (1) Childhood Nutrition for the Pediatrician, covering: Anemia; Breastfeeding; Calorie-protein requirements; Failure to thrive; Hyperlipidemia; Long-term TPN/complications; Malabsorption; Neonatal nutrition; Nutritional assessment; and Obesity; (2) Adult Nutrition for the Internist or General Surgeon, covering: Aging; AIDS and immunology; Alcohol and liver disease; Anemias; Cancer; Diabetes; Gastrointestinal disease; Hospital malnutrition/assessment; Hyperlipidemia; Hypertension; Malabsorption; Obesity; and Osteoporosis; and (3) Mixed Pediatric and Adult Nutrition. **Preparatory Materials:** Handbook, including sample questions, provided. **Examination Frequency:** Annual. **Examination Type:** Case study; matching; multiple-choice; true or false. **Waiting Period to Receive Scores:** 60 days. **Fees:** $1000.

Hypnotists

`917`

Certified Clinical Hypnotherapist
American Council of Hypnotist
  Examiners (ACHE)
700 S. Central Ave.
Glendale, CA 91204
Phone: (818)242-1159
Fax: (818)247-9379
Gil Boyne, Exec.Dir.

Recipient: Clinical hypnotherapists. **Certification Requirements:** Must meet one of the following requirements: (1)

Hold Certified Hypnotherapist designation (see separate entry) and have 250 hours of instruction in hypnosis; or (2) 150 hours of instruction and current state licensure as psychiatrist, psychologist, or marriage, family, or child counselor. **Renewal:** Every two years. Recertification based on accumulation of 30 hours of continuing education. **Fees:** $125.

`918`

Certified Hypnotherapist
American Council of Hypnotist
  Examiners (ACHE)
700 S. Central Ave.
Glendale, CA 91204
Phone: (818)242-1159
Fax: (818)247-9379
Gil Boyne, Exec.Dir.

Recipient: Hypnotherapists. **Certification Requirements:** Must meet one of the following requirements: (1) Hold Certified Master Hypnotist designation (see separate entry) and have 200 hours of instruction in hypnosis; or (2) 100 hours of instruction in hypnosis and current state licensure as psychiatrist, psychologist, or marriage, family, or child counselor. **Renewal:** Every two years. Recertification based on accumulation of 30 hours of continuing education. **Fees:** $125.

`919`

Certified Hypnotherapist (C.Ht.)
International Medical and Dental
  Hypnotherapy Association
  (IMDHA)
4110 Edgeland, Ste. 800
Royal Oak, MI 48073
Phone: (810)549-5594
Fax: (810)549-5421
Toll Free: (800)257-5467
Anne H. Spencer Ph.D., Exec.Dir.

Recipient: Professional hypnotherapists serving the general public and health care community. **Number of Certified Individuals:** 500. **Educational/Experience Requirements:** Graduate from state licensed or approved hypnosis training school with minimum of 120 hours of hands-on education. **Membership:** Required. **Certification Requirements:** Successful completion of written and oral exams. **Renewal:** Every year. Recertification based on continuing education. **Preparatory Materials:** Training materials available. **Examination Frequency:** quarterly. **Examination Sites:** Exam given at IMDHA headquarters and approved schools throughout the U.S. and internationally. **Examination Type:** Essay;

multiple-choice. **Pass/Fail Rate:** 90% pass exam the first time. **Waiting Period to Receive Scores:** 30 days. **Fees:** $50.

920

Certified Master Hypnotist
American Council of Hypnotist
    Examiners (ACHE)
700 S. Central Ave.
Glendale, CA 91204
Phone: (818)242-1159
Fax: (818)247-9379
Gil Boyne, Exec.Dir.

Recipient: Hypnotists. **Educational/ Experience Requirements:** Must meet the following requirements: (1) 150 hours of instruction in hypnosis; and (2) City business license, if necessary. **Certification Requirements:** Successful completion of exam. Exam may be waived for candidates with four consecutive years of experience. **Renewal:** Every two years. Recertification based on accumulation of 30 hours of continuing education. **Fees:** $125.

921

Clinical Associate in Hypnotherapy
Institute for Research in Hypnosis
    and Psychotherapy (IRHP)
1991 Broadway, Apt. 18B
New York, NY 10023
Phone: (212)874-5290
Fax: (914)238-1422
Dr. Milton V. Kline, Dir.

Recipient: Health care professionals in mental health medicine and allied health care professions. **Number of Certified Individuals:** 100. **Educational/Experience Requirements:** Master's degree or higher in related field and state license or certification. **Membership:** Required. **Certification Requirements:** Successful completion of application. **Renewal:** Every year. **Preparatory Materials:** none. **Fees:** $100.

922

**Diplomate in Clinical Hypnosis of
    the American Board of
    Psychological Hypnosis**
American Board of Psychological
    Hypnosis (ABPH)
c/o Dr. Samuel M. Migdole, APBH
23 Broadway
Beverly, MA 01915
Phone: (508)922-2280
Fax: (508)927-1758
Dr. Samuel M. Migdole APBH,
    Sec.

Recipient: Licensed psychologists specializing in clinical hypnosis. **Educational/Experience Requirements:** Must meet the following requirements: (1) Doctorate in psychology; and (2) Five years postdoctoral experience. **Membership:** Required. **Certification Requirements:** Must meet the following requirements: (1) Submission of work sample; and (2) Successful completion of oral exam. Exam covers theory, practice, and professional issues in psychology and hypnosis. **Renewal:** none. **Preparatory Materials:** Reading list provided. **Examination Frequency:** Three times per year. **Examination Sites:** Exam given at national meetings of American Psychological Association, American Society of Clinical Hypnosis, and Society of Clinical and Experimental Hypnosis, or by arrangement with proctor. **Pass/Fail Rate:** 60% pass exam the first time. **Waiting Period to Receive Scores:** Immediately-three months. **Re-examination:** There is no time limit to retake exam. **Fees:** $350.

923

**Diplomate in Experimental
    Hypnosis of the American Board
    of Psychological Hypnosis**
American Board of Psychological
    Hypnosis (ABPH)
c/o Dr. Samuel M. Migdole, APBH
23 Broadway
Beverly, MA 01915
Phone: (508)922-2280
Fax: (508)927-1758
Dr. Samuel M. Migdole APBH,
    Sec.

Recipient: Licensed psychologists specializing in experimental hypnosis. **Educational/Experience Requirements:** Must meet the following requirements: (1) Doctorate in psychology; and (2) Five years postdoctoral experience. **Membership:** Required. **Certification Requirements:** Must meet the following requirements: (1) Submission of work sample; and (2) Successful completion of oral exam. Exam covers theory, practice, and professional issues in psychology and hypnosis. **Renewal:** none. **Preparatory Materials:** Reading list provided. **Examination Frequency:** Three times per year. **Examination Sites:** Exam given at national meetings of American Psychological Association, American Society of Clinical Hypnosis, and Society of Clinical and Experimental Hypnosis, or by arrangement with proctor. **Pass/Fail Rate:** 60% pass exam the first time. **Waiting Period to Receive Scores:** Immediately-three months. **Re-examination:** There is no time limit to retake exam. **Fees:** $350.

Music Therapists

924

**Music Therapist - Board Certified
    (MT-BC)**
Certification Board for Music
    Therapists (CBMT)
1407 Huguenot Rd.
Midlothian, VA 23113-2644
Phone: (804)379-9497
Toll Free: (800)765-CBMT

Recipient: Music therapists. **Educational/Experience Requirements:** Academic and clinical training in approved music therapy curriculum. **Certification Requirements:** Successful completion of exam. Exam covers: (1) Music Theory/Skills, including: Applying music skills in clinical situations; and Applying music theory in clinical situations; (2) Assessment - Individual and Group, including: Interpreting data and making recommendations; and Obtaining data for assessment; (3) Treatment, including: Evaluation/documentation; Implementation; Planning; and Termination; and (4) Professional Responsibilities. **Renewal:** Every five years. Recertification based on either successful completion of exam or accumulation of 100 Continuing Music Therapy Education (CMTE) credits through approved educational activities, graduate coursework, self-study activities, professional activities, and short event activities. **Examination Frequency:** Annual - always November. **Examination Sites:** Exam given at sites throughout the U.S. **Examination Type:** Multiple-choice. **Waiting Period to Receive Scores:** Four weeks. **Fees:** $140. **Accredited By:** National Commission for Certifying Agencies. **Endorsed By:** American Association for Music Therapy; National Association for Music Therapy; National Organization for Competency Assurance.

Occupational Therapists

925

**Certified Occupational Therapy
    Assistant (COTA)**
American Occupational Therapy
    Certification Board (AOTCB)
Four Research Pl., Ste. 160
Rockville, MD 20850-3226
Phone: (301)990-7979
Fax: (301)869-8492

Recipient: Occupational therapy assistants. **Educational/Experience Require-**

ments: Successful completion of occupational therapy assistant program accredited by Accreditation Council for Occupational Therapy Education (see separate entry). Candidates of foreign programs are not eligible for exam. **Certification Requirements:** Successful completion of exam. Exam consists of following sections: Collect Data Regarding Individual's Occupational Performance; Develop Treatment Plan; Implement Treatment Plan; Evaluate Treatment Plan; Develop Discharge Plan; Support Service Management; and Promote Professional Practice. **Preparatory Materials:** *Uniform Terminology for Occupational Therapy,* Second Edition (reference). *Candidate Handbook,* including list of accredited programs, sample questions, and exam content outlines, and study guide available. **Examination Frequency:** semiannual - always January and July. **Examination Sites:** Exam given at sites throughout the U.S. and Canada and internationally. **Examination Type:** Multiple-choice. **Waiting Period to Receive Scores:** Four-five weeks. **Re-examination:** There is no limit on how many times exam may be retaken. **Fees:** $250. **Endorsed By:** American Occupational Therapy Association; National Organization for Competency Assurance.

▮926▮

Occupational Therapist, Registered (OTR)

American Occupational Therapy Certification Board (AOTCB)
Four Research Pl., Ste. 160
Rockville, MD 20850-3226
Phone: (301)990-7979
Fax: (301)869-8492

Recipient: Occupational therapists. **Educational/Experience Requirements:** Must meet following requirements: (1) Bachelor's or master's degree or post-baccalaureate certificate in occupational therapy; and (2) Successful completion of occupational therapy assistant program accredited by Accreditation Council for Occupational Therapy Education (see separate entry). **Certification Requirements:** Successful completion of exam. Exam consists of following sections: Assess Individual's Occupational Performance; Develop Treatment Plan; Implement Treatment Plan; Evaluate Treatment Plan; Develop Discharge Plan; Organize and Manage Services; and Promote Professional Practice. **Preparatory Materials:** *Candidate Handbook,* including list of accredited programs and exam content outline, sample questions, and study guide available. **Examination**

Frequency: semiannual - always January and July. **Examination Sites:** Exam given at sites throughout the U.S. and Canada and internationally. **Examination Type:** Multiple-choice. **Waiting Period to Receive Scores:** Four-five weeks. **Re-examination:** There is no limit on how many times exam can be retaken. **Fees:** $250. **Endorsed By:** American Occupational Therapy Association; National Organization for Competency Assurance.

▮927▮

Pediatric Occupational Therapy Board Certified in Pediatrics

American Occupational Therapy Association (AOTA)
1383 Piccard Dr.
PO Box 1725
Rockville, MD 20849-1725
Phone: (301)652-2682
Fax: (301)652-7711
Toll Free: (800)SAY-AOTA
Dr. Stephanie Hoover OTR, Assoc. Exec.Dir.

Recipient: Occupational therapists specializing in pediatrics. **Number of Certified Individuals:** 234. **Educational/Experience Requirements:** Five years experience in pediatric practice and documentation of professional development activities. **Membership:** Not required. **Certification Requirements:** Successful completion of exam. **Renewal:** Every five years. Recertification based on experience and professional development activities. **Preparatory Materials:** Candidate handbook, including exam content outline, sample questions, and study references, provided. Study guide available. **Examination Frequency:** Annual. **Examination Sites:** Exam given at annual conference and at four-five sites in the U.S. **Examination Type:** Multiple-choice. **Waiting Period to Receive Scores:** Six-eight weeks. **Re-examination:** Must wait one year to retake exam. **Fees:** $310 (members); $460 (nonmembers).

Oriental Medicine Practitioners

▮928▮

Diplomate in Acupuncture

National Commission for the Certification of Acupuncturists (NCCA)
1424 16th St., NW, Ste. 501
Washington, DC 20036
Phone: (202)232-1404
Fax: (202)462-6157

Recipient: Acupuncturists. **Number of Certified Individuals:** 4700. **Educational/Experience Requirements:** Must meet one of the following requirements: (1) Successful completion of acupuncture program and three years experience, including minimum of 1350 hours of acupuncture education and 500 clinic hours; (2) Successful completion of apprenticeship of at least 4000 contact hours in three to six year period with preceptor who has five years experience and practice that includes use of acupuncture with minimum of 100 different patients and has 500 patient visits per year during apprenticeship; (3) Four years experience in practice that includes use of acupuncture with minimum of 100 different patients and has 500 patient visits per year. Practice must be at least 70 percent general health care; (4) Accumulation of 40 points through combination of education, apprenticeships, and experience; or (5) Enrollment in third or fourth year of acupuncture program with successful completion of 1000 hours of schooling in no less than 18 academic months, including 250 clinic hours. **Certification Requirements:** Successful completion of CCAOM CNT course and written and practical exams. **Preparatory Materials:** Candidate handbook provided. **Examination Frequency:** semiannual - always spring and fall. **Examination Sites:** Exam given in San Francisco, CA, in the spring, and Ryebrook, NY, in the fall. **Fees:** $695. **Accredited By:** National Commission for Certifying Agencies. **Endorsed By:** National Organization for Competency Assurance.

▮929▮

Diplomate of Chinese Herbology

National Commission for the Certification of Acupuncturists (NCCA)
1424 16th St., NW, Ste. 501
Washington, DC 20036
Phone: (202)232-1404
Fax: (202)462-6157

Recipient: Professionals involved in Chinese herbology. **Number of Certified Individuals:** 200. **Educational/Experience Requirements:** Must meet one of the following requirements: (1) Successful completion of Oriental medicine program with three comprehensive curriculums consisting of 1800 hours of Oriental medicine education, including 500 clinic hours and 300 hours of Chinese herbology; (2) Successful completion of apprenticeship of 4000 contact hours in three to six year period. Twenty-five percent of training must be in combined apprenticeships of Chinese herbology and another Oriental medicine discipline; (3) Licensure, certification, or registration in any state in the U.S. to practice Chinese herbology that is based on eligibility requirements equivalent to NCCA standards and requires successful completion of exam which includes Chinese herbology at time of licensure; (4) Four years experience in practice that includes use of Chinese herbology with 100 different patients and has 500 patient visits per year; or (5) Certification, licensure, or successful completion of program in acupuncture and accumulation of 30 points through education, experience, and apprenticeships in Chinese herbology. **Certification Requirements:** Successful completion of exam. **Preparatory Materials:** Candidate handbook provided. **Examination Frequency:** semiannual - always spring and fall. **Examination Sites:** Exam given in San Francisco, CA, in the spring, and Ryebrook, NY, in the fall. **Fees:** $545. **Accredited By:** National Commission for Certifying Agencies. **Endorsed By:** National Organization for Competency Assurance.

Orthoptists

931 930

Certified Orthoptist
American Orthoptic Council (AOC)
3914 Nakoma Rd.
Madison, WI 53711
Phone: (608)233-5383
Fax: (608)263-7694

Recipient: Orthoptists. **Educational/Experience Requirements:** Successful completion of two years of orthoptic training. **Certification Requirements:** Successful completion of written and oral exams. **Renewal:** Every year. Recertification based on accumulation of continuing education through attendance at conferences, teaching or attending workshops, presentations, authoring articles, and self study activities. **Examination Frequency:**

Annual - always June (written) and fall (oral). **Examination Sites:** Written exam given at sites throughout the U.S. and oral exam given at one site in the U.S. **Endorsed By:** American Academy of Ophthalmology; American Association of Certified Orthoptists; American Association for Pediatric Ophthalmology and Strabismus; American Ophthalmological Society; Canadian Orthoptic Council.

Pharmacists

931

Board Certified Nuclear Pharmacist (BCNP)
Board of Pharmaceutical Specialties (BPS)
2215 Constitution Ave., NW
Washington, DC 20037-2985
Phone: (202)429-7591
Fax: (202)783-2351
Carla A. Hillyer, Adm.Asst.

Recipient: Pharmacists specializing in nuclear pharmacy. **Number of Certified Individuals:** 271. **Educational/Experience Requirements:** Must meet the following requirements: (1) Degree in pharmacy from program accredited by American Council on Pharmaceutical Education (see separate entry); (2) Current license to practice pharmacy; and (3) 4000 hours experience. Credit can be earned through education (maximum of 2000 hours) and training/practice, including residency and internships (maximum of 4000 hours). **Certification Requirements:** Successful completion of exam. Exam covers: Basic radiation protection procedures; Compounding; Consultation and education; Dispensing; Distribution; Procurement; and Routine quality control. **Renewal:** Every seven years. Recertification based on submission of self-evaluation and documentation of practice, continuing education, and successful completion of exam. **Preparatory Materials:** *Selected Bibliography on Nuclear Pharmacy Practice* (reference). *Candidate's Guide,* including exam content outline, list of reference materials, and sample questions, provided. **Examination Frequency:** Annual. **Examination Sites:** Exam given in conjunction with annual meeting. **Examination Type:** Multiple-choice. **Waiting Period to Receive Scores:** 90 days. **Re-examination:** May retake exam twice. Fee to retake exam is $275. **Fees:** $550. **Endorsed By:** American Pharmaceutical Association.

932

Board Certified Nutrition Support Pharmacist (BCNSP)
Board of Pharmaceutical Specialties (BPS)
2215 Constitution Ave., NW
Washington, DC 20037-2985
Phone: (202)429-7591
Fax: (202)783-2351
Carla A. Hillyer, Adm.Asst.

Recipient: Pharmacists specializing in nutrition support pharmacy. **Number of Certified Individuals:** 304. **Educational/Experience Requirements:** Must have degree in pharmacy from program accredited by American Council on Pharmaceutical Education (see separate entry), current license to practice pharmacy, and one of the following: (1) Three years experience; (2) One year of experience and successful completion of specialty residency in nutrition support pharmacy; or (3) One year of experience and successful completion of nutrition support fellowship. No additional year of experience required for candidates who successfully complete residency and fellowship. Experience must include substantial time spent in nutrition support pharmacy. Candidates who do not meet these requirements may qualify for exemption. **Certification Requirements:** Successful completion of exam. Exam covers the following domains: (1) Provision of Individualized Nutrition Support Care to Patients, including: Assessment; Development of therapeutic plan; Implementation; and Monitoring and management; (2) Management of Nutrition Support Services; and (3) Advancement of Nutrition Support Pharmacy Practice. **Renewal:** Every seven years. Recertification based on successful completion of exam, accumulation of three continuing education units (CEUs), maintenance of licensure, and documentation of practice. **Preparatory Materials:** *Candidate's Guide,* including exam content outline, list of reference materials, and sample questions, provided. Review courses available. **Examination Frequency:** Annual. **Examination Sites:** Exam given at two U.S. sites. **Examination Type:** Multiple-choice. **Waiting Period to Receive Scores:** 60 days. **Re-examination:** May retake exam twice. Fee to retake exam is $275. **Fees:** $550. **Endorsed By:** American Pharmaceutical Association.

933

Board Certified Pharmacotherapy Specialist (BCPS)

Board of Pharmaceutical Specialties (BPS)
2215 Constitution Ave., NW
Washington, DC 20037-2985
Phone: (202)429-7591
Fax: (202)783-2351
Carla A. Hillyer, Adm.Asst.

Recipient: Pharmacists specializing in pharmacotherapy. **Number of Certified Individuals:** 692. **Educational/ Experience Requirements:** Must have degree in pharmacy from program accredited by American Council on Pharmaceutical Education (see separate entry), current license to practice pharmacy, and successful completion of one of the following: (1) Pharmacy residency program with substantial component of patient-care activities in pharmacotherapy; (2) Fellowship program; or (3) Five years experience, with substantial component of patient-care activities in pharmacotherapy. Candidates who do not meet these requirements may qualify for exemption. **Certification Requirements:** Successful completion of exam. Exam covers: Collecting and interpreting data to design, recommend, implement, monitor, and modify patient-specific pharmacotherapy in collaboration with other health care professionals to optimize drug therapy; Designing, recommending, implementing, monitoring, and modifying system specific policies and procedures in collaboration with other professionals/administrators to optimize health care; and Interpreting, generating, and disseminating knowledge in pharmacotherapy. Exam will also cover patient-care problems in the following areas: Age-specific problems; Bone and joint; Cardiovascular; Dermatologic; Endocrine and exocrine; Eyes, ears, nose, and throat; Fluid and electrolyte/metabolic; Gastrointestinal; Genitourinary; Hematologic; Immunologic; Infectious diseases; Multi-system diseases (critical care, sepsis/shock, and toxicology); Neurological; Obstetrics/gynecology; Oncology; Perinatology; Psychiatric; Renal; and Respiratory. **Renewal:** Every seven years. Recertification based on either successful completion of exam or accumulation of 120 hours of continuing education. **Preparatory Materials:** *Candidate's Guide,* including exam content outline, list of reference materials, and sample questions, provided. Review courses also available. **Examination Frequency:** Annual. **Examination Sites:** Exam given at regional sites in the U.S. **Examination Type:** Multiple-choice. **Waiting Period to Receive Scores:** 60-90 days. **Re-**examination: May retake exam twice. Fee to retake exam is $275. **Fees:** $550. **Endorsed By:** American Pharmaceutical Association.

934

Board Certified Psychiatric Pharmacist

Board of Pharmaceutical Specialties (BPS)
2215 Constitution Ave., NW
Washington, DC 20037-2985
Phone: (202)429-7591
Fax: (202)783-2351
Carla A. Hillyer, Adm.Asst.

Recipient: Pharmacists specializing in psychiatric pharmacy. **Certification Requirements:** Successful completion of exam. **Renewal:** Every seven years. **Endorsed By:** American Pharmaceutical Association.

Physical Therapists

935

Nationally Certified in Therapeutic Massage and Bodywork (NCTMB)

National Certification Board for Therapeutic Massage and Bodywork (NCBTMB)
1735 N. Lynn St., Ste. 950
Arlington, VA 22209
Phone: (703)524-9563
Toll Free: (800)296-0664

Recipient: Professionals involved with traditional European, contemporary western, structural integration/ functional integration/movement integration, Oriental, energetic, and eclectic therapeutic massage and bodywork. **Educational/Experience Requirements:** Must earn 50 total points through: (1) Training from formal schools, seminars, workshops, training programs, and apprenticeships (ten points each); and (2) Years of experience (seven and one-half points per year; maximum of four years). Each year defined as at least 400 sessions/treatments performing massage and/or bodywork. **Certification Requirements:** Successful completion of exam. Exam covers: (1) Human Anatomy, Physiology, and Kinesiology, including: Cardiovascular; Digestive; Efficient and safe movement patterns; Endocrine; Lymphatic; Major organs; Musculoskeletal; Nervous; Origins, insertions, and actions of muscles; Relationship between anatomy and physiology; Respiratory; Skin/integumentary; and Urogenital; (2) Clinical Pathology and Recognition of Various Conditions, including: Circulatory conditions; Contraindications; Emotional states; Gastrointestinal disorders; Healing mechanisms of the body as they relate to various conditions; Hygiene and sanitation in massage therapy/bodywork; Injuries; Joint disorders; Medical terminology; Muscle/fascia conditions; Neurological disorders; Respiratory conditions; Signs and symptoms of disease; Skeletal dysfunction; and Skin conditions; (3) Massage/Bodywork Theory, Assessment, and Practice, including: Basic theory of massage/bodywork and massage/ bodywork hand movements; Client positioning, support draping, and turning; Endangerment sites; Interview techniques; Joint mobilization; Observation techniques; Palpation; Physiological rationale of massage/bodywork; Range of motion; and Technical descriptions of massage/bodywork; (4) Adjunct Techniques and Methods, including: Exercise methods; Hydrotherapy; and Stress management/relaxation techniques; and (5) Business Practices and Professionalism, including: Business and professional standards and ethical guidelines; CPR/ standard first aid; Scope of practice of healthcare disciplines outside massage therapy/bodywork for purposes of referral; and Scope of practice of other disciplines within massage therapy/bodywork for purposes of referral. **Renewal:** Every four years. Recertification based on either successful completion of exam or accumulation of 50 hours of continuing education. **Preparatory Materials:** Handbook, including exam content outline, sample questions, and list of suggested references, provided. **Examination Frequency:** semiannual. **Examination Sites:** Exam given at sites throughout the U.S. **Examination Type:** Multiple-choice. **Waiting Period to Receive Scores:** Six weeks. **Re-examination:** There is a $150 fee to retake exam. **Fees:** $150. **Accredited By:** National Commission for Certifying Agencies. **Endorsed By:** National Organization for Competency Assurance.

936

Physical Therapist, Cardiopulmonary Certified Specialist (PT, CCS)

American Board of Physical Therapy Specialties (ABPTS)
1111 N. Fairfax St.
Alexandria, VA 22314-1488
Phone: (703)706-3150
Fax: (703)684-7343

Toll Free: (800)999-APTA
Patrima L. Tice, Dir.

Recipient: Physical therapists specializing in cardiopulmonary physical therapy. **Number of Certified Individuals:** 45. **Educational/Experience Requirements:** Must meet the following requirements: (1) Current licensure to practice physical therapy; (2) Current Advanced Cardiac Life Support certification from American Heart Association; (3) 6240 hours of clinical practice in specialty area in last ten years, with 4160 hours of clinical practice experience in direct patient care in cardiopulmonary physical therapy; and (4) Submission of documentation of participation in research process directly related to specialty area. Clinical practice includes teaching, research, consultation, and administrative duties, in addition to patient care. Patient care experience includes evaluation and treatment, documentation, travel en route to patient care, education, and rounds/discharge planning conferences, and should involve patients with primary disease process involving cardiopulmonary system in both acute and rehabilitation settings. **Membership:** mnr **Certification Requirements:** Successful completion of exam. **Renewal:** Every ten years. Recertification based on current licensure, minimum of four hours clinical practice per week in specialty area, and either successful completion of exam or documentation of continued competence and professional development. **Preparatory Materials:** *Physical Therapy Advanced Clinical Competencies: Cardiopulmonary* and *Cardiopulmonary Patient Care Competency* (references). Application booklet, including exam content outline, provided. Reference materials, review courses, and study groups available. **Examination Frequency:** Annual. **Examination Sites:** Exam given at sites throughout the U.S. **Examination Type:** Multiple-choice. **Re-examination:** May retake exam four times. Fees to retake exam are: $250 (specialty section member); $265 (American Physical Therapy Association member); $310 (nonmembers). **Fees:** $960 (specialty section member); $990 (American Physical Therapy Association member); $1325 (nonmembers). **Endorsed By:** American Physical Therapy Association.

937

Physical Therapist, Clinical Electrophysiology Certified Specialist (PT, CECS)

American Board of Physical
Therapy Specialties (ABPTS)
1111 N. Fairfax St.
Alexandria, VA 22314-1488
Phone: (703)706-3150
Fax: (703)684-7343
Toll Free: (800)999-APTA
Patrima L. Tice, Dir.

Recipient: Physical therapists specializing in clinical electrophysiology. **Number of Certified Individuals:** 51. **Educational/Experience Requirements:** Must meet the following requirements: (1) Current licensure to practice physical therapy; (2) 6240 hours of direct patient care experience in specialty area in last ten years, with 2080 hours in area of electrophysiologic testing in last three years and 400 hours in last year; (3) Submission of evidence of supervised clinical education in electrophysiologic testing; and (4) Submission of case reports completed in last three years, including cases in required specialty areas. Patient care experience includes evaluation and treatment, documentation, travel en route to patient care, education, and rounds/discharge planning conferences.**Membership:** mnr **Certification Requirements:** Successful completion of exam. **Renewal:** Every ten years. Recertification based on current licensure, minimum of four hours clinical practice per week in specialty area, and either successful completion of exam or documentation of continued competence and professional development. **Preparatory Materials:** *Description of Advanced Clinical Practice: Clinical Electrophysiologic Physical Therapy* (reference). Application booklet, including exam content outline, provided. Reference materials, review courses, and study groups available. **Examination Frequency:** Annual. **Examination Sites:** Exam given at sites throughout the U.S. **Examination Type:** Multiple-choice. **Re-examination:** May retake exam four times. Fees to retake exam are: $250 (specialty section member); $265 (American Physical Therapy Association member); $310 (nonmembers). **Fees:** $960 (specialty section member); $990 (American Physical Therapy Association member); $1325 (nonmembers). **Endorsed By:** American Physical Therapy Association.

938

Physical Therapist, Geriatrics Certified Specialist (PT, GCS)

American Board of Physical
Therapy Specialties (ABPTS)
1111 N. Fairfax St.
Alexandria, VA 22314-1488
Phone: (703)706-3150
Fax: (703)684-7343
Toll Free: (800)999-APTA
Patrima L. Tice, Dir.

Recipient: Physical therapists specializing in geriatric physical therapy. **Number of Certified Individuals:** 75. **Educational/Experience Requirements:** Must meet the following requirements: (1) Current licensure to practice physical therapy; and (2) Four years (8320 hours) experience after successful completion of professional physical therapy education, with 6240 hours of clinical practice in specialty area in last ten years and 4160 hours of this practice in direct patient care in geriatric physical therapy in last six years. Clinical practice includes teaching, research, consultation, and administrative duties, in addition to patient care. Patient care experience includes evaluation and treatment, documentation, travel en route to patient care, education, and rounds/discharge planning conferences, and should be in at least two of the following areas of practice: Acute care; Home health care; Long-term care; Outpatient; Short-term rehabilitation; Subacute rehabilitation; and Wellness center. **Membership:** mnr **Certification Requirements:** Successful completion of exam. **Renewal:** Every ten years. Recertification based on current licensure, minimum of four hours clinical practice per week in specialty area, and either successful completion of exam or documentation of continued competence and professional development. **Preparatory Materials:** *Geriatric Physical Therapy Specialty* and *Geriatric Physical Therapy Specialty Competencies* (references). Application booklet, including exam content outline, provided. Reference materials, review courses, and study groups available. **Examination Frequency:** Annual. **Examination Sites:** Exam given at sites throughout the U.S. **Examination Type:** Multiple-choice. **Re-examination:** May retake exam four times. Fees to retake exam are: $250 (specialty section member); $265 (American Physical Therapy Association member); $310 (nonmembers). **Fees:** $960 (specialty section member); $990 (American Physical Therapy Association member); $1325 (nonmembers). **Endorsed By:** American Physical Therapy Association.

939

Physical Therapist, Neurology Certified Specialist (PT, NCS)

American Board of Physical
Therapy Specialties (ABPTS)
1111 N. Fairfax St.
Alexandria, VA 22314-1488
Phone: (703)706-3150
Fax: (703)684-7343
Toll Free: (800)999-APTA
Patrima L. Tice, Dir.

Recipient: Physical therapists specializing in neurological physical therapy. **Number of Certified Individuals:** 83. **Educational/Experience Requirements:** Must meet the following requirements: (1) Current licensure to practice physical therapy; and (2) 4160 hours of clinical practice experience in direct patient care of patients with neurologic deficit in last ten years, with 1248 of these hours in last three years. **Membership:** mnr **Certification Requirements:** Successful completion of exam. **Renewal:** Every ten years. Recertification based on current licensure, minimum of four hours of clinical practice per week in specialty area, and either successful completion of exam or documentation of continued competence and professional development. **Preparatory Materials:** *Description of Advanced Clinical Practice: Neurological Physical Therapy* (reference). Application booklet, including exam content outline, provided. Reference materials, review courses, and study groups available. **Examination Frequency:** Annual. **Examination Sites:** Exam given at sites throughout the U.S. **Examination Type:** Multiple-choice. **Re-examination:** May retake exam four times. Fees to retake exam are: $250 (specialty section member); $265 (American Physical Therapy Association member); $310 (nonmembers). **Fees:** $960 (specialty section member); $990 (American Physical Therapy Association member); $1325 (nonmembers). **Endorsed By:** American Physical Therapy Association.

940

Physical Therapist, Orthopaedics Certified Specialist (PT, OCS)

American Board of Physical
Therapy Specialties (ABPTS)
1111 N. Fairfax St.
Alexandria, VA 22314-1488
Phone: (703)706-3150
Fax: (703)684-7343
Toll Free: (800)999-APTA
Patrima L. Tice, Dir.

Recipient: Physical therapists specializ-

ing in orthopaedic physical therapy. **Number of Certified Individuals:** 485. **Educational/Experience Requirements:** Must meet the following requirements: (1) Current licensure to practice physical therapy; and (2) Five years (10,400 hours) experience in physical therapy after successful completion of professional physical therapy education, with three years (6240 hours) of direct patient care in orthopaedic physical therapy in last six years. Patient care experience includes evaluation and treatment, documentation, travel en route to patient care, education, and rounds/discharge planning conferences. **Membership:** mnr **Certification Requirements:** Successful completion of exam. **Renewal:** Every ten years. Recertification based on current licensure, minimum of four hours of clinical practice per week in specialty area, and either successful completion of exam or documentation of continued competence and professional development. **Preparatory Materials:** *Description of Advanced Clinical Practice: Orthopaedic Physical Therapy* (reference). Application booklet, including exam content outline, provided. Reference materials, review courses, and study groups available. **Examination Frequency:** Annual. **Examination Sites:** Exam given at sites throughout the U.S. **Examination Type:** Multiple-choice. **Re-examination:** May retake exam four times. Fees to retake exam are: $250 (specialty section member); $265 (American Physical Therapy Association member); $310 (nonmembers). **Fees:** $960 (specialty section member); $990 (American Physical Therapy Association member); $1325 (nonmembers). **Endorsed By:** American Physical Therapy Association.

941

Physical Therapist, Pediatrics Certified Specialist (PT, PCS)

American Board of Physical
Therapy Specialties (ABPTS)
1111 N. Fairfax St.
Alexandria, VA 22314-1488
Phone: (703)706-3150
Fax: (703)684-7343
Toll Free: (800)999-APTA
Patrima L. Tice, Dir.

Recipient: Physical therapists specializing in pediatric physical therapy. **Number of Certified Individuals:** 144. **Educational/Experience Requirements:** Must meet the following requirements: (1) Current licensure to practice physical therapy; and (2) 6240 hours of clinical practice in specialty area in last ten years, with 4160 hours of these hours in direct patient care and at least 1248 hours in

last three years. Clinical practice includes teaching, research, consultation, and administrative duties, in addition to patient care. Patient care experience includes evaluation and treatment, documentation, travel en route to patient care, education, and rounds/discharge planning conferences. **Membership:** mnr **Certification Requirements:** Successful completion of exam. **Renewal:** Every ten years. Recertification based on current licensure, minimum of four hours of clinical practice per week in specialty area, and either successful completion of exam or documentation of continued competence and professional development. **Preparatory Materials:** *Description of Advanced Clinical Practice: Pediatric Physical Therapy* (reference). Application booklet, including exam content outline, provided. Reference materials, review courses, and study groups available. **Examination Frequency:** Annual. **Examination Sites:** Exam given at sites throughout the U.S. **Examination Type:** Multiple-choice. **Re-examination:** May retake exam four times. Fees to retake exam are: $250 (specialty section member); $265 (American Physical Therapy Association member); $310 (nonmembers). **Fees:** $960 (specialty section member); $990 (American Physical Therapy Association member); $1325 (nonmembers). **Endorsed By:** American Physical Therapy Association.

942

Physical Therapist, Sports Certified Specialist (PT, SCS)

American Board of Physical
Therapy Specialties (ABPTS)
1111 N. Fairfax St.
Alexandria, VA 22314-1488
Phone: (703)706-3150
Fax: (703)684-7343
Toll Free: (800)999-APTA
Patrima L. Tice, Dir.

Recipient: Physical therapists specializing in sports-related physical therapy. **Number of Certified Individuals:** 148. **Educational/Experience Requirements:** Must meet the following requirements: (1) Current licensure to practice physical therapy; (2) Current certification in CPR Level B by American Heart Association or American Red Cross; (3) Either successful completion of American Red Cross Emergency Responder Course or equivalent, current or past certification (within last six years) as Emergency Medical Technician (EMT) or paramedic, or certification as Certified Athletic Trainer (C.A.T.) (see separate entry) by National Athletic Trainers Association; and (4) Five years (10,400 hours) experience after successful completion of professional physical therapy education, with 6240 hours of direct patient care in sports physical therapy in last six years. Patient care experience includes evaluation and treatment, documentation, travel en route to patient care, education, and rounds/discharge planning conferences, and must include patients with primary processes involving sports activity in both acute and rehabilitation settings. **Membership:** mnr **Certification Requirements:** Successful completion of exam. **Renewal:** Every ten years. Recertification based on current licensure, minimum of four hours of clinical practice per week in specialty area, and either successful completion of exam or documentation of continued competence and professional development. **Preparatory Materials:** *Description of Advanced Clinical Practice: Sports Physical Therapy* (reference). Application booklet, including exam content outline, provided. Reference materials, review courses, and study groups available. **Examination Frequency:** Annual. **Examination Sites:** Exam given at sites throughout the U.S. **Examination Type:** Multiple-choice. **Reexamination:** May retake exam four times. Fees to retake exam are: $250 (specialty section member); $265 (American Physical Therapy Association member); $310 (nonmembers). **Fees:** $960 (specialty section member); $990 (American Physical Therapy Association member); $1325 (nonmembers). **Endorsed By:** American Physical Therapy Association.

Physician Assistants

Physician Assistant - Certified (PA-C)
National Commission on
   Certification of Physician
   Assistants (NCCPA)
2845 Henderson Mill Rd., NE
Atlanta, GA 30341
Phone: (404)493-9100
David L. Glazer, Exec. VP

Recipient: Physician assistants. **Educational/Experience Requirements:** Successful completion of physician assistant or surgical assistant program accredited by Commission on Accreditation of Allied Health Education Programs (see separate entry) or its predecessor organization. **Certification Requirements:** Successful completion of three-part exam. Part one covers general practice, part two covers clinical skills, and part three covers either primary care or surgery. Certi-

fication required by 48 states and the District of Columbia. **Renewal:** Recertification required. **Examination Frequency:** Annual. **Examination Sites:** Exam given at sites throughout the U.S. and in Germany and South Korea. **Examination Type:** Multiple-choice. **Waiting Period to Receive Scores:** Three months. **Reexamination:** Must retake entire exam. **Fees:** $345. **Endorsed By:** American Academy of Family Physicians; American Academy of Pediatrics; American Academy of Physician Assistants; American College of Physicians; American College of Surgeons; American Hospital Association; American Medical Association; Association of American Medical Colleges; Association of Physician Assistant Programs; Federation of State Medical Boards of the U.S.; National Medical Association; U.S. Department of Defense.

Urology Physician's Assistant
American Board of Urologic Allied
   Health Professionals (ABUAHP)
1391 Delta Corners, SW
Lawrenceville, GA 30245

Recipient: Physician assistants working in the field of urology. **Educational/Experience Requirements:** Must meet one of the following requirements: (1) Successful completion of approved physician's assistant or registered nurse program and current licensure as physician's assistant; or (2) Successful completion of National Commission on Certification of Physician's Assistants' exam (see separate entry), current licensure, and one year of experience. **Membership:** Not required. **Certification Requirements:** Successful completion of written and oral exams. Exams covers: Anatomy; Catherization techniques; Concepts of sterilization and disinfection; Laboratory values; Physiology; Urine collection; X-ray procedures; and Other related procedures. **Preparatory Materials:** *Standards of Urologic Nursing* (reference). Study guide, including sample questions, list of required areas of study, and glossary of terms, and study courses, available. Curriculum guide being developed. **Examination Frequency:** Two times per year - usually April and May. **Examination Sites:** Exams given at annual assembly and at sites throughout the U.S. **Examination Type:** Multiple-choice. **Waiting Period to Receive Scores:** Six weeks. **Fees:** $175 (members); $235 (nonmembers). **Endorsed By:** American Urological Association Allied.

Practical Nurses

Certified Gastroenterology Licensed Vocational/Practical Nurse (CGN)
Certifying Board of
   Gastroenterology Nurses and
   Associates (CBGNA)
720 Light St.
Baltimore, MD 21230
Phone: (410)752-1808
Fax: (410)752-8295

Recipient: Licensed vocational and practical nurses specializing in gastroenterology and endoscopic procedures. **Educational/Experience Requirements:** Two years (4000 hours) experience within last five years in clinical, supervisory, or administrative capacities in institutional or private practice settings. **Membership:** Not required. **Certification Requirements:** Successful completion of exam. Exam covers: Education of the patient, family, and public healthcare professionals within the specialty; Patient care management; and Professional practice. **Renewal:** Every five years. Recertification based on either successful completion of exam or accumulation of 100 hours of continuing education through gastroenterology/endoscopy nursing seminars and workshops (minimum of 80 hours), other nursing seminars and workshops, presentations, publications authored, course work in medicine, health care, or health sciences, independent study, exam questions written, and research projects. Renewal fees are: $200 (members); $270 (nonmembers). **Preparatory Materials:** Handbook, including exam content outline and sample questions, provided. **Examination Frequency:** semiannual - always May and fall. **Examination Sites:** Exam given at annual education course, fall course, and at 15 sites throughout the U.S. **Examination Type:** Multiple-choice. **Fees:** $200 (members); $270 (nonmembers). **Endorsed By:** National Organization for Competency Assurance; Society of Gastroenterology Nurses and Associates.

Recreational Therapists

| 946 |

Activity Assistant Certified (AAC)
National Certification Council for
    Activity Professionals (NCCAP)
520 Stewart
Park Ridge, IL 60068
Phone: (708)698-4263
Fax: (708)698-9864
Marilyn Jaeger ACC, Admin.

Recipient: Individuals who can carry out, with supervision, activity programs in long-term facilities, retirement housing, adult daycare programs, and senior centers. **Membership:** Not required. **Certification Requirements:** Must meet one of the following requirements: (1) Thirty college semester credits in required areas, 2000 hours experience within last five years, and 20 clock hours of related continuing education; or (2) High school diploma or GED, successful completion of NCCAP 90 hour Basic Education Course or six college credits, 4000 hours experience in last five years, and 20 clock hours of related continuing education. Continuing education credits can be earned through adult education, workshops, seminars, college courses, association meetings, articles authored, speeches given, and presentations made. Continuing education topics are: (1) Working with Patients/Residents, including: Basic health; Biology of aging; Community services/support/relations; Group instruction/leadership; Human development and aging; Human development and late adult years; Interpersonal relationships; Leisure and aging; Motivation; Psychology of aging; Public relations; Public speaking; Regulations; Residents and staff; Sociology of aging; Spirituality of aging; and Therapy for disabled aging; (2) Programming, including: Individualized care planning; Program management; and Program types - theory and practice; and (3) Management/Personnel Legal and Ethical Issues, including: Consulting; Financial management; Management leadership; Management writing skills; Personnel employment; Professionalism; and Resources. **Renewal:** Every two years. Recertification based on accumulation of 20 hours of related continuing education. Renewal fee is $30. **Preparatory Materials:** List of applicable coursework areas provided. **Fees:** $30 (members); $35 (nonmembers). **Endorsed By:** National Association of Activity Professionals.

| 947 |

Activity Consultant Certified (ACC)
National Certification Council for
    Activity Professionals (NCCAP)
520 Stewart
Park Ridge, IL 60068
Phone: (708)698-4263
Fax: (708)698-9864
Marilyn Jaeger ACC, Admin.

Recipient: Consultants, trainers, and instructors for activity program, staff, or department in long-term facilities, retirement housing, adult day-care programs, and senior centers. **Membership:** Not required. **Certification Requirements:** Must meet one of the following requirements: (1) Master's degree with coursework in required areas, 2000 hours experience, 40 hours of related continuing education, and 200 hours of consulting experience in last five years; or (2) Bachelor's degree with coursework in required areas, 4000 hours experience, 40 hours of related continuing education, and 200 hours of consulting experience in last three years. Continuing education credits can be earned through adult education, workshops, seminars, college courses, association meetings, articles authored, speeches given, and presentations made. Continuing education topics are: (1) Working with Patients/Residents, including: Basic health; Biology of aging; Community services/support/relations; Group instruction/leadership; Human development and aging; Human development and late adult years; Interpersonal relationships; Leisure and aging; Motivation; Psychology of aging; Public relations; Public speaking; Regulations; Residents and staff; Sociology of aging; Spirituality of aging; and Therapy for disabled aging; (2) Programming, including: Individualized care planning; Program management; and Program types - theory and practice; and (3) Management/Personnel Legal and Ethical Issues, including: Consulting; Financial management; Management leadership; Management writing skills; Personnel employment; Professionalism; and Resources. **Renewal:** Every two years. Recertification based on accumulation of 40 hours of related continuing education. Renewal fee is $30. **Preparatory Materials:** List of applicable coursework areas provided. **Fees:** $50 (members); $55 (nonmembers). **Endorsed By:** National Association of Activity Professionals.

| 948 |

Activity Director Certified (ADC)
National Certification Council for
    Activity Professionals (NCCAP)
520 Stewart
Park Ridge, IL 60068
Phone: (708)698-4263
Fax: (708)698-9864
Marilyn Jaeger ACC, Admin.

Recipient: Individuals who direct, coordinate, or supervise activity program, staff, and department primarily in long-term facilities, retirement housing, adult day-care programs, and senior centers. **Membership:** Not required. **Certification Requirements:** Must meet one of the following requirements: (1) Bachelor's degree including coursework in required areas, 2000 hours experience in last five years, and 30 clock hours of related continuing education; (2) 60 college semester credits in required areas, 6000 hours experience within last five years, and 30 clock hours of related continuing education; or (3) Either 30 college semester credits in required areas or successful completion of NCCAP Basic Education Course, NCCAP Advanced Management Course, and 12 semester or 18 quarter credits, 10,000 hours experience in last five years, and 30 hours of related continuing education. Continuing education credits can be earned through adult education, workshops, seminars, college courses, association meetings, articles authored, speeches given, and presentations made. Continuing education topics are: (1) Working with Patients/Residents, including: Basic health; Biology of aging; Community services/support/relations; Group instruction/leadership; Human development and aging; Human development and late adult years; Interpersonal relationships; Leisure and aging; Motivation; Psychology of aging; Public relations; Public speaking; Regulations; Residents and staff; Sociology of aging; Spirituality of aging; and Therapy for disabled aging; (2) Programming, including: Individualized care planning; Program management; and Program types - theory and practice; and (3) Management/Personnel Legal and Ethical Issues, including: Consulting; Financial management; Management leadership; Management writing skills; Personnel employment; Professionalism; and Resources. Provisional certification available for candidates who do not meet all requirements. **Renewal:** Every two years. Recertification based on accumulation of 30 hours of continuing education. Renewal fee is $30. **Preparatory Materials:** List of applicable coursework areas provided. **Fees:** $40 (members); $45 (nonmembers). **Endorsed By:** National Association of Activity Professionals.

949

Certified Therapeutic Recreation Specialist (CTRS)

National Council for Therapeutic Recreation Certification (NCTRC)
PO Box 479
Thiells, NY 10984-0479
Phone: (914)947-4346

Recipient: Therapeutic recreation specialists. **Educational/Experience Requirements:** Must meet one of the requirements: (1) Bachelor's degree in therapeutic recreation or recreation with minor in therapeutic recreation and 360 hour field placement in clinical, community-based, or residential therapeutic recreation program; or (2) Five years experience and bachelor's degree in non-related field including 18 semester or 24 quarter hours of graduate coursework in therapeutic recreation and 24 semester or 36 quarter hours in three of the following areas: Adaptive physical education; Human services; Psychology; Related biological/physical sciences; Sociology; and Special education. **Certification Requirements:** Successful completion of exam. Exam covers: (1) Background, including: Leisure: theories and concepts; Service delivery systems; and Therapeutic recreation; (2) Diagnostic Groupings and Populations Served, including: Addictions; Cognitive; Emotional; Physical; Sensory and communication; and Social; (3) Assessment, including: Domains; Procedures; Process; and Purpose; (4) Planning the Program/Treatment, including: Professional standards of practice; Program design; Programming considerations; Types of programs; and Writing treatment plan; (5) Implementing the Program/Treatment, including: Education and integration of families and significant others; Intervention techniques; and Leadership principles; (6) Documentation and Managing Services, including: Documentation procedures for discharge/transition planning and program accountability; Methods for evaluating programs for efficiency and efficacy; and Methods of monitoring progress toward goals and behavioral objectives; (7) Organizing and Managing Services, including: Content of agency/department written plan of operation; Guidelines for administration; Knowledge of external regulations; Personnel supervision; Quality improvement; and Resources; and (8) Professional Issues, including: Advancement of profession; and Practice issues. **Renewal:** Recertification based on accumulation of 100 total points through: (1) Experience (50 points), including work in the following

therapeutic recreation positions: Administrator; Consultant; Direct service deliverer; Educator; Professional service provider; Student; Supervisor; or Volunteer; (2) Continuing Education (30 points minimum; 50 points maximum), including courses, seminars, and symposia, and professional publications and presentations; and (3) Successful completion of exam. **Preparatory Materials:** *Certification Standards and Eligibility Requirements* and *Study Guide for the NCTRC Therapeutic Recreation Specialist Certification Exam* (references). Bulletin, including exam content outline, list of suggested references, and sample questions, provided. **Examination Frequency:** semiannual - always May and November. **Examination Sites:** Exam given at sites throughout the U.S. **Examination Type:** Multiple-choice. **Waiting Period to Receive Scores:** Six weeks. **Fees:** $200. **Accredited By:** National Commission for Certifying Agencies. **Endorsed By:** National Organization for Competency Assurance; National Therapeutic Recreation Society.

Registered Nurses

950

Adult Nurse Practitioner (ANP)

Board on Certification for Primary Care in Adult and Family Nursing Practice
American Nurses Credentialing Center
600 Maryland Ave., SW, Ste. 100 West
Washington, DC 20024-2571
Toll Free: (800)284-CERT
Marie A. Reed R.N., Dir.

Recipient: Adult nurse practitioners. **Number of Certified Individuals:** 5667. **Educational/Experience Requirements:** Current licensure as registered nurse (R.N.) and master's or higher degree in nursing. Must also have been prepared as adult nurse practitioner in either: (1) Adult nurse practitioner or family nurse practitioner master's degree program within nursing program; or (2) Formal post-graduate adult nurse practitioner or family nurse practitioner track or program within a school of nursing granting graduate level academic credit. Educational program must include both didactic and clinical components. **Membership:** Not required. **Certification Requirements:** Successful completion of exam. Exam covers: Assessment and management of client illness in primary care; Evaluation and promotion of client

wellness in primary care; Issues and trends in primary care; and Nurse/client relationships. **Renewal:** Every five years. Recertification based on either successful completion of exam or continuing education. Continuing education requirement may be met using in-services, grand rounds, academic credits, continuing medical education (CME) credits, and other related programs. **Preparatory Materials:** "Guidelines for Educational Preparation of Adult Nurse Practitioners," *Directory of Certification Examination Review Courses,* and *How to Take ANCC Certification Examinations* (references). Handbook, including exam content outline and sample questions, provided. Review courses available. **Examination Frequency:** semiannual - always July and October. **Examination Sites:** Exam given at sites throughout the U.S. **Examination Type:** Multiple-choice. **Waiting Period to Receive Scores:** Six-eight weeks. **Fees:** $145 (members); $285 (nonmembers). **Accredited By:** American Board of Nursing Specialties. **Endorsed By:** American Nurses Association; National Organization for Competency Assurance.

951

Advanced Oncology Certified Nurse (AOCN)

Oncology Nursing Certification Corp. (ONCC)
501 Holiday Dr.
Pittsburgh, PA 15220-2749
Phone: (412)921-8597
Fax: (412)921-6565

Recipient: Oncology nurses. **Educational/Experience Requirements:** Must meet the following requirements: (1) Current licensure as registered nurse (R.N.); (2) Master's degree or higher in nursing or bachelor's degree in nursing and successful completion of nurse practitioner program; and (3) Thirty months experience within last five years, including 2000 hours experience within last 30 months. Experience may be in nursing administration, education, clinical practice, or research. Beginning in the year 2000, all candidates will be required to hold master's degree or higher in nursing. **Membership:** Not required. **Certification Requirements:** Successful completion of exam. Exam covers: (1) Direct Caregiver Role, including: Comprehensive assessment; Continuity of care; Evaluation; Managing clients receiving cancer treatment; Screening, prevention, and early detection; and Symptom management, including prevention, etiology, recommendations, interventions, pharmacology, patterns of symptoms, and self-care; (2) Administrator/ Coordinator Role, including: Administration and organizational theory; Community contact; Direct-care provision; Personnel management; Professional issues; and Reimbursement and care costs; (3) Consultant Role, including: Communication; Organizational analysis; and Theory; (4) Researcher Role, including: Application of research findings to practice; Critique of research; Dissemination of findings by incorporation into policies, procedures, and standards; Evaluation of data collection instruments; Identification of sampling strategy; Interpretation of data; Problem identification; Safeguarding of rights of human subjects; Selection of appropriate statistical techniques for data analysis; and Synthesis of relevant research literature; and (5) Educator Role, including both theory and process. **Renewal:** Every four years. Recertification based on successful completion of exam. **Preparatory Materials:** Bulletin, including exam content outline, list of suggested references, and sample questions, provided. **Examination Frequency:** Annual. **Examination Sites:** Exam given at annual congress. **Fees:** $210 (members); $285 (nonmembers). **Endorsed By:** Oncology Nursing Society.

952

Ambulatory Women's Health Care Nurse

National Certification Corp. for the Obstetric, Gynecologic, and Neonatal Nursing Specialties (NCC)
645 N. Michigan Ave., Ste. 900
Chicago, IL 60611
Phone: (312)951-0207
Toll Free: (800)367-5613
Suzanne Choiniere RNC, Pres.

Recipient: Reproductive endocrinology/ infertility nurses. **Educational/ Experience Requirements:** Must meet the following requirements: (1) Current licensure as registered nurse; and (2) Two years experience in ambulatory women's health care nursing, including 2000 hours of practice. **Certification Requirements:** Successful completion of exam. Exam covers: (1) General Assessment, covering: Diagnostic procedures and laboratory tests; General health supervision; and Recognition, basic management and /or referral of common health problems; (2) Gynecology Deviations, covering: Benign and malignant tumors of pelvis; Breast diseases and disorders; Diagnostic studies and laboratory tests; Ectopic pregnancy; Fertility control; Induced abortion; Infertility (screening and evalu-

ation); Menstrual and endocrinological disorders; Pelvic inflammatory disease/ salpingitis; Perimenopause/menopause concerns; Sexually transmitted diseases, including HIV and hepatitis; Toxic shock syndrome; Urinary tract disorders; and Vaginitis; (3) Gynecology - Normal, covering: Climacteric; Normal anatomy and physiology of reproductive organs; Puberty/adolescence; and Reproductive years; (4) Obstetrics, covering: Assessment of fetal well being; Health guidance; Maternal assessment, including diagnostic tests and studies, maternal complications of pregnancy, and pre-existing risk factors; and Normal anatomy and physiology of pregnancy and puerperium; and (5) Professional Issues, covering: Legal/ ethical issues; and Research terms. **Renewal:** Every three years. Recertification based on either successful completion of exam or continuing education. **Preparatory Materials:** Candidate guide, including bibliography of references and sample questions, provided. **Examination Frequency:** semiannual. **Examination Sites:** Exam given at sites throughout the U.S. **Examination Type:** Multiple-choice. **Waiting Period to Receive Scores:** Eight weeks. **Re-examination:** May retake the exam as many times as necessary. There is a $300 fee to retake exam. **Fees:** $300.

953

Cardiac Rehabilitation Nurse

American Nurses Credentialing Center (ANCC)
600 Maryland Ave., SW, Ste. 100 West
Washington, DC 20024-2571
Toll Free: (800)284-CERT
Marie A. Reed R.N., Dir.

Recipient: Cardiac rehabilitation nurses working in acute and ambulatory care, community-based facilities, and work-site and school-based programs. **Educational/Experience Requirements:** Must meet the following requirements: (1) Current licensure as registered nurse (R.N.); (2) Bachelor's degree or higher in nursing; (3) Two years experience as licensed R.N.; (4) Successful completion of American Heart Association ACLS (advanced cardiac life support) program; (5) Current practice of cardiac rehabilitation nursing for an average of eight hours per week; (6) 2000 hours of in-hospital experience either in critical or acute coronary care; and (7) 30 contact hours of related continuing education within last three years. Continuing education requirement may be met through inservices, grand rounds, academic credits, continuing medical education (CME) credits, and other related continuing education pro-

grams. Experience must be in direct patient care or direct clinical management, supervision, education, or direction of other persons to achieve or help achieve patient/client goals. **Membership:** Not required. **Certification Requirements:** Successful completion of exam. Exam covers: Cardiac rehabilitative care; Cardiovascular disorders; Issues and trends; Psychosocial aspects; and Special situations. **Renewal:** Every five years. Recertification based on either successful completion of exam or continuing education. Continuing education requirement may be met through in-services, grand rounds, academic credits, continuing medical education (CME) credits, and other related programs. **Preparatory Materials:** *Directory of Certification Examination Review Courses* and *How to Take ANCC Certification Examinations* (references). Handbook, including exam content outline and sample questions, provided. Review courses available. **Examination Frequency:** semiannual - always July and October. **Examination Sites:** Exam given at sites throughout the U.S. **Examination Type:** Multiple-choice. **Waiting Period to Receive Scores:** Six-eight weeks. **Fees:** $145 (members); $285 (nonmembers). **Endorsed By:** American Nurses Association; National Organization for Competency Assurance.

954

CCRN

American Association of Critical-Care Nurses (AACN)
101 Columbia
Aliso Viejo, CA 92656
Phone: (714)362-2000
Fax: (714)362-2022
Toll Free: (800)899-AACN
Diana Shuneson, Admin.

Recipient: Professionals involved with neonatal, pediatric, and/or adult critical-care nursing. **Educational/Experience Requirements:** Must meet the following requirements: (1) Current unrestricted licensure as registered nurse (R.N.); (2) One year of experience; and (3) 1750 hours experience within last two years, with 875 hours in last year. Experience must be in bedside care of critically ill patients requiring specific interventions. **Membership:** Not required. **Certification Requirements:** Successful completion of exam. Exams offered in adult, neonatal, and pediatric critical care nursing. Exams consist of the following patient care problem sections: Cardiovascular; Endocrine; Gastrointestinal; Hematology/ Immunology; Multi-System; Neurologic; Pulmonary; and Renal. **Renewal:** Every three years. Recertification based on either successful completion of exam or accumulation of 100 points through college courses, continuing education, authoring of publications, presentations, leadership positions held, and quality assurance activities. Renewal fees are: $120 (members); $195 (nonmembers). **Preparatory Materials:** Handbook, including list of suggested references and sample questions, provided. Review courses, sample questions, and study guides available. **Examination Frequency:** semiannual. **Examination Sites:** Exam given at sites throughout the U.S. **Examination Type:** Multiple-choice. **Waiting Period to Receive Scores:** Five weeks. **Fees:** $150 (members); $225 (nonmembers).

955

Certified Addictions Registered Nurse (CARN)

Addictions Nursing Certification Board (ANCB)
4101 Lake Boone Trail, Ste. 201
Raleigh, NC 27607
Phone: (919)783-5871
Fax: (919)787-4916
Sandra Tweed CARN, Chairperson

Recipient: Registered nurses (R.N.s) involved in addictions nursing. **Educational/Experience Requirements:** Must meet the following requirements: (1) Current unrestricted licensure as R.N. in the U.S. or Canada; (2) Three years experience as R.N.; and (3) Two years (4000 hours) addictions nursing experience as R.N. in staff, administrative, teaching, private practice, consultation, counseling, or research capacity. **Membership:** Not required. **Certification Requirements:** Successful completion of exam. Exam content areas are: (1) Concurrent Diagnoses; (2) Depressant Substances; (3) Stimulant Substances; (4) Process Addictions; and (5) Hallucinogenic Substances. **Renewal:** Every four years. Recertification based on either successful completion of exam or continuing education. **Preparatory Materials:** *Care of Client with Addictions* and *Standards of Addictions Nursing Practice with Selected Diagnoses and Criteria* (references). Information booklet, including list of reference materials and sample questions, provided. **Examination Frequency:** semiannual - always fourth Saturday in April and fall. **Examination Sites:** Exam given at sites throughout the U.S. in April and at annual educational conference in the fall. **Examination Type:** Multiple-choice. **Waiting Period to Receive Scores:** Six weeks. **Fees:** $165 (members); $250 (nonmembers). **Endorsed By:** National League for Nursing; National Nurses Society on Addictions.

956

Certified Ambulatory Perianesthesia Nurse (CAPA)

American Board of Post Anesthesia Nursing Certification (ABPANC)
475 Riverside Dr.
New York, NY 10115-0089
Phone: (212)870-3161
Fax: (212)870-3333
Toll Free: (800)6AB-PANC
Bonnie Niebuhr, Exec.Dir.

Recipient: Registered nurses (R.N.) working in ambulatory surgical units. **Number of Certified Individuals:** 500. **Educational/Experience Requirements:** Must meet the following requirements: (1) Current licensure as R.N.; and (2) 1800 hours experience within three consecutive years. **Membership:** Not required. **Certification Requirements:** Successful completion of exam. **Renewal:** Every three years. Recertification based on either successful completion of exam or continuing education. **Preparatory Materials:** Book, seminars, and videos available. **Examination Frequency:** semiannual - always spring and November. **Examination Sites:** Exam given at national conference and at sites throughout the U.S. **Examination Type:** Multiple-choice. **Pass/Fail Rate:** 80% pass exam the first time. **Waiting Period to Receive Scores:** Four-six weeks. **Fees:** $135 (members); $200 (nonmembers).

957

Certified Chemical Dependency Nurse (RN-CD)

National Consortium of Chemical Dependency Nurses (NCCDN)
1720 Willow Creek Cir., Ste. 519
Eugene, OR 97402
Phone: (503)485-4421
Fax: (503)485-7372
Toll Free: (800)87N-CCDN
Randy Bryson, Exec.Dir.

Recipient: Registered nurses (R.N.s) working in specialty of chemical dependency. **Number of Certified Individuals:** 1200. **Educational/Experience Requirements:** Must meet the following requirements: (1) Current licensure at R.N.; (2) Thirty hours of chemical dependency specific education; and (3) 4000 hours of chemical dependency nursing experience within past five years. **Membership:** Not required. **Certification Requirements:** Successful completion of exam. **Renewal:** Every two years. Renewal fees are: $75 (members); $150 (nonmembers). **Preparatory Materials:** Review course offered at NCCDN annual convention. Biblio-

graphical listing available. **Examination Frequency:** Fifteen times per year. **Examination Sites:** Exam given at sites throughout the U.S. **Examination Type:** Multiple-choice. **Waiting Period to Receive Scores:** Four-six weeks. **Re-examination:** Must wait 60 days to retake exam. **Fees:** $125 (members); $250 (nonmembers).

958

Certified Colon Hydrotherapist

International Association for Colon Hydrotherapy
2051 Hilltop Dr., Ste. A-11
Redding, CA 96002
Phone: (916)222-1498
Fax: (916)222-1497
Dollie I. Popoff, Sec.

Recipient: Colon hydrotherapists. **Educational/Experience Requirements:** Must meet the following requirements: (1) Current licensure as registered nurse (R.N.) or 45 hours of anatomy and physiology coursework; (2) Five hours of coursework in sanitation; (3) 25 hours of coursework in theory; (4) Documentation of 25 sessions of colon hydrotherapy as apprentice, including: Amount of release; Clients complaints; Color of release; History of problems; How many releases; Number of fills; Trigger point for release; Water temperature; and Other pertinent information; and (5) 100 sessions as colon hydrotherapist. **Membership:** Required. **Certification Requirements:** Successful completion of written, oral, and practical exams.

959

Certified Continence Care Nurse (CCCN)

Wound Ostomy and Continence Nurses Society (WOCN)
2755 Bristol St., Ste. 110
Costa Mesa, CA 92626
Phone: (714)476-0268
Toll Free: (800)228-4238
Lynne Greene RN, Pres.

Recipient: Continence care nurses who function in acute care, extended care, home health care, industry, outpatient facilities, private practice, and other settings. **Educational/Experience Requirements:** Bachelor's degree, current licensure as registered nurse (R.N.), and one of the following: (1) Successful completion of accredited enterstomal therapy nursing education program or specialty-training course and one year (2000 hours) of experience; or (2) Two years

(4000 hours) experience. **Certification Requirements:** Successful completion of exam. **Preparatory Materials:** Handbook, including sample questions and study references, provided. **Examination Frequency:** semiannual - always June and November. **Examination Sites:** Exam given at sites throughout the U.S. and Canada.

960

Certified Emergency Nurse (CEN)
Board of Certification for
   Emergency Nursing
216 Higgins Rd.
Park Ridge, IL 60068-5736
Phone: (708)698-9400
Toll Free: (800)243-8362

Recipient: Emergency nurses. **Number of Certified Individuals:** 21,000. **Educational/Experience Requirements:** Current licensure as registered nurse (R.N.). Two years experience recommended. **Membership:** Not required. **Certification Requirements:** Successful completion of exam. Exam covers professional issues and the following types of emergencies: Abdominal; Cardiovascular; Disaster management; Environmental; General; Genitourinary and gynecological; Maxillofacial; Mental health; Neurological; Obstetrical; Ocular; Orthopedic; Patient care management; Patient/community education; Respiratory emergencies; Shock/multisystem trauma emergencies; Stabilization and transfer; Substance abuse/toxicological; and Surface trauma. **Renewal:** Every four years. **Preparatory Materials:** Review manual, computer software, and video available. **Examination Sites:** Exam given at sites throughout the U.S. and Canada. **Examination Type:** Multiple-choice. **Fees:** $110 (members); $220 (nonmembers). **Endorsed By:** Emergency Nurses Association.

961

Certified Enterostomal Therapy Nurse (CETN)
Wound Ostomy and Continence
   Nurses Society (WOCN)
2755 Bristol St., Ste. 110
Costa Mesa, CA 92626
Phone: (714)476-0268
Toll Free: (800)228-4238
Lynne Grant RN, Pres.

Recipient: Enterostomal therapy nurses who function in acute care, extended care, home health care, industry, outpatient facilities, private practice, and other settings. **Educational/Experience Requirements:** Must meet the following requirements: (1) Current licensure as registered nurse (R.N.); and (2) Successful completion of accredited enterostomal therapy nursing education program. **Membership:** mnr **Certification Requirements:** Successful completion of exam. Exam covers: (1) Anatomy and Physiology - Normal, including: Anatomy and physiology of alimentary canal; Anatomy and physiology - genitourinary tract; Fluid balance; and Integumentary system; (2) Pathological States and Diagnostic Tests, including: Alimentary tract; Diagnostic techniques; Genitourinary system; and Skin; (3) Ostomy Surgery Perisurgery Care, including: Complications; Postoperative care; Preoperative care; and Surgical procedures - techniques, purpose, characteristics, and indications; (4) Wounds and Fistulas, including: Draining wounds and fistulas; Lower extremity ulcers; Management; Other wounds; and Pressure ulcers; (5) Urinary and Fecal Incontinence, including: Fecal incontinence; Management; and Urinary incontinence; and (6) Patient Rehabilitation, including: Discharge planning; Long-term complications; Patient care and teaching; Principles of rehabilitation; and Psychosocial and economic factors. **Renewal:** Recertification required. **Preparatory Materials:** Handbook, including sample questions and study references, provided. Manual, standards of care, video, and slide program available. **Examination Frequency:** semiannual - always June and November. **Examination Sites:** Exam given at sites throughout the U.S. and Canada. **Examination Type:** Multiple-choice. **Re-examination:** There is no limit to how many times exam may be retaken. Fees to retake exam are: $175 (members); $225 (nonmembers). **Fees:** $175 (members); $225 (nonmembers).

962

Certified Flight Registered Nurse (CFRN)
Board of Certification for
   Emergency Nursing (BCEN)
216 Higgins Rd.
Park Ridge, IL 60068-5736
Phone: (708)698-9409
Fax: (708)698-9406
Toll Free: (800)243-8362

Recipient: Flight nurses. **Educational/Experience Requirements:** Current licensure as registered nurse (R.N.) in the U.S. or Canada. Two years experience are recommended. **Membership:** Not required. **Certification Requirements:** Successful completion of exam. Exam covers: (1) Clinical Practice, including: Abdominal; Altitude physiology (pure mechanics); Cardiovascular; Communication; Critical incident stress debriefing; Disaster management; Environmental; Flight communication; Flight stressors; General medical; Genitourinary and gynecological; Maxillofacial; Medication administration; Mental health; Neurological; Obstetrical; Ocular; Organ procurement; Orthopedic; Patient care management; Patient/community education; Preparation for flight; Respiratory; Safety (including Hazmat); Shock/multisystem trauma; Stabilization and transfer; Substance abuse/toxicological; Surface trauma; Survival; and Triage/priority setting; and (2) Professional Issues, including: Legal; Organization issues; and Quality improvement. **Renewal:** Every four years. **Preparatory Materials:** Handbook provided. **Examination Frequency:** Annual - always February. **Examination Sites:** Exam given at sites throughout the U.S. and Canada. **Examination Type:** Multiple-choice. **Endorsed By:** National Flight Nurses Association.

963

Certified Gastroenterology Registered Nurse (CGRN)
Certifying Board of
   Gastroenterology Nurses and
   Associates (CBGNA)
720 Light St.
Baltimore, MD 21230
Phone: (410)752-1808
Fax: (410)752-8295

Recipient: Registered nurses specializing in gastroenterology and endoscopic procedures. **Educational/Experience Requirements:** Two years (4000 hours) experience within last five years in clinical, supervisory, or administrative capacities in institutional or private practice settings. **Membership:** Not required. **Certification Requirements:** Successful completion of exam. Exam covers: Education of the patient, family, and public healthcare professionals within the specialty; Patient care management; and Professional practice. **Renewal:** Every five years. Recertification based on either successful completion of exam or accumulation of 100 hours of continuing education through gastroenterology/endoscopy nursing seminars and workshops (minimum of 80 hours), other nursing seminars and workshops, presentations, publications authored, course work in medicine, health care, or health sciences, independent study, exam questions written, and research projects. Renewal fees are: $200 (members); $270 (nonmembers). **Preparatory Materials:**

Handbook, including exam content outline and sample questions, provided. **Examination Frequency:** semiannual - always May and fall. **Examination Sites:** Exam given at annual education course, fall course, and at 15 sites throughout the U.S. **Examination Type:** Multiple-choice. **Fees:** $200 (members); $270 (nonmembers). **Endorsed By:** National Organization for Competency Assurance; Society of Gastroenterology Nurses and Associates.

964

Certified Hemodialysis Nurse (CHN)
Board of Nephrology Examiners - Nursing and Technology (BONENT)
PO Box 15945-282
Lenexa, KS 66285
Phone: (913)541-9077
Fax: (913)541-0156

Recipient: Hemodialysis nurses. **Educational/Experience Requirements:** Must meet the following requirements: (1) Current licensure as registered nurse (R.N.); and (2) One year of experience in nephrology nursing in general staff, administrative, teaching, and/or research capacity. **Certification Requirements:** Successful completion of exam. Exam covers: (1) Supervision/Administration, including: Equipment and supplies; and Personnel management; (2) Dialysis and Related Issues, including: Dialyzer reuse; Home dialysis; Initiation of dialysis; Machine setup; Monitoring during dialysis; Patient care; Termination of dialysis procedure; and Water treatment; (3) Professional Development, including: Information sharing; Research; and Staff training; and (4) Environmental Control, including: Biological agents; Chemical agents; Hazards prevention and control; Infection control; and Occupational injuries. **Renewal:** Every four years. Recertification based on either successful completion of exam or accumulation of 45 hours of continuing education through academic courses, home study, seminars and workshops, publications authored, and presentations. Thirty hours must be nephrology-related. **Preparatory Materials:** Study guide, including exam content outline, list of suggested readings, and sample questions, provided. **Examination Frequency:** Throughout the year. **Examination Sites:** Exam given at sites throughout the U.S. **Examination Type:** Multiple-choice. **Re-examination:** May retake exam twice. There is a $140 fee to retake exam. **Fees:** $140.

965

Certified Holistic Nurse (CHN)
American Holistic Nurses' Association (AHNA)
4101 Lake Boone Trail, Ste. 201
Raleigh, NC 27607
Phone: (919)787-5181
Fax: (919)787-4916

Recipient: Holistic nurses. **Educational/Experience Requirements:** Must meet the following requirements: (1) Current licensure as registered nurse (R.N.); (2) Successful completion of Certificate Program in Holistic Nursing (CPHN); (3) Six months integrative period after successful completion of CPHN; and (4) Eight hours per week holistic nursing practice in employed or community role for six months. **Membership:** Not required. **Certification Requirements:** Submission of portfolio. Portfolio must include demonstrations of the following: (1) Patterns of self growth and transformation consistent with holistic nursing philosophy, demonstrated through poetry, mixed-media illustration, or other artistic expression; (2) Universality of application of holistic nursing, demonstrated by submission of two work examples and client and co-worker testimonial statements; (3) Leadership in holistic nursing community, demonstrated by written discussion of *ANHA Standards of Holistic Nursing Practice;* and (4) Educating communities about holistic nursing, demonstrated by written discussion of educational activities conducted with both lay and nursing communities. **Preparatory Materials:** *ANHA Standards of Holistic Nursing Practice* (reference). **Fees:** $150 (members); $225 (nonmembers).

966

Certified Nephrology Nurse (CNN)
Nephrology Nursing Certification Board (NNCB)
East Holly Ave.
Box 56
Pitman, NJ 08071-0056
Phone: (609)256-2321
Fax: (609)589-7463

Recipient: Nephrology nurses. **Educational/Experience Requirements:** Must meet the following requirements: (1) Current licensure as registered nurse (R.N.); and (2) Two years experience with at least 50 percent of time spent as R.N. in nephrology nursing in general staff, administrative, teaching, or research capacity. Beginning in the year 2000 must have bachelor's degree and 30

hours of related continuing education within last three years. **Membership:** Not required. **Certification Requirements:** Successful completion of exam. Exam covers: Concepts of renal failure; Conservative management; Hemodialysis; Peritoneal dialysis; Renal replacement therapies; and Transplant. **Renewal:** Every three years. Recertification based on successful completion of exam or continuing education. Renewal fees for continuing education option are: $75 (members); $100 (nonmembers). Renewal fees for exam option are: $175 (members); $225 (nonmembers). **Preparatory Materials:** *Core Curriculum for Nephrology Nursing, Nephrology Nursing Certification Review Guide,* and *Standards of Clinical Practice for Nephrology Nursing* (references). Sample questions provided. Review course and list of study references available. **Examination Frequency:** Exam given nine times per year. **Examination Sites:** Exam given at sites throughout the U.S. **Examination Type:** Multiple-choice. **Re-examination:** May retake exam once. Must successfully complete exam within two years. Fees to retake exam are: $75 (members); $100 (nonmembers). **Fees:** $175 (members); $225 (nonmembers). **Endorsed By:** American Nephrology Nurses' Association.

967

Certified in Nursing Administration
Board on Certification for Nursing Administration Practice
American Nurses Credentialing Center
600 Maryland Ave., SW, Ste. 100 West
Washington, DC 20024-2571
Toll Free: (800)284-CERT
Marie A. Reed R.N., Dir.

Recipient: Nurses who hold an administrative position at the nurse manager or nurse executive level. **Number of Certified Individuals:** 6824. **Educational/Experience Requirements:** Must meet the following requirements: (1) Current licensure as registered nurse (R.N.); (2) Bachelor's degree or higher; (3) Twenty-four months experience within last five years. Requirement may be met if engaged in education and supervision of graduate students in mid-level or executive level nursing administration tracks or programs for at least the equivalent of 24 months in last five years; and (4) 20 contact hours of related continuing education in last two years or hold master's degree in nursing administration. Continuing education requirement may be met using in-services, grand rounds, academic credits, continuing medical education (CME) credits, and other related continuing education programs. Beginning in 1998 bachelor's degree in nursing required. **Membership:** Not required. **Certification Requirements:** Successful completion of exam. Exam covers: Economics; Ethics; Human resources; Legal and regulatory; and Organization and structure. **Renewal:** Every five years. Recertification based on either successful completion of exam or continuing education. Continuing education requirement may be met using in-services, grand rounds, academic credits, continuing medical education (CME) credits, and other related programs. **Preparatory Materials:** *Directory of Certification Examination Review Courses* and *How to Take ANCC Certification Examinations* (references). Handbook, including exam content outline and sample questions, provided. Review courses available. **Examination Frequency:** semiannual - always July and October. **Examination Sites:** Exam given at sites throughout the U.S. **Examination Type:** Multiple-choice. **Waiting Period to Receive Scores:** Six-eight weeks. **Fees:** $145 (members); $285 (nonmembers). **Accredited By:** American Board of Nursing Specialties. **Endorsed By:** American Nurses Association; National Organization for Competency Assurance.

968

Certified in Nursing Administration, Advanced

Board on Certification for Nursing Administration Practice
American Nurses Credentialing Center
600 Maryland Ave., SW, Ste. 100 West
Washington, DC 20024-2571
Toll Free: (800)284-CERT
Marie A. Reed R.N., Dir.

Recipient: Nurse executives who are responsible for the management of organized nursing services and are accountable for the environment in which clinical nursing is practiced. **Number of Certified Individuals:** 2244. **Educational/ Experience Requirements:** Current licensure as registered nurse (R.N.) and 24 months experience in last five years. Must also meet one of the following educational requirements: (1) Master's degree in nursing administration; or (2) Master's degree in unrelated field, bachelor's degree in nursing, and 30 contact hours of related continuing education in last two years. Continuing education requirement may be met using in-services, grand rounds, academic credits, continuing medical education (CME) credits,

and other related continuing education programs. Educators and consultants may apply for certification if they have provided consultative services at the nurse executive level. **Membership:** Not required. **Certification Requirements:** Successful completion of exam. Exam covers: Economics; Ethics; Human resources; Legal and regulatory; and Organization and structure. **Renewal:** Every five years. Recertification based on either successful completion of exam or continuing education. Continuing education requirement may be met using in-services, grand rounds, academic credits, continuing medical education (CME) credits, and other related programs. **Preparatory Materials:** *Directory of Certification Examination Review Courses* and *How to Take ANCC Certification Examinations* (references). Handbook, including exam content outline and sample questions, provided. Review courses available. **Examination Frequency:** semiannual - always July and October. **Examination Sites:** Exam given at sites throughout the U.S. **Examination Type:** Multiple-choice. **Waiting Period to Receive Scores:** Six-eight weeks. **Fees:** $145 (members); $285 (nonmembers). **Accredited By:** American Board of Nursing Specialties. **Endorsed By:** American Nurses Association; National Organization for Competency Assurance.

969

Certified Nutrition Support Nurse (CNSN)

National Board of Nutrition Support Certification (NBNSC)
8630 Fenton St., Ste. 412
Silver Spring, MD 20910-3805
Phone: (301)587-6315
Janet Gannon, Dir.

Recipient: Registered nurses (R.N.s) specializing in nutrition support. **Number of Certified Individuals:** 250. **Educational/ Experience Requirements:** Current licensure as R.N. Two years experience recommended. **Membership:** Not required. **Certification Requirements:** Successful completion of exam. Exam covers: (1) Nutrition and Physiology Concepts, including: Fluid and electrolytes; Gastrointestinal anatomy and physiology; Macronutrients; and Micronutrients; (2) Assessment, including: Patient assessment; and Patient history; (3) Planning, including: Discharge planning/ continuity of care; Enteral delivery systems; Identification of risk factors; Indications for therapy; Nutritional support in specific disease states; and Parenteral delivery systems; (4) Intervention, including: Education; Patient care; and

Pharmacological interventions; and (5) Evaluation, including: Complications; Quality improvement/standards of care; Research; and Response to therapy. **Renewal:** Every five years. Recertification based on successful completion of exam. **Preparatory Materials:** *Nutrition Support Nurse Core Curriculum* (reference). Handbook, including exam content outline, list of suggested study references, and sample questions, provided. Self-assessment program, audio tapes, and review courses available. **Examination Frequency:** semiannual - always spring and fall. **Examination Sites:** Exam given at sites throughout the U.S. **Examination Type:** Multiple-choice. **Waiting Period to Receive Scores:** Six weeks. **Re-examination:** There is no limit to the number of times exam may be retaken. Fees to retake exam are: $190 (members); $250 (nonmembers). **Fees:** $190 (members); $250 (nonmembers). **Endorsed By:** American Society for Parenteral and Enteral Nutrition.

970

Certified Occupational Health Nurse (COHN)

American Board for Occupational Health Nurses (ABOHN)
9944 S. Roberts Rd., Ste. 205
Palos Hills, IL 60465
Phone: (708)598-6368

Recipient: Occupational health nurses. **Number of Certified Individuals:** 6100. **Educational/Experience Requirements:** Must meet the following requirements: (1) Current licensure as registered nurse (R.N.); (2) Bachelor's degree; (3) Five thousand hours of experience over last five years; and (4) Successful completion of 75 hours of continuing education in related field. Professional presentations and publications may be used to meet part of this requirement. Fifteen-hundred hours of graduate study may be substituted for part of experience requirement. **Certification Requirements:** Successful completion of exam. **Renewal:** Every five years. Recertification based on the following: (1) Current licensure as registered nurse (R.N.); (2) Five thousand hours of experience; and (3) Successful completion of 75 hours of continuing education. Professional presentations and publications may be used to meet part of this requirement. Fifteen-hundred hours of graduate study may be substituted for part of experience requirement. **Preparatory Materials:** List of suggested review courses and study references and sample questions provided. **Examination Frequency:** Annual - always April. **Examination Sites:** Exam given at American

Occupational Health Conference, Atlanta, GA, Boston, MA, Chicago, IL, Arlington, TX, and the San Francisco, CA area. **Examination Type:** Multiple-choice. **Fees:** $250. **Endorsed By:** American Board of Nursing Specialties.

971

Certified Ostomy Care Nurse (COCN)

Wound Ostomy and Continence
   Nurses Society (WOCN)
2755 Bristol St., Ste. 110
Costa Mesa, CA 92626
Phone: (714)476-0268
Toll Free: (800)228-4238
Lynne Greene RN, Pres.

Recipient: Ostomy care nurses who function in acute care, extended care, home health care, industry, outpatient facilities, private practice, and other settings. **Educational/Experience Requirements:** Bachelor's degree, current licensure as registered nurse (R.N.), and one of the following: (1) Successful completion of accredited enterstomal therapy nursing education program or specialty-training course and one year (2000 hours) of experience; or (2) Two years (4000 hours) experience. **Certification Requirements:** Successful completion of exam. **Preparatory Materials:** Handbook, including sample questions and study references, provided. **Examination Frequency:** semi-annual - always June and November. **Examination Sites:** Exam given at sites throughout the U.S. and Canada.

972

Certified Pediatric Nurse (CPN)

National Certification Board of
   Pediatric Nurse Practitioners and
   Nurses
416 Hungerford Dr., Ste. 222
Rockville, MD 20850-4127
Phone: (301)340-8213
Fax: (301)340-8604
Mary Jean Schumann, Exec.Dir.

Recipient: Pediatric nurses. **Educational/Experience Requirements:** Current licensure as registered nurse (R.N.) and meet one of the following requirements: (1) Bachelor's degree in nursing and two years experience (3500 hours) within last five years; or (2) Successful completion of non-baccalaureate nursing program and three years (5250 hours) experience within last six years. Experience must be in direct patient care, teaching, administration, research, or consultation in pediatric nursing. **Certification Require-**

ments: Successful completion of exam. Exam covers: Child with special needs; Family dynamics; Growth and development; Health promotion of children and their families; Pediatric nursing in various health care delivery systems; Principles and techniques of pediatric nursing; and Nursing process for common health problems associated with: Cardiovascular system; Endocrine systems; Gastrointestinal system; Hematologic/ oncologic system; Integumentary systems; Nervous system; Neuromuscular/ musculoskeletal system; Psychosocial issues; Renal/genitourinary system; Respiratory systems; and Sensory system. **Renewal:** Every five years. Recertification based on either successful completion of exam or accumulation of one continuing education unit (CEU) every year. **Preparatory Materials:** List of suggested study references provided. **Examination Frequency:** Annual - always October. **Examination Sites:** Exam given at sites throughout the U.S. **Examination Type:** Multiple-choice. **Pass/Fail Rate:** 80-85 percent pass exam the first time. **Waiting Period to Receive Scores:** Twelve weeks. **Re-examination:** May retake exam three times. There is a $200 fee to retake exam. **Fees:** $200. **Endorsed By:** National Association of Pediatric Nurse Associates and Practitioners.

973

Certified Pediatric Nurse Practitioner (CPNP)

National Certification Board of
   Pediatric Nurse Practitioners and
   Nurses
416 Hungerford Dr., Ste. 222
Rockville, MD 20850-4127
Phone: (301)340-8213
Fax: (301)340-8604
Mary Jean Schumann, Exec.Dir.

Recipient: Practical nurse practitioners. **Educational/Experience Requirements:** Current licensure as registered nurse and meet one of the following requirements: (1) Master's degree in nursing; or (2) Successful completion of approved post-master's pediatric nurse practitioner program. **Certification Requirements:** Successful completion of exam. Exam covers: (1) Health Care Delivery - Systems and Methods, including: Community resources systems; History interviewing; Physical assessment; and Role of pediatric nurse practitioner; (2) Growth and Development, including: Anticipatory guidance/teaching counseling; Interactive growth and development; Physical growth and development; and Specific findings/variations; (3) Health Maintenance, including: Dental; Family

dynamics; Immunizations; Injury prevention; Nutrition; Pharmacology/drug therapy; and Pregnancy and birth; and (4) Common Clinical Problems, including: Behavioral/psychiatric; Cardiovascular; Dermatologic; Digestive/ abdominal; EENT; Endocrine; Genitourinary/reproductive; Hematologic/immunologic/oncology; Infectious disease;Multi-system/genetics; Musculoskeletal/connective tissue; Nervous system; and Respiratory/ pulmonary. **Renewal:** Every six years. Recertification based on either successful completion of exam or continuing education. **Preparatory Materials:** List of references provided. **Examination Frequency:** Annual - always October. **Examination Sites:** Exam given at sites throughout the U.S. **Examination Type:** Multiple-choice. **Pass/Fail Rate:** 80-85 percent pass exam the first time. **Waiting Period to Receive Scores:** Twelve weeks. **Re-examination:** May retake exam three times. There is a $300 fee to retake exam. **Fees:** $300. **Endorsed By:** National Association of Pediatric Nurse Associates and Practitioners.

974

Certified Peritoneal Dialysis Nurse (CPDN)

Board of Nephrology Examiners -
   Nursing and Technology
   (BONENT)
PO Box 15945-282
Lenexa, KS 66285
Phone: (913)541-9077
Fax: (913)541-0156

Recipient: Peritoneal dialysis nurse. **Educational/Experience Requirements:** Must meet the following requirements: (1) Current licensure as registered nurse (R.N.); and (2) One year of experience in nephrology nursing in general staff, administrative, teaching, and/or research capacity. **Certification Requirements:** Successful completion of exam. Exam covers: (1) Nursing Process, including: Access; Acute peritoneal dialysis; Clinical manifestations of end stage renal disease; Complications; Contraindications to peritoneal dialysis; Diagnostic testing; Dialysis solutions; Dietary prescriptions for end stage renal disease patients; Etiologies of end stage renal disease; General principles of dialysis; Human anatomy and physiology; Interviewing techniques; Kinetics of peritoneal dialysis; Laboratory testing; Medical and surgical asepsis; Nursing assessment; Other treatment modalities; Outpatient nursing management of chronic peritoneal dialysis patient; Pathophysiology of kidney and urinary systems; Peritoneal dialysis systems; Peritoneal membrane characteristics; Pharmacology; Physical assessment; Prescription; Procedures; and Types of peritoneal disease; (2) Administration, including: Budgeting/financial planning; Environmental control; Equipment and supplies; Management; Quality assurance; and Staff training and development; (3) Education, including: Activities and teaching; Principles of learning; and Retention of learning; and (4) Professional Development, including: Ethics; Information sharing; and Research. **Renewal:** Every four years. Recertification based on either successful completion of exam or accumulation of 45 hours of continuing education through academic courses, home study, seminars and workshops, publications authored, and presentations. Thirty hours must be nephrology-related. **Preparatory Materials:** Study guide, including exam content outline, list of suggested readings, and sample questions, provided. **Examination Frequency:** Throughout the year. **Examination Sites:** Exam given at sites throughout the U.S. **Examination Type:** Multiple-choice. **Re-examination:** May retake exam twice. There is a $140 fee to retake exam. **Fees:** $140.

975

Certified Plastic Surgical Nurse (CPSN)

Plastic Surgical Nursing
  Certification Board (PSNCB)
N. Woodbury Rd.
Box 56
Pitman, NJ 08071
Phone: (609)589-1490
Fax: (609)589-7463
Susan J. Hockenberger CPSN, Pres.

Recipient: Registered nurses (R.N.) involved in plastic surgery. **Educational/Experience Requirements:** Must meet the following requirements: (1) Current licensure as R.N.; (2) Two years experience in general, staff, administrative, teaching, or research capacity in last five years; and (3) 50 percent of practice hours spent in plastic surgical nursing during two of preceding five years. **Membership:** Not required. **Certification Requirements:** Successful completion of exam. Exam covers: Abdomen/trunk; Breast; Extremities; Head and neck; and Urologic/genitalia. **Renewal:** Every three years. Recertification based on either successful completion of exam or continuing education. Renewal fees for exam option are: $175 (members); $275 (nonmembers). Renewal fees for continuing education option are: $125 (members); $175 (nonmembers). **Preparatory Materials:** *AORN Standards of Practice, ASPRSN*

Bibliography, and *Core Curriculum for Plastic and Reconstructive Surgical Nursing* (references). Exam content outline, references, standardized nursing care plans, and study questions available. **Examination Frequency:** Three times per year. **Examination Sites:** Exam given at three different sites per year. **Examination Type:** Multiple-choice. **Waiting Period to Receive Scores:** Four weeks. **Re-examination:** May retake exam once. Must successfully complete exam within two years. Fees to retake exam are: $100 (members); $150 (nonmembers). **Fees:** $200 (members); $300 (nonmembers). **Endorsed By:** American Society of Plastic and Reconstructive Surgical Nurses.

976

Certified Post Anesthesia Nurse (CPAN)

American Board of Post Anesthesia
  Nursing Certification (ABPANC)
475 Riverside Dr.
New York, NY 10115-0089
Phone: (212)870-3161
Fax: (212)870-3333
Toll Free: (800)6AB-PANC
Bonnie Niebuhr, Exec.Dir.

Recipient: Registered nurses (R.N.) specializing in post anesthesia recovery. **Number of Certified Individuals:** 5000. **Educational/Experience Requirements:** Must meet the following requirements: (1) Current licensure as R.N.; and (2) 1800 hours experience within three consecutive years. **Membership:** Not required. **Certification Requirements:** Successful completion of exam. **Renewal:** Every three years. Recertification based on either successful completion of exam or continuing education. **Preparatory Materials:** Book, seminars, and videos available. **Examination Frequency:** semiannual - always spring and November. **Examination Sites:** Exam given at national conference and at sites throughout the U.S. **Examination Type:** Multiple-choice. **Pass/Fail Rate:** 80% pass exam the first time. **Waiting Period to Receive Scores:** Four-six weeks. **Fees:** $135 (members); $200 (nonmembers).

977

Certified Registered Nurse Anesthetist (CRNA)

Council on Certification of Nurse
  Anesthetists (CCNA)
222 S. Prospect Ave.
Park Ridge, IL 60068-4001
Phone: (708)692-7050
Fax: (708)692-6968
Susan Smith Caulk CRNA, Dir.

Recipient: Nurse anesthetists who practice in hospital surgical suites and obstetrical delivery rooms, the offices of dentists, podiatrists, ophthalmologists, and plastic surgeons, ambulatory surgical centers, health maintenance organizations (HMOs), preferred provider organizations (PPOs), and U.S. military, Public Health Services, and Veterans Administration medical facilities. **Number of Certified Individuals:** 25,000. **Educational/Experience Requirements:** Must meet the following requirements: (1) Bachelor's degree in nursing or other appropriate baccalaureate degree; (2) Current licensure as registered nurse (R.N.); (3) One year of experience in acute care nursing setting; and (4) Successful completion of nurse anesthesia program accredited by Council on Accreditation of Nurse Anesthesia Educational Programs (see separate entry). Candidates whose graduation date is more than two years prior to taking exam must document successful completion of 20 hours of approved continuing education. **Certification Requirements:** Successful completion of exam. Exam covers: (1) Basic Sciences, including: Anatomy, physiology, and pathophysiology; Chemistry, biochemistry, and physics; and Pharmacology; (2) Equipment, Instrumentation, and Technology, including: Airway equipment; Anesthetic delivery systems; and Monitoring devices; (3) Basic Principles of Anesthesia, including: Airway management; Fluid/blood replacement; Interpretation of data; Local/regional anesthesia; Monitored anesthesia care/conscious sedation; Pain management; Positioning; Post-anesthesia care/respiratory therapy; Preoperative assessment; Preparation of patient; and Other related areas; (4) Advanced Principles of Anesthesia, including: Geriatrics; Obstetrics; Pediatrics; and Surgical procedures and procedures related to organ systems; and (5) Professional Issues, including: Legal; Quality improvement; and Safety standards (professional and organizational). **Renewal:** Every two years. Recertification based on maintaining licensure as registered nurse, evidence of continuing employment in the field, and the accumulation of 40 points through continuing education. **Preparatory Materials:** *Criteria for Recertification* (reference). Candidate handbook, including exam content outline, list of accredited programs, and sample questions, provided. **Examination Frequency:** semiannual - always June and December. **Examination Sites:** Exam given at sites throughout the U.S. **Examination Type:** Multiple-choice. **Waiting Period to Receive Scores:** Five weeks. **Fees:** $400. **Accredited By:** American Board of Nursing Specialties; National Commission for

Certifying Agencies. **Endorsed By:** American Association of Nurse Anesthetists; National Organization of Competency Assurance.

978

Certified Registered Nurse Hospice (CRNH)
National Board for Certification of
    Hospice Nurses (NBCHN)
5512 Northumberland St.
Pittsburgh, PA 15217-1131
Phone: (412)687-3231
Fax: (412)687-9095
Madalon O'Rawe Amenta R.N.,
    Exec.Dir.

Recipient: Hospice nurses who provide palliative nursing care for terminally ill and their families with emphasis on physical, psychosocial, emotional, and spiritual needs. **Educational/Experience Requirements:** Must meet the following requirements: (1) Current licensure as registered nurse (R.N.); and (2) Two years (4000 hours) experience as R.N. in hospice or palliative care. **Membership:** Not required. **Certification Requirements:** Successful completion of exam. Exam covers: (1) End-Stage Disease Process, covering: Diagnosis, including AIDS, cancer and hematologic malignancies, cardiovascular, congenital anomalies, neurological pulmonary, renal, and other conditions; and Impending death, including altered breathing patterns, altered elimination, changes in mentation, changes in reflex responses, circulatory changes, thermoregulatory changes, and other issues; (2) Palliative Therapeutics, covering: Pain management, including assessment, evaluation, and intervention; and Symptom management, including major symptoms and principles; (3) Interdisciplinary Collaborative Practice, covering: Process; Roles and responsibility; and Team assessment; (4) Education and Advocacy, covering focus and methods; and (5) Professional Issues, covering: Ethical issues; Historical perspective; Hospice philosophy; Legal issues; and Related issues, such as care delivery and nurse as caregiver. **Renewal:** Every four years. Recertification based on successful completion of exam or continuing education. **Preparatory Materials:** Handbook, including exam content outline, list of suggested references, and sample questions, provided. Review course available. **Examination Frequency:** semiannual - always March and August. **Examination Sites:** Exam given at sites throughout the U.S. **Examination Type:** Multiple-choice. **Waiting Period to Receive Scores:** Six weeks. **Reexamination:** Fees to retake exam are:

$200 (members); $275 (nonmembers). **Fees:** $200 (members); $275 (nonmembers). **Endorsed By:** Hospice Nurses Association.

979

Certified Registered Nurse Intravenous (CRNI)
Intravenous Nurses Society (INS)
Two Brighton St.
Belmont, MA 02178
Phone: (617)489-5205
Fax: (617)489-0656
Toll Free: (800)434-INCC
Cynthia Rutherford CRNI, Pres.

Recipient: Registered nurses (R.N.s) involved in clinical practice of intravenous therapies. **Educational/Experience Requirements:** Must meet the following requirements: (1) Current licensure as R.N.; and (2) 1600 hours experience as R.N. within last two years. Experience may be as R.N. functioning as administrator, educator, or researcher. **Membership:** Not required. **Certification Requirements:** Successful completion of exam. Exam covers: Antineoplastic therapy; Fluid and electrolyte therapy; Infection control; Parenteral nutrition; Pediatrics; Pharmacology; Quality assurance; Technology and clinical applications; and Transfusion therapy. **Renewal:** Every three years. Recertification based on successful completion of exam or accumulation of 40 units through attendance at the following: (1) INS meetings, academies, and educational programs (minimum of 30 units); (2) Exam item writing workshops (maximum of ten units); and (3) INS chapter educational programs (maximum of five units). Must also hold current licensure as R.N. and document 1000 hours of experience during recertification period. Renewal fee for unit option is $100. Renewal fees for exam option are: $325 (members); $480 (nonmembers). **Preparatory Materials:** *Guidelines for Preparing to Take the Intravenous Nurses Certification Examination* (reference). Bulletin, including exam content outline, list of study references, and sample questions, provided. *Preparation for Taking the Intravenous Nurses Certification Examination* (videotape program) available. **Examination Frequency:** semiannual. **Examination Sites:** Exam given at annual meeting and at sites throughout the U.S. **Examination Type:** Multiple-choice. **Waiting Period to Receive Scores:** Six weeks. **Fees:** $225 (member); $380 (nonmembers). **Endorsed By:** National Organization for Competency Assurance.

980

Certified Rehabilitation Registered Nurse (CRRN)
Rehabilitation Nursing Certification
    Board (RNCB)
5700 Old Orchard Rd., First Fl.
Skokie, IL 60077-1057
Phone: (708)966-3433
Fax: (708)966-9418
Linda L. Pierce CRRN, Chair

Recipient: Registered nurses (R.N.s) working in rehabilitation nursing. **Educational/Experience Requirements:** Must meet the following requirements: (1) Current unrestricted licensure as R.N.; and (2) Two years experience in last five years. Experience may include direct patient care, education, research, and supervision. One year of postbaccalaureate study in nursing may count toward experience. Beginning in the year 2000, must also have bachelor's degree in nursing and successfully complete one course in specialty of rehabilitation nursing. **Membership:** Not required. **Certification Requirements:** Successful completion of exam. Exam consists of the following sections: (1) Rehabilitation and Rehabilitation Nursing, covering models and theories; (2) Functional Health Patterns: Theories, Physiology, Assessment, Nursing Diagnoses, and Interventions, covering the following patterns: Activity-exercise; Cognitiveperceptual; Coping-stress tolerance; Elimination; Health perception-health management; Nutrition-metabolic; Role relationship; Self-perception/self-concept; Sexuality-reproductive; Sleep-rest; and Value-belief; (3) The Rehabilitation Team and Community, covering: Barriers in the community; Case management; Life skills and community living; and Rehabilitation teams; and (4) Legislation/Economic/Ethical/Legal Issues. **Renewal:** Every five years. Recertification based on either successful completion of exam or accumulation of 60 points through continuing education, course work, authoring professional publications, presentations, and submission of test items for exam. **Preparatory Materials:** *Specialty Practice of Rehabilitation Nursing - A Core Curriculum,* Third Edition (reference). Handbook, including exam content outline, list of suggested study resources, and sample questions, provided. *Application of Rehabilitation Concepts to Nursing Practice,* independent study program, available. Study groups also available. **Examination Frequency:** Annual - always first Saturday in December. **Examination Sites:** Exam given at sites throughout the U.S. **Examination Type:** Multiple-choice. **Waiting Period to Receive Scores:** Six weeks. **Re-

examination: There is no limit to how many times exam may be retaken. Fees to retake exam are: $185 (members); $265 (nonmembers). **Fees:** $185 (members); $265 (nonmembers). **Endorsed By:** American Board of Nursing Specialties; Association of Rehabilitation Nurses.

981

Certified School Nurse (CSN)
National Association of School
 Nurses (NASN)
PO Box 130
Scarborough, ME 04070-1300
Phone: (207)883-2117
Fax: (207)883-2683

Recipient: School nurses. **Educational/ Experience Requirements:** Bachelor's degree and current licensure as registered nurse (R.N.). Three years experience is recommended. **Membership:** mnr **Certification Requirements:** Successful completion of exam. Exam covers: (1) Health Appraisal, covering: General Health, including data collection, interpretation of data, and intervention/ referral; and Systems, including cardiovascular, ears, endocrine, eyes, gastrointestinal, musculoskeletal, neurodevelopmental, reproductive/ genitourinary, respiratory, skin and scalp, and nose, mouth, and throat; (2) Health Problems and Nursing Management, covering: Acute, episodic and chronic conditions; Communicable diseases; and Emergency care; (3) Health Promotion/Disease Prevention, covering: Community health needs; Counseling; Environmental health concerns; Health and safety education; Immunizations; and Risk reduction and infection control; (4) Special Health Issues, covering: Special health needs, including abuse and neglect, eating disorders, human sexuality, parenting, psychosocial problems, suicide, and substance use, abuse, and addiction; Educational/health management; and Legal considerations; and (5) Professional Issues, covering: Administrative; Consultation to administration on health issues; Ethics; Health records; Legal issues; Medication policy; Professional responsibilities and designations; and Treatment policy. **Renewal:** Every five years. Recertification based on either successful completion of exam or accumulation of 75 hours of continuing education through home-study courses, seminars, workshops, attendance at state and national conferences, or other professional development activities. **Preparatory Materials:** Handbook, including sample questions and list of study resources, provided. **Examination Frequency:** Three times per year - always

March, June, and August. **Examination Sites:** Exam given at sites throughout the U.S. **Examination Type:** Multiple-choice. **Waiting Period to Receive Scores:** Six weeks. **Fees:** $150 (members); $200 (nonmembers).

982

Certified Wound Care Nurse (CWCN)
Wound Ostomy and Continence
 Nurses Society (WOCN)
2755 Bristol St., Ste. 110
Costa Mesa, CA 92626
Phone: (714)476-0268
Toll Free: (800)228-4238
Lynne Greene RN, Pres.

Recipient: Wound nurses who function in acute care, extended care, home health care, industry, outpatient facilities, private practice, and other settings. **Educational/Experience Requirements:** Bachelor's degree, current licensure as registered nurse (R.N.), and one of the following: (1) Successful completion of accredited enterostomal therapy nursing education program or specialty-training course and one year (2000 hours) of experience; or (2) Two years (4000 hours) experience. **Certification Requirements:** Successful completion of exam. **Preparatory Materials:** Handbook, including sample questions and study references, provided. **Examination Frequency:** semiannual - always June and November. **Examination Sites:** Exam given at sites throughout the U.S. and Canada.

983

**Clinical Specialist in Adult
 Psychiatric and Mental Health
 Nursing**
Board on Certification for
 Psychiatric and Mental Health
 Nursing Practice
American Nurses Credentialing
 Center
600 Maryland Ave., SW, Ste. 100
 West
Washington, DC 20024-2571
Toll Free: (800)284-CERT
Marie A. Reed R.N., Dir.

Recipient: Clinical specialists in adult psychiatric and mental health nursing. **Number of Certified Individuals:** 5653. **Educational/Experience Requirements:** Must meet the following requirements: (1) Current licensure as registered nurse (R.N.); (2) Current involvement in direct patient contact in psychiatric and mental health nursing an average of four hours

per week. Administrators, educators, researchers, and consultants can meet this requirement if they are involved in direct patient contact; (3) Current involvement in clinical consultation or clinical supervision; (4) Experience in at least two different modalities; (5) Master's or higher degree in psychiatric and mental health nursing or master's or higher degree in nursing outside the psychiatric and mental health nursing field, 24 graduate or post-graduate level academic credits in courses which have a significant focus on psychiatric and mental health theory (12 of which must be in psychiatric mental health nursing theory), and supervised clinical training in two psychotherapeutic treatment modalities; (6) 800 hours of direct patient/client contact in advanced clinical practice of psychiatric and mental health nursing, with 400 of these hours being post-master's degree; and (7) 100 hours of individual or group clinical consultation/supervision with both nurse certified as clinical specialist in psychiatric and mental health nursing and mental health professionals. **Membership:** Not required. **Certification Requirements:** Successful completion of exam. Exam covers: Conceptual models of practice; Mental health disorders; Nursing intervention strategies/approaches; Professional issues; and Professional roles. **Renewal:** Every five years. Recertification based on either successful completion of exam or continuing education. Continuing education requirement may be met using in-services, grand rounds, academic credits, continuing medical education (CME) credits, and other related programs. **Preparatory Materials:** *Directory of Certification Examination Review Courses* and *How to Take ANCC Certification Examinations* (references). Handbook, including exam content outline and sample questions, provided. Review courses available. **Examination Frequency:** semiannual - always July and October. **Examination Sites:** Exam given at sites throughout the U.S. **Examination Type:** Multiple-choice. **Waiting Period to Receive Scores:** Six-eight weeks. **Fees:** $145 (members); $285 (nonmembers). **Accredited By:** American Board of Nursing Specialties. **Endorsed By:** American Nurses Association; National Organization for Competency Assurance.

984

Clinical Specialist in Child and Adolescent Psychiatric and Mental Health Nursing

Board on Certification for Psychiatric and Mental Health Nursing Practice
American Nurses Credentialing Center
600 Maryland Ave., SW, Ste. 100 West
Washington, DC 20024-2571
Toll Free: (800)284-CERT
Marie A. Reed R.N., Dir.

Recipient: Clinical specialists in child and adolescent psychiatric and mental health nursing. **Number of Certified Individuals:** 716. **Educational/Experience Requirements:** Must meet the following requirements: (1) Current licensure as registered nurse (R.N.); (2) Current involvement in direct patient contact in psychiatric and mental health nursing an average of four hours per week. Administrators, educators, researchers, and consultants can meet this requirement if they are involved in direct patient contact; (3) Current involvement in clinical consultation or clinical supervision; (4) Experience in at least two different modalities; (5) Master's or higher degree in psychiatric and mental health nursing or master's or higher degree in nursing outside the psychiatric and mental health nursing field, 24 graduate or post-graduate level academic credits in courses which have significant focus in psychiatric and mental health theory (12 of which must be in psychiatric mental health nursing theory), and supervised clinical training in two psychotherapeutic treatment modalities; (6) 800 hours of direct patient/client contact in advanced clinical practice of psychiatric and mental health nursing, with 400 of these hours being post-master's degree; and (7) 100 hours of individual or group clinical consultation/supervision with both nurse certified as clinical specialist in psychiatric and mental health nursing and mental health professionals. **Membership:** Not required. **Certification Requirements:** Successful completion of exam. Exam covers: Consultation and research; Education; Lifestyle and environment; Practice theories; Psychopathology; Treatment modalities; and Trends and issues. **Renewal:** Every five years. Recertification based on either successful completion of exam or continuing education. Continuing education requirement may be met using in-services, grand rounds, academic credits, continuing medical education (CME) credits, and other related programs. **Preparatory Materials:** *Directory of Certification Examination Review Courses* and *How to Take ANCC Certification Examinations* (references). Handbook, including exam content outline and sample questions, provided. Review courses available. **Examination Frequency:** semiannual - always July and October. **Examination Sites:** Exam given at sites throughout the U.S. **Examination Type:** Multiple-choice. **Waiting Period to Receive Scores:** Six-eight weeks. **Fees:** $145 (members); $285 (nonmembers). **Accredited By:** American Board of Nursing Specialties. **Endorsed By:** American Nurses Association; National Organization for Competency Assurance.

985

Clinical Specialist in Community Health Nursing

Board on Certification for Community Health Nursing Practice
American Nurses Credentialing Center
600 Maryland Ave., SW, Ste. 100 West
Washington, DC 20024-2571
Toll Free: (800)284-CERT
Marie A. Reed R.N., Dir.

Recipient: Clinical specialists in community health nursing. **Number of Certified Individuals:** 294. **Educational/Experience Requirements:** Must meet the following requirements: (1) Current licensure as registered nurse (R.N.); (2) Master's degree or higher in nursing, preferably with specialization in community/public health nursing practice, or bachelor's degree in nursing and master's or higher degree in public health; (3) Current practice of an average of 12 hours weekly in community/public health nursing; and (4) 800 hours of post-master's experience in community/public health nursing within last 24 months. Beginning in 1998 must have either master's degree or higher in nursing with a specialization in community/public health nursing or hold baccalaureate or higher degree in nursing and master's degree in public health with a specialization in community/public health nursing. **Membership:** Not required. **Certification Requirements:** Successful completion of exam. Exam covers: Community assessment process; Health care delivery system; Program administration; Public health sciences; Research; Theory; and Trends and issues. **Renewal:** Every five years. Recertification based on either successful completion of exam or continuing education. Continuing education requirement may be met using in-services, grand rounds, academic credits, continuing medical education (CME) credits, and other related programs. **Preparatory Materials:** *Directory of Certification Examination Review Courses* and *How to Take ANCC Certification Examinations* (references). Handbook, including exam content outline and sample questions, provided. Review courses available. **Examination Frequency:** semiannual - always July and October. **Examination Sites:** Exam given at sites throughout the U.S. **Examination Type:** Multiple-choice. **Waiting Period to Receive Scores:** Six-eight weeks. **Fees:** $145 (members); $285 (nonmembers). **Accredited By:** American Board of Nursing Specialties. **Endorsed By:** American Nurses Association; American Public Health Association; National Organization for Competency Assurance.

986

Clinical Specialist in Gerontological Nursing

Board on Certification for Gerontological Nursing Practice
American Nurses Credentialing Center
600 Maryland Ave., SW, Ste. 100 West
Washington, DC 20024-2571
Toll Free: (800)284-CERT
Marie A. Reed R.N., Dir.

Recipient: Clinical specialists in gerontological nursing who provide, direct, and influence the care of older adults and their families and significant others in a variety of settings. **Number of Certified Individuals:** 601. **Educational/Experience Requirements:** Current licensure as registered nurse (R.N.), master's degree or higher in nursing, preferably in gerontological nursing, one year of experience following completion of master's degree, and one of the following: (1) Clinical specialists must have 800 hours of post-master's direct patient care or clinical management experience in gerontological nursing within past 24 months; or (2) Consultants, researchers, educators, or administrators must have provided 400 hours of post-master's direct patient care or been involved in clinical management in gerontological nursing within past 24 months. Supervision of student's patient care fulfills the requirement for direct patient care or clinical management only when the supervisor intervenes with the patient/client and is personally responsible and accountable for the outcome of that intervention. Beginning in 1998 must hold master's or higher degree in gerontological nursing or master's degree or higher in nursing with a specialization in gerontological nursing. **Membership:** Not required. **Certification Requirements:** Successful completion of exam. Exam covers: Administration; Consultation; Education; Practice; and Research. **Renewal:** Every five years. Recertification based on either successful completion of exam or continuing education. Continuing education requirement may be met using in-services, grand rounds, academic credits, continuing medical education (CME) credits, and other related programs. **Preparatory Materials:** *Directory of Certification Examination Review Courses* and *How to Take ANCC Certification Examinations* (references). Handbook, including exam content outline and sample questions, provided. Review courses available. **Examination Frequency:** semiannual - always July and October. **Examination Sites:** Exam given at sites throughout the U.S. **Examination Type:** Multiple-choice. **Waiting Period to Receive Scores:** Six-eight weeks. **Fees:** $145 (members); $285 (nonmembers). **Accredited By:** American Board of Nursing Specialties. **Endorsed By:** American Nurses Association; National Organization for Competency Assurance.

987

Clinical Specialist in Medical-Surgical Nursing
Board on Certification for Medical-Surgical Nursing Practice
American Nurses Credentialing Center
600 Maryland Ave., SW, Ste. 100 West
Washington, DC 20024-2571
Toll Free: (800)284-CERT
Marie A. Reed R.N., Dir.

Recipient: Clinical specialists in medical-surgical nursing. **Number of Certified Individuals:** 1631. **Educational/Experience Requirements:** Must meet the following requirements: (1) Current licensure as registered nurse (R.N.); (2) Master's degree in nursing; (3) Current practice in direct patient care in medical-surgical nursing for an average of four hours or more weekly; (4) One year post-master's degree practice; and (5) 800 hours of direct patient care within last 24 months or post-master's employment as consultant, researcher, administrator, or educator for two of the past three years during which have provided direct patient care in medical-surgical nursing for 400 hours. Supervision of students' patient care fulfills the requirement for direct patient care or clinical management

only when the supervisor interacts with the patient/client and is personally responsible and accountable for the outcome of that interaction. **Membership:** Not required. **Certification Requirements:** Successful completion of exam. Exam covers: Clinical practice; Consultation; Education; Issues and trends; Management; and Research. **Renewal:** Every five years. Recertification based on either successful completion of exam or continuing education. Continuing education requirement may be met using in-services, grand rounds, academic credits, continuing medical education (CME) credits, and other related programs. **Preparatory Materials:** *Directory of Certification Examination Review Courses* and *How to Take ANCC Certification Examinations* (references). Handbook, including exam content outline and sample questions, provided. Review courses available. **Examination Frequency:** semiannual - always July and October. **Examination Sites:** Exam given at sites throughout the U.S. **Examination Type:** Multiple-choice. **Waiting Period to Receive Scores:** Six-eight weeks. **Fees:** $145 (members); $285 (nonmembers). **Accredited By:** American Board of Nursing Specialties. **Endorsed By:** American Nurses Association; National Organization for Competency Assurance.

988

CNOR
National Certification Board: Perioperative Nursing
2170 S. Parker Rd., Ste. 295
Denver, CO 80231
Phone: (303)369-9566
Fax: (303)695-8464
Mary O'Neale CNOR, Exec.Dir.

Recipient: Registered nurses whose practice emphasis is care of patients during the intraoperative period. **Number of Certified Individuals:** 25,000. **Educational/Experience Requirements:** Must meet the following requirements: (1) Current licensure as R.N.; and (2) Two years experience as R.N. in administrative, teaching, research, or general capacity in operating room nursing. **Membership:** Not required. **Certification Requirements:** Successful completion of exam. Exam covers preoperative, intra-operative, and postoperative procedures in: Patient care management; Management of materials; and Management of personnel/services. **Renewal:** Every five years. Recertification based on either successful completion of exam or accumulation of 150 hours of continuing education. Renewal fees are: $125 (members); $200 (nonmembers). **Preparatory Mate-**

rials: Self-assessment materials, review courses, study groups, and study guide, including list of suggested references, available. **Examination Frequency:** semiannual - always March and September. **Examination Sites:** Exam given at sites throughout the U.S. **Examination Type:** Multiple-choice. **Waiting Period to Receive Scores:** Eight weeks. **Fees:** $150 (members); $225 (nonmembers). **Endorsed By:** Association of Operating Room Nurses.

989

CNRN
American Board of Neuroscience Nursing (ABNN)
224 N. Des Plaines, Ste. 601
Chicago, IL 60661
Phone: (312)993-0256

Recipient: Neuroscience nurses involved in diagnosis and treatment of actual or potential patient and family responses to nervous dysfunction. **Educational/Experience Requirements:** Must meet the following requirements: (1) Current licensure as registered nurse (R.N.); and (2) Two years experience within last five years. Experience must be in clinical practice or as consultant, researcher, administrator, or educator with direct or indirect involvement in neuroscience nursing. **Membership:** Not required. **Certification Requirements:** Successful completion of exam. Exam consists of the following sections: (1) Human Responses to Problems, including: Cognition; Communication; Consciousness; Mobility; Nutrition; Sensation; and Social role; and (2) Neuroscience Health Problems (Disorders), including: Cerebrovascular; Infections; Metabolic; Seizures; Trauma; and Tumors. **Renewal:** Every five years. **Preparatory Materials:** Handbook, including sample questions and list of study references, provided. **Examination Frequency:** semiannual. **Examination Sites:** Exam given at sites throughout the U.S. **Examination Type:** Multiple-choice. **Waiting Period to Receive Scores:** Several weeks. **Fees:** $175 (members); $250 (nonmembers). **Endorsed By:** American Association of Neuroscience Nurses.

990

College Health Nurse
American Nurses Credentialing Center (ANCC)
600 Maryland Ave., SW, Ste. 100 West
Washington, DC 20024-2571
Toll Free: (800)284-CERT
Marie A. Reed R.N., Dir.

Recipient: Nurses working in areas such as case management, home health, long-term care, and extended care, and in settings such as community hospitals, ambulatory clinics, personnel resource pools, and nurse-managed centers. **Number of Certified Individuals:** 1365. **Educational/Experience Requirements:** Must meet the following requirements: (1) Current licensure as registered nurse (R.N.); (2) Bachelor's degree or higher in nursing; (3) 1500 hours of experience as licensed R.N. in college health nursing within last three years; and (4) Current practice of college health nursing for average of eight hours per week (minimum of 288 hours per year). Experience must be in direct patient care or direct clinical management, supervision, education, or direction of other persons to achieve or help achieve patient/client goals. Beginning in 1996 must have 30 contact hours of continuing education related to college health nursing within last three years. Continuing education requirement may be met through inservices, grand rounds, academic credits, continuing medical education (CME) credits, and other related continuing education programs. **Membership:** Not required. **Certification Requirements:** Successful completion of exam. Exam covers: Client care; Environment; Foundations of college health; Issues and trends; and Roles. **Renewal:** Every five years. Recertification based on either successful completion of exam or through continuing education. Continuing education requirement may be met through in-services, grand rounds, academic credits, continuing medical education (CME) credits, and other related programs. **Preparatory Materials:** *Directory of Certification Examination Review Courses* and *How to Take ANCC Certification Examinations* (references). Handbook, including exam content outline and sample questions, provided. Review courses available. **Examination Frequency:** semiannual - always July and October. **Examination Sites:** Exam given at sites throughout the U.S. **Examination Type:** Multiple-choice. **Waiting Period to Receive Scores:** Six-eight weeks. **Fees:** $145 (members); $285 (nonmembers). **Endorsed By:** American College Health Association; American Nurses Association; National Organization for Competency Assurance.

991

Community Health Nurse
Board on Certification for
  Community Health Nursing
  Practice
American Nurses Credentialing
  Center
600 Maryland Ave., SW, Ste. 100
  West
Washington, DC 20024-2571
Toll Free: (800)284-CERT
Marie A. Reed R.N., Dir.

Recipient: Community health nurses who work in ambulatory clinics, private offices, and occupational health, health department, school, health maintenance, home health agency, visiting nurse, correctional institution, camp, and other community-based settings. **Number of Certified Individuals:** 2433. **Educational/Experience Requirements:** Must meet the following requirements: (1) Current licensure as registered nurse (R.N.); (2) Bachelor's degree or higher in nursing; and (3) 24 months (1600 hours) experience as licensed registered nurse in community health nursing within last 48 months. Beginning in 1996 must have 30 contact hours of continuing education related to community health nursing within last three years. Continuing education requirement may be met using in-services, grand rounds, academic credits, continuing medical education (CME) credits, and other related continuing education programs. Consultants, researchers, administrators, or educators may also qualify. **Membership:** Not required. **Certification Requirements:** Successful completion of exam. Exam covers: Areas of practice; Community as client; Individual/family as client; Public health problems; Public health science; and Professional issues. **Renewal:** Every five years. Recertification based on either successful completion of exam or continuing education. Continuing education requirement may be met using in-services, grand rounds, academic credits, continuing medical education (CME) credits, and other related programs. **Preparatory Materials:** *Directory of Certification Examination Review Courses* and *How to Take ANCC Certification Examinations* (references). Handbook, including exam content outline and sample questions, provided. Review courses available. **Examination Frequency:** semiannual - always July and October. **Examination Sites:** Exam given at sites throughout the U.S. **Examination Type:** Multiple-choice. **Waiting Period to Receive Scores:** Six-eight weeks. **Fees:** $145 (members); $285 (nonmembers). **Accredited By:** American Board of Nursing Specialties. **Endorsed By:** American Nurses Association; Na-

tional Organization for Competency Assurance.

992

CRNFA
National Certification Board:
  Perioperative Nursing
2170 S. Parker Rd., Ste. 295
Denver, CO 80231
Phone: (303)369-9566
Fax: (303)695-8464
Mary O'Neale CNOR, Exec.Dir.

Recipient: Registered nurse (R.N.) first assistants. **Educational/Experience Requirements:** Must meet the following requirements: (1) Hold CNOR designation (see separate entry); (2) Current licensure as R.N.; and (3) 2000 hours experience, with 500 hours in last two years. Beginning in 1998 must have bachelor's degree in nursing. **Membership:** Not required. **Certification Requirements:** Successful completion of exam. Exam covers pre-op, intra-op, and post-op procedures in: Direct patient care management; and Collaborative patient care management. **Renewal:** Every five years. Recertification based on successful completion of exam. **Preparatory Materials:** *AORN Standards and Recommended Practices for Perioperative Nursing* and *A Job Analysis for the RN First Assistant* (references). Manual, including job analysis, provided. **Examination Frequency:** semiannual - always March and September. **Examination Sites:** Exam given at sites throughout the U.S. **Examination Type:** Multiple-choice. **Waiting Period to Receive Scores:** Eight weeks. **Fees:** $375 (members); $500 (nonmembers). **Endorsed By:** Association of Operating Room Nurses.

993

CRNO
National Certifying Board for
  Ophthalmic Registered Nurses
  (NCBORN)
PO Box 193030
San Francisco, CA 94119
Phone: (415)561-8513

Recipient: Ophthalmic registered nurses (R.N.S.). **Educational/Experience Requirements:** Must meet the following requirements: (1) Current licensure as R.N.; and (2) Two years experience (4000 hours) or equivalent. **Membership:** Not required. **Certification Requirements:** Successful completion of exam. Exam covers: (1) Nursing Assessment of the Ophthalmic Patient, including: Basic diagnostic tests and techniques; Health history; and Special diagnostic tests; (2) Ocular Conditions, including: Acquired; Congenital and hereditary; Developmental; Malignancies; Systemic; and Trauma; (3) Ophthalmic Nursing Interventions, including: Complications; Operative procedures; Perioperative procedures; Postoperative care; Trauma; and Visual impairment and blindness; (4) Pharmacology, including: Administration routes and techniques; Injections; Oral; and Types and effects of drugs; and (5) Professional Issues, including: Ethics; Legal aspects; Management and supervision; Patient and staff education; and Patient teaching. **Preparatory Materials:** Candidate handbook, including exam content outline, sample questions, and suggested bibliography, provided. **Examination Frequency:** semiannual - always February and August. **Examination Sites:** Exam given at 20 sites throughout the U.S. or by arrangement with proctor. **Examination Type:** Multiple-choice. **Reexamination:** Exam may be retaken as many times as necessary. Fees to retake exam are: $175 (members); $250 (nonmembers). **Fees:** $175 (members); $250 (nonmembers). **Endorsed By:** American Society of Ophthalmic Registered Nurses.

994

Family Nurse Practitioner (FNP)
Board on Certification for Primary
  Care in Adult and Family
  Nursing Practice
American Nurses Credentialing
  Center
600 Maryland Ave., SW, Ste. 100
  West
Washington, DC 20024-2571
Toll Free: (800)284-CERT
Marie A. Reed R.N., Dir.

Recipient: Family nurse practitioners. **Number of Certified Individuals:** 7593. **Educational/Experience Requirements:** Current licensure as registered nurse (R.N.) and master's or higher degree in nursing. Must also have been prepared as family nurse practitioner in either: (1) Family nurse practitioner master's degree program within nursing program; or (2) Formal postgraduate family nurse practitioner track or program within school of nursing granting graduate level academic credit. Educational program must include both didactic and clinical components. **Membership:** Not required. **Certification Requirements:** Successful completion of exam. Exam covers: Assessment and management of client illness in primary care; Evaluation and promotion of client wellness in primary care; Issues and trends in primary care;

and Nurse/client relationships. **Renewal:** Every five years. Recertification based on either successful completion of exam or continuing education. Continuing education requirement may be met using in-services, grand rounds, academic credits, continuing medical education (CME) credits, and other related programs. **Preparatory Materials:** "Guidelines for Educational Preparation of Family Nurse Practitioners," *Directory of Certification Examination Review Courses,* and *How to Take ANCC Certification Examinations* (references). Handbook, including exam content outline and sample questions, provided. Review courses available. **Examination Frequency:** semiannual - always July and October. **Examination Sites:** Exam given at sites throughout the U.S. **Examination Type:** Multiple-choice. **Waiting Period to Receive Scores:** Six-eight weeks. **Fees:** $145 (members); $285 (nonmembers). **Accredited By:** American Board of Nursing Specialties. **Endorsed By:** American Nurses Association; National Organization for Competency Assurance.

995

General Nursing Practice
Board on Certification for General
  Nursing Practice
American Nurses Credentialing
  Center
600 Maryland Ave., SW, Ste. 100
  West
Washington, DC 20024-2571
Toll Free: (800)284-CERT
Marie A. Reed R.N., Dir.

Recipient: Nurses working in areas or settings such as home health, long-term care, extended care, community hospitals, ambulatory clinics, case management, personnel resource pools, and nurse-managed centers. **Number of Certified Individuals:** 1112. **Educational/Experience Requirements:** Must meet the following requirements: (1) Hold current licensure as registered nurse (R.N.); and (2) 4000 hours of experience as licensed R.N. in general nursing, with 2000 hours in last three years. Experience must be in direct patient care or direct clinical management, supervision, education, or direction of other persons to achieve or help achieve patient/client goals. **Certification Requirements:** Successful completion of exam. Exam covers: Adaptation to illness; Health promotion, disease prevention, and control; Human sexuality and parenting; Professional issues; Psychological disturbance; Psychological responses to illness and change; and Physiological alterations: trauma/illness. **Renewal:** Every five years. Recer-

tification based on either successful completion of exam or continuing education. Continuing education requirement may be met using in-services, grand rounds, academic credits, continuing medical education (CME) credits, and other related programs. **Preparatory Materials:** *Directory of Certification Examination Review Courses* and *How to Take ANCC Certification Examinations* (references). Handbook, including exam content outline and sample questions, provided. Review courses available. **Examination Frequency:** semiannual - always July and October. **Examination Sites:** Exam given at sites throughout the U.S. **Examination Type:** Multiple-choice. **Waiting Period to Receive Scores:** Six-eight weeks. **Fees:** $145 (members); $285 (nonmembers). **Endorsed By:** American Nurses Association; National Organization for Competency Assurance.

996

Gerontological Nurse
Board on Certification for
  Gerontological Nursing Practice
American Nurses Credentialing
  Center
600 Maryland Ave., SW, Ste. 100
  West
Washington, DC 20024-2571
Toll Free: (800)284-CERT
Marie A. Reed R.N., Dir.

Recipient: Gerontological nurses. **Number of Certified Individuals:** 10,282. **Educational/Experience Requirements:** Must meet the following requirements: (1) Current licensure as registered nurse (R.N.); (2) 4000 hours experience as licensed R.N. in gerontological nursing practice, with 2000 hours in the last two years; and (3) 30 hours of continuing education related to gerontology/ gerontological nursing within last two years. Continuing education requirement may be met using in-services, grand rounds, academic credits, continuing medical education (CME) credits, and other related continuing education programs. Experience must be in direct patient care or direct clinical management, supervision, education, or direction of other persons to achieve or help achieve patient/client goals. Time spent in formal program of advanced nursing study may count toward 300 hours of experience requirement. **Membership:** Not required. **Certification Requirements:** Successful completion of exam. Exam covers: Education and advocacy; Management (administration); Nursing practice and policy issues; and Nursing process. **Renewal:** Every five years. Recertification based on either successful completion of exam or continuing education. Continuing education requirement may be met using in-services, grand rounds, academic credits, continuing medical education (CME) credits, and other related programs. **Preparatory Materials:** *Directory of Certification Examination Review Courses* and *How to Take ANCC Certification Examinations* (references). Handbook, including exam content outline and sample questions, provided. Review courses available. **Examination Frequency:** semiannual - always July and October. **Examination Sites:** Exam given at sites throughout the U.S. **Examination Type:** Multiple-choice. **Waiting Period to Receive Scores:** Six-eight weeks. **Fees:** $145 (members); $285 (nonmembers). **Accredited By:** American Board of Nursing Specialties. **Endorsed By:** American Nurses Association; National Organization for Competency Assurance.

997

Gerontological Nurse Practitioner
Board on Certification for
Gerontological Nursing Practice
American Nurses Credentialing
Center
600 Maryland Ave., SW, Ste. 100
West
Washington, DC 20024-2571
Toll Free: (800)284-CERT
Marie A. Reed R.N., Dir.

Recipient: Gerontological nurse practitioners providing primary health care for older adults and their families in a variety of settings. **Number of Certified Individuals:** 1698. **Educational/Experience Requirements:** Current licensure as registered nurse (R.N.) and master's degree in nursing. Must also have been prepared as nurse practitioner in either: (1) Gerontological nurse practitioner master's degree program within nursing program; or (2) Formal postgraduate gerontological nurse practitioner track or program within school of nursing granting graduate level academic credit. Education program must include both didactic and clinical components. **Membership:** Not required. **Certification Requirements:** Successful completion of exam. Exam covers: Health promotion; Illness management; Legal and ethical issues; Organizational and health policy issues; Professional issues and role functions in advanced practice; and Theoretical foundations in nursing and gerontology. **Renewal:** Every five years. Recertification based on either successful completion of exam or continuing education. Continuing education requirement may be met using in-services, grand rounds, academic credits, continuing medical education

(CME) credits, and other related programs. **Preparatory Materials:** "Guidelines for Educational Preparation of Gerontological Nurse Practitioners," *Directory of Certification Examination Review Courses,* and *How to Take ANCC Certification Examinations* (references). Handbook, including exam content outline and sample questions, provided. Review courses available. **Examination Frequency:** semiannual - always July and October. **Examination Sites:** Exam given at sites throughout the U.S. **Examination Type:** Multiple-choice. **Waiting Period to Receive Scores:** Six-eight weeks. **Fees:** $145 (members); $285 (nonmembers). **Accredited By:** American Board of Nursing Specialties. **Endorsed By:** American Nurses Association; National Organization for Competency Assurance.

998

High Risk Obstetric Nurse
National Certification Corp. for the
Obstetric, Gynecologic, and
Neonatal Nursing Specialties
(NCC)
645 N. Michigan Ave., Ste. 900
Chicago, IL 60611
Phone: (312)951-0207
Toll Free: (800)367-5613
Suzanne Choiniere RNC, Pres.

Recipient: High risk obstetric nurses. **Educational/Experience Requirements:** Must meet the following requirements: (1) Current licensure as registered nurse; and (2) Two years experience in inpatient obstetric nursing, including 2000 hours of practice. **Certification Requirements:** Successful completion of exam. Exam covers: (1) Normal Anatomy and Physiology of the Maternal/Fetal Unit; (2) Maternal Assessment, covering: Diagnostic tools; and Laboratory tests; (3) Fetal Assessment, covering: Diagnostic tools; and Laboratory tests; (4) Management of High Risk and Pathophysiologic States, covering: Amniotic fluid disorders; Blood disorders; Collagen vascular diseases; Diabetes; Hypertension; Infectious disease/sepsis; Labor assessment/abnormalities; Life style and environmental risks; Malignancies; Maternal cardiac disease/anomalies; Multiple gestation; Neurologic disorders; Pharmacology; Pulmonary disorders; Renal/GU diseases; Stabilization and resuscitation; Thyroid disorders; and Uteroplacental disorders; (5) Family Dynamics and High Risk Pregnancy, covering: Grieving; Prolonged hospitalization/prolonged bed rest; and Psychophysiology; and (6) Professional Issues, covering: Ethical issues and dilemmas; Practice; and Research. **Renewal:** Every three years. Re-

certification based on either successful completion of exam or continuing education. **Preparatory Materials:** Candidate guide, including bibliography of references and sample questions, provided. **Examination Frequency:** semiannual. **Examination Sites:** Exam given at sites throughout the U.S. **Examination Type:** Multiple-choice. **Waiting Period to Receive Scores:** Eight weeks. **Reexamination:** May retake the exam as many times as necessary. There is a $300 fee to retake exam. **Fees:** $300.

999

Home Health Nurse
American Nurses Credentialing
Center (ANCC)
600 Maryland Ave., SW, Ste. 100
West
Washington, DC 20024-2571
Toll Free: (800)284-CERT
Marie A. Reed R.N., Dir.

Recipient: Home health nurses working in the home, place of residence, or appropriate community site. **Number of Certified Individuals:** 450. **Educational/Experience Requirements:** Must meet the following requirements: (1) Current licensure as registered nurse (R.N.); (2) Bachelor's degree or higher in nursing; (3) Two years experience as licensed R.N.; (4) 2000 hours experience as licensed R.N. in home health nursing within last 48 months; and (5) Current practice of home health nursing for minimum of eight hours per week. Experience must be in direct patient care or clinical management, supervision, education, research, or direction of other persons to achieve or help achieve patient/client goals. Time spent in formal program of advanced nursing study may count toward 300 hours of experience requirement. Beginning in 1996 must have 20 contact hours of related continuing education within last two years. Continuing education requirement may be met through in-services, grand rounds, academic credits, continuing medical education (CME) credits, and other related continuing education programs. **Membership:** Not required. **Certification Requirements:** Successful completion of exam. Exam covers: Clinical management; Concepts and models; Program management; and Trends, issues and research. **Renewal:** Every five years. Recertification based on either successful completion of exam or continuing education. Continuing education requirement may be met through in-services, grand rounds, academic credits, continuing medical education (CME) credits, and other related programs. **Preparatory Ma-**

terials: *Directory of Certification Examination Review Courses* and *How to Take ANCC Certification Examinations* (references). Handbook, including exam content outline and sample questions, provided. Review courses available. **Examination Frequency:** semiannual - always July and October. **Examination Sites:** Exam given at sites throughout the U.S. **Examination Type:** Multiple-choice. **Waiting Period to Receive Scores:** Six-eight weeks. **Fees:** $145 (members); $285 (nonmembers). **Endorsed By:** American Nurses Association; National Organization for Competency Assurance.

1000

Informatics Nurse

Board on Certification for
    Informatics Nursing
American Nurses Credentialing
    Center
600 Maryland Ave., SW, Ste. 100
    West
Washington, DC 20024-2571
Toll Free: (800)284-CERT
Marie A. Reed R.N., Dir.

Recipient: Informatics nurses. **Membership:** Not required. **Certification Requirements:** Successful completion of exam. **Renewal:** Every five years. Recertification based on either successful completion of exam or continuing education. Continuing education requirement may be met using in-services, grand rounds, academic credits, continuing medical education (CME) credits, and other related programs. **Preparatory Materials:** *Directory of Certification Examination Review Courses* and *How to Take ANCC Certification Examinations* (references). Handbook, including exam content outline and sample questions, provided. Review courses available. **Examination Frequency:** semiannual - always July and October. **Examination Sites:** Exam given at sites throughout the U.S. **Examination Type:** Multiple-choice. **Waiting Period to Receive Scores:** Six-eight weeks. **Fees:** $145 (members); $285 (nonmembers). **Endorsed By:** American Nurses Association; National Organization for Competency Assurance.

1001

Inpatient Obstetric Nurse

National Certification Corp. for the
    Obstetric, Gynecologic, and
    Neonatal Nursing Specialties
    (NCC)
645 N. Michigan Ave., Ste. 900
Chicago, IL 60611
Phone: (312)951-0207
Toll Free: (800)367-5613
Suzanne Choiniere RNC, Pres.

Recipient: Inpatient obstetric nurses. **Educational/Experience Requirements:** Must meet the following requirements: (1) Current licensure as registered nurse; and (2) Two years experience in inpatient obstetric nursing, including 2000 hours of practice. **Certification Requirements:** Successful completion of exam. Exam covers: (1) Maternal Factors Affecting the Fetus and Newborn, covering: Disease processes and risk factors; Life style and environmental risks; and Pharmacology; (2) Fetal Assessment, covering: Acid-base assessment; Antepartum assessment; Electronic fetal monitoring; Non-electronic fetal monitoring; and Prenatal diagnosis; (3) Labor and Delivery, covering: Childbirth education; Labor management, including abnormal, induction of labor, normal, operative delivery, preterm labor, and post-term pregnancy; Pain management; and Physiology of labor; (4) Postpartum, covering: Complications of postpartum period; Discharge planning and teaching; Family adaption; Lactation; and Physiology of postpartum woman; (5) Newborn, covering: Adaptation to external life; Assessment; Pathophysiology; and Resuscitation; and (6) Professional Issues, covering: Ethical issues; Legal issues; Research; and Standards/quality assurance. **Renewal:** Every three years. Recertification based on either successful completion of exam or continuing education. **Preparatory Materials:** Candidate guide, including bibliography of references and sample questions, provided. **Examination Frequency:** semiannual. **Examination Sites:** Exam given at sites throughout the U.S. **Examination Type:** Multiple-choice. **Waiting Period to Receive Scores:** Eight weeks. **Re-examination:** May retake exam as many times as necessary. There is a $300 fee to retake exam. **Fees:** $300.

1002

Low Risk Neonatal Nurse

National Certification Corp. for the
    Obstetric, Gynecologic, and
    Neonatal Nursing Specialties
    (NCC)
645 N. Michigan Ave., Ste. 900
Chicago, IL 60611
Phone: (312)951-0207
Toll Free: (800)367-5613
Suzanne Choiniere RNC, Pres.

Recipient: Low risk neonatal nurses. **Educational/Experience Requirements:** Must meet the following requirements: (1) Current licensure as registered nurse; and (2) Two years experience in low risk neonatal nursing, including 2000 hours of practice. **Certification Requirements:** Successful completion of exam. Exam covers: (1) Family Integration, covering: Discharge planning; and Role adaptation; (2) Mother/Fetus, covering: Fetal physiology/assessment of fetal well being; and Maternal factors and complications; (3) Newborn, including: Assessment and management, covering behavioral/developmental, clinical laboratory and diagnostic data, gestational age, and thermoregulation; Neonatal nutrition, feeding, and lactation; Pharmacology; Resuscitation and stabilization; and Systems review and complications; and (4) Professional Issues, covering: Legal/ethical issues; and Research. **Renewal:** Every three years. Recertification based on either successful completion of exam or continuing education. **Preparatory Materials:** Candidate guide, including bibliography of references and sample questions, provided. **Examination Frequency:** semiannual. **Examination Sites:** Exam given at sites throughout the U.S. **Examination Type:** Multiple-choice. **Waiting Period to Receive Scores:** Eight weeks. **Re-examination:** May retake exam as many times as necessary. There is a $300 fee to retake exam. **Fees:** $300.

1003

Maternal Newborn Nurse

National Certification Corp. for the
    Obstetric, Gynecologic, and
    Neonatal Nursing Specialties
    (NCC)
645 N. Michigan Ave., Ste. 900
Chicago, IL 60611
Phone: (312)951-0207
Toll Free: (800)367-5613
Suzanne Choiniere RNC, Pres.

Recipient: Reproductive endocrinology/infertility nurses. **Educational/Experience Requirements:** Must meet the following requirements: (1) Current licensure as registered nurse; and (2) Two years experience in maternal newborn nursing, including 2000 hours of practice. **Certification Requirements:** Successful completion of exam. Exam covers: (1) Aspects of Professional Practice, covering: Ethical/legal issues; Research; and Standards of practice; (2) Factors Affecting Maternal/Neonatal Outcomes, covering: Antenatal factors; and Intrapartal factors; (3) Newborn Assessment and Management and Family Education, covering: Behavioral/developmental; Clinical laboratory and diagnostic data; Family education; Gestational age; Pharmacology; and Thermoregulation; (4) Nursing Management of Postpartum Complications, covering alterations in family dynamics and complications; (5) Postpartum Period, covering: Family dynamics after childbirth; Lactation and newborn feeding, including bottle and breastfeeding; Nursing assessment, management, and education; and Physiologic changes and laboratory values; and (6) System Review - Normal and Complication, covering: Cardiac; Endocrine/metabolic; Gastrointestinal; Genetic disorders; Genitourinary; Head, ears, eyes, nose, and throat; Hematopoietic; Infectious diseases; Integumentary; Jaundice and liver diseases; Musculoskeletal; Neurological; Respiratory; and Substance abused neonate. **Renewal:** Every three years. Recertification based on either successful completion of exam or continuing education. **Preparatory Materials:** Candidate guide, including bibliography of references and sample questions, provided. **Examination Frequency:** semiannual. **Examination Sites:** Exam given at sites throughout the U.S. **Examination Type:** Multiple-choice. **Waiting Period to Receive Scores:** Eight weeks. **Reexamination:** May retake exam as many times as necessary. There is a $300 fee to retake exam. **Fees:** $300.

1004

Medical-Surgical Nurse
Board on Certification for
　Medical-Surgical Nursing
　Practice
American Nurses Credentialing
　Center
600 Maryland Ave., SW, Ste. 100
　West
Washington, DC 20024-2571
Toll Free: (800)284-CERT
Marie A. Reed R.N., Dir.

Recipient: Medical-surgical nurses working where primary, acute, or long-term nursing care is delivered. **Number of Certified Individuals:** 27,033. **Educational/**

Experience Requirements: Must meet the following requirements: (1) Current licensure as registered nurse (R.N.); (2) 4000 hours of experience in medical surgical nursing, with 2000 hours in the last two years; and (3) Current practice of an average of eight hours per week. Experience must be in direct patient care or direct clinical management, supervision, education, or direction of other persons to achieve or help achieve patient/client goals. Beginning in 1996 must have had 30 contact hours of continuing education related to medical-surgical nursing within last three years. Continuing education requirement may be met using in-services, grand rounds, academic credits, continuing medical education (CME) credits, and other related continuing education programs. **Membership:** Not required. **Certification Requirements:** Successful completion of exam. Exam covers: Biophysical and psychosocial concepts; Client care issues; Issues and trends; and Pathophysiology of body systems. **Renewal:** Every five years. Recertification based on either successful completion of exam or continuing education. Continuing education requirement may be met using in-services, grand rounds, academic credits, continuing medical education (CME) credits, and other related programs. **Preparatory Materials:** *Directory of Certification Examination Review Courses* and *How to Take ANCC Certification Examinations* (references). Handbook, including exam content outline and sample questions, provided. Review courses available. **Examination Frequency:** semiannual - always July and October. **Examination Sites:** Exam given at sites throughout the U.S. **Examination Type:** Multiple-choice. **Waiting Period to Receive Scores:** Six-eight weeks. **Fees:** $145 (members); $285 (nonmembers). **Accredited By:** American Board of Nursing Specialties. **Endorsed By:** American Nurses Association; National Organization for Competency Assurance.

1005

Neonatal Intensive Care Nurse
National Certification Corp. for the
　Obstetric, Gynecologic, and
　Neonatal Nursing Specialties
　(NCC)
645 N. Michigan Ave., Ste. 900
Chicago, IL 60611
Phone: (312)951-0207
Toll Free: (800)367-5613
Suzanne Choiniere RNC, Pres.

Recipient: Neonatal intensive care nurses. **Educational/Experience Requirements:** Must meet the following re-

quirements: (1) Current licensure as registered nurse; and (2) Two years experience in neonatal intensive care nursing, including 2000 hours of practice. Level 2 and Level 3 NICU experience will be accepted. Level 1 experience may be accepted. **Certification Requirements:** Successful completion of exam. Exam covers: (1) General Assessment, including: Baseline laboratory (knowledge and interpretation); Gestational age; Maternal history and risk factors; Neurobehavioral assessment; and Physical assessment; (2) General Management, including: Fluids and electrolytes; Hygiene and routine care; Monitoring and equipment; Nutrition and feeding; Oxygenation and acid base homeostasis; Pharmacology; Resuscitation and stabilization; and Thermoregulation; (3) Access and Manage Pathophysiologic States, including: Cardiac; Genetic disorders; GI (gastrointestinal); GU (genital urinary); Head, eyes, ears, nose, and throat; Hematopoietic; Infectious diseases; Metabolic/endocrine; Neurological/neuromuscular; and Respiratory; (4) Assess and Manage Psychosocial/Behavioral Adjustments, including: Discharge planning; Family integration; Grieving process; Infant follow-up and outcome; and Promotion and development; and (5) Professional Issues. **Renewal:** Every three years. Recertification based on either successful completion of exam or continuing education. **Preparatory Materials:** Candidate guide, including bibliography of references and sample questions, provided. **Examination Frequency:** semiannual. **Examination Sites:** Exam given at sites throughout the U.S. **Examination Type:** Multiple-choice. **Waiting Period to Receive Scores:** Eight weeks. **Reexamination:** May retake exam as many times as necessary. There is a $300 fee to retake exam. **Fees:** $300.

1006

Neonatal Nurse Practitioner
National Certification Corp. for the
　Obstetric, Gynecologic, and
　Neonatal Nursing Specialties
　(NCC)
645 N. Michigan Ave., Ste. 900
Chicago, IL 60611
Phone: (312)951-0207
Toll Free: (800)367-5613
Suzanne Choiniere RNC, Pres.

Recipient: Neonatal nurse practitioners. **Educational/Experience Requirements:** Must meet the following requirements: (1) Current licensure as registered nurse; (2) Successful completion of nurse practitioner program in neonatal intensive care nursing leading to advanced nurse practitioner certificate or graduate nursing degree; and (3) Two years experience as neonatal nurse practitioner, including 2000 hours of practice. **Certification Requirements:** Successful completion of exam. Exam covers: (1) Neonatal Assessment, including: Behavioral assessment; Clinical laboratory tests; Diagnostic procedures and techniques; Gestational age; and Physical examination; (2) Perinatal Assessment, including: Antepartum; and Intrapartum; (3) General Management, covering: Equipment; Fluids and electrolytes; Nutrition; Pharmacology, including drug therapies and pharmacokinetics; Resuscitation and stabilization; and Thermoregulation; (4) Disease Process, covering: Cardiac; Ears, eyes, nose, and throat; Embryology; Gastrointestinal; Genetics; Hematopoietic and malignancies; Infectious diseases; Integumentary; Intrauterine drug exposure; Metabolic/endocrine; Musculoskeletal; Neurological; Pathophysiology; Physiology; Pulmonary; and Renal/genitourinary; (5) Family Integration, covering: Communication; Discharge planning and follow-up; and Grieving process; and (6) Professional Issues, covering: Legal/ethical problems; and Research, including advances in technology and practice and principles of nursing research. **Renewal:** Every three years. Recertification based on either successful completion of exam or continuing education. **Preparatory Materials:** Candidate guide, including bibliography of references and sample questions, provided. **Examination Frequency:** semiannual. **Examination Sites:** Exam given at sites throughout the U.S. **Examination Type:** Multiple-choice. **Waiting Period to Receive Scores:** Eight weeks. **Re-examination:** May retake exam as many times as necessary. There is a $300 fee to retake exam. **Fees:** $300.

`1007`

Nursing Continuing Education/Staff Development
Board on Certification for Nursing Continuing Education/Staff Development
American Nurses Credentialing Center
600 Maryland Ave., SW, Ste. 100 West
Washington, DC 20024-2571
Toll Free: (800)284-CERT
Marie A. Reed R.N., Dir.

Recipient: Nurses involved in providing non-academic learning activities intended to build upon the educational and experiential bases of professional nurses and

other personnel who assist in providing nursing care. **Number of Certified Individuals:** 18,901. **Educational/Experience Requirements:** Must meet the following requirements: (1) Current licensure as registered nurse (R.N.); (2) Bachelor's degree or higher in nursing; (3) 4000 hours experience as licensed R.N. in direct nursing continuing education and/or staff development within last five years; and (3) Current practice in nursing continuing education and/or staff development for an average of 20 hours per week. Experience must be in teaching, managing, or consulting in nursing continuing education/staff development. Beginning in 1996 must have 20 contact hours of related continuing education within last two years. Continuing education requirement may be met using in-services, grand rounds, academic credits, continuing medical education (CME) credits, and other related continuing education programs. **Membership:** Not required. **Certification Requirements:** Successful completion of exam. Exam covers: Educational process; Foundations of practice; Management of offerings and programs; and Roles. **Renewal:** Every five years. Recertification based on either successful completion of exam or continuing education. Continuing education requirement may be met using in-services, grand rounds, academic credits, continuing medical education (CME) credits, and other related programs. **Preparatory Materials:** *Directory of Certification Examination Review Courses* and *How to Take ANCC Certification Examinations* (references). Handbook, including exam content outline and sample questions, provided. Review courses available. **Examination Frequency:** semiannual - always July and October. **Examination Sites:** Exam given at sites throughout the U.S. **Examination Type:** Multiple-choice. **Waiting Period to Receive Scores:** Six-eight weeks. **Fees:** $145 (members); $285 (nonmembers). **Accredited By:** American Board of Nursing Specialties. **Endorsed By:** American Nurses Association; National Nursing Staff Development Organization; National Organization for Competency Assurance.

`1008`

Oncology Certified Nurse (OCN)
Oncology Nursing Certification Corp. (ONCC)
501 Holiday Dr.
Pittsburgh, PA 15220-2749
Phone: (412)921-8597
Fax: (412)921-6565

Recipient: Oncology nurses.

Educational/Experience Requirements: Must meet the following requirements: (1) Current licensure as registered nurse (R.N.); and (2) Thirty months experience within last five years, including 1000 hours experience within last 30 months. Experience may be in nursing administration, education, clinical practice, or research. **Membership:** Not required. **Certification Requirements:** Successful completion of exam. Exam covers: (1) Cancer Nursing Practice, including: Nursing management of response to cancer experience, including assessment, nursing diagnosis, intervention, and evaluation; Oncologic emergencies, including assessment, nursing diagnosis, intervention, and evaluation; Patient and family/social support systems; Professional issues; and Standards; (2) Major Cancers, including: Adaptation and rehabilitation; Characteristics/symptoms; Diagnostic measures, including metastatic work-up; Nursing care planning; Prognosis, including recurrence; and Standard methods of treatment; (3) Treatment of Cancer, including: General concepts of diagnosis and therapy; Supportive therapies and procedures; and Treatment modalities; (4) Issues and Trends in Cancer Care, including: Care delivery systems; Informed consent; Legal issues; and Survivorship; (5) Cancer Prevention and Detection, including: Early detection and screening measures; Prevention strategies; and Risk factors; (6) Pathophysiology of Cancer, including: Alterations in cellular biology; Carcinogenesis; Immunologic surveillance; and Tumor growth; and (7) Cancer Epidemiology, including: Cancer statistics; Cancer trends; Concepts; and Patterns of occurrence. **Renewal:** Every four years. Recertification based on successful completion of exam. Renewal fees are: $125 (members); $200 (nonmembers). **Preparatory Materials:** Bulletin, including exam content outline, list of suggested references, and sample questions, provided. **Examination Frequency:** semiannual. **Examination Sites:** Exam given at annual congress and at sites throughout the U.S. **Examination Type:** Multiple-choice. **Fees:** $175 (members); $250 (nonmembers). **Endorsed By:** Oncology Nursing Society.

`1009`

Orthopaedic Nurse Certified (ONC)
Orthopaedic Nurses Certification Board (ONCB)
E. Holly Ave.
Box 56
Pitman, NJ 08071-0056
Phone: (609)256-2311
Fax: (609)589-7463

Recipient: Orthopaedic nurses. **Educational/Experience Requirements:** Must meet the following requirements: (1) Current unrestricted licensure as registered nurse (R.N.); (2) Two years experience; and (3) 1000 hours of work experience as R.N. in orthopaedic nursing practice within past three years. Experience may be in the following areas: Administration; Adult care; Clinic; Critical care; Education; Emergency room; Home health care; Long term care; Medical-surgical nursing; Office practice; Oncology; Operating room; and Pediatrics. **Membership:** Not required. **Certification Requirements:** Successful completion of exam. Exam covers: Activity/positioning/use of assistive devices and equipment; Complications; Degenerative disease; Inflammatory disorders; Metabolic bone disease; Neuromuscular/pediatric/congenital; Nutrition; Oncology; Operative orthopaedics; Pain; Psychosocial/emotional support; Self care/wellness/patient education; Sports injuries; and Trauma. **Renewal:** Every five years. Recertification based on either successful completion of exam or continuing education. **Preparatory Materials:** Core curriculum and nursing practice guideline available. Pilot and self-assessment exams available. **Examination Frequency:** Throughout the year. **Examination Sites:** Exam given at sites throughout the U.S. **Examination Type:** Multiple-choice. **Waiting Period to Receive Scores:** Six weeks. **Reexamination:** There if no limit to how may times exam may be retaken. Fees to retake exam are: $180 (members); $225 (nonmembers). **Fees:** $180 (members); $225 (nonmembers). **Endorsed By:** National Association of Osteopathic Nurses.

1010

Pediatric Nurse
Board on Certification for
    Maternal-Child Nursing Practice
American   Nurses   Credentialing
    Center
600 Maryland Ave., SW, Ste. 100
    West
Washington, DC 20024-2571
Toll Free: (800)284-CERT
Marie A. Reed R.N., Dir.

Recipient: Pediatric nurses working in hospital, clinic, long-term care facility, community, and home settings. **Number of Certified Individuals:** 2937. **Educational/Experience Requirements:** Must meet the following requirements: (1) Current licensure as registered nurse (R.N.); (2) 2100 hours experience as licensed R.N. in pediatric nursing within last three years; and (3) 30 hours of

continuing education related to pediatric nursing within past three years. Continuing education requirement may be met using inservices, grand rounds, academic credits, continuing medical education (CME) credits, and other related continuing education programs. Experience must be in direct patient care or direct clinical management, supervision, education, or direction of other persons to achieve or help achieve patient/client goals. Time spent in formal program of advanced nursing study may count toward 300 hours of experience requirement. Beginning in 1998 bachelor's degree in nursing will be required. **Membership:** Not required. **Certification Requirements:** Successful completion of exam. Exam covers: Issues and trends; Major health problems; and Primary concepts of child health care. **Renewal:** Every five years. Recertification based on either successful completion of exam or continuing education. Continuing education requirement may be met using in-services, grand rounds, academic credits, continuing medical education (CME) credits, and other related programs. **Preparatory Materials:** *Directory of Certification Examination Review Courses* and *How to Take ANCC Certification Examinations* (references). Handbook, including exam content outline and sample questions, provided. Review courses available. **Examination Frequency:** semiannual - always July and October. **Examination Sites:** Exam given at sites throughout the U.S. **Examination Type:** Multiple-choice. **Waiting Period to Receive Scores:** Six-eight weeks. **Fees:** $145 (members); $285 (nonmembers). **Accredited By:** American Board of Nursing Specialties. **Endorsed By:** American Nurses Association; National Organization for Competency Assurance.

1011

Pediatric Nurse Practitioner
Board on Certification for
    Maternal-Child Nursing Practice
American   Nurses   Credentialing
    Center
600 Maryland Ave., SW, Ste. 100
    West
Washington, DC 20024-2571
Toll Free: (800)284-CERT
Marie A. Reed R.N., Dir.

Recipient: Pediatric nurse practitioners providing primary health care for children. **Number of Certified Individuals:** 1943. **Educational/Experience Requirements:** Current licensure as registered nurse (R.N.), master's degree in nursing, 600 hours experience within past three years, and preparation as pediatric nurse

practitioner in either: (1) Pediatric nurse practitioner or family nurse practitioner master's degree program within nursing program; or (2) Formal post-graduate pediatric nurse practitioner, family nurse practitioner, or school nurse practitioner track or program within school of nursing granting graduate level academic credit. Education program must include both didactic and clinical components. **Membership:** Not required. **Certification Requirements:** Successful completion of exam. Exam covers: Nursing practice; Patient care issues; Professional issues; Role development; and Trends and issues. **Renewal:** Every five years. Recertification based on either successful completion of exam or continuing education. Continuing education requirement may be met using in-services, grand rounds, academic credits, continuing medical education (CME) credits, and other related programs. **Preparatory Materials:** "Guidelines for Educational Preparation of Pediatric Nurse Practitioners," *Directory of Certification Examination Review Courses,* and *How to Take ANCC Certification Examinations* (references). Handbook, including exam content outline and sample questions, provided. Review courses available. **Examination Frequency:** semiannual - always July and October. **Examination Sites:** Exam given at sites throughout the U.S. **Examination Type:** Multiple-choice. **Waiting Period to Receive Scores:** Six-eight weeks. **Fees:** $145 (members); $285 (nonmembers). **Accredited By:** American Board of Nursing Specialties. **Endorsed By:** American Nurses Association; National Organization for Competency Assurance.

1012

Perinatal Nurse
Board on Certification for
    Maternal-Child Nursing Practice
American   Nurses   Credentialing
    Center
600 Maryland Ave., SW, Ste. 100
    West
Washington, DC 20024-2571
Toll Free: (800)284-CERT
Marie A. Reed R.N., Dir.

Recipient: Perinatal nurses. **Number of Certified Individuals:** 7831. **Educational/Experience Requirements:** Must meet the following requirements: (1) Current licensure as registered nurse (R.N.); (2) 2100 hours experience as licensed R.N. in perinatal nursing within last three years; and (3) 30 hours of continuing education related to perinatal nursing within past three years. Continuing education requirement may be met using in-services, grand rounds, academic credits, continuing medical education (CME) credits, and other related continuing education programs. Experience must be in direct patient care or direct clinical management, supervision, education, or direction of other persons to achieve or help achieve patient/client goals. Time spent in formal program of advanced nursing study may count toward 300 hours of experience requirement. Beginning in 1998 bachelor's degree in nursing will be required. **Membership:** Not required. **Certification Requirements:** Successful completion of exam. Exam covers: Antepartum; Intrapartum; Issues and trends; Neonatal; and Postpartum. **Renewal:** Every five years. Recertification based on either successful completion of exam or continuing education. Continuing education requirement may be met using in-services, grand rounds, academic credits, continuing medical education (CME) credits, and other related programs. **Preparatory Materials:** *Directory of Certification Examination Review Courses* and *How to Take ANCC Certification Examinations* (references). Handbook, including exam content outline and sample questions, provided. Review courses available. **Examination Frequency:** semiannual - always July and October. **Examination Sites:** Exam given at sites throughout the U.S. **Examination Type:** Multiple-choice. **Waiting Period to Receive Scores:** Six-eight weeks. **Fees:** $145 (members); $285 (nonmembers). **Accredited By:** American Board of Nursing Specialties. **Endorsed By:** American Nurses Association; National Organization for Competency Assurance.

1013

Psychiatric and Mental Health Nurse
Board on Certification for Psychiatric and Mental Health Nursing Practice
American Nurses Credentialing Center
600 Maryland Ave., SW, Ste. 100 West
Washington, DC 20024-2571
Toll Free: (800)284-CERT
Marie A. Reed R.N., Dir.

Recipient: Psychiatric and mental health nurses. **Number of Certified Individuals:** 18,901. **Educational/Experience Requirements:** Must meet the following requirements: (1) Current licensure as registered nurse (R.N.); (2) 24 months (1600 hours) experience as licensed R.N. in direct psychiatric and mental health nursing practice in last 48 months; (3)

Current practice in direct psychiatric and mental health nursing practice for an average of eight hours per week; (4) Current access to clinical consultation/supervision; and (5) 30 contact hours of related continuing education within past three years. Continuing education requirement may be met using in-services, grand rounds, academic credits, continuing medical education (CME) credits, and other related continuing education programs. **Membership:** Not required. **Certification Requirements:** Successful completion of exam. Exam covers: Concepts and theories; Professional issues and trends; Psychopathology; and Treatment modalities. **Renewal:** Every five years. Recertification based on either successful completion of exam or continuing education. Continuing education requirement may be met using in-services, grand rounds, academic credits, continuing medical education (CME) credits, and other related programs. **Preparatory Materials:** *Directory of Certification Examination Review Courses* and *How to Take ANCC Certification Examinations* (references). Handbook, including exam content outline and sample questions, provided. Review courses available. **Examination Frequency:** semiannual - always July and October. **Examination Sites:** Exam given at sites throughout the U.S. **Examination Type:** Multiple-choice. **Waiting Period to Receive Scores:** Six-eight weeks. **Fees:** $145 (members); $285 (nonmembers). **Accredited By:** American Board of Nursing Specialties. **Endorsed By:** American Nurses Association; National Organization for Competency Assurance.

1014

Reproductive Endocrinology/Infertility Nurse
National Certification Corp. for the Obstetric, Gynecologic, and Neonatal Nursing Specialties (NCC)
645 N. Michigan Ave., Ste. 900
Chicago, IL 60611
Phone: (312)951-0207
Toll Free: (800)367-5613
Suzanne Choiniere RNC, Pres.

Recipient: Reproductive endocrinology/infertility nurses. **Educational/Experience Requirements:** Must meet the following requirements: (1) Current licensure as registered nurse; and (2) Two years experience in reproductive endocrinology/infertility nursing, including 2000 hours of practice. **Certification Requirements:** Successful completion of exam. Exam covers: (1) Assessment and Management of Pathophysiologic States,

covering: Cervical disorders; Endocrine disorders; Male factors; Pregnancy complications; Tubal disorders; Unexplained infertility; and Uterine factors; (2) General Assessment, covering: History taking, including lifestyle, medical/family/genetic/sexual/psychosocial history, and reproductive history; Physical examination; and Psychosocial aspects of care, including closure, cultural factors, decision making, grief process, pregnancy after infertility, and stress management; (3) Professional Issues, covering: Ethical aspects; Legal aspects; Quality assurance; and Research; (4) Reproductive Physiology, covering: Female, including climacteric, puberty, and reproductive span; and Male, including puberty and reproductive span; and (5) Therapeutic Modalities: New Reproductive Technologies, covering: Cryopreservation of embryos; Donor gametes; Gestational carrier; GIFT; and IVF. **Renewal:** Every three years. Recertification based on either successful completion of exam or continuing education. **Preparatory Materials:** Candidate guide, including bibliography of references and sample questions, provided. **Examination Frequency:** semiannual. **Examination Sites:** Exam given at sites throughout the U.S. **Examination Type:** Multiple-choice. **Waiting Period to Receive Scores:** Eight weeks. **Reexamination:** May retake exam as many times as necessary. There is a $300 fee to retake exam. **Fees:** $300.

1015

School Nurse
American Nurses Credentialing Center (ANCC)
600 Maryland Ave., SW, Ste. 100 West
Washington, DC 20024-2571
Toll Free: (800)284-CERT
Marie A. Reed R.N., Dir.

Recipient: School nurses. **Number of Certified Individuals:** 143. **Educational/Experience Requirements:** Must meet the following requirements: (1) Current licensure as registered nurse (R.N.); (2) Bachelor's degree in nursing; (3) Minimum of 15 semester credit hours in the following curriculum areas with a minimum of two semester credit hours in each: Basic introduction to the education system; Children with special needs (handicapped); Growth and development; Human and intercultural relations; and School nursing and/or community health nursing; and (4) Successful completion of one of the following: 200-hour supervised college/university sponsored internship or practicum in school nursing; 3600 hours experience as R.N.

in school nursing, education supervision, or direction of other persons engaged in school nursing within last three years; or Combination of practicum hours and school nursing experience that totals 3600 hours. Fifty hours of practicum is equal to 900 hours of experience. **Membership:** Not required. **Certification Requirements:** Successful completion of exam. Exam covers: Children with special needs; Growth and development; Health assessment; Health counseling, education, and promotion; Professional issues in school nursing; Safety, injury prevention, and emergency care; School and community health; and Special health conditions. **Renewal:** Every five years. Recertification based on either successful completion of exam or continuing education. Continuing education requirement may be met through in-services, grand rounds, academic credits, continuing medical education (CME) credits, and other related programs. **Preparatory Materials:** *Directory of Certification Examination Review Courses* and *How to Take ANCC Certification Examinations* (references). Handbook, including exam content outline and sample questions, provided. Review courses available. **Examination Frequency:** semiannual - always July and October. **Examination Sites:** Exam given at sites throughout the U.S. **Examination Type:** Multiple-choice. **Waiting Period to Receive Scores:** Six-eight weeks. **Fees:** $145 (members); $285 (nonmembers). **Endorsed By:** American Nurses Association; American School Health Association; National Association of State School Nurse Consultants; National Organization for Competency Assurance.

1016

School Nurse Practitioner
Board on Certification for
　Community Health Nursing
　Practice
American Nurses Credentialing
　Center
600 Maryland Ave., SW, Ste. 100
　West
Washington, DC 20024-2571
Toll Free: (800)284-CERT
Marie A. Reed R.N., Dir.

Recipient: School nurse practitioners involved with the health care of preschool and school-age children and adolescents. **Number of Certified Individuals:** 326. **Educational/Experience Requirements:** Current licensure as registered nurse (R.N.) and graduate degree from school accredited by National League for Nursing (see separate entry). Must also have been prepared as school nurse practitio-

ner in either: (1) School nurse practitioner graduate nursing degree program; or (2) Formal post-graduate school nurse practitioner track or program within a school of nursing granting graduate level academic credit. Educational program must include both didactic and clinical components. **Membership:** Not required. **Certification Requirements:** Successful completion of exam. Exam covers: Health education; Nursing process; Professional issues/role development; and School and community health systems. **Renewal:** Every five years. Recertification based on either successful completion of exam or continuing education. Continuing education requirement may be met using in-services, grand rounds, academic credits, continuing medical education (CME) credits, and other related programs. **Preparatory Materials:** "Guidelines for Educational Preparation of School Nurse Practitioners," *Directory of Certification Examination Review Courses,* and *How to Take ANCC Certification Examinations* (references). Handbook, including exam content outline and sample questions, provided. Review courses available. **Examination Frequency:** semiannual - always July and October. **Examination Sites:** Exam given at sites throughout the U.S. **Examination Type:** Multiple-choice. **Waiting Period to Receive Scores:** Six-eight weeks. **Fees:** $145 (members); $285 (nonmembers). **Accredited By:** American Board of Nursing Specialties. **Endorsed By:** American Nurses Association; National Organization for Competency Assurance.

1017

Urology Registered Nurse
American Board of Urologic Allied
　Health Professionals (ABUAHP)
1391 Delta Corners, SW
Lawrenceville, GA 30245

Recipient: Urology nurses. **Educational/Experience Requirements:** Must meet the following requirements: (1) Successful completion of nursing program accredited by National League for Nursing (see separate entry) or approved by ABUAHP; and (2) One year of experience. **Membership:** Not required. **Certification Requirements:** Successful completion of exam. Exam covers: Anatomy; Catherization techniques; Concepts of sterilization and disinfection; Laboratory values; Physiology; Urine collection; X-ray procedures; and Other related procedures. **Renewal:** Every three years. Recertification based on successful completion of one of the following: (1) Exam; (2) Thirty updates; or (3) Twenty updates and 36 hours of continuing educa-

tion in urology. **Preparatory Materials:** *Standards of Urologic Nursing* (reference). Study guide, including sample questions, list of required areas of study, and glossary of terms, and study courses, available. Curriculum guide being developed. **Examination Frequency:** Two times per year - usually April and May. **Examination Sites:** Exam given at annual assembly and at sites throughout the U.S. **Examination Type:** Multiple-choice. **Waiting Period to Receive Scores:** Six weeks. **Fees:** $175 (members); $235 (nonmembers). **Endorsed By:** American Urological Association Allied.

1018

**Women's Health Care Nurse
　Practitioner**
National Certification Corp. for the
　Obstetric, Gynecologic, and
　Neonatal Nursing Specialties
　(NCC)
645 N. Michigan Ave., Ste. 900
Chicago, IL 60611
Phone: (312)951-0207
Toll Free: (800)367-5613
Suzanne Choiniere RNC, Pres.

Recipient: Women's health care nurse practitioners. **Educational/Experience Requirements:** Must meet the following requirements: (1) Current licensure as registered nurse; (2) Successful completion of nurse practitioner program in ob/gyn or women's health care leading to advanced nurse practitioner certificate or graduate nursing degree; and (3) Two years experience in women's health care nursing, including 2000 hours of practice. **Certification Requirements:** Successful completion of exam. Exam covers: (1) General Health Assessment, including: Diagnosis; Diagnostic studies/laboratory (non-gyn); Etiology; Health history; Health maintenance, education, and counseling; Management; Non-gyn medical problems; Pharmacology; and Physical examination; (2) Gynecology, including: Diagnostic studies and laboratory tests; Etiology; Fertility control; Male factors related to women's health; Management; and Pharmacology; (3) Obstetrics, including: Assessment of fetal well-being; Complications of pregnancy; Diagnosis; Etiology; Knowledge of Puerperium; Laboratory tests relevant to pregnancy; Management; Pharmacology; Physiology of pregnancy; Prenatal care; and Preparation of childbirth; and (4) Professional Issues, including: Basic research principles; and Ethical/legal issues. **Renewal:** Every three years. Recertification based on either successful completion of exam or continuing education. **Preparatory Materials:** Candidate guide, including bibliography of references and sample questions, provided. **Examination Frequency:** semiannual. **Examination Sites:** Exam given at sites throughout the U.S. **Examination Type:** Multiple-choice. **Waiting Period to Receive Scores:** Eight weeks. **Re-examination:** May retake exam as many times as necessary. There is a $300 fee to retake exam. **Fees:** $300.

Respiratory Therapists

▌1019▐

Certified Pulmonary Function Technologist (CPFT)
National Board for Respiratory
   Care (NBRC)
8310 Nieman Rd.
Lenexa, KS 66214
Phone: (913)599-4200

Recipient: Entry-level pulmonary function technologists. **Educational/ Experience Requirements:** Must meet one of the following requirements: (1) Successful completion of respiratory therapy technician or respiratory therapist educational program accredited by Joint Review Committee for Respiratory Therapy Education (see separate entry); (2) Successful completion of pulmonary function technology educational program approved by National Society for Pulmonary Technology; (3) Either Certified Respiratory Therapy Technician (CRTT) or Registered Respiratory Technician (RTT) designations (see separate entries); (4) Successful completion of 62 hours or college credit, including one course in biology, chemistry, and mathematics, and six months experience; or (5) High school diploma or equivalent and two years experience. Experience must be under supervision of medical director of pulmonary function laboratory or special care area. **Certification Requirements:** Successful completion of exam. Exam covers: Data management; Diagnostic procedures; and Equipment and instrumentation. **Examination Frequency:** Annual - always June. **Examination Type:** Multiple-choice. **Accredited By:** National Commission for Certifying Agencies. **Endorsed By:** American Association for Respiratory Care; American College of Chest Physicians; American Society of Anesthesiologists; American Thoracic Society; National Organization for Competency Assurance; National Society for Pulmonary Technology.

▌1020▐

Certified Respiratory Therapy Technician (CRTT)
National Board for Respiratory
   Care (NBRC)
8310 Nieman Rd.
Lenexa, KS 66214
Phone: (913)599-4200

Recipient: Entry-level respiratory therapy personnel. **Educational/ Experience Requirements:** Successful completion of respiratory therapy technician or respiratory therapist educational program accredited by Joint Review Committee for Respiratory Therapy Education (see separate entry). Canadian Registered Respiratory Therapists meet requirements. **Certification Requirements:** Successful completion of exam. Exam covers: Clinical data; Equipment; and Therapeutic procedures. **Renewal:** Every five years. Recertification based on successful completion of exam. **Preparatory Materials:** Study guide, including exam content outline and self-evaluation exam, available. **Examination Frequency:** Three times per year - always March, July, and November. **Examination Type:** Multiple-choice. **Accredited By:** National Commission for Certifying Agencies. **Endorsed By:** American Association for Respiratory Care; American College of Chest Physicians; American Society of Anesthesiologists; American Thoracic Society; National Organization for Competency Assurance; National Society for Pulmonary Technology.

▌1021▐

Perinatal/Pediatric Respiratory Care Specialist
National Board for Respiratory
   Care (NBRC)
8310 Nieman Rd.
Lenexa, KS 66214
Phone: (913)599-4200

Recipient: Perinatal and pediatric respiratory specialists. **Educational/ Experience Requirements:** Must meet one of the following requirements: (1) Hold Registered Respiratory Therapist (RRT) designation (see separate entry); or (2) Hold Certified Respiratory Therapy Technician (CRTT) designation (see separate entry) and one year of experience following certification in perinatal/pediatric respiratory care under supervision of medical director of respiratory care or special care area. **Certification Requirements:** Successful completion of exam. Exam covers: Clinical data; Equipment; and Therapeutic procedures. **Examination Frequency:**

Annual - always March. **Examination Type:** Multiple-choice. **Accredited By:** National Commission for Certifying Agencies. **Endorsed By:** American Association for Respiratory Care; American College of Chest Physicians; American Society of Anesthesiologists; American Thoracic Society; National Organization for Competency Assurance; National Society for Pulmonary Technology.

▌1022▐

Registered Pulmonary Function Technologist (RPFT)
National Board for Respiratory
   Care (NBRC)
8310 Nieman Rd.
Lenexa, KS 66214
Phone: (913)599-4200

Recipient: Advanced pulmonary function technologists. **Educational/ Experience Requirements:** Hold Certified Pulmonary Function Technologist (CPFT) designation (see separate entry). **Certification Requirements:** Successful completion of exam. Exam covers: Data management; Diagnostic procedures; and Equipment and instrumentation. **Examination Frequency:** Annual - always December. **Examination Type:** Multiple-choice. **Accredited By:** National Commission for Certifying Agencies. **Endorsed By:** American Association for Respiratory Care; American College of Chest Physicians; American Society of Anesthesiologists; American Thoracic Society; National Organization for Competency Assurance; National Society for Pulmonary Technology.

▌1023▐

Registered Respiratory Therapist (RRT)
National Board for Respiratory
   Care (NBRC)
8310 Nieman Rd.
Lenexa, KS 66214
Phone: (913)599-4200

Recipient: Advanced respiratory therapy practitioners. **Educational/Experience Requirements:** Hold Certified Respiratory Therapy Technician (CRTT) designation (see separate entry) and meet one of the following requirements: (1) Successful completion of respiratory therapy technician or respiratory therapist educational program accredited by Joint Review Committee for Respiratory Therapy Education (see separate entry), including 62 semester hours of college credit; (2) 62 semester hours of college credit, including courses in anatomy and physiology, chemistry, microbiology, physics, and mathematics, and four years experience; or (3) Bachelor's degree in area other than respiratory therapy, including college-level courses in anatomy and physiology, chemistry, microbiology, physics, and mathematics, and two years experience. Experience must be in clinical respiratory therapy under licensed medical supervision. **Certification Requirements:** Successful completion of written and clinical simulation exams. Written exam covers: Clinical data: Equipment; and Therapeutic procedures. Clinical simulation exam covers: Adult cardiovascular, COPD, neurological or neuromuscular, and trauma patients; Neonatal patients; Pediatric patients; and Patients with other medical and surgical conditions. Candidates who hold Canadian Society of Respiratory Therapists registry certificate must only successfully complete clinical simulation exam. **Examination Frequency:** semiannual - always June and December. **Examination Type:** Multiple-choice. **Accredited By:** National Commission for Certifying Agencies. **Endorsed By:** American Association for Respiratory Care; American College of Chest Physicians; American Society of Anesthesiologists; American Thoracic Society; National Organization for Competency Assurance; National Society for Pulmonary Technology.

Speech-Language Pathologists and Audiologists

1024

Board Certified - Hearing Instrument Specialist (BC-HIS)
National Board for Certification in Hearing Instrument Sciences (NBCHIS)
20361 Middlebelt Rd.
Livonia, MI 48152
Phone: (810)478-5712
Fax: (810)478-4520
Toll Free: (800)521-5247
Douglas C. Kelsey CAE, Admin.

Recipient: Health care professionals involved in testing of hearing, evaluation of hearing loss, and selection and fitting of hearing instruments. **Number of Certified Individuals:** 2200. **Educational/ Experience Requirements:** Two years hands-on experience with hearing impaired. **Membership:** Not required. **Certification Requirements:** Successful completion of exam. Exam covers the following skills: Assessing hearing; Educating patient/client and family; Eliciting patient/client history; Fitting hearing aid; and Maintaining professional standards. **Renewal:** Every three years. Recertification based on either successful completion of exam or accumulation of 24 continuing education units (CEUs). **Preparatory Materials:** *Training Manual for Professionals in the Field of Hearing Instrument Sciences* (reference). List of recommended readings, sample test, and study guide available. **Examination Frequency:** 40 times per year. **Examination Sites:** Exam given at annual meeting and at 20 sites throughout the U.S. and Canada. **Examination Type:** Multiple-choice. **Pass/Fail Rate:** 70% pass exam the first time. **Waiting Period to Receive Scores:** Six-eight weeks. **Re-examination:** There is no time limit to retake exam. Must successfully complete exam within two years. **Fees:** $105 (members); $185 (nonmembers). **Accredited By:** National Commission for Certifying Agencies. **Endorsed By:** International Hearing Society; National Organization for Competency Assurance.

1025

Certified Occupational Hearing Conservationist
Council for Accreditation in Occupational Hearing Conservation (CAOHC)
611 E. Wells St.
Milwaukee, WI 53202
Phone: (414)276-5338
Fax: (414)276-3349

Recipient: Occupational hearing conservationists. **Certification Requirements:** Successful completion of CAOHC-approved course. **Renewal:** Every five years. Renewal fee is $20. **Preparatory Materials:** Manual available. **Fees:** $50.

1026

Hearing Instrument Specialist
National Board for Certification in Hearing Instrument Sciences (NBCHIS)
20361 Middlebelt Rd.
Livonia, MI 48152
Phone: (810)478-5712
Fax: (810)478-4520
Toll Free: (800)521-5247
Douglas C. Kelsey CAE, Admin.

Recipient: Health care professionals involved in testing of hearing, evaluation of hearing loss, and selection and fitting of hearing instruments. **Membership:** Required. **Certification Requirements:** Must be legally able to dispense hearing instruments.

Communications Occupations

Public Relations Specialists

1027

Accredited in Public Relations (APR)
Public Relations Society of America (PRSA)
33 Irving Pl., 3rd Fl.
New York, NY 10003-2376
Phone: (212)995-2230
Fax: (212)995-0757
Ray Gaulke, COO

Recipient: Public relations professionals. **Number of Certified Individuals:** 4100. **Educational/Experience Requirements:** Five years experience. **Membership:** Required. **Certification Requirements:** Successful completion of exam. Exam covers: Crisis management; Evaluation; Law and professional ethics; Media relations; Planning; Public relations theories; Research; and Societal factors. **Renewal:** Every three years. Recertification based on continuing education, experience, and association activities. **Pass/Fail Rate:** 70% pass exam. **Fees:** $200.

Translators

1028

Accredited Translator
American Translators Association (ATA)
1735 Jefferson Davis Hwy., Ste. 903
Arlington, VA 22202-3413
Phone: (703)412-1500
Fax: (703)412-1501
John Ferreira, Mgr.

Recipient: Translators competent at translating written material from one language to another. **Number of Certified Individuals:** 1900. **Educational/Experience Requirements:** none. **Membership:** Required. **Certification Requirements:** Successful completion of exam. Exam covers translation techniques and the ability to successfully translate meaning and intent in the following areas: General; Legal/commercial; Literary; Scientific/medical; and Semi-technical. Certification offered in Arabic, Dutch, Finnish, French, German, Italian, Japanese, Polish, Portuguese, Russian, and Spanish into, and from, English. **Renewal:** none. **Preparatory Materials:** Practice test available. **Examination Frequency:** Throughout the year. **Examination Sites:** Exam given at sites throughout the U.S. **Examination Type:** Essay. **Waiting Period to Receive Scores:** Four weeks. **Re-examination:** Must wait one year to retake exam. **Fees:** $100.

1029

Certificate of Interpretation (CI)
Registry of Interpreters for the Deaf (RID)
8630 Fenton St., Ste. 324
Silver Spring, MD 20910
Phone: (301)608-0050
Fax: (301)608-0508

Recipient: Interpreters who have demonstrated ability to interpret between American Sign Language (ASL) and spoken English in both signto-voice and voice-to-sign. **Membership:** Not required. **Certification Requirements:** Successful completion of two-part written exam and practical exam. **Renewal:** Recertification required. **Preparatory Materials:** *Study Guide and Candidate Bulletin,* including exam content outline and sample exam, available. List of suggested study references provided. Videos available. Teletypewriter number is: (301)608-0562. **Ex-**amination Frequency: Throughout the year. **Examination Sites:** Exams given at sites throughout the U.S. **Examination Type:** Multiple-choice. **Waiting Period to Receive Scores:** Ten days (written); 90 days (practical). **Re-examination:** Must only retake part of written exam failed. Fees to retake each part of written exam are: $45 (members); $70 (nonmembers). **Fees:** $310 (members); $450 (nonmembers). **Endorsed By:** National Organization for Competency Assurance.

1030

Certificate of Interpretation/Certificate of Transliteration (CI/CT)
Registry of Interpreters for the Deaf (RID)
8630 Fenton St., Ste. 324
Silver Spring, MD 20910
Phone: (301)608-0050
Fax: (301)608-0508

Recipient: Individuals who have demonstrated ability to interpret between American Sign Language (ASL) and spoken English in both sign-to-voice and voice-to-sign and transliterate between English-based sign language and spoken English in both sign-to-voice and voice-to-sign. **Membership:** Not required. **Certification Requirements:** Successful completion of two-part written exam and practical exam in both interpretation and transliteration. **Renewal:** Recertification required. **Preparatory Materials:** *Study Guide and Candidate Bulletin,* including exam content outline and sample exam, available. List of suggested study references provided. Videos available. Teletypewriter number is: (301)608-0562. **Examination Frequency:** Throughout the year. **Examination Sites:** Exams given at sites throughout the U.S. **Examination Type:** Multiple-choice. **Waiting Period to**

Receive Scores: Ten days (written); 90 days (practical). **Re-examination:** Must only retake part of written exams failed. Fees to retake each part of written exams are: $75 (members); $100 (nonmembers). **Fees:** $620 (members); $900 (nonmembers). **Endorsed By:** National Organization for Competency Assurance.

`1031`

Certificate of Transliteration (CT)
Registry of Interpreters for the Deaf (RID)
8630 Fenton St., Ste. 324
Silver Spring, MD 20910
Phone: (301)608-0050
Fax: (301)608-0508

Recipient: Individuals who have demonstrated ability to transliterate between English-based sign language and spoken English in both sign-to-voice and voice-to-sign. **Membership:** Not required. **Certification Requirements:** Successful completion of two-part written exam and practical exam. **Renewal:** Recertification required. **Preparatory Materials:** *Study Guide and Candidate Bulletin,* including exam content outline and sample exam, available. List of suggested study references provided. Videos available. Teletypewriter number is: (301)608-0562. **Examination Frequency:** Throughout the year. **Examination Sites:** Exams given at sites throughout the U.S. **Examination Type:** Multiple-choice. **Waiting Period to Receive Scores:** Ten days (written); 90 days (practical). **Re-examination:** Must only retake part of written exam failed. Fees to retake each part of written exam are: $45 (members); $70 (nonmembers). **Fees:** $310 (members); $450 (nonmembers). **Endorsed By:** National Organization for Competency Assurance.

`1032`

Certified Deaf Interpreter - Provisional (CDI-P)
Registry of Interpreters for the Deaf (RID)
8630 Fenton St., Ste. 324
Silver Spring, MD 20910
Phone: (301)608-0050
Fax: (301)608-0508

Recipient: Interpreters for the deaf who are deaf or hard-of-hearing. **Certification Requirements:** Must meet the following requirements: (1) One year of experience; (2) Eight hours of training in RID Code of Ethics; and (3) Eight hours of training in general interpretation. **Renewal:** Recertification required. **Preparatory Mate-**

rials: Teletypewriter number is: (301)608-0562. **Endorsed By:** National Organization for Competency Assurance.

`1033`

Conditional Legal Interpreting Permit (CLIP)
Registry of Interpreters for the Deaf (RID)
8630 Fenton St., Ste. 324
Silver Spring, MD 20910
Phone: (301)608-0050
Fax: (301)608-0508

Recipient: Interpreters and transliterators working in legal settings. **Educational/Experience Requirements:** Hold Certificate of Interpretation and Certificate of Transliteration (CI and CT) designation (see separate entry). **Membership:** Not required. **Certification Requirements:** Successful completion of training program. **Renewal:** Recertification required. **Preparatory Materials:** Teletypewriter number is: (301)608-0562. **Endorsed By:** National Organization for Competency Assurance.

`1034`

Conditional Legal Interpreting Permit - Relay (CLIP-R)
Registry of Interpreters for the Deaf (RID)
8630 Fenton St., Ste. 324
Silver Spring, MD 20910
Phone: (301)608-0050
Fax: (301)608-0508

Recipient: Interpreters and transliterators for the deaf working in legal settings who are deaf or hard-of-hearing. **Educational/Experience Requirements:** Hold Certified Deaf Interpreter - Provisional (CDI-P) designation (see separate entry). **Membership:** Not required. **Certification Requirements:** Successful completion of training program. **Renewal:** Recertification required. **Preparatory Materials:** Teletypewriter number is: (301)608-0562. **Endorsed By:** National Organization for Competency Assurance.

Writers and Editors

`1035`

Certified Professional Resume Writer (CPRW)
Professional Association of Resume Writers (PARW)
3637 4th St., N., Ste. 330
St. Petersburg, FL 33704-1336
Phone: (813)821-2274
Fax: (813)894-1277
Toll Free: (800)822-7279
E-mail: NNFP 40A.@Prodigy.com
Paul R. Guzman, Test Coord.

Recipient: Professional resume writers. **Number of Certified Individuals:** 225. **Educational/Experience Requirements:** Submission of two client resumes. **Membership:** Required. **Certification Requirements:** Successful completion of exam. **Renewal:** none. **Preparatory Materials:** *How to Comply With Federal Employee Laws, The Overnight Resume,* and *The Perfect Resume* (references). Study guides available. **Examination Sites:** Exams given by fax, online, and at PARW convention. **Examination Type:** Multiple-choice; practical; proofreading; true or false. **Pass/Fail Rate:** 95% pass exam the first time. **Waiting Period to Receive Scores:** 30 days. **Re-examination:** There is no time limit to retake exam. **Fees:** $175.

Visual and Performing Arts Occupations

Designers, Including Interior Designers and Florists

1036

Certified Bathroom Designer (CBD)
National Kitchen and Bath
  Association (NKBA)
687 Willow Grove St.
Hackettstown, NJ 07840
Phone: (908)852-0033
Fax: (908)852-1695
Toll Free: (800)843-6522
John Spitz, Dir.

Recipient: Showroom salespersons, drafters, installers, and contractors involved in designing, planning, and supervising residential bathroom installations. **Number of Certified Individuals:** 96. **Educational/Experience Requirements:** Must meet one of the following requirements: (1) Two years experience and bachelor's degree; (2) Three years experience and associate's degree; (3) Four years experience and successful completion of NKBA Bathroom Designer Correspondence Course; (4) Six years experience and successful completion of NKBA Bathroom Design Preparatory Seminar; or (5) Seven years experience. **Membership:** Required. **Certification Requirements:** Must meet the following requirements: (1) Submission of two professional affidavits, client referrals, and work samples; and (2) Successful completion of exam based on current industry technical manuals. **Renewal:** none. **Preparatory Materials:** Technical manuals and other resources available. **Examination Frequency:** semiannual. **Examination Sites:** Exam given by NKBA local chapters. **Examination Type:** Multiple-choice; problem solving. **Pass/Fail Rate:** 65 percent pass exam. **Waiting Period to Receive Scores:** Ten weeks. **Fees:** $300. **Endorsed By:** National Organization for Competency Assurance.

1037

Certified Interior Designer (NCIDQ Certified)
National Council for Interior
  Design Qualification (NCIDQ)
50 Main St., 5th Fl.
White Plains, NY 10606
Phone: (914)948-9100
Fax: (914)948-9198
M. Todd Bostick, Exec. VP

Recipient: Interior designers. **Number of Certified Individuals:** 8000. **Educational/Experience Requirements:** Must meet one of the following requirements: (1) Bachelor's degree in interior design and two years experience; (2) Three-year certificate in interior design and three years experience; or (3) Two-year certificate in interior design and four years experience. **Membership:** Not required. **Certification Requirements:** Successful completion of six-part exam. Parts are: (1) Identification and Application; (2) Building and Barrier Free Codes, covering building code concepts and their effects on public health and safety; (3) Problem-Solving, requiring review of drawings; (4) Programming, covering: Conducting client interview; and Creating bubble diagram/schematic; (5) Three Dimensional Exercise, requiring application of interior design theory to three-dimensional volume; and (6) Project Scenario, requiring analysis of written project scenario and formulation of space plan. **Renewal:** Every year. Renewal fee is $25. **Preparatory Materials:** Examination guide available. **Examination Frequency:** semiannual - always spring and fall. **Examination Sites:** Exam given at 80 sites throughout the U.S. and Canada. **Examination Type:** Multiple-choice; problem solving. **Pass/Fail Rate:** 75 percent pass exam. **Waiting Period to Receive Scores:** Fourteen weeks. **Fees:** $450.

1038

Certified Kitchen Designer (CKD)
National Kitchen and Bath
  Association (NKBA)
687 Willow Grove St.
Hackettstown, NJ 07840
Phone: (908)852-0033
Fax: (908)852-1695
Toll Free: (800)843-6522
John Spitz, Dir.

Recipient: Showroom salespersons, drafters, installers, and contractors involved in designing, planning, and supervising residential kitchen installations. **Number of Certified Individuals:** 1569. **Educational/Experience Requirements:** Must meet one of the following requirements: (1) Two years experience and bachelor's degree; (2) Three years experience and associate's degree; (3) Four years experience and successful completion of NKBA Kitchen Designer Correspondence Course; (4) Six years experience and successful completion of NKBA Kitchen Design Preparatory Seminar; or (5) Seven years experience. **Membership:** Required. **Certification Requirements:** Must meet the following requirements: (1) Submission of two professional affidavits, client referrals, and work samples; and (2) Successful completion of exam based on current industry technical manuals. **Renewal:** none. **Preparatory Materials:** Technical manuals and other resources available. **Examination Frequency:** semiannual. **Examination Sites:** Exam given by NKBA local chapters. **Examination Type:** Multiple-choice; problem solving. **Pass/Fail Rate:** 65 percent pass exam. **Waiting Period to Receive Scores:** Ten weeks. **Fees:** $300. **Endorsed By:** National Organization for Competency Assurance.

1039

Registered/Certified Residential Interior Designer
Council for Qualifications of Residential Interior Designers
PO Box 1757
High Point, NC 27261
Phone: (910)883-1680
Fax: (910)883-1195
Faye Laverty, Exec.Dir.

Recipient: Interior designers who specialize in residential practice. **Educational/ Experience Requirements:** Must meet one of the following requirements: (1) Bachelor's degree in interior design and two years experience; (2) Three-year certificate in interior design and three years experience; (3) Two-year certificate in interior design and four years experience; or (4) High school diploma and eight years experience. **Certification Requirements:** Successful completion of exam. Exam covers all phases of residential interior design. **Renewal:** none. **Examination Type:** Multiple-choice; problem solving. **Fees:** $350.

Musicians

1040

Associate, American Guild of Organists
American Guild of Organists (AGO)
475 Riverside Dr., Ste. 1260
New York, NY 10115
Phone: (212)870-2310
Fax: (212)870-2163

Recipient: Organists. **Membership:** Required. **Certification Requirements:** Successful completion of two-section exam. Exam sections are paperwork and organ playing. Paperwork section covers: Analysis; Ear tests; Fugue; Harmonization-composition; and Questions. **Preparatory Materials:** *Examination Hymn Booklet* (reference). Bibliography of suggested study references and manual of procedure provided. Previous exams available. **Examination Frequency:** Annual. **Examination Sites:** Exam given at sites throughout the U.S. **Re-examination:** Must only retake section failed. Must successfully complete exam within five years. Fees to retake exam are: $80 (entire exam); $65 (single section). **Fees:** $80.

1041

Choir Master, American Guild of Organists
American Guild of Organists (AGO)
475 Riverside Dr., Ste. 1260
New York, NY 10115
Phone: (212)870-2310
Fax: (212)870-2163

Recipient: Organists. **Membership:** Required. **Certification Requirements:** Successful completion of two-section exam. Exam sections are paperwork and organ playing. Paperwork section covers: Analysis; Choir training; Choral repertoire; Ear tests; General musical knowledge; Gregorian chant; Hymnody; and Liturgy. **Preparatory Materials:** *Examination Hymn Booklet* (reference). Bibliography of suggested study references and manual of procedure provided. Previous exams available. **Examination Frequency:** Annual. **Examination Sites:** Exam given at sites throughout the U.S. **Re-examination:** Must only retake section failed. Must successfully complete exam within five years. Fees to retake exam are: $80 (entire exam); $65 (single section). **Fees:** $80.

1042

Colleague, American Guild of Organists
American Guild of Organists (AGO)
475 Riverside Dr., Ste. 1260
New York, NY 10115
Phone: (212)870-2310
Fax: (212)870-2163

Recipient: Organists. **Membership:** Required. **Certification Requirements:** Successful completion of exam. **Preparatory Materials:** *Colleague Examination Study Guide* and *Examination Hymn Booklet* (references). Bibliography of suggested study references and manual of procedure provided. Previous exams available. **Examination Frequency:** semiannual. **Examination Sites:** Exam given by local chapters. **Re-examination:** Fee to retake exam is $50. **Fees:** $50.

1043

Fellow, American Guild of Organists
American Guild of Organists (AGO)
475 Riverside Dr., Ste. 1260
New York, NY 10115
Phone: (212)870-2310
Fax: (212)870-2163

Recipient: Organists. **Membership:** Required. **Certification Requirements:** Successful completion of two-section exam. Exam sections are paperwork and organ playing. Paperwork section covers: Composition; Counterpoint; Ear tests; Essay; Fugue; and Orchestration. **Preparatory Materials:** *Examination Hymn Booklet* (reference). Bibliography of suggested study references and manual of procedure provided. Previous exams available. **Examination Frequency:** Annual. **Examination Sites:** Exam given at sites throughout the U.S. **Re-examination:** Must only retake section failed. Must successfully complete exam within five years. Fees to retake exam are: $100 (entire exam); $75 (single section). **Fees:** $100.

Painters

1044

Advanced Painter
National PlasterCraft Association (NPCA)
c/o George L. Kirkpatrick
0465 North 300 East
Albion, IN 46701
George L. Kirkpatrick, Sec.

Recipient: PlasterCraft painters. **Educational/Experience Requirements:** Must meet the following requirements: (1) Be 18 years old or older; and (2) Hold current employment or association with company, retailer, or supplier that is member or associate member of NPCA. **Membership:** Required. **Certification Requirements:** Submission of the following pieces of work: (1) One museum metallic finish; (2) One museum stone finish; (3) One marble finish; and (4) One gold leaf finish. **Preparatory Materials:** *Certification Program Manual* and *Entry Levels and Judging Criteria* (references). **Examination Sites:** Pieces judged at regional seminars and national conventions. **Re-examination:** There is a $7 fee for each piece of work resubmitted. **Fees:** $21.

1045

Certified Painter

National PlasterCraft Association (NPCA)
c/o George L. Kirkpatrick
0465 North 300 East
Albion, IN 46701
George L. Kirkpatrick, Sec.

Recipient: PlasterCraft painters. **Educational/Experience Requirements:** Must meet the following requirements: (1) Be 18 years old or older; and (2) Hold current employment or association with company, retailer, or supplier that is member or associate member of NPCA. **Membership:** Required. **Certification Requirements:** Submission of the following pieces of work: (1) One fruit or floral plaque or plate; (2) One dressed human figure; and (3) Realistic wood finish on plain, untextured plaster blank. **Preparatory Materials:** *Certification Program Manual* and *Entry Levels and Judging Criteria* (references). **Examination Sites:** Pieces judged at regional seminars and national conventions. **Re-examination:** There is a $7 fee for each piece of work resubmitted. **Fees:** $45.

1046

Certified Teacher

National PlasterCraft Association (NPCA)
c/o George L. Kirkpatrick
0465 North 300 East
Albion, IN 46701
George L. Kirkpatrick, Sec.

Recipient: PlasterCraft painting teachers. **Educational/Experience Requirements:** Must meet the following requirements: (1) Be 18 years old or older; (2) Hold current employment or association with company, retailer, or supplier that is member or associate member of NPCA; and (3) Hold either Advanced Painter or Master Painter designations (see separate entries). **Membership:** Required. **Certification Requirements:** Successful completion of exam and submission of painted fullface mask. Candidates who hold Master Painter designation are exempt from face mask requirement. **Preparatory Materials:** *Certification Program Manual* and *Teachers's Certification Manual* (references). **Examination Sites:** Exam given at annual convention and seminars and judging locations. **Fees:** $27.50.

1047

Master Certified Teacher

National PlasterCraft Association (NPCA)
c/o George L. Kirkpatrick
0465 North 300 East
Albion, IN 46701
George L. Kirkpatrick, Sec.

Recipient: PlasterCraft painting teachers. **Educational/Experience Requirements:** Must meet the following requirements: (1) Be 18 years old or older; (2) Hold current employment or association with company, retailer, or supplier that is member or associate member of NPCA; and (3) Hold Master Painter designation (see separate entry). **Membership:** Required. **Certification Requirements:** Successful completion of written exam and oral interview. **Preparatory Materials:** *Certification Program Manual* and *Teachers's Certification Manual* (references). **Examination Sites:** Exam given at annual convention and seminars and judging locations. **Fees:** $35.

1048

Master Painter

National PlasterCraft Association (NPCA)
c/o George L. Kirkpatrick
0465 North 300 East
Albion, IN 46701
George L. Kirkpatrick, Sec.

Recipient: PlasterCraft painters. **Educational/Experience Requirements:** Must meet the following requirements: (1) Be 18 years old or older; and (2) Hold current employment or association with company, retailer, or supplier that is member or associate member of NPCA. **Membership:** Required. **Certification Requirements:** Submission of the following pieces of work: (1) One full-face bust; (2) One animal or one bird; and (3) One hummel-type or royal doulton-type finish. **Preparatory Materials:** *Certification Program Manual* and *Entry Levels and Judging Criteria* (references). **Examination Sites:** Pieces judged at regional seminars and national conventions. **Re-examination:** There is a $7 fee for each piece of work resubmitted. **Fees:** $45.

Photographers and Camera Operators

1049

Certified Electronic Imager (CEI)

Professional Photographers of America (PP of A)
57 Forsythe St., Ste. 1600
Atlanta, GA 30303
Phone: (404)522-8600
Fax: (404)614-6405
Toll Free: (800)742-7468
LaRee Distasio, Standards Admin.

Recipient: Videographers involved in commercial, industrial, wedding/event, and computer graphics work and who are available on first-come, first-serve basis. **Educational/Experience Requirements:** Must meet one of the following requirements: (1) Two years experience; or (2) One year of experience and 60 college or school of photography semester hours. **Membership:** Required. **Certification Requirements:** Must meet the following requirements: (1) Submission of portfolio of four commercial assignments of no less than thirty seconds apiece; and (2) Successful completion of exam. **Renewal:** Every five years. Recertification based on accumulation of 10 days of acceptable continuing education and submission of portfolio of six examples of work completed during recertification cycle. **Preparatory Materials:** Study guide and list of suggested references provided. **Examination Sites:** Exam given at national headquarters, regional and state conventions and seminars, PPA Resource Center, and Winona International School of Professional Photography. **Examination Type:** Multiple-choice. **Fees:** $75.

1050

Certified Ophthalmic Photographer and Retinal Angiographer (COPRA)

Ophthalmic Photographers' Society (OPS)
c/o Terrance L. Tomer, COPRA
Wills Eye Hospital
900 Walnut St.
Philadelphia, PA 19107
Phone: (215)928-3405
Fax: (215)928-3123
Terrance L. Tomer COPRA, Chm.

Recipient: Ophthalmic photographers qualified in all aspects of ophthalmic photography and who have knowledge of general photographic and ophthalmic procedures and common ophthalmic findings. **Educational/Experience Requirements:** Must meet the following requirements: (1) Five years experience; and (2) Current CPR certification. **Membership:** Not required. **Certification Requirements:** Must meet the following requirements: (1) Successful completion of written and oral exams; and (2) Submission of portfolio of film, slides, and videotapes. Exams cover: Anatomy and physiology; Anterior segment angiography; Cinematography; Clinical pathology; External eye photography; Film processing and printing black and white and color; Fundus photography; Gonio photography; Monochromatic photography; Motility photography; Pharmacology; Photographic reproduction; Photographic theory; Photography through and operating microscope; Retinal fluorescein angiography; Slitlamp photography; Specular photomicrography; Terminology; and Videography. **Renewal:** Every three years. Recertification based on accumulation of 30 continuing education credits. **Examination Type:** Multiple-choice. **Waiting Period to Receive Scores:** Six weeks. **Fees:** $350 (members); $425 (nonmembers). **Endorsed By:** National Organization for Competency Assurance.

`1051`

Certified Professional Evidence Photographer (Civil Evidence Photography)

Evidence Photographers
    International Council (EPIC)
600 Main St.
Honesdale, PA 18431
Phone: (717)253-5450
Fax: (717)253-4398
Toll Free: (800)356-3742

Recipient: Civil evidence photographers. **Membership:** Required. **Certification Requirements:** Must meet the following requirements: (1) Submission of at least one article or research paper for publication in EPIC's *Journal of Evidence Photography* with supporting photographs; (2) Submission of at least seven cases with proper narrative summary or investigative report to support each case history and at least seven different photographic assignments with minimum of 30 prints. Pictures must cover many aspects of civil evidence photography and EPIC will accept any type of portfolio/assignment, including video; and (3) Successful completion of either oral or written exam. **Renewal:** Every two years. Recertification based on attendance at one EPIC seminar or publication of article or research paper in EPIC's *Journal of Evidence Photography*. **Fees:** $150.

`1052`

Certified Professional Evidence Photographer (Law Enforcement Photography)

Evidence Photographers
    International Council (EPIC)
600 Main St.
Honesdale, PA 18431
Phone: (717)253-5450
Fax: (717)253-4398
Toll Free: (800)356-3742

Recipient: Law enforcement evidence photographers. **Membership:** Required. **Certification Requirements:** Must meet the following requirements: (1) Submission of at least one article or research paper for publication in EPIC's *Journal of Evidence Photography* with supporting photographs; (2) Submission of at least seven cases with proper narrative summary or investigative report to support each case history and at least seven different photographic assignments with minimum of 30 prints. Pictures must cover many aspects of law enforcement photography and EPIC will accept any type of portfolio/assignment, including video; and (3) Successful completion of either oral or written exam. **Renewal:** Every two years. Recertification based on attendance at one EPIC seminar or publication of article or research paper in EPIC's *Journal of Evidence Photography*. **Fees:** $150.

`1053`

Certified Professional Photographer (CPP)

Professional Photographers of
    America (PP of A)
57 Forsythe St., Ste. 1600
Atlanta, GA 30303
Phone: (404)522-8600
Fax: (404)614-6405
Toll Free: (800)742-7468
LaRee Distasio, Standards Admin.

Recipient: Photographers involved in commercial, industrial, portrait, and wedding photography who are available on first-come, first-serve basis. **Educational/Experience Requirements:** Must meet one of the following requirements: (1) Two years experience; or (1) One year of experience and 60 college or school of photography semester hours. **Membership:** Required. **Certification Requirements:** Must meet the following requirements: (1) Submission of portfolio of ten prints or transparencies from ten different job assignments and four videos produced within last two years; and (2) Successful completion of exam. **Renewal:**

Every five years. Recertification based on accumulation of ten days of acceptable continuing education and submission of portfolio of six examples of work completed during recertification cycle. **Preparatory Materials:** Study guide and list of suggested references provided. **Examination Sites:** Exam given at national headquarters, regional and state conventions and seminars, PPA Resource Center, and Winona International School of Professional Photography. **Examination Type:** Multiple-choice. **Re-examination:** Must wait 30 days to retake exam. May retake exam twice. **Fees:** $75.

`1054`

Certified Retinal Angiographer (CRA)

Ophthalmic Photographers' Society
    (OPS)
c/o Terrance L. Tomer, COPRA
Wills Eye Hospital
900 Walnut St.
Philadelphia, PA 19107
Phone: (215)928-3405
Fax: (215)928-3123
Terrance L. Tomer COPRA, Chm.

Recipient: Ophthalmic photographers who have demonstrated proficiency in retinal photography and fluorescein angiography. **Number of Certified Individuals:** 450. **Educational/Experience Requirements:** Must meet the following requirements: (1) Two years experience; and (2) Current CPR certification. **Membership:** Not required. **Certification Requirements:** Must meet the following requirements: (1) Successful completion of written and practical exams; and (2) Submission of portfolio of photographs, contact sheets, paper prints, and slides. Written exam covers: Anatomy; Descriptive angiographic interpretation; Flashlight examination; Fluorescein angiography and complications; Fundus photography and artifacts; General photography; Ocular pharmacology; Ophthalmoscopic findings; and Terminology. Practical exam covers: Contraindications; Fluorescein angiography; Fundus photography; Patient management; Processing and printing; and Stereo slide editing. **Renewal:** Every three years. Recertification based on accumulation of 15 continuing education credits. **Examination Frequency:** semiannual. **Examination Sites:** Exam given at two sites in the U.S. **Examination Type:** Matching; multiple-choice. **Waiting Period to Receive Scores:** Six weeks. **Fees:** $300 (members); $375 (nonmembers). **Endorsed By:** National Organization for Competency Assurance.

1055

Registered Biological Photographer (RBP)
Biological Photographic Association (BPA)
1819 Peachtree St., NE, Ste. 712
Atlanta, GA 30309
Phone: (404)351-6300
Fax: (404)351-3348

Recipient: Biological photographers employed in medicine, dentistry, forensic medicine, natural sciences, ophthalmology, veterinary medicine, and other life sciences. **Educational/Experience Requirements:** Two years education, experience, and training. **Membership:** Not required. **Certification Requirements:** Successful completion of written, practical, and oral exams. Written exam covers basic and specialized photographic knowledge. Practical exam requires submission of portfolio. **Preparatory Materials:** Study guide, including list of suggested study references and sample questions, available. Mentorship program also available. **Examination Frequency:** Annual (oral exam). **Examination Sites:** Oral exam given at annual meeting. **Fees:** $200.

Technicians and Related Support Occupations

Health Technologists and Technicians

Cardiovascular Technologists and Technicians

1056

Certified Cardiovascular Technologist (CCT)
Cardiovascular Credentialing International (CCI)
4456 Corporation Ln., Ste. 120
Virginia Beach, VA 23462-3151
Phone: (804)497-3380
Fax: (804)497-3491
Toll Free: (800)326-0268

Recipient: Cardiovascular technologists. **Certification Requirements:** Successful completion of exam. Exam covers: Basic cardiovascular anatomy and physiology; Cardiac medications; ECG techniques and recognition; Electrophysiology; Holter monitoring; and Stress test techniques. **Renewal:** Every year. Recertification based on continuing education. **Examination Frequency:** Three times per year - always March, June, and September. **Examination Sites:** Exam given at sites throughout the U.S., Canada, and internationally. **Examination Type:** Multiple-choice. **Endorsed By:** American College of Cardiovascular Administrators; American College of Chest Physicians; American Council on Education; American Society of Cardiovascular Professionals; American Society of Echocardiography; National Society of Cardiovascular Technology/National Society for Pulmonary Technology; Society of Invasive Cardiovascular Professionals; Society of Vascular Technology; Surgeon Generals Office - U.S. Army/Air Force.

1057

Registered Cardiovascular Technologist (RCVT)
Cardiovascular Credentialing International (CCI)
4456 Corporation Ln., Ste. 120
Virginia Beach, VA 23462-3151
Phone: (804)497-3380
Fax: (804)497-3491
Toll Free: (800)326-0268

Recipient: Cardiovascular technologists. **Certification Requirements:** Successful completion of one registry specialty exam and cardiovascular science exam. Registry specialty exams are: (1) Invasive, including: Cardiac anatomy and physiology; Cardiovascular diseases/pathophysiology; Diagnostic techniques; Hemodynamic data; Instrumentation; Intervention; Patient care/patient assessment; and Pharmacology; (2) Noninvasive, including: Advanced techniques in echocardiography; Cardiac doppler and color flow echocardiography; Clinical medicine and therapeutic measures; Electrocardiography and holter monitoring; Exercise stress testing; Pathophysiology of cardiovascular diseases; Patient management and care/basic pharmacology; Two dimensional echocardiography; Ultrasound, doppler, and color flow physics/instrumentation; and Other noninvasive modalities; and (3) Vascular, including: Advanced techniques; Anatomy and physiology; Disease states; Evaluation of blood flow; Patient assessment; Physics/instrumentation; Quality assurance/quality control; and Vascular surgery/intervention. Cardiovascular Science exam covers: Basic chemistry and physics; Cardiovascular anatomy and physiology; Clinical chemistry; General anatomy and physiology; General mathematics; and Quality assurance/quality control. **Renewal:** Every year. Recertification based on continuing education. **Examination Frequency:** Three times per year - always March, June, and September. **Examination Sites:** Exam given at sites throughout the U.S., Canada, and internationally. **Examination Type:** Multiple-choice. **Endorsed By:** American College of Cardiovascular Administrators; American College of Chest Physicians; American Society of Cardiovascular Professionals; American Society of Echocardiography; National Society of Cardiovascular Technology/National Society for Pulmonary Technology; Society of Invasive Cardiovascular Professionals; Society of Vascular Technology; Surgeon Generals Office - U.S. Army/Air Force.

Clinical Consultants

1058

Clinical Consultant (CC)
American Board of Bioanalysis (ABB)
818 Olive St., Ste. 918
St. Louis, MO 63101-1598
Phone: (314)241-1445
Fax: (314)241-1449
Mark S. Birenbaum Ph.D., Admin.

Recipient: Bioanalysis clinical consultants. **Certification Requirements:** Must meet the following requirements: (1) Doctoral degree in the chemical, physical, or biological sciences, or clinical laboratory science; and (2) Hold High-Complexity Clinical Laboratory Director designation (see separate entry) from approved scientific board. **Renewal:** Every year. Recertification based on meeting requirements of Professional Enrichment/Education Renewal (PEER) continuing education program. **Fees:** $150. **Endorsed By:** American Association of Bioanalysts.

Clinical Laboratory Technologists and Technicians

1059

Assistant Laboratory Animal Technician (ALAT)

American Association for Laboratory Animal Science (AALAS)
70 Timber Creek Dr.
Cordova, TN 38018-4233
Phone: (901)754-8620
Fax: (901)753-0046

Recipient: Animal laboratory technicians. **Educational/Experience Requirements:** Must meet one of the following requirements: (1) Two years experience; (2) High school diploma or GED and one year of experience; or (3) Associate's degree or higher and one-half year of experience. **Membership:** Not required. **Certification Requirements:** Successful completion of exam. Exam covers: Animal health and welfare; Animal husbandry; and Facility management. **Preparatory Materials:** *AALAS Candidate Application Handbook* (reference). Study guides, role delineation documents, monographs, manuals, and sample tests available. (901)754-8620 (voice bulletin board). **Examination Frequency:** Throughout the year. **Examination Sites:** Exam given at 300 sites throughout the U.S. **Examination Type:** Multiple-choice. **Fees:** $125 (members); $250 (nonmembers).

1060

Certified Biomedical Equipment Technician (CBET)

International Certification Commission (ICC)
3330 Washington Blvd., Ste. 400
Arlington, VA 22201
Phone: (703)525-4890
Fax: (703)276-0793
Toll Free: (800)332-2264
Nancy Carney, Prog.Admin.

Recipient: Individuals who maintain, troubleshoot, and repair biomedical equipment. **Number of Certified Individuals:** 4450. **Educational/Experience Requirements:** Must meet one of the following requirements: (1) Four years experience; (2) Three years experience and associate's degree in electronics technology; or (3) Two years experience and associate's degree in biomedical equipment technology. **Membership:** Not required. **Certification Requirements:** Successful

completion of exam. Exam covers: Anatomy and physiology; Fundamentals of electricity and electronics; Health care facility safety; Medical equipment function and operation; and Medical equipment troubleshooting. **Renewal:** Every year. Recertification based on accumulation of continuing practice points. Renewal fee is $20. **Examination Frequency:** monthly. **Examination Sites:** Exam given at sites throughout the U.S. **Examination Type:** Multiple-choice. **Waiting Period to Receive Scores:** One month. **Re-examination:** Must wait six months to retake exam. **Fees:** $175.

1061

Certified Laboratory Equipment Specialist (CLES)

International Certification Commission (ICC)
3330 Washington Blvd., Ste. 400
Arlington, VA 22201
Phone: (703)525-4890
Fax: (703)276-0793
Toll Free: (800)332-2264
Nancy Carney, Prog.Admin.

Recipient: Individuals who maintain, troubleshoot, and repair medical laboratory equipment involved in chemistry and urinalysis, serology, hematology, histology, cytology, and bacteriology. **Number of Certified Individuals:** 50. **Educational/Experience Requirements:** Must meet one of the following requirements: (1) Four years experience; (2) Three years experience and associate's degree in electronics technology; or (3) Two years experience and associate's degree in biomedical equipment technology. **Membership:** Not required. **Certification Requirements:** Successful completion of exam. Exam covers: Anatomy and physiology; Fundamentals of electricity and electronics; Health care facility safety; Laboratory equipment function and operation; and Laboratory equipment troubleshooting. **Renewal:** Every year. Recertification based on accumulation of continuing practice points. Renewal fee is $20. **Examination Frequency:** monthly. **Examination Sites:** Exam given at sites throughout the U.S. **Examination Type:** Multiple-choice. **Waiting Period to Receive Scores:** One month. **Re-examination:** Must wait six months to retake exam. **Fees:** $175.

1062

Clinical Laboratory Phlebotomist (CLPlb)

National Certification Agency for Medical Laboratory Personnel (NCA)
Dept. 5022
Washington, DC 20061-5022
Phone: (301)654-1622

Recipient: Clinical laboratory personnel who specialize in phlebotomy. **Educational/Experience Requirements:** Must meet one of the following requirements: (1) Successful completion of program in phlebotomy, laboratory or medical assisting, or other related discipline; or (2) One year of experience. **Certification Requirements:** Successful completion of exam. **Renewal:** Recertification required. **Preparatory Materials:** *Candidate Handbook,* including exam content outline, sample questions, and study references, provided. Self-assessment exam available. **Examination Frequency:** semiannual - always January and July. **Examination Sites:** Exam given at 75 sites throughout the U.S. and internationally. **Fees:** $50. **Endorsed By:** American Society for Medical Technology.

1063

Clinical Laboratory Scientist (CLS)

National Certification Agency for Medical Laboratory Personnel (NCA)
Dept. 5022
Washington, DC 20061-5022
Phone: (301)654-1622

Recipient: Clinical laboratory scientists. **Educational/Experience Requirements:** Must meet one of the following requirements: (1) Bachelor's degree in clinical laboratory science, including clinical experience in each major discipline of laboratory practice; (2) Bachelor's degree, including 36 semester hours or equivalent in biological and physical sciences, and either successful completion of accredited clinical laboratory program or successful completion of advanced military medical laboratory specialist program; (3) Bachelor's degree, including 36 semester hours or equivalent in biological and physical sciences, and two years experience within last five years, including minimum of four months in each major discipline of laboratory practice. Laboratory work must be under supervision of appropriately certified clinical laboratory scientist or equivalent; (4) Clinical Laboratory Technician (CLT) designation (see separate entry), either associate's degree or 60 semester hours of college course work, including 36 semester or equivalent quarter hours in biological or physical sciences, and four years experience within last six years, including four months in each major discipline of laboratory practice. Two years of experience must be under supervision of appropriately certified clinical laboratory scientist or equivalent; (5) Associate's degree or 60 semester hours of college coursework, including 36 semester hours or equivalent quarter hours in biological or physical sciences, and six years experience within last eight years, including six months in each major discipline of laboratory practice. Two years of experience must be under supervision of appropriately certified clinical laboratory scientist or equivalent; (6) Registered Technologist (RT) designation from Canadian Society of Laboratory Technologists and six months experience in each major discipline of laboratory practice; or (7) Advanced Registered Technologist (ART) designation in cytogenetics form Canadian Society of Laboratory Technologists. Four major disciplines of laboratory practice are: Clinical chemistry; Hematology; Immunohematology; and Microbiology. **Certification Requirements:** Successful completion of exam. Exam covers: (1) Chemistry/Urinalysis; (2) Hematology, including hemostasis; (3) Immunohematology, including: Basic techniques in blood group serology; Donors and donor blood; and Issuing blood and blood products; (4) Microbiology, including: Bacteriology; Infection control; Mycology; Parasitology; and Virology; (5) Immunology, including: Cellular assays; Miscellaneous serological assays; and Serology; and (6) Laboratory Practice, including: Education; Information management; Instrumentation and equipment; Management; Reagent preparation; Safety; and Specimen collection and handling. **Renewal:** Recertification required. **Preparatory Materials:** *Candidate Handbook,* including exam content outline, sample questions, and study references, provided. Self-assessment exam available. **Examination Frequency:** semiannual - always January and July. **Examination Sites:** Exam given at 75 sites throughout the U.S. and internationally. **Fees:** $65. **Endorsed By:** American Society for Medical Technology.

1064

Clinical Laboratory Scientist in Clinical Chemistry (CLS(C))
National Certification Agency for Medical Laboratory Personnel (NCA)
Dept. 5022
Washington, DC 20061-5022
Phone: (301)654-1622

Recipient: Clinical laboratory scientists specializing in clinical chemistry. **Educational/Experience Requirements:** Must meet one of the following requirements: (1) Bachelor's degree in clinical laboratory science, including clinical experience in each of the following major disciplines of laboratory practice: Clinical chemistry; Hematology; Immunohematology; and Microbiology; (2) Bachelor's degree, including 36 semester hours or equivalent in biological and physical sciences, and either successful completion of accredited clinical laboratory program or advanced military medical laboratory specialist program; (3) Successful completion of categorical discipline of medical technology training program, including academic and clinical components; (4) Bachelor's degree, including 36 hours or equivalent in biological and physical sciences, and six months clinical laboratory experience within last two years; (5) Successful completion of 60 semester hours or equivalent quarter hours, including 36 hours in biological and physical sciences, and 18 months experience within last four years; or (6) Registered Technologist (RT) designation from Canadian Society of Laboratory Technologists and six months clinical laboratory experience within last two years. **Certification Requirements:** Successful completion of laboratory practice and specialty exams. Laboratory practice exam covers: (1) Chemistry/Urinalysis; (2) Hematology, including hemostasis; (3) Immunohematology, including: Basic techniques in blood group serology; Donors and donor blood; and Issuing blood and blood products; (4) Microbiology, including: Bacteriology; Infection control; Mycology; Parasitology; and Virology; (5) Immunology, including: Cellular assays; Miscellaneous serological assays; and Serology; and (6) Laboratory Practice, including: Education; Information management; Instrumentation and equipment; Management; Reagent preparation; Safety; and Specimen collection and handling. **Renewal:** Recertification required. **Preparatory Materials:** *Candidate Handbook,* including exam content outline, sample questions, and study references, provided. Self-assessment exam available. **Examination Frequency:** semiannual - always January and July. **Exam-**

ination Sites: Exam given at 75 sites throughout the U.S. and internationally. **Fees:** $65. **Endorsed By:** American Society for Medical Technology.

1065

Clinical Laboratory Scientist in Hematology (CLS(H))
National Certification Agency for Medical Laboratory Personnel (NCA)
Dept. 5022
Washington, DC 20061-5022
Phone: (301)654-1622

Recipient: Clinical laboratory scientists specializing in hematology. **Educational/Experience Requirements:** Must meet one of the following requirements: (1) Bachelor's degree in clinical laboratory science, including clinical experience in each of the following major disciplines of laboratory practice: Clinical chemistry; Hematology; Immunohematology; and Microbiology; (2) Bachelor's degree, including 36 semester hours or equivalent quarter hours in biological and physical sciences, and either successful completion of accredited clinical laboratory program or advanced military medical laboratory specialist program; (3) Successful completion of categorical discipline of medical technology training program, including academic and clinical components; (4) Bachelor's degree, including 36 semester hours or equivalent quarter hours in biological and physical sciences, and six months clinical laboratory experience within last two years; (5) Successful completion of 60 semester hours or equivalent quarter hours, including 36 hours in biological and physical sciences, and 18 months experience within last four years; or (6) Registered Technologist (RT) designation from Canadian Society of Laboratory Technologists and six months clinical laboratory experience within last two years. **Certification Requirements:** Successful completion of laboratory practice and specialty exams. Laboratory practice exam covers: (1) Chemistry/Urinalysis; (2) Hematology, including hemostasis; (3) Immunohematology, including: Basic techniques in blood group serology; Donors and donor blood; and Issuing blood and blood products; (4) Microbiology, including: Bacteriology; Infection control; Mycology; Parasitology; and Virology; (5) Immunology, including: Cellular assays; Miscellaneous serological assays; and Serology; and (6) Laboratory Practice, including: Education; Information management; Instrumentation and equipment; Management; Reagent preparation; Safety; and Specimen collection and handling. **Renewal:** Recertification required. **Preparatory Materials:** *Candidate Handbook,* including exam content outline, sample questions, and study references, provided. Self-assessment exam available. **Examination Frequency:** semiannual - always January and July. **Examination Sites:** Exam given at 75 sites throughout the U.S. and internationally. **Fees:** $65. **Endorsed By:** American Society for Medical Technology.

1066

Clinical Laboratory Scientist in Immunohematology (CLS(I))
National Certification Agency for Medical Laboratory Personnel (NCA)
Dept. 5022
Washington, DC 20061-5022
Phone: (301)654-1622

Recipient: Clinical laboratory scientists specializing in immunohematology. **Educational/Experience Requirements:** Must meet one of the following requirements: (1) Bachelor's degree in clinical laboratory science, including clinical experience in each the following major discipline of laboratory practice: Clinical chemistry; Hematology; Immunohematology; and Microbiology; (2) Bachelor's degree, including 36 semester hours or equivalent in biological and physical sciences, and either successful completion of accredited clinical laboratory program or advanced military medical laboratory specialist program; (3) Successful completion of categorical discipline of medical technology training program, including academic and clinical components; (4) Bachelor's degree, including 36 semester hours or equivalent in biological and physical sciences, and six months clinical laboratory experience within last two years; (5) Successful completion of 60 semester hours or equivalent, including 36 hours in biological and physical sciences, and 18 months experience within last four years; or (6) Registered Technologist (RT) designation from Canadian Society of Laboratory Technologists and six months clinical laboratory experience within last two years. **Certification Requirements:** Successful completion of laboratory practice and specialty exams. Laboratory practice exam covers: (1) Chemistry/Urinalysis; (2) Hematology, including hemostasis; (3) Immunohematology, including: Basic techniques in blood group serology; Donors and donor blood; and Issuing blood and blood products; (4) Microbiology, including: Bacteriology; Infection control; Mycology; Parasitology; and Virology; (5) Immunology, including: Cellular

assays; Miscellaneous serological assays; and Serology; and (6) Laboratory Practice, including: Education; Information management; Instrumentation and equipment; Management; Reagent preparation; Safety; and Specimen collection and handling. **Renewal:** Recertification required. **Preparatory Materials:** *Candidate Handbook,* including exam content outline, sample questions, and study references, provided. Self-assessment exam available. **Examination Frequency:** semiannual - always January and July. **Examination Sites:** Exam given at 75 sites throughout the U.S. and internationally. **Fees:** $65. **Endorsed By:** American Society for Medical Technology.

1067

Clinical Laboratory Scientist in Microbiology (CLS(M))
National Certification Agency for Medical Laboratory Personnel (NCA)
Dept. 5022
Washington, DC 20061-5022
Phone: (301)654-1622

Recipient: Clinical laboratory scientists specializing in microbiology. **Educational/Experience Requirements:** Must meet one of the following requirements: (1) Bachelor's degree in clinical laboratory science, including clinical experience in each the following major discipline of laboratory practice: Clinical chemistry; Hematology; Immunohematology; and Microbiology; (2) Bachelor's degree, including 36 semester hours or equivalent in biological and physical sciences, and either successful completion of accredited clinical laboratory program or advanced military medical laboratory specialist program; (3) Successful completion of categorical discipline of medical technology training program, including academic and clinical components; (4) Bachelor's degree, including 36 hours or equivalent in biological and physical sciences, and six months clinical laboratory experience within last two years; (5) Successful completion of 60 semester hours or equivalent, including 36 hours in biological and physical sciences, and 18 months experience within last four years; or (6) Registered Technologist (RT) designation from Canadian Society of Laboratory Technologists and six months clinical laboratory experience within last two years. **Certification Requirements:** Successful completion of laboratory practice and specialty exams. Laboratory practice exam covers: (1) Chemistry/Urinalysis; (2) Hematology, including hemostasis; (3) Immunohematology, including: Basic techniques in

blood group serology; Donors and donor blood; and Issuing blood and blood products; (4) Microbiology, including: Bacteriology; Infection control; Mycology; Parasitology; and Virology; (5) Immunology, including: Cellular assays; Miscellaneous serological assays; and Serology; and (6) Laboratory Practice, including: Education; Information management; Instrumentation and equipment; Management; Reagent preparation; Safety; and Specimen collection and handling. **Renewal:** Recertification required. **Preparatory Materials:** *Candidate Handbook,* including exam content outline, sample questions, and study references, provided. Self-assessment exam available. **Examination Frequency:** semiannual - always January and July. **Examination Sites:** Exam given at 75 sites throughout the U.S. and internationally. **Fees:** $65. **Endorsed By:** American Society for Medical Technology.

1068

Clinical Laboratory Specialist in Cytogenetics (CLSp(CG))
National Certification Agency for Medical Laboratory Personnel (NCA)
Dept. 5022
Washington, DC 20061-5022
Phone: (301)654-1622

Recipient: Clinical laboratory personnel who specialize in cytogenetics. **Educational/Experience Requirements:** Must meet one of the following requirements: (1) Bachelor's degree in medical technology or physical or natural sciences and one year of experience; (2) Successful completion of baccalaureate or post-baccalaureate cytogenetic education program (hospital or university based) and six months experience; (3) Registered Technologist (RT) designation awarded by Canadian Society of Laboratory Technologists and two years experience; or (4) Advanced Registered Technologist (ART) designation in cytogenetics awarded by Canadian Society of Laboratory Technologists. Experience must be in laboratory involved in all aspects of cytogenetic testing including culturing, harvesting, staining, photomicroscopy, and chromosome. **Certification Requirements:** Successful completion of exam. **Renewal:** Recertification required. **Preparatory Materials:** *Candidate Handbook,* including exam content outline, sample questions, and study references, provided. **Examination Frequency:** semiannual - always January and July. **Examination Sites:** Exam given at 75 sites throughout the U.S. and internationally. **Fees:** $85. **Endorsed By:** American Society for Medical Technology; Association of Cytogenetic Technologists.

Clinical Laboratory Specialist in Hematology (CLSp(H))

National Certification Agency for Medical Laboratory Personnel (NCA)
Dept. 5022
Washington, DC 20061-5022
Phone: (301)654-1622

Recipient: Clinical laboratory personnel who specialize in hematology. **Educational/Experience Requirements:** Must meet one of the following requirements: (1) Master's degree or higher in hematology and two years experience; or (2) Current licensure or certification by another credentialing agency and four years supervisory experience. Experience must be as clinical hematology practitioner or general or hematology categorical educator. **Certification Requirements:** Successful completion of exam. **Renewal:** Recertification required. **Preparatory Materials:** *Candidate Handbook,* including exam content outline, sample questions, and study references, provided. **Examination Frequency:** Annual - always January. **Examination Sites:** Exam given at 75 sites throughout the U.S. and internationally. **Fees:** $100. **Endorsed By:** American Society for Medical Technology.

Clinical Laboratory Technician (CLT)

National Certification Agency for Medical Laboratory Personnel (NCA)
Dept. 5022
Washington, DC 20061-5022
Phone: (301)654-1622

Recipient: Clinical laboratory technicians. **Educational/Experience Requirements:** Must meet one of the following requirements: (1) Successful completion of accredited clinical laboratory program; (2) Certificate from advanced military medical laboratory specialist agency; (3) Either associate's degree or 60 semester or 90 quarter hours of college course work, including 36 semester or 54 quarter hours in biological and physical sciences, successful completion of accredited program in medical office assisting which contains course(s) in clinical laboratory sciences, and three years experience within last ten years, including min-

imum of four months in each of the following disciplines of laboratory practice: Clinical chemistry; Hematology; Immunohematology; and Microbiology. At least two years of experience must be under supervision of individual certified as clinical laboratory scientist, clinical laboratory scientist consultant, clinical laboratory technician, or equivalent; (4) Equivalent credentials from foreign country; or (5) Four years experience within last seven years. **Certification Requirements:** Successful completion of exam. **Renewal:** Recertification required. **Preparatory Materials:** *Candidate Handbook,* including exam content outline, sample questions, and study references, provided. **Examination Frequency:** semiannual - always January and July. **Examination Sites:** Exam given at 75 sites throughout the U.S. and internationally. **Fees:** $65. **Endorsed By:** American Society for Medical Technology.

Cytotechnologist (CT(ASCP))

American Society of Clinical Pathologists (ASCP)
PO Box 12277
Chicago, IL 60612-0277
Phone: (312)738-1336
Fax: (312)738-1619
John R. Snyder Ph.D., Chair

Recipient: Cytotechnologists. **Educational/Experience Requirements:** Must meet one of the following requirements: (1) Bachelor's degree, including 20 semester hours (30 quarter hours) of biological sciences, eight semester hours (12 quarter hours) of chemistry, and three semester hours (four quarter hours) of mathematics, and successful completion of cytotechnology program accredited by either Commission on Accreditation of Allied Health Education Programs or National Accrediting Agency for Clinical Laboratory Sciences (see separate entries); or (2) Bachelor's degree, including 20 semester hours (30 quarter hours) of biological science, eight semester hours (12 quarter hours) of chemistry, and three semester hours (four quarter hours) or mathematics, and five years experience within last ten years, with two years under supervision of physician certified by American Board of Pathology in anatomic pathology or other suitable qualifications. Experience must include cytopreparatory techniques, microscopic analysis, and evaluation of body systems. **Certification Requirements:** Successful completion of exam. **Renewal:** none. **Preparatory Materials:** Exam content outline provided. **Examination Frequency:** Throughout the year.

Examination Sites: Exam given at sites throughout the U.S. **Examination Type:** Multiple-choice. **Waiting Period to Receive Scores:** Ten working days. **Reexamination:** May retake exam four times. There is a fee to retake exam. **Endorsed By:** American Academy of Microbiology; American Association of Blood Banks; American Society of Cytology; American Society of Hematology; Clinical Laboratory Management Association; National Registry in Clinical Chemistry; National Society for Histotechnology.

Diplomate of the American Board of Medical Laboratory Immunology

American Board of Medical Laboratory Immunology (ABMLI)
1325 Massachusetts Ave., NW
Washington, DC 20005
Phone: (202)737-3600
Rori B. Ferensic, Coord.

Recipient: Immunologists directing laboratories engaged in practice of medical laboratory immunology. **Number of Certified Individuals:** 134. **Educational/Experience Requirements:** Doctoral degree with special training and experience in immunology or clinical laboratory immunology and one of the following: (1) Six years experience as laboratory director or assistant director; (2) Successful completion of one year of postdoctoral training and four years experience; or (3) Successful completion of two years of postdoctoral training and two years experience. **Certification Requirements:** Successful completion of written and oral exams. Exams cover: Basic immunologic mechanisms; Clinical implications; Immunodiagnosis and clinical laboratory correlation; Laboratory practice; Methodology; and Technical aspects. **Renewal:** none. **Examination Type:** Multiple-choice.

Hemapheresis Practitioner (HP(ASCP))

American Society of Clinical Pathologists (ASCP)
PO Box 12277
Chicago, IL 60612-0277
Phone: (312)738-1336
Fax: (312)738-1619
John R. Snyder Ph.D., Chair

Recipient: Hemapheresis practitioners. **Educational/Experience Requirements:**

Must meet one of the following requirements: (1) Current licensure as registered nurse (R.N.) and three years experience; (2) Hold either Medical Technologist (MT(ASCAP)), Blood Banking (BB(ASCP)), or Specialist in Blood Banking (SBB(ASCP)) designations (see separate entries) and three years experience; or (3) Bachelor's degree, including combination of 24 semester hours (36 quarter hours) of biology and chemistry, and five years experience. Experience must be under supervision of medical director and in last ten years. Experience must include donor and therapeutic procedures and four of the following procedures: Clinical assessment; Donor selection; Fluid balance; Management of adverse reactions; Quality assurance procedures; and Vascular access. **Certification Requirements:** Successful completion of exam. **Renewal:** none. **Preparatory Materials:** Exam content outline provided. **Examination Frequency:** Throughout the year. **Examination Sites:** Exam given at sites throughout the U.S. **Examination Type:** Multiple-choice. **Waiting Period to Receive Scores:** Ten working days. **Re-examination:** May retake exam four times. There is a fee to retake exam. **Endorsed By:** American Academy of Microbiology; American Association of Blood Banks; American Society of Cytology; American Society of Hematology; Clinical Laboratory Management Association; National Registry in Clinical Chemistry; National Society for Histotechnology.

`1074`

Histologic Technician (HT(ASCP))
American Society of Clinical
 Pathologists (ASCP)
PO Box 12277
Chicago, IL 60612-0277
Phone: (312)738-1336
Fax: (312)738-1619
John R. Snyder Ph.D., Chair

Recipient: Histologic technicians. **Educational/Experience Requirements:** Must meet one of the following requirements: (1) Successful completion of histotechnology program accredited by either Commission on Accreditation of Allied Health Education Programs (CAAHEP) or National Accrediting Agency for Clinical Laboratory Sciences (NAACLS) (see separate entries); (2) Associate degree or at least 60 semester hours (90 quarter hours) of academic credit at accredited college or university with combination of 12 semester hours (18 quarter hours) of biology and chemistry and one year of experience within last ten years under supervision of pa-

thologist certified by American Board of Pathology (ABP) in anatomic pathology or appropriately certified medical scientist and certified medical technologist; or (3) High school diploma or equivalent and two years experience within last ten years under supervision of pathologist certified by ABP in anatomic pathology or appropriately certified medical scientist and certified medical technologist. **Certification Requirements:** Successful completion of written and practical exams. **Renewal:** none. **Preparatory Materials:** Exam content outline provided. **Examination Frequency:** Throughout the year. **Examination Sites:** Exams given at sites throughout the U.S. **Examination Type:** Multiple-choice. **Waiting Period to Receive Scores:** Ten working days. **Re-examination:** May retake exam four times. There is a fee to retake exam. **Endorsed By:** American Academy of Microbiology; American Association of Blood Banks; American Society of Cytology; American Society of Hematology; Clinical Laboratory Management Association; National Registry in Clinical Chemistry; National Society for Histotechnology.

`1075`

Histotechnologist (HTL(ASCP))
American Society of Clinical
 Pathologists (ASCP)
PO Box 12277
Chicago, IL 60612-0277
Phone: (312)738-1336
Fax: (312)738-1619
John R. Snyder Ph.D., Chair

Recipient: Histotechnologists. **Educational/Experience Requirements:** Bachelor's degree with combination of 30 semester hours (45 quarter hours) of biology and chemistry and meet one of the following requirements: (1) One year of experience in last ten years under supervision of pathologist certified by American Board of Pathology or appropriately certified medical scientist and certified medical technologist; or (2) Successful completion of histotechnology program accredited by either Commission on Accreditation of Allied Health Education Programs or National Accrediting Agency for Clinical Laboratory Sciences (see separate entries). **Certification Requirements:** Successful completion of written and practical exams. **Renewal:** none. **Preparatory Materials:** Exam content outline provided. **Examination Frequency:** Throughout the year. **Examination Sites:** Exams given at sites throughout the U.S. **Examination Type:** Multiple-choice. **Waiting Period to Receive Scores:** Ten working days. **Re-**

examination: May retake exams four times. There is a fee to retake exams. **Endorsed By:** American Academy of Microbiology; American Association of Blood Banks; American Society of Cytology; American Society of Hematology; Clinical Laboratory Management Association; National Registry in Clinical Chemistry; National Society for Histotechnology.

`1076`

Laboratory Animal Technician (LAT)
American Association for
 Laboratory Animal Science
 (AALAS)
70 Timber Creek Dr.
Cordova, TN 38018-4233
Phone: (901)754-8620
Fax: (901)753-0046

Recipient: Animal laboratory technicians. **Educational/Experience Requirements:** Must meet one of the following requirements: (1) High school diploma or GED and three years experience; (2) Associate's degree and two-and-one-half years experience; (3) Bachelor's degree or higher and two years experience; or (4) High school diploma or GED and hold Assistant Laboratory Animal Technician (ALAT) designation (see separate entry) for one year. Experience must be directly related to maintenance of health and well-being of laboratory animals, including: Cage wash operations; Care, use, handling, and treatment of animals; Clinical pathology laboratory duties; and Surgical or necropsy activities. **Membership:** Not required. **Certification Requirements:** Successful completion of exam. Exam covers: Animal health and welfare; Animal husbandry; and Facility management. **Preparatory Materials:** *AALAS Candidate Application Handbook* (reference). Study guides, role delineation documents, monographs, manuals, and sample tests available. (901)754-8620 (voice bulletin board). **Examination Frequency:** Throughout the year. **Examination Sites:** Exam given at 300 sites throughout the U.S. **Examination Type:** Multiple-choice. **Fees:** $150 (members); $300 (nonmembers).

1077

Laboratory Animal Technologist (LATG)

American Association for
  Laboratory Animal Science
  (AALAS)
70 Timber Creek Dr.
Cordova, TN 38018-4233
Phone: (901)754-8620
Fax: (901)753-0046

Recipient: Animal laboratory technicians. **Educational/Experience Requirements:** Must meet one of the following requirements: (1) High school diploma or GED and five years experience; (2) Associate's degree and four-and-one-half years experience; (3) Bachelor's degree or higher and four years experience; or (4) High school diploma or GED and hold Laboratory Animal Technician (LAT) designation (see separate entry) for one year. **Membership:** Not required. **Certification Requirements:** Successful completion of exam. Exam covers Animal health and welfare; Animal husbandry; and Facility management. **Preparatory Materials:** *AALAS Candidate Application Handbook* (reference). Study guides, role delineation documents, monographs, manuals, and sample tests available. (901)754-8620 (voice bulletin board). **Examination Frequency:** Throughout the year. **Examination Sites:** Exam given at 300 sites throughout the U.S. **Examination Type:** Multiple-choice. **Fees:** $175 (members); $350 (nonmembers).

1078

Medical Laboratory Technician (MLT)

American Medical Technologists
  (AMT)
710 Higgins Rd.
Park Ridge, IL 60068
Phone: (708)823-5169
Fax: (708)823-0458
Toll Free: (800)275-1268
James R. Fidler Ph.D., Dir.

Recipient: Individuals qualified by education, experience, and training to perform clinical laboratory tests requiring limited exercise of independent judgement and responsibility. Technicians ordinarily work only under immediate supervision, particularly when performing tests of other than routine nature. **Educational/ Experience Requirements:** Must meet one of the following requirements: (1) Associate's degree in medical technology from accredited college; (2) Two years of college coursework (60 semester hours),

with 25 semester hours in medical technology related subjects, including any chemical or biological science courses, as well as mathematics and/or courses in computer science, not to exceed six semester hours, and six months experience in a laboratory which performs chemical testing; (3) Degree from accredited medical laboratory school or program accredited by Accrediting Bureau of Health Education Schools (see separate entry) or other recognized accrediting agency; (4) Successful completion of military laboratory course (50 weeks) and Medical Laboratory Specialist designation (see separate entry); or (5) Certified Laboratory Assistant designation (see separate entry) and two years experience. All qualifying experience must be in an approved clinical or research laboratory which performs chemical, physical, biological, histological, or cytological examination of various body fluids and tissues. **Membership:** Required. **Certification Requirements:** Successful completion of exam. Exam covers: Chemistry; Hematology; Immunology/immunohematology; Microbiology; and Urinalysis. Candidates holding certifications obtained through examination in the medical laboratory technician category may be exempt from exam. **Renewal:** Every year. Recertification based on continuing education. **Preparatory Materials:** Reference list and study guide bibliography available. **Examination Frequency:** Three times per year - always March, June, and November. **Examination Sites:** Exam given at sites throughout the U.S. **Examination Type:** Multiple-choice. **Pass/Fail Rate:** 60% pass exam the first time. **Waiting Period to Receive Scores:** Four-six weeks. **Re-examination:** Must wait four-six months to retake exam. **Fees:** $95. **Accredited By:** National Commission for Certifying Agencies. **Endorsed By:** National Organization for Competency Assurance.

1079

Medical Laboratory Technician (MLT(ASCP))

American Society of Clinical
  Pathologists (ASCP)
PO Box 12277
Chicago, IL 60612-0277
Phone: (312)738-1336
Fax: (312)738-1619
John R. Snyder Ph.D., Chair

Recipient: Medial laboratory technicians. **Educational/Experience Requirements:** Must meet one of the following requirements: (1) Associate degree or at least 60 semester hours (90 quarter hours) at accredited college or university, including

successful completion of MLT program accredited by either Commission on Accreditation of Allied Health Education Programs (CAAHEP) or National Accrediting Agency for Clinical Laboratory Sciences (NAACLS) (see separate entries) and courses in biology and chemistry; (2) Associate degree or at least 60 semester hours (90 quarter hours) at accredited college or university, including six semester hours (nine quarter hours) of biology, and hold CLA(ASAP) certification; (3) 30 semester hours (45 quarter hours) at accredited college or university, including six semester hours (nine quarter hours) of chemistry and six semester hours (nine quarter hours) of biology, and either successful completion of MLT-C program accredited by CAAHEP or NAACLS or advanced 50 week military medical laboratory specialist program; (4) High school diploma or equivalent, successful completion of MLT-C program accredited by CAAHEP or NAACLS, and one year of experience within last ten years under supervision of pathologist certified by American Board of Pathology (ABP) or appropriately certified medical scientist and certified medical technologist; (5) High school diploma or equivalent, successful completion of advanced 50 week military medical laboratory specialist program, and one year of experience within last ten years under supervision of pathologist certified by ABP or appropriately certified medical scientist and certified medical technologist; or (6) Associate degree or at least 60 semester hours (90 quarter hours) at accredited college or university, including six semester hours (nine quarter hours) of chemistry and six semester hours (nine quarter hours) of biology, and five years acceptable clinical laboratory experience in blood banking, chemistry, clinical microscopy, hematology, immunology, and microbiology within last 10 years, two of which must be under supervision of pathologist certified by ABP or appropriately certified medical scientist and certified medical technologist. **Certification Requirements:** Successful completion of exam. **Renewal:** none. **Preparatory Materials:** Exam content outline provided. **Examination Frequency:** Throughout the year. **Examination Sites:** Exam given at sites throughout the U.S. **Examination Type:** Multiple-choice. **Waiting Period to Receive Scores:** Ten working days. **Re-examination:** May retake exam four times. There is a fee to retake exam. **Endorsed By:** American Academy of Microbiology; American Association of Blood Banks; American Society of Cytology; American Society of Hematology; Clinical Laboratory Management Association; National Registry in Clinical

Chemistry; National Society for Histotechnology.

`1080`

Medical Technologist (MT)
American Medical Technologists
 (AMT)
710 Higgins Rd.
Park Ridge, IL 60068
Phone: (708)823-5169
Fax: (708)823-0458
Toll Free: (800)275-1268
James R. Fidler Ph.D., Dir.

Recipient: Medical technologists who are capable of performing full range of technical, supervisory, and instructional responsibilities related to the clinical laboratory. **Educational/Experience Requirements:** Must meet one of the following requirements: (1) Bachelor's degree in medical technology or major in one of the biological or chemical sciences, and one year of experience; (2) Successful completion of 90 hours at accredited college and one year of experience. This can include community or junior college credit and must include 40 semester hours in those disciplines that comprise medical technology; or (3) Associate's degree from accredited college in medical technology or with major in one of the biological or chemical sciences, and five years experience. All qualifying experience must be in an approved clinical or research laboratory which performs chemical, physical, biological, histological, or cytological examination of various body fluids and tissues. **Membership:** Required. **Certification Requirements:** Successful completion of exam. Exam covers: (1) Administration, including: Bookkeeping; and Insurance; (2) Clinical Medical Assisting, including: Emergencies; Examination room; Laboratory; Medical instruments; and Pharmacology; and (3) General Medical Assisting, including: Anatomy and physiology; Ethics; Medical Law; Patient education; and Terminology. Candidates may be exempt from exam if they meet the following requirements: (1) Successfully complete the HHS(HEW) CLT Proficiency Exam and have five years experience; (2) Hold other certifications obtained through examination and approved by AMT; or (3) Successfully complete medical technologist level exam for state licensure approved by AMT. **Renewal:** Every year. Recertification based on continuing education. **Preparatory Materials:** Practice exam, reference list, and study guide bibliography available. **Examination Frequency:** Three times per year - March, June, and November. **Examination Sites:** Exam given

at sites throughout the U.S. and internationally. **Examination Type:** Multiple-choice. **Pass/Fail Rate:** 60% pass exam the first time. **Waiting Period to Receive Scores:** Four-six weeks. **Re-examination:** There is no time limit to retake exam. **Fees:** $95. **Accredited By:** National Commission for Certifying Agencies. **Endorsed By:** National Organization for Competency Assurance.

`1081`

Medical Technologist (MT(ASCP))
American Society of Clinical
 Pathologists (ASCP)
PO Box 12277
Chicago, IL 60612-0277
Phone: (312)738-1336
Fax: (312)738-1619
John R. Snyder Ph.D., Chair

Recipient: Medical technologists. **Educational/Experience Requirements:** Must meet one of the following requirements: (1) Bachelor's degree, including courses in biological science, chemistry, and mathematics, and successful completion of medical technology program accredited by either Commission on Accreditation of Allied Health Education Programs or National Accrediting Agency for Clinical Laboratory Sciences (see separate entries); (2) Hold Medical Laboratory Technician (MLT(ASCP)) designation (see separate entry), bachelor's degree, including 16 semester hours (24 quarter hours) of biological science (with one semester in microbiology), 16 semester hours (24 quarter hours) of chemistry (with one semester in organic or biochemistry), and one semester (one quarter) of mathematics, and three years clinical laboratory experience in blood banking, chemistry, clinical microscopy, hematology, immunology, and microbiology within last ten years, two of which must be under supervision of pathologist certified by American Board of Pathology (ABP) or appropriately certified medical scientist and certified medical technologist; (3) Hold CLA(ASCP) designation, bachelor's degree, including 16 semester hours (24 quarter hours) of biological science (with one semester in microbiology), 16 semester hours (24 quarter hours) of chemistry (with one semester in organic or biochemistry), and one semester (one quarter) of mathematics, and four years clinical laboratory experience in blood banking, chemistry, clinical microscopy, hematology, immunology, and microbiology within last ten years, two of which must be under supervision of pathologist certified by ABP or appropriately certified medical scientist and certified medical technologist; or (4)

Bachelor's degree, including 16 semester hours (24 quarter hours) of biological science (with one semester in microbiology), 16 semester hours (24 quarter hours) of chemistry (with one semester in organic or biochemistry), and one semester (one quarter) of mathematics, and five years clinical laboratory experience in blood banking, chemistry, clinical microscopy, hematology, immunology, and microbiology within last ten years, two of which must be under supervision of pathologist certified by ABP or appropriately certified medical scientist and certified medical technologist. **Certification Requirements:** Successful completion of exam. **Renewal:** none. **Preparatory Materials:** Exam content outline provided. **Examination Frequency:** Throughout the year. **Examination Sites:** Exam given at sites throughout the U.S. **Examination Type:** Multiple-choice. **Waiting Period to Receive Scores:** Ten working days. **Re-examination:** May retake exam four times. There is a fee to retake exam. **Endorsed By:** American Academy of Microbiology; American Association of Blood Banks; American Society of Cytology; American Society of Hematology; Clinical Laboratory Management Association; National Registry in Clinical Chemistry; National Society for Histotechnology.

`1082`

**Phlebotomy Technician
 (PBT(ASCP))**
American Society of Clinical
 Pathologists (ASCP)
PO Box 12277
Chicago, IL 60612-0277
Phone: (312)738-1336
Fax: (312)738-1619
John R. Snyder Ph.D., Chair

Recipient: Phlebotomy technicians. **Educational/Experience Requirements:** High school diploma or equivalent and one of the following requirements: (1) Successful completion of phlebotomy program approved by National Accrediting Agency for Clinical Laboratory Sciences (see separate entry); (2) Successful completion of approved structured phlebotomy program and 40 clock hours of didactic training including anatomy and physiology of circulatory system, specimen collection, specimen processing and handling, and laboratory operations at accredited college or laboratory within last five years; or (3) One year of experience in accredited laboratory within last five years. **Certification Requirements:** Successful completion of exam. **Renewal:** none. **Preparatory Materials:** Exam content outline provided. **Examination Fre-**

quency: Throughout the year. **Examination Sites:** Exams given at sites throughout the U.S. **Examination Type:** Multiple-choice. **Waiting Period to Receive Scores:** Ten working days. **Re-examination:** May retake exam four times. There is a fee to retake exam. **Endorsed By:** American Academy of Microbiology; American Association of Blood Banks; American Society of Cytology; American Society of Hematology; Clinical Laboratory Management Association; National Registry in Clinical Chemistry; National Society for Histotechnology.

1083

Physician Office Laboratory Technician (POLT)
International Society for Clinical Laboratory Technology (ISCLT)
818 Olive St., Ste. 918
St. Louis, MO 63101-1598
Phone: (314)241-1445
Fax: (314)241-1449
Mark S. Birenbaum Ph.D., Admin.

Recipient: Technicians who perform clinical laboratory procedures in offices and satellite laboratories. **Educational/ Experience Requirements:** High school diploma or equivalent and meet one of the following requirements: (1) Successful completion of approved clinical laboratory training program of at least six months in length; or (2) One year of experience in physicians' laboratory or other approved clinical laboratory. **Certification Requirements:** Successful completion of exam. Exam may be waived for candidates with more than two years acceptable experience. Candidates who have successfully completed other certification or licensure exams may be exempt from POLT exam. **Renewal:** Every year. **Re-examination:** May retake exam twice. There is a fee to retake exam. **Fees:** $75.

1084

Qualification in Cytometry
American Society of Clinical Pathologists (ASCP)
PO Box 12277
Chicago, IL 60612-0277
Phone: (312)738-1336
Fax: (312)738-1619
John R. Snyder Ph.D., Chair

Recipient: Individuals involved in cytometry. **Educational/Experience Requirements:** Must meet one of the following requirements: (1) Hold ASCP certifica-

tion as technologist or specialist (see separate entries) and six months experience; (2) Hold ASCP technician certification (see separate entries) and one year of experience; or (3) Bachelor's degree or higher and 18 months experience. Must have experience in: (1) Immunophenotyping, including one of the following: Immunodeficiencies; Immunoproliferative disorders (nonneoplastic and neoplastic conditions); and Transplant; (2) DNA Ploidy Analysis; (3) Cytometry, including all of the following: Data management; Instrument set-up; Interpretation of results; Specimen analysis; and Specimen processing; and (4) Quality Assurance, including all of the following: Assay selection, validation, and documentation; Instrument operation and maintenance; Quality control; Reagent selection, preparation, storage, and disposal; Safety; and Specimen collection, processing, and storage. **Certification Requirements:** Submission of Work Sample Project. Project covers: (1) Evaluation of DNA ploidy data; (2) Evaluation of immunophenotyping data; (3) Implementation of proper safety procedures for equipment use, infectious materials, laser hazards, reagent handling, and waste disposal; (4) Performance of DNA ploidy assays; (5) Performance of immunophenotyping assays; (6) Performance of quality control of reagents and specimen processing; (7) Quality control of flow cytometer and related computer functions to include software manipulation, alignment, calibration, and preventive maintenance; and (8) Selection of appropriate methods for immunophenotyping and DNA ploidy analysis. **Renewal:** Every five years. Recertification based on accumulation of 30 hours of related continuing education. Renewal fee is $50. **Preparatory Materials:** *Instruction Booklet for Qualification in Cytometry* provided. **Fees:** $85. **Endorsed By:** American Academy of Microbiology; American Association of Blood Banks; American Society of Cytology; American Society of Hematology; Clinical Laboratory Management Association; National Registry in Clinical Chemistry; National Society for Histotechnology.

1085

Qualification in Immunohistochemistry
American Society of Clinical Pathologists (ASCP)
PO Box 12277
Chicago, IL 60612-0277
Phone: (312)738-1336
Fax: (312)738-1619
John R. Snyder Ph.D., Chair

Recipient: Individuals specializing in immunohistochemistry. **Educational/ Experience Requirements:** Must meet one of the following requirements: (1) Hold ASCP certification as technologist or specialist (see separate entries) and six months experience; (2) Hold ASCP technician certification (see separate entries) and one year of experience; or (3) Bachelor's degree or higher and 18 months experience. Must have experience in: (1) Immunohistochemical and Immunofluorescence Preparation, including all of the following: Selection of proper control material; Staining technique; and Titration of immunologic reagents; (2) Immunophenotyping, including at least one of the following: Immunodeficiencies; Immunoproliferative disorders (neoplastic and non-neoplastic disorders); and Transplantation biopsies; and (3) Quality Assurance, including all of the following: Method selection, validation, and documentation; Quality control; Reagent selection, preparation, storage, and disposal; Safety; and Specimen fixation, processing, and microtomy. Experience must be in prior five years. **Certification Requirements:** Submission of Work Sample Project. Project covers: (1) Evaluating adequacy of staining results and identifying possible sources of error; (2) Obtaining properly fixed/processed and sectioned material; and (3) Selecting appropriate positive/negative controls and fixation/processing control. Project must include the following procedures: DNA probes; Estrogen receptors; Immunofluorescence; Immunohistochemical titration for primary antibodies; and Phenotype T/B cells. **Renewal:** Every five years. Recertification based on accumulation of 30 hours of related continuing education. Renewal fee is $50. **Preparatory Materials:** *Immunohistochemistry Instruction Booklet* provided. **Fees:** $85. **Endorsed By:** American Academy of Microbiology; American Association of Blood Banks; American Society of Cytology; American Society of Hematology; Clinical Laboratory Management Association; National Registry in Clinical Chemistry; National Society for Histotechnology.

1086

Registered Environmental Laboratory Technologist (RELT)
National Registry of Environmental Professionals (NREP)
PO Box 2068
Glenview, IL 60025
Phone: (708)724-6631
Fax: (708)724-4223
Richard A. Young, Exec.Dir.

Recipient: Environmental laboratory technologists. **Educational/Experience Requirements:** Must meet the following requirements: (1) Associate's degree in environmentally-related discipline; and (2) Two years experience of laboratory work conducting research and/or analyses of environmental contaminants and experience in use of wet chemistry and laboratory analytical devices. Four years experience performing laboratory analysis may be substituted for associate's degree. **Membership:** Not required. **Certification Requirements:** Successful completion of exam. Exam covers: Analytical techniques; Evidence handling; Laboratory practice involving gases, solids, and liquids from environmental samples; Liabilities; and Quality control. **Renewal:** Every year. Renewal fee is $75. **Preparatory Materials:** Lists of approved review workshops and recommended reading provided. **Examination Frequency:** Throughout the year. **Examination Sites:** Exam given at sites throughout the U.S. or by arrangement with proctor. **Examination Type:** Multiple-choice. **Pass/Fail Rate:** 70 percent pass exam the first time. **Waiting Period to Receive Scores:** Two-four weeks. **Re-examination:** There is no time limit to retake exam. There is a $75 fee to retake exam. **Fees:** $75.

1087

Registered Laboratory Technician (RLT)

International Society for Clinical
   Laboratory Technology (ISCLT)
818 Olive St., Ste. 918
St. Louis, MO 63101-1598
Phone: (314)241-1445
Fax: (314)241-1449
Mark S. Birenbaum, Admin.

Recipient: Laboratory technicians who perform tests under supervision in a medical laboratory. **Educational/Experience Requirements:** Must meet one of the following requirements: (1) Successful completion of accredited medical laboratory technician training program of at least 12 months in length; (2) Associate's degree or 60 semester credit hours majoring in laboratory science or medical technology; (3) Successful completion of one-year military laboratory procedures course; (4) Successful completion of 35 semester hours of college credit in biological science (16 hours), chemistry (16 hours), and math (three hours); or (5) Five years experience. **Certification Requirements:** Successful completion of general and specialty exams. Specialty exams are: (1) Chemistry, including: Endocrinology;

Radiobioassay; Routine chemistry; Toxicology; and Urinalysis; (2) Hematology; (3) Immunohematology (blood banking), including: ABO grouping and Rh typing; Compatibility testing; and Unexpected antibody detection and identification; (4) Microbiology, including: Bacteriology; Mycobacteriology; Mycology; Parasitology; and Virology; and (5) Serology, including general immunology and syphilis serology. Candidates who have successfully completed other certification or licensure exams may be exempt from RLT exam. Candidates who hold Physician Office Laboratory Technician (POLT) designation (see separate entry), have four years of experience, and accumulate six continuing education units (CEUs) will be upgraded to the RLT designation. **Renewal:** Every year. **Re-examination:** May retake exam twice. There is a $25 fee to retake each section of exam. **Fees:** $75.

1088

Registered Medical Technologist (RMT)

International Society for Clinical
   Laboratory Technology (ISCLT)
818 Olive St., Ste. 918
St. Louis, MO 63101-1598
Phone: (314)241-1445
Fax: (314)241-1449
Mark S. Birenbaum Ph.D., Admin.

Recipient: Medical technicians who perform tests with little supervision and may supervise technicians. **Educational/Experience Requirements:** Must meet one of the following requirements: (1) Bachelor's degree or higher or 90 semester hours with major in chemical, physical, or biological science; (2) Three years experience and associate's degree or 60 semester hours majoring in laboratory science; or (3) Qualification as medical technologist under revised Medicare/CLIA '67 regulations. **Certification Requirements:** Successful completion of general and specialty exams. Specialty exams are: (1) Chemistry, including: Endocrinology; Radiobioassay; Routine chemistry; Toxicology; and Urinalysis; (2) Hematology; (3) Immunohematology (blood banking), including: ABO grouping and Rh typing; Compatibility testing; and Unexpected antibody detection and identification; (4) Microbiology, including: Bacteriology; Mycobacteriology; Mycology; Parasitology; and Virology; and (5) Serology, including general immunology and syphilis serology. Candidates who have successfully completed other certification or licensure exams may be exempt from RLT exam. Candidates who hold the Registered Labora-

tory Technician (RLT) designation (see separate entry) and have three years experience may be upgraded to RMT designation. **Renewal:** Every year. **Re-examination:** May retake exam twice. There is a $25 fee to retake each section of exam. **Fees:** $75.

1089

Registered Phlebotomy Technician (RPT)

American Medical Technologists
   (AMT)
710 Higgins Rd.
Park Ridge, IL 60068
Phone: (708)823-5169
Fax: (708)823-0458
Toll Free: (800)275-1268
James R. Fidler Ph.D., Dir.

Recipient: Phlebotomy technicians whose primary function is the collection of blood samples from patients by venipuncture or microtechniques and facilitate the collection and transportation of laboratory specimens. **Educational/Experience Requirements:** Must meet one of the following requirements: (1) Successful completion phlebotomy course in program or school accredited by the Accrediting Bureau of Health Education Schools (see separate entry) or other recognized accrediting agency; (2) Successful completion of acceptable phlebotomy program which includes 120 hours each of didactic and clinical instruction; (3) Accumulation of 1040 hours of experience within last three years as phlebotomy technician performing venipunctures, skin punctures, specimen processing, and clerical duties; or (4) Successful completion of state phlebotomist licensure exam. All qualifying experience must be earned in approved clinical or research health care facility that engages in the collection, examination, or transportation of materials derived from the human body. **Membership:** Required. **Certification Requirements:** Successful completion of exam. Exam covers: Blood samples; Clerical; Ethical, legal, and professional considerations; Professional communications; Safety; Specimen collection; Terminology, anatomy, and physiology; and Time management. Candidates who hold other certifications in phlebotomy obtained through examination may be exempt from exam. **Renewal:** Every year. Recertification based on continuing education. **Preparatory Materials:** Reference list and study guide bibliography available. **Examination Frequency:** Throughout the year. **Examination Sites:** Exam given at sites throughout the U.S. **Examination Type:** Multiple-choice. **Pass/Fail Rate:** 92%

pass exam the first time. **Waiting Period to Receive Scores:** Four-six weeks. **Re-examination:** There is no time limit to retake exam. **Fees:** $59. **Accredited By:** National Commission for Certifying Agencies. **Endorsed By:** National Organization for Competency Assurance.

▮1090▮

Specialist in Blood Banking (SBB(ASCP))

American Society of Clinical
  Pathologists (ASCP)
PO Box 12277
Chicago, IL 60612-0277
Phone: (312)738-1336
Fax: (312)738-1619
John R. Snyder Ph.D., Chair

Recipient: Professionals specializing in blood banking. **Educational/Experience Requirements:** Must meet one of the following requirements: (1) Bachelor's degree, including biological science, chemistry, and mathematics courses, and successful completion of specialist in blood bank technology program accredited by either Commission on Accreditation of Allied Health Education Programs or National Accrediting Agency for Clinical Laboratory Sciences (see separate entries); (2) Hold Medical Technologist (MT(ASCP)) or Technologist in Blood Banking (BB(ASCP)) designations (see separate entries), bachelor's degree, including 16 semester hours (24 quarter hours) of biological science (with one semester in microbiology), 16 semester hours (24 quarter hours) of chemistry (with one semester in organic or biochemistry), and one semester (one quarter) of mathematics, and five years post-baccalaureate experience in last ten years under supervision of pathologist certified by American Board of Pathology (ABP) or appropriately certified medical scientist and certified medical technologist; or (3) Master's degree or higher in allied health, biology, chemistry, clinical laboratory sciences, immunohematology, immunology, microbiology, or related field, and three years post-baccalaureate experience in last ten years under supervision of pathologist certified by ABP or appropriately certified medical scientist and certified medical technologist. Experience must include the following procedures: ABO grouping; Antibody detection and identification; Autoimmune hemolytic anemias; Crossmatching; Direct antiglobulin tests; Donor blood processing; Donors and blood collection; Lab operations; Preparation and storage of blood components; Quality assurance procedure; Rh immune globulin studies; Rh typing; and Transfusion reactions.

Certification Requirements: Successful completion of exam. **Renewal:** none. **Preparatory Materials:** Exam content outline provided. **Examination Frequency:** Throughout the year. **Examination Sites:** Exam given at sites throughout the U.S. **Examination Type:** Multiple-choice. **Waiting Period to Receive Scores:** Ten working days. **Re-examination:** May retake exam four times. There is a fee to retake exam. **Endorsed By:** American Academy of Microbiology; American Association of Blood Banks; American Society of Cytology; American Society of Hematology; Clinical Laboratory Management Association; National Registry in Clinical Chemistry; National Society for Histotechnology.

▮1091▮

Specialist in Chemistry (SC(ASCP))

American Society of Clinical
  Pathologists (ASCP)
PO Box 12277
Chicago, IL 60612-0277
Phone: (312)738-1336
Fax: (312)738-1619
John R. Snyder Ph.D., Chair

Recipient: Professionals specializing in chemistry. **Educational/Experience Requirements:** Must meet one of the following requirements: (1) Master's degree or equivalent in allied health, biology, chemistry, clinical laboratory sciences, immunology, microbiology, or related field and four years post-baccalaureate experience in last ten years under supervision of pathologist certified by American Board of Pathology (ABP) or appropriately certified medical scientist and certified medical technologist; (2) Doctorate degree in allied health, biology, chemistry, clinical laboratory sciences, immunology, microbiology, or related field and two years post-baccalaureate experience in last ten years under supervision of pathologist certified by ABP or appropriately certified medical scientist and certified medical technologist; or (3) Hold Medical Technologist (MT(ASCP)) designation (see separate entry) or equivalent, bachelor's degree, and five years post-baccalaureate experience in last ten years under supervision of pathologist certified by ABP or appropriately certified medical scientist and certified medical technologist. Experience must include: (1) Eight of the following procedures: Blood gases; Carbohydrates; Electrolytes; Enzymes; Heme compounds; Hormones; Lipids; Non-protein nitrogen compounds; Proteins; Therapeutic drug monitoring; and Toxicology; and (2) Two of the following procedures: New test development; Procurement of

laboratory equipment; Quality control program; Supervisory experience; Teaching; and Work load analysis. **Certification Requirements:** Successful completion of exam. **Renewal:** none. **Preparatory Materials:** Exam content outline provided. **Examination Frequency:** Throughout the year. **Examination Sites:** Exam given at sites throughout the U.S. **Examination Type:** Multiple-choice. **Waiting Period to Receive Scores:** Ten working days. **Re-examination:** May retake exam four times. There is a fee to retake exam. **Endorsed By:** American Academy of Microbiology; American Association of Blood Banks; American Society of Cytology; American Society of Hematology; Clinical Laboratory Management Association; National Registry in Clinical Chemistry; National Society for Histotechnology.

▮1092▮

Specialist in Cytotechnology (SCT(ASCP))

American Society of Clinical
  Pathologists (ASCP)
PO Box 12277
Chicago, IL 60612-0277
Phone: (312)738-1336
Fax: (312)738-1619
John R. Snyder Ph.D., Chair

Recipient: Professionals specializing in cytotechnology. **Educational/Experience Requirements:** Must hold Cytotechnologist (CT(ASCP)) designation and meet one of the following requirements: (1) Bachelor's degree and five years experience within last ten years; (2) Master's degree and four years experience; or (3) Doctorate degree and three years experience. Experience must be within last ten years, after receiving CT(ASAP) designation, and under supervision of licensed physician certified by American Board of Pathology in anatomic pathology or having other acceptable qualifications. **Certification Requirements:** Successful completion of exam. **Renewal:** none. **Preparatory Materials:** Exam content outline provided. **Examination Frequency:** Throughout the year. **Examination Sites:** Exam given at sites throughout the U.S. **Examination Type:** Multiple-choice. **Waiting Period to Receive Scores:** Ten working days. **Re-examination:** May retake exam four times. There is a fee to retake exam. **Endorsed By:** American Academy of Microbiology; American Association of Blood Banks; American Society of Cytology; American Society of Hematology; Clinical Laboratory Management Association; National Registry in Clinical Chemistry; National Society for Histotechnology.

1093

Specialist in Hematology (SH(ASCP))

American Society of Clinical
  Pathologists (ASCP)
PO Box 12277
Chicago, IL 60612-0277
Phone: (312)738-1336
Fax: (312)738-1619
John R. Snyder Ph.D., Chair

Recipient: Professionals specializing in hematology. **Educational/Experience Requirements:** Must meet one of the following requirements: (1) Master's degree or equivalent in allied health, biology, chemistry, clinical laboratory sciences, immunology, microbiology, or related field and four years post-baccalaureate experience in last ten years under supervision of pathologist certified by American Board of Pathology (ABP) or appropriately certified medical scientist and certified medical technologist; (2) Doctorate degree in allied health, biology, chemistry, clinical laboratory sciences, immunology, microbiology, or related field and two years post-baccalaureate experience in last ten years under supervision of pathologist certified by ABP or appropriately certified medical scientist and certified medical technologist; or (3) Hold Medical Technologist (MT(ASCP)) designation (see separate entry) or equivalent, bachelor's degree, and five years post-baccalaureate experience in last ten years under supervision of pathologist certified by ABP or appropriately certified medical scientist and certified medical technologist. Experience must include: (1) All of the following procedures: Activated PTT; Blood smear evaluation and differential; ESR; HCT; HGB; Instrument maintenance; Platelet; Prothrombin time; Quality control/evaluation; RBC; RBC indices; Reticulocyte; WBC; and Wright/Giemsa stain; and (2) Seven of the following procedures: Body fluid evaluation; Bone marrow prep or evaluation; Budgeting/inventory control/purchasing; Cytochemical stains; Eosinophil count; FDP/D-dimer; Fibrinogen; Hemoglobinopathy evaluation; and PT/PTT substitution studies/factor assays. **Certification Requirements:** Successful completion of exam. **Renewal:** none. **Preparatory Materials:** Exam content outline provided. **Examination Frequency:** Throughout the year. **Examination Sites:** Exam given at sites throughout the U.S. **Examination Type:** Multiple-choice. **Waiting Period to Receive Scores:** Ten working days. **Re-examination:** May retake exam four times. There is a fee to retake exam. **Endorsed By:** American Academy of Microbiology; American Association of Blood Banks; American Society of Cytology; American Society of Hematology; Clinical Laboratory Management Association; National Registry in Clinical Chemistry; National Society for Histotechnology.

1094

Specialist in Immunology (SI(ASCP))

American Society of Clinical
  Pathologists (ASCP)
PO Box 12277
Chicago, IL 60612-0277
Phone: (312)738-1336
Fax: (312)738-1619
John R. Snyder Ph.D., Chair

Recipient: Professionals specializing in immunology. **Educational/Experience Requirements:** Must meet one of the following requirements: (1) Master's degree or equivalent in allied health, biology, chemistry, clinical laboratory sciences, immunology, microbiology, or related field and four years post-baccalaureate experience in last ten years under supervision of pathologist certified by American Board of Pathology (ABP) or appropriately certified medical scientist and certified medical technologist; (2) Doctorate degree in allied health, biology, chemistry, clinical laboratory sciences, immunology, microbiology, or related field and two years post-baccalaureate experience in last ten years under supervision of pathologist certified by ABP or appropriately certified medical scientist and certified medical technologist; or (3) Hold Medical Technologist (MT(ASCP)) designation (see separate entry) or equivalent, bachelor's degree, and five years post-baccalaureate experience in last ten years under supervision of pathologist certified by ABP or appropriately certified medical scientist and certified medical technologist. Experience must include four of the following procedures: Cellular components of immune response; Histocompatibility testing; Immunoassay; Immunochemical analysis of proteins; Immunomicroscopy; Infectious disease serology; and Other related procedures. **Certification Requirements:** Successful completion of exam. **Renewal:** none. **Preparatory Materials:** Exam content outline provided. **Examination Frequency:** Throughout the year. **Examination Sites:** Exam given at sites throughout the U.S. **Examination Type:** Multiple-choice. **Waiting Period to Receive Scores:** Ten working days. **Re-examination:** May retake exam four times. There is a fee to retake exam. **Endorsed By:** American Academy of Microbiology; American Association of Blood Banks; American Society of Cytology; American Society of Hematology; Clinical Laboratory Management Association; National Registry in Clinical Chemistry; National Society for Histotechnology.

1095

Specialist in Microbiology (SM(ASCP))

American Society of Clinical
  Pathologists (ASCP)
PO Box 12277
Chicago, IL 60612-0277
Phone: (312)738-1336
Fax: (312)738-1619
John R. Snyder Ph.D., Chair

Recipient: Professionals specializing in microbiology. **Educational/Experience Requirements:** Must meet one of the following requirements: (1) Master's degree or equivalent in allied health, biology, chemistry, clinical laboratory sciences, immunology, microbiology, or related field and four years post-baccalaureate experience in last ten years under supervision of pathologist certified by American Board of Pathology (ABP) or appropriately certified medical scientist and certified medical technologist; (2) Doctorate degree in allied health, biology, chemistry, clinical laboratory sciences, immunology, microbiology, or related field and two years post-baccalaureate experience in last ten years under supervision of pathologist certified by ABP or appropriately certified medical scientist and certified medical technologist; or (3) Hold Medical Technologist (MT(ASCP)) designation (see separate entry) or equivalent, bachelor's degree, and five years post-baccalaureate experience in last ten years under supervision of pathologist certified by ABP or appropriately certified medical scientist and certified medical technologist. Experience must include bacteriology and three of the following areas: Mycobacteriology; Mycology; Parasitology; and Virology. **Certification Requirements:** Successful completion of exam. **Renewal:** none. **Preparatory Materials:** Exam content outline provided. **Examination Frequency:** Throughout the year. **Examination Sites:** Exam given at sites throughout the U.S. **Examination Type:** Multiple-choice. **Waiting Period to Receive Scores:** Ten working days. **Re-examination:** May retake exam four times. There is a fee to retake exam. **Endorsed By:** American Academy of Microbiology; American Association of Blood Banks; American Society of Cytology; American Society of Hematology; Clinical Laboratory Management Association; National Registry in Clinical Chemistry; National Society for Histotechnology.

1096

Technologist in Blood Banking (BB(ASCP))

American Society of Clinical
   Pathologists (ASCP)
PO Box 12277
Chicago, IL 60612-0277
Phone: (312)738-1336
Fax: (312)738-1619
John R. Snyder Ph.D., Chair

Recipient: Blood banking technologists.
Educational/Experience Requirements:
Must meet one of the following requirements: (1) Hold Medical Technologist
(MT(ASCP)) designation (see separate
entry) and bachelor's degree; (2) Bachelor's degree with either major in biological science or chemistry or combination
of 30 semester hours (45 quarter hours)
of biology or chemistry and two years
clinical laboratory experience under supervision of pathologist certified by
American Board of Pathology (ABP) or
appropriately certified medical scientist
and certified medical technologist; (3)
Bachelor's degree including combination
of 30 semester hours (45 quarter hours)
of biology and chemistry and successful
completion of structured program in
blood banking in medical technology
program accredited by either Commission on Accreditation of Allied Health
Education Programs (CAAHEP) or National Accrediting Agency for Clinical
Laboratory Sciences (NAACLS) (see
separate entries); (4) Hold Medical Laboratory Technician (MLT(ASCP)) designation (see separate entry), bachelor's
degree, including 16 semester hours (24
quarter hours) of biological science (with
one semester in microbiology), 16 semester hours (24 quarter hours) of chemistry
(with one semester in organic or biochemistry), and one semester (one quarter) of mathematics, and successful
completion of structured program in
blood banking in medical technology
program accredited by either CAAHEP
or NAACLS; or (5) Master's degree or
higher in allied health, biology, chemistry, clinical laboratory sciences, immunohematology, immunology, microbiology,
or related field, and six months experience in last ten years under supervision
of pathologist certified by ABP or appropriately certified medical scientist and
certified medical technologist. Experience
must include work in each of the following areas in last ten years: (1) Component
Preparation for Storage and Administration, including: Cryoprecipitated AHF;
Fresh frozen plaza; Platlets; and Red
blood cell components; (2) Donor Blood,
including: Processing and confirmation
testing; and Selection, preparation, and
blood collection; (3) Quality Control, in-

cluding: Equipment; and Reagents; (4)
Routine Problem Solving, including: Hemolytic disease of the newborn; Immune
hemolytic anemias; Rh immune globulin
evaluation; and Transfusion reactions;
and (5) Serologic Testing, including:
ABO and Rh typing; Antibody detection
and identification; Crossmatching; Direct
antiglobulin tests; and Test for other
blood group antigens. **Certification Requirements:** Successful completion of
exam. **Renewal:** none. **Preparatory Materials:** Exam content outline provided.
Examination Frequency: Throughout the
year. **Examination Sites:** Exam given at
sites throughout the U.S. **Examination
Type:** Multiple-choice. **Waiting Period to
Receive Scores:** Ten working days. **Reexamination:** May retake exam four
times. There is a fee to retake exam.
Endorsed By: American Academy of Microbiology; American Association of
Blood Banks; American Society of Cytology; American Society of Hematology;
Clinical Laboratory Management Association; National Registry in Clinical
Chemistry; National Society for Histotechnology.

1097

Technologist in Chemistry (C(ASCP))

American Society of Clinical
   Pathologists (ASCP)
PO Box 12277
Chicago, IL 60612-0277
Phone: (312)738-1336
Fax: (312)738-1619
John R. Snyder Ph.D., Chair

Recipient: Chemistry technologists.
Educational/Experience Requirements:
Must meet one of the following requirements: (1) Hold Medical Technologist
(MT(ASCP)) designation (see separate
entry) and bachelor's degree; (2) Bachelor's degree with either major in chemistry or 24 semester hours (36 quarter
hours) of chemistry and one year of experience under supervision of pathologist
certified by American Board of Pathology (ABP) or appropriately certified
medical scientist and certified medical
technologist; (3) Bachelor's degree including 24 semester hours (36 quarter
hours) of chemistry and successful
completion of structured program in
clinical chemistry in medical technology
program accredited by either Commission on Accreditation of Allied Health
Education Programs (CAAHEP) or National Accrediting Agency for Clinical
Laboratory Sciences (NAACLS) (see
separate entries); (4) Hold Medical Laboratory Technician (MLT(ASCP)) designation (see separate entry), bachelor's

degree, including 16 semester hours (24
quarter hours) of biological science (with
one semester in microbiology), 16 semester hours (24 quarter hours) of chemistry
(with one semester in organic or biochemistry), and one semester (one quarter) of mathematics, and successful
completion of structured program in
clinical chemistry in medical technology
program accredited by either CAAHEP
or NAACLS; or (5) Master's degree or
equivalent in chemistry and six months
experience in last ten years under supervision of pathologist certified by ABP or
appropriately certified medical scientist
and certified medical technologist. Experience must be in last ten years and
include: (1) Experience in five of the following seven procedures: Carbohydrates;
Electrolytes; Enzymes; Heme compounds; Lipids; Non-protein nitrogen
compounds; and Proteins; and (2) Experience in three of the following five procedures: Blood gases; Hormones; Therapeutic drug monitoring; Toxicology; and
Vitamins. **Certification Requirements:**
Successful completion of exam. **Renewal:**
none. **Preparatory Materials:** Exam content outline provided. **Examination Frequency:** Throughout the year. **Examination Sites:** Exam given at sites
throughout the U.S. **Examination Type:**
Multiple-choice. **Waiting Period to Receive Scores:** Ten working days. **Reexamination:** May retake exam four
times. There is a fee to retake exam.
Endorsed By: American Academy of Microbiology; American Association of
Blood Banks; American Society of Cytology; American Society of Hematology;
Clinical Laboratory Management Association; National Registry in Clinical
Chemistry; National Society for Histotechnology.

1098

Technologist in Hematology (H(ASCP))

American Society of Clinical
   Pathologists (ASCP)
PO Box 12277
Chicago, IL 60612-0277
Phone: (312)738-1336
Fax: (312)738-1619
John R. Snyder Ph.D., Chair

Recipient: Hematology technologists.
Educational/Experience Requirements:
Must meet one of the following requirements: (1) Hold Medical Technologist
(MT(ASCP)) designation (see separate
entry) and bachelor's degree; (2) Bachelor's degree with either major in biological sciences or chemistry or combination
of 30 semester hours (45 quarter hours)
of biology and chemistry and two years

of experience in last ten years under supervision of pathologist certified by American Board of Pathology (ABP) or appropriately certified medical scientist and certified medical technologist; (3) Bachelor's degree including 30 semester hours (45 quarter hours) of biology and chemistry and successful completion of structured program in hematology in medical technology program accredited by either Commission on Accreditation of Allied Health Education Programs (CAAHEP) or National Accrediting Agency for Clinical Laboratory Sciences (NAACLS) (see separate entries); (4) Hold Medical Laboratory Technician (MLT(ASCP)) designation (see separate entry), bachelor's degree, including 16 semester hours (24 quarter hours) of biological science (with one semester in microbiology), 16 semester hours (24 quarter hours) of chemistry (with one semester in organic or biochemistry), and one semester (one quarter) of mathematics, and successful completion of structured program in hematology in medical technology program accredited by either CAAHEP or NAACLS; or (5) Master's degree or equivalent in biology, chemistry, or related field and six months experience in last ten years under supervision of pathologist certified by ABP or appropriately certified medical scientist and certified medical technologist. Experience must include all of the following procedures: Activated PTT; Blood smear evaluation and differential; ESR; HCT; HGB; Instrument maintenance; Platelet; Prothrombin time; Quality control/evaluation; RBC; RBC indices; Reticulocyte; WBC; and Wright/Giemsa stain. **Certification Requirements:** Successful completion of exam. **Renewal:** none. **Preparatory Materials:** Exam content outline provided. **Examination Frequency:** Throughout the year. **Examination Sites:** Exam given at sites throughout the U.S. **Examination Type:** Multiple-choice. **Waiting Period to Receive Scores:** Ten working days. **Re-examination:** May retake exam four times. There is a fee to retake exam. **Endorsed By:** American Academy of Microbiology; American Association of Blood Banks; American Society of Cytology; American Society of Hematology; Clinical Laboratory Management Association; National Registry in Clinical Chemistry; National Society for Histotechnology.

`1099`

Technologist in Immunology (I(ASCP))

American Society of Clinical
  Pathologists (ASCP)
PO Box 12277
Chicago, IL 60612-0277
Phone: (312)738-1336
Fax: (312)738-1619
John R. Snyder Ph.D., Chair

Recipient: Immunology technologists. **Educational/Experience Requirements:** Must meet one of the following requirements: (1) Hold Medical Technologist (MT(ASCP)) designation (see separate entry) and bachelor's degree; (2) Bachelor's degree with either major in biological sciences or chemistry or combination of 30 semester hours (45 quarter hours) of biology, chemistry, immunology, and microbiology, and two years experience in last ten years under supervision of pathologist certified by American Board of Pathology (ABP) or appropriately certified medical scientist and certified medical technologist; (3) Bachelor's degree including combination of 30 semester hours (45 quarter hours) of biology, chemistry, immunology, and microbiology, and successful completion of structured program in immunology in medical technology program accredited by either Commission on Accreditation of Allied Health Education Programs (CAAHEP) or National Accrediting Agency for Clinical Laboratory Sciences (NAACLS) (see separate entries); (4) Hold Medical Laboratory Technician (MLT(ASCP)) designation (see separate entry), bachelor's degree, including 16 semester hours (24 quarter hours) of biological science (with one semester in microbiology), 16 semester hours (24 quarter hours) of chemistry (with one semester in organic or biochemistry), and one semester (one quarter) of mathematics, and successful completion of structured program in hematology in medical technology program accredited by either CAAHEP or NAACLS; or (5) Master's degree or equivalent in biology, chemistry, or related field and six months experience in last ten years under supervision of pathologist certified by ABP or appropriately certified medical scientist and certified medical technologist. Experience must include four of the following seven procedures: Cellular components of immune response; Histocompatibility testing; Immunoassay; Immunochemical analysis of proteins; Immunomicroscopy; Infectious disease serology; and Other related procedures. **Certification Requirements:** Successful completion of exam. **Renewal:** none. **Preparatory Materials:** Exam content outline provided. **Examination Frequency:** Throughout the year. **Examination Sites:** Exam given at sites throughout the U.S. **Examination Type:** Multiple-choice. **Waiting Period to Receive Scores:** Ten working days. **Re-examination:** May retake exam four times. There is a fee to retake exam. **Endorsed By:** American Academy of Microbiology; American Association of Blood Banks; American Society of Cytology; American Society of Hematology; Clinical Laboratory Management Association; National Registry in Clinical Chemistry; National Society for Histotechnology.

`1100`

Technologist in Microbiology (M(ASCP))

American Society of Clinical
  Pathologists (ASCP)
PO Box 12277
Chicago, IL 60612-0277
Phone: (312)738-1336
Fax: (312)738-1619
John R. Snyder Ph.D., Chair

Recipient: Microbiology technologists. **Educational/Experience Requirements:** Must meet one of the following requirements: (1) Hold Medical Technologist (MT(ASCP)) designation (see separate entry) and bachelor's degree; (2) Bachelor's degree with major in microbiology or 30 semester hours (45 quarter hours) of biological science, including 20 semester hours (30 quarter hours) in microbiology, and one year of experience in last ten years under supervision of pathologist certified by American Board of Pathology (ABP) or appropriately certified medical scientist and certified medical technologist; (3) Bachelor's degree, with 30 semester hours (45 quarter hours) of biological sciences, including 20 semester hours (30 quarter hours) in microbiology, and successful completion of structured program in immunology in medical technology program accredited by either Commission on Accreditation of Allied Health Education Programs (CAAHEP) or National Accrediting Agency for Clinical Laboratory Sciences (NAACLS) (see separate entries); (4) Hold Medical Laboratory Technician (MLT(ASCP)) designation (see separate entry), bachelor's degree, including 16 semester hours (24 quarter hours) of biological science (with one semester in microbiology), 16 semester hours (24 quarter hours) of chemistry (with one semester in organic or biochemistry), and one semester (one quarter) of mathematics, and successful completion of structured program in microbiology in medical technology program accredited by either CAA-

HEP or NAACLS; or (5) Master's degree or equivalent in microbiology or related field and six months experience in last ten years under supervision of pathologist certified by ABP or appropriately certified medical scientist and certified medical technologist. Experience must be in bacteriology and two of the following areas: Mycobacteriology; Mycology; Parasitology; and Virology. **Certification Requirements:** Successful completion of exam. **Renewal:** none. **Preparatory Materials:** Exam content outline provided. **Examination Frequency:** Throughout the year. **Examination Sites:** Exam given at sites throughout the U.S. **Examination Type:** Multiple-choice. **Waiting Period to Receive Scores:** Ten working days. **Re-examination:** May retake exam four times. There is a fee to retake exam. **Endorsed By:** American Academy of Microbiology; American Association of Blood Banks; American Society of Cytology; American Society of Hematology; Clinical Laboratory Management Association; National Registry in Clinical Chemistry; National Society for Histotechnology.

1101

Urology Technician
American Board of Urologic Allied
   Health Professionals (ABUAHP)
1391 Delta Corners, SW
Lawrenceville, GA 30245

Recipient: Urology technicians. **Educational/Experience Requirements:** Must meet one of the following requirements: (1) Successful completion of accredited training program or current licensure as licensed practical nurse or registered nurse, and one year of experience; or (2) Three years in-service training under supervision of practicing urologist. **Membership:** Not required. **Certification Requirements:** Successful completion of exam. Exam covers: Anatomy; Catherization techniques; Concepts of sterilization and disinfection; Laboratory values; Physiology; Urine collection; X-ray procedures; and Other related procedures. **Preparatory Materials:** *Standards of Urologic Nursing* (reference). Study guide, including sample questions, list of required areas of study, and glossary of terms, and study courses, available. Curriculum guide being developed. **Examination Frequency:** Two times per year - usually April and May. **Examination Sites:** Exam given at annual assembly and at sites throughout the U.S. **Examination Type:** Multiple-choice. **Waiting Period to Receive Scores:** Six weeks. **Fees:** $175 (members); $235 (nonmembers). **Endorsed By:** American Urological Association Allied.

CPR and First Aid Practitioners

1102

Adult CPR Certification
American Red Cross (ARC)
431 18th St., NW
Washington, DC 20006
Phone: (202)737-8300

Recipient: Individuals trained in adult cardio-pulmonary resuscitation (CPR). **Certification Requirements:** Successful completion of course. Course covers: Breathing emergencies; Cardiac arrest; EMS system; Heart attacks; and Reducing heart attack risk. **Renewal:** Every year. **Preparatory Materials:** *Adult CPR* and *First Aid and CPR Instructor's Manual* (references). Video also available. **Examination Sites:** Courses given by local and state chapters.

1103

Adult Heartsaver
American Heart Association (AHA)
7272 Greenville Ave.
Dallas, TX 75231-4596
Phone: (214)373-6300
Fax: (214)706-1341
Toll Free: (800)242-8721

Recipient: Individuals trained in cardio-pulmonary resuscitation (CPR). **Certification Requirements:** Successful completion of course. **Examination Sites:** Courses given by local and state chapters.

1104

Advanced Cardiac Life Support
American Heart Association (AHA)
7272 Greenville Ave.
Dallas, TX 75231-4596
Phone: (214)373-6300
Fax: (214)706-1341
Toll Free: (800)242-8721

Recipient: Health professionals involved with cardiac life support. **Certification Requirements:** Successful completion of course. **Examination Sites:** Courses given by local and state chapters.

1105

**Basic Life Support for the
   Healthcare Provider**
American Heart Association (AHA)
7272 Greenville Ave.
Dallas, TX 75231-4596
Phone: (214)373-6300
Fax: (214)706-1341
Toll Free: (800)242-8721

Recipient: Healthcare providers trained in cardio-pulmonary resuscitation (CPR). **Certification Requirements:** Successful completion of course. **Examination Sites:** Courses given by local and state chapters.

1106

Community CPR Certification
American Red Cross (ARC)
431 18th St., NW
Washington, DC 20006
Phone: (202)737-8300

Recipient: Individuals trained in adult and infant and child cardiopulmonary resuscitation (CPR). **Certification Requirements:** Successful completion of course. Course covers: Breathing emergencies; Cardiac arrest; EMS system; Heart attacks; and Reducing illness and injury risks. **Renewal:** Every year. **Preparatory Materials:** *Community CPR* and *First Aid and CPR Instructor's Manual* (references). Video also available. **Examination Sites:** Courses given by local and state chapters.

1107

Community First Aid and Safety
American Red Cross (ARC)
431 18th St., NW
Washington, DC 20006
Phone: (202)737-8300

Recipient: Individuals trained in first aid. **Certification Requirements:** Successful completion of course. Course covers: EMS system; Identifying and caring for sudden illness, including poisoning and heat and cold emergencies; Identifying and caring for various soft tissue and musculoskeletal injuries; Identifying life-threatening bleeding and how to control it; Identifying signals of shock and minimizing its effects; Recognizing and caring for breathing emergencies, heart attacks, and cardiac arrest; and Recognizing emergencies and overcoming resistance to act. **Renewal:** Every three years. **Preparatory Materials:** *First Aid and CPR Instructor's Manual* and

Standard First Aid (references). Video also available. **Examination Sites:** Courses given by local and state chapters.

`1108`

Infant and Child CPR Certification

American Red Cross (ARC)
431 18th St., NW
Washington, DC 20006
Phone: (202)737-8300

Recipient: Individuals trained in infant and child cardio-pulmonary resuscitation (CPR). **Certification Requirements:** Successful completion of course. Course covers: Breathing emergencies; Cardiac arrest; EMS system; and Reducing injury risks. **Renewal:** Every year. **Preparatory Materials:** *Infant and Child CPR* and *First Aid and CPR Instructor's Manual* (references). Video also available. **Examination Sites:** Courses given by local and state chapters.

`1109`

Pediatric Advanced Life Support

American Heart Association (AHA)
7272 Greenville Ave.
Dallas, TX 75231-4596
Phone: (214)373-6300
Fax: (214)706-1341
Toll Free: (800)242-8721

Recipient: Healthcare providers trained in pediatric cardio-pulmonary resuscitation (CPR). **Certification Requirements:** Successful completion of course. **Examination Sites:** Courses given by local and state chapters.

`1110`

Pediatric Basic Life Support

American Heart Association (AHA)
7272 Greenville Ave.
Dallas, TX 75231-4596
Phone: (214)373-6300
Fax: (214)706-1341
Toll Free: (800)242-8721

Recipient: Individuals trained in pediatric cardio-pulmonary resuscitation (CPR). **Certification Requirements:** Successful completion of course. **Examination Sites:** Courses given by local and state chapters.

`1111`

Standard First Aid Certification

American Red Cross (ARC)
431 18th St., NW
Washington, DC 20006
Phone: (202)737-8300

Recipient: Individuals trained in first aid. **Certification Requirements:** Successful completion of course. Course covers: EMS system; Identifying and caring for sudden illness, including poisoning and heat and cold emergencies; Identifying and caring for various soft tissue and musculoskeletal injuries; Identifying life-threatening bleeding and how to control it; Identifying signals of shock and minimizing its effects; Recognizing and caring for breathing emergencies, heart attacks, and cardiac arrest; and Recognizing emergencies and overcoming resistance to act. **Renewal:** Every three years. **Preparatory Materials:** *First Aid and CPR Instructor's Manual* and *Standard First Aid* (references). Video also available. **Examination Sites:** Courses given by local and state chapters.

Dispensing Opticians

`1112`

American Board of Opticianry Certified

American Board of Opticianry (ABO)
10341 Democracy Ln.
Fairfax, VA 22030
Phone: (703)691-8356
Fax: (703)691-3929

Recipient: Dispensing opticians. **Educational/Experience Requirements:** Two-three years experience or training at optical school recommended. **Certification Requirements:** Successful completion of exam. Exam consists of the following sections: (1) Communicate with Patient/Customer, including: Articulating sales and service policies; Communication equipment; Determining needs and wants; Establishing rapport; Illustrating and demonstrating ophthalmic products; Instruction on use and care of ophthalmic products; Responding to complaints; and Selling ophthalmic products; (2) Analyze and Interpret Prescription, including: Analyzing prescription; Detecting and verifying prescription irregularities; and Determining relationship between prescription and patient/customer needs and wants; (3) Fit and Dispense Spectacles and Accessories, including: Adjusting product; Demonstrat-

ing product performance and applicability; Evaluating parameters of new and old eyewear; Making recommendations; Offering additional ophthalmic products; Providing follow-up services; Taking necessary measurements; and Verifying ordered product; (4) Utilization of Standard Ophthalmic Equipment, including: Computing and analyzing ophthalmic data; Maintaining equipment; and Operating equipment; and (5) Standards and Regulations. **Renewal:** Every three years. Recertification based on continuing education. **Preparatory Materials:** Handbook, including list of suggested references and sample questions, provided. Home study and review courses available. **Examination Sites:** Exam given at sites throughout the U.S. **Examination Type:** Multiple-choice. **Waiting Period to Receive Scores:** Seven weeks. **Re-examination:** There is a $95 fee to retake exam. **Fees:** $95. **Accredited By:** National Commission for Certifying Agencies. **Endorsed By:** National Organization for Competency Assurance

`1113`

National Contact Lens Certified (NCLC)

National Contact Lens Examiners (NCLE)
10341 Democracy Ln.
Fairfax, VA 22030
Phone: (703)691-1061
Fax: (703)691-3929
Nancy Roylance, Exec.Dir.

Recipient: Contact lens fitters. **Number of Certified Individuals:** 6500. **Educational/Experience Requirements:** none. **Membership:** Not required. **Certification Requirements:** Successful completion of exam. Exam covers: Determining type and specification; Follow-up; Patient/customer interaction; Practice management; and Prefit and evaluation. **Renewal:** Every three years. Recertification based on accumulation of 15 approved continuing education units (CEUs). Renewal fee is $66. **Preparatory Materials:** List of suggested reference books available. **Examination Frequency:** semiannual. **Examination Sites:** Exam given at 50 sites throughout the U.S. **Examination Type:** Multiple-choice. **Pass/Fail Rate:** 65% pass exam the first time. **Waiting Period to Receive Scores:** Six-eight weeks. **Re-examination:** Must wait six months to retake exam. **Fees:** $125. **Accredited By:** National Commission for Certifying Agencies. **Endorsed By:** Contact Lens Society of America; National Organization for Competency Assurance; and Opticians Association of America.

1114

Registered Optometric Assistant (Opt. A., R.)

National Paraoptometric Registry
243 N. Lindbergh Blvd.
St. Louis, MO 63141-7881
Phone: (314)991-4100
Fax: (314)991-4104

Recipient: Optometric assistants. **Educational/Experience Requirements:** Must meet one of the following requirements: (1) Two years of training and 24 hours of continuing education within last five years; (2) One year of experience in last five years and 12 hours of continuing education in last two years; or (3) Successful completion of one-year or two-year para-optometric training program within last five years. Education must be in the following areas: Anatomy and physiology; Frames dispensing and styling; Instrumentation - basic procedures; Ophthalmic optics; Practice management; Refractive status of the eye; and Special procedures blood pressure testing, contact lenses, first aid, low vision, tonometry, vision therapy, and visual fields. Optional methods of education, such as authoring articles or presenting lectures, may be considered on individual basis. **Membership:** Not required. **Certification Requirements:** Successful completion of exam. Exam covers: (1) Practice Management, including: Office finances; Office procedures; Patient handling; and Professional issues; (2) Ophthalmic Optics and Dispensing, including: Adjustment and dispensing; Frame selection; Lenses; and Prescriptions; (3) Basic Procedures, including: Basic concepts and procedures for preliminary testing; Case history; Color vision; Examination instrumentation (familiarity); Stereo acuity; and Visual acuity; (4) Special Procedures, including: Contact lenses; First aid; Sphygmomanometry; Tonometry; and Visual fields; (5) Refractive Status of the Eye and Binocularity, including: Binocular visions; Eye movements - terminology and definitions only; Refractive conditions; and Refractive errors; and (6) Basic Ocular Anatomy and Physiology, including: Basic conditions; Basic ocular pharmacology; Common pathological and functional disorders - causes and definitions; and Parts of the eye - definitions and location. **Renewal:** Every three years. Recertification based on accumulation of 16 hours of continuing education. **Preparatory Materials:** Handbook, including exam content outline, list of suggested study references, and sample questions, provided. Home study course also available. **Examination Frequency:** semiannual - usually April and November. **Examination Sites:** Exam given at 35 sites throughout the U.S. and Canada. **Examination Type:** Multiple-choice. **Pass/Fail Rate:** 75 percent pass exam the first time. **Waiting Period to Receive Scores:** Six weeks. **Re-examination:** There is no limit to how many times exam may be retaken. **Fees:** $135 (members); $190 (nonmembers); $75 (students). **Endorsed By:** American Optometric Association.

1115

Registered Optometric Technician (Opt. T., R.)

National Paraoptometric Registry
243 N. Lindbergh Blvd.
St. Louis, MO 63141-7881
Phone: (314)991-4100
Fax: (314)991-4101

Recipient: Optometric technicians. **Educational/Experience Requirements:** Must meet one of the following requirements: (1) Hold Registered Optometric Assistant (Opt. A., R.) designation (see separate entry), two years experience, and 24 hours of continuing education following receipt of Opt. A., R. designation; or (2) Successfully complete two-year technician program within last five years. Education must be in the following areas: Anatomy and physiology; Frames dispensing and styling; Instrumentation - basic procedures; Ophthalmic optics; Practice management; Refractive status of the eye; and Special procedures - blood pressure testing, contact lenses, first aid, low vision, tonometry, vision therapy, and visual fields. Optional methods of education, such as authoring articles or presenting lectures, may be considered on individual basis. **Membership:** Not required. **Certification Requirements:** Successful completion of exam. Exam covers: (1) Pre-Testing Procedures, including: Case history; Color vision; Stereo acuity; Vision screening and preliminary testing techniques; and Visual acuity; (2) Clinical Procedures, including: Contact lenses; Keratometry; Low vision; Special ocular procedures; Sphygmomanometry; Tonometry; Triage/first aid; Visual fields; and Vision therapy; (3) Ophthalmic Optics and Dispensing, including: Adjustment; Frame selection; Lenses; Optical principles of light; and Prescriptions; (4) Refractive Status of the Eye and Binocularity, including: Binocular vision; Eye movements; Refractive conditions; and Refractive errors; (5) Anatomy and Physiology, including: Eye; and General anatomy and physiology; and (6) Practice Management, including: Government rules and regulations; Office management; and Professional issues. **Renewal:** Every three years. Recertification based on accumulation of 16 hours of continuing education. **Preparatory Materials:** Handbook, including exam content outline, list of suggested study references, and sample questions, provided. **Examination Frequency:** semiannual - usually April and November. **Examination Sites:** Exam given at 35 sites throughout the U.S. and Canada. **Examination Type:** Multiple-choice. **Pass/Fail Rate:** 75 percent pass exam the first time. **Waiting Period to Receive Scores:** Six weeks. **Re-examination:** There is no limit to how many times exam may be retaken. **Fees:** $135 (members); $190 (nonmembers); $75 (students). **Endorsed By:** American Optometric Association.

Emergency Medical Technicians

1116

Registered EMT - Basic

National Registry of Emergency
    Medical Technicians (NREMT)
PO Box 29233
Columbus, OH 43229
Phone: (614)888-4484
William E. Brown Jr., Exec.Dir.

Recipient: Emergency medical technicians (EMTs). **Educational/Experience Requirements:** Must be 18 years old and meet the following requirements: (1) Successful completion of state-approved National Standard EMT-Basic training program within last two years or documentation of state certification; and (2) Current CPR certification in the following areas: Adult 1 and 2 Rescuer CPR; Adult Obstructed Airway; Child Obstructed Airway; Child 1 and 2 Rescuer CPR; Infant CPR; and Infant Obstructed Airway. **Certification Requirements:** Successful completion of written exam and state-approved practical exam. Written exam covers: Anatomy and physiology and patient assessment; Breathing, resuscitation, cardiac arrest, and CPR; Emergency childbirth; Environmental emergencies; Fractures and dislocations; Injuries: head, face, neck, spine, chest, abdomen, and genitalia; Medical emergencies; Patient handling and transportation; Psychological factors; and Soft tissue injuries, bleeding, shock, and pneumatic counter pressure device. Practical exam must cover: Bag-valve-mask apneic patient with pulse; Bleeding, wounds, and shock; Cardiac arrest management; Long bone fracture immobilization; Mouth-to-mask with supplemental oxygen; Oropharyngeal and nasopharyngeal airway; Patient assessment and management; Spinal immobilization (lying and seated patient); Supplemental oxygen administration; and Traction splinting. **Renewal:** Every two years. Recertification based on: (1) Successful completion of state-approved National Standard EMT-Basic Refresher training course, including written and practical exams; (2) Current CPR certification in same areas as initial certification; and (3) 48 hours of approved continuing education. Teaching EMT courses may be substituted for continuing education. **Examination Type:** Multiple-choice. **Waiting Period to Receive Scores:** Three-four weeks. **Re-examination:** May retake written exam two times. Fee to retake exam is $15. **Fees:** $15. **Endorsed By:** American Academy of Orthopaedic Surgeons; American Ambulance Association; American College of Surgeons; American College of Emergency Physicians; American Psychiatric Association; American Society of Anesthesiologists; International Association of Fire Chiefs; International Rescue and Emergency Care Association; National Association of Emergency Medical Service Physicians; National Association of Emergency Technicians; National Association of State EMS Directors; National Funeral Directors Association; National Sheriffs Association.

`1117`

Registered EMT - Intermediate
National Registry of Emergency
   Medical Technicians (NREMT)
PO Box 29233
Columbus, OH 43229
Phone: (614)888-4484
William E. Brown Jr., Exec.Dir.

Recipient: Emergency medical technicians (EMTs). **Educational/Experience Requirements:** Must be 18 years old and meet the following requirements: (1) Hold Registered EMT - Basic designation (see separate entry) or equivalent state certification; (2) Successfully complete state approved EMT - Intermediate training program within last two years; and (3) Hold current CPR certification. **Certification Requirements:** Successful completion of written and practical exams. Written exam covers: (1) EMT - Basic Reassessment, including: Breathing, resuscitation, and CPR; Emergency childbirth; Environmental emergencies, burns, and hazardous materials; Fractures and dislocations; Injuries to head, face, neck, spine, chest, abdomen, and genitalia; Medical emergencies; Patient handling and transportation; Psychologi-

cal factors; and Wounds, bleeding, and shock; and (2) EMT - Intermediate, including: Airway management and ventilation; Assessment and management of shock; EMS communications; EMS systems; General patient assessment and initial management; Medical legal considerations; Medical terminology; and Roles and responsibilities. Practical exam is scenario-based and covers: Bleeding, wounds, and shock; Intravenous therapy; Long bone splinting; Patient assessment and management; Spinal immobilization (lying and seated patients); Traction splinting; and Ventilatory management. **Renewal:** Every two years. Recertification based on the following: (1) Successful completion of National Standard EMT - Basic refresher Course; (2) Current CPR certification; (3) Successful completion of 12 hours of refresher training; and (4) Successful completion of 36 hours of related continuing education or National Standards Paramedic Curriculum. **Examination Type:** Multiple-choice. **Re-examination:** May retake exams two times. Must successfully complete exams within 12 months. Fee to retake written exam is $35. **Fees:** $35. **Endorsed By:** American Academy of Orthopaedic Surgeons; American Ambulance Association; American College of Surgeons; American College of Emergency Physicians; American Psychiatric Association; American Society of Anesthesiologists; International Association of Fire Chiefs; International Rescue and Emergency Care Association; National Association of Emergency Medical Service Physicians; National Association of Emergency Medical Technicians; National Association of State EMS Directors; National Funeral Directors Association; National Sheriffs Association.

`1118`

Registered EMT - Paramedic
National Registry of Emergency
   Medical Technicians (NREMT)
PO Box 29233
Columbus, OH 43229
Phone: (614)888-4484
William E. Brown Jr., Exec.Dir.

Recipient: Paramedics. **Educational/ Experience Requirements:** Must be 18 years old and meet the following requirements: (1) Hold Registered EMT - Basic designation (see separate entry) or equivalent state certification; (2) Successfully complete state approved EMT - Paramedic training program within last two years; and (3) Hold current CPR certification. **Certification Requirements:** Successful completion of written and practical exams. Written exam covers:

Cardiovascular; Medical emergencies; Obstetric, gynecologic, neonatal, and behavioral emergencies; Prehospital environment; Preparatory; and Trauma. Practical exam is scenario-based and covers: (1) Patient Assessment and Management, including: Primary survey and resuscitation; and Secondary survey; (2) Ventilatory Management; (3) Cardiac Arrest Skills, including: Dynamic cardiology; and State cardiology; (4) IV and Medication Skills, including: Intravenous bolus medications; Intravenous piggyback medications; and Intravenous therapy; (5) Spinal Immobilization (Seated Patient); and (6) Random Basic Skills, including: Bleeding, wounds, and shock; Long bone splinting; Spinal immobilization (lying patient); and Traction splinting. **Renewal:** Every two years. Recertification based on the following: (1) Successful completion of 48 hours of paramedic training; (2) Current CPR certification; and (3) Accumulation of 24 hours of related continuing education. **Examination Type:** Multiple-choice. **Re-examination:** May retake exams two times. Must successfully complete exams within 12 months. Fee to retake written exam is $35. **Fees:** $35. **Endorsed By:** American Academy of Orthopaedic Surgeons; American Ambulance Association; American College of Surgeons; American College of Emergency Physicians; American Psychiatric Association; American Society of Anesthesiologists; International Association of Fire Chiefs; International Rescue and Emergency Care Association; National Association of Emergency Medical Service Physicians; National Association of Emergency Medical Technicians; National Association of State EMS Directors; National Funeral Directors Association; National Sheriffs Association.

Hygienists

`1119`

Certified Industrial Hygienist (CIH)
American Board of Industrial
   Hygiene (ABIH)
4600 W. Saginaw, Ste. 101
Lansing, MI 48917-2737
Phone: (517)321-2638

Recipient: Industrial hygienists. **Educational/Experience Requirements:** Must meet the following requirements: (1) Bachelor's degree from accredited college or university in industrial hygiene, chemistry, physics, biology, or chemical, mechanical, or sanitary engineering, or bachelor's degree in non-related field with 60 semester credit hours earned in undergraduate or graduate level courses in science, mathematics, engineering, and technology, with at least 15 of those hours at the upper level; and (2) Five years post-degree experience. Graduate degree in industrial hygiene may be substituted for two years experience and master's degree may be substituted for one year of experience. Degrees in chemistry may be used only by candidates seeking chemical practice designation. Candidates seeking certification in comprehensive practice of industrial hygiene are expected to have performed broad range of functions. Candidates seeking certification in chemical practice must have spent 25 percent of total working time in industrial hygiene laboratory practice. Candidates with less than five years experience may qualify for Industrial Hygienist in Training (IHIT) designation (see separate entry). **Membership:** Not required. **Certification Requirements:** Successful completion of core exam and comprehensive practice or chemical practice exam. Must successfully complete core exam before attempting comprehensive practice or chemical practice exam. May seek certification in both designations. Candidates certified by Board of Certified Safety Professionals (see separate entry) or active with British Examining Board in Occupational Hygiene are exempt from core exam. Exam in sub-specialty of indoor environmental quality also offered. **Renewal:** Every six years. Recertification based on either successful completion of exam or accumulation of 60 points through experience, membership in professional societies, meeting attendance, seminars and short meetings, participation on technical committees, articles published, teaching, and other professional development activities. Lifetime certification available for retired CIHs. **Examination Frequency:** semiannual - always spring and fall. **Examination Sites:** Exam given at annual conference in the spring and at sites throughout the U.S. in the fall. **Re-examination:** Must wait 10 months to retake exams. Must only retake exam failed. May retake core exam once. Must successfully complete core exam within two years. **Endorsed By:** American Academy of Industrial Hygiene; American Conference of Governmental Industrial Hygienists; American Industrial Hygiene Association.

Industrial Hygienist in Training (IHIT)
American Board of Industrial Hygiene (ABIH)
4600 W. Saginaw, Ste. 101
Lansing, MI 48917-2737
Phone: (517)321-2638

Recipient: Industrial hygienists. **Educational/Experience Requirements:** Must meet the following requirements: (1) Bachelor's degree from accredited college or university in industrial hygiene, chemistry, physics, biology, or chemical, mechanical, or sanitary engineering, or bachelor's degree in non-related field with 60 semester credit hours earned in undergraduate or graduate level courses in science, mathematics, engineering, and technology, with at least 15 of those hours at the upper level; and (2) One year of post-degree experience. Master's degree in industrial hygiene may be substituted for experience requirement. **Membership:** Not required. **Certification Requirements:** Successful completion of exam. Must earn Certified Industrial Hygienist (CIA) designation (see separate entry) within six years. **Examination Frequency:** semiannual - always spring and fall. **Examination Sites:** Exam given at annual conference in the spring and at sites throughout the U.S. in the fall. **Re-examination:** Must wait 10 months to retake exam. **Endorsed By:** American Academy of Industrial Hygiene; American Conference of Governmental Industrial Hygienists; American Industrial Hygiene Association.

Laboratory Managers

Bioanalyst Clinical Laboratory Director (BCLD)
American Board of Bioanalysis (ABB)
818 Olive St., Ste. 918
St. Louis, MO 63101-1598
Phone: (314)241-1445
Fax: (314)241-1449
Mark S. Birenbaum Ph.D., Admin.

Recipient: Directors of bioanalysis clinical laboratories. **Certification Requirements:** Must meet the following requirements: (1) Doctoral degree in chemical, physical, or biological science, including 32 semester hours in chemistry or the biological sciences; and (2) Five years experience, with one year as supervisor and work in three of the following areas:

Clinical chemistry; Clinical microbiology; Hematology; and Immunohematology. **Renewal:** Every year. Recertification based on meeting requirements of Professional Enrichment/Education Renewal (PEER) continuing education program. **Fees:** $150. **Endorsed By:** American Association of Bioanalysts.

Bioanalyst Laboratory Manager (BLM)
American Board of Bioanalysis (ABB)
818 Olive St., Ste. 918
St. Louis, MO 63101-1598
Phone: (314)241-1445
Fax: (314)241-1449
Mark S. Birenbaum Ph.D., Admin.

Recipient: Bioanalyst laboratory managers. **Certification Requirements:** Must meet one of the following requirements: (1) Current licensure or qualification as laboratory supervisor and two years managerial and administrative experience; or (2) Master's degree in business administration and one year of managerial and administrative experience. **Renewal:** Every year. Recertification based on meeting requirements of Professional Enrichment/Education Renewal (PEER) continuing education program. **Fees:** $150. **Endorsed By:** American Association of Bioanalysts.

Clinical Laboratory Director (CLDir)
National Certification Agency for Medical Laboratory Personnel (NCA)
Dept. 5022
Washington, DC 20061-5022
Phone: (301)654-1622

Recipient: Clinical laboratory directors. **Educational/Experience Requirements:** Hold either another NCA designation or equivalent licensure or certification by credentialing agency recognized by NCA and meet one of the following requirements: (1) Master's degree or higher in health care management, education, medical technology, or business administration; (2) Master's degree or higher in biological, chemical, medical, or physical science and two years experience; or (3) Four experience. **Certification Requirements:** Successful completion of exam. **Renewal:** Recertification required. **Preparatory Materials:** *Candidate Handbook,* including exam content outline, sample questions, and study references, provided. **Examination Frequency:** Annual - always January. **Examination Sites:** Exam given at 75 sites throughout the U.S. and internationally. **Fees:** $150. **Endorsed By:** American Society for Medical Technology.

1124

Clinical Laboratory Supervisor (CLSup)

National Certification Agency for Medical Laboratory Personnel (NCA)
Dept. 5022
Washington, DC 20061-5022
Phone: (301)654-1622

Recipient: Clinical laboratory supervisors. **Educational/Experience Requirements:** Must meet one of the following requirements: (1) Hold another NCA certification; or (2) Current licensure or certification by another credentialing agency and four years supervisory experience. **Certification Requirements:** Successful completion of exam. **Renewal:** Recertification required. **Preparatory Materials:** *Candidate Handbook,* including exam content outline, sample questions, and study references, provided. **Examination Frequency:** Annual - always January. **Examination Sites:** Exam given at 75 sites throughout the U.S. and internationally. **Fees:** $100. **Endorsed By:** American Society for Medical Technology.

1125

Diplomate, American Board of Medical Microbiology

American Board of Medical Microbiology (ASM)
1325 Massachusetts Ave., NW
Washington, DC 20005
Phone: (202)737-3600
Rori B. Ferensic, Coord.

Recipient: Microbiologists directing public health and clinical microbiology laboratories. **Number of Certified Individuals:** 842. **Educational/Experience Requirements:** Doctoral degree in biological science and one of the following: (1) Five years postdoctoral employment as laboratory director or assistant director; or (2) Successful completion of two-year approved training program and one year of experience. **Certification Requirements:** Successful completion of written and oral exams. Exams cover: Associated scientific titles; Infection control; Laboratory management; and Technical proce-

dures and equipment. Certification available in the following specialty areas: Medical and Public Health Microbiology; Mycology; Parasitology; and Virology. **Renewal:** Every three years. Recertification based on either successful completion of exam or professional education. **Examination Type:** Multiple-choice. **Endorsed By:** American Society for Microbiology.

1126

Diplomate in Laboratory Management (DLM(ASCP))

American Society of Clinical Pathologists (ASCP)
PO Box 12277
Chicago, IL 60612-0277
Phone: (312)738-1336
Fax: (312)738-1619
John R. Snyder Ph.D., Chair

Recipient: Clinical laboratory managers. **Educational/Experience Requirements:** Must spend 50 percent of time in clinical management or supervisory positions and meet one of the following requirements: (1) Master's degree in management related field, ASCP technologist or specialist certification, and two years experience; (2) Master's of Business Administration (MBA), Master's of Health Administration (MHA), or other management related master's degree, and three years experience; (3) Master's degree, ASCP technologist or specialist certification, and three years experience; (4) Bachelor's degree, ASCP technologist or specialist certification, and five years experience; (5) Doctorate degree in allied health, biology, chemistry, clinical laboratory sciences, immunology, medicine, microbiology, or related field, and three years experience; (6) Bachelor's degree in management or business related field and six years experience; or (7) Bachelor's degree and six years experience. Candidates with non-management related degrees must document one of the following: (1) Six semester hours of business or management courses, three semester hours of statistics, and one semester hour of computer information systems; or (2) 150 hours of continuing education in management, statistics, and computer information systems within last ten years. Acceptable on-the-job experience in statistics and computers may be substituted for academic or continuing education requirements. Experience must be within last ten years and include the following areas: (1) Financial Management, including seven of the following: Billing and collection; Budgets; Capital equipment acquisition; Cash flow analysis; Contract negotiations; Cost analysis; Financial ac-

counting; Inventory control; Purchasing; and Reimbursement issues; (2) Marketing Management, including one of the following: Consumer relations; Market relations; and Product development; (3) Operations Management, including six of the following: Data processing; Facilities management; Flowcharting; Intra/interdepartmental relations; Licensure/accreditation; Medical legal issues; Quality assurance; and Safety; and (4) Personnel Management, including six of the following: Counseling/disciplinary action; Education and training/continuing education; Job descriptions; Motivation; Performance standards/evaluations; Personnel negotiations; Staffing/scheduling; and Wage and salary administration. **Certification Requirements:** Successful completion of exam. **Renewal:** none. **Preparatory Materials:** Exam content outline provided. **Examination Frequency:** Throughout the year. **Examination Sites:** Exam given at sites throughout the U.S. **Examination Type:** Multiple-choice. **Waiting Period to Receive Scores:** Ten working days. **Re-examination:** May retake exam four times. There is a fee to retake exam. **Endorsed By:** American Academy of Microbiology; American Association of Blood Banks; American Society of Cytology; American Society of Hematology; Clinical Laboratory Management Association; National Registry in Clinical Chemistry; National Society for Histotechnology.

1127

General Supervisor (GS)

American Board of Bioanalysis (ABB)
818 Olive St., Ste. 918
St. Louis, MO 63101-1598
Phone: (314)241-1445
Fax: (314)241-1449
Mark S. Birenbaum Ph.D., Admin.

Recipient: Bioanalysis general supervisors. **Certification Requirements:** Must qualify as general supervisor or meet one of the following requirements: (1) Doctoral, master's, or bachelor's degree in the chemical, physical, or biological sciences, or clinical laboratory sciences, and one year of experience; or (2) Bachelor's degree in laboratory science or medical laboratory technology and one year of experience. Experience must be in high complexity testing at acceptable clinical laboratory. **Renewal:** Every year. Recertification based on meeting requirements of Professional Enrichment/Education Renewal (PEER) continuing education program. **Fees:** $150. **Endorsed By:** American Association of Bioanalysts.

1128

High-Complexity Clinical Laboratory Director (HCLD)
American Board of Bioanalysis
(ABB)
818 Olive St., Ste. 918
St. Louis, MO 63101-1598
Phone: (314)241-1445
Fax: (314)241-1449
Mark S. Birenbaum Ph.D., Admin.

Recipient: Directors of bioanalysis clinical laboratories performing high complexity testing. **Educational/Experience Requirements:** Must be qualified as laboratory director or meet the following requirements: (1) Doctoral degree in the chemical, physical, or biological sciences, including 32 semester hours in chemistry or the biological sciences; and (2) Four years clinical laboratory training or experience, including two years experience directing or supervising high complexity testing. For specialty of embryology, experience must include 60 personally performed, successfully completed, assisted reproductive procedures in humans. **Certification Requirements:** Successful completion of exam. Acceptable exams include: (1) Federal, state, and city licensure exams; (2) Exams given by certifying boards; and (3) ABB exams. ABB exams cover general laboratory knowledge and one of the following laboratory disciplines: Andrology; Bacteriology, including mycobacteriology; Clinical cytogenetics; Clinical molecular biology; Embryology; Endocrinology; Hematology, including flow cytometry; Immunohematology; Immunology/serology; Mycology; Parasitology; Routine chemistry, including urinalysis; Toxicology; and Virology. **Renewal:** Every year. Recertification based on meeting requirements of Professional Enrichment/Education Renewal (PEER) continuing education program. **Fees:** $150; there are additional fees for ABB exams. **Endorsed By:** American Association of Bioanalysts.

1129

Moderate-Complexity Clinical Laboratory Director (MCLD)
American Board of Bioanalysis
(ABB)
818 Olive St., Ste. 918
St. Louis, MO 63101-1598
Phone: (314)241-1445
Fax: (314)241-1449
Mark S. Birenbaum Ph.D., Admin.

Recipient: Directors of bioanalysis clinical laboratories performing moderate complexity testing. **Educational/**

Experience Requirements: Must be qualified as laboratory director or meet the following requirements: (1) Bachelor's or master's degree in the chemical, physical, or biological sciences, or clinical laboratory science, including minimum of 16 semester hours in both chemistry and biological sciences and three semester hours of mathematics; and (2) Four years experience, including two years as supervisor. Master's degree may be substituted for one year of both laboratory and supervisory experience. **Certification Requirements:** Successful completion of exam. Acceptable exams include: (1) Federal, state, and city licensure exams; (2) Exams given by certifying boards; and (3) ABB exams. ABB exams cover general laboratory knowledge and one of the following laboratory disciplines: Andrology; Bacteriology, including mycobacteriology; Clinical cytogenetics; Clinical molecular biology; Embryology; Endocrinology; Hematology, including flow cytometry; Immunohematology; Immunology/serology; Mycology; Parasitology; Routine chemistry, including urinalysis; Toxicology; and Virology. **Renewal:** Every year. Recertification based on meeting requirements of Professional Enrichment/Education Renewal (PEER) continuing education program. **Fees:** $150; there are additional fees for ABB exams. **Endorsed By:** American Association of Bioanalysts.

1130

Technical Supervisor (TS)
American Board of Bioanalysis
(ABB)
818 Olive St., Ste. 918
St. Louis, MO 63101-1598
Phone: (314)241-1445
Fax: (314)241-1449
Mark S. Birenbaum Ph.D., Admin.

Recipient: Technical bioanalysis supervisors in the specialties of chemistry, diagnostic immunology, hematology, andrology, clinical molecular biology, embryology, and endocrinology, and the subspecialties of bacteriology, mycobacteriology, mycology, parasitology, and virology. **Educational/Experience Requirements:** Must meet one of the following requirements: (1) Doctoral degree in a chemical, physical, biological, or clinical laboratory science or medical technology and one year of laboratory training or experience in specialty and six months in subspecialty; (2) Certification in anatomic or clinical pathology by the American Board of Pathology (see separate entry) or equivalent; (3) Current licensure to practice medicine or osteopathy and one year laboratory training or

experience in specialty and six months in subspecialty; (4) Master's degree in chemical, physical, biological, or clinical laboratory sciences or medical technology and two years laboratory training or experience in specialty and six months in subspecialty; or (5) Bachelor's degree in chemical, physical, or biological sciences or medical technology and four years laboratory training or experience in specialty and six months in subspecialty. For the specialty of clinical cytogenetics the following requirements apply: (1) Doctoral degree in a biological science, including biochemistry, medicine, or osteopathy, or clinical laboratory science; and (2) Four years of training or experience in genetics, two of which are in clinical cytogenetics. For the specialty of immunohematology the following requirements apply: (1) Current licensure to practice medicine or osteopathy; and (2) One year of laboratory training or experience. Experience for the specialty of embryology must include 60 personally performed, completed assisted reproductive procedures in humans. Training and experience in specialty must be in high complexity testing. Requirement for six months of experience in subspecialty is not required for the specialties of chemistry, diagnostic immunology, and hematology. **Certification Requirements:** Successful completion of exam. Acceptable exams include: (1) Federal, state, and city licensure exams; (2) Exams given by certifying boards; and (3) ABB exams. ABB exams cover general laboratory knowledge and one of the following laboratory disciplines: Andrology; Bacteriology (including mycobacteriology); Clinical cytogenetics; Clinical molecular biology; Embryology; Endocrinology; Hematology (including flow cytometry); Immunohematology; Immunology/serology; Mycology; Parasitology; Routine chemistry (including urinalysis); Toxicology; and Virology. **Renewal:** Every year. Recertification based on meeting requirements of Professional Enrichment/Education Renewal (PEER) continuing education program. **Fees:** $150; there is an additional fee for ABB exams. **Endorsed By:** American Association of Bioanalysts.

Medical Record Technicians

`1131`

Accredited Record Technician (ART)

American Health Information Management Association (AHIMA)
919 N. Michigan Ave., Ste. 1400
Chicago, IL 60611-1683
Phone: (312)787-2672

Recipient: Health information record technicians. **Educational/Experience Requirements:** Associate's degree or successful completion of AHIMA's Independent Study Program consisting of the following modules: (1) Orientation to the Healthcare Field; (2) Health Record Content and Format; (3) Medical Terminology; (4) Medical Transcription; (5) Numbering and Filing Systems: Indexes, Registers; (6) Legal Aspects of Health Information; (7) Health Statistics; (8) Medical Staff; (9) Basic Pathology of Disease Process; (10) ICD-9-CM; (11) Healthcare Environment; (12) Quality Management; (13) Nomenclatures, Classification Systems, and Coding for Reimbursement; (14) Supervisory Principles and Practices; (15) Management Principles and Practices; (16) Directed Clinical Practice; and (17) Health Information Management Technology. Candidates enrolled in the program must also complete 30 semester credits (45 quarter credits), including the following required courses: (1) English composition; (2) College level mathematics; (3) Human anatomy and physiology; and (4) Introductory computer course. Additional courses can be in any field except physical education. **Certification Requirements:** Successful completion of exam. **Preparatory Materials:** Study modules available. **Examination Frequency:** Annual - always fall. **Examination Sites:** Exam given at sites throughout the U.S.

`1132`

Certified Coding Specialist (CCS)

American Health Information Management Association (AHIMA)
919 N. Michigan Ave., Ste. 1400
Chicago, IL 60611-1683
Phone: (312)787-2672

Recipient: Individuals involved in analyzing health records and assigning classifications to medical data. **Educational/Experience Requirements:** Must meet the following requirements: (1) High school diploma or equivalent; (2) Coding experience; and (3) Coding education through workshops, seminars, and college courses. **Certification Requirements:** Successful completion of exam. **Preparatory Materials:** Study modules available.

`1133`

Certified Medical Transcriptionist (CMT)

American Association for Medical Transcription (AAMT)
3460 Oakdale Rd., Ste. M
PO Box 576187
Modesto, CA 95357-6187
Phone: (209)551-0883
Fax: (209)551-9317
Toll Free: (800)982-2182
Claudia Tessier CAE, Exec.Dir.

Recipient: Medical transcriptionists. **Membership:** Not required. **Certification Requirements:** Successful completion of written and practical exams. Written exam consists of the following sections: (1) Medical Terminology; (2) English Language and Usage; (3) Anatomy and Physiology; (4) Disease Processes; (5) Healthcare Record; and (6) Professional Development. Practical exam tests ability to successfully complete medical transcriptions in several medical specialty areas and report types. Must successfully complete written exam before attempting practical exam. **Renewal:** Every three years. Recertification based on accumulation of 30 continuing education credits (CECs), with minimum of 20 CECs in medical science. Credits can be earned through successful completion of one or both exams, college courses, educational programs, presentations, observations of medical procedures, and authoring publications. **Preparatory Materials:** *COMPRO* and *Style Guide for Medical Transcription* (texts). Exam guide, including suggested reference materials and sample questions, provided. **Examination Frequency:** Throughout the year (written); quarterly (practical) - always February, May, August, and November. **Examination Sites:** Written exam given at sites throughout the U.S. **Examination Type:** Multiple-choice. **Waiting Period to Receive Scores:** Immediately (written); 12 weeks (practical). **Re-examination:** There is no waiting period to retake exams. **Fees:** $300.

`1134`

Certified Professional Coder (CPC)

American Academy of Procedural Coders (AAPC)
2144 S. Highland Dr., Ste. 100
Salt Lake City, UT 84106
Phone: (801)487-5590
Fax: (801)485-7803
Toll Free: (800)626-CODE
Kathy D. England, Exec.Dir.

Recipient: Procedural coders, medical records coders, health claims examiners, patient accounts billers, consultants, reimbursement managers, office managers, and administrators who work for physicians, clinics, payers, and consulting firms. **Educational/Experience Requirements:** Must meet the following requirements: (1) One year of experience; and (2) Successful completion of medical terminology course. Medical terminology course requirement may be waived for candidates with two or more years of experience. **Membership:** Not required. **Certification Requirements:** Successful completion of exam. Exam covers the following: Anatomy; Facility; Global surgery; ICD-9 medical necessity issues; Insurance payer issues; Medical terminology; Procedural coding; and Techniques and equipment. **Renewal:** Every year. Recertification based on accumulation of 18 hours of continuing education credits through successful completion of courses, seminars, and workshops, or subscriptions to approved periodicals and texts. Renewal fee is $50. **Preparatory Materials:** *Study Guide for the Certified Procedural Coder CPC and CPC-H Examinations,* including study questions, available. *Discussion Leader's Guide* and independent study programs also available. **Examination Frequency:** Throughout the year. **Examination Sites:** Exam given by arrangement with proctor. **Examination Type:** Multiple-choice. **Pass/Fail Rate:** 66% pass exam the first time. **Waiting Period to Receive Scores:** 20 days. **Re-examination:** Must wait 30 days to retake exam. May retake exam two times. Must successfully complete exam within one year. **Fees:** $250 (members); $350 (nonmembers).

`1135`

Certified Professional Coder - Hospital (CPC-H)

American Academy of Procedural Coders (AAPC)
2144 S. Highland Dr., Ste. 100
Salt Lake City, UT 84106
Phone: (801)487-5590
Fax: (801)485-7803

Toll Free: (800)626-CODE
Kathy D. England, Exec.Dir.

Recipient: Procedural coders, medical records coders, health claims examiners, patient accounts billers, consultants, reimbursement managers, office managers, administrators, and physicians who work in hospitals and outpatient facilities. **Educational/Experience Requirements:** Must meet the following requirements: (1) One year of experience; and (2) Successful completion of medical terminology course. Medical terminology course requirement may be waived for candidates with two or more years of experience. **Membership:** Not required. **Certification Requirements:** Successful completion of exam. Exam covers the following: Anatomy; Facility; Global surgery; ICD-9 medical necessity; Insurance payer; Medical terminology; Procedural coding; and Techniques and equipment. **Renewal:** Every year. Recertification based on accumulation of 18 hours of continuing education credits through successful completion of courses, seminars, and workshops, or subscriptions to approved periodicals and texts. Renewal fee is $50. **Preparatory Materials:** *Study Guide for the Certified Procedural Coder CPC and CPC-H Examinations,* including study questions, available. *Discussion Leader's Guide* and independent study programs also available. **Examination Frequency:** Throughout the year. **Examination Sites:** Exam given by arrangement with proctor. **Examination Type:** Multiple-choice. **Pass/Fail Rate:** 66% pass exam the first time. **Waiting Period to Receive Scores:** 20 days. **Re-examination:** Must wait 30 days to retake exam. May retake exam two times. Must successfully complete exam within one year. **Fees:** $250 (members); $350 (nonmembers).

1136

Registered Record Administrator (RRA)
American Health Information
  Management Association
  (AHIMA)
919 N. Michigan Ave., Ste. 1400
Chicago, IL 60611-1683
Phone: (312)787-2672

Recipient: Health information record managers. **Educational/Experience Requirements:** Bachelor's degree. **Certification Requirements:** Successful completion of exam. **Preparatory Materials:** Study modules available.

Nuclear Medicine Technologists

1137

Certified Nuclear Medicine Technologist (CNMT)
Nuclear Medicine Technology
  Certification Board (NMTCB)
2970 Clairmont Rd., Ste. 610
Atlanta, GA 30329
Phone: (404)315-1740
Fax: (404)315-6502
E-mail: REGJEG@GSUVM1.GSU.EDU
Dr. James E. Greene Jr., Exec.Dir.

Recipient: Medical professionals who utilize radio pharmaceuticals for diagnosis and treatment of patients. **Number of Certified Individuals:** 15,800. **Educational/Experience Requirements:** Successful completion of accredited nuclear medicine technology program. **Membership:** Required. **Certification Requirements:** Successful completion of exam. **Renewal:** Every year. Renewal fee is $30. **Preparatory Materials:** Study guides and sample questions available. **Examination Frequency:** semiannual - always June and September. **Examination Sites:** Exam given at 80 sites throughout the U.S. **Examination Type:** Multiple-choice. **Pass/Fail Rate:** 75% pass exam the first time. **Waiting Period to Receive Scores:** 30 days. **Re-examination:** Must wait three-nine months to retake exam. **Fees:** $80. **Endorsed By:** Technologists Section, Society of Nuclear Medicine.

Orthopaedic Technologists

1138

Certified Orthopaedic Technologist
National Board for Certification of
  Orthopaedic Technologists
  (NBCOT)
c/o Columbia Assessment Services
3725 National Dr., Ste. 213
Raleigh, NC 27615
Phone: (919)787-2721
Fax: (919)781-3186
Paul Grace, Exec.Dir.

Recipient: Orthopaedic technicians. **Number of Certified Individuals:** 1600. **Educational/Experience Requirements:** Must meet one of the following requirements: (1) Two years experience; or (2) Successful completion of orthopaedic program and six months experience.

Membership: Not required. **Certification Requirements:** Successful completion of exam. **Renewal:** Every six years. Recertification based on either successful completion of exam or accumulation of required number of continuing education units (CEUs). **Preparatory Materials:** Study guide available. **Examination Frequency:** semiannual. **Examination Sites:** Exam given at 20 sites throughout the U.S. **Examination Type:** Multiple-choice. **Pass/Fail Rate:** 63% pass exam the first time. **Waiting Period to Receive Scores:** Two weeks. **Re-examination:** There is no time limit to retake exam.

1139

Certified Orthopaedic Technologist
National Board for Certification of
  Orthopaedic Technologists
  (NBCOT)
3725 National Dr., Ste. 213
Raleigh, NC 27612
Phone: (919)787-2721
Fax: (919)781-3186

Recipient: Orthopaedic technologists. **Educational/Experience Requirements:** Must meet one of the following requirements: (1) Two years experience; (2) Successful completion of orthopaedic technology training program; or (3) Successful completion of related allied health program and one year of experience. Experience must be in clinic, hospital, or office, or as independent contractor. **Membership:** Not required. **Certification Requirements:** Successful completion of exam. Exam covers: (1) Assessment, including: Anatomy; Diagnostic procedures; Orthopaedic conditions; and Physiology; (2) Casting, Splinting, and Orthopaedic Appliances, including; Patient safety; and Potential complications; (3) Practice Management, including: Sensitivity to needs of patient; and Understanding of orthopaedic technologist's position and responsibilities in medical hierarchy; (4) Surgery, covering common orthopaedic surgery procedures; and (5) Traction, including: Methods; Procedures; and Types. **Preparatory Materials:** Study guide, including exam content outline, list of study references, and sample questions, available. **Examination Frequency:** semiannual - always February and August. **Examination Sites:** Exam given at sites throughout the U.S. **Examination Type:** Multiple-choice. **Re-examination:** There is no limit to how many times exam may be retaken. **Fees:** $285 (members); $360 (nonmembers). **Endorsed By:** National Association of Orthopaedic Technologists.

Orthotists and Prosthetists

1140

BOC Orthotist
Board for Orthotist Certification (BOC)
Allied Health Bldg., Rm. 234
100 Penn St.
Baltimore, MD 21201-1082
Phone: (410)539-3910
Dr. Donald O. Fedder BSP, Exec. Dir.

Recipient: Orthotists. **Educational/Experience Requirements:** High school diploma, 40 hours of education, and meet one of the following requirements: (1) Two years experience; or (2) Hold Registered Orthotic Fitter (ROF) designation (see separate entry) and documentation of experience in fitting orthoses. May fulfill educational requirement through coursework or submission of Life Learning Paper, documenting education and experience. **Certification Requirements:** Successful completion of written and practical exams. Written exam covers: (1) Facilities Management, including: Elements of fitting room; Environmental safety; Equipment, tools, and materials; and Policies and procedures; (2) Assessment, including: Patients; and Prescriptions; (3) Communications/Patient Education, including: Interprofessional communications; Oral and written communications; Patient follow-up; Psychological impact; and Purpose of orthosis; (4) Select Product/Model/Type of Orthoses, including: Abdominal and pelvic; Ankle foot orthoses; Cervical orthoses; Compression devices; Elbow and shoulder orthoses; Foot orthoses; Functional fracture bracing; Head; Hip abduction orthoses; Hip knee ankle foot orthoses; Knee ankle foot orthoses; Knee orthoses; Lumbo-sacral orthoses; Spinal deformity braces/scoliosis jackets; Thoraco-lumbo-sacral-hip orthoses; Thoraco-lumbo-sacral orthoses; and Wrist/hand orthoses; (5) Breast Prostheses and Bras, including: Evaluating systems; and Selecting product/model/type; (6) Casting, including: Foot only; Lower extremity; Modifications; Serial; Spinal (including cervical); and Upper extremity; (7) Product Application, including: Adjustment and alternations; Fitting product; and Follow-up procedures; and (8) Professional Ethics, including: Performance; and Quality Assurance. Practical exam requires fitting models with any of the following types of orthoses: Extremity supports and orthoses; Flexible spinal orthoses; Mastectomy products; Miscellaneous, including abdominal supports, clavicle supports, and rib supports; and Rigid spinal orthoses. Practical exam covers: (1) Adjustment/Alteration; (2) Application, including: Centering; Even/parallel; Length/edge; Steels shaping; and Tightness; (3) Overall Technique; (4) Patient Instruction; (5) Patient Preparation; and (6) Selection, including: Appropriate model; Correct orthoses; and Measurements and sizes correct. **Renewal:** Every year. Recertification based on accumulation of 12 hours of related continuing education through attendance at grand rounds, authorship of articles, educational programs, subscriptions to professional journals, and teaching. **Preparatory Materials:** Handbook, including exam content outline and sample questions, provided. Study guide available. **Examination Frequency:** Annual (written) - always fall. Practical exam given throughout the year. **Examination Sites:** Exams given at sites throughout the U.S. **Examination Type:** Multiple-choice. **Waiting Period to Receive Scores:** Six-eight weeks. **Fees:** $400. **Accredited By:** National Commission for Certifying Agencies **Endorsed By:** Health Care Industry Foundation; Health Industry Distributors Association; National Organization for Competency Assurance.

1141

Certified Orthotist (CO)
American Board for Certification in Orthotics and Prosthetics (ABC)
1650 King St., Ste. 500
Alexandria, VA 22314-2747
Phone: (703)836-7114
Fax: (703)836-0838

Recipient: Orthotists in private practice or working for privately owned facilities, laboratories, hospitals, or government agencies. **Educational/Experience Requirements:** Must meet the following requirements: (1) Bachelor's degree in orthotics, prosthetics, or related discipline; (2) Successful completion of certificate program in orthotics and/or prosthetics; and (3) One year (1900 hours) of supervised experience. **Certification Requirements:** Successful completion of written, simulation, and practical exams. **Renewal:** Every five years. Recertification based on continuing education. **Accredited By:** National Commission for Certifying Agencies. **Endorsed By:** American Academy of Orthotists and Prosthetists; American Orthotic and Prosthetic Association; National Organization for Competency Assurance.

1142

Certified Pedorthist (C.Ped.)
Board for Certification of Pedorthics (BCP)
9861 Broken Land Pkwy., Ste. 255
Columbia, MD 21046-1151
Phone: (410)381-5729
Fax: (410)381-1167

Recipient: Individuals involved in pedorthics or design, manufacture, fit, or modification of shoes or related foot orthoses to alleviate foot pain caused by disease, overuse, or injury. **Educational/Experience Requirements:** High school diploma or equivalent and meet one of the following requirements: (1) Associate's degree in health or science-related field; (2) Bachelor's degree; or (3) Accumulation of 300 points through successful completion of college science courses (20 points per credit hour), internships within last five years (one point per each six and two-thirds hours), and successful completion of BCP-approved courses and seminars within last five years (point totals vary). **Certification Requirements:** Successful completion of exam. **Renewal:** Recertification based on continuing education. **Preparatory Materials:** *Foot and Ankle Pain, The Foot - Examination and Diagnosis,* and *Professional Shoe Fitting* (references). Study guide, including sample questions, available. Role delineation study also available. **Examination Frequency:** quarterly. **Examination Sites:** Exam given at sites throughout the U.S. **Examination Type:** Multiple-choice. **Waiting Period to Receive Scores:** 90 days. **Re-examination:** There is a $225 fee to retake exam. **Fees:** $350. **Accredited By:** National Commission for Certifying Agencies. **Endorsed By:** National Organization for Competency Assurance; Pedorthic Footwear Association.

1143

Certified Prosthetist (CP)
American Board for Certification in Orthotics and Prosthetics (ABC)
1650 King St., Ste. 500
Alexandria, VA 22314-2747
Phone: (703)836-7114
Fax: (703)836-0838

Recipient: Prosthetists in private practice or working for privately owned facilities, laboratories, hospitals, or government agencies. **Educational/Experience Requirements:** Must meet the following requirements: (1) Bachelor's degree in orthotics, prosthetics, or related discipline; (2) Successful completion of certificate program in orthotics and/or prosthetics; and (3) One year (1900 hours) of supervised experience. **Certification Requirements:** Successful completion of written, simulation, and practical exams. **Renewal:** Every five years. Recertification based on continuing education. **Accredited By:** National Commission for Certifying Agencies. **Endorsed By:** American Academy of Orthotists and Prosthetists; American Orthotic and Prosthetic Association; National Organization for Competency Assurance.

1144

Certified Prosthetist/Orthotist (CPO)

American Board for Certification in Orthotics and Prosthetics (ACC)
1650 King St., Ste. 500
Alexandria, VA 22314-2747
Phone: (703)836-7114
Fax: (703)836-0838

Recipient: Orthotists and prosthetists in private practice or working for privately owned facilities, laboratories, hospitals, or government agencies. **Educational/Experience Requirements:** Must meet the following requirements: (1) Bachelor's degree in orthotics, prosthetics, or related discipline; (2) Successful completion of certificate program in orthotics and/or prosthetics; and (3) One year (1900 hours) of supervised experience. **Certification Requirements:** Successful completion of written, simulation, and practical exams. **Renewal:** Every five years. Recertification based on continuing education. **Accredited By:** National Organization for Certifying Agencies. **Endorsed By:** American Academy of Orthotists and Prosthetists; American Orthotic and Prosthetic Association; National Organization for Competency Assurance.

1145

Registered Orthotic Fitter (ROF)

Board for Orthotist Certification (BOC)
Allied Health Bldg., Suite 234
100 Penn St.
Baltimore, MD 21201-1082
Phone: (410)539-3910
Dr. Donald O. Fedder BSP, Exec. Dir.

Recipient: Professionals who fit orthoses. **Certification Requirements:** Successful completion of 40 hours of education and assessment and submission of log book of orthoses fitted. Assessment covers: Contraindications; Definitions; Elastic stocking fitting knowledge; Fitting positions;

General skeletal anatomy; Hernia knowledge; Muscle terminology; Orthosis terminology; Pathophysiology; Pelvic anatomy; Physiology; Prescription assessment; Production application; Spinal conditions; Terminology; and Vertebrae knowledge. **Examination Frequency:** Throughout the year. **Examination Sites:** Assessment given at sites throughout the U.S. **Fees:** $75. **Accredited By:** National Commission for Certifying Agencies **Endorsed By:** Health Care Industry Foundation; Health Industry Distributors Association; National Organization for Competency Assurance.

Radiologic Technologists

1146

Certified Chiropractic Radiologic Technologist

American Chiropractic Registry of Radiologic Technologists (ACRRT)
2330 Gull Rd.
Kalamazoo, MI 49001
Phone: (616)343-6666

Recipient: Chiropractic radiologic technologists employed in chiropractic offices. **Certification Requirements:** Successful completion of exam. **Endorsed By:** National Organization for Competency Assurance.

1147

Certified Radiology Equipment Specialist (CRES)

International Certification Commission (ICC)
3330 Washington Blvd., Ste. 400
Arlington, VA 22201
Phone: (703)525-4890
Fax: (703)276-0793
Toll Free: (800)332-2264
Nancy Carney, Prog.Admin.

Recipient: Individuals who maintain, troubleshoot, and repair radiology equipment. **Number of Certified Individuals:** 150. **Educational/Experience Requirements:** Must meet one of the following requirements: (1) Four years experience; (2) Three years experience and associate's degree in electronics technology; or (3) Two years experience and associate's degree in biomedical equipment technology. **Membership:** Not required. **Certification Requirements:** Successful completion of exam. Exam covers: Anat-

omy and physiology; Fundamentals of electricity and electronics; Radiologic equipment function and operation; Medical equipment troubleshooting; and Radiology safety. **Renewal:** Every year. Recertification based on accumulation of continuing practice points. Renewal fee is $20. **Examination Frequency:** monthly. **Examination Sites:** Exam given at sites throughout the U.S. **Examination Type:** Multiple-choice. **Waiting Period to Receive Scores:** One month. **Re-examination:** Must wait six months to retake exam. **Fees:** $175.

1148

Registered Technologist (Cardiovascular-Interventional Technology) (R.T.(CV)(ARRT))

American Registry of Radiologic Technologists (ARRT)
1255 Northland Dr.
St. Paul, MN 55120-1155
Phone: (612)687-0048

Recipient: Cardiovascular-interventional technology technologists. **Educational/Experience Requirements:** Must hold Registered Technologist (Radiography) (R.T.)(R)(ARRT) designation (see separate entry) for one year. **Certification Requirements:** Successful completion of exam. **Renewal:** Every two years. Recertification based on either successful completion of exam in additional discipline or accumulation of 24 continuing education credits. **Preparatory Materials:** Handbook, including sample questions, provided. **Examination Frequency:** Three times per year - March, July, and October. **Examination Sites:** Exam given at sites throughout the U.S. **Examination Type:** Multiple-choice. **Re-examination:** May retake exam twice. Must successfully complete exam within three years. There is a fee to retake exam. **Endorsed By:** American College of Radiology; American Society of Radiologic Technologists.

1149

Registered Technologist (Commuted Tomography)

American Registry of Radiologic Technologists (ARRT)
1255 Northland Dr.
St. Paul, MN 55120-1155
Phone: (612)687-0048

Recipient: Commuted tomography technologists. **Educational/Experience Requirements:** Must hold Registered Technologist (Radiography)

(R.T.)(R)(ARRT) or Registered Technologist (Radiation Therapy Technology) (R.T.)(T)(ARRT) designations (see separate entries) for one year. **Certification Requirements:** Successful completion of exam. **Renewal:** Every two years. Recertification based on either successful completion of exam in additional discipline or accumulation of 24 continuing education credits. **Preparatory Materials:** Handbook, including sample questions, provided. **Examination Frequency:** Three times per year - March, July, and October. **Examination Sites:** Exam given at sites throughout the U.S. **Examination Type:** Multiple-choice. **Waiting Period to Receive Scores:** Five weeks. **Reexamination:** May retake exam twice. Must successfully complete exam within three years. There is a fee to retake exam. **Endorsed By:** American College of Radiology; American Society of Radiologic Technologists.

▮1150▮

Registered Technologist (Magnetic Resonance Imaging)

American Registry of Radiologic
   Technologists (ARRT)
1255 Northland Dr.
St. Paul, MN 55120-1155
Phone: (612)687-0048

Recipient: Magnetic resonance imaging technologists. **Educational/Experience Requirements:** Must hold Registered Technologist (Nuclear Medicine Technology) (R.T.)(N)(AART), Registered Technologist (Radiography) (R.T.)(R)(ARRT) or Registered Technologist (Radiation Therapy Technology) (R.T.)(T)(ARRT) designations (see separate entries) for one year. **Certification Requirements:** Successful completion of exam. **Renewal:** Every two years. Recertification based on either successful completion of exam in additional discipline or accumulation of 24 continuing education credits. **Preparatory Materials:** Handbook, including sample questions, provided. **Examination Frequency:** Three times per year - March, July, and October. **Examination Sites:** Exam given at sites throughout the U.S. **Examination Type:** Multiple-choice. **Waiting Period to Receive Scores:** Five weeks. **Reexamination:** May retake exam twice . Must successfully complete exam within three years. There is a fee to retake exam. **Endorsed By:** American College of Radiology; American Society of Radiologic Technologists.

▮1151▮

Registered Technologist (Mammography) (R.T.(M)(ARRT))

American Registry of Radiologic
   Technologists (ARRT)
1255 Northland Dr.
St. Paul, MN 55120-1155
Phone: (612)687-0048

Recipient: Mammography technologists. **Educational/Experience Requirements:** Must hold Registered Technologist (Radiography) (R.T.)(R)(ARRT) designation (see separate entry) for one year. **Certification Requirements:** Successful completion of exam. **Renewal:** Every two years. Recertification based on either successful completion of exam in additional discipline or accumulation of 24 continuing education credits. **Preparatory Materials:** Handbook, including sample questions, provided. **Examination Frequency:** Three times per year - March, July, and October. **Examination Sites:** Exam given at sites throughout the U.S. **Examination Type:** Multiple-choice. **Waiting Period to Receive Scores:** Five weeks. **Reexamination:** May retake exam twice. Must successfully complete exam within three years. There is a fee to retake exam. **Endorsed By:** American College of Radiology; American Society of Radiologic Technologists.

▮1152▮

Registered Technologist (Nuclear Medicine Technology) (R.T.(N)(ARRT))

American Registry of Radiologic
   Technologists (ARRT)
1255 Northland Dr.
St. Paul, MN 55120-1155
Phone: (612)687-0048

Recipient: Nuclear medicine technologists who use radioactive materials in specialized studies of body organs and/or laboratory analysis to assist the physician in the diagnosis and treatment of disease. **Educational/Experience Requirements:** Successful completion of accredited program in nuclear medicine technology or equivalent. **Certification Requirements:** Successful completion of exam. Exam covers: (1) Diagnostic Procedures, including: Administration of radiopharmaceuticals; Computerized data processing; Evaluation of image quality; Gated procedures; Image management; Patient - camera positioning and monitoring; Parameter selection; Radiopharmaceutical selection; Scintillation camera and collimator selection; Selected therapeutic pro-

cedures; and Specific diagnostic procedures; (2) Instrumentation Quality Control, including: Documentation; Dose calibrator quality control; Gamma camera quality control; Gas and aerosol delivery systems; Scintillation detector system; and Survey meter quality control; (3) Patient Care, including: Emergency situations and adverse reactions; Infection control; Monitoring vital signs; Patient considerations; Patient identification and requisition forms; Patient scheduling; Patient transport; and Support systems; (4) Radiation Protection, including: Areas/facilities monitoring; Biological effects of radiation; Disposal of radioactive waste; Misadministrations and recordable events; Packaging and storage of radioactive materials; Personnel protection and monitoring; and Radioactive contamination; and (5) Radiopharmaceutical Preparation, including: Dosage determination; Dosage preparation; Elution of Mo99/Tc-99m generator; Kit preparation; Quality control of Tc-99m eluate; and Radiopharmaceutical identification. **Renewal:** Every two years. Recertification based on either successful completion of exam in additional discipline or accumulation of 24 continuing education credits. **Preparatory Materials:** Handbook, including sample questions, provided. **Examination Frequency:** Three times per year - March, July, and October. **Examination Sites:** Exam given at sites throughout the U.S. **Examination Type:** Multiple-choice. **Waiting Period to Receive Scores:** Five weeks. **Reexamination:** May retake exam twice. Must successfully complete exam within three years. There is a $40 fee to retake exam. **Fees:** $50. **Endorsed By:** American College of Radiology; American Society of Radiologic Technologists.

▮1153▮

Registered Technologist (Radiation Therapy Technology) (R.T.(T)(ARRT))

American Registry of Radiologic
   Technologists (ARRT)
1255 Northland Dr.
St. Paul, MN 55120-1155
Phone: (612)687-0048

Recipient: Radiation therapy technologists who use ionizing radiation producing equipment to administer therapeutic doses of radiation as prescribed by the physician for the treatment of disease. **Educational/Experience Requirements:** Successful completion of accredited program in radiation therapy or equivalent. **Certification Requirements:** Successful completion of exam. Exam covers: (1) Patient Care, Management, and Education, including: Assessment, care, and management; Ethics; Medical emergencies; Physical assistance of patients; Professional interactions; and Universal precautions and infection control; (2) Radiation Protection and Quality Assurance, including: Environmental protection; Quality assurance procedures and assessment; Radiation protection; and Theory and principles of equipment operation; and (3) Treatment Planning and Delivery, including: Dose to critical structures; Elements of treatment planning; Factors affecting simulation and treatment; Monitoring patient and treatment room; Monitoring treatment machine; Radiation treatment record keeping; Set-up of treatment machine; Treatment accessories; Treatment volume localization; and Verification imaging. **Renewal:** Every two years. Recertification based on either successful completion of exam in additional discipline or accumulation of 24 continuing education credits. **Preparatory Materials:** Handbook, including sample questions, provided. **Examination Frequency:** Three times per year - March, July, and October. **Examination Sites:** Exam given at sites throughout the U.S. **Examination Type:** Multiple-choice. **Waiting Period to Receive Scores:** Five weeks. **Re-examination:** May retake exam twice. Must successfully complete exam within three years. There is a $40 fee to retake exam. **Fees:** $50. **Endorsed By:** American College of Radiology; American Society of Radiologic Technologists.

1154

Registered Technologist (Radiography) (R.T.(R)(ARRT))
American Registry of Radiologic
Technologists (ARRT)
1255 Northland Dr.
St. Paul, MN 55120-1155
Phone: (612)687-0048

Recipient: Radiographers responsible for applying ionizing radiation to demonstrate portions of the human body on a radiograph, fluoroscopic screen, or other imaging modalities to assist the physician in the diagnosis of disease and injury. **Educational/Experience Requirements:** Successful completion of accredited program in radiography or equivalent. **Certification Requirements:** Successful completion of exam. Exam covers: (1) Equipment Operation and Maintenance, including: Evaluation of radiographic equipment and accessories; and Radiographic equipment; (2) Image Production and Evaluation, including: Evaluation of radiographs; Film processing and quality assurance; and Selection of technical fac-

tors; (3) Patient Care, including: Contrast media; Legal and professional responsibilities; Patient education, safety, and control; and Prevention and control of infection; (4) Radiation Protection, including: Patient protection; Personnel protection; and Radiation exposure and monitoring; and (5) Radiographic Procedures, including: General procedural considerations; and Specific imaging procedures. **Renewal:** Every two years. Recertification based on either successful completion of exam in additional discipline or accumulation of 24 continuing education credits. **Preparatory Materials:** Handbook, including sample questions, provided. **Examination Frequency:** Three times per year - March, July, and October. **Examination Sites:** Exam given at sites throughout the U.S. **Examination Type:** Multiple-choice. **Waiting Period to Receive Scores:** Five weeks. **Re-examination:** May retake exam twice. Must successfully complete exam within three years. There is a $40 fee to retake exam. **Fees:** $50. **Endorsed By:** American College of Radiology; American Society of Radiologic Technologists.

Sonographers

1155

Certified Echocardiographic Technologist (CET)
National Foundation for
Non-Invasive Diagnostics
(NFNID)
103 Carnegie Center, Ste. 311
Princeton, NJ 08540
Phone: (609)520-1300
Fax: (609)452-8544
Dr. Benedict Kingsley, Prog.Dir.

Recipient: Echocardiographic technologists. (Echocardiography is noninvasive test used in diagnosing heart disease.) **Number of Certified Individuals:** 325. **Educational/Experience Requirements:** Must meet one of the following requirements: (1) Successful completion of training course in echocardiography; or (2) Two years experience in ultrasound. **Membership:** Not required. **Certification Requirements:** Successful completion of course and oral, practical, and written exams. **Renewal:** Every three years. Recertification based on successful completion of course. **Preparatory Materials:** Instructional books, videos, and special handouts available. **Examination Frequency:** Throughout the year. **Examination Sites:** Exams given in either Atlantic City or Princeton, NJ. **Pass/Fail Rate:** 90% pass exams the first time. **Waiting**

Period to Receive Scores: Three weeks. **Re-examination:** Must wait two months to retake exams. **Fees:** $395. **Endorsed By:** American Hospital Association.

1156

Professional Ultrasound Technologist
National Foundation for
Non-Invasive Diagnostics
(NFNID)
103 Carnegie Center, Ste. 311
Princeton, NJ 08540
Phone: (609)520-1300
Fax: (609)452-8544
Dr. Benedict Kingsley, Prog.Dir.

Recipient: Ultrasound technologists. **Certification Requirements:** Successful completion of Echocardiography Course for Physicians and Technologists. Course consists of the following sections: Basic Interpretation Procedures; Basic Physical Principles of Ultrasound and Instrumentation; Basic Transesophageal Echocardiography; Cardiac Anatomy; Clinical Applications; Examination Techniques; Geriatric Echocardiography; M-Mode, 2D, Doppler, and Color Flow Artifacts and Limitations; Pediatric Echocardiology; and Practical Quantitative Analytical Methods - Mode, 2D, and Doppler. **Fees:** $595.

1157

Registered Diagnostic Cardiac Sonographer (RDCS)
American Registry of Diagnostic
Medical Sonographers (ARDMS)
2368 Victory Pkwy., Ste. 510
Cincinnati, OH 45206
Phone: (513)281-7111
Fax: (513)281-7524
Toll Free: (800)541-9754

Recipient: Diagnostic cardiac sonographers. **Educational/Experience Requirements:** Must meet one of the following requirements: (1) Successful completion of two-year American Medical Association or equivalent allied health training program that is patient care related, and twelve months experience; (2) Successful completion of accredited educational program in diagnostic medical sonography or vascular technology; (3) Bachelor's degree in sonography/vascular technology or in a radiology degree program with a minor in sonography and twelve months experience; (4) Current licensure as medical or osteopathic doctors or equivalent and 12 months experience; (5) Two years formal post-high school education and 24 months experience; or (6) Twenty-four months of training in allied health field that is patient care related and 24 months experience. Experience must be in clinical ultrasound/vascular settings at hospitals, clinics, or private practices under the supervision of a physician and/or registered sonographer or vascular technologist. **Certification Requirements:** Successful completion of Cardiovascular Principles and Instrumentation exam and a specialty exam in adult or pediatric echocardiography. Cardiovascular Principles and Instrumentation exam covers: Anatomy of the heart; Basic embryology; Bioeffects and safety; Cardiac catheterization; Cardiac evaluation methods; Cardiac physiology; Congenital defects; Doppler; EKG; Elementary principles; Image features and artifacts; Images, storage, and display; Phonocardiography; Principles of cardiac hemodynamics; Principles of pulse echo imaging; Propagation of ultrasound through tissues; Pulse echo instruments; Quality assurance of ultrasound; and Ultrasound transducers. Adult echocardiography exam covers: Anatomy and physiology; Cardiac tumors; Cardiomyopathies; Congenital heart disease in the adult; Diseases of the aorta; Doppler; Ischemic heart disease; Pericardial disease; Systematic and pulmonary hypertensive heart disease; Technique; Valvular heart disease; and Miscellaneous items. Pediatric echocardiography exam covers: Acquired pathology; Congenital pathology; Functional assessment; Instrumentation; Normal anatomy; Normal hemodynamics; Phases of the cardiac cycle; and Scanning technique. **Renewal:** Every three years. Recertification based on either successful completion of exam or accumulation of 30 credits of approved continuing education. **Preparatory Materials:** Lists of accredited schools and training programs, review courses, sample questions, and exam content outlines provided. **Examination Frequency:** Annual. **Examination Sites:** Exam given at sites throughout the U.S. and Canada. **Examination Type:** Multiple-choice. **Waiting Period to Receive Scores:** Two months. **Re-examination:** Must only retake exam failed. **Fees:** $155. **Accredited By:** National Commission for Certifying Agencies. **Endorsed By:** National Organization for Competency Assurance.

1158

Registered Diagnostic Medical Sonographer (RDMS)

American Registry of Diagnostic Medical Sonographers (ARDMS)
2368 Victory Pkwy., Ste. 510
Cincinnati, OH 45206
Phone: (513)281-7111
Fax: (513)281-7524
Toll Free: (800)541-9754

Recipient: Diagnostic medical sonographers. **Educational/Experience Requirements:** Must meet one of the following requirements: (1) Successful completion of two-year American Medical Association or equivalent allied health training program that is patient-care related, and twelve months experience; (2) Successful completion of accredited educational program in diagnostic medical sonography or vascular technology; (3) Bachelor's degree in sonography/vascular technology or in a radiology degree program with a minor in sonography, and twelve months experience; (4) Current licensure as medical or osteopathic doctor or equivalent and 12 months experience; (5) Two years formal post-high school education and 24 months experience; or (6) 24 months of training in allied health field that is patient care related and 24 months experience. Experience must be in clinical ultrasound/vascular settings at hospitals, clinics, or private practices under the supervision of a physician and/or registered sonographer or vascular technologist. **Certification Requirements:** Successful completion of Ultrasound Physics and Instrumentation exam and one specialty exam. Ultrasound Physics and Instrumentation exam covers: Bioeffects and safety; Doppler; Elementary principles; Image features and artifacts; Images, storage, and display; Principles of pulse echo imaging; Propagation of ultrasound through tissues; Pulse echo instruments; Quality assurance of ultrasound instruments; and Ultrasound transducers. Specialty exams are: (1) Abdomen, including: Biliary tree; GI tract; Liver; Neck; Pancreas; Retroperitoneum; Spleen; Superficial structures; Urinary tract; and General and miscellaneous items; (2) Obstetrics and Gynecology, including: Gynecology; Obstetrics; and Patient-care preparation/technique; (3) Neurosonology, including: Anatomy and physiology; Medical care of the neonate during scanning; Physics and instrumentation; Recognition of pathology and differential diagnosis; and Technique in neurosonography; and (4) Ophthalmology, including: Anatomy and physiology; Biometry; Exam techniques; Instrumentation; Pathology; and Physics. **Renewal:**

Every three years. Recertification based on successful completion of exam or accumulation of 30 credits of approved continuing education. **Preparatory Materials:** Lists of accredited schools and training programs, review courses, sample questions, and exam content outlines provided. **Examination Frequency:** Annual. Ultrasonic Physics and Instrumentation exam given throughout the year. **Examination Sites:** Exams given at sites throughout the U.S. and Canada. **Examination Type:** Multiple-choice. **Waiting Period to Receive Scores:** Two months. **Re-examination:** Must only retake exam failed. **Fees:** $155; $230 (computer testing option). **Accredited By:** National Commission for Certifying Agencies. **Endorsed By:** National Organization for Competency Assurance.

1159

Registered Vascular Technologist (RVT)

American Registry of Diagnostic Medical Sonographers (ARDMS)
2368 Victory Pkwy., Ste. 510
Cincinnati, OH 45206
Phone: (513)281-7111
Fax: (513)281-7524
Toll Free: (800)541-9754

Recipient: Vascular technologists. **Educational/Experience Requirements:** Must meet one of the following requirements: (1) Successful completion of two-year American Medical Association or equivalent allied health training program that is patient care related and twelve months experience; (2) Successful completion of accredited educational program in diagnostic medical sonography or vascular technology; (3) Bachelor's degree in sonography/vascular technology or in a radiology degree program with a minor in sonography and twelve months experience; (4) Current licensure as medical or osteopathic doctor or equivalent and 12 months experience; (5) Two years formal post-high school formal education and 24 months experience; or (6) Twenty-four months of training in allied health field that is patient care related and 24 months experience. Experience must be in clinical ultrasound/vascular settings at hospitals, clinics, or private practices under the supervision of a physician and/or registered sonographer or vascular technologist. **Certification Requirements:** Successful completion of the following exams: (1) Vascular Physical Principles and Instrumentation, including: Physical principles; Physiology and fluid dynamic; Ultrasonic imaging; Ultrasound physics; and Ultrasound safety and quality assurance; and (2) Vascular Technology, including: Arterial disease testing; Cerebral artery disease testing; Gross anatomy (vessel routes, variations, and collaterals); Test validation; Therapeutic intervention; Venous disease testing; and Other conditions. **Renewal:** Every three years. Recertification based on either successful completion of exam or accumulation of 30 credits of approved continuing education. **Preparatory Materials:** Lists of accredited schools and training programs, review courses, sample questions, and exam content outlines provided. **Examination Frequency:** Annual. **Examination Sites:** Exam given at sites throughout the U.S. and Canada. **Examination Type:** Multiple-choice. **Waiting Period to Receive Scores:** Two months. **Re-examination:** Must only retake exam failed. **Fees:** $155. **Accredited By:** National Commission for Certifying Agencies. **Endorsed By:** National Organization for Competency Assurance.

Surgical Technicians

1160

Certified Clinical Perfusionist (CCP)
American Board of Cardiovascular
    Perfusion (ABCP)
207 N. 25th Ave.
Hattiesburg, MS 39401
Phone: (601)582-3309

Recipient: Clinical perfusionists. **Educational/Experience Requirements:** Must meet the following requirements: (1) Graduation from accredited program; (2) Six months experience; and (3) Performance of 50 clinical perfusions of the following types: Acquired heart diseases in adults (20 perfusions); Myocardial revascularizations (20 perfusions); and Pediatric perfusions (ten perfusions). **Certification Requirements:** Successful completion of written and oral exams. Written exam covers: Anatomy and pathology; Perfusion; Pharmacology; and Physiology. **Renewal:** Every three years. Recertification based on accumulation of 150 points, with 90 points in professional activities and 60 points in clinical activities. Professional activity points earned through continuing education, attendance at meetings, hospital medical conferences, seminars, presentations, teaching, and reading and authoring publications in the field. Clinical activity points earned by participating in 40 clinical perfusions per year. **Preparatory Materials:** *Guidebook for the Examination Process* (reference). **Examination Fre-**

quency: Annual. **Examination Type:** Multiple-choice. **Re-examination:** May retake exams three times. **Fees:** $500.

1161

Certified Surgical Technologist (CST)
Liaison Council on Certification for
    the Surgical Technologist
    (LCC-ST)
7108-C S. Alton Way
Englewood, CO 80112
Phone: (303)694-9264
Fax: (303)694-9169
Toll Free: (800)637-7433

Recipient: Surgical technologists. **Educational/Experience Requirements:** Successful completion of surgical technology program or equivalent that includes both classroom and clinical education and 125 total cases scrubbed in the areas of general, genitourinary, gynecological, orthopedic, and otorhinolaryngology surgery. Graduates of registered nurse (R.N.), licensed practical nurse (L.P.N.), or licensed vocational nurse (L.V.N.) programs with sufficient scrub experience may meet requirement. **Certification Requirements:** Successful completion of exam. Exam covers: Fundamental knowledge; Intraoperative and postoperative procedures; and Preoperative preparation. **Renewal:** Every six years. Recertification based on either successful completion of exam or accumulation of 80 hours of related continuing education. **Examination Frequency:** semiannual - always March and September. **Examination Type:** Multiple-choice. **Accredited By:** National Commission for Certifying Agencies. **Endorsed By:** Association of Surgical Technologists; National Organization for Competency Assurance.

1162

Certified Surgical Technologist/Certified First Assistant (CST/CFA)
Liaison Council on Certification for
    the Surgical Technologist
7108-C S. Alton Way
Englewood, CO 80112
Phone: (303)694-9264
Fax: (303)694-9169
Toll Free: (800)637-7433

Recipient: Surgical first assistants. **Educational/Experience Requirements:** Hold Certified Surgical Technologist (CST) designation (see separate entry) and meet one of the following require-

ments: (1) Two years experience in last four years; or (2) Successful completion of first assistant training program. **Certification Requirements:** Successful completion of exam. Exam covers: (1) Application and Usage of Surgical Equipment, Supplies, and Medications, including: Supplies (types and usage); Surgical equipment; and Surgical pharmacology; (2) Surgical Anatomy and Physiology, including: Body systems; Surgical pathology; Surgical principles of wound healing; and Tissue assessment; (3) Surgical Patient Care, including: Cardiopulmonary resuscitation; Catheterization techniques; Evaluation of diagnostic results; Legal aspects of surgery; Patient transfer principles; Positioning principles; and Surgical hazards and emergencies; and (4) Surgical Skills, including: Hemostasis; Insertion; Instrumentation; Ligation; Placement; Principles of tissue handling; Retraction and visualization; Securing of drains; and Suturing. **Renewal:** Every six years. Recertification based on either successful completion of exam or accumulation of 100 hours of related continuing education. **Examination Frequency:** Annual - always September. **Examination Type:** Multiple-choice. **Accredited By:** National Commission for Certifying Agencies. **Endorsed By:** Association of Surgical Technologists; National Organization for Competency Assurance.

Technical Consultants

1163

Technical Consultant (TC)
American Board of Bioanalysis
    (ABB)
818 Olive St., Ste. 918
St. Louis, MO 63101-1598
Phone: (314)241-1445
Fax: (314)241-1449
Mark S. Birenbaum Ph.D., Admin.

Recipient: Bioanalysis technical consultants. **Certification Requirements:** Must be qualified as technical consultant or meet one of the following requirements: (1) Doctoral or master's degree in the chemical, physical, or biological sciences, or clinical laboratory science, and one year of laboratory training in designated specialty or subspecialty area; (2) Certification in anatomic or clinical pathology by American Board of Pathology (see separate entries) or equivalent; (3) Current licensure to practice medicine and one year of laboratory training in designated specialty or subspecialty area; or (4) Bachelor's degree in the chemical, physical, or biological sciences, or medical technology, and two years training or experience in designated specialty or subspecialty area. **Renewal:** Every year. Recertification based on meeting requirements of Professional Enrichment/ Education Renewal (PEER) continuing education program. **Fees:** $150. **Endorsed By:** American Association of Bioanalysts.

Technologists, Except Health

Broadcast Technicians

1164

Broadband Communications Technician (BCT)
Society of Cable Television Engineers (SCTE)
669 Exton Commons
Exton, PA 19341
Phone: (610)363-6888
Fax: (610)363-5898
Toll Free: (800)542-5040
E-mail: MarvinSCTE@AOL.com
Marvin Nelson, Dir.

Recipient: Cable television technical professionals. **Number of Certified Individuals:** 250. **Educational/Experience Requirements:** Two years experience. **Membership:** Required. **Certification Requirements:** Successful completion of seven exams. Exams consist of the following sections: Data Networking and Architecture; Distribution Systems; Engineering Management and Professionalism; Signal Processing Centers; Terminal Devices; Transportation Systems; and Video and Audio Signals and Systems. **Renewal:** Every three years. Recertification based on either successful completion of exam or accumulation of 12 recertification units through: (1) SCTE national and local chapter membership (one unit per year); (2) Seminars and meetings (one unit per day); (3) Successful completion of approved courses (one unit per credit hour); (4) Speaking engagements or presenting papers (four units at national level; two units at local level); (5) Publication of articles (four units per article); and (6) Service as officer or on committee (one unit per year). Renewal fee is $15. **Preparatory Materials:** Bibliography available. **Examination Frequency:** Three-six times per year. **Examination Sites:** Exams given at SCTE chapter meetings and regional shows.

Examination Type: Multiple choice. **Pass/Fail Rate:** 55% pass the exams the first time. **Waiting Period to Receive Scores:** Two weeks. **Re-examination:** There is no waiting period to retake exams. **Fees:** $70.

1165

Certified Broadcast Technologist (CBT)
Society of Broadcast Engineers (SBE)
8455 Keystone Crossing, Ste. 140
Indianapolis, IN 46240
Phone: (317)253-1640
Fax: (317)253-0418
Linda L. Godby, Exec. Officer

Recipient: Broadcast engineers involved in design, operation, maintenance, or administration of broadcast facility or related technology. **Educational/Experience Requirements:** none. **Membership:** Not required. **Certification Requirements:** Must meet one of the following requirements: (1) Successfully complete exam on radio or television covering: Electronic fundamentals; FCC rules pertaining to operating tolerances; and Safety; or (2) Hold life-time General Class license, FCC Amateur Extra Class license, or equivalent, with either two years continuous experience or three years experience in last five years in broadcast engineering or related technology. **Renewal:** Every five years. Recertification based on meeting service requirement. **Preparatory Materials:** Study guide, including sample questions, and study course available. **Examination Frequency:** quarterly. **Examination Sites:** Exams given at National Association of Broadcasters annual convention, SBE annual conference, and by chapters throughout the U.S. **Examination Type:** Multiple-choice. **Fees:** $35 (members); $90 (nonmembers).

1166

Certified Radio Operator
Society of Broadcast Engineers (SBE)
8455 Keystone Crossing, Ste. 140
Indianapolis, IN 46240
Phone: (317)253-1640
Fax: (317)253-0418
Linda L. Godby, Exec. Officer

Recipient: Entry-level radio station operators. **Certification Requirements:** Successful completion of course.

1167

Electromagnetic Compatibility Technicians
National Association of Radio and Telecommunications Engineers (NARTE)
PO Box 678
Medway, MA 02053
Phone: (508)533-8333
Fax: (508)533-3815
Toll Free: (800)89N-ARTE

Recipient: Electromagnetic compatibility (EMC) technicians. **Educational/Experience Requirements:** Six years experience. Graduation from school or college approved by NARTE, including successful completion of course in electronics technology or applied electronics, may be substituted for two years of experience. Each year of study in noncompleted program may be substituted for one year of experience. Teaching in engineering may be substituted for up to one year of experience. **Certification Requirements:** Successful completion of exam. Exam covers: Bonding; Conducted interference; Electromagnetic pulse; Electrostatic discharge; EMC test plans; Filtering; Grounding; Interface control; Lightning protection; Materials and special devices; Mathematics/spectrum analysis; Military specification standards and handbooks; Radiated interference; Safety; Shielding; Terminology; Test equipment; and Test facilities. Each year of additional experience may add one percent to exam score. **Renewal:** Every year. Recertification based on continuing education. Renewal fee is $40. **Preparatory Materials:** Study guide, including list of suggested study references, available. **Examination Frequency:** quarterly - always March, May, September, and December. **Examination Sites:** Exam given at sites throughout the U.S. **Examination Type:** Multiple-choice. **Waiting Period to Receive Scores:** Four weeks. **Re-examination:** Must wait 90 days to retake exam. There is a $20 fee to retake exam. **Fees:** $40.

`1168`

Electrostatic Discharge Control Technician

National Association of Radio and Telecommunications Engineers (NARTE)
PO Box 678
Medway, MA 02053
Phone: (508)533-8333
Fax: (508)533-3815
Toll Free: (800)89N-ARTE

Recipient: Electrostatic discharge control (ESDC) technicians. **Educational/Experience Requirements:** Six years experience. Graduation from school or college approved by NARTE, including successful completion of course in electronics technology or applied electronics, may be substituted for two years of experience. Each year of study in non-completed program may be substituted for one year of experience. Teaching in engineering may be substituted for up to one year of experience. **Certification Requirements:** Successful completion of exam. Exam covers: Body charge evaluation and control; Clean room equipment and material control; ESD control material in-field testing; ESD loss analysis; ESD program design and management; ESD shielding analysis; ESD theory; Flooring; Garment control and evaluation; Grounding technology; In field ESD controls; Ionization devices and systems; Laboratory test and analysis of ESDC packaging materials; Manufacturing plant handling procedures; Manufacturing/repair facility evaluation, survey, and auditing; Materials tests and measurement; Math/physics; Plant equipment ESD control and evaluation; Production aids and tool evaluation; Safety; Standards/specifications; System test and measurement; Terminology; and

Workstations. Each year of additional experience may add one percent to exam score. **Renewal:** Every year. Recertification based on continuing education. Renewal fee is $40. **Examination Frequency:** quarterly - always March, May, September, and December. **Examination Sites:** Exam given at sites throughout the U.S. **Examination Type:** Multiple-choice. **Waiting Period to Receive Scores:** Four weeks. **Re-examination:** Must wait 90 days to retake exam. There is a $20 fee to retake exam. **Fees:** $40.

`1169`

NABER Technician Certification

National Association for Business and Educational Radio (NABER)
1501 Duke St.
Alexandria, VA 22314
Phone: (703)739-0300
Fax: (703)683-1608
Toll Free: (800)759-0300
Jan Jensen, Coord.

Recipient: Mobile two-way radio technicians. **Membership:** Not required. **Certification Requirements:** Successful completion of exam. Exam covers: Component installation and repairs, uses of hand tools, soldering, and safety precautions; Fault analysis, methodology, and instrumentation; FCC rules and regulations; and Theory of two-way radio and communication systems technology. **Preparatory Materials:** *NABER Resource: FCC Rules, Regulations, and Licensing* (reference). Study guide, including list of reference books and sample questions, available. **Examination Frequency:** Throughout the year. **Examination Sites:** Exam given at sites throughout the U.S. **Examination Type:** Multiple-choice. **Waiting Period to Receive Scores:** Immediately. **Fees:** $125.

`1170`

Radio and Telecommunications Technician, Class I

National Association of Radio and Telecommunications Engineers (NARTE)
PO Box 678
Medway, MA 02053
Phone: (508)533-8333
Fax: (508)533-3815
Toll Free: (800)89N-ARTE

Recipient: Radio and telecommunications technicians working with either non RF radiating or RF radiating systems and equipment. **Educational/Experience Requirements:** Eight years experience

and successful completion of coursework in telecommunications offered by educational institutions and/or through corporate training programs. Bachelor's degree in electrical engineering, electrical engineering technology, or physical science may be substituted for four years of experience. Candidates with less experience may qualify for either Radio and Telecommunications Technician, Class II, III, or IV designations (see separate entries). **Certification Requirements:** Successful completion of exam. Must also earn one endorsement in either RF radiating or non-RF radiating systems and equipment through either successful completion of exam or credential review. RF endorsements are: Administrative/Regulatory; Aeronautical/Marine; Antenna Systems; Broadcast AM; Broadcast FM; Broadcast TV; Cellular Radio Systems; Control Systems (including SCADA); Education; Frequency Coordination (Class I and II Engineer only); Interference Analysis/Suppression; International Broadcast; International Public Fixed; Landmobile Systems; LF, MF, and HF Radio (Non Broadcast); Microwave Systems; Millimeter Wave Systems; Power Line Carrier; Radar Systems; Satellite Systems; Scatter Systems; Special Field Test; and Telegraphy. Non-RF endorsements are: Administrative/Regulatory; Cable Transmission Systems; Circuit Design; Common Channel Signaling (CCS); Computer Telecommunications; Control Systems; Education; Encryption, Voice, and Data; Equipment Appraiser; Fiber Optic Splicing; Lightwave Systems; Multiplex Systems; Operations; Power Systems; Station Equipment; Switching Systems; Telephone Inside Plant; Telephone Local Outside Plant; Telephone Toll Outside Plant; Test Equipment Calibration; Traffic Engineering; and Wire Transmission Systems. May also earn Master endorsements with proof of proficiency in six endorsements. **Renewal:** Every year. Renewal fee is $30. **Preparatory Materials:** Reference guides and study materials available. **Examination Frequency:** quarterly - always March, May, September, and December. **Examination Sites:** Exam given at sites throughout the U.S. **Fees:** $30; $5 (per endorsement).

1171

Radio and Telecommunications Technician, Class II

National Association of Radio and Telecommunications Engineers (NARTE)
PO Box 678
Medway, MA 02053
Phone: (508)533-8333
Fax: (508)533-3815
Toll Free: (800)89N-ARTE

Recipient: Radio and telecommunications technicians working with either non RF radiating or RF radiating systems and equipment. **Educational/Experience Requirements:** Six years experience and successful completion of coursework in radio or telecommunications offered by educational institutions and/or through corporate training programs. Bachelor's degree in electrical engineering, electrical engineering technology, or physical science may be substituted for four years of experience. May qualify for Radio and Telecommunications Technician, Class I designation (see separate entry) with more experience. Candidates with less experience may qualify for Radio and Telecommunications Technician, Class III or IV designations (see separate entries). **Certification Requirements:** Successful completion of exam. Must also earn one endorsement in either RF radiating or non-RF radiating systems and equipment through either successful completion of exam or credential review. RF endorsements are: Administrative/Regulatory; Aeronautical/Marine; Antenna Systems; Broadcast AM; Broadcast FM; Broadcast TV; Cellular Radio Systems; Control Systems (including SCADA); Education; Frequency Coordination (Class I and II Engineer only); Interference Analysis/Suppression; International Broadcast; International Public Fixed; Landmobile Systems; LF, MF, and HF Radio (Non Broadcast); Microwave Systems; Millimeter Wave Systems; Power Line Carrier; Radar Systems; Satellite Systems; Scatter Systems; Special Field Test; and Telegraphy. Non-RF endorsements are: Administrative/Regulatory; Cable Transmission Systems; Circuit Design; Common Channel Signaling (CCS); Computer Telecommunications; Control Systems; Education; Encryption, Voice, and Data; Equipment Appraiser; Fiber Optic Splicing; Lightwave Systems; Multiplex Systems; Operations; Power Systems; Station Equipment; Switching Systems; Telephone Inside Plant; Telephone Local Outside Plant; Telephone Toll Outside Plant; Test Equipment Calibration; Traffic Engineering; and Wire Transmission Systems. May also earn Master endorsements with proof of proficiency in six endorsements. **Renewal:** Every year. Renewal fee is $25. **Preparatory Materials:** Reference guides and study materials available. **Examination Frequency:** quarterly - always March, May, September, and December. **Examination Sites:** Exam given at sites throughout the U.S. **Fees:** $25; $5 (per endorsement).

1172

Radio and Telecommunications Technician, Class III

National Association of Radio and Telecommunications Engineers (NARTE)
PO Box 678
Medway, MA 02053
Phone: (508)533-8333
Fax: (508)533-3815
Toll Free: (800)89N-ARTE

Recipient: Radio and telecommunications technicians working with either non RF radiating or RF radiating systems and equipment. **Educational/Experience Requirements:** Two years experience and successful completion of coursework in radio and telecommunications electronics offered by educational institutions and/or through corporate training programs. Bachelor's degree in electrical engineering, electrical engineering technology, or physical science may be substituted for four years of experience. May qualify for Radio and Telecommunications Technician, Class I or II designations (see separate entries) with more experience. Candidates with less experience may qualify for Radio and Telecommunications Technician, Class IV designation (see separate entry). **Certification Requirements:** Successful completion of one of the following: (1) Either NARTE Class III exam or FCC General Radiotelephone exam; or (2) Two-year ASEE program from approved college or university. **Renewal:** Every year. Renewal fee is $20. **Preparatory Materials:** Reference guides and study materials available. **Examination Frequency:** quarterly - always March, May, September, and December. **Examination Sites:** Exam given at sites throughout the U.S. **Fees:** $20; $5 (per endorsement).

1173

Radio and Telecommunications Technician, Class IV

National Association of Radio and Telecommunications Engineers (NARTE)
PO Box 678
Medway, MA 02053
Phone: (508)533-8333
Fax: (508)533-3815
Toll Free: (800)89N-ARTE

Recipient: Radio and telecommunications technicians working with either non RF radiating or RF radiating systems and equipment. **Educational/Experience Requirements:** Less than two years of experience and successful completion of coursework in radio and/or telecommunications electronics offered by educational institutions and/or through corporate training programs. May qualify for Radio and Telecommunications Technician, Class I, II, or III designations (see separate entries) with more experience. **Certification Requirements:** Successful completion of exam. **Renewal:** Every year. Renewal fee is $15. **Preparatory Materials:** Reference guides and study materials available. **Examination Frequency:** quarterly - always March, May, September, and December. **Examination Sites:** Exam given at sites throughout the U.S. **Fees:** $15; $5 (per endorsement).

Computer Programmers

1174

Certified Data Educator (CDE)

Data Education Certification Council (DECC)
c/o Dr. Robert Behling
Bryant Coll.
Smithfield, RI 02917
Dr. Robert Behling, Exec. Officer

Recipient: Educational professionals qualified to instruct data processing in industrial, institutional, or educational environments. **Number of Certified Individuals:** 800. **Educational/Experience Requirements:** One year experience (one course in two semesters, three quarters, or 100 hours) and successful completion of two courses in either accounting, management, mathematics, or systems. **Membership:** Not required. **Certification Requirements:** Successful completion of exam. Exam covers: Basic information systems; Management of information systems; Teaching of concepts for information systems and data processing; and Telecommunications. **Renewal:** none.

Pass/Fail Rate: 50% pass exam. **Fees:** $60.

Drafters

1175

Certified Drafter (CD)
American Design Drafting
   Association (ADDA)
PO Box 799
Rockville, MD 20848
Phone: (301)460-6875
Fax: (301)460-8591
Rachel H. Howard, Exec.Dir.

Recipient: Professional drafters. **Membership:** Not required. **Certification Requirements:** Successful completion of exam. **Renewal:** none. **Preparatory Materials:** none. **Examination Frequency:** Throughout the year. **Examination Sites:** Exam given at sites throughout the U.S. **Examination Type:** Multiple-choice; true or false. **Pass/Fail Rate:** 75% pass exam the first time. **Waiting Period to Receive Scores:** One month. **Re-examination:** There is no waiting period to retake exam. **Fees:** $55.

Engineering Technicians

1176

**Associate Engineering Technician
   (AET)**
National Institute for Certification
   in Engineering Technologies
   (NICET)
1420 King St.
Alexandria, VA 22314-2794
Phone: (703)684-2835

Recipient: Intermediate-level engineering technicians working within specified field under general supervision. **Educational/Experience Requirements:** Two years experience. Candidates with less experience may qualify for Technician Trainee (TT) designation (see separate entry). May qualify for Engineering Technician (ET) designation (see separate entry) with increased experience. **Membership:** Not required. **Certification Requirements:** Successful completion of either job task competency exam or two-part general knowledge exam. Exams available in the following job task competencies: (1) Building Construction, including the following subfields: Code and specification compliance; and Water and wastewater plants; (2) Computer Engineering Tech-

nology; (3) Construction Materials Testing, including the following subfields: Asphalt; Concrete; and Soils; (4) Electric Power Engineering Technology, including the subfield of substation; (5) Engineering Model Technology, including the subfield of piping; (6) Fire Protection Engineering Technology, including the following subfields: Automatic sprinkler system layout; Fire alarm systems; Inspection of fire suppression systems; and Special hazard systems layout; (7) Geosynthetic Materials Installation Inspection, including the following subfields: CSPE geomembranes; Geogrids; Geonets; Geosynthetic appurtenances; Geosynthetic clay liners; Geotextiles; HDPE geomembranes; PVC geomembranes; and VLDPE Geomembranes; (8) Geotechnical Engineering Technology, including the following subfields: Construction; Exploration; Generalist; Laboratory; and Waste containment; (9) Hydro Projects; (10) Industrial Instrumentation; (11) Land Management and Water Control, including the subfield of erosion and sediment control; (12) Mechanical Engineering Technology, including the following subfields: HVAC; and Industrial plant process piping; (13) Site Development; (14) Telecommunications Engineering Technology; (15) Transportation Engineering Technology, including: Bridge safety inspection; Highway bridge layout; Highway construction; Highway design; Highway maintenance; Highway materials; Highway surveys; Highway traffic operations; and Roadway layout; and (16) Underground Utilities Construction, including the subfield of water and sewer lines. General knowledge exam consists of general and technical parts. General part covers: (1) Communications, including: Basic communications skills; Basic drafting; and Business communications; (2) Mathematics, including: Advanced mathematics; Algebra; and Trigonometry; and (3) Physical Science, including: Basic physical science; Intermediate mechanics; and Intermediate non-mechanical physical science. Technical part of exam offered in following specialties: (1) Architectural/Building Construction Engineering Technology, including: Architectural types; Building materials; Carpentry fundamentals; Concrete design; Conductance; Cooling; Drafting; Estimating; Foundations; Heating; Legal aspects; Loads; Plaster design; Site preparation; Stresses; Structural concrete design; Structural steel design; Structural wood design; and Ventilation; (2) Civil Engineering Technology, including: Blueprint reading; Concrete mixtures and quantities; Construction equipment and functions; Cost estimating; Drafting; Environmental (air, water,

and sewage); Excavation and fill computations and planning; Foundation design; Highway design; Inspection and materials testing; Mapping; Materials inspection and analysis; Photogrammetry; Pilings; Piping design (basic); Soils analysis; Statics and dynamics; Structural steel design; Surveying; and Water control design; (3) Electrical/Electronics Engineering Technology, including: Basic electrical units (various meters, curve tracers, amplifiers, transformers, tubes, switches, capacitors, resistors, and transistors); Communications electronics; Computers and controls; Digital; Electric power systems (generators, transformers, relays, and controls); Electrical schematics; Pulse; Resistance; Switching electronics; Test equipment and measurement; Voltage; and Wattage; (4) Electrical Power Engineering Technology, including exams in the following areas: (A) Distribution, covering: Calibration; Diagnostics; Dispatching; Economics; Inspection; Instrumentation; Layout; Load flow; Protection; Protection device coordination; Repair; Safety; Scheduling; Testing; and Troubleshooting; (B) Production, covering: Auxiliary systems; Calibration; Control systems; Diagnostics; Dispatching; Economics; Generator design; Inspection; Instrumentation; Layout; Protection; Protection device coordination; Repair; Safety; Scheduling; Shift operations; Startup; Testing; and Troubleshooting; (C) Substation, covering: Calibration; Communication; Control; Diagnostics; Dispatching; Economics; Equipment; Inspection; Instruments; Layout (grounding and profile); Protection; Protection device coordination; Repair; Safety; Scheduling; Testing; and Troubleshooting; and (D) Transmission, covering: Codes and standards; Conductor selection and spacing; Economics; Inspection; Insulator requirements; Phasing; Potential problem analysis; Repair; Safety; Scheduling; Startup; System studies (load flow, fault, and stability); Testing; and Troubleshooting; (5) Electrical Testing Engineering Technology, including: Cable testing; Relaying and protective equipment; Switch gear testing; and Transformer testing; (6) Industrial Engineering Technology, including: Basic management; Computer concepts; Engineering economy; Inventory analysis; Linear programming; Manufacturing process and basic accounting; Plant layout; Production control; Quality control concepts; Statistics and probability; and Time study; (7) Mechanical Engineering Technology, including: Air conditioning and heating systems and theory; Basic electricity; Characteristics of materials; Drafting; Energy conversion and transmission; Fluid power systems and theory; Gear systems; Gears; Hydraulics; Inspection; Instrumentation; Measurement instruments; Levers; Motors; Piping design; Pneumatics; Pressure vessels; Production machines; Production methods (casting, drawing, extrusion, and stamping); Pumps; Riveting; Systems; Tolerances; and Welding; and (8) Telecommunications Engineering Technology, including: Basic electricity, covering AC/DC fundamentals, active circuits, electronic devices, and passive networks; Communications (transmission), covering antennas, devices, transmission lines, and waveguides; Communications (2-way radio), covering AM/FM, communications circuits, modulation/detection, noise, and receivers/transmitter; FCC regulations, covering land-based communications, rules and regulations, and station operation; and Test equipment and measurements, covering measurements, test equipment operation, and types of test equipment. Electrical Testing Engineering Technology specialty requires successful completion of different general exam that covers: (1) Communication Skills, including: Basic graphics; Grammar; Logic; Reading; Report writing; and Vocabulary; (2) Electricity, including: Current and voltage relationships; Kirchhoff's Laws; Ohm's Law; Power and power factor; and Resistance and conductance; and (3) Mathematics, including: Algebra; Analytic geometry; Arithmetic; Basic calculus; Geometry; and Trigonometry. **Renewal:** Every five years. Recertification based on professional activities such as experience, management activities, continuing education, research, additional certifications, and successful completion of exam. **Preparatory Materials:** Program detail manual, including list of job task competencies, provided. Study guide available. Computer bulletin board numbers are: (703)519-8094 (2400 baud); (703)519-8095 (9600 baud). TDD number is: (703)684-2887. **Examination Frequency:** quarterly - always Saturday. **Examination Sites:** Exam given at sites throughout the U.S. **Examination Type:** Multiple-choice. **Pass/Fail Rate:** 20% pass exam the first time. **Waiting Period to Receive Scores:** Three weeks. **Reexamination:** Must wait six months to retake exam. May retake exam twice. **Fees:** $90. **Endorsed By:** American Society for Certified Engineering Technicians; National Society of Professional Engineers.

1177

Associate Engineering Technologist (ACT)
National Institute for Certification in Engineering Technologies (NICET)
1420 King St.
Alexandria, VA 22314-2794
Phone: (703)684-2835

Recipient: Engineering technologists. **Educational/Experience Requirements:** Graduation from engineering program accredited by Technology Accreditation Commission of the Accreditation Board for Engineering and Technology (see separate entry). May qualify for Certified Engineering Technologist (CET) designation (see separate entry) with increased experience. **Membership:** Not required. **Certification Requirements:** Successful completion of exam. **Renewal:** Every five years. Recertification based on professional activities such as experience, management activities, continuing education, research, additional certifications, and successful completion of exam. **Preparatory Materials:** Computer bulletin board numbers are: (703)519-8094 (2400 baud); (703)519-8095 (9600 baud). TDD number is: (703)684-2887. **Fees:** $35. **Endorsed By:** National Society of Professional Engineers.

1178

Certified Engineering Technologist (CT)
National Institute for Certification in Engineering Technologies (NICET)
1420 King St.
Alexandria
VA 22314-2794
Phone: (703)684-2835

Recipient: Engineering technologists. **Educational/Experience Requirements:** Must meet the following requirements: (1) Graduation from engineering program accredited by Technology Accreditation Commission of the Accreditation Board for Engineering and Technology (see separate entry); and (2) Five years experience. Candidates with less experience may qualify for Associate Engineering Technologist (AT) designation (see separate entry). **Membership:** Not required. **Certification Requirements:** Successful completion of exam. **Renewal:** Every five years. Recertification based on professional activities such as experience, management activities, continuing education, research, additional certifications, and successful completion of exam. **Pre-

---

paratory Materials:** Computer bulletin board numbers are: (703)519-8094 (2400 baud); (703)519-8095 (9600 baud). TDD number is: (703)684-2887. **Fees:** $35. **Endorsed By:** American Society of Certified Engineering Technicians; National Society of Professional Engineers.

1179

Certified Manufacturing Technologist (CMfgT)
Manufacturing Engineering Certification Institute (MECI)
Society of Manufacturing Engineers
One SME Dr.
PO Box 930
Dearborn, MI 48121-0930
Phone: (313)271-1500
Fax: (313)271-2861
Toll Free: (800)733-4763
John Covalchuck CMfgE, Chair

Recipient: Manufacturing technologists. **Educational/Experience Requirements:** Four years experience. **Membership:** Not required. **Certification Requirements:** Successful completion of exam. Exam covers: Applied sciences; Computer applications and engineering design; and Mathematics. **Renewal:** Every three years. Recertification based on either successful completion of exam or accumulation of 36 credits through continuing education, patents earned, technical papers published and presented, teaching, and other significant accomplishments in the field. Renewal fees are: Credit option: $40 (members); $50 (nonmembers); Exam option: $70 (members); $130 (nonmembers). **Preparatory Materials:** *Fundamentals of Manufacturing* (reference). Study guide, including list of references and sample questions, provided. Review courses and practice exams available. **Examination Frequency:** semiannual - always May and December. **Examination Sites:** Exam given at chapters and universities throughout the U.S. **Examination Type:** Multiple-choice. **Waiting Period to Receive Scores:** 60 days. **Fees:** $70 (members); $130 (nonmembers). **Endorsed By:** Society of Manufacturing Engineers.

1180

Engineering Technician (ET)
National Institute for Certification in Engineering Technologies (NICET)
1420 King St.
Alexandria, VA 22314-2794
Phone: (703)684-2835

Recipient: Engineering technicians working independently on jobs covered by standard and complete plans, specs, or instructions. **Educational/Experience Requirements:** Five years experience. Candidates with less experience may qualify for Associate Engineering Technician (AET) designation (see separate entry). May qualify for Senior Engineering Technician (SET) designation (see separate entry) with increased experience. **Membership:** Not required. **Certification Requirements:** Successful completion of either job task competency exam or two-part general knowledge exam. Exams available in the following job task competencies: (1) Building Construction, including the following subfields: Code and specification compliance; and Water and wastewater plants; (2) Computer Engineering Technology; (3) Construction Materials Testing, including the following subfields: Asphalt; Concrete; and Soils; (4) Electric Power Engineering Technology, including the subfield of substation; (5) Engineering Model Technology, including the subfield of piping; (6) Fire Protection Engineering Technology, including the following subfields: Automatic sprinkler system layout; Fire alarm systems; Inspection of fire suppression systems; and Special hazard systems layout; (7) Geosynthetic Materials Installation Inspection, including the following subfields: CSPE geomembranes; Geogrids; Geonets; Geosynthetic appurtenances; Geosynthetic clay liners; Geotextiles; HDPE geomembranes; PVC geomembranes; and VLDPE Geomembranes; (8) Geotechnical Engineering Technology, including the following subfields: Construction; Exploration; Generalist; Laboratory; and Waste containment; (9) Hydro Projects; (10) Industrial Instrumentation; (11) Land Management and Water Control, including the subfield of erosion and sediment control; (12) Mechanical Engineering Technology, including the following subfields: HVAC; and Industrial plant process piping; (13) Site Development; (14) Telecommunications Engineering Technology; (15) Transportation Engineering Technology, including: Bridge safety inspection; Highway bridge layout; Highway construction; Highway design; Highway maintenance; Highway materials; Highway surveys; Highway traffic operations; and Roadway layout; and (16) Underground Utilities Construction, including the subfield of water and sewer lines. General knowledge exam consists of general and technical parts. General part covers: (1) Communications, including: Basic communications skills; Basic drafting; and Business communications; (2) Mathematics, including: Advanced mathematics; Algebra; and Trigonom-

etry; and (3) Physical Science, including: Basic physical science; Intermediate mechanics; and Intermediate nonmechanical physical science. Technical part of exam offered in following specialties: (1) Architectural/Building Construction Engineering Technology, including: Architectural types; Building materials; Carpentry fundamentals; Concrete design; Conductance; Cooling; Drafting; Estimating; Foundations; Heating; Legal aspects; Loads; Plaster design; Site preparation; Stresses; Structural concrete design; Structural steel design; Structural wood design; and Ventilation; (2) Civil Engineering Technology, including: Blueprint reading; Concrete mixtures and quantities; Construction equipment and functions; Cost estimating; Drafting; Environmental (air, water, and sewage); Excavation and fill computations and planning; Foundation design; Highway design; Inspection and materials testing; Mapping; Materials inspection and analysis; Photogrammetry; Pilings; Piping design (basic); Soils analysis; Statics and dynamics; Structural steel design; Surveying; and Water control design; (3) Electrical/Electronics Engineering Technology, including: Basic electrical units (various meters, curve tracers, amplifiers, transformers, tubes, switches, capacitors, resistors, and transistors); Communications electronics; Computers and controls; Digital; Electric power systems (generators, transformers, relays, and controls); Electrical schematics; Pulse; Resistance; Switching electronics; Test equipment and measurement; Voltage; and Wattage; (4) Electrical Power Engineering Technology, including exams in the following areas: (A) Distribution, covering: Calibration; Diagnostics; Dispatching; Economics; Inspection; Instrumentation; Layout; Load flow; Protection; Protection device coordination; Repair; Safety; Scheduling; Testing; and Troubleshooting; (B) Production, covering: Auxiliary systems; Calibration; Control systems; Diagnostics; Dispatching; Economics; Generator design; Inspection; Instrumentation; Layout; Protection; Protection device coordination; Repair; Safety; Scheduling; Shift operations; Startup; Testing; and Troubleshooting; (C) Substation, covering: Calibration; Communication; Control; Diagnostics; Dispatching; Economics; Equipment; Inspection; Instruments; Layout (grounding and profile); Protection; Protection device coordination; Repair; Safety; Scheduling; Testing; and Troubleshooting; and (D) Transmission, covering: Codes and standards; Conductor selection and spacing; Economics; Inspection; Insulator requirements; Phasing; Potential problem analysis; Repair; Safety; Scheduling; Startup;

System studies (load flow, fault, and stability); Testing; and Troubleshooting; (5) Electrical Testing Engineering Technology, including: Cable testing; Relaying and protective equipment; Switch gear testing; and Transformer testing; (6) Industrial Engineering Technology, including: Basic management; Computer concepts; Engineering economy; Inventory analysis; Linear programming; Manufacturing process and basic accounting; Plant layout; Production control; Quality control concepts; Statistics and probability; and Time study; (7) Mechanical Engineering Technology, including: Air conditioning and heating systems and theory; Basic electricity; Characteristics of materials; Drafting; Energy conversion and transmission; Fluid power systems and theory; Gear systems; Gears; Hydraulics; Inspection; Instrumentation; Measurement instruments; Levers; Motors; Piping design; Pneumatics; Pressure vessels; Production machines; Production methods (casting, drawing, extrusion, and stamping); Pumps; Riveting; Systems; Tolerances; and Welding; and (8) Telecommunications Engineering Technology, including: Basic electricity, covering AC/DC fundamentals, active circuits, electronic devices, and passive networks; Communications (transmission), covering antennas, devices, transmission lines, and waveguides; Communications (2-way radio), covering: AM/FM, communications circuits, modulation/detection, noise, and receivers/transmitter; FCC regulations, covering land-based communications, rules and regulations, and station operation; and Test equipment and measurements, covering measurements, test equipment operation, and types of test equipment. Electrical Testing Engineering Technology specialty requires successful completion of different general exam that covers: (1) Communication Skills, including: Basic graphics; Grammar; Logic; Reading; Report writing; and Vocabulary; (2) Electricity, including: Current and voltage relationships; Kirchhoff's Laws; Ohm's Law; Power and power factor; and Resistance and conductance; and (3) Mathematics, including: Algebra; Analytic geometry; Arithmetic; Basic calculus; Geometry; and Trigonometry. **Renewal:** Every five years. Recertification based on professional activities such as experience, management activities, continuing education, research, additional certifications, and successful completion of exam. **Preparatory Materials:** Program detail manual available, including list of job task competencies, provided. Computer bulletin board numbers are: (703)519-8094 (2400 baud); (703)519-8095 (9600 baud). TDD number is: (703)684-2887. **Examination**

Frequency: quarterly - always Saturday. **Examination Sites:** Exam given at sites throughout the U.S. **Examination Type:** Multiple-choice. **Waiting Period to Receive Scores:** Three weeks. **Reexamination:** Must wait six months to retake exam. May retake exam twice. **Fees:** $90. **Endorsed By:** American Society for Certified Engineering Technicians; National Society of Professional Engineers.

1181

Senior Engineering Technician (SET)

National Institute for Certification in Engineering Technologies (NICET)
1420 King St.
Alexandria, VA 22314-2794
Phone: (703)684-2835

Recipient: Engineering technicians working independently. **Educational/Experience Requirements:** Ten to 15 years experience. Candidates with less experience may qualify for Engineering Technician (ET) designation (see separate entry). **Membership:** Not required. **Certification Requirements:** Successful completion of either job task competency exam or two-part general knowledge exam. Exams available in the following job task competencies: (1) Building Construction, including the following subfields: Code and specification compliance; and Water and wastewater plants; (2) Computer Engineering Technology; (3) Construction Materials Testing, including the following subfields: Asphalt; Concrete; and Soils; (4) Electric Power Engineering Technology, including the subfield of substation; (5) Engineering Model Technology, including the subfield of piping; (6) Fire Protection Engineering Technology, including the following subfields: Automatic sprinkler system layout; Fire alarm systems; Inspection of fire suppression systems; and Special hazard systems layout; (7) Geosynthetic Materials Installation Inspection, including the following subfields: CSPE geomembranes; Geogrids; Geonets; Geosynthetic appurtenances; Geosynthetic clay liners; Geotextiles; HDPE geomembranes; PVC geomembranes; and VLDPE Geomembranes; (8) Geotechnical Engineering Technology, including the following subfields: Construction; Exploration; Generalist; Laboratory; and Waste containment; (9) Hydro Projects; (10) Industrial Instrumentation; (11) Land Management and Water Control, including the subfield of erosion and sediment control; (12) Mechanical Engineering Technol-

ogy, including the following subfields: HVAC; and Industrial plant process piping; (13) Site Development; (14) Telecommunications Engineering Technology; (15) Transportation Engineering Technology, including: Bridge safety inspection; Highway bridge layout; Highway construction; Highway design; Highway maintenance; Highway materials; Highway surveys; Highway traffic operations; and Roadway layout; and (16) Underground Utilities Construction, including the subfield of water and sewer lines. General knowledge exam consists of general and technical parts. General part covers: (1) Communications, including: Basic communications skills; Basic drafting; and Business communications; (2) Mathematics, including: Advanced mathematics; Algebra; and Trigonometry; and (3) Physical Science, including: Basic physical science; Intermediate mechanics; and Intermediate nonmechanical physical science. Technical part of exam offered in following specialties: (1) Architectural/Building Construction Engineering Technology, including: Architectural types; Building materials; Carpentry fundamentals; Concrete design; Conductance; Cooling; Drafting; Estimating; Foundations; Heating; Legal aspects; Loads; Plaster design; Site preparation; Stresses; Structural concrete design; Structural steel design; Structural wood design; and Ventilation; (2) Civil Engineering Technology, including: Blueprint reading; Concrete mixtures and quantities; Construction equipment and functions; Cost estimating; Drafting; Environmental (air, water, and sewage); Excavation and fill computations and planning; Foundation design; Highway design; Inspection and materials testing; Mapping; Materials inspection and analysis; Photogrammetry; Pilings; Piping design (basic); Soils analysis; Statics and dynamics; Structural steel design; Surveying; and Water control design; (3) Electrical/Electronics Engineering Technology, including: Basic electrical units (various meters, curve tracers, amplifiers, transformers, tubes, switches, capacitors, resistors, and transistors); Communications electronics; Computers and controls; Digital; Electric power systems (generators, transformers, relays, and controls); Electrical schematics; Pulse; Resistance; Switching electronics; Test equipment and measurement; Voltage; and Wattage; (4) Electrical Power Engineering Technology, including exams in the following areas: (A) Distribution, covering: Calibration; Diagnostics; Dispatching; Economics; Inspection; Instrumentation; Layout; Load flow; Protection; Protection device coordination; Repair; Safety; Scheduling; Testing; and Troubleshoot-

ing; (B) Production, covering: Auxiliary systems; Calibration; Control systems; Diagnostics; Dispatching; Economics; Generator design; Inspection; Instrumentation; Layout; Protection; Protection device coordination; Repair; Safety; Scheduling; Shift operations; Startup; Testing; and Troubleshooting; (C) Substation, covering: Calibration; Communication; Control; Diagnostics; Dispatching; Economics; Equipment; Inspection; Instruments; Layout (grounding and profile); Protection; Protection device coordination; Repair; Safety; Scheduling; Testing; and Troubleshooting; and (D) Transmission, covering: Codes and standards; Conductor selection and spacing; Economics; Inspection; Insulator requirements; Phasing; Potential problem analysis; Repair; Safety; Scheduling; Startup; System studies (loadflow, fault, and stability); Testing; and Troubleshooting; (5) Electrical Testing Engineering Technology, including: Cable testing; Relaying and protective equipment; Switch gear testing; and Transformer testing; (6) Industrial Engineering Technology, including: Basic management; Computer concepts; Engineering economy; Inventory analysis; Linear programming; Manufacturing process and basic accounting; Plant layout; Production control; Quality control concepts; Statistics and probability; and Time study; (7) Mechanical Engineering Technology, including: Air conditioning and heating systems and theory; Basic electricity; Characteristics of materials; Drafting; Energy conversion and transmission; Fluid power systems and theory; Gear systems; Gears; Hydraulics; Inspection; Instrumentation; Measurement instruments; Levers; Motors; Piping design; Pneumatics; Pressure vessels; Production machines; Production methods (casting, drawing, extrusion, and stamping); Pumps; Riveting; Systems; Tolerances; and Welding; and (8) Telecommunications Engineering Technology, including: Basic electricity, covering AC/DC fundamentals, active circuits, electronic devices, and passive networks; Communications (transmission), covering antennas, devices, transmission lines, and waveguides; Communications (2-way radio), covering: AM/FM, communications circuits, modulation/detection, noise, and receivers/transmitter; FCC regulations, covering land-based communications, rules and regulations, and station operation; and Test equipment and measurements, covering measurements, test equipment operation, and types of test equipment. Electrical Testing Engineering Technology specialty requires successful completion of different general exam that covers: (1) Communication Skills, including: Basic graphics; Grammar; Logic; Reading; Report writing; and Vocabulary; (2) Electricity, including: Current and voltage relationships; Kirchhoff's Laws; Ohm's Law; Power and power factor; and Resistance and conductance; and (3) Mathematics, including: Algebra; Analytic geometry; Arithmetic; Basic calculus; Geometry; and Trigonometry. **Renewal:** Every five years. Recertification based on professional activities such as experience, management activities, continuing education, research, additional certifications, and successful completion of exam. **Preparatory Materials:** Program detail manual available, including list of job competencies, provided. Computer bulletin board numbers are: (703)519-8094 (2400 baud); (703)519-8095 (9600 baud). TDD number is: (703)684-2887. **Examination Frequency:** quarterly - always Saturday. **Examination Sites:** Exam given at sites throughout the U.S. **Examination Type:** Multiple-choice. **Waiting Period to Receive Scores:** Three weeks. **Reexamination:** Must wait six months to retake exam. May retake exam twice. **Fees:** $90. **Endorsed By:** American Society for Certified Engineering Technicians; National Society of Professional Engineers.

`1182`

Technician Trainee (TT)
National Institute for Certification in Engineering Technologies (NICET)
1420 King St.
Alexandria, VA 22314-2794
Phone: (703)684-2835

Recipient: Entry-level engineering technicians working under direct supervision. **Educational/Experience Requirements:** none. May qualify for Associate Engineering Technician (AET) designation (see separate entry) with increased experience. **Membership:** Not required. **Certification Requirements:** Successful completion of either job task competency exam or general knowledge exam. Exams available in the following job task competencies: (1) Building Construction, including the following subfields: Code and specification compliance; and Water and wastewater plants; (2) Computer Engineering Technology; (3) Construction Materials Testing, including the following subfields: Asphalt; Concrete; and Soils; (4) Electric Power Engineering Technology, including the subfield of substation; (5) Engineering Model Technology, including the subfield of piping; (6) Fire Protection Engineering Technology, including the following subfields: Automatic sprinkler system layout; Fire

alarm systems; Inspection of fire suppression systems; and Special hazard systems layout; (7) Geosynthetic Materials Installation Inspection, including the following subfields: CSPE geomembranes; Geogrids; Geonets; Geosynthetic appurtenances; Geosynthetic clay liners; Geotextiles; HDPE geomembranes; PVC geomembranes; and VLDPE Geomembranes; (8) Geotechnical Engineering Technology, including the following subfields: Construction; Exploration; Generalist; Laboratory; and Waste containment; (9) Hydro Projects; (10) Industrial Instrumentation; (11) Land Management and Water Control, including the subfield of erosion and sediment control; (12) Mechanical Engineering Technology, including the following subfields: HVAC; and Industrial plant process piping; (13) Site Development; (14) Telecommunications Engineering Technology; (15) Transportation Engineering Technology, including: Bridge safety inspection; Highway bridge layout; Highway construction; Highway design; Highway maintenance; Highway materials; Highway surveys; Highway traffic operations; and Roadway layout; and (16) Underground Utilities Construction, including the subfield of water and sewer lines. General knowledge exam covers: (1) Communications, including: Basic communications skills; Basic drafting; and Business communications; (2) Mathematics, including: Advanced mathematics; Algebra; and Trigonometry; and (3) Physical Science, including: Basic physical science; Intermediate mechanics; and Intermediate non-mechanical physical science. **Renewal:** Every five years. Recertification based on professional activities such as experience, management activities, continuing education, research, additional certifications, and successful completion of exam. **Preparatory Materials:** Program detail manual, including list of job task competencies, available. Computer bulletin board numbers are: (703)519-8094 (2400 baud); (703)519-8095 (9600 baud). TDD number is: (703)684-2887. **Examination Frequency:** quarterly - always Saturday. **Examination Sites:** Exam given at sites throughout the U.S. **Examination Type:** Multiple-choice. **Waiting Period to Receive Scores:** Three weeks. **Reexamination:** Must wait six months to retake exam. May retake exam twice. **Fees:** $90. **Endorsed By:** American Society of Certified Engineering Technicians; National Society of Professional Engineers.

Paralegals

`1183`

Certified Legal Assistant (CLA)
National Association of Legal Assistants (NALA)
1516 S. Boston, Ste. 200
Tulsa, OK 74119
Phone: (918)587-6828
Fax: (918)582-6772

Recipient: Paralegals. **Number of Certified Individuals:** 6700. **Educational/Experience Requirements:** Must meet one of the following requirements: (1) Associate's degree in legal assisting; (2) Post-baccalaureate certificate in legal assistant studies; (3) Bachelor's degree in legal assistant studies; (4) Successful completion of legal assistant program which consists of minimum of 60 semester (90 quarter) hours of which at least 15 semester (22 and one-half quarter) hours are substantive legal courses; (5) Bachelor's degree in any field and one year of experience. Successful completion of 15 semester hours (22 and one-half quarter or 225 clock) hours of substantive legal assistant courses is equivalent to one year of experience; or (6) High school diploma or equivalent, seven years experience, and 20 hours of continuing education within last two years. **Membership:** Not required. **Certification Requirements:** Successful completion of exam. Exam consists of the following sections: (1) Communications, including: Capitalization; Concise writing; Correspondence; Grammar; Nonverbal communication; Punctuation; Rules of composition; Vocabulary; and Word usage; (2) Ethics, including: Confidentiality; Practice rules; and Unauthorized practice; (3) Human Relations and Interviewing Techniques, including: Communication and interaction with clients and fellow employees; and Techniques for both initial and subsequent and client and witness interviews; (4) Judgment and Analytical Analysis, including: Analysis of research request; Analyzing and categorizing facts and evidence; Handling telephone situations; Memo writing; Reading comprehension and data; and Relationship with the lawyer, legal secretary, client, courts, and other law firms; (5) Legal Research, including: Case reports; Digests; Research procedure; Shepardizing; State and federal codes; and Statutes; (6) Legal Terminology, including: Latin phrases; Legal phrases or terms; and Utilization and understanding of common legal terms; and (7) Substantive Law, in which candidate must successfully complete General section (on American legal system) and four of the following parts: Administrative Law;

Bankruptcy; Contract; Business Organizations; Criminal; Litigation; Probate and Estate Planning; and Real Estate. **Renewal:** Every five years. Recertification based on accumulation of five units through: (1) Successful completion of specialty exam (two units); (2) Successful completion of college course (two units per course); (3) Attendance at conferences, seminars, workshops, or other related educational functions (one unit per event); and (4) Teaching, research, and publications (two units maximum). Renewal fee is $50. **Preparatory Materials:** *CLA Review Manual, A Practical Guide, NALA CLA Exam Preparation Manual,* and *NALA Manual for Legal Assistants* (references). Review seminar, mock exam, and study guides available. **Examination Frequency:** Three times per year - always spring, July, and December. **Examination Sites:** Exam given at sites throughout the U.S. **Examination Type:** Essay; matching; multiple-choice; short answer; true or false. **Pass/Fail Rate:** 40% pass exam. **Re-examination:** Candidates who successfully complete four sections must only retake sections failed. May retake exam five times. Must successfully complete exam within three years. There is a fee to retake exam. **Fees:** $225 (members); $240 (nonmembers).

1184

Certified Legal Assistant Specialist
National Association of Legal
    Assistants (NALA)
1516 S. Boston, Ste. 200
Tulsa, OK 74119
Phone: (918)587-6828
Fax: (918)582-6772

Recipient: Paralegals. **Educational/ Experience Requirements:** Hold Certified Legal Assistant (CLA) designation (see separate entry). Substantial experience in specialty areas is required to successfully complete exams. **Membership:** Not required. **Certification Requirements:** Successful completion of one of the following specialty exams: (1) Bankruptcy, including: Bankruptcy Code (Title II U.S.C. and Title 28 U.S.C.); Bankruptcy rules and procedures; Federal rules of civil procedure; and Federal rules of evidence; (2) Civil Litigation, including: Abstracting information; Civil procedure; Document control; Drafting of pleadings; Federal rules of civil, evidence, and appellate procedure; General litigation techniques; Legal research and terminology; and Substantive law and litigation techniques; (3) Corporate and Business Law, including: Administrative, agency, contract, corporate, employment, partnership, property, tax, and tort

law; Federal regulatory agencies; Model Business Corporate Act; Uniform Commercial Code; Uniform Limited Partnership Act; and Uniform Partnership Act; (4) Criminal Law and Procedure, including: Components of substantive criminal law; Constitutional rights guaranteed to defendants; Evidence; Federal rules of criminal procedure; Procedural matters; and U.S. Supreme Court cases; (5) Probate and Estate Planning, including: Drafting wills and trusts; Estate planning concepts; Federal estate tax; Fiduciary income tax; and General probate and trust law; and (6) Real Estate, including: Abstracts; Actions affecting title; Cluster developments; Easements; Landlord/ tenant relations; Legal remedies associated with real estate and legal descriptions of real estate; Liens; Methods of passing title included in conveyances; Oil and gas; Purchases; Sales; Terminology; Title insurance; and Types of conveyances. **Examination Frequency:** Three times per year - always spring, July, and December. **Examination Sites:** Exam given at sites throughout the U.S.

Photographic Process Workers

1185

**Member, Society of Photo
    Finishing Engineers**
Society of Photo Finishing
    Engineers (SPFE)
3000 Picture Pl.
Jackson, MI 49201
Phone: (517)788-8100
Fax: (517)788-8371
Roy S. Pung PMA, Exec.Dir.

Recipient: Wholesale and professional film processors or lab technicians. **Educational/Experience Requirements:** Two years experience or equivalent training from school of photofinishing or photography. **Certification Requirements:** Successful completion of exam. Exam covers: Administration; Film processing and printing; Health/safety; and Quality Control. **Preparatory Materials:** *Photofinishing Color Printing* (manual). Resource guide and sample questions available. **Examination Frequency:** Throughout the year. **Examination Sites:** Exam given at annual convention, seminars, division meetings, and by arrangement with proctor.

Quality Control Engineers and Technicians

1186

**Certified Mechanical Inspector
(CMI)**
American Society for Quality
    Control (ASQC)
611 E. Wisconsin Ave.
PO Box 3005
Milwaukee, WI 53201-3005
Phone: (414)272-8575
Fax: (414)272-1734
Toll Free: (800)248-1946
Sally M. Harthun, Mgr.

Recipient: Mechanical inspectors who, under direction of quality engineers, supervisors, or technicians, evaluate hardware documentation, perform laboratory procedures, inspect products, measure process performance, record data, and prepare formal reports. **Educational/ Experience Requirements:** High school diploma, two years experience, and document professionalism in one of the following ways: (1) Registration as professional engineer (P.E.); and (2) Membership in ASQC or related association. Three years additional experience may be substituted for high school diploma. **Membership:** Not required. **Certification Requirements:** Successful completion of exam. Exam consists of the following sections: (1) Technical Mathematics; (2) Blueprint Reading; (3) Inspection Tools and Equipment; (4) Materials and Processes; (5) Inspection Planning; (6) Inspection Technology; (7) Statistics; and (8) Sampling and Sampling Plans. **Renewal:** none. **Preparatory Materials:** Study guide, including bibliography and sample questions, provided. Review courses available. **Examination Frequency:** semiannual - always March and October. **Examination Sites:** Exam given at ASQC sections and internationally. **Examination Type:** Multiple-choice. **Waiting Period to Receive Scores:** Four weeks. **Re-examination:** Must retake exam within 18 months. There is a fee to retake exam. **Fees:** $60.

1187

Certified Quality Auditor (CQA)
American Society for Quality
    Control (ASQC)
611 E. Wisconsin Ave.
PO Box 3005
Milwaukee, WI 53201-3005
Phone: (414)272-8575
Fax: (414)272-1734
Toll Free: (800)248-1946
Sally M. Harthun, Mgr.

Recipient: Quality auditors who apply standards and principles of auditing and auditing techniques for examining, questioning, evaluating, and reporting to determine adequacy and deficiencies of quality control systems. **Educational/ Experience Requirements:** Eight years experience, three years of which must be in professional, decision-making technical, or management position, and document professionalism in one of the following ways: (1) Registration as professional engineer (P.E.); or (2) Membership in ASQC or related association. One of the following educational achievements may be substituted for experience as follows: (1) Master's or doctorate degree (five years); (2) Bachelor's degree (four years); (3) Associate's degree (two years); and (4) Successful completion of quality technology program at community college or vocational school (one year). **Membership:** Not required. **Certification Requirements:** Successful completion of exam. Exam consists of the following sections: (1) General Knowledge, Conduct, Ethics, and Audit Administration, including: Audit administration; General knowledge; and Professional conduct and ethics; (2) Audit Preparation, including: Audit plan communication and distribution; Audit plan preparation and documentation; Audit team selection criteria; Checklists/ guidelines/log sheets; Development of data collection models; Importance and utility of quality documentation; Requirements against which to audit; and Sources of authority for conducting audits; (3) Audit Performance, including: Audit analysis; Audit implementation; Audit team management; Closing/exit meeting; and Conducting opening/ entrance meeting; (4) Audit Reporting, Corrective Active, Follow-up, and Closure; and (5) Auditing Tools and Techniques. **Renewal:** Every three years. Recertification based on accumulation of 18 units through experience, continuing education, attendance at technical conferences, symposia, workshops, and ASQC section meetings, teaching courses, publishing articles or papers, or other educational programs. **Preparatory Materials:** Study guide, including bibliography, glossary, and sample questions, provided. Review courses available. **Examination Frequency:** semiannual - always June and December. **Examination Sites:** Exam given at ASQC sections and internationally. **Examination Type:** Multiple-choice. **Waiting Period to Receive Scores:** Four weeks. **Re-examination:** Must retake exam within 18 months. There is a fee to retake exam. **Fees:** $90.

1188

Certified Quality Engineer (CQE)
American Society for Quality
  Control (ASQC)
611 E. Wisconsin Ave.
PO Box 3005
Milwaukee, WI 53201-3005
Phone: (414)272-8575
Fax: (414)272-1734
Toll Free: (800)248-1946
Sally M. Harthun, Mgr.

Recipient: Quality engineers who understand principles of product and service quality evaluation and control. **Educational/Experience Requirements:** Bachelor's, master's, or doctoral degree and document professionalism in one of the following ways: (1) Registration as professional engineer (P.E.); and (2) Membership in ASQC or related association. **Membership:** Not required. **Certification Requirements:** Successful completion of exam. Exam covers: (1) General Knowledge, Conduct, and Ethics; (2) Quality Practices and Applications, including: Continuous improvement tools; Cost of quality; Human resource management; Quality audits; Quality planning; Quality systems; and Supplier management; (3) Statistical Principles and Applications, including: Acceptance sampling; Correlation and regression analysis; Distributions; Experimental design; Statistical inference; and Terms and concepts; (4) Product, Process, and Materials Control, including: Classification of characteristics and defects; Identification of materials and status; Lot traceability; Materials Review Board criteria and procedures; Materials segregation practices; Sample integrity and control; Statistical process control; and Work instructions; (5) Measurement Systems, including: Destructive and nondestructive testing concepts; Metrology; Repeatability and reproducibility studies; and Terms and definitions; and (6) Safety and Reliability, including: Product traceability systems and recall procedures; Reliability life characteristic concepts; Risk assessment tools and risk prevention; Terms and definitions; and Types of reliability systems. Must earn Certified Quality Engineer (CQE) designation (see separate entry) within six years. **Preparatory Materials:** Study guide, including bibliography and sample questions, provided. Review courses available. **Examination Frequency:** semiannual - always June and December. **Examination Sites:** Exam given at ASQC sections and internationally. **Examination Type:** Multiple-choice. **Waiting Period to Receive Scores:** Four weeks. **Re-examination:** Must retake exam within 18 months. There is a fee to retake exam.

1189

Certified Quality Engineer (CQE)
American Society for Quality
  Control (ASQC)
611 E. Wisconsin Ave.
PO Box 3005
Milwaukee, WI 53201-3005
Phone: (414)272-8575
Fax: (414)272-1734
Toll Free: (800)248-1946
Sally M. Harthun, Mgr.

Recipient: Quality engineers who apply principles of product and service quality evaluation and control. **Educational/ Experience Requirements:** Eight years experience, three years of which must be in professional, decision-making technical, or management position, and document professionalism in one of the following ways: (1) Registration as professional engineer (P.E.); and (2) Membership in ASQC or related association. One of the following educational achievements may be substituted for experience as follows: (1) Master's or doctorate degree (five years); (2) Bachelor's degree (four years); (3) Associate's degree (two years); and (4) Successful completion of quality technology program at community college or vocational school (one year). **Membership:** Not required. **Certification Requirements:** Successful completion of exam. Exam covers: (1) General Knowledge, Conduct, and Ethics; (2) Quality Practices and Applications, including: Continuous improvement tools; Cost of quality; Human resource management; Quality audits; Quality planning; Quality systems; and Supplier management; (3) Statistical Principles and Applications, including: Acceptance sampling; Correlation and regression analysis; Distributions; Experimental design; Statistical inference; and Terms and concepts; (4) Product, Process, and Materials Control, including: Classification of characteristics and defects; Identification of materials and status; Lot traceability; Materials Review Board criteria and procedures; Materials segregation practices; Sample integrity and control; Statistical process control; and Work instructions; (5) Measurement Systems, including: Destructive and nondestructive testing concepts; Metrology; Repeatability and reproducibility studies; and Terms and definitions; and (6) Safety and Reliability, including: Product traceability systems and recall procedures; Reliability life characteristic concepts; Risk assessment tools and risk prevention; Terms and definitions; and Types of reliability systems. **Renewal:** Every three years. Recertification based on accumulation of 18 units through experience, continuing education, attendance at technical conferences, symposia, workshops, and ASQC section meetings, teaching courses, publishing articles or papers, or other educational programs. **Preparatory Materials:** Study guide, including bibliography and sample questions, provided. Review courses available. **Examination Frequency:** semiannual - always June and December. **Examination Sites:** Exam given at ASQC sections and internationally. **Examination Type:** Multiple-choice. **Waiting Period to Receive Scores:** Four weeks. **Re-examination:** Must retake exam within 18 months. There is a fee to retake exam. **Fees:** $90.

1190

Certified Quality Manager (CQM)
American Society for Quality
    Control (ASQC)
611 E. Wisconsin Ave.
PO Box 3005
Milwaukee, WI 53201-3005
Phone: (414)272-8575
Fax: (414)272-1734
Toll Free: (800)248-1946
Sally M. Harthun, Mgr.

Recipient: Quality managers. **Educational/Experience Requirements:** Ten years experience, five of which must be in management or decision-making position. **Membership:** Not required. **Certification Requirements:** Successful completion of exam. Exam consists of the following sections: (1) Quality Standards; (2) Organizations and Their Functions; (3) Quality Needs and Overall Strategic Plans; (4) Customer Satisfaction and Focus; (5) Project Management; (6) Continuous Improvement; (7) Human Resource Management; and (8) Training and Education.

1191

Certified Quality Technician (CQT)
American Society for Quality
    Control (ASQC)
611 E. Wisconsin Ave.
PO Box 3005
Milwaukee, WI 53201-3005
Phone: (414)272-8575
Fax: (414)272-1734
Toll Free: (800)248-1946
Sally M. Harthun, Mgr.

Recipient: Quality technicians who, under direction of quality engineers or supervisors, analyze and solve quality problems, prepare inspection plans and instruction, select sampling plan applications, prepare procedures, train inspectors, perform audits, analyze quality

costs and other quality data, and apply fundamental statistical methods for process control. **Educational/Experience Requirements:** Four years experience and document professionalism in one of the following ways: (1) Registration as professional engineer (P.E.); or (2) Membership in ASQC or related association. One of the following educational achievements may be substituted for experience as follows: (1) Bachelor's degree (three years); (2) Associate's degree (two years); or (3) Successful completion of quality technology program at community college or vocational school (one year). **Membership:** Not required. **Certification Requirements:** Successful completion of exam. Exam covers: (1) Quality Control Concepts and Techniques, including: Classification of characteristics and nonconformances; Determination of inspection points and methods; Inspection methods; Nonconforming material control; Quality data; and Total quality control concepts; (2) Fundamentals of Practical Statistical Methods, including: Control charts; Presentation, description, and analysis of data; Sampling distributions; and Statistical inference; (3) Application of Sampling Principles, including: Alpha and beta risks; Concept of sampling based on hypergeometric distribution; Definitions and selection of AQL, LTPD, and AOQL; Economics of selection of sampling plan; Limitations and applications; Principles of homogeneity; Producer and consumer risks; Use of MIL-STD-105D and MIL-STD-414; and Use of O.C. curves; (4) Reliability Principles, Applications, and Simple Calculations, including calculations and concepts; (5) Meteorology and Calibration Fundamentals, including: Calibration control systems; Calibration error effect on product acceptance; Calibration labels; Common international standards of measurement; Definitions; Levels of accuracy and hierarchy of standards and instruments; Measurement standards and traceability; MIL-STD-45662; and Statistical tolerancing measurement uncertainties; (6) Quality Data, Analysis, Problem Solving, and Cost Methodology, including: Comparing needs with resources; Economics of quality costs (nonconformance); Profit and productivity improvement by use and application of quality cost data; and Using and analyzing quality cost data; (7) Quality Audit Concepts and Principles, including: Application of statistics to auditing; Audit principles and methods; Audit purposes; Audit vs. inspection; Audit reporting; Corrective actions based on audits; Methods of audit follow-up and closure; and Types of audits; and (8) Geometry, Trigonometry, and Metric Conversion, including: Common formulas; Metric conversion factors

and applications; Problems; and Simple algebra. **Renewal:** none. **Preparatory Materials:** Study guide, including bibliography and sample questions, provided. Review courses available. **Examination Frequency:** semiannual - always March and October. **Examination Sites:** Exam given at ASQC sections and internationally. **Examination Type:** Multiple-choice. **Waiting Period to Receive Scores:** Four weeks. **Re-examination:** Must retake exam within 18 months. There is a fee to retake exam. **Fees:** $60 (members); $125 (nonmembers).

1192

Certified Reliability Engineer (CRE)
American Society for Quality
    Control (ASQC)
611 E. Wisconsin Ave.
PO Box 3005
Milwaukee, WI 53201-3005
Phone: (414)272-8575
Fax: (414)272-1734
Toll Free: (800)248-1946
Sally M. Harthun, Mgr.

Recipient: Reliability engineers who apply principles of performance evaluation and prediction to improve product/systems safety, reliability, and maintainability. **Educational/Experience Requirements:** Eight years experience, three years of which must be in professional, decision-making technical, or management position, and document professionalism in one of the following ways: (1) Registration as professional engineer (P.E.); or (2) Membership in ASQC or related association. One of the following educational achievements may be substituted for experience as follows: (1) Master's or doctorate degree (five years); (2) Bachelor's degree (four years); (3) Associate's degree (two years); and (4) Successful completion of quality technology program at community college or vocational school (one year). **Membership:** Not required. **Certification Requirements:** Successful completion of exam. Exam consists of the following sections: (1) Basic Principles, Concepts, and Definitions; (2) Management Control; (3) Prediction, Estimation, and Apportionment Methods; (4) Failure Mode, Effect, and Criticality Analysis (Hardware and Software); (5) Part Selection and Derating; (6) Reliability Design Review; (7) Maintainability and Availability; (8) Product Safety; (9) Human Factors in Reliability; (10) Reliability Testing and Planning; (11) Data Collection, Analysis, and Reporting; and (12) Mathematical Models. **Renewal:** Every three years. Recertification based on successful completion of exam or accumulation of 18 units through experience, continuing education, attendance at technical conferences, symposia, workshops, and ASQC section meetings, teaching courses, publishing articles or papers, or other professional development activities. **Preparatory Materials:** Study guide, including bibliography and sample questions, provided. Review courses available. **Examination Frequency:** semiannual - always March and October. **Examination Sites:** Exam given at ASQC sections and internationally. **Examination Type:** Multiple-choice. **Waiting Period to Receive Scores:** Four weeks. **Re-examination:** Must retake exam within 18 months. There is a fee to retake exam. **Fees:** $90.

Science Technicians

1193

Certification in Infection Control (CIC)
Certification Board of Infection Control (CBIC)
PO Box 14661
Lenexa, KS 66285-4661
Phone: (913)541-9077
Fax: (913)541-0156
Deborah M. Hamlin CAE, Exec. Dir.

Recipient: Infection control practitioners. **Educational/Experience Requirements:** Must meet the following requirements: (1) Bachelor's degree or higher in healthcare-related field; and (2) Two years practice within last four years. Experience must include analysis and interpretation of collected infection control data, investigation and surveillance of suspected outbreaks of infection, and three of the following: Development and revision of infection control policies and procedures; Education of individuals about infection risk, prevention, and control; Management of infection prevention and control activities; Planning, implementation, and evaluation of infection prevention and control measures; and Provision of consultation of infection risk assessment, prevention, and control strategies. **Certification Requirements:** Successful completion of exam. Exam covers: (1) Infectious Process, including: Clinical findings and diagnostic tests; Host factors; and Microbiologic agents; (2) Surveillance and Epidemiologic Investigation, including: Data analysis; Data collection; and Data reporting; (3) Transmission of Infection, including: Prevention and intervention; and Risks; (4) Management and Communication,

including: Human relations skills; Influence of organization and regulation of the healthcare system; Personnel and financial resource management; Program planning and evaluation; Role of infection control personnel; and (5) Education, including: Instructional methods; Principles of adult learning; and Program planning and evaluation. **Renewal:** Every five years. Recertification based on successful completion of exam. Renewal fee is $155. **Preparatory Materials:** Handbook, including exam content outline, list of suggested study references, and sample questions, provided. **Examination Frequency:** semiannual - always spring and fall. **Examination Sites:** Exam given at annual conference in the spring and at sites throughout the U.S. and Canada in the fall. **Examination Type:** Multiple-choice. **Waiting Period to Receive Scores:** Six weeks. **Fees:** $230. **Endorsed By:** National Organization for Competency Assurance.

1194

Certified Electron Microscopy Technologist
Microscopy Society of America (MSA)
PO Box MSA
Woods Hole, MA 02543
Phone: (508)540-7639
Fax: (508)548-9053
Toll Free: (800)538-3672
E-mail: bozzola@qm.c-chom.siu.edu
Dr. John Bozzola, Contact

Recipient: Electron microscope technologists involved in the biological sciences. **Educational/Experience Requirements:** Must meet one of the following requirements: (1) Two years (60 credits) of college with one semester of mathematics and two semesters each in transmission electron microscopy (TEM), biology, chemistry, and physics; (2) One year of experience and one year of college including two semesters of laboratory courses each in chemistry and physics; (3) Two years experience and high school diploma; or (4) Three years experience. **Membership:** Not required. **Certification Requirements:** Successful completion of written and practical exams. Written exam covers: Instrumentation; Sectioning and staining; Special techniques and photography; Tissue processing; and General, covering: Chemistry; Cytology; Safety; and Other areas of electron microscopy. Practical exam consists of preparing blocks, sections, and micrographs from three different tissues. **Renewal:** Every five years. Recertification based on continued employment in the field. **Preparatory Materials:** Study guide, reading

list, and sample questions provided. **Examination Frequency:** semiannual. **Examination Type:** Matching; multiple-choice; true or false. **Fees:** $50 (members); $100 (nonmembers).

1195

Certified Eye Bank Technician
Eye Bank Association of America (EBAA)
1001 Connecticut Ave., NW, Ste. 601
Washington, DC 20036-5504
Phone: (202)775-4999
Fax: (202)429-6036

Recipient: Eye bank technicians. **Educational/Experience Requirements:** Must meet one of the following requirements: (1) High school diploma or equivalent, one year of experience, and successful completion of EBAA Technician Training Course; (2) Hold either Certified Ophthalmic Technician (COT) (see separate entry), medical laboratory technician, or licensed vocational/practical nurse designations, six months experience, and successfully complete of EBAA Technician Training Course; or (3) Bachelor's degree or higher, hold either physician assistant, registered nurse, or Certified Ophthalmic Technologist (COMT) designation (see separate entry), and three months experience. **Membership:** Not required. **Certification Requirements:** Successful completion of written and practical exams. Written exam covers: (1) Donor Related Procedures, covering: Blood drawing procedures; History screening, evaluation, and documentation; *In situ* corneal excision procedure and documentation; *In situ* examination of corneal eye tissue; Informed consent procedures and documentation; Notification protocols; Preparation procedures; Restoration; and Whole eye enucleation procedure and documentation; (2) Tissue Related Procedures, including: Distribution of tissue and documentation required; Intermediate and permanent labeling; Microbiologic culturing of tissue; Packaging of tissue for transport to and from eye bank; Preservation of tissue in laboratory; Required documentation to be completed and sent with tissue; Slit lamping biomicroscopy; and Specular microscopy; (3) Quality Assurance and Quality Control Issues in the Laboratory, including: Back-up fail-safe systems/corrective procedures; Cleaning documentation; EBAA Medical Standards and Procedures; Infection control, including biohazardous waste handling and disposal and Universal Precautions Guidelines; Instrument handling, cleaning, and inspection; Maintenance documentation; Quality assurance monitoring activities; Serology; and Temperature recording; (4) Scientific Basis for Practice, including: Asepsis and aseptic technique; Current viral and bacterially transmitted diseases of import, including hepatitis, HIV, septicemia, and slow viruses; Disease transmission; History of eye banking; and Ocular and corneal anatomy and physiology; (5) Use of Tissue for Transplantation and Research; (6) Legislated Statutory Requirements, including: OBRA of 1987; Required request; and Uniform Anatomical Gift Act; and (7) Accrediting and Certifying Requirements. **Renewal:** Every three years. Recertification based on accumulation of 16 continuing credit credits through: (1) Attendance at EBAA annual meetings, educational conferences, scientific sessions, and technical skills workshops; (2) Successful completion of programs or courses related directly or indirectly to the field; (3) Ophthalmology lectures presented; (4) Publication of journal articles, chapters, or similar scholarly works; (5) Summarizations of self-study courses or journal articles and books; and (6) Association participation. Renewal fees are: $125 (members); $200 (nonmembers). **Re-examination:** Must successfully complete exams within 60 days. There is a fee to retake exams. **Fees:** $200 (members); $300 (nonmembers).

1196

Certified Genetic Counselor (CGC)
American Board of Genetic
 Counseling
9650 Rockville Pike
Bethesda, MD 20814-3998
Phone: (301)571-1825
Fax: (301)571-1895
Sharon Robinson, Admin.

Recipient: Professionals involved in genetic counseling. **Number of Certified Individuals:** 814. **Educational/ Experience Requirements:** Must meet the following requirements: (1) Graduate degree in genetic counseling; and (2) Submission of logbook of 50 distinct supervised genetic counseling cases. Candidates with equivalent training may qualify. **Membership:** Not required. **Certification Requirements:** Successful completion of general exam and genetic counseling exam. **Renewal:** Every ten years. **Preparatory Materials:** none. **Examination Frequency:** triennial - always June. Next exam 1996. **Examination Sites:** Exams given in Chicago, IL; Atlanta, GA; Los Angeles, CA; and Philadelphia, PA. **Examination Type:** Multiple-choice. **Waiting Period to Receive Scores:** Four months. **Re-**

examination: Must wait three years to retake exams. Must only retake exam failed. May retake exams two times. **Fees:** $900.

1197

Certified Sterile Processing and Distribution Technician (CSPDT)
National Institute for the
 Certification of Healthcare Sterile
 Processing and Distribution
 Personnel (NICHSPDP)
PO Box 558
Annandale, NJ 08801

Recipient: Technicians in healthcare sterile processing and distribution departments. **Educational/Experience Requirements:** Must meet one of the following requirements: (1) One year of experience; (2) Successful completion of related allied health program and six months experience; (3) One year of experience in healthcare product sales or service; or (4) Successful completion of Central Service/SPD Training Course. **Certification Requirements:** Successful completion of exam. Exam covers: (1) Roles and Responsibilities, including: Administration organization; Inventory control and distribution; and Quality assurance; (2) Life Sciences, including: Anatomy and physiology; and Microbiology and infection control; (3) Decontamination, including: Objectives and purpose; Procedures for handling infectious waste (medical waste management); and Selection of appropriate decontamination methods; (4) Sterilization, including: Safety considerations; Selection of sterilization methods; Sterilization parameters; Terminal sterilization process; and Types of equipment; and (5) Preparation and Handling, including: Assembly and packaging; Instrumentation; and Sterile storage. **Renewal:** Every five years. Recertification based on accumulation of 100 points through: (1) Successful completion of exam (75 points); (2) Continuing education (one point per contact hour); (3) Successful completion of college courses in anatomy/physiology, chemistry, communication, computers, English, environmental control, finance, microbiology, psychology, and safety (45 points per three credit hour course); and (4) Experience (ten points per year of full-time employment; five points per year of part-time employment; three points per year for per diem workers). **Preparatory Materials:** Bulletin, including exam content outline, glossary of terms, list of suggested references, and sample questions, provided. Study guide available. **Examination Frequency:** semi-annual - always April and October. **Ex-**

amination Sites: Exam given at sites throughout the U.S. and internationally. **Waiting Period to Receive Scores:** Three-four weeks. **Re-examination:** There is a $95 fee to retake exam. **Fees:** $95. **Accredited By:** National Commission for Certifying Agencies. **Endorsed By:** American Society for Healthcare Central Service Personnel; National Organization for Competency Assurance.

1198

Certified Tumor Registrar (CTR)
National Cancer Registrars
 Association (NCRA)
505 E. Hawley St.
Mundelein, IL 60060
Phone: (708)566-0833
Fax: (708)566-7282

Recipient: Professionals involved in hospital-wide cancer tumor registries. **Educational/Experience Requirements:** Must meet one of the following requirements: (1) Two years experience; (2) Successful completion of college level curriculum in cancer data management/cancer registry; or (3) One year of experience and either successful completion of college level curriculum in medical records, nursing, or other allied health field or current licensure in recognized allied health field. **Membership:** Not required. **Certification Requirements:** Successful completion of two-part exam. Part one covers: (1) Abstracting and Coding, including: Content; Principles of abstracting and coding; and Staging concepts; (2) Anatomy, Physiology, and Histology, including: Body locations and position; Characteristics of cancer; Derivation of cells and tissues; and Tissues, body systems, and neoplasms; (3) Computer Principles, including: Basic concepts; and System analysis; (4) Registry Organization and Operation, including: Cancer program activities; Cancer registry files; Case-finding; Commission on Cancer; Confidentiality of information; Follow-up methodology; Health care delivery systems; Health facility relationships; Management principles; Patient care evaluations; Quality control; and Reports; and (5) Statistics and Epidemiology, including: Epidemiology; Preparation of reports; Statistical techniques; and Study design. Part two covers International Classification of Diseases for Oncology coding exercises and staging exercises by site for the following areas: Bones, joints, and articular cartilage; Breast; Connective, subcutaneous, and other soft tissues; Digestive organs and peritoneum; Endocrine glands; Eye and lacrimal gland; Genitourinary organs; Hematopoietic and reticuloendothelial systems; Lip, oral cavity, and pharynx; Lymph nodes; Nervous system; Respiratory system and intrathoracic organs; Skin; and Other body areas. **Renewal:** Recertification based on continuing education. **Preparatory Materials:** Handbook, including list of suggested study references and sample questions, provided. **Examination Frequency:** semiannual - always January and July. **Examination Sites:** Exam given at sites throughout the U.S. **Examination Type:** Multiple-choice. **Waiting Period to Receive Scores:** Six weeks. **Re-examination:** There is no limit to how many times exam may be retaken. Fees to retake exam are: $175 (members); $250 (nonmembers). **Fees:** $175 (members); $250 (nonmembers).

1199

Registered Electroencephalographic Technologist (REEGT)

American Board of Registration of Electroencephalographic and Evoked Potential Technologists (ABRET)
PO Box 11434
Norfolk, VA 23517
Phone: (804)627-5503
Patricia Smith, Exec.Dir.

Recipient: Professionals involved in evoked potential technology. **Educational/Experience Requirements:** Must meet the following requirements: (1) High school diploma or equivalent; and (2) One year of experience in any combination of experience, formal schooling, or on-the-job training. **Certification Requirements:** Successful completion of written and oral/practical exams. Written exam covers: (1) Basic Science, including: Clinical neurology; Electricity and electronic concepts; Neuroanatomy; and Neurophysiology; (2) EEG Instrumentation, including: Calibration; Differential amplifiers; Digital; Filters; Sensitivity calculations; Troubleshooting; and Waveform measurements; (3) EEG Recording Techniques, including: Activation procedures; AEEGS guidelines; Artifacts; Electrode placement; Localization and polarity; Montages; and Uses of instrument setting changes; (4) EEG Pattern Recognition, including: Abnormal patterns; Artifacts; Medication and drug effects; Normal awake patterns; Normal sleep patterns; and Normal variants; (5) Clinical Conditions and EEG Correlates, including: Apnea; Brain tumors; Cerebrovascular disease; Congenital and developmental disorders; Head trauma; Headaches; Narcolepsy; Neuro-degenerative diseases; Psychiatric and psychological disorders;

Seizures; and Toxic, metabolic, and infectious conditions; and (6) Patient Protection, Safety, and Environmental Issues, including: Cardiopulmonary resuscitation; Electrical safety; Hazardous items; Infection control; Patient rights and confidentiality; Patient sedation; and Seizure management and precautions. **Preparatory Materials:** Handbook, including exam content outline, list of suggested references, and sample questions, provided. **Examination Frequency:** semiannual (written) - always May and October. Oral/practical exam given throughout year. **Examination Sites:** Exams given at sites throughout the U.S. **Examination Type:** Multiple-choice. **Waiting Period to Receive Scores:** Six weeks. **Re-examination:** May retake oral/practical exam three times. Must successfully complete exams within five years. **Fees:** $150. **Endorsed By:** American Society of Electroneurodiagnostic Technologists.

1200

Registered Electroencephalographic Technologists (REPT)

American Board of Registration of Electroencephalographic and Evoked Potential Technologists (ABRET)
PO Box 11434
Norfolk, VA 23517
Phone: (804)627-5503
Patricia Smith, Exec.Dir.

Recipient: Professionals involved in electroencephalographic technology. **Educational/Experience Requirements:** Must meet the following requirements: (1) High school diploma or equivalent; and (2) One year of experience in any combination of experience, formal schooling, or on-the-job training. **Certification Requirements:** Successful completion of written and oral/practical exams. Written exam covers: (1) Technical Sciences, including: Analog to digital conversion; Calibration; Differential amplifier; Electrical concepts; Evoked potential validation and criteria for reproducibility - normative data; Filters; Noise reduction; Patient grounding and electrical safety; Recording techniques; Signal averaging; Signal to noise ratio; and Types of noise in evoked potential recording; (2) Anatomy and Neurophysiology, including: Anatomical correlates of evoked potential; Auditory; Basic neurophysiology; Clinical neurology and medicine; Evoked potential maturation; General anatomy; Somatosensory system; Terminology; and Visual; (3) Evoked Potentials, including: Brainstem auditory; Generator sources; Somatosensory; Surgical; Visual; and Other evoked poten-

tials; and (4) Clinical Conditions, including: Coma; Degenerative diseases; Demyelinating disease; Infections; Medications; Trauma; Tumors; Vascular disease; and Other diagnostic procedures. **Preparatory Materials:** Handbook, including exam content outline, list of suggested references, and sample questions, provided. **Examination Frequency:** semiannual (written) - always May and October. Oral/practical exam given throughout the year. **Examination Sites:** Exams given at sites throughout the U.S. **Examination Type:** Multiple-choice. **Waiting Period to Receive Scores:** Six weeks. **Re-examination:** May retake oral/practical exam three times. Must successfully complete exams within five years. **Fees:** $150. **Endorsed By:** American Society of Electroneurodiagnostic Technologists.

1201

Registered Polysomnographic Technologist (RPSGT)

Association of Polysomnographic Technologists (APT)
PO Box 14861
Lenexa, KS 66285-4861
Phone: (913)541-1991
Fax: (913)541-0156
Gary Hansen, Chair

Recipient: Polysomnographic technologists. **Educational/Experience Requirements:** Must meet the following requirements: (1) One year of clinical or research laboratory human polysomnography experience; and (2) Certification in Basic Cardiac Life Support (BCLS). **Membership:** Not required. **Certification Requirements:** Successful completion of three-part exam. Part I covers: (1) Overnight Testing Procedures, including: Gathering and analyzing information; Monitoring, recording, and ending tests; Recording scoring; and Setting-up and calibrating equipment; (2) Patient and Equipment Safety, including: Equipment safety, handling, and cleaning; and Patient safety and emergency procedures; and (3) Special Procedures, including: Continuous positive airway pressure; Infant/pediatric polysomnography; Multiple sleep latency testing; Nocturnal penile tumescence; and Supplemental oxygen administration. Part II covers: (1) Calibrations, including: Machine; and Physiologic; (2) Events and Artifacts; and (3) Scoring, including: MSLT and NPT; and Sleep stage. Part III is practical exam requiring set-up, equipment calibration, and conduct of overnight polysomnographic study. Must successfully complete Parts I and II before attempting Part III. **Preparatory Materials:** *Candidate Handbook and Study*

Guide for the Registry Examination, including exam content outline, list of suggested readings, and sample questions, provided. **Examination Frequency:** semi-annual (Parts I and II); three times per year (Part III). **Examination Sites:** Exam given at sites throughout the U.S. **Examination Type:** Multiple-choice. **Waiting Period to Receive Scores:** 45 days. **Re-examination:** Must only retake part failed. Must successfully complete Parts I and II within two years. Must successfully complete Part III within two years of successfully completing Parts I and II. Fees to retake Part I or Part II are: $125 (members); $150 (nonmembers). Fees to retake Part III are: $150 (members); $200 (nonmembers).

Marketing and Sales Occupations

Auctioneers

1202

Certified Auctioneer (CA)
National Auctioneers Association
(NAI)
8880 Ballentine
Overland Park, KS 66214
Phone: (913)541-8084
Fax: (913)894-5281
Joseph G. Keefhaver, Exec. VP

Recipient: Auctioneers. **Certification Requirements:** Successful completion of course held at Indiana University. **Renewal:** Every three years.

Cashiers

1203

Certified Store Professional (CSP)
National Association of College
Stores (NACS)
500 E. Lorain St.
Oberlin, OH 44074
Phone: (216)775-7777
Fax: (216)775-4769
Toll Free: (800)622-7498
E-mail: mbecker@nacs.org
Marcia Becker, Coord.

Recipient: Professional college store personnel. **Educational/Experience Requirements:** Accumulation of points through education, experience, bookstore and industry activities, and community involvement. **Membership:** Not required. **Certification Requirements:** Successful completion of exam. **Renewal:** Every five years. Recertification based on point system. **Preparatory Materials:** *Principles of College Bookstore Management* (refer-

ence). Reading list available. **Examination Frequency:** Throughout the year. **Examination Sites:** Exam given at sites throughout the U.S. **Examination Type:** Essay; fill-in the blank; matching; multiple-choice; true or false. **Waiting Period to Receive Scores:** Six weeks. **Fees:** $125 (members); $225 (nonmembers).

Insurance Agents and Brokers

1204

Accredited Adviser in Insurance (AAI)
Insurance Institute of America
(IIA)
720 Providence Rd.
PO Box 3016
Malvern, PA 19355-0716
Phone: (610)644-2100
Fax: (610)640-9576
Toll Free: (800)644-2101
Daniel P. Hussey Jr., Dir.

Recipient: Insurance agency managers, production personnel, and field representative supervisors. **Educational/Experience Requirements:** none. **Membership:** Not required. **Certification Requirements:** Successful completion the of following courses, including exams, covering major coverages: (1) Agency Operations and Sales Management; (2) Multiple-Lines Insurance Production; and (3) Principles of Insurance Production, including: Commercial insurance; Insurance sales; Legal liability; and Personal lines. Courses can be taken through group- or independent-study. Candidates who have successfully completed IIA Program in General Insurance or certain CPCU courses, or hold the Certified In-

surance Counselor (CIC) designation (see separate entry), are exempt from Agency Operations and Sales Management course. **Renewal:** Every three years. Recertification based on continuing education. **Examination Type:** Essay. **Pass/Fail Rate:** 70-72% pass exams. **Endorsed By:** American Council on Education; Independent Insurance Agents of America.

1205

Accredited Customer Service Representative (ACSR)
Independent Insurance Agents of
America (IIAA)
127 S. Peyton St.
PO Box 1497
Alexandria, VA 22314
Phone: (703)683-4422
Fax: (703)688-7556
Toll Free: (800)221-7917
Trelle Shaw, Admin.

Recipient: Insurance customer service representatives. **Educational/Experience Requirements:** One year of experience recommended. **Certification Requirements:** Successful completion of study modules and exams. Certification available in commercial or personal lines. Must successfully complete Errors and Omissions Loss Control and Professional Development and Account Management core modules for each designation. Personal Line candidates must successfully complete following modules: (1) Homeowners, covering: Eligibility requirements; Endorsements; Exclusions and limitations; HO forms for tenants and condo owners; and Section I and II coverage features; (2) Personal Auto, covering: Coverages; Endorsements; Legal liability and automobile exposures; and Specific coverages, including damage to auto, liability, medical payments, and uninsured/underinsured motorists; and

(3) Personal Lines Related Coverages, covering: Dwelling policy forms; Floater policies; Flood insurance; Personal umbrella policies; and Variations in boat policies. Commercial Line candidates must successfully complete following modules: (1) Commercial Property, covering: Business income forms and options; Loss forms; and Property conditions and forms; (2) Commercial Liability, covering: CGL; Commercial umbrella policies; Liability endorsements; and Occurrence and claims made forms; (3) Auto and Garage Policies, covering: Business auto coverage; Endorsements; Garage forms; and Truckers forms; and (4) Commercial Lines Related Coverages, covering: Bonds; BOP and other package policies; Crime policies; Inland marine coverage; and Workers' compensation. Candidates seeking both designations must only complete core modules once. May choose from classroom or self-study options. **Renewal:** Every year. Recertification based on accumulation of six hours of continuing education. **Endorsed By:** American Institute for CPCU; Insurance Institute of America.

1206

Associate in Automation Management (AAM)

Insurance Institute of America (IIA)
720 Providence Rd.
PO Box 3016
Malvern, PA 19355-0716
Phone: (610)644-2100
Fax: (610)640-9576
Toll Free: (800)644-2101
Dr. Robert J. Gibbons CPCU, VP

Recipient: Professionals in insurance automation management. **Educational/Experience Requirements:** none. **Membership:** Not required. **Certification Requirements:** Successful completion of the following three courses, including exams: (1) Automation in Insurance; (2) Essentials of Automation; and (3) Managing Automated Activities. Courses can be taken through group- or independent-study. **Renewal:** none. **Examination Type:** Essay. **Endorsed By:** American Council on Education; National Association of Insurance Women (International).

1207

Associate, Customer Service (ACS)

Life Office Management Association (LOMA)
5770 Powers Ferry Rd.
Atlanta, GA 30327-4308
Phone: (404)951-1770
Fax: (404)984-0441

Recipient: Customer service professionals in life and health insurance and financial services industries. **Membership:** Not required. **Certification Requirements:** Successful completion of the following courses, including exams: (1) Principles of Life and Health Insurance, including: Application, underwriting, and policy issues; Basic types of life insurance products; Beneficiaries and their rights; Contractual requirements; Group insurance principles and group life insurance; Group retirement plans; Individual annuities and investment products; Insurance and insurance industry; Life insurance policy provisions; Managed care coverages and providers; Meeting needs for life insurance; Paying life insurance proceeds; Policy ownership rights; Pricing life insurance; and Traditional health insurance coverages and providers; (2) Life and Health Insurance Company Operations, including: Accounting functions; Actuarial functions; Additional distribution systems; Agency building distribution systems; Claim administration; Customer service; Ethics and professionalism; Formation of life and health insurance companies; Human resources information systems; Insurance companies and their environment; Internal organization of insurance companies; International operations; Investment operations; Legal operations; Marketing fundamentals; and Underwriting functions; (3) Legal Aspects of Life and Health Insurance, including: Annuity contracts; Assignments and other transfers; Beneficiary designations and changes; Contracts and agency; Formation and structure of life insurance policy; Group insurance and health insurance; Insurance advertising and privacy; Insurers and agents as employers; Lapse and reinstatement; Legal environment; Life and health insurance agency; Nonforfeiture provisions and policy loans; Policy provisions, benefits, and limitations; Premiums and dividends; Property rights in life insurance policy; Remedies, policy contests, and contract performance; Settlement options, trusts, and wills; and Waiver and estoppel; (4) Marketing Life and Health Insurance, including: Advertising, personal selling, sales promotion, and publicity; Basic product concepts; Consumer behavior; Distribution channel concepts; Informa-

tion management and marketing research; Introduction to marketing; Life and health insurance distribution systems; Managing customer relationship; Market segmentation and target marketing; Marketing environment; Marketing to organizational buyers; Organizing, implementing, and controlling marketing activities; Persistency, replacement, and customer service; Price and pricing; Product development and management; Regulatory influences on marketing; and Strategic planning and marketing planning; and (5) Foundations of Customer Service, including: Building customer service culture; Customer expectations and perceptions; Customer service research; Developing customer service strategy; Developing dedicated customer service staff; Establishing customer service system; Measuring customer service system's performance; Preparing to help customer; Staying ready to help customer; Understanding communication process; and Working with customer. **Preparatory Materials:** Catalog, including lists of required study aids and texts and course learning outcomes provided. Student and test preparation guides, instructors' manuals, study groups, and mentors available. **Examination Frequency:** semiannual - always May and November. Exams also given by computer throughout the year. **Examination Sites:** Exam given at sites throughout the U.S. **Waiting Period to Receive Scores:** One month.

1208

Associate in Fidelity and Surety Bonding (AFSB)

Insurance Institute of America (IIA)
720 Providence Rd.
PO Box 3016
Malvern, PA 19355-0716
Phone: (610)644-2100
Fax: (610)640-9576
Toll Free: (800)644-2101
S. Wesley Porter AFSB, Dir.

Recipient: Professionals in the fidelity and surety bond industry. **Educational/Experience Requirements:** none. **Membership:** Not required. **Certification Requirements:** Successful completion of the following courses, including exams: (1) Accounting and Finance, including basic accounting and property and casualty insurance company accounting requirements; (2) Contract Surety; (3) Fidelity and Noncontract Surety; (4) Legal Environment of Insurance, covering the application of business law to insurance situations; and (5) Principles of Suretyship. Courses can be taken through group- or independent-study. **Renewal:** none. **Examination Type:** Essay. **Endorsed By:** American Council on Education; National Association of Surety Bond Producers; Surety Association of America.

1209

Associate, Insurance Agency Administration (AIAA)

Life Office Management Association (LOMA)
5770 Powers Ferry Rd.
Atlanta, GA 30327-4308
Phone: (404)951-1770
Fax: (404)984-0441

Recipient: Non-sales and company home or regional office employees for life and health insurance agencies. **Membership:** Not required. **Certification Requirements:** Successful completion of the following courses, including exams: (1) Principles of Life and Health Insurance, including: Application, underwriting, and policy issues; Basic types of life insurance products; Beneficiaries and their rights; Contractual requirements; Group insurance principles and group life insurance; Group retirement plans; Individual annuities and investment products; Insurance and insurance industry; Life insurance policy provisions; Managed care coverages and providers; Meeting needs for life insurance; Paying life insurance proceeds; Policy ownership rights; Pricing life insurance; and Traditional health insurance coverages and providers; (2) Life and Health Insurance Company Operations, including: Accounting functions; Actuarial functions; Additional distribution systems; Agency building distribution systems; Claim administration; Customer service; Ethics and professionalism; Formation of life and health insurance companies; Human resources information systems; Insurance companies and their environment; Internal organization of insurance companies; International operations; Investment operations; Legal operations; Marketing fundamentals; and Underwriting functions; (3) Marketing Life and Health Insurance, including: Advertising, personal selling, sales promotion, and publicity; Basic product concepts; Consumer behavior; Distribution channel concepts; Information management and marketing research; Introduction to marketing; Life and health insurance distribution systems; Managing customer relationship; Market segmentation and target marketing; Marketing environment; Marketing to organizational buyers; Organizing, implementing, and controlling marketing activities; Persistency, replacement, and customer service; Price and pricing;

Product development and management; Regulatory influences on marketing; and Strategic planning and marketing planning; (4) Foundations of Customer Service, including: Building customer service culture; Customer expectations and perceptions; Customer service research; Developing customer service strategy; Developing dedicated customer service staff; Establishing customer service system; Measuring customer service system's performance; Preparing to help customer; Staying ready to help customer; Understanding communication process; and Working with customer; and (5) Agency Administration, including: Agency office automation; Agency office management concepts; Agency organization and structure; Communication and professional image; Compliance and sales practices; Introduction to agency law; Marketing insurance products; Office productivity and budgetary control; Salary administration and employee benefits; Solving problems in agency office; Supervisory skills; Supporting sales function; and Working with people. **Preparatory Materials:** Catalog, including lists of required study aids and texts and course learning outcomes, provided. **Examination Frequency:** semiannual - always May and November. Exams also given by computer throughout the year. **Examination Sites:** Exam given at sites throughout the U.S. **Waiting Period to Receive Scores:** One month.

1210

Associate in Insurance Services (AIS)

Insurance Institute of America (IIA)
720 Providence Rd.
PO Box 3016
Malvern, PA 19355-0716
Phone: (610)644-2100
Fax: (610)640-9576
Toll Free: (800)644-2101
Warren T. Hope Ph.D., VP

Recipient: Professionals in insurance or related businesses. **Educational/Experience Requirements:** none. **Membership:** Not required. **Certification Requirements:** Successful completion of the following courses, including exams: (1) Commercial Insurance; (2) Delivering Insurance Services; (3) Personal Insurance; and (4) Property and Liability Insurance Principles. Courses can be taken through group- or independent-study. **Renewal:** none. **Examination Type:** Essay. **Endorsed By:** American Council on Education; Life Office Management Association; Society of Insurance Research.

1211

Associate in Marine Insurance Management (AMIM)

Insurance Institute of America (IIA)
720 Providence Rd.
PO Box 3016
Malvern, PA 19355-0716
Phone: (610)644-2100
Fax: (610)640-9576
Toll Free: (800)644-2101
Arthur L. Flitner CPCU, Dir.

Recipient: Marine insurance professionals. **Educational/Experience Requirements:** none. **Membership:** Not required. **Certification Requirements:** Successful completion of the following courses, including exams: (1) Ethics, Insurance Perspectives, and Insurance Contract Analysis; (2) Inland Marine Insurance; (3) Insurance Operations; (4) Legal Environment of Insurance; (5) Management, covering basic management concepts and how they apply in insurance organizations; and (6) Ocean Marine Insurance. Courses can be taken through group or independent-study. **Renewal:** none. **Examination Type:** Essay. **Endorsed By:** American Council on Education; American Institute of Marine Underwriters; Inland Marine Underwriters Association.

1212

Associate in Reinsurance (ARe)

Insurance Institute of America (IIA)
720 Providence Rd.
PO Box 3016
Malvern, PA 19355-0716
Phone: (610)644-2100
Fax: (610)640-9576
Toll Free: (800)644-2101
Michael W. Elliott AIAF, Asst.VP

Recipient: Insurance professionals involved in reinsurance. **Educational/Experience Requirements:** none. **Membership:** Not required. **Certification Requirements:** Successful completion of the following courses, including exams: (1) Accounting and Finance, including basic accounting and property and casualty insurance company accounting requirements; (2) Insurance Operations; (3) Principles of Reinsurance; and (4) Reinsurance Practices. Courses can be taken through group- or independent-study. **Renewal:** none. **Examination Type:** Essay. **Endorsed By:** American Council on Education; Brokers and Reinsurance Markets Association; CPCU Society.

█1213█

Certified Insurance Counselor (CIC)
Society of Certified Insurance
   Counselors (CIC)
PO Box 27027
Austin, TX 78755-1027
Phone: (512)345-7932
Fax: (512)343-2167
William T. Hold Ph.D., Pres.

Recipient: Insurance counselors. **Educational/Experience Requirements:** Must meet one of the following requirements: (1) Hold license as insurance agent, broker, or solicitor; (2) Two years experience in insurance industry; or (3) Two years experience as college/university insurance instructor. **Membership:** Not required. **Certification Requirements:** Successful completion of the following classes, including exams: (1) Commercial Property Institute, covering: Commercial inland marine coverages; Commercial property causes of loss forms; Commercial property coverages; Commercial property endorsements; and Time element coverages; (2) Commercial Casualty Institute, covering: Business automobile coverages; Commercial general liability; Excess liability/commercial umbrella coverages; and Workers compensation; (3) Personal Lines Institute, including the following coverages: Condominium; Homeowners; Personal automobile; and Personal umbrella/excess; (4) Agency Management Institute, covering: Agency planning; Financial management; Group discussions on marketing and sales management; Human resource management; Internal systems and automation; Legal and ethical responsibilities; and Marketing and sales management; and (5) Life and Health Institute, covering: Applications of life and health insurance to business and personal needs; Essentials of group, individual disability income, health, and life insurance; and Organizational structure and marketing techniques for life and health insurance. **Renewal:** Every year. Recertification based on attendance at one Society sponsored seminar program or institute. **Examination Frequency:** Throughout the year. **Examination Sites:** Courses given at sites throughout the U.S., Puerto Rico, and internationally.

█1214█

Certified Insurance Service Representative (CISR)
Society of Certified Insurance
   Service Representatives
PO Box 27028
3630 North Hills Dr.
Austin, TX 78755-1028
Phone: (512)346-7358
William T. Hold Ph.D., Pres.

Recipient: Insurance customer service representatives. **Number of Certified Individuals:** 5075. **Membership:** Not required. **Certification Requirements:** Successful completion of the following courses, including exams: (1) Agency Operations, covering: Agency systems, including applications, billing, binders, cancellations, certificates of insurance, claims processing, policy issuance, and renewals; Automation in the agency; Ethics and legal obligations; Independent agency relations with companies and customers; and Professionalism and professional relationships; (2) Insuring Personal Auto Exposures, covering: Coverage of personal auto policies; Endorsements to personal auto policies, including no-fault; and Personal umbrella coverages; (3) Insuring Personal Residential Property, covering: Comparing dwelling fire and homeowners policies; and Homeowner's policies and all major endorsements; (4) Introduction to Commercial Casualty Insurance, covering: Commercial automobile and garage insurance; Endorsements and risks; General liability; and Workers compensation; and (5) Introduction to Commercial Property Coverages, covering: Coverage provided by commercial property policy, including buildings and contents; Endorsements; and Essentials of commercial property insurance. Credit for courses from programs from other related associations may be accepted as replacements for CISR courses. **Renewal:** Every year. Recertification based on attendance at one of the following: (1) One CISR course; (2) Advanced Lecture Series course; or (3) Certified Insurance Counselor Institute. This option fulfills requirement for two years. **Examination Frequency:** Throughout the year. **Examination Sites:** Courses given at sites throughout the U.S. **Re-examination:** Must successfully complete all exams within three years.

█1215█

**Certified Professional Insurance
   Agent (CPIA)**
Certified Professional Insurance
   Agents Society (CPIA Society)
400 N. Washington St.
Alexandria, VA 22314
Phone: (703)836-0834
Fax: (703)836-1279
Kathleen McCarty, Dir.

Recipient: Individuals licensed in, or associated with casualty/property insurance sales and marketing. **Number of Certified Individuals:** 700. **Educational/Experience Requirements:** none. **Membership:** Required. **Certification Requirements:** Successful completion of three modules on sales and three modules in the following specialized areas: Commercial lines; Loss prevention; Marketing; and Risk management. **Renewal:** Every year. Recertification based on accumulation of eight hours of approved continuing education. **Preparatory Materials:** none.

█1216█

**Certified Professional Insurance
   Man (CPIM)**
National Association of Insurance
   Women - International (NAIW)
1847 E. 15th
PO Box 4410
Tulsa, OK 74159
Phone: (918)744-5195
Fax: (918)743-1968
Toll Free: (800)766-6249
Kay O'Bryant, Exec. Officer

Recipient: Insurance professionals. **Membership:** Required. **Certification Requirements:** Must meet the following requirements: (1) Three years membership in NAIW; (2) Five years experience; (3) Successful completion of NAIW education program; and (4) Recognized insurance-related designation or membership. **Renewal:** none. **Fees:** $15.

█1217█

**Certified Professional Insurance
   Woman (CPIW)**
National Association of Insurance
   Women - International (NAIW)
1847 E. 15th
PO Box 4410
Tulsa, OK 74159
Phone: (918)744-5195
Fax: (918)743-1968
Toll Free: (800)766-6249
Kay O'Bryant, Exec. Officer

Recipient: Insurance professionals. **Membership:** Required. **Certification Requirements:** Must meet the following requirements: (1) Three years membership in NAIW; (2) Five years experience; (3) Successful completion of NAIW education program; and (4) Recognized insurance-related designation or membership. **Renewal:** none. **Fees:** $15.

1218

Fellow, Life Management Institute (FLMI)

Life Office Management Association (LOMA)
5770 Powers Ferry Rd.
Atlanta, GA 30327-4308
Phone: (404)951-1770
Fax: (404)984-0441

Recipient: Professionals in life and health insurance and financial services industries. **Membership:** Not required. **Certification Requirements:** Successful completion of the following courses, including exams: (1) Principles of Life and Health Insurance, including: Application, underwriting, and policy issues; Basic types of life insurance products; Beneficiaries and their rights; Contractual requirements; Group insurance principles and group life insurance; Group retirement plans; Individual annuities and investment products; Insurance and insurance industry; Life insurance policy provisions; Managed care coverages and providers; Meeting needs for life insurance; Paying life insurance proceeds; Policy ownership rights; Pricing life insurance; and Traditional health insurance coverages and providers; (2) Life and Health Insurance Company Operations, including: Accounting functions; Actuarial functions; Additional distribution systems; Agency building distribution systems; Claim administration; Customer service; Ethics and professionalism; Formation of life and health insurance companies; Human resources information systems; Insurance companies and their environment; Internal organization of insurance companies; International operations; Investment operations; Legal operations; Marketing fundamentals; and Underwriting functions; (3) Legal Aspects of Life and Health Insurance, including: Annuity contracts; Assignments and other transfers; Beneficiary designations and changes; Contracts and agency; Formation and structure of life insurance policy; Group insurance and health insurance; Insurance advertising and privacy; Insurers and agents as employers; Lapse and reinstatement; Legal environment; Life and health insurance agency;

Nonforfeiture provisions and policy loans; Policy provisions, benefits, and limitations; Premiums and dividends; Property rights in life insurance policy; Remedies, policy contests, and contract performance; Settlement options, trusts, and wills; and Waiver and estoppel; (4) Marketing Life and Health Insurance, including: Advertising, personal selling, sales promotion, and publicity; Basic product concepts; Consumer behavior; Distribution channel concepts; Information management and marketing research; Introduction to marketing; Life and health insurance distribution systems; Managing customer relationship; Market segmentation and target marketing; Marketing environment; Marketing to organizational buyers; Organizing, implementing, and controlling marketing activities; Persistency, replacement, and customer service; Price and pricing; Product development and management; Regulatory influences on marketing; and Strategic planning and marketing planning; (5) Management of Organizations and Human Resources, including: Authority, delegation, and decentralization; Control methods; Controlling; Emerging concepts in management; Evolution of management theory; Groups and communication; Human resource management; Interpersonal and organizational communication; Leadership; Motivation, performance, and satisfaction; Organizing for stability and change; Planning; Problem solving and decision making; Social responsibility and ethics; and Strategic planning and strategic management; (6) Information Management in Insurance Companies, including: Artificial intelligence in business; Business information systems; Computer hardware and software; Database management; Descriptive and inductive statistics; End user computing and office automation; Information systems for operations, management, and strategic advantage; International and ethical dimensions of information technology; Introduction to information systems; Management science models and concepts; Managerial decision making and executive support; Measuring, graphing, and describing data; Planning, implementing, and controlling information technology; Solving business problems with information systems; Telecommunications; Time series analysis, regression analysis, probability, and sampling; and Transaction processing and information reporting; (7) Accounting in Life and Health Insurance Companies, including: Accounting information systems; Accounting for investments; Capital and surplus; Claim and contract settlement; Cost accounting; Financial accounting fundamentals; Financial statements used by U.S. and Cana-

dian life and health insurers; GAAP and statutory accounting; Internal control and auditing; Introduction to life and health insurance accounting; Planning and budgeting; Policy benefit accounting; Premium and commission accounting; Separate accounts; and Tax accounting; (8) Economics and Investments, including: Bond investment, valuation, and analysis; Common stock investment and analysis; Economics; Government intervention in marketplace; International trade; Investment markets and transactions; Labor market; Market structures and competition; Measuring investment return and risk; Money, monetary policy, and banking; Mutual funds; Planning, building, and managing portfolio; Productivity and economic growth; Real estate investments; Role and scope of investments; Supply and demand; and U.S. and Canadian economies; and (9) Mathematics of Life and Health Insurance, including: Accumulated value of annuities certain; Accumulated value of money; Dividends; Fundamentals of mathematics; Group life insurance premiums, reserves, and dividends; Health insurance premiums, reserves, and dividends; Life annuities; Life insurance premiums; Modified reserve methods; Mortality tables; Net level premium reserves; Nonforfeiture values; Present value of annuities certain; Present value of money; and Role of actuary. Must also successfully complete one of the following elective courses: (1) Financial Management, including: Capital budgeting and cash flow principles; Capital budgeting in insurance companies; Cash and marketable securities; Cost of capital and short-term financing; Financial planning and decision-making; Financial ratio analysis in insurance companies; Financial statements, analysis, and planning; Insurance investment operations and practices; International finance; Long-term financing: expansion and failure; Operating environment of firm; Role of finance and financial manager; and Time value of money, risk/return, and valuation; (2) Group Insurance, including: Actuarial aspects of group insurance; Cafeteria plans; Creditor, association, and Taft-Hartley groups; Government environment; Government social insurance programs; Group benefit plan design; Group disability income insurance; Group insurance in Canada; Group long-term care insurance; Group marketing and administration; Group medical expense insurance; Group reinsurance; Methods of funding group insurance; Post-retirement coverage; and Team coverage and group life underwriting; (3) Human Resources Administration, including: Appraising and improving performance; Auditing human resources management program; Creating productive work environment; Employee benefits; Human resource planning; International human resources management; Managing employee compensation; Measuring compensation and benefits; Measuring employee relations and activities; Measuring planning and staffing; Measuring training and development; Nondiscriminatory employment laws and regulations; Recruitment and selection; Safety and health; and Training and career development; (4) Information Systems (IS), including: Analyzing systems; Decision support systems; Designing and formatting systems; Electronic document management; Executive information systems; Expert systems; Group support systems; Information requirements analysis; IS implementation; Managing end user computing, mobile computing, and multimedia; Managing essential IS technologies; Managing human side of systems; Managing system development; Managing systems analysis and design activities; Prototyping; Quality assurance and software engineering; Strategic role of IS and IS planning; Systems analysis fundamentals; and Systems proposals; (5) Management Science, including: Basic concepts of probability; Case studies in management science; Decision making using probabilities; Distribution models: transportation and assignment problems; Forecasting; Goal programming; Insurance applications of management science techniques; Integar programming; Inventory models; Linear programming; Management science in life and health insurance companies; Management science/operations research; Markov analysis; Network models: Pert, CPM, and dynamic programming; Probability distributions; Simulation; and Waiting lines and queuing theory; and (6) Managerial Accounting, including: Applications of managerial accounting concepts; Capital budgeting and other investment decisions; Case studies in managerial accounting; Control of decentralized operations and service department cost allocations; Cost terms, cost behavior, and cost measurement systems design; Cost-volume-profit relationships; Financial statement analysis; Financial statements, profit centers, pricing, and expense allocation; Flexible budgets and overhead analysis; Managerial accounting in life and health insurance companies; Pricing products and services; Profit planning and cost control; Segmented reporting and contribution approach to costing; and Using cost data in decision making. Candidates who hold either Associate, Life and Health Claims (ALHC) or Fellow, Academy of Life Underwriting (FALU) designations (see separate entries) are given credit for elective. **Pre-**

paratory Materials: Catalog, including lists of required study aids and texts and course learning outcomes, provided. **Examination Frequency:** semiannual - always May and November. Exams also given by computer throughout the year. **Examination Sites:** Exam given at sites throughout the U.S. **Waiting Period to Receive Scores:** One month.

`1219`

Health Insurance Associate (HIA)
Health Insurance Association of America (HIAA)
555 13th St., NW, Ste. 600 E.
Washington, DC 20004-1109
Phone: (202)223-7789
Fax: (202)824-1800

Recipient: Professionals involved in health insurance. **Educational/Experience Requirements:** none. **Membership:** Not required. **Certification Requirements:** Successful completion of the following self-study courses, including exams: (1) Group Life and Health Insurance, Group A, covering: Basic underwriting; Concept and history of group insurance; Contracts; Group medical coverages: types of benefits; Marketing; Other group insurance coverages; Pricing; and Special underwriting situations; (2) Group Life and Health Insurance, Group B, covering: Claim administration and examination; Claim processing and related issues; Experience refunds; Government activity related to insurance; Group insurance in Canada; Issue and basic administration; Other aspects of administration; and Reporting and interpreting financial results; (3) Group Life and Health Insurance, Group C, covering: Computers in insurance; Current industry challenges; Employer viewpoints in structuring a group plan; Flexible benefit plans; Funding benefits; Group universal life; Long-term care; Managing health care costs; Meeting insurance needs of retired employees; and Rehabilitation and managing disability income claims; (4) Individual Health Insurance, Individual A, covering: Contracts; Development of health insurance; Disability income insurance; Marketing; Medical expense insurance; Need for health insurance; Policy issue, renewal, and service; and Underwriting; and (5) Individual Health Insurance, Individual B, covering: Challenges in health care; Controlling health care costs; Data processing and information systems; Health insurance claims; Investments; Pricing health insurance product; Regulation; and Reports. **Preparatory Materials:** Course texts and study guides provided. Audio- and video-tapes available. **Examination**

Frequency: Throughout the year. **Examination Sites:** Exams given by arrangement with proctor. **Waiting Period to Receive Scores:** Four-six weeks. **Reexamination:** Fees to retake each course are: $50 (members); $75 (nonmembers). **Fees:** $300 (members); $425 (nonmembers).

`1220`

Managed Healthcare Professional (MHP)
Health Insurance Association of America (HIAA)
555 13th St., NW, Ste. 600 E.
Washington, DC 20004-1109
Phone: (202)223-7780
Fax: (202)824-1800

Recipient: Professionals involved in managed healthcare insurance. **Educational/Experience Requirements:** none. **Membership:** mnr **Certification Requirements:** Successful completion of five self-study courses, including exams. Required courses are: (1) Managed Care, Part A, covering: Administrative systems and practices; Development of managed care; Employer and managed care; Government as managed care sponsor; Government as regulator; Individual and managed care; Managed care structure and organization; Medical management; Need for strategy to contain rising health care costs; Overview and summary; Physicians and managed care; and Quality; (2) Managed Care, Part B, covering: Administrative structures; Benefit design and plan offerings; Customer service; Developing network; Financial structures; Marketing; and Risk sharing; and (3) Long-Term Care, covering: Future of financing; Government programs; Group insurance products; Methods of long-term care protection; Private insurance; Services and costs; and What is long-term care and who needs it? Must also successfully complete either Group life and health insurance or individual health insurance courses. Group life and health insurance courses are: (1) Group Life and Health Insurance, Group A, covering: Basic underwriting; Concept and history of group insurance; Contracts; Group medical coverages: types of benefits; Marketing; Other group insurance coverages; Pricing; and Special underwriting situations; and (2) Group Life and Health Insurance, Group B, covering: Claim administration and examination; Claim processing and related issues; Experience refunds; Government activity related to insurance; Group insurance in Canada; Issue and basic administration; Other aspects of administration; and Reporting and interpreting financial results. Individual health insurance courses are: (1) Individual Health Insurance, Individual A, covering: Contracts; Development of health insurance; Disability income insurance; Marketing; Medical expense insurance; Need for health insurance; Policy issue, renewal, and service; and Underwriting; and (2) Individual Health Insurance, Individual B, covering: Challenges in health care; Controlling health care costs; Data processing and information systems; Health insurance claims; Investments; Pricing health insurance product; Regulation; and Reports. **Preparatory Materials:** Course texts and study guides provided. Audio- and videotapes available. **Examination Frequency:** Throughout the year. **Examination Sites:** Exams given by arrangement with proctor. **Waiting Period to Receive Scores:** Four-six weeks. **Re-examination:** Fees to retake each course are: $50 (members); $75 (nonmembers). **Fees:** $300 (members); $425 (nonmembers).

Manufacturers' and Wholesale Sales Representatives

1221

Certified Machine Tool Sales Engineer (CMTSE)
American Machine Tool Distributors' Association (AMTDA)
1335 Rockville Pike, Ste. 300
Rockville, MD 20852
Phone: (301)738-1200
Fax: (301)738-9499
Barbra A. Laird, Mgr.

Recipient: Machine tool sales engineers. **Number of Certified Individuals:** 465. **Educational/Experience Requirements:** One year of outside sales experience and one of the following: (1) Four years related machine tool employment in applications, inside or outside sales, service, and training; or (2) Bachelor's degree and two years related experience. **Membership:** Not required. **Certification Requirements:** Successful completion of exam. Exam covers: (1) Planning and Organizing, including: Establishing priorities; Goal measurement; Relevant technical material; and Reviewing customer base; (2) Developing Plan of Action, including: Analyzing information; Communicating with customer; Formulating preliminary plan of action; Preparing and verifying proposal accuracy and format; and Selecting appropriate selling strategy; (3) Implementing Plan of Action, including: Concluding sales proce-

dure; Initiating selling strategy; and Responding to customer feedback; (4) Managing Results, including: Coordinating requirements and progress; and Verifying purchase order and proposal information; and (5) Legal and Ethical Issues. **Renewal:** Every three years. Recertification based on accumulation of Professional Development Points through related continuing education, attendance at technical conferences, symposia, and workshops, teaching, publishing articles and papers, experience, and other professional activities. **Preparatory Materials:** Study guide, including glossary, list of suggested study references, and sample questions, provided. Reference bibliography and study material available. **Examination Frequency:** semiannual - always April and November. **Examination Sites:** Exam given at regional sites in the U.S. **Examination Type:** Multiple-choice. **Waiting Period to Receive Scores:** Four weeks. **Re-examination:** May retake exam one time. Fee to retake exam is $75. **Fees:** $750 (members); $950 (nonmembers). **Endorsed By:** Association for Manufacturing Technology; National Tooling and Machining Association.

1222

Certified Medical Representative (CMR)
Certified Medical Representatives Institute (CMRI)
4950 Brambleton Ave., SE
Roanoke, VA 24018
Toll Free: (800)274-2674

Recipient: Pharmaceutical representatives. **Membership:** Not required. **Certification Requirements:** Must accumulate 36 credits through successful completion of prerequisite and elective CMRI correspondence courses, including exams. Prerequisite courses are: (1) Human Body, Pathology, and Treatment (four credits), including: Body systems and diagnostic tools; Health professional's perspective; Introduction to pathology; and Treatment approaches; and (2) Introduction to Pathology (four credits), including: Basic principles of drug actions and interactions; and Therapeutic classes. Scientific/medical elective courses, covering anatomy and physiology, disorders, and pharmacology of drugs of the following systems: Cardiovascular (four credits); Digestive (three credits); Endocrine (two credits); Immune (three credits); Integumentary (two credits); Musculoskeletal (three credits); Nervous (three credits); Reproductive (three credits); Respiratory (three credits); Sensory organs (two credits); and Urinary (two credits). Trends and Issues

in Healthcare elective courses (maximum of six credits) are: (1) Biomedical Ethics (one credit), including: Economic issues in biomedical ethics; Issues of life and death; and Overview of biomedical ethics; (2) Epidemic and Catastrophic Disease (two credits), including: AIDS; Immunization and preventable diseases; Overview of epidemiology; and Streptococcal virulence and related diseases; (3) Nutrition and Disease, including: Diseases related to nutrition; and Role of nutrition in severely ill patients; (4) Nutrition and Good Health, including: Functions of nutrients in the body; Importance of healthy diet and lifestyle; and Nutrient standards and food guides for health promotion; and (5) Quality-of-Life Issues, including: Health and quality of life; Impact on quality-of-life issues on healthcare; Quality-of-life measurements; and Utility and quality of life. Other elective courses are: (1) Behavioral Pathology and Treatment (three credits), including: Behavioral disorders; Pharmacology related to behavioral disorders; and Psychotherapy; (2) Changing Roles of Healthcare Providers (one credit); (3) Formulatory Process - Challenges and Opportunities (one credit); (4) Healthcare Community (three credits), including: Healthcare delivery; Healthcare funding; and Healthcare providers; (5) Impact of Drug Resistance on Antibiotic Therapy (two credits); (6) Managed Healthcare (three credits), including: Changing roles of physician and hospital; Delivery systems; Impact of managed healthcare on key accounts; Key players; and Managed pharmacy; (7) Medical Applications of Biotechnology (two credits); (8) Pain Management (one credit); (9) Pharmaceutical Industry (three credits), including: Development and distribution of pharmaceutical products; Evolution of pharmaceutical industry; and Pharmaceutical industry and society; (10) Pharmaceutical and Medical Research (three credits), including: Design, methodology, and analysis of research; and Research costs and constraints; (11) Pharmacoeconomics (three credits), including: Case study review of key pharmacoeconomic models; Components of pharmacoeconomic research; Context of pharmacoeconomics; and Review of pharmacoeconomic methods; (12) Total Disease Management (three credits); and (13) Women's Health Issues (one credit). May challenge courses through successful completion of exams. **Examination Frequency:** Three times per year. **Examination Sites:** Exams given at sites throughout the U.S. **Waiting Period to Receive Scores:** 30 days. **Re-examination:** There is no limit to how many times exams may be retaken. **Fees:** $2160 (members); $3240 (nonmembers). **Endorsed By:** American Council on Education.

`1223`

Certified Professional Food Broker (CPFB)

Manufacturers Representatives Educational Research Foundation (MRERF)
PO Box 247
Geneva, IL 60134
Phone: (708)208-1466
Fax: (708)208-1475
Toll Free: (800)346-7373
Marilyn Stephens Ed.D., Exec. VP

Recipient: Owners of food broker firms or the heir for ownership. **Educational/Experience Requirements:** High school diploma or equivalent and five years experience. **Membership:** Required. **Certification Requirements:** Successful completion of course of study, including exams. **Renewal:** Every five years. Recertification based on accumulation of three continuing education units (CEUs). Renewal fee is $100. **Preparatory Materials:** Textbooks for each course and list of suggested reading available. **Examination Frequency:** semiannual - always January and August. **Examination Sites:** Exams given at Arizona State University in January and Indiana University in August. **Examination Type:** Multiple-choice. **Pass/Fail Rate:** 95% pass exams the first time. **Waiting Period to Receive Scores:** Three weeks. **Re-examination:** There is no time limit to retake exams. **Fees:** $995.

`1224`

Certified Professional Manufacturers Representative (CPMR)

Manufacturers Representatives Educational Research Foundation (MRERF)
PO Box 247
Geneva, IL 60134
Phone: (708)208-1466
Fax: (708)208-1475
Toll Free: (800)346-7373
Marilyn Stephens Ed.D., Exec. VP

Recipient: Owners of manufacturers representative firms or the heir for ownership. **Educational/Experience Requirements:** High school diploma or equivalent and five years experience. **Membership:** Required. **Certification Requirements:** Successful completion of course of study, including exams. **Renewal:** Every five years. Recertification based on accumulation of three continuing education units (CEUs). Renewal fee is $100. **Preparatory Materials:** Textbooks for each course and list of sug-

gested reading available. **Examination Frequency:** semiannual - always January and August. **Examination Sites:** Exams given at Arizona State University in January and Indiana University in August. **Examination Type:** Multiple-choice. **Pass/Fail Rate:** 95% pass exams the first time. **Waiting Period to Receive Scores:** Three weeks. **Re-examination:** There is no time limit to retake exams. **Fees:** $995.

Real Estate Agents, Brokers, and Appraisers

`1225`

Accredited in Appraisal Review (AAR)

Accredited Review Appraisers Council (ARAC)
303 W. Cypress St.
PO Box 12528
San Antonio, TX 78212
Phone: (210)225-2897
Fax: (210)225-8450
Toll Free: (800)486-3676
Deborah J. Deane AAR, Pres.

Recipient: Individuals who analyze and review real estate appraisal reports. **Membership:** Required. **Certification Requirements:** Successful completion of Principles of Appraisal Review course, including demonstration report and exam. Course covers: Analysis of expenses; Appraisal management; Basic principles of real property values; Capitalization techniques; Discounted cash flow; FDIC appraisal rules; FNMA guidelines; Gross income estimates; Lease valuation; Relating income to value; Review of appraisal process; Reviewing narrative report; Uniform standards; and URAR appraisal report. **Renewal:** none. **Preparatory Materials:** *Principles of Appraisal Review* (text). Bibliography and copies of current laws and regulations available. **Examination Frequency:** Throughout the year. **Examination Sites:** Course and exam given at sites throughout the U.S. **Fees:** $345.

`1226`

Accredited Land Consultant (ALC)

Realtors Land Institute (RLI)
430 N. Michigan Ave.
Chicago, IL 60611
Phone: (312)329-8440
Toll Free: (800)441-LAND

Recipient: Land brokers involved with

investment land and development in both rural and urban areas. **Educational/Experience Requirements:** Must meet the following requirements: (1) Submission of resume of professional, business, and civic background; (2) Submission of one narrative report describing most difficult non-residential transaction; (3) Service for one year on RLI Board of Governors or national committee, and attendance at two national meetings; (4) Either service for one year as elected RLI chapter officer or one year as active committee member for RLI state chapter, and attendance at two meetings; and (5) Sponsorship of two new RLI members. Educational requirements are as follows: (1) Candidates with less than five years experience or less than $5 million nonresidential sales production must successfully complete seven RLI Land University courses; or (2) Candidates with five years experience and more than $5 million non-residential sales or sales supervision must successfully complete three RLI Land University courses. **Membership:** Required. **Certification Requirements:** Successful completion of exam and oral interview. **Renewal:** Recertification based on continuing education. **Examination Sites:** Exam and oral interview given at RLI national meeting. **Endorsed By:** National Association of Realtors.

`1227`

Accredited Rural Appraiser (ARA)

American Society of Farm Managers and Rural Appraisers (ASFMRA)
950 S. Cherry St., Ste. 508
Denver, CO 80222
Phone: (303)758-3513
Fax: (303)758-0190
Cheryl L. Cooley, Coord.

Recipient: Real estate review appraisers specializing in rural property. **Educational/Experience Requirements:** Must meet the following requirements: (1) Five years experience; (2) Bachelor's degree or equivalent; and (3) Submission of narrative appraisal demonstration report. **Membership:** Not required. **Certification Requirements:** Successful completion of the following courses, including exams, and written and oral exams. Courses are: (1) Advanced Rural Appraisal, covering: Cost approach; Income approach; Lease analysis; and Sales comparison approach; (2) Eminent Domain, covering: Bundle of rights; Condemnation; Damages and benefits; Easements; Highest and best use zoning; Just compensation; Larger parcel; Law; Partial takings; and Trial preparation and participation; (4) Fundamentals of Rural

Appraisal, covering: Appraisal concepts; Area descriptions; Cost approach; Ethics; Income approach; Legal descriptions; Sales comparison approach; Uniform Standards of Professional Appraisal Practice; and Valuation process; (5) Highest and Best Use, covering principles behind various types of land use; (6) Income Capitalization-Unleveraged, covering: Direct capitalization; Financial functions; Lease valuation; and Unleveraged yield capitalization; (7) Principles of Rural Appraisal, covering: Annuity capitalization; Cash equivalency; Cost approach; Depreciation; Direct and straight line capitalization; Highest and best use; Income approach; Market abstraction; and Sales comparison approach; (8) Report Writing School, covering: Grammar; Letter writing; Persuasion and argumentation; Reader's goals; Report content; and Writing styles; and (9) Standards and Ethics. Courses may be challenged by exam with ASFMRA approval. **Renewal:** Every three years. Recertification based on accumulation of 60 continuing education credits. **Preparatory Materials:** Study guides and reference publications available. **Examination Frequency:** semiannual. **Examination Sites:** Exam given at two sites in the U.S. every year. **Re-examination:** May retake exams one time. **Fees:** $4265 (members); $5130 (nonmembers).

1228

Assessment Administration Specialist (AAS)
International Association of Assessing Officers (IAAO)
130 E. Randolph St., Ste. 850
Chicago, IL 60601
Phone: (312)819-6104
Fax: (312)819-6149
Karen Graf, Coord.

Recipient: Assessors and appraisers specializing in valuation of business personal property or personal property assessment administration. **Educational/Experience Requirements:** Must meet the following requirements: (1) High school diploma or equivalent; (2) Three years experience; (3) Successful completion of IAAO Standards of Practice and Professional Ethics Workshop, including exam, or equivalent; (4) Successful completion of the following IAAO courses, including exams: Assessment Administration; Fundamentals of Real Property Appraisal; Income Approach to Value; and Tax Appraisal; and (5) Successful completion of either seminars, workshops, or courses related to mass appraisal or public administration. Educational requirements must have been successfully completed within

last ten years. IAAO courses may be challenged through successful completion of exams. Courses given by other associations may be substituted for IAAO courses. **Membership:** Required. **Certification Requirements:** Successful completion of the following: (1) Either assessment administration case study or administration research project; and (2) Exam. Oral exam may be required. **Renewal:** Every five years. Recertification based on accumulation of 45 hours of continuing education. **Preparatory Materials:** *Professional Designation Program Requirements* (reference). Demonstration appraisal report writing guides available. **Examination Frequency:** Throughout the year. **Examination Sites:** Exam given by arrangement with proctor. **Re-examination:** Must wait 30 days to retake exam.

1229

Board Certified in Business Appraisal (BCBA)
Real Estate Law Institute (RELI)
303 W. Cypress
PO Box 12528
San Antonio, TX 78212
Phone: (210)225-2897
Fax: (210)225-8450
Gary T. Deane, Exec. Officer

Recipient: Business real estate appraisers. **Number of Certified Individuals:** 160. **Certification Requirements:** Must meet the following requirements: (1) Successful completion of Principles of Business Appraisal course, including exam; and (2) Submission of business appraisal report. **Renewal:** none. **Fees:** $100.

1230

Board Certified in Business Valuation
Professional Certification Board (PCB)
303 W. Cypress
PO Box 12528
San Antonio, TX 78212-0528
Phone: (210)271-0781
Fax: (210)225-8450
Toll Free: (800)486-3676
Gary T. Deane Ed.D., Exec.Dir.

Recipient: Real estate professionals involved in business valuation. **Educational/Experience Requirements:** none. **Membership:** Not required. **Certification Requirements:** Must meet the following requirements: (1) Successful completion of Principles of Business Appraisal course, including exam; and

(2) Presentation of demonstration business appraisal report. **Examination Frequency:** Throughout the year. **Examination Sites:** Course given at sites throughout the U.S. **Examination Type:** Multiple-choice. **Waiting Period to Receive Scores:** Two weeks. **Fees:** $370. **Endorsed By:** Real Estate Law Institute.

1231

Board Certified in Manufactured Housing Valuation
Professional Certification Board (PCB)
303 W. Cypress
PO Box 12528
San Antonio, TX 78212-0528
Phone: (210)271-0781
Fax: (210)225-8450
Toll Free: (800)486-3676
Gary T. Deane Ed.D., Exec.Dir.

Recipient: Real estate professionals involved in manufactured housing valuation. **Educational/Experience Requirements:** none. **Membership:** Not required. **Certification Requirements:** Must meet the following requirements: (1) Successful completion of Principles of Manufactured Housing Appraisal course, including exam; and (2) Presentation of demonstration manufactured housing valuation report. **Examination Frequency:** Throughout the year. **Examination Sites:** Course given at sites throughout the U.S. **Examination Type:** Multiple-choice. **Waiting Period to Receive Scores:** Two weeks. **Fees:** $370. **Endorsed By:** Real Estate Law Institute.

1232

Board Certified in Real Estate Litigation Management (RLM)
Real Estate Law Institute (RELI)
303 W. Cypress
PO Box 12528
San Antonio, TX 78212
Phone: (210)225-2897
Fax: (210)225-8450
Gary T. Deane, Exec. Officer

Recipient: Real estate litigation management appraisers. **Number of Certified Individuals:** 100. **Certification Requirements:** Must meet the following requirements: (1) Successful completion of Effective Court Testimony course, including exam; and (2) Submission of business appraisal report. **Renewal:** none. **Fees:** $100.

〖1233〗

Cadastral Mapping Specialist (CMS)

International Association of
Assessing Officers (IAAO)
130 E. Randolph St., Ste. 850
Chicago, IL 60601
Phone: (312)819-6104
Fax: (312)819-6149
Karen Graf, Coord.

Recipient: Assessors specializing in development and maintenance of cadastral mapping system. **Educational/ Experience Requirements:** Must meet the following requirements: (1) High school diploma or equivalent; (2) Three years experience; (3) Successful completion of both seminar or workshop and course related to cadastral mapping or geographical information systems; and (4) Successful completion of the following IAAO courses, including exams: Fundamentals of Mapping; and Fundamentals of Real Property Appraisal. Educational requirements must have been successfully completed within last ten years. IAAO courses may be challenged through successful completion of exams. Courses given by other associations may be substituted for IAAO courses. **Membership:** Required. **Certification Requirements:** Successful completion of the following: (1) Case Problem on Cadastral Mapping; and (2) Exam. Oral exam may be required. **Renewal:** Every five years. Recertification based on accumulation of 45 hours of continuing education. **Preparatory Materials:** *Professional Designation Program Requirements* (reference). Demonstration appraisal report writing guides available. **Examination Frequency:** Throughout the year. **Examination Sites:** Exam given by arrangement with proctor. **Re-examination:** Must wait 30 days to retake exam.

〖1234〗

Certified Appraiser Consultant (CA-C)

American Association of Certified
Appraisers (AACA)
800 Compton Rd., Ste. 10
Cincinnati, OH 45231
Phone: (513)729-1400
Fax: (513)729-1401
Toll Free: (800)543-AACA

Recipient: Commercial and industrial appraiser consultants. **Educational/ Experience Requirements:** Must meet the following requirements: (1) College degree; and (2) Hold Certified Appraiser Senior (CA-S) designation (see separate entry)

for two years; and (3) Successfully complete 15 hours of study in Uniform Standards of Professional Appraisal Practice (USPAR). **Membership:** Required. **Certification Requirements:** Successful completion of consultant thesis based on evaluation process as presented in the USPAR. **Renewal:** Every three years. Recertification based on accumulation of 30 contact hours of continuing education. **Fees:** $275. **Endorsed By:** Appraisal Foundation.

〖1235〗

Certified Appraiser Farm and Land (CA-FL)

American Association of Certified
Appraisers (AACA)
800 Compton Rd., Ste. 10
Cincinnati, OH 45231
Phone: (513)729-1400
Fax: (513)729-1401
Toll Free: (800)543-AACA

Recipient: Farm and land appraisers. **Educational/Experience Requirements:** Must meet the following requirements: (1) Two years experience; and (2) Either 120 hours of appraisal education, including 15 hours in Uniform Standards of Professional Appraisal Review (US-PAR), or state licensure or certification as appraiser. Candidates whose education does not meet AACA or state requirements must successfully complete entrance exam. **Membership:** Required. **Certification Requirements:** Submission of farm and land narrative report based on market comparison and/or income valuation. **Renewal:** Every three years. Recertification based on accumulation of 30 contact hours of continuing education. **Fees:** $275. **Endorsed By:** Appraisal Foundation.

〖1236〗

Certified Appraiser of Personal Property (CAPP)

International Society of Appraisers
(ISA)
Riverview Plaza Office Park, Ste. 320
16040 Christensen Rd.
Seattle, WA 98188
Phone: (206)241-0359
Fax: (206)241-0436
Chris Coleman CAPP, Exec.Dir.

Recipient: Personal property appraisers. **Educational/Experience Requirements:** Successful completion of the following core courses: (1) 101, consisting of the following parts: Definitions of Value and

Markets; Intended Uses of Appraisals; Methods and Principles of Appraising; and Professional Appraisal Practice; (2) 102, consisting of the following parts: The Appraiser and the Law; Basic Appraiser Techniques; Code of Ethics and Professional Conduct, USPAP, and Other Standards; Identification and Authentication; and Market and Value Research; and (3) 103, consisting of the following parts: Advanced Report Writing; and Basic Report Writing. **Membership:** Required. **Certification Requirements:** Successful completion of the following courses: (1) Advanced Appraisal Studies; (2) Advanced Report Writing; (3) Identification and Authentication; (4) Laws, Case Law, and Regulations; (5) Market Identification and Analysis; (6) Methodology; (7) Research; and (8) Specialty Knowledge. **Preparatory Materials:** *ISA Standards* (reference). Seminars and workshops available. **Examination Sites:** Courses given at sites throughout the U.S. **Examination Frequency:** Five times per year.

〖1237〗

Certified Appraiser Residential (CA-R)

American Association of Certified
Appraisers (AACA)
800 Compton Rd., Ste. 10
Cincinnati, OH 45231
Phone: (513)729-1400
Fax: (513)729-1401
Toll Free: (800)543-AACA

Recipient: Residential appraisers. **Educational/Experience Requirements:** Must meet the following requirements: (1) Two years experience; and (2) Either 120 hours of appraisal education, including 15 hours in Uniform Standards of Professional Appraisal Review (US-PAR), or state licensure or certification as appraiser. Candidates whose education does not meet AACB or state requirements must successfully complete entrance exam. **Membership:** Required. **Certification Requirements:** Submission of either residential narrative report written to specific professional standards or seven form appraisal reports. **Renewal:** Every three years. Recertification based on accumulation of 30 contact hours of continuing education. **Fees:** $275 **Endorsed By:** Appraisal Foundation.

1238

Certified Appraiser Senior (CA-S)
American Association of Certified
    Appraisers (AACA)
800 Compton Rd., Ste. 10
Cincinnati, OH 45231
Phone: (513)729-1400
Fax: (513)729-1401
Toll Free: (800)543-AACA

Recipient: Commercial and industrial appraisers. **Educational/Experience Requirements:** Must meet the following requirements: (1) Five years experience in commercial/industrial appraising; and (2) Either 165 hours of appraisal education, including successful completion of 15 hours in Uniform Standards of Professional Appraisal Review (USPAR), or state certification as general appraiser. Candidates whose education does not meet AACA or state qualifications must successfully complete entrance exam. **Membership:** Required. **Certification Requirements:** Submission of commercial/industrial narrative report written to specific professional standards. **Renewal:** Every three years. Recertification based on accumulation of 30 contact hours of continuing education. **Fees:** $275. **Endorsed By:** Appraisal Foundation.

1239

Certified Assessment Evaluator (CAE)
International Association of
    Assessing Officers (IAAO)
130 E. Randolph St., Ste. 850
Chicago, IL 60601
Phone: (312)819-6104
Fax: (312)819-6149
Karen Graf, Coord.

Recipient: Assessors involved in single property and mass appraisals and assessment administration. **Educational/Experience Requirements:** Must meet the following requirements: (1) High school diploma or equivalent; (2) Five years experience; (3) Successful completion of IAAO Standards of Practice and Professional Ethics Workshop, including exam, or equivalent; and (4) Successful completion of the following IAAO courses, including exams: Assessment Administration; Fundamentals of Real Property Appraisal; Income Approach to Value; and Mass Appraisal of Residential Property. Educational requirements must have been successfully completed within last ten years. IAAO courses may be challenged through successful completion of exams. Courses given by other associations may be substituted for IAAO

courses. Successful completion of four additional courses may be substituted for one year of experience. **Membership:** Required. **Certification Requirements:** Successful completion of the following: (1) Either residential demonstration appraisal report, using all recognized approaches to value, on single-family residence, or residential demonstration appraisal report on computer-assisted valuation of group of residential properties; (2) Either commercial demonstration appraisal report, using all recognized approaches to value, on income-producing property, or Mass Appraisal Case Study Exam; and (3) Comprehensive Exam. Comprehensive Exam covers: Appraisal principles and techniques; and Assessment theory, practice, procedures, standards, and administration. Oral exam may be required. **Renewal:** Every five years. Recertification based on accumulation of 45 hours of continuing education. **Preparatory Materials:** *Professional Designation Program Requirements* (reference). Demonstration appraisal report writing guides available. **Examination Frequency:** Throughout the year. **Examination Sites:** Exam given by arrangement with proctor. **Re-examination:** Must wait 30 days to retake exam.

1240

Certified Commercial Investment Member (CCIM)
Commercial Investment Real Estate
    Institute (CIREI)
430 N. Michigan Ave., Ste. 600
Chicago, IL 60611-4092
Phone: (312)321-4485
Fax: (312)321-4530
Toll Free: (800)621-7027

Recipient: Real estate professionals involved in commercial real estate asset management, brokerage, investment analysis, leasing, and valuation. **Number of Certified Individuals:** 4000. **Educational/Experience Requirements:** Must meet the following requirements: (1) Successful completion of five graduate level courses (18 credits) including the following core requirements: Financial Analysis for Commercial Real Estate; Market Analysis for Commercial Real Estate; and Decision Analysis for Commercial Real Estate; and (2) Submission of Resume of Qualifying Experience documenting transactions involving commercial real estate. May substitute successful completion of exams for course credit. **Membership:** Required. **Certification Requirements:** Successful completion of exam. **Preparatory Materials:** *CCIM Designation Handbook* (ref-

erence). Course outlines and review and audio home-study courses available. **Examination Sites:** Exam given at Institute meetings. **Pass/Fail Rate:** 92% pass exam. **Waiting Period to Receive Scores:** Immediately. **Re-examination:** There is no waiting period to retake exam. **Endorsed By:** International Association of Corporate Real Estate Executives; International Council of Shopping Centers; International Development Research Council; National Association of Realtors.

1241

Certified Commercial Real Estate Appraiser (CCRA)
National Association of Real Estate
    Appraisers (NAREA)
8383 E. Evans Rd.
Scottsdale, AZ 85260
Phone: (602)948-8000
Fax: (602)998-8022
Toll Free: (800)537-2069
E. Kenneth Twichell, Mng.Dir.

Recipient: Real estate appraisers. **Membership:** Required. **Certification Requirements:** Hold general real estate property state license or certificate and meet experience requirements. **Renewal:** none. **Fees:** $195.

1242

Certified Exchanger
Certified Exchangers (CE)
PO Box 12490
Scottsdale, AZ 85267-2490
Phone: (602)860-8838

Recipient: Real estate exchanging professionals. **Educational/Experience Requirements:** Must demonstrate competency in field. **Certification Requirements:** Successful completion of exam program.

1243

Certified Form Appraiser (CF-A)
American Association of Certified
    Appraisers (AACA)
800 Compton Rd., Ste. 10
Cincinnati, OH 45231
Phone: (513)729-1400
Fax: (513)729-1401
Toll Free: (800)543-AACA

Recipient: Form appraisers. **Educational/Experience Requirements:** Must meet the following requirements: (1) Two years experience; and (2) Either

120 hours of appraisal education, including 15 hours in Uniform Standards of Professional Appraisal Review (US-PAR), or state licensure or certification as appraiser. Candidates whose education does not meet AACA standards or state requirements must successfully complete entrance exam. **Membership:** Required. **Certification Requirements:** Submission of five acceptable appraisal form reports. **Renewal:** Every three years. Recertification based on accumulation of 30 contact hours of continuing education. **Fees:** $275. **Endorsed By:** Appraisal Foundation.

▪1244▪

Certified International Property Specialist (CIPS)

International Real Estate Section, National Association of Realtors
430 N. Michigan Ave.
Chicago, IL 60611-4087
Phone: (312)329-3278
Fax: (312)329-8338
Toll Free: (800)874-6500

Recipient: Real estate professionals specializing in international real estate. **Educational/Experience Requirements:** Must accumulate 100 total points through: (1) Education, including: College degrees; Educational programs attended; and Successful completion of courses; (2) Association Participation, including: Attendance at conferences and meetings; Designations earned; and Offices held; (3) Experience, including: Closed international transactions successfully completed; and Overseas business trips conducted; and (4) Foreign Languages Spoken. **Membership:** Required. **Certification Requirements:** Successful completion of the following courses and exams: (1) Essentials of International Real Estate, including: Capital flow; Cultures; Currencies; Government regulations; International brokerage; International real estate environment; Marketing; Networking; and Selling; (2) Europe and International Real Estate, covering property and people of European Economic Community and Eastern Europe; (3) Asia Pacific and International Real Estate; (4) The Americas and International Real Estate, covering Latin America, Canada, the Caribbean, and the U.S.; and (5) Investment and Financial Analysis for International Real Estate, including: Development of international business and marketing plans; and Evaluation of international opportunities. Must also submit three international transaction sheets involving citizen or property from foreign country. **Preparatory Materials:** Course

books provided. **Examination Frequency:** Throughout the year. **Examination Sites:** Courses given at sites throughout the U.S.

▪1245▪

Certified Market Data Analyst (CMDA)

National Residential Appraisers Institute (NRAI)
2001 Cooper Foster Park Rd.
Amherst, OH 44001
Phone: (216)282-7925
Fax: (216)282-8072
Toll Free: (800)331-2732
Ade Schreiber, Pres.

Recipient: Real estate sales professionals involved in single family residential market analysis. **Educational/Experience Requirements:** Must meet one of the following requirements: (1) Successful completion of NRAI Single Family Appraisal course, including exam. Course covers: Cost, sales comparison, and income approaches to value; Freddie Mac/Fannie Mae URAR forms; and NRAI's *Reproduction Cost Guide,*; (2) Successful completion of appraisal course at college, university, or real estate school or institute; or (3) One year of experience and successful completion of training in market data analyzation of single family properties. **Membership:** Required. **Certification Requirements:** Submission of two correlated market data analysis reports or equivalent. **Examination Sites:** Courses offered throughout Ohio. **Fees:** $265.

▪1246▪

Certified Real Estate Appraiser (CREA)

National Association of Real Estate Appraisers (NAREA)
8383 E. Evans Rd.
Scottsdale, AZ 85260
Phone: (602)948-8000
Fax: (602)998-8022
Toll Free: (800)537-2069
E. Kenneth Twichell, Mng.Dir.

Recipient: Real estate appraisers. **Membership:** Required. **Certification Requirements:** Hold General Real Property, Real Property, or Residential Real Property state license or certificate and meet experience requirements. **Renewal:** none. **Fees:** $195.

▪1247▪

Certified Real Estate Brokerage Manager (CRB)

Real Estate Brokerage Managers Council (RBMC)
430 N. Michigan Ave.
Chicago, IL 60611-4092
Phone: (312)670-3780
Fax: (312)329-8882
Toll Free: (800)621-8738

Recipient: Real estate brokerage managers, including general managers, branch and sales managers, administrative and department managers, recruitment and training specialists, CEOs, presidents, firm owners, and sales associates who manage personal consultants. **Educational/Experience Requirements:** Two consecutive years of experience. **Membership:** Required. **Certification Requirements:** Must meet one of the following requirements: (1) Successful completion of eighteen credits of approved CRB courses, including Decision Making: The Ultimate Challenge course (four credits); or (2) Ten years experience and successful completion of ten credits of approved CRB courses, including exams. Experience must be in position directly responsible for effective management of real estate business as active principal, in brokerage management capacity, or in real estate related management or administrative position. Courses can be chosen from the following different categories: Changing Markets; Increasing Productivity; Increasing Profitability; and Winning Markets Each one-day course equals one credit. Courses include case studies, group activities, problem solving sessions, role playing, and simulations for hands-on training. **Preparatory Materials:** List of required reading provided. Cassette and software programs available. **Examination Frequency:** Throughout the year. **Examination Sites:** Courses given at sites throughout the U.S. **Waiting Period to Receive Scores:** Four-six weeks. **Endorsed By:** National Association of Realtors; Realtors National Marketing Institute.

▪1248▪

Certified Residential Specialist (CRS)

Residential Sales Council (RSC)
430 N. Michigan Ave.
Chicago, IL 60611-4092
Phone: (312)321-4448
Fax: (312)321-4520
Toll Free: (800)462-8841

Recipient: Sales associates in residential

sales field. **Educational/Experience Requirements:** Membership with local board of realtors. **Membership:** Required. **Certification Requirements:** Candidates with less than five years experience must earn total of 85 points, hold Graduate, Realtor Institute (GRI) designation, document either 50 transactions or 25 transactions totaling $3 million in volume, and successfully complete three of the following residential specialist courses, including exams: (1) Building Wealth Through Residential Real Estate Investments, covering: Advantages and disadvantages of housing as investment; Investment concepts; Matching investors to properties; Positioning homes as investments; Salesperson role; and Servicing investors; (2) Business Development, covering: Business budgeting and plan development; Marketing plans; Personal promotion; Personality trait analysis; and Prospecting techniques; (3) Computer Applications, covering: Choosing right computer; Saving money when purchasing or upgrading computer system; and Word processing and graphics programs; (4) Financial Skills, covering: Financing; Introduction to taxes; Personal financial planning; Taxes affecting homeowner; and Taxes affecting real estate professional; (5) Listing Strategies, covering: Closing techniques; Handling objections; Marketing techniques; Preparation for and conducting listing presentation; Pricing; Seller counseling; and Servicing during listing term; (6) Personal and Career Management, covering: Assertiveness development; Goal setting; Life planning; Self-image development; Stress management; and Time management; (7) Sales and Marketing Strategies, covering: Essential ingredients of builders' presentation book; Identifying builders and potential clients; and Servicing techniques; and (8) Sales Strategies, including: Buyer counseling; Communication; Establishing rapport; Motivation; Negotiation strategies; Obtaining buyer decision; and Showing and demonstrating property. Points may also be earned through college degrees, continuing education, experience, other professional certifications, office holding in professional societies, publication of articles, awards received, and presentations given. Candidates with five-nine years experience must meet the following requirements: (1) Hold GRI designation; (2) Successfully complete two of the courses listed above; (3) Document either 75 closed listings or sales or minimum of 40 transactions totaling $1 million in volume per year of experience. Candidates with ten years experience must meet the following requirements: (1) Successfully complete one of the courses listed above and document either 150 close listings or sales, or minimum of 40 transactions totaling $1 million in volume per year of experience; or (2) Successfully complete two of the courses listed above and document either 75 closed listings or sales transactions or minimum of $10 million in sales with minimum of 40 transactions. **Renewal:** Recertification may be required. **Examination Frequency:** Throughout the year. **Examination Sites:** Courses given at sites throughout the U.S. **Waiting Period to Receive Scores:** Four-six weeks. **Re-examination:** May retake exams one time. **Endorsed By:** National Association of Realtors.

`1249`

Certified Review Appraiser (CRA)
National Association of Review
  Appraisers and Mortgage
  Underwriters (NARA/MU)
8383 E. Evans Rd.
Scottsdale, AZ 85260
Phone: (602)998-3000
Fax: (602)998-8022
Robert G. Johnson, Exec.Dir.

Recipient: Review appraisers. **Membership:** Required. **Certification Requirements:** Hold current state appraiser license or certificate. **Renewal:** none. **Fees:** $265.

`1250`

**Certified Review Appraiser -
  Administrative (CRA-A)**
National Association of Review
  Appraisers and Mortgage
  Underwriters (NARA/MU)
8383 E. Evans Rd.
Scottsdale, AZ 85260
Phone: (602)998-3000
Fax: (602)998-8022
Robert G. Johnson, Exec.Dir.

Recipient: Review appraisers who do not hold state license or certificate. **Membership:** Required. **Certification Requirements:** Five years experience in appraisal review. CRA-As are not authorized to change a valuation. **Renewal:** none. **Fees:** $265.

`1251`

Counselor of Real Estate (CRE)
Counselors of Real Estate
430 N. Michigan Ave.
Chicago, IL 60611-4089
Phone: (312)329-8427
Fax: (312)329-8881
Mary Walker Fleischmann, Exec.V. Pres.

Recipient: Real estate professionals who provide counseling services for which they are compensated by pre-arranged fee or salary for services, as opposed to commission or contingent fee. **Membership:** Required. **Certification Requirements:** Ten years experience and demonstration of leadership and commitment to counseling. Post-baccalaureate credentials may be substituted if the candidate has acted as real estate counselor in three of the last ten years. **Endorsed By:** National Association of Realtors.

`1252`

**Designated Real Estate Instructor
  (DREI)**
Real Estate Educators Association
  (REEA)
11 S. LaSalle St., Ste. 1400
Chicago, IL 60603
Phone: (312)201-0101
Fax: (312)201-0214
Cindy Clark, Mng.Dir.

Recipient: Individuals involved in real estate education and training. **Educational/Experience Requirements:** Three years experience, 200 hours as real estate instructor, and accumulation of 125 points through combination of education and experience. **Membership:** Required. **Certification Requirements:** Successful completion of the following: (1) Teaching skills evaluation based on videotape of instructional session. Evaluation covers: Instructional environment and quality; Real estate knowledge; Teaching aids used; and Verbal presentation; and (2) Exam. Exam covers: Broker-level real estate knowledge; and Instructional methodology. **Renewal:** Every three years. Recertification based on accumulation of 85 points through continuing education, experience, and industry participation. **Fees:** $175.

`1253`

Forestland Appraiser (FLA)
Association of Consulting Foresters
  of America (ACF)
5400 Grosvenor Ln., Ste. 300
Bethesda, MD 20814-2198
Phone: (301)530-6795
Fax: (301)530-5128

Recipient: Appraisers qualified to appraise forestland. **Certification Requirements:** Must meet the following requirements: (1) Successful completion of the following courses, including exams: Forestland Appraisal I; Forestland Appraisal II; Forestland Appraisal III (report writing); Real Estate Appraisal Principles 1; Real Estate Appraisal Principles 2; and Uniform Standards of Professional Appraisal Practice; (2) Submission of demonstration forestland appraisal; (3) One year as state-certified general real estate appraiser; (4) Bachelor's or higher degree in forestry from program accredited by Society of American Foresters (see separate entry) or approved by ACF; and (5) Five years (2880 hours) experience, with 200 hours in forestland appraising. Candidate may substitute prior education, appraiser certification, or successful completion of exams for course requirement. Program currently undergoing reorganization. **Renewal:** Every three years. Recertification based on accumulation of 60 hours of continuing education, with 30 hours in forestland appraisal. Must also successfully complete Uniform Standards of Professional Appraisal Practice course every five years. Renewal fee is $250. **Preparatory Materials:** Manual (reference). **Re-examination:** May retake exams two times.

1254

Graduate Senior Appraiser (GSA)
National Residential Appraisers
 Institute (NRAI)
2001 Cooper Foster Park Rd.
Amherst, OH 44001
Phone: (216)282-7925
Fax: (216)282-8072
Toll Free: (800)331-2732
Ade Schreiber, Pres.

Recipient: Real estate professionals involved in one- to four-family residence appraisals in areas such as probate, tax valuations, divorce settlements for attorneys and other legal situations, and listing and selling. **Educational/Experience Requirements:** Two years experience and meet one of the following requirements: (1) Successful completion of NRAI Single Family Appraisal course, including exam. Course covers: Cost, sales comparison, and income approaches to value; Freddie Mac/Fannie Mae URAR forms; and NRAI's *Reproduction Cost Guide,*; (2) Successful completion of appraisal course covering URAR forms; or (3) Earning other real estate designation. **Membership:** Required. **Certification Requirements:** Submission of two Uniform Residential Appraisal Reports (URARs). **Examination Sites:** Courses offered throughout Ohio. **Fees:** $265.

1255

Independent Fee Appraiser (IFA)
National Association of
 Independent Fee Appraisers
 (NAIFA)
7501 Murdoch Ave.
St. Louis, MO 63119
Phone: (314)781-6688
Fax: (314)781-2872
Robert G. Kaestner, Exec.V.Pres.

Recipient: Independent residential real estate fee appraisers. **Educational/Experience Requirements:** Must meet the following requirements: (1) Two years of college or equivalent; (2) 2000 hours of experience; and (3) 120 hours of coursework in subjects related to real-estate appraisal, including coverage of *Uniform Standards of Professional Appraisal Practice* (USPAP). **Membership:** Required. **Certification Requirements:** Successful completion of NAIFA-approved residential appraising course, exam, and submission of narrative residential appraisal report or five URAR appraisal reports. Reports must be on one- to four- family residences, which may include residential condominiums. One report must cover: (1) Cost Approach, including: Acceptable method of accrued depreciation; Basis or source of cost data; and Land value justification; (2) Market Data Comparison, covering comparable sales used, including but not limited to: Description of property; Explanation and justification for all adjustments made, by market extraction or justification by cost; Recordation data; and Terms and conditions of sale; and (3) Income Approach, including: Rental comparison to justify economic rent; and Sales comparison to justify gross monthly multiplier. Exam will be waived for candidates with state license or certification in residential appraisal. **Renewal:** Recertification based on continuing education. **Preparatory Materials:** Review courses available. **Endorsed By:** Appraisal Foundation.

1256

**Independent Fee
 Appraiser/Agricultural (IFAA)**
National Association of
 Independent Fee Appraisers
 (NAIFA)
7501 Murdoch Ave.
St. Louis, MO 63119
Phone: (314)781-6688
Fax: (314)781-2872
Robert G. Kaestner, Exec.V.Pres.

Recipient: Independent agricultural real estate fee appraisers. **Educational/**

Experience Requirements: Two years of college or equivalent and appraisal experience. **Membership:** Required. **Certification Requirements:** Submission of narrative demonstration appraisal report on agricultural property and successful completion of exam. Exam will be waived for candidates with state general certification. **Renewal:** Recertification based on continuing education. **Preparatory Materials:** Review courses available. **Endorsed By:** Appraisal Foundation.

1257

**Independent Fee
 Appraiser/Counselor (IFAC)**
National Association of
 Independent Fee Appraisers
 (NAIFA)
7501 Murdoch Ave.
St. Louis, MO 63119
Phone: (314)781-6688
Fax: (314)781-2872
Robert G. Kaestner, Exec.V.Pres.

Recipient: Independent real estate fee appraiser consultants. **Educational/Experience Requirements:** Five years experience and hold Independent Fee Appraiser/Senior designation (see separate entry) for three years. **Membership:** Required. **Certification Requirements:** Submission of thesis demonstrating counseling experience. **Renewal:** Recertification based on continuing education. **Preparatory Materials:** Review courses available. **Endorsed By:** Appraisal Foundation.

1258

**Independent Fee Appraiser/Senior
 (IFAS)**
National Association of
 Independent Fee Appraisers
 (NAIFA)
7501 Murdoch Ave.
St. Louis, MO 63119
Phone: (314)781-6688
Fax: (314)781-2872
Robert G. Kaestner, Exec.V.Pres.

Recipient: Independent commercial real estate fee appraisers. **Educational/Experience Requirements:** Must meet the following requirement: (1) Two years of college or equivalent; (2) 2000 hours of experience with at least one thousand hours appraising other than one- to four-family residential properties; and (3) 165 classroom hours in related subjects, including coverage of the *Uniform Standards of Professional Appraisal Practice* (USPAP). **Membership:** Required.

Certification Requirements: Successful completion of NAIFA-approved income-property appraising course and exam, and submission of narrative demonstration appraisal report on income-producing property such as an apartment complex with minimum of eight units, warehouse, industrial building, office complex, shopping center, or special purpose building. Report must cover: (1) Cost Approach, including: Acceptable method of accrued depreciation; Basis or source of cost data; and Land value justification; (2) Market Data Comparison, covering comparable sales used, including but not limited to: Description of property; Explanation and justification for all adjustments made, by market extraction or justification by cost; Recordation data; and Terms and conditions of sale; and (3) Income Approach, including: Rental comparison to justify economic rent; and Sales comparison to justify gross monthly multiplier. Exam will be waived for candidates with state general certification. **Renewal:** Recertification based on continuing education. **Preparatory Materials:** Review courses available. **Endorsed By:** Appraisal Foundation.

1259

Master of Corporate Real Estate (MCR)
Institute for Corporate Real Estate
440 Columbia Dr., Ste. 100
West Palm Beach, FL 33409
Phone: (407)683-8111
Fax: (407)697-4853

Recipient: Real estate professionals specializing in corporate real estate. **Educational/Experience Requirements:** NACORE International. **Membership:** Required. **Certification Requirements:** Must accumulate points through education, experience, and association participation.

1260

Master Farm and Land Appraiser (MFLA)
National Association of Master Appraisers (NAMA)
303 W. Cypress St.
PO Box 12617
San Antonio, TX 78212-0617
Phone: (210)271-0781
Fax: (210)225-8450
Toll Free: (800)229-6262
Harry B. Joachim, Exec.Dir.

Recipient: Farm and land real estate ap-

praisers. **Certification Requirements:** Must meet one of the following requirements: (1) Hold state certified residential appraisal certification, with at least one course in Farm and Land Appraisal; or (2) Two years experience, 120 hours of approved education, including 15 hours each of farm and land appraisal and standards of professional appraisal practice courses, and submission of acceptable residential and farm property demonstration appraisal report. **Renewal:** Every two years. Recertification based on accumulation of 20 hours of continuing education and attendance at Standards of Professional Appraisal Practice course every five years. **Preparatory Materials:** Preparation courses available. **Fees:** $275.

1261

Master Residential Appraiser (MRA)
National Association of Master Appraisers (NAMA)
303 W. Cypress St.
PO Box 12617
San Antonio, TX 78212-0617
Phone: (210)271-0781
Fax: (210)225-8450
Toll Free: (800)229-6262
Harry B. Joachim, Exec.Dir.

Recipient: Residential real estate appraisers. **Membership:** Required. **Certification Requirements:** Must meet one of the following requirements: (1) Hold state appraiser license or equivalent; or (2) Two years experience, 75 hours of education, including 15 hours of standards of professional appraisal practice courses, and submission of residential demonstration appraisal report. **Renewal:** Every two years. Recertification based on accumulation of 20 hours of continuing education and attendance at Standards of Professional Appraisal Practice course every five years. **Preparatory Materials:** Preparation courses available. **Fees:** $275.

1262

Master Senior Appraiser (MSA)
National Association of Master Appraisers (NAMA)
303 W. Cypress St.
PO Box 12617
San Antonio, TX 78212-0617
Phone: (210)271-0781
Fax: (210)225-8450
Toll Free: (800)229-6262
Harry B. Joachim, Exec.Dir.

Recipient: General real estate appraisers. **Membership:** Required. **Certification Re-**

quirements: Must meet one of the following requirements: (1) Hold state Certified General Appraiser designation; or (2) Two years experience, 165 hours of education, including 15 hours of standards of professional appraisal practice courses, and submission of acceptable commercial, farm property, and residential demonstration appraisal report. **Renewal:** Every two years. Recertification based on accumulation of 20 hours of continuing education and attendance at Standards of Professional Appraisal Practice course every five years. **Preparatory Materials:** Preparation courses available. **Fees:** $275.

1263

Member, Appraisal Institute (MAI)
Appraisal Institute (AI)
875 N. Michigan Ave., Ste. 2400
Chicago, IL 60611-1980
Phone: (312)335-4100
Fax: (312)335-4480

Recipient: Real estate appraisers involved in commercial, industrial, residential, and other types of properties. **Educational/Experience Requirements:** Must meet the following requirements: (1) Bachelor's degree; (2) One year as Appraisal Institute candidate; and (3) 4500 hours specialized appraisal experience in other than one-to-four family properties. **Membership:** Required. **Certification Requirements:** Must meet the following requirements: (1) Attendance at the Standards of Professional Practice and Report Writing and Valuation Analysis courses; (2) Successful completion of demonstration report; and (3) Successful completion of ten approved General Appraiser exams and comprehensive exam. **Renewal:** Recertification based on continuing education.

1264

Member, International Society of Appraisers
International Society of Appraisers (ISA)
Riverview Plaza Office Park, Ste. 320
16040 Christensen Rd.
Seattle, WA 98188
Phone: (206)241-0359
Fax: (206)241-0436
Chris Coleman CAPP, Exec.Dir.

Recipient: Personal property appraisers. **Educational/Experience Requirements:** Successful completion of the following core courses: (1) 101, consisting of the following parts: Definitions of Value and Markets; Intended Uses of Appraisals; Methods and Principles of Appraising; and Professional Appraisal Practice; (2) 102, consisting of the following parts: The Appraiser and the Law; Basic Appraiser Techniques; Code of Ethics and Professional Conduct, USPAP, and Other Standards; Identification and Authentication; and Market and Value Research; and (3) 103, consisting of the following parts: Advanced Report Writing; and Basic Report Writing. **Membership:** Required. **Certification Requirements:** Successful completion of the following courses, including exams: (1) Identification and Authentication; (2) Market Identification and Analysis; (3) Methodology and Terminology; (4) Report Writing; (5) Research; (6) Rules and Regulations; and (7) Theory and Principles. **Preparatory Materials:** *ISA Standards* (reference). Seminars available. **Examination Sites:** Courses given at sites throughout the U.S. **Examination Frequency:** Five times per year.

`1265`

Professional Real Estate Executive (PRE)

Society of Industrial and Office Realtors (SIOR)
777 Fourteenth St., NW, Ste. 400
Washington, DC 20005-3271
Phone: (202)737-1150
Fax: (202)737-3142
Nancy B. Bryant, Exec.VP

Recipient: Real estate brokers specializing in industrial and office properties. **Educational/Experience Requirements:** Must meet the following requirements: (1) Six years SIOR membership; (2) Fifteen years experience; and (3) Attendance at four of last eight national and/or regional SIOR conferences. **Membership:** Required. **Certification Requirements:** Successful completion of exam or approved courses. **Endorsed By:** National Association of Realtors.

`1266`

Real Estate Consulting Professional (RECP)

International College of Real Estate Consulting Professionals
297 Dakota St.
Le Sueur, MN 56058
Phone: (612)665-6280
Fax: (612)665-6280

Recipient: Individuals involved in fields related to real estate industry. **Membership:** Required.

`1267`

Real Property Review Appraiser (RPRA)

American Society of Farm Managers and Rural Appraisers (ASFMRA)
950 S. Cherry St., Ste. 508
Denver, CO 80222
Phone: (303)758-3513
Fax: (303)758-0190
Cheryl L. Cooley, Coord.

Recipient: Real estate review appraisers specializing in rural property. **Educational/Experience Requirements:** Must meet the following requirements: (1) One year of experience; (2) Bachelor's degree or equivalent; (3) Current state General Appraiser certification; and (4) Submission of appraisal reviews. **Membership:** Not required. **Certification Requirements:** Successful completion of the following courses, including exams, and written and oral exams. Courses are: (1) Advanced Appraisal Review, covering: Common deficiencies; Procedures and methods of review; Resolving divergences; Use of SARR, UAAR, URAR, and FmHA rural forms; and Writing review report; (2) Advanced Resource Appraisal, covering: Analysis of sales; Cost approach; Income approach; and Sales approach; (3) Advanced Rural Appraisal, covering: Cost approach; Income approach; Lease analysis; and Sales comparison approach; (4) Eminent Domain, covering: Bundle of rights; Condemnation; Damages and benefits; Easements; Highest and best use zoning; Just compensation; Larger parcel; Law; Partial takings; and Trial preparation and participation; (5) Fundamentals of Rural Appraisal, covering: Appraisal concepts; Area descriptions; Cost approach; Ethics; Income approach; Legal descriptions; Sales comparison approach; Uniform Standards of Professional Appraisal Practice; and Valuation process; (6) Highest and Best Use, covering: principles behind various types of land use; (7) Income Capitalization-Unleveraged, covering: Direct capitalization; Financial functions; Lease valuation; and Unleveraged yield capitalization; (8) Principles of Rural Appraisal, covering: Annuity capitalization; Cash equivalency; Cost approach; Depreciation; Direct and straight line capitalization; Highest and best use; Income approach; Market abstraction; and Sales comparison approach; (9) Report Writing, covering: Grammar; Letter writing; Persuasion and Argumentation; Reader's Goals; Report content; and Writing Styles; and (10) Standards and Ethics. Courses may be challenged by exam with ASFMRA approval. **Renewal:** Every three years. Recertification based

on accumulation of 60 continuing education credits. **Preparatory Materials:** Study guides and reference publications available. **Examination Frequency:** semi-annual. **Examination Sites:** Exam given at two sites in the U.S. every year. **Re-examination:** May retake exams one time. **Fees:** $4760 (members); $5755 (nonmembers).

`1268`

Realtor Association Certified Executive (RCE)

National Association of Realtors (NAR)
430 N. Michigan Ave.
Chicago, IL 60610-4087
Phone: (312)329-8200
Fax: (312)329-8391
Mary T. Krukoff, Mgr.

Recipient: Real estate association executives. **Educational/Experience Requirements:** Must meet the following requirements: (1) Employment by local or state association of realtors, wholly owned realtor association subsidiary corporation, or regional multiple listing service owned by realtor association; (2) Be full-time employee of NAR, or real estate board, provincial association, or other organization affiliated with Canadian Real Estate Association; and (3) Accumulate minimum of 350 points (maximum of 575) in the following categories: (A) Experience (50 points minimum; 90 points maximum); (B) Education (280 points minimum; 545 points maximum); (C) Involvement in national, regional, state, or local realtor association activities (180 points minimum; 323 points maximum); (D) Involvement in association management activities outside NAR (40 points minimum; 75 points maximum); and (E) Major accomplishments (25 points maximum). **Membership:** Required. **Certification Requirements:** Successful completion of exam. Exam covers: (1) Association Law and Governance, including: Fair housing/VAMA; Governing documents and policy; Legal and regulatory activities; Member policies and procedures; Political and governmental affairs; and Trademark policies; (2) Realtor Association Management, including: Budget and financial affairs; Computers and technology; Facilities and equipment; General management; General real estate practices; Marketing; Meeting management; Membership development; and Working with volunteers; and (3) Member Services, including: Affiliates, institutes, societies, and councils; Communications and publications; Education programs; MLS; Professional standards; Programming; and Public relations programs. **Renewal:** Every four years. Recertification based on accumulation of 75 points in same areas as initial certification. Renewal fee is $100. Lifetime certification available for retired RCEs. **Preparatory Materials:** Exam content outline and reference list provided. Study guide available. **Examination Sites:** Exam given at annual convention and annual Association Executives Institute. **Examination Type:** Essay; short answer. **Re-examination:** Must wait one year to retake exam. There is a $75 fee to retake exam. **Fees:** $250.

1269

Registered Professional Member of the National Association of Real Estate Appraisers (RPM)

National Association of Real Estate Appraisers (NAREA)
8383 E. Evans Rd.
Scottsdale, AZ 85260
Phone: (602)948-8000
Fax: (602)998-8022
Toll Free: (800)537-2069
E. Kenneth Twichell, Mng.Dir.

Recipient: Real estate appraisers. **Membership:** Required. **Certification Requirements:** One year of experience. **Renewal:** none. **Fees:** $195.

1270

Residential Evaluation Specialist (RES)

International Association of Assessing Officers (IAAO)
130 E. Randolph St., Ste. 850
Chicago, IL 60601
Phone: (312)819-6104
Fax: (312)819-6149
Karen Graf, Coord.

Recipient: Assessors involved in single and mass real property appraisal specializing in valuation of residential properties. **Educational/Experience Requirements:** Must meet the following requirements: (1) High school diploma or equivalent; (2) Three years experience; (3) Successful completion of IAAO Standards of Practice and Professional Ethics Workshop, including exam, or equivalent; and (4) Successful completion of the following IAAO courses, including exams: Fundamentals of Real Property Appraisal; Income Approach to Value; and Mass Appraisal of Residential Property. Educational requirements must have been successfully completed within last ten years. IAAO courses may be challenged through successful completion of

exams. Courses given by other associations may be substituted for IAAO courses. **Membership:** Required. **Certification Requirements:** Successful completion of the following: (1) Either residential demonstration appraisal report, using all recognized approaches to value, on single-family residence, or residential demonstration appraisal report on computer-assisted valuation of group of residential properties; and (2) Exam. Oral exam may be required. **Renewal:** Every five years. Recertification based on accumulation of 45 hours of continuing education. **Preparatory Materials:** *Professional Designation Program Requirements* (reference). Demonstration appraisal report writing guides available. **Examination Frequency:** Throughout the year. **Examination Sites:** Exam given by arrangement with proctor. **Re-examination:** Must wait 30 days to retake exam.

1271

Senior Certified Appraiser (SCA)

National Residential Appraisers Institute (NRAI)
2001 Cooper Foster Park Rd.
Amherst, OH 44001
Phone: (216)282-7925
Fax: (216)282-8072
Toll Free: (800)331-2732
Ade Schreiber, Pres.

Recipient: Real estate fee appraisers. **Educational/Experience Requirements:** Must meet the following requirements: (1) Three years experience; and (2) Current state appraisers certification. **Membership:** Required. **Certification Requirements:** Submission of sample residential, condominium, small income, and commercial appraisal report. **Examination Sites:** Courses offered throughout Ohio. **Fees:** $100.

1272

Senior Licensed Appraiser (SLA)

National Residential Appraisers Institute (NRAI)
2001 Cooper Foster Park Rd.
Amherst, OH 44001
Phone: (216)282-7925
Fax: (216)282-8072
Toll Free: (800)331-2732
Ade Schreiber, Pres.

Recipient: Real estate single family and one- to four-unit single family fee appraisers. **Educational/Experience Requirements:** Must meet the following requirements: (1) Three years experience;

and (2) Current state appraisal licensure. **Membership:** Required. **Certification Requirements:** Submission of sample residential, condominium, and small income appraisal report. **Examination Sites:** Courses offered throughout Ohio. **Fees:** $100.

1273

Senior Real Estate Counselor (SRC)

National Association of Counselors (NAC)
303 W. Cypress
Box 12528
San Antonio, TX 78212-0528
Phone: (210)225-2897
Fax: (210)225-8450
Toll Free: (800)531-5333
Marvin T. Deane, CEO

Recipient: Real estate counselors. **Membership:** Required. **Certification Requirements:** Successful completion of the following courses, including exams: (1) Principles of Real Estate Counseling; (2) Principles of Real Estate Appraisal; and (3) Practice of Real Estate Appraisal. **Renewal:** none. **Fees:** $100.

1274

Specialist, Industrial/Office Real Estate (SIOR)

Society of Industrial and Office Realtors (SIOR)
777 Fourteenth St., NW, Ste. 400
Washington, DC 20005-1150
Phone: (202)737-1150
Fax: (202)737-3142
Nancy B. Bryant, Exec.VP

Recipient: Real estate brokers specializing in industrial and office properties. **Number of Certified Individuals:** 1300. **Educational/Experience Requirements:** Must meet the following requirements: (1) Seven years SIOR membership; (2) Twenty years experience; and (3) Successful completion of two SIOR sponsored courses. **Membership:** Required. **Certification Requirements:** Successful completion of exam or approved course. **Renewal:** Every three years. Recertification based on continuing education. **Examination Sites:** Exam given at SIOR sponsored programs and at national headquarters. **Examination Type:** Essay; multiple-choice; true or false. **Pass/Fail Rate:** 90% pass exam the first time. **Waiting Period to Receive Scores:** Two weeks. **Fees:** $165. **Endorsed By:** National Association of Realtors.

1275

Specialist in Residential Appraisal (SRA)

Appraisal Institute (AI)
875 N. Michigan Ave., Ste. 2400
Chicago, IL 60611-1980
Phone: (312)335-4100
Fax: (312)335-4480

Recipient: Real estate appraisers involved in residential (one-to-four family) properties. **Educational/Experience Requirements:** Must meet the following requirements: (1) Bachelor's degree (or accepted equivalent); (2) One year as an Appraisal Institute candidate; and (3) 3000 hours of residential appraisal experience in one-to-four family properties. **Membership:** Required. **Certification Requirements:** Must meet the following requirements: (1) Successful completion of Advanced Residential Form and Narrative Report Writing and Standards of Professional Practice courses; (2) Successful completion of demonstration report; and (3) Successful completion of four approved exams. **Renewal:** Recertification based on continuing education.

Retail Sales Workers

1276

Certified Photographic Counselor (CPC)

Society of Photographic Counselors
3000 Picture Pl.
Jackson, MI 49201
Phone: (517)788-8100
Fax: (517)788-8371
Roy S. Pung PMA, Exec.Dir.

Recipient: Photography shop sales and service professionals. **Educational/Experience Requirements:** One year of photography counter sales experience or equivalent training from recognized school of photography or photofinishing. **Certification Requirements:** Successful completion of exam. Exam covers: Darkroom; Film; Retail techniques; Still cameras and accessories; and Video, movies, and screens. **Preparatory Materials:** *A Better Understanding of Photo Hardware* and *Sales and Customer Relations* (manuals). Sample questions available. **Examination Frequency:** Throughout the year. **Examination Sites:** Exam given at annual convention, seminars, division meetings, and by arrangement with proctor. **Endorsed By:** Photo Marketing Association International.

1277

NADA Certified

National Automobile Dealers Association (NADA)
8400 Westpark Dr.
McLean, VA 22102
Phone: (703)821-7124
Fax: (703)821-7075
Toll Free: (800)252-6232

Recipient: Automotive showroom salespersons and dealers and sales managers. **Educational/Experience Requirements:** Must meet the following requirements: (1) Successful completion of manufacturer product training; (2) Employment with dealership registered in program; and (3) Six months experience. **Certification Requirements:** Successful completion of training curriculum and exam. Training curriculum consists of the following modules: (1) Automotive Sales Leadership (except salespersons); (2) Automotive Sales Today: Ethical and Legal Practices, including: Ethics; Federal and state laws; and Personal development; (3) Consumer Psychology and Customer Loyalty, including: Building career; Customers and earning their loyalty; and Providing customer benefits; and (4) Professional Automotive Selling Techniques. **Renewal:** Every three years. Recertification based on successful completion of annual manufacturer product training and continuing education. **Examination Type:** Multiple-choice. **Endorsed By:** Society of Automotive Sales Professionals.

Securities and Financial Services Sales Representatives

1278

Chartered Financial Analyst (CFA)

Association for Investment Management and Research (AIMR)
Five Boar's Head Ln.
PO Box 3668
Charlottesville, VA 22903-0668
Phone: (804)980-3668
Fax: (804)980-3670

Recipient: Security analysts, portfolio managers, and other investment professionals. **Number of Certified Individuals:** 18,000. **Educational/Experience Requirements:** Must meet the following requirements: (1) Bachelor's degree. Study in capital markets, corporate finance, elementary statistics, financial economics, macroeconomics, and microeconomics recommended; (2) Three years experience; and (3) Membership in local financial analyst society. **Membership:** Required. **Certification Requirements:** Successful completion of the following three levels of exams: (1) Level 1, covering: Asset and investment valuation; Financial markets and instruments; Financial statement analysis; Fundamental investment valuation; Investment analysis and management; Macro and microeconomics; Portfolio management; Quantitative methods and statistics; and Securities law; (2) Level 2, covering: Accounting in analyzing and valuing investments; Capital market theory; Economics; Industry and company analysis; Quantitative techniques; Real estate; Specific equity and fixed income securities; and Valuation case study applications; and (3) Level 3, covering: Capital markets expectations; Different asset classes; Investor constraints and objectives; and Portfolio management. The exams must be taken in order and only one can be taken per year. **Renewal:** none. **Preparatory Materials:** Required readings, textbooks, and study guides and groups available. **Examination Frequency:** Annual - always June. **Examination Sites:** Exam given at sites throughout the U.S. and internationally. **Examination Type:** Multiple-choice; problem-solving; short essay. **Waiting Period to Receive Scores:** 90 days. **Re-examination:** Must wait one year to retake exams. Must successfully complete Level I exam within three years and all three exams within seven years. There is a fee to retake exams. **Fees:** $950. **Endorsed By:** Financial Analysts Federation; Institute of Chartered Financial Analysts.

Services Sales Representatives

1279

Certified Graphic Arts Sales Representative (CGASR)

Graphic Arts Sales Foundation (GASF)
Matlack Bldg., Ste. A
113 E. Evans St.
West Chester, PA 19380
Phone: (610)431-9780
Fax: (610)436-5238
Judy M. Warren, Admin.

Recipient: Sales and marketing professionals in graphic arts industry. **Number of Certified Individuals:** 17. **Educational/Experience Requirements:** Successful completion of 50 hours of study in GASF sponsored programs. Programs include: (1) Customer Service Representative Institute; (2) In-House custom seminars, tailored to company's needs; (3) One-day seminars (seven hours); (4) Print Marketing Institute (40 hours), covering: Analysis of company's sales history; Developing sound marketing plan; Gathering customer information; Preparing mission statement and self-promotion program; and Primary and secondary research; (5) Sales Institute (40 hours), covering: Annual account review; Buyer behavior; Development of existing customers; Identifying prospects; Market conditions; and Proposals to do business; (6) Sales Management Institute (40 hours); and (7) Trade Show Seminars (maximum of 15 hours). **Membership:** Not required. **Certification Requirements:** Successful completion of exam. Exam covers graphic arts sales concepts. **Renewal:** none. **Examination Frequency:** By arrangement. **Examination Sites:** Exam given by arrangement with proctor. **Endorsed By:** Graphic Arts Institute of America.

1280

Certified Sales Representative (CSR)
Water Quality Association (WQA)
4151 Naperville Rd.
Lisle, IL 60532
Phone: (708)505-0160
Fax: (708)505-9637
Dr. Judith A. Grove, Dir.

Recipient: Individuals responsible for face-to-face sale of water quality improvement products. **Educational/Experience Requirements:** none. **Membership:** Not required. **Certification Requirements:** Successful completion of exam. **Renewal:** Every three years. Recertification based on accumulation of two Continuing Professional Development credits through: (1) Attendance at Seminars, Workshops, or Convention Sessions (one credit per ten hours); (2) Attendance at WQA-Approved Educational Sessions; (3) Attendance at Educational Sessions Sponsored by Other Organizations; (4) Successful Completion of Measured Learning Sessions, including: Courses taken at colleges or trade schools; Exams successfully completed; or Home study or correspondence courses; and (5) Experiential Learning Experiences, including: Committee service; Individual learning; Presentations; Speeches; and Voluntary service. Renewal fees are: $60 (members); $135 (nonmembers). **Preparatory Materials:** List of suggested study references provided. Seminars and study kit available.

Examination Frequency: Throughout the year. **Examination Sites:** Exam given at annual convention, mid-year conference, seminars, state and regional conventions, or by arrangement with proctor. **Examination Type:** Matching; multiple-choice; true or false. **Re-examination:** Fees to retake exam are: $60 (members); $90 (nonmembers). **Fees:** $60 (members); $90 (nonmembers).

Travel Agents

1281

Certified Corporate Travel Executive (CCTE)
National Business Travel Association (NBTA)
1650 King St., Ste. 301
Alexandria, VA 22314
Phone: (703)684-0836
Fax: (703)684-0263

Recipient: Business management travel professionals. **Educational/Experience Requirements:** Two years experience and meet the following requirements: (1) Submission of thesis on issue related to candidate's corporation; and (2) Successful completion of courses held at Cornell University and five elective courses. Core courses are: (1) Automation and Information Systems, covering: Information utilization; Methods and systems available to track and measure travel programs; and Strategic thinking; (2) Business Travel Law, covering: Contractual issues; Legal aspects of travel relating to travel agencies, airlines, hotels, rental cars, and rail travel arrangement; and Legal liability; (3) Finance Systems and Management, covering: Departmental budgeting; General finance and accounting concepts; and Tracking travel expenditures; (4) Negotiation and Purchasing, covering: Skills for negotiating favorable rates and services; and Strategies for productive relationships with travel and accommodation providers; (5) Travel Industry Operations, including service providers and vendors; and (6) Corporate Application Project, requiring application of information learned in other courses to candidate's own corporation. Elective courses are: (1) Achieving Personal Excellence; (2) Corporate Communication Skills; (3) Leadership and Management; (4) Managing T & E Information; (5) Marketing in Travel Programs; (6) Meeting Facilitation; (7) Procurement Management; (8) Travel Industry Ethics; (9) Travel Patterns and Needs; (10) Travel Policy Compliance; and (11) Using Internal Corporate Re-

sources. Elective courses held at selected locations. **Certification Requirements:** Successful completion of exam. **Renewal:** Every year. Recertification based on successful completion of one elective course per year. **Fees:** $3100.

1282

Certified Incentive Travel Executive (CITE)
Society of Incentive Travel Executives (SITE)
21 W. 38th St., 10th Fl.
New York, NY 10018-5584
Phone: (212)575-0910
Fax: (212)575-1838
Maureen P. Mangan, Dir.

Recipient: Individuals responsible for administration or sale of incentive travel, including corporate users, incentive travel houses, cruise lines, hotel chains, resort operators, airlines, and tourist boards. **Educational/Experience Requirements:** Must earn 100 points through association participation, academic and professional education, publications, and experience. **Membership:** Required. **Certification Requirements:** Must meet the following requirements: (1) Submission of research paper; and (2) Successful completion of exam. **Examination Type:** Essay; short-answer.

1283

Certified Travel Counselor (CTC)
Institute of Certified Travel Agents (ICTA)
148 Linden St.
PO Box 812059
Wellesley, MA 02181-0012
Phone: (617)237-0280
Fax: (617)237-3860
Toll Free: (800)542-4282
Stevan K. Trooboff DBA, CEO

Recipient: Travel agency owners, managers, counselors, and individuals who sell to or work with travel agencies. **Number of Certified Individuals:** 18,000. **Educational/Experience Requirements:** Five years experience. Experience requirement can be reduced to two years by earning one year of credit for each of the following: (1) Successful completion of travel program using ICTA's *Travel Career Development* text and accompanying exam; (2) Every four years of non-travel experience in public contact related activity; (3) Associate's degree in travel or tourism; (4) Bachelor's degree in travel and tourism, business administration, or travel related disciplines; or

(5) Master's degree. **Certification Requirements:** Successful completion of the following courses: (1) Communications for the Travel Professional, covering the fundamentals of oral and written communication; (2) Travel Industry in the '90's and Beyond, including the following units: History and Trends; Psychology of Travel; Government and Public Policy; Destination Development; Social Issues; Land and Sea Travel; Air Travel; Hotel, Food, and Beverage; and Attraction Marketing; (3) The Travel Professional: Selling in a Competitive Service Environment, including the following units: The Role of the Professional Agent; The Sales Cycle; Understanding Customer Needs; Meeting Customer Needs; Customer-Focused Selling; and Customer Service; (4) Challenges in Leadership and Management, including the following units: Strategy; Leadership vs. Management; Recruitment and Selection; Goal Setting; Performance Appraisal; Teamwork; Compensation; Organizational Climate; and Total Quality Management; and (5) Issues in Agency Management, covering: Accounting; Business strategies; Legal considerations; and Planning. Programs use articles, case studies, role plays, and group discussions. Each course ends with an exam or paper and presentation. Courses may be completed through independent or group study, or in licensed schools. **Renewal:** Every five years. Recertification based on accumulation of 50 points through attendance at national, regional, and local forums, meetings, seminars, and workshops, continuing education, and industry participation in leadership positions and service on advisory boards. **Preparatory Materials:** Audio tapes, exercises, reading materials, study guides, and unit booklets. **Examination Frequency:** By arrangement. **Examination Sites:** Exam given by arrangement with proctor. **Fees:** $1075.

Administrative Support Occupations, Including Clerical

Adjusters, Investigators, and Collectors

1284

Accredited Insurance Examiner (AIE)
Insurance Regulatory Examiners Society
130 N. Cherry, Ste. 202
Olathe, KS 66061
Phone: (913)768-4700
Fax: (913)768-4900
David V. Chartrand, Exec.Sec.

Recipient: Insurance regulators working for state or federal insurance agencies. **Educational/Experience Requirements:** Two years experience. **Membership:** Required. **Certification Requirements:** Successful completion of one of two paths. Property and Casualty path requires successful completion of eight of the following ten courses: (1) Personal Insurance; (2) Commercial Insurance; (3) Claims Person and the Public; (4) Commercial Liability Risk Management and Insurance; (5) Insurance Company Operations; (6) Legal Environment of Insurance; (7) Management; (8) Accounting and Finance; (9) Economics; and (10) Business Research Methods. Life and Health path requires successful completion of the following courses: (1) Principles of Life and Health Insurance; (2) Life and Health Insurance Company Operations; (3) Legal Aspects of Life and Health Insurance; (4) Marketing Life and Health Insurance; (5) Management of Organizations and Human Resources; (6) Information Management in Insurance Companies; (7) Accounting in Life and Health Insurance Companies; and (8) Claim Administration. Candidates who hold Chartered Property Casualty Underwriter (CPCU), Chartered Life Underwriter (CLU), or Fellow, Life Management Institute designations (see

separate entries) are exempt from course work. **Endorsed By:** National Association of Insurance Commissioners.

1285

Advanced Certified Collector
American Collectors Association (ACA)
ASAE Bldg.
4040 W. 70th St.
Minneapolis, MN 55435-4199
Phone: (612)926-6547
Fax: (612)926-1624

Recipient: Telephone debt collection professionals. **Certification Requirements:** Successful completion of exam.

1286

Associate in Claims (AIC)
Insurance Institute of America (IIA)
720 Providence Rd.
PO Box 3016
Malvern, PA 19355-0716
Phone: (610)644-2100
Fax: (610)640-9576
Toll Free: (800)644-2101
James J. Markham AIC, VP

Recipient: Claims adjusters, supervisors and examiners, and others working with property loss and liability claims. **Educational/Experience Requirements:** none. **Membership:** Not required. **Certification Requirements:** Successful completion of the following courses, including exams: (1) Claims Environment, covering the claims process and types; (2) Liability Claims Adjusting; (3) Property Loss Adjusting; and (4) Workers Compensation and Medical Aspects of Claims. Courses can be taken through group- or independent-study. **Renewal:**

none. **Examination Type:** Essay. **Endorsed By:** American Council on Education; National Association of Independent Insurance Adjusters.

1287

Associate, Life and Health Claims (ALHC)
International Claims Association (ICA)
2300 Windy Ridge Pkwy., Ste. 600
Atlanta, GA 30339-8443
Phone: (770)951-1770
Fax: (770)984-0441

Recipient: Professionals involved in life and health insurance claims. **Number of Certified Individuals:** 8100. **Educational/Experience Requirements:** Successful completion of introductory courses and exams offered by one of the following organizations: (1) American College, including: Group Benefits; and either Individual Life and Health Insurance or Insurance Environment and Operations; (2) Health Insurance Association of America, including: Individual Health Insurance (Part A or B); and Group Life/Health Insurance (Part A or B); (3) Life Office Management Association, including: Life and Health Insurance Company Operations; and Principles of Life and Health Insurance; or (4) Life Underwriters Association of Canada, including: CLU Subject 122; and CLU Subject 128. **Certification Requirements:** Successful completion of the following self-study courses, including exams: (1) Medical and Dental Aspects of Claims, covering: Anatomy and physiology; Dental insurance plans; Diagnostic and preventive services; Disorders of body systems; Medical terminology; Oral structures and associated disorders; and Substance abuse; (2) Life and Health Insurance Law, covering: Basic principles of contract and agency law; Conflict of laws; Exclusions and limitations; Fair claim settlement practices and consumerism; Government regulation; Group policy owner as agent; Health policies; Insurance operations framework; Law and courts in the U.S.; Life policies; Remedies; Tax aspects; and Wills and estates; (3) Claim Administration, covering the following types of claims: Annuity and endowment; Creditor insurance; Dental expense; Disability; General; Life; Medical; and Reinsurance; and (4) Management of Claim Operation, covering: Managing claim area; Managing claim operation; and Managing claim staff. **Preparatory Materials:** Textbooks provided. Study aids available. **Examination Frequency:** semiannual - always May and November. **Examination Sites:** Exams given by arrangement with proctor. **Waiting Period to Receive Scores:** Four-six weeks. **Endorsed By:** Life Office Management Association.

1288

Associate in Loss Control Management (ALCM)

Insurance Institute of America (IIA)
720 Providence Rd.
PO Box 3016
Malvern, PA 19355-0716
Phone: (610)644-2100
Fax: (610)640-9576
Toll Free: (800)644-2101
Dr. George L. Head CPCU, VP

Recipient: Insurance professionals involved in loss control management. **Educational/Experience Requirements:** none. **Membership:** Not required. **Certification Requirements:** Successful completion of the following courses: (1) Accident Prevention; (2) Property Protection; and (3) Occupational Health and Hygiene. Must also successfully complete two of the following courses: (1) Ethics, Insurance Perspectives, and Insurance Contract Analysis; (2) Insurance Operations; and (3) Management, which covers basic management concepts and how they apply in insurance organizations. Courses can be taken through group- or independent-study. **Renewal:** none. **Examination Type:** Essay. **Endorsed By:** American Council on Education.

1289

Associate in Risk Management (ARM)

Insurance Institute of America (IIA)
720 Providence Rd.
PO Box
Malvern, PA 19355-0716
Phone: (610)644-2100
Fax: (610)640-9576
Toll Free: (800)644-2101
Dr. George L. Head CPCU, VP

Recipient: Insurance professionals involved in risk management. **Educational/Experience Requirements:** none. **Membership:** Not required. **Certification Requirements:** Successful completion of the following courses, including exams: (1) Essentials of Risk Control; (2) Essentials of Risk Financing; and (3) Essentials of Risk Management. Courses can be taken through group- or independent-study. **Renewal:** none. **Examination Type:** Essay. **Endorsed By:** American Council on Education; Risk and Insurance Management Society.

1290

Certified Civil and Criminal Investigator (C.C.C.I.)

International Security and Detective Alliance (ISDA)
Box 6303
Corpus Christi, TX 78466-6303
Phone: (512)888-6164
Fax: (512)888-6164
H. Roehm Ph.D., Dir.

Recipient: Civil and criminal investigators. **Membership:** Not required. **Certification Requirements:** Submission of resume including education and experience and description of case. **Renewal:** Every three years. **Fees:** $36 (members); $45 (nonmembers).

1291

Certified Civil Process Officer (C.C.P.O.)

International Security and Detective Alliance (ISDA)
Box 6303
Corpus Christi, TX 78466-6303
Phone: (512)888-6164
Fax: (512)888-6164
H. Roehm Ph.D., Dir.

Recipient: Civil process officers. **Membership:** Not required. **Certification Requirements:** Submission of resume in-

cluding education and experience and description of case. **Renewal:** Every three years. **Fees:** $36 (members); $45 (nonmembers).

1292

Certified Collection Sales Professional

American Collectors Association (ACA)
ASAE Bldg.
4040 W. 70th St.
Minneapolis, MN 55435-4199
Phone: (612)926-6547
Fax: (612)926-1624

Recipient: Telephone debt collection services salespeople. **Certification Requirements:** Successful completion of exam.

1293

Certified Collector

American Collectors Association (ACA)
ASAE Bldg.
4040 W. 70th St.
Minneapolis, MN 55435-4199
Phone: (612)926-6547
Fax: (612)926-1624

Recipient: Telephone debt collection professionals. **Certification Requirements:** Successful completion of exam.

1294

Certified Financial Fraud Investigator (C.F.F.I.)

International Security and Detective Alliance (ISDA)
Box 6303
Corpus Christi, TX 78466-6303
Phone: (512)888-6164
Fax: (512)888-6164
H. Roehm Ph.D., Dir.

Recipient: Financial fraud investigators. **Membership:** Not required. **Certification Requirements:** Submission of resume including education and experience and description of case. **Renewal:** Every three years. **Fees:** $36 (members); $45 (nonmembers).

1295

Certified Fire and Arson Investigator (C.F.A.I.)
International Security and Detective Alliance (ISDA)
Box 6303
Corpus Christi, TX 78466-6303
Phone: (512)888-6164
Fax: (512)888-6164
H. Roehm Ph.D., Dir.

Recipient: Fire and arson investigators. **Membership:** Not required. **Certification Requirements:** Submission of resume including education and experience and description of case. **Renewal:** Every three years. **Fees:** $36 (members); $45 (nonmembers).

1296

Certified Fraud Examiner (CFE)
Association of Certified Fraud Examiners (ACFE)
716 West Ave.
Austin, TX 78701
Phone: (512)478-9070
Fax: (512)478-9297
Toll Free: (800)245-3321
Helen Clem, Prog.Admin.

Recipient: Experts in fraud and white collar crime who are qualified to detect, investigate, and deter fraud, including fraud auditors and investigators, forensic accountants, loss prevention professionals, public accountants, law enforcement personnel, researchers, and academicians. **Number of Certified Individuals:** 12,000. **Educational/Experience Requirements:** Must meet the following requirements: (1) Bachelor's degree; and (2) Two years experience in the following areas: Academic/research; Auditing and accounting; Criminology and sociology; Crime investigation; and Loss prevention. **Membership:** Required. **Certification Requirements:** Successful completion of four-section exam. Exam sections are: (1) Financial Transactions, including: Accounting theory; Auditing theory; Financial statement analysis; Internal controls; Proving illicit transactions; and Other accounting and auditing matters; (2) Investigation, including: Evaluating deception; Evidence gathering; Interviewing; Public records; and Report writing; (3) Legal Elements, including: Civil law; Criminal law; Expert witness matters; Rules of evidence; and Other legal matters; and (4) Criminology, including: Administration of criminal justice; Crime statistics; Ethics; Traditional crime; White-collar crime; and Other criminological matters. Exam re-

quirement may be waived if following requirements are met: (1) Bachelor's degree; (2) Twelve or more years experience in related field including, but not limited to: Auditing and accounting (except for tax preparation); Criminology or sociology, with an emphasis on white-collar crime; Fraud or white-collar crime investigation; Law, as it relates to civil or criminal fraud; Loss prevention or internal crime; or Academic or research experience in one of the above fields; and (3) Experience uncovering, documenting, or investigating fraud matters. Two years of experience can be substituted for each year of academic qualifications. **Renewal:** Every three years. Recertification based on accumulation of 60 hours of continuing education. At least fifty percent of these hours must relate directly to the detection and deterrence of fraud. **Preparatory Materials:** *Fraud Examiners Manual* (reference). List of study references provided. Self-study course available. **Examination Frequency:** By arrangement. **Examination Sites:** Exam given on computer diskette only and is taken at candidate's home or workplace. **Examination Type:** Multiple-choice; true or false. **Pass/Fail Rate:** 20% pass exam the first time. **Waiting Period to Receive Scores:** Two-three weeks. **Reexamination:** Must only retake sections failed. May retake exam twice. **Fees:** $200 (exam option); $250 (exam exempt option).

1297

Certified Insurance Examiner (CIE)
Insurance Regulatory Examiners Society
130 N. Cherry, Ste. 202
Olathe, KS 66061
Phone: (913)768-4700
Fax: (913)768-4900
David V. Chartrand, Exec.Sec.

Recipient: Insurance regulators working for state or federal insurance agencies. **Educational/Experience Requirements:** Two years experience and hold Accredited Insurance Examiner designation (see separate entry). **Membership:** Required. **Certification Requirements:** Successfully completion of one of two paths. Property and Casualty path requires successful completion of the following courses: (1) Principles of Life and Health Insurance; (2) Life and Health Insurance Company Operations; (3) Marketing Life and Health Insurance; and (4) Information Management in Insurance Companies. Life and Health path requires successful completion of the following courses: (1) Principles of Insurance; (2) Insurance Company Operations; (3) Legal Environ-

ment of Insurance; and (4) Business Research Methods. **Endorsed By:** National Association of Insurance Commissioners.

1298

Certified Insurance Investigator (C.I.I.)
International Security and Detective Alliance (ISDA)
Box 6303
Corpus Christi, TX 78466-6303
Phone: (512)888-6164
Fax: (512)888-6164
H. Roehm Ph.D., Dir.

Recipient: Insurance investigators. **Membership:** Not required. **Certification Requirements:** Submission of resume including education and experience and description of case. **Renewal:** Every three years. **Fees:** $36 (members); $45 (nonmembers).

1299

Certified International Courier (C.I.C.)
International Security and Detective Alliance (ISDA)
Box 6303
Corpus Christi, TX 78466-6303
Phone: (512)888-6164
Fax: (512)888-6164
H. Roehm Ph.D., Dir.

Recipient: International couriers. **Membership:** Not required. **Certification Requirements:** Submission of resume including education and experience and description of case. **Renewal:** Every three years. **Fees:** $36 (members); $45 (nonmembers).

1300

Certified Investigator/Inspector, Level I
Council on Licensure, Enforcement, and Regulation (CLEAR)
201 W. Short St., Ste. 410
Lexington, KY 40507
Phone: (606)231-1901
Fax: (606)231-1943
E-mail: CLEAR1@UKCC.UKY. EDU
Pam Brinegar, Exec.Dir.

Recipient: Regulatory inspectors and investigators. **Number of Certified Individuals:** 1450. **Educational/Experience Requirements:** One year of experience. **Membership:** Not required. **Certification**

Requirements: Successful completion of course and exam. **Renewal:** none. **Preparatory Materials:** Instruction guide available. **Examination Frequency:** Six-ten times per year. **Examination Sites:** Exam given at sites throughout the U.S. **Examination Type:** Multiple-choice. **Pass/Fail Rate:** 97% pass exam the first time. **Waiting Period to Receive Scores:** Six weeks. **Re-examination:** There is no time limit to retake exam. **Fees:** $300. **Endorsed By:** National Organization for Competency Assurance.

1301

Certified Investigator/Inspector, Level II

Council on Licensure, Enforcement, and Regulation (CLEAR)
201 W. Short St., Ste. 410
Lexington, KY 40507
Phone: (606)231-1901
Fax: (606)231-1943
E-mail: CLEAR1@UKCC.UKY.EDU
Pam Brinegar, Exec.Dir.

Recipient: Regulatory inspectors and investigators. **Number of Certified Individuals:** 44. **Educational/Experience Requirements:** Hold Certified Investigator/ Inspector, Level I designation (see separate entry). **Membership:** Not required. **Certification Requirements:** Successful completion of three exams. **Renewal:** none. **Preparatory Materials:** Instructional guide available. **Examination Frequency:** Six-ten times every year. **Examination Sites:** Exams given at sites throughout the U.S. **Examination Type:** Multiple-choice. **Pass/Fail Rate:** 94% pass exams the first time. **Waiting Period to Receive Scores:** Six weeks. **Re-examination:** There is no time limit to retake exams. **Fees:** $375. **Endorsed By:** National Organization for Competency Assurance.

1302

Certified Legal Investigator (CLI)

National Association of Legal Investigators (NALI)
c/o Lynne K. Curtis, CLI
Posner and Houghton
1230 Market St., Ste. 420
San Francisco, CA 94102
Phone: (415)292-5513
Fax: (415)292-6052
Lynne K. Curtis CLI, Chair

Recipient: Legal investigators who gather evidence and aid attorneys in preparing for litigation. **Educational/Experience**

Requirements: Must meet the following requirements: (1) Documentation of majority of practice in negligence investigations for plaintiff and/or criminal defense; (2) Employment by private practice law firm or investigative firm; (3) Current licensure, if required by state; and (4) Either accumulation of 60 semester or 90 quarter hours of college coursework or two years experience. **Membership:** Not required. **Certification Requirements:** Must meet the following requirements: (1) Submission of white paper on investigative subject; and (2) Successful completion of written and oral exams. **Renewal:** Every two years. Recertification based on accumulation of two continuing education units (CEUs). **Preparatory Materials:** List of manuals and publications and sample exam provided. **Examination Frequency:** semiannual - always summer and winter. **Examination Sites:** Exams given at summer conference and winter meeting. **Examination Type:** Definition; essay; fill-in-the-blank; multiple-choice; true or false. **Fees:** $125 (members); $225 (nonmembers).

1303

Certified Liquidator

Association of Certified Liquidators (A.C.L.)
1476 Clara Ave.
Columbus, OH 43211-2624
Phone: (614)291-1461
Fax: (614)291-2060
Mitch Klass, Exec. Officer

Recipient: Liquidators. **Membership:** Required. **Certification Requirements:** Successful completion of exam. Exam covers pricing, reselling, techniques, and other aspects of the liquidation industry. **Preparatory Materials:** Training manual and tapes available.

1304

Certified Professional Public Adjuster (CPPA)

National Association of Public Insurance Adjusters (NAPIA)
1767 Business Center Dr., Ste. 302
Reston, VA 22090
Phone: (703)438-8254
Fax: (703)438-3113
David W. Barrack, Admin.

Recipient: Public insurance adjusters in public practice dealing with fire and allied coverages. **Educational/Experience Requirements:** Five years experience. **Membership:** Required. **Certification Requirements:** Successful completion of

exam. **Renewal:** Recertification based on continuing education.

1305

Certified Skiptracer

American Collectors Association (ACA)
ASAE Bldg.
4040 W. 70th St.
Minneapolis, MN 55435-4199
Phone: (612)926-6547
Fax: (612)926-1624

Recipient: Telephone debt collection professionals. **Certification Requirements:** Successful completion of exam.

1306

Certified Supervisor

American Collectors Association (ACA)
ASAE Bldg.
4040 W. 70th St.
Minneapolis, MN 55435-4199
Phone: (612)926-6547
Fax: (612)926-1624

Recipient: Telephone debt collection company supervisors. **Certification Requirements:** Successful completion of exam.

1307

Senior Professional Public Adjuster (SPPA)

National Association of Public Insurance Adjusters (NAPIA)
1767 Business Center Dr., Ste. 302
Reston, VA 22090
Phone: (703)438-8254
Fax: (703)438-3113
David W. Barrack, Admin.

Recipient: Public insurance adjusters in public practice dealing with fire and allied coverages. **Educational/Experience Requirements:** Ten years experience. **Membership:** Required. **Certification Requirements:** Successful completion of exam. **Renewal:** Recertification based on continuing education.

Appraisers, Other Than Real Estate

1308

Accredited Machinery and Equipment Appraiser (AMEA)
Association of Machinery and Equipment Appraisers (AMEA)
1110 Spring St.
Silver Spring, MD 20910
Phone: (301)587-9335
Fax: (301)588-7830

Recipient: Individuals who buy, sell, and appraise used machinery and equipment. **Educational/Experience Requirements:** Five years experience. **Membership:** Required. **Certification Requirements:** Must meet the following requirements: (1) Attendance at two seminars; (2) Submission of appraisal; and (3) Successful completion of exam. **Renewal:** Every two years.

1309

Accredited Member, American Society of Appraisers (AM)
American Society of Appraisers (ASA)
PO Box 17265
Washington, DC 20041
Phone: (703)478-2228
Fax: (703)742-8471
Toll Free: (800)ASA-VALU
A.W. Carson, Exec.Dir.

Recipient: Appraisers. **Educational/Experience Requirements:** Must meet the following requirements: (1) Two years experience; (2) College degree or equivalent; (3) Successful completion of ASA Ethics exam; and (4) Successful completion of Uniform Standards of Professional Appraisal Practice (USPAP) exam. Holders of designations from other appraisal organizations may submit resume for approval. **Membership:** Required. **Certification Requirements:** Must meet one of the following requirements: (1) Successful completion of ethical and technical exams and submission of two appraisal reports; or (2) Successful completion of four specialized courses, including exams, and submission of two appraisal reports. Certification available in general appraisal or one of the following specialties: (1) Appraisal Review and Management, including: Functions related to the administration of appraisal activities within the private or public sectors that frequently involve the management of professional staff; Coordination of diverse valuation disciplines; Review of valuation estimates prepared by oth-

ers; and Reconciliation of valuation concepts with requirements of financial accounting, government rulings, and professional standards; (2) Business Valuation, including appraisal of closely held businesses of all sizes - from small proprietorships such as medical practices to large, multi-national corporations; (3) Gems and Jewelry, including: Collateral loans; Estates; Insurance replacement; Liquidation; and Purchase; (4) Machinery and Technical Specialties, including: Agricultural chattels; Aircraft; Arboriculture; Computers and high-tech personal property; Cost surveys; Industrials; Machinery and equipment; Marine-Survey commercial; Marine-survey yachts; Mines and quarries; Oil and gas; Public utilities; and Railroads; (5) Personal Property, including: Antiques and decorative art; Classified specialties; Fine arts; and Residential contents - general; and (6) Real Property, including: Ad valorem; Residential; Rural; Timber and timberland; and Urban. **Preparatory Materials:** *Uniform Standards of Professional Appraisal Practice* (USOAP) (reference). Study packages available. **Examination Frequency:** Throughout the year. **Examination Sites:** Exam given at sites throughout the U.S. **Re-examination:** May retake exam once.

1310

Accredited Senior Appraiser (ASA)
American Society of Appraisers (ASA)
PO Box 17265
Washington, DC 20041
Phone: (703)478-2228
Fax: (703)742-8471
Toll Free: (800)ASA-VALU
A.W. Carson, Exec.Dir.

Recipient: Appraisers. **Educational/Experience Requirements:** Must meet the following requirements: (1) Two years experience; (2) College degree or equivalent; (3) Successful completion of ASA Ethics exam; and (4) Successful completion of the Uniform Standards of Professional Appraisal Practice (USPAP) exam. Holders of designations from other appraisal organizations may submit resume for approval. **Membership:** Required. **Certification Requirements:** Must meet one of the following requirements: (1) Successful completion of ethical and technical exams and submission of two appraisal reports; or (2) Successful completion of four specialized courses, including exams, and submission of two appraisal reports. Certification available in general appraisal or one of the following specialties: (1) Appraisal Review and Management, including: Functions re-

lated to the administration of appraisal activities within the private or public sectors that frequently involve the management of professional staff; Coordination of diverse valuation disciplines; Review of valuation estimates prepared by others; and Reconciliation of valuation concepts with requirements of financial accounting, government rulings, and professional standards; (2) Business Valuation, including appraisal of closely held businesses of all sizes - from small proprietorships such as medical practices to large, multi-national corporations; (3) Gems and Jewelry, including: Collateral loans; Estates; Insurance replacement; Liquidation; and Purchase; (4) Machinery and Technical Specialties, including: Agricultural chattels; Aircraft; Arboriculture; Computers and high-tech personal property; Cost surveys; Industrials; Machinery and equipment; Marine-Survey commercial; Marine-survey yachts; Mines and quarries; Oil and gas; Public utilities; and Railroads; (5) Personal Property, including: Antiques and decorative art; Classified specialties; Fine arts; and Residential contents - general; and (6) Real Property, including: Ad valorem; Residential; Rural; Timber and timberland; and Urban. **Renewal:** Every five years. Recertification based on continuing education through professional courses or seminars, publishing technical articles and textbooks, and teaching. **Preparatory Materials:** *Uniform Standards of Professional Appraisal Practice* (USOAP) (reference). Study packages available. **Examination Frequency:** Throughout the year. **Examination Sites:** Exam given at sites throughout the U.S. **Re-examination:** May retake exam once.

1311

Certified Business Appraiser (CBA)
Institute of Business Appraisers (IBA)
PO Box 1447
Boynton Beach, FL 33425
Phone: (407)732-3202
Kenneth F. MacKenzie, Asst.Exec. Dir.

Recipient: Business appraisers qualified to value closely held businesses. **Number of Certified Individuals:** 200. **Educational/Experience Requirements:** Bachelor's degree or equivalent. **Membership:** Required. **Certification Requirements:** Must meet the following requirements: (1) Successful completion of exam; and (2) Submission of two business appraisal reports. **Renewal:** Every five years. Recertification based on attendance at conferences and seminars and submission of work product. **Preparatory**

Materials: Self-study course and suggested reading list available. **Examination Frequency:** 20 times/year. **Examination Sites:** Exam given at selected IBA seminars and national conference. **Examination Type:** Essay; multiple-choice; problem-solving; short answer; true or false. **Pass/Fail Rate:** 80% pass exam the first time. **Waiting Period to Receive Scores:** Two weeks. **Re-examination:** There is no waiting period to retake exam. **Fees:** $200.

1312

Certified Gemologist Appraiser (CGA)

American Gem Society (AGS)
8881 W. Sahara Ave.
Las Vegas, NV 89117
Phone: (702)255-6500
Fax: (702)255-7420
Tina L. LeDuc, Educ.Coord.

Recipient: Jewelry appraisers. **Educational/Experience Requirements:** Must hold Certified Gemologist (CG) designation (see separate entry) and maintain Accredited Gem Laboratory (see separate entry) in store. **Membership:** Required. **Certification Requirements:** Successful completion of exam. **Renewal:** Every year. Recertification based on successful completion of exam. **Preparatory Materials:** *Handbook of Jewelry and Gemstone Appraising* (reference). **Examination Frequency:** Annual. **Examination Sites:** Exam given at annual conclave.

1313

Certified Machinery and Equipment Appraiser (CMEA)

Association of Machinery and Equipment Appraisers (AMEA)
1110 Spring St.
Silver Spring, MD 20910
Phone: (301)587-9335
Fax: (301)588-7830

Recipient: Individuals who buy, sell, and appraise used machinery and equipment. **Educational/Experience Requirements:** Hold Accredited Machinery and Equipment Appraiser (AMEA) designation (see separate entry) for two years. **Membership:** Required. **Certification Requirements:** Must meet the following requirements: (1) Successful completion of course; (2) Submission of acceptable appraisal; and (3) Successful completion of exam. **Renewal:** Every two years.

1314

Certified Valuation Analyst (CVA)

National Association of Certified Valuation Analysts (NACVA)
Brickyard Towers, Ste. 110
1245 E. Brickyard Rd.
Salt Lake City, UT 84106
Phone: (801)486-7500
Fax: (801)486-7500
Toll Free: (800)677-2009
Parnell Black CVA, Pres./Exec.Dir.

Recipient: Practicing certified public accountants (CPAs) involved in small business valuations. **Educational/Experience Requirements:** Hold valid and unrevoked CPA certificate and/or license issued by legally constituted state authority. **Membership:** Required. **Certification Requirements:** Successful completion of exam. Exam covers: Economic financial statements; Ethics; Methods of valuation; Ratio, trend, and comparative analysis; Report writing; Theory and practice; and Valuation of intangible assets. Candidates who have successfully completed state or American Institute of Certified Public Accountants sponsored Certificate of Educational Achievement (CEA) programs may qualify for certification after successful completion of special requirements. **Preparatory Materials:** List of study references provided. Training program available. **Examination Type:** Case study; multiple-choice; short essay; true or false. **Waiting Period to Receive Scores:** 30 days. **Re-examination:** May retake exam twice. There is a $50 fee to retake exam. **Fees:** $300.

1315

Fellow of the American Society of Appraisers (FASA)

American Society of Appraisers (ASA)
PO Box 17265
Washington, DC 20041
Phone: (703)478-2228
Fax: (703)742-8471
Toll Free: (800)ASA-VALU
A.W. Carson, Exec.Dir.

Recipient: Appraisers. **Educational/Experience Requirements:** Must hold Accredited Senior Appraiser (ASA) designation (see separate entry). **Membership:** Required. **Certification Requirements:** Must provide outstanding service to the profession and/or ASA.

1316

Master Gemologist Appraiser (MGA)

American Society of Appraisers (ASA)
PO Box 17265
Washington, DC 20041
Phone: (703)478-2228
Fax: (703)742-8471
Toll Free: (800)ASA-VALU
A.W. Carson, Exec.Dir.

Recipient: Gem and jewelry appraisers. **Educational/Experience Requirements:** Must meet the following requirements: (1) Hold Accredited Senior Appraiser (ASA) designation (see separate entry); (2) Hold Graduate Gemologist (GS) designation from Gemological Institute of America, or Fellow, Gemological Association of Great Britain (FGA) designation; (3) Be employed at approved gemological laboratory; and (4) Successfully complete Farnsworth-Munsell 100-hue test for color discrimination. **Membership:** Required. **Certification Requirements:** Successfully complete program that includes hands-on test of ability to correctly identify and qualitatively rank gemstones and jewelry.

1317

Master Governmental Appraiser (MGA)

American Society of Appraisers (ASA)
PO Box 17265
Washington, DC 20041
Phone: (703)478-2228
Fax: (703)742-8471
Toll Free: (800)ASA-VALU
A.W. Carson, Exec.Dir.

Recipient: Governmental appraisers. **Membership:** Required.

1318

Personal Property Specialist (PPS)

International Association of Assessing Officers (IAAO)
130 E. Randolph St., Ste. 850
Chicago, IL 60601
Phone: (312)819-6104
Fax: (312)819-6149
Karen Graf, Coord.

Recipient: Assessors and appraisers specializing in valuation of business personal property or personal property assessment administration. **Educational/Experience Requirements:** Must meet the following requirements: (1) High school diploma or equivalent; (2) Three years experience; (3) Successful completion of IAAO Standards of Practice and Professional Ethics Workshop, including exam, or equivalent; (4) Successful completion of the following IAAO courses, including exams: Fundamentals of Real Property Appraisal; and Personal Property Appraisal; and (5) Attendance at seminar or workshop on appraising personal property. Educational requirements must have been successfully completed within last ten years. IAAO courses may be challenged through successful completion of exams. Courses given by other associations may be substituted for IAAO courses. **Membership:** Required. **Certification Requirements:** Successful completion of the following: (1) Demonstration appraisal report, using recognized approaches to value, on retail, service, or manufacturing business; and (2) Exam. Oral exam may be required. **Renewal:** Every five years. Recertification based on accumulation of 45 hours of continuing education. **Preparatory Materials:** *Professional Designation Program Requirements* (reference). Demonstration appraisal report writing guides available. **Examination Frequency:** Throughout the year. **Examination Sites:** Exam given by arrangement with proctor. **Re-examination:** Must wait 30 days to retake exam.

Computer and Peripheral Equipment Operators

1319

Certified Professional Credential (CPC)
Wordperfect
c/o Novell
122 East 1700 South
Provo, UT 84606-6194
Phone: (801)429-5508
Fax: (801)429-5363
Toll Free: (800)233-EDUC

Recipient: Professionals who assist, consult with, or train WordPerfect software users to accomplish common tasks within a business environment. **Certification Requirements:** Successful completion of exam. Exams available in: WordPerfect 6.0 DOS; and WordPerfect 6.0 for Windows. **Preparatory Materials:** List of test objectives, study guides and kits, and practice exams available. **Examination Frequency:** Throughout the year. **Examination Sites:** Exam given at sites throughout the U.S. **Examination Type:** Multiple-choice. **Fees:** $100.

1320

Electronic Document and Printing Professional (EDPP)
Xplor International
24238 Hawthorne Blvd.
Torrance, CA 90505-6505
Phone: (310)373-3633
Fax: (310)375-4240
Toll Free: (800)669-7567
Jim Parker, Mgr.

Recipient: Individuals responsible for using and managing electronic document and printing systems. **Number of Certified Individuals:** 59. **Membership:** Not required. **Certification Requirements:** Must earn 1500 points through submission of personal data form (minimum of 670 points; maximum of 1150 points) and three work examples (minimum of 350 points; maximum of 925 points). Personal data form covers education, experience, and industry participation. Each work example must cover one identified area from *Body of Knowledge for Electronic Document Systems* and describe candidate's role, obstacles to completion, and equipment used. **Renewal:** Every five years. Recertification based on accumulation of 250 points. Lifetime certification available to EDPPs at age of 60 with ten years experience. **Fees:** $235.

Credit Clerks and Authorizers

1321

Certified Credit Executive (CCE)
National Association of Credit Management (NACM)
8815 Centre Park Dr., Ste. 200
Columbia, MD 21045-2158
Phone: (410)740-5560
Fax: (410)740-5574

Recipient: Business credit administration professionals. **Educational/Experience Requirements:** Must have six years experience in managerial role in the field of credit and financial management or five years experience in managerial role in the field and one year of experience in general management. Must also meet one of the following requirements: (1) Hold Certified Business Associate (CBA) and Credit Business Fellow (CBF) designations (see separate entry) and earn 25 points above those required for the CBF; or (2) Document 125 points. Points can be earned in the following ways: (1) College course work (one point per three credit hours); (2) Attendance at NACM

Credit Management Leadership Institute (CMLI), Mid-School Career School (MCS), Advanced Credit Executives Studies (ACES) program, or Graduate School of Credit and Financial Management (GSCFM) (ten points per year attended); (3) Attendance at local and regional conferences, seminars and workshops, company-sponsored educational sessions, and nationally sponsored meetings, conferences, seminars, and workshops (one point per ten hours of continuing education); (4) Successful completion of self-study course (point totals vary); (5) Experience (two points per year); (6) Mentoring and training provided (point totals vary); (7) Speeches, serving as panelist, articles published, and outstanding contributions to the field (point totals vary); (8) Association participation (point totals vary); and (9) Earning Credit Business Associate (CBA) and Credit Business Fellow (CBF) designations (see separate entries). Candidates with less education and experience may qualify for CBA or CBF designations. **Membership:** Not required. **Certification Requirements:** Successful completion of exam. **Renewal:** Every three years. Recertification based on accumulation of six points in same areas as initial certification. Lifetime certification available to CCEs age 60 or older. **Preparatory Materials:** *Credit Executives Handbook, Credit Management Review: A Guide to Professional Accreditation,* and *Effective Supervision: Frontline Management for the '90s* (references). **Examination Frequency:** semiannual - always May or June and December. **Examination Sites:** Exam given at NACM annual convention and affiliated association offices. **Re-examination:** Must wait six months to retake exam. There is a fee to retake exam.

1322

Credit Associate (CA)
Society of Certified Credit Executives (SCCE)
PO Box 419057
St. Louis, MO 63141-1757
Phone: (314)991-3030
Fax: (314)991-3029
Sandra K. Weber, Assoc.Admin.

Recipient: Entry-level professionals in credit field. **Membership:** Required. **Certification Requirements:** One year of experience within credit granting/credit services operation, credit reporting agency, collection agency or collection division of credit reporting agency, or organization offering budget and/or credit counseling to consumers. May be eligible for Associate Credit Executive designation (see separate entry) with increased experience. **Fees:** $50. **Endorsed By:** International Credit Association.

1323

Credit Business Associate (CBA)
National Association of Credit
  Management (NACM)
8815 Centre Park Dr., Ste. 200
Columbia, MD 21045-2158
Phone: (410)740-5560
Fax: (410)740-5574

Recipient: Professionals at supervisory level in the field of credit and financial management. **Educational/Experience Requirements:** Successful completion of one of two educational plans. Plan A requires successful completion of the following college or NACM self-study courses: (1) Either Introductory Accounting (100 level course) or NACM Keeping Score course; (2) Either Intermediate Accounting (200 level course) or NACM Beyond Basics course; (3) Macroeconomics; (4) Microeconomics; (5) Either Credit and Collection Principles, NACM Introduction to Credit Management course, or Credit Management Leadership Institute; (6) Either Financial Analysis (Applied Credit Management), NACM How to Read and Interpret Financial Statements course, or NACM Mid-Career School; and (7) NACM Business Communications course. Plan B requires three years experience and successful completion of Credit Administration Program (CAP), including the following courses: (1) Applied Credit Management; (2) Credit Management Cases; (3) Intermediate Credit Management; and (4) Introduction to Credit Management. Candidates must also accumulate 50 total points through: (1) College course work (one point per three credit hours); (2) Attendance at NACM Credit Management Leadership Institute (CMLI), Mid-School Career School (MCS), Advanced Credit Executives Studies (ACES) program, or Graduate School of Credit and Financial Management (GSCFM) (ten points per year attended); (3) Attendance at local and regional conferences, seminars and workshops, company-sponsored educational sessions, and nationally sponsored meetings, conferences, seminars, and workshops (one point per ten hours of continuing education); (4) Successful completion of self-study course (point totals vary); (5) Experience (two points per year); (6) Mentoring and training provided (point totals vary); (7) Speeches, serving as panelist, articles published, and outstanding contributions to the field (point totals vary); and (8)

Association participation (point totals vary). Candidates with more education and experience may qualify for Credit Business Fellow (CBF) or Certified Credit Executive (CCE) designations (see separate entries). **Membership:** Not required. **Certification Requirements:** Successful completion of exam. **Preparatory Materials:** *Credit Executive's Handbook* and *Credit Management Review: A Guide to Professional Accreditation* (references). Handbook, including sample questions, available. **Examination Frequency:** semiannual - always May or June and December. **Examination Sites:** Exam given at NACM annual convention and affiliated association offices. **Re-examination:** Must wait six months to retake exam. There is a fee to retake exam.

1324

Credit Business Fellow (CBF)
National Association of Credit
  Management (NACM)
8815 Centre Park Dr., Ste. 200
Columbia, MD 21045-2158
Phone: (410)740-5560
Fax: (410)740-5574

Recipient: Professionals in credit and financial management. **Educational/Experience Requirements:** Hold Credit Business Associate (CBA) designation (see separate entry) and three to five years experience. Must also successfully complete one of two educational plans. Plan A requires successful completion of the following college or NACM home-study courses: (1) Either Business Law I or NACM Credit and Commercial Laws in Review course; (2) Business Law II; (3) Either Public Speaking or Fundamentals of Public Speaking; (4) Principles of Marketing; (5) Either NACM Credit Management Cases or Credit Management Review courses; (6) Either Psychology or General Psychology; (7) Either Management or Principles of Management; and (8) Elective business courses, including: Advanced Accounting; Business Finance (NACM); Business Policy; Business and Society (NACM); Computer Application (NACM); Corporate Finance; Cost Accounting; Credit Insurance; Credit Law; Financial Analysis II (NACM); Financial Management; International Marketing; and Organizational Development. Successful completion of NACM's Mid-Career School meets part of requirement. Plan B requires one of the following: (1) Five years experience; (2) Bachelor's degree in business and three years college teaching experience; or (3) Master's of Business Administration degree. Both plans require accumulation of 100 total points through: (1)

College course work (one point per three credit hours); (2) Attendance at either NACM Credit Management Leadership Institute (CMLI), Mid-School Career School (MCS), Advanced Credit Executives Studies (ACES) program, or Graduate School of Credit and Financial Management (GSCFM) (ten points per year attended); (3) Attendance at local and regional conferences, seminars and workshops, company-sponsored educational sessions, and nationally sponsored meetings, conferences, seminars, and workshops (one point per ten hours of continuing education); (4) Successful completion of self-study course (point totals vary); (5) Experience (two points per year); (6) Mentoring and training provided (point totals vary); (7) Speeches, serving as panelist, articles published, and outstanding contributions to the field (point totals vary); (8) Association participation (point totals vary); and (9) Earning Certified Business Associate (CBA) designation (see separate entry). Candidates with less education and experience may qualify for CBA designation. Candidates with more education and experience may qualify for Certified Credit Executive (CCE) designation (see separate entry). **Membership:** Not required. **Certification Requirements:** Successful completion of exam. Exam covers: Credit management problems; Human relations in credit; and Legal aspects of credit. **Renewal:** none. **Preparatory Materials:** *Credit Executives Handbook, Credit Management Review: A Guide to Professional Accreditation, Credit Manual of Commercial Laws, Effective Supervision: Front-line Management for the '90s,* and *NACM Bankruptcy Reorganization Guide* (references). **Examination Frequency:** semiannual - always May or June and December. **Examination Sites:** Exam given at NACM annual convention and affiliated association offices. **Re-examination:** Must wait six months to retake exam. There is a fee to retake exam.

General Office Clerks

1325

**Certified Educational Office
  Employee (CEOE)**
National Association of Educational
  Office Professionals (NAEOP)
PO Box 12619
Wichita, KS 67277
Phone: (316)942-4822
Fax: (316)942-7100

Recipient: Secretaries, stenographers, administrative assistants, bookkeepers, receptionists, and other office workers employed by schools, colleges and universities, educational associations, and county and state departments of education. **Membership:** Required. **Certification Requirements:** Minimum of three years experience and meet educational, experience, and professional activity requirements. Educational requirement met by earning bachelor's, master's, or doctoral degree, or in one of the following ways: (1) Continuing education, in-service courses, and business college, institute, and college and university courses; (2) Adult Education in subject areas such as: Business; Business administration; Communications/media; Computer science; Cultural/historical; Education; Engineering; Health/physical education; Language; Management; Mathematics; Science; and Social science; and (3) Successful completion of exams in the following subjects: American government; Business law (school law); College composition (report writing); Computers and data processing; Freshman English; General psychology; History of American education; Human growth and development; and Introductory accounting. Adult and continuing education must be in 13 different areas. Experience requirement met by working in educational or other office or teaching. Professional activity requirement met in the following ways: (1) Attendance at related seminars, workshops, conferences, conventions, institutes, and noncredit courses; and (2) Membership in associations in the field and official positions held in those associations. **Endorsed By:** American Association for Adult and Continuing Education; American Association of School Administrators; Association of School Business Officials; National Academy for School Executives; National Association of Elementary School Principles; National Association of Secondary School Principles; National Business Education Association.

Material Recording, Scheduling, and Distributing Occupations

1326

Certified Claims Professional (CCP)
Certified Claims Professional
    Accreditation Council (CCPAC)
PO Box 441110
Fort Washington, MD 20744
Phone: (301)292-1988
Fax: (301)292-1787
Dale L. Anderson, Admin.

Recipient: Transportation professionals specializing in freight claims management. **Educational/Experience Requirements:** Must accumulate 200 totals points through: (1) Experience (50 points minimum), with 50% of time performing related functions (20 points per year); (2) Experience, with less than 50% of time performing related functions (ten points per year); (3) Arbitrating claims (ten points per case); (4) Association membership (up to ten points per year); (5) Academic education, including: Bachelor's degree (50 points); Master's degree (25 points); Graduate degree (25 points); and Years of full-time schooling (12 points per year); and (6) Related courses (one point per course). **Membership:** Not required. **Certification Requirements:** Successful completion of exam. Must complete general section and two of the following mode sections: Air; Rail; Truck; and Water. Exam covers: Agents and insurance; Bills of lading; Claims, including adjudication, arbitration, documentation, filing, prevention, and settlements; Laws, tariffs, and statutes; and Liability, including carrier, forwarder, and warehouse. **Renewal:** Every three years. Recertification based on either successful completion of exam or continuing education. **Examination Type:** Multiple-choice. **Pass/Fail Rate:** 64% pass exam. **Fees:** $125.

1327

**Certified Director of
    Equipment/Maintenance**
National Committee for Motor
    Fleet Supervisor Training
    (NCMFST)
2200 Mill Rd.
Alexandria, VA 22314-4677
Phone: (703)838-7952
Fax: (703)836-6070
Jeff Arnold, Dir.

Recipient: Motor fleet directors of equipment and/or maintenance. **Educational/Experience Requirements:** Must meet following requirements: (1) Successful completion of Maintenance Management and Maintenance of Commercial Vehicles, Phases A and B, workshops; and (2) Five years experience with current employer. Bachelor's degree may be substituted for one year of experience. Candidates with two-and-a-half to five years of experience with one employer may apply for waiver. **Certification Requirements:** Must meet following requirements: (1) Submission of exhibit documenting experience, education, and professional activities and designations; and (2) Successful completion of exam. **Preparatory Materials:** *Motor Carrier*

Safety Regulations, Motor Fleet Safety Supervision: Principles and Practices, and *Occupational Safety and Health Regulations* (references). Manuals and study group materials available. **Examination Frequency:** Throughout the year. **Examination Sites:** Exam given at sites throughout the U.S. **Examination Type:** Essay; multiple-choice; true or false. **Waiting Period to Receive Scores:** 24 hours. **Re-examination:** Must wait three months to retake exam.

1328

**Certified Expediting Manager
    (CEM)**
Expediting Management Association
    (EMA)
40 Irwin St.
New Hyde Park, NY 11040
Phone: (516)746-7438
Fax: (516)746-7438
James P. Hughes, Exec.Admin.

Recipient: Professionals responsible for ensuring prompt delivery of products and materials. **Educational/Experience Requirements:** Must earn 150 total points in the following categories: (1) Associate's degree (20 points); (2) Bachelor's degree (20 points); (3) Masters degree (20 points); (4) Experience (ten points per year); (5) EMA membership (ten points per year); (6) EMA association positions held (20 points per year); (7) EMA seminars attended and presentations given (20 points each); and (8) Papers written and published (ten points each). **Membership:** Required. **Certification Requirements:** Successful completion of exam. **Renewal:** Every five years. Recertification based on accumulation of points through continuing education and professional development activities. **Preparatory Materials:** *Expediting Manager's Manual* (reference). **Examination Frequency:** Annual. **Examination Sites:** Exam given at general conference. **Re-examination:** Must wait one year to retake exam.

1329

Certified Mail Manager (CMM)
International Publishing
    Management Association (IPMA)
1205 W. College St.
Liberty, MO 64068-3733
Phone: (816)781-1111
Fax: (816)781-2790
E-mail: CompuServe 71674.1647
Larry E. Aaron CAE, Exec.Dir.

Recipient: In-house mail managers. **Number of Certified Individuals:** 5.

Educational/Experience Requirements: Five years experience. **Membership:** Not required. **Certification Requirements:** Successful completion of six-part exam. Exam parts are: (1) Computer Skills, including: Computer system hardware and software; Concepts; and Purchasing; (2) Financial Management, including: Accounting; Budgeting; Inventory; and Management reports; (3) General Management, including: Controls; Objectives; Organization, Planning, and Principles; (4) Personnel Management, including: Development; Employee relations; Hiring; Pay and benefits; and Personnel records; (5) General Mail Management, including: Functions; Mail flow and mail room problems; and Operations; and (6) Technical Skills, including: Alternate carrier services; Mail classification; and U.S. Postal Service operations and automation. **Renewal:** Every five years. Recertification based on accumulation of 15 professional credits through membership in IPMA or other professional mail manager associations, attendance at IPMA conference or other related seminars, writing articles, participating as volunteer in association activities, or instructing or lecturing on mail management. Lifetime certification available for CMMs age 60 or older after initial renewal. **Preparatory Materials:** *Complete Reference to Postal Knowledge, Computers: The Plain English Guide, First Book of Personal Computing, Professional Mail Management,* and *Small Business Management* (references). List of suggested study references provided. **Examination Frequency:** Throughout the year. **Examination Sites:** Exam given at IPMA annual conference, regional conferences, and other sites throughout the U.S. **Examination Type:** Multiple-choice. **Pass/Fail Rate:** 48% pass exam the first time. **Waiting Period to Receive Scores:** Four weeks. **Fees:** $225 (members); $450 (non-members).

`1330`

Certified Maintenance Supervisor
National Committee for Motor
   Fleet Supervisor Training
   (NCMFST)
2200 Mill Rd.
Alexandria, VA 22314-4677
Phone: (703)838-7952
Fax: (703)836-6070
Jeff Arnold, Dir.

Recipient: Motor fleet maintenance supervisors. **Educational/Experience Requirements:** Must meet the following requirements: (1) Successful completion of Maintenance or Commercial Vehicles, Phase A and B, workshops; and (2)

Three years experience with current employer. **Certification Requirements:** Must meet following requirements: (1) Submission of exhibit documenting experience, education, and professional activities and designations; and (2) Successful completion of exam. **Preparatory Materials:** *Motor Carrier Safety Regulations, Motor Fleet Safety Supervision: Principles and Practices,* and *Occupational Safety and Health Regulations* (references). Manuals and study group materials available. **Examination Frequency:** Throughout the year. **Examination Sites:** Exam given at sites throughout the U.S. **Examination Type:** Essay; multiple-choice; true or false. **Waiting Period to Receive Scores:** 24 hours. **Re-examination:** Must wait three months to retake exam.

`1331`

Certified Moving Consultant (CMC)
National Institute of Certified
   Moving Consultants (NICMC)
11150 Main St., Ste. 402
Fairfax, VA 22030
Phone: (703)934-9111
Fax: (703)934-9712
Toll Free: (800)538-6672
Dr. Gary Frank Petty, Pres.

Recipient: Individuals involved directly or indirectly in sales and marketing of moving and storage services. **Number of Certified Individuals:** 3000. **Educational/Experience Requirements:** Six months experience. **Membership:** Not required. **Certification Requirements:** Successful completion of exam. **Renewal:** Every three years. Recertification based on accumulation of 15 hours of continuing education and training. Renewal fees are: $75 (members); $75 (international members); $150 (nonmembers). **Preparatory Materials:** Manual and exam booklet available. **Re-examination:** Fees to retake exams are: $50 (members); $75 (international members); $100 (nonmembers). **Fees:** $200 (members); $250 (international members); $350 (nonmembers).

`1332`

Certified Packaging Professional (CPP)
Institute of Packaging Professionals
   (IoPP)
481 Carlisle Dr.
Herndon, VA 22070
Phone: (703)318-8970
Fax: (703)318-0310
William C. Pflaum, Exec.Dir.

Recipient: Packaging and handling pro-

fessionals. **Educational/Experience Requirements:** Must meet one of the following requirements: (1) Six years experience or; (2) Two years experience and bachelor's degree in packaging technology. One additional year of credit will be given for postgraduate degree. **Membership:** Not required. **Certification Requirements:** Must complete the following requirements: (1) Successful completion of exam. Candidates may take Commercial/Distribution or Military version of exam; and (2) Submission of technical paper. Paper must cover area of packaging. Previously published paper or U.S. patent (within the previous twelve months) may be substituted for paper. **Renewal:** Every five years. Recertification based on either successful completion of exam or meeting professional advancement requirements. Lifetime certification available after second renewal. **Examination Sites:** Exam given by correspondence. **Examination Type:** Multiple-choice. **Pass/Fail Rate:** 75% pass exam. **Fees:** $75 (members); $175 (nonmembers).

`1333`

Certified Professional in Healthcare Materials Management (CPHM)
Health Care Material Management
   Society (HCMMS)
306 Crestview Dr.
Grapevine, TX 76051-3569
Phone: (817)421-8517
Fax: (817)421-8971
Toll Free: (800)543-5885
Richard D. Warmanen FDPHM,
   Exec.Dir.

Recipient: Health care material management directors and peer group professionals. **Number of Certified Individuals:** 200. **Membership:** Not required. **Certification Requirements:** Successful completion of one of the following: (1) Exam; or (2) Three programs required for Recognition of Expertise, Health Care Material Management Society designation (see separate entry). **Renewal:** Every three years. Recertification based on either successful completion of exam or accumulation of 200 points through course work, association and professional activities, written materials published, seminars, speaking engagements, and special projects. **Preparatory Materials:** Bibliography, sample questions, study guide, and self-study courses available. **Examination Frequency:** Throughout the year. **Examination Sites:** Exam given at HCMMS annual meeting or by arrangement with proctor. **Examination Type:** Essay; multiple-choice; true or false. **Pass/Fail Rate:** 80% pass exam the first time. **Waiting Period to Receive Scores:** Ten days. **Re-examination:** There is no time limit to retake exam. **Fees:** $100 (members); $200 (nonmembers).

1334

Certified Safety Supervisor
National Committee for Motor
   Fleet Supervisor Training
   (NCMFST)
2200 Mill Rd.
Alexandria, VA 22314-4677
Phone: (703)838-7952
Fax: (703)836-6070
Jeff Arnold, Dir.

Recipient: Motor fleet safety supervisors. **Educational/Experience Requirements:** Must meet the following requirements: (1) Successful completion of Fleet Supervisor and one other workshop; and (2) Three years experience with current employer. **Certification Requirements:** Must meet following requirements: (1) Submission of exhibit documenting experience, education, and professional activities and designations; and (2) Successful completion of exam. **Preparatory Materials:** *Motor Carrier Safety Regulations, Motor Fleet Safety Supervision: Principles and Practices,* and *Occupational Safety and Health Regulations* (references). Manuals and study group materials available. **Examination Frequency:** Throughout the year. **Examination Sites:** Exam given at sites throughout the U.S. **Examination Type:** Essay; multiple-choice; true or false. **Waiting Period to Receive Scores:** 24 hours. **Re-examination:** Must wait three months to retake exam.

1335

Certified Senior Member of the American Society of Healthcare Materials Management
American Society of Healthcare
   Materials Management
   (ASHMM)
c/o American Hospital Association
One N. Franklin
Chicago, IL 60606
Phone: (312)280-6155

Recipient: Professionals involved in healthcare materials management. **Educational/Experience Requirements:** Must accumulate points through: (1) Continuing Education (five points minimum), including: ASHMM seminars (two points per day); ASHMM annual conference (four points); Health care programs (one point per day); and College courses (one point per credit); and

(2) Experience (three points minimum) in the following health care purchasing or materials management positions: Manager/director (three points per year); and Staff member (two points per year). May also earn points as Manager/director of purchasing and materials management in another field (one point per year) or as vendor, manufacturer, distributor, or consultant to the healthcare field (one point per year). **Membership:** Required. **Certification Requirements:** Successful completion of exam. **Re-examination:** May retake exam twice. **Fees:** $75. **Endorsed By:** American Hospital Association.

1336

Certified Shop Service Managers
National Committee for Motor
   Fleet Supervisor Training
   (NCMFST)
2200 Mill Rd.
Alexandria, VA 22314-4677
Phone: (703)838-7952
Fax: (703)836-6070
Jeff Arnold, Dir.

Recipient: Motor fleet shop service managers. **Educational/Experience Requirements:** Must meet the following requirements: (1) Successful completion of Maintenance of Commercial Vehicles, Phases A and B, workshops; and (2) Three years experience with current employer. **Certification Requirements:** Must meet following requirements: (1) Submission of exhibit documenting experience, education, and professional activities and designations; and (2) Successful completion of exam. **Preparatory Materials:** *Motor Carrier Safety Regulations, Motor Fleet Safety Supervision: Principles and Practices,* and *Occupational Safety and Health Regulations* (references). Manuals and study group materials available. **Examination Frequency:** Throughout the year. **Examination Sites:** Exam given at sites throughout the U.S. **Examination Type:** Essay; multiple-choice; true or false. **Waiting Period to Receive Scores:** 24 hours. **Re-examination:** Must wait three months to retake exam.

1337

Certified Sterile Processing and Distribution Manager (CSPDM)
National Institute for the
   Certification of Healthcare Sterile
   Processing and Distribution
   Personnel (NICHSPDP)
PO Box 558
Annandale, NJ 08801

Recipient: Managers of healthcare sterile processing and distribution departments. **Educational/Experience Requirements:** Three years experience. **Certification Requirements:** Successful completion of exam. Exam covers: (1) Fiscal Management, including: Developing departmental budget; and Monitoring budget against actual expenses; (2) Personnel Management, including: Approving worker time schedule; Arbitrating conflicts; Developing employee job descriptions; Evaluating employee performance; Hiring and labor laws; Personnel training; Productivity monitoring of staff; Providing education; Resolving and mediating personnel conflicts; and Staffing decisions; (3) Compliance with Standards, including: Insuring compliance with relevant guidelines, recommendations, regulations, and standards; and Maintaining safe work environment; (4) Sterile Processing and Distribution/Central Service Responsibilities, including: Operations performed in sterile processing; Operations of sterile storage and distribution; and Procedures performed in decontamination department; (5) Anatomy, Microbiology, and Infection Control, including: Disease transmission and preventative measures; Relationship between human anatomy and physiology and work performed in sterile processing and distribution; and Relationship between microbiology and infection control and work performed in sterile processing and distribution; (6) Administration of Sterile Processing and Distribution, including: Assisting in development of policies and procedures; Assisting in planning for emergencies and disasters; Assuring implementation of policies and procedures; Implementation of facility recall procedures; Maintaining ethics and standards; Monitoring compliance to policies and procedures; Responding to emergencies; Testing of procedures and results; and (7) Inventory Control and Distribution, including: Assisting in development of procedures for storage; Assisting in implementation of storage method; Ensuring that equipment, instruments, and medical devices are kept in working order; Establishing supply distribution system; Maintaining adequate quantities of supplies, equipment, instruments, and medical devices; Monitoring storage methods; Ordering supplies; and Use of computers. **Renewal:** Every five years. Recertification based on accumulation of 150 points through: (1) Successful completion of exam (75 points); (2) Continuing education (one point per contact hour); (3) Successful completion of college courses in anatomy/physiology, chemistry, communication, computers, English, environmental control, finance, microbiology, psychology, and safety (seven points per credit hour); (4) Experience (five points per year of full-time employment; two-and-one-half points per year of part-time employment); (5) Holding committee chairperson position at local, state, or national level (five points per year); (6) Holding leadership position in local, state, or national chapter related to healthcare (five points per year); (7) Authoring of published papers related to healthcare (10 points per paper); and (8) Making presentations on related subjects (one point per hour; maximum of ten points per year). **Preparatory Materials:** Bulletin, including exam content outline, list of suggested references, and sample questions, provided. Study guide available. **Examination Frequency:** semiannual - always April and October. **Examination Sites:** Exam given at sites throughout the U.S. and internationally. **Waiting Period to Receive Scores:** Three-four weeks. **Re-examination:** There is a $130 fee to retake exam. **Fees:** $130. **Accredited By:** National Commission for Certifying Agencies. **Endorsed By:** American Society for Healthcare Central Service Personnel; National Organization for Competency Assurance.

1338

Certified Trainer of Commercial Drivers

National Committee for Motor Fleet Supervisor Training (NCMFST)
2200 Mill Rd.
Alexandria, VA 22314-4677
Phone: (703)838-7952
Fax: (703)836-6070
Jeff Arnold, Dir.

Recipient: Motor fleet commercial driver trainers. **Educational/Experience Requirements:** Must meet the following requirements: (1) Successful completion of Motor Fleet Trainer workshop; and (2) Three years experience with current employer. **Certification Requirements:** Must meet following requirements: (1) Submission of exhibit documenting experience, education, and professional activities and designations; and (2) Successful completion of exam. **Preparatory Materials:**

Motor Carrier Safety Regulations, Motor Fleet Safety Supervision: Principles and Practices, and *Occupational Safety and Health Regulations* (references). Manuals and study group materials available. **Examination Frequency:** Throughout the year. **Examination Sites:** Exam given at sites throughout the U.S. **Examination Type:** Essay; multiple-choice; true or false. **Waiting Period to Receive Scores:** 24 hours. **Re-examination:** Must wait three months to retake exam.

1339

Distinguished Professional in Healthcare Materials Management (DPHM)

Health Care Material Management Society (HCMMS)
306 Crestview Dr.
Grapevine, TX 76051-3569
Phone: (817)421-8517
Fax: (817)421-8971
Toll Free: (800)543-5885
Richard D. Warmanen FDPHM, Exec.Dir.

Recipient: Health care material management directors and peer group professionals. **Membership:** Not required. **Certification Requirements:** Hold Certified Professional in Healthcare Materials Management (CPHM) designation and successfully renew four times. **Renewal:** Every three years. Recertification based on providing verification of involvement in the field.

1340

Military Packaging Professional (MPP)

School of Military Packaging Technology (SMPT)
U.S. Army Logistics Mgt. Coll.
Aberdeen Proving Grounds, MD 21005
Phone: (410)278-4770
Fax: (410)278-2176
Joseph Wise, Training Specialist

Recipient: Military personnel, Department of Defense civilian employees, non-Department of Defense agencies, and employees of private contractors bidding or planning to bid on military contracts. **Educational/Experience Requirements:** Five years experience. **Membership:** Not required. **Certification Requirements:** Successful completion of three core courses and six additional elective courses on packaging. Core courses are: (1) Defense Packaging Design; (2) Defense Packing and Utilization; and (3)

Defense Preservation and Intermediate Protection. Other service or civilian courses related to military packaging may be accepted as electives upon petition to SMPT. **Renewal:** none.

1341

Professional Certified in Materials Handling (PCMH)

Materials Handling and Management Society (MHMS)
8720 Red Oak Blvd., Ste. 224
Charlotte, NC 28217-3990
Phone: (704)525-4667
Fax: (704)525-2880

Recipient: Professionals involved in materials handling, a function of materials management, centering on actual handling of products and materials between procurement and shipping. **Educational/Experience Requirements:** Eight years experience. Education and professional activities can be substituted for up to five years of experience in the following ways: (1) Four years for bachelor's degree; (2) Two years for associate degree if credit not applied to higher degree; (3) Two years for graduate degree related to materials handling or management; and (4) Two years for holding Registered Professional Engineer designation. **Membership:** Not required. **Certification Requirements:** Successful completion of exam. Exam covers: Applications and systems planning; Environmental control; Integrated computer applications; Packaging (industrial); Plant layout; Safety; Transportation; and Work measurement/economic justification. **Renewal:** Every three years. Recertification based on either successful completion of exam or accumulation of 180 professional credits through experience, participation in professional societies, speaking engagements, published works, seminar attendance, formal course work, self-study, and special projects. **Preparatory Materials:** Study guide, including bibliography, exam content outline, and sample questions, provided. **Examination Frequency:** Throughout the year. **Examination Sites:** Exam given at sites throughout the U.S. **Examination Type:** Multiple-choice. **Fees:** $50 (members); $100 (nonmembers).

1342

Professional Certified in Materials Management (PCMM)
Materials Handling and
    Management Society (MHMS)
8720 Red Oak Blvd., Ste. 224
Charlotte, NC 28217-3990
Phone: (704)525-4667
Fax: (704)525-2880

Recipient: Professionals involved in materials handling, a function of materials management, centering on actual handling of products and materials between procurement and shipping. **Educational/ Experience Requirements:** Eight years experience. Education and professional activities can be substituted for up to five years of experience in the following ways: (1) Four years for bachelor's degree; (2) Two years for associate degree if credit not applied to higher degree; (3) Two years for graduate degree related to materials handling or management; and (4) Two years for holding Registered Professional Engineer designation. **Membership:** Not required. **Certification Requirements:** Successful completion of exam. Exam covers: Information systems and computer applications; In-plant handling; Inventory control; Planning materials flow; Production control; Purchasing; Traffic and distribution; and Value techniques. **Renewal:** Every three years. Recertification based on either successful completion of exam or accumulation of 180 professional credits through experience, participation in professional societies, speaking engagements, published works, seminar attendance, formal course work, self-study, and special projects. **Preparatory Materials:** Study guide, including bibliography, exam content outline, and sample questions, provided. **Examination Frequency:** Throughout the year. **Examination Sites:** Exam given at sites throughout the U.S. **Examination Type:** Multiple-choice. **Fees:** $50 (members); $100 (nonmembers).

1343

Recognition of Expertise, Health Care Materials Management Society
Health Care Material Management
    Society (HCMMS)
306 Crestview Dr.
Grapevine, TX 76051-3569
Phone: (817)421-8517
Fax: (817)421-8971
Toll Free: (800)543-5885
Richard D. Warmanen FDPHM,
    Exec.Dir.

Recipient: Health care material manage-

ment directors and peer group professionals. **Membership:** Not required. **Certification Requirements:** Successful completion of exam. Certification available in the following areas: (1) Purchasing and Inventory Control; (2) Supply Processing and Infection Control; and (3) Supply Storage and Distribution. Candidates who successfully complete all three areas earn Certified Professional in Health Care Material Management (CPHM) designation (see separate entry). **Renewal:** Every three years. Recertification based on successful completion of exam or accumulation of 100 points through course work, association and professional activities, written materials published, seminars, speaking engagements, and special projects. **Preparatory Materials:** Bibliography, sample questions, study guide, and self-study courses available. **Examination Frequency:** Throughout the year. **Examination Sites:** Exam given at HCMMS annual meeting or by arrangement with proctor. **Fees:** $50 (members); $100 (nonmembers).

Payroll and Timekeeping Clerks

1344

Certified Payroll Professional (CPP)
American Payroll Association
    (APA)
30 E. 33rd St., 5th Fl.
New York, NY 10016
Phone: (212)686-2030
Fax: (212)686-2789
Rosemary Birardi, Mgr.

Recipient: Payroll employees. **Number of Certified Individuals:** 3750. **Educational/ Experience Requirements:** Direct involvement with payroll for three of the preceding five years. **Membership:** Not required. **Certification Requirements:** Successful completion of exam. Exam covers: Accounting; Federal tax and social security; Fundamentals of the practice of payroll, including federal regulations and legislation, benefits, deductions, record-keeping, and payment options; General management; Payroll systems; and Recertification. **Renewal:** Every five years. Recertification based on either successful completion of exam or accumulation of 120 hours of related continuing education. **Preparatory Materials:** Reference materials available. **Examination Frequency:** semiannual. **Examination Sites:** Exam given at APS annual meeting and sites throughout the U.S. **Examination Type:** Multiple-choice. **Pass/Fail**

Rate: 55% pass exam the first time. **Waiting Period to Receive Scores:** Six weeks. **Re-examination:** Must wait six months to retake exam. **Fees:** $230 (members); $290 (nonmembers).

Record Clerks

1345

Associate in State Filings (ASF)
Society of State Filers (SSF)
3101 Broadway, Ste. 585
Kansas City, MO 64111
Phone: (816)931-4800
Fax: (816)561-7765
Michelle Groner, Exec.Dir.

Recipient: Individuals involved or interested in filing of rates, rules, and forms with state regulatory departments. **Educational/Experience Requirements:** Five years experience, with three years involved in state filing functions. **Membership:** Not required. **Certification Requirements:** Successful completion of the following courses, including exams: (1) Chartered Property Casualty Underwriter (CPCU) 1: Ethics, Insurance Perspectives, and Insurance Contract Analysis, offered by American Institute for CPCU (AICPCU), including: Common insurance policy provisions; Ethics and professional movement; External factors affecting insurance policy analysis; Insurable interests and insured parties; Insured events; Loss sharing provisions; Multiple sources of recovery; and Policy limits and loss valuation provisions; (2) Chartered Property Casualty Underwriter (CPCU) 5: Insurance Company Operations, including: Claims adjusting; Loss control; Marketing; Premium auditing; Ratemaking; Reinsurance; and Underwriting; and (3) Associate in Insurance Accounting and Finance (AIAF) 111: Statutory Accounting for Property and Liability Insurers, offered by Insurance Institute of America (IIA). **Preparatory Materials:** Review materials and study groups available. **Examination Frequency:** semiannual - always June and January (AICPCU exams) and June and December (AIAF exams). **Examination Type:** Essay (AICPCU exams).

1346

Certified Records Manager (CRM)
Institute of Certified Records
    Managers (ICRM)
PO Box 8188
Prairie Village, KS 66208
Toll Free: (800)825-4276
Isabelle R. Peterson CRM, Sec.

Recipient: Professional records and information managers. **Educational/ Experience Requirements:** Must meet one of the following requirements: (1) Bachelor's degree or equivalent and three years experience; (2) Three years college education and five years experience; (3) Two years college education and seven years experience; (4) One year of college education and nine years experience; or (5) High school diploma and 11 years experience. Experience must be in at least three of the following areas: Active records systems; Inactive records systems; Management of records management program; Records appraisal, retention, disposition; Records creation and use; Records and information management and technology; and Records protection. Acceptable experience may come from conducting studies and surveys, designing, developing, and implementing records systems, or teaching college courses in records management. Consultants and vendors must have at least two clients describe their work in writing. Teachers must submit the syllabi of courses taught and letter from school official substantiating experience. Specialized equipment operations and traditional librarian functions are not acceptable. Medical records experience may be accepted based on the actual tasks performed. **Certification Requirements:** Successful completion of six-part exam. Exam parts are: (1) Equipment, Supplies, and Technology, including: Computers; Ergonomics; Micrographics; Optical disks/image systems; Reprographics; Telecommunications; Word processing; and Other filing and preservation equipment; (2) Management Principles and the Records Management Program, including: Developing, planning, organizing, directing, and controlling records management program; Legal and ethical responsibilities; Outside resources; and Principles of management; (3) Records Appraisal, Retention, Protection, and Disposition, including: Archives; Disaster recovery; Implementing and administering schedules; Records inventory; Retention schedules; and Vital records programs; (4) Records Creation and Use, covering: Correspondence; Directives; Forms; Mail; Reports; Reproduction; and Special media management; (5) Records Systems, Storage, and Retrieval, including: Active file, filing, and information retrieval systems; Active and inactive file operations; Automated paper and film systems; and Converting files to new systems; and (6) Case studies. Parts one-five must be successfully completed before part six may be attempted. **Renewal:** Every five years. Recertification based on accumulation of 100 contact hours of continuing education through

college coursework, conferences and seminars, correspondence courses, association educational activities, teaching, lecturing, and giving presentations, publication of articles, books, and manuals, review of professional books, and design of records retention schedules, software, file or disaster plans, or records management systems. Lifetime certification available for retired CRMs. Renewal fee is $100. **Preparatory Materials:** *Preparing for the CRM Examination: A Handbook* (reference). Study materials available. **Examination Frequency:** semiannual - always May and November. **Examination Sites:** Exam given at sites throughout the U.S. **Examination Type:** Essay; multiple-choice. **Re-examination:** Must only retake parts of exam failed. Must successfully complete exam within five years. **Fees:** $320.

1347

Certified State Filer (CSF)
Society of State Filers (SSF)
3101 Broadway, Ste. 585
Kansas City, MO 64111
Phone: (816)931-4800
Fax: (816)561-7765
Michelle Groner, Exec.Dir.

Recipient: Individuals involved or interested in filing of rates, rules, and forms with state regulatory departments. **Educational/Experience Requirements:** Must hold Associate in State Filings (ASF) designation (see separate entry). **Certification Requirements:** Successfully completion of the following courses given through American Institute of CPCU (AICPCU): (1) Insurance Regulation, including: Current regulatory environment; Evolution of insurance regulation; Impact of regulation on insurance industry; International issues; Operation of state regulation and insurance; and Theory of insurance regulation; and (2) Ratemaking - What the State Filer Needs to Know, including: Background; Calendar year vs. policy year; Development of final rates; Property and liability ratemaking; and Words and phrases. **Examination Frequency:** semiannual - always January and June. **Examination Type:** Essay.

Secretaries

1348

Accredited Legal Secretary (ALS)
National Association of Legal
  Secretaries (International)
  (NALS)
2250 E. 73rd St., Ste. 550
Tulsa, OK 74136
Phone: (918)493-3540
Fax: (918)493-5784
Toll Free: (800)756-NALS
Gretta Kontas CAE, Dir.

Recipient: Legal secretaries. **Educational/Experience Requirements:** Must meet one of the following requirements: (1) Successful completion of acceptable secretarial course; (2) Successful completion of NALS Legal Training Course; or (3) One year of experience. **Membership:** Not required. **Certification Requirements:** Successful completion of exam. Exam covers: Ethics, human relations, and applied office procedures; Office administration, legal terminology, and accounting; and Written communication comprehension and application. **Renewal:** Every five years. **Preparatory Materials:** *Career Legal Secretary, Essentials of Accounting,* and *The Gregg Reference Manual* (references). **Examination Frequency:** semiannual - always March and September; exam also given at special times for schools and colleges. **Examination Sites:** Exam given at sites throughout the U.S. **Fees:** $35 (students); $50 (members); $75 (nonmembers).

1349

**Certified Professional Legal
  Secretary (PLS)**
National Association of Legal
  Secretaries (International)
  (NALS)
2250 E. 73rd St., Ste. 550
Tulsa, OK 74136
Phone: (918)493-3540
Fax: (918)493-5784
Toll Free: (800)756-NALS
Gretta Kontas CAE, Dir.

Recipient: Legal secretaries. **Number of Certified Individuals:** 3799. **Educational/ Experience Requirements:** Three years experience under direct supervision of lawyer or judge. Approved postsecondary degrees may be substituted for up to one year of experience requirement. **Membership:** Not required. **Certification Requirements:** Successful completion of exam. Exam covers: Accounting; Ethics; Office procedures; Exercise in judgement;

Legal secretarial skills; Legal terminology, techniques, and procedures; and Written communication skills and knowledge. **Renewal:** Every five years. Recertification based on articles or texts authored, college course work, continuing education, exam construction and monitoring, self-study courses, seminars and workshops attended, and teaching. Renewal fee is $75. **Preparatory Materials:** *Career Legal Secretary, Gregg Reference Manual,* and *PLS Resource Manual* (texts). Legal training course, reference bibliography, and study materials available. **Examination Frequency:** semiannual - always March and September. **Examination Sites:** Exam given at 100 sites throughout the U.S. **Examination Type:** Multiple-choice. **Waiting Period to Receive Scores:** Eight-ten weeks. **Re-examination:** Must wait six months to retake exam. May retake exam four times in three years. **Fees:** $100 (members); $200 (nonmembers).

1350

Certified Professional Secretary (CPS)
Professional Secretaries
  International (PSI)
10502 N.W. Ambassador Dr.
PO Box 20404
Kansas City, MO 64195-0404
Phone: (816)891-6600
Fax: (816)891-9118

Recipient: Secretaries. **Educational/ Experience Requirements:** Twelve months continuous experience with one employer in past five years and meet one of the following requirements: (1) Bachelor's degree and two years experience; (2) Associate's degree and three years experience; or (3) Four years experience. Experience must be as executive assistant with mastery of office skills and ability to assume responsibility without direct supervision, exercise initiative and judgment, and make decisions. Students and business educators may also qualify to take exam. **Membership:** Not required. **Certification Requirements:** Successful completion of three-part exam. Exam parts are: (1) Finance and Business Law, including: Accounting; Business law; and Economics; (2) Office Systems and Administration, including: Business communications; Office administration; and Office technology; and (3) Management, including: Behavioral science in business; Human resources management; and Organizations and management. **Renewal:** Every five years. Recertification based on accumulation of 120 points through: College courses (90 point maximum); Seminars, workshops, or company training

(60 points maximum); Conducting seminars, workshops, or courses (30 points maximum); Continuing education units (CEUs) (60 points maximum); Published articles (50 points maximum); Association leadership (35 points maximum); and CPS review courses (ten points maximum). **Preparatory Materials:** *CPS Exam Review, CPS Outline and Bibliography, CPS: A Sampling of Questions, CPS Video Review,* and *Suggested Plans and Procedures for CPS Review Courses* (manuals). Self-study guides, review and self-study courses, and seminars available. **Examination Frequency:** semiannual - always May and November. **Examination Sites:** Exam given at 250 sites in the U.S., Canada, Jamaica, Malaysia, Hong Kong, and other international locations. **Examination Type:** Multiple-choice. **Waiting Period to Receive Scores:** 45 days. **Re-examination:** Must only retake sections failed. Must successfully complete exam within three years. **Fees:** $110 (members); $135 (nonmembers).

Stenographers and Court Reporters

1351

Certified Legal Video Specialist (CLVS)
National Court Reporters
  Association (NCRA)
8224 Old Courthouse Rd.
Vienna, VA 22182
Phone: (703)556-6272
Fax: (703)556-6291
Toll Free: (800)272-6272
Karen S. Jacoby, Dir.

Recipient: Legal videographers who participate in video depositions with court reporter. **Number of Certified Individuals:** 450. **Educational/Experience Requirements:** none. **Membership:** Not required. **Certification Requirements:** Successful completion of seminar and two-part exam. Part one of exam covers: Duplication; Editing; Legal and judicial procedures; Legal requirements; Operating practices; Playbacks; Professional conduct; and Videotaping techniques. Second part of exam covers video skills. **Renewal:** Every year. Renewal fee is $35. **Preparatory Materials:** *Today's Video* (text). **Examination Frequency:** semiannual - always May and November (Part one) and April and October (Part two). **Examination Sites:** Part one given at over 100 sites throughout the U.S. and part two given at sites on east and west coasts of the U.S. **Examination Type:**

Multiple-choice; practical. **Pass/Fail Rate:** 50 percent pass part one of exam; 65 percent pass part two of exam. **Waiting Period to Receive Scores:** Six-eight weeks. **Re-examination:** Must wait six months to retake exam. **Fees:** $720 (members); $920 (nonmembers).

1352

Certified Manager of Reporting Services (CMRS)
National Court Reporters
  Association (NCRA)
8224 Old Courthouse Rd.
Vienna, VA 22182
Phone: (703)556-6272
Fax: (703)556-6291
Toll Free: (800)272-6272
Karen S. Jacoby, Dir.

Recipient: Managers of court reporting services in both freelance and court areas. **Number of Certified Individuals:** 43. **Educational/Experience Requirements:** none. **Membership:** Not required. **Certification Requirements:** Completion of two modules and independent study project. Modules are: (1) Management Concepts and Applications; and (2) Financial Concepts and Marketing Practices. Must submit professional paper after each module. **Renewal:** none. **Preparatory Materials:** *Developing Management Skills, Finance and Accounting for Nonfinancial Manager, The Marketing Guide,* and *What Every Supervisor Should Know* (texts). *The Balance Sheet Barrier* (video) also available. **Fees:** $930 (members); $990 (nonmembers).

1353

Certified Real time Reporter (CRR)
National Court Reporters
  Association (NCRA)
8224 Old Courthouse Rd.
Vienna, VA 22182
Phone: (703)556-6272
Fax: (703)556-6291
Toll Free: (800)272-6272
Karen S. Jacoby, Dir.

Recipient: Court reporters who instantaneously translate spoken word to print. **Number of Certified Individuals:** 137. **Educational/Experience Requirements:** Hold Registered Professional Reporter (RPR) designation (see separate entry). **Membership:** Required. **Certification Requirements:** Successful completion of exam. Must translate variable speed (189-200 words per minute) spoken presentation with 96 percent accuracy. **Renewal:** none. **Preparatory Materials:** Seminars and workshops available. **Examination Frequency:** quarterly. **Examination Sites:** Exam given at NACR midyear meeting and convention and at sites throughout the U.S. **Pass/Fail Rate:** 25 percent pass exam. **Waiting Period to Receive Scores:** Six-eight weeks. **Re-examination:** Must wait four months to retake exam. **Fees:** $125.

1354

Registered Professional Reporter (RPR)
National Court Reporters
  Association (NCRA)
8224 Old Courthouse Rd.
Vienna, VA 22182
Phone: (703)556-6272
Fax: (703)556-6291
Toll Free: (800)272-6272
Kris R. Mitchell, Asst.Dir.

Recipient: Court reporters. **Number of Certified Individuals:** 12,000. **Educational/Experience Requirements:** none. **Membership:** Required. **Certification Requirements:** Successful completion of two-part exam. Part one covers: Court system; Legal terminology and procedures; Operating practices and professional issues; Reporting actions; Role of the reporter; Transcript production; and Verification. Part two includes three five-minute dictation segments that must be successfully completed with 95 percent accuracy. **Renewal:** Every three years. Recertification based on accumulation of 30 continuing education credits. **Preparatory Materials:** Practice tapes and study guide available. **Examination Frequency:** semiannual - always May and November. **Examination Sites:** Exam given at 110 sites throughout the U.S. **Examination Type:** Multiple-choice. **Pass/Fail Rate:** 60 percent pass part one of exam; 34 percent pass part two of exam. **Waiting Period to Receive Scores:** Eight weeks. **Re-examination:** Must wait six months to retake exam. **Fees:** $85

Service Occupations

Protective Service Occupations

Criminalists

1355

Diplomate of the American Board of Criminalistics
American Board of Criminalistics (ABC)
PO Box 669
Colorado Springs, CO 80901-0669

Recipient: Criminalists involved in examination of physical evidence, interpretation of data, and/or technical consultation for litigation purposes. **Educational/Experience Requirements:** Must meet the following requirements: (1) Bachelor's degree in a natural science or related field; and (2) Two years experience. **Certification Requirements:** Successful completion of exam. Exam covers: Applicable areas of civil and criminal law; Ethics; Philosophical and scientific concepts; and Questions on techniques. **Endorsed By:** American Academy of Forensic Sciences; California Association of Criminalistics; Mid-Atlantic Association of Forensic Scientists; Midwestern Association of Forensic Scientists; Northeastern Association of Forensic Scientists; Southern Association of Forensic Scientists.

1356

Fellow of the American Board of Criminalistics
American Board of Criminalistics (ABC)
PO Box 669
Colorado Springs, CO 80901-0669

Recipient: Criminalists involved in examination of physical evidence, interpretation of data, and/or technical consultation for litigation purposes. **Educational/Experience Requirements:** Must meet the

following requirements: (1) Bachelor's degree in a natural science or related field; and (2) Two years experience. **Certification Requirements:** Successful completion of general exam and one specialty exam. General exam covers: Applicable areas of civil and criminal law; Ethics; Philosophical and scientific concepts; and Questions on techniques. Specialty exams are offered in: Drug chemistry; Fire debris analysis; Forensic biology; and Trace evidence. Specialty exams in other areas under development. **Endorsed By:** American Academy of Forensic Sciences; California Association of Criminalistics; Mid-Atlantic Association of Forensic Scientists; Midwestern Association of Forensic Scientists; Northeastern Association of Forensic Scientists; Southern Association of Forensic Scientists.

Firefighting Occupations

1357

Associate Fire Alarm Technician
International Municipal Signal Association (IMSA)
165 E. Union St.
PO Box 539
Newark, NY 14513
Phone: (315)331-2182
Fax: (315)331-8205
Toll Free: (800)723-4672

Recipient: Entry-level fire alarm technicians. **Educational/Experience Requirements:** Hold Associate Work Zone Safety Specialist designation (see separate entry). **Membership:** Not required. **Certification Requirements:** Successful completion of exam. Exam covers: Fundamentals of fire alarm wiring, wiring practices, and line construction; Fundamentals of work area safety and liability;

Testing techniques; Understanding fire alarm circuit wiring; and Volt Ohm meter and its use. **Renewal:** Recertification required. **Preparatory Materials:** *IMSA Official Fire Alarm Manual* (reference). Handbook, including list of suggested references, provided. Study guide and review program available. **Examination Frequency:** Throughout the year. **Examination Sites:** Exam given by arrangement with proctor. **Re-examination:** Must wait three months to retake exam. There is no fee to retake exam.

1358

Associate Interior Fire Alarm Technician
International Municipal Signal Association (IMSA)
165 E. Union St.
PO Box 539
Newark, NY 14513
Phone: (315)331-2182
Fax: (315)331-8205
Toll Free: (800)723-4672

Recipient: Fire inspectors, fire marshals, installers, electrical contractors, systems designers, and other individuals involved with interior fire alarms. **Membership:** Not required. **Certification Requirements:** Successful completion of exam. Exam may cover: (1) Fire Alarm Wiring and Methods, including: Conductivity; Current; National Electrical Code; Ohm's Law; Properties of matter; Resistor identification; Series and parallel circuits; and Wire and cable; (2) Fire Detection Systems Design, including: Auxiliary circuits; Code and standards references; Detector installation; Detector overview; Fire terminology; Municipal connections; Systems overview; Systems wiring; UL listings; and Zoning; (3) Testing Techniques, including: Fire inspector; Inspections; Maintenance; Permits; Records; and Testing methods; and (4) Understanding Blueprints and Specifications, including: Scaling; Specifications; Symbols; Title block views of building; Wiring diagrams; and Working drawings. **Renewal:** Recertification required. **Preparatory Materials:** *IMSA Official Fire Alarm Manual* (reference). Handbook, including list of suggested references, provided. Study guide and review program available. **Examination Frequency:** Throughout the year. **Examination Sites:** Exam given by arrangement with proctor. **Re-examination:** Must wait three months to retake exam. There is no fee to retake exam.

`1359`

Certified Fire and Explosion Investigator (CFEI)

National Association of Fire
 Investigators (NAFI)
PO Box 957257
Hoffman Estates, IL 60195
Phone: (312)427-6320
John Kennedy CFEI, Pres.

Recipient: Individuals investigating fires and explosions for fire and police departments, insurance companies, attorneys, and businesses. **Educational/Experience Requirements:** Must meet the following requirements: (1) Successful completion of formal fire, arson, and explosion investigation instruction from recognized training organization, college, or municipality. On-scene experience may contribute to portion of requirement; and (2) Demonstration of proper application and use of fire investigative principles by conducting acceptable number of on-site investigations. **Membership:** Required. **Certification Requirements:** Successful completion of general exam and professional preference section. General exam consists of the following sections: (1) Basic Fire and Explosion Investigation Core Knowledge; (2) Chemistry, Physics, and Behavior of Fires and Explosions; (3) Fuels and Ignition Sources; (4) General Fire and Explosion Investigation Techniques; and (5) Law, Testifying, and Court Procedure. Professional preference sections are: (1) Fire Department Operations; (2) Fire Safety, Prevention, and Codes; (3) Forensic Engineering and Science; (4) Insurance and Subrogation; (5) Law Enforcement Procedures; and (6) Products and Liability. **Preparatory Materials:** List of suggested study references available. **Examination Frequency:** Throughout the year. **Examination Sites:** Exam given by correspondence. **Waiting Period to Receive Scores:** Two weeks. **Re-examination:** Must wait six months to retake exam. **Fees:** $100.

`1360`

Certified Fire Investigation Instructor

National Association of Fire
 Investigators (NAFI)
PO Box 957257
Hoffman Estates, IL 60195
Phone: (312)427-6320
John Kennedy CFEI, Pres.

Recipient: Fire investigation instructors. **Educational/Experience Requirements:** Hold Certified Fire and Explosion Investigator (CFEI) designation (see separate entry). **Membership:** Required. **Certification Requirements:** Successful completion of course, including exam. Course covers: Classroom teaching techniques; Curriculum and lesson planning; Fire investigation technology; Planning and preparation of demonstration burns; Testing and student evaluation methods; and Theory and methodology of education. **Examination Sites:** Course given at NAFI seminars.

`1361`

Certified Fire Investigator (CFI)

International Association of Arson
 Investigators (IAAI)
300 S. Broadway, Ste. 100
St. Louis, MO 63102-2808
Phone: (314)621-1966
Fax: (314)621-5125

Recipient: Arson investigators. **Educational/Experience Requirements:** Must earn 150 total points from the following: (1) Education, including highest degree earned (10 points minimum; 50 points maximum); (2) Training, including college courses, police academies, fire investigation training programs and seminars, and other related training (20 points minimum; 90 points maximum); and (3) Experience, including years involved in fire investigation related positions, membership in professional associations, articles and books published, lectures given, courses taught, and occasions testifying as expert witness (40 points minimum). **Membership:** Not required. **Certification Requirements:** Successful completion of exam. **Renewal:** Every five years. Recertification based on accumulation of 50 points, 20 of which must be in training. **Preparatory Materials:** List of recommended study references provided. **Examination Frequency:** Annual. **Re-examination:** May retake exam once. **Fees:** $60 (members); $100 (nonmembers).

`1362`

Certified Fire Protection Specialist (CFPS)

Fire Protection Specialist
 Certification Board
c/o EMACS
PO Box 198
Ashland, MA 01721
Phone: (508)881-6044
Fax: (508)881-6829
Robert Robitaille, Dir.

Recipient: Insurance loss prevention/control specialists, fire marshals, and fire inspectors. **Number of Certified Individuals:** 600. **Educational/Experience Requirements:** High school diploma and two to six years experience. **Membership:** Not required. **Certification Requirements:** Successful completion of exam. **Renewal:** Every year. **Preparatory Materials:** *NFPA Fire Protection Handbook*, 17th edition (reference). **Examination Frequency:** quarterly. **Examination Sites:** Exam given at sites throughout the U.S. **Examination Type:** Multiple-choice. **Pass/Fail Rate:** 65% pass exam the first time. **Waiting Period to Receive Scores:** Four weeks. **Re-examination:** Must wait six months to retake exam. **Fees:** $150. **Endorsed By:** Emergency Management Accreditation and Certification System.

`1363`

Fire Alarm Engineering Technician

International Municipal Signal
 Association (IMSA)
165 E. Union St.
PO Box 539
Newark, NY 14513
Phone: (315)331-2182
Fax: (315)331-8205
Toll Free: (800)723-4672

Recipient: Fire alarm engineering technicians involved in installing, servicing, maintaining, and operating fire alarm reporting systems and devices. **Educational/Experience Requirements:** Must meet the following requirements: (1) Hold Associate Certified Electronics Technician and Municipal Fire Alarm Technician designations (see separate entries); and (2) Five years experience. **Membership:** Not required. **Certification Requirements:** Successful completion of exams. **Renewal:** Recertification required. **Preparatory Materials:** *IMSA Official Fire Alarm Manual* (reference). Handbook, including list of suggested references, provided. Study guide and review program available. **Examination Frequency:** Throughout the year. **Examination Sites:** Exams given by arrangement with proctor. **Re-examination:** Must wait three months to retake exams. There are no fees to retake exams.

1364

Municipal Fire Alarm Technician
International Municipal Signal
  Association (IMSA)
165 E. Union St.
PO Box 539
Newark, NY 14513
Phone: (315)331-2182
Fax: (315)331-8205
Toll Free: (800)723-4672

Recipient: Municipal fire alarm technicians. **Educational/Experience Requirements:** Must meet the following requirements: (1) Hold either Associate Fire Alarm Technician or Associate Interior Fire Alarm Technician designations (see separate entries); and (2) Two years experience. **Membership:** Not required. **Certification Requirements:** Successful completion of exam. Exam covers: Arrangement of fire alarm systems; Boxes; Cable information; Control equipment; Devices; Field related operations; Fire alarm reporting; Layout and installation; Multiple use of cable plants; Municipal Fire Alarm system (100 MA); Municipal reporting systems; Power sources; Remote and central systems; Review and testing procedures; and Troubleshooting techniques. **Renewal:** Recertification required. **Preparatory Materials:** *IMSA Official Fire Alarm Manual* (reference). Handbook, including list of suggested references, provided. Study guide and review program available. **Examination Frequency:** Throughout the year. **Examination Sites:** Exam given by arrangement with proctor. **Re-examination:** Must wait three months to retake exam. There is no fee to retake exam.

Forensic Experts and Investigators

1365

Board Certified Forensic Examiner
  (BCFE)
American Board of Forensic
  Examiners (ABFE)
300 S. Jefferson Ave., Ste. 411
Springfield, MO 65806
Phone: (417)863-8930
Fax: (417)863-8941
Toll Free: (800)4AE-XPERT

Recipient: Forensic examiners and con-

sultants involved in accounting, criminalistics, document examination, engineering, fingerprint identification, forensic hypnosis, fraud examination, law, medicine, psychiatry, psychology, toxicology, and other forensic areas. **Educational/Experience Requirements:** Must meet the following requirements: (1) Submit documentation of qualifications to serve as trial forensic expert by reason of knowledge, skill, experience, training, and education under Federal Rules of Evidence 702; and (2) Hold required licenses and certifications in respective fields. **Membership:** Required. **Certification Requirements:** Must meet the following requirements: (1) Submission of sample copy of work product; and (2) Successful completion of ethics exam. **Examination Frequency:** Throughout the year. **Examination Sites:** Exam given by arrangement with proctor. **Examination Type:** Multiple-choice; true and false. **Waiting Period to Receive Scores:** Two weeks. **Fees:** $350.

1366

Diplomate of the American Board
  of Forensic Anthropology
  (DABFA)
American Board of Forensic
  Anthropology (ABFA)
Sorg Associates
91 Mill St.
PO Box 70
Orono, ME 04473-0070
Phone: (207)866-7865
Fax: (207)866-3608
Marcella H. Sorg Ph.D., Pres.

Recipient: Forensic anthropologists. **Educational/Experience Requirements:** Must meet the following requirements: (1) Doctoral degree in anthropology with emphasis in physical anthropology and advanced study in human anatomy, human osteology, and dental anthropology; (2) Three years experience. Experience may include: Post-doctoral training in forensic anthropology or closely related discipline; Practice of forensic anthropology; Research in one or more areas of forensic anthropology; or Teaching of courses in forensic anthropology or osteology; and (3) Submission of five professional case reports. **Certification Requirements:** Successful completion of written and practical exams. Exams cover dental anatomy and skeletal biology. **Renewal:** Every year. **Examination Frequency:** Annual. **Examination Sites:** Exams given at annual meeting. **Re-examination:** Must wait one year to retake exams. May retake exams one time. **Fees:** $100. **Endorsed By:** American

Academy of Forensic Sciences; Forensic Sciences Foundation.

1367

Diplomate of the American Board
  of Forensic Document Examiners
American Board of Forensic
  Document Examiners (ABFDE)
7887 San Felipe, Ste. 122
Houston, TX 77063
Phone: (417)863-8930
Fax: (417)863-8941
Dan C. Purdy, Pres.

Recipient: Specialists in forensic document examination. **Number of Certified Individuals:** 220. **Educational/Experience Requirements:** Bachelor's degree and one of the following: (1) Successful completion of two-year training program recognized by the ABFDE; or (2) Two years experience. **Membership:** Not required. **Certification Requirements:** Successful completion of written, practical, and oral exams. Exams cover: Comparing ink, paper, and writing instruments; Detecting document alterations; Handwriting and signature examination; and Identifying devices (such as rubber stamps, typewriters, and photocopiers) used to produce certain documents. **Renewal:** Every five years. Recertification based on successful completion of three exams or accumulation of 50 continuing education credits. **Preparatory Materials:** *Objectives for Training* (reference). **Examination Frequency:** Throughout the year. **Examination Sites:** Practical and written exams given by arrangement with proctor. Oral exam given in conjunction with scientific meetings. **Examination Type:** Multiple-choice; problem solving. **Fees:** $150. **Endorsed By:** American Academy of Forensic Science; American Society of Questioned Document Examiners; Canadian Society of Forensic Science.

1368

Fellow, American Board of Forensic
  Examiners
American Board of Forensic
  Examiners (ABFE)
300 S. Jefferson Ave., Ste. 411
Springfield, MO 65806
Phone: (417)863-8930
Fax: (417)863-8941
Toll Free: (800)4AE-XPERT

Recipient: Forensic examiners and consultants involved in accounting, criminalistics, document examination, engineering, fingerprint identification, forensic hypnosis, fraud examination, law, medicine, psychiatry, psychology, toxicology, and other forensic areas. **Educational/Experience Requirements:** Must meet the following requirements: (1) Hold Board Certified Forensic Examiner (BCFE) designation (see separate entry); and (2) Either life membership in ABFE or three years membership in ABFE. **Membership:** Required. **Certification Requirements:** Must have made outstanding contributions to the ABFE and to forensic examining field. Examples include: (1) Five years experience in field; (2) Research; (3) Development of theory in field; (4) Leadership positions held in ABFE or other associations; (5) Awards and honors received; (6) Presentations and speeches given and workshops conducted; (7) Holding Fellow status in related scientific societies; (8) Service on association or government committees; (9) Publications and serving as editor of publications; (10) Teaching and instruction; (11) Serving as mentor to apprentice; (12) Writing curriculum, especially at college level, and developing new courses of instruction; (13) Consulting services provided to courts, legislatures, and criminal justice system; (14) Professional position held at college or university; (15) Administration of forensic documents; and (16) Pro Bono work for just causes.

1369

Fellow of the National Academy of Forensic Engineers (NAFE)
National Academy of Forensic Engineers
174 Brady Ave.
Hawthorne, NY 10532
Phone: (914)741-0633
Fax: (914)747-2988
E. Joyce Dixon, Exec.Dir.

Recipient: Engineers who serve as engineering consultants to members of legal profession and as expert witnesses in courts of law, arbitration proceedings, and administrative adjudication proceedings. **Certification Requirements:** Must meet the following requirements: (1) Hold professional engineer (P.E.) designation; (2) Membership in National Society of Professional Engineers and appropriate level of membership in national engineering technical society; (3) 20 years experience, with two in forensic engineering; (4) Experience in case preparation as forensic engineer in at least 50 cases; and (5) Experience in actual courtroom testimony as engineering expert in at least ten cases. **Renewal:** Recertification based on continuing professional development. **Endorsed By:** Council of Engineering

Specialty Boards; National Society of Professional Engineers.

1370

Member, National Academy of Forensic Engineers (NAFE)
National Academy of Forensic Engineers
174 Brady Ave.
Hawthorne, NY 10532
Phone: (914)741-0633
Fax: (914)747-2988
E. Joyce Dixon, Exec.Dir.

Recipient: Engineers who serve as engineering consultants to members of legal profession and as expert witnesses in courts of law, arbitration proceedings, and administrative adjudication proceedings. **Certification Requirements:** Must meet the following requirements: (1) Hold professional engineer (P.E.) designation; (2) Membership in National Society of Professional Engineers and appropriate level of membership in national engineering technical society; (3) Five years experience, with two in forensic engineering; (4) Experience in case preparation as forensic engineer in at least two cases; and (5) Experience in actual courtroom testimony as engineering expert in at least two cases. **Renewal:** Recertification based on continuing professional development. **Endorsed By:** Council of Engineering Specialty Boards; National Society of Professional Engineers.

1371

Senior Member, National Academy of Forensic Engineers (NAFE)
National Academy of Forensic Engineers
174 Brady Ave.
Hawthorne, NY 10532
Phone: (914)741-0633
Fax: (914)747-2988
E. Joyce Dixon, Exec.Dir.

Recipient: Engineers who serve as engineering consultants to members of legal profession and as expert witnesses in courts of law, arbitration proceedings, and administrative adjudication proceedings. **Certification Requirements:** Must meet the following requirements: (1) Hold professional engineer (P.E.) designation; (2) Membership in National Society of Professional Engineers and appropriate level of membership in national engineering technical society; (3) 12 years experience, with two in forensic engineering; (4) Experience in case preparation as

forensic engineer in at least ten cases; and (5) Experience in actual courtroom testimony as engineering expert in at least five cases. **Renewal:** Recertification based on continuing professional development. **Endorsed By:** Council of Engineering Specialty Boards; National Society of Professional Engineers.

Guards

1372

Certified Financial Services Security Professional (CFSSP)
Institute for Certified Bankers (ICB)
1120 Connecticut Ave., NW, Ste. 600
Washington, DC 20036
Phone: (202)663-5380
Fax: (202)663-7543
Toll Free: (800)338-0626

Recipient: Financial service security professionals. **Educational/Experience Requirements:** Must meet one of the following requirements: (1) High school diploma or equivalent and three years experience; (2) Associate's degree and two years experience; or (3) Bachelor's degree and one year of experience. **Membership:** Not required. **Certification Requirements:** Successful completion of exam. Exam consists of the following sections: (1) Crimes Investigation, including: Burglary; Check fraud; Conflict of interest; Credit card fraud; Drugs; Embezzlement; Falsification of records; Insurance fraud; Larceny; Loan fraud; Robbery; and Wire fraud; (2) Investigations, including: Conduct of investigations; Due diligence investigations; Employee screening; Incident investigations; Investigative techniques; Parameters for cooperation with law enforcement agencies; and Polygraph and drug analysis; (3) Legal, Regulatory, and Administrative Responsibilities, including: Budgeting; Personnel training and management; Planning and managing external relationships; Regulatory requirements; and Risk assessment; (4) Life Safety, including: Employee training; Evacuation procedures; First aid and emergency medical assistance; Natural disaster plans; and Prevention programs and equipment; and (5) Security Devices, including: Access controls; Alarms; ATMs and after-hours depositories; Bait money; Barriers; Cameras; Communication devices; Dye packs; Technical devices; and Vaults and safes. **Renewal:** Every three years. Recertification based on accumulation 24 continuing education hours through conferences, seminars, and workshops, in-bank training programs, college courses, teaching, audio- and video-tape programs, authoring of books or articles, or writing exam questions. **Preparatory Materials:** Handbook, including study questions, list of suggested readings, and sample test, available. List of recommended study materials and programs provided. **Examination Frequency:** Three times per year. **Examination Sites:** Exam given at sites throughout the U.S. **Examination Type:** Multiple-choice. **Waiting Period to Receive Scores:** Six-eight weeks. **Fees:** $425. **Endorsed By:** American Bankers Association.

1373

Certified Jail Technician
National Sheriffs' Association
    (NSA)
1450 Duke St.
Alexandria, VA 22314-3490
Phone: (703)836-7827
Fax: (703)683-6541
Toll Free: (800)424-7827

Recipient: Jail technicians. **Educational/Experience Requirements:** CPR, emergency cardiac care, and basic first aid certifications. Other related documents concerning education, experience, and training may be required. **Certification Requirements:** Successful completion of the following: (1) Jail Officers' Training Program; (2) Certified Jail Technician Program; (3) Exam; and (4) Hands-on evaluation. **Preparatory Materials:** *Competency Based Certifiers Guide* (reference). **Examination Frequency:** Throughout the year. **Examination Sites:** Exam given by arrangement with proctor. **Fees:** $75.

1374

Certified Protection Officer (CPO)
International Foundation for
    Protection Officers (IFPO)
4200 Meridian, Ste. 200
Bellingham, WA 98226
Phone: (206)733-1571
Fax: (206)671-4329
Sandi Davies, Exec.Dir.

Recipient: Private security and protection professionals. **Number of Certified Individuals:** 3200. **Educational/Experience Requirements:** Six months experience. **Membership:** Not required. **Certification Requirements:** Successful completion of exam. **Renewal:** none. **Preparatory Materials:** *Protection Officer Training Manual* (reference). **Examination Type:** Multiple-choice; true or false.

Pass/Fail Rate: 75% pass exam. **Waiting Period to Receive Scores:** One week. **Re-examination:** Must wait 30 days to retake exam. **Fees:** $205.

1375

Certified Protection Professional (CPP)
American Society for Industrial
    Security (ASIS)
1655 N. Ft. Myer Dr., Ste. 1200
Arlington, VA 22209
Phone: (703)522-5800
Fax: (703)243-4954
Gail Garnett, Dir.

Recipient: Security managers and directors responsible for loss prevention and security for private and public organizations. **Number of Certified Individuals:** 2800. **Educational/Experience Requirements:** Ten years experience, including seven years in responsible position, or acceptable combination of education and experience. **Membership:** Not required. **Certification Requirements:** Successful completion of exam. **Renewal:** Every three years. Recertification based on accumulation of nine credits through security related activities. Renewal fee is $30. **Preparatory Materials:** Brochures, planning guide, reading list, and review program available. **Examination Frequency:** Three times per year - always May, September, and November. **Examination Sites:** Exam given at sites throughout the U.S. and Canada. **Examination Type:** Multiple-choice. **Pass/Fail Rate:** 70% pass exam the first time. **Waiting Period to Receive Scores:** Four-six weeks. **Re-examination:** Must wait six months to retake exam. There is a $100 fee to retake exam. **Fees:** $200.

1376

Certified Security Supervisor (CSS)
International Foundation for
    Protection Officers (IFPO)
4200 Meridian, Ste. 200
Bellingham, WA 98226
Phone: (206)733-1571
Fax: (206)671-4329
Sandi Davies, Exec.Dir.

Recipient: Private security managers and supervisors. **Number of Certified Individuals:** 350. **Membership:** Not required. **Certification Requirements:** Successful completion of home-study course and written and practical exams. **Renewal:** none. **Preparatory Materials:** *Security Supervisors Training Manual* (reference). **Examination Type:** Multiple-choice; true

or false. **Pass/Fail Rate:** 80% pass. **Waiting Period to Receive Scores:** One week. **Re-examination:** Must wait 30 days to retake exam. **Fees:** $160.

1377

Certified Security Trainer (CST)
Academy of Security Educators and
    Trainees (ASET)
c/o Dr. Richard W. Kobetz
Rte. 2, Box 3644
Berryville, VA 22611
Phone: (703)955-1129
Dr. Richard W. Kobetz, Pres.

Recipient: Individuals who develop and present security training. **Number of Certified Individuals:** 70. **Educational/Experience Requirements:** Background check and successful completion of qualifying essay questions in security training. **Certification Requirements:** Successful completion of seven day assessment and evaluation program, including exams, training exercises, and personal interviews. Must present three training sessions. **Renewal:** none. **Pass/Fail Rate:** 95% pass course.

1378

Personal Protection Specialist (PPS)
Nine Lives Associates (NLA)
Executive Protection Institute
Arcadia Manor
Rte. 2, Box 3645
Berryville, VA 22611
Phone: (703)955-1128
Dr. Richard W. Kobetz, Exec.Sec.

Recipient: Law enforcement, correctional, military, and security professionals. **Number of Certified Individuals:** 1100. **Educational/Experience Requirements:** Must complete 110 hours of training covering all areas of personal protection, including: Driving; Planning; Special events and procedures; and Weapons use. **Certification Requirements:** Successful completion of exam. **Pass/Fail Rate:** 90% pass exam. **Fees:** $2900.

Investigators

1379

Certified International Investigator (C.I.I.)

International Security and Detective Alliance (ISDA)
Box 6303
Corpus Christi, TX 78466-6303
Phone: (512)888-6164
Fax: (512)888-6164
H. Roehm Ph.D., Dir.

Recipient: International investigators. **Membership:** Not required. **Certification Requirements:** Submission of resume including education and experience and description of case. **Renewal:** Every three years. **Fees:** $36 (members); $45 (nonmembers).

1380

Certified Missing Persons Investigator (C.M.P.I.)

International Security and Detective Alliance (ISDA)
Box 6303
Corpus Christi, TX 78466-6303
Phone: (512)888-6164
Fax: (512)888-6164
H. Roehm Ph.D., Dir.

Recipient: Missing person investigators. **Membership:** Not required. **Certification Requirements:** Submission of resume including education and experience and description of case. **Renewal:** Every three years. **Fees:** $36 (members); $45 (nonmembers).

1381

Certified Professional Investigator (C.P.I.)

International Security and Detective Alliance (ISDA)
Box 6303
Corpus Christi, TX 78466-6303
Phone: (512)888-6164
Fax: (512)888-6164
H. Roehm Ph.D., Dir.

Recipient: Investigators. **Membership:** Not required. **Certification Requirements:** Submission of resume including education and experience and description of case. **Renewal:** Every three years. **Fees:** $36 (members); $45 (nonmembers).

Police, Detectives, and Special Agents

1382

Certified Protection Specialist (C.P.S.)

International Security and Detective Alliance (ISDA)
Box 6303
Corpus Christi, TX 78466-6303
Phone: (512)888-6164
Fax: (512)888-6164
H. Roehm Ph.D., Dir.

Recipient: Protection specialists. **Membership:** Not required. **Certification Requirements:** Submission of resume including education and experience and description of case. **Renewal:** Every three years. **Fees:** $36 (members); $45 (nonmembers).

1383

Certified Security Consultant (C.S.C.)

International Security and Detective Alliance (ISDA)
Box 6303
Corpus Christi, TX 78466-6303
Phone: (512)888-6164
Fax: (512)888-6164
H. Roehm Ph.D., Dir.

Recipient: Security consultants. **Membership:** Not required. **Certification Requirements:** Submission of resume including education and experience and description of case. **Renewal:** Every three years. **Fees:** $36 (members); $45 (nonmembers).

1384

Certified Security Specialist (C.S.S.)

International Security and Detective Alliance (ISDA)
Box 6303
Corpus Christi, TX 78466-6303
Phone: (512)888-6164
Fax: (512)888-6164
H. Roehm Ph.D., Dir.

Recipient: Security specialists. **Membership:** Not required. **Certification Requirements:** Submission of resume including education and experience and description of case. **Renewal:** Every three years. **Fees:** $36 (members); $45 (nonmembers).

1385

Industrial Counter-Espionage Specialist (I.C.E.S.)

International Security and Detective Alliance (ISDA)
Box 6303
Corpus Christi, TX 78466-6303
Phone: (512)888-6164
Fax: (512)888-6164
H. Roehm Ph.D., Dir.

Recipient: Industrial counter-espionage specialists. **Membership:** Not required. **Certification Requirements:** Submission of resume including education and experience and description of case. **Renewal:** Every three years. **Fees:** $36 (members); $45 (nonmembers).

1386

OPSEC Certified Professional (OCP)

OPSEC Professionals Society
7519 Ridge Rd.
Frederick, MD 21702-3519
Phone: (301)663-1418

Recipient: OPSEC professionals. OPSEC is process by which the U.S. Government and its supporting contractors deny to potential adversaries information about capabilities and intentions by identifying, controlling, and protecting generally unclassified evidence of planning and execution of sensitive government activities. **Educational/Experience Requirements:** Must meet the following requirements: (1) Bachelor's degree or equivalent; (2) Forty-eight hours of professional training, including courses, conferences, seminars, and symposia, within last ten years; and (3) Five years experience, including at least two years direct experience as OPSEC professional. Direct experience includes: Carrying out OPSEC planning; Conducting OPSEC surveys; Developing OPSEC training manuals; Managing organization OPSEC program; Providing assistance in OPSEC program development; and Providing instruction. Years of indirect experience may be substituted on two-for-one basis. Indirect experience includes: Clandestine operations; Classification guide development; Conduct of limited vulnerability analysis or risk analysis; Deception analysis and planning; Development of intelligence trade craft; Intelligence threat analysis; and Single security discipline countermeasure application. Experience may be substituted for years of college degree. **Membership:** Required. **Certification Requirements:** Submission of paper dealing with OPSEC-related topic. **Renewal:** Every three years. Recertification based on accumulation of credits for professional activities. **Fees:** $75.

Public Safety Dispatchers and Technicians

1387

Apprentice Signs and Markings Specialist

International Municipal Signal Association (IMSA)
165 E. Union St.
PO Box 539
Newark, NY 14513
Phone: (315)331-2182
Fax: (315)331-8205
Toll Free: (800)723-4672

Recipient: Individuals responsible for fabrication, installation, and maintenance of traffic signs and markings. **Educational/Experience Requirements:** Must meet the following requirements: (1) Hold Work Zone Traffic Safety Specialist designation (see separate entry); and (2) One year of experience. **Membership:** Not required. **Certification Requirements:** Successful completion of seminar and exam. Seminar covers: (1) Alternative Resources, including: Maintenance management of street and highway signs; Standard alphabets for highway signs and pavement markings; and Standard highway signs; (2) Basic Signing and Marking Principles, including: Applications/usage; Common materials used; Physical characteristics; and Purpose of various types of traffic control devices; and (3) Using the *Manual on Uniform Traffic Control Devices* (MUTCD), including: Language interpretation; Legal significance; Organizational structure; and Purpose. **Renewal:** Recertification required. **Preparatory Materials:** *Manual on Uniform Traffic Control Devices* (MUTCD) (reference). Handbook, including list of suggested references, provided. **Examination Frequency:** Throughout the year. **Examination Type:** Multiple-choice. **Re-examination:** Must wait 60 days to retake exam.

1388

Associate Signs and Markings Specialist

International Municipal Signal Association (IMSA)
165 E. Union St.
PO Box 539
Newark, NY 14513
Phone: (315)331-2182
Fax: (315)331-8205
Toll Free: (800)723-4672

Recipient: Individuals responsible for fabrication, installation, and maintenance of traffic signs and markings. **Educational/Experience Requirements:** Must meet the following requirements: (1) Hold Apprentice Signs and Markings Specialist designation (see separate entry); and (2) Two years experience. **Membership:** Not required. **Certification Requirements:** Successful completion of seminar and exam. Seminar covers: *Manual on Uniform Traffic Control Devices* (MUTCD) sign identification system; Pavement marking methods and materials; Principles of reflectivity; Recognizing common signing mistakes; Sign fabrication methods and materials; Tort liability; and Warning sign placement. **Renewal:** Recertification required. **Preparatory Materials:** *Manual on Uniform Traffic Control Devices* (MUTCD) (reference). Handbook, including list of suggested references, provided. **Examination Frequency:** Throughout the year. **Examination Type:** Multiple-choice. **Re-examination:** Must wait 60 days to retake exam.

1389

Associate Traffic Signal Technician

International Municipal Signal Association (IMSA)
165 E. Union St.
PO Box 539
Newark, NY 14513
Phone: (315)331-2182
Fax: (315)331-8205
Toll Free: (800)723-4672

Recipient: Traffic signal technicians. **Educational/Experience Requirements:** Hold Work Zone Traffic Safety Specialist designation (see separate entry). **Membership:** Not required. **Certification Requirements:** Successful completion of exam. Exam may cover: (1) Field Maintenance of Traffic Signals, including: Controller cabinet group; Detector/sensor group; Emergency maintenance effort; Equipment requirements; Field equipment; Particular problem areas; Results of maintenance deficiencies; Signal head group; Signal support group; Sources of malfunction; Types of maintenance; and Typical preventive maintenance effort; (2) Fundamentals of Signal Installation, including: Documentation; Equipment installation requirements; Final inspection; Finish work; Job records; Overall installation requirements; Pre-construction activities; Safety; Signal turn-on; Testing; and Workmanship; (3) Introduction to Signal System Design, including: Advantages of systems control; Modes of system operation; System coordination methods; Systems concept description; Type of signal systems; and Understanding time-space diagrams; (4) Introduction to Traffic Control Signals, including: Advantages of signals; Basic control/detection equipment; Basic display design standards; Disadvantages of signals; Keys to effective signal program; Modes of signal control; Need for intersection traffic control; Purpose of sponsoring agencies; Relevant traffic terminology; Requests for signalization; Targeted training audience; and Types of signals; (5) Signal Justification and Study Requirements, including: Aspects of safety and liability; Field site investigation; Legal basis for installation; MUTCD overview; Reevaluation of traffic signals; Traffic studies for signals; and Warrants for traffic signal installation; (6) Signal Operations Planning/Design, including: Analyzing intersection data; Calculating timing; General elements; Identifying controller types; and Selection of phasing; and (7) Traffic Signal Configuration Design, including: Base plan elements; Examples of current practice; Need to P.S. and E.; Preparing estimates; Proposed improvements plans; and Typical specification elements. **Renewal:** Recertification required. **Preparatory Materials:** *Manual on Uniform Traffic Control Devices* (MUTCD) (reference). Handbook, including list of suggested references, provided. Study guide and review program available. **Examination Frequency:** Throughout the year. **Examination Sites:** Exam given by arrangement with proctor. **Re-examination:** Must wait 60 days to retake exam. There is no fee to retake exam.

1390

EMS Dispatcher

International Municipal Signal Association (IMSA)
165 E. Union St.
PO Box 539
Newark, NY 14513
Phone: (315)331-2182
Fax: (315)331-8205
Toll Free: (800)723-4672

Recipient: Emergency medical service (EMS) dispatchers. **Membership:** Not required. **Certification Requirements:** Successful completion of exam. **Renewal:** Recertification required. **Examination Frequency:** Throughout the year. **Examination Sites:** Exam given by arrangement with proctor.

1391

Fire Service Dispatcher
International Municipal Signal
 Association (IMSA)
165 E. Union St.
PO Box 539
Newark, NY 14513
Phone: (315)331-2182
Fax: (315)331-8205
Toll Free: (800)723-4672

Recipient: Fire service dispatchers. **Membership:** Not required. **Certification Requirements:** Successful completion of exam. **Renewal:** Recertification required. **Examination Frequency:** Throughout the year. **Examination Sites:** Exam given by arrangement with proctor.

1392

**Flagging and Traffic Control
 Certification**
International Municipal Signal
 Association (IMSA)
165 E. Union St.
PO Box 539
Newark, NY 14513
Phone: (315)331-2182
Fax: (315)331-8205
Toll Free: (800)723-4672

Recipient: Traffic control flaggers. **Membership:** Not required. **Certification Requirements:** Successful completion of exam. Exam may cover: (1) Channelization, including: Additional tools; Channelizing devices; Taper length; and Traffic control zone; (2) Flagger, including: Clothing and equipment; Positioning; and Safety; (3) Flagging Procedures, including: Directing traffic to another lane; One-way traffic control; Releasing traffic; Slowing traffic; and Stopping traffic; (4) Motoring Public, including: Road conditions; Stopping distances; and Traffic elements; (5) Signs, including: Guide signs; Regulatory signs; Sign placement; and Warning signs; and (6) Special Conditions, including: Flagging at night; and Freeway flagging. **Renewal:** Recertification required. **Preparatory Materials:** Handbook, including list of suggested references, provided. Study guide and review program available. **Examination**

Frequency: Throughout the year. **Examination Sites:** Exam given by arrangement with proctor. **Re-examination:** Must wait 60 days to retake exam. There is no fee to retake exam.

1393

Law Enforcement Dispatcher
International Municipal Signal
 Association (IMSA)
165 E. Union St.
PO Box 539
Newark, NY 14513
Phone: (315)331-2182
Fax: (315)331-8205
Toll Free: (800)723-4672

Recipient: Law enforcement dispatchers. **Membership:** Not required. **Certification Requirements:** Successful completion of exam. **Renewal:** Recertification required. **Examination Frequency:** Throughout the year. **Examination Sites:** Exam given by arrangement with proctor.

1394

Public Safety Dispatcher, Level I
International Municipal Signal
 Association (IMSA)
165 E. Union St.
PO Box 539
Newark, NY 14513
Phone: (315)331-2182
Fax: (315)331-8205
Toll Free: (800)723-4672

Recipient: Public safety dispatchers. **Membership:** Not required. **Certification Requirements:** Successful completion of program and exam. Program covers: Basic communications; Basic principles of communications; Basic 911 systems; Call processing; Communications process; Communications techniques; Consolidated dispatch centers; Cooperative dispatch centers; Dispatch center; Emergency call guidelines; Emergency medical dispatch protocols; Enhanced 911 systems; Liability; Non-emergency call guidelines; Objectives of public safety dispatch centers; Operating systems; Organizational models of public safety dispatch centers; Role of public safety dispatcher within dispatch center; and Roles and responsibilities of public safety dispatchers. **Renewal:** Recertification required. **Examination Frequency:** Throughout the year. **Examination Sites:** Exam given by arrangement with proctor.

1395

Public Safety Dispatcher, Level II
International Municipal Signal
 Association (IMSA)
165 E. Union St.
PO Box 539
Newark, NY 14513
Phone: (315)331-2182
Fax: (315)331-8205
Toll Free: (800)723-4672

Recipient: Public safety dispatchers. **Educational/Experience Requirements:** Hold Public Safety Dispatcher, Level I designation (see separate entry). **Membership:** Not required. **Certification Requirements:** Successful completion of program and exam. Program covers: Applications; Automatic alarm systems; Basic theory of radio systems; CAD system theory; Central stations; Computer aided dispatching; Data base development and maintenance; Development of standard operating procedures; Dispatch center reporting systems; Documentation; Emergency Medical Dispatching (EMD); Equipment; Hazardous materials (HAZMAT); Incident Command System (ICS); Keeping standard operating procedure current; Methods of dispatching; Municipal reporting systems; Paging systems; Propagation; Public safety dispatch center procedures; Quality control; Radio communications systems; Requirements of standard operating procedures; Response determination; Special applications; Standard operating procedures; Status and control; System operation; Telephone; and Trunking systems. **Renewal:** Recertification required. **Examination Frequency:** Throughout the year. **Examination Sites:** Exam given by arrangement with proctor.

1396

**Roadway Lighting Certification,
 Level I**
International Municipal Signal
 Association (IMSA)
165 E. Union St.
PO Box 539
Newark, NY 14513
Phone: (315)331-2182
Fax: (315)331-8205
Toll Free: (800)723-4672

Recipient: Individuals involved with roadway lighting. **Membership:** Not required. **Certification Requirements:** Successful completion of exam. Exam may cover: (1) Basic Electricity, including: Circuits; and Laws; (2) Basic Maintenance, including: Circuits; Controls; and Luminaries; (3) Electric Codes, including: Equipment; Overhead; and Underground; and (4) One Call System, including: Conduit and wire; Equipment operations; and Overhead/underground; and (5) Safety, including: Electrical hazards; Equipment safe operations; and Overhead/underground. **Renewal:** Recertification required. **Preparatory Materials:** Handbook, including list of suggested references, provided. Study guide and review program available. **Examination Frequency:** Throughout the year. **Examination Sites:** Exam given by arrangement with proctor. **Reexamination:** Must wait 60 days to retake exam. There is no fee to retake exam.

1397

Roadway Lighting Certification, Level II
International Municipal Signal
  Association (IMSA)
165 E. Union St.
PO Box 539
Newark, NY 14513
Phone: (315)331-2182
Fax: (315)331-8205
Toll Free: (800)723-4672

Recipient: Individuals involved with roadway lighting. **Membership:** Not required. **Certification Requirements:** Successful completion of exam. **Renewal:** Recertification required. **Preparatory Materials:** Handbook, including list of suggested references, provided. Study guide and review program available. **Examination Frequency:** Throughout the year. **Examination Sites:** Exam given by arrangement with proctor. **Reexamination:** Must wait 60 days to retake exam. There is no fee to retake exam.

1398

Signs and Markings Specialist
International Municipal Signal
  Association (IMSA)
165 E. Union St.
PO Box 539
Newark, NY 14513
Phone: (315)331-2182
Fax: (315)331-8205
Toll Free: (800)723-4672

Recipient: Individuals responsible for fabrication, installation, and maintenance of traffic signs and markings. **Educational/Experience Requirements:** Must meet the following requirements: (1) Hold Associate Signs and Markings Specialist designation (see separate entry); and (2) Five years experience. **Membership:** Not required. **Certification Re-**

quirements: Successful completion of seminar and exam. **Renewal:** Recertification required. **Preparatory Materials:** *Manual on Uniform Traffic Control Devices* (MUTCD) and *NCHRP Synthesis 157: Maintenance and Management of Street and Highway Signs* (references). Handbook, including list of suggested references, provided. **Examination Frequency:** Throughout the year. **Examination Type:** Multiple-choice. **Reexamination:** Must wait 60 days to retake exam.

1399

Traffic Signal Electrician
International Municipal Signal
  Association (IMSA)
165 E. Union St.
PO Box 539
Newark, NY 14513
Phone: (315)331-2182
Fax: (315)331-8205
Toll Free: (800)723-4672

Recipient: Traffic signal electricians. **Educational/Experience Requirements:** Must meet the following requirements: (1) Hold Associate Traffic Signal Technician designation (see separate entry); and (2) Two years experience. **Membership:** Not required. **Certification Requirements:** Successful completion of general exam and National Electrical Code exam. General exam may cover: (1) Auxiliary Equipment, including: Auxiliary logic; Conflict monitor; Flasher; Grounding; Load switch; Radio interference suppressor; Relays; Surge arrestor; and Switches; (2) Communications Concepts, including: Alternative communication links; Basic communications concepts; and Basic interface equipment; (3) Controller Equipment, including: Actuated controllers; Models 170 and 179 controllers; Pre-timed controllers; Time base coordinators; and Types of controller hardware; (4) Detector Equipment, including: Detector design applications; Detector operations; Types of detectors; and Types of loop electronics; (5) Electronics and Troubleshooting, including: Basic electricity; Conflict monitor testing; Introduction to digital circuits; Numbering systems; and Troubleshooting and repair; (6) National Electrical Code Review, including: Ampacity of wiring; Circuit fusing and protection; Conduit; Grounding; Insulation of wiring; Service entrances; and Wiring methods; (7) Signal Display Design and Operational Standards, including: Applications of traffic control signal indications; Arrangement of lenses in signal faces; Illumination of lenses; Lane use control signals; Number and location of signal faces; Number/size/

design of signal lenses; Operational requirements; Pedestrian signals; Unexpected conflicts; Vehicle change interval; and Visibility and shielding of signal faces; and (8) Test Equipment, including: AC instruments; Meter theory; Meters; Use of equipment measurement parameters; and Volumeters. **Renewal:** Recertification required. **Preparatory Materials:** *Manual on Uniform Traffic Control Devices* (MUTCD) (reference). Handbook, including list of suggested references, provided. Study guide and review program available. **Examination Frequency:** Throughout the year. **Examination Sites:** Exams given by arrangement with proctor. **Reexamination:** Must wait 60 days to retake exams. There are no fees to retake exams.

1400

Traffic Signal Technician
International Municipal Signal
  Association (IMSA)
165 E. Union St.
PO Box 539
Newark, NY 14513
Phone: (315)331-2182
Fax: (315)331-8205
Toll Free: (800)723-4672

Recipient: Traffic signal technicians. **Educational/Experience Requirements:** Must meet the following requirements: (1) Hold Associate Traffic Signal Technician designation (see separate entry); and (2) Two years experience. **Membership:** Not required. **Certification Requirements:** Successful completion of general and electronics exams. General exam may cover: (1) Auxiliary Equipment, including: Auxiliary logic; Conflict monitor; Flasher; Grounding; Load switch; Radio interference suppressor; Relays; Surge arrestor; and Switches; (2) Communications Concepts, including: Alternative communication links; Basic communications concepts; and Basic interface equipment; (3) Controller Equipment, including: Actuated controllers; Models 170 and 179 controllers; Pre-timed controllers; Time base coordinators; and Types of controller hardware; (4) Detector Equipment, including: Detector design applications; Detector operations; Types of detectors; and Types of loop electronics; (5) Electronics and Troubleshooting, including: Basic electricity; Conflict monitor testing; Introduction to digital circuits; Numbering systems; and Troubleshooting and repair; (6) National Electrical Code Review, including: Ampacity of wiring; Circuit fusing and protection; Conduit; Grounding; Insulation of wiring; Service entrances; and Wiring methods; (7) Signal Display

Design and Operational Standards, including: Applications of traffic control signal indications; Arrangement of lenses in signal faces; Illumination of lenses; Lane use control signals; Number and location of signal faces; Number/size/design of signal lenses; Operational requirements; Pedestrian signals; Unexpected conflicts; Vehicle change interval; and Visibility and shielding of signal faces; and (8) Test Equipment, including: AC instruments; Meter theory; Meters; Use of equipment measurement parameters; and Volumeters. **Renewal:** Recertification required. **Preparatory Materials:** *Manual on Uniform Traffic Control Devices* (MUTCD) (reference). Handbook, including list of suggested references, provided. Study guide and review program available. **Examination Frequency:** Throughout the year. **Examination Sites:** Exams given by arrangement with proctor. **Re-examination:** Must wait 60 days to retake exams. There are no fees to retake exams.

1401

Traffic Signal Technician, Level III
International Municipal Signal
   Association (IMSA)
165 E. Union St.
PO Box 539
Newark, NY 14513
Phone: (315)331-2182
Fax: (315)331-8205
Toll Free: (800)723-4672

Recipient: Traffic signal technicians involved in installing, maintaining, and operating traffic control devices. **Educational/Experience Requirements:** Must meet the following requirements: (1) Hold either Traffic Signal Technician or Traffic Signal Electrician designations (see separate entries); and (2) Five years experience. **Membership:** Not required. **Certification Requirements:** Successful completion of Microprocessors in Traffic Signals (MITS), general, and electrical exams. Electrical exam requirement can be met through one of the following: (1) Successful completion of IMSA exam; (2) Associate Certified Electronics Technician designation (see separate entry); or (3) Documentation of class room hours of electronic theory and lab from either vocational, technical, military, or trade school. **Renewal:** Recertification required. **Preparatory Materials:** *Manual on Uniform Traffic Control Devices* (MUTCD) (reference). Handbook, including list of suggested references, provided. Study guide and review program available. **Examination Frequency:** Throughout the year. **Examination Sites:** Exams given by arrangement with proc-

tor. **Re-examination:** Must wait 60 days to retake exams. There are no fees to retake exams.

1402

Work Zone Traffic Safety Specialist
International Municipal Signal
   Association (IMSA)
165 E. Union St.
PO Box 539
Newark, NY 14513
Phone: (315)331-2182
Fax: (315)331-8205
Toll Free: (800)723-4672

Recipient: Individuals involved with work zone traffic control and safety. **Educational/Experience Requirements:** One year of experience recommended. **Membership:** Not required. **Certification Requirements:** Successful completion of exam. Exam may cover: (1) Flagging, including: Functions; Safety; and Standards; (2) Guidelines for Using Traffic Control Devices, including: Applications; MUTCD standards; Objectives; and Safety; (3) Traffic Control Devices, including: Channelization and barricades; Lighting; MUTCD standards; Planning and design; and Signing; (4) Typical Construction Situations; and (5) Typical Work Situations, including the following applications: Continuous; Mobile; and Stationary. **Renewal:** Recertification required. **Preparatory Materials:** *Manual on Uniform Traffic Control Devices* (MUTCD) (reference). Handbook, including list of suggested references, provided. Study guide and review program available. **Examination Frequency:** Throughout the year. **Examination Sites:** Exam given by arrangement with proctor. **Re-examination:** Must wait 60 days to retake exam. There is no fee to retake exam.

Safety Professionals

1403

Certified Director of Safety
National Committee for Motor
   Fleet Supervisor Training
   (NCMFST)
2200 Mill Rd.
Alexandria, VA 22314-4677
Phone: (703)838-7952
Fax: (703)836-6070
Jeff Arnold, Dir.

Recipient: Directors of motor fleet safety. **Educational/Experience Requirements:**

Must meet following requirements: (1) Successful completion of Fleet Supervisor and one other workshop; and (2) Five years experience with current employer. Bachelor's degree may be substituted for one year of experience. Candidates with two-and-a-half to five years of experience with one employer may apply for waiver. **Certification Requirements:** Must meet the following requirements: (1) Submission of exhibit documenting experience, education, and professional activities and designations; and (2) Successful completion of exam. **Preparatory Materials:** *Motor Carrier Safety Regulations, Motor Fleet Safety Supervision: Principles and Practices,* and *Occupational Safety and Health Regulations* (references). Manuals and study group materials available. **Examination Frequency:** Throughout the year. **Examination Sites:** Exam given at sites throughout the U.S. **Examination Type:** Essay; multiple-choice; true or false. **Waiting Period to Receive Scores:** 24 hours. **Re-examination:** Must wait three months to retake exam.

1404

**Certified Hazard Control Manager,
   Associate Level (CHCM)**
Board of Hazard Control
   Management
8009 Carita Ct.
MD 20817
Phone: (301)984-8969

Recipient: Hazard control managers. **Educational/Experience Requirements:** Must meet one of the following requirements: (1) Associate's degree in safety, fire, or occupational health, and one year of experience; (2) Two years of college education and four years experience; or (3) Bachelor's degree in safety, fire, industrial hygiene, or occupational health and one year of experience. May substitute each full year (30 semester hours) of graduate study for one year of experience up to two years. Achievements in field such as holding leadership positions in professional associations, delivering papers or having them published, and conducting research activities may be substituted for up to one year of experience. May qualify for either Certified Hazard Control Manager, Senior or Master Level designations (see separate entries) with increased education and/or experience. Candidates with less education and/or experience may qualify for Registered Hazard Control Technician designation (see separate entry). **Certification Requirements:** Successful completion of exam. Exam covers: Communication and report writing; Hazard control program disciplines and source of information;

Hazard control program techniques; Interfacing staff functions; Legislative and regulation requirements and standards-setting organizations; and Management principles and techniques. Candidates may be required to submit examples of reports on hazard evaluation surveys or case study documenting hazard control management abilities. **Examination Sites:** Exam given by arrangement with proctor. **Fees:** $150.

1405

Certified Hazard Control Manager, Master Level (CHCM)
Board of Hazard Control
   Management
8009 Carita Ct.
MD 20817
Phone: (301)984-8969

Recipient: Hazard control managers. **Educational/Experience Requirements:** Must meet one of the following requirements: (1) Bachelor's degree and four years experience; or (2) 15 years experience. May substitute each full year (30 semester hours) of graduate study for one year of experience up to two years. Achievements in field such as holding leadership positions in professional associations, delivering papers or having them published, and conducting research activities may be substituted for up to one year of experience. Candidates with less education and/or experience may qualify for either Certified Hazard Control Manager, Associate or Senior Level, or Registered Hazard Control Technician designations (see separate entries). **Certification Requirements:** Successful completion of exam. Exam covers: Communication and report writing; Hazard control program disciplines and source of information; Hazard control program techniques; Interfacing staff functions; Legislative and regulation requirements and standards-setting organizations; and Management principles and techniques. Candidates with bachelor's degree in safety, health, or management and six years experience are exempt from exam. Candidates may be required to submit examples of reports on hazard evaluation surveys or case study documenting hazard control management abilities. **Examination Sites:** Exam given by arrangement with proctor. **Fees:** $150 (exam option); $75 (exam exempt option).

1406

Certified Hazard Control Manager, Senior Level (CHCM)
Board of Hazard Control
   Management
8009 Carita Ct.
MD 20817
Phone: (301)984-8969

Recipient: Hazard control managers. **Educational/Experience Requirements:** Must meet one of the following requirements: (1) Bachelor's degree and two years experience; (2) Associate's degree and four years experience; or (3) Eight years experience. Each year of college may be substituted for one year of experience. May substitute each full year (30 semester hours) of graduate study for one year of experience up to two years. Achievements in field such as holding leadership positions in professional associations, delivering papers or having them published, and conducting research activities may be substituted for up to one year of experience. May qualify for Certified Hazard Control Manager, Master Level designation (see separate entry) with increased education and/or experience. Candidates with less education and/or experience may qualify for Certified Hazard Control Manager, Associate Level or Registered Hazard Control Technician designations (see separate entries). **Certification Requirements:** Successful completion of exam. Exam covers: Communication and report writing; Hazard control program disciplines and source of information; Hazard control program techniques; Interfacing staff functions; Legislative and regulation requirements and standards-setting organizations; and Management principles and techniques. Candidates with bachelor's degree in safety, health, or management and three years experience are exempt from exam. Candidates may be required to submit examples of reports on hazard evaluation surveys or case study documenting hazard control management abilities. **Examination Sites:** Exam given by arrangement with proctor. **Fees:** $150 (exam option); $75 (exam exempt option).

1407

Certified Hazardous Materials Executive (CHME)
World Safety Organization (WSO)
WSO World Mgmt. Center
305 E. Market St.
PO Box 518
Warrensburg, MO 64093
Phone: (816)747-3132
Fax: (816)747-2647

Recipient: Senior professionals responsible for hazardous materials program design and implementation or emergency response programs. **Educational/Experience Requirements:** Must meet the following requirements: (1) Hold Certified Hazardous Materials Supervisor (CHMS) designation (see separate entry) or equivalent; (2) One year of experience; and (3) Successfully complete 100-150 hours of advanced training in the following areas: Cleanup planning and response; Emergency response programs; Evaluating and purchasing protection equipment; Hazard material regulations; Local, state, national, and international emergency support services; Procedures development; Safety programs; and Storage, handling, disposal, and incidents requirements. **Membership:** Required. **Certification Requirements:** Successful completion of two-part exam. First part covers professional expertise and accomplishments. Second part covers: Emergency response; Environmental safety; Ethics; Hazardous materials and waste operations; Law and regulations; Management; Occupational health and safety; Professional liability; Risk management; and Safety and loss control. **Renewal:** Every three years. Recertification based on accumulation of 30 points through continuing education, professional accomplishments, training, and other related activities. Renewal fee is $155. **Examination Type:** Essay; fill-in-the-blank; multiple-choice; true or false. **Pass/Fail Rate:** 50% pass exam the first time. **Fees:** $300. **Endorsed By:** U.N. Economic and Social Council.

1408

Certified Hazardous Materials Manager (Master Level)
Institute of Hazardous Materials
   Management (IHMM)
11900 Parklawn Dr., Ste. 450
Rockville, MD 20852
Phone: (301)984-8969

Recipient: Hazardous materials managers. **Educational/Experience Requirements:** Must meet the following requirements: (1) Bachelor's degree in related field; and (2) Seven years experience, including major responsibility for developing, implementing, directing, and/or evaluating one or more program activities relating to hazardous materials management/engineering. Graduate degree in related field may be substituted for up to two years of experience. **Certification Requirements:** Successful completion of exam. Exam covers: Laws and regulations; Compliance standards, work practices, and state of the art; (3) Management of hazardous materials programs; and (4) Science and technology. **Renewal:** Every year. Renewal fee is $45. **Fees:** $165.

█1409█

Certified Hazardous Materials Manager (Senior Level)
Institute of Hazardous Materials Management (IHMM)
11900 Parklawn Dr., Ste. 450
Rockville, MD 20852
Phone: (301)984-8969

Recipient: Hazardous materials managers. **Educational/Experience Requirements:** Must meet one of the following requirements: (1) Bachelor's degree in related field and three years experience; or (2) Eleven years experience. Graduate degree in related field may be substituted for one year of experience. Each full year of college (30 semester hours) in related fields may be substituted for experience on a year-for-year basis up to a maximum of three years. **Certification Requirements:** Successful completion of exam. Exam covers: Laws and regulations; Compliance standards, work practices, and state of the art; Management of hazardous materials programs; and Science and technology. **Renewal:** Every year. Renewal fee is $45. **Fees:** $165.

█1410█

Certified Hazardous Materials Supervisor (CHMS)
World Safety Organization (WSO)
WSO World Mgmt. Center
305 E. Market St.
PO Box 518
Warrensburg, MO 64093
Phone: (816)747-3132
Fax: (816)747-2647

Recipient: Professionals responsible for hazardous materials storage and handling, and supervisors of multiple emergency response teams. **Educational/Experience Requirements:** Must meet the

following requirements: (1) Hold Certified Hazardous Materials Technician, Level II (CHMT II) designation (see separate entry) or equivalent; (2) One year of experience in response or operations program; and (3) Successfully complete 40-60 hours of advanced training in the following areas: Emergency response; Hazard material regulations; Hazardous material and waste operations; Incident planning, command, resources, and reports; Operations supervision; Program and procedure evaluation; Purchasing; Recording and documentation; Safety department organization, structure, and personnel; and Safety management. **Membership:** Required. **Certification Requirements:** Successful completion of two-part exam. First part covers professional expertise and accomplishments. Second part covers: Emergency response; Environmental safety; Ethics; Hazardous materials and waste operations; Law and regulations; Management; Occupational health and safety; Professional liability; Risk management; and Safety and loss control. **Renewal:** Every three years. Recertification based on accumulation of 30 points through continuing education, professional accomplishments, training, and other related activities. Renewal fee is $155. **Examination Type:** Essay; fill-in-the-blank; multiple-choice; true or false. **Pass/Fail Rate:** 50% pass exam the first time. **Fees:** $300. **Endorsed By:** U.N. Economic and Social Council.

█1411█

Certified Hazardous Materials Technician, Level I (CHMT I)
World Safety Organization (WSO)
WSO World Mgmt. Center
305 E. Market St.
PO Box 518
Warrensburg, MO 64093
Phone: (816)747-3132
Fax: (816)747-2647

Recipient: Hazardous materials workers and first responders. **Educational/Experience Requirements:** Successful completion of the following: (1) 30-40 hours of training in basic hazardous materials recognition, classification, identification, and safety considerations, incident response, and control; and (2) Six months of field work. **Membership:** Required. **Certification Requirements:** Successful completion of exam. First part covers professional expertise and accomplishments. Second part covers: Emergency response procedures; Ethics; Hazardous materials and waste operations; Law and regulations; Management; Occupational health and safety; Professional liability; Risk management; and Safety

and loss control. **Renewal:** Every three years. Recertification based on accumulation of 30 points through continuing education, professional accomplishments, training, and other related activities. Renewal fee is $155. **Examination Type:** Essay; fill-in-the-blank; multiple-choice; true or false. **Pass/Fail Rate:** 50% pass exam the first time. **Fees:** $300. **Endorsed By:** U.N. Economic and Social Council.

█1412█

Certified Hazardous Materials Technician, Level II (CHMT II)
World Safety Organization (WSO)
WSO World Mgmt. Center
305 E. Market St.
PO Box 518
Warrensburg, MO 64093
Phone: (816)747-3132
Fax: (816)747-2647

Recipient: Hazardous materials workers and first responders. **Educational/Experience Requirements:** Must meet the following requirements: (1) Hold Certified Hazardous Materials Technician, Level I (CHMT I) designation (see separate entry); (2) Successfully complete six month internship; and (3) Successfully complete 140-150 hours of training in the following areas: Agricultural and pest-control chemicals; Characteristics and detection of combustible, explosive, flammable, and toxic materials; Chemistry; Containers; Control, containment, and handling methods; Emergency response procedures; Hazardous materials and waste operations; Operations and incident management procedures; Protection and decontamination; and Toxicology. **Membership:** Required. **Certification Requirements:** Successful completion of exam. First part covers professional expertise and accomplishments. Second part covers: Emergency response procedures; Ethics; Hazardous materials and waste operations; Law and regulations; Management; Occupational health and safety; Professional liability; Risk management; and Safety and loss control. **Renewal:** Every three years. Recertification based on accumulation of 30 points through continuing education, professional accomplishments, training, and other related activities. Renewal fee is $155. **Examination Type:** Essay; multiple-choice. **Pass/Fail Rate:** 50% pass exam the first time. **Fees:** $300. **Endorsed By:** U.N. Economic and Social Council.

1413

Certified Occupational Health and Safety Technologist (OHST)
Board of Certified Safety Professionals (BCSP)
208 Burwash Ave.
Savoy, IL 61874
Phone: (217)359-2686
Fax: (217)359-0055
Michael K. Orn, Exec.Dir.

Recipient: Professionals who perform safety inspections, monitor industrial hygiene, maintain occupational accident and illness records, and provide health and safety training. **Number of Certified Individuals:** 1200. **Educational/Experience Requirements:** High school diploma and five years experience. Bachelor's degree, or associate's degree in health and safety or a technical/scientific area, may be substituted for two years of experience. **Certification Requirements:** Successful completion of exam. Exam covers: Basic and applied sciences; Control concepts, including personal protective equipment; Data computation and record keeping; Education, training, and instruction; Incident/illness/injury/fire investigation; Occupational health and safety laws standards, certifications, and regulations; and Survey and inspection techniques. **Examination Type:** Multiple-choice. **Fees:** $170. **Endorsed By:** American Board of Industrial Hygiene; National Organization for Competency Assurance.

1414

Certified Product Safety Manager, Associate Level (CPSM)
Board of Certified Product Safety Management (BCPSM)
8009 Carita Ct.
Bethesda, MD 20817
Phone: (301)984-8969

Recipient: Professional managers and engineers involved in product safety and liability. **Educational/Experience Requirements:** Combination of college level education and experience equaling five years. May qualify for either Certified Product Safety Manager, Executive or Senior Level designations (see separate entries) with more education and/or experience. **Certification Requirements:** Successful completion of exam. Exam covers: Analytical and system safety techniques; Organization, operation, and audit product safety programs; Product safety and the law; Product safety liability and insurance; and Regulations and standards. Candidates who have made

outstanding contributions to field may be exempt from exam. **Preparatory Materials:** Examination guide available. **Fees:** $150.

1415

Certified Product Safety Manager, Executive Level (CPSM)
Board of Certified Product Safety Management (BCPSM)
8009 Carita Ct.
Bethesda, MD 20817
Phone: (301)984-8969

Recipient: Professional managers and engineers involved in product safety and liability. **Educational/Experience Requirements:** Must meet the following requirements: (1) Bachelor's degree in science, safety/health, engineering, medicine, business administration, law, behavioral science, or other related field; and (2) Six years experience. Candidates with less education and/or experience may qualify for either Certified Product Safety Manager, Associate Level or Senior Level designations (see separate entries). **Certification Requirements:** Successful completion of exam. Exam covers: Analytical and system safety techniques; Organization, operation, and audit product safety programs; Product safety and the law; Product safety liability and insurance; and Regulations and standards. Candidates who have made outstanding contributions to field may be exempt from exam. **Preparatory Materials:** Examination guide available. **Fees:** $150.

1416

Certified Product Safety Manager, Senior Level (CPSM)
Board of Certified Product Safety Management (BCPSM)
8009 Carita Ct.
Bethesda, MD 20817
Phone: (301)984-8969

Recipient: Professional managers and engineers involved in product safety and liability. **Educational/Experience Requirements:** Must meet one of the following requirements: (1) Bachelor's degree in related field and four years experience; (2) Two years of college education and six years experience; or (3) Eight years experience. May qualify for Certified Product Safety Manager, Executive Level designation (see separate entry) with increased education and/or experience. Candidates with less education and/or experience may qualify for Certified Product Safety Manager, Associate

Level designation (see separate entry). **Certification Requirements:** Successful completion of exam. Exam covers: Analytical and system safety techniques; Organization, operation, and audit product safety programs; Product safety and the law; Product safety liability and insurance; and Regulations and standards. Candidates who have made outstanding contributions to field may be exempt from exam. **Preparatory Materials:** Examination guide available. **Fees:** $150.

1417

Certified Safety Executive (CSE)
World Safety Organization (WSO)
WSO World Mgmt. Center
305 E. Market St.
PO Box 518
Warrensburg, MO 64093
Phone: (816)747-3132
Fax: (816)747-2647
Dr. G.E. Hudson, Chm.

Recipient: Corporate, government, and organizational executives responsible for setting occupational safety, health, environmental safety, and health policies. **Educational/Experience Requirements:** Must meet one of the following requirements: (1) College degree and four years experience; or (2) 11 years experience. **Membership:** Required. **Certification Requirements:** Successful completion of two-part exam. First part covers professional expertise or contributions. Second part covers: Ethics; Law and regulations; Management; Occupational health and safety; Product safety; Professional liability; Risk management; Safety and loss control; and Security. **Renewal:** Every three years. Recertification based on accumulation of 30 points through continuing education, professional accomplishments, training, and other related activities. Renewal fee is $155. **Preparatory Materials:** Sample questions and study guide available. **Examination Frequency:** Throughout the year. **Examination Sites:** Exam given by arrangement with proctor. **Examination Type:** Essay; fill-in-the-blank; multiple-choice; true or false. **Pass/Fail Rate:** 50% pass exam the first time. **Waiting Period to Receive Scores:** Three weeks. **Fees:** $300. **Endorsed By:** U.N. Economic and Social Council.

1418

Certified Safety Manager (CSM)

World Safety Organization (WSO)
WSO World Mgmt. Center
305 E. Market St.
PO Box 518
Warrensburg, MO 64093
Phone: (816)747-3132
Fax: (816)747-2647

Recipient: Safety practitioners in mid-level management who supervise safety training, enforce safety requirements, and coordinate safety programs. **Educational/Experience Requirements:** Must meet one of the following requirements: (1) Bachelor's degree in safety or related area, such as management, security, or engineering, and four years experience; (2) Master's degree and two years experience; or (3) Doctoral degree and one year of experience. Recognized professional certifications, licenses, or registrations may be substituted for up to two years of four-year requirement. Candidates may substitute two years of professional experience for each academic year of bachelor's degree. **Membership:** Required. **Certification Requirements:** Successful completion of two-part exam. First part covers professional expertise or contributions. Second part covers: Ethics; Law and regulations; Management; Occupational health and safety; Product safety; Professional liability; Risk management; Safety and loss control; and Security. **Renewal:** Every three years. Recertification based on accumulation of 30 points through continuing education, professional accomplishments, training, and other related activities. Renewal fee is $155. **Examination Type:** Essay; fill-in-the-blank; multiple-choice; true or false. **Pass/Fail Rate:** 50% pass exam the first time. **Fees:** $300. **Endorsed By:** U.N. Economic and Social Council.

1419

Certified Safety and Security Director (CSSD)

World Safety Organization (WSO)
WSO World Mgmt. Center
305 E. Market St.
PO Box 518
Warrensburg, MO 64093
Phone: (816)747-3132
Fax: (816)747-2647

Recipient: Security professionals concerned with safety and security of people, property, resources, or the environment. **Educational/Experience Requirements:** Must meet one of the following requirements: (1) Bachelor's degree in safety or

related area, such as management, security, or engineering, and four years experience; (2) Master's degree and two years experience; or (3) Doctoral degree and one year of experience. Recognized professional certifications, licenses, or registrations may be substituted for up to two years of four-year requirement. Candidates may substitute two years of professional experience for each academic year of bachelor's degree. **Membership:** Required. **Certification Requirements:** Successful completion of two-part exam. First part covers professional expertise or contributions. Second part covers: Ethics; Law and regulations; Management; Occupational health and safety; Product safety; Professional liability; Risk management; Safety and loss control; and Security. **Renewal:** Every three years. Recertification based on accumulation of 30 points through continuing education, professional accomplishments, training, and other related activities. Renewal fee is $155. **Examination Type:** Essay; fill-in-the-blank; multiple-choice; true or false. **Pass/Fail Rate:** 50% pass exam the first time. **Fees:** $300. **Endorsed By:** U.N. Economic and Social Council.

1420

Certified Safety Specialist (CSS)

World Safety Organization (WSO)
WSO World Mgmt. Center
305 E. Market St.
PO Box 518
Warrensburg, MO 64093
Phone: (816)747-3132
Fax: (816)747-2647

Recipient: Safety practitioners specializing in specific areas who perform both technical and managerial functions. **Educational/Experience Requirements:** Must meet one of the following requirements: (1) Bachelor's degree in safety or related area, such as management, security, or engineering, and four years experience; (2) Master's degree and two years experience; or (3) Doctoral degree and one year of experience. Recognized professional certifications, licenses, or registrations may be substituted for up to two years of four-year requirement. Candidates may substitute two years of professional experience for each academic year of bachelor's degree. **Membership:** Required. **Certification Requirements:** Successful completion of a two-part exam. First part covers professional expertise or contributions. Second part covers: General safety; Legal and regulatory issues; Professional ethics; and Specialization. **Renewal:** Every three years. Recertification based on accumulation of 30 points through continuing education, profes-

sional accomplishments, training, and other related activities. Renewal fee is $155. **Examination Type:** Essay; fill-in-the-blank; multiple-choice; true or false. **Pass/Fail Rate:** 50% pass exam the first time. **Fees:** $300. **Endorsed By:** U.N. Economic and Social Council.

1421

Certified Safety Technician (CST)

World Safety Organization (WSO)
WSO World Mgmt. Center
305 E. Market St.
PO Box 518
Warrensburg, MO 64093
Phone: (816)747-3132
Fax: (816)747-2647

Recipient: Entry-level safety and safety-related professionals. **Membership:** Required. **Certification Requirements:** Must meet one of the following requirements: (1) Bachelor's degree in safety or related area; (2) Associate's degree in safety or related field and three years experience; or (3) Five years related experience. **Renewal:** Every year. Renewal fee is $155. **Fees:** $300. **Endorsed By:** U.N. Economic and Social Council.

1422

Registered Hazard Control Technician

Board of Hazard Control
  Management
8009 Carita Ct.
MD 20817
Phone: (301)984-8969

Recipient: Hazard control technicians. **Educational/Experience Requirements:** Must meet one of the following requirements: (1) Associate's degree in safety, fire, or occupational health and one year of experience; (2) Successful completion of approved hazard control training course and two years experience; (3) Two years of college education and three years experience; or (4) Bachelor's degree and six months experience. May substitute each full year (30 semester hours) of graduate study for one year of experience up to two years. Achievements in field such as holding leadership positions in professional associations, delivering papers or having them published, and conducting research activities may be substituted for up to one year of experience. May qualify for either Certified Hazard Control Manager, Associate, Senior, or Master Level designations (see separate entries) with increased education and/or experience. **Certification Requirements:**

Successful completion of exam. Exam covers: Communication and report writing; Hazard control program disciplines and source of information; Hazard control program techniques; Interfacing staff functions; Legislative and regulation requirements and standards setting organizations; and Management principles and techniques. Candidates may be required to submit examples of reports on hazard evaluation surveys or case study documenting hazard control management abilities. **Examination Sites:** Exam given by arrangement with proctor. **Fees:** $150.

Food and Beverage Preparation and Service Occupations

Chefs, Cooks, and Other Kitchen Workers

1423

Certified Cook (CC)
American Culinary Federation (ACF)
10 San Bartola Rd.
PO Box 3466
St. Augustine, FL 32085-3466
Phone: (904)824-4468
Fax: (904)825-4758
Toll Free: (800)624-9458
Stephen Fernald CCC, Dir.

Recipient: Professional chefs. **Number of Certified Individuals:** 7800. **Educational/ Experience Requirements:** Successful completion of one of the following: (1) ACF apprenticeship program; (2) Culinary trade school program and documented work experience; or (3) Exam and three years experience. Must successfully complete acceptable courses in nutrition, sanitation, and supervisory development. **Membership:** Required. **Certification Requirements:** Must earn 44 total points through: (1) Education (20 points); (2) Experience (20 points); and (3) Association activities (four points). **Renewal:** Every five years. Recertification based on continuing education. **Preparatory Materials:** *The Art and Science of Culinary Preparation* (textbook). Handbook also available. **Examination Frequency:** Throughout the year. **Examination Sites:** Exam given at sites throughout the U.S. **Examination Type:** Multiple-choice. **Pass/Fail Rate:** 80% pass exam the first time. **Waiting Period to Receive Scores:** Immediately. **Reexamination:** There is no time limit to retake exam. **Fees:** $60.

1424

Certified Master Chef (CMC)
American Culinary Federation (ACF)
10 San Bartola Rd.
PO Box 3466
St. Augustine, FL 32085-3466
Phone: (904)824-4468
Fax: (904)825-4758
Toll Free: (800)624-9458
Stephen C. Fernald CCC, Dir.

Recipient: Professional chefs. **Educational/Experience Requirements:** Must hold Certified Executive Chef (CEC) designation (see separate entry). **Membership:** Required. **Certification Requirements:** Successful completion of practical and theoretical exams. **Renewal:** Every five years. Recertification based on continuing education. Renewal fee is $100. **Preparatory Materials:** Candidate's manual and reading list available. **Examination Frequency:** Throughout the year. **Examination Sites:** Exam given at Culinary Institute of America. **Pass/Fail Rate:** 30% pass exams the first time. **Waiting Period to Receive Scores:** Immediately. **Fees:** $3000.

1425

Certified Master Pastry Chef (CMPC)
American Culinary Federation (ACF)
10 San Bartola Rd.
PO Box 3466
St. Augustine, FL 32085-3466
Phone: (904)824-4468
Fax: (904)825-4758
Toll Free: (800)624-9458
Stephen C. Fernald CCC, Dir.

Recipient: Professional pastry chefs. **Educational/Experience Requirements:** Must hold Certified Executive Pastry Chef (CEPC) designation (see separate entry). **Membership:** Required. **Certification Requirements:** Successful completion of practical and theoretical exams. **Renewal:** Every five years. Recertification based on continuing education. Renewal fee is $100. **Preparatory Materials:** Candidate's manual and reading list available. **Examination Frequency:** Throughout the year. **Examination Sites:** Exam given at Culinary Institute of America. **Pass/Fail Rate:** 30% pass exams the first time. **Waiting Period to Receive Scores:** Immediately. **Fees:** $3000.

1426

Certified Pastry Cook (CPC)
American Culinary Federation (ACF)
10 San Bartola Rd.
PO Box 3466
St. Augustine, FL 32085-3466
Phone: (904)824-4468
Fax: (904)825-4758
Toll Free: (800)624-9458
Stephen Fernald CCC, Dir.

Recipient: Professional pastry chefs. **Educational/Experience Requirements:** Must successfully complete one of the following: (1) ACF apprenticeship program; (2) Culinary trade school program and documented work experience; or (3) Exam and three years experience. Must have successfully completed acceptable courses in nutrition, sanitation, and supervisory development. **Membership:** Required. **Certification Requirements:** Must earn 44 total points through: (1) Education (20 points); (2) Experience (20 points); and (3) Association activities (four points). **Renewal:** Every five years. Recertification based on continuing education. **Preparatory Materials:** *The Art and Science of Culinary Preparation* (textbook). Handbook also available. **Examination Frequency:** Throughout the year. **Examination Sites:** Exam given by arrangement with proctor. **Examination Type:** Multiple-choice. **Pass/Fail Rate:** 85% pass exam the first time. **Waiting Period to Receive Scores:** Two weeks. **Re-examination:** There is no time limit to retake exam. **Fees:** $60.

Restaurant and Food Service Managers

`1427`

Certified Church Food Service Director

National Association of Church
  Food Service (NACFS)
76 Ivy Pkwy., NE
Atlanta, GA 30342-4241
Phone: (404)261-1794

Recipient: Church food service directors. **Certification Requirements:** Must accumulate 75 total points in the following ways: (1) High school diploma (two points); (2) Bachelor's degree (five points); (3) Master's degree (ten points); (4) Successful completion of course in food service and management (ten points) or course from local or state health department (five points); (5) Attendance at NACFS national conference (20 points), food shows (two points), local chapter meetings with programs (three points), state meetings (five points), or classes at national conference (one point per class); (6) Experience (one point per year; maximum of ten points); (7) Continuing Education Units (CEUs) earned from colleges or food shows (five points); (8) Meritorious community work related to food service (five points); (9) Membership in food service related associations (one point); (10) Conference displays (ten points); (11) Submission of five quality-quantity recipes to conference (one point); and (12) Sponsoring new NACFS members (five points each). Five extra points awarded if college degree related to food. Ten points awarded for attendance at or teaching of food service courses that are more than four hours in length. Must also have formal training in food service. **Renewal:** Every three years. Recertification based on accumulation of 75 points in areas listed above. Renewal fee is $15. **Fees:** $15.

`1428`

Certified Concession Manager (CCM)

National Association of
  Concessionaires (NAC)
35 E. Wacker Dr., Ste. 1545
Chicago, IL 60601
Phone: (312)236-3858
Fax: (312)236-7809
Shelley Feldman, Dir. of Educ.

Recipient: Operators of food and beverage concessions in theaters, amusement parks, sports arenas, and other recreational facilities. **Number of Certified Individuals:** 350. **Membership:** Not required. **Certification Requirements:** Must meet the following requirements: (1) Successful completion of the following courses: Cost Control Systems; Event Planning, including preparation of simulated event; Management, covering management basics and their applications in recreational food service; Profit Planning, including production of budget and completion of case studies; and Sanitation; (2) Successful completion of exam; and (3) Membership in NAC or attendance at three NAC functions within two years. **Renewal:** none. **Preparatory Materials:** *Recreational Foodservice* (reference). **Examination Frequency:** Five-six times per year. **Examination Sites:** Exam given at NAC programs. **Examination Type:** Multiple-choice; problem solving. **Pass/Fail Rate:** 95% pass exam the first time. **Waiting Period to Receive Scores:** Two weeks. **Re-examination:** There is no time limit to retake exam. **Fees:** $350 (members); $475 (nonmembers).

`1429`

Certified Food Executive (CFE)

International Food Service
  Executives Association (IFSEA)
1100 S. State Rd. 7, Ste. 103
Margate, FL 33068
Phone: (305)977-0767
Fax: (305)977-0874
Ed Manley CFE, Exec.Dir.

Recipient: Proprietors, executives, managers, educators, and consultants for hotels, restaurants, clubs, institutions, caterers, military, cruise lines, and airlines. **Membership:** Not required. **Certification Requirements:** Must earn 1250 total points in the following categories: (1) Experience (minimum of 200 points), including positions held, lectures given, articles and books published, and teaching; (2) Education (minimum of 350 points), including college degrees and courses, technical training, correspondence

courses, apprenticeship programs, and seminars, educational programs, and trade shows; and (3) Association Participation (no minimum), including years as member, conferences attended, and leadership positions held. Candidates with only 900 points may qualify for Certified Food Manager designation (see separate entry). **Renewal:** Every five years. Recertification based on accumulation of 700 points in same categories as initial certification. Lifetime certification available for retired CFEs. Renewal fees are: $40 (members); $110 (nonmembers). **Fees:** $80 (members); $150 (nonmembers).

`1430`

Certified Food Manager (CFM)

International Food Service
  Executives Association (IFSEA)
1100 S. State Rd. 7, Ste. 103
Margate, FL 33068
Phone: (305)977-0767
Fax: (305)977-0874
Ed Manley CFE, Exec.Dir.

Recipient: Proprietors, executives, managers, educators, and consultants for hotels, restaurants, clubs, institutions, caterers, military, cruise lines, and airlines. **Membership:** Not required. **Certification Requirements:** Must earn 900 total points in the following categories: (1) Experience (minimum of 150 points), including internships, culinary competitions and demonstrations, positions held, lectures, published articles and books, awards, and teaching; (2) Education (minimum of 350 points), including high school diploma, college degrees and courses, technical training, correspondence courses, apprenticeship programs, and seminars, educational programs, and trade shows; and (3) Association Participation (no minimum), including years as member, conferences attended, and leadership positions held. Candidates with 1250 points may qualify for Certified Food Executive designation (see separate entry). **Fees:** $60 (members); $130 (nonmembers).

`1431`

Certified Foodservice Professional (CFSP)

National Association of Food
  Equipment Manufacturers
  (NAFEM)
401 N. Michigan Ave.
Chicago, IL 60611-4267
Phone: (312)644-6610
Fax: (312)245-1080
Patty Urell, Admin.

Recipient: Foodservice professionals. **Educational/Experience Requirements:** Must earn 165 total points in the following areas: (1) Education, including one of the following: High school diploma (one point); Associate's degree (four points); Bachelor's degree (eight points for related degree; six points for unrelated degree); Master's degree (ten points for related degree; eight points for unrelated degree); and Doctorate degree (12 points for related degree; ten points for unrelated degree); (2) Industry Service, including: Association membership (one point); Association official positions held (one-three points); Articles written and published (two points); Speeches given or instruction provided on industry topics (two points); and Volunteer/leadership roles in business, professional, or community service organizations (one point); (3) Industry Related Activities, including: Attendance at NAFEM Trade Show (six points); Attendance at seminars (two-eight points); Attendance at other trade association conventions, seminars, or chapter meetings (one-two points); and Industry awards, honors, and other achievements (one-two points); and (4) Foodservice Industry Experience (one-eighteen points based on years of experience). Candidates with fewer points may qualify for Certified Foodservice Professional Associate (CFSP Associate) designation (see separate entry). **Certification Requirements:** Successful completion of exam. Exam covers: Cook-chill; Dining room; Dishroom; Equipment; Facility design; Food preparation; Foodservice industry; Receiving/storage; Service area; and Utility. **Renewal:** Every two years. Recertification based on accumulation of ten points in same categories as initial certification. Renewal fee is $25. **Preparatory Materials:** Seminars and reference guide available. **Examination Frequency:** Throughout the year. **Examination Sites:** Exam given at industry shows throughout the U.S. or by arrangement with proctor. **Examination Type:** Fill-in-the-blank; multiple-choice; true or false. **Waiting Period to Receive Scores:** Three weeks. **Fees:** $125.

1432

Certified Foodservice Professional Associate (CFSP Associate)
National Association of Food Equipment Manufacturers (NAFEM)
401 N. Michigan Ave.
Chicago, IL 60611-4267
Phone: (312)644-6610
Fax: (312)245-1080
Patty Urell, Admin.

Recipient: Individuals who interface with, but are not employed in, foodservice industry. **Educational/Experience Requirements:** Must earn 35 total points in the following areas: (1) Education, including one of the following: High school diploma (one point); Associate's degree (four points); Bachelor's degree (eight points for related degree; six points for unrelated degree); Master's degree (ten points for related degree; eight points for unrelated degree); and Doctorate degree (twelve points for unrelated degree; ten points for related degree); (2) Industry Service, including: Association membership (one point); Association official positions held (one-three points); Articles written and published (two points); Speeches given or instruction provided on industry topics (two points); and Volunteer/leadership roles in business, professional, or community service organizations (one point); (3) Industry Related Activities, including: Attendance at NAFEM Trade Show (six points); Attendance at seminars (two-eight points); Attendance at other trade association conventions, seminars, or chapter meetings (one-two points); and Industry awards, honors, and other achievements (one-two points); and (4) Foodservice Industry Experience (one-eighteen points based on years of experience). Candidates with more points may qualify for Certified Foodservice Professional (CFSP) designation (see separate entry). **Certification Requirements:** Successful completion of exam. Exam covers: Cook-chill; Dining room; Dishroom; Equipment; Facility design; Food preparation; Foodservice industry; Receiving/storage; Service area; and Utility. **Renewal:** Every two years. Recertification based on accumulation of ten points in same categories as initial certification. Renewal fee is $25. **Preparatory Materials:** Seminars and reference guide available. **Examination Frequency:** Throughout the year. **Examination Sites:** Exam given at industry shows throughout the U.S. or by arrangement with proctor. **Examination Type:** Fill-in-the-blank; multiple-choice; true or false. **Waiting Period to Receive Scores:** Three weeks. **Fees:** $125.

1433

Certified Professional Catering Executive (CPCE)
National Association of Catering Executives (NACE)
60 Revere Dr., Ste. 500
Northbrook, IL 60062
Phone: (708)480-9080
Fax: (708)480-9282
Ellen Berger CPCE, Chair

Recipient: Catering executives. **Certification Requirements:** Successful completion of exam. **Preparatory Materials:** Study materials provided. **Examination Sites:** Exam given at annual educational conference and at sites throughout the U.S.

1434

Foodservice Management Professional (FMP)
National Restaurant Association Educational Foundation
250 S. Wacker Dr., Ste. 1400
Chicago, IL 60606-5834
Phone: (312)715-1010
Toll Free: (800)765-2122
Kathleen Wood FMP, Dir.

Recipient: Foodservice unit managers, multi-unit managers, corporate executives and trainers, and hospitality educators. **Educational/Experience Requirements:** Foodservice unit managers, multi-unit managers, or corporate executives must meet one of the following requirements: (1) Ten years experience, with at least five years at unit manager or corporate level, and either successful completion of one Foundation Management Development course or attendance at FMP review session; (2) Five years experience, with at least three years at unit manager or corporate level, and either bachelor's or associate's degree and successful completion of one Foundation Management Development Course or successful completion of three Foundation Management Development courses; (3) Three years experience, with at least one year at unit manager or corporate level, and bachelor's or associate's degree, postsecondary certificate, or diploma with hospitality, foodservice, culinary, or equivalent major; (4) Three years experience, with at least one year at unit manager or corporate level, bachelor's or associate's degree, postsecondary certificate, or diploma with business or equivalent major, and successful completion of one Foundation foodservice operations course; (5) Three years experience, with at least one year at unit manager or corporate level, and successful completion of Foundation's eight-course Management Development Program; or (6) Three years experience, with at least one year at unit manager or corporate level, and successful completion of five management-area exams from Foundation's Management Skills Program. Corporate trainers from foodservice management companies with at least three units must have three years experience, with at least two years in foodservice operations. Hospitality educators must meet the following requirements: (1) Three years experience as educator in hospitality, foodservice, culinary, or equivalent program at accredited post-secondary degree-, certificate-, or diploma-granting school; and (2) Two years experience in foodservice operations. Experience must be in supervisory or management positions. **Certification Requirements:** Successful completion of exam. Exam covers: Human resources/diversity management; Marketing; Operations; Risk management; and Unit revenue/cost management. **Renewal:** Every three years. Recertification based on accumulation of points through continuing education, industry involvement, professional development activities, and work experience. **Preparatory Materials:** Review notebook and review sessions available. **Examination Sites:** Exam given at sites throughout the U.S. **Reexamination:** May retake exam twice. There is a $25 fee to retake exam. **Fees:** $250. **Endorsed By:** National Restaurant Association.

Health Service Occupations

Dental Assistants

1435

Certified Dental Assistant (CDA)
Dental Assisting National Board
  (DANB)
216 E. Ontario St.
Chicago, IL 60611
Phone: (312)642-3368

Recipient: Dental assistants. **Educational/Experience Requirements:** Current CPR certification and meet one of the following requirements: (1) Successful completion of dental assisting or dental hygiene program accredited by Commission on Dental Accreditation (see separate entry); or (2) High school diploma or equivalent and two years (3500 hours) experience. **Certification Requirements:** Successful completion of exam. Exam consists of the following sections: Dental Radiation Health and Safety; General Chairside; and Infection Control. Exam covers: Chairside dental materials and procedures; Collection and recording of clinical data; Dental radiography; Lab materials and procedures; Occupational safety; Office management procedures; Patient education and oral health management; Prevention and management of emergencies; and Universal precautions and the prevention of disease transmission. **Renewal:** Every year. Recertification based on either successful completion of exam or continuing education. **Preparatory Materials:** *Dental Assisting National Board's Task Analysis* (reference). Handbook, including exam content outline, list of references, sample questions, and study hints, provided. **Examination Frequency:** quarterly. **Examination Sites:** Exam given at sites throughout the U.S. **Examination Type:** Matching; multiple-choice. **Waiting Period to Receive Scores:** Four-six weeks. **Re-examination:** Must only retake sec-

tions failed. May retake exam twice. There is a $25 fee to retake each section of exam. **Accredited By:** National Commission for Certifying Agencies. **Endorsed By:** Academy of Oral and Maxillofacial Radiology; American Association of Dental Examiners; American Association of Dental Schools; American Association of Oral and Maxillofacial Surgery; American Association of Orthodontists; American Dental Assistants Association; American Dental Association; National Organization for Competency Assurance.

1436

**Certified Dental Practice
  Management Assistant (CDPMA)**
Dental Assisting National Board
  (DANB)
216 E. Ontario St.
Chicago, IL 60611
Phone: (312)642-3368

Recipient: Dental practice management assistants. **Educational/Experience Requirements:** Current CPR certification and one of the following requirements: (1) Work experience in dental office; or (2) Successful completion of practice management course at institution having dental assisting program accredited by the Commission on Dental Accreditation (see separate entry). **Certification Requirements:** Successful completion of exam. Exam covers: Chairside dental procedures; Collection and recording of clinical data; Dental radiography; Occupational safety; Office management procedures; Patient education and oral health management; Prevention and management of emergencies; and Universal precautions and prevention of disease transmission. **Renewal:** Every year. Recertification based on either successful completion of exam or continuing education. **Preparatory Materials:** *Dental As-*

sisting National Board's Task Analysis (reference). Handbook, including exam content outline, list of references, sample questions, and study hints, provided. **Examination Frequency:** quarterly. **Examination Sites:** Exam given at sites throughout the U.S. **Examination Type:** Matching; multiple-choice. **Waiting Period to Receive Scores:** Four-six weeks. **Re-examination:** May retake exam twice. **Accredited By:** National Commission for Certifying Agencies. **Endorsed By:** Academy of Oral and Maxillofacial Radiology; American Association of Dental Examiners; American Association of Dental Schools; American Association of Oral and Maxillofacial Surgery; American Association of Orthodontists; American Dental Assistants Association; American Dental Association; National Organization for Competency Assurance.

1437

**Certified Oral and Maxillofacial
  Surgery Assistant (COMSA)**
Dental Assisting National Board
  (DANB)
216 E. Ontario St.
Chicago, IL 60611
Phone: (312)642-3368

Recipient: Oral and maxillofacial surgery assistants. **Educational/Experience Requirements:** High school diploma or equivalent, current CPR certification, and one of the following requirements: (1) Successfully complete 500 hours of post-secondary education in oral and maxillofacial surgery assisting and six months (875 hours) experience in the last three years; (2) Hold Certified Dental Assistant (CDA) designation (see separate entry) or related certification and have work experience; or (3) Two years (3500 hours) experience in last three years. **Certification Requirements:** Successful completion of exam. Exam consists of following sections: Infection Control; and Oral and Maxillofacial Surgery Assisting. Exam covers: Chairside dental materials and procedures; Collection and recording of clinical data; Dental radiography; General anesthesia, sedation, and analgesia; Lab materials and procedures; Occupational safety; Office management procedures; Oral and maxillofacial procedures; Patient education and oral health management; Prevention and management of emergencies; and Universal precautions and prevention of disease transmission. **Renewal:** Every year. Recertification based on either successful completion of exam or continuing education. **Preparatory Materials:** *Dental Assisting National Board's Task Analysis* (reference). Handbook, including exam content outline, list of references, sample questions, and study hints, provided. **Examination Frequency:** quarterly. **Examination Sites:** Exam given at sites throughout the U.S. **Examination Type:** Matching; multiple-choice. **Waiting Period to Receive Scores:** Four-six weeks. **Re-examination:** Must only retake sections failed. May retake exam twice. There is a $75 fee to retake entire exam. **Accredited By:** National Commission for Certifying Agencies. **Endorsed By:** Academy of Oral and Maxillofacial Radiology; American Association of Dental Examiners; American Association of Dental Schools; American Association of Oral and Maxillofacial Surgery; American Association of Orthodontists; American Dental Assistants Association; American Dental Association; National Organization for Competency Assurance.

Certified Orthodontic Assistant (COA)

Dental Assisting National Board (DANB)
216 E. Ontario St.
Chicago, IL 60611
Phone: (312)642-3368

Recipient: Orthodontic assistants. **Educational/Experience Requirements:** Current CPR certification and one of the following requirements: (1) High school diploma or equivalent, work experience in orthodontic office, and Certified Dental Assistant (CDA) designation (see separate entry) or related certification; (2) High school diploma and two years (3500 hours) experience; or (3) Successful completion of orthodontic assisting preparation course at institution having dental assisting program accredited by Commission on Dental Accreditation (see separate entry) and CDA designation. **Certification Requirements:** Suc-

cessful completion of exam. Exam consists of following sections: Infection Control; and Orthodontic Assisting. Exam covers: Chairside dental materials and procedures; Collection and recording of clinical data; Dental radiography; Lab materials and procedures; Occupational safety; Office management procedures; Patient education and oral health management; Prevention and management of emergencies; and Universal precautions and prevention of disease transmission. **Renewal:** Every year. Recertification based on either successful completion of exam or continuing education. **Preparatory Materials:** *Dental Assisting National Board's Task Analysis* (reference). Handbook, including exam content outline, list of references, sample questions, and study hints, provided. **Examination Frequency:** quarterly. **Examination Sites:** Exam given at sites throughout the U.S. **Examination Type:** Matching; multiple-choice. **Waiting Period to Receive Scores:** Four-six weeks. **Re-examination:** Must only retake sections failed. May retake exam twice. There is a $75 fee to retake entire exam. **Accredited By:** National Commission for Certifying Agencies. **Endorsed By:** Academy of Oral and Maxillofacial Radiology; American Association of Dental Examiners; American Association of Dental Schools; American Association of Oral and Maxillofacial Surgery; American Association of Orthodontists; American Dental Assistants Association; American Dental Association; National Organization for Competency Assurance.

Registered Dental Assistant (RDA)

American Medical Technologists (AMT)
710 Higgins Rd.
Park Ridge, IL 60068
Phone: (708)823-5169
Fax: (708)823-0458
Toll Free: (800)275-1268
James R. Fidler Ph.D., Dir.

Recipient: Dental assistants qualified to provide support in administrative duties, and chairside, laboratory, and radiological procedures. **Educational/Experience Requirements:** Current CPR certification and meet one of the following requirements: (1) Graduate from dental assisting program accredited by Accrediting Bureau of Health Education Schools (see separate entry) or other recognized accrediting agency; or (2) Graduate from U.S. Armed Forces dental assisting program and one year of experience. Programs must include office assisting, dental sciences, clinical procedures, and

radiology. **Membership:** Required. **Certification Requirements:** Successful completion of exam. Exam covers: Clinical procedures; Dental sciences; Office assisting skills; and Radiology. **Renewal:** Every year. Recertification based on continuing education. **Preparatory Materials:** Reference list and study guide bibliography available. **Examination Frequency:** Throughout the year. **Examination Sites:** Exam given at sites throughout the U.S. **Examination Type:** Multiple-choice. **Pass/Fail Rate:** 55% pass exam the first time. **Waiting Period to Receive Scores:** Four-six weeks. **Re-examination:** There is no time limit to retake exam. **Fees:** $59. **Accredited By:** National Commission for Certifying Agencies. **Endorsed By:** National Committee for Clinical Laboratory Standards; National Organization for Competency Assurance.

Dental Laboratory Technicians

Certified Dental Technician (CDT)

National Board for Certification in Dental Technology (NBC)
3801 Mt. Vernon Ave.
Alexandria, VA 22305
Phone: (703)683-5310
Fax: (703)549-4788
Toll Free: (800)950-1150
Sandra C. Stewart, Dir.

Recipient: Dental laboratory technicians. **Number of Certified Individuals:** 8000. **Educational/Experience Requirements:** Must meet one of the following requirements: (1) Successful completion of accredited two-year dental technology program and Recognized Graduate (RG) exam and two years post-graduation experience; (2) Successful completion of accredited two-year dental technology program, two years post-graduation experience, and successful completion of Comprehensive Examination; or (3) Five years combined education and experience in dental technology and successful completion of Comprehensive Examination. **Certification Requirements:** Successful completion of written and practical exams in specialty. Specialties are: Complete Dentures; Partial Dentures; Crown and Bridge; Ceramics; and Orthodontics. **Renewal:** Every two years. Recertification based on accumulation of at least ten hours of continuing education every year through: (1) Approved technical clinics and courses and technical education videotapes; (2) Management and finance, communication skills, and instructional technique courses; and (3) Non-documented studies, including non-approved courses and clinics, independent study of publications or videotapes, and other related activities. Renewal fee is $95. **Preparatory Materials:** Manual, pamphlets, and brochures provided. Instructional texts available from U.S. government. Study groups available. **Examination Frequency:** 14-20 times per year. **Examination Sites:** Exam given at 20 sites throughout the U.S. **Examination Type:** Multiple-choice. **Fees:** $200. **Endorsed By:** American Dental Association; National Association of Dental Laboratories.

Medical Assistants

1441

Certified Gastroenterology Associate (CGA)
Certifying Board of Gastroenterology Nurses and Associates (CBGNA)
720 Light St.
Baltimore, MD 21230
Phone: (410)752-1808
Fax: (410)752-8295

Recipient: Medical professionals specializing in gastroenterology and endoscopic procedures. **Educational/Experience Requirements:** Two years (4000 hours) experience within last five years in clinical, supervisory, or administrative capacities in institutional or private practice settings. **Membership:** Not required. **Certification Requirements:** Successful completion of exam. Exam covers: Education of the patient, family, and public healthcare professionals within the specialty; Patient care management; and Professional practice. **Renewal:** Every five years. Recertification based on either successful completion of exam or accumulation of 100 hours of continuing education through gastroenterology/endoscopy nursing seminars and workshops (minimum of 80 hours), other nursing seminars and workshops, presentations, publications authored, course work in medicine, health care, or health sciences, independent study, exam questions written, and research projects. Renewal fees are: $200 (members); $270 (nonmembers). **Preparatory Materials:** Handbook, including exam content outline and sample questions, provided. **Examination Frequency:** semiannual - always May and fall. **Examination Sites:** Exam given at annual education course, fall course, and at 15 sites throughout the

U.S. **Examination Type:** Multiple-choice. **Fees:** $200 (members); $270 (nonmembers). **Endorsed By:** National Organization for Competency Assurance; Society of Gastroenterology Nurses and Associates.

1442

Certified Gastroenterology Technologist/Technician (CGT)
Certifying Board of Gastroenterology Nurses and Associates (CBGNA)
720 Light St.
Baltimore, MD 21230
Phone: (410)752-1808
Fax: (410)752-8295

Recipient: Medical professionals specializing in gastroenterology and endoscopic procedures. **Educational/Experience Requirements:** Two years (4000 hours) experience within last five years in clinical, supervisory, or administrative capacities in institutional or private practice settings. **Membership:** Not required. **Certification Requirements:** Successful completion of exam. Exam covers: Education of the patient, family, and public healthcare professionals within the specialty; Patient care management; and Professional practice. **Renewal:** Every five years. Recertification based on either successful completion of exam or accumulation 100 hours of continuing education through gastroenterology/endoscopy nursing seminars and workshops (minimum of 80 hours), other nursing seminars and workshops, presentations, publications authored, course work in medicine, health care, or health sciences, independent study, exam questions written, and research projects. Renewal fees are: $200 (members); $270 (nonmembers). **Preparatory Materials:** Handbook, including exam content outline and sample questions, provided. **Examination Frequency:** semiannual - always May and fall. **Examination Sites:** Exam given at annual education course, fall course, and at 15 sites throughout the U.S. **Examination Type:** Multiple-choice. **Fees:** $200 (members); $270 (nonmembers). **Endorsed By:** National Organization for Competency Assurance; Society of Gastroenterology Nurses and Associates.

1443

Certified Hemodialysis Technician (CHT)
Board of Nephrology Examiners - Nursing and Technology (BONENT)
PO Box 15945-282
Lenexa, KS 66285
Phone: (913)541-9077
Fax: (913)541-0156

Recipient: Hemodialysis technicians. **Educational/Experience Requirements:** Must meet the following requirements: (1) High school diploma or equivalent; and (2) One year of experience in dialysis setting in administrative, equipment maintenance/repair, patient care, teaching, and/or research capacity. **Certification Requirements:** Successful completion of exam. Exam covers: (1) Supervision/Administration, including: Equipment and supplies; and Personnel management; (2) Patient Care and Machine Related Issues, including: Anatomy and physiology of renal system; Complications during dialysis; Dialyzer reuse; Documentation; Home dialysis; Initiation of dialysis; Machine set-up; Medications and renal patient; Monitoring during dialysis; Nutrition in renal patient; Pathophysiology of renal system; Patient assessment; Principles of dialysis; Psychosocial problems of renal patient; Termination of dialysis procedure; and Water treatment; (3) Professional Development, including: Information sharing; Professional relationships; Research; and Staff training; and (4) Environmental Control, including: Air quality; Infection control; and Safety. **Renewal:** Every four years. Recertification based on either successful completion of exam or accumulation of 45 hours of continuing education through academic courses, home study, seminars and workshops, publications authored, and presentations. Thirty hours must be nephrology-related. **Preparatory Materials:** Study guide, including exam content outline, list of suggested readings, and sample questions, provided. **Examination Frequency:** Throughout the year. **Examination Sites:** Exam given at sites throughout the U.S. **Examination Type:** Multiple-choice. **Reexamination:** May retake exam twice. There is a $140 fee to retake exam. **Fees:** $140.

`1444`

Certified Medical Assistant (CMA)

American Association of Medical
  Assistants (AAMA)
20 N. Wacker Dr., Ste. 1575
Chicago, IL 60606-2903
Phone: (312)424-3100
Fax: (312)899-1259
Toll Free: (800)228-2262

Recipient: Medical assistants. **Educational/Experience Requirements:** Must meet one of the following requirements: (1) Student in or graduate from medical assisting program accredited by Commission on Accreditation of Allied Health Education Programs (see separate entry); (2) Graduate from non-accredited medical assisting program and twelve months experience; (3) Graduate from allied health profession program or be military applicant, and twelve months experience; or (4) Current employment as instructor in accredited post-secondary institution. **Membership:** Not required. **Certification Requirements:** Successful completion of exam. Exam covers: (1) General, including: Anatomy and physiology; Communication; Medical terminology; Medicolegal guidelines and requirements; and Professionalism; (2) Administrative, including: Computer concepts; Equipment; Managing the office; Managing physician's professional schedule and travel; Managing practice finances; Office policies and procedures; Records management; Resource information and community services; Scheduling and monitoring appointments; Screening and processing mail; and Typing and data entry; and (3) Clinical, including: Collecting and processing specimens; Emergencies; First-aid; Patient history interview; Patient preparation and assisting physician; Preparing and administering medications; Principles of infection control; and Treatment area. **Renewal:** Every five years. Recertification based on either successful completion of exam or continuing education. **Preparatory Materials:** *A Candidate's Guide to the AAMA Certification Examination,* including bibliography of study and reference aids and sample exam, available. **Examination Frequency:** semiannual - always January and June. **Examination Sites:** Exam given at 100 test sites throughout the U.S. **Waiting Period to Receive Scores:** Twelve weeks. **Fees:** $70 (members); $145 (nonmembers).

`1445`

Certified Ophthalmic Assistant (COA)

Joint Commission on Allied Health
  Personnel in Ophthalmology
  (JCAHPO)
2025 Woodlane Dr.
St. Paul, MN 55125-2995
Phone: (612)731-2944
Fax: (612)731-0410
Toll Free: (800)284-3937

Recipient: Ophthalmic assistants. **Educational/Experience Requirements:** High school diploma or equivalent, one year of experience, current CPR certification, and successful completion of one of the following: (1) Program for ophthalmic assistants within past three years; (2) Independent/home study course for ophthalmic assistants within past three years; or (3) Program for ophthalmic assistants more than three years ago and 18 hours of continuing education. **Certification Requirements:** Successful completion of exam. Exam covers following content areas: (1) History Taking, including: Allergies and drug reaction; Family history; Medications; Partially sighted patients; Past ocular history; Presenting complaint/history of presenting illness; and Systemic illness, past and present; (2) Basic Skills and Lensometry, including: Amsler grid; Color vision testing; Estimation of anterior chamber depth; Evaluation of pupil; Exophthalmometry; Lensometry; Method of measuring/recording acuity; and Schirmer tests; (3) Patient Services, including: Assisting patient; Drug delivery (advantages/disadvantages); Ocular dressings and shields; and Spectacle principles; (4) Basic Tonometry, including: Applanation; Complications/contraindications; Factors altering intraocular pressure; Indentation; Non-contact; and Scleral rigidity; (5) Instrument Maintenance, including: Acuity projectors; Keratometers; Lenses; Lensometers; Muscle light; Ophthalmoscopes; Perimeters; Phoropters; Retinoscopes; Slit lamps; Special instruments (equipment); Surgical instruments; Tangent screen; Tonometers; and Ultrasound; and (6) General Medical Knowledge, including: Anatomy; Cardiopulmonary resuscitation; Fundamentals of microbial control; Metric conversions; Ocular diseases; Ocular emergencies; Physiology; and Systemic diseases. **Renewal:** Every three years. Recertification based on maintenance of CPR certification and accumulation of 18 continuing education hours through JCAHPO courses and seminars, other ophthalmology-related courses, self-study in ophthalmology including listen-ing to tapes, reading books, and attendance at non-JCAHPO approved courses, teaching, presentations, and authoring scientific publications. **Preparatory Materials:** *JCAHPO Standards, Procedures, and Sanctions Pertaining to Certification and Recertification* (reference). List of basic study materials provided. **Examination Sites:** Exam given at 80 sites throughout the U.S. and Canada. **Examination Type:** Multiple-choice. **Accredited By:** National Commission for Certifying Agencies. **Endorsed By:** Association of Technical Personnel in Ophthalmology; National Organization for Competency Assurance.

`1446`

Certified Ophthalmic Medical Technologist (COMT)

Joint Commission on Allied Health
  Personnel in Ophthalmology
  (JCAHPO)
2025 Woodlane Dr.
St. Paul, MN 55125-2995
Phone: (612)731-2944
Fax: (612)731-0410
Toll Free: (800)284-3937

Recipient: Ophthalmic medical technologists. **Educational/Experience Requirements:** Current CPR certification and meet one of the following requirements: (1) Successful completion of four-year college degree program in ophthalmic technology accredited by Commission on Accreditation of Allied Health Education Programs (CAAHEP) (see separate entry); (2) Successful completion of two or more years of college/university courses (90 quarter or 60 semester credits) in non-technical and/or non/vocational programs, successful completion of CAAHEP-accredited program for ophthalmic medical technologists within last five years, and 12 hours of approved continuing education for each year after graduation; (3) High school diploma or equivalent, less than two years of experience, successful completion of CAAHEP-accredited two-year ophthalmic medical technology program, two years experience within last five years, and 12 hours of approved continuing education for each year following graduation; (4) Hold Certified Ophthalmic Technician (COT) designation (see separate entry), three years experience as COT within last five years, and 36 hours of approved continuing education within last three years; or (5) Certification as orthoptist by the American or Canadian Orthoptic Council, two years experience within past five years, and 24 hours of continuing education credit within last three years. All experience must be under

ophthalmological supervision.
Certification Requirements: Successful completion of written and practical performance exams. Written exam consists of following sections: (1) History Taking, including: Allergies and drug reaction; Family history; Medications; Partially sighted patients; Past ocular history; Presenting complaint/history of presenting illness; and Systemic illness, past and present; (2) Basic Skills and Lensometry, including: Amsler grid; Color vision testing; Estimation of anterior chamber depth; Evaluation of pupil; Exophthalmometry; Lensometry; Method of measuring/recording acuity; and Schirmer tests; (3) Patient Services, including: Assisting patient; Drug delivery (advantages/disadvantages); Ocular dressings and shields; and Spectacle principles; (4) Basic Tonometry, including: Applanation; Complications/contraindications; Factors altering intraocular pressure; Indentation; Noncontact; and Scleral rigidity; (5) Instrument Maintenance, including: Acuity projectors; Keratometers; Lenses; Lensometers; Muscle light; Ophthalmoscopes; Perimeters; Phoropters; Retinoscopes; Slit lamps; Special instruments (equipment); Surgical instruments; Tangent screen; Tonometers; and Ultrasound; (6) General Medical Knowledge, including: Anatomy; Cardiopulmonary resuscitation; Fundamentals of microbial control; Metric conversions; Ocular diseases; Ocular emergencies; Physiology; and Systemic diseases; (7) Clinical Optics, including: Advanced Spectacle Principles; Low Vision Aids; Optics; Refractometry; and Retinoscopy; (8) Basic Ocular Motility, including: Amblyopia detection; Evaluation assessment methods; Extraocular muscle actions; and Strabismus; (9) Visual Fields, including: Calibration; Error factors; Methods; Techniques; and Visual pathways; (10) Contact Lenses, including: Basic principles; Fitting procedures; Patient instruction; Troubleshooting problems; and Verification of lenses; (11) Intermediate Tonometry, including: Aqueous Humor Dynamics; and Glaucoma; (12) Ocular Pharmacology (types, strengths, actions, and complications), including: Anesthetics; Antibiotics; Antihistamines; Beta-blockers; Carbonic anhydrase inhibitors; Epinephrine; Miotics; Mydriatics and cycloplegics; Nonsteroidal anti-inflammatories; Osmotic agents; Steroids; Vasoconstrictors; and Other related pharmaceuticals; (13) Microbiology, including: Culture media; Inflammatory response; Microscopy; Specimen collection and processing; and Staining; (14) Advanced Tonometry, including: Managing tonometry problems; Pathophysiology of glaucoma; and Tonometry theory; (15)

Advanced Visual Fields, including: Advanced principles of visual field testing; and Etiology and description of less common defects; (16) Advanced Color Vision, including: Advanced testing techniques; Defects; and Physiology/Theory; (17) Advanced Clinical Optics, including: Advanced optics; and Advanced refractometry; (18) Advanced Ocular Motility, including: Advanced strabismus; Amblyopia; Anatomy and physiology of the extraocular muscles; and Binocular function; (19) Photography, including: Basics of photography; Clinical photography; Defects; Film processing; and Fluorescein angiography; (20) Advanced Pharmacology, including: Basic concepts of topical medications; and Mechanism of action and desired effects; (21) Special Instruments and Techniques, including: Contrast sensitivity; Dark adaptometry; Electrodiagnostics; Imaging techniques; IOL power computation; Low vision equipment; Macular function testing; Ophthalmic lasers; Ophthalmoscope; Pachymetry; Pupillography; and Slit lamp; and (22) Advanced General Medical Knowledge, including: Low vision/blindness; Ocular disease; Ocular manifestation of systemic diseases; and Trauma. Practical performance test covers following areas: Advanced color vision testing; Advanced tonometry; Clinical optics; Microbiology; Ocular motility; Photography; Special instrument and techniques; and Visual fields. Candidates who fail practical performance test will be awarded Certified Ophthalmic Assistant (COA) designation (see separate entry). **Renewal:** Every three years. Recertification based on maintenance of CPR certification and accumulation of 36 continuing education hours through JCAHPO courses and seminars, other ophthalmology-related courses, self-study in ophthalmology including listening to tapes, reading books, and attendance at non-JCAHPO approved courses, teaching, presentations, and authoring scientific publications. **Preparatory Materials:** *JCAHPO Standards, Procedures, and Sanctions Pertaining to Certification and Recertification* (reference). List of basic study materials provided. **Examination Sites:** Exam given at 80 sites throughout the U.S. and Canada. **Examination Type:** Multiple-choice. **Reexamination:** May retake practical performance test one time. Must complete practical performance test within five years of successful completion of written exam. **Accredited By:** National Commission for Certifying Agencies. **Endorsed By:** Association of Technical Personnel in Ophthalmology; National Organization for Competency Assurance.

Certified Ophthalmic Technician (COT)

Joint Commission on Allied Health Personnel in Ophthalmology (JCAHPO)
2025 Woodlane Dr.
St. Paul, MN 55125-2995
Phone: (612)731-2944
Fax: (612)731-0410
Toll Free: (800)284-3937

Recipient: Ophthalmic technicians.
Educational/Experience Requirements: High school diploma, current CPR certification, and successful completion of ophthalmic technician program accredited by Commission on Accreditation of Allied Health Education Programs (CAAHEP) (see separate entry) or have one year of supervised experience and meet one of the following requirements: (1) Successfully complete ophthalmic technician program accredited by CAAHEP more than one year ago and accumulation of 18 hours of approved continuing education credits within past two years; (2) Hold Certified Ophthalmic Assistant designation (see separate entry) and accumulate 18 hours of approved continuing education credits within past two years; or (3) Hold current certification as an orthoptist by the American or Canadian Orthoptic Council and accumulate 12 hours of approved continuing education credits within past two years.
Certification Requirements: Successful completion of skill evaluation and exam. Skill evaluation covers: Clinical optics; Contact lens; Ocular Motility; Tonometry; and Visual fields. Exam covers: (1) History Taking, including: Allergies and drug reaction; Family history; Partially sighted patients; Past ocular history; Presenting complaint/history of presenting illness; and Systemic illness, past and present; (2) Basic Skills and Lensometry, including: Amsler grid; Color vision testing; Estimation of anterior chamber depth; Evaluation of pupil; Exophthalmometry; Lensometry; Method of measuring/recording acuity; and Schirmer tests; (3) Patient Services, including: Assisting patient; Drug delivery (advantages/disadvantages); Ocular dressings and shields; and Spectacle principles; (4) Basic Tonometry, including: Applanation; Complications/contraindications; Factors altering intraocular pressure; Indentation; Noncontact; and Scleral rigidity; (5) Instrument Maintenance, including: Acuity projectors; Keratometers; Lenses; Lensometers; Muscle light; Ophthalmoscopes; Perimeters; Phoropters; Retinoscopes; Slit lamps; Special instruments (equipment); Surgical instruments; Tan-

gent screen; Tonometers; and Ultrasound; (6) General Medical Knowledge, including: Anatomy; Cardiopulmonary resuscitation; Fundamentals of microbial control; Metric conversions; Ocular diseases; Ocular emergencies; Physiology; and Systemic diseases; (7) Clinical Optics, including: Advanced Spectacle Principles; Low Vision Aids; Optics; Refractometry; and Retinoscopy; (8) Basic Ocular Motility, including: Amblyopia detection; Evaluation assessment methods; Extraocular muscle actions; and Strabismus; (9) Visual Fields, including: Calibration; Error factors; Methods; Techniques; and Visual pathways; (10) Contact Lenses, including: Basic principles; Fitting procedures; Patient instruction; Trouble shooting problems; and Verification of lenses; (11) Intermediate Tonometry, including: Aqueous Humor Dynamics; and Glaucoma; and (12) Ocular Pharmacology (types, strengths, actions, and complications), including: Anesthetics; Antibiotics; Antihistamines; Beta-blockers; Carbonic anhydrase inhibitors; Epinephrine; Miotics; Mydriatics and cycloplegics; Nonsteroidal anti-inflammatories; Osmotic agents; Steroids; Vasoconstrictors; and Other related pharmaceuticals. **Renewal:** Every three years. Recertification based on maintenance of CPR certification and accumulation of 27 continuing education hours through JCAHPO courses and seminars, other ophthalmology-related courses, self-study in ophthalmology including listening to tapes, reading books, and attendance at non-JCAHPO approved courses, teaching, presentations, and authoring scientific publications. **Preparatory Materials:** *JCAHPO Standards, Procedures, and Sanctions Pertaining to Certification and Recertification* (reference). List of basic study materials provided. **Examination Sites:** Exam given at 80 sites throughout the U.S. and Canada. **Examination Type:** Multiple-choice. **Accredited By:** National Commission for Certifying Agencies. **Endorsed By:** Association of Technical Personnel in Ophthalmology; National Organization for Competency Assurance.

`1448`

Certified Podiatric Medical Assistant

American Society of Podiatric
  Medical Assistants (ASPMA)
c/o Joyce Burton
145 W. Mechanic St.
Shelbyville, IN 46176
Joyce Burton PMAC, Chm.

Recipient: Podiatric medical assistants. **Membership:** Required. **Certification Re-**

quirements: Successful completion of exam. **Renewal:** Every year. Recertification based on accumulation of 15 total credits through the following: (1) Attendance at local, state, regional, or national meetings (2-15 points per meeting); (2) Postgraduate course (ten points); (3) Lectures (ten points); (4) Articles published in professional journals (five points); (5) ASPMA questionnaire submitted (five points); (6) Articles read and summarized (two points); and (7) Community service projects attended such as career day, health fair, podiatry blood pressure clinic, or other such activity (two points). **Preparatory Materials:** Study reference list available.

`1449`

Ophthalmic Surgical Assisting (OSA)

Joint Commission on Allied Health
  Personnel in Ophthalmology
  (JCAHPO)
2025 Woodlane Dr.
St. Paul, MN 55125-2995
Phone: (612)731-2944
Fax: (612)731-0410
Toll Free: (800)284-3937

Recipient: Ophthalmic surgical assistants. **Educational/Experience Requirements:** Hold Certified Ophthalmic Assistant (COA) designation (see separate entry) and current CPR certificate and meet one of the following requirements: (1) Successful completion of nine-month hospital based surgical technologist (operating room technician) course, including six months of satisfactory on-the-job instruction and experience in accredited operating suite under the supervision of regularly scheduling ophthalmic surgeons; or (2) Successful completion of 18 months on-the-job instruction and experience in accredited operating suite under the supervision of regularly scheduled ophthalmic surgeons and functioning as any of the following: Sterile first assistant; Sterile scrub assistant; or Non-sterile circulator. **Certification Requirements:** Successful completion of exam. Exam covers: (1) Aseptic Technique, including: Assisting; Circulating; General knowledge; and Scrubbing/gowning/gloving/prepping; (2) Instruments, including: Function; Identification; Maintenance; Selection/setup; Sterilization; and Sutures/supplies; (3) Ophthalmic Surgical Pharmacology, including: Enzymes; Miotics; Mydriatics; Narcotics; Osmotic diuretics; Viscoelastics; and Other related issues; (4) Pre-Operative Preparation of Patient, including: Consent; and Intraoperative monitoring; and (5) Surgical Procedures, including anes-

thesia, complications, and the following types of surgery: Cataract; Corneal; Glaucoma; Lacrimal; Laser; Oculoplastics; Orbital; Refractive; Retinal; and Strabismus. **Renewal:** Every three years. Recertification based on maintenance of CPR certification and accumulation of 18 continuing education hours through JCAHPO courses and seminars, other ophthalmology-related courses, self-study in ophthalmology including listening to tapes, reading books, and attendance at non-JCAHPO approved courses, teaching, presentations, and authoring scientific publications. **Preparatory Materials:** *JCAHPO Standards, Procedures, and Sanctions Pertaining to Certification and Recertification* (reference). List of basic study materials provided. **Examination Sites:** Exam given at 80 sites throughout the U.S. and Canada. **Examination Type:** Multiple-choice. **Accredited By:** National Commission for Certifying Agencies. **Endorsed By:** Association of Technical Personnel in Ophthalmology; National Organization for Competency Assurance.

`1450`

Registered Medical Assistant (RMA)

American Medical Technologists
  (AMT)
710 Higgins Rd.
Park Ridge, IL 60068
Phone: (708)823-5169
Fax: (708)823-0458
Toll Free: (800)275-1268
James R. Fidler Ph.D., Dir.

Recipient: Medical professionals who work in medical offices, examining rooms, or laboratories and act as liaison between doctor and patient. **Educational/Experience Requirements:** Must meet one of the following requirements: (1) Graduate from medical assisting program accredited by Accrediting Bureau of Health Education Schools (see separate entry) or other recognized accrediting agency; (2) Graduate from formal U.S. Armed Forces medical services training program; or (3) Five years experience, with no more than two years as an instructor in postsecondary medical assistant program. **Membership:** Required. **Certification Requirements:** Successful completion of exam. Exam covers: (1) Administration, including: Bookkeeping; and Insurance; (2) Clinical Medical Assisting, including: Emergencies; Examination room; Laboratory; Medical instruments; and Pharmacology; and (3) General Medical Assisting, including: Anatomy and physiology; Ethics; Medical law; Patient education; and

Terminology. **Renewal:** Every year. Recertification based on continuing education. **Preparatory Materials:** Reference list and study guide bibliography available. **Examination Frequency:** Throughout the year. **Examination Sites:** Exam given at sites throughout the U.S. **Examination Type:** Multiple-choice. **Pass/Fail Rate:** 91% pass exam the first time. **Waiting Period to Receive Scores:** Four-six weeks. **Re-examination:** There is no time limit to retake exam. **Fees:** $59. **Accredited By:** National Commission for Certifying Agencies. **Endorsed By:** National Organization for Competency Assurance.

1451

Registered Medical Assistant (R.M.A.)
American Registry of Medical Assistants (ARMA)
69 Southwick Rd.
Westfield, MA 01085
Phone: (413)562-7336
Toll Free: (800)527-2762
Annette H. Heyman, Dir.

Recipient: Medical assistants. **Number of Certified Individuals:** 3000. **Membership:** Required. **Certification Requirements:** Must meet one of the following requirements: (1) Graduation from accredited medical assisting program at licensed college or training school; (2) Employment as medical assistant or aid with one year of on-the-job training; or (3) Current licensure as registered nurse (R.N.), licensed practical nurse (L.P.N.), or allied health professional. **Renewal:** Every year. Recertification based on accumulation five points through continuing education. Renewal fee is $25. **Examination Frequency:** Throughout the year. **Examination Sites:** Exam given at schools throughout the U.S. **Fees:** $45.

Medical Illustrators

1452

Certified Medical Illustrator
Association of Medical Illustrators (AMI)
1819 Peachtree St., NE, Ste. 712
Atlanta, GA 30309
Phone: (404)747-9682
Fax: (404)965-0619
Toll Free: (800)747-9682
Sue Seif, Chair

Recipient: Medical illustrators. **Number of Certified Individuals:** 375. **Educational/Experience Requirements:** Must meet one of the following requirements: (1) Successful completion of graduate program accredited by AMI in medical/biological illustration; or (2) Five years experience and successful completion of human gross anatomy dissection course. **Membership:** Not required. **Certification Requirements:** Successful completion of exam and submission of illustration portfolio. **Renewal:** Every five years. Recertification based on accumulation of 35 hours of continuing education. Renewal fee is $50. **Examination Frequency:** Annual. **Examination Sites:** Exam given at annual meeting. **Pass/Fail Rate:** 85% pass exam the first time. **Waiting Period to Receive Scores:** Three months. **Re-examination:** Must wait one year to retake exam. **Fees:** $100.

Nursing Aides and Psychiatric Aides

1453

Nationally Certified Psychiatric Technician, Level 1 (NCPT1)
American Association of Psychiatric Technicians (AAPT)
PO Box 14014
Phoenix, AZ 85063-4014
Phone: (602)873-1890
Fax: (602)873-1890
Toll Free: (800)391-7589
George Blake, Pres.

Recipient: Psychiatric technicians or other mental health workers involved with mentally ill or developmentally disabled in inpatient or outpatient settings. **Educational/Experience Requirements:** High school diploma or equivalent and experience. May qualify for Nationally Certified Psychiatric Technician, Level 2 (NCPT2) designation (see separate entry) with increased education and experience. **Membership:** Required. **Certification Requirements:** Successful completion of exam. **Renewal:** Every year. Recertification based on continuing education. Renewal fee is $24. **Preparatory Materials:** *Outline of Knowledge for Psychiatric Technicians* and *Training Manual - Textbook for Psychiatric Technicians* (references). **Examination Sites:** Exam given by arrangement with proctor. **Examination Frequency:** Throughout the year. **Examination Type:** Multiple-choice. **Waiting Period to Receive Scores:** Six months. **Re-examination:** Must wait three-six weeks to retake exam. **Fees:** $45.

1454

Nationally Certified Psychiatric Technician, Level 2 (NCPT2)
American Association of Psychiatric Technicians (AAPT)
PO Box 14014
Phoenix, AZ 85063-4014
Phone: (602)873-1890
Fax: (602)873-1890
Toll Free: (800)391-7589
George Blake, Pres.

Recipient: Psychiatric technicians or other mental health workers involved with mentally ill or developmentally disabled in inpatient or outpatient settings. **Educational/Experience Requirements:** Must meet the following requirements: (1) Thirty college credits in psychology or related field; (2) One year of experience; and (3) Hold Nationally Certified Psychiatric Technician, Level 1 (NCST1) designation for one year. May qualify for Nationally Certified Psychiatric Technician, Level 3 (NCST3) or Level 4 (NCST4) designations (see separate entries) with increased education and experience. **Membership:** Required. **Certification Requirements:** Successful completion of exam. **Renewal:** Every year. Recertification based on continuing education. Renewal fee is $24. **Preparatory Materials:** *Outline of Knowledge for Psychiatric Technicians* and *Training Manual - Textbook for Psychiatric Technicians* (references). **Examination Sites:** Exam given by arrangement with proctor. **Examination Frequency:** Throughout the year. **Examination Type:** Essay. **Waiting Period to Receive Scores:** Six months. **Re-examination:** Must wait three-six weeks to retake exam. **Fees:** $65.

1455

Nationally Certified Psychiatric Technician, Level 3 (NCPT3)
American Association of Psychiatric Technicians (AAPT)
PO Box 14014
Phoenix, AZ 85063-4014
Phone: (602)873-1890
Fax: (602)873-1890
Toll Free: (800)391-7589
George Blake, Pres.

Recipient: Psychiatric technicians or other mental health workers involved with mentally ill or developmentally disabled in inpatient or outpatient settings. **Educational/Experience Requirements:** Must meet the following requirements: (1) Associate' degree in psychology or related field; (2) Two years experience; and

(3) Hold Nationally Certified Psychiatric Technician, Level 2 (NCPT2) designation (see separate entry) for one year. Candidates with less education and experience may qualify for Nationally Certified Psychiatric Technician, Level 1 (NCPT1) designation (see separate entry). May qualify for Nationally Certified Psychiatric Technician, Level 4 (NCPT4) designation (see separate entry) with increased education and experience. **Membership:** Required. **Certification Requirements:** Successful completion of exam. **Renewal:** Every year. Recertification based on continuing education. Renewal fee is $24. **Preparatory Materials:** *Outline of Knowledge for Psychiatric Technicians* and *Training Manual - Textbook for Psychiatric Technicians* (references). **Examination Sites:** Exam given by arrangement with proctor. **Examination Frequency:** Throughout the year. **Examination Type:** Essay. **Waiting Period to Receive Scores:** Six months. **Re-examination:** Must wait three-six weeks to retake exam. **Fees:** $55.

1456

Nationally Certified Psychiatric Technician, Level 4 (NCPT4)

American Association of Psychiatric Technicians (AAPT)
PO Box 14014
Phoenix, AZ 85063-4014
Phone: (602)873-1890
Fax: (602)873-1890
Toll Free: (800)391-7589
George Blake, Pres.

Recipient: Psychiatric technicians or other mental health workers involved with mentally ill or developmentally disabled in inpatient or outpatient settings. **Educational/Experience Requirements:** Must meet the following requirements: (1) Bachelor's degree in psychology or related field; (2) Three years experience; and (3) Hold Nationally Certified Psychiatric Technician, Level 3 (NCPT3) designation (see separate entry) for one year. Candidates with less education and experience may qualify for Nationally Certified Psychiatric Technician, Level 1 (NCPT1) or Level 2 (NCPT2) designations (see separate entries). **Membership:** Required. **Certification Requirements:** Successful completion of exam. **Renewal:** Every year. Recertification based on continuing education. Renewal fee is $24. **Preparatory Materials:** *Outline of Knowledge for Psychiatric Technicians* and *Training Manual - Textbook for Psychiatric Technicians* (references). **Examination Sites:** Exam given by arrangement with proctor. **Examination Frequency:** Throughout the year. **Examination Type:** Essay. **Waiting Period to Receive Scores:** Six months. **Re-examination:** Must wait three-six weeks to retake exam. **Fees:** $75.

Personal Service and Building and Grounds Service Occupations

Animal Caretakers and Trainers, Except Farm

1457

Advanced Pet Care Technician
American Boarding Kennels
    Association (ABKA)
4575 Galley Rd., No. 400-A
Colorado Springs, CO 80915
Phone: (719)591-1113
Fax: (719)595-0006

Recipient: Professionals involved in commercial pet care. **Educational/ Experience Requirements:** Must meet the following requirements: (1) Hold Pet Care Technician designation (see separate entry); and (2) One year of experience. **Membership:** Not required. **Certification Requirements:** Successful completion of home-study Advanced Pet Care Technician Program, covering: Basic principles of animal care; Customer relations procedures; Kennel office; and Personnel management and business development. **Preparatory Materials:** *Emergency Care for Cats and Dogs* (text). **Examination Sites:** Exam given at ABKA national convention, regional meetings, and seminars. **Fees:** $125 (members); $175 (nonmembers).

1458

Certified Avian Specialist (CAS)
Pet Industry Joint Advisory Council
    (PIJAC)
1220 19th St., NW, Ste. 400
Washington, DC 20036
Phone: (202)452-1525
Fax: (202)293-4377
Toll Free: (800)553-PETS
James A. Tolliver, Dir.

Recipient: Pet store owners and managers; pet store maintenance supervisors or staff; pet store sales personnel; veterinary technicians; animal control staff personnel; and animal breeders. **Educational/ Experience Requirements:** Successful completion of seminar, including exam. Seminar topics include: Disease recognition and prevention; Health maintenance; Housing; Illness and disorder identification and treatment; Nutrition; Routine care; and Sanitation. **Certification Requirements:** Successful completion of the following: (1) Maintenance Care and Breed/Species Identifications home study materials; and (2) Exam. Home study materials cover: Behavior traits; Breed and species identification; and Facility maintenance. **Renewal:** Every three years. Recertification based on successful completion of exam and accumulation of ten hours of continuing education. Renewal fee is $15. **Fees:** $100.

1459

Certified Canine Specialist (CCS)
Pet Industry Joint Advisory Council
    (PIJAC)
1220 19th St., NW, Ste. 400
Washington, DC 20036
Phone: (202)452-1525
Fax: (202)293-4377
Toll Free: (800)553-PETS
James A. Tolliver, Dir.

Recipient: Pet store owners and managers; pet store maintenance supervisors or staff; pet store sales personnel; veterinary technicians; animal control staff personnel; and animal breeders. **Educational/ Experience Requirements:** Successful completion of seminar, including exam. Seminar topics include: Disease recognition and prevention; Health maintenance; Housing; Illness and disorder identification and treatment; Nutrition; Routine care; and Sanitation. **Certification Requirements:** Successful completion of the following: (1) Maintenance Care and Breed/Species Identifications home study materials; and (2) Exam. Home study materials cover: Behavior traits; Breed and species identification; and Facility maintenance. **Renewal:** Every three years. Recertification based on successful completion of exam and accumulation of ten hours of continuing education. Renewal fee is $15. **Fees:** $100.

1460

Certified Farrier
American Farrier's Association
    (AFA)
4059 Iron Works Pike
Lexington, KY 40511
Phone: (606)233-7411
Fax: (606)231-7862
E-mail: AFA@WORLD.STD.COM
Allen Smith, Pres.

Recipient: Farriers. **Educational/ Experience Requirements:** One year of experience. **Membership:** Required. **Certification Requirements:** Successful completion of written and practical exams and shoe display with various modifications made to either machine or hand made horseshoes. Written exam covers: Bones; Circulation; Conformation; Gait problems; Hoof structures; Horseshoes; Leg problems; Ligaments; and Tendons. **Renewal:** none. **Preparatory Materials:** Study guide, including exam content outline and list of suggested study references, provided. Clinics and study groups also available. **Examination Sites:** Exams given at sites throughout the U.S. **Examination Type:** Multiple-choice; true or false. **Re-examination:** There is no waiting period to retake exams. Must successfully complete exams within two years. **Fees:** $25.

1461

Certified Freshwater Fish Specialist (CFFS)
Pet Industry Joint Advisory Council (PIJAC)
1220 19th St., NW, Ste. 400
Washington, DC 20036
Phone: (202)452-1525
Fax: (202)293-4377
Toll Free: (800)553-PETS
James A. Tolliver, Dir.

Recipient: Pet store owners and managers; pet store maintenance supervisors or staff; pet store sales personnel; veterinary technicians; animal control staff personnel; and animal breeders. **Educational/Experience Requirements:** Successful completion of seminar, including exam. Seminar topics include: Disease recognition and prevention; Health maintenance; Housing; Illness and disorder identification and treatment; Nutrition; Routine care; and Sanitation. **Certification Requirements:** Successful completion of the following: (1) Maintenance Care and Breed/Species Identifications home study materials; and (2) Exam. Home study materials cover: Behavior traits; Breed and species identification; and Facility maintenance. **Renewal:** Every three years. Recertification based on successful completion of exam and accumulation of ten hours of continuing education. Renewal fee is $15. **Fees:** $100.

1462

Certified Journeyman Farrier
American Farrier's Association (AFA)
4059 Iron Works Pike
Lexington, KY 40511
Phone: (606)233-7411
Fax: (606)231-7862
E-mail: AFA@WORLD.STD.COM
Allen Smith, Pres.

Recipient: Farriers. **Educational/Experience Requirements:** Two years experience. **Membership:** Required. **Certification Requirements:** Successful completion of written and practical exams and shoe display with various modifications made to either machine or hand made horseshoes. Written exam covers: Bones; Circulation; Gaits of the horse; Hoof structures; Horseshoes; Ligaments; Pathology; and Tendons. **Renewal:** none. **Preparatory Materials:** Study guide, including exam content outline and list of suggested study references, provided. Clinics and study groups also available. **Examination Sites:** Exams given at sites throughout the U.S. **Examination Type:** Multiple-choice; true or false. **Re-examination:** There is no waiting period to retake exams. Must successfully complete exams within two years. **Fees:** $25.

1463

Certified Kennel Operator (CKO)
American Boarding Kennels Association (ABKA)
4575 Galley Rd., No. 400-A
Colorado Springs, CO 80915
Phone: (719)591-1113
Fax: (719)595-0006

Recipient: Kennel operators and managers trained in both animal care and business. **Educational/Experience Requirements:** Must meet the following requirements: (1) Three years experience; (2) Hold Advanced Pet Care Technician designation (see separate entry); and (3) Earn 100 total points through industry service and education. Service points can be earned in the following ways: (1) Experience (one point per year; maximum of ten points); (2) ABKA Membership (ten points per year); (3) Attendance at ABKA Convention (ten points per convention); (4) Attendance at ABKA Regional Meeting (five points per meeting); (5) Serving as ABKA Area Representative (five points per year); (6) Serving as ABKA Director (ten points); (7) Presentations Given at ABKA Convention (ten points per presentation); (8) Presentations Given at ABKA Regional Meeting (five points per presentation); (9) Published Articles in Industry Publications (five points per article); and (10) Miscellaneous Industry Activities (five points per activity). Education points can be earned in the following ways: (1) Seminar Attendance at ABKA Convention (five points per seminar); (2) Seminar Attendance at ABKA Regional Meeting (five points per seminar); (3) Seminar Cassettes Ordered (five points per cassette); and (4) Miscellaneous Educational Activities (five points per activity). **Membership:** Not required. **Certification Requirements:** Successful completion of written and oral exams. **Renewal:** Every two years. Recertification based on accumulation of 20 points (ten points per year minimum) through continuing education, including attendance at at least one ABKO national convention or regional meeting. Points can also be accumulated through earning Accredited Boarding Kennel designation (see separate entry), attendance at ABKO meetings, association service, continuing education, membership recruitment, presentations, publications reviewed and written, and other miscellaneous activities. Lifetime certification available at age 62. **Examination Frequency:** Annual. **Examination Sites:** Exams given at ABKA national convention. **Fees:** $145 (members); $225 (non-members).

1464

Certified Reptile Specialist (CRS)
Pet Industry Joint Advisory Council (PIJAC)
1220 19th St., NW, Ste. 400
Washington, DC 20036
Phone: (202)452-1525
Fax: (202)293-4377
Toll Free: (800)553-PETS
James A. Tolliver, Dir.

Recipient: Pet store owners and managers; pet store maintenance supervisors or staff; pet store sales personnel; veterinary technicians; animal control staff personnel; and animal breeders. **Educational/Experience Requirements:** Successful completion of seminar, including exam. Seminar topics include: Disease recognition and prevention; Health maintenance; Housing; Illness and disorder identification and treatment; Nutrition; Routine care; and Sanitation. **Certification Requirements:** Successful completion of the following: (1) Maintenance Care and Breed/Species Identifications home study materials; and (2) Exam. Home study materials cover: Behavior traits; Breed and species identification; and Facility maintenance. **Renewal:** Every three years. Recertification based on successful completion of exam and accumulation of ten hours of continuing education. Renewal fee is $15. **Fees:** $100.

1465

Certified Small Animal Specialist (CSAS)
Pet Industry Joint Advisory Council (PIJAC)
1220 19th St., NW, Ste. 400
Washington, DC 20036
Phone: (202)452-1525
Fax: (202)293-4377
Toll Free: (800)553-PETS
James A. Tolliver, Dir.

Recipient: Pet store owners and managers; pet store maintenance supervisors or staff; pet store sales personnel; veterinary technicians; animal control staff personnel; and animal breeders. **Educational/Experience Requirements:** Successful completion of seminar, including exam. Seminar topics include: Disease recognition and prevention; Health maintenance; Housing; Illness and disorder identification and treatment; Nutrition; Routine care; and Sanitation. **Certification Requirements:** Successful completion of the following: (1) Maintenance Care and Breed/Species Identifications home study materials; and (2) Exam. Home study materials cover: Behavior traits; Breed and species identification; and Facility maintenance. **Renewal:** Every three years. Recertification based on successful completion of exam and accumulation of ten hours of continuing education. Renewal fee is $15. **Fees:** $100.

1466

National Certified Groomer
National Dog Groomers
  Association of America
  (NDGAA)
PO Box 101
Clark, PA 16113
Phone: (412)962-2711
Fax: (412)962-1919
Jeffrey L. Reynolds, Exec.Dir.

Recipient: Professional pet groomers. **Membership:** Not required. **Certification Requirements:** Successful completion of practical and written exams. Certification available in any or all of the following breed areas: (1) Non-Sporting, including: Bichon Frise; Boston Terrier; Bulldog; Chinese Shar-Pei; Chow Chow; Dalmatian; Finnish Spitz; French Bulldog; Keeshond; Lhasa Apso; Poodle; Schipperke; Tibetan Spaniel; and Tibetan Terrier; (2) Sporting, including: American Spaniel; American Water Spaniel; Brittany; Chesapeake Bay Retriever; Clumber Spaniel; Cocker Spaniel; Curly and Flat Coated Retriever; English, Gordon, and Irish Setter; English Spaniel; English Springer Spaniel; Field Spaniel; German Shorthaired Pointer; German Wirehaired Pointer; Golden Retriever; Irish Water Spaniel; Labrador Retriever; Pointer; Sussex Spaniel; Vizala; Weimaraner; Welsh Springer Spaniel; and Wire Haired Pointing Griffon; and (3) Terrier, including: Airedale; American Staffordshire; Australian; Bedlington; Border; Bull; Cairn; Dandie Dinmont; Fox (Smooth); Fox (Wire Haired); Irish; Kerry Blue; Lakeland; Manchester; Miniature Bull; Miniature Schnauzer; Norfolk; Norwich; Scottish; Sealyham; Skye; Soft Coated Wheaten; Staffordshire Bull; Welsh; and West Highland White. **Preparatory Materials:** *AKC Complete Dog Book,* 18th Edition (reference). Breed profile guidelines, study aids and guides, and workshops available. **Examination Frequency:** 15-20 times per year. **Examination Sites:** Exams given at sites throughout the U.S.

Examination Type: Fill-in-the-blanks; multiple-choice; true or false. **Pass/Fail Rate:** 70 percent pass exam the first time. **Waiting Period to Receive Scores:** Immediately. **Re-examination:** There is a $100 fee to retake exams. **Fees:** $100 (each breed area).

1467

National Certified Master Groomer (NCMG)
National Dog Groomers
  Association of America
  (NDGAA)
PO Box 101
Clark, PA 16113
Phone: (412)962-2711
Fax: (412)962-1919
Jeffrey L. Reynolds, Exec.Dir.

Recipient: Professional pet groomers. **Number of Certified Individuals:** 750. **Educational/Experience Requirements:** Successful completion of exams in all three breed areas offered for National Certified Groomer designation (see separate entry). **Membership:** Not required. **Certification Requirements:** Successful completion of exam. Exam covers: Anatomy; Breed identification; Breed standards; Cat questions; Clipper identification; External head; External and internal; Eyes, tails, bites, and feet; General health; Glossary of canine terms; Pesticides; and Working, herding, toy, and hound groups. **Preparatory Materials:** *AKC Complete Dog Book,* 18th Edition (reference). Breed profile guidelines, study aids and guides, and workshops available. **Examination Frequency:** 15-20 times per year. **Examination Sites:** Exam given at sites throughout the U.S. **Examination Type:** Fill-in-the-blanks; multiple-choice; true or false. **Pass/Fail Rate:** 70 percent pass exam the first time. **Waiting Period to Receive Scores:** Immediately. **Re-examination:** There is a $100 fee to retake exam. **Fees:** $100.

1468

Pet Care Technician
American Boarding Kennels
  Association (ABKA)
4575 Galley Rd., No. 400-A
Colorado Springs, CO 80915
Phone: (719)591-1113
Fax: (719)595-0006

Recipient: Professionals involved in commercial pet care. **Educational/Experience Requirements:** Current employment in the field. **Membership:** Not required. **Certification Requirements:**

Successful completion of home-study Pet Care Technician Program, covering: Basic principles of animal care; Customer relation procedures; and Kennel office. **Fees:** $90 (members); $150 (nonmembers).

Barbers and Cosmetologists

1469

Certified Trichologist
International Association of
  Trichologists
1511 W. Florence St.
Los Angeles, CA 90047
Marlene Hansen, Exec. Officer

Recipient: Trichologists who assist persons with hair or scalp problems. **Educational/Experience Requirements:** Successful completion of correspondence course and 100 hours of clinical training. Course consists of following modules, including exams: (1) Basic Chemistry and Hair Care Processes, covering structure of protein and possible damage caused by permanent waving and bleaching; (2) Body Systems, covering imbalances that affect hair and skin; (3) Clinical Organization, covering operation of trichology clinic; (4) Electrotherapy, covering: Effects, indications, and contra-indication of ultraviolet rays, infra-red rays, and galvanic and high-frequency machines with regard to hair and scalp problems; and Electrotherapeutic machines and how different types of current are produced; (5) Hair Loss, covering different types of hair loss and baldness and their treatment; (6) Hair and Scalp, covering structure of skin, hair follicles, hair, sebaceous glands, sweat glands, and nails, their function, and how they link with other systems of the body; (7) Microdiagnostic Techniques, covering use of microscopes in trichology; (8) Nutrition, covering values and purposes of different groups of foods with particular reference to hair and skin; (9) Problems of the Scalp, covering scaling, itching, and excessive oiliness and their causes, recognition, and treatment; (10) Trichological Preparations, covering drugs used for trichological purposes; and (11) Trichological Procedures/Hair Shaft Problems, covering procedures for questioning and examining clients with trichological problems and problems that affect the hair shaft. Candidates who have extensive education and/or experience in trichology may be exempt from course. **Certification Requirements:** Successful completion of written and practical exams. **Endorsed By:** Institute of Trichologists.

Busdrivers

1470

Certified Director of Pupil Transportation

National Committee for Motor
  Fleet Supervisor Training
  (NCMFST)
2200 Mill Rd.
Alexandria, VA 22314-4677
Phone: (703)838-7952
Fax: (703)836-6070
Jeff Arnold, Dir.

Recipient: Motor fleet directors of pupil transportation. **Educational/Experience Requirements:** Must meet the following requirements: (1) Successful completion of Pupil Transportation Supervisor and one other workshop; and (2) Five years experience with current employer. Bachelor's degree may be substituted for one year of experience. Candidates with two-and-a-half to five years of experience with one employer may apply for waiver. **Certification Requirements:** Must meet following requirements: (1) Submission of exhibit documenting experience, education, and professional activities and designations; and (2) Successful completion of exam. **Preparatory Materials:** *Motor Carrier Safety Regulations, Motor Fleet Safety Supervision: Principles and Practices,* and *Occupational Safety and Health Regulations* (references). Manuals and study group materials available. **Examination Frequency:** Throughout the year. **Examination Sites:** Exam given at sites throughout the U.S. **Examination Type:** Essay; multiple-choice; true or false. **Waiting Period to Receive Scores:** 24 hours. **Re-examination:** Must wait three months to retake exam.

1471

Certified Pupil Transportation Supervisor

National Committee for Motor
  Fleet Supervisor Training
  (NCMFST)
2200 Mill Rd.
Alexandria, VA 22314-4677
Phone: (703)838-7952
Fax: (703)836-6070
Jeff Arnold, Dir.

Recipient: Motor fleet pupil transportation supervisors. **Educational/**

Experience Requirements: Must meet following requirements: (1) Successful completion of Pupil Transportation Supervisor and one other workshop; and (2) Three years experience with current employer. **Certification Requirements:** Must meet following requirements: (1) Submission of exhibit documenting experience, education, and professional activities and designations; and (2) Successful completion of exam. **Preparatory Materials:** *Motor Carrier Safety Regulations, Motor Fleet Safety Supervision: Principles and Practices,* and *Occupational Safety and Health Regulations* (references). Manuals and study group materials available. **Examination Frequency:** Throughout the year. **Examination Sites:** Exam given at sites throughout the U.S. **Examination Type:** Essay; multiple-choice; true or false. **Waiting Period to Receive Scores:** 24 hours. **Re-examination:** Must wait three months to retake exam.

1472

Certified School Bus Driver Trainer

National Committee for Motor
  Fleet Supervisor Training
  (NCMFST)
2200 Mill Rd.
Alexandria, VA 22314-4677
Phone: (703)838-7952
Fax: (703)836-6070
Jeff Arnold, Dir.

Recipient: Motor fleet school bus driver trainers. **Educational/Experience Requirements:** Must meet the following requirements: (1) Successful completion of Motor Fleet Trainer workshop; and (2) Three years experience with current employer. **Certification Requirements:** Must meet following requirements: (1) Submission of exhibit documenting experience, education, and professional activities and designations; and (2) Successful completion of exam. **Preparatory Materials:** *Motor Carrier Safety Regulations, Motor Fleet Safety Supervision: Principles and Practices,* and *Occupational Safety and Health Regulations* (references). Manuals and study group materials available. **Examination Frequency:** Throughout the year. **Examination Sites:** Exam given at sites throughout the U.S. **Examination Type:** Essay; multiple-choice; true or false. **Waiting Period to Receive Scores:** 24 hours. **Re-examination:** Must wait three months to retake exam.

Cleaning and Restoration Technicians

1473

Carpet Cleaning Technician

Institute of Inspection, Cleaning,
  and Restoration Certification
2715 E. Mill Plain Blvd.
Vancouver, WA 98661
Phone: (206)693-5675
Fax: (206)693-4858

Recipient: Carpet cleaning technicians. **Educational/Experience Requirements:** Successful completion of coursework at approved schools. **Certification Requirements:** Successful completion of exam. **Renewal:** Every four years. Recertification based on accumulation of two continuing education credits (CECs) through coursework, seminars, workshops, or attendance at national or regional conventions or markets. **Fees:** $40.

1474

Carpet Repair and Reinstallation Technician

Institute of Inspection, Cleaning,
  and Restoration Certification
2715 E. Mill Plain Blvd.
Vancouver, WA 98661
Phone: (206)693-5675
Fax: (206)693-4858

Recipient: Carpet repair and reinstallation technicians. **Educational/Experience Requirements:** Successful completion of coursework at approved schools. **Certification Requirements:** Successful completion of exam. **Renewal:** Every four years. Recertification based on accumulation of two continuing education credits (CECs) through coursework, seminars, workshops, or attendance at national or regional conventions or markets. **Fees:** $40.

1475

Certified Restoration Technician

National Institute of Fire
  Restoration (NIFR)
10830 Annapolis Junction Rd., Ste.
  312
Annapolis Junction, MD
  20701-1120
Phone: (301)604-4411
Fax: (301)604-4713

Recipient: Fire restoration technicians. **Membership:** Not required. **Certification Requirements:** Successful completion of course and exam. Course covers fire, water, and smoke damage basics, including: Deodorization; Structure and contents cleaning, including wood, wood furniture, books, and duct cleaning; and Ultrasonics. **Fees:** $495 (members); $695 (nonmembers). **Endorsed By:** Association of Specialists in Cleaning and Restoration.

1476

Color Repair Technician
Institute of Inspection, Cleaning,
    and Restoration Certification
2715 E. Mill Plain Blvd.
Vancouver, WA 98661
Phone: (206)693-5675
Fax: (206)693-4858

Recipient: Color repair technicians. **Educational/Experience Requirements:** Successful completion of coursework at approved schools. **Certification Requirements:** Successful completion of exam. **Renewal:** Every four years. Recertification based on accumulation of two continuing education credits (CECs) through coursework, seminars, workshops, or attendance at national or regional conventions or markets. **Fees:** $40.

1477

**Fire and Smoke Restoration
    Technician**
Institute of Inspection, Cleaning,
    and Restoration Certification
2715 E. Mill Plain Blvd.
Vancouver, WA 98661
Phone: (206)693-5675
Fax: (206)693-4858

Recipient: Fire and smoke restoration technicians. **Educational/Experience Requirements:** Successful completion of coursework at approved schools. **Certification Requirements:** Successful completion of exam. **Renewal:** Every four years. Recertification based on accumulation of two continuing education credits (CECs) through coursework, seminars, workshops, or attendance at national or regional conventions or markets. **Fees:** $40.

1478

Odor Control Technician
Institute of Inspection, Cleaning,
    and Restoration Certification
2715 E. Mill Plain Blvd.
Vancouver, WA 98661
Phone: (206)693-5675
Fax: (206)693-4858

Recipient: Odor control technicians. **Educational/Experience Requirements:** Successful completion of coursework at approved schools. **Certification Requirements:** Successful completion of exam. **Renewal:** Every four years. Recertification based on accumulation of two continuing education credits (CECs) through coursework, seminars, workshops, or attendance at national or regional conventions or markets. **Fees:** $40.

1479

Senior Carpet Inspector
Institute of Inspection, Cleaning,
    and Restoration Certification
2715 E. Mill Plain Blvd.
Vancouver, WA 98661
Phone: (206)693-5675
Fax: (206)693-4858

Recipient: Carpet inspectors. **Educational/Experience Requirements:** Successful completion of coursework at approved schools. **Certification Requirements:** Successful completion of exam. **Renewal:** Every two years. Recertification based on accumulation of two continuing education credits (CECs) through coursework, seminars, workshops, or attendance at national or regional conventions or markets. **Fees:** $40.

1480

**Upholstery and Fabric Cleaning
    Technician**
Institute of Inspection, Cleaning,
    and Restoration Certification
2715 E. Mill Plain Blvd.
Vancouver, WA 98661
Phone: (206)693-5675
Fax: (206)693-4858

Recipient: Upholstery and fabric cleaning technicians. **Educational/Experience Requirements:** Successful completion of coursework at approved schools. **Certification Requirements:** Successful completion of exam. **Renewal:** Every four years. Recertification based on accumulation of two continuing education credits (CECs) through coursework, seminars, workshops, or attendance at national or

regional conventions or markets. **Fees:** $40.

1481

**Water Damage Restoration
    Technician**
Institute of Inspection, Cleaning,
    and Restoration Certification
2715 E. Mill Plain Blvd.
Vancouver, WA 98661
Phone: (206)693-5675
Fax: (206)693-4858

Recipient: Water damage restoration technicians. **Educational/Experience Requirements:** Successful completion of coursework at approved schools. **Certification Requirements:** Successful completion of exam. **Renewal:** Every four years. Recertification based on accumulation of two continuing education credits (CECs) through coursework, seminars, workshops, or attendance at national or regional conventions or markets. **Fees:** $40.

Electrologists

1482

**Certified Clinical Electrologist
    (C.C.E.)**
National Commission for
    Electrologist Certification
    (NCEC)
Six Abbott Rd. Annex
Wellesley Hills, MA 02181
Phone: (617)431-7263
Fax: (617)237-9039

Recipient: Electrologists. **Educational/Experience Requirements:** One year of experience recommended. **Membership:** Not required. **Certification Requirements:** Successful completion of exam. Exam covers: (1) Assessment, including: Evaluating data; Making appropriate referrals; Nature and extent of hair problems; Patient history; Screening for underlying conditions; and Treatment considerations; (2) Treatment, including: Application of topical agents; Comfort considerations; Counseling; Draping; Positioning; Preparation of patient; Psychological evaluation; and Use of relaxation techniques; (3) Examination, including: Equipment selection, preparation, and procedures; Hair; Proper sterilization and sanitation; and Skin; (4) Epilation Techniques, including: Anatomy and physiology of hair and follicle; Appropriate reactions; Use of electric current; and

Use of equipment; (5) Post-Treatment Care, including: Documentation; Instructions to patient; Scheduling; and Topical; and (6) Equipment, including: Adjustment and repair; Documentation; Inspection; and Maintenance. **Renewal:** Every five years. Recertification based on either successful completion of exam or continuing education. **Preparatory Materials:** List of suggested readings and sample questions provided. Review seminars available. **Examination Sites:** Exam given at sites throughout the U.S. **Examination Type:** Multiple-choice. **Waiting Period to Receive Scores:** 90 days. **Fees:** $150 (members); $200 (nonmembers). **Endorsed By:** International Electrology Educators; International Guild of Professional Electrologists; Society of Clinical and Medical Electrologists.

1483

Certified Medical Electrologist (C.M.E.)
National Commission for
    Electrologist Certification
    (NCEC)
Six Abbott Rd. Annex
Wellesley Hills, MA 02181
Phone: (617)431-7263
Fax: (617)237-9039

Recipient: Medical electrologists. **Educational/Experience Requirements:** Must meet one of the following requirements: (1) Associate's degree in medical electrology; or (2) Hold Certified Clinical Electrologist (CCE) designation (see separate entry) for five years and accumulate post-secondary credits in the following areas: Anatomy and Physiology, I, II, and III; Business mathematics; English composition and literature; General psychology; Medical terminology; Microbiology; and Philosophy. **Membership:** Not required. **Certification Requirements:** Successful completion of exam. Exam covers: (1) Assessment, including: Evaluating data; Making appropriate referrals; Nature and extent of hair problems; Patient history; Screening for underlying conditions; and Treatment considerations; (2) Treatment, including: Application of topical agents; Comfort considerations; Counseling; Draping; Positioning; Preparation of patient; Psychological evaluation; and Use of relaxation techniques; (3) Examination, including: Equipment selection, preparation, and procedures; Hair; Proper sterilization and sanitation; and Skin; (4) Epilation Techniques, including: Anatomy and physiology of hair and follicle; Appropriate reactions; Use of electric current; and Use of equipment; (5) Post-Treatment Care, including:

Documentation; Instructions to patient; Scheduling; and Topical; and (6) Equipment, including: Adjustment and repair; Documentation; Inspection; and Maintenance. **Renewal:** Every five years. Recertification based on either successful completion of exam or continuing education. **Preparatory Materials:** Review sessions available. **Examination Sites:** Exam given at sites throughout the U.S. **Examination Type:** Multiple-choice. **Waiting Period to Receive Scores:** 90 days. **Fees:** $150 (members); $200 (nonmembers). **Endorsed By:** International Electrology Educators; International Guild of Professional Electrologists; Society of Clinical and Medical Electrologists.

1484

Certified Professional Electrologist (C.P.E.)
International Board of Electrology
    Certification
106 Oak Ridge Rd.
Trumbull, CT 06611
Phone: (203)374-6667
Fax: (203)372-7134

Recipient: Electrologists. **Educational/Experience Requirements:** Must meet one of the following requirements: (1) Current licensure; (2) Successful completion of school of electrology; or (3) One year as apprenticed electrologist. **Membership:** Not required. **Certification Requirements:** Successful completion of exam. Exam covers: (1) Anatomy of Physiology of Skin and Hair, including: Anatomy of the pilosebaceous unit; Hair growth cycle; Reasons for excessive hair growth; Structure, function, and disorders of the skin; and Types of hair; (2) Infection Control, including: *AEA Infection Control Standards for the Practice of Electrology;* Personal hygiene; and Transmittable diseases; (3) Clinical Observation, including: Patient/client assessment; Patient/client reaction; and Skin reactions; (4) Equipment Operation, including: Electrical current; Methods and techniques of permanent hair removal; Periodic epilator testing; Positioning, draping, and lighting; Sterilizer temperature testing; and Tuning, calibration, and timing; (5) Supplies, including: Cleaning; Inventory; Selection; and Updating and disposal; and (6) Professional, Ethical, and Legal Considerations. **Renewal:** Every five years. Recertification based on either successful completion of exam or accumulation of 7.5 continuing education units (CEUs) through approved lectures, seminars, courses, home study, and other educational activities. **Preparatory Materials:** "Compendium of Study" and "CPE's Guide to Recertification" (refer-

ences). Bulletin, including sample questions, provided. **Examination Frequency:** semiannual - always spring and fall. **Examination Sites:** Exam given at annual convention and sites throughout the U.S. and internationally. **Examination Type:** Multiple-choice. **Waiting Period to Receive Scores:** Four weeks. **Fees:** $165 (members); $215 (nonmembers). **Endorsed By:** American Electrology Association.

Gardeners, Horticulture Workers, and Groundskeepers

1485

Certified Golf Course Superintendent (CGCS)
Golf Course Superintendents
    Association of America (GCSAA)
1421 Research Park Dr.
Lawrence, KS 66049-3859
Phone: (913)841-2240
Fax: (913)832-4455
Toll Free: (800)472-7878

Recipient: Golf course superintendents. **Educational/Experience Requirements:** Must meet one of the following requirements: (1) Bachelor's degree in turf management, three years experience, and 4.2 GCSAA continuing education units (CEUs); (2) Bachelor's degree in non-turf management field, five years experience, and seven GCSAA CEUs; (3) Associate's degree in turf management, five years experience, and seven GCSAA CEUs; (4) Turf certificate from program that is two years in length and offered by four-year institution, five years experience, and seven GCSAA CEUs; (5) Associate's degree in non-turf related field, seven years experience, and 9.8 GCSAA CEUs; (6) Turf certificate from program with at least 400 contact hours, seven years experience, and 9.8 GCSAA CEUs; or (7) Eight years experience and 31.5 GCSAA CEUs. **Certification Requirements:** Successful completion of the following requirements: (1) Six-part exam. Exam parts are: Knowledge of GCSAA and the Certification Program; The Game and Rules of Golf; Turf-grass Management; Pest Control, Safety, and Compliance; Financial Management; and Organizational Management; and (2) Golf course operation review. Review must be conducted during course's growing season and involves tour of course and facilities. **Renewal:** Every five years. Recertification based on either successful completion of exam or accumulation of CEUs through successful completion of GCS-

SA's Continuing Education Curriculum courses, college course work, or attendance at seminars sponsored by other organizations. **Re-examination:** Must only retake sections failed. May retake each section two times.

┃1486┃

Certified Grounds Manager (CGM)

Professional Grounds Management Society (PGMS)
120 Cockeysville Rd., Ste. 104
Hunt Valley, MD 21031
Phone: (410)584-9754
Fax: (410)584-9756
Toll Free: (800)609-7567
John Gillan, Exec.Dir.

Recipient: Grounds managers of large institutions and independent landscape contractors. **Number of Certified Individuals:** 50. **Educational/Experience Requirements:** Must meet one of the following requirements: (1) Bachelor's degree or higher in related field and four years experience, with two years in supervisory position; (2) Associate's degree and six years experience, with three years in supervisory position; or (3) Eight years experience, with four years in supervisory position. Experience must include installing and removing outdoor and indoor foliage. **Membership:** Not required. **Certification Requirements:** Successful completion of two-part exam. Part one covers: Design and management relationships; Energy and water conservation; Environmental issues; Equipment management; Financial management; Grounds management principles; Materials and supplies management; Personnel management; and Technical considerations. Part two covers: Budget and finance; Management systems and skills; Operations inventory; Pavings and structures; Site management; Trees, shrubs, and other plantings; and Turf care and irrigation. **Renewal:** Every five years. Recertification based on accumulation of 50 points in the following areas: (1) PGMS Conference (ten points/year); (2) PGMS Management seminars (five points/seminar); and (3) Other national/state conferences related to grounds management (five points/conference). No more than 20 points may be earned in any one year. **Examination Sites:** Exam given by arrangement with proctor. **Examination Type:** Multiple-choice; true or false. **Pass/Fail Rate:** 80% pass exam the first time. **Fees:** $150 (members); $300 (nonmembers).

┃1487┃

Certified Landscape Management Technician (CLMT)

American Landscape Horticulture Association (ALHA)
3124 Gray Fox Ln.
Paso Robles, CA 93446
Phone: (805)238-7921
Toll Free: (800)359-6647
James C. Keener, Dir.

Recipient: Landscape management technicians. **Number of Certified Individuals:** 35. **Educational/Experience Requirements:** 2000 hours of experience in 16 landscaping work processes. **Membership:** Not required. **Certification Requirements:** Successful completion of practical exam based on industry work processes. **Renewal:** none. **Preparatory Materials:** List of recommended study references available. **Examination Frequency:** Throughout the year. **Examination Sites:** Exam given at sites throughout the U.S. and Canada. **Pass/Fail Rate:** 85% pass exam the first time. **Waiting Period to Receive Scores:** 30 days. **Re-examination:** There is no time limit to retake exam. **Fees:** $100.

┃1488┃

Certified Landscape Professional (CLP)

American Landscape Horticulture Association (ALHA)
3124 Gray Fox Ln.
Paso Robles, CA 93446
Phone: (805)238-7921
Toll Free: (800)359-6647
James C. Keener, Dir.

Recipient: Supervisors, sales persons, designers, and managers in landscaping; landscape architects and contractors; arborists, horticulturists, and nursery persons; interiorscapers; and lawn care and pest control specialists. **Number of Certified Individuals:** 25. **Membership:** Not required. **Certification Requirements:** Submission of biography listing qualifications and experience. Classroom training, correspondence courses, educational programs, specialty certification or licensing, hands-on training, and experience are all considered as qualifications for certification. **Renewal:** Every two years. Recertification based on meeting requirements in the following areas: (1) Education (56 hours), which can include courses on business administration, pest control, sprinkler system design, industry related technical subjects, and water management; and (2) Personal Development (24 hours), which can include self-

motivation, time management, wealth building, and general educational courses. Continuing education sources can be organized classroom or educational programs, including adult education, audio or video programs, correspondence courses, industry organizations, manufacturer, or supplier sponsored programs, and seminars. Renewal fee is $100. **Preparatory Materials:** List of recommended study resources available. **Examination Frequency:** Throughout the year. **Examination Sites:** Exam given at sites throughout the U.S. and Canada. **Pass/Fail Rate:** 85% pass exam the first time. **Waiting Period to Receive Scores:** 30 days. **Re-examination:** There is no time limit to retake exam. **Fees:** $100.

┃1489┃

Certified Landscape Technician (CLT)

American Landscape Horticulture Association (ALHA)
3124 Gray Fox Ln.
Paso Robles, CA 93446
Phone: (805)238-7921
Toll Free: (800)359-6647
James C. Keener, Dir.

Recipient: Landscape technicians. **Number of Certified Individuals:** 50. **Educational/Experience Requirements:** 4000 hours of experience in 13 landscaping work processes. **Membership:** Not required. **Certification Requirements:** Successful completion of practical exam. **Renewal:** none. **Preparatory Materials:** List of recommended books available. **Examination Frequency:** Throughout the year. **Examination Sites:** Exam given at sites throughout the U.S. and Canada. **Pass/Fail Rate:** 90% pass exam the first time. **Waiting Period to Receive Scores:** 30 days. **Re-examination:** There is no time limit to retake exam. **Fees:** $100.

┃1490┃

Certified Turfgrass Professional (CTP)

Professional Lawn Care Association of America (PLCAA)
Principles of Turfgrass Mgmt. 23106
Community Learning Resources, Ste. 191
Georgia Center for Continuing Educ.
Univ. of Georgia
Athens, GA 30602-3603
Phone: (706)542-1756
Fax: (706)542-5990
Toll Free: (800)542-8097
Karen Bishop, Prog.Coord.

Recipient: Lawn care professionals involved with lawn care companies, public parks, school grounds maintenance, sod production, landscape management firms, golf courses, cemeteries, athletic fields, and other turf facilities. **Number of Certified Individuals:** 20. **Membership:** Not required. **Certification Requirements:** Successful completion of the following: (1) Principles of Turfgrass Management correspondence course, which covers turfgrass management practices and procedures and principles of warm- and cool-season turfgrass establishment, growth, maintenance, and troubleshooting. Course consists of the following chapters: Customer Relations; Establishment; Fertilization; Insects; Irrigation; Mowing; Pesticides; Soils; Turfgrass Characterization, Identification, and Adaptation; Turfgrass Diseases; Turfgrass and the Environment; Turfgrass Growth, Development, and Physiology; Turfgrass Troubleshooting; and Weeds; and (3) Two exams. **Renewal:** Every five years. Recertification based on successful completion of exam. **Preparatory Materials:** Study texts provided. **Examination Frequency:** Throughout the year. **Examination Sites:** Exams given at sites throughout the U.S. **Examination Type:** Multiple-choice. **Pass/Fail Rate:** 70% pass exams the first time. **Waiting Period to Receive Scores:** One-two weeks. **Reexamination:** There is no time limit to retake exams. **Fees:** $275.

General Maintenance Mechanics

▮1491▮

Certified Apartment Maintenance Technician (CAMT)
National Apartment Association (NAA)
1111 Fourteenth St., NW, Ste. 900
Washington, DC 20005
Phone: (202)842-4050
Fax: (202)842-4056

Recipient: Apartment maintenance professionals. **Educational/Experience Requirements:** One year of experience. **Certification Requirements:** Successful completion of the following: (1) 156-hour comprehensive training program, including exams. Program covers: Appliances; Electricity; Grounds; HVAC; Interior and exterior maintenance; Maintenance operations; Pest control; Plumbing; Pools; Preventive maintenance; and Safety and first aid; and (2) Exam. **Renewal:** Every year. Recertification based on accumulation of five continuing credits. There is a renewal fee.

▮1492▮

Systems Maintenance Technician (SMT)
Building Owners and Managers Institute (BOMI)
1521 Ritchie Hwy.
Arnold, MD 21012
Phone: (410)974-1410
Fax: (410)974-1935
Toll Free: (800)235-2664

Recipient: Building maintenance technicians. **Certification Requirements:** Successful completion of the following courses: (1) Air Handling, Water Treatment, and Plumbing Systems, covering: Air properties; Air distribution, humidification, and dehumidification; Basic air conditioning systems; Fans and air ducts; Fire protection; Indoor air quality; Internal water treatment of boilers and cooling water treatment; Microbiological water treatment, chemical feed equipment, and cleaning heat exchangers; Piping and valves; Plumbing systems; Psychometric chart; Testing and pretreatment of water; and Water terminology, chemistry, and problems; (2) Basic Mathematics, Boilers, and Heating Systems, covering: Automatic boiler components; Boiler components; Boiler operation and maintenance; Boiler types; Energy sources; Hydronic (hot water) heating systems; Mathematics and conversion factors; Measurements and mechanical forces; Pumps; Steam heating systems; Thermodynamics; and Warm air and radiant heating systems; (3) Control Systems, covering: Auxiliary control devices; Central HVAC system control applications; Computers and microprocessors in control systems; Control system basics and the pneumatic control system; Controlled devices; Controllers; Cooling, humidification, and dehumidification control applications; Electric and electronic control systems; Fan modulation and building pressurization control; Heating control applications; and VAV design, application, and control; (4) Electrical Systems and Illumination, covering: Basic electricity; Basics of lighting; Building electrical service; Electrical boxes, receptacles, switches, and solenoids; Electrical conductors, insulation, and raceways; Electrical meters; Electrical motors; Light sources, fixtures, and maintenance; Measuring electrical energy consumption and electrical circuits; Motors and starters, maintenance, and safety; Protective devices (fuses and circuit breakers) and electrical symbols; and Sources of electricity; (5) Refrigeration Systems and Accessories, covering: Absorption refrigeration systems; Basic refrigeration cycle; Centrifugal refrigeration machines; Compressors and metering devices; Cooling

towers; Evaporators and condensers; General maintenance requirements; Leak testing, evacuation, and charging; Operating and safety controls; Reciprocating refrigeration systems; Refrigerants and lubricants; and Refrigeration accessories. Comparable experience or education related to a course subject may receive credit for up to three courses. Courses may be taken in instructor-led local classes, accelerated courses, and self-study courses. **Examination Frequency:** Three times per year (self-study) - January, May, and September. **Examination Sites:** Exams given at courses or at local sites throughout the U.S. for self-study courses. **Endorsed By:** Building Owners and Managers Association International; Society of Property Professionals.

Homemaker-Home Health Aides

▮1493▮

Certified Home Care Aide
Foundation for Hospice and Homecare (FHH)
513 C St., NE
Washington, DC 20002-5809
Phone: (202)547-6586
Fax: (202)546-8968

Recipient: Home care aides. **Educational/Experience Requirements:** Successful completion of 75 hour training program based on *Model Curriculum and Teaching Guide for the Instruction of the Home Care Aide.* **Certification Requirements:** Successful completion of performance evaluation and exam. Performance evaluation requires demonstrating skills in 17 different areas. **Preparatory Materials:** *Model Curriculum and Teaching Guide for the Instruction of the Home Care Aide* (reference). **Examination Sites:** Exam given at sites throughout the U.S. **Waiting Period to Receive Scores:** Four weeks. **Reexamination:** There is a $32 fee to retake exam. **Endorsed By:** National Association for Home Care; National HomeCaring Council.

1494

Certified Home Economist (CHE)
American Association of Family
  and Consumer Sciences (AAFCS)
1555 King St.
Alexandria, VA 22314
Phone: (703)706-4600
Fax: (703)706-4663
Dr. Mary Jane Kolar CAE, Exec.
  Officer

Recipient: Family and consumer sciences professionals. **Number of Certified Individuals:** 7500. **Educational/Experience Requirements:** Must meet one of the following requirements: (1) Bachelor's degree in family and consumer sciences or related field; or (2) Bachelor's degree in unrelated field and two years experience. **Membership:** Not required. **Certification Requirements:** Successful completion of exam. Exam consists of the following sections: Family Resource Management; The Family System; Impact of Apparel and Textiles; Lifespan Human Development; Nutrition; Professional Roles; and Technology and the Impact of Change. **Renewal:** Every three years. Recertification based on system of points called Professional Development Units. Units earned through internships, professional workshops, and college course work. **Preparatory Materials:** Examination study manual available. **Examination Frequency:** Throughout the year. **Examination Sites:** Exam given at sites throughout the U.S. **Examination Type:** Multiple-choice. **Re-examination:** There is no time limit to retake exam. **Fees:** $150 (members); $200 (nonmembers); $85 (senior-level family and consumer sciences majors).

Janitors and Cleaners

1495

Custodial Maintenance Supervisor
Cleaning Management Institute
  (CMI)
13 Century Hill Dr.
Latham, NY 12110-2197
Phone: (518)783-1281
Fax: (518)783-1386
Tara Leigh Martin, Coord.

Recipient: Custodial maintenance supervisors. **Membership:** Not required. **Certification Requirements:** Successful completion of home-study course and exam. Course consists of the following sections, including exams: (1) What Is a Supervisor?, including: Developing potential; Functions of management; Objec-

tives of supervision; Qualifications; and Supervisor on the job; (2) Basis Tools and Techniques, including: Bloodborne pathogens and right to know; Building exterior and grounds; Cleaning chemicals; Equipment and supplies; Floors and floor maintenance; Preventive maintenance; Recycling; Stock rooms and storage facilities; Washroom sanitation; and Windows, walls, ceilings, and light fixtures; and (3) Application of Supervisory Principles, including: Onward and upward; Personnel relations; Preparing cleaning schedule; Purchasing; Record keeping; Safety and security; Staffing; Time study; and Training. **Examination Frequency:** Throughout the year. **Examination Type:** Essay; multiple-choice; true or false. **Re-examination:** May retake exam one time. **Fees:** $165 (members); $215 (nonmembers).

1496

Custodial Technician, Level I
Cleaning Management Institute
  (CMI)
13 Century Hill Dr.
Latham, NY 12110-2197
Phone: (518)783-1281
Fax: (518)783-1386
Tara Leigh Martin, Coord.

Recipient: Custodial technicians. **Membership:** Not required. **Certification Requirements:** Successful completion of course, including exam. Course consists of the following sections: (1) Basic Cleaning for Carpeted Floor Surfaces; (2) Basic Cleaning for Hard Floor Surfaces; (3) Basic Cleaning for Rest Rooms and Shower Rooms; (4) Chemistry of Cleaning, including: Acidity and alkalinity; Cleaning agents; Identification and control methods for germ control; Removal processes; Treatment with disinfectant chemicals; and Types of soil; (5) Equipment and Supplies Storage; and (6) Handling of Hazardous and Infectious Waste. Course may be taken through independent study or at community colleges, place of employment, or CMI training centers. **Preparatory Materials:** Handbook, study guide, and trainer manual available. **Examination Frequency:** Throughout the year. **Examination Sites:** Exam given at annual conference or by arrangement with proctor. **Examination Type:** Multiple choice; true or false. **Re-examination:** Must retake exam within six months. Fee to retake exam is $35. **Fees:** $89.95 (members); $99.95 (nonmembers).

1497

Custodial Technician, Level II
Cleaning Management Institute
  (CMI)
13 Century Hill Dr.
Latham, NY 12110-2197
Phone: (518)783-1281
Fax: (518)783-1386
Tara Leigh Martin, Coord.

Recipient: Custodial technicians. **Membership:** Not required. **Certification Requirements:** Successful completion of course, including exam. Course consists of the following sections: (1) Advanced Cleaning for Carpeted Floor Surfaces, including: Carpet cleaning tools; Materials; Mop buckets and wringers; Supplies; Tank and pump-up sprayers; Types of floor machines; Vacuums; Wet extractors; and Work procedures; (2) Advanced Cleaning for Hard Floor Surfaces, including: Equipment; Floor machines; Floor strippers for both resilient floor and tile, wood, and concrete; Machineless stripping process; Materials; Mop buckets, wringers, wet mop holders, and other hand equipment; Mop heads, floor machine pads, and finish applicator pads; Stripping with floor machine; Surface chemicals; and Wet and dry stripping; (3) Chemistry of Cleaning, including: Floor finishes; Governmental regulations; High speed floor finish chemistry and characteristics; Identifying stains; Terminology; and Treatment of stains for stain-resistant and regular carpets; (4) Floor Covering Types: A Simple Analysis, including: Masonry, resilient, and wood floor types; and Methods for identifying various carpet fibers; and (5) Hard Surface Floors Requiring Special Procedures, including: Ceramic tile, concrete, cork, marble, and quarry tile; Equipment; Maintenance; Materials; Procedures; Proper care techniques for asphalt tile, rubber, terrazzo, and wood; Sealing; Stripping; and Supplies. Course may be taken through independent study or at community colleges, place of employment, or CMI training centers. **Preparatory Materials:** Handbook, study guide, and trainer manual available. **Examination Frequency:** Throughout the year. **Examination Sites:** Exam given at annual conference or by arrangement with proctor. **Examination Type:** Multiple choice; true or false. **Re-examination:** Must retake exam within six months. Fee to retake exam is $35. **Fees:** $99.95 (members); $109.95 (nonmembers).

Private Household Workers

1498

Certified Executive Housekeeper (CEH)

National Executive Housekeepers
   Association (NEHA)
1001 Eastwind Dr., Ste. 301
Westerville, OH 43081-3361
Phone: (614)895-7166
Fax: (614)895-1248
Toll Free: (800)200-6342
Beth B. Risinger, Exec.Dir.

Recipient: Middle managers responsible for directing housekeeping programs in commercial, institutional, medical, or industrial facilities, including managing staff and budgets. **Educational/ Experience Requirements:** Must meet the following requirements: (1) High school diploma or equivalent; and (2) One year of experience. **Membership:** Required. **Certification Requirements:** Must meet one of the following requirements: (1) Successful completion of 330 hour CEH program, including 70 hours in the following areas: Behavioral sciences; Communications; Environmental controls; Housekeeping techniques; Introduction to business; and Personnel management; (2) Successful completion of Collegiate Program, including 60 hours of college coursework, 39 of which must be in courses required by NEHA; or (3) Successful completion of NEHA Training and Certification Program, a two-part self-study program. Part one consists of the following modules: Communication; Continuous Improvement; Management Philosophy and Style; Planning and Organizing; and Staffing and Staff Development. Part Two, Technical and Administrative Series, covers various specific areas of housekeeping management. **Renewal:** Every two years. Recertification based on continuing education.

1499

Registered Executive Housekeeper (REH)

National Executive Housekeepers
   Association (NEHA)
1001 Eastwind Dr., Ste. 301
Westerville, OH 43081
Phone: (614)895-7166
Fax: (614)895-1248
Beth B. Risinger, Exec.Dir.

Recipient: Middle managers responsible for directing housekeeping programs in commercial, institutional, medical, or industrial facilities, including managing staff and budgets. **Educational/ Experience Requirements:** Must meet the following requirements: (1) High school diploma or equivalent; and (2) One year of experience. **Membership:** Required. **Certification Requirements:** Must meet the following requirements: (1) Be associate member of NEHA or hold Certified Executive Housekeeper (CEH) designation (see separate entry) for one year; and (2) Bachelor's degree, including 39 hours in classes required by NEHA. **Renewal:** Every two years. Recertification based on continuing education.

Mechanics, Installers, and Repairers

Automotive Body Repairers and Mechanics

1500

ASE Certified Alternative Fuels Technician
National Institute for Automotive Service Excellence (ASE)
13505 Dulles Technology Dr.
Herndon, VA 22071-3415
Phone: (703)713-3800
Fax: (703)713-0727
Ronald H. Weiner, Pres.

Recipient: Alternative fuels technicians. **Educational/Experience Requirements:** Two years experience. May substitute the following for experience: (1) One year of experience for three years of high school training in either automobile/truck repair or collision repair and refinish; (2) One year of experience for two years of post-high school training in a public or private trade school, technical institute, community or four-year college, or in an apprenticeship program; (3) One month of experience for two months of post-high school training; or (4) Two years experience for successful completion of three- or four-year apprenticeship program. **Certification Requirements:** Successful completion of Light Vehicle Compressed Natural Gas exam. Exam covers: Engine performance diagnosis; Equipment installation; Initial adjustments; Leak testing and repairs; Parts fabrication; System diagnosis and repair; and Vehicle compatibility analysis. **Renewal:** Every five years. Recertification based on successful completion of exam. Renewal fee is $40. **Preparatory Materials:** Preparation guides, including sample questions, provided. **Examination Frequency:** semiannual - always May and November. **Examination Sites:** Exam given at sites throughout the U.S. **Examination Type:** Multiple-choice. **Waiting Period to Receive Scores:** Eight-ten weeks. **Reexamination:** There is a $35 fee to retake exam. **Fees:** $35.

1501

ASE Certified Collision Repair and Refinish Technician
National Institute for Automotive Service Excellence (ASE)
13505 Dulles Technology Dr.
Herndon, VA 22071-3415
Phone: (703)713-3800
Fax: (703)713-0727
Ronald H. Weiner, Pres.

Recipient: Collision repair and refinishing specialists. **Educational/Experience Requirements:** Two years experience. May substitute the following for experience: (1) One year of experience for three years of high school training in either automobile/truck repair or collision repair and refinish; (2) One year of experience for two years of post-high school training in a public or private trade school, technical institute, community or four-year college, or in an apprenticeship program; (3) One month of experience for two months of post-high school training; or (4) Two years experience for successful completion of three- or four-year apprenticeship program. **Certification Requirements:** Successful completion of one of the following exams: (1) Painting and Refinishing, covering: Finish defects, causes, and cures; Paint mixing, matching, and applying; Safety precautions and miscellaneous; Solving paint application problems; Spray gun operation and related equipment; and Surface preparation; (2) NonStructural Analysis and Damage Repair, covering: Metal finishing and body filling; Movable glass and hardware; Outer body panel repairs, replacements, and adjustments; Plastic repair; Preparation; and Welding and cutting; (3) Structural Analysis and Damage Repair, covering: Frame inspection and repair; Metal welding and cutting; Stationary glass; and Unibody inspection, measurement, and repair; and (4) Mechanical and Electrical Components, covering: Brakes; Drive train; Electrical; Engine cooling systems; Fuel, intake, and exhaust systems; Heating and air conditioning; Restraint systems; and Suspension and steering. **Renewal:** Every five years. Recertification based on successful completion of exam. Renewal fee is $40. **Preparatory Materials:** Preparation guides, including sample questions, provided. **Examination Frequency:** semiannual - always May and November. **Examination Sites:** Exams given at sites throughout the U.S. **Examination Type:** Multiple-choice. **Waiting Period to Receive Scores:** Eight-ten weeks. **Reexamination:** There is a $35 fee to retake exams. **Fees:** $35.

1502

ASE Certified Engine Machinist
National Institute for Automotive Service Excellence (ASE)
13505 Dulles Technology Dr.
Herndon, VA 22071-3415
Phone: (703)713-3800
Fax: (703)713-0727
Ronald H. Weiner, Pres.

Recipient: Engine machinists. **Educational/Experience Requirements:** Two years experience. May substitute the following for experience: (1) One year of experience for three years of high school training in either automobile/truck repair or collision repair and refinish; (2) One year of experience for two years of post-high school training in a public or private trade school, technical institute, community or four-year college, or in an apprenticeship program; (3) One month of experience for two months of post-high school training; or (4) Two years experience for successful completion of three- or four-year apprenticeship program. **Certification Requirements:** Successful completion of one of the following exams: (1) Cylinder Head, covering: Cylinder head assembly; and Cylinder head crack repair; Cylinder head disassembly and cleaning; Cylinder head inspection and machining; (2) Cylinder Block, covering: Balancing; Connecting rods and piston inspection and machining; Crankshaft inspection and machining; Cylinder block crack repair; Cylinder block disassembly and cleaning; Cylinder block machining; and Cylinder block preparation; and (3) Assembly, covering: Engine disassembly, inspection, and cleaning; Engine preparation; Final assembly; Long block assembly; and Short block assembly. **Renewal:** Every five years. Recertification based on successful completion of exam. Renewal fee is $40. **Preparatory Materials:** Preparation guides, including sample questions, provided. **Examination Frequency:** semiannual - always May and November. **Examination Sites:** Exams given at sites throughout the U.S. **Examination Type:** Multiple-choice. **Waiting Period to Receive Scores:** Eight-ten weeks. **Reexamination:** There is a $35 fee to retake exam. **Fees:** $35.

1503

ASE Certified Master Engine Machinist

National Institute for Automotive Service Excellence (ASE)
13505 Dulles Technology Dr.
Herndon, VA 22071-3415
Phone: (703)713-3800
Fax: (703)713-0727
Ronald H. Weiner, Pres.

Recipient: Engine machinists. **Educational/Experience Requirements:** Hold ASE Certified Engine Machinist designation (see separate entry). **Certification Requirements:** Successful completion of the following exams: (1) Cylinder Head, covering: Cylinder head assembly; Cylinder head crack repair; Cylinder head disassembly and cleaning; and Cylinder head inspection and machining; (2) Cylinder Block, covering: Balancing; Connecting rods and piston inspection and machining; Crankshaft inspection and machining; Cylinder block crack repair; Cylinder block disassembly and cleaning; Cylinder block machining; and Cylinder block preparation; and (3) Assembly, covering: Engine disassembly, inspection, and cleaning; Engine preparation; Final assembly; Long block assem-

bly; and Short block assembly. **Renewal:** Every five years. **Preparatory Materials:** Preparation guides, including sample questions, provided. **Examination Frequency:** semiannual - always May and November. **Examination Sites:** Exams given at sites throughout the U.S. **Examination Type:** Multiple-choice. **Waiting Period to Receive Scores:** Eight-ten weeks.

1504

ASE Certified Parts Specialist

National Institute for Automotive Service Excellence (ASE)
13505 Dulles Technology Dr.
Herndon, VA 22071-3415
Phone: (703)713-3800
Fax: (703)713-0727
Ronald H. Weiner, Pres.

Recipient: Automobile and truck parts specialists. **Educational/Experience Requirements:** Two years experience. May substitute the following for experience: (1) One year of experience for three years of high school training in either automobile or truck parts; (2) One year of experience for two years of post-high school training as a parts specialist in a public or private trade school, technical institute, community or four-year college, or in an apprenticeship program; (3) One month of experience for two months of post-high school training as a parts specialist; or (4) Two years experience for successful completion of three- or four-year parts specialist apprenticeship program. **Certification Requirements:** Successful completion of the following specialist exams: (1) Medium/Heavy Truck Parts, covering: Communications skills; Inventory management; Sales skills; and Vehicle systems; and (2) Automobile Parts, covering: Cataloging skills; Customer relations and sales skills; General operations; Inventory management; Merchandising; Vehicle identification; and Vehicle systems knowledge. **Renewal:** Every five years. Recertification based on successful completion of exam. Renewal fee is $40. **Preparatory Materials:** Preparation guides, including sample questions, provided. **Examination Frequency:** semiannual - always May and November. **Examination Sites:** Exams given at sites throughout the U.S. **Examination Type:** Multiple-choice. **Waiting Period to Receive Scores:** Eight-ten weeks. **Fees:** $50.

1505

Automotive Advanced Engine Performance Specialist

National Institute for Automotive Service Excellence (ASE)
13505 Dulles Technology Dr.
Herndon, VA 22071-3415
Phone: (703)713-3800
Fax: (703)713-0727
Ronald H. Weiner, Pres.

Recipient: Engine performance specialists. **Educational/Experience Requirements:** Two years experience. May substitute the following for experience: (1) One year of experience for three years of high school training in either automobile/truck repair or collision repair and refinish; (2) One year of experience for two years of post-high school training in a public or private trade school, technical institute, community or four-year college, or in an apprenticeship program; (3) One month of experience for two months of post-high school training; or (4) Two years experience for successful completion of three- or four-year apprenticeship program. **Certification Requirements:** Successful completion of the following exams: (1) Engine Performance, covering the following diagnosis and repair areas: Computerized engine controls; Emissions control systems; Engine electrical systems; Fuel, air induction, and exhaust systems; General engine; and Ignition system; and (2) Automobile Advanced Engine Performance Specialist, covering the following diagnosis areas: Computerized engine controls; Emissions control systems; Fuel systems and air induction systems; General power train; Ignition system; and IM Failure. **Renewal:** Every five years. Recertification based on successful completion of exam. Renewal fee is $40. **Preparatory Materials:** Preparation guides, including sample questions, provided. **Examination Frequency:** semiannual - always May and November. **Examination Sites:** Exams given at sites throughout the U.S. **Examination Type:** Multiple-choice. **Waiting Period to Receive Scores:** Eight-ten weeks. **Fees:** $60.

Automotive Mechanics

1506

ASE Certified Automobile Technician
National Institute for Automotive Service Excellence (ASE)
13505 Dulles Technology Dr.
Herndon, VA 22071-3415
Phone: (703)713-3800
Fax: (703)713-0727
Ronald H. Weiner, Pres.

Recipient: Automotive technicians. **Educational/Experience Requirements:** Two years experience. May substitute the following for experience: (1) One year of experience for three years of high school training in either automobile/truck repair or collision repair and refinish; (2) One year of experience for two years of post-high school training in public or private trade school, technical institute, community or four-year college, or in apprenticeship program; (3) One month of experience for two months of post-high school training; or (4) Two years experience for successful completion of three- or four-year apprenticeship program. **Certification Requirements:** Successful completion of at least one of the following diagnostic and repair exams: (1) Engine Repair, covering: Battery and starting systems; Cylinder head and valve train; Engine block; Fuel and exhaust systems; General engine; Ignition system; and Lubrication and cooling systems; (2) Automatic Transmission/Transaxle, covering: General transmission/transaxle; In-vehicle transmission/transaxle; Transmission/transaxle maintenance and adjustment; Off-vehicle transmissions/transaxle; Oil pump and converter; and Removal, disassembly, and assembly; (3) Manual Drive Train and Axles, covering: Clutch; Drive (half) shaft and universal joint; Four-wheel drive component; Transaxle; Transmission; and Real axle; (4) Suspension and Steering, covering: Steering systems; Suspension systems; Wheel alignment; and Wheel and tire; (5) Brakes, covering: Anti-lock brake system; Disc brake; Drum brake; Hydraulic system; Miscellaneous; and Power assist units; (6) Electrical/Electronic Systems, covering: Accessories; Battery; Charging systems; Gages, warning devices, and driver information systems; General electrical/electronic systems; Horn and wiper/washer; Lighting systems; and Starting systems; (7) Heating and Air Conditioning, covering: A/C system; Heating and engine cooling systems; Operating systems and related controls; Refrigerant recovery, recycling, and handling; and Refrigeration system; and (8) Engine Performance, covering: Computerized engine controls; Emissions control systems; Engine electrical systems; Fuel, air induction, and exhaust systems; General engine; and Ignition system. **Renewal:** Every five years. Recertification based on successful completion of exam. Renewal fee is $40. **Preparatory Materials:** Preparation guides, including sample questions, provided. **Examination Frequency:** semiannual - always May and November. **Examination Sites:** Exams given at sites throughout the U.S. **Examination Type:** Multiple-choice. **Waiting Period to Receive Scores:** Eight-ten weeks. **Re-examination:** There is a $35 fee to retake exams. **Fees:** $35.

1507

ASE Certified Master Autobody/Paint Technician
National Institute for Automotive Service Excellence (ASE)
13505 Dulles Technology Dr.
Herndon, VA 22071-3415
Phone: (703)713-3800
Fax: (703)713-0727
Ronald H. Weiner, Pres.

Recipient: Collision repair and refinishing specialists. **Educational/Experience Requirements:** Hold ASE Certified Collision Repair and Refinish Technician designation (see separate entry). **Certification Requirements:** Successful completion of the following exams: (1) Painting and Refinishing, covering: Finish defects, causes, and cures; Paint mixing, matching, and applying; Safety precautions and miscellaneous; Solving paint application problems; Spray gun operation and related equipment; and Surface preparation; (2) NonStructural Analysis and Damage Repair, covering: Metal finishing and body filling; Movable glass and hardware; Outer body panel repairs, replacements, and adjustments; Plastic repair; Preparation; and Welding and cutting; (3) Structural Analysis and Damage Repair, covering: Frame inspection and repair; Metal welding and cutting; Stationary glass; and Unibody inspection, measurement, and repair; and (4) Mechanical and Electrical Components, covering: Brakes; Drive train; Electrical; Engine cooling systems; Fuel, intake, and exhaust systems; Heating and air conditioning; Restraint systems; and Suspension and steering. **Renewal:** Every five years. **Preparatory Materials:** Preparation guides, including sample questions, provided. **Examination Frequency:** semiannual - always May and November. **Examination Sites:** Exams given at sites throughout the U.S. **Examination Type:** Multiple-choice. **Waiting Period to Receive Scores:** Eight-ten weeks.

1508

ASE Certified Master Automobile Technician
National Institute for Automotive Service Excellence (ASE)
13505 Dulles Technology Dr.
Herndon, VA 22071-3415
Phone: (703)713-3800
Fax: (703)713-0727
Ronald H. Weiner, Pres.

Recipient: Automotive technicians. **Educational/Experience Requirements:** Hold ASE Certified Automobile Technician designation (see separate entry). **Certification Requirements:** Successful completion of the following diagnostic and repair exams: (1) Engine Repair, covering: Battery and starting systems; Cylinder head and valve train; Engine block; Fuel and exhaust systems; General engine; Ignition system; and Lubrication and cooling systems; (2) Automatic Transmission/Transaxle, covering: General transmission/transaxle; In-vehicle transmission/transaxle; Transmission/transaxle maintenance and adjustment; Off-vehicle transmissions/transaxle; Oil pump and converter; and Removal, disassembly, and assembly; (3) Manual Drive Train and Axles, covering: Clutch; Drive (half) shaft and universal joint; Four-wheel drive component; Transaxle; Transmission; and Real axle; (4) Suspension and Steering, covering: Steering systems; Suspension systems; Wheel alignment; and Wheel and tire; (5) Brakes, covering: Anti-lock brake system; Disc brake; Drum brake; Hydraulic system; Miscellaneous; and Power assist units; (6) Electrical/Electronic Systems, covering: Accessories; Battery; Charging systems; Gages, warning devices, and driver information systems; General electrical/electronic systems; Horn and wiper/washer; Lighting systems; and Starting systems; (7) Heating and Air Conditioning, covering: A/C system; Heating and engine cooling systems; Operating systems and related controls; Refrigerant recovery, recycling, and handling; and Refrigeration system; and (8) Engine Performance, covering: Computerized engine controls; Emissions control systems; Engine electrical systems; Fuel, air induction, and exhaust systems; General engine; and Ignition system. **Renewal:** Every five years. **Preparatory Materials:** Preparation guides, including sample questions, provided. **Examination Frequency:** semiannual - always May and November. **Examination Sites:** Exams given at sites throughout the U.S. **Examination Type:** Multiple-choice. **Waiting Period to Receive Scores:** Eight-ten weeks.

1509

ASE Certified Master Medium/Heavy Truck Technician

National Institute for Automotive Service Excellence (ASE)
13505 Dulles Technology Dr.
Herndon, VA 22071-3415
Phone: (703)713-3800
Fax: (703)713-0727
Ronald H. Weiner, Pres.

Recipient: Truck technicians. **Educational/Experience Requirements:** Hold ASE Certified Medium/Heavy Truck Technician designation (see separate entry). **Certification Requirements:** Successful completion of Gasoline Engines or Diesel Engines exams and four specialty exams. Gasoline Engines exam covers: Battery and starting systems; Cylinder head and valve train; Emission control systems; Engine block; Fuel and exhaust systems; General engine; Ignition systems; and Lubrication and cooling systems. Diesel Engines exam covers: Air induction and exhaust systems; Cylinder head and valve train; Engine block; Engine brakes; Fuel system; General engine; Lubrication and cooling systems; and Starting systems. Specialty exams are: (1) Drive Train, covering: Clutch; Drive axle; Drive shaft and universal joint; and Transmission; (2) Brakes, covering: Air brakes; Hydraulic brakes; and Wheel bearings; (3) Suspension and Steering, covering: Frame service; Steering system; Suspension system; Wheel alignment; and Wheels and tires; and (4) Electrical/Electronic Systems, covering: Battery; Charging system; Gauges and warning; General electrical; Lighting systems; Miscellaneous; and Starting system. **Renewal:** Every five years. **Preparatory Materials:** Preparation guides, including sample questions, provided. **Examination Frequency:** semiannual - always May and November. **Examination Sites:** Exams given at sites throughout the U.S. **Examination Type:** Multiple-choice. **Waiting Period to Receive Scores:** Eight-ten weeks.

1510

ASE Certified Medium/Heavy Truck Technician

National Institute for Automotive Service Excellence (ASE)
13505 Dulles Technology Dr.
Herndon, VA 22071-3415
Phone: (703)713-3800
Fax: (703)713-0727
Ronald H. Weiner, Pres.

Recipient: Truck technicians.

Educational/Experience Requirements: Two years experience. May substitute the following for experience: (1) One year of experience for three years of high school training in either automobile/truck repair or collision repair and refinish; (2) One year of experience for two years of post-high school training in public or private trade school, technical institute, community or four-year college, or in an apprenticeship program; (3) One month of experience for two months of post-high school training; or (4) Two years experience for successful completion of three- or four-year apprenticeship program. **Certification Requirements:** Successful completion of at least one of the following diagnostic and repair exams: (1) Gasoline Engines, covering: Battery and starting systems; Cylinder head and valve train; Emission control systems; Engine block; Fuel and exhaust systems; General engine; Ignition systems; and Lubrication and cooling systems; (2) Diesel Engines, covering: Air induction and exhaust systems; Cylinder head and valve train; Engine block; Engine brakes; Fuel system; General engine; Lubrication and cooling systems; and Starting systems; (3) Drive Train, covering: Clutch; Drive axle; Drive shaft and universal joint; and Transmission; (4) Brakes, covering: Air brakes; Hydraulic brakes; and Wheel bearings; (5) Suspension and Steering, covering: Frame service; Steering system; Suspension system; Wheel alignment; and Wheels and tires; and (6) Electrical/Electronic Systems, covering: Battery; Charging system; Gauges and warning; General electrical; Lighting systems; Miscellaneous; and Starting system. **Renewal:** Every five years. Recertification based on successful completion of exam. Renewal fee is $40. **Preparatory Materials:** Preparation guides, including sample questions, provided. **Examination Frequency:** semiannual - always May and November. **Examination Sites:** Exams given at sites throughout the U.S. **Examination Type:** Multiple-choice. **Waiting Period to Receive Scores:** Eight-ten weeks. **Re-examination:** There is a $35 fee to retake exams. **Fees:** $35.

Automotive Part Suppliers

1511

Import Parts Specialist

Auto International Association
PO Box 4910
Diamond Bar, CA 91765-0910
Phone: (909)396-0289
Fax: (909)860-0184
Karen Yin, Coord.

Recipient: Individuals involved in the import parts industry. **Number of Certified Individuals:** 3000. **Membership:** Not required. **Certification Requirements:** Successful completion of exam. Exam covers the fundamentals necessary for working with import parts. **Renewal:** none. **Preparatory Materials:** none. **Examination Frequency:** Throughout the year. **Examination Sites:** Exam given by correspondence **Examination Type:** Fill-in-the-blanks; matching; multiple-choice. **Pass/Fail Rate:** 90% pass exam the first time. **Waiting Period to Receive Scores:** Three weeks. **Re-examination:** There is no time limit to retake exam. There is no fee to retake exam. **Fees:** $20 (members); $40 (nonmembers).

1512

Master's Level Import Parts Specialist

Auto International Association
PO Box 4910
Diamond Bar, CA 91765-0910
Phone: (909)396-0289
Fax: (909)860-0184
Karen Yin, Coord.

Recipient: Individuals involved in the import parts industry. **Number of Certified Individuals:** 500. **Educational/Experience Requirements:** Hold Import Parts Specialist designation (see separate entry). **Membership:** Not required. **Certification Requirements:** Successful completion of exam. Exam covers: Brake systems; Electrical; Math and ignition; and Suspension. **Renewal:** none. **Preparatory Materials:** none. **Examination Frequency:** Throughout the year. **Examination Sites:** Exam given by correspondence. **Examination Type:** Fill-in-the-blanks; matching; multiple-choice. **Pass/Fail Rate:** 60% pass exam the first time. **Waiting Period to Receive Scores:** Three weeks. **Re-examination:** There is no time limit to retake exam. There is no fee to retake exam. **Fees:** $35 (members); $50 (nonmembers).

Commercial and Industrial Electronic Equipment Repairers

1513

NETA Certified Test Technician
International Electrical Testing
  Association (NETA)
106 Stone St.
PO Box 687
Morrison, CO 80465
Phone: (303)697-8441
Fax: (303)697-8431
Mary R. Jordan Ed.D., Exec.Dir.

Recipient: Electrical testing technicians. **Number of Certified Individuals:** 319. **Educational/Experience Requirements:** Two years experience and 4000 hours in testing and maintenance of electrical power distribution systems. **Membership:** Required. **Certification Requirements:** Successful completion of exam. Exam covers: Maintenance; Power theory; Testing; and Troubleshooting skills. **Renewal:** none. **Preparatory Materials:** Training books and NETA Specifications available. **Examination Frequency:** semiannual. **Examination Sites:** Exam given by arrangement with proctor. **Examination Type:** Multiple-choice. **Pass/Fail Rate:** 54% pass exam the first time. **Waiting Period to Receive Scores:** Two weeks. **Fees:** $100.

Computer and Office Machine Repairers

1514

A Certified Service Technician
Computing Technology Industry
  Association (CompTIA)
450 E. 22nd St., Ste. 230
Lombard, IL 60148-6158
Phone: (708)268-1818
Fax: (708)268-1384
Toll Free: (800)77M-ICRO

Recipient: Computer service technicians. **Membership:** Not required. **Certification Requirements:** Successful completion of exam. Exam covers: Configuration; Customer relations; Data communications; Diagnostics; Displays; Electronics; Ethics; Installation; Major operating systems, including DOS, Macintosh, and Windows; Microcomputers; PC architecture; Peripherals; Preventative maintenance; Printers; Relationship skills; Repair; Safety; Storage devices; and Upgrading and maintaining PCs. **Prepa-**ratory Materials: *Twenty Things You Need to Know to Prepare for the CompTIA A Certification Exam,* including list of suggested references and sample questions, available. Self-study training kit also available. **Examination Frequency:** Throughout the year. **Examination Sites:** Exam given at 300 sites throughout the U.S. **Waiting Period to Receive Scores:** Immediately. **Fees:** $150 (member); $165 (nonmembers).

Electronic Home Entertainment Equipment Repairers

1515

Associate Electronics Technician
Electronics Technicians Association,
  International (ETA-I)
602 N. Jackson
Greencastle, IN 46135
Phone: (317)653-8262
Fax: (317)653-8262
Anne Voiles, Admin.

Recipient: Electronics technicians. **Certification Requirements:** Successful completion of exam. Exam covers: AC-DC circuits; Antennas-wave propagation; Audio; Basic math; Batteries; Block diagrams; Decibels; Digital concepts; Electronic component nomenclature; Inductance-capacitance-reactance; Integrated circuits; Safety Precautions - ESD; Semiconductors; Test equipment; and Video. May qualify for Certified Electronics Technician designation (see separate entry) with more education and experience. **Preparatory Materials:** *CET Exam Book,* Third Edition and *Improving TV Signal Reception* (study manuals). Training programs, monographs, videotapes, and seminars available. **Examination Frequency:** Throughout the year. **Examination Sites:** Exam given at sites throughout the U.S. **Re-examination:** May retake exam once. **Fees:** $30.

1516

Certified Customer Service Specialist (CSS)
Electronics Technicians Association,
  International (ETA-I)
602 N. Jackson
Greencastle, IN 46135
Phone: (317)653-8262
Fax: (317)653-8262
Anne Voiles, Admin.

Recipient: Electronics service specialists. **Educational/Experience Requirements:** Four years combined education and experience. **Certification Requirements:** Successful completion of exam. Exam covers: Amps-preamps; Customer relations; Frequency bands; MATV; RF components; Rotors towers; and Telephone systems. **Preparatory Materials:** *CET Exam Book,* Third Edition and *Improving TV Signal Reception* (study manuals). Training programs, monographs, videotapes, and seminars available. **Examination Frequency:** Throughout the year. **Examination Sites:** Exam given at sites throughout the U.S. **Re-examination:** May retake exam once. **Fees:** $30.

1517

Certified Electronics Technician (CET)
Electronics Technicians Association,
  International (ETA-I)
602 N. Jackson
Greencastle, IN 46135
Phone: (317)653-8262
Fax: (317)653-8262
Anne Voiles, Admin.

Recipient: Electronics technicians. **Educational/Experience Requirements:** Four years combined education and experience. **Certification Requirements:** Successful completion of general exam and one specialty exam. General exam covers: AC-DC circuits; Antennas - wave propagation; Audio; Basic math; Batteries; Block diagrams; Decibels; Digital concepts; Electronic component nomenclature; Inductance capacitance-reactance; Integrated circuits; Safety Precautions ESD; Semiconductors; Test equipment; and Video. Specialty exams are: (1) Avionics; (2) Biomedical; (3) Computer; (4) Consumer Electronics; (5) Industrial; (6) Radio Communications; (7) Satellite; (8) Telecommunications; and (9) Video Distribution. **Preparatory Materials:** *CET Exam Book,* Third Edition and *Improving TV Signal Reception* (study manuals). Training programs, monographs, videotapes, and seminars available. **Examination Frequency:** Throughout the year. **Examination Sites:** Exam given at sites throughout the U.S. **Re-examination:** May retake exam once. **Fees:** $40.

■ 1518 ■

Certified Electronics Technician (Associate) (CET)

International Society of Certified
    Electronics Technicians (ISCET)
2708 W. Berry St.
Fort Worth, TX 76109
Phone: (817)921-9101
Fax: (817)921-3741
Clyde W. Nabors, Exec.Dir.

Recipient: Electronics technicians. **Educational/Experience Requirements:** Less than four years experience. Candidates with more than four years experience may qualify for Certified Electronics Technician (Journeyman) designation (see separate entry). **Certification Requirements:** Successful completion of exam. Exam covers: Basic electronics; DC and AC circuits; Math; Transistors; and Troubleshooting. **Renewal:** Every four years. **Preparatory Materials:** Study guides, practice exams, books, tapes, service aids, and training kits available. **Examination Sites:** Exam given at sites throughout the U.S. and internationally, or by arrangement with proctor. **Examination Type:** Multiple-choice. **Fees:** $25.

■ 1519 ■

Certified Electronics Technician (Journeyman) (CET)

International Society of Certified
    Electronics Technicians (ISCET)
2708 W. Berry St.
Fort Worth, TX 76109
Phone: (817)921-9101
Fax: (817)921-3741
Clyde W. Nabors, Exec.Dir.

Recipient: Electronics technicians. **Educational/Experience Requirements:** Four years experience. Candidates with less than four years experience may qualify for Certified Electronics Technician (Associate) designation (see separate entry). **Certification Requirements:** Successful completion of general exam and one specialty exam. General exam covers: Basic electronics; DC and AC circuits; Math; Transistors; and Troubleshooting. Specialty exams are: (1) Audio, covering: Amplifiers and sound quality; Compact disc and tape players; Digital and analog; Radio; Speaker installation; System set-up; Troubleshooting; and Turntables; (2) Communications, covering servicing two-way transceivers (basic communication theory, deviation, quieting, receivers, sensitivity, theory, transmitters, and troubleshooting); (3) Computer, covering: Basic arithmetic and logic operations as related to computer theory; Computer organiza-

tion; Input and output equipment; Memory and storage; Operation of computer systems, with emphasis on hardware; Software and programming; and Troubleshooting; (4) Consumer, covering: Antennas and transmission lines; Digital and linear circuits in consumer electronics; Servicing problems on televisions and VCRs; Troubleshooting consumer products; and Use of test equipment; (5) Industrial, covering: Basic logic circuits and functions; Differential amplifiers; Elements of numeric control; Items and circuits, including closed loop feedback, thyratons, and SCR control; Power factor; Switches; and Transducers; (6) Medical, covering: Differential amplifier applications; Electrical safety and accuracy of calibration for electromedical instruments; Instrumentation; Measurements; Need for prompt in-house service; Operational amplifier applications; and Telemetry; (7) Radar, covering: Antennas; Continuous wave radar operation; CRT display systems and their power supplies; Pulse radar; Receivers; Transmission lines; and Transmitters; and (8) Video, covering: Camcorders; Cameras and monitors; 8mm video; Microprocessors used in video operations; NTSC standards; Operations of electronics and mechanical systems in video cassette recorders; Test signals; and Video basics. **Renewal:** Every four years. **Preparatory Materials:** Study guides, practice exams, books, tapes, service aids, and training kits available. **Examination Sites:** Exam given at sites in the U.S., Canada, and internationally, or by arrangement with proctor. **Examination Type:** Multiple-choice. **Re-examination:** There is a $12.50 fee to retake exam. **Fees:** $25.

■ 1520 ■

Certified Satellite Installer (CSI)

Electronics Technicians Association,
    International (ETA-I)
602 N. Jackson
Greencastle, IN 46135
Phone: (317)653-8262
Fax: (317)653-8262
Anne Voiles, Admin.

Recipient: Satellite installers. **Educational/Experience Requirements:** Four years combined education and experience. **Certification Requirements:** Successful completion of exam. Exam covers: Amps-preamps; Cable leakage; EMI-TI; Frequency bands; MATV; Radar basics; RF components; and TVRO. **Preparatory Materials:** *CET Exam Book*, Third Edition and *Improving TV Signal Reception* (study manuals). Training programs, monographs, videotapes, and seminars available. **Examination**

Frequency: Throughout the year. **Examination Sites:** Exam given at sites throughout the U.S. **Re-examination:** May retake exam once. **Fees:** $40.

■ 1521 ■

Master Certified Electronics Technician (MASTER CET)

Electronics Technicians Association,
    International (ETA-I)
602 N. Jackson
Greencastle, IN 46135
Phone: (317)653-8262
Fax: (317)653-8262
Anne Voiles, Admin.

Recipient: Electronics technicians. **Educational/Experience Requirements:** Four years combined education and experience. **Certification Requirements:** Successful completion of exam. Must complete general exam and six specialty exams. General exam covers: AC-DC circuits; Antennas - wave propagation; Audio; Basic math; Batteries; Block diagrams; Decibels; Digital concepts; Electronic component nomenclature; Inductance-capacitance-reactance; Integrated circuits; Safety Precautions - ESD; Semiconductors; Test equipment; and Video. Specialty exams are: (1) Biomedical; (2) Computer; (3) Consumer Electronics; (4) Industrial; (5) Radio Communications; (6) Satellite; (7) Telecommunications; and (8) Video Distribution. **Preparatory Materials:** *CET Exam Book*, Third Edition and *Improving TV Signal Reception* (study manuals). Training programs, monographs, videotapes, and seminars available. **Examination Frequency:** Throughout the year. **Examination Sites:** Exam given at sites throughout the U.S. **Re-examination:** May retake exam once. **Fees:** $90.

■ 1522 ■

Senior Certified Electronics Technician (SCET)

Electronics Technicians Association,
    International (ETA-I)
602 N. Jackson
Greencastle, IN 46135
Phone: (317)653-8262
Fax: (317)653-8262
Anne Voiles, Admin.

Recipient: Electronics technicians. **Educational/Experience Requirements:** Eight years experience and hold Certified Electronics Technician (CET) designation (see separate entry). **Certification Requirements:** Successful completion of specialty exam not taken when awarded

CET designation. Specialty exams are: (1) Avionics; (2) Biomedical; (3) Computer; (4) Consumer Electronics; (5) Industrial; (6) Radio Communications; (7) Satellite; (8) Telecommunications; and (9) Video Distribution. **Preparatory Materials:** *CET Exam Book,* Third Edition and *Improving TV Signal Reception* (study manuals). Training programs, monographs, videotapes, and seminars available. **Examination Frequency:** Throughout the year. **Examination Sites:** Exam given at sites throughout the U.S. **Fees:** $65.

Electroplaters and Surface Finishers

1523

Certified Electroplater-Finisher (CEF)

American Electroplaters and Surface Finishers Society (AESF) 12644 Research Pkwy. Orlando, FL 32826-3298 Phone: (407)281-6441 Fax: (407)281-6446

Recipient: Electroplaters and surface finishers. **Educational/Experience Requirements:** High school diploma and three years experience. **Membership:** Not required. **Certification Requirements:** Successful completion of exam. Exam covers: Alloy plating; Anodizing of aluminum; Art and science of rinsing; Bright acid copper; Carbon treatment and filtration; Chemistry 1 and 2; Chromate conversion coatings; Cleaning and pickling; Cyanide copper; Decorative chromium; Electricity; Electrochemistry; Electroless plating; Electroplating plastics; Hard chromium; Hull cell tests; Metallic corrosion; Metallic and inorganic finishes; Nickel plating; Phosphating; Precious metals; Recycle and recovery; Testing and evaluation; Treating CN and chromate rinses; and Zinc and cadmium. **Renewal:** none. **Preparatory Materials:** AESF Illustrated Lectures Series, Training Course in Electroplating and Surface Finishing, or home study course available. AESF branches and community colleges and universities offer courses. Correspondence courses also available. **Examination Frequency:** Throughout the year. **Examination Sites:** Exam given at sites throughout the U.S. or by arrangement with proctor. **Re-examination:** There is a $50 fee to retake exam. **Fees:** $100.

1524

Certified Electroplater Finisher - Specialist in Electronics (CEF-SE)

American Electroplaters and Surface Finishers Society (AESF) 12644 Research Pkwy. Orlando, FL 32826-3298 Phone: (407)281-6441 Fax: (407)281-6446

Recipient: Electroplaters and surface finishers who specialize in electronic applications. **Educational/Experience Requirements:** Must hold Certified Electroplater-Finisher (CEF) designation (see separate entry) and meet experience criteria. **Membership:** Not required. **Certification Requirements:** Successful completion of exam. **Examination Frequency:** Throughout the year. **Examination Sites:** Exam given at sites throughout the U.S.

1525

Electronics Specialist, Certified (ESC)

American Electroplaters and Surface Finishers Society (AESF) 12644 Research Pkwy. Orlando, FL 32826-3298 Phone: (407)281-6441 Fax: (407)281-6446

Recipient: Electroplaters and surface finishers who specialize in electronic applications. **Membership:** Not required. **Certification Requirements:** Successful completion of exam. **Examination Frequency:** Throughout the year. **Examination Sites:** Exam given at sites throughout the U.S.

Heating, Air-Conditioning, and Refrigeration Mechanics

1526

CFC Technician Certification, Type I

National Association of Plumbing-Heating-Cooling Contractors (NAPHCC) 180 S. Washington St. PO Box 6808 Falls Church, VA 22046-1148 Phone: (703)237-8100 Fax: (703)237-7442 Toll Free: (800)533-7694

Recipient: Technicians approved by U.S. Environmental Protection Agency to perform installation, service, maintenance, or repair functions on small/home air conditioning and refrigeration appliances. **Membership:** Not required. **Certification Requirements:** Successful completion of exam. Exam covers: Clean Air Act/EPA requirements; Dehydration; Global warming; Leak detection; Montreal Protocol; Ozone depletion; Recovery, recycling, and reclamation; Recovery techniques; Refrigeration; Safety; Shipping; and Substitute refrigerants and oils. **Preparatory Materials:** *Responsible CFC Technician's Handbook* (reference). Seminar also available. **Examination Sites:** Exam given by correspondence. **Waiting Period to Receive Scores:** 30 days. **Fees:** $15 (members); $25 (nonmembers).

1527

CFC Technician Certification, Type II

National Association of Plumbing-Heating-Cooling Contractors (NAPHCC) 180 S. Washington St. PO Box 6808 Falls Church, VA 22046-1148 Phone: (703)237-8100 Fax: (703)237-7442 Toll Free: (800)533-7694

Recipient: Technicians approved by U.S. Environmental Protection Agency to perform installation, service, maintenance, or repair functions on high pressure air conditioning and refrigeration appliances. **Membership:** Not required. **Certification Requirements:** Successful completion of exam. **Preparatory Materials:** *Responsible CFC Technician's Handbook* (reference). Seminar also available. **Examination Sites:** Exam given by arrangement with proctor.

1528

CFC Technician Certification, Type III

National Association of Plumbing-Heating-Cooling Contractors (NAPHCC) 180 S. Washington St. PO Box 6808 Falls Church, VA 22046-1148 Phone: (703)237-8100 Fax: (703)237-7442 Toll Free: (800)533-7694

Recipient: Technicians approved by U.S. Environmental Protection Agency to perform installation, service, maintenance, or repair functions on low pressure air conditioning and refrigeration appliances. **Membership:** Not required. **Certification Requirements:** Successful completion of exam. **Preparatory Materials:** *Responsible CFC Technician's Handbook* (reference). Seminar also available. **Examination Sites:** Exam given by arrangement with proctor.

1529

CFC Technician Certification, Universal

National Association of
    Plumbing-Heating-Cooling
    Contractors (NAPHCC)
180 S. Washington St.
PO Box 6808
Falls Church, VA 22046-1148
Phone: (703)237-8100
Fax: (703)237-7442
Toll Free: (800)533-7694

Recipient: Technicians approved by U.S. Environmental Protection Agency to perform installation, service, maintenance, or repair functions on small/home, high pressure, and low pressure air conditioning and refrigeration appliances. **Membership:** Not required. **Certification Requirements:** Successful completion of exam. **Preparatory Materials:** *Responsible CFC Technician's Handbook* (reference). Seminar also available. **Examination Sites:** Exam given by arrangement with proctor.

1530

Refrigerant Recovery Certification

North American Retail Dealers
    Association (NARDA)
Ten E. 22nd St.
Lombard, IL 60148
Phone: (708)953-8956
Fax: (708)953-9510
Toll Free: (800)394-TEST
Gail Hoppe, Admin.

Recipient: Professionals who recover refrigerant from small appliances defined as Type I by U.S. Environmental Protection Administration (EPA). **Certification Requirements:** Successful completion of self-study course and two-section exam. **Preparatory Materials:** Training manual provided. **Examination Frequency:** Throughout the year. **Examination Sites:** Exam given by correspondence. **Re-examination:** Must only retake section failed. **Fees:** $22. **Endorsed By:** Association of Home Appliance Manufacturers.

1531

Refrigerant Transition and Recovery Type I Certification

Air Conditioning Contractors of
    America (ACCA)
1712 New Hampshire Ave., NW
Washington, DC 20009
Phone: (202)483-9370
Fax: (202)232-8545
Lisa Wolf CAE, Exec.Dir.

Recipient: HVACR technicians who recover and contain refrigerant from small appliances defined as Type I by U.S. Environmental Protection Agency (EPA). **Membership:** Not required. **Certification Requirements:** Successful completion of course of study and four-section exam. Course of study covers: (1) Refrigerant Chemistry and Applications, including: Blend fractionation; Blend temperature glide; Molecular structure: CFCs, HCFCs, and HFCs; Origin and destination; Refrigerant blends; Refrigerant nomenclature; and Superheat and supercooling calculation methods for near azeotropic blends; (2) Refrigerant Oils and Their Applications, including: Alkylbenzene; Estors; Glycols; Mineral oils; Oil additives; Oil groups; Oil properties; and Synthetic oils; (3) Ozone Depletion, including: Effects on environment; Effects on human health, including cataracts, immune system, and skin cancer; Global warming; Sources of CFCs; Stratospheric and atmospheric ozone; Stratospheric ozone depletion; and Other impacts; (4) Montreal Protocol, including: Chemicals included in Protocol; Early concerns and controls; Ozone depletion potential (ODP); and Reassessments and updates to Protocol; (5) Legislation and Regulation, including: CFC excise tax; Clean Air Act Amendment (Class I and II substances); National recycling and emission reduction program, including enforcement and recommended forms; and Phaseout of production and consumption of Class I and II substances; (6) Recovery, Recycling, and Reclamations, including: Changing storage tanks during recovery; Equipment used for recovery and recycling; Process definitions; Recovery and recycling equipment standards; Refrigerant containment options; Refrigerant reclamation; Refrigerant recovery; and Refrigerant recycling; (7) Containers Safe Handling and Transport of Refrigerants, including: ARI Guideline "K"; CFC and HCFC warning labels; Cylinders used in recovery; Disposable and returnable cylinders; Handling of recovered refrigerants; Refillable cylinders, including filling cylinders and refilling precautions; Safe disposal requirements; and Vehicular transportation; (8) Conservation - Servic-

ing and Testing, including: CFC demand in 2000; Installation requirements; Leak detectors for alternative refrigerants; Leak testing; Prohibition against venting; Refrigerant leaks; Service aperture; Service practice requirements; Service-related suggestions; and Soldering and brazing techniques; (9) Waste Oil, including: Categories of waste oil; and Disposal; and (10) High Pressure and Low Pressure Industrial/Commercial Chillers, including: Common safety related questions; Equipment room/job site requirements; Oil/refrigerant relationships; Planning and acting for the future; R-12/R-134a procedure for retrofit; R-123, including compatibility and handling and performance; Recovery; Refrigeration decomposition; Retrofitting chillers with alternative refrigerants; Retrofitting existing equipment to R134a; Safety group classification system; Safety and handling procedures; and Transition refrigerants. **Preparatory Materials:** Instructor, refresher, and training manuals available. Video guide also available. **Examination Frequency:** Throughout the year. **Examination Sites:** Exam given by arrangement with proctor. **Examination Type:** Multiple-choice. **Re-examination:** Must only retake section failed. Fees to retake exam are: $65 (one to two sections); $70 (three sections); $75 (four sections). **Endorsed By:** U.S. Environmental Protection Agency.

1532

Refrigerant Transition and Recovery Type II Certification

Air Conditioning Contractors of
    America (ACCA)
1712 New Hampshire Ave., NW
Washington, DC 20009
Phone: (202)483-9370
Fax: (202)232-8545
Lisa Wolf CAE, Exec.Dir.

Recipient: HVACR technicians who recover and contain refrigerant from high pressure and very high pressure air conditioning and refrigeration systems defined as Type II by U.S. Environmental Protection Agency (EPA). **Membership:** Not required. **Certification Requirements:** Successful completion of course of study and four-section exam. Course of study covers: (1) Refrigerant Chemistry and Applications, including: Blend fractionation; Blend temperature glide; Molecular structure: CFCs, HCFCs, and HFCs; Origin and destination; Refrigerant blends; Refrigerant nomenclature; and Superheat and supercooling calculation methods for near azeotropic blends; (2) Refrigerant Oils and Their Applications, including: Alkylbenzene; Estors;

Glycols; Mineral oils; Oil additives; Oil groups; Oil properties; and Synthetic oils; (3) Ozone Depletion, including: Effects on environment; Effects on human health, including cataracts, immune system, and skin cancer; Global warming; Sources of CFCs; Stratospheric and atmospheric ozone; Stratospheric ozone depletion; and Other impacts; (4) Montreal Protocol, including: Chemicals included in Protocol; Early concerns and controls; Ozone depletion potential (ODP); and Reassessments and updates to Protocol; (5) Legislation and Regulation, including: CFC excise tax; Clean Air Act Amendment (Class I and II substances); National recycling and emission reduction program, including enforcement and recommended forms; and Phaseout of production and consumption of Class I and II substances; (6) Recovery, Recycling, and Reclamations, including: Changing storage tanks during recovery; Equipment used for recovery and recycling; Process definitions; Recovery and recycling equipment standards; Refrigerant containment options; Refrigerant reclamation; Refrigerant recovery; and Refrigerant recycling; (7) Containers Safe Handling and Transport of Refrigerants, including: ARI Guideline "K"; CFC and HCFC warning labels; Cylinders used in recovery; Disposable and returnable cylinders; Handling of recovered refrigerants; Refillable cylinders, including filling cylinders and refilling precautions; Safe disposal requirements; and Vehicular transportation; (8) Conservation - Servicing and Testing, including: CFC demand in 2000; Installation requirements; Leak detectors for alternative refrigerants; Leak testing; Prohibition against venting; Refrigerant leaks; Service aperture; Service practice requirements; Service-related suggestions; and Soldering and brazing techniques; (9) Waste Oil, including: Categories of waste oil; and Disposal; and (10) High Pressure and Low Pressure Industrial/ Commercial Chillers, including: Common safety related questions; Equipment room/job site requirements; Oil/ refrigerant relationships; Planning and acting for the future; R-12/R-134a procedure for retrofit; R-123, including compatibility and handling and performance; Recovery; Refrigeration decomposition; Retrofitting chillers with alternative refrigerants; Retrofitting existing equipment to R134a; Safety group classification system; Safety and handling procedures; and Transition refrigerants. **Preparatory Materials:** Instructor, refresher, and training manuals available. Video guide also available. **Examination Frequency:** Throughout the year. **Examination Sites:** Exam given by arrangement with proctor. **Examination Type:**

Multiple-choice. **Re-examination:** Must only retake section failed. Fees to retake exam are: $65 (one to two sections); $70 (three sections); $75 (four sections). **Endorsed By:** U.S. Environmental Protection Agency.

1533

Refrigerant Transition and Recovery Type III Certification
Air Conditioning Contractors of America (ACCA)
1712 New Hampshire Ave., NW
Washington, DC 20009
Phone: (202)483-9370
Fax: (202)232-8545
Lisa Wolf CAE, Exec.Dir.

Recipient: HVACR technicians who recover and contain refrigerant from low pressure air conditioning and refrigeration systems defined as Type III by U.S. Environmental Protection Agency (EPA). **Membership:** Not required. **Certification Requirements:** Successful completion of course of study and four-section exam. Course of study covers: (1) Refrigerant Chemistry and Applications, including: Blend fractionation; Blend temperature glide; Molecular structure: CFCs, HCFCs, and HFCs; Origin and destination; Refrigerant blends; Refrigerant nomenclature; and Superheat and supercooling calculation methods for near azeotropic blends; (2) Refrigerant Oils and Their Applications, including: Alkylbenzene; Estors; Glycols; Mineral oils; Oil additives; Oil groups; Oil properties; and Synthetic oils; (3) Ozone Depletion, including: Effects on environment; Effects on human health, including cataracts, immune system, and skin cancer; Global warming; Sources of CFCs; Stratospheric and atmospheric ozone; Stratospheric ozone depletion; and Other impacts; (4) Montreal Protocol, including: Chemicals included in Protocol; Early concerns and controls; Ozone depletion potential (ODP); and Reassessments and updates to Protocol; (5) Legislation and Regulation, including: CFC excise tax; Clean Air Act Amendment (Class I and II substances); National recycling and emission reduction program, including enforcement and recommended forms; and Phaseout of production and consumption of Class I and II substances; (6) Recovery, Recycling, and Reclamations, including: Changing storage tanks during recovery; Equipment used for recovery and recycling; Process definitions; Recovery and recycling equipment standards; Refrigerant containment options; Refrigerant reclamation; Refrigerant recovery; and Refrigerant recycling; (7) Containers Safe

Handling and Transport of Refrigerants, including: ARI Guideline "K"; CFC and HCFC warning labels; Cylinders used in recovery; Disposable and returnable cylinders; Handling of recovered refrigerants; Refillable cylinders, including filling cylinders and refilling precautions; Safe disposal requirements; and Vehicular transportation; (8) Conservation - Servicing and Testing, including: CFC demand in 2000; Installation requirements; Leak detectors for alternative refrigerants; Leak testing; Prohibition against venting; Refrigerant leaks; Service aperture; Service practice requirements; Service-related suggestions; and Soldering and brazing techniques; (9) Waste Oil, including: Categories of waste oil; and Disposal; and (10) High Pressure and Low Pressure Industrial/Commercial Chillers, including: Common safety related questions; Equipment room/job site requirements; Oil/refrigerant relationships; Planning and acting for the future; R-12/R-134a procedure for retrofit; R-123, including compatibility and handling and performance; Recovery; Refrigeration decomposition; Retrofitting chillers with alternative refrigerants; Retrofitting existing equipment to R134a; Safety group classification system; Safety and handling procedures; and Transition refrigerants. **Preparatory Materials:** Instructor, refresher, and training manuals available. Video guide also available. **Examination Frequency:** Throughout the year. **Examination Sites:** Exam given by arrangement with proctor. **Examination Type:** Multiple-choice. **Re-examination:** Must only retake section failed. Fees to retake exam are: $65 (one to two sections); $70 (three sections); $75 (four sections). **Endorsed By:** U.S. Environmental Protection Agency.

1534

Refrigerant Transition and Recovery Universal Certification
Air Conditioning Contractors of America (ACCA)
1712 New Hampshire Ave., NW
Washington, DC 20009
Phone: (202)483-9370
Fax: (202)232-8545
Lisa Wolf CAE, Exec.Dir.

Recipient: HVACR technicians who recover and contain refrigerant from both low and high pressure air conditioning and refrigeration systems defined as Type I, II, or III by U.S. Environmental Protection Administration (EPA). **Membership:** Not required. **Certification Requirements:** Successful completion of course of study and four-section exam. Course of study covers: (1) Refrigerant

Chemistry and Applications, including: Blend fractionation; Blend temperature glide; Molecular structure: CFCs, HCFCs, and HFCs; Origin and destination; Refrigerant blends; Refrigerant nomenclature; and Superheat and supercooling calculation methods for near azeotropic blends; (2) Refrigerant Oils and Their Applications, including: Alkylbenzene; Estors; Glycols; Mineral oils; Oil additives; Oil groups; Oil properties; and Synthetic oils; (3) Ozone Depletion, including: Effects on environment; Effects on human health, including cataracts, immune system, and skin cancer; Global warming; Sources of CFCs; Stratospheric and atmospheric ozone; Stratospheric ozone depletion; and Other impacts; (4) Montreal Protocol, including: Chemicals included in Protocol; Early concerns and controls; Ozone depletion potential (ODP); and Reassessments and updates to Protocol; (5) Legislation and Regulation, including: CFC excise tax; Clean Air Act Amendment (Class I and II substances); National recycling and emission reduction program, including enforcement and recommended forms; and Phaseout of production and consumption of Class I and II substances; (6) Recovery, Recycling, and Reclamations, including: Changing storage tanks during recovery; Equipment used for recovery and recycling; Process definitions; Recovery and recycling equipment standards; Refrigerant containment options; Refrigerant reclamation; Refrigerant recovery; and Refrigerant recycling; (7) Containers Safe Handling and Transport of Refrigerants, including: ARI Guideline "K"; CFC and HCFC warning labels; Cylinders used in recovery; Disposable and returnable cylinders; Handling of recovered refrigerants; Refillable cylinders, including filling cylinders and refilling precautions; Safe disposal requirements; and Vehicular transportation; (8) Conservation - Servicing and Testing, including: CFC demand in 2000; Installation requirements; Leak detectors for alternative refrigerants; Leak testing; Prohibition against venting; Refrigerant leaks; Service aperture; Service practice requirements; Service-related suggestions; and Soldering and brazing techniques; (9) Waste Oil, including: Categories of waste oil; and Disposal; and (10) High Pressure and Low Pressure Industrial/Commercial Chillers, including: Common safety related questions; Equipment room/job site requirements; Oil/refrigerant relationships; Planning and acting for the future; R-12/R-134a procedure for retrofit; R-123, including compatibility and handling and performance; Recovery; Refrigeration decomposition; Retrofitting chillers with alternative refrigerants; Retrofitting ex-

isting equipment to R134a; Safety group classification system; Safety and handling procedures; and Transition refrigerants. **Preparatory Materials:** Instructor, refresher, and training manuals available. Video guide also available. **Examination Frequency:** Throughout the year. **Examination Sites:** Exam given by arrangement with proctor. **Examination Type:** Multiple-choice. **Re-examination:** Must only retake section failed. Fees to retake exam are: $65 (one to two sections); $70 (three sections); $75 (four sections). **Endorsed By:** U.S. Environmental Protection Agency.

Home Appliance and Power Tool Repairers

1535

Certified Appliance Technician (CAT)
International Society of Certified Electronics Technicians (ISCET)
2708 W. Berry St.
Fort Worth, TX 76109
Phone: (817)921-9101
Fax: (817)921-3741
Clyde W. Nabors, Exec.Dir.

Recipient: Appliance technicians. **Educational/Experience Requirements:** Four years experience. **Certification Requirements:** Successful completion of exam. Exam covers: Cooking equipment; Dishwashers; Electrical circuits and components; Laundry equipment; Refrigeration systems; and Trash compactors. **Renewal:** Every four years. **Preparatory Materials:** Study guides, practice exams, books, tapes, service aids, and training kits available. **Examination Sites:** Exam given at sites throughout the U.S. and internationally, or by arrangement with proctor. **Examination Type:** Multiple-choice. **Re-examination:** There is a $12.50 fee to retake exam. **Fees:** $25.

Hydraulic or Pneumatic Product Technicians and Engineers

1536

Fluid Power Electrician
Fluid Power Society (FPS)
2433 N. Mayfair Rd., Ste. 111
Milwaukee, WI 53226
Phone: (414)257-0910
Fax: (414)257-4092

Recipient: Fluid power electricians. **Membership:** Not required. **Certification Requirements:** Successful completion of exam. **Renewal:** Every five years. Recertification based on experience, continuing education, courses taught, and professional involvement in fluid power organizations. **Preparatory Materials:** Review manual, including exam content outline, list of suggested study references, and sample questions, provided. Review training sessions available. **Examination Frequency:** Throughout the year. **Examination Sites:** Exam given at sites throughout the U.S. **Examination Type:** Multiple-choice.

1537

Fluid Power Engineer
Fluid Power Society (FPS)
2433 N. Mayfair Rd., Ste. 111
Milwaukee, WI 53226
Phone: (414)257-0910
Fax: (414)257-4092

Recipient: Fluid power engineers. **Membership:** Not required. **Certification Requirements:** Successful completion of exam. **Renewal:** Every five years. Recertification based on experience, continuing education, courses taught, and professional involvement in fluid power organizations. **Preparatory Materials:** Review manual, including exam content outline, list of suggested study references, and sample questions, provided. Review training sessions available. **Examination Frequency:** Throughout the year. **Examination Sites:** Exam given at sites throughout the U.S. **Examination Type:** Multiple-choice.

1538

Fluid Power Specialist
Fluid Power Society (FPS)
2433 N. Mayfair Rd., Ste. 111
Milwaukee, WI 53226
Phone: (414)257-0910
Fax: (414)257-4092

Recipient: Individuals involved in systems design, selection, and application of hydraulic and/or pneumatic products, including system design and installation supervision. **Membership:** Not required. **Certification Requirements:** Successful completion of exam. Exam covers: Electrical control; Fluid power fundamentals; Hydraulics and pneumatics; Relay logic; Specialized fluid power topics; and Systems. **Renewal:** Every five years. **Preparatory Materials:** Study course and guide, including exam content outline, list of study references, and sample questions, provided. Review sessions available. **Examination Frequency:** Throughout the year. **Examination Sites:** Exam given at sites throughout the U.S. **Examination Type:** Multiple-choice. **Waiting Period to Receive Scores:** Four-six weeks. **Re-examination:** Fee to retake exam is $35. **Fees:** $110 (members); $160 (nonmembers); $45 (students).

1539

Hydraulic Technician
Fluid Power Society (FPS)
2433 N. Mayfair Rd., Ste. 111
Milwaukee, WI 53226
Phone: (414)257-0910
Fax: (414)257-4092

Recipient: Individuals responsible for developing hydraulic fluid power circuit specifications, testing and modifying circuits and systems, writing technical reports, and preparing graphs and schematics. **Membership:** Not required. **Certification Requirements:** Successful completion of exam. **Renewal:** Every five years. Recertification based on experience, continuing education, courses taught, and professional involvement in fluid power organizations. **Preparatory Materials:** Review manual, including exam content outline, list of suggested study references, and sample questions, provided. Review training sessions available. **Examination Frequency:** Throughout the year. **Examination Sites:** Exam given at sites throughout the U.S. **Examination Type:** Multiple-choice. **Waiting Period to Receive Scores:** Four-six weeks. **Re-examination:** Fee to retake exam is $35. **Fees:** $110 (members); $160 (nonmembers); $45 (students).

1540

Industrial Hydraulic Mechanic
Fluid Power Society (FPS)
2433 N. Mayfair Rd., Ste. 111
Milwaukee, WI 53226
Phone: (414)257-0910
Fax: (414)257-4092

Recipient: Mechanics who install, maintain, and repair industrial hydraulic systems and components. **Membership:** Not required. **Certification Requirements:** Successful completion of written and practical exams. Practical exam consists of six hands-on performance exercises. Exercises may include: Bending and flaring tubing; Drawing fluid power circuits; Identification of fittings, fasteners, and fluid power symbols; Making hose connections; and Setting pressure relief and pressure reducing valves. Candidates

who hold either Mobile Hydraulic Technician or Pneumatic Technician designations (see separate entries) must only successfully complete written exam. **Renewal:** Every five years. Recertification based on experience, continuing education, courses taught, and professional involvement in fluid power organizations. **Preparatory Materials:** Review manual, including exam content outline, list of suggested study references, and sample questions, provided. Review training sessions available. **Examination Frequency:** Throughout the year. **Examination Sites:** Exam given at sites throughout the U.S. **Examination Type:** Multiple-choice. **Waiting Period to Receive Scores:** One month. **Re-examination:** Must only retake exam failed. Fees to retake exams are: $35 (written); $50 (practical). **Fees:** $95 (members); $130 (nonmembers); $45 (students).

1541

Mobile Hydraulic Mechanic
Fluid Power Society (FPS)
2433 N. Mayfair Rd., Ste. 111
Milwaukee, WI 53226
Phone: (414)257-0910
Fax: (414)257-4092

Recipient: Mechanics who install, maintain, and repair mobile hydraulic systems and components. **Membership:** Not required. **Certification Requirements:** Successful completion of written and practical exams. Practical exam consists of six hands-on performance exercises. Exercises may include: Bending and flaring tubing; Drawing fluid power circuits; Identification of fittings, fasteners, and fluid power symbols; Making hose connections; and Setting pressure relief and pressure reducing valves. Candidates who hold either Industrial Hydraulic Technician or Pneumatic Technician designations (see separate entries) must only successfully complete written exam. **Renewal:** Every five years. Recertification based on experience, continuing education, courses taught, and professional involvement in fluid power organizations. **Preparatory Materials:** Review manual, including exam content outline, list of suggested study references, and sample questions, provided. Review training sessions available. **Examination Frequency:** Throughout the year. **Examination Sites:** Exam given at sites throughout the U.S. **Examination Type:** Multiple-choice. **Waiting Period to Receive Scores:** One month. **Re-examination:** Must only retake exam failed. Fees to retake exams are: $35 (written); $50 (practical). **Fees:** $95 (members); $130 (nonmembers); $45 (students).

1542

Pneumatic Mechanic
Fluid Power Society (FPS)
2433 N. Mayfair Rd., Ste. 111
Milwaukee, WI 53226
Phone: (414)257-0910
Fax: (414)257-4092

Recipient: Mechanics who install, maintain, and repair pneumatic systems and components. **Membership:** Not required. **Certification Requirements:** Successful completion of written and practical exams. Practical exam consists of six hands-on performance exercises. Exercises may include: Bending and flaring tubing; Drawing fluid power circuits; Identification of fittings, fasteners, and fluid power symbols; Making hose connections; and Setting pressure relief and pressure reducing valves. Candidates who hold either Industrial Hydraulic Technician or Mobile Hydraulic Technician designations (see separate entries) must only successfully complete written exam. **Renewal:** Every five years. Recertification based on experience, continuing education, courses taught, and professional involvement in fluid power organizations. **Preparatory Materials:** Review manual, including exam content outline, list of suggested study references, and sample questions, provided. Review training sessions available. **Examination Frequency:** Throughout the year. **Examination Sites:** Exam given at sites throughout the U.S. **Examination Type:** Multiple-choice. **Waiting Period to Receive Scores:** One month. **Re-examination:** Must only retake exam failed. Fees to retake exams are: $35 (written); $50 (practical). **Fees:** $95 (members); $130 (nonmembers); $45 (students).

1543

Pneumatic Technician
Fluid Power Society (FPS)
2433 N. Mayfair Rd., Ste. 111
Milwaukee, WI 53226
Phone: (414)257-0910
Fax: (414)257-4092

Recipient: Individuals responsible for developing pneumatic fluid power circuit specifications, testing and modifying circuits and systems, writing technical reports, and preparing graphs and schematics. **Membership:** Not required. **Certification Requirements:** Successful completion of exam. **Renewal:** Every five years. Recertification based on experience, continuing education, courses taught, and professional involvement in fluid power organizations. **Preparatory**

Materials: Review manual, including exam content outline, list of suggested study references, and sample questions, provided. Review training sessions available. **Examination Frequency:** Throughout the year. **Examination Sites:** Exam given at sites throughout the U.S. **Examination Type:** Multiple-choice. **Waiting Period to Receive Scores:** Four-six weeks. **Re-examination:** Fee to retake exam is $35. **Fees:** $110 (members); $160 (nonmembers); $45 (students).

Line Installers and Cable Splicers

1544

Installer Certification
Society of Cable Television
   Engineers (SCTE)
669 Exton Commons
Exton, PA 19341
Phone: (610)363-6888
Fax: (610)363-5898
Toll Free: (800)542-5040
E-mail: MarvinSCTE@AOL.com
Marvin Nelson, Dir.

Recipient: Entry-level cable television installers. **Number of Certified Individuals:** 2900. **Educational/Experience Requirements:** Successful completion of classroom and hands-on training in cable installation. **Membership:** Required. **Certification Requirements:** Successful completion of three exams. **Renewal:** Every three years. Recertification based on successful completion of exam or receiving letter of recommendation from supervisor. There is no renewal fee. **Preparatory Materials:** *Installer Certification Manual* (reference). **Examination Frequency:** Six-12 times per year. **Examination Sites:** Exams given at SCTE chapter meetings. **Pass/Fail Rate:** 60% pass exams the first time. **Waiting Period to Receive Scores:** Two weeks. **Re-examination:** There is no waiting period to retake exams. **Fees:** $25.

Machinists

1545

Certified Forms Press Operator
IBFI - The International
   Association
2111 Wilson Blvd., Ste. 350
Arlington, VA 22201-3042
Phone: (703)841-9191
Fax: (703)522-5750
Cathleen R. Marros, Contact

Recipient: Forms press operators. **Membership:** Not required. **Certification Requirements:** Successful completion of Forms Press Operator Training Course and exam. Course covers: Business and printing basics; Controls; Finishing; Multi-color printing; Press components; Processing; Safety; Total quality management (TQM); UV printing; and Webbing. **Preparatory Materials:** *Business Forms Glossary of Design and Production Terms, Color and Its Reproduction,* and *Lithography Primer* (texts). Operator's Trainee's Package, glossary of terms, instructor' manual, and one thousand four-color 35mm slides and illustrations provided. **Examination Frequency:** monthly. **Waiting Period to Receive Scores:** One week.

Nondestructive Testing Personnel

1546

Nondestructive Testing Level III
American Society for
   Nondestructive Testing (ASNT)
1711 Arlingate Ln.
PO Box 28518
Columbus, OH 43228-0518
Phone: (614)274-6003
Fax: (614)274-6899
Toll Free: (800)222-2768
Robert T. Anderson, Mgr.

Recipient: Nondestructive testing professionals. **Educational/Experience Requirements:** Must meet one of the following requirements: (1) Bachelor's degree in engineering or a physical science and one year of experience; (2) Successful completion of two years of college coursework in engineering or a physical science and two years experience; or (3) Four years experience. Experience must be in position where candidate set up and calibrated equipment and interpreted and evaluated results with respect to applicable codes, standards, and specifications. **Membership:** Not required. **Certification Requirements:** Successful

completion of basic exam and one method exam. Basic exam covers: (1) Administration of *SNT-TC-IA,* 1992 Edition, and *ASNT CP-189,* 1991, NDT Personnel Certification Programs; (2) Basic Materials, Fabrication, and Production Technology, including: Dimensional metrology; Materials processing (adhesive bonding, brazing, casting, forging, heat treatment, machining, soldering, surface treatment, welding, and other methods); and Properties of materials, origin of discontinuities, and failure modes; and (3) General Familiarity with Other NDT Methods, including: Acoustic emission testing; Eddy current and flux leakage testing; Leak testing; Liquid penetrant testing; Magnetic particle testing; Neutron radiography; Radiography (isotope methods, safety, and X-ray); Ultrasonic testing; and Visual testing. Method exams are: (1) Acoustic Emission, covering: Acoustic emission procedures, codes, standards and specifications, and health and safety considerations; Acoustic emission test techniques and applications; Equipment, instrumentation, and signal processing; Interpretation/evaluation of indications; Kaiser and felicity effects; Materials and deformation; Principles and theory; Sensing acoustic emissions; and Sources of acoustic emission; (2) Dye Penetrant, covering: Control and measurement of process variables; Effect of discontinuities; Equipment and materials; Interpretation/evaluation of indications; Principles and theory; Procedures, codes, standards and specifications, and health and safety considerations; Selection of test techniques; and Techniques and calibrations; (3) Eddy Current, covering: Applications; Control and measurement of process variables; Coupling, magnetization, and field strength; Effect of discontinuities; Interpretation/evaluation of indications; Principles and theory; Procedures, codes, standards and specifications, and health and safety considerations; Selection of techniques; and Techniques/calibrations; (4) Infrared/Thermal, covering: Equipment/material systems; Exothermic/endothermic investigations; Personal safety; Physical principles and theory; Procedures; and Techniques; (5) Leak, including: Bubble tests; Evacuated and pressurized systems; Halogen diode detector test; Interpretation/evaluation; Mass spectrometer test; Personnel safety considerations; Physical principles and theory; Pressure change/measurement test; Procedures, codes, standards and specifications, and health and safety considerations; Systems principles; Techniques and calibration of test equipment; and Test equipment and materials; (6) Magnetic Particle, covering: Effects and discontinuities; Equipment and materials;

Inspection of materials, interpretation, and evaluation; Magnetization by electric current; Principles and theory; Procedures, codes, standards and specifications, and health and safety considerations; Selection of proper method; and Types of discontinuities indicated; (7) Neutron Radiography, covering: Interpretation/evaluation; Neutron detectors and detection; Neutron imaging considerations; Neutron radiographic process; Neutron sources; Personnel safety and neutron radiation protection; Physical principles and theory; Procedures, codes, standards and specifications, and health and safety considerations; and Techniques and calibrations; (8) Radiographic, covering: Effects of discontinuities; Interpretation and evaluation; Personnel safety and radiation protection; Physical principles and theory; Procedures, codes, standards and specifications, and health and safety considerations; Radiation detectors and detection; Radiation sources, equipment, and materials; Radiographic process; and Techniques and calibration; (9) Ultrasonic, covering: Effect of discontinuities; Equipment (instruments and transducers); Immersion and contact techniques and applications; Interpretation/ evaluation; Material and transducer manipulation; Principles and theory; Procedures, codes, standards and specifications, and health and safety considerations; Reference reflectors for calibration; and Test result variability causes; and (10) Visual, covering: Equipment/material; Health and safety; Interpretation/evaluation; Principles/ theory; Procedures; and Techniques/ calibration. May attempt up to six method exams. **Renewal:** Recertification based on either successful completion of exam or submission of application. **Preparatory Materials:** *A Guide to Personnel Qualification and Certification, ASNT Standard for Qualification and Certification of Nondestructive Testing Personnel,* and *Introduction to Nondestructive Testing: A Training Guide* (references). List of suggested references, refresher courses, and study guides available. **Examination Frequency:** Throughout the year. **Examination Sites:** Exam given at sites throughout the U.S. and internationally. **Re-examination:** Must wait one year to retake exams.

Picture Framers

1547

Certified Picture Framer (CPF)
Professional Picture Framers
  Association (PPFA)
4305 Sarellen Rd.
Richmond, VA 23231-4311
Phone: (804)226-0430
Fax: (804)222-2175
Rex P. Boynton, Exec.Dir.

Recipient: Picture framers who frame or are consulted on presentation and preservation of wide range of artwork. **Educational/Experience Requirements:** One year of experience. **Membership:** Not required. **Certification Requirements:** Successful completion of exam. Exam covers: Conservation techniques; Fitting and backing; Frame cutting, joining, and finishing; Glazing; Handling; Lining; Materials; Matting techniques; Moulding/frame selection; Mounting; and Storage. **Renewal:** Every four years. **Preparatory Materials:** Study guide, including sample questions and list of suggested references, provided. Seminars and workshops available. **Examination Frequency:** Throughout the year. **Examination Sites:** Exam given at sites throughout the U.S. **Examination Type:** Multiple-choice. **Waiting Period to Receive Scores:** Four-six weeks. **Fees:** $200 (members); $300 (nonmembers).

Safety Equipment Installers

1548

LPI Certified Designer/Inspector
Lightning Protection Institute (LPI)
3365 N. Arlington Heights Rd., Ste.
  J
Arlington Heights, IL 60004
Phone: (708)255-3003
Fax: (708)577-7276
Toll Free: (800)488-6864
Andy Larsen, Exec.Dir.

Recipient: Lightning protection equipment designers and inspectors. **Educational/Experience Requirements:** Experience in the field. **Membership:** Not required. **Certification Requirements:** Successful completion of two exams. **Preparatory Materials:** List of study references provided. **Fees:** $150 (members); $300 (nonmembers).

1549

LPI Certified Journeyman Installer
Lightning Protection Institute (LPI)
3365 N. Arlington Heights Rd., Ste.
  J
Arlington Heights, IL 60004
Phone: (708)255-3003
Fax: (708)577-7276
Toll Free: (800)488-6864
Andy Larsen, Exec.Dir.

Recipient: Lightning protection equipment installers. **Membership:** Not required. **Certification Requirements:** Successful completion of two exams. **Renewal:** Every year. Recertification based on successful completion of exam. **Preparatory Materials:** List of study references provided. **Examination Frequency:** By arrangement. **Examination Type:** Multiple-choice; short answer. **Waiting Period to Receive Scores:** 30 days. **Fees:** $150 (members); $300 (nonmembers).

1550

LPI Certified Master Installer
Lightning Protection Institute (LPI)
3365 N. Arlington Heights Rd., Ste.
  J
Arlington Heights, IL 60004
Phone: (708)255-3003
Fax: (708)577-7276
Toll Free: (800)488-6864
Andy Larsen, Exec.Dir.

Recipient: Lightning protection equipment installers. **Educational/Experience Requirements:** Experience in the field. **Membership:** Not required. **Certification Requirements:** Successful completion of two exams. **Preparatory Materials:** List of study references provided. **Fees:** $150 (members); $300 (nonmembers).

1551

**LPI Certified Master
  Installer/Designer**
Lightning Protection Institute (LPI)
3365 N. Arlington Heights Rd., Ste.
  J
Arlington Heights, IL 60004
Phone: (708)255-3003
Fax: (708)577-7276
Toll Free: (800)488-6864
Andy Larsen, Exec.Dir.

Recipient: Lightning protection equipment installers and designers. **Educational/Experience Requirements:** Experience in the field. **Membership:** Not required. **Certification Requirements:** Successful completion of exam. **Preparatory Materials:** List of study references provided. **Fees:** $150 (members); $300 (nonmembers).

Construction Trades and Extractive Occupations

Bricklayers and Stonemasons

1552

Certified Fireplace Hearth Specialist
Hearth Education Foundation
3019 Perry Ln.
Austin, TX 78731
Phone: (512)450-0987
Fax: (512)450-1649
Tracy Wurzel, Exec.Dir.

Recipient: Professionals involved in residential fireplace hearth installation. **Membership:** Not required. **Certification Requirements:** Successful completion of exam. **Renewal:** Every three years. Recertification based on successful completion of exam. Renewal fees are: $60 (members); $75 (nonmembers). **Preparatory Materials:** *Fireplace Installer Training Manual* (reference). **Examination Type:** Multiple-choice; true or false. **Fees:** $150 (members); $195 (nonmembers). **Endorsed By:** National Fire Protection Association.

1553

Certified Gas Appliance Hearth Specialist
Hearth Education Foundation
3019 Perry Ln.
Austin, TX 78731
Phone: (512)450-0987
Fax: (512)450-1649
Tracy Wurzel, Exec.Dir.

Recipient: Professionals involved in residential gas appliance hearth installation. **Membership:** Not required. **Certification Requirements:** Successful completion of exam. **Renewal:** Every three years. Recertification based on successful comple-

tion of exam. Renewal fees are: $60 (members); $75 (nonmembers). **Preparatory Materials:** Manual (reference). **Examination Type:** Multiple-choice; true or false. **Fees:** $245 (members); $320 (nonmembers). **Endorsed By:** National Fire Protection Association.

1554

Certified Pellet Appliance Hearth Specialist
Hearth Education Foundation
3019 Perry Ln.
Austin, TX 78731
Phone: (512)450-0987
Fax: (512)450-1649
Tracy Wurzel, Exec.Dir.

Recipient: Professionals involved in residential pellet appliance hearth installation. **Membership:** Not required. **Certification Requirements:** Successful completion of exam. **Renewal:** Every three years. Recertification based on successful completion of exam. **Preparatory Materials:** Manual (reference). **Examination Type:** Multiple-choice; true or false. **Endorsed By:** National Fire Protection Association.

1555

Certified Woodstove Hearth Specialist
Hearth Education Foundation
3019 Perry Ln.
Austin, TX 78731
Phone: (512)450-0987
Fax: (512)450-1649
Tracy Wurzel, Exec.Dir.

Recipient: Professionals involved in residential woodstove hearth installation. **Membership:** Not required. **Certification Requirements:** Successful completion of

exam. **Renewal:** Every three years. Recertification based on successful completion of exam. Renewal fees are: $60 (members); $75 (nonmembers). **Preparatory Materials:** Manual (reference). **Examination Type:** Multiple-choice; true or false. **Fees:** $245 (members); $320 (nonmembers). **Endorsed By:** National Fire Protection Association.

Concrete Masons and Terrazzo Workers

1556

Concrete Field Testing Technician - Grade I
American Concrete Institute (ACI)
PO Box 19150
Detroit, MI 48219-0150
Phone: (313)532-2600
Fax: (313)538-0655
Richard F. Heitzmann, Dir.

Recipient: Professionals working with freshly mixed concrete. **Membership:** Not required. **Certification Requirements:** Successful completion of written and performance exams. Exams cover the following American Society for Testing and Materials (ASTM) standards: (1) Sampling Freshly Mixed Concretes; (2) Slump of Hydraulic Cement Concrete; (3) Unit Weight, Yield, and Air Content (Gravimetric) of Concrete; (4) Air Content of Freshly Mixed Concrete by the Pressure Method; (5) Air Content of Freshly Mixed Concrete by the Volumetric Method; (6) Making and Curing Concrete Test Specimens in the Field; and (7) Temperature of Freshly Mixed Portland-Cement Concrete. Performance exam requires demonstration of six of the standards and verbal description of sampling freshly mixed concretes. **Renewal:** Every five years. Recertification based on successful completion of written and performance exams. **Preparatory Materials:** Training course available. **Examination Type:** Multiple-choice.

`1557`

Concrete Flatwork Finisher
American Concrete Institute (ACI)
PO Box 19150
Detroit, MI 48219-0150
Phone: (313)532-2600
Fax: (313)538-0655
Richard F. Heitzmann, Dir.

Recipient: Professionals involved in concrete flatwork. **Educational/Experience Requirements:** One year (1500 hours) experience. Experience must include placing, finishing, edging, jointing, curing, and protection of concrete flatwork. May qualify for Concrete Flatwork Technician designation (see separate entry) with less experience. **Membership:** Not required. **Certification Requirements:** Must successfully complete the following: (1) Written or oral exam. Exam covers: Basic concrete technology; Concrete materials and mix proportioning; Concrete control tests; Proper use of finishing tools; Placing, consolidating, and finishing; and Edging, jointing, curing, and protection; and (2) Performance evaluation. Requirement can be met either by demonstrating technique or providing documentation of two additional years (3000 hours) experience and competency in the field. **Renewal:** Every five years. Recertification based on successful completion of exam. **Preparatory Materials:** List of required reading provided. Training course available. **Examination Type:** Multiple-choice; true or false.

`1558`

Concrete Flatwork Technician
American Concrete Institute (ACI)
PO Box 19150
Detroit, MI 48219-0150
Phone: (313)532-2600
Fax: (313)538-0655
Richard F. Heitzmann, Dir.

Recipient: Professionals involved in concrete flatwork. **Membership:** Not required. **Certification Requirements:** Successful completion of written or oral exam. Exam covers: Basic concrete technology; Concrete materials and mix proportioning; Concrete control tests; Proper use of finishing tools; Placing, consolidating, and finishing; and Edging, jointing, curing, and protection. May qualify for Concrete Flatwork Finisher

designation (see separate entry) with increased experience. **Renewal:** Every five years. Recertification based on successful completion of exam. **Preparatory Materials:** List of required reading provided. Training course available. **Examination Type:** Multiple-choice; true or false.

`1559`

Concrete Laboratory Testing Technician - Grade I
American Concrete Institute (ACI)
PO Box 19150
Detroit, MI 48219-0150
Phone: (313)532-2600
Fax: (313)538-0655
Richard F. Heitzmann, Dir.

Recipient: Professionals working with aggregates and concrete. **Membership:** Not required. **Certification Requirements:** Successful completion of written and performance exams. Exams cover the following American Society for Testing and Materials (ASTM) standards: (1) Capping Cylindrical Concrete Specimens; (2) Compressive Strength of Cylindrical Concrete Specimens; (3) Sampling Aggregates; (4) Reducing Field Samples of Aggregate to Testing Size; (5) Materials Finer than Number 200 Sieve for Mineral Aggregates by Washing; (6) Sieve Analysis of Fine and Coarse Aggregates; (7) Unit Weight and Voids in Aggregate; (8) Specific Gravity and Absorption of Coarse Aggregate; (9) Specific Gravity and Absorption of Fine Aggregate; (10) Total Moisture Content of Aggregate by Drying; and (11) Organic Impurities in Fine Aggregates for Concrete. **Renewal:** Every six years. Recertification based on successful completion of written and performance exams. **Preparatory Materials:** Training course available. **Examination Type:** Multiple-choice.

`1560`

Concrete Laboratory Testing Technician - Grade II
American Concrete Institute (ACI)
PO Box 19150
Detroit, MI 48219-0150
Phone: (313)532-2600
Fax: (313)538-0655
Richard F. Heitzmann, Dir.

Recipient: Professionals working with aggregates and concrete. **Educational/Experience Requirements:** One year of experience and/or education and hold Concrete Laboratory Testing Technician - Grade I designation (see separate entry). **Membership:** Not required.

Certification Requirements: Successful completion of written and performance exams. Exams cover the following ACI and American Society for Testing and Materials (ASTM) standards: (1) Evaluation of Strength Test Results of Concrete; (2) Selecting Proportions for Concrete; (3) Soundness of Aggregates by Use of Sodium Sulfate or Magnesium Sulfate; (4) Lightweight Pieces of Aggregate; (5) Resistance to Degradation of Small-Size Coarse Aggregates by Abrasion and Impact in the Los Angeles Machine; (6) Resistance to Degradation of Large-Size Coarse Aggregates by Abrasion and Impact in the Los Angeles Machine; (7) Clay Lumps and Friable Particles in Aggregate; (8) Flexural Strength of Concrete (Using Simple Method with Third-Point Loading); (9) Making and Curing Concrete Test Specimens in the Laboratory; (10) Molds for Forming Concrete Test Cylinders Vertically; (11) Splitting Tensile Strength of Cylindrical Concrete Specimens; and (12) Obtaining and Testing Drilled Cores and Sawed Beams. **Renewal:** Every six years. Recertification based on successful completion of written and performance exams. **Preparatory Materials:** Training course available. **Examination Type:** Multiple-choice.

Handlers, Equipment Cleaners, Helpers, and Laborers

`1561`

Certified Chimney Sweep
Chimney Sweep Institute of America (CSIA)
16021 Industrial Dr., Ste. 8
Gaithersburg, MD 20877
Phone: (301)963-6900
Fax: (301)963-0838
John E. Bittner, Exec.Dir.

Recipient: Individuals involved in chimney service industry. **Membership:** Not required. **Certification Requirements:** Successful completion of exam. **Renewal:** Recertification based on accumulation of 40 continuing education units (CEUs). **Preparatory Materials:** Study manual available. **Examination Frequency:** Eight times per year or by arrangement. **Examination Sites:** Exam given at CSIA seminars and sites throughout the U.S. **Examination Type:** Multiple-choice. **Pass/Fail Rate:** 54% pass exam the first time. **Waiting Period to Receive Scores:** Immediately. **Re-examination:** Must wait 30 days to retake exam. **Fees:** $60 (members); $95 (nonmembers).

Plumbers and Pipefitters

1562

Certified Irrigation Designer (CID)
Irrigation Association (IA)
8260 Wilow Oak Corp Dr.
Fairfax, VA 22031
Phone: (703)573-3551
Fax: (703)573-1913
Charles Putnam, Exec.Dir.

Recipient: Irrigation system designers. **Educational/Experience Requirements:** Must meet one of the following requirements: (1) Three years experience; (2) Two years experience and 60 points earned through college courses (five points each), IA Short Course (one point per day), and manufacturer's course (one point per day); or (3) Hold Certified Irrigation Contractor (CIC) or Certified Irrigation Manager (CIM) designations (see separate entries). **Membership:** Not required. **Certification Requirements:** Successful completion of irrigation industry, general, and specialty exams. Irrigation industry exam covers: Basic electricity and hydraulics; Irrigation scheduling and terminology; Pumps; and Soil/water/plant relationships. General and specialty exams are given in agriculture and landscape/turf specialties. General agriculture and landscape/turf specialty exams cover: Electrical; Hydraulics; Irrigation equipment; Precipitation/application rates; Pumps; Scheduling; Soil/water/plant relationships; and Spacing. Specialty agricultural exams are: Drip/Micro-Irrigation; Sprinkler; and Surface. General landscape/turf specialty exams are: Commercial; Golf Course; and Residential. Candidates who hold Certified Irrigation Manager (CIM) or Certified Irrigation Contractor (CIC) designations (see separate entries) are exempt from irrigation industry exam. **Renewal:** Every three years. Recertification based on accumulation of continuing education units (CEUs). **Preparatory Materials:** *Irrigation,* Fifth Edition. Study materials available. **Examination Frequency:** Throughout the year. **Examination Sites:** Exam given at annual exposition, IA headquarters, and by arrangement with proctor. **Examination Type:** Multiple-choice. **Re-examination:** Must wait 30 days to retake exams. May retake exams three times. There is a $75 fee to retake each exam. **Fees:** $250 (members); $350 (affiliate society/organization member); $450 (nonmembers).

1563

Certified in Plumbing Engineering (CIPE)
American Society of Plumbing Engineers (ASPE)
3617 Thousand Oaks Blvd., No. 210
Westlake Village, CA 91362-3649
Phone: (805)495-7120
Fax: (805)495-4861
John S. Shaw CAE, Exec.Dir.

Recipient: Plumbing engineers. **Number of Certified Individuals:** 1515. **Membership:** Not required. **Certification Requirements:** Successful completion of exam. Exam covers: Scope of work; System design; Specifications; and Construction services. **Renewal:** none. **Examination Type:** Multiple-choice. **Fees:** $110 (member); $170 (nonmembers).

1564

Certified Plumbing Inspector
International Association of Plumbing and Mechanical Officials (IAPMO)
20001 Walnut Dr., S.
Walnut, CA 91789-2825
Phone: (909)595-8449
Fax: (909)594-1537
George H. Howe, Mgr.

Recipient: Plumbing inspectors. **Number of Certified Individuals:** 3000. **Educational/Experience Requirements:** none. **Membership:** Not required. **Certification Requirements:** Successful completion of exam. Exam covers the Uniform Plumbing Code. **Renewal:** Every three years. Recertification based on successful completion of exam. Renewal fee is $45. **Examination Frequency:** monthly. **Examination Sites:** Exam given at sites throughout the U.S. **Examination Type:** Multiple-choice. **Pass/Fail Rate:** 70% pass exam. **Waiting Period to Receive Scores:** 60 days. **Re-examination:** Must wait 120 days before retaking exam.

1565

Certified Pump Installer (CPI)
National Ground Water Association (NGWA)
6375 Riverside Dr.
PO Box 9050
Dublin, OH 43017-0950
Phone: (614)761-1711
Fax: (614)761-3446
Toll Free: (800)551-7379

Recipient: Ground water pump installers. **Educational/Experience Require-**ments: Two years experience. **Membership:** Not required. **Certification Requirements:** Successful completion of general exam and exam in one of the following pump installation specialty areas: (1) Domestic one to three horsepower; (2) Domestic three to 20 horsepower; and (3) Industrial and municipal, more than 20 horsepower. **Renewal:** Every year. Recertification based on accumulation of seven hours of continuing education. Renewal fees are: $25 (members); $200 (nonmembers). **Preparatory Materials:** Study guide available. **Examination Frequency:** Throughout the year. **Examination Sites:** Exam given at 20 sites throughout the U.S. **Examination Type:** Multiple-choice; true or false. **Re-examination:** Must wait 90 days to retake exam. Must successfully complete both exams within one year. **Fees:** $55 (members); $155 (nonmembers).

1566

Certified Well Driller (CWD)
National Ground Water Association (NGWA)
6375 Riverside Dr.
PO Box 9050
Dublin, OH 43017-0950
Phone: (614)761-1711
Fax: (614)761-3446
Toll Free: (800)551-7379

Recipient: Ground water well drillers. **Educational/Experience Requirements:** Two years experience. **Membership:** Not required. **Certification Requirements:** Successful completion of general exam and exam in one of the following specialty areas: (1) Air rotary drilling in rock material; (2) Air rotary drilling in unconsolidated material; (3) Boring and auguring in unconsolidated material; (4) Cable tool drilling in rock material; (5) Cable tool drilling in unconsolidated material; (6) Jetting and driving wells in unconsolidated material; (7) Monitoring and construction; (8) Mud rotary drilling in rock material; (9) Mud rotary drilling in unconsolidated material; (10) Reverse rotary drilling in unconsolidated material; and (11) Well servicing and maintenance. **Renewal:** Every year. Recertification based on accumulation of seven hours of continuing education through attendance at conventions and meetings, successful completion of college and correspondence courses, seminars, speaking engagements or teaching, conducting safety programs, and presenting slide shows, demonstrations, or talks to community service groups, schools, and other organizations. Renewal fees are: $25 (members); $200 (nonmembers). **Preparatory Materials:** Study guides available.

Examination Frequency: Throughout the year. **Examination Sites:** Exam given at 20 sites throughout the U.S. **Examination Type:** Multiple-choice; true or false. **Re-examination:** Must wait 90 days to retake exam. Must successfully complete both exams within one year. **Fees:** $55 (members); $155 (nonmembers).

`1567`

Certified Well Driller/Pump Installer (CWD/PI)
National Ground Water Association (NGWA)
6375 Riverside Dr.
PO Box 9050
Dublin, OH 43017-0950
Phone: (614)761-1711
Fax: (614)761-3446
Toll Free: (800)551-7379

Recipient: Ground water pump installers and well drillers. **Educational/ Experience Requirements:** Two years experience. **Membership:** Not required. **Certification Requirements:** Must hold both Certified Pump Installer (CPI) and Certified Well Driller (CWD) designations (see separate entries). **Renewal:** Every year. Recertification based on accumulation of seven hours of continuing education. Renewal fees are: $25 (members); $200 (nonmembers). **Preparatory Materials:** Study guides available. **Examination Frequency:** Throughout the year. **Examination Sites:** Exam given at 20 sites throughout the U.S. **Examination Type:** Multiple-choice; true or false.

`1568`

Master Ground Water Contractor (MGWC)
National Ground Water Association (NGWA)
6375 Riverside Dr.
PO Box 9050
Dublin, OH 43017-0950
Phone: (614)761-1711
Fax: (614)761-3446
Toll Free: (800)551-7379

Recipient: Ground water contractors involved in pump installation or well construction. **Educational/Experience Requirements:** Must meet the following requirements: (1) Five years experience in operational or supervisory capacity; and (2) Successful completion of general and specialty exams (except monitoring well construction) required to earn Certified Pump Installer (CPI) and Certified Well Driller (CWD) designations (see separate entries). **Membership:** Not required. **Certification Requirements:** Successful completion of exam. **Renewal:** Every year. Recertification based on accumulation of seven hours of continuing education. Renewal fees are: $25 (members); $200 (nonmembers). **Preparatory Materials:** Study guide available. **Examination Frequency:** Throughout the year. **Examination Sites:** Exam given at 20 sites throughout the U.S. **Examination Type:** Essay; multiple-choice. **Re-examination:** Must wait 90 days to retake exam.

Production Occupations

Metalworking and Plastics-Working Occupations

Jewelers

1569

Advanced Executive Manager
Diamond Council of America
(DCA)
9140 Ward Pkwy.
Kansas City, MO 64114
Phone: (816)444-3500
Fax: (816)444-0330
Jerry Fogel CAE, Exec.Dir.

Recipient: Jewelry store executives.
Membership: Required. **Certification Requirements:** Successful completion of correspondence course series. **Endorsed By:** Distance Education and Training Council; Gemological Institute of America.

1570

Certified Clockmaker (CC)
American
  Watchmakers-Clockmakers
  Institute (AWI)
3700 Harrison Ave.
Cincinnati, OH 45211
Phone: (513)661-3838
Fax: (513)661-3131

Recipient: Clockmakers. **Membership:** Not required. **Certification Requirements:** Successful completion of written and practical exams. **Preparatory Materials:** Handbook, including list of suggested references and sample questions, provided. Video tapes available. **Examination Frequency:** By arrangement. **Examination Sites:** Exam given by arrangement with proctor. **Examination Type:** Completion; essay; matching; multiple-choice; short answer; true or false. **Pass/Fail Rate:** Must only retake exam failed. May retake exams one time. Must suc-

cessfully complete exams within one year. **Fees:** $75 (members); $120 (non-members).

1571

Certified Diamontologist
Diamond Council of America
(DCA)
9140 Ward Pkwy.
Kansas City, MO 64114
Phone: (816)444-3500
Fax: (816)444-0330
Jerry Fogel CAE, Exec.Dir.

Recipient: Diamontologists. **Membership:** Required. **Certification Requirements:** Successful completion of 26 lesson correspondence course and exam. Course covers all aspects of diamontology. Each lesson is followed by either exam or self-study test. **Preparatory Materials:** Supplemental reading packet and overview of course provided. **Endorsed By:** Distance Education and Training Council; Gemological Institute of America.

1572

Certified Gemologist (CG)
American Gem Society (AGS)
8881 W. Sahara Ave.
Las Vegas, NV 89117
Phone: (702)255-6500
Fax: (702)255-7420
Tina L. LeDuc, Educ.Coord.

Recipient: Gemologists. **Educational/Experience Requirements:** Hold either Registered Jeweler (RJ) or Registered Supplier (RS) designation (see separate entries) for one year. **Membership:** Required. **Certification Requirements:** Successful completion of Gemological Institute of America's (GIA) Diamond Program and hold one of the following:

(1) Graduate Gemologist designation or Gemology Diploma from GIA; (2) Fellow of the Gemological Association of Great Britain designation; or (3) Graduate certificate from Texas Institute of Jewelry Technology/Paris Junior College. **Renewal:** Every year. Recertification based on successful completion of exam.

1573

Certified Managerial Associate
Diamond Council of America
(DCA)
9140 Ward Pkwy.
Kansas City, MO 64114
Phone: (816)444-3500
Fax: (816)444-0330
Jerry Fogel CAE, Exec.Dir.

Recipient: Jewelry store middle-managers. **Membership:** Required. **Certification Requirements:** Successful completion of correspondence course series. **Endorsed By:** Distance Education and Training Council; Gemological Institute of America.

1574

Certified Master Clockmaker (CMC)
American
  Watchmakers-Clockmakers
  Institute (AWI)
3700 Harrison Ave.
Cincinnati, OH 45211
Phone: (513)661-3838
Fax: (513)661-3131

Recipient: Clockmakers. **Membership:** Not required. **Certification Requirements:** Successful completion of written and practical exams. Candidates who hold Certified Clockmaker (CC) designation (see separate entry) may upgrade to CMC designation by meeting the following requirements: (1) 18 months experience as CC; (2) Successful completion of written exam; and (3) Successful completion of fabrication project. **Preparatory Materials:** Handbook, including list of suggested references and sample questions, provided. Video tapes available. **Examination Frequency:** By arrangement. **Examination Sites:** Exam given by arrangement with proctor. **Examination Type:** Completion; matching; multiple-choice; short answer; true or false. **Re-examination:** Must only retake exam failed. May retake exams one time. Must successfully complete exams within one year. **Fees:** $100 (members); $145 (non-members).

1575

Certified Master Electronic Watchmaker (CMEW)

American Watchmakers-Clockmakers Institute (AWI)
3700 Harrison Ave.
Cincinnati, OH 45211
Phone: (513)661-3838
Fax: (513)661-3131

Recipient: Makers of electronic and quartz watches. **Membership:** Not required. **Certification Requirements:** Successful completion of written and practical exams. **Preparatory Materials:** Handbook, including list of suggested references and sample questions, provided. Video tapes available. **Examination Frequency:** By arrangement. **Examination Sites:** Exam given by arrangement with proctor. **Examination Type:** Completion; matching; multiple-choice; short answer; true or false. **Re-examination:** Must only retake exam failed. May retake exams one time. Must successfully complete exams within one year. **Fees:** $75 (members); $120 (non-members).

1576

Certified Master Watchmaker (CMW)

American Watchmakers-Clockmakers Institute (AWI)
3700 Harrison Ave.
Cincinnati, OH 45211
Phone: (513)661-3838
Fax: (513)661-3131

Recipient: Watchmakers. **Membership:** Not required. **Certification Require-**

ments: Successful completion of written and practical exams. Candidates who hold Certified Watchmaker (CW) designation (see separate entry) may upgrade to CMW designation by meeting the following requirements: (1) 18 months experience as CW; (2) Successful construction of watch stem; and (3) Successful repair of automatic watch. **Preparatory Materials:** Handbook, including list of suggested references and sample questions, provided. Video tapes available. **Examination Frequency:** By arrangement. **Examination Sites:** Exam given by arrangement with proctor. **Examination Type:** Completion; matching; multiple-choice; short answer; true or false. **Pass/Fail Rate:** Must only retake exam failed. May retake exams one time. Must successfully complete exams within one year. **Fees:** $75 (members); $120 (non-members).

1577

Certified Watchmaker (CW)

American Watchmakers-Clockmakers Institute (AWI)
3700 Harrison Ave.
Cincinnati, OH 45211
Phone: (513)661-3838
Fax: (513)661-3131

Recipient: Watchmakers. **Membership:** Not required. **Certification Requirements:** Successful completion of written and practical exams. **Preparatory Materials:** Handbook, including list of suggested references and sample questions, provided. Video tapes available. **Examination Frequency:** By arrangement. **Examination Sites:** Exam given by arrangement with proctor. **Examination Type:** Completion; matching; multiple-choice; short answer; true or false. **Re-examination:** Must only retake exam failed. May retake exams one time. Must successfully complete exams within one year. **Fees:** $50 (members); $95 (non-members).

1578

Guild Gemologist

Diamond Council of America (DCA)
9140 Ward Pkwy.
Kansas City, MO 64114
Phone: (816)444-3500
Fax: (816)444-0330
Jerry Fogel CAE, Exec.Dir.

Recipient: Gemologists. **Membership:** Required. **Certification Requirements:**

Successful completion of 26 lesson correspondence course and exam. Course covers all aspects of gemology. **Preparatory Materials:** Supplemental reading packet and overview of course provided. **Endorsed By:** Distance Education and Training Council; Gemological Institute of America.

1579

Professional Sales Associate

Diamond Council of America (DCA)
9140 Ward Pkwy.
Kansas City, MO 64114
Phone: (816)444-3500
Fax: (816)444-0330
Jerry Fogel CAE, Exec.Dir.

Recipient: Jewelry store salespersons. **Membership:** Required. **Certification Requirements:** Successful completion of correspondence course series. **Endorsed By:** Distance Education and Training Council; Gemological Institute of America.

1580

Registered Jeweler (RJ)

American Gem Society (AGS)
8881 W. Sahara Ave.
Las Vegas, NV 89117
Phone: (702)255-6500
Fax: (702)255-7420
Tina L. LeDuc, Educ.Coord.

Recipient: Jewelers involved only in retail industry. **Educational/Experience Requirements:** Two years experience. **Membership:** Required. **Certification Requirements:** Successful completion of American Gem Society Way course and Diamonds or Colored Stones course offered by Gemological Institute of America. **Renewal:** Every year. Recertification based on successful completion of exam.

1581

Registered Supplier (RS)

American Gem Society (AGS)
8881 W. Sahara Ave.
Las Vegas, NV 89117
Phone: (702)255-6500
Fax: (702)255-7420
Tina L. LeDuc, Educ.Coord.

Recipient: Suppliers involved in wholesale phase of jewelry industry. **Educational/Experience Requirements:** Two years experience. **Membership:** Required. **Certification Requirements:** Successful completion of either American Gem Society Way course or Diamonds or Colored Stones course offered by Gemological Institute of America. **Renewal:** Every year. Recertification based on successful completion of exam.

Welders, Cutters, and Welding Machine Operators

1582

Certified Associate Welding Inspector (CAWI)
American Welding Society (AWS)
550 LeJeune Rd., NW
Miami, FL 33126
Phone: (305)443-9353
Fax: (305)443-7559
Toll Free: (800)443-9353
Dr. Frank G. DeLaurier, Exec.Dir.

Recipient: Welding inspectors who determine if a weldment meets the acceptance criteria of specific code, standard, or other document. Inspections must be done under the supervision of Certified Welding Instructor (CWI) (see separate entry). **Educational/Experience Requirements:** Must meet one of the following requirements: (1) Two years post-high school education in welding curriculum or engineering, engineering technology, or physical sciences, and six months experience; (2) High school diploma or equivalent and two years experience; (3) Eighth grade level of schooling and four years experience; (4) Less than eighth grade level of schooling and six years experience; or (5) Eighth grade level of schooling, one year of vocational education and training in a welding curriculum, and three years experience. All candidates must have understanding of SMAW, SAW, OFW, GTAW, FCAW, GMAW, SW, B, ESW, Thermal Cutting, and Mechanical Cutting, meet AWS's visual acuity standards, and have written verification of documented employment completed and signed by candidate's supervisor. Experience must be in occupational function that has direct relationship to weldments fabricated to code or standard and directly involved in one or more of the following: Construction; Design; Inspection; Production; and Repair. Trade/vocational courses and teaching experience can be substituted for up to two years of the five year experience requirement. **Certification Requirements:** Successful completion of exams which cover: (1) Code or standard; (2) Fundamentals, including: Basic on-the-job arithmetic; Inspector's duties; Mechanical properties of metals; Safety; Symbols; Weld discontinuities; and Welding and nondestructive testing processed; and (3) Practical application of welding inspection knowledge, including: Drawing/specification compliance; Mechanical testing; Nondestructive testing processes; Welding inspection; Welding procedure qualification; and Welder qualification. Candidates who hold designations awarded by other countries may be considered for certification. **Renewal:** Every three years. Recertification based on meeting AWS visual acuity standards and one of the following requirements: (1) Successful completion of exam; (2) Two years experience as welding inspector; or (3) One year experience as welding inspector and successful completion of AWS course. Nine years from the date of initial certification, and each nine years thereafter, recertification based on successful completion of practical section of CAWI exam.

1583

Certified Pipe Welder
United Association of Journeymen and Apprentices of the Plumbing and Pipe Fitting Industry of the United States and Canada
PO Box 37800
Washington, DC 20013
Phone: (202)628-5823
Fax: (202)628-5024

Recipient: Pipe welders. **Certification Requirements:** Successful completion of exam. **Endorsed By:** Mechanical Contractors Association of America.

1584

Certified Welder
American Welding Society (AWS)
550 LeJeune Rd., NW
Miami, FL 33126
Phone: (305)443-9353
Fax: (305)443-7559
Toll Free: (800)443-9353
Dr. Frank G. DeLaurier, Exec.Dir.

Recipient: Welders. **Educational/Experience Requirements:** Meet AWS minimum visual acuity standards (corrected or uncorrected). **Certification Requirements:** Successful completion of performance test in specific nondestructive or mechanical welding area. Must perform test welds under observation. **Renewal:** Every year. Recertification based on either successful completion of exam or employer certification of continued work performing welding in the de-fined area. **Re-examination:** May retake exam once. Must successfully complete exam within 30 days.

1585

Certified Welding Educator (CWE)
American Welding Society (AWS)
550 LeJeune Rd., NW
Miami, FL 33126
Phone: (305)443-9353
Fax: (305)443-7559
Toll Free: (800)443-9353
Dr. Frank G. DeLaurier, Exec.Dir.

Recipient: Classroom and hands-on welding instructors who have the responsibility to direct and perform operations associated with welder training classroom instruction. **Educational/Experience Requirements:** Must meet the following requirements: (1) High school diploma or equivalent; (2) Five years welding experience in occupational function that has direct relationship to weldments fabricated to code or standard and directly involved with either production, construction, inspection, or repair; and (3) Documentation of instructional experience and background meeting the requirements of the school or college where presently employed. **Membership:** Not required. **Certification Requirements:** Successful completion of the following three tests: (1) Certified Welding Inspector (CWI) or Certified Associate Welding Inspector (CAWI) (see separate entries) Practical exam or practical welding inspection including determining qualification standards from code or specification; (2) CWI or CAWI Inspector Fundamentals exam or written exam on fundamental welding principles including welding processes, nondestructive testing processes, safety, basic welding metallurgy, welding symbols, print reading, equipment, process/equipment troubleshooting, and basic arithmetic; and (3) Certified Welder (CW) (see separate entry) exam. **Renewal:** Every four years. Recertification based on two years employment in welding education.

1586

Certified Welding Inspector (CWI)
American Welding Society (AWS)
550 LeJeune Rd., NW
Miami, FL 33126
Phone: (305)443-9353
Fax: (305)443-7559
Toll Free: (800)443-9353
Dr. Frank G. DeLaurier, Exec.Dir.

Recipient: Welding inspectors who determine if a weldment meets the acceptance criteria of a specific code, standard, or other document. **Educational/ Experience Requirements:** Must meet one of the following requirements: (1) Associate degree or higher in engineering, engineering technology, physics, or physical sciences, and three years experience; (2) High school diploma or equivalent and five years experience; (3) Eighth grade level schooling with not less than ten years work experience in welding functions described above; or (4) Less than eighth grade level schooling and 15 years experience. All candidates must have understanding of SMAW, SAW, OFW, GTAW, FCAW, GMAW, SW, B, ESW, Thermal Cutting, and Mechanical Cutting and written verification of documented employment completed and signed by candidate's supervisor. Experience must be in occupational function that has direct relationship to weldments fabricated to code or standard and directly involved in one or more of the following: Construction; Design; Inspection; Production; and Repair. Trade/ vocational courses and teaching experience can be substituted for up to two years of the five year experience requirement. **Certification Requirements:** Successful completion of exams which cover: (1) Code or standard; (2) Fundamentals, including: Basic on-the-job arithmetic; Inspector's duties; Mechanical properties of metals; Safety; Symbols; Weld discontinuities; and Welding and nondestructive testing processes; and (3) Practical application of welding inspection knowledge, including: Drawing/ specification compliance; Mechanical testing; Nondestructive testing processes; Welding inspection; Welding procedure qualification; and Welder qualification. Candidates who hold designations awarded by other countries may be considered for certification. **Renewal:** Every three years. Recertification based on meeting AWS visual acuity standards and one of the following requirements: (1) Successful completion of exam; (2) Two years experience as welding inspector; or (3) One year experience as welding inspector and successful completion of AWS course. Nine years from the date of initial certification, and each nine years thereafter, recertification based on successful completion of practical section of CWI exam.

Accreditation Programs

Accreditation Programs

Accreditation

1587

Commission on Recognition of Postsecondary Accreditation (CORPA)
One Dupont Circle, NW, Ste. 305
Washington, DC 20036
Phone: (202)452-1433
Fax: (202)331-9571

Recipient: National private-sector agencies offering accreditation for postsecondary institutions and programs. 56. **Accreditation Requirements:** Accrediting agencies must document compliance with criteria in the following areas: (1) General Eligibility, requiring that agencies: Be non-governmental; Evaluate institution or program only by invitation and using stated purposes of institution or program; Maintain written policies and procedures; and Require self-assessment; (2) Protection of the Public, requiring that agencies: Have mechanisms to provide public correction of misleading or incorrect statements regarding accreditation status and content or reports and actions; Make available qualifications of individuals involved in agency's accreditation activities; and Make public current listing of institutions and/or programs affiliated with agency; (3) Protection of Interests of Institutions and Programs, requiring that agencies: Apply standards and criteria consistently; Encourage discussion during on-site review between site visitors and faculty, staff, administrators, students, and other interested parties; Provide fair appeals process; Provide fair and appropriate procedures for acting upon applications; and Provide written report and opportunity to respond to report; (4) General Accrediting Practices, requiring that agencies: Provide advance notice of proposed changes in objectives, criteria, and evaluating policies, and provide opportunity for comment on those proposed changes; Provide balance between academic and administrative personnel and between educators and practitioners in evaluation, policy, and decision making processes; and Provide written policies regarding conflict of interest which apply to all stages of accreditation process; (5) General Acceptance, requiring that agencies: Demonstrate there is demand for accrediting agency activity; and Demonstrate that various communities of interest, such as educators, practitioners, employers, and professional and public organizations, accept agency as authoritative; and (6) Professional Standing, requiring that agencies: Develop and apply accreditation policies and procedures to protect interests of students, benefit public, and improve quality of teaching, learning, and professional practice; Develop and interpret evaluative criteria to encourage institutional freedom and autonomy, improvement of institutions and programs, and sound educational experimentation and constructive innovation; and Require institution or program to evaluate on ongoing basis extent to which it achieves its purposes using data concerning educational outcomes and other indicators as appropriate to document how it uses results of evaluations for institutional and program improvement. **Preparatory Materials:** *Accredited Institutions of Postsecondary Education* and *Directory of Recognized Agencies and Supporters of Accreditation* (references).

Acupuncture

1588

National Accreditation Commission for Schools and Colleges of Acupuncture and Oriental Medicine (NACSCAOM)
8403 Colesville Rd., Ste. 370
Silver Spring, MD 20910
Phone: (301)608-9680
Fax: (301)608-9576
Penelope Ward, Dir.

Recipient: First professional master's degree and professional master's level certification and diploma programs in acupuncture or Oriental medicine with concentrations in both acupuncture and herbal therapies. **Number of Accredited Institutions:** 30. **Application Procedures:** Self-assessment required. Must document compliance with criteria in the following areas: (1) Purpose; (2) Legal Organization, including adherence to local, state, and federal laws and regulations; (3) Governance, including public representation; (4) Administration, including: Administrative staff; Chief administrative officer; and Organizational structure; (5) Records, covering accuracy and completeness of record keeping system; (6) Admissions, covering requirements; (7) Evaluation, including: Clinical acupuncture competence; Herbal therapy competence; Program; and Students; (8) Program of Staff, including: Clinical component; Core curriculum; Length; Professional competence; and Resident program; (9) Faculty, including: Qualifications; and Staff size; (10) Student Services and Activities, including: Objectives; Student assistance; and Student morale; (11) Library and Learning Resources, including: Equipment; and Objectives; (12) Physical Facilities and Equipment, including: Accessibility; Clinic; Herbal dispensary; Maintenance;

Media; and Safety; (13) Financial Resources, including: Accounting; Financial base; Financial management system; and Financial planning; and (14) Publications and Advertising, including: Catalog; and Dissemination of policies and procedures. **Accreditation Requirements:** Programs in acupuncture must be at least three years in length and follow at least two years of accredited postsecondary education. Programs in Oriental medicine must be at least four years in length and follow at least two years of accredited postsecondary education. Programs must: Be resident program; Demonstrate attainment of professional competence; Have adequate clinical component; and Include minimum core curriculum. On-site review required. Review includes discussion with faculty, staff, administrators, students, and other interested parties. May respond to on-site review. Programs must consider criticism and suggestions of visiting team, determine internal procedures for corrective action, and maintain self-assessment and improvement mechanisms. May respond to on-site review. **Renewal:** Every five years. Must also submit annual reports. **State Requirements:** Must meet all local, state, and federal regulations. **Preparatory Materials:** *Accreditation Handbook* (reference). **Fees:** Actual cost of on-site review; must also submit annual fee. **Accredited By:** Commission on Recognition of Postsecondary Accreditation; U.S. Department of Education. **Endorsed By:** Association of Specialized and Professional Accreditors; Council of Colleges of Acupuncture and Oriental Medicine.

Allied Health

1589

Accreditation Commission - Perfusion Education (AC-PE)
7108-C S. Alton Way
Englewood, CO 80112-2106
Phone: (303)741-3598
Fax: (303)741-3655
Annamarie Dubies-Appel, Exec.Dir.

Recipient: Review committee of Commission on Accreditation of Allied Health Education Programs (CAAHEP) (see separate entry) for one- to four-year training programs for perfusionists. **Number of Accredited Institutions:** 68. **Application Procedures:** Self-assessment, conducted by program faculty with input from administrators, students, employers of graduates, and other interested parties, required. Must address strengths and weaknesses of program, cover entire

range of educational operations, including ancillary services, and document compliance with criteria in the following areas: (1) Sponsorship; (2) Resources, including: Financial resources; General resources; Personnel, covering administrative personnel, clerical and support staff, faculty and instructional staff, medical director, professional development, and program director; and Physical resources, covering affiliated institutions, equipment and supplies, facilities, and learning resources, including instructional aids and library; (3) Students, including: Admission policies and procedures; Appeals; Evaluation; Guidance; and Health; (4) Operational Policies, including: Fair practices; and Student records; (5) Program Evaluation, including: Outcomes; and Results of ongoing program evaluation; (6) Curriculum, including: Instructional plan; Program organizational structure; and Required knowledge and skills; and (7) Maintaining and Administering Accreditation. **Accreditation Requirements:** Sponsoring institutions must assume primary responsibility for the following: Academic, didactic, and clinical educational experiences; Appointing qualified faculty; Ensuring financial support necessary for meeting commitments to matriculating and accepted students; Selecting students; and Granting degrees. Curriculum must include: Heart-lung bypass for adult, pediatric, and infant patients undergoing heart surgery; Long-term supportive extracorpeal circulation; and Special applications of technology. Program must include clinical experience and performance of circulation procedures. On-site review, verifying information provided in self-assessment, required. Review includes tour of facilities and interviews with chief executive officer, administrators of educational program, instructors, students, medical director, and members of admissions committee. May respond to on-site review. Possible accreditation decisions are: (1) Accreditation; (2) Probationary Accreditation, requiring correction of deficiencies; or (3) Withholding Accreditation, for programs in substantial noncompliance with standards. **Renewal:** Every five years (maximum). Renewal based on self-assessment and on-site review. **Preparatory Materials:** *Essentials and Guidelines for an Accredited Educational Program for the Perfusionist* (reference). **Accredited By:** Commission for Recognition of Postsecondary Accreditation; U.S. Department of Education. **Endorsed By:** American Association for Thoracic Surgery; American Board of Cardiovascular Perfusion; American Medical Association; American Society of Extra-Corporeal Technology; Commission on Accreditation of Allied Health Education Programs; Council on Medical Education; Council of Perfusion Program Directors; Society of Thoracic Surgeons; Society of Cardiovascular Anesthesiologists.

1590

Accreditation Council for Occupational Therapy Education (ACOTE)
American Occupational Therapy Association (AOTA)
4720 Montgomery Ln.
PO Box 31220
Bethesda, MD 20824-1220
Phone: (301)652-2682
Fax: (301)652-7711
Martha S. O'Connor, Dir.

Recipient: Educational programs for occupational therapists and therapy assistants at colleges, universities, medical schools, community, technical, and junior colleges, and post-secondary vocational technical schools and institutions. **Number of Accredited Institutions:** 168. **Application Procedures:** Self-assessment required. Must document compliance with standards. Must also formulate development plan and propose changes to improve program. **Accreditation Requirements:** Curriculum for occupational therapy assistants must include instruction in the following areas: Direction of program activity; Documentation of services; Field work education; Implementation of skills and knowledge; Management of assistive services; Normal and abnormal conditions across life span; Occupational therapy process; and Treatment planning. Curriculum for occupational therapists must include instruction in the following areas: Basic human sciences; Health and illness; Human development process; Specific life tasks and activities; and Theory and practice. Students must also successfully complete six months of supervised field experiences. On-site review required. May respond to on-site review. **Renewal:** Every five years (initial); every seven years thereafter. Renewal based on self-assessment and on-site review. **Preparatory Materials:** *Essentials and Guidelines for an Accredited Educational Program for the Occupational Therapist or Occupational Therapy Assistant* (reference). **Fees:** $6850; $850 (annual fee). **Accredited By:** Commission on Recognition of Postsecondary Accreditation; U.S. Department of Education.

1591

Accreditation Review Committee on Education for the Anesthesiologist's Assistant
515 N. State St., Ste. 7530
Chicago, IL 60610-4377
Phone: (312)464-4623
Fax: (312)464-5830
Lawrence M. Detmer, Dir.

Recipient: Review committee of Commission on Accreditation of Allied Health Education Programs (CAAHEP) (see separate entry) for two-year training programs for anesthesiologist's assistants. **Application Procedures:** Self-assessment, conducted by program faculty with input from administrators, students, employers of graduates, and other interested parties, required. Must address strengths and weaknesses of program, cover entire range of educational operations, including ancillary services, and document compliance with criteria in the following areas: (1) Sponsorship; (2) Resources, including: Financial resources; General resources; Personnel, including administrative personnel, clerical and support staff, faculty and instructional staff, medical director, professional development, and program director; and Physical resources, covering affiliated institutions, equipment and supplies, facilities, and learning resources, including instructional aids and library; (3) Students, including: Admission policies and procedures; Appeals; Evaluation; Guidance; and Health; (4) Operational Policies, including: Fair practices; and Student records; (5) Program Evaluation, including: Outcomes; and Results of ongoing program evaluation; (6) Curriculum, including: Instructional plan; Program organizational structure; and Required knowledge and skills; and (7) Maintaining and Administering Accreditation. **Accreditation Requirements:** Sponsoring institutions must assume primary responsibility for the following: Academic, didactic, and clinical educational experiences; Appointing qualified faculty; Ensuring financial support necessary for meeting commitments to matriculating and accepted students; Selecting students; and Granting degrees. On-site review, verifying information provided in self-assessment, required. Review includes tour of facilities and interviews with chief executive officer, administrators of educational program, instructors, students, medical director, and members of admissions committee. May respond to on-site review. Possible accreditation decisions are: (1) Accreditation; (2) Probationary Accreditation, requiring correction of deficiencies; or (3) Withholding Accreditation, for programs in substantial noncompliance with standards. **Renewal:** Five years (maximum). Renewal based on self-assessment and on-site review. **Preparatory Materials:** *Essentials and Guidelines* (reference). **Fees:** $1000, plus actual cost of on-site review. **Accredited By:** Commission on Recognition of Postsecondary Accreditation; U.S. Department of Education. **Endorsed By:** American Academy of Anesthesiologists' Assistants Education; American Medical Association; Association for Anesthesiologists Assistants Education; Commission on Accreditation of Allied Health Education Programs; Council on Medical Education.

1592

Accreditation Review Committee on Education for the Physician Assistant (ARC-PA)
1000 N. Oak Ave.
Marshfield, WI 54449-5788
Phone: (715)389-3785
Fax: (715)389-3131
John McCarty, Exec.Dir.

Recipient: Review committee of Commission on Accreditation of Allied Health Education Programs (CAAHEP) (see separate entry) for two-year training programs for physician and surgical assistants. **Number of Accredited Institutions:** 59. **Application Procedures:** Self-assessment, conducted by program faculty with input from administrators, students, employers of graduates, and other interested parties, required. Must address strengths and weaknesses of program, cover entire range of educational operations, including ancillary services, and document compliance with criteria in the following areas: (1) Sponsorship; (2) Resources, including: Financial resources; General resources; Personnel, covering administrative personnel, clerical and support staff, faculty and instructional staff, medical director, professional development, and program director; and Physical resources, covering affiliated institutions, equipment and supplies, facilities, and learning resources, including instructional aids and library; (3) Students, including: Admission policies and procedures; Appeals; Evaluation; Guidance; and Health; (4) Operational Policies, including: Fair practices; and Student records; (5) Program Evaluation, including: Outcomes; and Results of ongoing program evaluation; (6) Curriculum, including: Instructional plan; Program organizational structure; and Required knowledge and skills; and (7) Maintaining and Administering Accreditation. **Accreditation Requirements:** Sponsoring institutions must assume primary responsibility for the following: Academic, didactic, and clinical educational experiences; Appointing qualified faculty; Ensuring financial support necessary for meeting commitments to matriculating and accepted students; Selecting students; and Granting degrees. Program must include clinical didactic and practice components that cover: Anatomy; Applied behavioral science; Microbiology; Pharmacology; and Physiology. Clinical practice must be in the following areas: Family medicine; Geriatrics; Internal medicine; Obstetrics and gynecology; Pediatrics; and Surgery. On-site review, verifying information provided in self-assessment, required. Review includes tour of facilities and interviews with chief executive officer, administrators of educational program, instructors, students, medical director, and members of admissions committee. May respond to on-site review. Possible accreditation decisions are: (1) Accreditation; (2) Probationary Accreditation, requiring correction of deficiencies; or (3) Withholding Accreditation, for programs in substantial noncompliance with standards. **Renewal:** Every five years (maximum). Renewal based on self-assessment and on-site review. **Preparatory Materials:** *Essentials and Guidelines for an Accredited Educational Program for the Physician Assistant* (reference). **Fees:** $1750, plus actual cost of on-site review. **Accredited By:** Commission on Recognition of Postsecondary Accreditation; U.S. Department of Education. **Endorsed By:** American Academy of Family Physicians; American Academy of Pediatrics; American Academy of Physician Assistants; American College of Physicians; American College of Surgeons; American Medical Association; Association of Physician Assistant Programs; Commission on Accreditation of Allied Health Education Programs; Council on Medical Education.

1593

Accreditation Review Committee on Education in Surgical Technology (ARC-ST)
Association of Surgical Technologists (AST)
7108-C S. Alton Way
Englewood, CO 80112
Phone: (303)694-9262
Fax: (303)694-9169
Annamarie Dubies-Appel, Mgr.

Recipient: Review committee of Commission on Accreditation of Allied Health Education Programs (CAAHEP) (see separate entry) for nine- to 24-month training programs in surgical services. **Number of Accredited Institutions:** 131. **Application Procedures:** Self-assessment, conducted by program faculty with input from administrators, students, employers of graduates, and other interested parties, required. Must address strengths and weaknesses of program, cover entire range of educational operations, including ancillary services, and document compliance with criteria in the following areas: (1) Sponsorship; (2) Resources, including: Financial resources; General resources; Personnel, covering administrative personnel, clerical and support staff, faculty and instructional staff, medical director, professional development, and program director; and Physical resources, covering affiliated institutions, equipment and supplies, facilities, and learning resources, including instructional aids and library; (3) Students, including: Admission policies and procedures; Appeals; Evaluation; Guidance; and Health; (4) Operational Policies, including: Fair practices; and Student records; (5) Program Evaluation, including: Outcomes; and Results of ongoing program evaluation; and (6) Curriculum, including: Instructional plan; Program organizational structure; and Required knowledge and skills; and (7) Maintaining and Administering Accreditation. **Accreditation Requirements:** Sponsoring institutions must assume primary responsibility for the following: Academic, didactic, and clinical educational experiences; Appointing qualified faculty; Ensuring financial support necessary for meeting commitments to matriculating and accepted students; Selecting students; and Granting degrees. Must provide classroom education and supervised clinical experience. Curriculum must include: Anatomy and physiology; Anesthesia; Basic sciences; Behavioral sciences; Communications; Fundamentals of surgical care; Instruments, supplies, and equipment used in surgery; Legal aspects of surgical patient; Medical terminology; Microbiology; Operative procedures; Orientation to surgical care; Pharmacology; Preparation for surgery; Professional ethics; Sterilization methods and aseptic technique; Surgical patient care and safety precautions; and Surgical procedures. Clinical practice in operating room must include commonly performed procedures in: Cardiovascular and peripheral vascular surgery; General surgery; Neurosurgery; Obstetrics and gynecology; Ophthalmology; Orthopedics; Otorhinolaryngology; Plastic surgery; Thoracic surgery; and Urology. On-site review, verifying information provided in self-assessment, required. Review includes tour of facilities and interviews with chief executive officer, administrators of educational program, instructors, students, medical director, and members of admissions committee. May respond

to on-site review. Possible accreditation decisions are: (1) Accreditation; (2) Probationary Accreditation, requiring correction of deficiencies; or (3) Withholding Accreditation, for programs in substantial noncompliance with standards. **Renewal:** Every six years (maximum). Renewal based on self-assessment and on-site review. **Preparatory Materials:** *Essentials and Guidelines for Accredited Educational Programs in Surgical Technology* (reference). **Fees:** $500, plus actual cost of on-site review. **Accredited By:** Commission on Recognition of Postsecondary Accreditation; U.S. Department of Education. **Endorsed By:** American College of Surgeons; American Hospital Association; American Medical Association; Association of Surgical Technologists; Commission on Accreditation of Allied Health Education Programs; Council on Medical Education.

<hr>

1594

Accreditation Review Committee for the Medical Illustrator (ARC-MI)

Association of Medical Illustrators (AMI)
1819 Peachtree, NE, Ste. 560
Atlanta, GA 30309
Phone: (404)350-7900
Fax: (404)351-3348

Recipient: Review committee of Commission on Accreditation of Allied Health Education Programs (CAAHEP) (see separate entry) for master's degree programs for medical illustrators. **Number of Accredited Institutions:** 68. **Application Procedures:** Self-assessment, conducted by program faculty with input from administrators, students, employers of graduates, and other interested parties, required. Must address strengths and weaknesses of program, cover entire range of educational operations, including ancillary services, and document compliance with criteria in the following areas: (1) Sponsorship; (2) Resources, including: Financial resources; General resources; Personnel, covering administrative personnel, clerical and support staff, faculty and instructional staff, medical director, professional development, and program director; and Physical resources, covering affiliated institutions, equipment and supplies, facilities, and learning resources, including instructional aids and library; (3) Students, including: Admission policies and procedures; Evaluation; Guidance; and Health; (4) Operational Policies, including: Fair practices; and Student records; (5) Program Evaluation, including: Outcomes; and Results of ongoing program evaluation; (6) Curriculum, including:

Instructional plan; Program organizational structure; and Required knowledge and skills; and (7) Maintaining and Administering Accreditation. **Accreditation Requirements:** Sponsoring institutions must assume primary responsibility for the following: Academic, didactic, and clinical educational experiences; Appointing qualified faculty; Ensuring financial support necessary for meeting commitments to matriculating and accepted students; Selecting students; and Granting degrees. Curriculum may include: Anatomical illustration; Business management; Computer graphics; Design for charts, graphs, and statistical data; Embryology; Exhibit design and construction; Histology; Human gross anatomy (with detailed dissection); Illustration techniques; Instructional design; Medical photography; Neuroanatomy; Pathology; Physiology; Production technology; Prosthetics; Surgical illustration; Television and film production; and Three-dimensional modeling. On-site review, verifying information provided in self-assessment, required. Review includes tour of facilities and interviews with chief executive officer, administrators of educational program, instructors, students, medical director, and members of admissions committee. May respond to on-site review. Possible accreditation decisions are: (1) Accreditation; (2) Probationary Accreditation, requiring correction of deficiencies; or (3) Withholding Accreditation, for programs in substantial noncompliance with standards. **Renewal:** Every eight years (maximum). Renewal based on self-assessment and on-site review. **Preparatory Materials:** *Essentials and Guidelines* (reference). **Fees:** $750, plus actual cost of on-site review. **Accredited By:** Commission on Recognition of Postsecondary Accreditation; U.S. Department of Education. **Endorsed By:** American Medical Association; Commission on Accreditation of Allied Health Education Programs; Council on Medical Education.

<hr>

1595

Commission on Accreditation of Allied Health Education Programs (CAAHEP)

515 N. State St., Ste. 7530
Chicago, IL 60610-4377
Phone: (312)464-4636
Fax: (312)464-5830
Lawrence M. Detmer, Dir.

Recipient: Umbrella organization of 17 review committees accrediting training programs in allied health in medical schools; junior and community colleges; senior colleges and universities; vocational and technical schools and institutions; consortia; proprietary schools; military training institutions; and hospitals, clinics, and other healthcare institutions. **Accreditation Requirements:** CAAHEP grants or denies accreditation based on recommendation of review committees. Review committees are: Accreditation Committee Perfusion Education; Accreditation Review Committee on Education for the Anesthesiologist's Assistant; Accreditation Review Committee on Education for the Physician Assistant; Accreditation Review Committee on Education in Surgical Technology; Accreditation Review Committee for the Medical Illustrator; Committee on Accreditation of Specialists in Blood Bank Schools; Council on Accreditation, American Health Information Management Association; Curriculum Review Board, American Association of Medical Assistants; Cytotechnology Programs Review Committee; Joint Review Committee on Education in Cardiovascular Technology; Joint Review Committee on Education in Diagnostic Medical Sonography; Joint Review Committee on Education in Electroneurodiagnostic Technology; Joint Review Committee on Educational Programs in Athletic Training; Joint Review Committee on Educational Programs for the EMT-Paramedic; Joint Review Committee for Ophthalmic Medical Personnel; Joint Review Committee for Respiratory Therapy Education; and National Commission on Orthotic and Prosthetic Education (see separate entries). **Accredited By:** Commission on Recognition of Postsecondary Accreditation; U.S. Department of Education. **Endorsed By:** American Medical Association; Council on Medical Education.

1596

Committee on Accreditation of Specialists in Blood Bank Schools
American Association of Blood Banks (AABB)
8101 Glenbrook Rd.
Bethesda, MD 20814-2749
Phone: (301)907-6977
Fax: (301)907-6895
Helen Bishop, Dir.

Recipient: Review committee of Commission on Accreditation of Allied Health Education Programs (CAAHEP) (see separate entry) for 12-month training programs for blood bank technicians. **Application Procedures:** Self-assessment, conducted by program faculty with input from administrators, students, employers of graduates, and other interested parties, required. Must address strengths and

weaknesses of program, cover entire range of educational operations, including ancillary services, and document compliance with criteria in the following areas: (1) Sponsorship; (2) Resources, including: Financial resources; General resources; Personnel, covering administrative personnel, clerical and support staff, faculty and instructional staff, medical director, professional development, and program director; and Physical resources, covering affiliated institutions, equipment and supplies, facilities, and learning resources, including instructional aids and library; (3) Students, including: Admission policies and procedures; Appeals; Evaluation; Guidance; and Health; (4) Operational Policies, including: Fair practices; and Student records; (5) Program Evaluation, including: Outcomes; and Results of ongoing program evaluation; (6) Curriculum, including: Instructional plan; Program organizational structure; and Required knowledge and skills; and (7) Maintaining and Administering Accreditation. **Accreditation Requirements:** Sponsoring institutions must assume primary responsibility for the following: Academic, didactic, and clinical educational experiences; Appointing qualified faculty; Ensuring financial support necessary for meeting commitments to matriculating and accepted students; Selecting students; and Granting degrees. On-site review, verifying information provided in self-assessment, required. Review includes tour of facilities and interviews with chief executive officer, administrators of educational program, instructors, students, medical director, and members of admissions committee. May respond to on-site review. Possible accreditation decisions are: (1) Accreditation; (2) Probationary Accreditation, requiring correction of deficiencies; or (3) Withholding Accreditation, for programs in substantial noncompliance with standards. **Renewal:** Every five years (maximum). Renewal based on self-assessment and on-site review. **Preparatory Materials:** *Essentials and Guidelines* (reference). **Accredited By:** Commission on Recognition of Postsecondary Accreditation; U.S. Department of Education. **Endorsed By:** American Medical Association; Commission on Accreditation of Allied Health Education Programs; Council on Medical Education.

1597

Council on Education of American Health Information Management Association
American Health Information Management Association (AHIMA)
919 N. Michigan Ave., Ste. 1400
Chicago, IL 60611
Phone: (312)787-2672
Fax: (312)787-5926
Shirley Eichenwald, Dir.

Recipient: Review committee of Commission on Accreditation of Allied Health Education Programs (CAAHEP) (see separate entry) for baccalaureate and post-baccalaureate degree programs for medical record administrators and associate degree programs for medical record technicians involved in health information management. **Number of Accredited Institutions:** 84. **Application Procedures:** Self-assessment, conducted by program faculty with input from administrators, students, employers of graduates, and other interested parties, required. Must address strengths and weaknesses of program, cover entire range of educational operations, including ancillary services, and document compliance with criteria in the following areas: (1) Sponsorship; (2) Resources, including: Financial resources; General resources; Personnel, covering administrative personnel, clerical and support staff, faculty and instructional staff, medical director, professional development, and program director; and Physical resources, covering affiliated institutions, equipment and supplies, facilities, and learning resources, including instructional aids and library; (3) Students, including: Admission policies and procedures; Appeals; Evaluation; Guidance; and Health; (4) Operational Policies, including: Fair practices; and Student records; (5) Program Evaluation, including: Outcomes; and Results of ongoing program evaluation; (6) Curriculum, including: Instructional plan; Program organizational structure; and Required knowledge and skills; and (7) Maintaining and Administering Accreditation. **Accreditation Requirements:** Sponsoring institutions must assume primary responsibility for the following: Academic, didactic, and clinical educational experiences; Appointing qualified faculty; Ensuring financial support necessary for meeting commitments to matriculating and accepted students; Selecting students; and Granting degrees. Curriculum for medical record administrators (bachelor's degree program) must include: Computerized health information systems; Disease classification systems; Fundamentals of medical science; Healthcare statistics; Medical terminology; Organization of healthcare institutions; Principles of law as applied to health field; Principles of organization, administration, supervision, and human relations; Supervised practice in health information departments or healthcare facilities and agencies; and Use of medical records. Curriculum for medical record technicians (associate's degree program) must include: Anatomy and physiology; Diagnostic and procedural coding; Directed clinical practice; Filing systems; General business and healthcare-specific computer applications; Healthcare statistics; Medical record documentation systems and standards; Medical terminology; Medico-legal principles; and Specialized clinical registries. On-site review, verifying information provided in self-assessment, required. Review includes tour of facilities and interviews with chief executive officer, administrators of educational program, instructors, students, medical director, and members of admissions committee. May respond to on-site review. Possible accreditation decisions are: (1) Accreditation; (2) Probationary Accreditation, requiring correction of deficiencies; or (3) Withholding Accreditation, for programs in substantial noncompliance with standards. **Renewal:** Every five years (initial); every eight years thereafter. Renewal based on self-assessment and on-site review. **Preparatory Materials:** *Essentials and Guidelines* (reference). **Fees:** $600, plus actual cost of on-site review. **Accredited By:** Commission on Recognition of Postsecondary Accreditation; U.S. Department of Education. **Endorsed By:** American Medical Association; Commission on Accreditation of Allied Health Education Programs; Council on Medical Education.

`1598`

Curriculum Review Board of the American Association of Medical Assistants

American Association of Medical
Assistants (AAMA)
20 N. Wacker Dr., Ste. 1575
Chicago, IL 60606-2903
Phone: (312)899-1500
Fax: (312)899-1259
Toll Free: (800)228-2262
Monique M. Buckner, Dir.

Recipient: Review committee of Commission on Accreditation of Allied Health Education Programs (CAAHEP) (see separate entry) for two- or four-year training programs for medical assistants. **Number of Accredited Institutions:** 216. **Application Procedures:** Self-assessment, conducted by program faculty with input

from administrators, students, employers of graduates, and other interested parties, required. Must address strengths and weaknesses of programs, cover entire range of educational operations, including ancillary services, and document compliance with criteria in the following areas: (1) Sponsorship; (2) Resources, including: Financial resources; General resources; Personnel, covering administrative personnel, clerical and support staff, faculty and instructional staff, medical director, professional development, and program director; and Physical resources, covering affiliated institutions, equipment and supplies, facilities, and learning resources, including instructional aids and library; (3) Students, including: Admission policies and procedures; Appeals; Evaluation; Guidance; and Health; (4) Operational Policies, including: Fair practices; and Student records; (5) Program Evaluation, including: Outcomes; and Results of ongoing program evaluation; (6) Curriculum, including: Instructional plan; Program organizational structure; and Required knowledge and skills; and (7) Maintaining and Administering Accreditation. **Accreditation Requirements:** Sponsoring institutions must assume primary responsibility for the following: Academic, didactic, and clinical educational experiences; Appointing qualified faculty; Ensuring financial support necessary for meeting commitments to matriculating and accepted students; Selecting students; and Granting degrees. Program must have graduated one class, be competency based, and include externship. Curriculum must include: Anatomy and physiology; Communications (oral and written); Medical assisting administrative procedures; Medical assisting clinical procedures; Medical law and ethics; Medical terminology; and Psychology. Program must include internship that provides practical experience in qualified physicians' offices, accredited hospitals, or other healthcare facilities. On-site review, verifying information provided in self-assessment, required. Review includes tour of facilities and interviews with chief executive officer, administrators of educational program, instructors, students, medical director, and members of admissions committee. May respond to on-site review. Possible accreditation decisions are: (1) Accreditation; (2) Probationary Accreditation, requiring correction of deficiencies; or (3) Withholding Accreditation, for programs in substantial noncompliance with standards. **Renewal:** Every seven years (maximum). Renewal based on self-assessment and on-site review. Renewal fee is $400, plus actual costs of on-site review. **Preparatory Materials:** *Essentials and Guide-*

lines for an Accredited Educational Program for the Medical Assistant (reference). **Length of Process:** One year. **Fees:** $800, plus actual cost of on-site review; $700 (annual fee). **Accredited By:** Commission on Recognition of Postsecondary Accreditation; U.S. Department of Education. **Endorsed By:** American Medical Association; Commission on Accreditation of Allied Health Education Programs; Council on Medical Education.

`1599`

Cytotechnology Programs Review Committee (ASC)

American Society of Cytopathology
400 W. Ninth St., Ste. 201
Wilmington, DE 19801
Phone: (302)429-8802
Fax: (302)429-8807
Shirley Indictor, Sec.

Recipient: Review committee of Commission on Accreditation of Allied Health Education Programs (CAAHEP) (see separate entry) for training programs in cytopathology. **Number of Accredited Institutions:** 68. **Application Procedures:** Self-assessment, conducted by program faculty with input from administrators, students, employers of graduates, and other interested parties, required. Must address strengths and weaknesses of program, cover entire range of educational operations, including ancillary services, and document compliance with standards in the following areas: (1) Sponsorship; (2) Resources, including: Financial resources; Personnel, covering administrative personnel, clerical, and support staff, faculty and instructional staff, medical director, professional development, and program director; and Physical resources, covering affiliated institutions, equipment and supplies, facilities, and learning resources, including instructional aids and library; (3) Students, including: Admission policies and procedures; Evaluation; Guidance; and Health; (4) Operational Policies, including: Fair practices; and Student records; (5) Program Evaluation, including: Outcomes; and Results of ongoing program evaluation; (6) Curriculum, including: Instructional plan; Program organizational structure; and Required knowledge and skills; and (7) Maintaining and Administering Accreditation. **Accreditation Requirements:** Sponsoring institutions must assume primary responsibility for the following: Academic, didactic, and clinical educational experiences; Appointing qualified faculty; Ensuring financial support necessary for meeting commitments to matriculating and accepted students; Selecting students; and

Granting degrees. Curriculum must include: Anatomy; Cytochemistry; Cytology as applied in clinical medicine; Cytology in screening of tumor cells obtained following spontaneous exfoliation or by needle aspiration biopsy; Cytophysiology; Embryology; Endocrinology; Histology; Historical background of cytology; and Inflammatory diseases. On-site review, verifying information provided in self-assessment, required. Review includes tour of facilities and interviews with chief executive officer, administrators of educational program, instructors, students, medical director, and members of admissions committee. May respond to on-site review. Possible accreditation decisions are: (1) Accreditation; (2) Probationary Accreditation, requiring correction of deficiencies; or (3) Withholding Accreditation, for programs in substantial noncompliance with standards. **Renewal:** Every five years (maximum). Renewal based on self-assessment and on-site review. **Preparatory Materials:** *Essentials and Guidelines for an Accredited Educational Program for the Cytotechnologist* (reference). **Fees:** $600. **Accredited By:** Commission on Recognition of Postsecondary Accreditation; U.S. Department of Education. **Endorsed By:** American Medical Association; Commission on Accreditation of Allied Health Education Programs; Council on Medical Education.

1600

Joint Review Committee on Education in Cardiovascular Technology (JRC-CVT)
9111 Old Georgetown Rd.
Bethesda, MD 20814
Phone: (301)493-2334
Fax: (301)897-9745
Rebecca A. Trachtman, Exec.Dir.

Recipient: Review committee of Commission on Accreditation of Allied Health Education Programs (CAAHEP) (see separate entry) for one- to four-year training programs in invasive cardiology, noninvasive cardiology, and peripheral vascular programs. **Application Procedures:** Self-assessment, conducted by program faculty with input from administrators, students, employers of graduates, and other interested parties, required. Must address strengths and weaknesses of program, cover entire range of educational operations, including ancillary services, and document compliance with standards in the following areas: (1) Resources, including: Financial resources, including budgets and financial assistance; General resources; Personnel, including instructional staff and program directors; and Physical resources, includ-

ing equipment and supplies, facilities, and library; (2) Curriculum, including: Clinical skills and knowledge; Didactic courses and clinical experiences; Length; Structure; and Units of instruction; (3) Students, including: Admission; Evaluation; Guidance; Health; and Information; (4) Operational Policies, including: Fair practices; Financial aid; Student records; Tuition and credit; and Withdrawal; (5) Program Evaluation, including system for periodic self-assessment; (6) Curriculum, including: Instructional plan; Program organizational structure; and Required knowledge and skills; and (7) Maintaining and Administering Accreditation. **Accreditation Requirements:** Sponsoring institutions must assume primary responsibility for the following: Academic, didactic, and clinical educational experiences; Appointing qualified faculty; Ensuring financial support necessary for meeting commitments to matriculating and accepted students; Selecting students; and Granting degrees. Programs must include both didactic instruction and formal laboratory experiences. Core curriculum should include: Basic medical electronics; Basic pharmacology; General and/or applied sciences; Human anatomy and physiology; Introduction to field of cardiovascular technology; and Medical instrumentation. On-site review, verifying information provided in self-assessment, required. Review includes tour of facilities and interviews with chief executive officer, administrators of educational program, instructors, students, medical director, and members of admissions committee. May respond to on-site review. Possible accreditation decisions are: (1) Accreditation; (2) Probationary Accreditation, requiring correction of deficiencies; or (3) Withholding Accreditation, for programs in substantial noncompliance with standards. **Renewal:** Every five years (maximum). Renewal based on self-assessment and on-site review. Must also submit annual report. **Restrictions:** Must report key personnel changes and additions of clinical affiliates. **Preparatory Materials:** *Accreditation Procedures for Cardiovascular Technology Educational Programs, Essentials and Guidelines of an Accredited Educational Program for the Cardiovascular Technologist,* and *Guide to Self-Study Report* (references). **Fees:** $100, plus actual cost of on-site review; $300 (annual fee). **Accredited By:** Commission on Recognition of Postsecondary Accreditation; U.S. Department of Education. **Endorsed By:** American College of Cardiology; American College of Chest Physicians; American College of Radiology; American Institute of Ultrasound in Medicine; American Medical Association; American Society of Echocardiography; Com-

mission on Accreditation of Allied Health Education Programs; Council on Medical Education; National Society for Cardiovascular Technology; National Society for Pulmonary Technology; Society of Diagnostic Medical Sonographers; Society for Vascular Surgery and International Society for Cardiovascular Surgery; Society of Vascular Technology.

1601

Joint Review Committee on Education in Diagnostic Medical Sonography (JRCDMS)
7108-C S. Alton Way
Englewood, CO 80112-2106
Phone: (303)741-3533
Fax: (303)741-3655
Annamarie Dubies-Appel, Exec.Dir.

Recipient: Review committee of Commission on Accreditation of Allied Health Education Programs (CAAHEP) (see separate entry) for one-, two-, or four-year training programs for diagnostic medical sonographers. **Number of Accredited Institutions:** 68. **Application Procedures:** Self-assessment, conducted by program faculty with input from administrators, students, employers of graduates, and other interested parties, required. Must address strengths and weaknesses or program, cover entire range of educational operations, including ancillary services, and document compliance with criteria in the following areas: (1) Sponsorship; (2) Resources, including: Financial resources; General resources; Personnel, covering administrative personnel, clerical and support staff, faculty and instructional staff, medical director, professional development, and program director; and Physical resources, covering affiliated institutions, equipment and supplies, facilities, and learning resources, including instructional aids and library; (3) Students, including: Admission policies and procedures; Evaluation; Guidance; and Health; (4) Operational Policies, including: Fair practices; and Student records; (5) Program Evaluation, including: Outcomes; and Results of ongoing program evaluation; (6) Curriculum, including: Instructional plan; Program organizational structure; and Required knowledge and skills; and (7) Maintaining and Administering Accreditation. **Accreditation Requirements:** Sponsoring institutions must assume primary responsibility for the following: Academic, didactic, and clinical educational experiences; Appointing qualified faculty; Ensuring financial support necessary for meeting commitments to matriculating and accepted students; Selecting students; and Granting degrees. Curriculum should include: Applications of ultrasound; Applied biological sciences; Clinical medicine; Image evaluation; Instrumentation; Patient care; Physical sciences; and Related diagnostic procedures. On-site review, verifying information provided in self-assessment, required. Review includes tour of facilities and interviews with chief executive officer, administrators of educational program, instructors, students, medical director, and members of admissions committee. May respond to on-site review. Possible accreditation decisions are: (1) Accreditation; (2) Probationary Accreditation, requiring correction of deficiencies; or (3) Withholding Accreditation, for programs in substantial noncompliance with standards. **Renewal:** Every five years (maximum). Renewal based on self-assessment and on-site review. **Preparatory Materials:** *Essentials and Guidelines of an Accredited Educational Program for the Diagnostic Medical Sonographer* (reference). **Fees:** $600, plus actual cost of on-site review. **Accredited By:** Commission on Recognition of Postsecondary Accreditation; U.S. Department of Education. **Endorsed By:** American College of Cardiology; American College of Radiology; American Institute of Ultrasound in Medicine; American Medical Association; American Society of Echocardiography; American Society of Radiologic Technologists; Commission on Accreditation of Allied Health Education Schools; Society of Diagnostic Medical Sonographers; Society of Vascular Technology.

`1602`

Joint Review Committee on Education in Electroneurodiagnostic Technology

PO Box 11434
Norfolk, VA 23517
Phone: (804)627-6791
Fax: (804)627-0713
Patricia Smith, Exec. Officer

Recipient: Review committee of Commission on Accreditation of Allied Health Education Programs (CAAHEP) (see separate entry) for 12-month or longer training programs for electroneurodiagnostic technicians. **Application Procedures:** Self-assessment, conducted by program faculty with input from administrators, students, employers of graduates, and other interested parties, required. Must address strengths and weaknesses of program, cover entire range of educational operations, including ancillary services, and document compliance with criteria in the following areas: (1) Sponsorship; (2) Resources, in-

cluding: Financial resources; General resources; Personnel, covering administrative personnel, clerical and support staff, faculty and instructional staff, medical director, professional development, and program director; and Physical resources, covering affiliated institutions, equipment and supplies, facilities, and learning resources, including instructional aids and library; (3) Students, including: Admission policies and procedures; Appeals; Evaluation; Guidance; and Health; (4) Operational Policies, including: Fair practices; and Student records; (5) Program Evaluation, including: Outcomes; and Results of ongoing program evaluation; (6) Curriculum, including: Instructional plan; Program organizational structure; and Required knowledge and skills; and (7) Maintaining and Administering Accreditation. **Accreditation Requirements:** Sponsoring institutions must assume primary responsibility for the following: Academic, didactic, and clinical educational experiences; Appointing qualified faculty; Ensuring financial support necessary for meeting commitments to matriculating and accepted students; Selecting students; and Granting degrees. Curriculum must include: Anatomy; Electronics; Instrumentation; Neuroanatomy; Personal and patient safety; and Physiology. On-site review, verifying information provided in self-assessment, required. Review includes tour of facilities and interviews with chief executive officer, administrators of educational program, instructors, students, medical director, and members of admissions committee. May respond to on-site review. Possible accreditation decisions are: (1) Accreditation; (2) Probationary Accreditation, requiring correction of deficiencies; or (3) Withholding Accreditation, for programs in substantial noncompliance with standards. **Renewal:** Every seven years (maximum). Renewal based on self-assessment and on-site review. **Fees:** $1000. **Accredited By:** Commission on Accreditation of Postsecondary Education; U.S. Department of Education. **Endorsed By:** American Electroencephalographic Society; American Medical Association; American Medical Electroencephalographic Association; American Society of Electroneurodiagnostic Technologists; Commission on Accreditation of Allied Health Education Schools; Council on Medical Education.

`1603`

Joint Review Committee on Education in Radiologic Technology (JRCERT)

20 N. Wacker Dr., Ste. 900
Chicago, IL 60606-2901
Phone: (312)704-5300
Fax: (312)704-5304
Marilyn Fay, Exec.Dir.

Recipient: Educational programs for radiation therapists and radiographers at hospitals, two- and four-year colleges and universities, postsecondary vocational and technical schools and institutions, proprietary institutions, and government and military facilities. **Number of Accredited Institutions:** 820. **Application Procedures:** Self-assessment required. Must document compliance with standards in the following areas: (1) Sponsorship, including: Accreditation; Policies and procedures; and Responsibilities; (2) Resources, including: Financial resources, including budget planning and objectives; General resources; Personnel qualifications and responsibilities, including clinical coordinator, clinical instructor, clinical staff, didactic faculty, medical director/advisor, and program director; Physical resources, including clinical, equipment and supplies, general, and library; Professional development; and Student/faculty ratio; (3) Curriculum, including: Course syllabi; Grading policy; Graduate competencies; Institution and program philosophies and goals; Learning objectives and competencies; Outcomes assessment methods; Professional values; Program policies; Sequence; Teaching strategies; and Textbooks; (4) Student, including: Admission; Evaluation; Guidance; Health services; and Program description; (5) Operational Policies, including: Fair practices; and Student records; and (6) Continuing Program Evaluation, including: Attrition, retention, and academic delinquency rates; Curriculum; Graduates; Interactions and relationships; Knowledge; Skills; and Values and beliefs. Must make the following materials available: Affiliation agreements for clinical education centers; Course syllabi for all curriculum content areas; Curricula vitae and position descriptions for faculty and officials; Evaluation instruments; Forms and evaluations used in student selection process; Index of library holdings; Inventory of equipment and instructional aids; Policies and procedures; Student handbook; and Student records. **Accreditation Requirements:** Program must include didactic and supervised clinical education components. Programs for radiographers must include instruction in the following areas: Equipment maintenance; Evaluation of radiographs; Human structure and function; Imaging equipment; Imaging procedures; Interpersonal communication; Introduction to computer literacy; Introduction to quality assurance; Introduction to radiography; Medical ethics and law; Medical terminology; Methods of patient care; Patient care and management; Principles of radiation biology; Principles of radiation protection; Principles of radiographic exposure; Professional responsibility; Quality assurance; Radiation physics; Radiation protection; Radiographic film processing; Radiographic pathology; Radiographic procedures; Recording media processing; and Structured competency-based clinical education. Programs for radiation therapists must include instruction in the following areas: Clinical dosimetry; Human structure and function; Introduction to computers; Introduction to hyperthermia; Mathematics; Medical ethics and law; Medical terminology; Methods of patient care; Oncologic pathology; Orientation to radiation therapy technology; Patient care and management; Quality assurance; Radiation oncology; Radiation oncology techniques; Radiation physics; Radiation protection; Radiobiology; Radiographic imaging; Simulation procedures; and Treatment procedures. On-site review, verifying information provided in self-assessment, required. Review includes: Interviews with administrator, faculty, students, and other interested parties; and Review of materials. May respond to on-site review. Possible accreditation decisions are: (1) Accreditation; (2) Probationary Accreditation, requiring correction of deficiencies; or (3) Withholding Accreditation, for programs in substantial non-compliance with standards. **Renewal:** Every five years (maximum). Renewal base on self-assessment and on-site review. Must also submit annual reports. **Restrictions:** Must report changes in administrative positions and length of program. **State Requirements:** Must be licensed by state. **Preparatory Materials:** *Essentials and Guidelines of an Accredited Educational Program for the Radiation Therapist* and *Essentials and Guidelines of an Accredited Educational Program for the Radiographer* (references). Seminars and workshops available. **Length of Process:** 18 months. **Fees:** $725, plus actual cost of on-site review; must also submit annual fee. **Accredited By:** Commission on Recognition of Postsecondary Accreditation. **Endorsed By:** American College of Radiology; American Society of Radiologic Technologists; Association of Educators in Radiological Sciences.

1604

Joint Review Committee on Educational Programs in Athletic Training
Physical Educ. Dept.
Indiana State Univ.
Terre Haute, IN 47809-3026
Phone: (812)237-3026
Fax: (812)237-4338
Linda Syster, Exec. Officer

Recipient: Review committee of Commission on Accreditation of Allied Health Education Programs (CAAHEP) (see separate entry) for baccalaureate and post-baccalaureate training programs in athletic training. **Application Procedures:** Self-assessment, conducted by program faculty with input from administrators, students, employers of graduates, and other interested parties, required. Must address strengths and weaknesses of program, cover entire range of educational operations, including ancillary services, and document compliance with criteria in the following areas: (1) Sponsorship; (2) Resources, including: Financial resources; General resources; Personnel, covering administrative personnel, clerical and support staff, faculty and instructional staff, medical director, professional development, and program director; and Physical resources, covering affiliated institutions, equipment and supplies, facilities, and learning resources, including instructional aids and library; (3) Students, including: Admission policies and procedures; Appeals; Evaluation; Guidance; and Health; (4) Operational Policies, including: Fair practices; and Student records; (5) Program Evaluation, including: Outcomes; and Results of ongoing program evaluation; (6) Curriculum, including: Instructional plan; Program organizational structure; and Required knowledge and skills; and (7) Maintaining and Administering Accreditation. **Accreditation Requirements:** Sponsoring institutions must assume primary responsibility for the following: Academic, didactic, and clinical educational experiences; Appointing qualified faculty; Ensuring financial support necessary for meeting commitments to matriculating and accepted students; Selecting students; and Granting degrees. Curriculum must include structured laboratory and clinical experiences and formal instruction in the following areas: Administration of athletic training programs; Exercise physiology; First aid and emergency care; Human anatomy; Human physiology; Kinesiology and biomechanics; Nutrition; Personal and community health; Prevention and evaluation of athletic injuries and illnesses; Psychology; and Therapeutic exercise. On-site review,

verifying information provided in self-assessment, required. Review includes tour of facilities and interviews with chief executive officer, administrators of educational program, instructors, students, medical director, and members of admissions committee. May respond to on-site review. Possible accreditation decisions are: (1) Accreditation; (2) Probationary Accreditation, requiring correction of deficiencies; or (3) Withholding Accreditation, for programs in substantial non-compliance with standards. **Renewal:** Every seven years (maximum). Renewal based on self-assessment and on-site review. **Preparatory Materials:** *Essentials and Guidelines* (reference). **Fees:** $200, plus actual cost of on-site review. **Accredited By:** Commission on Recognition of Postsecondary Accreditation; U.S. Department of Education. **Endorsed By:** American Academy of Family Physicians; American Academy of Pediatrics; American Medical Association; Commission on Accreditation of Allied Health Education Programs; Council on Medical Education; National Athletic Trainers' Association.

1605

Joint Review Committee on Educational Programs for the EMT Paramedic (JRCEMT-P)
1701 W. Euless Blvd., Ste. 300
Euless, TX 76040
Phone: (817)283-2836
Fax: (817)354-8519
Phillip von der Heydt RRT, Exec. Sec.

Recipient: Review committee of Commission on Accreditation of Allied Health Education Programs (CAAHEP) (see separate entry) for training programs for emergency medical technicians (EMTs) and paramedics. **Number of Accredited Institutions:** 87. **Application Procedures:** Self-assessment, conducted by program faculty with input from administrators, students, employers of graduates, and other interested parties, required. Must address strengths and weaknesses of program, cover entire range of educational operations, including ancillary services, and document compliance with criteria in the following areas: (1) Sponsorship; (2) Resources, including: Financial resources; General resources; Personnel, covering administrative personnel, clerical and support staff, faculty and instructional staff, medical director, professional development, and program director; and Physical resources, covering affiliated institutions, equipment and supplies, facilities, and learning resources, including instructional aids and library; (3) Students, including: Admission policies and procedures; Appeals; Evaluation; Guidance; and Health; (4) Operational Policies, including: Fair practices; and Student records; (5) Program Evaluation, including: Outcomes; and Results of ongoing program evaluation; (6) Curriculum, including: Instructional plan; Program organizational structure; and Required knowledge and skills; and (7) Maintaining and Administering Accreditation. **Accreditation Requirements:** Sponsoring institutions must assume primary responsibility for the following: Academic, didactic, and clinical educational experiences; Appointing qualified faculty; Ensuring financial support necessary for meeting commitments to matriculating and accepted students; Selecting students; and Granting degrees. Curriculum must include didactic clinical instruction, in-hospital clinical practice, and supervised field internship in advanced life-support unit that functions under emergency medical services command authority. On-site review, verifying information provided in self-assessment, required. Review includes tour of facilities and interviews with chief executive officer, administrators of educational program, instructors, students, medical director, and members of admissions committee. May respond to on-site review. Possible accreditation decisions are: (1) Accreditation; (2) Probationary Accreditation, requiring correction of deficiencies; or (3) Withholding Accreditation, for programs in substantial noncompliance with standards. **Renewal:** Every five years. Renewal based on self-assessment and on-site review. **Preparatory Materials:** *Accreditation Handbook* and *Essentials and Guidelines* (references). **Length of Process:** Eight months-one year. **Fees:** $100, plus actual cost of on-site review. **Accredited By:** Commission on Recognition of Postsecondary Accreditation; U.S. Department of Education. **Endorsed By:** American Academy of Pediatrics; American College of Cardiology; American College of Emergency Physicians; American College of Surgeons; American Medical Association; American Society of Anesthesiologists; Commission on Accreditation of Allied Health Education Programs; Council on Medical Education; National Association of Emergency Medical Technicians; National Council of State EMS Training Coordinators; National Registry of Emergency Medical Technicians.

`1606`

Joint Review Committee on Educational Programs in Nuclear Medicine Technology

1144 West 3300 South
Salt Lake City, UT 84119-3330
Phone: (801)975-1144
Fax: (801)975-7872
Cuklanz, Exec.Dir.

Recipient: One-, two-, or four-year programs in nuclear medicine technology at colleges, universities, medical schools, community, technical, and junior colleges, and post-secondary vocational technical schools and institutions. **Application Procedures:** Self-assessment, including faculty, administrators, students, employers of graduates, and other interested parties, required. Must address strengths and weaknesses and cover entire range of educational operations, including ancillary services, and document compliance with standards in the following areas: (1) Sponsorship; (2) Resources, including: Financial resources; Personnel, covering administrative personnel, faculty and instructional staff, medical director, and program director; and Physical resources, covering affiliated institutions, equipment and supplies, facilities, and learning resources, including instructional aids and library; (3) Students, including: Admission policies and procedures; Evaluation; Guidance; and Health; (4) Operational Policies, including: Fair practices; and Student records; (5) Program Evaluation, including: Outcomes; and Results of ongoing program evaluation; (6) Curriculum; and (7) Maintaining and Administering Accreditation. **Accreditation Requirements:** Sponsoring institutions must assume primary responsibility for the following: Academic, didactic, and clinical educational experiences; Appointing qualified faculty; Ensuring financial support necessary for meeting commitments to matriculating and accepted students; Selecting students; and Granting degrees. Curriculum must include: Administrative procedures; Imaging procedures; Non-imaging *in-vivo* procedures; Patient care; Physical science; Radiation biology, safety, and protection; Radiopharmaceuticals; and Therapeutic uses of radionuclides. On-site review, verifying information provided in self-assessment, required. Review includes tour of facilities and interviews with chief executive officer, administrators of educational program, instructors, students, medical director, and members of admissions committee. May respond to on-site review. Possible accreditation decisions are: (1) Accreditation; (2) Probationary Accreditation, requiring correction of deficiencies; or (3)

Withholding Accreditation, for programs in substantial noncompliance with standards. **Renewal:** Every five years (maximum). Renewal based on self-assessment and on-site review. Must also submit annual report. **Preparatory Materials:** *Essentials and Guidelines of an Accredited Educational Program for the Nuclear Technologist* and *Manual of Program Evaluation Procedures* (references). **Fees:** $1350, plus actual cost of on-site review; $600 (annual fee). **Accredited By:** Commission on Recognition of Postsecondary Accreditation; U.S. Department of Education. **Endorsed By:** American College of Radiology; American Society for Clinical Laboratory Science; American Society of Clinical Pathologists; American Society of Radiologic Technologists; Society of Nuclear Medicine.

`1607`

Joint Review Committee for Ophthalmic Medical Personnel (JRCOMP)

Joint Commission on Allied Health Personnel in Ophthalmology (JCAHPO)
2025 Woodlane Dr.
St. Paul, MN 55125-2995
Phone: (612)731-2944
Fax: (612)731-0410
Toll Free: (800)284-3937
Alice Gelinas, Exec.Dir.

Recipient: Review committee of Commission on Accreditation of Allied Health Education Programs (CAAHEP) (see separate entry) for one- to two-year training programs for ophthalmic medical personnel. **Application Procedures:** Self-assessment, conducted by program faculty with input from administrators, students, employers of graduates, and other interested parties, required. Must address strengths and weaknesses of program, cover entire range of educational operations, including ancillary services, and document compliance with criteria in the following areas: (1) Sponsorship; (2) Resources, including: Financial resources; Personnel, covering administrative personnel, faculty and instructional staff, medical director, and program director; and Physical resources, covering affiliated institutions, equipment and supplies, facilities, and learning resources, including instructional aids and library; (3) Students, including: Admission policies and procedures; Evaluation; Guidance; and Health; (4) Operational Policies, including: Fair practices; and Student records; (5) Program Evaluation, including: Outcomes; and Results of ongoing program evaluation; (6) Curriculum, including: Instructional plan; Program organizational structure; and Required knowledge and skills; and (7) Maintaining and Administering Accreditation. **Accreditation Requirements:** Sponsoring institutions must assume primary responsibility for the following: Academic, didactic, and clinical educational experiences; Appointing qualified faculty; Ensuring financial support necessary for meeting commitments to matriculating and accepted students; Selecting students; and Granting degrees. Curriculum should include: Anatomy and physiology; Diseases of the eye; Medical law and ethics; Medical terminology; Microbiology; Ocular anatomy and physiology; Ocular motility; Ophthalmic optics; Ophthalmic pharmacology and toxicology; and Psychology. Curriculum must also cover diagnostic and treatment procedures, including: (1) Care and maintenance of ophthalmic instruments and equipment; (2) Contact lenses; and (3) Visual field testing. Students must also successfully complete supervised clinical experience. On-site review, verifying information provided in self-assessment, required. Review includes tour of facilities and interviews with chief executive officer, administrators of educational program, instructors, students, medical director, and members of admissions committee. May respond to on-site review. Possible accreditation decisions are: (1) Accreditation; (2) Probationary Accreditation, requiring correction of deficiencies; or (3) Withholding Accreditation, for programs in substantial noncompliance with standards. **Renewal:** Every five years (maximum). Renewal based on self-assessment and on-site review. **Preparatory Materials:** *Essentials and Guidelines* (reference). **Fees:** Actual cost of on-site review. **Accredited By:** Commission on Recognition of Postsecondary Accreditation; U.S. Department of Education. **Endorsed By:** American Medical Association; Association of Technical Personnel in Ophthalmology; Commission on Accreditation of Allied Health Education Programs; Council on Medical Education.

1608

Joint Review Committee for Respiratory Therapy Education (JRCRTE)
1701 W. Euless Blvd., Ste. 300
Euless, TX 76040
Phone: (817)283-2836
Fax: (817)354-8519
Toll Free: (800)874-5615
Phillip von der Heydt RRT, Exec. Sec.

Recipient: Review committee of Com-

mission on Accreditation of Allied Health Education Programs (CAAHEP) (see separate entry) for associate's degree programs for respiratory therapists and one-year certificate programs for respiratory therapy technicians. **Number of Accredited Institutions:** 376. **Application Procedures:** Self-assessment, conducted by program faculty with input from administrators, students, employers of graduates, and other interested parties, required. Must address strengths and weaknesses of program, cover entire range of educational operations, including ancillary services, and document compliance with criteria in the following areas: (1) Sponsorship; (2) Resources, including: Financial resources; General resources; Personnel, covering administrative personnel, clerical and support staff, faculty and instructional staff, medical director, professional development, and program director; and Physical resources, covering affiliated institutions, equipment and supplies, facilities, and learning resources, including instructional aids and library; (3) Students, including: Admission policies and procedures; Appeals; Evaluation; Guidance; and Health; (4) Operational Policies, including: Fair practices; and Student records; (5) Program Evaluation, including: Outcomes; and Results of ongoing program evaluation; (6) Curriculum, including: Instructional plan; Program organizational structure; and Required knowledge and skills; and (7) Maintaining and Administering Accreditation. **Accreditation Requirements:** Sponsoring institutions must assume primary responsibility for the following: Academic, didactic, and clinical educational experiences; Appointing qualified faculty; Ensuring financial support necessary for meeting commitments to matriculating and accepted students; Selecting students; and Granting degrees. Program must include clinical, didactic, and laboratory preparation. Curriculum must include: Anatomy; Chemistry; Clinical expressions; Clinical medicine; Communication skills; Mathematics; Medical ethics; Medical terminology; Microbiology; Physics; Physiology; Psychology; and Therapeutic procedures. On-site review, verifying information provided in self-assessment, required. Review includes tour of facilities and interviews with chief executive officer, administrators of educational program, instructors, students, medical director, and members of admissions committee. May respond to on-site review. Possible accreditation decisions are: (1) Accreditation; (2) Probationary Accreditation, requiring correction of deficiencies; or (3) Withholding Accreditation, for programs in substantial noncompliance with stan-

dards. **Renewal:** Every five years (maximum). Renewal based on self-assessment and on-site review. **Preparatory Materials:** *Accreditation Handbook* and *Essentials and Guidelines* (references). **Length of Process:** Eight months-one year. **Fees:** $825, plus actual cost of on-site review. **Accredited By:** Commission on Accreditation of Postsecondary Accreditation; U.S. Department of Education. **Endorsed By:** American Association for Respiratory Care; American College of Chest Physicians; American Medical Association; American Society of Anesthesiologists; American Thoracic Society; Commission on Accreditation of Allied Health Education Programs; Council on Medical Education.

1609

National Accrediting Agency for Clinical Laboratory Sciences (NAACLS)
8410 W. Bryn Mawr Ave., Ste. 670
Chicago, IL 60631
Phone: (312)714-8886
Fax: (312)714-8886
E-mail: OKIMBALLdelawarephi. com
Olive M. Kimball Ed.D., Exec.Dir.

Recipient: Training programs for histologic technicians (one year) and technologists (bachelor's degree), medical laboratory technicians (associate's degree and certificate), and medical technologists (one year). **Number of Accredited Institutions:** 700. **Application Procedures:** Self-assessment required. Must document compliance with standards. **Accreditation Requirements:** Program for histologic technicians and technologists should include didactic instruction and practical demonstration in the following areas: Anatomy; Chemistry; Histochemistry; Histology; Instrumentation; Laboratory mathematics; Medical ethics; Medical terminology; Microscopy; Preparation of museum specimens; Processing techniques; Quality control; and Record and administration procedures. Programs for medical laboratory technicians should focus on: Clinical chemistry; Communications skills; Hematology; Immunohematology; Immunology; Interpersonal relationships; Microbiology; Procedures of laboratory testing; Social responsibilities; and Urinalysis. Program for medical technologists must be structured laboratory programs, including instruction in the following: Clinical chemistry; Immunohematology; Immunology; Microbiology; and Theory and practice in hematology. On-site review required. May respond to on-site review. **Renewal:** Every five years (initial); every seven years thereafter. Renewal based on self-assessment and on-site review. **Preparatory Materials:** *Essentials and Guidelines* (reference). Publications, guides, handbooks, and other materials available. **Length of Process:** Six months-one year. **Fees:** $300, plus actual cost of on-site review. **Accredited By:** Commission on Recognition of Postsecondary Accreditation; U.S. Department of Education. **Endorsed By:** American Society for Clinical Laboratory Science; American Society of Clinical Pathologists; National Society for Histotechnology.

`1610`

National Commission on Orthotic and Prosthetic Education (NCOPE)

1650 King St., Ste. 500
Alexandria, VA 22314
Phone: (703)836-7114
Robin C. Seabrook, Dir.

Recipient: Review committee of Commission on Accreditation of Allied Health Education Programs (CAAHEP) (see separate entry) for one- to four-year training programs in orthotics and prosthetics. **Application Procedures:** Self-assessment, conducted by program faculty with input from administrators, students, employers of graduates, and other interested parties, required. Must address strengths and weaknesses of program, cover entire range of educational operations, including ancillary services, and document compliance with criteria in the following areas: (1) Sponsorship; (2) Resources, including: Financial resources; General resources; Personnel, covering administrative personnel, clerical and support staff, faculty and instructional staff, medical director, professional development, and program director; and Physical resources, covering affiliated institutions, equipment and supplies, facilities, and learning resources, including instructional aids and library; (3) Students, including: Admission policies and procedures; Appeals; Evaluation; Guidance; and Health; (4) Operational Policies, including: Fair practices; and Student records; (5) Program Evaluation, including: Outcomes; and Results of on-going program evaluation; (6) Curriculum, including: Instructional plan; Program organizational structure; and Required knowledge and skills; and (7) Maintaining and Administering Accreditation. **Accreditation Requirements:** Sponsoring institutions must assume primary responsibility for the following: Academic, didactic, and clinical educational experiences; Appointing qualified faculty; Ensuring financial support necessary for meeting commitments to matriculating

and accepted students; Selecting students; and Granting degrees. Curriculum must include: Biomechanics gait analysis/pathomechanics; Diagnostic fitting; Diagnostic imaging techniques; External power; Fitting and alignment of orthoses for lower limb, upper limb, and spine with various systems to be included; Impression taking; Kinesiology; Materials science; Measurement; Model rectification; Pathology; Postoperative management; Research methods; and Static and dynamic alignment of sockets related to various amputation levels. Program must include clinical experience. On-site review, verifying information provided in self-assessment, required. Review includes tour of facilities and interviews with chief executive officer, administrators of educational program, instructors, students, medical director, and members of admissions committee. May respond to on-site review. Possible accreditation decisions are: (1) Accreditation; (2) Probationary Accreditation, requiring correction of deficiencies; or (3) Withholding Accreditation, for programs in substantial noncompliance with standards. **Renewal:** Every five years (maximum). Renewal based on self-assessment and on-site review. **Fees:** $1000, plus actual cost of on-site review. **Accredited By:** Commission on Recognition of Postsecondary Accreditation; U.S. Department of Education. **Endorsed By:** American Academy of Orthotists and Prosthetists; American Medical Association; American Orthotic and Prosthetic Association; Commission on Accreditation of Allied Health Education Programs; Council on Medical Education.

`1611`

Psychiatric Technician Training Program Accreditation

American Association of Psychiatric Technicians (AAPT)
PO Box 14014
Phoenix, AZ 85063-4014
Phone: (602)873-1890
Fax: (602)873-1890
Toll Free: (800)371-7589
George Blake, Pres.

Recipient: Psychiatric technician programs at colleges, universities, private business schools, and hospitals and other medical facilities. **Accreditation Requirements:** General and specific self-assessments required. General self-assessment requires documentation of compliance with standards in the following areas: Admissions and student services; Board of trustees; Catalogs and other publications; Faculty; Financing and accounting; Innovation and experi-

mentation; Institutional mission or purpose; Library/learning center; Objectives or goals; Organization and administration and top officers; Outcomes; Planning; Plant and equipment; Program in general; Program specific to allied mental health paraprofessionals and psychiatric technicians; and Resources. Specific self-assessment requires documentation of compliance with standards concerning learning objectives. Must submit brochure and catalog and/or curriculum. On-site review may be required. **Renewal:** Every ten years. Renewal based on self-assessment. Must also submit annual report. **Fees:** $2950.

Ambulatory Health Care

`1612`

Accreditation Association for Ambulatory Health Care (AAAHC)

9933 Lawler Ave.
Skokie, IL 60077-3708
Phone: (708)676-9610
Fax: (708)676-9628
Christopher Damon, Exec.Dir.

Recipient: Ambulatory health care organizations. **Accreditation Requirements:** On-site review required. **Renewal:** Every three years (maximum). Renewal based on on-site review. **Preparatory Materials:** *Accreditation Handbook for Ambulatory Health Care* (reference). **Length of Process:** Nine months. **Fees:** Varies.

`1613`

American Association for Accreditation of Ambulatory Plastic Surgery Facilities (AAAAPSF)

1020 Allanson Rd.
Mundelein, IL 60060
Phone: (708)949-6058
Fax: (708)566-4580

Recipient: Ambulatory plastic surgery facilities. **Number of Accredited Institutions:** 400. **Accreditation Requirements:** On-site review required. **Endorsed By:** American Society of Plastic and Reconstructive Surgeons.

Architecture

1614

National Architectural Accrediting Board (NAAB)
1735 New York Ave., NW
Washington, DC 20006
Phone: (202)783-2007
Fax: (202)783-2822
John Maudlin-Jeronimo, Exec.Dir.

Recipient: Bachelor's and master's degree programs in architecture. **Number of Accredited Institutions:** 102. **Application Procedures:** Self-assessment required. Must document compliance with 13 conditions and 54 performance-oriented criteria. **Accreditation Requirements:** On-site review required. May respond to on-site visit. **Renewal:** Every five years (maximum). Renewal based on self-assessment and on-site review. **Preparatory Materials:** *NAAB Conditions and Procedures* and *Visiting Team Handbook* (references). Video available. **Fees:** Actual cost of on-site review and document review. **Accredited By:** U.S. Department of Education.

Art

1615

Commission on Accreditation, National Association of Schools of Art and Design
National Association of Schools of Art and Design (NASAD)
11250 Roger Bacon Dr., Ste. 21
Reston, VA 22090
Phone: (703)437-0700
Fax: (703)437-6312
Samuel Hope, Exec.Dir.

Recipient: Institutions and units within institutions offering associate, baccalaureate, and/or graduate degree programs in art, design, and related disciplines; and non-degree-granting institutions offering programs in these areas. **Application Procedures:** Self-assessment required. Must document compliance with standards in the following areas: (1) Mission, Goals, and Objectives, including: Appropriateness; Creative work and research; Dissemination; Educational and artistic decision-making; Evaluation; Institutional objectives; Long-range planning; Operational decision-making; Performance; Policies and procedures; Resources; Service; Students; Teaching; and Written statement; (2) Size and Scope, including: Enrollment; Objectives; Re-

sources; and Staff size; (3) Finances, including: Allocation of resources; Audits; Financial management; Financial records; Financial statements; Long-range planning; Objectives; and Tuition, fees, and other charges; (4) Governance and Administration, including: Administrative personnel; Autonomy; Board of trustees; Communications; Continuity; Faculty input; Long-range planning; Objectives; Organization; Policies and procedures; Public representation; and Student input; (5) Faculty and Staff, including: Appointment, evaluation, and advancement; Faculty development; Graduate teaching assistants; Loads; Number and distribution; Qualifications; Student/faculty ratios; and Support staff; (6) Facilities, Equipment, and Safety, including: Accessibility; Administrative offices; Budget; Classrooms; Faculty teaching studios and offices; Maintenance; Planning; Safety; Storage facilities; Student practice rooms; Supplies; and Ventilation and safety; (7) Library, including: Collections; Facilities; Finance; Governance; Personnel; and Services; (8) Recruitment, Admission-Retention, Record Keeping, and Advisement, including: Counseling services; Objectives; Requirements; and Student records; (8) Published Materials, including: Catalog; and Published documents; (9) Community Involvement and Articulation with Other Schools, including: Arts agencies; Local schools; and Performing organizations; (10) Evaluation, Planning, and Projections, including: Assessment techniques; Curriculum; Objectives; Operational conditions; Programs and services; Resource allocation and development; Size and scope; and Student achievement and evaluation; and (11) Credit and Time Requirements, including: Awarding credit; Program lengths; Published policies; and Transfer of credit. Proprietary schools must meet additional standards. **Accreditation Requirements:** Degree-granting-institutions must have graduated one class; non-degree-granting institutions must have been in operation for three years. Two-year degree-granting colleges must document compliance with standards in the following areas: Articulation; Objectives; Published materials; and Standards. Undergraduate programs must document compliance with standards in the following areas: Admissions; Advanced standing; General studies; Liberal arts degrees; Majors and areas of emphasis; Professional degrees; Residence; and Studies in the visual arts. Liberal arts degrees offered in the following areas: Art conversation; Art education; Art history; Art therapy; Medical illustration; Museum studies; and Studio art or design. Professional degrees offered in the following areas: Ceramics; Drawing;

Fashion design; Film and video; General crafts; General design; General fine arts; Glass; Graphic design; Illustration; Industrial design; Interior design; Jewelry and metals; Painting; Photography; Printmaking; Sculpture; Studio and art history; Textile design; Theatre design; Weaving and fibers; and Woodworking. Graduate programs must document compliance with standards in the following areas: Admissions; Advisement; Breadth of competence; Course work; Evaluations; Faculty; Final project; Functions of graduate study; Graduation requirements; Language or other proficiencies; Practice-oriented degrees; Preparation for the profession; Publication of degree requirements and procedures; Research-oriented degrees; Residence; Resources; Standardized national examinations; and Statement and publication of objectives and resources. Standards also available for programs in the following areas: Arts administration; Business of visual arts and design; Management or administration; and Support services. On-site review, verifying information provided in self-assessment, required. Review includes interviews with administrators, faculty, students, and other interested parties. May respond to on-site review. Possible accreditation decisions are: (1) Accreditation; (2) Probationary Status, requiring correction of deficiencies within five years; or (3) Denial, for programs in substantial noncompliance with standards. **Renewal:** Every five years (initial); every ten years thereafter. Renewal based on self-assessment and on-site review. **Restrictions:** Must report changes in curriculum. **State Requirements:** Must hold appropriate licenses or charters. **Preparatory Materials:** *Handbook of the National Association of Schools of Art and Design* (reference). **Fees:** $500, plus actual cost of on-site review; must also submit annual fee based on enrollment. **Accredited By:** Commission on Recognition of Postsecondary Accreditation; U.S. Department of Education.

Automotive and Truck Repair

1616

Automobile Technician Training Certification Program
National Automotive Technicians Education Foundation (NATEF)
13505 Dulles Technology Dr., Ste. 2
Herndon, VA 22071-3421
Phone: (703)713-0100
Fax: (703)713-0727

Recipient: Secondary and post-secondary institutions, community colleges, and technical institutes offering National Institute for Automotive Service Excellence courses leading to ASE certifications (see separate entries). **Application Procedures:** Self-assessment required. Must document compliance with standards in the following areas: (1) Purpose, including: Employment potential; and Program description and goals; (2) Administration, including: Administrative support; Advisory committee; Chain of command; Live work; Public and community relations; Student competency certification; and Written policies; (3) Learning Resources, including: Instructional development services; Multimedia; Periodicals; Service information; and Student materials; (4) Finances, including: Budget; Budget preparation; Program training cost; and Status reports; (5) Student Services, including: Follow-up; Legal requirements; Placement; Pre-admission interviews; Pretesting; and Student records; (6) Instruction, including: Articulation; Curriculum; Evaluation of instruction; Live work; Performance standards; Personal characteristics; Preparation time; Program plan; Provision for individual differences; Related instruction; Safety standards; Student progress; Student training plan; Teaching load; Testing; and Work habits and ethics; (7) Equipment, including: Consumable supplies; Hand tools; Inventory; Maintenance; Parts purchasing; Quantity and quality; Replacement; and Safety; (8) Facilities, including: Facility evaluation; First aid; Housekeeping; Instructional area; Maintenance; Office space; Safety; Storage; Support facilities; Training stations; and Ventilation; (9) Instructional Staff, including: First aid; Instructional competency and certification; Substitutes; Technical competency; and Technical updating; and (10) Cooperative Agreements, including: Agreements; Standards; and Supervision. Must identify strengths and weaknesses of program and submit course of study, including: Areas and sequence of instruction; List of training and audio-visual materials; Number of contact hours for each area; Sample evaluation form; Syllabus for each class; and Tasks to be taught. **Accreditation Requirements:** Schools may be accredited in one or all of the following: Automobile; Collision repair and refinish; and Medium and heavy truck. Automobile programs may provide instruction in the following diagnostic and repair areas: (1) Automatic Transmission and Transaxle, including: General; In-vehicle; Maintenance and adjustment; and Off-vehicle. (2) Brakes, including: Anti-lock brake systems; Disc brake; Drum brake; Electrical; Hydraulic system; Parking brakes;

Power assist units; and Wheel bearings; (3) Electrical and Electronic Systems, including: Accessories; Battery; Charging system; Gauges, warning devices, and driver information systems; General electrical system; Horn and wiper and washer; Lighting systems; and Starting system; (4) Engine Performance, including: Computerized engine controls; Emissions control systems; Engine related service; Fuel, air induction, and exhaust systems; General engine; and Ignition system; (5) Engine Repair, including: Cylinder head and valve train; Engine block; General engine diagnosis; Lubrication and cooling systems; and Removal and reinstallation; (6) Heating and Air Conditioning, including: Air conditioning system; Heating and engine cooling systems; Operating systems and related controls; Refrigerant recovery, recycling, and handling; and Refrigeration system components; (7) Manual Drive Train and Axles, including: Clutch; Drive and half shaft universal and constant-velocity joint; Four-wheel drive component; Rear axle; Transaxle; and Transmission; and (8) Suspension and Steering, including: Steering systems; Suspension systems; Wheel alignment; and Wheel and tire. Automobile programs must also provide instruction in the following workplace skills areas: Accepting employment; Adapting and coping with change; Communicating on the job; Demonstrating team work; Demonstrating technology literacy; Demonstrating work ethics and behavior; Developing employment plan; Interpreting economics of work; Maintaining interpersonal relationships; Maintaining professionalism; Maintaining safe and healthy environment; Seeking and applying for employment opportunities; and Solving problems and critical thinking. Collision repair and refinish programs may provide instruction in the following diagnostic and repair areas: (1) Mechanical and Electrical Components, including: Brakes; Cooling systems; Drive train; Electrical; Fuel, intake, and exhaust systems; Heating and air conditioning; Restraint systems; and Suspension and steering; (2) Non-Structural Analysis and Damage Repair, including: Metal finishing and body filling; Metal welding and cutting; Movable glass and hardware; Outer body panel; and Preparation; (3) Painting and Refinishing, including: Final detail; Finish defects, causes, and cures; Paint mixing, matching, and applying; Safety precautions; Solving paint application problems; Spray gun and related equipment; and Surface preparation; (4) Plastics and Adhesives; and (5) Structural Analysis and Damage Repair, including: Fixed glass; Frame; Metal welding and cutting; and Unibody. Medium and heavy truck pro-

grams may provide instruction in the following diagnostic and repair areas: (1) Brakes, including: Air brakes; and Hydraulic brakes; (2) Diesel Engines, including: Air induction and exhaust systems; Cooling system; Cylinder head and valve train; Engine block; Engine brakes; Fuel system; General engine; and Lubrication systems; (3) Drive Train, including: Clutch; Drive axle; Drive shaft and universal joint; and Transmission; (4) Electrical and Electronic Systems, including: Battery; Charging system; Gauges and warning devices; General electrical systems; Lighting systems; and Starting system; (5) Gasoline Engines, including: Cylinder head and valve train; Emissions control systems; Engine block; Fuel and exhaust systems; General engine; Ignition system; Lubrication and cooling systems; and Removal and reinstallation; (6) Heating and Air Conditioning, including: Air conditioning systems; Heating system; Operating systems and related controls; Refrigerant recovery, recycling, and handling; and Refrigeration system component; (7) Preventive Maintenance Inspection, including: Cab and body; Chassis and undercarriage; Electrical and electronic; Engine compartment; and Tires and wheels; and (8) Suspension and Steering, including: Steering systems; Suspension systems; Wheel alignment; and Wheels and tires. On-site review required. **Renewal:** Every five years. Renewal based on self-assessment and on-site review. Must also submit compliance reports. Renewal fee is $445. **Preparatory Materials:** *ASE Program Certification Standards* (reference). **Fees:** $720.

Birth Centers

1617

Commission for the Accreditation of Freestanding Birth Centers (CAFBC)
3121 Gottschall Rd.
Perkomenville, PA 18074
Phone: (215)234-0564
Fax: (215)234-8829
Mary Lou Longeway RN, Chair

Recipient: Freestanding birth centers. **Number of Accredited Institutions:** 36. **Application Procedures:** Self-assessment required. Must document compliance with eight standards. Must also submit policies and procedures manual. **Accreditation Requirements:** On-site review required. May respond to on-site review. **Renewal:** Every three years. Renewal based on self-assessment and on-site review. **Restrictions:** Must be autonomous and self-governing. **State Requirements:** Must hold state license, if required. **Preparatory Materials:** *Standards for Freestanding Birth Centers* (reference). Manual and video available. **Length of Process:** Four-six months. **Fees:** $2500.

Blind and Visually Handicapped

1618

National Accreditation Council for Agencies Serving the Blind and Visually Handicapped (NAC)
15 E. 40th St., Ste. 1004
New York, NY 10016
Phone: (212)683-5068
Fax: (212)683-4475
Ruth T. Westman, Exec.Dir.

Recipient: Private and public schools, agencies, and programs serving children and adults who are blind or visually disabled. **Number of Accredited Institutions:** 74. **Application Procedures:** Self-assessment required. Must document compliance with standards in the following areas: Accountability; Consumer satisfaction; Management; and Services. Must submit completed manuals, narratives, and supporting documentation. **Accreditation Requirements:** On-site review required. May respond to on-site review. **Renewal:** Every five years. Renewal based on self-assessment and on-site review. **Preparatory Materials:** Standards and procedural guidelines available. **Length of Process:** Every year. **Fees:** Actual cost of materials and on-site review.

Business

1619

Accrediting Council, American Assembly of Collegiate Schools of Business
American Assembly of Collegiate Schools of Business (AACSB)
600 Emerson Rd., Ste. 300
St. Louis, MO 63141-6762
Phone: (314)872-8481
Fax: (314)872-8495
Milton R. Blood, Dir.

Recipient: Baccalaureate, master's, and doctoral degree programs in business administration and management and ac-

counting. **Number of Accredited Institutions:** 305. **Application Procedures:** Self-assessment required. Must document compliance with standards in the following areas: (1) Mission and Objective, including: Appropriateness; Educational objectives; Emphasis on teaching, intellectual contributions, and service; Periodic review; and Student characteristics; (2) Faculty Composition and Development, including: Development, promotion, retention, and renewal; Experience; Planning; Qualifications; Recruitment, selection, and orientation; and Size, composition, and deployment; (3) Curriculum Content and Evaluation, including: Content; Evaluation; Majors; Planning; and Requirements; (4) Instructional Resources and Responsibilities, including: Collective faculty responsibilities; Individual instructional responsibilities; and Management; (5) Students, including: Admissions; Career planning and placement; Diversity; and Selection; and (6) Intellectual Contributions, including: Applied scholarship; Basic scholarship; and Instructional development. Must document strengths and weaknesses of program and develop plan for the future. **Accreditation Requirements:** Programs must have administrative support, support policy of diversity, and have been in operation for sufficient length of time. Both undergraduate and graduate business curriculums must cover: Ethical and global issues; Impact of demographic diversity on organizations; and Influence of political, social, legal and regulatory, environmental, and technological issues. Undergraduate business curriculum should include: Accounting; Communications (written and oral); Behavioral science; Economics; Mathematics; and Statistics. Core curriculum for Master's of Business Administration (MBA) and other general management master's degree programs should include instruction in the following areas: Creation and distribution of goods and services; Domestic and global economic environments of organizations; Financial reporting, analysis, and markets; and Human behavior in organizations. Curriculum for business doctoral programs should include: Acquisition of advanced knowledge; Development of advanced research; Managerial and organizational contexts; and Teaching experience. Undergraduate accounting curriculum should include instruction in the following areas: Arts; Auditing; Communication (written and oral); Computer-based technology; Critical thinking; Financial accounting; Governmental accounting; History; Information systems; Legal, international, and multi-cultural environment of society; Literature; Managerial accounting; Non-for-profit accounting; Operations and

technology management; Science; Taxation; and Value systems. On-site review, verifying information provided in self-assessment, required. Review includes tour of facilities and meetings with administrators, faculty, students, and other interested individuals. May respond to on-site review. Possible accreditation decisions are: (1) Accreditation; (2) Accreditation Deferred, requiring correction of deficiencies; or (3) Accreditation Denied, for programs in substantial non-compliance with standards. **Renewal:** Every ten years. Renewal based on self-assessment and on-site review. Must also submit interim reports. Renewal fees are: $7000 (business or accounting); $9500 (business and accounting). **Preparatory Materials:** *Guidance for Self-Evaluation, Peer Review Process Manual,* and *Standards for Accreditation in Business Administration and Accounting* (references). Video available. **Length of Process:** Two years. **Fees:** $3000 (business or accounting) or $5000 (business and accounting), plus actual cost of on-site review. Annual fees are: $2100 (business); $4400 (business and accounting). **Accredited By:** Commission on Recognition of Postsecondary Accreditation; U.S. Department of Education.

1620

Association of Collegiate Business Schools and Programs (ACBSP)
7007 College Blvd., Ste. 420
Overland, KS 66211
Phone: (913)339-9356
Fax: (913)339-6226
Dr. John L. Green Jr., Exec.Dir.

Recipient: Business schools and programs operating at degree granting colleges and universities in the U.S. **Application Procedures:** Self-assessment required. Must document compliance with standards. **Accreditation Requirements:** On-site review required. May respond to on-site review. **Renewal:** Every seven years. Must also submit annual report. **Preparatory Materials:** Publications and training sessions available. **Length of Process:** One year. **Fees:** $5000. **Accredited By:** U.S. Department of Education.

1621

International Federation for Business Education (IFBE)
7007 College Blvd., Ste. 420
Overland, KS 66211
Phone: (913)339-9356
Fax: (913)339-6226
Dr. John L. Green Jr., Exec.Dir.

Recipient: Business schools and programs operating at degree granting colleges and universities outside the U.S. **Application Procedures:** Self-assessment required. Must document compliance with standards. **Accreditation Requirements:** On-site review required. May respond to on-site review. **Renewal:** Every seven years. Must also submit annual report. **Preparatory Materials:** Publications and training sessions available. **Length of Process:** One year. **Fees:** $10,000.

Camping

▊1622▊

Accredited Camp
American Camping Association
  (ACA)
5000 State Rd. 67 N.
Martinsville, IN 46151-7902
Phone: (317)342-8456
Fax: (317)342-2065
Toll Free: (800)428-CAMP

Recipient: Day and resident camps. **Application Procedures:** Self-assessment required. Must attend Basic Standards Course. **Accreditation Requirements:** Must meet the following requirements: (1) Provide creative, recreational, and educational opportunities in group living in the out-of-doors; (2) Utilize trained leadership and resources of natural surroundings; and (3) Contribute to each camper's mental, physical, social, and spiritual growth. Program operators must hire staff and plan program and have operating season consisting of sessions, a majority of which are at least five consecutive days in length. Day camps must have operating season consisting of sessions, a majority of which are at least five days in length in a period of not more than 14 days. Accredited camps may operate on their own property or on property belonging to someone else. On-site review required. Review covers the following areas: (1) Site, including: Bathing and toilet facilities; Fire protection; Food service; and Sleeping quarters; (2) Administration, including: Administrative concerns; Child protection; and Overall site safety; (3) Transportation, including: Drivers; Traffic on site; and Vehicles; (4) Personnel, including: Staff qualifications; and Training and supervision ratios and procedures; (5) Program, including: Activity leadership qualifications; Facility and equipment requirements; Procedures for conducting program activities; and Safety regulations; (6) Health Care, including: Facility requirements; Health information; Record-

keeping; and Staff qualifications; (7) Aquatics, including: Facility and equipment requirements; Leadership qualifications; and Safety regulations and procedures; (8) Trip/Travel Camping, including: Camping practices; Communication; Leadership qualifications; and Training; (9) Horseback Riding, including: Facility and equipment requirements; Leadership qualifications; and Safety regulations; and (10) Mandatory standards, including: Aquatic-certified personnel; Emergency exits; Emergency transportation; First aid; Obtaining appropriate health information; and Storage and use of flammables and firearms. **Preparatory Materials:** *Standards for Day and Resident Camps and Guide to Accredited Camps* (reference). **Length of Process:** Six months.

▊1623▊

Accredited Conference/Retreat Center
American Camping Association
  (ACA)
5000 State Rd. 67 N.
Martinsville, IN 46151-7902
Phone: (317)342-8456
Fax: (317)342-2065
Toll Free: (800)428-CAMP

Recipient: Conference/retreat centers for adults and other groups who hold meetings, training sessions, and educational or inspirational programs. **Application Procedures:** Self-assessment required. Must document compliance with standards in the following areas: (1) Administration and Hospitality Services, including: Administrative policies; Personnel; and Risk management; (2) Recreation and Leisure Services, including: Aquatics; General recreation; and Horseback riding; and (3) Site and Food Service, including: Food service; Meeting rooms; Sleeping quarters; and Transportation. Must attend Basic Standards Course and hold membership in one of the following: American Camping Association; Christian Camping International; or International Association of Conference Center Administrators. **Accreditation Requirements:** Centers operate three seasons per year, are designed to minimize outside distractions, and provide: Access to facilities and natural environments for release and diversion; Dedicated meeting space; Food service; Hospitality and support services; and Housing styles appropriate to target clientele. Must meet the following requirements: (1) Operate at least 60 days per year; (2) Provide indoor space specifically suited for group meetings, in addition to space used for dining; (3) Provide hospitality and support services for groups that include staff on-site and

staffed food service; and (4) Operate facility and services primarily for group programs, not for individual hospitality, as in resorts and hotels. On-site review required. **Renewal:** Every three years. Renewal based on on-site review. **Preparatory Materials:** *Standards for Conference and Retreat Centers* (reference). **Fees:** $300-$1500 (based on gross operating income or expenses).

▊1624▊

Accredited Site
American Camping Association
  (ACA)
5000 State Rd. 67 N.
Martinsville, IN 46151-7902
Phone: (317)342-8456
Fax: (317)342-2065
Toll Free: (800)428-CAMP

Recipient: Camp-style facilities utilized by youth, family, and adult groups seeking rustic setting for retreats, environmental and outdoor education, youth and family camping, and other organized activities. **Application Procedures:** Self-assessment required. Must attend Basic Standards Course. **Accreditation Requirements:** Must lease, rent, or otherwise make available site and/or facilities to other program operators or sponsors who are responsible for their own staffing and programming. Although some sites may offer limited program services to groups, most groups using approved sites retain responsibility for their own staffing and activities. On-site review required. Review includes the following areas: (1) Site, including: Bathing and toilet facilities; Fire protection; Food service; Maintenance; and Sleeping quarters; (2) Administration, including procedures for: Health care; Personnel; Site safety; and Transportation; (3) Aquatics, including: Facility and equipment requirements; Leadership qualifications; and Safety procedures; (4) Horseback Riding, including: Facility and equipment requirements; Leadership qualifications; and Safety procedures; and (5) Mandatory Standards, including: Aquatic-certified personnel; Emergency exits; Emergency transportation; First aid; Meeting commonly accepted business practices; Obtaining appropriate health information; and Storage and use of flammables and firearms. **Preparatory Materials:** *Standards for Day and Resident Camps and Guide to Accredited Camps* (reference). **Length of Process:** Six months.

Certification

National Commission for Certifying Agencies (NCCA)
1200 19th St., NW, Ste. 300
Washington, DC 20036-2401
Phone: (202)857-1165
Fax: (202)223-4579
Michael S. Hamm, Exec.Dir.

Recipient: National certifying agencies. **Number of Accredited Institutions:** 28. **Accreditation Requirements:** Must be non-governmental and non-profit, and have successfully completed two national exam administrations. Must document compliance with standards in the following areas: (1) Purpose; (2) Structure, including: Autonomy; Governing body; Incorporation; Public involvement; and Scope; (3) Resources, including: Financial resources; and Knowledge and skills; (4) Candidate Testing Mechanism, including: Exam records; Objectiveness; Pass/fail levels; Policies and procedures; Reliability and validity; and Periodic review; (5) Public Information, including: Certification responsibilities; Eligibility requirements and determination procedures; Exam administration; Exam construction and validation; Information, knowledge, or functions covered by exam; Other activities of organization; and Summary of certification activities; (6) Responsibilities to Applicants for Certification or Recertification, including: Alternate eligibility pathways; Appeal procedures; Compliance with federal and state laws; Confidentiality; Dissemination of procedures; Exam site availability; Feedback for failing students; Nondiscrimination; Periodic review of eligibility criteria and application procedures; and Reporting exam results; (7) Responsibilities to Public and Employers of Certified Practitioners, including: Adequacy of testing mechanism; Discipline procedures; Lists of certified practitioners; Requirements for certification or recertification; and Titles; and (8) Recertification Program, requiring that program measures continued competence. Must undergo evaluation of written materials. **Renewal:** Every five years (maximum). Must submit annual reports. **Restrictions:** Must report changes in the following areas: Activities; Exam administration; Exam techniques; Purpose; Scope or objectives of exam; or Structure. **Preparatory Materials:** "Standards for Accreditation of National Certification Organizations" (reference). **Fees:** $500; $3000 (annual fee). **Endorsed By:** National Organization for Competency Assurance.

Chemistry

Commission on Accreditation in Clinical Chemistry (ComACC)
c/o American Association for Clinical Chemistry
2101 L St., NW, Ste. 202
Washington, DC 20037-1526

Recipient: Master's, Ph.D., and post-doctoral degree programs in clinical chemistry. **Number of Accredited Institutions:** 32. **Application Procedures:** Self-assessment required. **Accreditation Requirements:** On-site review required. May respond to on-site review. **Renewal:** Every three years. Renewal based on self-assessment and on-site review. **Endorsed By:** Academy of Clinical Laboratory Physicians and Scientists; American Association for Clinical Chemistry; Association of Clinical Scientists; National Academy of Clinical Biochemistry.

Childhood

National Academy of Early Childhood Programs
National Association for the Education of Young Children (NAEYC)
1509 16th St., NW
Washington, DC 20036-1426
Phone: (202)328-2601
Fax: (202)328-1846
Toll Free: (800)424-2460
Sue Bredekamp, Dir.

Recipient: Early childhood group programs. **Number of Accredited Institutions:** 3500. **Application Procedures:** Self-assessment required. Must document compliance with standards in the following areas: Administration; Curriculum; Health and safety; Interactions among staff and children; Nutrition and food service; Physical environment; Program evaluation; Staff and parent interactions; Staff qualifications and development; and Staffing patterns. Must include: Administrative evaluation; Classroom observation; Internal evaluation; and Parent and staff questionnaires. Must make needed improvements based on self-assessment. **Accreditation Requirements:** Must meet needs of, and promote physical, social, emotional, and cognitive development of, children involved in program. On-site review required. May respond to on-site review. **Renewal:** Every three years. Renewal based on self-assessment and on-site review. **Restrictions:** Accreditation not transferrable if program changes ownership or location. **State Requirements:** Must meet local/state licensing requirements or demonstrate compliance if exempt. **Preparatory Materials:** *Accreditation Criteria and Procedures of the National Academy of Early Childhood Programs* and *Guide to Accreditation* (references). Brochures and videotape available. **Fees:** $350-$850 (based on size of program).

Chiropractic

Council on Chiropractic Education (CCE)
7975 N. Hayden Rd., Ste. A-210
Scottsdale, AZ 85258
Phone: (602)443-8877
Fax: (602)483-7333

Recipient: Chiropractic programs and institutions awarding Doctor of Chiropractic (D.C.) degree. **Number of Accredited Institutions:** 20. **Application Procedures:** Self-assessment required. Must document compliance with standards in the following areas: Academic calendars; Advertising; Catalogs and publications; Curriculum; Evaluation; Facilities, equipment, and supplies; Faculty; Fiscal and administrative capacity; Recruiting an admissions practices; Student support services. **Accreditation Requirements:** Applicants to programs must meet following requirements: (1) Sixty semester hours or equivalent of college credit leading toward baccalaureate degree at accredited university, with grade point average of at least 2.25 on 4.00 scale; and (2) Coursework in the following: Biological sciences; Chiropractic theory; Communication and/or language skills; Diagnostic procedures; General or inorganic chemistry; Humanities; Organic chemistry; Physics; Psychology; Social studies; and Treatment procedures. Curriculum should consist of five academic years and include classroom and laboratory work in basic sciences such as anatomy, biochemistry, and physiology. Onsite review required. **Accredited By:** Commission on Recognition of Postsecondary Accreditation; U.S. Department of Education.

Cleaning and Restoration

1629

Cleaning Equipment Trade Association (CETA)
2535 Pilot Knob Rd., Ste. 105
St. Paul, MN 55120
Phone: (612)686-7086
Fax: (612)686-7088
Toll Free: (800)441-0111
John Hoppenstedt, Exec.Dir.

Recipient: Pressure washer distributors. **Membership:** Required. **Accreditation Requirements:** Must meet the following requirements: (1) Hold membership in CETA; (2) Have been in operation for two years; and (3) Have at least one employee who has received factory (manufacturer) service training. Must also accumulate 100 total points through: (1) CETA-sanctioned seminars or state, regional, or national meetings; (2) Factory and supplier training programs or seminars, or courses at community colleges or vocational-technical schools; and (3) Years of operation. Points for seminars and training may be earned by any employee of company. **Renewal:** Every two years. Renewal based on accumulation of 100 points. **Fees:** $100.

1630

Institute of Inspection, Cleaning, and Restoration Certification Certified Firm
Institute of Inspection, Cleaning, and Restoration Certification (IICRC)
2715 E. Mill Plain Blvd.
Vancouver, WA 98661
Phone: (206)693-5675
Fax: (206)693-4858
Toll Free: (800)835-4624

Recipient: Carpet inspection, cleaning, and restoration firms. **Accreditation Requirements:** Firms must: (1) Carry adequate insurance coverage; (2) Employ, or have on staff, technicians certified by IICRC (see separate entries) in areas in which firm offers services; (3) Maintain appropriate licenses; (4) Maintain payroll procedure paying certified technicians at higher rate than non-certified technicians; (5) Maintain written complaint procedure; and (6) Provide continuous education program for technicians.

Clinical Pastoral Education

1631

Association for Clinical Pastoral Education Accreditation Commission
Association for Clinical Pastoral Education (ACPE)
1549 Clairmont Rd., Ste. 103
Decatur, GA 30033
Phone: (404)320-1472

Recipient: Clinical pastoral centers and clusters. Clusters are groups of at least three centers in same region related to one theological school. **Application Procedures:** Feasibility study, requiring input from supervisors, chaplaincy staff members, and administration, required. Must document compliance with standards in the following areas: (1) Rationale and Objectives; (2) Administrative Structure and Support, including: Budget; Secretarial support; Space; and Structure; (3) Curriculum, including: Methodology of educational programs; and Philosophy; (4) Clinical and Educational Resources, including: Faculty; Ministry of students; and Seminars; (5) Policies and Procedures, including: Admission; Complaint resolution; Program evaluation; Rights and responsibilities; Student records; and Tuition; and (6) Strengths and Limitations of Program, including proposed corrective action. **Accreditation Requirements:** On-site review, verifying compliance with feasibility study, required. Review includes meetings with administrator, chaplaincy staff members, past and present students, supervisors, and other educational personnel. May respond to on-site review. Possible accreditation decisions are: (1) Accreditation Granted; (2) Accreditation Deferred, requiring correction of deficiencies; or (3) Accreditation Denied, for centers or clusters in substantial noncompliance with standards. **Renewal:** Every seven years (maximum). Renewal based on self-assessment and on-site review. **Restrictions:** Must have each new program accredited.

Community Association Management

1632

Accredited Association Management Company (AAMC)
Community Associations Institute (CAI)
1630 Duke St.
Alexandria, VA 22314
Phone: (703)548-8600
Fax: (703)684-1581

Recipient: Community association management companies. **Membership:** Required. **Accreditation Requirements:** Management company must: (1) Employ supervisor who holds Professional Community Association Manager (PCAM) designation (see separate entry); (2) Have been in operation for three years; (3) Maintain minimum of $100,000 of fidelity insurance and general liability, worker's compensation, and other insurance as may be required by statute; (4) Maintain separate bank accounts for each of its clients and reconcile them monthly; (5) Provide, at least quarterly, a balance sheet, budget comparison, income statement, receivables reports, and statement of disbursements; and (6) Require boards to acknowledge investments and disbursements of reserve funds. **Restrictions:** Must report changes in name or address. **State Requirements:** Must comply with all local, state, and federal laws. **Fees:** $200; $100 (annual fee).

Computer Science

1633

Computing Science Accreditation Commission (CSAC)
Computing Sciences Accreditation Board (CSAB)
Two Landmark Sq., Ste. 209
Stamford, CT 06901
Phone: (203)975-1117
Fax: (203)975-1222
E-mail: csab@uconnvm.uconn.edu
Patrick M. LaMalva, Exec.Dir.

Recipient: Baccalaureate degree programs designated as computer science programs preparing students for entry into computer science profession. **Number of Accredited Institutions:** 126. **Application Procedures:** Self-assessment, involving administrators, faculty, and students, required. Must document compliance with standards in the following areas: (1) Faculty, including: Continuing education; Continuity and stability; Evaluation; Full-time faculty; Input on curriculum; Professional development; Qualifications; Scholarly activities; Staff size; Student/faculty ratio; and Teaching load; (2) Curriculum, including: Communication skills; Computer science; Electives; General education; Length; and Social and ethical implications of computing; (3) Laboratory and Computing Resources, including: Accessibility; Equipment; Instructional assistance; Maintenance; Scholarly activities; Software; and Support personnel; (4) Students, including: Advising; Evaluation; Graduation requirements; and Student progress; (5) Institutional Support, including: Administration; Faculty support; Laboratory and computing support; Library; and Office secretarial support; and (6) Innovative, Experimental, and Non-Day Programs. **Accreditation Requirements:** On-site review, verifying information provided in self-assessment, required. Review includes interviews with faculty, staff, administrators, students, and other interested parties. May respond to on-site review. Possible accreditation decisions are: (1) Accreditation; (2) 3V Action, requiring correction of deficiencies within three years; or (3) Not to Accredit, for programs in substantial noncompliance with standards. **Renewal:** Every six years (maximum). Renewal based on self-assessment and on-site review. **Fees:** $6100. **Accredited By:** Commission on Recognition of Postsecondary Accreditation; U.S. Department of Education.

Construction

1634

American Council for Construction Education (ACCE)
1300 Hudson Ln., Ste. 3
Monroe, LA 71201-6054
Phone: (318)323-2413
Daniel E. Dupress, Exec.V.Pres.

Recipient: Associate degree programs in construction and baccalaureate degree programs in construction, construction science, construction management, and construction technology. **Number of Accredited Institutions:** 44. **Application Procedures:** Self-assessment required. **Accreditation Requirements:** On-site review required. Review includes discussion with faculty, staff, administrators, students, and other interested parties. May respond to on-site review. **Renewal:** Every six years. **Accredited By:** Commission on Recognition of Postsecondary Accreditation.

Continuing Education

1635

Accrediting Council for Continuing Education and Training (ACCET)
1560 Wilson Blvd., Ste. 900
Arlington, VA 22209
Phone: (703)525-3000
Fax: (703)525-3339

Recipient: Institutions offering postsecondary non-degree continuing education and training programs. **Number of Accredited Institutions:** 1034. **Application Procedures:** Self-assessment required. Must document compliance with standards. Must attend pre-accreditation workshop. **Accreditation Requirements:** Must meet the following requirements: (1) Be in operation for two years; (2) Document financial and administrative capability; and (3) Document educational mission within ACCET's guidelines. On-site review required. May respond to on-site review. **Renewal:** Every five years (maximum). Renewal based on self-assessment and on-site review. **Restrictions:** May not add programs or locations during review process or for one year after initial accreditation. **Preparatory Materials:** Information packet provided. **Length of Process:** 12-18 months. **Fees:** $5450; must also submit annual fee. **Accredited By:** U.S. Department of Education.

Correspondence Education

1636

Accrediting Commission of the Distance Education and Training Council
Distance Education and Training Council (DETC)
1601 18th St., NW
Washington, DC 20009-2529
Phone: (202)234-5100
Fax: (202)332-1386
Michael P. Lambert, Exec.Sec.

Recipient: Postsecondary distance or correspondence/home study education institutions offering non-degree and degree courses and programs through master's degree level. **Number of Accredited Institutions:** 88. **Application Procedures:** Self-assessment required. Must document compliance with standards in the following areas: Advertising; Curriculum; Educational services; Faculty; Finance; Student success and satisfaction; and

Students. Must also submit instructional material for review. **Accreditation Requirements:** On-site review required. Review includes discussion with faculty, staff, administrators, students, and other interested parties. May respond to on-site review. **Accredited By:** Commission on Recognition of Postsecondary Accreditation; U.S. Department of Education.

Cosmetology

1637

National Accrediting Commission of Cosmetology Arts and Sciences (NACCAS)
901 N. Stuart St., Ste. 900
Arlington, VA 22203-1816
Phone: (703)527-7600
Fax: (703)527-8811

Recipient: Postsecondary schools and departments of cosmetology arts and sciences, including specialized schools. **Number of Accredited Institutions:** 1500. **Application Procedures:** Self-assessment required. Must demonstrate compliance with standards in the following areas: Administration; Ethics; Financial responsibility; and Good practice. **Accreditation Requirements:** Curriculum may include: Advanced cosmetology beauty school management and administration of salon management; Barbering; Cosmetology (basic); Esthetics; Ethnic hair studies; Hair coloring; Hair removal (temporary or permanent); Make-up specialties, including stage and theatrical; Manicuring sculptured nails; Modeling; Permanent waving; Platform artistry; Shampoo specialties; Skin care; Small equipment repair; Spa/health club management; Teacher training; and Wig specialties. **Preparatory Materials:** *Rules of Practice and Procedure, Self-Evaluation Report,* and *Standards and Criteria* (references). **Accredited By:** U.S. Department of Education. **Endorsed By:** American Association of Cosmetology Schools; National Cosmetology Association; National Interstate Council of State Boards of Cosmetology.

Counseling

1638

Community and Junior College Counseling Services Board of Accreditation of the International Association of Counseling Services
International Association of
Counseling Services (IACS)
101 S. Whiting St., Ste. 211
Alexandria, VA 22304
Phone: (703)823-9840
Fax: (703)823-9843

Recipient: Community and junior college counseling services. **Application Procedures:** Self-assessment required. Must document compliance with standards in the following areas: (1) Professional Education, Supervised Practice, and Experience, including: Counseling staff; and Director of counseling; (2) Professional Association Membership; (3) Professional Practices, including: Caseloads; Client records; Community articulation; Ethics; Informational materials; Intracollege articulation; Procedural flexibility; Procedures and policies; Professional development; Program accountability system; Source of professional decisions; and Tests; (4) Administrative Criteria, including: Fees; Publicity; and Stability; and (5) Counseling Center Effectiveness. **Accreditation Requirements:** On-site review, verifying information provided in self-assessment, required. May respond to on-site review. Possible accreditation decisions are: (1) Fully Accredited; (2) Provisionally Accredited, requiring correction of deficiencies within three years; or (3) Deny Accreditation, for services in substantial non-compliance with standards. **Renewal:** Every four years. Renewal based on submission of annual reports. On-site review required every eight years. **Preparatory Materials:** *Guidelines for Community and Junior Colleges Counseling Services* (reference). Consultants available.

1639

Council for Accreditation of Counseling and Related Educational Programs (CACREP)
American Counseling Association
(ACA)
5999 Stevenson Ave.
Alexandria, VA 22304
Phone: (703)823-9800
Fax: (703)823-0252
Toll Free: (800)347-6647
Carol L. Bobby, Exec.Dir.

Recipient: Master's degree programs designed to prepare individuals for community, marriage and family, mental health, and school counseling, and careers in student affairs practice in higher education, and doctoral level programs in counselor education and supervision. **Number of Accredited Institutions:** 91. **Application Procedures:** Self-assessment required. Must document compliance with standards. **Accreditation Requirements:** Successful completion of three-stage review process, including on-site review. Review includes discussion with faculty, staff, administrators, students, and other interested parties. May respond to on-site review. Possible accreditation decisions are: (1) Accreditation; (2) Accreditation With Conditions, requiring correction of deficiencies within two years; or (3) Accreditation Denied, for programs in substantial noncompliance with standards. **Renewal:** Every seven years. Renewal based on self-assessment and on-site review. **Preparatory Materials:** *CACREP Accreditation Standards and Procedures Manual* (reference). Self-assessment writing workshop available. **Length of Process:** One year. **Accredited By:** Commission on Recognition of Postsecondary Accreditation.

1640

Public and Private Counseling Services Board of Accreditation of the International Association of Counseling Services
International Association of
Counseling Services (IACS)
101 S. Whiting St., Ste. 211
Alexandria, VA 22304
Phone: (703)823-9840
Fax: (703)823-9843

Recipient: Public and private counseling services. **Application Procedures:** Self-assessment required. Must document compliance with standards in the following areas: (1) Organization, including: Affirmative action; Articles of incorporation and by-laws; Board of directors or governing body; Conflict of interest; Meeting minutes; Organizational chart; and Tax exempt status; (2) Fiscal Management, including: Annual budget; Audit report; and Financial statements; (3) Counseling Agency Functions, Roles, and Scope, including: Mission and objectives statement; and Referrals to professionals and agencies; (4) Ethical Standards, including: Disposition of client and agency records; Preparation, use, and distribution of psychological tests; Release forms; State data privacy laws; and Utilizing clients as subjects for research; (5) Counseling and Professional Practices, including: Case records; Counseling and testing by mail or telephone; Follow-up procedures; and Procedural flexibility; (6) Informational Materials, including: Adequacy of materials; and Use of library; (7) Personnel Policies, including: Code of personnel policies, including employee benefits, employee categories, employment practices and procedures, general policy statements, and termination of service procedures; Counseling staff, including education and supervised practice; Director of counseling program, including: education, experience, licensure or certification, and supervised practice; Paraprofessional staff; Personnel files; Professional association membership criteria; Support staff; and Trainees; (8) Staff Development, including: Case conferences and seminars; Continuing professional education; and Observation and other supervision of counseling interviews; (9) Physical Facilities, including: Accessibility; Safety; and Space considerations; (10) Marketing and Public Relations, including: Brochures; Forms; News releases; and Telephone directory listing; and (11) Fees. **Accreditation Requirements:** On-site review, verifying information provided in self-assessment, required. May respond to on-site review. Possible accreditation decisions are: (1) Fully Accredited; (2) Provisionally Accredited, requiring correction of deficiencies within three years; or (3) Deny Accreditation, for services in substantial non-compliance with standards. **Renewal:** Every four years. Renewal based on submission of annual reports. On-site review required every eight years. **Preparatory Materials:** *Criteria and Standards for Accreditation of Public and Private Counseling Services* (reference). Consultants available.

1641

University and College Counseling Centers Board of Accreditation of the International Association of Counseling Services
International Association of
Counseling Services (IACS)
101 S. Whiting St., Ste. 211
Alexandria, VA 22304
Phone: (703)823-9840
Fax: (703)823-9843

Recipient: University and college counseling centers. **Application Procedures:** Self-assessment required. Must document compliance with standards in the following areas: (1) Relationship of the Counseling Center to the University and College Community; (2) Counseling Services Roles and Functions, including: Consultation services; Crisis intervention and emergency services; Individual and group counseling and psychotherapy; Outreach programming; Research; and Training; (3) Ethical Standards; (4) Counseling Services Personnel, including: Duties of director; Duties of professional staff; Duties of trainees and paraprofessionals; Equivalency criteria of nondoctorate directors; Professional staff; Qualifications and competencies of director; Qualifications and competencies of professional staff; Status of professional staff within university or college; and Support staff; and (5) Related Guidelines, including: Compensation-salary; Multiple counseling agencies; Physical facilities; Professional development; Size of staff; Staffing practices; and Workload. **Accreditation Requirements:** On-site review, verifying information provided in self-assessment, required. May respond to on-site review. Possible accreditation decisions are: (1) Fully Accredited; (2) Provisionally Accredited, requiring correction of deficiencies within three years; or (3) Deny Accreditation, for centers in substantial non-compliance with standards. **Renewal:** Every four years. Renewal based on submission of annual reports. On-site review required every eight years. **Preparatory Materials:** *Accreditation of College and University Counseling Centers* and *Accreditation Standards for University and College Counseling Centers* (references). Consultants available.

Culinary Arts

1642

American Culinary Federation Educational Institute Accrediting Commission
American Culinary Federation (ACF)
PO Box 3466
St. Augustine, FL 32085-3466
Phone: (904)824-4468
Fax: (904)832-4758

Recipient: Culinary arts educational programs. **Number of Accredited Institutions:** 65. **Application Procedures:** Self-assessment required. Must document compliance with standards in the following areas: Curriculum; Facilities; Faculty; Organizational structure; Resources; and Support staff. **Accreditation Requirements:** On-site review, verifying information provided in self-assessment, required. May respond to on-site review. **Accredited By:** U.S. Department of Education.

Dance

1643

Commission on Accreditation, National Association of Schools of Dance
National Association of Schools of Dance (NASD)
11250 Roger Bacon Dr., Ste. 21
Reston, VA 22090
Phone: (703)437-0700
Fax: (703)437-6312
Samuel Hope, Exec.Dir.

Recipient: Institutions and units within institutions offering associate, baccalaureate, and/or graduate programs in dance and related disciplines; and non-degree granting institutions sponsoring similar programs. **Application Procedures:** Self-assessment required. Must document compliance with standards in the following areas: (1) Mission, Goals, and Objectives, including: Appropriateness; Creative work and research; Dissemination; Educational and artistic decision-making; Evaluation; Institutional objectives; Long-range planning; Music and music-related fields; Operational decision-making; Performance; Policies and procedures; Resources; Service; Students; Teaching; and Written statement; (2) Size and Scope, including: Enrollment; Objectives; Resources; and Staff size; (3) Finances, including: Allocation of resources; Audits; Financial management; Financial records; Financial statements; Long-range planning; Objectives; and Tuition, fees, and other charges; (4) Governance and Administration, including: Administrative personnel; Autonomy; Board of trustees; Communications; Continuity; Faculty input; Long-range planning; Objectives; Organization; Policies and procedures; Public representation; and Student input; (5) Faculty and Staff, including: Appointment, evaluation, and advancement; Class size; Faculty development; Graduate teaching assistants; Loads; Music staff; Number and distribution; Qualifications; Student/faculty ratios; Support staff; and Technical staff; (6) Facilities, Equipment, and Safety, including: Access; Equipment; Health and safety hazards; Office and administrative space; Studio, rehearsal, and performance space; and Technical space; (7) Library, including: Collections; Facilities; Finance; Governance; Personnel; and Services; (8) Recruitment, Admission-Retention, Record Keeping, and Advisement, including: Counseling services; Objectives; Requirements; and Student records; (8) Published Materials, including: Catalog; and Published docu-

ments; (9) Community Involvement and Articulation with Other Schools, including: Arts agencies; Local schools; and Performing organizations; (10) Evaluation, Planning, and Projections, including: Assessment techniques; Curriculum; Objectives; Operational conditions; Programs and services; Resource allocation and development; Size and scope; and Student achievement and evaluation; (11) Credit and Time Requirements, including: Awarding credit; Program lengths; Published policies; and Transfer of credit; (12) Training Programs, including: Certificate program; General standards; and Program strengths; and (13) Specific Aspects of Theatre in General Education, including: Faculty; General college student; Local community; Media; Policy development; and Training of the theatre professional. Proprietary institutions must meet additional standards. **Accreditation Requirements:** Degree-granting institutions must have graduated one class; professional studio schools must have been in operation for five years. Undergraduate programs must document compliance with standards in the following areas: Admissions; Choreography; Curricular structure; Dance aptitudes; Dance studies; General studies; Performance; Preparation for teaching; and Theoretical studies. Graduate programs must document compliance with standards in the following areas: Admissions; Breadth of competence; Degree requirements and procedures; Faculty; Functions of graduate study; Preparation for teaching; Resources; and Statement and publications of objectives and resources. On-site review, verifying information provided in self-assessment, required. May respond to on-site review. Possible accreditation decisions are: (1) Accreditation; (2) Probationary Status, requiring correction of deficiencies within five years; or (3) Denial, for programs in substantial noncompliance with standards. **Renewal:** Every five years (initial); every ten years thereafter. Renewal based on self-assessment and on-site review. Must also submit annual reports. **Restrictions:** Must report changes in curriculum. **State Requirements:** Must be state approved or licensed. **Preparatory Materials:** *Handbook of the National Association of Schools of Dance* (reference). **Fees:** $500, plus actual cost of on-site review; must also submit annual fee. **Accredited By:** Commission on Recognition of Postsecondary Accreditation; U.S. Department of Education.

Dentistry

1644

Commission on Dental Accreditation (CDA)
American Dental Association (ADA)
211 E. Chicago Ave.
Chicago, IL 60611
Phone: (312)440-4660
Fax: (312)440-2915
Toll Free: (800)621-8099
E-mail: davenpor@ada.org
Neal D. Bellariti, Dir.

Recipient: First professional degree programs in dental education; degree, certificate, and diploma programs in allied dental education, including dental assisting, dental hygiene, and dental laboratory technology; and advanced degree and certificate programs in dental education, including dental public health, endodontics, oral and maxillofacial surgery, oral pathology, orthodontics, pediatric dentistry, periodontics, prosthodontics, general practice residency, and general dentistry. **Number of Accredited Institutions:** 1300. **Application Procedures:** Self-assessment required. Must document compliance with standards in the following areas: Administration; Curriculum; Faculty; Financial support; Operational policies and practices; Physical facilities; and Student policies and practices. **Accreditation Requirements:** On-site review, verifying information provided in self-assessment, required. Review includes: Examination of documents; and Interviews with administrators, faculty, staff, and students. Report lists strengths and weaknesses of program. May respond to on-site review. Possible accreditation decisions are: (1) Approval; (2) Conditional Approval, requiring correction of deficiencies within two years; (3) Provisional Approval, requiring correction of deficiencies within one year; and (4) Not Approved, for programs in substantial non-compliance with standards. **Renewal:** Every seven years (maximum). Renewal based on on-site review. **Restrictions:** Must report major changes to program. **Preparatory Materials:** Preparatory materials available. **Length of Process:** Six months-two years. **Fees:** Actual cost of on-site review; $130-$1300 (annual fee). **Accredited By:** Commission on Recognition of Postsecondary Accreditation; U.S. Department of Education. **Endorsed By:** American Association of Dental Examiners; American Association of Dental Schools; American Dental Assistants Association; American Dental Hygienists' Association; National Association of Dental Laboratories.

Diaper Services

1645

Diaper Service Accreditation Council (DSAC)
2017 Walnut St.
Philadelphia, PA 19103

Recipient: Diaper services. **Accreditation Requirements:** Must demonstrate compliance with standards in the following areas: (1) Product, including sanitary score covering: Absorbency; Antiseptics; Appearance; pH reading; and Softness of diapers; (2) Plant Layout and Equipment, including: Airflow; Lighting; Maintenance; Packaging materials; Restrooms; Work and airflow; and Other materials used in cleaning and delivery process; (3) Plant Procedures, including: Cleaning; Employee training; Infection control and sanitation; Pest control; and Quality control records; (4) Personnel, including: Employee manuals; and Training; (5) Routesalesmen, including: Customer relations; and Diaper delivery; (6) Delivery Equipment, including vehicles used to transport clean and soiled diapers; (7) Marketing Practices, including: Advertising and literature; and Face-to-face and/or telephone selling; and (8) Record Keeping, including: Employees; Equipment and vehicle maintenance; Production; Quality control; Safety and sanitation procedures; and Training. Must submit one random sample per month from finished package of diapers to specified independent medical laboratory for analysis. **Endorsed By:** National Association of Diaper Services.

Dietetics

1646

Commission on Accreditation/Approval for Dietetics Education (CAADE)
American Dietetic Association (ADA)
216 W. Jackson Blvd.
Chicago, IL 60606-6995
Phone: (312)899-0040
Fax: (312)899-1979
Toll Free: (800)877-1600
Beverly E. Mitchell MBA, Exec. Officer

Recipient: Coordinated bachelor's degree programs; post-baccalaureate dietetic internship programs;, coordinated master's degree programs in dietetics; dietetic technician programs; didactic programs in dietetics; and preprofessional practice programs in dietetics. **Number of Accredited Institutions:** 179. **Application Procedures:** Self-assessment required. Must document compliance with standards in the following areas: (1) Philosophy and Goals, including: Environment in which program exists; Evaluation; Measurable goals and objectives; and Mission of sponsoring institution; (2) Students, including: Accountability; Admissions; Cost to student; Disciplinary and termination procedures; Evaluation; Graduation and/or program completion requirements; Grievance procedures; Insurance requirements; Non-discrimination; Student records; Student support services; and Tuition; (3) Resources, including: Administrative support; Faculty qualifications; Faculty/student ratio; Financial support; Learning resources; Physical facilities; Program Director; and Support services; (4) Curriculum, including: Didactic and practice-related learning experiences; Expected competence of program graduate; Experience with other disciplines; Objectives; Personal and professional attitudes and values; Requirements; Sequence; and Supervised practice; and (5) Managing and Evaluating Program, including: Administrator, faculty, and student input; Graduate outcome measures; Long- and short-range planning; Policies and procedures; Program Director; and Student competence. **Accreditation Requirements:** On-site review required. Review involves interviews with faculty, staff, administrators, students, and other interested parties. May respond to on-site review. Didactic programs in dietetics do not require on-site review. **Renewal:** Every ten years. Renewal based on self-assessment and on-site review. Renewal fee is $300. Must also submit annual reports. **Preparatory Materials:** *Accreditation/Approval Manual for Dietetics Education Programs,* Third Edition and *Standards of Education for Dietetics Programs* (references). **Length of Process:** Nine months. **Fees:** Application fee, plus actual cost of on-site review; $375 (annual fee). **Accredited By:** Commission on Recognition of Postsecondary Accreditation; U.S. Department of Education.

Disability Services

1647

Accreditation Council on Services for People with Disabilities
8100 Professional Pl., Ste. 204
Landover, MD 20785-2225
Phone: (410)583-0060
Fax: (410)583-0063
Catherine E. Parsons, Dir.

Recipient: Organizations providing services and support to people with disabilities. **Number of Accredited Institutions:** 135. **Application Procedures:** Self-assessment required. Must document compliance with standards. **Accreditation Requirements:** On-site review required. May respond to on-site review. **Renewal:** Every three years (maximum). Renewal based on self-assessment and on-site review. **State Requirements:** Accreditation required in some states and voluntary in others. **Preparatory Materials:** Manuals and other publications available.

Engineering

1648

Committee on Engineering Related Specialty Certification
Council of Engineering Specialty Boards (CESB)
130 Holiday Ct., Ste. 100
Annapolis, MD 21401
Phone: (410)266-3766
Fax: (410)266-7653

Recipient: Certification programs for professionals in engineering-related fields. **Application Procedures:** Must document compliance with standards in following areas: (1) Purpose of Specialty Certification Program, including: Evaluation of individuals who practice in specialized area; and Issuance of credentials to individuals who meet requirements; (2) Structure of Certifying Body; (3) Resources, covering: Financial; and Knowledge and skill requirements; (4) Certification Program Operation, covering evaluation methods; (5) Public Disclosure of Certification, including: Listing of certified individuals; and Requirements; (6) Responsibilities to Applicants, including: Appeal procedures; Certification policies and procedures; Confidentiality; and Non-discrimination; (7) Responsibilities to the Public and Consumers, including: Adequacy of certification requirements; and Disciplinary procedures;

(8) Recertification; and (9) Titles. **Accreditation Requirements:** Applicants to certification programs must meet following requirements: (1) Bachelor's degree in physics, chemistry, biology, mathematics, or engineering technology; and (2) Four years experience in engineering related specialty. Program must have required body of knowledge, include comprehensive exam, and require recertification every five years.

1649

Committee on Engineering Technician Specialty Certification
Council of Engineering Specialty Boards (CESB)
130 Holiday Ct., Ste. 100
Annapolis, MD 21401
Phone: (410)266-3766
Fax: (410)266-7653

Recipient: Certification programs for engineering technicians. **Application Procedures:** Must document compliance with standards in following areas: (1) Purpose of Specialty Certification Program, including: Evaluation of individuals who practice in specialized area; and Issuance of credentials to individuals who meet requirements; (2) Structure of Certifying Body; (3) Resources, covering: Financial; and Knowledge and skill requirements; (4) Certification Program Operation, covering evaluation methods; (5) Public Disclosure of Certification, including: Listing of certified individuals; and Requirements; (6) Responsibilities to Applicants, including: Appeal procedures; Certification policies and procedures; Confidentiality; and Non-discrimination; (7) Responsibilities to the Public and Consumers, including: Adequacy of certification requirements; and Disciplinary procedures; (8) Recertification; and (9) Titles. **Accreditation Requirements:** Applicants for certification programs must meet following requirements: (1) Associate's degree in engineering technology or equivalent; and (2) Two years experience. Program must have required body of knowledge, include comprehensive exam, and require recertification every five years.

1650

Committee on Graduate Engineer Specialty Certification
Council of Engineering Specialty Boards (CESB)
130 Holiday Ct., Ste. 100
Annapolis, MD 21401
Phone: (410)266-3766
Fax: (410)266-7653

Recipient: Engineering specialty certification programs. **Application Procedures:** Must document compliance with standards in following areas: (1) Purpose of Specialty Certification Program, including: Evaluation of individuals who practice in specialized area; and Issuance of credentials to individuals who meet requirements; (2) Structure of Certifying Body; (3) Resources, covering: Financial; and Knowledge and skill requirements; (4) Certification Program Operation, covering evaluation methods; (5) Public Disclosure of Certification, including: Listing of certified individuals; and Requirements; (6) Responsibilities to Applicants, including: Appeal procedures; Certification policies and procedures; Confidentiality; and Non-discrimination; (7) Responsibilities to the Public and Consumers, including: Adequacy of certification requirements; and Disciplinary procedures; (8) Recertification; and (9) Titles. **Accreditation Requirements:** Applicants to certification programs must meet following requirements: (1) Degree in engineering from program accredited by Engineering Accreditation Commission of the Accreditation Board for Engineering and Technology (see separate entry); and (2) Four years post-degree experience. Program must have required body of knowledge, include comprehensive exam, and require recertification every five years.

1651

Committee on Professional Engineering Specialty Certification
Council of Engineering Specialty Boards (CESB)
130 Holiday Ct., Ste. 100
Annapolis, MD 21401
Phone: (410)266-3766
Fax: (410)266-7653

Recipient: Engineering specialty certification programs. **Application Procedures:** Must document compliance with standards in following areas: (1) Purpose of Specialty Certification Program, including: Evaluation of individuals who practice in specialized area; and Issuance of credentials to individuals who meet requirements; (2) Structure of Certifying Body; (3) Resources, covering: Financial; and Knowledge and skill requirements; (4) Certification Program Operation, covering evaluation methods; (5) Public Disclosure of Certification, including: Listing of certified individuals; and Requirements; (6) Responsibilities to Applicants, including: Appeal procedures; Certification policies and procedures; Confidentiality; and Non-discrimination; (7) Responsibilities to the Public and

Consumers, including: Adequacy of certification requirements; and Disciplinary procedures; (8) Recertification; and (9) Titles. **Accreditation Requirements:** Applicants to certification programs must meet following requirements: (1) License or registration as professional engineer (P.E.); and (2) Six years of experience following baccalaureate degree or two years experience following licensure or registration. Program must have required body of knowledge and require recertification every five years.

1652

Engineering Accreditation Commission of the Accreditation Board for Engineering and Technology (EAC/ABET)

Accreditation Board for Engineering and Technology (ABET)
111 Market Pl., Ste. 1050
Baltimore, MD 21202-4012
Phone: (410)347-7727
Fax: (410)625-2238

Recipient: Engineering programs. **Application Procedures:** Self-assessment required. Must document compliance with criteria in the following areas: Computer and library facilities; Curriculum; Equipment; Faculty; Laboratories; and Student performance. **Accreditation Requirements:** Curriculum must include: Basic sciences; Engineering design and synthesis; Engineering sciences; Humanities and social sciences; and Mathematical foundations. On-site review, verifying information provided in self-assessment, required. Review includes interviews with administrators, faculty, students, and departmental personnel. May respond to on-site review. **Renewal:** Every six years (maximum). Renewal based on self-assessment and on-site review. **Preparatory Materials:** Preparatory publications available. **Accredited By:** Commission on Recognition of Postsecondary Accreditation; U.S. Department of Education. **Endorsed By:** American Academy of Environmental Engineers; American Congress on Surveying and Mapping; American Consulting Engineers Council; American Institute of Aeronautics and Astronautics; American Institute of Chemical Engineers; American Institute of Mining, Metallurgical, and Petroleum Engineers; American Nuclear Society; American Society of Agricultural Engineers; American Society of Civil Engineers; American Society for Engineering Education; American Society of Heating, Refrigerating, and Air-Conditioning Engineers; American Society of Mechanical Engineers; American Society of Nondestructive Testing; American Society of

Safety Engineers; Instrument Society of America; Institute of Electrical and Electronics Engineers; Institute of Industrial Engineers; Minerals, Metals, and Materials Society; National Council of Examiners for Engineering and Surveying; National Institute of Ceramic Engineers; National Society of Professional Engineers; Society of Automotive Engineers; Society of Manufacturing Engineers; Society for Mining, Metallurgy, and Exploration; Society of Naval Architects and Marine Engineers; Society of Petroleum Engineers; Society of Plastics Engineers.

1653

Related Accreditation Commission of the Accreditation Board for Engineering and Technology (RAC/ABET)

Accreditation Board for Engineering and Technology (ABET)
111 Market Pl., Ste. 1050
Baltimore, MD 21202-4012

Recipient: Programs in engineering-related technology. **Application Procedures:** Self-assessment required. Must document compliance with criteria in the following areas: Computer and library facilities; Curriculum; Equipment; Faculty; Laboratories; and Student performance. **Accreditation Requirements:** Curriculum must include: Basic sciences; Engineering design and synthesis; Engineering sciences; Humanities and social sciences; and Mathematical foundations. On-site review, verifying information provided in self-assessment, required. Review includes interviews with administrators, faculty, students, and departmental personnel. May respond to on-site review. **Renewal:** Every six years (maximum). Renewal based on self-assessment and on-site review. **Preparatory Materials:** Preparatory publications available. **Accredited By:** Commission on Recognition of Postsecondary Accreditation; U.S. Department of Education. **Endorsed By:** American Academy of Environmental Engineers; American Congress on Surveying and Mapping; American Consulting Engineers Council; American Institute of Aeronautics and Astronautics; American Institute of Chemical Engineers; American Institute of Mining, Metallurgical, and Petroleum Engineers; American Nuclear Society; American Society of Agricultural Engineers; American Society of Civil Engineers; American Society for Engineering Education; American Society of Heating, Refrigerating, and Air-Conditioning Engineers; American Society of Mechanical Engineers; American Society of Nondestructive Testing; American Society of Safety Engineers; Instrument Society of Amer-

ica; Institute of Electrical and Electronics Engineers; Institute of Industrial Engineers; Minerals, Metals, and Materials Society; National Council of Examiners for Engineering and Surveying; National Institute of Ceramic Engineers; National Society of Professional Engineers; Society of Automotive Engineers; Society of Manufacturing Engineers; Society for Mining, Metallurgy, and Exploration; Society of Naval Architects and Marine Engineers; Society of Petroleum Engineers; Society of Plastics Engineers.

1654

Technology Accreditation Commission of the Accreditation Board for Engineering and Technology (TAC/ABET)

Accreditation Board for Engineering and Technology (ABET)
111 Market Pl., Ste. 1050
Baltimore, MD 21202-4012

Recipient: Engineering technology programs. **Application Procedures:** Self-assessment required. Must document compliance with criteria in the following areas: Computer and library facilities; Equipment; Curriculum; Faculty; Laboratories; and Student performance. **Accreditation Requirements:** Curriculum must include: Basic sciences; Engineering design and synthesis; Engineering sciences; Humanities and social sciences; and Mathematical foundations. On-site review, verifying information provided in self-assessment, required. Review includes interviews with administrators, faculty, students, and departmental personnel. May respond to on-site review. **Renewal:** Every six years (maximum). Renewal based on self-assessment and on-site review. **Preparatory Materials:** Preparatory publications available. **Accredited By:** Commission on Recognition of Postsecondary Accreditation; U.S. Department of Education. **Endorsed By:** American Academy of Environmental Engineers; American Congress on Surveying and Mapping; American Consulting Engineers Council; American Institute of Aeronautics and Astronautics; American Institute of Chemical Engineers; American Institute of Mining, Metallurgical, and Petroleum Engineers; American Nuclear Society; American Society of Agricultural Engineers; American Society of Civil Engineers; American Society for Engineering Education; American Society of Heating, Refrigerating, and Air-Conditioning Engineers; American Society of Mechanical Engineers; American Society of Nondestructive Testing; American Society of Safety Engineers; Instrument Society of America; Institute of Electrical and Electronics Engineers; Institute of Industrial Engineers; Minerals, Metals, and Materials Society; National Council of Examiners for Engineering and Surveying; National Institute of Ceramic Engineers; National Society of Professional Engineers; Society of Automotive Engineers; Society of Manufacturing Engineers; Society for Mining, Metallurgy, and Exploration; Society of Naval Architects and Marine Engineers; Society of Petroleum Engineers; Society of Plastics Engineers.

Environmental Health Science

`1655`

International Accrediting Commission for Safety and Environmental Education/Training (IACSEET)
PO Box 516
Doniphan, MO 63935
Phone: (314)996-3438
Fax: (314)996-4398
Dr. Al Mims, Pres.

Recipient: Courses and bachelor's, master's, and doctorate degree programs in safety and environmental education and training. **Application Procedures:** Self-assessment required. Must document compliance with standards concerning course/program syllabus, instructor qualifications, facilities, and other areas. Must also submit reports, data on course/program, and other materials. **Accreditation Requirements:** Programs must have stated goals, written exam, and practical exercise (when applicable). On-site review may be required. May respond to on-site review. **Renewal:** Every three years (program); every year (course). **Restrictions:** Must report modifications or changes to course or program. **Preparatory Materials:** Preparatory literature available. **Length of Process:** 45 days (course); 180 days (program). **Fees:** $500-$5000.

`1656`

National Environmental Health Science and Protection Accreditation Council (NEHAC)
c/o John B. Conway
School of Public Health
Univ. at Albany
Exec. Park, S., Rm. 159
Albany, NY 12203-3727
Phone: (518)485-5548
Fax: (518)485-5565
John B. Conway, Chair

Recipient: Institutions offering bachelor's and master's degree programs in environmental science. **Number of Accredited Institutions:** 25. **Application Procedures:** Self-assessment required. Must document compliance with standards in the following areas: Curriculum; Facilities and resources; Faculty and administrative evaluation; Financial information; Funding; General information; and Student data. **Accreditation Requirements:** Must offer the following core requirements: (1) Two years of basic sciences; (2) Epidemiology, statistical methods, and toxicology; and (3) Technical offerings in environmental health. On-site review required. May respond to on-site review. **Renewal:** Every six years (maximum). Renewal based on self-assessment and on-site review. Must also submit annual reports. **Restrictions:** Changes in curriculum or personnel must be reported. **Preparatory Materials:** *Guidelines* (booklet). **Fees:** $500; $200 (annual fee).

Family and Consumer Sciences

`1657`

Council for Accreditation of the American Association of Family and Consumer Sciences
American Association of Family and Consumer Sciences (AAFCS)
1555 King St.
Alexandria, VA 22314
Phone: (703)706-4600
Fax: (703)706-HOME
Jenny Hemphill, Coord.

Recipient: Undergraduate home economics programs. **Application Procedures:** Self-assessment required. Must document compliance with standards. **Accreditation Requirements:** On-site review required. Review includes discussion with faculty, staff, administrators, students, and other interested parties. May respond to on-site review. **Preparatory Materials:** *Accreditation Documents for Undergraduate Programs in Home Economics* (reference). **Accredited By:** Commission on Recognition of Postsecondary Accreditation.

Family Service

`1658`

Council on Accreditation of Services for Families and Children (COA)
520 Eight Ave., Ste. 2202B
New York, NY 10018-6507
Phone: (212)714-9399
Fax: (212)967-8624
David P. Shover, Exec.Dir.

Recipient: Social service and mental health agencies offering services in organized care setting. **Number of Accredited Institutions:** 3600. **Application Procedures:** Self-assessment required. **Accreditation Requirements:** Must be in operation for one year. On-site review required. May respond to on-site review. **Renewal:** Every four years. Renewal based on on-site review. Must also submit annual report. **Restrictions:** Self-assessment must include all services for which Council has standards. **State Requirements:** Must hold all applicable licenses. **Preparatory Materials:** *Guidelines for Accreditation, Manual for Agency Accreditation,* and *Standards for Agency Management and Service Delivery* (references). **Length of Process:** 12-15 months. **Fees:** $4400 (minimum fee).

Forestry

`1659`

Academic Accreditation for Programs Leading to Degrees in Urban Forestry
Society of Municipal Arborists (SMA)
c/o Leonard E. Phillips, Jr.
Superintendent-Operations
Wellesley Park and Tree Divisions
56 Woodlawn Ave.
Wellesley Hills, MA 02181-3123
Phone: (617)235-7600
Fax: (617)237-1936
Leonard E. Phillips Jr., Chair

Recipient: Institutions offering associate's, bachelor's, or master's degrees in urban forestry. **Application Procedures:** Self-assessment required. Must document compliance with standards in the following areas: Administration; Curriculum; Facilities; Goals and objectives; Professionals; and Students. **Accreditation Requirements:** Must offer minimum course requirements. On-site review required. May respond to on-site review. **Renewal:** Every five years. Renewal based on self-assessment. **Restrictions:** Must report changes to: Administrator; Curriculum; Degree programs; and Parent institution. **Preparatory Materials:** *Accreditation Procedures and Standards Report* (reference). **Length of Process:** Three months. **Fees:** $1000.

1660

Committee on Accreditation, Society of American Foresters (SAF)
5400 Grosvenor Ln.
Bethesda, MD 20814
Phone: (301)897-8720
Fax: (301)897-3690
P. Gregory Smith, Dir.

Recipient: First professional degree programs, baccalaureate or graduate, in forestry education. **Number of Accredited Institutions:** 47. **Application Procedures:** Self-assessment required. Must document compliance with standards in the following areas: Academic calendars; Advertising; Catalogs and publications; Curriculum; Evaluation; Facilities, equipment, and supplies; Faculty; Fiscal and administrative capacity; Recruiting an admissions practices; and Student support services. **Accreditation Requirements:** On-site review required. Review includes interviews with administrators, faculty, students, and other interested parties. May respond to on-site review. **Renewal:** Every five years. Renewal based on submission of interim status report and documentation of continued compliance with standards. **Preparatory Materials:** *Accreditation Handbook* (reference). **Accredited By:** Commission on Recognition of Postsecondary Accreditation.

1661

County Forestry Department Accreditation Program
Society of Municipal Arborists (SMA)
c/o Leonard E. Phillips, Jr.
Superintendent-Operations
Wellesley Park and Tree Divisions
56 Woodlawn Ave.
Wellesley Hills, MA 02181-3123
Phone: (617)235-7600
Fax: (617)237-1936
Leonard E. Phillips Jr., Chair

Recipient: Counties with forestry departments. **Application Procedures:** Self-assessment required. Must document compliance with standards in the following areas: Budget; Evaluation of forestry program; Evaluation and summary of tree inventory; Personnel; Plans; Planting

list; and Regulations for tree protection. Must meet standards on per capita or per tree basis. **Accreditation Requirements:** On-site review required. May respond to on-site review. **Renewal:** Every five years. Renewal based on self-assessment. **Length of Process:** One month. **Fees:** $180.

1662

Municipal Forestry Department Accreditation Program
Society of Municipal Arborists (SMA)
c/o Leonard E. Phillips, Jr.
Superintendent-Operations
Wellesley Park and Tree Divisions
56 Woodlawn Ave.
Wellesley Hills, MA 02181-3123
Phone: (617)235-7600
Fax: (617)237-1936
Leonard E. Phillips Jr., Chair

Recipient: Municipalities with forestry departments. **Application Procedures:** Self-assessment required. Must document compliance with standards in the following areas: Budget; Evaluation of forestry program; Evaluation and summary of tree inventory; Personnel; Plans; Planting list; and Regulations for tree protection. Must meet standards on per capita or per tree basis. **Accreditation Requirements:** On-site review required. May respond to on-site review. **Renewal:** Every five years. Renewal based on self-assessment. **Length of Process:** One month. **Fees:** $180.

Funeral Service

1663

Commission on Accreditation, American Board of Funeral Service Education
American Board of Funeral Service Education (ABFSE)
13 Gurnet Rd., No. 316
PO Box 1305
Brunswick, ME 04011
Phone: (207)798-5801
Fax: (207)798-5988
Gordon Bigelow Ph.D., Exec.Dir.

Recipient: Institutions and programs offering diplomas and associate and baccalaureate degrees in funeral service education and mortuary science education. **Application Procedures:** Self-assessment required. Must document compliance with standards in the following areas: (1) Sponsorship, including: Financial sup-

port; Institutional responsibilities; and Policies and procedures; (2) Organization and Administration, including: Chief administrative officer or director; Constitution or by-laws; Governing board; Resource management; and Student involvement; (3) Aims and Purposes, including: Community needs; Curriculum; Ethics; Objectives; and Research; (4) Administrative Practices and Ethical Standards, including: Catalog; Due process and grievances; Nondiscrimination; Publications; and Records; (5) Finance, including: Accounting; Financial statements; Library budget; and Resources; (6) Curriculum, including: Assigning credit; Course objectives; Curriculum plan; Evaluation; Prerequisites; and Sequence; (7) Faculty, including: Academic requirements; Experience requirements; Instructional support; Licensure; Professional development; Staff size; and Student-faculty ratios; (8) Facilities, including: Classrooms; Equipment; Fire and safety codes; Heating; Laboratories; Lavatories; Lighting; Locker facilities; Off-campus instructional sites; and Ventilation; (9) Library, including: Acquisitions; Cataloging; Materials; Space; and Staff; (10) Students, including: Admissions; Attendance; Extracurricular activities; Graduation; Guidance; Health and safety; Records and reports; Requirements; and Student involvement; and (11) Program Planning and Evaluation, including: Graduate and employer assessment; Self-evaluation; and Student evaluation of courses and faculty. **Accreditation Requirements:** Program must include instruction in the following areas: (1) Business Management, including: Accounting; Computer application; Funeral directing; Funeral home management and merchandising; and Small business management; (2) Legal, Ethical, and Regulatory, including: Business law; Ethics; and Mortuary law; (3) Public Health and Technical, including: Anatomy; Chemistry; Embalming; Microbiology and public health; Pathology; and Restorative art; and (4) Social Sciences, including: Communications skills (oral and written); Counseling; Dynamics of grief; History of funeral service; and Sociology of funeral service. On-site review, verifying information provided in self-assessment, required. Review includes discussion with faculty, staff, administrators, students, and other interested parties. May respond to on-site review. **State Requirements:** Must have state approval to grant diplomas or degrees. **Accredited By:** Commission on Recognition of Postsecondary Accreditation; U.S. Department of Education.

Genetics

1664

American Board of Genetic Counseling (ABGC)
9650 Rockville Pike
Bethesda, MD 20814-3998
Phone: (301)571-1825
Fax: (301)571-1895
E-mail: srobinson@abmg.faseb.org
Sharon Robinson, Admin.

Recipient: Master's degree and clinical training programs in genetic counseling. **Application Procedures:** Self-assessment required. **Accreditation Requirements:** On-site review required. May respond to on-site review. **Renewal:** Every six years. Renewal based on on-site review. Must also submit annual reports. Renewal fee is $3000. **Preparatory Materials:** none. **Length of Process:** Six months-one year. **Fees:** $3000.

Health Care Organizations

1665

Community Health Accreditation Program (CHAP)
350 Hudson St.
New York, NY 10014
Phone: (212)989-9393
Toll Free: (800)669-1656

Recipient: Home and community-based health care organizations in one of the following categories: Clinics; Community nursing center; Home health aide; Home medical equipment; Homemaker; Hospice; Infusion therapy; Management services; Nursing; Nutrition counseling; Occupational therapy; Pharmacy; Physical therapy; Public health nursing; Respiratory therapy; Social work; Speech therapy; and other services. **Application Procedures:** Self-assessment required. Must document compliance with standards in the following areas: Budget development; Cash flow; Company diversification; Financial, human, and physical resources; Long-term viability; Marketing strategies; Philosophy and purpose; Products; Quality of products and services; Recruiting techniques; Reimbursement techniques; and Strategic development and planning. **Accreditation Requirements:** On-site review, verifying information provided in self-assessment, required. Review includes: Administration, client, and staff interviews; Assessment of client satisfaction; Evaluation of documents, policies, procedures, and

clinical records; Home visits; and Tour of facilities. Review evaluates strengths and weaknesses of organization. Possible accreditation decisions are: (1) Accreditation; (2) Defer Accreditation, requiring correction of deficiencies within specified time period; or (3) Deny Accreditation, for programs in substantial noncompliance with standards. **Renewal:** Every year. Renewal based on on-site review. **Preparatory Materials:** *In Search of Excellence in Home Care* and *Standards of Excellence for Home Care Organizations* (references). Self-study references, finance institute, and workshop also available. **Fees:** $1500, plus actual cost of on-site review; must also submit annual fee based on gross revenues.

1666

Joint Commission on Accreditation of Healthcare Organizations (JCAHO)
One Renaissance Blvd.
Oakbrook Terrace, IL 60181
Phone: (708)916-5639
Fax: (708)916-5644
Charles Bair, V.Pres.

Recipient: Children's, mental health, and rehabilitation hospitals; health care networks, including HMOs, PPOs, physician networks, and comprehensive delivery systems for defined populations; home care agencies and organizations, including those providing home health, personal care and support, home infusion, and/or durable medical equipment services; nursing homes and long-term care facilities; mental health, chemical dependency, and mental retardation/developmental disability services; ambulatory health care providers, including outpatient facilities, rehabilitation centers, infusion centers, group practices, and other providers; and clinical and pathology laboratories. **Number of Accredited Institutions:** 11,000. **Accreditation Requirements:** Must have provided care to patients for six months. On-site review required. Review includes interviews with administration, clinical staff, and patients, and may include interviews with public and organization staff. Must carry out policies for measuring, assessing, and improving performance, and demonstrate improvement in areas of weakness. May respond to on-site review. Possible accreditation decisions are: (1) Accreditation With Commendation; (2) Accreditation; (3) Provisional Accreditation; (4) Conditional Accreditation; or (5) Not Accredited. **Renewal:** Every three years. Renewal based on on-site review. **Restrictions:** Must report new components or services. New branch of home care organization must be sepa-

rately accredited. **Preparatory Materials:** Standards manuals, educational publications, seminars, and videos available. **Fees:** Varies. **Endorsed By:** American College of Physicians; American College of Surgeons; American Dental Association; American Hospital Association; American Medical Association.

1667

National Committee for Quality Assurance (NCQA)
1350 New York Ave., NW, Ste. 700
Washington, DC 20005
Phone: (202)662-1888
Fax: (202)637-0445

Recipient: Managed care health care insurance organizations providing comprehensive services through defined delivery system to specific population. **Application Procedures:** Self-assessment required. Must document compliance with standards in the following areas: Credentialing; Medical records; Members' rights and responsibilities; Preventive health services; Quality improvement; and Utilization management. **Accreditation Requirements:** Must be in operation for 18 months. On-site review required. Review verifies that organizations verify credentials of physicians, maintain quality records, and provide preventive health services to members. Report documents strengths and weaknesses of organization. **Renewal:** Every three years (maximum). **Preparatory Materials:** *Standards for Accreditation of Managed Care Organizations* (reference). **Fees:** $23,000-$96,000.

Homecare Organizations

1668

National HomeCaring Council
513 C St., NE
Washington, DC 20002-5809
Phone: (202)547-6586
Fax: (202)546-8968
Marian Brown, Assoc.Dir.

Recipient: Voluntary, governmental, or proprietary agencies employing home care aides who deliver all homemaker and personal tasks in a home for individuals unable to provide these tasks for themselves. **Application Procedures:** Self-assessment required. Must document compliance with standards in the following areas: (1) Governing Body, including: Assessment and evaluation of community needs and demographic data; Bylaws; Financial oversight; and Policies for quality assessment; (2) Non-Discrimination; (3) Fiscal Management, including: Financial records; and Planning and provision of financial support; (4) Personnel Management, including: Job descriptions; Personnel policies; Recruitment; Retention; Selection; Termination; and Wage scales; (5) Training, including each task to be performed by Home Care Aides; (6) Eligibility Criteria for Service and Procedures for Referral to Other Resources, including such factors as: Age group; Crisis or emergency services; Funding sources; Geographical area; Hours of service; Income; Referral sources; and Social and health needs; (7) Supervision of Service, including: Assessment of needs; Development of plan of care; Keeping records on each client; and Reassessment of plan of care; (8) Evaluation of Service, including setting and monitoring short- and long-term goals; (9) Ongoing Evaluation of Service to Community, including: Communication through media; Distribution of written material; Participation in community meetings; and Submission of annual reports; and (10) Maintenance of Written Statement of Clients' Rights, including: Billing; Confidentiality; Development, implementation, and discontinuation of care plan; Explanations of agency policies; and Grievances. Must request related agencies in community and consumers to complete questionnaires about agency. **Accreditation Requirements:** Must employ home care aides for at least one fiscal year. On-site review required. Review involves overview of entire program. Possible accreditation decisions are: (1) Accreditation; (2) Provisional Status, requiring correction of deficiencies; or (3) Denial of Accreditation, for agencies in substantial non-compliance with standards. **Renewal:** Every three years. Renewal based on self-assessment and onsite review. **Preparatory Materials:** Self-study materials available. **Fees:** Actual cost of on-site review; must also submit annual fee based on gross home care aide salaries. **Endorsed By:** Foundation for Hospice and Homecare.

Hotel and Restaurant Management

1669

Council on Hotel, Restaurant, and Institutional Education (CHRIE)
1200 17th St., NW
Washington, DC 20036-3097
Phone: (202)331-5990
Fax: (202)785-2511

Recipient: Two- and four-year programs

in cooking, baking, tourism, and hotel, restaurant, and institutional administration.

Independent Schools

1670

Arizona Association of Independent Schools (AAIS)
c/o Todd R. Horn
The Orme School
HC 63, Box 3040
Mayer, AZ 86333
Phone: (602)632-7601
Fax: (602)632-7605
Todd R. Horn, Pres.

Recipient: Elementary and secondary independent schools in Arizona. **Application Procedures:** Self-assessment required. Must document compliance with standards. **Accreditation Requirements:** On-site review required. **Endorsed By:** National Association of Independent Schools.

1671

Association of Colorado Independent Schools (ACIS)
1236 Third Ave.
Longmont, CO 80501
Phone: (303)442-5252
Fax: (303)442-5252
Rhoney DuQuesne, Exec.Dir.

Recipient: Elementary and secondary independent schools in Colorado. **Application Procedures:** Self-assessment required. Must document compliance with standards in the following areas: (1) Purpose, Goals, and Philosophy; (2) Community of the School, including: Admissions policies and procedures; Alumni; Financial aid; Gender and diversity issues; Local community; Parent organizations and programs; Public relations; School climate and morale; and Student demographics; (3) Program, Activities, and Student Services, including: Curriculum and overall program; Extracurricular activities; and Student services; (4) Governance and Administration, including: Business and financial management; Governance and decision-making; and School facilities, including buildings, equipment, grounds, maintenance, safety provisions, and transportation; (5) Personnel, including: Administration; Faculty; and Staff; and (6) Other Required Areas, including: Boarding and residential life; Early childhood programs; Religious programs; Special education and

instruction; Special programs; and Volunteer/service programs. Must submit audit, identify strengths and weaknesses of school, and develop plan for improvement. **Accreditation Requirements:** Must document compliance with the following requirements: (1) Three years of operation; (2) Not-for-profit status; (3) Nondiscrimination policy in admissions and employment; (4) Operational independence; (5) Disclosure of information; and (6) Maintenance of policy of freedom of inquiry. On-site review, verifying information provided in self-assessment, required. Review includes classroom visits, meetings with faculty, and reviewing materials. May respond to on-site review. **Renewal:** Every seven years. Renewal based on self-assessment and on-site review. Must also submit progress report every three years. **Endorsed By:** National Association of Independent Schools.

1672

Association of Independent Maryland Schools (AIMS)
PO Box 813
Millersville, MD 21108
Phone: (410)987-7025
Fax: (410)987-7133
Sarah Ann M. Donnelly, Exec.Dir.

Recipient: Elementary and secondary independent schools in Maryland. **Application Procedures:** Self-assessment, involving administrators, faculty, staff, and students, required. Must document compliance with standards in the following areas: (1) Purposes and Objectives; (2) Students and Parents, including: Admission; Community involvement; Nondiscrimination; Parental involvement; Public relations; and Records; (3) Professional Staff, including: Qualifications; Recruitment; Staffing changes; Supervision and evaluation; and Teaching loads; (4) Program, including: Counseling and guidance; Curriculum; Extracurricular programs; Library materials, objectives, and staff; Objectives; Placement counseling; Residential program; Residential staff; Review; School climate; School day and year; Special needs and abilities; Student achievement; Student assessment; and Student needs; (5) Decision Making Process, including: Alumni involvement; Chief administrative officer; Community involvement; Evaluation; Faculty involvement; Gender issues; Governing body; Long-range planning; Multi-cultural issues; Parental involvement; and Student involvement; and (6) Administration of the Institution, including: Administration; Financial management; Food services; Health services; Legal and regulatory compliance; and

Physical plant. **Accreditation Requirements:** Schools must be not for profit. On-site review, verifying information provided in self-assessment, required. May respond to on-site review. **Endorsed By:** National Association of Independent Schools.

1673

Association of Independent Schools in New England (AISNE)
100 Grossman Dr., Ste. 301
Braintree, MA 02184
Phone: (617)849-3080
Fax: (617)849-1618

Recipient: Independent elementary schools in Maine, Massachusetts, New Hampshire, Rhode Island, and Vermont. **Application Procedures:** Self-assessment required. Must document compliance with standards in the following areas: (1) Mission and Philosophy, including: Decision-making; Dissemination; Evaluation; Objectives; Planning; and Program; (2) School Community, including: Admissions; Communications; Matriculation; Parent guidance; and Record keeping; (3) Professional Staff, including: Composition; Decision making; Professional development; Programs; Schools with internship/apprentice teaching; and Supervision and evaluation; (4) Program, including: Before or after school programs; Content; Extracurricular activities; Implementation; Library; Residential program; School programs; Student guidance; Summer camp or program; (5) Administration, including: Development; Financial management; Food service; Health services; Organization; Personnel policies; and Physical plant; and (6) Governance, including: Conflict of interest; Evaluation; Equity and openness; and Organization and delegation. May be required to submit: Admission catalog; Admission folder; Audit report; Board policy manual; Campus map; Conflict of interest policy statement; Constitution and by-laws; Current operating budget; Curriculum and program goals; Emergency plans; Enrollment agreements; Evaluation procedures; Feasibility study; Financial aid materials; Health-related inspections; Job descriptions; Long-range financial plan; Marketing and recruiting materials; Non-discrimination policy statement; Orientation materials; Organizational chart; Parent handbook; Personnel policy manual; Personnel files; Press releases; Promotion goals; Publications and informational materials; School calendar; Sexual harassment policy; Student folder; Student handbook; Student publications; and Trustee handbook. **Accreditation Requirements:** Schools must: (1) Be incorporated as not-for-profit organization; (2) Consist of three or more consecutive grades in kindergarten through grade nine or equivalent; and (3) Maintain policy of non-discrimination. On-site review, verifying information provided in self-assessment, required. **Endorsed By:** National Association of Independent Schools.

1674

California Association of Independent Schools (CAIS)
1351 Third St., Promenade No. 303
Santa Monica, CA 90401
Phone: (310)375-7711
Mimi S. Baer, Exec.Dir.

Recipient: Independent, academic elementary and secondary schools in California. **Application Procedures:** Self-assessment required. Must document compliance with standards in the following areas: (1) Philosophy, Purposes, and Methods; (2) Governing Body; (3) Finances, including: Annual audit; Budget-making process; Credit rating; Financial stability; Financial statements; Long range financial planning; and Management of financial resources; (4) Administration, Faculty, and Staff, including: Administrative staff; Alumni involvement; Evaluation; Governing board; Non-discrimination; Organization; Parental involvement; Qualifications; Recordkeeping for staff, students, and graduates; School head administrator; Staffing; Teaching faculty; and Working conditions and salaries; (5) Students; (6) Community of the School; (7) Program; (8) School Library; (9) School Plant; and (10) Health and Safety. Secondary schools must: (1) Be accredited by Western Association of Schools and Colleges (see separate entry); (2) Be college preparatory in stated goals and purposes; (3) Require graduates to successfully complete courses meeting minimum course requirements for freshman admissions to University of California system; (4) Prepare annual college profile for graduates, including SAT scores and achievement scores and college acceptances; and (5) Provide adequate facilities and equipment for student laboratory experience in at least one field of science. Elementary schools must participate in testing program and issue student progress reports at least twice during school year. **Accreditation Requirements:** Must have been in operation for six years, be non-profit, and maintain policy of non-discrimination. On-site review required. **Renewal:** Every six years (maximum). **Restrictions:** May not transfer membership. Must report change of head administrator. **Endorsed By:** National Association of Independent Schools.

1675

Commission on College Accreditation, Accrediting Council for Independent Colleges and Schools (COCA)
Accrediting Council for
Independent Colleges and Schools
750 First St., NE, Ste. 980
Washington, DC 20002-6780
Phone: (202)336-6780

Recipient: Independent junior and senior colleges offering primarily business or business-related programs or career-enhancement instruction in the U.S., Puerto Rico, Guam, the Cayman Islands, England, France, Spain, Germany, Switzerland, and Italy. **Application Procedures:** Self-assessment required. Must document compliance with standards and submit catalog, supporting exhibits, and audited financial statements. **Accreditation Requirements:** Must have offered programs for two years. Programs must be residential and enrollment must be sufficient to support regularly scheduled classes, laboratory work, or study sessions. On-site review, verifying information provided in self-assessment, required. Review includes interviews with faculty, staff, administrators, students, and other interested parties. May respond to on-site review. **Renewal:** Every six years (maximum). **State Requirements:** Must be locally or state licensed. **Preparatory Materials:** *Accreditation Criteria* and *Directory of Accredited Institutions* (references). Workshops available. **Accredited By:** Commission on Recognition of Postsecondary Accreditation; U.S. Department of Education.

1676

Commission on Postsecondary Schools Accreditation, Accrediting Council for Independent Colleges and Schools (COPSA)
Accrediting Council for
Independent Colleges and Schools
750 First St., NE, Ste. 980
Washington, DC 20002-6780
Phone: (202)336-6780

Recipient: Independent non-collegiate, postsecondary institutions offering programs of two years or less primarily in business or business-related programs or career-enhancement instruction in the U.S., Puerto Rico, Guam, the Cayman Islands, England, France, Spain, Germany, Switzerland, and Italy. **Application Procedures:** Self-assessment required. Must document compliance with standards and submit catalog, supporting exhibits, and audited financial statements. **Accreditation Requirements:** Must have offered programs for two years. Programs must be residential and enrollment must be sufficient to support regularly scheduled classes, laboratory work, or study sessions. On-site review, verifying information provided in self-assessment, required. Review includes discussion with faculty, staff, administrators, students, and other interested parties. May respond to on-site review. **Renewal:** Every six years (maximum). **Restrictions:** Must be locally or state licensed. **Preparatory Materials:** *Accreditation Criteria* and *Directory of Accredited Institutions* (references). Workshops available. **Accredited By:** Commission on Recognition of Postsecondary Accreditation; U.S. Department of Education.

1677

Connecticut Association of Independent Schools (CAIS)
PO Box 159
Mystic, CT 06355
Phone: (203)572-2950
Fax: (203)572-2938

Recipient: Independent elementary and middle schools in Connecticut. **Application Procedures:** Self-assessment required. Must document compliance with standards in the following areas: (1) Purposes and Objectives, including: Dissemination to administration, governing body, parents and students; Evaluation; Planning; and Professional staff; (2) Community of the School, including: Admissions; Community involvement; Nondiscrimination; Parental involvement; Public relations materials; Recordkeeping; and Student requirements; (2) Professional Staff, including: Qualifications; Recruitment, screening, and interviewing staff; Staffing changes; Staffing requirements; Supervision and evaluation of professional staff; and Teaching conditions and teaching load; (3) Program, including: Academic progress of students; Adherence to rules and procedures; Assessment of students, diagnosis of special needs and abilities, and appropriate placement; College or school placement counseling; Concern for property within school community; Counseling and guidance; Curriculum; Evaluation of educational program and student achievement; Extracurricular programs; Instructional materials and equipment; Library organization, supply, and staffing; Mutual respect between students and teachers; Objectives; Residential program and staff; Residential schools; School atmosphere; School day and year; Student involvement in learning activities; and Student requirements; (4) Decision Making Prog-

ress, including: Alumni involvement; Chief administrative officer; Community involvement; Faculty involvement in program planning and development; Gender issues; Governing body; Long-range planning; Multicultural issues; and Student involvement in program planning and development; and (5) Administration of the Institution, including: Administration; Financial management; Food services; Health services; Legal and regulatory compliance; Personnel; and Physical plant. **Accreditation Requirements:** Must be in operation for three years, offer four or more grade levels or their equivalent, and support policy of nondiscrimination. On-site review required. Review includes meetings with faculty, administration, trustees, and other interested parties. May respond to on-site review. Possible accreditation decisions are: (1) Accreditation; (2) Institutional Member, requiring correction of deficiencies; or (3) Denial, for schools in substantial noncompliance with standards. **Renewal:** Every six years (maximum). On-site review required every ten years. **Restrictions:** Must report substantive changes. **Preparatory Materials:** *Handbook for the Chair of the Visiting Committee, Manual on School Evaluation,* and *Standards for Membership* (references). **Fees:** $700-$1100 (evaluation fee based on enrollment); $600-$4700 (annual fee based on enrollment). **Endorsed By:** National Association of Independent Schools.

1678

Florida Council of Independent Schools (FCIS)
Team Staff Bldg., Ste. 612
1211 N. Westshore Blvd., Ste. 612
Tampa, FL 33607
Phone: (813)287-2820

Recipient: Independent co-ed, day, boarding, and single sex schools in grades pre-kindergarten through twelve in Florida. **Number of Accredited Institutions:** 125. **Application Procedures:** Self-assessment, including administrators and faculty, required. All schools must document compliance with standards in the following areas: (1) Organization, including governance; (2) Philosophy and Objectives, including: Administrative policies; Compliance with standards; Dissemination of statement; Evaluation; Planning; Professional growth; Supervision of dormitory life; and Written statement; (3) Course of Study, including: Curriculum; Evaluation; and Philosophy and objectives; (4) Professional Staff, including: Abilities, needs, and interests of individual students; Class size; Methods; Staffing; Teacher-student ratio; and Teaching conditions; (5) Records, includ-

ing: Data on former students; Grade and progress reports; Standardized tests; and Student records; (6) School Sessions, including: Activities; School day; and School year; (7) Business and Finance, including: Compensation policy; Dealing with financial difficulties; Financial reports; Financial resources; Financial stability; Fund raising; Liability insurance; and Retirement program; (8) Health, including: Contagious diseases; First aid administrator; and State and county health, safety, and sanitation codes; (9) Transportation, including: Drivers; Insurance; and Vehicles; (10) Parent Organizations, including parent participation; (11) Student Discipline and Morale, including: Policies and procedures; and Self-discipline, care and concern for students and teachers; (12) Physical Facilities and Equipment, including: Equipment; Maintenance; and Plant; (13) Facilities, including: Air conditioning; Art and music studios; Auditorium or meeting room; Chalkboards, bulletin boards, and display spaces; Classrooms; Dining area; Dormitories; Electrical outlets; Fire codes; Floors; Food serving and preparation areas; Health office or infirmary; Health, safety, and sanitation codes; Heating; Kitchen equipment; Laboratories; Library; Light and ventilation; Lockers; Offices; Recreation area; Stairways; State and federal environmental laws; Storage space; Toilets and facilities; and Walls and ceilings; (14) Equipment, including: Bathrooms; Classroom furniture and equipment; Dining and kitchen areas; Drinking fountains; Fire extinguishers; Laboratories; Playground equipment; and Studios; (15) Maintenance, including: Cleaning; Grounds; and Repair; (16) Grounds, including: Outdoor instruction; Outdoor play and recreational areas; and Safety; (17) Library/Media Center, including: Catalogue record and inventory; Elementary schools; Librarian; Library and research skills; Objectives; and Secondary school instructional aids; (18) Code of Ethics; and (19) Moral and Ethical Development. Pre-schools must document compliance with standards in the following areas: Buildings and equipment; Health and safety; Organization and administration; Pre-school introduction; and Program and curriculum. Elementary schools must document compliance with standards in the following areas: Instructional aids; and Programs. Secondary schools must document compliance with standards in the following areas: Course of study; Instructional aids; Program; and Student services. Must address strengths and weaknesses and develop plan for the future. **Accreditation Requirements:** On-site review. Review includes: Examination of promotional material and copies of school publications; Interviews with administrators, faculty, and students; and Tour of classrooms. Possible accreditation decisions are: (1) Accredited; (2) Probation, requiring correction of deficiencies within one year; (3) Accredited Warned, requiring correction of serious deficiencies; or (4) Denied, for schools in substantial noncompliance with standards. **Renewal:** Every five years (maximum). Renewal based on self-assessment and on-site review. **Fees:** Actual cost of on-site review; must also submit annual fee. **Endorsed By:** Council of American Private Education; Florida Association of Academic Non-Public Schools; National Association of Independent Schools.

1679

Independent Schools Association of the Central States (ISACS)
1400 W. Maple Ave.
Downers Grove, IL 60515-4828
Phone: (708)971-3581
Fax: (708)971-3574

Recipient: Independent elementary and secondary schools in Arkansas, Illinois, Indiana, Iowa, Kansas, Kentucky, Michigan, Minnesota, Missouri, Nebraska, North Dakota, Ohio, South Dakota, West Virginia, and Wisconsin. **Application Procedures:** Self-assessment required. Must document compliance with standards in the following areas: (1) Purpose, Goals, and Philosophy; (2) Community of the School, including: Admissions policies and procedures; Alumni; Financial aid; Gender and diversity issues; Local community; Parent organizations and programs; Public relations; School climate and morale; and Student demographics; (3) Program, Activities, and Student Services, including: Curriculum and overall program; Extracurricular activities; and Student services; (4) Governance and Administration, including: Business and financial management; Governance and decision-making; and School facilities, including buildings, equipment, grounds, maintenance, safety provisions, and transportation; (5) Personnel, including: Administration; Faculty; and Staff; and (6) Other Required Areas, including: Boarding and residential life; Early childhood programs; Religious programs; Special education and instruction; Special programs; and Volunteer/service programs. Must submit audit, identify strengths and weaknesses of school, and develop plan for improvement. On campus workshop required. **Accreditation Requirements:** Must document compliance with the following requirements: (1) Three years of operation; (2) Not-for-profit status; (3)

Nondiscrimination policy in admissions and employment; (4) Operational independence; (5) Disclosure of information; and (6) Freedom of inquiry. On-site review, verifying information provided in self-assessment, required. Review includes classroom visits, meetings with faculty, and reviewing materials. May respond to on-site review. Possible accreditation decisions are: (1) Accreditation; (2) Accreditation Delayed, requiring correction of deficiencies; or (3) Accreditation Denied, for schools in substantial noncompliance with standards. **Renewal:** Every seven years. Renewal based on self-assessment and on-site review. Must also submit progress report every three years. **Preparatory Materials:** *ISACS Evaluation Guide,* Fifth Edition, *ISACS Evaluation Manual for School Self-Study, ISACS Manual for Evaluation Visiting Team Leaders,* and *ISACS Standards of Membership* (references). **Fees:** $1250-$5000 (annual fee based on enrollment). **Endorsed By:** College Board; Council for American Private Education; National Association of Independent Schools.

1680

Independent Schools Association of the Southwest (ISAS)
PO Box 52297
Tulsa, OK 74152-0297
Phone: (918)749-5927
Fax: (918)749-5937
Richard W. Ekdahl, Exec.Dir.

Recipient: Independent schools in Kansas, Louisiana, New Mexico, Oklahoma, and Texas. **Application Procedures:** Self-assessment required. Must document compliance with standards in the following areas: (1) Organization and Governance, including: Good faith efforts towards diversity; Governing body; Legal entity; Non-discriminatory practices; Non-profit status; and Statement of educational philosophy and goals and objectives; (2) Program, including: Freedom of inquiry; Learning assumptions; Offerings (elementary and secondary); Program support; State education authorities; and Student development; (3) Administration, including: Evaluation process; Financial management, including annual audit, control of funds, and procedures; Follow-up studies; Full disclosure of mission, policies, program, and practices; ISAS Code of Ethics; Physical plant and facilities; and School admissions; and (4) Faculty and Staff, including: Involvement in program development; Personnel policies; Procedural fairness; Professional growth and development; Qualifications; and Supervision and evaluation. Must submit: Audited financial statement; List of faculty salaries; school catalog; and

Tuition schedule. **Accreditation Requirements:** On-site review, verifying information provided in self-assessment, required. Review includes: Class visits; Evaluation of school publications, standard forms, and textbooks; and Interviews with administrators, faculty, parents, students, and trustees. May respond to on-site review. Possible accreditation decisions are: (1) Accredited; (2) Warned, requiring correction of deficiencies regarding one or more standards within one year; or (3) Dropped, for schools in substantial noncompliance with standards. **Renewal:** Every ten years (maximum). Renewal based on self-assessment and on-site review. Must also submit interim reports every three, five, and eight years. **Preparatory Materials:** *Membership Information* (reference). **Fees:** Application fee, plus actual cost of on-site review. Must also submit annual fee based on enrollment. **Endorsed By:** National Association of Independent Schools.

1681

New York State Association of Independent Schools (NYSAIS)
287 Pawling Ave.
Troy, NY 12180-5238
Phone: (518)274-0184
Fax: (518)274-0185
Frederick C. Calder, Exec.Dir.

Recipient: Elementary and secondary independent schools in New York State. **Application Procedures:** Self-assessment, involving faculty, parents, staff, students, and trustees, required. Must document compliance with standards in the following areas: (1) Statement of Purposes and Objectives; (2) Admissions, including: Non-discrimination; Objectives; and Prospectus; (3) Tuition and Fees, including: Financial responsibilities; and Tuition refund and insurance plan; (4) Professional Staff, including: Evaluation; Faculty and staff assignments; Non-discrimination; Professional development; Qualifications; Salaries and benefits; and Staff size; (4) Educational Program, including: Academic program; Assumptions about nature of learning process; Evaluation; Extracurricular program; School and class size; and Student performance; (5) Program Resources, including: Equipment; Guidance and counseling program; Library/learning center; and Physical facilities; (6) Governing Body, including: Fiduciary responsibility; Policies and procedures; and Relations with school administration; (7) Administration, including: Administrative staff; Alumni involvement; Faculty involvement; Parent involvement; and Student involvement; (8) Resources and Service Management, including: Accounting; Auditing; Budget; Financial resources; Food service; Health care; Insurance; Long-range financial planning; and Physical facilities; (9) Service Personnel, including: Non-discrimination; Qualifications; and Salaries and benefits; (10) Staff, Student, and Graduate Records, including: Confidentiality; Fire; and Theft; (11) Boarding School, including: Day students; Health; Residential staff; and Safety; and (12) Technology Issues, including: Classroom management; Computers; Faculty training; Funding; and Multi-media literacy. **Accreditation Requirements:** Must be not-for-profit. On-site review, verifying information provided in self-assessment, required. Review includes: Interviews with administrators, parents, students, teachers, and trustees; Review of school materials; and Visits to classrooms. Must work to implement recommendations made in on-site review report. **Renewal:** Every ten years. Renewal based on self-assessment and on-site review. **State Requirements:** Must document compliance with New York State law, rules, and regulations. **Preparatory Materials:** "Guidelines of Good Practice for Governance and the Headship" (reference). **Endorsed By:** National Association of Independent Schools.

▮**1682**▮

Pacific Northwest Association of Independent Schools (PNAIS)
1906 42nd Ave., E.
Seattle, WA 98112
Phone: (206)323-6137
Fax: (206)324-4863

Recipient: Independent elementary and secondary schools in Alaska, Idaho, Montana, Nevada, Oregon, Utah, and Washington. **Number of Accredited Institutions:** 56. **Application Procedures:** Self-assessment required. Must document compliance with standards covering mission and objectives and resources necessary to carry out these objectives. **Accreditation Requirements:** Must maintain policy of diversity and non-discrimination in the following areas: Admissions policies; Athletic and school administered programs; Educational policies; Hiring practices; and Scholarship and loan programs. On-site review required. **Endorsed By:** National Association of Independent Schools.

▮**1683**▮

Pennsylvania Association of Private Academic Schools (PAPAS)
PO Box 511
Bryn Mawr, PA 19010
Phone: (215)836-7429
Fax: (215)836-7429
Linda Phelps, Exec.Dir.

Recipient: Elementary and secondary independent schools in Pennsylvania. **Application Procedures:** Self-assessment required. Must document compliance with standards. **Accreditation Requirements:** On-site review required. **Endorsed By:** National Association of Independent Schools.

▮**1684**▮

Virginia Association of Independent Schools (VAIA)
101 N. Mooreland Rd.
Richmond, VA 23229
Phone: (804)282-3592
Sally Boese, Exec.Dir.

Recipient: Elementary and secondary independent schools in Virginia. **Application Procedures:** Self-assessment required. Must document compliance with standards. **Accreditation Requirements:** On-site review required. **Endorsed By:** National Association of Independent Schools.

Industrial Technology

▮**1685**▮

National Association of Industrial Technology (NAIT)
3157 Packard, Ste. A
Ann Arbor, MI 48198-1900
Phone: (313)677-0720
Fax: (313)677-2407
Dr. Clois E. Kicklighter, Chair

Recipient: Institutions offering associate's and/or baccalaureate degrees in industrial technology. **Number of Accredited Institutions:** 48. **Application Procedures:** Self-assessment required. Must document compliance with standards in the following areas: (1) Philosophy and Objectives, including: Mission; Program acceptance; Program definition; and Program goals; (2) Major Programs, including: Applications of mathematics and science; Communications; Competency identification; Computer applications; Course sequencing; Foundation requirements; Industrial experiences;

Institutional course work; Legal authorization; Level of instruction; Program definition; Program development; Program emphasis; Program level; Program name; Program publicity; Program validation; and Transfer course work; (3) Instruction, including: Motivation of students; Problem-solving activities; Program balance; Reference materials; Scheduling of instruction; Study guides; and Supervision of instruction; (4) Faculty, including: Faculty loads; Full-time faculty; Minimum faculty qualifications; Selection and appointment policies; and Tenure and reappointment policies; (5) Students, including: Ability to benefit students; Admission and retention standards; Advanced study; Advisory and counseling services; Ethical practices; Placement of graduates; Scholastic success of students; Student enrollment; and Student evaluation of program; (6) Administration, including: Administrative leadership; Administrative support; and Program administration; (7) Facilities and Equipment, including: Adequacy of facilities and equipment; Appropriateness of equipment; and Support for facilities and equipment; (8) Computer Systems, including: Availability; and Utilization; (9) Financial Resources, including: External financial support; and Financial support; (10) Library Services, including: Resources; and Utilization; (11) Support Personnel; (12) Placement Services, including cooperative education; and (13) Industrial Advisory Committee, including: Advisory committee meetings; Assessment; Educational innovation; and Program advisory committee. **Accreditation Requirements:** Associate degree programs must include instruction in the following areas: Communications; Management; Mathematics; Physical sciences; and Technical-computer integrated manufacturing. Associate's degree programs accredited in the following technologies: Communications; Computer Aided Manufacturing (CAM); Construction; Design; Electronics; Industrial safety; Manufacturing; Polymer; Production; and Robotics. Baccalaureate programs must include instruction in the following areas: General education; Management; Mathematics; Physical sciences; and Technical-computer integrated manufacturing. Baccalaureate degree programs accredited in the following technologies: Aerospace; Communications; Computer; Computer Aided Design (CAD); Computer integrated manufacturing; Construction; Electronics; Industrial distribution; Manufacturing/production; and Packaging. On-site review required. Review includes: Interviews with administrators, faculty, and students; Review of course outlines, exams, student assignments, and textbooks; and Tour of classrooms, laboratories, physical plant, and other facilities. May respond to on-site review. Possible accreditation decisions are: (1) Accreditation-Full; (2) Accreditation-Provisional, requiring correction of deficiencies within two years; (3) Accreditation-Conditional, requiring correction of major deficiencies within two years; or (4) Non-Accreditation, for programs in substantial non-compliance with standards. **Renewal:** Every four years (initial); every six years thereafter. Renewal based on self-assessment and on-site review. Renewal fee is $3000. **Restrictions:** Must report program changes. **Preparatory Materials:** *Accreditation Handbook* (reference). **Fees:** $1000, plus actual cost of on-site review; $400 (annual fee).

Interior Design

1686

Foundation for Interior Design Education Research (FIDER)
60 Monroe Center, NW, Ste. 300
Grand Rapids, MI 49503-2920
Phone: (616)458-0400
Fax: (616)458-0460
Kayem Dunn, Exec.Dir.

Recipient: Programs offering pre-professional assistant level (two-year) and first professional degree level (four-to five-year) programs in interior design. **Number of Accredited Institutions:** 108. **Application Procedures:** Self-assessment required. Must document compliance with standards in the following areas: Administration; Educational program; Faculty; Program, philosophy, mission, and goals; Relations to outside community; Resources and facilities; and Students. **Accreditation Requirements:** On-site review required. Review includes discussion with faculty, staff, administrators, students, and other interested parties. May respond to on-site review. **Renewal:** Every six years (maximum). Renewal based on self-assessment and on-site review. Renewal fee is $2750. **Preparatory Materials:** Accreditation application package available. **Length of Process:** Eighteen months. **Fees:** $2750; $800 (annual fee). **Accredited By:** Commission on Recognition of Postsecondary Accreditation; U.S. Department of Education.

Journalism

1687

Accrediting Council on Education in Journalism and Mass Communications (ACEJMC)
Univ. of Kansas School of Journalism
Stauffer-Flint Hall
Lawrence, KS 66045
Phone: (913)864-3973
Fax: (913)864-5225
Susanne Shaw, Exec.Dir.

Recipient: Colleges, schools, and departments whose major focus is offering professional programs in journalism and mass communications. **Number of Accredited Institutions:** 98. **Application Procedures:** Self-assessment required. Must document compliance with standards in the following areas: (1) Governance/Administration, including: Administrative structure; Chief administrative officer; Faculty governance; Objectives; and Student involvement; (2) Budget, including: Equipment; Faculty research; Faculty salaries; Financial assistance; Financial support; Library resources; Office and instructional space; Support services; and Travel; (3) Curriculum, including: Content; Degree requirements; Educational program; and Skill and knowledge skills and training; (4) Student Records/Advising, including: Academic and career advising; Curriculum pre-requisites and requirements; Distribution requirements; and Enrollment records; (5) Instruction/Evaluation, including: Evaluation; Professional development; Student-teacher ratio; and Teaching strategies; (6) Faculty: Full-Time/Part-Time, including: Diversity; Faculty academic and practical experience qualifications; Professional activities; Research; and Scholarly writing; (7) Internships/Work Experience, including: Academic credit; Practicums; Student publications; and Supervision; (8) Equipment/Facilities, including: Laboratories; Library, including accessibility, collections, and use; Offices; and Objectives; (9) Faculty: Scholarship/Research/ Professional Activities, including: Academic scholarship; Dissemination of results; Institutional support; and Promotion and tenure; (10) Public Service, including: Community outreach; Conferences; Continuing education programs; Demonstrations; High school and community college outreach; Lectures; Seminars; Short-courses; and Simulations; (11) Graduate/Alumni, including: Alumni records; Degree requirements and job expectations; and Job placement; and (12) Minority/Female Representa-

tion, including: Course content; Faculty; and Student body. Must also submit: Budget; Catalog; Course syllabi; Degree requirements; Faculty vitae; Minutes of committee reports and faculty meetings; and Outlines of courses. **Accreditation Requirements:** On-site review, verifying information provided in self-assessment, required. Review includes: Classroom visits; Inspection of equipment; Interviews with administrators, faculty, and students; and Tour of facilities. Review report includes strengths and weaknesses of program. May respond to on-site review. Possible accreditation decisions are: (1) Accreditation; (2) Provisional Accreditation, requiring correction of deficiencies; or (3) Denial, for programs in substantial non-compliance with standards. **Renewal:** Every six years. Renewal based on self-assessment and on-site review. **Fees:** Actual cost of on-site review and presentation of report; $400 (annual dues). **Accredited By:** Commission on Recognition of Postsecondary Accreditation; U.S. Department of Education.

Kennels

1688

Accredited Boarding Kennel
American Boarding Kennels Association (ABKA)
4575 Galley Rd., No. 400-A
Colorado Springs, CO 80915
Phone: (719)591-1113
Fax: (719)595-0006

Recipient: Pet boarding kennels. **Membership:** Not required. **Accreditation Requirements:** On-site review required. **Fees:** $300 (members); $600 (nonmembers).

Laboratories

1689

Accreditation Council, American Association for Laboratory Accreditation
American Association for Laboratory Accreditation (AALA)
656 Quince Orchard Rd.
Gaithersburg, MD 20878-1409
Phone: (301)670-1377
Fax: (301)869-1495
John Locke, Pres.

Recipient: Testing and calibration laboratories in private and governmental sectors. **Number of Accredited Institutions:** 603. **Accreditation Requirements:** Accreditation offered in the following fields of testing: Acoustical and vibration; Biological; Chemical; Construction materials; Electrical; Environmental; Geotechnical; Mechanical; Metrology (calibration); Nondestructive; and Thermal. Must document compliance with standards in the following areas: (1) Organization and Management, including: Confidentiality; Conflict of interest; Independence of judgement and integrity; Inter-laboratory comparisons; Managerial staff; Policies and procedures; Proficiency testing; Quality manager; and Technical manager; (2) Quality System, Audit, and Review, including: Confidentiality; Evaluation; Grievance procedures; Policies and objectives; Quality manager; Quality manual; Scope of calibrations and tests; and Traceability of measurements; (3) Personnel, including: Qualifications; Records; Staff size; and Training; (4) Accommodation and Environment, including: Access and use; Calibration and test areas; Control and recording; Energy sources; Heating; Housekeeping; Lighting; Monitoring; and Ventilation; (5) Equipment and Reference Materials, including: Labelling; Maintenance; and Recordkeeping; (6) Measurement Traceability and Calibration, including: In-service checks; International standards; National standards; and Reference standards; (7) Calibration and Test Methods, including: Calculations and data transfers; Computers and automated equipment; Consumable materials; Instructions; Methods and procedures; and Sampling; (8) Handling of Calibration and Test Items, including: Condition of calibration or test item; Deterioration or damage to calibration or test item; Identifying items to be calibrated or tested; and Receipt, retention, or safe disposal of calibration or test items; (9) Records, including: Recordkeeping system; and Safety; (10) Certificates and Reports; (11) Sub-Contracting of Calibration or Testing; (12) Outside Support and Supplies; and (13) Complaints. May also need to document compliance with standards in specific calibration and testing areas. On-site review and proficiency testing required. Review includes: Demonstration of selected tests or calibrations; Examination of equipment and calibration records; Interviews with technical staff; and Review of quality documentation, sample handling, and records. Must correct all deficiencies discovered during review. May respond to on-site review. Possible accreditation decisions are: (1) Accreditation; and (2) Accreditation Denied, for laboratories in substantial noncompliance with standards. **Renewal:** Every two years. Renewal based on on-site review. Must also submit annual reports. **Restrictions:** Must report changes in any of the following: Equipment; Facilities; Laboratory's status or operation affecting legal, commercial, or organizational standing; Organization or management; Personnel; Policies or procedures; Premises; and Working environment. **Preparatory Materials:** *General Requirements for Accreditation* (reference). Training courses available.

1690

Certified Dental Laboratory (CDL)
National Board for Certification of Dental Laboratories
555 E. Braddock Rd.
Alexandria, VA 22314-2106
Phone: (703)683-5263
Fax: (703)549-4788

Recipient: Dental laboratories engaged in fabricating prosthetic devices or appliances according to prescriptions or work authorizations from legally authorized sources. **Application Procedures:** Must submit the following information: (1) Basic identification of laboratory and its principles; (2) Two professional references; (3) Affidavit attesting to legal and ethical operation of business; (4) List of personnel responsible for production/quality control in each specialty; and (5) Photographs or videotape documenting laboratory's compliance with facility standards. **Accreditation Requirements:** Must meet standards in the following areas: (1) Personnel; (2) Infection Control, including: Facility; Personnel training; and Processes; and (3) Facility, including facilities for: Ceramics Complete dentures; Crown and bridge; Orthodontics; and Partial dentures. On-site review required. **Renewal:** Every year. Renewal based on continued compliance with standards. **Restrictions:** Must report changes in personnel or facilities. Significant changes in facility (remodelling or relocation) require new photographic documentation. Adding new specialties requires written request, photographs, identification of individual responsible for new specialty, and fee. **Fees:** Application fee.

1691

Certified Laboratory of the American Oil Chemists' Society
American Oil Chemists' Society (AOCS)
PO Box 3489
Champaign, IL 61826-3489
Phone: (217)359-2344
Fax: (217)351-8091

Recipient: Laboratories proficient in use of AOCS methodology for analysis of soybean meal. **Accreditation Requirements:** Must meet the following requirements: (1) Have AOCS Approved Chemist (see separate entry) on staff who is approved in oilseed cake and meal analysis; (2) Have adequate facility in which to perform analysis, including all apparatus and reagents; (3) Successfully participate in Smalley soybean meal series for one year; (4) Successfully complete analysis of 12 soybean meal samples per year; and (5) Use AOCS methods for referee analysis of soybean meal. Laboratory inspection required. **Restrictions:** Accreditation not transferable. **Fees:** Application and administrative fees. **Endorsed By:** National Oilseed Processors Association.

1692

Commission on Laboratory Accreditation, College of American Pathologists
College of American Pathologists (CAP)
325 Waukegan Rd.
Northfield, IL 60093-2750
Phone: (708)446-8800
Fax: (708)446-9044
Toll Free: (800)323-4040

Recipient: Clinical laboratories. **Number of Accredited Institutions:** 4600. **Application Procedures:** Must complete application and document compliance with standards in the following areas: Director and personnel requirements; Inspector requirements; Quality assurance; Quality control; and Resources and facilities. **Accreditation Requirements:** Must be enrolled in CAP program of proficiency testing and meet quality assurance standards concerning: Control media; Equipment; Management principles; Methodology; Personnel; Procedure manuals; Reagents; Reports and proficiency testing; Safety; and Specimen handling. On-site review required. Review includes meeting with administrators and inspection of laboratory that may include the following areas: (1) Laboratory General, including: Computer-generated reports; Handwritten reports; Personnel; Quality assurance; Quality control; Space and facilities; and Specimen collection; (2) Safety, including: Chemical hazards; Disaster preparedness; Electrical hazards; Fire protection; General safety; Microbiologic hazards; Radioactive hazards; and Waste disposal; (3) Hematology, including: Abnormal hemoglobin detection; Automated blood cell counting; Automated differential counters; Automated reticulocytes; Body fluids; Bone marrow preparations; Coagulation tests; Manual blood films; Manual CBC Methods; and Manual Reticulocytes; (4) Clinical Chemistry; (5) Urinalysis, including: Automated/semiautomated tests; Manual tests; and Specimens; (6) Therapeutic Drug Monitoring; (7) Microbiology, including: Bacteriology; Mycobacteriology and mycology; Parasitology; and Quality control; (8) Transfusion Medicine, including: Component accession and disposition records; Donor procedures; Technical procedures; and Transfusion and apheresis; (9) Diagnostic Immunology and Syphilis Serology; (10) Nuclear Medicine; (11) Anatomic Pathology and Cytopathology; (12) Cytogenetics; (13) Histocompatibility; (14) Flow Cytometry; (15) Molecular Pathology; (16) Limited Service Laboratories; (17) Small Laboratory Inspections; (18) Special Function Laboratories; (19) Affiliated Laboratories; (20) Satellite Laboratories; and (21) Ancillary Testing. Review report addresses deficiencies and suggestions for their correction. May respond to on-site review. **Renewal:** Every two years. Renewal based on self-assessment. Must also participate in surveys and provide on-site review team. **Restrictions:** Must report: Adverse media attention related to laboratory performance; Changes in laboratory's director, location, and/or ownership; and Investigations by state or federal agencies. **Preparatory Materials:** *Standards for Accreditation* (reference). List of suggested references provided. **Fees:** Must submit annual fee.

1693

Council on Accreditation, American Association for the Accreditation of Laboratory Animal Care

American Association for the
   Accreditation of Laboratory
   Animal Care (AAALAC)
11300 Rockville Pike, Ste. 1211
Rockville, MD 20852-3035
Phone: (301)231-5353
Fax: (301)231-8282

Recipient: Public and private organizations using animals in research, teaching, and testing in the U.S., Canada, and Europe. **Number of Accredited Institu-**

tions: 600. **Membership:** Not required. **Application Procedures:** Self-assessment required. Must document compliance with standards in the following areas: (1) Institutional Policies, including: Monitoring care and use of animals; Occupational health; Personal hygiene; Personnel qualifications, including animal care and technical personnel, animal resource professional personnel, personnel using hazardous agents, and research staff; Special considerations, including multiple major surgical procedures and physical restraint; and Veterinary care; (2) Laboratory Animal Husbandry, including: Animal environment, including illumination, micro and macroenvironments, noise, temperature and humidity, and ventilation; Bedding; Emergency, weekend, and holiday care; Food; Housing, including activity, caging or housing system, social environment, and space recommendations for laboratory animals; Identification and records; Sanitation, including cleanliness, vermin, and waste disposal; and Water; (3) Veterinary Care, including: Anesthesia and analgesia; Euthanasia; Preventive medicine, including animal procurement, quarantine and stabilization, and separation by species, source, and health status; Surveillance, diagnosis, treatment, and control of disease; and Surgery and post-surgical care; (4) Physical Plant, including: Aseptic surgery; Construction guidelines, including animal room doors, ceilings, corridors, doors, exterior windows, facilities for sanitizing equipment and supplies, floors, noise control, power and lighting, storage areas, temperature and humidity control, ventilation, and walls; Functional area; and Relationship of animal facilities to laboratories; and (5) Special Considerations, including: Facilities and procedures for animal research with hazardous agents; Farm animals; and Genetics and nomenclature. Must identify strengths and weaknesses of program and submit the following: Animal inventory; Cage inventory and description; Description of research, testing, and teaching programs involving animals; Floor plans; List of personnel; Meeting minutes; Organizational chart; Report of annual research funding; Statement of purpose; and Summary of heating, ventilation, and air conditioning systems. **Accreditation Requirements:** Active animal care and use program must be operational. Onsite review, verifying information provided in self-assessment, required. Review includes: Interviews with administrators and animal program and research staffs; Review of programmic information; and Tour of animal holding rooms, laboratory or use areas, and support areas. May respond to on-site review. Possible accreditation decisions are: (1) Full Ac-

creditation; (2) Provisional Accreditation, requiring correction of deficiencies within two years; or (3) Withhold Accreditation, for organizations in substantial non-compliance with standards. **Renewal:** Every three years. Renewal based on self-assessment and on-site review. Must also submit annual reports. **Restrictions:** Must observe all statutes and governmental regulations. **Preparatory Materials:** *Guide for the Care and Use of Laboratory Animals* (reference). **Fees:** Application fee; must also submit annual fees. **Endorsed By:** Academy of Surgical Research; American Association for the Advancement of Science; American Association of Colleges of Pharmacy; American Association of Dental Schools; American Association for Laboratory Animal Science; American Association of Pharmaceutical Scientists; American College of Laboratory Animal Medicine; American College of Physicians; American College of Surgeons; American College of Toxicology; American Dairy Science Association; American Dental Association; American Diabetes Association; American Heart Association; American Hospital Association; American Institute of Nutrition; American Medical Association; American Physiological Society; American Psychological Association; American Psychological Society; American Society of Animal Science; American Society of Laboratory Animal Practitioners; American Society for Pharmacology and Experimental Therapeutics; American Veterinary Medical Association; Association of American Medical Colleges; Association of American Veterinary Medical Colleges; Association of Gnotobiotics; Behavioral Toxicology Society; Cystic Fibrosis Foundation; Endocrine Society; Federation of American Societies for Experimental Biology; National Association of State Universities and Land Grant Colleges; Pharmaceutical Manufacturers Association; Poultry Science Association; Shock Society; Society for Neuroscience; Society for Pediatric Research; Society of Toxicology; and Teratology Society.

Landscape Architecture

▮1694▮

Landscape Architectural Accreditation Board
American Society of Landscape Architects (ASLA)
4401 Connecticut Ave., NW, Fifth Fl.
Washington, DC 20008-2302
Phone: (202)686-2752
Fax: (202)686-1001
Ronald C. Leighton, Mgr.

Recipient: First professional degree programs in landscape architecture at bachelor's and master's degree levels. **Number of Accredited Institutions:** 71. **Application Procedures:** Self-assessment, involving administrators, faculty, and students, required. Must document compliance with standards in the following areas: (1) Program Mission and Objectives, including: Academic mission; Curriculum; Institutional resources; Learning opportunities; Long-range plan; Program disclosure; and Program relationships; (2) Governance/Administration, including: Equal opportunity and affirmative action; Faculty evaluation; Faculty number; Faculty participation; Faculty responsibility; Faculty workload; Funding; Instructional effectiveness; Program administration; Program administrator; and Support staff; (3) Professional Curriculum, including: Content; Course evaluation; and Syllabus; (4) Bachelor's Level, including: Coursework; Program interaction; Student opportunities; and Student perspective; (5) Master's Level, including: Independent study; Program concentration; Research and scholarly methods; and Thesis or terminal project; (6) Faculty and Other Instructional Personnel, including: Continued academic and professional development; Credentials; Evaluation; Extra-instructional faculty involvement; Faculty diversity and balance; Faculty rank; Faculty travel support; Professional resources; Rank and salary equivalence; and Teaching assistants; (7) Students, including: Advising; Career options; Communication; Diversity; Educational perspective; Professional commitment; Student abilities; Student attitudes; and Student participation; (8) Alumni, including: Alumni evaluation; Alumni relations; and Graduate accomplishments; (9) Practitioners, including: Community of practice; and Local/regional practitioners; (10) Relation to University, Community, and Profession, including: Service activities; and Visibility; (11) Facilities and Equipment, including: Access to facilities; Adequate space; Configuration; Faculty offices;

Furniture and equipment; Permanent work stations; and Technical equipment; and (12) Library, including: Acquisition of collection; Areas of concentration; Extent of collection; and Integration with curriculum. **Accreditation Requirements:** Program title and degree description must incorporate the term "Landscape Architecture". On-site review, verifying information provided in self-assessment, required. Review includes: Discussion with faculty, staff, administrators, students, and other interested parties; Review of curriculum; and Tour of facilities. May respond to on-site review. Possible accreditation decisions are: (1) Full Accreditation; (2) Provisional Accreditation, requiring correction of deficiencies within two years; or (3) Accreditation Denied, for programs in substantial non-compliance with standards, **Renewal:** Every five years (maximum). Renewal based on self-assessment and on-site review. Must also submit annual reports. **Restrictions:** Must report changes in: Administration; Curriculum; Fiscal support; Personnel; and Physical facilities. **Preparatory Materials:** *Accreditation Standards and Procedures* (reference). **Fees:** $1000 (annual fee). **Accredited By:** Commission on Recognition of Postsecondary Accreditation.

Law

▮1695▮

Accreditation Committee, Association of American Law Schools
Association of American Law Schools (AALS)
1201 Connecticut Ave., NW, Ste 800
Washington, DC 20036-2605
Phone: (202)296-8851
Fax: (202)296-8869

Recipient: Programs leading to first professional degree in law. **Application Procedures:** Self-assessment required. Must document compliance with standards in the following areas: (1) Program Objectives; (2) Admissions, including: Evaluation of applicants; Fairness; Financial considerations; Recruitment; Requirements; and Transfer students; (3) Design and Mission of Juris Doctor Degree Program, including: Class schedule; Credit transfer; Curriculum; Joint degree programs; Length of program; Required hours and credit hours; Special circumstances; Student employment; and Written exams; (4) Diversity: Non-Discrimination and Affirmative Action,

covering: Admissions; and Employment policies; (5) Faculty, including: Dean; Full-time faculty; and Qualifications; (6) Law School Governance, requiring faculty control of program; (7) Faculty Development, including: Academic freedom; Class schedule and size; Compensation; Research; Secretarial and library staff; and Teaching responsibilities; (8) Curriculum and Pedagogy, including: Bar exam courses; Content; Foreign study programs; Review; Teaching law school outside law school; and Teaching methods; (9) Library, including: Access; Budget; Conditions; Organization; Physical condition of collection; Planning; Research needs; and Staff; (10) Physical Facilities, including: Classrooms; Office space; and Physical plant; (11) Financial Resources, including: Fundraising; and Institutional support; and (12) Records and Reports, including: Compliance reports; Individual records; and Retention. **Accreditation Requirements:** Program must have been in operation for five years and graduated three classes. On-site review required. May respond to on-site review. **Restrictions:** Must report significant institutional, locational, or programmic changes. **Fees:** $10,000, plus actual cost of on-site review. **Accredited By:** Commission on Recognition of Postsecondary Accreditation.

▮1696▮

Accreditation Committee of the Council of the Section of Legal Education and Admissions to the Bar
American Bar Association (ABA)
735 W. New York St.
Indianapolis, IN 46202

Recipient: Law schools. **Number of Accredited Institutions:** 175. **Application Procedures:** Self-assessment required. Must document compliance with standards in the following areas: (1) Academic Program and Curriculum, including: Core curriculum; and Professional responsibility and skills; (2) Faculty, including: Education; Faculty/student ratio; Professional activities outside law school; Salaries; Scholarly research and writing; Service to the law school community; Teaching ability; and Tenure; (3) Finances; (4) Library Resources, including: Appropriate technological resources; Content and size of collection; Materials that meet demands of curriculum; and Research needs of faculty and students; (5) Physical Plant, including: Classrooms; and Faculty offices; and (6) Students, including: Admissions; and Retention policy. **Accreditation Requirements:** Must have completed one full year of operation. On-site review, verifying information provided in self-assessment, required. Review includes: Class visits; Conferences with faculty members, law school administrators, and students; and Review of law school rules and procedures. Possible accreditation decisions are: (1) Full Accreditation; (2) Provisional Accreditation, requiring correction of deficiencies; or (3) Denial, for schools in substantial non-compliance with standards. **Renewal:** Every seven years (maximum). Renewal based on on-site review. Must also submit annual reports. **Preparatory Materials:** *Standards for the Approval of Law Schools* (reference). **Accredited By:** Commission on Recognition of Postsecondary Accreditation; U.S. Department of Education.

Law Enforcement

1697

Commission on Accreditation for Law Enforcement Agencies (CALEA)
10306 Eaton Pl., Ste. 320
Fairfax, VA 22030-2201
Phone: (703)352-4225
Fax: (703)591-2206
Toll Free: (800)368-3757

Recipient: Law enforcement agencies. **Application Procedures:** Self-assessment required. Must document compliance with standards in the following areas: Auxiliary and technical services; Law enforcement operations, operational support, and traffic law enforcement; Organization, management, and administration; Personnel administration; Prisoner and court-related services; and Role, responsibilities, and relationships with other agencies. Must also submit information on: Functions; Management; Organizational structure; Responsibilities; and Size of agency. **Accreditation Requirements:** Agency must accept precepts of community-oriented policing. Written directives and training required in the following areas: Facilities and equipment to ensure employees' safety; Informing employees about policies and practices; and Processes to safeguard employees' rights. On-site review required. Review includes: Inspection of facilities; Interviews with operations and management personnel; and Public hearing. Review report addresses areas needing improvement. May respond to on-site review. Possible accreditation decisions are: (1) Accreditation; (2) Accreditation Deferred, requiring correction of deficiencies; or (3) Accreditation Denied, for agencies in substantial noncompliance

with standards. **Renewal:** Every three years. Renewal based on on-site review. Must also submit annual reports. **Preparatory Materials:** *Accreditation Program Book, Accreditation Program Overview, Self-Assessment Manual,* and *Standards for Law Enforcement Agencies* (references). Training, technical assistance, and practice on-site reviews available. **Length of Process:** 24 months. **Fees:** $250 (application fee); $4675-16,150 (self-assessment and on-site review fees based on size of agency). **Endorsed By:** International Association of Chiefs of Police; National Organization of Black Law Enforcement Executives; National Sheriffs' Association; Police Executive Research Forum.

Librarianship

1698

Committee on Accreditation, American Library Association
American Library Association (ALA)
50 E. Huron St.
Chicago, IL 60611-2795
Phone: (312)280-2435
Fax: (312)280-2433
Toll Free: (800)545-2433
E-mail: U36765@UICVM.UIC. EDU
Prudence W. Dalrymple Ph.D., Dir.

Recipient: Programs leading to Master's in Library Science (MLS) degree. **Application Procedures:** Self-assessment required. Must document compliance with standards in the following areas: (1) Mission, Goals, and Objectives, including: Evaluation; Needs of constituencies; Philosophy, principles, and ethics; Planning; Role of library and information sciences; and Value of research and teaching; (2) Curriculum, including: Acquisitions; Analysis of information; Communication; Course content and sequence; Evaluation; Identification of information sources; Individual needs, goals, and objectives; Information and knowledge creation and dissemination; Information management; Interpretation of information; Organization and description; Preservation; Professional practice and principles; Review; Selection of information sources; Specialized learning experiences; Storage and retrieval; Synthesis of information; Theory; and Values; (3) Faculty, including: Appointments and promotions; Diversity; Professional development; Qualifications; Recruitment and retention policies; Research; Service activities; Specialties; and Student counsel-

ing; (4) Students, including: Admissions; Counseling and guidance; Diversity; Evaluation; Financial aid; Placement; Programs of study; and Recruitment; (5) Administration and Financial Support, including: Administrative support; Autonomy; Compensation; Executive officers; Interdisciplinary relations; Resources; and Staffing; and (6) Physical Resources and Facilities, including: Computer and other information technologies; Library; Media production facilities; Multimedia resources and services; and Staff. **Accreditation Requirements:** Students entering program must have bachelor's degree. On-site review, verifying information provided in self-assessment, required. Review includes meetings with faculty, school and university administrative personnel, and students. May respond to on-site review. Possible accreditation decisions are: (1) Accredited; and (2) Conditional Accreditation, requiring improvements in specific areas. **Renewal:** Renewal based on self-assessment and on-site review. Must also submit annual statistical reports and biennial narrative reports. **Preparatory Materials:** *Standards for Accreditation of Master's Programs in Library and Information Studies* (reference). **Length of Process:** Two-three years. **Fees:** $1750, plus actual cost of on-site review; $2000 (annual fee). **Accredited By:** Commission on Recognition of Postsecondary Accreditation; U.S. Department of Education.

Library Binding

1699

Library Binding Institute (LBI)
7401 Metro Blvd., No. 325
Edina, MN 55439
Phone: (612)835-4707
Fax: (612)835-4780

Recipient: Firms and library binders involved in rebinding of worn volumes, prebinding of new volumes, initial hardcover binding of periodicals, and other binding principally for libraries and schools. **Accreditation Requirements:** Must meet LBI Standard for Library Binding. LBI examines work and investigates experience, insurance for protection of customers' property, and bank and library references. On-site review required.

Marriage and Family Therapy

1700

Commission on Accreditation for Marriage and Family Therapy Education

American Association for Marriage and Family Therapy (AAMFT)
1100 17th St., NW, 10th Fl.
Washington, DC 20036
Phone: (202)452-0109
Fax: (202)232-2329
Denise Heaman Calvert, Exec.Dir.

Recipient: Master's and doctoral degree, and post-graduate degree clinical training, programs in marriage and family therapy. **Number of Accredited Institutions:** 75. **Application Procedures:** Self-assessment required. Must document compliance with standards in the following areas: Administrative and organization structure; Clinical and training facilities; Curriculum requirements; Eligibility; Entrance requirements; Evaluation; Professional staff and resources; and Supervision. **Accreditation Requirements:** On-site review required. Review includes interviews with faculty, staff, administrators, students, and other interested parties. May respond to on-site review. **Renewal:** Every five years (maximum). Renewal based on self-assessment and on-site review. **Preparatory Materials:** *Manual on Accreditation* (reference). **Accredited By:** Commission on Recognition of Postsecondary Accreditation; U.S. Department of Education.

Medicine

1701

Accreditation Council for Continuing Medical Education (ACCME)

515 N. State St., Ste. 7340
Chicago, IL 60610
Phone: (312)464-2500
Fax: (312)464-2586
John Fauser Ph.D., Interim Sec.

Recipient: Sponsors of continuing medical education. **Number of Accredited Institutions:** 537. **Application Procedures:** Self-assessment required. Must document compliance with standards in the following areas: (1) Statement of Mission, including: Characteristics of potential participants; Description of activities and services provided; Goals of program; and Scope of program; (2) Identifying and

Analyzing Needs and Interests of Prospective Participants, including: Data sources used; Planning educational activities; Processes used to identify needs; and Statement of overall needs; (3) Objectives for Each Activity, including: Disseminating objectives to prospective participants; Identifying physicians for whom activity is designed; Instructional content and/or expected learning outcomes in terms of knowledge, skills, and/or attitudes; Meeting individual educational needs; and Special background requirements of prospective participants; (4) Design and Implementation of Educational Activities, including: Educational content and methods; Responsiveness of educational programs to prospective participants in areas such as knowledge levels, preferred learning styles, and professional experience; and Systematic planning procedures; (5) Evaluating Effectiveness of Overall Program and Planning, including: Evaluation data; Evaluation of educational activities, quality of instructional process, and participant satisfaction; and Evaluation methods; (6) Management Procedures and Resources, including: Administration; Budget for program and components; Facilities; Faculty; Internal review and control procedure; Organizational structure; and Recordkeeping; and (7) Educational Activities Jointly Sponsored with Non-Accredited Entities, including evaluation and planning of these activities. Separate standards cover commercial sponsors of and materials for continuing education programs. **Accreditation Requirements:** On-site review required. May not respond to on-site review. **Renewal:** Every four years. Renewal based on on-site review. Renewal fee is $1750. **Preparatory Materials:** *Essentials, Guidelines, and Standards for the Accreditation of Sponsors of Continuing Medical Education, Standards for Commercial Support of Continuing Medical Education,* and *Standards for Interpreting the Essentials as Applied to Continuing Medical Education Enduring Materials* (references). **Length of Process:** Six months-one year. **Fees:** $2600; $500 (annual fee). **Endorsed By:** American Medical Association.

1702

Accreditation Council for Graduate Medical Education (ACGME)

515 N. State St.
Chicago, IL 60610
Phone: (312)464-4920
Fax: (312)464-4098
John C. Gienapp Ph.D., Exec.Dir.

Recipient: Medical specialty residency programs. **Application Procedures:** Self-

assessment required. Must document compliance with general standards for residency programs and requirements for specialty area. General standards cover: (1) Institutional Organization and Commitment, including: Accreditation for patient care; Compliance with ACGME policies and procedures; Educational administration; Institutional agreements; Responsibilities to residents; and Sponsoring institution; (2) Institutional Policies and Procedures, including: Ancillary support; Conditions of resident employment; Counseling and support services; Quality assurance; Resident financial support and benefits; and Resident supervision and working environment; (3) Program Goals and Objectives, including: Program design; and Program evaluation; (4) Program Personnel, including: Program director; Teaching staff; and Other program personnel; (5) Program Research and Scholarly Activity, including: Library; and Scholarly activity; and (6) Resident Eligibility, including: Enrollment of non-eligibles; Resident eligibility; and Resident selection. Specialty standards cover: Educational content; Facilities; Instructional activities; and Responsibilities of patient care and supervision. Standards for each specialty developed by Residency Review Committees in the following areas: Allergy and immunology; Anesthesiology; Colon and rectal surgery; Dermatology; Emergency medicine; Family practice; Internal medicine; Medical genetics; Neurological surgery; Neurology; Nuclear medicine; Obstetrics and gynecology; Ophthalmology; Orthopaedic surgery; Otolaryngology; Pathology; Pediatrics; Physical medicine and rehabilitation; Plastic surgery; Preventive medicine; Psychiatry; Radiology; Surgery; Thoracic surgery; and Urology (see separate entries). **Accreditation Requirements:** On-site review, verifying information provided in self-assessment, required. Review includes interviews with program directors, administrators, key faculty, and residents. May respond to on-site review. Possible accreditation decisions are: (1) Accreditation; (2) Provisional Accreditation, requiring correction of deficiencies within two years; or (3) Withhold Accreditation, for programs in substantial non-compliance with standards. **Renewal:** Every five years (maximum). Renewal based on self-assessment and on-site review. **Preparatory Materials:** *Essentials of Accredited Residencies in Graduate Medical Education* (reference). **Fees:** $1000 (application fee); $2375 (on-site review fee); must also submit annual fee based on number of residents. **Endorsed By:** American Board of Medical Specialties; American Hospital Association; American Medical Association; Association of American Medical Colleges; Council of Medical Specialty Societies.

1703

Accrediting Bureau of Health Education Schools (ABHES)

2700 S. Quincy St., Ste. 210
Arlington, VA 22206
Phone: (703)998-1200
Fax: (703)998-2550
Carol A. Moneymaker, Exec.Dir.

Recipient: Private, postsecondary institutions offering educational programs exclusively in allied health and medical assisting; and private and public institutions offering medical laboratory technician programs. **Number of Accredited Institutions:** 165. **Application Procedures:** Self-assessment, involving administrator, chief executive officer, or program director, consultants or advisors, faculty, students, and other interested parties, required. Must document compliance with standards in the following areas: (1) Philosophy and Objectives, including: Appropriate objectives; and Written objectives; (2) Instruction, Curriculum, and Programs, including: Clinical experience; Comprehensive instruction; Instructional content and materials; Library; Orientation of incoming students and study instructions; Organization of instruction; Standards of instruction; Supplementary printed materials; and Teaching methods and instructional materials; (3) Examination and Student Achievement, including: Encouragement of students; Examination service; Handling failures; Individual differences; Student evaluation of courses; and Student experience; (4) Student Services, including: Counseling assistance; Employment assistance; Grading of examinations; and Student progress; (5) Student Satisfaction, including: Student progress and completion rate; and Student success and satisfaction; (6) Faculty, including: Benefits; Faculty involvement in decision-making; Instructional approaches and methods; Medical supervisor/director; Professional dedication; Professional development; Qualifications; Recruitment; Staff size; Student/faculty ratio; Teaching load; and Working conditions; (7) Admission Practices and Enrollment Agreements, including: Admissions; Catalog and promotional literature; and Enrollment agreements; (8) Advertising and Promotion, including: Comparisons to competitors; Literature; Sales techniques; and Truthfulness; (9) Financial Responsibility, including: Demonstrated operation; Financial reporting; and Financial responsibility; (10) Tuition Policies, including: Reasonable tuition; Tuition collection procedures; and Tuition

refund policies; (11) Plant and Equipment, including: Building; Classrooms; Equipment; Health; Laboratories; Record protection; Safety; Ventilating and heating; and Workspace; (12) Assessment of Educational Outcomes, including: Alumni assessment; Curriculum; Employer assessment; Materials; and Objectives; and (13) Professional Growth, including: Faculty; Operating efficiency; and Service. Must also submit catalogs, course materials, financial statements, and promotional material. **Accreditation Requirements:** Must be in operation for two years. Medical assistant curriculum should include instruction in the following areas: Anatomy and basic human systems; Medical law and ethics; Medical laboratory procedures; Medical office business procedures; Medical office clinical procedures; Medical terminology; Pharmacology; and Psychology of human relations. Medical laboratory technician curriculum should include instruction in the following areas: Anatomy and physiology; Clinical chemistry; ECG; General chemistry; General orientation; Hematology; Immunohematology; Medical ethics; Microbiology; Quality control; Serology; Special laboratory procedures and registry review; and Urinalysis and gastric analysis. On-site review required. Review includes interviews with faculty, staff, administrators, students, and other interested parties. Review report addresses strengths and weaknesses of program. May respond to on-site review. Possible accreditation decisions are: (1) Accreditation; (2) Defer Accreditation, requiring correction of deficiencies; or (3) Deny Accreditation, for programs in substantial non-compliance with standards. **Restrictions:** Must report changes in ownership. **Accredited By:** Commission on Recognition of Postsecondary Accreditation; U.S. Department of Education.

1704

Accrediting Commission on Education for Health Services Administration (ACEHSA)

1911 N. Fort Myer Dr., Ste. 503
Arlington, VA 22209
Phone: (703)524-0511
Fax: (703)525-4791
Dr. Sherril B. Gelmon, Exec.Dir.

Recipient: Master's degree level health administration programs in schools of business, medicine, public health, public administration, allied health sciences, and graduate studies, and other institutions in the U.S. and Canada. **Number of Accredited Institutions:** 65. **Application Procedures:** Self-assessment required. Must document compliance with stan-

dards in the following areas: Curriculum; Faculty; Program mission, goals, objectives, and evaluation; Research and scholarship; Resources and academic relationships; and Student and the graduate. **Accreditation Requirements:** Must have graduated two classes and offer major course of study lasting beyond baccalaureate level in at least one of the following: Health care administration; Health planning and evaluation; Health policy; Health services management; Hospital or other health care organization-specific administration and management; or Other related areas. On-site review required. Review includes interviews with faculty, staff, administrators, students, and other interested parties. May respond to on-site review. **Renewal:** Renewal required. Must also submit periodic progress reports. **Preparatory Materials:** *Criteria for Accreditation* (reference). **Accredited By:** Commission on Recognition of Postsecondary Accreditation. **Endorsed By:** American College of Health Care Administrators; American College of Healthcare Executives; American College of Medical Practice Executives; American Hospital Association; American Public Health Association; Association of Mental Health Administrators; Association of University Programs in Health Administration; Canadian College of Health Service Executives.

1705

American Board of Medical Genetics (ABMG)

9650 Rockville Pike
Bethesda, MD 20814-3998
Phone: (301)571-1825
Fax: (301)571-1895
E-mail: srobinson@abmg.faseb.org
Sharon Robinson, Admin.

Recipient: Two-year postdoctoral fellowships in medical genetics. **Number of Accredited Institutions:** 80. **Accreditation Requirements:** Must document compliance with standards. Must maintain accredited clinical genetics program to be accredited in laboratory specialties. **Renewal:** Every five years. Must also submit annual report. Renewal fee is $1000-$1500. **Preparatory Materials:** none. **Length of Process:** One year. **Fees:** $1000-$1500.

1706

Council on Education for Public Health (CEPH)

1015 15th St., NW, Ste. 403
Washington, DC 20005
Phone: (202)789-1050
Fax: (202)289-8274
Patricia P. Evans, Exec.Dir.

Recipient: Graduate schools of public health and graduate programs outside schools of public health in community health education and community health/preventive medicine. **Application Procedures:** Self-assessment, involving administrative officers and staff, alumni, faculty, students, and other interested parties, required. Must document compliance with standards in the following areas: (1) Mission, Goals, and Objectives, including: Community service; Evaluation of outcomes; Instruction; Mission of public health; Research; and Resources; (2) Organizational Setting, including: Accountability; Ethical standards; Evaluation; Faculty and student participation; Interdisciplinary coordination; and Objectives; (3) Governance, including: Academic standards and policy; Autonomy; Budget and resource allocation; Faculty involvement; Faculty recruitment, retention, promotion, and tenure; General program policy development; Planning; Research and service; Student involvement; and Student recruitment, admissions, and award of degree; (4) Resources, including: Administration; Classrooms; Community resources; Computer facilities; Faculty; Field experience sites; Financial; Laboratories; Library facilities and holdings; Offices; Outcome measures; Staff; and Student/faculty ratio; (5) Instructional Programs, including: Academic and professional degrees; Application of concepts and knowledge to solution of community health problems; Culminating experience; Curriculum; Evaluation; Joint degree programs; Knowledge basic to public health; Learning objectives; Non-traditional degree programs; Policies and procedures; Practice experience; School bulletin; Specialization; and Student progress; (6) Research, including: Basic and applied topics; Community based research activities; Faculty; Objectives; Policies and procedures; and Students; (7) Service, including: Community involvement; Community linkages; Community needs; Continuing or outreach education; Evaluation; Objectives; Policies, procedures, and practices; Professional needs; and Student involvement; (8) Faculty, including: Evaluation; Faculty involvement; Non-discrimination and diversity; Polices and procedures; Practice experience; Professional devel-

opment; Promotions; Qualifications; Recruitment; Research; Staff size; Student involvement; Teaching competence; and Tenure; and (9) Evaluation and Planning, including: Alumni involvement; Data collection mechanisms; Employer involvement; Objectives; and Planning. Must submit: Budget statement; Committee minutes; Faculty curricula vitae; Faculty handbook; Student and alumni survey instruments; Student papers and theses; and University reports. **Accreditation Requirements:** Must have graduated one class. Programs must include instruction in the following areas: Biostatistics; Environmental health services; Epidemiology; Health services administration; and Social and behavioral sciences. On-site review required. Review includes: Evaluation of documents; Interviews with alumni, community representatives, faculty, staff, administrators, students, and other interested parties; and Tour of campus facilities. May respond to on-site review. Possible accreditation decisions are: (1) Accreditation; (2) Probationary Accreditation, requiring correction of deficiencies within three years; or (3) Denial of Accreditation, for schools or programs in substantial non-compliance with standards. **Renewal:** Every five years (initial); every seven years thereafter. Renewal based on self-assessment and on-site review. Must also submit annual reports. **Preparatory Materials:** *Accredtitation Criteria* and *Accreditation Procedures* (references). **Fees:** Application fee, plus actual cost of on-site review. **Accredited By:** U.S. Department of Education.

1707

Liaison Committee on Medical Education (LCME)

American Medical Association (AMA)
515 N. State St.
Chicago, IL 60610
Phone: (312)464-4933
Fax: (312)464-5830

Recipient: Medical programs leading to medical doctor (M.D.) degree in the U.S. and Canada. **Application Procedures:** Self-assessment required. Must document compliance with standards in the following areas: (1) Objectives, including: Defined goals and objectives; Enrollment and class sizes; and Reporting goals and objectives to faculty, students, and public; (2) Governance, including: Accreditation; Administrators; and Educational environment; (3) Administration, including: Educational and experience requirements for deans and other administrators; Medical school or university bylaws; and Organization; (4) Educa-

tional Program for M.D. Degree, including: Academic counseling and career guidance; Content; Design and management; Duration; and Evaluation of student achievement and due process; (5) Medical Students, including: Admissions; Amenities for students; Financial aid; Personal counseling; and Student health services; and (6) Resources for Educational Program, including: Clinical teaching facilities; Faculty; Finances; General facilities; and Library. Must also prepare database cataloging program of medical education. **Accreditation Requirements:** On-site review, verifying information provided in self-assessment, required. Review includes interviews with administrators, faculty, students, and other interested parties. May respond to on-site review. Possible accreditation decisions are: (1) Full Accreditation; (2) Probation, requiring correction of deficiencies within limited time period; or (3) Denial of Accreditation, for programs in substantial non-compliance with standards. **Renewal:** Every seven years (maximum). Renewal based on self-assessment, preparation of database cataloging program of medical education, and on-site review. Must also submit annual reports. **Fees:** Administrative fee, plus actual cost of on-site review. **Accredited By:** U.S. Department of Education. **Endorsed By:** American Medical Association; Association of American Medical Colleges; Committee on Accreditation of Canadian Medical Schools; Council on Medical Education.

1708

Residency Review Committee for Allergy and Immunology

American Board of Allergy and Immunology (ABAI)
3624 Market St.
Philadelphia, PA 19104-2675
Phone: (215)349-9466
Fax: (215)222-8669
Dr. Herbert C. Mansmann Jr., Exec.Sec.

Recipient: Residency review committee of Accreditation Council for Graduate Medical Education (see separate entry) for residency programs in medical institutions for medical doctors (M.D.s) specializing in allergy and immunology and the specialty area of clinical and laboratory immunology. **Accreditation Requirements:** Residencies in allergy and immunology must be two years in length; residencies in clinical and laboratory immunology require an additional year of training. Programs must provide instruction in all aspects of allergy and immunological medicine. Residents evaluated in the following: Attitudes and professional behavior; Clinical judgment; Clinical skills of history taking; Commitment to scholarship; Humanistic qualities; Medical care, including utilization of laboratory tests and diagnostic procedures; Medical knowledge; Physical examination; Procedural skills; and Work habits. Program director must submit semiannual reports on each resident. **Endorsed By:** American Board of Internal Medicine; American Board of Pediatrics; American Medical Association; Council on Medical Education.

`1709`

Residency Review Committee for Anesthesiology
American Board of Anesthesiology (ABA)
100 Constitution Plaza
Hartford, CT 06103-1796
Phone: (203)522-9857
Fax: (203)522-6626
Francis P. Hughes Ph.D., Exec.Sec.

Recipient: Residency review committee of Accreditation Council for Graduate Medical Education (see separate entry) for residency programs in medical institutions for medical doctors (M.D.s) specializing in anesthesiology and the specialty areas of: Critical care medicine; and Pain management. **Accreditation Requirements:** Residencies in anesthesiology must be three years in length; residencies in critical care medicine or pain management require an additional year of training. Program must include instruction in the following: (1) Basic Anesthesia Training; (2) Subspecialty Anesthesia Training, including: Anesthesia for outpatient surgery; Cardiothoracic anesthesia; Critical care medicine; Neuroanesthesia; Obstetric anesthesia; Pain management; Pediatric; Recovery room care; and Regional anesthesia; and (3) Advanced Anesthesia Training, including the following tracks: Advanced clinical; Clinical scientist; and Subspecialty clinical. Must maintain leave of absence policy. **Endorsed By:** American Medical Association; American Society of Anesthesiologists; Council on Medical Education.

`1710`

Residency Review Committee for Colon and Rectal Surgery
American Board of Colon and Rectal Surgery (ABCRS)
20600 Eureka Rd., Ste. 713
Taylor, MI 48180
Phone: (313)282-9400
Fax: (313)282-9402
Herand Abcarian M.D., Exec.Dir.

Recipient: Residency review committee of Accreditation Council for Graduate Medical Education (see separate entry) for residency programs in medical institutions for medical doctors (M.D.s) specializing in colon and rectal surgery. **Accreditation Requirements:** Residencies must be one year in length. Program must include instruction in the following: Abscesses; Colon and rectal cancer; Diverticulitis; Endoscopic procedures; Fissures; Fistulas; Hemorrhoids; Inflammatory bowel disease; Intestinal and anorectal physiology; Medical and surgical management of diseases; Minimally invasive abdominal surgery; and Polyps. **Endorsed By:** American College of Surgeons; American Medical Association; Council on Medical Education.

`1711`

Residency Review Committee for Dermatology
American Board of Dermatology (ABD)
Henry Ford Hospital
Detroit, MI 48202-2689
Phone: (313)874-1088
Fax: (313)872-3221
Harry J. Hurley M.D., Exec.Dir.

Recipient: Residency review committee of Accreditation Council for Graduate Medical Education (see separate entry) for residency programs in medical institutions for medical doctors (M.D.s) specializing in dermatology and the specialty areas of: Clinical and laboratory dermatological immunology; and Dermatopathology. **Accreditation Requirements:** Residencies in dermatology must be three years in length; residencies in clinical and laboratory dermatological immunology must be one year in length. At least 75 percent of resident's time must be related to direct care of dermatologic outpatients and inpatients. Program directors must submit annual report on each resident. **Endorsed By:** American College of Surgeons; American Medical Association; Council on Medical Education.

`1712`

Residency Review Committee for Emergency Medicine
American Board for Emergency Medicine (ABEM)
3000 Coolidge Rd.
East Lansing, MI 48823
Phone: (517)332-4800
Fax: (517)332-2234

Recipient: Residency review committee of Accreditation Council for Graduate Medical Education (see separate entry) for residency programs in medical institutions for medical doctors (M.D.s) specializing in emergency medicine. **Accreditation Requirements:** Residencies must be 36 months in length. **Endorsed By:** American College of Emergency Physicians; American Medical Association; Council on Medical Education.

`1713`

Residency Review Committee for Family Practice
American Board of Family Practice (ABFP)
2228 Young Dr.
Lexington, KY 40505-4294
Phone: (606)269-5626

Recipient: Residency review committee of Accreditation Council for Graduate Medical Education (see separate entry) for residency programs in medical institutions for medical doctors (M.D.s) specializing in family practice and the specialty area of geriatric medicine. **Accreditation Requirements:** Residencies in family practice must be 36 months in length; residencies in geriatric medicine must be two years in length. Must maintain transfer policy. **Endorsed By:** American Academy of Family Physicians; American Board of Family Practice; American Medical Association; Council on Medical Education.

`1714`

Residency Review Committee for Internal Medicine
American Board of Internal Medicine (ABIM)
3624 Market St.
Philadelphia, PA 19104-2675
Phone: (215)243-1500
Fax: (215)382-4702
Toll Free: (800)441-ABIM

Recipient: Residency review committee of Accreditation Council for Graduate Medical Education (see separate entry) for residency programs in medical institutions for medical doctors (M.D.s) specializing in internal medicine and the specialty areas of: Cardiology; Critical care medicine; Endocrinology and metabolism; Gastroenterology; Geriatric medicine; Hematology; Hematology and oncology; Infectious diseases; Nephrology; Oncology; Pulmonary diseases; Pulmonary diseases and critical care; and Rheumatology. **Accreditation Requirements:** Residencies in internal medicine must be 36 months in length, including 24 months of patient responsibility in the following areas: Dermatology or neurology services; Emergency medicine, general medical, or subspecialty ambulatory settings; Inpatient services in which disorders or general internal medicine are managed; and Inpatient services in which disorders of one or more subspecialties of internal medicine are managed. Residencies in cardiovascular disease must be three years in length; residencies in the following specialty areas must be two years in length: Diabetes and metabolism; Endocrinology; Gastroenterology; Hematology; Infectious disease; Medical oncology; Nephrology; Pulmonary disease; and Rheumatology. Residents evaluated in the following areas: Clinical judgment; Clinical skills; Humanistic qualities; Medical knowledge; Professionalism; and Provision of medical care. Must maintain transfer policies. Program director must submit annual reports for each resident. **Endorsed By:** American College of Physicians; American Medical Association; Council on Medical Education.

1715

Residency Review Committee for Medical Genetics
American Board of Medical Genetics (ABMG)
9650 Rockville Pike
Bethesda, MD 20814-3998
Phone: (301)571-1825
Fax: (301)571-1825

Recipient: Residency review committee of Accreditation Council for Graduate Medical Education (see separate entry) for residency programs in medical institutions for medical doctors (M.D.s) specializing in medical genetics. **Accreditation Requirements:** Residencies must be two years in length. **Endorsed By:** American College of Medical Genetics; American Medical Association; Council on Medical Education.

1716

Residency Review Committee for Neurological Surgery
American Board of Neurological Surgery (ABNS)
6550 Fannin St., Ste. 2139
Houston, TX 77030
Phone: (713)790-6015
Fax: (713)794-0207
Mary Louise Sanderson, Admin.

Recipient: Residency review committee of Accreditation Council for Graduate Medical Education (see separate entry) for residency programs in medical institutions for medical doctors (M.D.s) specializing in neurological surgery. **Accreditation Requirements:** Residencies must be 60 months in length, including 36 months in clinical neurosurgery. Program must include instruction in the following: Basic neurosciences; Neuropathology; Neuroradiology; Research; and Related disciplines. Must maintain transfer policy. **Endorsed By:** American College of Surgeons; American Medical Association; Council on Medical Education.

1717

Residency Review Committee for Neurology
American Board of Psychiatry and Neurology (ABPN)
500 Lake Cook Rd., Ste. 335
Deerfield, IL 60015-5249
Phone: (708)945-7900
Fax: (708)945-1146

Recipient: Residency review committee of Accreditation Council for Graduate Medical Education (see separate entry) for residency programs in medical institutions for medical doctors (M.D.s) specializing in neurology and the specialty area of child neurology. **Accreditation Requirements:** Residencies in neurology must be three years in length; residencies in child neurology must be two years in length. **Endorsed By:** American Academy of Neurology; American Medical Association; Council on Medical Education.

1718

Residency Review Committee for Nuclear Medicine
American Board of Nuclear Medicine (ABNM)
900 Veteran Ave.
Los Angeles, CA 90024
Phone: (310)825-6787

Recipient: Residency review committee

of Accreditation Council for Graduate Medical Education (see separate entry) for residency programs in medical institutions for medical doctors (M.D.s) specializing in nuclear medicine. **Accreditation Requirements:** Residencies must be two years in length, including 18 months of training in clinical nuclear medicine and six months of training in allied sciences. Programs must include instruction in the following: Computer sciences; Direction of radiation safety programs; *in vitro* and *in vivo* measurements; Instrumentation; Medical management of individuals exposed to ionizing radiation; Medical nuclear physics; Nuclear imaging; Nuclear magnetic resonance imaging; Pathology; Physiology; Positron emission tomography; Radiation biology; Radiation protection; Radiobioassay; Radiopharmaceutical chemistry; Safe management and disposal of radioactive substances; Single photon emission computed tomography; Statistics; and Therapy with unsealed radionuclides. **Endorsed By:** American Academy of Neurology; American Medical Association; Council on Medical Education.

1719

Residency Review Committee for Obstetrics and Gynecology
American Board of Obstetrics and Gynecology (ABOG)
2915 Vine St.
Dallas, TX 75204-1069
Phone: (214)871-1619
Fax: (214)871-1943
Norman F. Gant M.D., Exec.Dir.

Recipient: Residency review committee of Accreditation Council for Graduate Medical Education (see separate entry) for residency programs in medical institutions for medical doctors (M.D.s) specializing in obstetrics and gynecology. **Accreditation Requirements:** Residencies must be 36 months in length. Programs must include inpatient and ambulatory primary preventive care, provide continuity of care, and include instruction in the following areas: Diagnosis and management of breast disease; Diagnosis and management of lower urinary tract dysfunction in women; Diagnostic procedures; Major gynecologic operations; Managing complications; Performance and interpretation of diagnostic pelvic and transvaginal ultrasound; and Spontaneous and operative obstetric deliveries. Must also maintain policies concerning leaves of absence and transfers. **Endorsed By:** American College of Obstetricians and Gynecologists; American Medical Association; Council on Medical Education.

1720

Residency Review Committee for Ophthalmology

American Board of Ophthalmology
111 Presidential Blvd., Ste. 241
Bala Cynwyd, PA 19004
Phone: (610)664-1175

Recipient: Residency review committee of Accreditation Council for Graduate Medical Education (see separate entry) for residency programs in medical institutions for medical doctors (M.D.s) specializing in ophthalmology. **Accreditation Requirements:** Residencies must be 36 months in length. **Endorsed By:** American Academy of Ophthalmology; American Medical Association; Council on Medical Education.

1721

Residency Review Committee for Orthopaedic Surgery

American Board of Orthopaedic Surgery (ABOS)
400 Silver Cedar Ct.
Chapel Hill, NC 27514
Phone: (919)929-7103
Fax: (919)942-8988

Recipient: Residency review committee of Accreditation Council for Graduate Medical Education (see separate entry) for residency programs in medical institutions for medical doctors (M.D.s) specializing in orthopaedic surgery and the specialties of: Adult reconstructive orthopaedics; Hand surgery; Musculoskeletal oncology; Orthopaedic sports medicine; Orthopaedic surgery of the spine; Orthopaedic trauma; and Pediatric orthopaedics. **Accreditation Requirements:** Residencies in orthopaedic surgery must be five years in length, including three years in orthopaedic surgery. Program must include instruction in the following: (1) Acute and Chronic Care, including diagnosis and care, both operative and nonoperative, of the following: Acute trauma; Chronic orthopaedic problems, including benign and malignant tumors, metabolic bone disease, neuromuscular disease, reconstructive surgery, and rehabilitation; Infectious disease; and Neurovascular impairment; (2) Adult Orthopaedics; (3) Anatomic Areas, including: Bones; Bony pelvis; Joints; Soft tissues of upper and lower extremities, including the hand and foot; and Spine, including intervertebral discs; (4) Basic Science, including: Anatomy; Biochemistry; Biomaterials; Biomechanics; Microbiology; Pathology; Pharmacology; and Physiology; (5) Children's Orthopaedics; (6) Fractures and Trauma; (7) Related Clini-

cal Subjects, including: Musculoskeletal imaging procedures; Neurological and rheumatological disorders; Orthotics; Physical modalities and exercises; Prosthetics; and Use and interpretation of clinical laboratory tests; and (8) Research, including: Clinical; and Laboratory. Must maintain policy concerning leaves of absence. Program directors must submit annual reports on each resident. **Endorsed By:** American Academy of Orthopaedic Surgeons; American Medical Association; Council on Medical Education.

1722

Residency Review Committee for Otolaryngology

American Board of Otolaryngology (ABO)
5615 Kirby Dr., Ste. 936
Houston, TX 77005-2452
Robert W. Cantrell M.D., Exec.V. Pres.

Recipient: Residency review committee of Accreditation Council for Graduate Medical Education (see separate entry) for residency programs in medical institutions for medical doctors (M.D.s) specializing in otolaryngology. **Accreditation Requirements:** Residencies must be five years in length, including one year of general surgery and four years in otolaryngology-head and neck surgery. Program must include instruction in the following: Basic medical sciences; Chemical senses; Clinical aspects of diagnosis and medical and/or surgical therapy or prevention for deformities, diseases, disorders, and/or injuries; Communication sciences, including audiology and speech-language pathology; Endocrinology; Facial plastic and reconstructive surgery; Head and neck oncology; Neurology; and Respiratory and upper alimentary systems. Must maintain policies concerning leaves of absence and transfers. Program directors must submit annual reports on each resident. **Endorsed By:** American College of Surgeons; American Medical Association; Council on Medical Education.

1723

Residency Review Committee for Pathology

American Board of Pathology (ABP)
PO Box 25915
Tampa, FL 33622-5915
Phone: (813)286-2444
Fax: (813)289-5279

Recipient: Residency review committee

of Accreditation Council for Graduate Medical Education (see separate entry) for residency programs in medical institutions for medical doctors (M.D.s) specializing in anatomic and/or clinical pathology and the following specialties: Blood banking; Chemical pathology; Cytopathology; Dermatopathology; Forensic pathology; Hematology; Immunopathology; Medical microbiology; and Neuropathology. **Accreditation Requirements:** Residencies in anatomic and/or clinical pathology may be either three or four years in length; residencies in specialty areas must be one year in length. Must maintain leave of absence policy. **Endorsed By:** American Medical Association; Council on Medical Education.

1724

Residency Review Committee for Pediatrics

American Board of Pediatrics (ABP)
111 Silver Cedar Ct.
Chapel Hill, NC 27514-1651
Phone: (919)929-0461
Fax: (919)929-9255

Recipient: Residency review committee of Accreditation Council for Graduate Medical Education (see separate entry) for residency programs in medical institutions for medical doctors (M.D.s) specializing in pediatrics and the specialty areas of: Neonatal-perinatal medicine; Pediatric cardiology; Pediatric critical-care medicine; Pediatric endocrinology; Pediatric gastroenterology; Pediatric hematology and oncology; Pediatric nephrology; and Pediatric pulmonology. **Accreditation Requirements:** Residencies in pediatrics must be three years in length; residencies in specialties vary in length. Residents evaluated in following areas: Assessing data and arriving at diagnosis; Gathering data by history, laboratory studies, and physical examination; Interpersonal relationships with other members of health team; Interpersonal relationships with patients and families; Managing problems and maintaining health; and Work habits and personal qualities. Must maintain leave of absence and transfer policies. Program directors must submit annual reports and develop evaluation procedures for residents. **Endorsed By:** American Academy of Pediatrics; American Medical Association; Council on Medical Education.

1725

Residency Review Committee for Physical Medicine and Rehabilitation

American Board of Physical
Medicine and Rehabilitation
(ABPMR)
Norwest Center, Ste. 674
21 First St., SW
Rochester, MN 55902-3009
Phone: (507)282-1776
Fax: (507)282-9242
Joachim L. Opitz M.D., Exec.Dir.

Recipient: Residency review committee of Accreditation Council for Graduate Medical Education (see separate entry) for residency programs in medical institutions for medical doctors (M.D.s) specializing in physical medicine and rehabilitation. **Accreditation Requirements:** Residencies must be 48 months in length. Programs must include instruction in clinical skills, physical medicine and rehabilitation, and the following: Brain lesions; Cardiac rehabilitation; Electrodiagnosis; Electromyography; Geriatrics; Inpatient and outpatient pediatric rehabilitation; Musculoskeletal and neuromuscular problems; Nerve conduction studies; Psychosocial aspects of patients with disabilities; Somatosensory evoked potentials; Spinal cord-injured patients; and Sports medicine. Must maintain policy concerning transfers. **Endorsed By:** American Academy of Physical Medicine and Rehabilitation; American Medical Association; Council on Medical Education.

1726

Residency Review Committee for Plastic Surgery

American Board of Plastic Surgery
(ABPS)
Seven Penn Center, Ste. 400
1635 Market St.
Philadelphia, PA 19103-2204
Phone: (215)587-9322

Recipient: Residency review committee of Accreditation Council for Graduate Medical Education (see separate entry) for residency programs in medical institutions for medical doctors (M.D.s) specializing in plastic surgery and the specialty of hand surgery. **Accreditation Requirements:** Residencies in plastic surgery may be either two or three years in length. Program must include instruction in the following areas: Anesthetics; Basic sciences, including anatomy, biochemistry, microbiology, pathology, and physiology; Blood replacement; Care of emergencies; Chemotherapy; Fluid and electrolyte balance; Functional and aesthetic management of congenital and acquired defects of head and neck, trunk, and extremities; Pharmacology; Shock; and Wound healing. **Endorsed By:** American College of Surgeons; American Medical Association; Council on Medical Education.

1727

Residency Review Committee for Preventive Medicine

American Board of Preventive
Medicine (ABPM)
9950 W. Lawrence Ave., Ste. 106
Schiller Park, IL 60176
Phone: (708)671-1750
Fax: (708)671-1751
Dr. Alice R. Ring M.P.H., Exec.
Dir.

Recipient: Residency review committee of Accreditation Council for Graduate Medical Education (see separate entry) for residency programs in medical institutions for medical doctors (M.D.s) specializing in preventive medicine and the specialty areas of: Aerospace medicine; Occupational medicine; Preventive medicine; and Public health. **Accreditation Requirements:** Residencies must be at least one year in length. **Endorsed By:** American Medical Association; Council on Medical Education.

1728

Residency Review Committee for Psychiatry

American Board of Psychiatry and
Neurology (ABPN)
500 Lake Cook Rd., Ste. 335
Deerfield, IL 60015-5249
Phone: (708)945-7900
Fax: (708)945-1146

Recipient: Residency review committee of Accreditation Council for Graduate Medical Education (see separate entry) for residency programs in medical institutions for medical doctors (M.D.s) specializing in psychiatry and the specialty areas of: Child and adolescent psychiatry; and Geriatric psychiatry. **Accreditation Requirements:** Residencies in psychiatry must be three years in length; residencies in child and adolescent psychiatry must be two years in length; residencies in geriatric psychiatry must be one year in length. Must maintain leave of absence policy. **Endorsed By:** American Medical Association; American Psychiatric Association; Council on Medical Education.

1729

Residency Review Committee for Radiation Oncology

American Board of Radiology
(ABR)
5255 E. Williams Circle, Ste. 6800
Tucson, AZ 85711
Phone: (520)790-2900
Fax: (520)790-3200
M. Paul Capp M.D., Exec.Dir.

Recipient: Residency review committee of Accreditation Council for Graduate Medical Education (see separate entry) for residency programs in medical institutions for medical doctors (M.D.s) specializing in radiation oncology. **Accreditation Requirements:** Residencies must be four years in length. Programs in radiation biology must provide instruction in the following: Cell and tissue kinetics; Chemotherapeutic agents used as adjuvant with radiation; Factors that modify radiation response; Hyperthermia; Interaction of radiation with matter; Late effects; Linear energy transfer; Mammalian cell radiosensitivity; New radiation modalities; Radiation effects in developing embryo and fetus; Radiophysiology of human tissues; Relative biological effectiveness; Solid tumor systems; Time-dose and fractionation; Tissue radiosensitivity; and Total body irradiation. Programs in radiological physics must provide instruction in the following: Atomic and nuclear structure; Calibration of high energy photon and electron beams; Computerized treatment planning; Dose distributions for external beam therapy; Dose distributions for sealed source therapy; High energy treatment machines; Interactions of particulate radiations; Interactions of x- and gamma-rays; Measurement of absorbed dose; Measurement of radiation exposure; Production of x-rays; Radiation protection from external sources; Radiation protection from internal sources; Radiation quality; and Radioactive decay. Must maintain leave of absence policy. **Endorsed By:** American College of Radiology; American Medical Association; Council on Medical Education.

1730

Residency Review Committee for Radiology-Diagnostic

American Board of Radiology
(ABR)
5255 E. Williams Circle, Ste. 6800
Tucson, AZ 85711
Phone: (520)790-2900
Fax: (520)790-3200
M. Paul Capp M.D., Exec.Dir.

Recipient: Residency review committee

of Accreditation Council for Graduate Medical Education (see separate entry) for residency programs in medical institutions for medical doctors (M.D.s) specializing in diagnostic radiology and the specialty areas of: Neuroradiology and nuclear radiology; Pediatric radiology; and Vascular and interventional radiology. **Accreditation Requirements:** Residencies in diagnostic radiology must be four years in length, including six months in nuclear radiology; residencies in specialty areas must be one year in length. Programs in diagnostic radiology must provide instruction in the following: Atomic and nuclear structure; Body section radiography; Computerized tomography; Computers; Film and other recording media; Filters and beam limiting devices; Fluoroscopy; Imaging concepts; Interactions of radiation with matter; Interactions of radiation in the patient; Magnetic resonance; Nature of radiation; Nuclear radiology; Production of x-rays; Quality assurance; Radiation quantities and units; Radiobiology and radiation control; Radiographic image; Reduction of scattered radiation; Screens; Special radiographic techniques; Ultrasonography; X-ray generator; and X-ray tube. Must maintain transfer policy. **Endorsed By:** American College of Radiology; American Medical Association; Council on Medical Education.

1731

Residency Review Committee for Surgery

American Board of Surgery (ABS)
1617 John F. Kennedy Blvd., Ste. 860
Philadelphia, PA 19103-1847
Phone: (215)568-4000
Dr. Wallace P. Ritchie Jr., Exec. Dir.

Recipient: Residency review committee of Accreditation Council for Graduate Medical Education (see separate entry) for residency programs in medical institutions for medical doctors (M.D.s) specializing in surgery and the specialty areas of: General vascular surgery; Hand surgery; Pediatric surgery; and Surgical critical care. **Accreditation Requirements:** Residencies in general surgery must be five years in length, including 48 weeks in surgery; residencies in pediatric surgery and hand surgery must be two years in length. Residents in general surgery must participate in 500 operative procedures, including procedures in each of the following anatomical areas: Abdomen and its contents; Alimentary tract; Complete care of critically ill patients; Comprehensive management of trauma; Endocrine system; Head and neck; Surgi-

cal oncology; and Vascular system. Programs in general surgery must include instruction in the following: Administration of anesthetic agents; Anatomy; Cardiac surgery; Diagnosis; Endoscopic techniques; General thoracic surgery; Gynecologic surgery; Immunology; Intensive care; Metabolism; Neoplasia; Neurologic surgery; Nutrition; Orthopedic surgery; Pathology; Pediatric surgery; Physiology; Plastic surgery; Preoperative, operative, and postoperative management; Shock and resuscitation; Transplant surgery; Urologic surgery; and Wound healing. Must maintain leave of absence policy. **Endorsed By:** American College of Surgeons; American Medical Association.

1732

Residency Review Committee for Thoracic Surgery

American Board of Thoracic Surgery (ABTS)
One Rotary Center, Ste. 803
Evanston, IL 60201
Richard J. Cleveland M.D., Sec.

Recipient: Residency review committee of Accreditation Council for Graduate Medical Education (see separate entry) for residency programs in medical institutions for medical doctors (M.D.s) specializing in thoracic surgery. **Accreditation Requirements:** Residencies must be 24 months in length and include thoracic and cardiovascular surgery. Residencies must prepare students for preoperative evaluation, operative management, and post-operative care of patients with pathologic conditions involving thoracic structures. Curriculum should include instruction in the following: (1) Normal and Pathologic Conditions of Cardiovascular and General Thoracic Structures, including: Congenital and acquired lesions of both heart and blood vessels in thorax, including infections, metabolic disorders, trauma, and tumors; and Diseases involving chest wall, diaphragm, esophagus, lungs, mediastinum, and pleura; and (2) Diagnosis, including: Angiography; Biologic and biochemical tests; Cardiac; Catheterization; Electrocardiography; Endoscopy; Imaging techniques; Laser therapy; Thoracoscopic surgery; Thoracoscopy; and Tissue biopsy. Must also meet operating case criteria concerning volume and distribution of cases. **Endorsed By:** American College of Surgeons; American Medical Association; Council on Medical Education.

1733

Residency Review Committee for Urology

American Board of Urology (ABU)
31700 Telegraph Rd., Ste. 150
Bingham Farms, MI 48025
Phone: (810)646-9720
Alan D. Perlmutter M.D., Exec.Sec.

Recipient: Residency review committee of Accreditation Council for Graduate Medical Education (see separate entry) for residency programs in medical institutions for medical doctors (M.D.s) specializing in urology and the specialty area of pediatric urology. **Accreditation Requirements:** Residencies in urology must be at least five years in length, including: (1) 12 months in general surgery; (2) 36 months in clinical urology; and (3) Six months in general surgery, urology, or other clinical disciplines relevant to urology. Must maintain policies concerning leaves of absence and transfers. **Endorsed By:** American College of Surgeons; American Medical Association; Council on Medical Education.

Microbiology

1734

Committee on Postdoctoral Educational Programs of the American Academy of Microbiology

American Academy of Microbiology (ACM)
1325 Massachusetts Ave., NW
Washington, DC 20005-4174
Fax: (202)942-9335

Recipient: Two-year postdoctoral training programs for medical microbiologists and immunologists. **Application Procedures:** Self-assessment required. Must document compliance with standards and evaluate strengths and weaknesses of program. Must submit biographical sketches of principal staff members. **Accreditation Requirements:** Applicants must have doctoral degree (Ph.D., M.D., Sc.D., O.D., Dr., P.H., or other degree) with graduate education in microbiology and/or immunology. Programs must include training in the following areas: Designing and conducting microbiological research to solve medical and public health problems; Developing and communicating reliable interpretations of microbiological data and other relevant information; Developing and managing microbiology diagnostic service supporting clinical diagnostic and epidemiological data; and Planning and conducting effective training programs to fill needs in microbiology and immunology. Must have complete clinical laboratory or reference laboratories that perform clinical and/or public health microbiology procedures. On-site review required. **State Requirements:** Institution must be accredited, certified, or licensed as required by law. **Fees:** Actual cost of on-site review and expenses. **Endorsed By:** American Society for Microbiology.

Montessori

1735

American Montessori Society School Accreditation Commission (ACSSAC)
American Montessori Society (AMS)
150 Fifth Ave.
New York, NY 10011
Phone: (212)924-3209
Fax: (212)727-2254
Dottie S. Feldman, Dir.

Recipient: Montessori schools at the following age levels: Infant and toddler; Preprimary; Lower elementary; Upper elementary; Lower secondary; and Upper secondary. **Membership:** Required. **Application Procedures:** Self-assessment, involving administrators, academic directors, governing body, parents, students, and teaching staff, required. Must document compliance with standards in the following areas: (1) Organization and Stability, including: Legal counsel; Legal identity and ownership; Organizational chart; Record of school's history; Role of ownership or governing board; and Roles of administrator and administrative staff; (2) Financial Management, including: Annual financial reports or external audit; Assessment of assets and liabilities; Budget; Insurance coverage; and Records of collections and disbursements; (3) Facilities, including: Buildings and grounds; Classrooms; Clinics; Equipment inventory; Faculty offices and lounges; Indoor and outdoor physical activity areas; Lockers; Maintenance; Safety and emergency procedures; Site risks and hazards; Sterilization of foodservice equipment; and Storage; (4) Enrollment, including: Admission criteria and procedures; Expectations and responsibilities of school, family, and child; Financial policies; Non-discrimination; School services; Student assessment; Truth-in-advertising; and Withdrawal policy and procedures; (5) Child Records, including: Attendance; Child abuse; Confidentiality; De-

velopmental progress; Emergency medical information; First aid treatment; Health information; Maintenance of records; Medication administered at school; and Parent's rights; (6) Personnel, including: Assessment; Benefits; Employment agreement; Job descriptions; Membership in AMS; Personnel policies; and Professional development; (7) Community, including: Community involvement; Dissemination of information; Parent involvement; and Support services and agencies; (8) Transportation, including: Equipment maintenance; Insurance; and Policies and procedures; (9) Goals and Philosophy, including: Appropriateness; Evaluation; and Written statement; (10) Policies, including: Class ground rules; Classroom procedures; Discipline and support strategies; Orientation; Schedules; Observation, planning, and record keeping policies; Ownership and reimbursement for teacher-made materials; Student/faculty ratio; Teacher participation; and Vertical grouping; (11) Staff Qualifications, including: Assistant teachers; Certification; and Educational supervisor or coordinator; (12) Material Resources, including: Curriculum materials; Furnishings; Instructional materials and library collections; Montessori apparatus; Practical life resource materials; and Water and disposal systems; (13) Program and Implementation, including: Community expectations; Curriculum; and Physical, socio-emotional, and cognitive development; (14) Organization and Environments, including: Appropriateness of activities and materials; Arrangement of furnishings; Child behavior; Display of visual stimuli and children's projects; Individual activities; Lesson structure; and Organization of curriculum materials; (15) Staff Behavior, including: Child participation; Child selection of activities; Demonstration and encouragement; Expression of child emotional needs; Group leadership; Maintenance of equipment; Modeling appropriate behaviors; Monitoring of learning; Preparation of classroom; Responsiveness to child self-expression; Rules and procedures; and Strategies for use of equipment; and (16) Auxiliary Programs. **Accreditation Requirements:** Curriculum should promote age-appropriate development in the following areas: Acquisition of practical skills; Awareness of order and sequence; Concentration; Critical thinking and problem solving techniques; Experience with creative arts; Language skills, including opportunities for listening, self-expression, and instruction in writing, reading, and other language arts; Large muscle coordination; Mathematical and quantitative concepts; Observation skills; Perceptual awareness and discrimination, including ability to

recognize and identify attributes of objects; Small muscle coordination; Social sciences; and World of nature and physical universe. On-site review, verifying information provided in self-assessment, required. Review includes interviews with school personnel. May respond to on-site review. **Renewal:** Every seven years. Renewal based on self-assessment and on-site review. Must also submit annual reports. **State Requirements:** Must hold appropriate local, county, and state licenses. **Fees:** Application fee, plus actual cost of on-site review; must also submit annual fee.

Monument Construction

1736

Monument Builders of North America (MBNA)
1740 Ridge Ave.
Evanston, IL 60201
Phone: (212)628-3465
Fax: (708)869-2056
Toll Free: (800)233-4472

Recipient: Monument retailers, manufacturers, and wholesalers. **Membership:** Required.

Museums

1737

American Association of Museums (AAM)
1225 Eye St., NW, Ste. 200
Washington, DC 20005
Phone: (202)289-1818
Fax: (202)289-6578

Recipient: Public and private art, history, and science museums; art centers, historic sites, nature centers, planetariums, and science and technology centers; and arboreta and botanical gardens, zoos, and aquariums. **Number of Accredited Institutions:** 700. **Application Procedures:** Self-assessment required. Must document compliance with standards concerning all aspects of museum's operations and facilities. Must identify areas which need improvement and develop plan for the future. **Accreditation Requirements:** Museum must: (1) Have been in operation for two years; (2) Have operating budget of $25,000; (3) Be organized and permanent non-profit institution essentially educational or aesthetic in purpose; (4) Maintain professional staff; and (5)

Own or utilize tangible objects, care for them, and exhibit them to public on some regular schedule. On-site review, verifying information provided in self-assessment, required. Review includes evaluation of facilities. Possible accreditation decisions are: (1) Accreditation; (2) Table Decision, requiring further information, clarification, or correction of deficiencies; or (3) Accreditation Denied, for institutions in substantial noncompliance with standards. **Renewal:** Every ten years (maximum). **Preparatory Materials:** *Accreditation: A Handbook for the Visiting Committee, Accreditation: Self-Study and On-site Evaluation Questionnaire,* and *Museum Accreditation: A Handbook for the Institution* (references). Museum Assessment Program available to aid in self-assessment. **Fees:** $200, plus actual cost of on-site review; $170 (annual fee).

Music

1738

Commission on Accreditation, National Association of Schools of Music

National Association of Schools of Music (NASM)
11250 Roger Bacon Dr., Ste. 21
Reston, VA 22090
Phone: (703)437-0700
Fax: (703)437-6312
Samuel Hope, Exec.Dir.

Recipient: Institutions and units within institutions offering associate, baccalaureate, and/or graduate degree programs in music and/or music-related disciplines; and non-degree-granting institutions offering programs in these areas. **Application Procedures:** Self-assessment required. Must document compliance with standards in the following areas: (1) Mission, Goals, and Objectives, including: Appropriateness; Creative work and research; Dissemination; Educational and artistic decision-making; Evaluation; Institutional objectives; Long-range planning; Music and music-related fields; Operational decision-making; Performance; Policies and procedures; Resources; Service; Students; Teaching; and Written statement; (2) Size and Scope, including: Enrollment; Ensemble experience; Objectives; Resources; and Staff size; (3) Finances, including: Allocation of resources; Audits; Financial management; Financial records; Financial statements; Long-range planning; Objectives; and Tuition, fees, and other charges; (4) Governance and Administration, including:

Administrative personnel; Autonomy; Board of trustees; Communications; Continuity; Faculty input; Long-range planning; Music executive and other administrators; Objectives; Organization; Policies and procedures; Public representation; and Student input; (5) Faculty and Staff, including: Appointment, evaluation, and advancement; Faculty development; Graduate teaching assistants; Loads; Number and distribution; Qualifications; Student/faculty ratios; and Support staff; (6) Facilities, Equipment, and Safety, including: Accessibility; Administrative offices; Audio and video playback equipment; Audio/visual aids; Auditoriums; Budget; Classrooms; Computers; Electronic instruments and equipment; Ensemble rehearsal rooms; Faculty teaching studios and offices; Grand pianos; Maintenance; Music library; Orchestral and band instruments; Pipe and electronic organs; Planning; Recording equipment; Safety; Storage facilities; Student practice rooms; Supplies; and Upright pianos; (7) Library, including: Collections; Facilities; Finance; Governance; Personnel; and Services; (8) Recruitment, Admission, Retention, Record Keeping, and Advisement, including: Counseling services; Objectives; Requirements; and Student records; (8) Published Materials, including: Catalog; and Published documents; (9) Community Involvement and Articulation with Other Schools, including: Arts agencies; Local schools; and Performing organizations; (10) Evaluation, Planning, and Projections, including: Assessment techniques; Curriculum; Objectives; Operational conditions; Programs and services; Resource allocation and development; Size and scope; and Student achievement and evaluation; (11) Credit and Time Requirements, including: Awarding credit; Program lengths; Published policies; and Transfer of credit; and (12) Music in General Education, including: Arts and arts education policy development; Faculty and administrative involvement; Local community; Media; Music education for general college student; and Training of professional musician. Proprietary schools must meet additional standards. **Accreditation Requirements:** Undergraduate programs must have 25 candidates; graduate programs must have 15 candidates. Bachelor's degree programs must document compliance with standards in the following areas: Admission policy; Aural skills and analysis; Composition and improvisation; General studies; Musicianship, including content and purpose; Performance; Repertory and history; Synthesis; and Technology. Graduate programs must document compliance with standards in the following areas: Admissions; Breadth of competence; Evaluation of

creative work; Faculty; Functions of graduate study; General degree requirements and procedures; Preparation for teaching; Resources; and Statement and publication of objectives and resources. Bachelor's and master's degree programs offered in the following areas: Composition; Jazz studies; Music education; Music history and literature; Music theory; Music therapy; Pedagogy; Performance; and Sacred music. Master's degree programs offered in the following areas: Accompanying; Conducting; Music history and musicology; Opera performance; and Theory-composition. Doctorate degree programs must document compliance with standards in the following areas: Composition; Music education; Music theory; Musicology; Performance; and Sacred music. Standards and guidelines also available for the following programs: Music, business, and arts administration; Music and electrical engineering; Opera and musical theatre; and Orchestral conducting. On-site review, verifying information provided in self-assessment, required. Review includes interviews with administrators, faculty, students, and other interested parties. May respond to on-site review. Possible accreditation decisions are: (1) Accreditation; (2) Probationary Status, requiring correction of deficiencies within five years; or (3) Denial, for programs in substantial noncompliance with standards. **Renewal:** Every five years (initial); every ten years thereafter. Renewal based on self-assessment and on-site review. Must also submit annual reports. **Restrictions:** Must report changes in curriculum. **State Requirements:** Must be state approved or licensed. **Preparatory Materials:** *National Association of Schools of Music Handbook* (reference). **Fees:** $400, plus actual cost of on-site review; must also submit annual fee. **Accredited By:** Commission on Recognition of Postsecondary Accreditation; U.S. Department of Education. **Endorsed By:** American Council on Education.

1739

Commission on Community/Junior College Accreditation, National Association of Schools of Music

National Association of Schools of Music (NASM)
11250 Roger Bacon Dr., Ste. 21
Reston, VA 22090
Phone: (703)437-0700
Fax: (703)437-6312
Samuel Hope, Exec.Dir.

Recipient: Institutions and units within institutions offering associate degree programs in music and/or music-related disciplines. **Application Procedures:** Self-assessment required. Must document compliance with standards in the following areas: (1) Mission, Goals, and Objectives, including: Appropriateness; Creative work and research; Dissemination; Educational and artistic decision-making; Evaluation; Institutional objectives; Long-range planning; Music and music-related fields; Operational decision-making; Performance; Policies and procedures; Resources; Service; Students; Teaching; and Written statement; (2) Size and Scope, including: Enrollment; Ensemble experience; Objectives; Resources; and Staff size; (3) Finances, including: Allocation of resources; Audits; Financial management; Financial records; Financial statements; Long-range planning; Objectives; and Tuition, fees, and other charges; (4) Governance and Administration, including: Administrative personnel; Autonomy; Board of trustees; Communications; Continuity; Faculty input; Long-range planning; Music executive and other administrators; Objectives; Organization; Policies and procedures; Public representation; and Student input; (5) Faculty and Staff, including: Appointment, evaluation, and advancement; Faculty development; Graduate teaching assistants; Loads; Number and distribution; Qualifications; Student/faculty ratios; and Support staff; (6) Facilities, Equipment, and Safety, including: Accessibility; Administrative offices; Audio and video playback equipment; Audio/visual aids; Budget; Classrooms; Computers; Electronic instruments and equipment; Ensemble rehearsal rooms; Faculty teaching studios and offices; Grand pianos; Maintenance; Music library; Orchestral and band instruments; Pipe and electronic organs; Planning; Recording equipment; Safety; Storage facilities; Student practice rooms; Supplies; and Upright pianos; (7) Library, including: Collections; Facilities; Finance; Governance; Personnel; and Services; (8) Recruitment, Admission-Retention, Record Keeping, and Advisement, including: Counseling services; Objectives; Requirements; and Student records; (8) Published Materials, including: Catalog; and Published documents; (9) Community Involvement and Articulation with Other Schools, including: Arts agencies; Local schools; and Performing organizations; (10) Evaluation, Planning, and Projections, including: Assessment techniques; Curriculum; Objectives; Operational conditions; Programs and services; Resource allocation and development; Size and scope; and Student achievement and evaluation; (11) Credit and Time Requirements, including: Awarding credit; Program lengths; Published policies; and Transfer of credit;

(12) Two-Year Degree Granting Programs, including: Commission responsibility; Objectives; and Standards applicability; (13) General Enrichment Program, including: Basic musical studies; and Performance; and (14) Music Major Transfer Program, including: Basic analysis; Basic musicianship; General studies; Music education; and Performance. Proprietary schools must meet additional standards. **Accreditation Requirements:** Must have been in operation for three years and have 20 candidates. On-site review, verifying information provided in self-assessment, required. Review includes interviews with administrators, faculty, students, and other interested parties. May respond to on-site review. Possible accreditation decisions are: (1) Accreditation; (2) Probationary Status, requiring correction of deficiencies within five years; or (3) Denial, for programs in substantial non-compliance with standards. **Renewal:** Every five years (initial); every ten years thereafter. Renewal based on self-assessment and on-site review. Renewal fee is $100. Must also submit annual reports. **Restrictions:** Must report changes in curriculum. **State Requirements:** Must be state approved or licensed. **Preparatory Materials:** *National Association of Schools of Music Handbook* (reference). **Fees:** $400, plus actual cost of on-site review; must also submit annual fee. **Accredited By:** Commission on Recognition of Postsecondary Accreditation; U.S. Department of Education.

1740

Commission on Non-Degree-Granting Accreditation, National Association of Schools of Music
National Association of Schools of Music (NASM)
11250 Roger Bacon Dr., Ste. 21
Reston, VA 22090
Phone: (703)437-0700
Fax: (703)437-6312
Samuel Hope, Exec.Dir.

Recipient: Institutions and units within institutions offering nondegree-granting programs in music and/or music-related disciplines. **Application Procedures:** Self-assessment required. Must document compliance with standards in the following areas: (1) Mission, Goals, and Objectives, including: Appropriateness; Creative work and research; Dissemination; Educational and artistic decision-making; Evaluation; Institutional objectives; Long-range planning; Music and music-related fields; Operational decision-making; Performance; Policies

and procedures; Resources; Service; Students; Teaching; and Written statement; (2) Size and Scope, including: Enrollment; Ensemble experience; Objectives; Resources; and Staff size; (3) Finances, including: Allocation of resources; Audits; Financial management; Financial records; Financial statements; Long-range planning; Objectives; and Tuition, fees, and other charges; (4) Governance and Administration, including: Administrative personnel; Autonomy; Board of trustees; Communications; Continuity; Faculty input; Long-range planning; Music executive and other administrators; Objectives; Organization; Policies and procedures; Public representation; and Student input; (5) Faculty and Staff, including: Appointment, evaluation, and advancement; Faculty development; Graduate teaching assistants; Loads; Number and distribution; Qualifications; Student/faculty ratios; and Support staff; (6) Facilities, Equipment, and Safety, including: Accessibility; Administrative offices; Audio and video playback equipment; Audio/visual aids; Budget; Classrooms; Computers; Electronic instruments and equipment; Ensemble rehearsal rooms; Faculty teaching studios and offices; Grand pianos; Maintenance; Music library; Orchestral and band instruments; Pipe and electronic organs; Planning; Recording equipment; Safety; Storage facilities; Student practice rooms; Supplies; and Upright pianos; (7) Library, including: Collections; Facilities; Finance; Governance; Personnel; and Services; (8) Recruitment, Admission-Retention, Record Keeping, and Advisement, including: Counseling services; Objectives; Requirements; and Student records; (8) Published Materials, including: Catalog; and Published documents; (9) Community Involvement and Articulation with Other Schools, including: Arts agencies; Local schools; and Performing organizations; (10) Evaluation, Planning, and Projections, including: Assessment techniques; Curriculum; Objectives; Operational conditions; Programs and services; Resource allocation and development; Size and scope; and Student achievement and evaluation; (11) Curricula Common to All Non-Degree-Granting Programs, including: Appreciation; Basic musicianship; and Performance; (12) Specific Non-Degree-Granting Programs, including: Certificate programs; College preparatory certificate programs; and Postsecondary diploma programs; and (13) Boarding or Day Schools Offering General Education. Proprietary schools must meet additional standards. **Accreditation Requirements:** Must have been in operation for three years. On-site review, verifying information provided in self-assessment, required. Review includes interviews with administrators, faculty, students, and other interested parties. May respond to on-site review. Possible accreditation decisions are: (1) Accreditation; (2) Probationary Status, requiring correction of deficiencies within five years; or (3) Denial, for programs in substantial noncompliance with standards. **Renewal:** Every five years (initial); every ten years thereafter. Renewal based on self-assessment and on-site review. Renewal fee is $100. Must also submit annual reports. **Restrictions:** Must report changes in curriculum. **State Requirements:** Must be state approved or licensed. **Preparatory Materials:** *National Association of Schools of Music Handbook* (reference). **Fees:** $400, plus actual cost of on-site review; must also submit annual fee. **Accredited By:** Commission on Recognition of Postsecondary Accreditation; U.S. Department of Education.

Naturopathy

1741

Commission on Accreditation, Council on Naturopathic Medical Education
Council on Naturopathic Medical Education
PO Box 11426
Eugene, OR 97440-3626
Phone: (503)484-6028

Recipient: Programs leading to Doctor of Naturopathy (N.D.) or Doctor of Naturopathic Medicine (N.M.D.) degrees in the U.S. and Canada. **Number of Accredited Institutions:** 2. **Application Procedures:** Self-assessment required. Must document compliance with standards in the following areas: Academic calendars; Advertising; Catalogs and publications; Curriculum; Evaluation; Facilities, equipment, and supplies; Faculty; Fiscal and administrative capacity; Recruiting and admissions practices; Student support services. **Accreditation Requirements:** On-site review required. May respond to on-site review. **Renewal:** Renewal required. **Restrictions:** Must report substantive changes in the following areas: Addition of branch campus, courses, or programs; Legal status or control of institution; Length of program; and Mission or objectives. **Preparatory Materials:** Handbook available. **Accredited By:** U.S. Department of Education.

Nontraditional Schools and Colleges

1742

Accrediting Commission for Higher Education of the National Association of Private Nontraditional Schools and Colleges
National Association of Private, Nontraditional Schools and Colleges (NAPNSC)
182 Thompson Rd.
Grand Junction, CO 81503
Phone: (303)243-5441
Dolly Heusser, Co-Dir.

Recipient: Private, nontraditional colleges and universities offering bachelor's, master's, and doctoral degree programs. **Application Procedures:** Self-assessment required. Must document compliance with standards in the following areas: (1) Nontraditional or Alternate Character, including: Curricular identity; Rationale of need and effectiveness of nontraditional delivery; and Statement of objectives; (2) Governing Board; (3) Chief Executive Officer; (4) Faculty, including: Academic, professional, and technical education; Basic skills; and Size of staff; (5) Educational Programs, including: Planning and structure; and Student enrollment; (6) Admission Policies; (7) Catalog or Bulletin; (8) Physical Facilities, including: Electronic communication and retrieval equipment; Learning areas; Learning resources; and Offices; (9) Educational Records, including: Archiving and uses of records; Student information; and Student learning achievement; (10) Tuition, Fees, and Refund Schedules, including: Costs per term; Equitable return of unused funds; and Revenues; (11) Financial Base and Fiscal policy, including documentation of financial viability; (12) Identification of Students Served, including student body variables; (13) Educational Needs of Students, including: Instruction and independent learning modules; Job placement; and Student needs and aspirations; (14) General Institutional Goals; (15) Student and Public Services; (16) General Program Goals, including: Institutional philosophy; and Preparation for career and lifelong learning; (17) Specific Program Objectives and Assessment, including: Degree programs; Examinations; Learning programs; and Performance objectives; (18) Assessment Standards, including: Instruments; and Procedures; (19) Objective-Goal Relationship; (20) Resources Required, including: Facility resources; Literary resources; Human resources; and Material

resources; and (21) Cost Effectiveness and Benefits. **Accreditation Requirements:** Schools must: (1) Be free standing; (2) Have been in operation for two years; (3) Maintain nonprofit or proprietary status; and (4) Qualify as alternative or nontraditional in delivery system. On-site review required. **Renewal:** Every five years. Renewal based on self-assessment and on-site review. Must also submit annual reports. **Restrictions:** Must hold state registration, charter, corporation certificate, or other required state authority. **Preparatory Materials:** *Handbook for Accreditation* and *NAPNSC Accreditation Fact Sheet* (references).

Nursing

1743

American Board of Nursing Specialties (ABNS)
600 Maryland Ave., SW, Ste. 100 West
Washington, DC 20024-2571
Phone: (202)554-2054
Janice Camp R.N., Pres.

Recipient: Nursing specialty certification programs. **Number of Accredited Institutions:** 14. **Accreditation Requirements:** Applicants to certification programs must meet one of the following requirements: (1) Bachelor's degree in nursing and successful completion of educational program in specialty; or (2) Advanced specialty nursing certification that requires graduate degree in nursing or equivalent, including content in specialty. These requirements must either be in place or scheduled to take effect by the year 2000. Must document compliance with the following standards: (1) Have clearly defined specialty within nursing; (2) Adhere to overall licensure requirements of nursing profession; (3) Be national in scope with identified need and demand; (4) Have substantial number of nurses devote most of their time to specialty; (5) Have collaborative relationship with nursing specialty association in order to set standards; (6) Be autonomous body with administrative independence pertaining to certification; (7) Have existing mechanisms for supporting, reviewing, and disseminating research to support knowledge base of specialty; (8) Have educational programs that prepare nurses in specialty; (9) Incorporate peer review process that reflects standards and scope of practice of specialty and provides for validity, reliability, and integrity of process; and (10) Allow public member to sit on certifying board.

1744

Board of Review for Associate Degree Programs, National League for Nursing
National League for Nursing (NLN)
360 Hudson St.
New York, NY 10014
Phone: (212)989-9393
Fax: (212)989-9256
Toll Free: (800)669-1656

Recipient: Associate degree programs in nursing. **Application Procedures:** Self-assessment required. Must document compliance with standards in the following areas: Academic calendars; Advertising; Catalogs and publications; Curriculum; Evaluation; Facilities, equipment, and supplies; Faculty; Fiscal and administrative capacity; Recruiting and admissions practices; and Student support services. **Accreditation Requirements:** On-site review required. Review includes interviews with administrators, faculty, students, and other interested parties. May respond to on-site review. **Renewal:** Renewal required. **Restrictions:** Must report substantive changes in the following areas: Addition of branch campus, courses, or programs; Legal status or control of institution; Length of program; and Mission or objectives. **Accredited By:** Commission on Recognition of Postsecondary Accreditation; U.S. Department of Education.

1745

Board of Review for Baccalaureate and Higher Degree Programs, National League for Nursing
National League for Nursing (NLN)
360 Hudson St.
New York, NY 10014
Phone: (212)989-9393
Fax: (212)989-9256
Toll Free: (800)669-1656

Recipient: Baccalaureate and higher degree programs in nursing. **Application Procedures:** Self-assessment required. Must document compliance with standards in the following areas: Academic calendars; Advertising; Catalogs and publications; Curriculum; Evaluation; Facilities, equipment, and supplies; Faculty; Fiscal and administrative capacity; Recruiting and admissions practices; and Student support services. **Accreditation Requirements:** On-site review required. Review includes interviews with administrators, faculty, students, and other interested parties. May respond to on-site review. **Renewal:** Renewal required. **Re-**strictions: Must report substantive changes in the following areas: Addition of branch campus, courses, or programs; Legal status or control of institution; Length of program; and Mission or objectives. **Accredited By:** Commission on Recognition of Postsecondary Accreditation; U.S. Department of Education.

1746

Board of Review for Diploma Programs, National League for Nursing
National League for Nursing (NLN)
360 Hudson St.
New York, NY 10014
Phone: (212)989-9393
Fax: (212)989-9256
Toll Free: (800)669-1656

Recipient: Diploma programs in nursing. **Application Procedures:** Self-assessment required. Must document compliance with standards in the following areas: Academic calendars; Advertising; Catalogs and publications; Curriculum; Evaluation; Facilities, equipment, and supplies; Faculty; Fiscal and administrative capacity; Recruiting and admissions practices; and Student support services. **Accreditation Requirements:** On-site review required. Review includes interviews with administrators, faculty, students, and other interested parties. May respond to on-site review. **Renewal:** Renewal required. **Restrictions:** Must report substantive changes in the following areas: Addition of branch campus, courses, or programs; Legal status or control of institution; Length of program; and Mission or objectives. **Accredited By:** Commission on Recognition of Postsecondary Accreditation; U.S. Department of Education.

1747

Board of Review for Practical Nursing Programs, National League for Nursing
National League for Nursing (NLN)
360 Hudson St.
New York, NY 10014
Phone: (212)989-9393
Fax: (212)989-9256
Toll Free: (800)669-1656

Recipient: Practical nursing programs. **Application Procedures:** Self-assessment required. Must document compliance with standards in the following areas: Academic calendars; Advertising; Catalogs and publications; Curriculum; Evaluation; Facilities, equipment, and supplies; Faculty; Fiscal and administrative capacity; Recruiting and admissions practices; and Student support services. **Accreditation Requirements:** On-site review required. Review includes interviews with administrators, faculty, students, and other interested parties. May respond to on-site review. **Renewal:** Renewal required. **Restrictions:** Must report substantive changes in the following areas: Addition of branch campus, courses, or programs; Legal status or control of institution; Length of program; and Mission or objectives. **Accredited By:** Commission on Recognition of Postsecondary Accreditation; Education; U.S. Department of Education.

1748

Council on Accreditation of Nurse Anesthesia Educational Programs
American Association of Nurse Anesthetists (AANA)
222 S. Prospect Ave., Ste. 304
Park Ridge, IL 60068-4010
Phone: (708)692-7050
Fax: (708)693-7137
Betty J. Horton, Dir.

Recipient: Nurse anesthesia programs preparing graduates for entry-level practice at certificate, baccalaureate, master's, or doctorate degree levels. **Number of Accredited Institutions:** 90. **Application Procedures:** Self-assessment required. Must document compliance with standards in the following areas: Administrative policies and procedures; Curriculum and instruction; Ethics; Evaluation; Faculty; and Institutional support. **Accreditation Requirements:** On-site review required. Review includes discussion with faculty, staff, administrators, students, and other interested parties. May respond to on-site review. **Renewal:** Every six years. Renewal based on self-assessment and on-site review. **Restrictions:** Director must hold Certified Registered Nurse Anesthetist (CRNA) designation (see separate entry). **Preparatory Materials:** *Standards for Accreditation of Nurse Anesthesia Educational Programs* (reference). Self-assessment documents available. **Length of Process:** Six years (maximum). **Fees:** $200, plus actual cost of on-site review; must also submit annual fee. **Accredited By:** Commission on Recognition of Postsecondary Accreditation; U.S. Department of Education.

1749

Division of Accreditation, American College of Nurse-Midwives

American College of
Nurse-Midwives (ACNM)
818 Connecticut Ave., NW, Ste. 900
Washington, DC 20006
Lara Slattery, Dir.

Recipient: Basic certificate, graduate, and pre-certification programs in nurse-midwifery, and programs in basic midwifery. **Number of Accredited Institutions:** 44. **Application Procedures:** Self-assessment required. Must address compliance with criteria in the following areas: Curriculum; Faculty and faculty administration; Organization and administration; Philosophy, goals, and objectives; Resources, facilities, and services; and Students. **Accreditation Requirements:** On-site review, verifying information provided in self-assessment, required. May respond to on-site review. **Renewal:** Every five years (initial); every eight years thereafter. Renewal based on self-assessment and on-site review. **Preparatory Materials:** Manuals, competencies, and criteria and standards available for all program accreditation areas. **Accredited By:** U.S. Department of Education.

1750

Wound Ostomy and Continence Nurses Society (WOCN)

2755 Bristol St., Ste. 110
Costa Mesa, CA 92626
Phone: (714)476-0268
Ruth Bryant R.N., Pres.

Recipient: Enterostomal therapy nursing training programs. **Number of Accredited Institutions:** 7. **Accreditation Requirements:** Applicants to program must meet the following requirements: (1) Current licensure as registered nurse (R.N.); (2) Bachelor's degree with major in nursing; and (3) One year of clinical experience in medical-surgical nursing. Programs must meet criteria in the following areas: Clinical experience; Course content; Faculty; and Student/faculty ratio. Programs can be on- or off-site and may be taken for graduate credit as part of master's degree program. On-site review required.

Opticianry

1751

Commission on Opticianry Accreditation (COA)

10111 Martin Luther King, Jr. Hwy., Ste. 100
Bowie, MD 20720
Phone: (301)459-8075
Fax: (301)577-3880
Dr. Floyd H. Holmgrain Jr., Exec. Dir.

Recipient: Institutions or programs offering associate degrees in ophthalmic dispensing and certificates in ophthalmology laboratory technology. **Number of Accredited Institutions:** 31. **Application Procedures:** Self-assessment required. Must document compliance with standards concerning facilities, finances, and staff. **Accreditation Requirements:** Must have graduated at least one class of students. On-site review required. May respond to on-site review. **Renewal:** Every six years. Renewal based on self-assessment and on-site review. **Restrictions:** Must notify COA of any major curriculum changes or replacement of program director. Program director must be employed full-time. **State Requirements:** Must be state approved. **Preparatory Materials:** *Guide to Accreditation* (manual). **Length of Process:** Six months-one year. **Fees:** Actual cost of on-site review; $650 (annual fee). **Accredited By:** U.S. Department of Education.

Optometry

1752

Council on Optometric Education (COE)

American Optometric Association
243 N. Lindbergh Ave.
St. Louis, MO 63141
Phone: (314)991-4100
Fax: (314)991-4101
Joyce Urbeck, Adm.Dir.

Recipient: Optometric technician associate degree programs; professional optometric doctoral degree programs; and optometric post-doctoral residency programs. **Application Procedures:** Self-assessment, involving administrators, alumni, faculty, students, support staff, trustees, and other interested individuals, required. Must evaluate strengths and weaknesses of program and document compliance with standards in the following areas: (1) Mission Statement, Goals,

Objectives, and Outcomes, including: Dissemination; Educational; Evaluation; Outcomes; Processes; Programs; Resources; and Scope of practice; (2) Administration, including: Administrative staff; Chief academic officer; Chief executive officer; Communication; Catalog; Evaluation of administrators and staff; Financial development; Financial support; Fiscal management; Governing board; Long-range academic and economic planning; Non-discrimination; Organization; Outcomes assessments; and Policy formation; (3) Resources and Facilities, including: Access to library and other learning resources and technologies; Financial resources; Instructional and office equipment; Laboratory; Library; Maintenance; Objectives; Physical environment; and Planning; (4) Faculty, including: Academic assignments and responsibilities; Benefits; Evaluation; Faculty governance mechanism; Grievances; Handbook or guide; Nondiscrimination; Professional development; Promotion; Qualifications; Recruitment; Research and scholarly activity; Staff size; Support staff; and Tenure; (5) Students, including: Academic standards and regulations; Admissions; Counseling; Financial aid; Job placement; Non-discrimination; Prerequisites; Recruitment; Registration; Student affairs policy; Student government and involvement; Student handbook; Student records; Transfers; and Tuition; (6) Curriculum, including: Autonomy; Behavioral, biological, and physical sciences; Didactic and laboratory instruction; Educational expectations; Evaluation; External clinical programs; Length; Objectives; Scientific methods of inquiry; and Supervised diagnosis and treatment of patients; (7) Clinic Management and Patient Care, including: Internal and external clinic programs; Objectives; Patient care policies; and Student interaction with health care professionals; (8) Research and Scholarship, including: Basic and applied research; Faculty resources; Objectives; and Planning; and (9) Postgraduate Optometric Education and Training, including: Continuing education; Evaluation; and Residencies. Must submit or make available: Budget information; College or school bulletin; Course outlines; Curriculum; Description of physical plant; Documentation describing evaluation process; Faculty evaluation procedure; Faculty handbook; Faculty, graduate, and student data; Financial records; List of committees, faculty, and governing board members; Minutes of meetings; Mission statement; Outcomes assessments of course, faculty, and student evaluations; Planning documents; Report on library services, resources, staff, and usage; Organizational chart; Student and faculty publications; and Student handbook. **Accreditation Requirements:** Must demonstrate feasibility and need and be non-profit. Onsite review, verifying information provided in on-site review, required. Review includes: Interviews with faculty, staff, administrators, students, and other interested parties; Review of materials, records, and student work; and Tour of physical plant. May respond to on-site review. Possible accreditation decisions are: (1) Accredited; (2) Accredited with Conditions, requiring correction of deficiencies within two years; or (3) Denial of Accreditation, for programs in substantial non-compliance with standards. **Renewal:** Every seven years. Renewal based on self-assessment and on-site review. Must also submit annual reports. **Restrictions:** Must report substantive changes in the following areas: Institutional mission, goals, and objectives; Organizational relationship of school or college with parent institution; Resources; and Scope, length, and/or content of program. **Preparatory Materials:** *Accreditation Manual: Professional Optometric Degree Programs* (reference). **Accredited By:** Commission on Recognition of Postsecondary Accreditation; U.S. Department of Education. **Endorsed By:** International Association of Boards of Examiners of Optometry.

Orthotics and Prosthetics

1753

American Board for Certification in Orthotics and Prosthetics (ABC)
1650 King St., Ste. 500
Alexandria, VA 22314
Phone: (703)836-7114
Fax: (703)836-0838

Recipient: Orthotics and prosthetics facilities. **Accreditation Requirements:** Facilities must: (1) Have full-time staff of certified practitioners; (2) Meet service standards; and (3) Offer patients safe and professional environment, **Renewal:** Every five years. **Endorsed By:** American Academy of Orthotists and Prosthetists; American Orthotic and Prosthetic Association; National Commission on Orthotic and Prosthetic Education.

1754

Board for Orthotist Certification
Allied Health Bldg., Rm. 234
100 Penn St.
Baltimore, MD 21201-1082
Phone: (410)539-3910
Dr. Donald O. Fedder BSP, Exec. Dir.

Recipient: Facilities used for delivery of orthotic services. **Accreditation Requirements:** Facility must employ at least one certified orthotist, provide alterations and off-premises fitting, and maintain sufficient stock of merchandise. Must also have the following: (1) Office/reception area with area for patient records; (2) Halls and doorways that accommodate adult wheelchair patients; (3) Ramps and/or elevators; (4) Private fitting rooms; (5) Accessible lavatories; and (6) Separate laboratory facility. On-site review may be required.

Osteopathy

1755

Bureau of Professional Education, American Osteopathic Association
American Osteopathic Association (AOA)
142 E. Ontario St.
Chicago, IL 60611-2864
Phone: (312)280-5800
Fax: (312)280-5893
Toll Free: (800)621-1773

Recipient: Colleges or schools of osteopathic medicine conferring Doctor of Osteopathy (D.O.) degree. **Application Procedures:** Self-assessment required. Must document compliance with standards in the following areas: (1) Organization, Administration, and Finance, including: Allocation of resources; Audits; Catalog; Chief executive officer; Conflict of interest; Governing body; Mission and objectives; Planning; and Policies and guidelines; (2) Faculty and Instruction, including: Academic freedom; Appointing faculty; Benefits; Faculty development program; Faculty organization; Faculty selection; Insurance; Leaves of absence; Nondiscrimination; Personal policies and procedures; Promotion; Responsibilities; Retirement; Staff size; Tenure; and Termination; (3) Student Status and Services, including: Academic counseling; Admission policies; Financial aid counseling; Non-discrimination; Number of students; Physical and mental health care; Policies and procedures handbook;

Prerequisites; Student assessment; Student involvement; Student records; and Transfer credit and waiver policies; (4) Curriculum, including: Content; Evaluation and review; Objectives; and Planning; and (5) Facilities, including: Clinical teaching facilities; Learning resource centers; and Learning resources. Must also conduct financial feasibility study. **Accreditation Requirements:** Must be non-profit. On-site review required. May respond to on-site review. Possible accreditation decisions are: (1) Accreditation; (2) Accreditation With Warning, requiring correction of deficiencies within one year; (3) Accreditation With Probation, requiring correction of major deficiencies within one year; or (4) Withdrawal of Accreditation, for colleges in substantial noncompliance with standards. **Renewal:** Every seven years (maximum). Renewal based on self-assessment and on-site review. Must also submit annual reports. **State Requirements:** Must hold appropriate charter and licenses. **Preparatory Materials:** *Accreditation of Colleges of Osteopathic Medicine* and *Accreditation Handbook for the Accreditation of Colleges of Osteopathic Medicine* (references). **Accredited By:** Commission for Recognition of Postsecondary Accreditation; U.S. Department of Education.

1756

Committee on Continuing Medical Education, American Osteopathic Association
American Osteopathic Association (AOA)
142 E. Ontario
Chicago, IL 60611
Phone: (312)280-5839
Fax: (312)280-5893
Toll Free: (800)621-1773
Delores J. Rodgers, Coord.

Recipient: Providers of continuing osteopathic medical education. **Accreditation Requirements:** Programs must: Evaluate program on on-going basis; Provide statement of educational objectives; and Utilize faculty, formal, and educational modalities best suited to topic. Must also document compliance with standards in the following areas: Attendance records; Audience; Educational objectives; Evaluation; Facilities and equipment; Faculty; Organization and administration, including needs assessment; Quality standards; and Students.

1757

Committee on Hospital Accreditation, American Osteopathic Association (COHA)

American Osteopathic Association (AOA)
142 E. Ontario St.
Chicago, IL 60611
Phone: (312)289-5849
Fax: (312)280-5893
Toll Free: (800)621-1773
George A. Reuther, Asst.Dir.

Recipient: Osteopathic acute care hospitals. **Application Procedures:** Must engage in consultation and submit the following: Bylaws; List of professional staff; and Rules and regulations. **Accreditation Requirements:** Hospital must: (1) Be designated as osteopathic institution; (2) Have been in operation for 12 months; (3) Have minimum of 25 adult and pediatric beds; (4) Meet all state and local licensing requirements; and (5) Provide professional care and hospital service on 24-hour basis. On-site review required. Must document compliance with standards in the following areas: (1) Governing Body, including: Appointment of administrator; Bylaws; Committees; Duties of administrators; Meetings; Physical plant; Professional staff appointments; Professional staff liaison; Responsibilities; and Self evaluation; (2) Patient Rights and Advance Medical Directives, including: Advance medical directives; General patient rights; and Policies and procedures; (3) Physical Plant, including: Federal, state, and local laws; Fire protection; Hazardous waste management; Maintenance; Medical facilities; Patient rooms; and Safety control; (4) Quality Assurance Program, including: Committees, departments, and services; Evaluation of medical records; Evaluation of physicians; Plan; and Program; (5) Professional Staff, including: Governing body responsibilities; Optional committees; Organized departments; Required committees; Staff bylaws rules and regulations; Staff meetings; Staff membership and privileges; and Staff organization; (6) Required Facilities and Services, including: Anesthesiology department and services; Dietetic department and services; Discharge planning process; Emergency department and services; Medical records department; Nursing department and services; Pathology and laboratory medicine service; Pharmacy department and service; Professional library services; Radiology department and services; and Surgical department and services; (7) Optional Facilities and Services, including the following departments or services: Dedicated rehabilitation medicine unit; Drug abuse and alcoholism; Emergency;

General practice; Intensive care; Internal medicine; Nuclear medicine; Obstetrics and gynecology; Outpatient ambulatory care; Outpatient surgical; Physical medicine; Psychiatric; Recovery room; Respiratory therapy; and Social service; and (8) Allied Health Professions, including: Allied health assistants; and Podiatrists. May respond to on-site review. Possible accreditation decisions are: (1) Full Compliance; (2) Essential Compliance; (3) Marginal Compliance; and (4) Non-Compliance, for hospitals in substantial noncompliance with standards. **Renewal:** Every three years (maximum). Renewal based on on-site review. Must also submit annual reports. **Preparatory Materials:** *Accreditation Requirements* (reference). Fees: $1900, plus actual cost of on-site review.

1758

Council on Postdoctoral Training of the American Osteopathic Association

American Osteopathic Association (AOA)
142 E. Ontario St.
Chicago, IL 60611-2864
Phone: (312)280-5800
Fax: (312)280-5893
Toll Free: (800)621-1773

Recipient: Osteopathic medical internships and residencies. **Accreditation Requirements:** Intern training programs must include appropriate professional staff, operate in hospital or college of osteopathic medicine accredited by AOA, and document compliance with standards in the following areas: (1) Faculty and Administrative Staff, including: Administrative Director of Medical Education; Affiliate institutions; Associate institutions; Director of Medical Education; Education committee; and Professional staff; (2) Administration of Educational Program, including: Credit for previous training; Intern manual; Laboratory studies; Length of internship; Medical evaluation; and Orientation; (3) Clinical and Educational Resources, including: Clinical texts; Conference rooms; Educational; Facilities; Financial; Learning environment; Medical library; Scope, volume, and variety of rotation; Teaching aids; and Technical; (4) Curriculum and Instruction, including: Ambulatory rotations; Assignment of patients; Autopsies; Bio-psychosocial knowledge; Clinical conferences; Content; Daily rounds; Duties and responsibilities; Formal and informal methodology; Goals and objectives; Inpatient and outpatient settings; Log of activities; Osteopathic principles; Reading program; Record

keeping; Rotating internships; Special emphasis internships; Specialty internships; Staff activities; Staff obligations; and Surgical procedures; (5) Evaluation of Interns, including: Counseling; End of internship; Quarterly reviews; Termination of internship; and Transfer of credit; (6) Evaluation of the Program, including: Director of Medical Education evaluation of program; Intern evaluation of program; and Quarterly evaluation of program; and (7) Recruitment of Interns, including: Admissions; Non-discrimination; Policies and procedures; and Requirements. Residency training programs must operate in institution accredited by AOA, have been in operation for one year, and document compliance with standards in the following areas: (1) Concept of Residency Training, including: Attitudes towards patients, professional staff, and administration of institution; Basic science knowledge; Clinical application of knowledge; Clinical review of work; Philosophy of specialty training; Prerequisites; Specialty procedures and techniques; and Teaching staff; (2) Training Requirements, including: Credit for previous training; Equipment and facilities; Evaluation of program director and residents; In-hospital evaluation of program; Pathologic and radiologic services; Patient load of program; Required organized committees or departments; Teaching; and Termination; (3) Qualifications and Responsibilities of Program Director; (4) Requirements for Residents, including: AOA membership; Laws, rules, and regulations; Length of residency; Outside activities; Pre-requisites; Professional staff responsibilities; Reports; and Responsibilities to public and governmental agencies, training institution, program director, professional staff, and patients; (5) Teaching Case Load; (6) Outside Rotations; and (7) Resident Contracts, including: Resident responsibilities; and Responsibilities of institution. On-site review required. May respond to on-site review. **Renewal:** Every five years (maximum) for residency programs.

Pet Cemeteries

1759

Accredited Pet Cemetery Society (APCS)
139 Rush Rd.
West Rush, NY 14543
Phone: (716)533-1685
Fax: (716)533-2540
Jean Lawton, Exec. Officer

Recipient: Pet cemeteries. **Number of Ac-**

credited Institutions: 5. **Accreditation Requirements:** Must meet the following requirements: (1) Submit video for review of cemetery, crematory, office, and other facilities; (2) Endorse and support deed restriction of pet cemetery property and meaningful legislation; (3) Maintain irrevocable endowment care trust fund for pet cemetery; and (4) Document compliance with standards. **Preparatory Materials:** Standards and videos available. **Fees:** $50; $150 (annual fee).

Pharmacy

1760

American Council on Pharmaceutical Education (ACPE)
311 W. Superior St., Ste. 512
Chicago, IL 60610
Phone: (312)664-3575
Fax: (312)664-4652
Daniel A. Nona, Exec.Dir.

Recipient: Programs leading to bachelor's degree in pharmacy or Doctor of Pharmacy degree. **Number of Accredited Institutions:** 126. **Application Procedures:** Self-assessment required. Must document compliance with standards in the following areas: Academic calendars; Advertising; Catalogs and publications; Curriculum; Evaluation; Facilities, equipment, and supplies; Faculty; Fiscal and adminstrative capacity; Recruiting an admissions practices; Student support services. Must address strengths and weaknesses of program. **Accreditation Requirements:** Baccalaureate programs are five years in length and Doctor of Pharmacy programs are six years in length. On-site review, verifying information provided in self-assessment, required. Review includes: Interviews with dean, faculty, pharmacy practitioners, students, alumni, and university administrators; and Survey of physical facilities, library and other learning resources, and clinical facilities. May respond to on-site review. Possible accreditation decisions are: (1) Accreditation; (2) Probation, requiring correction of deficiencies; or (3) Denial of Accreditation, for programs in substantial non-compliance with standards. **Renewal:** Every six years (maximum). Renewal based on self-assessment and on-site review. **Preparatory Materials:** *ACPE Accreditation Manual* (reference). **Fees:** Application fee, plus actual cost of on-site review. **Accredited By:** U.S. Department of Education. **Endorsed By:** American Association of Colleges of Pharmacy; American Council on Educa-

tion; American Foundation for Pharmaceutical Education; American Pharmaceutical Association; National Association of Boards of Pharmacy.

1761

Continuing Education Division, American Council on Pharmaceutical Education
American Council on Pharmaceutical Education (ACPE)
311 W. Superior St., Ste. 512
Chicago, IL 60610
Phone: (312)664-3575
Fax: (312)664-4652
Daniel A. Nona, Exec.Dir.

Recipient: Providers of continuing pharmaceutical education. **Number of Accredited Institutions:** 336. **Accreditation Requirements:** Must document compliance with standards in the following areas: (1) Administration and Organization, including: Administrative responsibility; Administrator qualifications; Certificates of credit; Continuing education credit; Cosponsorship with non-APCE-approved providers; Cosponsorship with other ACPE approved providers; Grievance policy and procedures; Program announcement literature; and Recordkeeping; (2) Budget and Resources, including: Adequate financial resources; and Identifiable budget; (3) Faculty and Staff, including: Faculty: qualitative and quantitative considerations; and Support staff; (4) Education Program Development, including: Appropriate subject matter; Educational needs assessment; Educational objectives; Instructional materials; Non-commercialism; and Topic development; (5) Methods of Delivery, including: Instructional delivery; and Participant involvement in learning; (6) Facilities, including: Matching facilities to audience and objectives; and Matching facilities to content and method; and (7) Evaluation, including: Learning assessment; and Program evaluation. Program must conduct: Participant surveys; Periodic self-assessments; Reviews of selected educational activities; and Third-party peer reviews. **Renewal:** Every six years (maximum). Renewal based on participant survey, review of selected educational activities, self-assessment, and third-party peer review. **Preparatory Materials:** *Criteria for Quality and Interpretive Guidelines* and *Policy and Procedures for Approval of Providers of Continuing Education* (references). **Endorsed By:** American Association of Colleges of Pharmacy; American Council on Education; American Foundation for Pharma-

ceutical Education; American Pharmaceutical Association; National Association of Boards of Pharmacy.

Physical Therapy

1762

Commission on Accreditation in Physical Therapy Education (CAPTE)
American Physical Therapy Association (APTA)
1111 N. Fairfax St.
Alexandria, VA 22314
Phone: (703)706-3245
Fax: (703)684-7343
Virginia Nieland, Dir.

Recipient: Physical therapist assistant programs at associate's degree level and physical therapist programs at baccalaureate, post-baccalaureate certificate, master's degree, and clinical doctorate degree levels. **Number of Accredited Institutions:** 276. **Application Procedures:** Self-assessment required. Must document compliance with standards in the following areas: (1) Organization, including: Faculty policies and procedures; Institution; Program goals and objectives; and Student policies and procedures; (2) Resources, including: Equipment and supplies; Facilities; Faculty; Finances; Library and learning resources; Staff; Student services; and Students; (3) Curriculum, including: Clinical education; Comprehensive curriculum; Curriculum content in patient care; Curriculum content in physical therapy delivery system; and Curriculum development, content, and evaluation; and (4) Performance of Program Graduates, including: Patient care; and Physical therapy delivery system. **Accreditation Requirements:** On-site review required. May respond to on-site review. **Renewal:** Every five years (initial); every eight years thereafter. Renewal based on self-assessment and on-site review. **Preparatory Materials:** *Accreditation Handbook, Evaluative Criteria for Accreditation of Education Programs for the Preparation of Physical Therapist Assistants,* and *Evaluative Criteria for Accreditation of Education Programs for the Preparation of Physical Therapists* (references). **Fees:** $7500. **Accredited By:** Commission on Recognition of Postsecondary Accreditation; U.S. Department of Education.

Planning

Planning Accreditation Board
Research Park
Iowa State Univ.
2501 N. Loop Dr., Ste. 800
Ames, IA 50010
Phone: (515)296-7030
Fax: (515)296-9910
Beatrice Clupper Ph.D., Dir.

Recipient: Programs leading to bachelor's and master's degrees in planning. **Number of Accredited Institutions: 82. Application Procedures:** Self-assessment required. Must document compliance with standards in the following areas: (1) Goals and Objectives, including: Academic excellence; Assessment and participation; Clarity; Dissemination; Diversity; Focus; Planning documents; Program descriptions in school catalogues, bulletins, brochures, and other publications; and Surveys of program graduates; (2) Institutional Relations, including: Contributions to institution; Opportunities within institution; and Organization; (3) Academic Autonomy and Governance, including: Administrative location; Administrator's qualifications; Governance; Leadership; Participation in governance; and Program autonomy; (4) Curriculum, including: Experience; Goals; Knowledge components; Quality; Skill Components; and Values; (5) Faculty Resources and Composition, including: Administration, including non-instructional matters and student recruitment; Advising; Concentration of resources; Continuing academic and professional development; Educational attainment; Educational diversity; External funding; Normal teaching assignments; Planning procedures; Practice; Practitioners; Public service; Publication; Qualifications; Research activities; Service to institution; Service to profession; Size; Student/faculty ratio; and Visiting faculty; (6) Teaching, Advising, and Student Services, including: Advising; Course scheduling; Faculty qualifications; Financial aid; Placement; Specializations; and Teaching quality; (7) Research and Scholarly Activities, including: Dissemination; Link with practice; Link with teaching; Policy; and Quality; (8) Public and Professional Service, including: Continuing education; Link to professional and scholarly communities; Link with teaching; Policy; and Quality; (9) Students, including: Admission standards; Composition; Quality; Recruitment; and Size; (10) Resources, including: Institutional resources; and Use and generation of resources; and (11) Administrative and

Fair Practices, including: Accuracy and comprehensiveness of information; Affirmative action; Confidentiality of student records; Non-discrimination; On-going monitoring and evaluation; and Student and faculty grievance procedures. **Accreditation Requirements:** Programs must meet the following requirements: (1) Have graduated at least one class of 25 students; (2) Include word "planning" in formal titles of degrees and programs; (3) Have undergraduate programs of minimum of four years in length and graduate programs of minimum of two years in length; and (4) Have primary purpose of preparing students to become practitioners in planning profession. Curriculum should include coursework in the following areas: Administrative, legal, and political aspects of plan-making and policy implementation; Collaborative problem-solving, plan-making, and program design; Familiarity with at least one area of specialized knowledge of particular subject or set of issues; History and theory of planning processes and practices; Problem formulation, research skills, and data gathering; Quantitative analysis and computers; Structure and functions of urban settlements; Synthesis and application of knowledge to practice; and Written, oral, and graphic communications. On-site review, verifying information provided in self-assessment, required. Review includes: Interviews with administrative officials of institution, and administrator, faculty, students, and alumni of program; Inspection of library and other facilities; and Review of student work. Review report will include evaluation of strengths and weaknesses of program. May respond to on-site review. Possible accreditation decisions are: (1) Accreditation; (2) Probationary Accreditation, requiring correction of deficiencies within two years; or (3) Denial of Accreditation, for programs in substantial non-compliance with standards. **Renewal:** Every five years (maximum). Renewal based on self-assessment and on-site review. Must also submit annual reports. **Preparatory Materials:** *Accreditation Document: Criteria and Procedures of the Planning Accreditation Program* and *Site Visit Manual* (references). **Fees:** Application fee, plus actual cost of on-site review; must also submit annual fee. **Accredited By:** Commission on Recognition of Postsecondary Accreditation. **Endorsed By:** American Institute of Certified Planners; American Institute of Planners; American Planning Association; Association of Collegiate Schools of Planning.

Podiatry

Council on Podiatric Medical Education (CPME)
American Podiatric Medical Association (APMA)
9312 Old Georgetown Rd.
Bethesda, MD 20814-1621
Phone: (301)571-9200
Fax: (301)530-2752

Recipient: Colleges, schools, and educational programs leading to first professional degree in podiatric medicine, Doctor of Podiatric Medicine (D.P.M.). **Application Procedures:** Self-assessment required. Must document compliance with standards in the following areas: (1) Administration, including: Assessment; Fiscal responsibility; Governing body; Planning; and Policy formation; (2) Degree Programs; (3) Educational Program, including: Ethics; Knowledge, skills, and values; and Mission, goals, and objectives; (4) Faculty, including: Credentials; Diversity; Educational background; Experience; Patient care; and Research and scholarly activity; (5) Mission, Goals, and Objectives; (6) Physical Plant; (7) Student/Patient Interaction, including supervised diagnosis and treatment of patients; (8) Student Policies; and (9) Student Services. Must provide plan for continuing self-assessment and correcting weaknesses of program. **Accreditation Requirements:** Must meet requirements in the following areas: (1) Demonstration of Need, including: Availability of podiatric pathology; Demographics; Public need; and Student interest; (2) Educational Setting, including: Environment conducive to scholarly inquiry; and Research specific to biomedical sciences; (3) Goals and Objectives, including: Clearly articulated mission for educational program; and Plan of evaluation; (4) Four-Year Curriculum, requiring at least four years of study and appropriate tuition; and (5) Resources, including: Facilities and equipment; Financial capability; Human resources; and Student services and policies. On-site review, verifying information provided in self-assessment, required. Review identifies strengths and weaknesses of programs. Review includes: Interviews with administrators, faculty, students, and other interested individuals; and Tours physical facilities. May respond to on-site review. Possible accreditation decisions are: (1) Accreditation; (2) Probationary Accreditation, requiring correction of deficiencies within two years; or (3) Accreditation Withheld, for programs or schools in substantial noncompliance with standards. **Renewal:**

Every eight years (maximum). Renewal based on self-assessment and on-site review. Must also submit annual reports. **Restrictions:** Must report changes of affiliation or ownership or major changes to program. Accreditation not extended to branch campuses. **Preparatory Materials:** *Procedures for Accrediting Colleges of Podiatric Medicine* and *Standards, Requirements, Guidelines, and Self-Study Design for Colleges of Podiatric Medicine* (references). List of suggested resource materials available. **Fees:** Actual cost of on-site review; must also submit annual fee. **Accredited By:** Commission on Recognition of Postsecondary Accreditation; U.S. Department of Education. **Endorsed By:** American Association of Colleges of Podiatric Medicine; American Podiatric Medical Students' Association.

Psychoanalysis

1765

American Board for Accreditation in Psychoanalysis (ABAP)
80 Eighth Ave., Ste. 1501
New York, NY 10011-1501
Phone: (212)741-0515
Fax: (212)741-0515
Dean Davis Ph.D., Dir.

Recipient: Institutes granting certificates in psychoanalysis. **Number of Accredited Institutions:** 19. **Application Procedures:** Self-assessment required. Must submit catalog and fact sheet. **Accreditation Requirements:** On-site review required. May respond to on-site review. **Renewal:** Every five years. Renewal based on self-assessment and on-site review. **Preparatory Materials:** *Handbook on Accreditation* (reference). **Length of Process:** Five years. **Fees:** $250; $2000 (annual fee). **Endorsed By:** National Association for the Advancement of Psychoanalysis.

Psychology

1766

Committee on Accreditation, American Psychological Association
American Psychological Association (APA)
Office of Program Consultation and Accreditation
750 First St., NE
Washington, DC 20002-4242
Phone: (202)336-5979
Fax: (202)336-5978
E-mail: pdn.apa@mail.apa.org
Paul D. Nelson, Dir.

Recipient: Doctoral programs in professional specialties of psychology and predoctoral internship training programs in professional psychology. **Number of Accredited Institutions:** 720. **Application Procedures:** Self-assessment required. Must document compliance with standards in the following areas: (1) Eligibility, including: Academic admissions and degree requirements; Administrative and financial assistance; Advising; Diversity; Due process and grievance procedures for students and faculty; Faculty and student rights, responsibilities, and personal development; Length of program; Policies and procedures; Prerequisites; Relationship with sponsoring institution; Retention and termination decisions; Scope; and Student performance evaluation and feedback; (2) Program Philosophy, Objectives, and Curriculum Plan, including: Curriculum content; Diversity; Education and training objectives; Life-long learning; Philosophy and training model; Practicum experiences; Professional issues, including ethical, legal, and quality assurance principles; Psychological practice; Substantive areas of professional psychology; and Training procedures and sequence; (3) Program Resources, including: Clerical and technical support; Consortia; Faculty qualifications and responsibilities; Financial support; Physical facilities; Professional development; Staffing size; and Training materials and equipment; (4) Cultural and Individual Differences and Diversity, including: Attracting and retaining faculty and students; and Knowledge and experiences about role of cultural and individual diversity; (5) Student-Faculty Relations, including: Diversity; Faculty accessibility; Feedback; Guidance; Polices and procedures; and Student requirements; (6) Program Self-Assessment and Quality Enhancement, including: Graduate job placement and career paths; National standards; Needs for psychological services; Scientific and professional knowledge; and Sponsor institution's missions and goals; (7) Public Disclosure, including: Accreditation status; Administrative policies and procedures; Curriculum; Education and training outcomes; Faculty, students, facilities, and other resources; Goals, objectives, and training model; Requirements for admission and graduation; and Research and practicum experiences; and (8) Relationship with Accrediting Body. **Accreditation Requirements:** On-site review required. Review includes discussion with faculty, staff, administrators, students, and other interested parties. May respond to on-site review. Possible accreditation decisions are: (1) Accredited; (2) Accredited, On Probation, requiring correction of deficiencies within one-three years; or (3) Denial of Accreditation, for programs in substantial noncompliance with standards. **Renewal:** Every seven years (maximum) for doctoral programs; every five years (maximum) for internship programs. Renewal based on self-assessment and on-site review. Must also submit annual reports. Renewal fee is $1100. **Restrictions:** Must report changes in learning environment, plans, resources, or operations. **Preparatory Materials:** "Accreditation Operating Procedures" and "Guidelines and Principles for Accreditation of Programs in Professional Psychology" (references). **Fees:** $1200. **Accredited By:** Commission on Recognition of Postsecondary Accreditation; U.S. Department of Education.

Public Affairs and Administration

1767

Commission on Peer Review and Accreditation of the National Association of Schools of Public Affairs and Administration
National Association of Schools of Public Affairs and Administration (NASPAA)
1120 G St., NW, Ste. 730
Washington, DC 20005
Phone: (202)628-8965
Fax: (202)626-4978

Recipient: Master's degree programs in public affairs, policy, and administration. **Number of Accredited Institutions:** 124. **Application Procedures:** Self-assessment required. Must document compliance with standards in the following areas: (1) Program Mission, including: Assessment; Educational philosophy and mission; and Strategies for carrying out objectives consistent with mission, resources, and constituencies; (2) Program Jurisdiction, including: Administrative organization; Identifiable faculty; Program administration; and Scope of influence of administration and faculty over the following: Admissions; Appointment, promotion, and tenuring of program faculty; Certification of degree candidates; Course scheduling and teaching assignment; Degree requirements; General program policy and planning; New courses and curriculum changes; and Use of financial and other resources; (3) Curriculum, including: Curriculum components; Internships; Minimum degree requirements; and Purpose of curriculum; (4) Faculty, including: Diversity; Faculty nucleus; Practitioner involvement; and Professional qualifications; (5) Admission of Students, including: Admission factors; Goals and standards; and Baccalaureate requirement; (6) Student Services, including: Advisement and appraisal; and Placement services; (7) Supportive Services and Facilities, including: Budget; Classrooms; Faculty offices; Instructional equipment; Library services; Meeting areas; and Supportive personnel; and (8) Off-Campus Programs, including: Academic support services; Authorization; Definition; Faculty involvement; Program equivalency; and Quality of work. Must submit faculty data sheets and course abstracts. **Accreditation Requirements:** Program must be four years in length and have primary objective of professional education preparing persons for leadership and management roles in public affairs, policy, or administration. On-site review, verifying information provided in self-assessment, required. Review includes interviews with university and program administrators, faculty, alumni, and students. May respond to on-site review. Possible accreditation decisions are: (1) Accreditation; (2) Delayed Accreditation, requiring correction of deficiencies within one or two years; or (3) Deny Accreditation, for programs in substantial non-compliance with standards. **Renewal:** Every seven years (maximum). Renewal based on self-assessment and on-site review. **Preparatory Materials:** *Policies and Procedures for Peer Review and Accreditation* and *Standards for Professional Master's Degree Programs in Public Affairs, Policy, and Administration* (references). Manuals and workshops available. **Fees:** Must submit annual fee based on enrollment. **Accredited By:** Commission on Recognition of Postsecondary Accreditation.

Real Estate

1768

Accredited Management Organization (AMO)

Institute of Real Estate
    Management (IREM)
430 N. Michigan Ave.
PO Box 109025
Chicago, IL 60610-9025
Phone: (312)661-0004
Fax: (312)661-1936

Recipient: Real estate management firms. **Accreditation Requirements:** Must meet the following requirements: (1) Three years of operation; (2) Have Certified Property Manager (CPM) (see separate entry) in charge of firm's management operation as "Executive CPM" for at least 180 days; (3) Document that Executive CPM has successfully completed IREM's Managing the Management Company course, which covers: Acquiring new business; Allocating real estate managers' workloads; Analyzing income, expenses, and profits; Compensating real estate managers; Enhancing business relationships; Negotiating contracts; Networking; Rightsizing; Selecting, keeping, and motivating employees; Setting prices; and Strategic planning; (4) Maintain following types of insurance: Fidelity bond covering all management employees, officer, and owners of firm in amount equal to at least ten percent of firm's gross monthly collections, with value of at least $10,000 but not exceeding $500,000; and Depositor's forgery and alterations insurance, with minimum coverage of at least $25,000; and (5) Maintain high operating and financial standards. Must be verified by independent credit check and submission of all forms used in connection with management, including sample statement to property owners of income and expenses. Must also supply firm history. Accreditation of firm applies to principal office and every branch office, providing branch meets requirements. Must receive approval from IREM chapter, including interview of executive CPM and on-site review of property firm manages. Firm may have undergone one name change or ownership change equal to 50 percent or less prior to initial accreditation. **Renewal:** Every three years. Renewal based on meeting same requirements as initial accreditation. **Restrictions:** Must notify IREM if name, ownership, or organizational structure change. **Endorsed By:** National Association of Realtors.

Recreation

1769

Council on Accreditation, National Recreation and Park Association

National Recreation and Park
    Association (NRPA)
2775 S. Quincy St., Ste. 300
Arlington, VA 22206
Phone: (703)820-4940
Fax: (703)671-NRPA
Jeanne Houghton, Coord.

Recipient: Baccalaureate programs in recreation, park resources, and leisure services. **Number of Accredited Institutions:** 99. **Application Procedures:** Self-assessment required. Must document compliance with standards. **Accreditation Requirements:** On-site review required. Review includes interviews with administrators, faculty, students, and other interested parties. May respond to on-site review. **Preparatory Materials:** *Standards and Evaluative Criteria for Baccalaureate Programs in Recreation, Park Resources, and Leisure Services* (reference). **Accredited By:** Commission on Recognition of Postsecondary Accreditation. **Endorsed By:** American Association for Health, Physical Education, Recreation, and Dance; American Association for Leisure and Recreation.

1770

North American Riding for the Handicapped Association (NARHA)

PO Box 33150
Denver, CO 80233
Phone: (303)452-1212
Toll Free: (800)369-RIDE

Recipient: Centers teaching horseback riding to the handicapped. **Membership:** Required. **Accreditation Requirements:** Must submit the following: Instructor resumes; Lesson plan; Photographs of facilities; and Videotape of instructors and therapists conducting lessons. Must also meet criteria in the following areas: (1) Administration, including: Emergency plan; First aid; Insurance; List of riders; Medical releases; and Volunteers; (2) Equipment, including: Bridles; Helmets; Saddles; Special equipment; and Stirrups; (3) Facility, including: Bathroom facilities; Entrance to stable area and riding arena; Equipment used for special disciplines; Fire extinguishers; Grooming and tacking areas; Location of phone in facility; Lounge, offices, and classrooms; Mounting blocks; Mounting ramps; Parking area; Riding areas: indoor and outdoor; Stabling; and Tack room; (4)

Horses, including: First aid; and Number of horses; (5) Instructor and Instruction, including: Education; Equestrian background; Instructional background; and Lesson plans; (6) Mounting and Dismounting; (7) Therapist and Therapy; and (8) Volunteers. Centers must have insurance coverage. **Renewal:** Every five years (maximum). Must also submit annual report. **Fees:** Must submit annual fee.

Regional Institutional Accrediting Associations

`1771`

Accrediting Commission for Community and Junior Colleges, Western Association of Schools and Colleges (ACCJC)
Western Association of Schools and
    Colleges (WASC)
PO Box 70
3060 Valencia Rd.
Aptos, CA 95003
Phone: (408)688-7575
Fax: (408)688-1841
John C. Petersen, Exec.Dir.

Recipient: Institutions offering one or more educational programs of two academic years in length and awarding associate's degree in American Samoa, California, Commonwealth of the Northern Marianas, Federated States of Micronesia, Hawaii, Guam, Republic of the Marshall Islands, and Republic of Palau, and any American/International schools in East Asia or Pacific area. **Number of Accredited Institutions:** 136. **Application Procedures:** Self-assessment required. Must clearly define appropriate educational goals and objectives, create short- and long-range plans for achieving these goals, and demonstrate compliance with criteria in the following areas: Educational programs and resources; Financial support; Legal authority; Mission; Organization; and Public disclosure. Must submit the following supporting documents: Audited financial statement; Biographical information on board members; Budget; Bylaws; Catalog; Charter or articles of incorporation; Documentation of state authority to grant associate degrees; Planning studies; and Roster of full and part time faculty and administrative staff. **Accreditation Requirements:** On-site review, verifying information provided in self-assessment, required. Review includes interviews with administrators, faculty, students, and other interested parties. Review report includes recommendations for improvement. **Re-newal:** Every six years. Renewal based on self-assessment and on-site review. Must also submit annual reports. **Fees:** Application fee, plus actual cost of on-site review; must also submit annual fee based on enrollment. **Accredited By:** Commission on Recognition of Postsecondary Accreditation; U.S. Department of Education.

`1772`

Accrediting Commission for Schools of the Western Association of Schools and Colleges
Western Association of Schools and
    Colleges (WASC)
533 Airport Blvd., Ste. 200
Burlingame, CA 94010
Phone: (415)375-7711
Fax: (415)375-7790

Recipient: Public, independent, church-related, and proprietary elementary schools, junior high/middle/intermediate schools, comprehensive/college preparatory high schools, continuation high schools, alternative high schools, occupational/vocational high schools, regional occupational programs/centers, adult schools, and vocational skills centers in American Samoa, California, Commonwealth of the Northern Marianas, Federated States of Micronesia, Hawaii, Guam, Republic of the Marshall Islands, and Republic of Palau, and any American/International schools in East Asia or the Pacific area. **Number of Accredited Institutions:** 2300. **Application Procedures:** Self-assessment required. Must clearly define appropriate educational goals and objectives, create short- and long-range plans for achieving these goals, and document compliance with standards in the following areas: Co-curricular program; Curricular program; Finance; Organization; Philosophy, goals, and objectives; Student support services; School plant; and Staff. **Accreditation Requirements:** On-site review, verifying information provided in self-assessment, required. Review includes: Interviews with administrators, teachers, students, and others; Observation of school in operation; and Visits to classes. Review report includes recommendations for improvement. **Renewal:** Every six years (maximum). Renewal based on self-assessment and on-site review. Must also submit annual reports. **Restrictions:** Must meet local and state requirements. **Preparatory Materials:** Self-study coordinator workshops available. **Accredited By:** U.S. Department of Education. **Endorsed By:** California Association of California School Administrators; California Association of Independent Schools; California Association of Private School Organizations; California Congress of Parents and Teachers; California Federation of Teachers; California School Boards Association; California Teachers Association; East Asia Regional Council of Overseas Schools; Hawaii Association of Independent Schools; Hawaii Government Employees' Association; Hawaii State Teachers Association; Pacific Union Conference of Seventh-Day Adventists; Western Catholic Educational Association.

`1773`

Accrediting Commission for Senior Colleges and Schools of the Western Association of Schools and Colleges
Western Association of Schools and
    Colleges (WASC)
Box 9990
Mills College
Oakland, CA 94613
Phone: (510)632-5000
Fax: (510)632-8361

Recipient: Colleges and universities in American Samoa, California, Commonwealth of the Northern Marianas, Federated States of Micronesia, Hawaii, Guam, Republic of the Marshall Islands, and Republic of Palau, and any American/International schools in East Asia or the Pacific area. **Application Procedures:** Self-assessment required. Must clearly define appropriate educational goals and objectives, create short- and long-range plans for achieving these goals, and document compliance with standards in the following areas: Academic calendars; Advertising; Catalogs and publications; Curriculum; Evaluation; Facilities, equipment, and supplies; Faculty; Fiscal and adminstrative capacity; Recruiting an admissions practices; Student support services. **Accreditation Requirements:** Must have graduated at least one class in principal programs. On-site review, verifying information provided in self-assessment, required. Review includes interviews with administrators, faculty, students, and other interested parties. Review report includes recommendations for improvement. May respond to on-site review. **Renewal:** Every eight years (maximum). Renewal based on self-assessment and on-site review. Must also submit annual reports. **Restrictions:** Must meet local and state requirements. **Preparatory Materials:** Self-study coordinator workshops available. **Length of Process:** Six years (maximum). **Accredited By:** Commission on Recognition of Postsecondary Accreditation; U.S. Department of Education.

1774

Commission on Colleges, Northwest Association of Schools and Colleges

Northwest Association of Schools and Colleges (NASC)
3700 University Way, NE
Seattle, WA 98105
Phone: (206)543-0195
Fax: (206)685-4621

Recipient: Colleges and universities in Alaska, Idaho, Montana, Nevada, Oregon, Utah, and Washington. **Application Procedures:** Self-assessment required. Must document compliance with standards in the following areas: (1) Institutional Mission and Objectives, including: Curriculum objectives; Dissemination of objectives; Evaluation; Institutional character; and Unit objectives; (2) Finance, including: Accounting systems; Audits; Autonomy; Budgets; Capital outlay; Chief business officer; Debt; Distribution of expenditures; Endowments; Financial aid; Financial management; Financial planning; Financial reserves; Financial resources; Indebtedness; Operating budget; Sources of income; and Surpluses; (3) Physical Plant, Materials, and Equipment, including: Buildings; Campus; Classrooms; Equipment; Heating; Laboratories; Landscaping; Lighting; Maintenance; Materials; Parking space; Pedestrian areas; Planning; Scheduling for maximum utilization; and Ventilation; (4) Library and Information Resources, including: Facilities and access; Information services; Personnel and management; Planning and evaluation; and Purpose and scope; (5) Educational Program and Its Effectiveness, including: Alumni assessment; Assessment; Employer assessment; General education and related instruction requirements; Institutional analysis and appraisal; Institutional description; Internal academic unit analysis and appraisal; and Student assessment; (6) Continuing Education and Special Instructional Activities, including: Administration; Advertising and promotional information; Assessment of needs; Continuing Education Units (CEUs); Evaluation; Facilities; Faculty qualifications; Fee structure and refund policy; Financial aid; Financial support; Granting of credit; Objectives; Off-campus units; Size of staff; Student needs; and Student services; (7) Instructional Staff, including: Academic freedom; Benefits; Communication; Evaluation; Faculty input in development of academic policies; Professional development; Recruitment; Retention; Salaries; and Selection; (8) Administration, including: Administrative officer; Business office; Communica-

tion; Faculty manuals and handbooks; Fire protection; Governing board; Nondiscrimination; Organization; Plant and campus maintenance; Policies and procedures; Security; and Traffic safety; (9) Students, including: Academic advising; Admissions; Alumni; Bookstore; Career guidance; Catalog and student handbook; Cocurricular activities; Counseling and testing; Diversity and nondiscrimination; Evaluation; Financial aid; Food services; Grievances; Housing; Intercollegiate athletics; Objectives; Orientation; Physical and mental health services; Recreational sports; Resources; Rights and responsibilities; Safety and security; Student involvement; Student media; Student records and registration services; and Transfers; (10) Scholarship and Research, including: Freedom of inquiry and dissemination; Objectives; and Resources; and (11) Graduate Program, including: Admissions; Graduate credit; Graduation requirements; and Instruction. **Accreditation Requirements:** On-site review required. May respond to on-site review. Possible accreditation decisions are: (1) Accreditation; (2) Probation, requiring correction of deficiencies within specific period of time; or (3) Terminate Accreditation, for schools in substantial noncompliance with standards. **Renewal:** Every ten years (maximum). Renewal based on self-assessment and on-site review. Must also submit annual reports and interim report every five years. **Restrictions:** Must report significant changes in the following areas: Control; Geographic area; Objectives; Offerings; Scope; and Other significant matters. **Preparatory Materials:** *Accreditation Handbook* (reference). **Fees:** $1000, plus actual cost of on-site review; must also submit annual dues based on expenditures. **Accredited By:** Commission on Recognition of Postsecondary Accreditation; U.S. Department of Education.

1775

Commission on Colleges, Southern Association of Colleges and Schools

Southern Association of Colleges and Schools (SACS)
1866 Southern Ln.
Decatur, GA 30033-4097
Phone: (404)679-4500
Fax: (404)679-4556
Toll Free: (800)248-7701
Dr. Harry L. Bowman, Exec.Dir.

Recipient: Postsecondary degree-granting institutions in the U.S. states of Alabama, Florida, Georgia, Kentucky, Louisiana, Mississippi, North Carolina,

South Carolina, Tennessee, Texas, and Virginia, and Latin America. **Application Procedures:** Self-assessment, involving administrators, faculty, staff, and students, required. Must document compliance with standards in the following areas: Academic calendars; Advertising; Catalogs and publications; Curriculum; Evaluation; Facilities, equipment, and supplies; Faculty; Fiscal and adminstrative capacity; Recruiting an admissions practices; Student support services. **Accreditation Requirements:** On-site review, verifying information provided in self-assessment, required. Review includes interviews with administrators, faculty, students, and other interested parties. May respond to on-site review. **Renewal:** Renewal required. Renewal based on self-assessment and on-site review. **Preparatory Materials:** List of preparatory materials provided. **Accredited By:** Council on Postsecondary Accreditation; **Endorsed By:** Council on Regional School Accrediting Commissions. U.S. Department of Education.

1776

Commission on Elementary Schools of the Middle States Association of Colleges and Schools (CES)

Middle States Association of Colleges and Schools (MSA)
GSB Bldg., Ste. 618
One Belmont Ave.
Bala Cynwyd, PA 19004
Phone: (610)617-1100
Howard L. Simmons, Exec.Dir.

Recipient: Public, independent, church related, or proprietary elementary and middle schools, nursery schools, and special education schools in Delaware, the District of Columbia, Maryland, New Jersey, New York, Pennsylvania, Puerto Rico, the Virgin Islands, and American and International educational institutions in Europe, Africa, and Asia. **Application Procedures:** Self-assessment, involving teachers, administrators, parents, and school board members, required. Must document compliance with standards in the following areas: (1) Candidacy, including: Administration and staff; Philosophy and goals; Resources; and Safety and health; (2) Self-Study and Evaluation, including: Areas of learning; Community and student needs; Evaluation; Outcomes; Philosophy, purposes, and goals; Publicity materials; Pupil services; and Resources; (3) Operations, including: Communications; Evaluation; Governance; Physical and personnel resources; Policies and procedures; and Professional relationships; and (4) Development, including: Analysis of student experience;

Outcomes; Planning; Policy-making; and Projections of enrollment, expenditures, income, and sub-populations. **Accreditation Requirements:** On-site review, verifying information provided in self-assessment, required. Review includes: Interviews with administrators, faculty, students, and parents; and Tour of classrooms and teaching settings. Must develop plan for further development and improvement. **Renewal:** Every ten years. Renewal based on self-assessment and on-site review. Must also submit reports every third and sixth years. **State Requirements:** Must be state licensed. **Preparatory Materials:** Self-study materials and workshops available. **Length of Process:** Two years. **Fees:** Actual cost of on-site review; must also submit annual fee.

`1777`

Commission on Elementary Schools, Southern Association of Colleges and Schools

Southern Association of Colleges and Schools (SACS)
1866 Southern Ln.
Decatur, GA 30033-4097
Phone: (404)679-4500
Fax: (404)679-4556
Toll Free: (800)248-7701
Dr. Harry L. Bowman, Exec.Dir.

Recipient: Elementary schools in the U.S. states of Alabama, Florida, Georgia, Kentucky, Louisiana, Mississippi, North Carolina, South Carolina, Tennessee, Texas, and Virginia, and Latin America. **Application Procedures:** Self-assessment, involving administrators, faculty, staff, and students, required. Must document compliance with standards in the following areas: (1) Self-Study and Evaluation, requiring continuous evaluation of school; (2) School and Community, including: Effective school-community interaction; Learning community needs; Parent education and involvement; Public dissemination of purposes and program; School improvement; and Use of school facilities; (3) Philosophy, Objectives, and Commitments; (4) Design for Learning and Curriculum, including: Administrative and supervisory practices; Content; Curriculum balance; Diversity; Evaluation; Human development; Human, natural, and material resources; Instructional technologies; Planning; Scheduling; School climate; School improvement; Student performance; and Teaching strategies; (4) Areas of Learning, including: Aesthetic development; Assessment of children; Basic skills development; Citizenship; Cognitive development; Curriculum goals; Guidance of social-emotional develop-

ment; Health and safety; Intellectual development; Language development and literacy; Motivation; Parent-teacher relations; Personal, social, moral, and ethical development; Physical development; Program entry; and Teaching strategies; (5) School Staff, Administration, and Coordination, including: Board policies and procedures; Communication; Emergency plans; Financial record keeping; Financial support; Guidance; Instructional equipment and materials; Leadership training; Principles; Roles of professional and nonprofessional personnel; Salaries; School climate; School management principles; School policies; Staff development; Staffing; Student-teacher ratio; and Substitute teachers; (6) Faculty Qualifications, including: Administrators and supervisory staff; Guidance counselors; Librarian and media specialists; Paraprofessionals; and Teachers; (7) Learning Media Services, including: Book collection; Financial support; Learning materials and equipment; Multi-media materials; Physical facilities; and Teaching programs; (8) Student Services and Activities, including: Activity programs; Emergency plan; Exceptional children; First aid and health services; Guidance services; Nutrition; Placement of transfer students; Recreation; Safety; School, home, and community resources; Student records; Testing program; and Transportation; and (9) School Plant and Facilities, including: Buildings; Drinking water; Grounds; Lighting, ventilation, and temperature; Maintenance and housekeeping; Plant; and Toilet facilities. Must also develop plan for continued improvement. **Accreditation Requirements:** On-site review, verifying information provided in self-assessment, required. May respond to on-site review. Possible accreditation decisions are: (1) Accreditation; (2) Notified or Warning, requiring correction of deficiencies in one area; (3) Probation, requiring correction of deficiencies; or (4) Dropped From Accreditation, for schools in substantial noncompliance with standards. **Renewal:** Every ten years. Renewal based on self-assessment and on-site review. Must also submit annual reports and undergo interim review every five years. **Preparatory Materials:** *Guide to Initial Accreditation of Schools* and *Policies, Principles, and Standards for Schools Accredited by the Commission on Elementary Schools* (references). List of preparatory materials provided. **Fees:** $100-$250 (annual fee). **Endorsed By:** Council on Regional School Accrediting Commissions.

`1778`

Commission on Higher Education of the Middle States Association of Colleges and Schools (CHE)

Middle States Association of Colleges and Schools (MSA)
3624 Market St.
Philadelphia, PA 19104
Phone: (215)662-5606
Fax: (215)662-5950
Howard L. Simmons, Exec.Dir.

Recipient: Colleges and universities in Delaware, the District of Columbia, Maryland, New Jersey, New York, Pennsylvania, Puerto Rico, the Virgin Islands, and American and International educational institutions in Europe, Africa, and Asia. **Application Procedures:** Self-assessment, involving teachers, administrators, parents, and school board members, required. Must document compliance with standards in the following areas: (1) Institutional Integrity, including: Admissions; Allocation of resources; Curriculum; Equity and diversity issues; Fields of service; Goals; Institutional autonomy; Intellectual and academic freedom; Programs of research; Public service; Requirements for degrees; and Selecting and retaining faculty; (2) Missions, Goals, and Objectives, including: Evaluation and review; Institutional goals; Outcomes; Program goals; and Stating goals; (3) Students, including: Advising; Alumni; Athletic activities; Campus climate; Child care; Confidentiality; Counseling; Cultural programming; Discipline; Diversity; Financial aid; Health; Housing; Information and record keeping; Orientation; Placement; Policies and procedures; Recruitment; Registration; Retention; Rights and responsibilities; Security; Special needs of students; Student characteristics; Student organizations and activities; and Tutoring; (4) Faculty, including: Academic freedom; Appointment procedures; Diversity; Evaluation and supervision; Full- and part-time faculty; Nondiscrimination; Professional development; Promotion procedures; Qualifications; Recruitment; Retention; Retirement; Roles and responsibilities; Salaries; Support services; Teaching resources; and Teaching strategies; (5) Educational Program and Curricula, including: Community education and service; Content; Degree programs; Evaluation; Experimentation; Faculty control; General education; Goals and objectives; Requirements; Special programs; Specialized areas; Teaching strategies; Technology; and Transfer credit; (6) Library and Learning Resources: Access and Utilization, including: Building; Evaluation; Information literacy; Orientation; Print, non-print, and electronic media; Remote information services; Resources; Size of collection; and Staffing; (7) Institutional Effectiveness and Outcomes, including: Assessment; Data collection methods; Objectives; and Planning; (8) Planning and Resource Allocation, including: Adequate and appropriate data; Assessment; Assumptions and priorities; Budgeting; Constituent participation; Criteria; External forces; Fundraising; Implementation and evaluation; and Public appropriations; (9) Financial Resources, including: Accounting and financial reporting; Budget; Income and expenditure; Institutional autonomy; Planning; Priorities; and Resource allocation; (10) Organization, Administration, and Governance, including: Administrative staff; Chief executive officer; Communication; Constitution or by-laws; Governing board; Planning; and Support staff; (11) Governing Board, including: Authority; Chief executive officer; Communication; Decision-making; Diversity; Institutional policies; Member selection and qualifications; Planning and operations; Responsibilities; Rotation; and Terms of service; (12) Facilities, Equipment, and Other Resources, including: Athletic facilities; Audio-visual aids; Computers; Energy needs and utilization; Equipment; Financial resources; Instructional buildings; Instructional materials; Laboratories; Maintenance; Media centers; Planning; Residences; Safety and security requirements; and Student activity buildings; (13) Catalogs, Publications, and Promotional Materials, including: Advertisements; Basic academic policies; Costs and refund policies; Course and educational programs; Current roster of faculty; Films; Rights and responsibilities; Tapes; and View books; and (14) Institutional Change and Renewal. **Accreditation Requirements:** On-site review, verifying information provided in self-assessment, required. Review includes: Interviews with administrators, faculty, students, and parents; and Tour of classrooms and teaching settings. Must develop plan for further development and improvement. **Renewal:** Every five years (maximum). **Preparatory Materials:** *Characteristics of Excellence in Higher Education: Standards for Accreditation* (reference). List of suggested preparatory materials provided. **Accredited By:** Commission on Postsecondary Accreditation; U.S. Department of Education.

1779

Commission on Independent Schools of the New England Association of Schools and Colleges
New England Association of
Schools and Colleges (NEASC)
209 Burlington Rd.
Bedford, MA 01730-1433
Phone: (617)271-0022
Fax: (617)271-0950

Recipient: Independent schools in Connecticut, Maine, Massachusetts, New Hampshire, Rhode Island, and Vermont. **Application Procedures:** Self-assessment, involving administrators, faculty, staff, and students, required. Must document compliance with standards in the following areas: (1) Purposes and Objectives; (2) Students and Parents, including: Admission; Community involvement; Non-discrimination; Parental involvement; Public relations; and Records; (3) Professional Staff, including: Qualifications; Recruitment; Staffing changes; Supervision and evaluation; and Teaching loads; (4) Program, including: Counseling and guidance; Curriculum; Extracurricular programs; Library materials, objectives, and staff; Objectives; Placement counseling; Residential program; Residential staff; Review; School climate; School day and year; Special needs and abilities; Student achievement; Student assessment; and Student needs; (5) Decision Making Process, including: Alumni involvement; Chief administrative officer; Community involvement; Evaluation; Faculty involvement; Gender issues; Governing body; Long-range planning; Multicultural issues; Parental involvement; and Student involvement; and (6) Administration of the Institution, including: Administration; Financial management; Food services; Health services; Legal and regulatory compliance; and Physical plant. **Accreditation Requirements:** Schools must be not for profit. On-site review, verifying information provided in self-assessment, required. May respond to on-site review. **Preparatory Materials:** *Manual for School Evaluation* and *Standards for Accreditation* (references). **Accredited By:** Council on Recognition of Postsecondary Accreditation; U.S. Department of Education. **Endorsed By:** Council on Regional School Accrediting Commissions.

1780

Commission on Institutions of Higher Education, New England Association of Schools and Colleges
New England Association of
Schools and Colleges (NEASC)
209 Burlington Rd.
Bedford, MA 01730-1433
Phone: (617)271-0022
Fax: (617)271-0950
Charles M. Cook, Dir.

Recipient: Institutions awarding bachelor's, master's, or doctoral degrees; and two-year institutions that include in their offerings degrees in liberal arts and general studies in Connecticut, Maine, Massachusetts, New Hampshire, Rhode Island, and Vermont. **Number of Accredited Institutions:** 200. **Application Procedures:** Self-assessment, involving administration, faculty, staff, and students, required. Must document compliance with standards in the following areas: (1) Mission and Purposes, including: Acceptance by administration, faculty, and trustees; Curriculum; Distinctive character of institution; Evaluation; Institution's traditions; Mission statement; Needs of society; Planning; and Students; (2) Planning and Evaluation, including: Data collection and use; Financial and other contingencies; Input; Internal and external opportunities and restraints; Priorities; and Resources; (3) Organization and Governance, including: Achieving goals and objectives; Administration; Chief executive officer; Communication; Constitution or by-laws; Evaluation; Faculty; Governing board; Faculty, staff, and student involvement; Quality and integrity; and Staff; (4) Programs and Instruction, including: Academic planning and evaluation; Admissions; Allocation of human, financial, and physical resources; Conferences, institutes, workshops, or other instructional or enrichment activities; Course content; Degree objectives and requirements; Delivery of instructional program; Evaluation and planning; Financial resources; Graduate degree programs; Instruction; Instructional methods and procedures; Mission and purpose; Off-campus and continuing education programs; Program content and design; Registration; Scholarship and research; Selection and approval of faculty; Structure; Student learning and achievement; Student retention; and Undergraduate degree programs; (5) Faculty, including: Academic freedom; Academic support staff; Assignments and workloads; Evaluation; Graduate teaching assistants; Policies and procedures; Qualifications; Recruiting and appointing; Salaries and benefits; Scholarship, research, and service; Staff development; and Staffing; (6) Student Services, including: Academic advisement; Career development and placement counseling; Co-curricular activities; Diversity; Evaluation; Financial aid; Grievance procedures; Health education and care; Non-academic needs; Orientation; Philosophy; Psychological health care; Recreation and athletics; School environment; Student characteristics and learning needs; Student leadership and participation; Student records; and Student rights and responsibilities; (7) Library and Information Resources, including: Academic and research program; Access; Collections; Computer centers; Evaluation; Facilities; Financial support; Intellectual and cultural development of students, faculty, and staff; Language libraries; Libraries; Maintenance; Media centers; Museums; Orientation and training; Policies and procedures; Scholarly support services; Security; and Staff; (8) Physical Resources, including: Access; Buildings and grounds; Classrooms; Environmental and ecological concerns; Equipment; Health; Laboratories; Maintenance; Materials; Planning; Safety; and Security; (9) Financial Resources, including: Allocation of resources; Audits; Autonomy; Budget; Contracts and grants; Control mechanisms; Financial emergencies; Financial planning; Financial reporting; Financial stability; Fund-raising; Insurance; Objectives; Operating deficits; Policies and procedures; Record keeping; Risk management; and Transfers and inter-fund borrowing; (10) Public Disclosure, including: Catalog; Dissemination of policies and procedures; Evaluation; and Publications; and (11) Integrity, including: Academic freedom; Ethical standards; Legal requirements; Nondiscrimination; Policies and procedures; and Truthfulness, clarity, and fairness. Must address strengths and weaknesses of institution and develop plan for the future. **Accreditation Requirements:** On-site review required. May respond to on-site review. **Renewal:** Every ten years. Renewal based on self-assessment and on-site review. **Preparatory Materials:** *Self-Study Guide* and *Standards for Accreditation* (references). Self-assessment workshop available. **Accredited By:** Commission on Recognition of Postsecondary Accreditation; U.S. Department of Education.

1781

Commission on Institutions of Higher Education, North Central Association of Colleges and Schools

North Central Association of
Colleges and Schools (NCACS)
30 N. LaSalle St., Ste. 2400
Chicago, IL 60602
Phone: (312)263-0456
Fax: (312)263-7462
Toll Free: (800)621-7440
Patricia A. Thrash, Dir.

Recipient: Institutions of higher learning in Arizona, Arkansas, Colorado, Illinois, Indiana, Iowa, Kansas, Michigan, Minnesota, Missouri, Nebraska, New Mexico, North Dakota, Ohio, Oklahoma, South Dakota, West Virginia, Wisconsin, and Wyoming. **Application Procedures:** Self-assessment required. Must document compliance with standards in the following areas: Academic calendars; Advertising; Catalogs and publications; Curriculum; Evaluation; Facilities, equipment, and supplies; Faculty; Fiscal and administrative capacity; Recruiting and admissions practices; and Student support services. **Accreditation Requirements:** On-site review required. Review includes interviews with administrators, faculty, students, and other interested parties. May respond to on-site review. **Renewal:** Renewal required. **Restrictions:** Must report substantive changes in the following areas: Addition of branch campus, courses, or programs; Legal status or control of institution; Length of program; and Mission or objectives. **Accredited By:** Commission on Recognition of Postsecondary Accreditation; U.S. Department of Education.

1782

Commission on Occupational Education Institutions, Southern Association of Colleges and Schools (COEI)

Southern Association of Colleges
and Schools (SACS)
1866 Southern Ln.
Decatur, GA 30033-4097
Phone: (404)679-4500
Fax: (404)679-4556
Toll Free: (800)248-7701
Dr. Harry L. Bowman, Exec.Dir.

Recipient: Non-degree-granting postsecondary institutions in the U.S. states of Alabama, Florida, Georgia, Kentucky, Louisiana, Mississippi, North Carolina, South Carolina, Tennessee, Texas, and Virginia, and Latin America. **Application**

Procedures: Self-assessment, involving administrators, faculty, staff, and students, required. Must document compliance with standards in the following areas: (1) Mission of Institution; (2) Organization and Administration, including: Administrative personnel; Faculty, staff, and student involvement; Governing body; Organizational chart; and Policies and procedures; (3) Long-Range Planning, including: Cost estimates; Curriculum development; Demographic studies; Evaluation; Facility and equipment needs; Instructor availability; New program development; Occupational surveys; and Potential enrollment figures; (4) Educational Programs, including: Admissions; Associate degree programs; Externships; Instruction; Off-campus programs; and Programs offered by telecommunications and other nontraditional modes; (5) Staff, including: Administrative and supervisory staff; Faculty; Faculty involvement with business and industry; Non-instructional staff; Professional growth; Professional staff selection and preparation; and Teaching load; (6) Media Services, including: Accessibility; Budget; Evaluation; Facilities; Nature of services; Resources; and Staff; (7) Financial Resources, including: Budget preparation and control; Financial stability; Proper administration of finances; Purchasing policies; and Refund policy; (8) Physical Facilities, including: Existing facilities; Lighting and ventilation; Operation and maintenance; and Safety and emergency procedures; (9) Equipment and Supplies, including: Equipment; Funding; Inventory; Safety; and Supplies; (10) Student Personnel Services, including: Counseling; Health; Orientation program; Recruitment; Special student services; Student activities; Student financial assistance; Student grievances and complaints; and Student records; (11) Placement and Follow-Up; and (12) Public Information and Community Relations, including: Advertising; Data collection; Community involvement and outreach; Media; and Policies and procedures. Must attend self-study workshop. **Accreditation Requirements:** Must be in operation for one year. On-site review, verifying information provided in self-assessment, required. May respond to on-site review. Possible accreditation decisions are: (1) Accreditation; (2) Notified or Warning, requiring correction of deficiencies in one area; (3) Probation, requiring correction of deficiencies; or (4) Dropped From Accreditation, for schools in substantial noncompliance with standards. **Renewal:** Every six years (maximum). Renewal based on self-assessment and on-site review; must also submit annual reports, including most recent audit and financial statements. **Restrictions:** Must report changes in the following areas: Addition of new programs; Change in existing educational program; Change in ownership; Establishment of branches; or Other substantive administrative changes. **Preparatory Materials:** *Handbook of Accreditation* (reference). List of preparatory materials provided. **Fees:** $500, plus actual cost of on-site review. Must also submit annual fee based on enrollment. **Accredited By:** Council on Postsecondary Accreditation; U.S. Department of Education. **Endorsed By:** Council on Regional Schools Accrediting Commissions.

▪1783▪

Commission on Public Elementary Schools, New England Association of Schools and Colleges

New England Association of
Schools and Colleges (NEASC)
209 Burlington Rd.
Bedford, MA 01730-1433
Phone: (617)271-0022
Fax: (617)271-0950

Recipient: Public elementary schools in Connecticut, Maine, Massachusetts, New Hampshire, Rhode Island, and Vermont. **Application Procedures:** Self-assessment required. Must document compliance with standards in the following areas: (1) Philosophy and Goals; (2) School and Community, including: Community involvement; Community support; Outreach program; and Parental involvement; (3) Curriculum and Instruction, including: Content; Diversity; Evaluation; Integrated/interdisciplinary teaching; Instructional strategies; Objectives; and Outcomes; (4) Student Support Programs, including: Health and well-being of students; Non-academic needs; Resources; and Student records; (5) Monitoring and Assessment of Student Programs, including: Evaluation; Policies and procedures; Student progress; and Review; (6) Library/Learning Media, including: Administrator; Communication; Faculty and administrative input; Materials; Objectives; Personnel; Resources; and Volunteers; (7) Faculty, Staff, and Administration, including: Cooperation and communication; Evaluation and supervision; Orientation of new staff; Personnel records; and Professional development; (8) Climate for Learning and Growth, including: Morale; and Student-teacher interaction; and (9) School Facilities and Related Services, including: Building; Equipment; Fire, health, and safety regulations; Food service; Maintenance; Site; and Transportation services.

Accreditation Requirements: On-site review, verifying information provided in self-assessment, required. **Preparatory Materials:** *Standards for Accreditation* (reference).

▪1784▪

Commission on Public Secondary Schools, New England Association of Schools and Colleges

New England Association of
Schools and Colleges (NEASC)
209 Burlington Rd.
Bedford, MA 01730-1433
Phone: (617)271-0022
Fax: (617)271-0950

Recipient: Public secondary schools in Connecticut, Maine, Massachusetts, New Hampshire, Rhode Island, and Vermont. **Application Procedures:** Self-assessment required. Must document compliance with standards in the following areas: (1) Statement of Purpose; (2) Curriculum and Instruction, including: Curricular coordination and articulation; Curriculum development; Diversity; Evaluation; Instructional strategies and practices; Instructional technology; Program of studies; Staff development programs; Student activities; Student assessment data; and Teacher supervision and evaluation; (3) Student Support Services, including: Community agencies and resources; Guidance and health services; Materials; Personnel; and Student confidentiality and records; (4) Library Technology and Media Services, including: Access; Equipment; Materials and information resources; and Personnel and support staff; (5) Administration, Faculty, and Support Staff, including: Autonomy; Clerical; Food services; Health and nursing; Maintenance; Policies and procedures; Records; Staff development; and Transportation; (6) School Facilities, including: Buildings; Equipment; Fire, health, and safety regulations; Maintenance and repair; Plant; and Site; (7) Community Support and Involvement, including: Community participation; Parent involvement and partnership; and School-community partnerships; (8) Financial Support, including: Budget; and Resources; (9) School Climate, including: Communication; Safety; and School rules and standards; and (10) Assessment of Student Learning and School Performance, including: Assessment methods; Criteria for assessing student and school performance; and Strategies for improving performance. **Accreditation Requirements:** On-site review, verifying information provided in self-assessment, required. **Preparatory Materials:** *Standards for Accreditation* (reference).

▪1785▪

Commission on Schools, North Central Association of Colleges and Schools

North Central Association of
Colleges and Schools (NCA)
Box 873011
Arizona State University
Tempe, AZ 85287-3011
Phone: (602)965-8700
Fax: (602)965-9423
Toll Free: (800)525-9517

Recipient: Elementary, middle, secondary, unit, and vocational and adult schools in Arizona, Arkansas, Colorado, Illinois, Indiana, Iowa, Kansas, Michigan, Minnesota, Missouri, Nebraska, New Mexico, North Dakota, Ohio, Oklahoma, South Dakota, West Virginia, Wisconsin, and Wyoming. **Application Procedures:** Self-assessment, involving administrators, faculty, staff, and students, required. Must document compliance with standards in the following areas: (1) Philosophy and Goals; (2) Administration and Organization, including: Administrative and supervisory services; Governing board/staff relationships; and School reports and records; (3) Curriculum and Instruction, including: Assessment; Climate; Curriculum; and Instruction; (4) School Staff, including: Administrative; Qualifications; Staff development programs; and Support staffing; (5) Pupil Personnel Services; (6) Media Program, including: Collection; Evaluation; Selection; and Staff responsibilities; (7) Student Activities Program; (8) Financial Support; (9) School Facilities, including: Building; Safety; and Site; (10) Institutional Evaluation and School Improvement; (11) School/Community Relationships; and (12) Residential Provisions, including: Dormitory duties; Dormitory provisions; Food services; Health services; and Program for resident students. Adult education programs must meet standards in the following areas: Adult students; Annual report; Awarding of credit; Counseling and library services; Credit and residence requirements for graduation; Curriculum and schedule; Professional staff; and Units of credit. **Accreditation Requirements:** On-site review, verifying information provided in self-assessment, required. May respond to on-site review. Possible accreditation decisions are: (1) Accredited; (2) Accredited Warned, requiring correction of deficiencies; or (3) Dropped, for schools in substantial noncompliance with standards. **Preparatory Materials:** *Policies and Standards for Schools* (reference). **Fees:** $150, plus actual cost of on-site review. Annual fees are: $250 (elementary schools); $300 (all schools except elementary).

▮1786▮

Commission on Schools, Northwest Association of Schools and Colleges

Northwest Association of Schools
and Colleges (NASC)
Boise State Univ.
1910 University Dr.
Boise, ID 83725
Phone: (208)334-3210
Fax: (208)334-3228

Recipient: Elementary, middle, and secondary schools, and special purpose schools in Alaska, Idaho, Montana, Nevada, Oregon, Utah, and Washington. **Application Procedures:** Self-assessment required. Must document compliance with standards. **Accreditation Requirements:** On-site review required. May respond to on-site review. Possible accreditation decisions are: (1) Approved; (2) Advised, requiring correction of deficiencies concerning one standard within two years; (3) Warned, requiring correction of deficiencies concerning more than one standard; or (4) Dropped, for schools in substantial noncompliance with standards. **Renewal:** Every ten years (maximum). Renewal based on self-assessment and on-site review. Must also submit annual report. **Fees:** $250 (annual fee).

▮1787▮

Commission on Secondary Schools, Middle States Association of Colleges and Schools

Middle States Association of
Colleges and Schools (MSA)
3624 Market St.
Philadelphia, PA 19104
Phone: (215)662-5606
Fax: (215)662-5950
Howard L. Simmons, Exec.Dir.

Recipient: Secondary and public vocational-technical schools offering non-degree, post-secondary education in Delaware, the District of Columbia, Maryland, New Jersey, New York, Pennsylvania, Puerto Rico, the Virgin Islands, and American and International educational institutions in Europe, Africa, and Asia. **Application Procedures:** Self-assessment, involving teachers, administrators, parents, and school board members, required. Must document compliance with standards in the following areas: (1) Philosophy and Objectives, including: Development; Evaluation; Identified needs of school community; Nondiscrimination; Role of school; and Written statement; (2) Educational Program, including: Evaluation; Instructional guides; Instructional materials;

Objectives and philosophy; Policies and procedures; Resources; and Student abilities and learning styles; (3) Learning Media Services, including: Catalog; Curriculum development activities; Facilities; Maintenance; Objectives; Orientation; and Resources: (4) Student Services, including: Dissemination of information; Graduates; Guidance services; Health services and staff; Student data; and Support services; (5) Student Activities; (6) School Facilities, including: Maintenance; Safety and health; and School and class enrollment; (7) School Staff and Administration, including: Evaluation; Organizational structure; Planning; Policies and procedures; Professional growth; Qualifications; School climate; Staff size; Teaching assignments; and Work schedules; and (8) Finance, including: Budget; Business practices; Control of financial operations; Financial planning; Financial resources; and Policies and procedures. Must identify strengths and weaknesses and develop plan for the future. **Accreditation Requirements:** Must have been in operation for two years. On-site review, verifying information provided in self-assessment, required. **Renewal:** Every ten years (maximum). Renewal based on self-assessment and on-site review. Must also submit progress reports. **State Requirements:** Must have charter, license, or formal authority to operate. **Preparatory Materials:** *Policies and Procedures Manual* (reference). Workshop available. **Fees:** Actual cost of on-site review; must also submit annual fee.

▮1788▮

Commission on Secondary Schools, Southern Association of Colleges and Schools

Southern Association of Colleges
and Schools (SACS)
1866 Southern Ln.
Decatur, GA 30033-4097
Phone: (404)679-4500
Fax: (404)679-4556
Toll Free: (800)248-7701
Dr. Harry L. Bowman, Exec.Dir.

Recipient: Secondary schools in the U.S. states of Alabama, Florida, Georgia, Kentucky, Louisiana, Mississippi, North Carolina, South Carolina, Tennessee, Texas, and Virginia, and Latin America. **Application Procedures:** Self-assessment, involving administrators, faculty, staff, and students, required. Must document compliance with standards in the following areas: (1) Purposes and Objectives; (2) Instructional Program Design, including: Design; Experimental programs; School evaluation; and School improvement and accountability; (3) Governance

and Organization, including: Daily schedule; Granting credit; Policies and procedures; School records; Summer session; and Yearly calendar; (4) Personnel, including: Administrative head of school and school system; Administrative or supervisory assistants; Central office staff; Guidance/pupil personnel specialists; Instructional personnel; Librarian or media specialist; Minimum personnel requirements; Standards affecting personnel; and Support personnel; (5) Services, including: Guidance; Health; and Library/materials, including circulation, collection, nonprint materials, and periodicals; (6) Plant Operations and Facilities, including: Buildings; Equipment and furniture; Inspections; Maintenance; Safety; School site; and Supplies; and (7) Finance and Business Operations, including: Allocation of resources; Budget; and Financial records. Non-public schools must also meet standards in the following areas: Admissions; Alumni affairs; Development; Dormitory life; Finance and business operations; and Public relations. **Accreditation Requirements:** On-site review, verifying information provided in self-assessment, required. May respond to on-site review. Possible accreditation decisions are: (1) Accreditation; (2) Notified or Warning, requiring correction of deficiencies in one area; (3) Probation, requiring correction of deficiencies; or (4) Dropped From Accreditation, for schools in substantial noncompliance with standards. **Renewal:** Renewal required. Renewal based on self-assessment and on-site review. **Preparatory Materials:** *Standards of the Commission on Secondary Schools* (reference). List of preparatory materials provided. **Endorsed By:** Council on Regional School Accrediting Commissions.

▮1789▮

Commission on Technical and Career Institutions, New England Association of Schools and Colleges

New England Association of
Schools and Colleges (NEASC)
209 Burlington Rd.
Bedford, MA 01730-1433
Phone: (617)271-0022
Fax: (617)271-0950

Recipient: Non-profit and privately owned one- or two-year degree and non-degree-granting institutions, and three- and/or four-year degree and non-degree-granting institutions which offer general or specialized programs leading to career opportunities in Connecticut, Maine, Massachusetts, New Hampshire, Rhode Island, and Vermont. **Application Proce-**

dures: Self-assessment, involving administrators, faculty, staff, and students, required. Secondary vocational technical schools must document compliance with standards in the following areas: (1) Philosophy and Goals; (2) Program of Studies/Curriculum, including: Co-curricular activities; Content; Evaluation; and Needs of students, business, and industry; (3) Program of Studies for Schools with Postsecondary Curricula, including: Advisory committees; Assessment; Licensure and certification; and Objectives; (4) Student Services, including: Counseling; Financial arrangements; Health services; and Personnel services; (5) Educational Media Services/Library and Audio-Visual, including: Auditory and visual aids; Book collection; Periodicals; and Reference and library materials; (6) School Staff, including: Clerical; and Custodial; (7) Records, including: Grade reports; Permanent files; Placement data; and Student records; (8) Administration, including: Administrative and supervisory personnel; and Autonomy; (9) Plant and Equipment/School Facilities, including: Equipment; Safety and health; and Space; (10) School and Community Relations, including: Communication with community, business, and industry; and Dissemination of information; (11) Financial Support, including: Financial reporting; and Resources; and (12) School Atmosphere, including: Intellectual atmosphere; and Staff and student morale. Post-secondary schools must meet standards in the following areas: (1) Purposes and Objectives; (2) Control and Administration, including: Administrative staff; Faculty involvement; and Governing board; (3) Finance, including: Audits; Financial officer or department; Financial records; and Resources; (4) Faculty, including: Conditions of employment and services; Effectiveness of teaching; Policies and procedures; Qualifications; Student-faculty ratio; and Teaching loads and schedules; (5) Students, including: Admission; Student personnel policies; and Student records; (6) Program of Studies, including: Career/vocational/technical specialties; Content; Degrees; General education, including sciences, social sciences, and the humanities; Licensure; Objectives; Program recognition; and Use of advisory committees; (7) Physical Facilities, including: Buildings; Classrooms; Dormitories; Equipment; Furnishings; Grounds; Laboratories; Safety; and Sanitation; (8) Library, including: Access; Collections; and Staff; and (9) Publications, including: Advertising and promotional materials; Catalog; and Tapes and films. **Accreditation Requirements:** On-site review, verifying information provided in self-assessment, required. May respond to on-site review.

Restrictions: Must report changes in ownership. **Accredited By:** Council on Recognition of Postsecondary Accreditation; U.S. Department of Education. **Endorsed By:** Council on Regional School Accrediting Commissions.

Rehabilitation

1790

Commission on Accreditation of Rehabilitation Facilities (CARF)
101 N. Wilmot Rd., Ste. 500
Tucson, AZ 85711-3335
Phone: (602)748-1212
Fax: (602)571-1601

Recipient: Rehabilitation facilities in behavioral health, employment and community support, and medical rehabilitation. **Number of Accredited Institutions:** 4366. **Application Procedures:** Self-assessment required. Must document compliance with standards. Must also submit budget, brochures and publications, business license, and organizational chart. **Accreditation Requirements:** Behavioral and employment and community support programs are: (1) Alcohol and Other Drug Programs, including: Detoxification services; Outpatient services; and Residential treatment programs (including inpatient); (2) Mental Health Programs, including: Case management; Community housing; Emergency/crisis intervention; Inpatient psychiatric; Outpatient therapy; Partial hospitalization; and Residential treatment; (3) Psychosocial Rehabilitation Programs, including the following models: Clubhouse; Consumer-guided; High-expectancy/education; and Intensive case management; (4) Employment Services, including: Community; Job placement; Occupational skill training; Supported; Vocational evaluation; Work adjustment; and Work services; (5) Community Support Services, including: Family; Host family; Living; Personal, social, and community; and Respite; and (6) Early Intervention and Preschool Development Programs. Medical rehabilitation programs are: (1) Comprehensive Inpatient, including: Hospital; Hospital-based skilled nursing facility; and Skilled nursing facility; (2) Spinal Cord Injury Programs; (3) Comprehensive Pain Management Programs, including: Acute; Cancer-related; Chronic - inpatient; and Chronic - outpatient; (4) Brain Injury Programs, including: Community integrated; and Medical inpatient; (5) Outpatient Medical Rehabilitation Programs; and (6) Occupational Rehabilitation Programs, including: Acute; and Work specific. On-site review, verifying information provided in self-assessment, required. **Preparatory Materials:** *Standards Manual and Interpretive Guidelines for Behavioral Health, Standards Manual and Interpretive Guidelines for Employment and Community Support,* and *Standards Manual and Interpretive Guidelines for Medical Rehabilitation* (references). Preparatory literature and audiotapes also available. **Fees:** $550, plus actual cost of on-site review. **Endorsed By:** American Academy of Neurology; American Academy of Orthopaedic Surgeons; American Academy of Orthotists and Prosthetists; American Academy of Pain Medicine; American Academy of Physical Medicine and Rehabilitation; American Association for Partial Hospitalization; American Association on Mental Retardation; American Congress of Rehabilitation Medicine; American Hospital Association; American Network of Community Options and Resources; American Occupational Therapy Association; American Osteopathic College of Rehabilitation Medicine; American Psychological Association; American Physical Therapy Association; American Rehabilitation Association; American Speech-Language-Hearing Association; American Spinal Injury Association; American Therapeutic Recreation Association; Association of Mental Health Administrators; Association of Rehabilitation Nurses; Federation of American Health Systems; Goodwill Industries International; International Association of Business, Industry, and Rehabilitation; International Association of Jewish Vocational Services; International Association of Psychosocial Rehabilitation Services; National Association of Addiction Treatment Providers; National Association of Alcoholism and Drug Abuse Counselors; National Association for the Dually Diagnosed; National Association of Social Workers; National Association of State Mental Health Program Directors; National Coalition of Arts Therapies Associations; National Council of Community Mental Health Centers; National Easter Seal Society; National Head Injury Foundation; National Multiple Sclerosis Society; National Rehabilitation Association; National Spinal Cord Injury Association; National Therapeutic Recreation Society; and United Cerebral Palsy Associations.

`1791`

Commission on Standards and Accreditation, Council on Rehabilitation Education

Council on Rehabilitation
  Education (CORE)
1835 Rohlwing Rd., Ste. E
Rolling Meadows, IL 60008
Phone: (708)394-1785
Fax: (708)394-2108
Jeanne Boland Patterson, Dir.

Recipient: Master's degree programs in rehabilitation counselor education. **Application Procedures:** Self-assessment required. Must document compliance with standards in the following areas: (1) Mission and Objectives, including: Community needs; Dissemination; Professional issues; and Written statement; (2) Program Evaluation, including: Content and design of academic curriculum; Faculty composition, qualifications, and performance; Graduate achievement; Practicum and internship instruction; Professional and community contributions; Program objectives compared to mission; Program recognition, support, and resources; and Recruitment and retention of students; (3) Curriculum, including: Assessment; Case management; Counseling services; Course or unit syllabi; Electives; Experiences with disabled individuals; Foundations of rehabilitation counseling; Job development and placement; Length of program; Research; and Vocational and career development; (4) Clinical Experience, including: Internships; Policies and procedures; and Practicum; (5) Educational Outcomes, including: Career and vocational development; Ethical and legal principles and standards; History, philosophy, and structure of rehabilitation delivery systems; Identification and utilization of assessment information; Job development, placement, and retention; Practice rehabilitation counseling with individuals, groups, and/or families; Rehabilitation planning and case management; and Rehabilitation research; (6) Administration and Faculty, including: Admissions; Communication between students and faculty; Faculty composition and responsibilities; Faculty qualifications, including certification, education, experience, presentations, professional activities, publications, and research; Financial assistance; Full- and part-time faculty; Introducing students to profession; Program coordinator; Recruitment and retention policies and procedures; Representation of students with disabilities and minority students; and Student-to-advisor ratio; and (7) Program Support and Resources, including: Accessibility for disabled individuals; Classrooms; Equipment; Graduate assistantships; Institutional recognition; Library and information service materials; Office space; Staff; Student and research facilities; and Travel resources. **Accreditation Requirements:** On-site review required. Review includes discussion with faculty, staff, administrators, students, and other interested parties. May respond to on-site review. **Accredited By:** Commission on Recognition of Postsecondary Accreditation.

Religion

`1792`

Accreditation Commission of the Association of Advanced Rabbinical and Talmudic Schools

Association of Advanced Rabbinical
  and Talmudic Schools (AARTS)
175 Fifth Ave., Rm. 711
New York, NY 10010
Phone: (212)447-0950
Fax: (212)533-5335
Bernard Fryshman, Exec.V.Pres.

Recipient: Rabbinical and Talmudic schools that offering rabbinical degrees, ordination, and appropriate undergraduate and graduate degrees in field of rabbinical and Talmudic education. **Number of Accredited Institutions:** 53. **Application Procedures:** Self-assessment, involving administrators, faculty, and students, required. Must document compliance with standards in the following areas: (1) Purpose, including: Dissemination; Evaluation; Objectives; Philosophy; and Role of school; (2) Organization and Administration, including: Administrative staff; Responsibilities of Board of Directors; and Role of Rosh Yeshiva; (3) Finance, including: Budget; Control; Decision-making; Expenditures; Financial aid; Income; Long-range planning; Private and public sources of income; Reporting; and Tuition; (4) Physical Plant, Materials, and Equipment, including: Classrooms; Dining facilities; Dormitory; Maintenance; and Parking facilities; (5) Library, including: Accessibility and student use; Ordering; and Size of collection; (6) Educational Program, including: Admissions; Curriculum; Degree requirements; Details; Evaluation; Goals; Length; Review process; and Student achievement; (7) Faculty, including: Compensation; Counseling and guidance; Input; Professional growth; Qualifications; Recruitment; and Retention; (8) Students and Student Services, including: Behavior codes; Character development; Counseling services; Dormitory; Extra-curricular activities; Financial advice and assistance; Food; Guidance; Health; Interpersonal attitudes; Job placement; Room and board; Safety; and Tutorial services; (9) Records, including: Academic records; Class lists; Evaluation; Financial statements; and Student files; (10) Graduate Program; and (11) Other Institutional Activities, including: Community service; and Experimental and innovative programs. The following materials may be requested: Admission requirements; Annual calendar; Budget; Certified audit; Charter; Constitution and bylaws; Curriculum for each program; Description of alumni organization activities; Donations and contributions; Evidence of community service; Faculty rules and regulations; Faculty vitae; List of recent graduates; Map of campus; Organizational chart; Publications; Sample transcript and record forms; Schedule of fees; School catalog; Statistical data on program and students; and Tuition refund policy. May also be required to submit information on the following: Academic offerings; Admission policies; Catalogs; Degree requirements; Educational effectiveness; Fees and refund structures; Graduation rates; Placement of graduates; Program and faculty resources; Promotional material; Public documents; and Satisfactory progress policies. Must address strengths and weaknesses of program and develop plan for the future. **Accreditation Requirements:** Students must meet the following prerequisites: (1) Talmudic high school graduation or equivalent; (2) Competence in entire Pentateuch and Commentaries; (3) Successful completion of 150 folio pages of Talmud; and (4) Competence in laws and custom of Code of Law (Orach Chaim) and personal commitment to their observance. School must have been in operation for two years, graduated one class, and have at least three faculty and 50 students. On-site review, verifying information provided in self-assessment, required. Review includes tour of facilities and interviews with administrators, faculty, and students. May respond to on-site review. Possible accreditation decisions are: (1) Accreditation; (2) Status with Conditions; (3) Accreditation Status for less than seven years; or (4) Accreditation Denied, for schools in substantial noncompliance with standards. **Renewal:** Every seven years (maximum). **Preparatory Materials:** *Guide to the Self-Study* and *Interpretive Guidelines to the Standards of the Accreditation Committee* (references). **Length of Process:** Six months. **Fees:** $2000, plus actual cost of on-site review; $3000 (annual fee). **Accredited By:** Commission on Recognition of Postsecondary Education; U.S. Department of Education. **Endorsed By:** Council of Independent Colleges; Independent Sector; NAFSA: Association of International Educators; National Association of Independent Colleges and Universities.

1793

Accrediting Association of Bible Colleges
130F N. College Ave.
Fayetteville, AR 72702
Phone: (501)521-8164
Fax: (501)521-9202
Randall E. Bell, Exec.Dir.

Recipient: Colleges offering certificates, diplomas, and associate's and/or baccalaureate degrees aimed at preparing students for Christian ministries through Biblical, church/vocational, and general studies. **Number of Accredited Institutions:** 89. **Application Procedures:** Self-assessment required. Must describe mission and objectives and document compliance with standards. Must submit planning document and financial audit. **Accreditation Requirements:** Program should consist of biblical/theological, general, and professional studies. Active student involvement in ministry is required. On-site review, verifying information provided in self-assessment, required. Review includes interviews with faculty, staff, administrators, students, and other interested parties. May respond to on-site review. **Renewal:** Every five years (initial). Renewal based on self-assessment, submission of planning document, and on-site review. Renewal fees are: $3000-$5000. **State Requirements:** Must have state authorization, if necessary, to award credentials. **Preparatory Materials:** *A Guide to Conducting Self Evaluation* and *Manual* (references). **Length of Process:** Eight-ten years. **Fees:** $1000-$3500 (annual fee). **Accredited By:** Commission on Recognition of Postsecondary Accreditation; U.S. Department of Education.

1794

Accrediting Commission, Transnational Association of Christian Colleges and Schools
Transnational Association of
Christian Colleges and Schools
2114 Arrow Ct.
Murfreesboro, TN 37130
Phone: (615)890-8384

Recipient: Christian postsecondary institutions offering certificates, diplomas, and associate, baccalaureate, and graduate degrees. **Application Procedures:** Self-assessment required. Must document

compliance with standards in the following areas: Academic calendars; Advertising; Catalogs and publications; Curriculum; Evaluation; Facilities, equipment, and supplies; Faculty; Fiscal and administrative capacity; Recruiting and admissions practices; and Student support services. **Accreditation Requirements:** On-site review required. May respond to on-site review. **Renewal:** Renewal required. **Restrictions:** Must report substantive changes in the following areas: Addition of branch campus, courses, or programs; Legal status or control of institution; Length of program; and Mission or objectives. **Accredited By:** U.S. Department of Education.

1795

American Association of Christian Schools (AACS)
PO Box 2189
Independence, MO 64055
Phone: (816)795-7709
Fax: (816)795-7462

Recipient: Christian schools. **Application Procedures:** Self-assessment, involving faculty, staff, and constituents, required. Must develop policy manuals in the following areas: Academic; Administrative; Faculty; and Student/Parent. Must also document compliance with standards in the following areas: Parents; Personnel; Philosophy; Plant; Program; and Pupils. **Accreditation Requirements:** On-site review required. Review includes recommendations for improving quality in operational aspects of program. Must implement internal school improvement program based on on-site review and research. **Renewal:** Every six years. Renewal fee is $50. Must also submit annual reports. **Fees:** $500, plus actual cost of on-site review; $50 (annual fee).

1796

Commission on Accrediting, Association of Theological Schools in the United States and Canada
Association of Theological Schools
in the United States and Canada
(ATS)
Ten Summit Park Dr.
Pittsburgh, PA 15275-1103
Phone: (412)788-6505
Fax: (412)788-6510
Daniel O. Aleshire, Assoc.Dir.

Recipient: Graduate professional schools of theology, theological seminaries, and graduate programs in theology in the U.S. and Canada. **Number of Accredited Institutions:** 189. **Application Proce-**

dures: Self-assessment, involving administrators and faculty, required. Must document compliance with standards in the following areas: (1) Institutional Purpose, including: Development; Evaluation; and Goals and objectives; (2) Students, including Admissions; Diversity; Financial assistance; Requirements; and Size of enrollment; (3) Faculty, including: Academic freedom; Attendance at professional meetings; Diversity; Institutional policies; Involvement in curriculum development; Qualifications; Salaries; Security, promotion, and tenure; Staffing; Study leaves; Support services; Work load; and Working conditions; (4) Governance and Administration, including: Administrative officers; Conditions of employment; Diversity; Governing board; Grievance procedures; Institutional integrity; Internal administration; Policies and procedures; and Published materials; (5) Finances, including: Accounting and reporting systems; Changes in financial resources; Financial planning; and Income; (6) Library, including: Administrator; Budget; Clerical staff; Collection; Course and research needs; Librarians; Maintenance; Objectives; Reference services and printed guides; Resources; and Scope of services; (7) Buildings and Plant, including: Capital plant; Equipment; Expenditures; Facilities; Investments; and Maintenance and repair; (8) Evaluation, including: Administration; Curriculum; Educational methodology; Faculty; Governing board; and Students; (9) Globalization of Theological Education; (10) Responsiveness to Minority and Women's Concerns; (11) Educational Programs Conducted Off-Campus; and (12) Institutional Policies Regarding Placement, including: Equal opportunity; and Vocational opportunities. Individual degree programs must meet standards in all or some of the following areas: (1) Program Goals; (2) Program Content, Location, and Duration, including: Academic support services; Content; Context; Duration; Location; Personal and spiritual formation; Practice; and Structure; and (3) Resource Requirements, including: Admissions; Aids to learning; Community resources; Faculty; Library; and Students. Clusters of schools and distance and extension educational programs must meet additional criteria. Must evaluate strengths and weaknesses of school or program. **Accreditation Requirements:** On-site review required. Review includes: Interviews with administrators, faculty, students, recent graduates, and field supervisors; Review of administrative materials, budget, faculty and student manuals, and student work; and Tours of physical facilities. May respond to on-site review. Possible accreditation decisions are: (1) Accreditation; (2) Provisional Accreditation, requiring correction of deficiencies; or (3) Denial, for schools in substantial noncompliance with standards. **Renewal:** Every ten years (maximum). Renewal based on self-assessment and on-site review. **Preparatory Materials:** *Handbook of Accreditation* and *Procedures, Standards, and Criteria for Membership* (references). Must also submit annual reports. **Fees:** Actual cost of on-site review. **Accredited By:** Commission on Recognition of Postsecondary Accreditation; U.S. Department of Education.

1797

Commission on Certification and Accreditation, United States Catholic Conference
United States Catholic Conference
4455 Woodson Rd.
St. Louis, MO 63134-0889
Phone: (314)428-2000

Recipient: Centers and programs awarding certificates and baccalaureate and master's degrees for training for specialized ministries in Catholic Church. **Application Procedures:** Self-assessment required. Must document compliance with standards in the following areas: Academic calendars; Advertising; Catalogs and publications; Curriculum; Evaluation; Facilities, equipment, and supplies; Faculty; Fiscal and administrative capacity; Recruiting and admissions practices; and Student support services. **Accreditation Requirements:** On-site review required. May respond to on-site review. **Renewal:** Renewal required. **Restrictions:** Must report substantive changes in the following areas: Addition of branch campus, courses, or programs; Legal status or control of institution; Length of program; and Mission or objectives. **Accredited By:** U.S. Department of Education.

1798

International Christian Accrediting Association (ICAA)
7777 S. Lewis Ave.
Tulsa, OK 74171
Phone: (918)495-7054
Fax: (918)495-6191
David B. Hand, Dir.

Recipient: Charismatic/Pentecostal Christian preschools, Christian elementary/secondary schools, and Bible schools and colleges. **Number of Accredited Institutions:** 85. **Application Procedures:** Self-assessment required. Must document compliance with standards in the following areas: Administrative; Educational programs; Facilities and support services; Faculty and support staff; and Institutional purpose and description. **Accreditation Requirements:** On-site review required. May respond to on-site review. **Renewal:** Every five years. Renewal based on self-assessment and on-site review. Must also submit annual reports. **Preparatory Materials:** *ICAA Standards and Procedures Manual* and *Reevaluation Manual* (references). **Length of Process:** Three-seven years. **Fees:** $250 (application fee); $200 (candidate fee); $300 (provisional fee); $500 (annual fee). **Endorsed By:** National Council for Private School Accreditation.

1799

National Lutheran School Accreditation
1333 S. Kirkwood
St. Louis, MO 63122
Phone: (314)965-9000
Carl Moser, Exec.Dir.

Recipient: Early childhood, elementary, and secondary schools recognized by Lutheran Church Missouri Synod. **Number of Accredited Institutions:** 200. **Application Procedures:** Self-assessment required. Must document compliance with standards in the following areas: (1) Philosophy; (2) School and Congregation; (3) School and Community; (4) School Climate; (5) Administration, including: Administrator; and Governing board; (6) Professional Personnel; (7) Curriculum; (8) Instruction; (9) Instructional Materials; (10) Student Services, including: Activities; Childcare; Food services; Guidance; and Health and safety; (11) Physical facilities; and (12) Finance. **Accreditation Requirements:** On-site review, verifying information provided in self-assessment, required. **Renewal:** Every seven years (maximum). Renewal based on self-assessment and on-site review. **Preparatory Materials:** *Standards for Lutheran Schools* (reference). **Fees:** Application fee, plus actual cost of on-site review; must also submit annual fee.

1800

Southwest Association of Episcopal Schools (SAES)
PO Box 945
Addison, TX 75001
Phone: (214)484-4554
Rev. William P. Scheel, Exec.Dir.

Recipient: Elementary and secondary Episcopal schools in Arkansas, Louisiana, New Mexico, Oklahoma, and Texas.

Application Procedures: Self-assessment required. Must document compliance with standards. **Accreditation Requirements:** On-site review required. **Endorsed By:** National Association of Independent Schools.

Sailing

1801

National Association of Sailing Instructors and Sailing Schools (NASISS)
15 Reiner Ct.
Middletown, NJ 07748-1612
Phone: (908)671-6190
Richard A. Herbst, Exec.Dir.

Recipient: Recreational sailing schools and charter operators teaching people to sail boats ranging from 12-60 feet in length. **Number of Accredited Institutions:** 11. **Application Procedures:** Self-assessment required. Must document compliance with standards in the areas of course content, faculty, and school operations. Must include instructor credentials, course descriptions, lesson plans, and facility description. **Accreditation Requirements:** On-site review required. May respond to on-site review. **Renewal:** Every three years. Renewal based on self-assessment and telephone interview. Renewal fee is $25. **Restrictions:** May add or change courses, instructors, and boats in fleet with notification to NASISS. **State Requirements:** Federal or state vessel operator licenses necessary in some states. Vessels may require documentation. **Preparatory Materials:** Publications, tests, and on-the-water evaluations available. **Length of Process:** Six months-three years. **Fees:** $175; must also submit annual fee.

Sleep Disorders Centers

1802

American Sleep Disorders Association Accreditation Committee
American Sleep Disorders Association (ASDA)
1610 14th St., NW, Ste. 300
Rochester, MN 55901
Phone: (507)287-6006
Fax: (507)287-6008

Recipient: Sleep disorders centers and laboratories. Centers are medical facilities providing clinical diagnostic services and treatment to patients; laboratories provide diagnostic and treatment services limited to sleep-related breathing disorders. **Application Procedures:** Self-assessment required. Must document compliance with standards in the following areas: (1) History and Goals; (2) Administration of the Center and Its Relationship to a Host Institution; (3) Medical Structure, including: Consultative evaluations and procedures; Emergency medical plan; Laboratory tests; Medical and sleep history; Medical supervision; Medico-legal responsibility; Patient evaluation; and Physical examination; (4) Facility - Physical Plant, including: Bedrooms; Location; and Personal amenities for patients; (5) Budget - Finances, including: Billing procedures; Fees; Funds to maintain center; Receipts; and Utilization of receipts; (6) Personnel, including: Clerical; Consultants; Professionals; and Technical; (7) Patient Referral, Handling, and Follow-Up, including: Final diagnosis; Follow-up plans and care; Patient acceptance criteria; Patient charts; Patient contact by telephone; Referral sources; Reports from patient evaluation; Scheduling procedures; and Statement of follow-up plan; (8) Polysomnography and Other Monitoring Procedures, including: Criteria for other diagnostic procedures; Recording of PSG; and Use of multiple sleep latency tests; (9) Scoring and Interpretation of Polysomnographic Data, including: Archival storage; and Automated scoring; (10) Equipment, including: Audio/visual monitoring and recording equipment; Emergency resuscitation equipment and supplies; Fire detection; and Polygraphs and other monitoring devices; (11) Experience of the Center; and (12) Educational and Research Activities, including: Continuing education for staff, non-center professionals, students, and the public; and Public relations **Accreditation Requirements:** On-site review required. **Renewal:** Every five years. Renewal based on self-assessment and on-site review. **Preparatory Materials:** *Accreditation Standards and Guidelines* (reference). Accreditation packages for centers and laboratories available.

Social Work

1803

Council on Social Work Education (CSWE)
1600 Duke St., Ste. 300
Alexandria, VA 22314
Phone: (703)683-8080
Fax: (703)683-8099
E-mail: cswo@access.digex.net
Dr. Nancy Randolph, Dir.

Recipient: Baccalaureate and master's degree programs in social work education. **Number of Accredited Institutions:** 511. **Application Procedures:** Self-assessment required. Must document compliance with six standards. Must also submit feasibility information. **Accreditation Requirements:** Must have approval of parent institution, including commitment of resources. On-site review required. Review includes discussion with faculty, staff, administrators, students, and other interested parties. May respond to on-site review. **Renewal:** Every four years (initial); every eight years thereafter. Renewal based on self-assessment and on-site review. Renewal fee is $2525. **Restrictions:** Must report significant changes. **Preparatory Materials:** *Handbook on Accreditation Standards and Procedures* (reference). **Fees:** $5000. **Accredited By:** Commission on Recognition of Postsecondary Accreditation. **Endorsed By:** National Association of Social Workers.

Speech-Language Pathology and Audiology

1804

Educational Standards Board, American Speech-Language-Hearing Association
American Speech-Language-Hearing Association (ASHA)
10801 Rockville Pike
Rockville, MD 20852
Phone: (301)897-5700
Fax: (301)571-0457
Zenobia Bagli Ph.D., Dir.

Recipient: Graduate programs that provide entry-level professional preparation with major emphasis in speech-language pathology and/or audiology. **Number of Accredited Institutions:** 220. **Application Procedures:** Self-assessment, involving administration, instructional staff, students, graduates, employers of graduates,

and other interested parties, required. Must document compliance with standards in the following areas: (1) Administration, including: Administrator qualifications; Admission criteria; Autonomy; Budget; Curriculum; Equipment; Information dissemination; Instructional materials; Library holdings; Non-discrimination policy; Physical facilities, including classrooms, clinic rooms, offices, and research laboratories; Resources; Student evaluation and records; and Support services; (2) Instructional Staff, including: Number of staff; Professional development; Qualifications; and Staff/student ratio; (3) Curriculum, including: Competencies; Evaluation; Faculty input; Scientific and research base of profession; and Sequence; (4) Clinical Education, including: Client base; Clinical observations; Competencies; Guidance and feedback; Supervision; and Welfare of patient; and (5) Program Self-Analysis, including: Evaluation of program; Goals and objectives; and Planning. Must document strengths and weaknesses of program and develop plan for the future. **Accreditation Requirements:** On-site review required. Review includes: Meetings with institution and program administrators and academic and clinical staff; Review of materials and records; and Tour of facilities and library holdings. May respond to on-site review. Possible accreditation decisions are: (1) Award Accreditation; (2) Defer Accreditation Decision, requiring correction of deficiencies within six months; or (3) Withhold Accreditation, for programs in substantion noncompliance with standards. **Renewal:** Every five years (initial); every eight years thereafter. Renewal based on self-assessment and on-site review. Must also submit annual report. **Preparatory Materials:** *ESB Accreditation Manual* and *Standards for Accreditation of Educational Programs in Speech-Language Pathology and Audiology* (references). **Length of Process:** 12-18 months. **Fees:** $2500; $607-$875 (annual fee). **Accredited By:** Commission on Recognition of Postsecondary Accreditation; U.S. Department of Education.

Teacher Education

1805

National Council for Accreditation of Teacher Education (NCATE)
2010 Massachusetts Ave., NW, Ste. 500
Washington, DC 20036-1023
Phone: (202)466-7496
Fax: (202)296-6620
Arthur E. Wise, Pres.

Recipient: Units, within institutions, offering professional teacher education programs at basic and advanced levels. **Number of Accredited Institutions:** 500. **Application Procedures:** Self-assessment required. Must document compliance with standards in the following areas: Academic calendars; Advertising; Catalogs and publications; Curriculum; Evaluation; Facilities, equipment, and supplies; Faculty; Fiscal and administrative capacity; Recruiting and admissions practices; and Student support services. **Accreditation Requirements:** On-site review, verifying information provided in self-assessment, required. Review includes interviews with administrators, faculty, students, and other interested parties. May respond to on-site review. **Renewal:** Renewal based on self-assessment and on-site review. **Restrictions:** Must report substantive changes in the following areas: Addition of branch campus, courses, or programs; Legal status or control of institution; Length of program; and Mission or objectives. **Accredited By:** Commission on Recognition of Postsecondary Accreditation; U.S. Department of Education.

Telephone Helplines

1806

Contact USA Telephone Helpline Accreditation Program
Contact USA
Pouch A
Harrisburg, PA 17105-1300
Phone: (717)232-3501
Fax: (717)232-3505
Joseph M. Lang, Coord.

Recipient: Twenty-four hour telephone helplines and crisis intervention centers. **Number of Accredited Institutions:** 64. **Application Procedures:** Self-assessment required. Must document compliance with standards. **Accreditation Requirements:** On-site review required. May respond to on-site review. **Renewal:** Every five years. Must also submit annual reports. **Preparatory Materials:** *Contact USA Accreditation Manual* (reference). **Fees:** $300.

Television Marketing

1807

NIMA International Self-Certification Program
NIMA International
1201 New York Ave., NW, Ste. 1000
Washington, DC 20005
Phone: (202)962-8342
Fax: (202)962-8300

Recipient: Electronic retailers selling products through "infomercials." **Membership:** Required. **Accreditation Requirements:** Most document compliance with standards in the following areas: (1) Sponsorship and Identification, requiring each "infomercial" to announce that it is a paid advertisement and to clearly identify sponsor; (2) Program Production, requiring: Adequate inventory; Age appropriateness; Conformation to community standards regarding indecent or offensive material; and Truthfulness; (3) Product/Claims Substantiation, including: Proof of expert, objective, and comparative advertising claims; and Truthfulness regarding demonstrations of quality of product or competition; (4) Testimonials and Endorsements, including: Disclosure of material connection between endorser and product; Identifying credentials of experts; and Testimonials from consumers; (5) Ordering Prices, 900 Numbers, and Continuity Programs, including: Disclosure of additional costs; Disclosure of costs of 900 number phone calls; and Informing consumers of possible future required or voluntary purchases; and (6) Warranties, Guarantees, and Refunds, requiring accurate portrayal of warranties, refund policies, and money-back guarantees. Must submit videotape of "infomercial." **Preparatory Materials:** *Marketing Guidelines* (reference). **Fees:** $100 (per "infomercial").

Theater

1808

Commission on Accreditation, National Association of Schools of Theatre
National Association of Schools of Theatre (NAST)
11250 Roger Bacon Dr., Ste. 21
Reston, VA 22090
Phone: (703)437-0700
Fax: (703)437-6312
Samuel Hope, Exec.Dir.

Recipient: Institutions and units within institutions offering associate, baccalaureate, and/or graduate degree programs in theatre and theatre-related disciplines; and non-degree granting institutions offering programs in these areas. **Application Procedures:** Self-assessment required. Must document compliance with standards in the following areas: (1) Mission, Goals, and Objectives, including: Appropriateness; Creative work and research; Dissemination; Educational and artistic decision-making; Evaluation; Institutional objectives; Long-range planning; Operational decision-making; Performance; Policies and procedures; Resources; Service; Students; Teaching; and Written statement; (2) Size and Scope, including: Enrollment; Objectives; Resources; and Staff size; (3) Finances, including: Allocation of resources; Audits; Financial management; Financial records; Financial statements; Long-range planning; Objectives; and Tuition, fees, and other charges; (4) Governance and Administration, including: Administrative personnel; Autonomy; Board of trustees; Communications; Continuity; Faculty input; Long-range planning; Objectives; Organization; Policies and procedures; Public representation; and Student input; (5) Faculty and Staff, including: Appointment, evaluation, and advancement; Faculty development; Graduate teaching assistants; Loads; Number and distribution; Qualifications; Student/faculty ratios; and Support staff; (6) Facilities, Equipment, and Safety, including: Accessibility; Acoustical treatments; Administrative offices; Audio and video playback equipment; Audio/visual aids; Auditoriums; Budget; Classrooms; Computers; Electronic instruments and equipment; Faculty teaching studios and offices; Lighting equipment; Maintenance; Planning; Safety; Sets and costumes; Storage facilities; Student practice rooms; and Supplies; (7) Library, including: Collections; Facilities; Finance; Governance; Personnel; and Services; (8) Recruitment, Admission-Retention, Record Keeping, and Advisement, including:

Counseling services; Objectives; Requirements; and Student records; (8) Published Materials, including: Catalog; and Published documents; (9) Community Involvement and Articulation with Other Schools, including: Arts agencies; Local schools; and Performing organizations; (10) Evaluation, Planning, and Projections, including: Assessment techniques; Curriculum; Objectives; Operational conditions; Programs and services; Resource allocation and development; Size and scope; and Student achievement and evaluation; and (11) Credit and Time Requirements, including: Awarding credit; Program lengths; Published policies; and Transfer of credit. Proprietary schools must meet additional standards. **Accreditation Requirements:** Degree granting institutions must have graduated one class; non-degree-granting institutions must have been in operation for three years. Undergraduate programs must meet standards in the following areas: Academic studies; Admissions; Advanced standing; Curricular studies; Electives; General studies; Liberal arts degrees; Majors and areas of emphasis; Performance; Professional degrees; Repertory; Residence; Theatre studies; and Theoretical studies. Undergraduate degrees offered in the following areas: Acting; Design and Technology; Directing; Drama therapy; Film and video production; History and criticism; Playwriting; Theatre education; Theatre and Music; and Theatre for Youth. Graduate programs must meet standards in the following areas: Admissions; Breadth of competence; Course work; Credits; Degree requirements and procedures; Evaluation of performance and production; Faculty; Final project; Functions of graduate study; Graduation requirements; Language or other proficiencies; Practice-oriented degrees; Preparation for teaching; Research-oriented degrees; Residence; Resources; Standardized national examination; and Statement and publication of objectives and resources. Master's degrees offered in the following areas: Acting; Arts management; Costume design; Directing; Film and video production; Lighting design; Musical theatre; Playwriting; Scene design; Stage design (general); Theatre technology (design, costume, or sound); and Theatre for youth. Doctorate degrees offered in the following areas: Education in theatre; and Philosophy in theatre. Standards also available for programs in the following areas: Arts administration; Business; Musical theatre; Opera; Singer-actor; and Voice. On-site review, verifying information provided in self-assessment, required. Review includes interviews with administrators, faculty, students, and other interested parties. May respond to

on-site review. Possible accreditation decisions are: (1) Accreditation; (2) Probationary Status, requiring correction of deficiencies within five years; or (3) Denial, for programs in substantial non-compliance with standards. **Renewal:** Every five years (initial); every ten years thereafter. Renewal based on self-assessment and on-site review. Must also submit annual reports. **Restrictions:** Must report changes in curriculum. **State Requirements:** Must hold appropriate licenses or charters. **Preparatory Materials:** *Handbook of the National Association of Schools of Theatre* (reference). **Fees:** Application fee, plus actual cost of on-site review; must also submit annual fee. **Accredited By:** Commission on Recognition of Postsecondary Accreditation; U.S. Department of Education.

Trade and Technical Schools

1809

Accrediting Commission of Career Schools and Colleges of Technology (ACCSCT)
Career College Association
750 First St., NE, Ste. 905
Washington, DC 20002-4242
Phone: (202)336-6743
Fax: (202)842-2585
Alan Rosebrook, Dir.

Recipient: Private, residential two-year colleges and schools offering instruction in occupational, trade, and technical education. **Application Procedures:** Self-assessment required. Must document compliance with standards in the following areas: (1) Admissions Policies and Practices, including: Educational qualifications of potential students; and Responsibilities and demands of educational program; (2) Advertising and Promotion, including: Employment information; Ethical standards; Financial aid; and Recruitment; (3) Employment Qualifications, requiring that education offered by institution prepare students for employment in their field; (4) Enrollment Agreement, requiring that enrollment agreements clearly outline obligations and responsibilities of institution and students; (5) Faculty, including: Credentials; Retention; and Training; (6) Financial Stability and Responsibility, requiring institution to be financially sound with resources necessary to carry out educational objectives; (7) Instructional Materials, including: Library resources; and Training materials; (8) Placement, covering employment of graduates; (9)

Student Complaints, requiring published procedures for handling student complaints; (10) Student Progress, including: Retention rates; and Student attendance; (11) Student Recruitment, covering recruiting practices and procedures; and (12) Tuition and Refund Policies, requiring disclosure of tuition and refund policies. Self-assessment must include the following: Admissions and advising/testing procedures; Advertising samples; Complaints filed against institution in past five years; Current financial statements; Educational courses and program syllabi; Enrollment agreement; Enrollment completion data; Government initiated investigations of institution; Instructor qualifications and evaluations; Mission statement; Most recent state or regional program review; Organizational charts; Personnel reports for each instructor, listing educational backgrounds and work experience; Published student complaint procedures; School catalog; and Student graduation and job placement rates. Must attend accreditation seminar. **Accreditation Requirements:** Programs must: (1) Be open to public; (2) Have been in operation for two years; (3) Have graduated one class of students from its longest program; and (4) Have private pay tuition-based students. May offer both academic and occupational degree programs. On-site review, verifying information provided in self-assessment, required. Review team interviews institution's administration and staff, instructors, students, graduates, and employers to evaluate conditions, educational programs, and effectiveness. May respond to on-site review. Possible accreditation decisions are: (1) Full Accreditation; (2) Accreditation With Stipulations, requiring correction of deficiencies; (3) Denial of Accreditation, for schools in substantial non-compliance with standards. **Renewal:** Every six years (maximum). Must also submit annual reports. **Restrictions:** Must report: Addition of any branch or separate classroom facilities; Change of name, location, or ownership; and New educational programs. **State Requirements:** Must be licensed by state. **Fees:** $5000; must also submit annual fee based on gross tuition. **Accredited By:** Commission on Recognition of Postsecondary Accreditation; U.S. Department of Education.

1810

Accrediting Commission for Trade and Technical Schools (ACTTS)

Career College Association
750 First St., NE, Ste. 905
Washington, DC 20002-4242
Phone: (202)336-6743
Fax: (202)842-2585

Recipient: Private, postsecondary career colleges and schools. **Application Procedures:** Self-assessment required. Must document compliance with standards in the following areas: (1) Admissions Policies and Practices, including: Educational qualifications of potential students; and Responsibilities and demands of educational program; (2) Advertising and Promotion, including: Employment information; Ethical standards; Financial aid; and Recruitment; (3) Employment Qualifications, requiring that education offered by institution prepare students for employment in their field; (4) Enrollment Agreement, requiring that enrollment agreements clearly outline obligations and responsibilities of institution and students; (5) Faculty, including: Credentials; Retention; and Training; (6) Financial Stability and Responsibility, requiring institution to be financially sound with resources necessary to carry out educational objectives; (7) Instructional Materials, including: Library resources; and Training materials; (8) Placement, covering employment of graduates; (9) Student Complaints, requiring published procedures for handling student complaints; (10) Student Progress, including: Retention rates; and Student attendance; (11) Student Recruitment, covering recruiting practices and procedures; and (12) Tuition and Refund Policies, requiring disclosure of tuition and refund policies. Self-assessment must include the following: Admissions and advising/testing procedures; Advertising samples; Complaints filed against institution in past five years; Current financial statements; Educational courses and program syllabi; Enrollment agreement; Enrollment completion data; Government initiated investigations of institution; Instructor qualifications and evaluations; Mission statement; Most recent state or regional program review; Organizational charts; Personnel reports for each instructor listing educational backgrounds and work experience; Published student complaint procedures; School catalog; and Student graduation and job placement rates. Must attend accreditation seminar. **Accreditation Requirements:** Programs must: (1) Be open to public; (2) Have been in operation for two years; (3) Have graduated one class of students from its longest program; and (4) Have private

pay tuition-based students. May offer both academic and occupational degree programs. On-site review, verifying information provided in self-assessment, required. Review team interviews institution's administration and staff, instructors, students, graduates, and employers to evaluate conditions, educational programs, and effectiveness. May respond to on-site review. Possible accreditation decisions are: (1) Full Accreditation; (2) Accreditation With Stipulations, requiring correction of deficiencies; and (3) Denial of Accreditation, for schools in substantial noncompliance with standards. **Renewal:** Every six years (maximum). Must also submit annual reports. **Restrictions:** Must report: Addition of any branch or separate classroom facilities; Change of name, location, or ownership; and New educational programs. **State Requirements:** Must be licensed by state. **Fees:** $5000; must also submit annual fee based on enrollment.

Truck Driving

1811

Professional Truck Driver Institute of America (PTDIA)

8788 Elk Grove Blvd., Ste. 20
Elk Grove, CA 95624
Phone: (916)686-5146
Fax: (916)686-4878
Edward E. Kynaston, Pres.

Recipient: Public and private vocational truck driving schools. **Number of Accredited Institutions:** 34. **Application Procedures:** Must document compliance with 107 standards and submit exhibits. **Accreditation Requirements:** On-site review required. May respond to on-site review. **Renewal:** Every two years. Renewal based on review of training program. Renewal fee is $1500. **Preparatory Materials:** Curriculum manual and procedures and standards. **Length of Process:** 30-60 days. **Fees:** $3500.

Veterinary Medicine

1812

Committee on Veterinary Technician Education and Activities of the American Veterinary Medical Association (CVTEA)

American Veterinary Medical Association (AVMA)
1931 N. Meacham Rd., Ste. 100
Schaumburg, IL 60173-4360
Phone: (708)925-8070
Fax: (708)925-1329
Toll Free: (800)248-AVMA

Recipient: Two-year programs for veterinary technicians. **Number of Accredited Institutions:** 66. **Accreditation Requirements:** Core curriculum includes: Applied mathematics; Biological science; Communication skills; Fundamentals of chemistry; and Humanities or liberal arts. Required areas of study are: Anesthetic nursing and monitoring, including instrumentation; Animal care and management; Animal husbandry, including restraint, sex determination, and species and breed identification; Animal microbiology and sanitation; Animal nutrition and feeding; Biochemistry; Clinical experience in veterinary practice; Comparative animal husbandry; Diseases and nursing of companion animals, food production animals, horses, and laboratory animals; Ethics and jurisprudence in veterinary medicine; Medical terminology; Necroscopy techniques; Orientation to vocation; Pharmacology for animal technicians; Principles of veterinary anatomy and physiology; Radiography using live animal patients; Surgical nursing and assisting, including instrumentation; Veterinary clinical biochemistries; Veterinary office management; Veterinary parasitology; and Veterinary urinalysis. Possible accreditation decisions are: (1) Full Accreditation; (2) Provisional Accreditation, requiring progress toward correcting deficiencies; (3) Probational Accreditation, requiring progress toward correcting deficiencies; or (4) Accreditation Withheld, for programs in substantial noncompliance with standards. **Accredited By:** U.S. Department of Education.

1813

Council on Education of the American Veterinary Medical Association
American Veterinary Medical Association (AVMA)
1931 N. Meacham Rd., Ste. 100
Schaumburg, IL 60173-4360
Phone: (708)925-8070
Fax: (708)925-1329
Toll Free: (800)248-AVMA
Dr. Edward R. Ames Ph.D., Dir.

Recipient: Programs leading to Doctor of Veterinary Medicine (DVM) degree. **Number of Accredited Institutions:** 31. **Application Procedures:** Self-assessment, including administration, alumni, faculty, and students, required. Must document compliance with standards in the following areas: (1) Organization, including: Nondiscrimination policies; and Relationship with parent institution; (2) Finances, including: Acquisition and maintenance of necessary equipment; Auxiliary operations; Expenditures; Financial resources; and Revenue; (3) Physical Facilities and Equipment, including: Buildings; Classrooms; Equipment; Hospital affiliation; Isolation facilities; Library; Maintenance; Offices; Research laboratories; Safety; Seminar rooms; Storage space; and Teaching laboratories; (4) Clinical Resources, including: Ambulatory/field service program; Central supply; Client relations; Clinical experiences; Clinical laboratories; Clinical rotations; Evaluation; Goals and expectations; Herd/flock health program; Medical records; Necropsy; Patient availability; Patient management; Pharmacy; Radiology; Satellite clinics; Student participation; Teaching hospital; Teaching methods; and Teaching subsidies; (5) Library and Learning Resources, including: Accessibility; Budget; Collection; Hours; Instructional and research materials; Location; Organization; Relation to university library; Space and seating capacity; and Staff; (6) Enrollment, including: Graduate students; Interns and residents; Other educational programs; Students from non-veterinary programs; Undergraduates; and Veterinary medical program; (7) Admission, including: Policies and procedures; Requirements; and Student selection process; (8) Faculty, including: Compensation; Professional growth; Public service; Qualifications; Research; Retention; Teaching skills; and Tenure; (9) Curriculum, including: Content; Courses; Diversity; Evaluation; Humane animal care; Length; Objectives; Planning; Preceptorship and externship programs; Review; and Values, attitudes, and behaviors; (10) Continuing Education, including: Programs held on campus; and Programs presented by faculty; and (11) Research and Postgraduate Education, including: Advanced degrees; Internships; Research facilities and resources; Research programs; Residencies; and Specialty board certification. Must document strengths and weaknesses of program and describe plan for improvement. **Accreditation Requirements:** Curriculum should cover: Analysis of population characteristics of animal biology and clinical medicine; Biological basis of normal function; Biological mechanisms by which disordered states are returned to normal; Diagnosis and prevention of disease; Mechanisms that establish homeostasis; Natural history and manifestations of disease in individual animals and in populations of animals; Pathophysiology of organ systems; Principles of maintenance of health; Relationships between human and animal health; and Therapeutic and management strategies. On-site review, verifying information provided in self-assessment, required. Review includes: Meetings with dean, department heads, faculty members, librarian, and students; Review of case records; and Tour of buildings and facilities. On-site review report documents strengths and weaknesses of program. May respond to on-site review. Possible accreditation decisions are: (1) Accreditation; (2) Limited Accreditation, requiring correction of deficiencies within five years; or (3) Accreditation Withheld, for programs in substantial noncompliance with standards. **Renewal:** Every seven years (maximum). Renewal based on self-assessment and on-site review. Must also submit annual reports. **Restrictions:** Must report fundamental changes in administration, organization, association with parent institution, curriculum, faculty, instructional program, or stated objectives. **Preparatory Materials:** *Accreditation Policies and Procedures* and *Essentials of an Accredited or Approved College of Veterinary Medicine* (references). **Fees:** $5000, plus actual cost of on-site review. **Accredited By:** Commission on Recognition of Post-secondary Accreditation; U.S. Department of Education.

Profiles of Certifying Bodies

This section lists, in alphabetical order, the certifying bodies covered in the *Certification Programs* section. Following each certifying body is an alphabetical list of the certifications offered.

AACE International
209 Prairie Ave., Ste. 100
Morgantown, WV 26507
Phone: (304)296-8444
Fax: (304)291-5728
Toll Free: (800)858-COST

- Certified Cost Consultant (CCC)
- Certified Cost Engineer (CCE)

Academy of Board Certified Environmental Professionals (ABCEP)
5165 MacArthur Blvd., NW
Washington, DC 20016-3315
Phone: (202)966-8974
Fax: (202)966-1977

- Certified Environmental Professional (CEP)

Academy of Certified Archivists (ACA)
600 S. Federal St., Ste. 504
Chicago, IL 60605
Phone: (312)922-0140
Fax: (312)347-1452

- Certified Archivist (CA)

Academy of Certified Baccalaureate Social Workers (ACBSW)
National Association of Social Workers
750 First St., NE
Washington, DC 20002
Phone: (202)336-8232
Fax: (202)336-8327
Toll Free: (800)638-8799

- Member, Academy of Certified Baccalaureate Social Workers

Academy of Certified Social Workers (ACSW)
c/o National Association of Social Workers
750 First St., NE, Ste. 700
Washington, DC 20002
Phone: (202)336-8222
Fax: (202)336-8313
Toll Free: (800)638-8799

- Member of the Academy of Certified Social Workers

Academy of Health Information Professionals
c/o Medical Library Association
Six N. Michigan Ave., Ste. 300
Chicago, IL 60602-4805
Phone: (312)419-9094
Fax: (312)419-8950

- Distinguished Member, Academy of Health Information Professionals
- Member, Academy of Health Information Professionals
- Provisional Member, Academy of Health Information Professionals
- Senior Member, Academy of Health Information Professionals

Academy of Laser Dentistry (ALD)
401 N. Michigan Ave.
Chicago, IL 60611-4267
Phone: (312)644-6610
Fax: (312)321-6869

- Academy of Laser Dentistry, Category I Certification
- Academy of Laser Dentistry, Category II Certification
- Academy of Laser Dentistry, Category III (Master Status) Certification

Academy of Life Underwriting
c/o Karl Friedman, AALU
Allstate Insurance Company
1411 Lake Cook Rd.
Deerfield, IL 60015
Phone: (708)948-6702

- Associate, Academy of Life Underwriting (AALU)
- Certificate in Life Underwriting
- Fellow, Academy of Life Underwriting (FALU)

Academy of Security Educators and Trainees (ASET)
c/o Dr. Richard W. Kobetz
Rte. 2, Box 3644
Berryville, VA 22611
Phone: (703)955-1129

- Certified Security Trainer (CST)

Accreditation Council for Accountancy and Taxation (ACAT)
1010 N. Fairfax St.
Alexandria, VA 22314-1574
Phone: (703)549-2228
Fax: (703)549-2984

- Accredited in Accountancy
- Accredited Tax Advisor
- Accredited Tax Preparer

Accredited Review Appraisers Council (ARAC)
303 W. Cypress St.
PO Box 12528
San Antonio, TX 78212
Phone: (210)225-2897
Fax: (210)225-8450
Toll Free: (800)486-3676

- Accredited in Appraisal Review (AAR)

Addictions Nursing Certification Board (ANCB)
4101 Lake Boone Trail, Ste. 201
Raleigh, NC 27607
Phone: (919)783-5871
Fax: (919)787-4916

- Certified Addictions Registered Nurse (CARN)

Aerobics and Fitness Association of America (AFAA)
15250 Ventura Blvd., Ste. 200
Sherman Oaks, CA 91403-3297
Phone: (818)905-0040
Fax: (818)990-5468

- Adaptive Fitness Instructor Certification
- AFAA Primary Certification
- Certification for Personal Trainers and Fitness Counselors
- First-Aid and Emergency Response Certification
- Low Impact/Weighted Workout Certification
- Step Reebok Certification
- Teaching the Overweight Certification
- Weightroom/Resistance Training Certification

Air Conditioning Contractors of America (ACCA)
1712 New Hampshire Ave., NW
Washington, DC 20009
Phone: (202)483-9370
Fax: (202)232-8545

- Refrigerant Transition and Recovery Type I Certification
- Refrigerant Transition and Recovery Type II Certification
- Refrigerant Transition and Recovery Type III Certification
- Refrigerant Transition and Recovery Universal Certification

American Academy of Environmental Engineers (AAEE)
130 Holiday Ct., Ste. 100
Annapolis, MD 21401
Phone: (410)266-3311
Fax: (410)266-7653

- Diplomate, Environmental Engineer

American Academy of Environmental Medicine
4510 W. 89th St.
Prairie Village, KS 66207
Phone: (913)341-0765
Fax: (913)341-3625

- Fellow of the American Academy of Environmental Medicine (AAEM)

American Academy of Procedural Coders (AAPC)
2144 S. Highland Dr., Ste. 100
Salt Lake City, UT 84106
Phone: (801)487-5590
Fax: (801)485-7803
Toll Free: (800)626-CODE

- Certified Professional Coder (CPC)
- Certified Professional Coder - Hospital (CPC-H)

American Academy of Sanitarians (AAS)
829 Brookside Dr.
Miami, OK 74354
Phone: (918)540-2025

- Diplomate of the American Academy of Sanitarians (DAAS)

American Amateur Racquetball Association (AARA)
1685 W. Uintah
Colorado Springs, CO 80904-2921
Phone: (719)635-5396
Fax: (719)635-0685

- National Referee (Level III)
- Regional Referee (Level II)
- State Referee (Level I)

American Association of Airport Executives (AAAE)
4212 King St.
Alexandria, VA 22303
Phone: (703)824-0504
Fax: (703)820-1395

- Accredited Airport Executive (A.A.E.)

American Association of Automatic Door Manufacturers (AAADM)
1300 Sumner Ave.
Cleveland, OH 44115-2851
Phone: (216)241-7333
Fax: (216)241-0105

- Certified Automatic Door Installation Inspector

American Association of Certified Appraisers (AACA)
800 Compton Rd., Ste. 10
Cincinnati, OH 45231
Phone: (513)729-1400
Fax: (513)729-1401
Toll Free: (800)543-AACA

- Certified Appraiser Consultant (CA-C)
- Certified Appraiser Farm and Land (CA-FL)
- Certified Appraiser Residential (CA-R)
- Certified Appraiser Senior (CA-S)
- Certified Form Appraiser (CF-A)

American Association of Code Enforcement (AACE)
5360 Workman Mill Rd.
Whittier, CA 90601-2298

- AACE Housing Officer
- AACE Zoning Officer

American Association of Critical-Care Nurses (AACN)
101 Columbia
Aliso Viejo, CA 92656
Phone: (714)362-2000
Fax: (714)362-2022
Toll Free: (800)899-AACN

- CCRN

American Association of Dental Consultants (AADC)
919 Deer Park Ave.
North Babylon, NY 11703
Phone: (516)587-5049
Fax: (913)749-1140
Toll Free: (800)896-0707

- Certified Dental Consultant

American Association of Direct Human Service Personnel (AADHSP)
1832 Little Rd.
Parma, MI 49269
Phone: (517)531-5820
Toll Free: (800)333-6894

- Certified Human Service Provider (CHSP)
- Certified Service Facilitator (CSF)

American Association of Family and Consumer Sciences (AAFCS)
1555 King St.
Alexandria, VA 22314
Phone: (703)706-4600
Fax: (703)706-4663

- Certified Home Economist (CHE)

American Association for Laboratory Animal Science (AALAS)
70 Timber Creek Dr.
Cordova, TN 38018-4233
Phone: (901)754-8620
Fax: (901)753-0046

- Assistant Laboratory Animal Technician (ALAT)
- Laboratory Animal Technician (LAT)
- Laboratory Animal Technologist (LATG)

American Association of Medical Assistants (AAMA)
20 N. Wacker Dr., Ste. 1575
Chicago, IL 60606-2903
Phone: (312)424-3100
Fax: (312)899-1259
Toll Free: (800)228-2262

- Certified Medical Assistant (CMA)

American Association for Medical Transcription (AAMT)

3460 Oakdale Rd., Ste. M
PO Box 576187
Modesto, CA 95357-6187
Phone: (209)551-0883
Fax: (209)551-9317
Toll Free: (800)982-2182

- Certified Medical Transcriptionist (CMT)

American Association of Nutritional Consultants (AANC)

880 Canarios Ct., No. 210
Chula Vista, CA 91910
Phone: (619)482-8533

- Certified Nutritional Consultant (CNC)

American Association of Professional Landmen

4100 Fossil Creek Blvd.
Ft. Worth, TX 76137-2791
Phone: (817)847-7700
Fax: (817)847-7704

- Certified Professional Landman (CPL)

American Association of Psychiatric Technicians (AAPT)

PO Box 14014
Phoenix, AZ 85063-4014
Phone: (602)873-1890
Fax: (602)873-1890
Toll Free: (800)391-7589

- Nationally Certified Psychiatric Technician, Level 1 (NCPT1)
- Nationally Certified Psychiatric Technician, Level 2 (NCPT2)
- Nationally Certified Psychiatric Technician, Level 3 (NCPT3)
- Nationally Certified Psychiatric Technician, Level 4 (NCPT4)

American Board of Abdominal Surgery

675 Main St.
Melrose, MA 02176
Phone: (617)655-6101

- Diplomate of the American Board of Abdominal Surgery

American Board of Allergy and Immunology (ABAI)

3624 Market St.
Philadelphia, PA 19104-2675
Phone: (215)349-9466
Fax: (215)222-8669

- Certificate of Added Qualification in Clinical and Laboratory Immunology
- Diplomate of the American Board of Allergy and Immunology

American Board of Anesthesiology (ABA)

100 Constitution Plaza
Hartford, CT 06103-1796
Phone: (203)522-9857
Fax: (203)522-6626

- Board Eligible, American Board of Anesthesiology
- Diplomate of the American Board of Anesthesiology
- Diplomate of the American Board of Anesthesiology with Special Qualifications in Critical Care Medicine
- Diplomate of the American Board of Anesthesiology with Special Qualifications in Pain Management

American Board of Behavioral Psychology

2100 E. Broadway, Ste. 313
Columbia, MO 65201-6082
Phone: (314)875-1267
Fax: (314)443-1199
Toll Free: (800)255-7792

- Diplomate in Behavioral Psychology

American Board of Bioanalysis (ABB)

818 Olive St., Ste. 918
St. Louis, MO 63101-1598
Phone: (314)241-1445
Fax: (314)241-1449

- Bioanalyst Clinical Laboratory Director (BCLD)
- Bioanalyst Laboratory Manager (BLM)
- Clinical Consultant (CC)
- General Supervisor (GS)
- High-Complexity Clinical Laboratory Director (HCLD)
- Moderate-Complexity Clinical Laboratory Director (MCLD)
- Technical Consultant (TC)
- Technical Supervisor (TS)

American Board of Cardiovascular Perfusion (ABCP)

207 N. 25th Ave.
Hattiesburg, MS 39401
Phone: (601)582-3309

- Certified Clinical Perfusionist (CCP)

American Board of Certification in Anesthesiology

804 Main St., Ste. D
Forest Park, GA 30050
Phone: (404)363-8263
Fax: (404)361-2285
Toll Free: (800)447-9397

- Diplomate of the American Board of Certification in Anesthesiology
- Diplomate of American Board of Certification in Anesthesiology with Added Qualifications in Pain Management

American Board of Certification in Dermatology

804 Main St., Ste. D
Forest Park, GA 30050
Phone: (404)363-8263
Fax: (404)361-2285
Toll Free: (800)447-9397

- Diplomate of the American Board of Certification in Dermatology

American Board of Certification in Family Practice

804 Main St., Ste. D
Forest Park, GA 30050
Phone: (404)363-8263
Fax: (404)361-2285
Toll Free: (800)447-9397

- Certification in Sports Medicine

American Board of Certification in Internal Medicine

804 Main St., Ste. D
Forest Park, GA 30050
Phone: (404)363-8263
Fax: (404)361-2285
Toll Free: (800)447-9397

- Diplomate of the American Board of Certification in Internal Medicine

American Board of Certification in Neurology/Psychiatry

804 Main St., Ste. D
Forest Park, GA 30050
Phone: (404)363-8263
Fax: (404)361-2285
Toll Free: (800)447-9397

- Diplomate of the American Board of Certification in Neurology/Psychiatry

American Board of Certification in Orthopedic Surgery

804 Main St., Ste. D
Forest Park, GA 30050
Phone: (404)363-8263
Fax: (404)361-2285
Toll Free: (800)447-9397

- Diplomate of the American Board of Certification in Orthopedic Surgery

American Board for Certification in Orthotics and Prosthetics (ABC)

1650 King St., Ste. 500
Alexandria, VA 22314-2747
Phone: (703)836-7114
Fax: (703)836-0838

- Certified Orthotist (CO)
- Certified Prosthetist (CP)
- Certified Prosthetist/Orthotist (CPO)

American Board of Certification in Radiology
804 Main St., Ste. D
Forest Park, GA 30050
Phone: (404)363-8263
Fax: (404)361-2285
Toll Free: (800)447-9397

- Diplomate of the American Board of Certification in Radiology
- Diplomate in Radiation Oncology of the American Board of Certification in Radiology

American Board of Chelation Therapy (ABCT)
70 W. Huron St.
Chicago, IL 60610
Phone: (312)787-ABCT
Fax: (312)266-7291

- Diplomate of the American Board of Chelation Therapy

American Board of Chiropractic Orthopedics
c/o James Brandt, DC
330 Northdale Blvd.
Coon Rapids, MN 55448
Phone: (612)755-4300

- Board Eligible, American Board of Chiropractic Orthopedics
- Diplomate of the American Board of Chiropractic Orthopedics (DABCO)

American Board of Chiropractic Thermologists
c/o Phillip L. Smith, DC
318 S. Burnside Ave.
Gonzales, LA 70737
Phone: (504)644-8671

- Board Certified Thermographer

American Board of Clinical Chemistry (ABCC)
2101 L St., NW, Ste. 202
Washington, DC 20037-1526
Fax: (202)887-5093
Toll Free: (800)892-1400

- Diplomate of the American Board of Clinical Chemistry (DABCC)

American Board of Clinical Neuropsychology
2100 E. Broadway, Ste. 313
Columbia, MO 65201-6082
Phone: (314)875-1267
Fax: (314)443-1199
Toll Free: (800)255-7792

- Diplomate in Clinical Neuropsychology

American Board of Clinical Psychology
2100 E. Broadway, Ste. 313
Columbia, MO 65201-6082
Phone: (314)875-1267
Fax: (314)443-1199
Toll Free: (800)255-7792

- Diplomate in Clinical Psychology

American Board of Colon and Rectal Surgery (ABCRS)
20600 Eureka Rd., Ste. 713
Taylor, MI 48180
Phone: (313)282-9400
Fax: (313)282-9402

- Diplomate of the American Board of Colon and Rectal Surgery

American Board of Counseling Psychology
2100 E. Broadway, Ste. 313
Columbia, MO 65201-6082
Phone: (314)875-1267
Fax: (314)443-1199
Toll Free: (800)255-7792

- Diplomate in Counseling Psychology

American Board of Criminalistics (ABC)
PO Box 669
Colorado Springs, CO 80901-0669

- Diplomate of the American Board of Criminalistics
- Fellow of the American Board of Criminalistics

American Board of Dental Public Health
1321 NW 47th Terrace
Gainesville, FL 32605
Phone: (904)378-6301

- Diplomate of the American Board of Dental Public Health

American Board of Dermatology (ABD)
Henry Ford Hospital
Detroit, MI 48202-2689
Phone: (313)874-1088
Fax: (313)872-3221

- Diplomate of the American Board of Dermatology
- Diplomate of the American Board of Dermatology with Special Qualification in Clinical and Laboratory Dermatological Immunology
- Diplomate of the American Board of Dermatology with Special Qualification in Dermatopathology

American Board of Emergency Medicine (ABEM)
3000 Coolidge Rd.
East Lansing, MI 48823-6319
Phone: (517)332-4800
Fax: (517)332-2234

- Diplomate of the American Board of Emergency Medicine

American Board of Endodontics (ABE)
211 E. Chicago Ave., Ste. 100
Chicago, IL 60611
Phone: (312)266-7310

- Board Eligible, American Board of Endodontics
- Diplomate of the American Board of Endodontics

American Board of Environmental Medicine (ABEM)
4510 W. 89th St.
Prairie Village, KS 66207
Phone: (913)341-0765
Fax: (913)341-3625

- Diplomate of the American Board of Environmental Medicine

American Board of Examiners in Pastoral Counseling (ABEPC)
261 Spring St.
Cheshire, CT 06410
Phone: (203)271-3733
Toll Free: (800)358-9966
E-mail: CompuServe 72163,2447

- Counselor, American Board of Examiners in Pastoral Counseling
- Diplomate, American Board of Examiners in Pastoral Counseling
- Fellow, American Board of Examiners in Pastoral Counseling

American Board of Examiners in Psychodrama, Sociometry, and Group Psychotherapy (ABEPSGP)
PO Box 15572
Washington, DC 20003-0572
Phone: (202)483-0514

- Certified Practitioner (CP)
- Trainer, Educator, Practitioner (TEP)

American Board of Family Practice (ABFP)
2228 Young Dr.
Lexington, KY 40505-4294
Phone: (606)269-5626
Fax: (606)266-9699

- American Board of Family Practice Certificate of Added Qualification in Geriatric Medicine
- American Board of Family Practice Certificate of Added Qualification in Sports Medicine
- Diplomate of the American Board of Family Practice

American Board of Family Psychology

2100 E. Broadway, Ste. 313
Columbia, MO 65201-6082
Phone: (314)875-1267
Fax: (314)443-1199
Toll Free: (800)255-7792

- Diplomate in Family Psychology

American Board of Forensic Anthropology (ABFA)

Sorg Associates
91 Mill St.
PO Box 70
Orono, ME 04473-0070
Phone: (207)866-7865
Fax: (207)866-3608

- Diplomate of the American Board of Forensic Anthropology (DABFA)

American Board of Forensic Document Examiners (ABFDE)

7887 San Felipe, Ste. 122
Houston, TX 77063
Phone: (417)863-8930
Fax: (417)863-8941

- Diplomate of the American Board of Forensic Document Examiners

American Board of Forensic Examiners (ABFE)

300 S. Jefferson Ave., Ste. 411
Springfield, MO 65806
Phone: (417)863-8930
Fax: (417)863-8941
Toll Free: (800)4AE-XPERT

- Board Certified Forensic Examiner (BCFE)
- Fellow, American Board of Forensic Examiners

American Board of Forensic Psychology

2100 E. Broadway, Ste. 313
Columbia, MO 65201-6082
Phone: (314)875-1267
Fax: (314)443-1199
Toll Free: (800)255-7792

- Diplomate in Forensic Psychology

American Board of Genetic Counseling

9650 Rockville Pike
Bethesda, MD 20814-3998
Phone: (301)571-1825
Fax: (301)571-1895

- Certified Genetic Counselor (CGC)

American Board of Health Physics (ABHP)

1313 Dolley Madison Blvd., Ste. 402
McLean, VA 22101
Phone: (703)790-1745
Fax: (703)790-9063

- Certified Health Physicist (CHP)

American Board of Health Psychology

2100 E. Broadway, Ste. 313
Columbia, MO 65201-6082
Phone: (314)875-1267
Fax: (314)443-1199
Toll Free: (800)255-7792

- Diplomate in Health Psychology

American Board of Industrial Hygiene (ABIH)

4600 W. Saginaw, Ste. 101
Lansing, MI 48917-2737
Phone: (517)321-2638

- Certified Industrial Hygienist (CIH)
- Industrial Hygienist in Training (IHIT)

American Board of Industrial/Organizational Psychology

2100 E. Broadway, Ste. 313
Columbia, MO 65201-6082
Phone: (314)875-1267
Fax: (314)443-1199
Toll Free: (800)255-7792

- Diplomate in Industrial/Organizational Psychology

American Board of Internal Medicine (ABIM)

3624 Market St.
Philadelphia, PA 19104-2675
Phone: (215)243-1500
Fax: (215)382-4702
Toll Free: (800)441-ABIM

- Board Eligible, American Board of Internal Medicine
- Diplomate of the American Board of Internal Medicine
- Diplomate of the American Board of Internal Medicine with Added Qualifications in Adolescent Medicine
- Diplomate of the American Board of Internal Medicine with Added Qualifications in Clinical and Laboratory Immunology
- Diplomate of the American Board of Internal Medicine with Added Qualifications in Critical Care Medicine
- Diplomate of the American Board of Internal Medicine with Added Qualifications in Geriatric Medicine
- Diplomate of the American Board of Internal Medicine with Added Qualifications in Sports Medicine
- Diplomate in Cardiovascular Disease of the American Board of Internal Medicine
- Diplomate in Cardiovascular Disease of the American Board of Internal Medicine with Added Qualifications in Clinical Cardiac Electrophysiology
- Diplomate in Endocrinology, Diabetes, and Metabolism of the American Board of Internal Medicine
- Diplomate in Gastroenterology of the American Board of Internal Medicine
- Diplomate in Hematology of the American Board of Internal Medicine
- Diplomate in Hematology and Medical Oncology of the American Board of Internal Medicine
- Diplomate in Infectious Disease of the American Board of Internal Medicine
- Diplomate in Medical Oncology of the American Board of Internal Medicine
- Diplomate in Nephrology of the American Board of Internal Medicine
- Diplomate in Pulmonary Disease of the American Board of Internal Medicine
- Diplomate in Rheumatology and Allergy and Immunology of the American Board of Internal Medicine
- Diplomate in Rheumatology of the American Board of Internal Medicine

American Board of Medical Genetics (ABMG)

9650 Rockville Pike
Bethesda, MD 20814-3998
Phone: (301)571-1825
Fax: (301)571-1895

- Certified Clinical Biochemical Geneticist
- Certified Clinical Cytogeneticist
- Certified Clinical Geneticist
- Certified Clinical Molecular Geneticist
- Certified Ph.D. Medical Geneticist

American Board of Medical Laboratory Immunology (ABMLI)

1325 Massachusetts Ave., NW
Washington, DC 20005
Phone: (202)737-3600

- Diplomate of the American Board of Medical Laboratory Immunology

American Board of Medical Management (ABMM)

4890 W. Kennedy Blvd., Ste. 200
Tampa, FL 33609-2815
Phone: (813)287-2815
Fax: (813)287-8993

- Diplomate of the American Board of Medical Management

American Board of Medical Microbiology (ASM)
1325 Massachusetts Ave., NW
Washington, DC 20005
Phone: (202)737-3600

- Diplomate, American Board of Medical Microbiology

American Board of Medical Psychotherapists (ABMP)
Physicians' Park B, Ste. 11
345 24th Ave., N.
Nashville, TN 37203-1519
Phone: (615)327-2978
Fax: (615)327-9235

- Clinical Associate of the American Board of Medical Psychotherapists
- Fellow and Diplomate of the American Board of Medical Psychotherapists

American Board of Neurological Surgery (ABNS)
6550 Fannin St., Ste. 2139
Houston, TX 77030
Phone: (713)790-6015
Fax: (713)794-0207

- Diplomate of the American Board of Neurological Surgery (DABNS)

American Board of Neuroscience Nursing (ABNN)
224 N. Des Plaines, Ste. 601
Chicago, IL 60661
Phone: (312)993-0256

- CNRN

American Board of Nuclear Medicine (ABNM)
900 Veteran Ave.
Los Angeles, CA 90024
Phone: (310)825-6787
Fax: (310)825-9433

- Diplomate of the American Board of Nuclear Medicine

American Board of Nutrition (ABN)
Univ. of Alabama at Birmingham
Dept. of Nutrition Sciences
1675 University Blvd., WEBB 234
Birmingham, AL 35294-3360
Phone: (205)975-8788
Fax: (205)934-7049

- Specialist in Clinical Nutrition
- Specialist in Human Nutrition

American Board of Obstetricians and Gynecologists for Osteopathic Specialists
804 Main St., Ste. F
Forest Park, GA 30050
Phone: (404)363-8263
Fax: (404)361-2285
Toll Free: (800)447-9397

- Diplomate of the American Board of Obstetricians and Gynecologists for Osteopathic Specialists

American Board of Obstetrics and Gynecology (ABOG)
2915 Vine St.
Dallas, TX 75204-1069
Phone: (214)871-1619
Fax: (214)871-1943

- Diplomate of the American Board of Obstetrics and Gynecology
- Diplomate of the American Board of Obstetrics and Gynecology with Added Qualification in Critical Care

American Board for Occupational Health Nurses (ABOHN)
9944 S. Roberts Rd., Ste. 205
Palos Hills, IL 60465
Phone: (708)598-6368

- Certified Occupational Health Nurse (COHN)

American Board of Ophthalmology (ABO)
111 Presidential Blvd., Ste. 241
Bala Cynwyd, PA 19004
Phone: (610)664-1175

- Diplomate of the American Board of Ophthalmology

American Board of Opticianry (ABO)
10341 Democracy Ln.
Fairfax, VA 22030
Phone: (703)691-8356
Fax: (703)691-3929

- American Board of Opticianry Certified

American Board of Oral and Maxillofacial Surgery (ABOMS)
625 N. Michigan Ave., Ste. 1820
Chicago, IL 60611
Phone: (312)642-0070
Fax: (312)642-8584

- Board Eligible, American Board of Oral and Maxillofacial Surgery
- Diplomate of the American Board of Oral and Maxillofacial Surgery

American Board of Oral Pathology (ABOP)
One Urban Centre, Ste. 690
4830 W. Kennedy Blvd.
PO Box 25915
Tampa, FL 33622-5915
Phone: (813)286-2444
Fax: (813)289-5279

- Diplomate of the American Board of Oral Pathology

American Board of Orthodontics (ABO)
401 N. Lindbergh Blvd., Ste. 308
St. Louis, MO 63141
Phone: (314)432-6130
Fax: (314)432-8170

- Board Eligible, American Board of Orthodontics
- Diplomate of the American Board of Orthodontics

American Board of Orthopaedic Surgery (ABOS)
400 Silver Cedar Ct.
Chapel Hill, NC 27514
Phone: (919)929-7103
Fax: (919)942-8988

- Diplomate of the American Board of Orthopaedic Surgery
- Diplomate of the American Board of Orthopaedic Surgery with Added Qualifications in Surgery of the Hand

American Board of Otolaryngology (ABO)
5615 Kirby Dr., Ste. 936
Houston, TX 77005-2452
Phone: (713)528-6200

- Diplomate of the American Board of Otolaryngology

American Board of Pain Medicine
5700 Old Orchard Rd., First Fl.
Skokie, IL 60077-1057
Phone: (708)966-0459
Fax: (708)966-9418

- Diplomate of the American Board of Pain Medicine

American Board of Pathology (ABP)
PO Box 25915
Tampa, FL 33622-5915
Phone: (813)286-2444
Fax: (813)289-5279

- Diplomate of the American Board of Pathology with Added Qualification in Cytopathology
- Diplomate of the American Board of Pathology with Special Qualification in Blood Banking/Transfusion Medicine
- Diplomate of the American Board of Pathology with Special Qualification in Chemical Pathology
- Diplomate of the American Board of Pathology with Special Qualification in Dermatopathology
- Diplomate of the American Board of Pathology with Special Qualification in Forensic Pathology
- Diplomate of the American Board of Pathology with Special Qualification in Hematology
- Diplomate of the American Board of

Pathology with Special Qualification in Immunopathology
- Diplomate of the American Board of Pathology with Special Qualification in Medical Microbiology
- Diplomate of the American Board of Pathology with Special Qualification in Neuropathology
- Diplomate of the American Board of Pathology with Special Qualification in Pediatric Pathology
- Diplomate in Anatomic Pathology of the American Board of Pathology
- Diplomate in Clinical Pathology of the American Board of Pathology
- Diplomate in Combined Anatomic and Clinical Pathology of the American Board of Pathology

American Board of Pediatric Dentistry (ABPD)
1193 Woodgate Dr.
Carmel, IN 46033-9232
Phone: (317)573-0877
Fax: (317)846-7235

- Board Eligible, American Board of Pediatric Dentistry
- Diplomate of the American Board of Pediatric Dentistry

American Board of Pediatrics (ABP)
111 Silver Cedar Ct.
Chapel Hill, NC 27514-1651
Phone: (919)929-0461
Fax: (919)929-9255

- Diplomate of the American Board of Pediatrics
- Diplomate of the American Board of Pediatrics with Special Qualifications in Adolescent Medicine
- Diplomate of the American Board of Pediatrics with Special Qualifications in Neonatal-Perinatal Medicine
- Diplomate of the American Board of Pediatrics with Special Qualifications in Pediatric Cardiology
- Diplomate of the American Board of Pediatrics with Special Qualifications in Pediatric Critical Care Medicine
- Diplomate of the American Board of Pediatrics with Special Qualifications in Pediatric Emergency Medicine
- Diplomate of the American Board of Pediatrics with Special Qualifications in Pediatric Endocrinology
- Diplomate of the American Board of Pediatrics with Special Qualifications in Pediatric Gastroenterology
- Diplomate of the American Board of Pediatrics with Special Qualifications in Pediatric Hematology-Oncology
- Diplomate of the American Board of Pediatrics with Special Qualifications in Pediatric Infectious Diseases
- Diplomate of the American Board of Pediatrics with Special Qualifications in Pediatric Nephrology
- Diplomate of the American Board of

Pediatrics with Special Qualifications in Pediatric Pulmonology
- Diplomate of the American Board of Pediatrics with Special Qualifications in Pediatric Rheumatology

American Board of Periodontology (ABP)
c/o Gerald M. Bowers, D.D.S.
University of Maryland
Baltimore Coll. of Dental Surgery
666 W. Baltimore St., Rm. 3-C-08
Baltimore, MD 21201
Phone: (410)706-2432
Fax: (410)706-0074

- Board Eligible, American Board of Periodontology
- Diplomate of the American Board of Periodontology

American Board of Physical Medicine and Rehabilitation
Norwest Center, Ste. 674
21 First St., SW
Rochester, MN 55902-3009
Phone: (507)282-1776
Fax: (507)282-9242

- Diplomate of the American Board of Physical Medicine and Rehabilitation (ABPMR)

American Board of Physical Therapy Specialties (ABPTS)
1111 N. Fairfax St.
Alexandria, VA 22314-1488
Phone: (703)706-3150
Fax: (703)684-7343
Toll Free: (800)999-APTA

- Physical Therapist, Cardiopulmonary Certified Specialist (PT, CCS)
- Physical Therapist, Clinical Electrophysiology Certified Specialist (PT, CECS)
- Physical Therapist, Geriatrics Certified Specialist (PT, GCS)
- Physical Therapist, Neurology Certified Specialist (PT, NCS)
- Physical Therapist, Orthopaedics Certified Specialist (PT, OCS)
- Physical Therapist, Pediatrics Certified Specialist (PT, PCS)
- Physical Therapist, Sports Certified Specialist (PT, SCS)

American Board of Plastic Surgery (ABPS)
Seven Penn Center, Ste. 400 1635 Market St.
Philadelphia, PA 19103-2204
Phone: (215)587-9322

- Diplomate of the American Board of Plastic Surgery

American Board of Podiatric Orthopedics and Primary Medicine (ABPOPM)
401 N. Michigan Ave., Ste. 2400
Chicago, IL 60611-4267
Phone: (312)321-5139
Fax: (312)644-1815

- Board Qualified, American Board of Podiatric Orthopedics and Primary Medicine
- Diplomate of the American Board of Podiatric Orthopedics and Primary Medicine

American Board of Podiatric Surgery (ABPS)
1601 Dolores St.
San Francisco, CA 94110-4906
Phone: (415)826-3200
Fax: (415)826-4640

- Board Qualified, American Board of Podiatric Surgery
- Diplomate of the American Board of Podiatric Surgery with Certification in Foot and Ankle Surgery
- Diplomate of the American Board of Podiatric Surgery with Certification in Foot Surgery

American Board of Post Anesthesia Nursing Certification (ABPANC)
475 Riverside Dr.
New York, NY 10115-0089
Phone: (212)870-3161
Fax: (212)870-3333
Toll Free: (800)6AB-PANC

- Certified Ambulatory Perianesthesia Nurse (CAPA)
- Certified Post Anesthesia Nurse (CPAN)

American Board of Preventive Medicine (ABPM)
9950 W. Lawrence Ave., Ste. 106
Schiller Park, IL 60176
Phone: (708)671-1750
Fax: (708)671-1751

- Diplomate of the American Board of Preventive Medicine

American Board of Professional Disability Consultants (ABPDC)
1350 Beverly Rd., Ste. 115-327
McClean, VA 22101
Phone: (703)790-8644

- Certified Disability Consultant
- Diplomate, American Board of Professional Disability Consultants

American Board of Professional Liability Attorneys (ABPLA)
175 E. Shore Rd.
Great Neck, NY 11023
Phone: (516)487-1990
Fax: (516)487-4304
Toll Free: (800)633-6255

- Diplomate of the American Board of Professional Liability Attorneys

American Board of Prosthodontics
PO Box 8437
Atlanta, GA 30306

- Board Eligible, American Board of Prosthodontics
- Diplomate of the American Board of Prosthodontics

American Board of Psychiatry and Neurology (ABPN)
500 Lake Cook Rd., Ste. 335
Deerfield, IL 60015-5249
Phone: (708)945-7900
Fax: (708)945-1146

- Diplomate of the American Board of Psychiatry and Neurology with Added Qualifications in Clinical Neurophysiology
- Diplomate in Child and Adolescent Psychiatry of the American Board of Psychiatry and Neurology
- Diplomate in Neurology of the American Board of Psychiatry and Neurology
- Diplomate in Neurology of the American Board of Psychiatry and Neurology with Special Qualification in Child Neurology
- Diplomate in Psychiatry of the American Board of Psychiatry and Neurology
- Diplomate in Psychiatry of the American Board of Psychiatry and Neurology with Added Qualifications in Addiction Psychiatry
- Diplomate in Psychiatry of the American Board of Psychiatry and Neurology with Added Qualifications in Forensic Psychiatry
- Diplomate in Psychiatry of the American Board of Psychiatry and Neurology with Added Qualifications in Geriatric Psychiatry

American Board of Psychological Hypnosis (ABPH)
c/o Dr. Samuel M. Migdole, APBH
23 Broadway
Beverly, MA 01915
Phone: (508)922-2280
Fax: (508)927-1758

- Diplomate in Clinical Hypnosis of the American Board of Psychological Hypnosis
- Diplomate in Experimental Hypnosis of the American Board of Psychological Hypnosis

American Board of Quality Assurance and Utilization Review Physicians (ABQAURP)
4890 W. Kennedy Blvd., Ste. 260
Tampa, FL 33609
Phone: (813)286-4411
Fax: (813)286-4387

- Certified in Quality Assurance and Utilization Review (CQUAR)

American Board of Radiology (ABR)
5255 E. Williams Circle, Ste. 6800
Tucson, AZ 85711
Phone: (520)790-2900
Fax: (520)790-3200

- Added Qualifications in Neuroradiology of the American Board of Radiology
- Added Qualifications in Pediatric Radiology of the American Board of Radiology
- Certificate of Added Qualifications in Vascular and Interventional Radiology of the American Board of Radiology
- Diplomate in Diagnostic Radiology of the American Board of Radiology
- Diplomate in Diagnostic Radiology with Special Competence in Nuclear Radiology of the American Board of Radiology
- Diplomate in Radiation Oncology of the American Board of Radiology
- Diplomate in Radiological Physics of the American Board of Radiology

American Board of Registration of Electroencephalographic and Evoked Potential Technologists (ABRET)
PO Box 11434
Norfolk, VA 23517
Phone: (804)627-5503

- Registered Electroencephalographic Technologist (REEGT)
- Registered Electroencephalographic Technologists (REPT)

American Board of School Psychology
2100 E. Broadway, Ste. 313
Columbia, MO 65201-6082
Phone: (314)875-1267
Fax: (314)443-1199
Toll Free: (800)255-7792

- Diplomate in School Psychology

American Board of Sleep Medicine
1610 14th St., NW, Ste. 302
Rochester, MN 55901
Phone: (507)287-9819
Fax: (507)287-6008

- Diplomate of the American Board of Sleep Medicine

American Board of Surgery (ABS)
1617 John F. Kennedy Blvd., Ste. 860
Philadelphia, PA 19103-1847
Phone: (215)568-4000

- Diplomate of the American Board of Surgery
- Diplomate of the American Board of Surgery with Added Qualifications in General Vascular Surgery
- Diplomate of the American Board of Surgery with Added Qualifications in Surgery of the Hand
- Diplomate of the American Board of Surgery with Added Qualifications in Surgical Critical Care
- Diplomate of the American Board of Surgery with Special Qualifications in Pediatric Surgery

American Board of Thoracic Surgery (ABTS)
One Rotary Center, Ste. 803
Evanston, IL 60201
Phone: (708)475-1520
Fax: (708)474-6240

- Diplomate of the American Board of Thoracic Surgery

American Board of Toxicology (ABA)
PO Box 30054
Raleigh, NC 27622-0054
Phone: (919)782-0036
Fax: (919)782-0036

- Diplomate of the American Board of Toxicology

American Board of Urologic Allied Health Professionals (ABUAHP)
1391 Delta Corners, SW
Lawrenceville, GA 30245

- Urology Physician's Assistant
- Urology Registered Nurse
- Urology Technician

American Board of Urology (ABU)
31700 Telegraph Rd., Ste. 150
Bingham Farms, MI 48025
Phone: (810)646-9720

- Diplomate of the American Board of Urology

American Board of Veterinary Practitioners (ABVP)
530 Church St., Ste. 300
Nashville, TN 37219-2394
Phone: (615)254-3687
Fax: (615)254-7047

- Diplomate of the American Board of Veterinary Practitioners

American Board of Veterinary Toxicology (ABVT)

c/o Dr. Robert H. Poppenga, DVM
School of Veterinary Medicine, New
  Bolton Center
Univ. of Pennsylvania
383 W. Street Rd.
Kennett Square, PA 19348
Phone: (610)444-5800

- Diplomate of the American Board of Veterinary Toxicology

American Board of Vocational Experts (ABVE)

5700 Old Orchard Rd., 1st Fl.
Skokie, IL 60077-1057
Phone: (708)966-0074
Fax: (708)966-9418

- Diplomate of the American Board of Vocational Experts
- Fellow of the American Board of Vocational Experts

American Boarding Kennels Association (ABKA)

4575 Galley Rd., No. 400-A
Colorado Springs, CO 80915
Phone: (719)591-1113
Fax: (719)595-0006

- Advanced Pet Care Technician
- Certified Kennel Operator (CKO)
- Pet Care Technician

American BRD of Chiropractic Internists

c/o Brian K. Wilson, DC
3601 S. Broadway
Englewood, CO 80110
Phone: (303)761-8521

- Diplomate of the American Board of Chiropractic Internists (DABCI)

American Center for the Alexander Technique (ACAT)

129 W. 67th St.
New York, NY 10023
Phone: (212)799-0468

- American Center for the Alexander Technique Teacher Certification

American Chiropractic Board of Nutrition

c/o Donald E. Huml, DC
430 79th St.
Brooklyn, NY 11209
Phone: (718)748-6644

- Board Eligible, American Chiropractic Board of Nutrition
- Diplomate of the American Chiropractic Board of Nutrition (DACBN)

American Chiropractic Board of Occupational Health

c/o David Gilkey, DC
9975 N. Wardsworth Pkwy., Ste. J2
Broomfield, CO 80021
Phone: (303)425-5723

- Board Eligible, American Chiropractic Board of Occupational Health
- Diplomate of the American Chiropractic Board of Occupational Health (DACBOH)

American Chiropractic Board of Radiology

c/o Gary Casper, DC
6361 Washington Ave.
University City, MO 63130
Phone: (314)726-2939

- Diplomate of the American Chiropractic Board of Radiology (DACBR)

American Chiropractic Board of Sports Physicians

c/o John G. Scaringe, DC
2740 S. Bristol, Ste. 104
Santa Ana, CA 92704-6232
Phone: (310)947-8755

- Certified Chiropractic Sports Physician (CCSP)
- Diplomate of the American Chiropractic Board of Sports Physicians (DACBSP)

American Chiropractic Neurology Board

c/o Stephen Taylor, DC
2720 San Pedro, NE
Albuquerque, NM 87110

- Board Eligible, American Chiropractic Neurology Board
- Diplomate of the American Chiropractic Neurology Board (DACNB)

American Chiropractic Registry of Radiologic Technologists (ACRRT)

2330 Gull Rd.
Kalamazoo, MI 49001
Phone: (616)343-6666

- Certified Chiropractic Radiologic Technologist

American Collectors Association (ACA)

ASAE Bldg.
4040 W. 70th St.
Minneapolis, MN 55435-4199
Phone: (612)926-6547
Fax: (612)926-1624

- Advanced Certified Collector
- Certified Collection Sales Professional
- Certified Collector
- Certified Skiptracer
- Certified Supervisor

American College (AC)

270 S. Bryn Mawr Ave.
Bryn Mawr, PA 19010
Phone: (215)526-1490

- Chartered Financial Consultant (CFC)
- Chartered Life Underwriter (CLU)

American College of Childbirth Educators (ACCE)

c/o Amer. Soc. for
  Psychoprophylaxis in Obstetrics
1101 Connecticut Ave., NW, Ste.
  700
Washington, DC 20036
Phone: (202)857-1128
Fax: (202)857-1130
Toll Free: (800)368-4404

- Fellow of the American College of Childbirth Educators (FACCE)

American College of Health Care Administrators (ACHCA)

325 S. Patrick St.
Alexandria, VA 22314-3571
Phone: (703)549-5822
Fax: (703)739-7901

- Certified Nursing Home Administrator (CNHA)
- Fellow of the American College of Health Care Administrators (FACHCA)

American College of Laboratory Animal Medicine (ACLAM)

200 Summerwinds Dr.
Cary, NC 27511
Phone: (919)859-5985
Fax: (919)851-3126

- Diplomate of the American College of Laboratory Animal Medicine

American College of Medical Practice Executives (ACMPE)

104 Inverness Terrace, E.
Englewood, CO 80112-5306
Phone: (303)397-7869
Fax: (303)643-4427

- Certified Member of the American College of Medical Practice Executives
- Fellow of the American College of Medical Practice Executives

American College of Nurse-Midwives (ACNM)

8401 Corporate Dr., Ste. 630
Landover, MD 20785
Phone: (301)459-1321
Fax: (301)731-7825

- Certified Nurse-Midwife (CNM)

American College of Physician Executives (ACPE)

4890 W. Kennedy Blvd., Ste. 200
Tampa, FL 33609-2575
Phone: (813)287-2000
Fax: (813)287-8993
Toll Free: (800)562-8088

- Distinguished Fellow of the American College of Physician Executives (FACPE)
- Fellow of the American College of Physician Executives (FACPE)

American College of Poultry Veterinarians (ACPV)

Box 1227
Fayetteville, AR 72702-1227
Phone: (501)575-4390
Fax: (501)521-1810

- Diplomate of the American College of Poultry Veterinarians

American College of Sports Medicine (ACSM)

PO Box 1440
Indianapolis, IN 46206-1440
Phone: (317)637-9200
Fax: (317)634-7817

- ACSM Exercise Leader
- ACSM Exercise Program Director
- ACSM Exercise Specialist
- ACSM Exercise Test Technologist
- ACSM Health/Fitness Director
- ACSM Health/Fitness Instructor

American College of Theriogenologists

2727 W. Second St., Ste. 450
PO Box 2118
Hastings, NE 68902-2118
Phone: (402)463-0392
Fax: (402)463-5683

- Diplomate of the American College of Theriogenologists

American College of Veterinary Anesthesiologists (ACVA)

c/o Ann E. Wagner, DVM
Coll. of Veterinary Medicine
Colorado State Univ.
Fort Collins, CO 80523-1275
Phone: (303)491-0346
Fax: (303)491-1275

- Diplomate of the American College of Veterinary Anesthesiologists

American College of Veterinary Behaviorists (ACVB)

c/o Dr. K. Houpt
Dept. of Physiology
Coll. of Veterinary Medicine
Cornell Univ.
Ithaca, NY 14853-6401
Phone: (607)253-3450
Fax: (607)253-3846

- Diplomate of the American College of Veterinary Behaviorists

American College of Veterinary Clinical Pharmacology (ACVCP)

c/o Dr. Cyril R. Clarke, MRCVS
Dept. of Physiological Sciences
Coll. of Veterinary Medicine
Oklahoma State Univ.
Stillwater, OK 74078-0353
Phone: (405)744-8093
Fax: (405)744-8263

- Diplomate of the American College of Veterinary Clinical Pharmacology

American College of Veterinary Dermatology (ACVD)

c/o Craig E. Griffin, DVM
Animal Dermatology Clinic
13240 Evening Creek Dr.
San Diego, CA 92128
Phone: (619)486-4600
Fax: (619)486-4681

- Diplomate of the American College of Veterinary Dermatology

American College of Veterinary Emergency and Critical Care (ACVECC)

c/o James N. Ross, DVM
School of Veterinary Medicine
Tufts Univ.
200 Westboro Rd.
North Grafton, MA 01536
Phone: (508)839-7950
Fax: (508)839-7922

- Diplomate of the American College of Veterinary Emergency and Critical Care

American College of Veterinary Internal Medicine (ACVIM)

7175 W. Jefferson Ave., Ste. 2125
Lakewood, CO 80235
Phone: (303)980-7136
Fax: (303)980-7137
Toll Free: (800)245-9081

- Diplomate of the American College of Veterinary Internal Medicine
- Diplomate in Cardiology of the American College of Veterinary Internal Medicine
- Diplomate in Neurology of the American College of Veterinary Internal Medicine
- Diplomate in Oncology of the

American College of Veterinary Internal Medicine

American College of Veterinary Microbiologists (ACVM)

c/o Dr. H. G. Purchase
Coll. of Veterinary Medicine
Mississippi State Univ.
PO Box 9825
Mississippi State, MS 38762-9825
Phone: (601)325-1205
Fax: (601)325-1066

- Diplomate of the American College of Veterinary Microbiologists

American College of Veterinary Nutrition (ACVN)

c/o Dr. John Bauer, DACVN
College of Veterinary Medicine
Texas A & M Univ.
College Station, TX 77843-4461

- Diplomate of the American College of Veterinary Nutrition (DACVN)

American College of Veterinary Ophthalmologists (AVMO)

c/o Dr. Mary B. Glaze
Veterinary Clinical Sciences
Louisiana State Univ.
Baton Rouge, LA 70803
Phone: (504)346-3333
Fax: (504)346-3295

- Diplomate of the American College of Veterinary Ophthalmologists

American College of Veterinary Pathologists (ACVP)

875 Kings Hwy., Ste. 200
Woodbury, NJ 08096
Phone: (609)848-7784
Fax: (609)853-0411

- Diplomate in Veterinary Clinical Pathology of the American College of Veterinary Pathologists
- Diplomate in Veterinary Pathology of the American College of Veterinary Pathologists

American College of Veterinary Preventive Medicine (ACVPM)

c/o Dr. Stanley O. Hewins
3126 Morning Creek
San Antonio, TX 78247
Fax: (210)524-3944
Toll Free: (800)374-4944

- Diplomate of the American College of Veterinary Preventive Medicine
- Diplomate in Epidemiology of the American College of Veterinary Preventive Medicine

American College of Veterinary Radiology (ACVR)

PO Box 87
Glencoe, IL 60022
Phone: (708)251-5517
Fax: (708)446-8618

- Diplomate of the American College of Veterinary Radiology

American College of Veterinary Surgeons (ACVS)

4330 East-West Hwy., Ste. 1117
Bethesda, MD 20814
Phone: (301)718-6504
Fax: (301)656-0989

- Diplomate of the American College of Veterinary Surgeons

American College of Zoological Medicine (ACZM)

c/o Dr. George Kollias, Jr.
Dept. of Clinical Services
Sec. of Wildlife Medicine
New York State Veterinary Coll.
Cornell, NY 14853
Phone: (607)253-3049
Fax: (607)253-3708

- Diplomate of the American College of Zoological Medicine

American Compensation Association (ACA)

14040 N. Northsight Blvd.
Scottsdale, AZ 85260
Phone: (602)951-9191
Fax: (602)483-8352

- Certified Benefits Professional (CBP)
- Certified Compensation Professional (CCP)

American Concrete Institute (ACI)

PO Box 19150
Detroit, MI 48219-0150
Phone: (313)532-2600
Fax: (313)538-0655

- Concrete Construction Inspector-in-Training
- Concrete Construction Inspector - Level II
- Concrete Field Testing Technician - Grade I
- Concrete Flatwork Finisher
- Concrete Flatwork Technician
- Concrete Laboratory Testing Technician - Grade I
- Concrete Laboratory Testing Technician - Grade II
- Concrete Transportation Construction Inspector
- Concrete Transportation Construction Inspector-in-Training

American Congress on Surveying and Mapping (ACSM)

5410 Grosvenor Ln.
Bethesda, MD 20814-2122
Phone: (301)493-0200
Fax: (301)493-8245

- Certified Hydrographer

American Consultants League (ACL)

1290 Palm Ave.
Sarasota, FL 34236
Phone: (813)952-9290
Fax: (813)925-3670

- Certified Professional Consultant (CPC)

American Council of Applied Clinical Nutrition (ACACN)

PO Box 509
Florissant, MO 63032
Phone: (314)921-3997

- Fellow of the American Council of Applied Clinical Nutrition (FACACN)

American Council on Exercise (ACE)

5820 Oberlin Dr., Ste. 102
San Diego, CA 92121
Toll Free: (800)825-3636

- Certified Aerobics Instructor
- Certified Personal Trainer

American Council of Hypnotist Examiners (ACHE)

700 S. Central Ave.
Glendale, CA 91204
Phone: (818)242-1159
Fax: (818)247-9379

- Certified Clinical Hypnotherapist
- Certified Hypnotherapist
- Certified Master Hypnotist

American Culinary Federation (ACF)

10 San Bartola Rd.
PO Box 3466
St. Augustine, FL 32085-3466
Phone: (904)824-4468
Fax: (904)825-4758
Toll Free: (800)624-9458

- Certified Cook (CC)
- Certified Master Chef (CMC)
- Certified Master Pastry Chef (CMPC)
- Certified Pastry Cook (CPC)

American Design Drafting Association (ADDA)

PO Box 799
Rockville, MD 20848
Phone: (301)460-6875
Fax: (301)460-8591

- Certified Drafter (CD)

American Economic Development Council (AEDC)

9801 W. Higgins Rd., Ste. 540
Rosemont, IL 60018-4726
Phone: (708)692-9944
Fax: (708)696-2990

- Certified Economic Developer (CED)

American Educational Institute (AEI)

179 Mt. Airy Rd.
PO Box 356
Basking Ridge, NJ 07920-0356
Phone: (908)766-0909
Fax: (908)766-9710
Toll Free: (800)631-8183

- Casualty Claim Law Associate (CCLA)
- Casualty Claim Law Specialist (CCLS)
- Casualty-Fraud Claim Law Associate (CCLA/FCLA)
- Casualty-Property Claim Law Associate (CCLA/PCLA)
- Casualty-Workers' Compensation Claim Law Associate (CCLA/WCLA)
- Fraud Claim Law Associate (FCLA)
- Fraud Claim Law Specialist (FCLS)
- Property Claim Law Associate (PCLA)
- Property Claim Law Specialist (PCLS)
- Property-Fraud Claim Law Associate (PCLA/FCLA)
- Property-Workers' Compensation Claim Law Associate (PCLA/WCLA)
- Senior Claim Law Associate (SCLA)
- Workers' Compensation Claim Law Associate (WCLA)
- Workers' Compensation Claim Law Specialist (WCLS)
- Workers' Compensation-Fraud Claim Law Associate (WCLA/FCLA)

American Electroplaters and Surface Finishers Society (AESF)

12644 Research Pkwy.
Orlando, FL 32826-3298
Phone: (407)281-6441
Fax: (407)281-6446

- Certified Electroplater-Finisher (CEF)
- Certified Electroplater Finisher - Specialist in Electronics (CEF-SE)
- Electronics Specialist, Certified (ESC)

American Farrier's Association (AFA)

4059 Iron Works Pike
Lexington, KY 40511
Phone: (606)233-7411
Fax: (606)231-7862
E-mail: AFA@WORLD.STD.COM

- Certified Farrier
- Certified Journeyman Farrier

American Fence Association (AFA)
5300 Memorial Dr., Ste. 116
Stone Mountain, GA 30083
Phone: (404)299-5413
Fax: (404)299-8927
Toll Free: (800)822-4342

- Certified Fence Professional (CFP)

American Fisheries Society (AFS)
5410 Grosvenor Ln., Ste. 110
Bethesda, MD 20814
Phone: (301)897-8616
Fax: (301)897-8096

- Associate Fisheries Scientist (AFS)
- Certified Fisheries Scientist (CFS)

American Gem Society (AGS)
8881 W. Sahara Ave.
Las Vegas, NV 89117
Phone: (702)255-6500
Fax: (702)255-7420

- Certified Gemologist (CG)
- Certified Gemologist Appraiser (CGA)
- Registered Jeweler (RJ)
- Registered Supplier (RS)

American Guild of Organists (AGO)
475 Riverside Dr., Ste. 1260
New York, NY 10115
Phone: (212)870-2310
Fax: (212)870-2163

- Associate, American Guild of Organists
- Choir Master, American Guild of Organists
- Colleague, American Guild of Organists
- Fellow, American Guild of Organists

American Health Information Management Association (AHIMA)
919 N. Michigan Ave., Ste. 1400
Chicago, IL 60611-1683
Phone: (312)787-2672

- Accredited Record Technician (ART)
- Certified Coding Specialist (CCS)
- Registered Record Administrator (RRA)

American Heart Association (AHA)
7272 Greenville Ave.
Dallas, TX 75231-4596
Phone: (214)373-6300
Fax: (214)706-1341
Toll Free: (800)242-8721

- Adult Heartsaver
- Advanced Cardiac Life Support
- Basic Life Support for the Healthcare Provider
- Pediatric Advanced Life Support
- Pediatric Basic Life Support

American Holistic Nurses' Association (AHNA)
4101 Lake Boone Trail, Ste. 201
Raleigh, NC 27607
Phone: (919)787-5181
Fax: (919)787-4916

- Certified Holistic Nurse (CHN)

American Horticultural Therapy Association (AHTA)
362A Christopher Ave.
Gaithersburg, MD 20879-3660
Phone: (301)948-3010
Fax: (301)869-2397

- Horticultural Therapist Registered (HTR)
- Horticultural Therapist Technician (HTR)
- Master Horticultural Therapist (HTM)

American Institute of Certified Planners (AICP)
1776 Massachusetts Ave., NW
Washington, DC 20036
Phone: (202)872-0611
Fax: (202)872-0643

- Certified Planner

American Institute of Certified Public Accountants (AICPA)
1211 Avenue of the Americas
New York, NY 10036
Phone: (212)596-6200
Fax: (201)938-3329
Toll Free: (800)862-4272

- Personal Financial Specialist (PFS)

American Institute of Constructors (AIC)
9887 N. Gandy, Ste. 104
St. Petersburg, FL 33702
Phone: (813)578-0317
Fax: (813)578-9982

- Certified Professional Constructor (CPC)

American Institute for CPCU (AICPCU)
720 Providence Rd.
PO Box 3016
Malvern, PA 19355-0716
Phone: (610)644-2100
Fax: (610)640-9576
Toll Free: (800)644-2101

- Chartered Property Casualty Underwriter (CPCU)

American Institute of Hydrology (AIH)
3416 University Ave., SE
Minneapolis, MN 55414-3328
Phone: (612)379-1030
Fax: (612)379-0169

- Professional Hydrogeologist (PHG)
- Professional Hydrologist (PH)
- Professional Hydrologist - Ground Water (PH-GW)
- Professional Hydrologist - Water Quality (PH-WQ)

American Institute of Parliamentarians (AIP)
10535 Metropolitan Ave.
Kensington, MD 20895-2627
Phone: (301)946-9220
Fax: (301)949-5255

- Certified Parliamentarian (CP)
- Certified Professional Parliamentarian (CPP)

American Institute of Plant Engineers (AIPE)
8189 Corporate Park Dr., Ste. 305
Cincinnati, OH 45242
Phone: (513)489-2473
Fax: (513)247-7422

- Certified Facilities Environmental Professional (CFEP)
- Certified Plant Engineer (CPE)

American Institute of Professional Geologists (AIPG)
7828 Vance Dr., Ste. 103
Arvada, CO 80003-2125
Phone: (303)431-0831
Fax: (303)431-1332

- Certified Professional Geologist (CPG)

American Landscape Horticulture Association (ALHA)
3124 Gray Fox Ln.
Paso Robles, CA 93446
Phone: (805)238-7921
Toll Free: (800)359-6647

- Certified Landscape Management Technician (CLMT)
- Certified Landscape Professional (CLP)
- Certified Landscape Technician (CLT)

American Machine Tool Distributors' Association (AMTDA)
1335 Rockville Pike, Ste. 300
Rockville, MD 20852
Phone: (301)738-1200
Fax: (301)738-9499

- Certified Machine Tool Sales Engineer (CMTSE)

**American Managed Care and
Review Association (AMCRA)**
1200 19th St., Ste. 200
Washington, DC 20036-2437
Phone: (202)728-0506
Fax: (202)728-0609

- Certified Managed Care Executives
(CMCE)

**American Medical Technologists
(AMT)**
710 Higgins Rd.
Park Ridge, IL 60068
Phone: (708)823-5169
Fax: (708)823-0458
Toll Free: (800)275-1268

- Medical Laboratory Technician
(MLT)
- Medical Technologist (MT)
- Registered Dental Assistant (RDA)
- Registered Medical Assistant (RMA)
- Registered Phlebotomy Technician
(RPT)

**American Meteorological Society
(AMS)**
45 Beacon St.
Boston, MA 02108
Phone: (617)227-2425
Fax: (617)742-8718
E-mail: hallgren@aip.org

- Certified Consulting Meteorologist
(CCM)

**American Nurses Credentialing
Center (ANCC)**
600 Maryland Ave., SW, Ste. 100
West
Washington, DC 20024-2571
Toll Free: (800)284-CERT

- Cardiac Rehabilitation Nurse
- College Health Nurse
- Home Health Nurse
- School Nurse

**American Occupational Therapy
Association (AOTA)**
1383 Piccard Dr.
PO Box 1725
Rockville, MD 20849-1725
Phone: (301)652-2682
Fax: (301)652-7711
Toll Free: (800)SAY-AOTA

- Pediatric Occupational Therapy Board
Certified in Pediatrics

**American Occupational Therapy
Certification Board (AOTCB)**
Four Research Pl., Ste. 160
Rockville, MD 20850-3226
Phone: (301)990-7979
Fax: (301)869-8492

- Certified Occupational Therapy
Assistant (COTA)
- Occupational Therapist, Registered
(OTR)

**American Oil Chemists' Society
(AOCS)**
PO Box 3489
Champaign, IL 61826-3489
Phone: (217)359-2344
Fax: (217)351-8091

- Approved Chemist

American Orthoptic Council (AOC)
3914 Nakoma Rd.
Madison, WI 53711
Phone: (608)233-5383
Fax: (608)263-7694

- Certified Orthoptist

**American Osteopathic Board of
Anesthesiology**
17201 E. U.S. Hwy. 40, Ste. 204
Independence, MO 64055
Phone: (816)373-4700
Toll Free: (800)842-2622

- Board Eligible, American Osteopathic
Board of Anesthesiology
- Diplomate of the American
Osteopathic Board of Anesthesiology

**American Osteopathic Board of
Dermatology (AOBD)**
25510 Plymouth Rd.
Redford, MI 48239
Phone: (313)937-1200

- Board Eligible, American Osteopathic
Board of Dermatology
- Diplomate of the American
Osteopathic Board of Dermatology
- Diplomate of the American
Osteopathic Board of Dermatology
with Added Qualifications in MOHS
Micrographic Surgery

**American Osteopathic Board of
Emergency Medicine (AOBEM)**
142 E. Ontario St., Ste. 217
Chicago, IL 60611
Phone: (312)335-1065
Fax: (312)335-5489
Toll Free: (800)847-0057

- Board Eligible, American Osteopathic
Board of Emergency Medicine
- Diplomate of the American
Osteopathic Board of Emergency
Medicine

**American Osteopathic Board of
Family Practice (AOBFP)**
330 E. Algonquin Rd., Ste 2
Arlington Heights, IL 60005
Phone: (708)640-8477

- Board Eligible, American Osteopathic
Board of Family Practice
- Diplomate of the American
Osteopathic Board of Family Practice
- Diplomate of the American
Osteopathic Board of Family Practice

with Added Qualifications in
Adolescent and Young Adult
Medicine
- Diplomate of the American
Osteopathic Board of Family Practice
with Added Qualifications in
Geriatric Medicine
- Diplomate of the American
Osteopathic Board of Family Practice
with Added Qualifications in Sports
Medicine

**American Osteopathic Board of
Internal Medicine**
5200 S. Ellis Ave.
Chicago, IL 60615
Phone: (312)947-4881

- Board Eligible, American Osteopathic
Board of Internal Medicine
- Diplomate in Allergy and
Immunology of the American
Osteopathic Board of Internal
Medicine
- Diplomate of the American
Osteopathic Board of Internal
Medicine
- Diplomate of the American
Osteopathic Board of Internal
Medicine with Added Qualifications
in Critical Care Medicine
- Diplomate of the American
Osteopathic Board of Internal
Medicine with Added Qualifications
in Geriatric Medicine
- Diplomate in Cardiology of the
American Osteopathic Board of
Internal Medicine
- Diplomate in Endocrinology of the
American Osteopathic Board of
Internal Medicine
- Diplomate in Gastroenterology of the
American Osteopathic Board of
Internal Medicine
- Diplomate in Hematology of the
American Osteopathic Board of
Internal Medicine
- Diplomate in Hematology and
Oncology of the American
Osteopathic Board of Internal
Medicine
- Diplomate in Infectious Disease of the
American Osteopathic Board of
Internal Medicine
- Diplomate in Nephrology of the
American Osteopathic Board of
Internal Medicine
- Diplomate in Oncology of the
American Osteopathic Board of
Internal Medicine
- Diplomate in Pulmonary Disease of
the American Osteopathic Board of
Internal Medicine
- Diplomate in Rheumatology of the
American Osteopathic Board of
Internal Medicine

American Osteopathic Board of Neurology and Psychiatry

2250 Chapel Ave., W., Ste. 100
Cherry Hill, NJ 08002-2000
Phone: (609)482-9000

- Diplomate in Child Neurology of the American Osteopathic Board of Neurology and Psychiatry
- Diplomate in Child Psychiatry of the American Osteopathic Board of Neurology and Psychiatry
- Diplomate in Neurology of the American Osteopathic Board of Neurology and Psychiatry
- Diplomate in Psychiatry of the American Osteopathic Board of Neurology and Psychiatry

American Osteopathic Board of Nuclear Medicine

5200 S. Ellis Ave.
Chicago, IL 60615
Phone: (312)947-4490

- Board Eligible, American Osteopathic Board of Nuclear Medicine
- Diplomate of the American Osteopathic Board of Nuclear Medicine
- Diplomate of the American Osteopathic Board of Nuclear Medicine with Added Qualifications in *In Vivo* and *In Vitro* Nuclear Medicine
- Diplomate of the American Osteopathic Board of Nuclear Medicine with Added Qualifications in Nuclear Cardiology
- Diplomate of the American Osteopathic Board of Nuclear Medicine with Added Qualifications in Nuclear Imaging and Therapy

American Osteopathic Board of Obstetrics and Gynecology (AOBOG)

5200 S. Ellis Ave.
Chicago, IL 60615
Phone: (312)947-4630

- Board Eligible, American Osteopathic Board of Obstetrics and Gynecology
- Diplomate of the American Osteopathic Board of Obstetrics and Gynecology
- Diplomate in Gynecologic Oncology of the American Osteopathic Board of Obstetrics and Gynecology
- Diplomate in Maternal-Fetal Medicine of the American Osteopathic Board of Obstetrics and Gynecology
- Diplomate in Reproductive Endocrinology of the American Osteopathic Board of Obstetrics and Gynecology

American Osteopathic Board of Ophthalmology and Otorhinolaryngology

Three Mackoil Ave.
Dayton, OH 45403
Phone: (513)252-0868

- Board Eligible, American Osteopathic Board of Ophthalmology and Otorhinolaryngology
- Diplomate in Facial Plastic Surgery of the American Osteopathic Board of Ophthalmology and Otorhinolaryngology
- Diplomate in Ophthalmology of the American Osteopathic Board of Ophthalmology and Otorhinolaryngology
- Diplomate in Otorhinolaryngology of the American Osteopathic Board of Ophthalmology and Otorhinolaryngology
- Diplomate in Otorhinolaryngology and Facial Plastic Surgery of the American Osteopathic Board of Ophthalmology and Otorhinolaryngology

American Osteopathic Board of Orthopaedic Surgery

450 Powers Ave., Ste. 105
Harrisburg, PA 17109
Phone: (717)561-8560

- Board Eligible, American Osteopathic Board of Orthopaedic Surgery
- Diplomate of the American Osteopathic Board of Orthopaedic Surgery

American Osteopathic Board of Pathology

450 Powers Ave., Ste. 105
Harrisburg, PA 17109
Phone: (717)561-8560

- Board Eligible, American Osteopathic Board of Pathology
- Diplomate in Anatomic Pathology of the American Osteopathic Board of Pathology
- Diplomate in Anatomic Pathology and Laboratory Medicine of the American Osteopathic Board of Pathology
- Diplomate in Forensic Pathology of the American Osteopathic Board of Pathology
- Diplomate in Laboratory Medicine of the American Osteopathic Board of Pathology

American Osteopathic Board of Pediatrics (AOBP)

142 E. Ontario St., Sixth Fl.
Chicago, IL 60611
Phone: (312)280-5881

- Board Eligible, American Osteopathic Board of Pediatrics
- Diplomate of the American Osteopathic Board of Pediatrics
- Diplomate of the American Osteopathic Board of Pediatrics with Special Qualifications in Adolescent and Young Adult Medicine
- Diplomate of the American Osteopathic Board of Pediatrics with Special Qualifications in Neonatology
- Diplomate of the American Osteopathic Board of Pediatrics with Special Qualifications in Pediatric Allergy/Immunology
- Diplomate of the American Osteopathic Board of Pediatrics with Special Qualifications in Pediatric Cardiology
- Diplomate of the American Osteopathic Board of Pediatrics with Special Qualifications in Pediatric Hematology/Oncology
- Diplomate of the American Osteopathic Board of Pediatrics with Special Qualifications in Pediatric Infectious Diseases
- Diplomate of the American Osteopathic Board of Pediatrics with Special Qualifications in Pediatric Intensive Care
- Diplomate of the American Osteopathic Board of Pediatrics with Special Qualifications in Pediatric Nephrology
- Diplomate of the American Osteopathic Board of Pediatrics with Special Qualifications in Pediatric Pulmonary

American Osteopathic Board of Preventive Medicine

Box 226
U.S. Air Force Academy, CO 80840-2200
Phone: (719)472-3560

- Board Eligible, American Osteopathic Board of Preventive Medicine
- Certification of Added Qualifications in Occupational Medicine
- Diplomate in Aerospace Medicine of the American Osteopathic Board of Preventive Medicine
- Diplomate in Occupational-Environmental Medicine of the American Osteopathic Board of Preventive Medicine
- Diplomate in Public Health of the American Osteopathic Board of Preventive Medicine

American Osteopathic Board of Proctology

104A Kings Way West
Sewell, NJ 08080
Phone: (609)582-7900

- Board Eligible, American Osteopathic Board of Proctology
- Diplomate of the American Osteopathic Board of Proctology

American Osteopathic Board of Radiology
119 E. Second St.
Milan, MO 63556
Phone: (816)265-4011

- Board Eligible, American Osteopathic Board of Radiology
- Diplomate of the American Osteopathic Board of Radiology with Added Qualifications in Angiography and Interventional Radiology
- Diplomate of the American Osteopathic Board of Radiology with Added Qualifications in Body Imaging
- Diplomate of the American Osteopathic Board of Radiology with Added Qualifications in Diagnostic Ultrasound
- Diplomate of the American Osteopathic Board of Radiology with Added Qualifications in Neuroradiology
- Diplomate of the American Osteopathic Board of Radiology with Added Qualifications in Nuclear Radiology
- Diplomate of the American Osteopathic Board of Radiology with Added Qualifications in Pediatric Radiology
- Diplomate in Diagnostic Radiology of the American Osteopathic Board of Radiology
- Diplomate in Radiation Oncology of the American Osteopathic Board of Radiology

American Osteopathic Board of Rehabilitation Medicine
9058 W. Church St.
Des Plaines, IL 60016
Phone: (708)699-0048

- Board Eligible, American Osteopathic Board of Rehabilitation Medicine
- Diplomate of the American Osteopathic Board of Rehabilitation Medicine

American Osteopathic Board of Special Proficiency in Osteopathic Manipulative Medicine
3500 DePauw Blvd., Ste. 1080
Indianapolis, IN 46268
Phone: (317)879-1881

- Certification of Special Proficiency in Osteopathic Manipulative Medicine

American Osteopathic Board of Surgery
Three MacKoil Ave.
Dayton, OH 45403
Phone: (513)252-0868

- Board Eligible, American Osteopathic Board of Surgery
- Certificate of Added Qualifications in Surgical Critical Care
- Diplomate of the American Osteopathic Board of Surgery
- Diplomate in General Vascular Surgery of the American Osteopathic Board of Surgery
- Diplomate in Neurological Surgery of the American Osteopathic Board of Surgery
- Diplomate in Plastic and Reconstructive Surgery of the American Osteopathic Board of Surgery
- Diplomate in Thoracic Cardiovascular Surgery of the American Osteopathic Board of Surgery
- Diplomate in Urological Surgery of the American Osteopathic Board of Surgery

American Payroll Association (APA)
30 E. 33rd St., 5th Fl.
New York, NY 10016
Phone: (212)686-2030
Fax: (212)686-2789

- Certified Payroll Professional (CPP)

American Petroleum Institute (API)
1220 L St., NW
Washington, DC 20005
Phone: (202)682-8000
Fax: (202)962-4776

- Aboveground Storage Tank Inspector Certification
- Pressure Vessel Inspector Certification

American Purchasing Society (APS)
11910 Oak Trail Way
Port Richey, FL 34668
Phone: (813)862-7998
Fax: (813)862-8199

- Certified Purchasing Executive (CPE)
- Certified Purchasing Professional (CPP)

American Red Cross (ARC)
431 18th St., NW
Washington, DC 20006
Phone: (202)737-8300

- Adult CPR Certification
- Community CPR Certification
- Community First Aid and Safety
- Community Water Safety Certification
- Head Lifeguard
- Infant and Child CPR Certification
- Lifeguard
- Lifeguarding Instructor
- Standard First Aid Certification
- Water Safety Instructor

American Registry of Diagnostic Medical Sonographers (ARDMS)
2368 Victory Pkwy., Ste. 510
Cincinnati, OH 45206
Phone: (513)281-7111
Fax: (513)281-7524
Toll Free: (800)541-9754

- Registered Diagnostic Cardiac Sonographer (RDCS)
- Registered Diagnostic Medical Sonographer (RDMS)
- Registered Vascular Technologist (RVT)

American Registry of Medical Assistants (ARMA)
69 Southwick Rd.
Westfield, MA 01085
Phone: (413)562-7336
Toll Free: (800)527-2762

- Registered Medical Assistant (R.M.A.)

American Registry of Radiologic Technologists (ARRT)
1255 Northland Dr.
St. Paul, MN 55120-1155
Phone: (612)687-0048

- Registered Technologist (Cardiovascular-Interventional Technology) (R.T.(CV)(ARRT))
- Registered Technologist (Commuted Tomography)
- Registered Technologist (Magnetic Resonance Imaging)
- Registered Technologist (Mammography) (R.T.(M)(ARRT))
- Registered Technologist (Nuclear Medicine Technology) (R.T.(N)(ARRT))
- Registered Technologist (Radiation Therapy Technology) (R.T.(T)(ARRT))
- Registered Technologist (Radiography) (R.T.(R)(ARRT))

American Riding Instructor Certification Program (ARICP)
PO Box 282
Alton Bay, NH 03810
Phone: (603)875-4000
Fax: (603)875-7771

- Instructor of Beginner Through Advanced (IBA)
- Instructor of Beginner Through Intermediate (IBI)
- Instructor in Training (IT)

American Society of Agronomy (ASA)

677 S. Segoe Rd.
Madison, WI 53711
Phone: (608)273-8080
Fax: (608)273-2021

- Associate Professional Agronomist (APA)
- Associate Professional Crop Scientist (APCS)
- Associate Professional Crop Specialist (APCS)
- Associate Professional in Horticulture (APH)
- Associate Professional Plant Pathologist (APPP)
- Associate Professional Soil Classifier (APSC)
- Associate Professional Soil Scientist (APSS)
- Associate Professional Soil Specialist (APSS)
- Associate Professional in Weed Science (APWS)
- Certified Crop Adviser (CCA)
- Certified Professional Agronomist (CPA)
- Certified Professional Crop Scientist (CPCS)
- Certified Professional Horticulturist (CPH)
- Certified Professional Plant Pathologist (CPPP)
- Certified Professional Soil Classifier (CPSC)
- Certified Professional Soil Scientist (CPSS)
- Certified Professional Soil Specialist (CPSS)
- Certified Professional in Weed Science (CPWS)

American Society of Appraisers (ASA)

PO Box 17265
Washington, DC 20041
Phone: (703)478-2228
Fax: (703)742-8471
Toll Free: (800)ASA-VALU

- Accredited Member, American Society of Appraisers (AM)
- Accredited Senior Appraiser (ASA)
- Fellow of the American Society of Appraisers (FASA)
- Master Gemologist Appraiser (MGA)
- Master Governmental Appraiser (MGA)

American Society of Asset Managers (ASAM)

303 W. Cypress
Box 12528
San Antonio, TX 78212
Phone: (210)225-2897
Fax: (210)225-8450
Toll Free: (800)486-3676

- Senior Asset Manager (SAM)

American Society of Association Executives (ASAE)

1575 Eye St., NW
Washington, DC 20005-1168
Phone: (202)626-2821
Fax: (202)289-4049

- Certified Association Executive (CAE)

American Society of Clinical Pathologists (ASCP)

PO Box 12277
Chicago, IL 60612-0277
Phone: (312)738-1336
Fax: (312)738-1619

- Cytotechnologist (CT(ASCP))
- Diplomate in Laboratory Management (DLM(ASCP))
- Hemapheresis Practitioner (HP(ASCP))
- Histologic Technician (HT(ASCP))
- Histotechnologist (HTL(ASCP))
- Medical Laboratory Technician (MLT(ASCP))
- Medical Technologist (MT(ASCP))
- Phlebotomy Technician (PBT(ASCP))
- Qualification in Cytometry
- Qualification in Immunohistochemistry
- Specialist in Blood Banking (SBB(ASCP))
- Specialist in Chemistry (SC(ASCP))
- Specialist in Cytotechnology (SCT(ASCP))
- Specialist in Hematology (SH(ASCP))
- Specialist in Immunology (SI(ASCP))
- Specialist in Microbiology (SI(ASCP))
- Technologist in Blood Banking (BB(ASCP))
- Technologist in Chemistry (C(ASCP))
- Technologist in Hematology (H(ASCP))
- Technologist in Immunology (I(ASCP))
- Technologist in Microbiology (M(ASCP))

American Society of Farm Managers and Rural Appraisers (ASFMRA)

950 S. Cherry St., Ste. 508
Denver, CO 80222
Phone: (303)758-3513
Fax: (303)758-0190

- Accredited Farm Manager (AFM)
- Accredited Rural Appraiser (ARA)
- Real Property Review Appraiser (RPRA)

American Society of Healthcare Materials Management (ASHMM)

c/o American Hospital Association
One N. Franklin
Chicago, IL 60606
Phone: (312)280-6155

- Certified Senior Member of the American Society of Healthcare Materials Management

American Society for Industrial Security (ASIS)

1655 N. Ft. Myer Dr., Ste. 1200
Arlington, VA 22209
Phone: (703)522-5800
Fax: (703)243-4954

- Certified Protection Professional (CPP)

American Society for Microbiology (ASM)

1325 Massachusetts Ave., NW
Washington, DC 20005
Phone: (202)737-3600

- Registered Microbiologist (RM)
- Specialist Microbiologist (SM)

American Society for Nondestructive Testing (ASNT)

1711 Arlingate Ln.
PO Box 28518
Columbus, OH 43228-0518
Phone: (614)274-6003
Fax: (614)274-6899
Toll Free: (800)222-2768

- Nondestructive Testing Level III

American Society of Pension Actuaries (ASPA)

4350 N. Fairfax Dr., Ste. 820
Arlington, VA 22203
Phone: (703)516-9300
Fax: (703)516-9308

- Associated Professional Member, American Society of Pension Actuaries (APM)
- Certified Pension Consultant (CPC)
- Fellow, Society of Pension Actuaries (FSPA)
- Member, Society of Pension Actuaries (MSPA)
- Qualified Pension Administrator (QPA)

American Society of Petroleum Operations Engineers (ASPOE)

PO Box 6174
Arlington, VA 22206
Phone: (703)768-4159
Fax: (703)684-7476

- Petroleum Operations Engineer (POE)

American Society for Photogrammetry and Remote Sensing (ASPRS)

5410 Grosvenor Ln., Ste. 210
Bethesda, MD 20814-2160
Phone: (301)493-0290
Fax: (301)493-0208

- Certified Mapping Scientist - GIS/LIS
- Certified Mapping Scientist-In-Training
- Certified Mapping Scientist - Remote Sensing
- Certified Photogrammetrist
- Certified Photogrammetrist-In-Training

American Society of Plumbing Engineers (ASPE)
3617 Thousand Oaks Blvd., No. 210
Westlake Village, CA 91362-3649
Phone: (805)495-7120
Fax: (805)495-4861

- Certified in Plumbing Engineering (CIPE)

American Society of Podiatric Medical Assistants (ASPMA)
c/o Joyce Burton
145 W. Mechanic St.
Shelbyville, IN 46176

- Certified Podiatric Medical Assistant

American Society of Professional Estimators (ASPE)
11141 Georgia Ave., Ste. 412
Wheaton, MD 20902
Phone: (301)929-8848
Fax: (301)929-0231

- Certified Professional Estimator (CPE)

American Society for Psychoprophylaxis in Obstetrics (ASPO)
1200 19th St., NW, Ste. 300
Washington, DC 20036
Phone: (202)857-1128
Fax: (202)857-1130
Toll Free: (800)368-4404

- ASPO-Certified Childbirth Educators

American Society for Quality Control (ASQC)
611 E. Wisconsin Ave.
PO Box 3005
Milwaukee, WI 53201-3005
Phone: (414)272-8575
Fax: (414)272-1734
Toll Free: (800)248-1946

- Certified Mechanical Inspector (CMI)
- Certified Quality Auditor (CQA)
- Certified Quality Engineer (CQE)
- Certified Quality Engineer (CQE)
- Certified Quality Manager (CQM)
- Certified Quality Technician (CQT)
- Certified Reliability Engineer (CRE)

American Society of Transportation and Logistics (AST&L)
216 E. Church St.
Lock Haven, PA 17745
Phone: (717)748-8515
Fax: (717)748-9118

- Certification in Transportation and Logistics (CTL)

American Society of Tropical Medicine and Hygiene (ASTMH)
60 Revere Dr., Ste. 500
Northbrook, IL 60062
Phone: (708)480-9592
Fax: (708)480-9282

- Diplomate in Clinical Tropical Medicine

American Sports Medicine Association Board of Certification (ASMABOC)
660 Duarte Rd.
Arcadia, CA 91007
Phone: (818)445-1978

- Active Sports Medicine Trainer
- Certified Sports Medicine Trainer (CSMT)
- Certified Student Trainer
- Pre-Active Sports Medicine Trainer
- Student Trainer

American Translators Association (ATA)
1735 Jefferson Davis Hwy., Ste. 903
Arlington, VA 22202-3413
Phone: (703)412-1500
Fax: (703)412-1501

- Accredited Translator

American Veterinary Dental College (AVDC)
c/o Dr. Sandra Manfra Marretta
Coll. of Veterinary Medicine
Univ. of Illinois
1008 W. Hazelwood Dr.
Urbana, IL 61801
Phone: (217)333-5300
Fax: (217)244-1475

- Diplomate of the American Veterinary Dental College

American Watchmakers-Clockmakers Institute (AWI)
3700 Harrison Ave.
Cincinnati, OH 45211
Phone: (513)661-3838
Fax: (513)661-3131

- Certified Clockmaker (CC)
- Certified Master Clockmaker (CMC)
- Certified Master Electronic Watchmaker (CMEW)
- Certified Master Watchmaker (CMW)
- Certified Watchmaker (CW)

American Welding Society (AWS)
550 LeJeune Rd., NW
Miami, FL 33126
Phone: (305)443-9353
Fax: (305)443-7559
Toll Free: (800)443-9353

- Certified Associate Welding Inspector (CAWI)
- Certified Welder
- Certified Welding Educator (CWE)
- Certified Welding Inspector (CWI)

APICS-The Educational Society for Resource Management
500 W. Annandale Rd.
Falls Church, VA 22046
Phone: (703)237-8344
Fax: (703)237-4316
Toll Free: (800)444-2742

- Certified Fellow in Production and Inventory Management (CFPIM)
- Certified in Integrated Resource Management (CIRM)
- Certified in Production and Inventory Management (CPIM)

Appraisal Institute (AI)
875 N. Michigan Ave., Ste. 2400
Chicago, IL 60611-1980
Phone: (312)335-4100
Fax: (312)335-4480

- Member, Appraisal Institute (MAI)
- Specialist in Residential Appraisal (SRA)

Aquatic Exercise Association (AEA)
PO Box 1609
Nokomis, FL 34274
Phone: (813)486-8600
Fax: (813)486-8820

- Aquatic Fitness Instructor Certification
- Personal Pool Specialty Certification

Association of Certified Fraud Examiners (ACFE)
716 West Ave.
Austin, TX 78701
Phone: (512)478-9070
Fax: (512)478-9297
Toll Free: (800)245-3321

- Certified Fraud Examiner (CFE)

Association of Certified Liquidators (A.C.L.)
1476 Clara Ave.
Columbus, OH 43211-2624
Phone: (614)291-1461
Fax: (614)291-2060

- Certified Liquidator

Association of Consulting Foresters of America (ACF)
5400 Grosvenor Ln., Ste. 300
Bethesda, MD 20814-2198
Phone: (301)530-6795
Fax: (301)530-5128

- Forestland Appraiser (FLA)

Association of Energy Engineers (AEE)

4025 Pleasantdale Rd., Ste. 420
Atlanta, GA 30340
Phone: (404)447-6415
Fax: (404)446-3969

- Certified Cogeneration Professional (CCP)
- Certified Demand-Side Management Professional (CDSM)
- Certified Energy Manager (CEM)
- Certified Indoor Air Quality Professional (CIAQP)
- Certified Lighting Efficiency Professional (CLEP)

Association of Ground Water Scientists and Engineers (AGWSE)

6375 Riverside Dr.
Dublin, OH 43017
Phone: (614)761-1711
Fax: (614)761-3446
Toll Free: (800)551-7379

- Certified Ground Water Professional (CGWP)

Association for Horsemanship Safety and Education

5318 Old Bullard Rd.
Tyler, TX 75703
Phone: (903)509-2473
Fax: (903)509-2474
Toll Free: (800)399-0138

- Certified Riding Instructor

Association of Incentive Marketing (AIM)

1620 Rte. 22 E.
Union, NJ 07083
Phone: (908)687-3090
Fax: (908)687-0977

- Certified Incentive Professional (CIP)

Association of Insolvency Accountants (AIA)

31312 Via Colinas, Ste. 101
Westlake Village, CA 91362
Phone: (818)889-8317
Fax: (818)889-5107

- Certified Insolvency and Reorganization Accountant (CIRA)

Association for Investment Management and Research (AIMR)

Five Boar's Head Ln.
PO Box 3668
Charlottesville, VA 22903-0668
Phone: (804)980-3668
Fax: (804)980-3670

- Chartered Financial Analyst (CFA)

Association for Lactation Consultant Certification (ALCC)

PO Box 2348
Falls Church, VA 22042-0348
Phone: (703)560-7330
Fax: (703)560-7332

- International Board Certified Lactation Consultant (IBCLC)

Association of Machinery and Equipment Appraisers (AMEA)

1110 Spring St.
Silver Spring, MD 20910
Phone: (301)587-9335
Fax: (301)588-7830

- Accredited Machinery and Equipment Appraiser (AMEA)
- Certified Machinery and Equipment Appraiser (CMEA)

Association of Medical Illustrators (AMI)

1819 Peachtree St., NE, Ste. 712
Atlanta, GA 30309
Phone: (404)747-9682
Fax: (404)965-0619
Toll Free: (800)747-9682

- Certified Medical Illustrator

Association of Polysomnographic Technologists (APT)

PO Box 14861
Lenexa, KS 66285-4861
Phone: (913)541-1991
Fax: (913)541-0156

- Registered Polysomnographic Technologist (RPSGT)

Association for Volunteer Administration (AVA)

PO Box 4584
Boulder, CO 80306
Phone: (303)541-0238
Fax: (303)541-0277

- Certified in Volunteer Administration (CVA)

Auto International Association

PO Box 4910
Diamond Bar, CA 91765-0910
Phone: (909)396-0289
Fax: (909)860-0184

- Import Parts Specialist
- Master's Level Import Parts Specialist

Bank Administration Institute (BAI)

One Franklin St.
Chicago, IL 60606
Phone: (312)683-2339
Fax: (312)683-2426
Toll Free: (800)323-8552

- Certified Bank Auditor (CBA)
- Certified Bank Compliance Officer (CBCO)

Biological Photographic Association (BPA)

1819 Peachtree St., NE, Ste. 712
Atlanta, GA 30309
Phone: (404)351-6300
Fax: (404)351-3348

- Registered Biological Photographer (RBP)

Birth Support Providers, International (BSPI)

Four David Ct.
Novato, CA 94947
Toll Free: (800)818-BSPI

- Guided Self-Hypnosis Educator

Board on Certification for Community Health Nursing Practice

American Nurses Credentialing Center
600 Maryland Ave., SW, Ste. 100 West
Washington, DC 20024-2571
Toll Free: (800)284-CERT

- Clinical Specialist in Community Health Nursing
- Community Health Nurse
- School Nurse Practitioner

Board of Certification in Emergency Medicine

804 Main St., Ste. D
Forest Park, GA 30050
Phone: (404)363-8263
Fax: (404)361-2285
Toll Free: (800)447-9397

- Diplomate of the Board of Certification in Emergency Medicine

Board of Certification for Emergency Nursing

216 Higgins Rd.
Park Ridge, IL 60068-5736
Phone: (708)698-9400
Toll Free: (800)243-8362

- Certified Emergency Nurse (CEN)
- Certified Flight Registered Nurse (CFRN)

Board of Certification in Family Practice

804 Main St., Ste. D
Forest Park, GA 30050
Phone: (404)363-8263
Fax: (404)361-2285
Toll Free: (800)447-9397

- Diplomate of the Board of Certification in Family Practice

Board for Certification of Genealogists (BCG)

PO Box 5816
Falmouth, VA 22403-5816

- Certified American Indian Lineage Specialist
- Certified American Lineage Specialist
- Certified Genealogical Instructor
- Certified Genealogical Lecturer
- Certified Genealogical Record Searcher
- Certified Genealogist

Board on Certification for General Nursing Practice

American Nurses Credentialing Center
600 Maryland Ave., SW, Ste. 100 West
Washington, DC 20024-2571
Toll Free: (800)284-CERT

- General Nursing Practice

Board of Certification in Geriatric Medicine

804 Main St., Ste. D
Forest Park, GA 30050
Phone: (404)363-8263
Fax: (404)361-2285
Toll Free: (800)447-9397

- Diplomate of the Board of Certification in Geriatric Medicine

Board on Certification for Gerontological Nursing Practice

American Nurses Credentialing Center
600 Maryland Ave., SW, Ste. 100 West
Washington, DC 20024-2571
Toll Free: (800)284-CERT

- Clinical Specialist in Gerontological Nursing
- Gerontological Nurse
- Gerontological Nurse Practitioner

Board on Certification for Informatics Nursing

American Nurses Credentialing Center
600 Maryland Ave., SW, Ste. 100 West
Washington, DC 20024-2571
Toll Free: (800)284-CERT

- Informatics Nurse

Board on Certification for Maternal-Child Nursing Practice

American Nurses Credentialing Center
600 Maryland Ave., SW, Ste. 100 West
Washington, DC 20024-2571
Toll Free: (800)284-CERT

- Pediatric Nurse
- Pediatric Nurse Practitioner
- Perinatal Nurse

Board on Certification for Medical-Surgical Nursing Practice

American Nurses Credentialing Center
600 Maryland Ave., SW, Ste. 100 West
Washington, DC 20024-2571
Toll Free: (800)284-CERT

- Clinical Specialist in Medical-Surgical Nursing
- Medical-Surgical Nurse

Board on Certification for Nursing Administration Practice

American Nurses Credentialing Center
600 Maryland Ave., SW, Ste. 100 West
Washington, DC 20024-2571
Toll Free: (800)284-CERT

- Certified in Nursing Administration
- Certified in Nursing Administration, Advanced

Board on Certification for Nursing Continuing Education/Staff Development

American Nurses Credentialing Center
600 Maryland Ave., SW, Ste. 100 West
Washington, DC 20024-2571
Toll Free: (800)284-CERT

- Nursing Continuing Education/Staff Development

Board for Certification of Pedorthics (BCP)

9861 Broken Land Pkwy., Ste. 255
Columbia, MD 21046-1151
Phone: (410)381-5729
Fax: (410)381-1167

- Certified Pedorthist (C.Ped.)

Board on Certification for Primary Care in Adult and Family Nursing Practice

American Nurses Credentialing Center
600 Maryland Ave., SW, Ste. 100 West
Washington, DC 20024-2571
Toll Free: (800)284-CERT

- Adult Nurse Practitioner (ANP)
- Family Nurse Practitioner (FNP)

Board of Certification in Professional Ergonomics (BCPE)

PO Box 2811
Bellingham, WA 98227
Phone: (206)671-7601
Fax: (206)671-7681

- Certified Human Factors Professional (CHFP)
- Certified Professional Ergonomist (CPE)

Board on Certification for Psychiatric and Mental Health Nursing Practice

American Nurses Credentialing Center
600 Maryland Ave., SW, Ste. 100 West
Washington, DC 20024-2571
Toll Free: (800)284-CERT

- Clinical Specialist in Adult Psychiatric and Mental Health Nursing
- Clinical Specialist in Child and Adolescent Psychiatric and Mental Health Nursing
- Psychiatric and Mental Health Nurse

Board of Certification in Surgery

804 Main St., Ste. D
Forest Park, GA 30050
Phone: (404)363-8263
Fax: (404)361-2285
Toll Free: (800)447-9397

- Diplomate of the Board of Certification in Surgery
- Diplomate in Critical Care Medicine of the Board of Certification in Surgery
- Diplomate in Ophthalmology of the Board of Certification in Surgery
- Diplomate in Otorhinolaryngology of the Board of Certification in Surgery

Board of Certified Healthcare Safety (BCHSP)

8009 Carita Ct.
Bethesda, MD 20817

- Certified Healthcare Safety Professional, Associate Level (CHSP)
- Certified Healthcare Safety Professional, Master Level (CHSP)
- Certified Healthcare Safety Professional, Senior Level (CHSP)

Board of Certified Product Safety Management (BCPSM)

8009 Carita Ct.
Bethesda, MD 20817
Phone: (301)984-8969

- Certified Product Safety Manager, Associate Level (CPSM)
- Certified Product Safety Manager, Executive Level (CPSM)
- Certified Product Safety Manager, Senior Level (CPSM)

Board of Certified Safety Professionals (BCSP)
208 Burwash Ave.
Savoy, IL 61874
Phone: (217)359-2686
Fax: (217)359-0055

- Certified Occupational Health and Safety Technologist (OHST)

Board of Hazard Control Management
8009 Carita Ct.
MD 20817
Phone: (301)984-8969

- Certified Hazard Control Manager, Associate Level (CHCM)
- Certified Hazard Control Manager, Master Level (CHCM)
- Certified Hazard Control Manager, Senior Level (CHCM)
- Registered Hazard Control Technician

Board of Nephrology Examiners - Nursing and Technology (BONENT)
PO Box 15945-282
Lenexa, KS 66285
Phone: (913)541-9077
Fax: (913)541-0156

- Certified Hemodialysis Nurse (CHN)
- Certified Hemodialysis Technician (CHT)
- Certified Peritoneal Dialysis Nurse (CPDN)

Board for Orthotist Certification (BOC)
Allied Health Bldg., Rm. 234
100 Penn St.
Baltimore, MD 21201-1082
Phone: (410)539-3910

- BOC Orthotist
- Registered Orthotic Fitter (ROF)

Board of Pharmaceutical Specialties (BPS)
2215 Constitution Ave., NW
Washington, DC 20037-2985
Phone: (202)429-7591
Fax: (202)783-2351

- Board Certified Nuclear Pharmacist (BCNP)
- Board Certified Nutrition Support Pharmacist (BCNSP)
- Board Certified Pharmacotherapy Specialist (BCPS)
- Board Certified Psychiatric Pharmacist

Building Owners and Managers Institute (BOMI)
1521 Ritchie Hwy.
Arnold, MD 21012
Phone: (410)974-1410
Fax: (410)974-1935
Toll Free: (800)235-2664

- Facilities Management Administrator (FMA)
- Real Property Administrator (RPA)
- Systems Maintenance Administrator (SMA)
- Systems Maintenance Technician (SMT)

Building Service Contractors Association International (BSCAI)
10201 Lee Hwy., Ste. 225
Fairfax, VA 22030
Phone: (703)359-7090
Fax: (703)352-0493
Toll Free: (800)368-3414

- Certified Building Service Executives (CBSE)
- Certified Sanitary Supply Professional (CSSP)
- Registered Building Service Manager (RBSM)

Business Espionage Controls and Countermeasures Association (BECCA)
PO Box 55582
Seattle, WA 98155-0582
Phone: (206)364-4672
Fax: (206)367-3316

- Certified Confidentiality Officer (CCO)

Business Marketing Association (BMA)
150 N. Wacker Dr., Ste. 1760
Chicago, IL 60606
Phone: (312)409-4262

- Certified Business Communicator (CBC)

Cardiovascular Credentialing International (CCI)
4456 Corporation Ln., Ste. 120
Virginia Beach, VA 23462-3151
Phone: (804)497-3380
Fax: (804)497-3491
Toll Free: (800)326-0268

- Certified Cardiovascular Technologist (CCT)
- Registered Cardiovascular Technologist (RCVT)

Casualty Actuarial Society (CAS)
1110 N. Glebe Rd., Ste. 600
Arlington, VA 22201
Phone: (703)276-3100
Fax: (703)276-3108

- Associate, Casualty Actuarial Society (ACAS)
- Fellow, Casualty Actuarial Society (FCAS)

Certification Board of Infection Control (CBIC)
PO Box 14661
Lenexa, KS 66285-4661
Phone: (913)541-9077
Fax: (913)541-0156

- Certification in Infection Control (CIC)

Certification Board for Music Therapists (CBMT)
1407 Huguenot Rd.
Midlothian, VA 23113-2644
Phone: (804)379-9497
Toll Free: (800)765-CBMT

- Music Therapist - Board Certified (MT-BC)

Certification of Insurance Rehabilitation Specialists Commission (CIRSC)
1835 Rohlwing Rd., Ste. D
Rolling Meadows, IL 60008
Phone: (708)818-0292

- Certified Case Manager (CCM)
- Certified Insurance Rehabilitation Specialist (CIRS)

Certified Claims Professional Accreditation Council (CCPAC)
PO Box 441110
Fort Washington, MD 20744
Phone: (301)292-1988
Fax: (301)292-1787

- Certified Claims Professional (CCP)

Certified Exchangers (CE)
PO Box 12490
Scottsdale, AZ 85267-2490
Phone: (602)860-8838

- Certified Exchanger

Certified Financial Planner Board of Standards
1660 Lincoln St., Ste. 3050
Denver, CO 80264
Phone: (303)830-7543
Fax: (303)860-7388

- Certified Financial Planner (CFP)

Certified Medical Representatives Institute (CMRI)
4950 Brambleton Ave., SE
Roanoke, VA 24018
Toll Free: (800)274-2674

- Certified Medical Representative (CMR)

Certified Perinatal Educators Association (CPEA)
Four David Ct.
Novato, CA 94947
Phone: (415)893-0439

- Childbirth Educator

Certified Professional Insurance Agents Society (CPIA Society)
400 N. Washington St.
Alexandria, VA 22314
Phone: (703)836-0834
Fax: (703)836-1279

- Certified Professional Insurance Agent (CPIA)

Certified Strength and Conditioning Specialist Agency
PO Box 83469
Lincoln, NE 68501
Phone: (402)476-6669
Fax: (403)476-7141

- Certified Personal Trainer (CPT)
- Certified Strength and Conditioning Specialist (CSCS)

Certifying Board for Dietary Managers (CBDM)
One Pierce Pl., Ste. 1220W
Itasca, IL 60143
Phone: (708)775-9200
Fax: (708)775-9250

- Certified Dietary Manager (CDM)

Certifying Board of Gastroenterology Nurses and Associates (CBGNA)
720 Light St.
Baltimore, MD 21230
Phone: (410)752-1808
Fax: (410)752-8295

- Certified Gastroenterology Associate (CGA)
- Certified Gastroenterology Licensed Vocational/Practical Nurse (CGN)
- Certified Gastroenterology Registered Nurse (CGRN)
- Certified Gastroenterology Technologist/Technician (CGT)

Chimney Sweep Institute of America (CSIA)
16021 Industrial Dr., Ste. 8
Gaithersburg, MD 20877
Phone: (301)963-6900
Fax: (301)963-0838

- Certified Chimney Sweep

Cleaning Management Institute (CMI)
13 Century Hill Dr.
Latham, NY 12110-2197
Phone: (518)783-1281
Fax: (518)783-1386

- Custodial Maintenance Supervisor
- Custodial Technician, Level I
- Custodial Technician, Level II

Club Managers Association of America (CMAA)
1733 King St.
Alexandria, VA 22314
Phone: (703)739-9500
Fax: (703)739-0124

- Certified Club Manager (CCM)
- Master Club Manager (MCM)

Commercial Investment Real Estate Institute (CIREI)
430 N. Michigan Ave., Ste. 600
Chicago, IL 60611-4092
Phone: (312)321-4485
Fax: (312)321-4530
Toll Free: (800)621-7027

- Certified Commercial Investment Member (CCIM)

Commission on Dietetic Registration (CDR)
216 W. Jackson Blvd., Ste. 800
Chicago, IL 60606-6995
Phone: (312)899-0040
Fax: (312)899-1772

- Registered Dietetic Technician (RDT)
- Registered Dietician (RD)

Commission on Disability Examiner Certification (CDEC)
9101 Midlothian Tpke., Ste. 200
PO Box 35407
Richmond, VA 23235-0407
Phone: (804)378-8809

- Certified Disability Examiner (CDE)

Commission on Rehabilitation Counselor Certification (CRCC)
1835 Rohlwing Rd., Ste. E
Rolling Meadows, IL 60008
Phone: (708)394-2104

- Certified Rehabilitation Counselor (CRC)

Community Associations Institute (CAI)
1630 Duke St.
Alexandria, VA 22314
Phone: (703)548-8600
Fax: (703)684-1581

- Association Management Specialist (AMS)
- Professional Community Association Manager (PCAM)

Computing Technology Industry Association (CompTIA)
450 E. 22nd St., Ste. 230
Lombard, IL 60148-6158
Phone: (708)268-1818
Fax: (708)268-1384
Toll Free: (800)77M-ICRO

- A Certified Service Technician

Convention Liaison Council (CLC)
1575 Eye St., NW, Ste. 1190
Washington, DC 20005
Phone: (202)626-2764
Fax: (202)408-9652

- Certified Meeting Professional (CMP)

Cooper Institute for Aerobics Research
12330 Preston Rd.
Dallas, TX 75230
Phone: (214)386-0306
Toll Free: (800)635-7050

- Advanced Physical Fitness Specialist (Adv. PFS)
- Group Exercise Leadership (GEL)
- Physical Fitness Specialist (PFS)
- Program Director Specialist (PDS)

Council for Accreditation in Occupational Hearing Conservation (CAOHC)
611 E. Wells St.
Milwaukee, WI 53202
Phone: (414)276-5338
Fax: (414)276-3349

- Certified Occupational Hearing Conservationist

Council of American Building Officials (CABO)
5203 Leesburg Piike, Ste. 708
Falls Church, VA 22041
Phone: (703)931-4533
Fax: (703)379-1546

- Certified Building Official

Council on Certification of Nurse Anesthetists (CCNA)
222 S. Prospect Ave.
Park Ridge, IL 60068-4001
Phone: (708)692-7050
Fax: (708)692-6968

- Certified Registered Nurse Anesthetist (CRNA)

Council for Early Childhood Professional Recognition (CECPR)
1341 G St., NW, Ste. 400
Washington, DC 20005
Phone: (202)265-9090
Fax: (202)265-9161
Toll Free: (800)424-4310

- Child Development Associate (CDA)

Council on Licensure, Enforcement, and Regulation (CLEAR)
201 W. Short St., Ste. 410
Lexington, KY 40507
Phone: (606)231-1901
Fax: (606)231-1943
E-mail: CLEAR1@UKCC.UKY.EDU

- Certified Investigator/Inspector, Level I
- Certified Investigator/Inspector, Level II

Council for Qualifications of Residential Interior Designers
PO Box 1757
High Point, NC 27261
Phone: (910)883-1680
Fax: (910)883-1195

- Registered/Certified Residential Interior Designer

Counselors of Real Estate
430 N. Michigan Ave.
Chicago, IL 60611-4089
Phone: (312)329-8427
Fax: (312)329-8881

- Counselor of Real Estate (CRE)

Credit Union National Association (CUNA)
Human Resource Development Division
PO Box 431
Madison, WI 53701-0431
Phone: (608)231-4000
Toll Free: (800)358-5710

- Certified Credit Union Executive (CCUE)

Data Education Certification Council (DECC)
c/o Dr. Robert Behling
Bryant Coll.
Smithfield, RI 02917

- Certified Data Educator (CDE)

Dental Assisting National Board (DANB)
216 E. Ontario St.
Chicago, IL 60611
Phone: (312)642-3368

- Certified Dental Assistant (CDA)
- Certified Dental Practice Management Assistant (CDPMA)
- Certified Oral and Maxillofacial Surgery Assistant (COMSA)
- Certified Orthodontic Assistant (COA)

Diamond Council of America (DCA)
9140 Ward Pkwy.
Kansas City, MO 64114
Phone: (816)444-3500
Fax: (816)444-0330

- Advanced Executive Manager
- Certified Diamontologist
- Certified Managerial Associate
- Guild Gemologist
- Professional Sales Associate

Educational Institute of the American Hotel and Motel Association
1407 S. Harrison Rd.
PO Box 1240
East Lansing, MI 48826-1240
Phone: (517)353-5500
Fax: (517)353-5527

- Certified Engineering Operations Executive (CEOE)
- Certified Food and Beverage Executive (CFBE)
- Certified Hospitality Educator (CHE)
- Certified Hospitality Housekeeping Executive (CHHE)
- Certified Hospitality Sales Professional (CHSP)
- Certified Hospitality Supervisor (CHS)
- Certified Hotel Administrator (CHA)
- Certified Human Resources Executive (CHRE)
- Certified Rooms Division Executive (CRDE)
- Master Hotel Supplier (MHS)

Electronics Technicians Association, International (ETA-I)
602 N. Jackson
Greencastle, IN 46135
Phone: (317)653-8262
Fax: (317)653-8262

- Associate Electronics Technician
- Certified Customer Service Specialist (CSS)
- Certified Electronics Technician (CET)
- Certified Satellite Installer (CSI)
- Master Certified Electronics Technician (MASTER CET)
- Senior Certified Electronics Technician (SCET)

Employee Assistance Professionals Association (EAPA)
2101 Wilson Blvd., Ste. 500
Arlington, VA 22201
Phone: (703)522-6272
Fax: (703)522-4585

- Certified Employee Assistance Professional (CEAP)

Employee Relocation Council (ERC)
1720 N St., NW
Washington, DC 20036
Phone: (202)857-0857
Fax: (202)467-4012

- Certified Relocation Professional (CRP)
- Senior Certified Relocation Professional (SCRP)

Entomological Society of America (ESA)
9301 Annapolis Rd.
Lanham, MD 20706-3115
Phone: (301)731-4535
Fax: (301)731-4538

- Board Certified Entomologist (BCE)

Evidence Photographers International Council (EPIC)
600 Main St.
Honesdale, PA 18431
Phone: (717)253-5450
Fax: (717)253-4398
Toll Free: (800)356-3742

- Certified Professional Evidence Photographer (Civil Evidence Photography)
- Certified Professional Evidence Photographer (Law Enforcement Photography)

Expediting Management Association (EMA)
40 Irwin St.
New Hyde Park, NY 11040
Phone: (516)746-7438
Fax: (516)746-7438

- Certified Expediting Manager (CEM)

Eye Bank Association of America (EBAA)
1001 Connecticut Ave., NW, Ste. 601
Washington, DC 20036-5504
Phone: (202)775-4999
Fax: (202)429-6036

- Certified Eye Bank Technician

Fire Protection Specialist Certification Board
c/o EMACS
PO Box 198
Ashland, MA 01721
Phone: (508)881-6044
Fax: (508)881-6829

- Certified Fire Protection Specialist (CFPS)

Fluid Power Society (FPS)
2433 N. Mayfair Rd., Ste. 111
Milwaukee, WI 53226
Phone: (414)257-0910
Fax: (414)257-4092

- Fluid Power Electrician
- Fluid Power Engineer
- Fluid Power Specialist
- Hydraulic Technician
- Industrial Hydraulic Mechanic
- Mobile Hydraulic Mechanic
- Pneumatic Mechanic
- Pneumatic Technician

Foundation for Hospice and Homecare (FHH)
513 C St., NE
Washington, DC 20002-5809
Phone: (202)547-6586
Fax: (202)546-8968

- Certified Home Care Aide

Golf Course Superintendents Association of America (GCSAA)
1421 Research Park Dr.
Lawrence, KS 66049-3859
Phone: (913)841-2240
Fax: (913)832-4455
Toll Free: (800)472-7878

- Certified Golf Course Superintendent (CGCS)

Graphic Arts Sales Foundation (GASF)
Matlack Bldg., Ste. A
113 E. Evans St.
West Chester, PA 19380
Phone: (610)431-9780
Fax: (610)436-5238

- Certified Graphic Arts Sales Representative (CGASR)

Health Care Material Management Society (HCMMS)
306 Crestview Dr.
Grapevine, TX 76051-3569
Phone: (817)421-8517
Fax: (817)421-8971
Toll Free: (800)543-5885

- Certified Professional in Healthcare Materials Management (CPHM)
- Distinguished Professional in Healthcare Materials Management (DPHM)
- Recognition of Expertise, Health Care Materials Management Society

Health Insurance Association of America (HIAA)
555 13th St., NW, Ste. 600 E.
Washington, DC 20004-1109
Phone: (202)223-7789
Fax: (202)824-1800

- Health Insurance Associate (HIA)
- Managed Healthcare Professional (MHP)

Healthcare Financial Management Association (HFMA)
Two Westbrook Corporate Center, Ste. 700
Westchester, IL 60154
Phone: (708)531-9600
Fax: (708)531-0032
Toll Free: (800)252-HFMA

- Certified Manager of Patient Accounts (CMPA)
- Fellow, Healthcare Financial Management Association (FHFMA)

Healthcare Quality Certification Board (HQCB)
JLM Associates
PO Box 1880
San Gabriel, CA 91778
Phone: (818)286-8074
Fax: (818)286-9415
Toll Free: (800)346-4722

- Certified Professional in Healthcare Quality (CPHQ)

Hearth Education Foundation
3019 Perry Ln.
Austin, TX 78731
Phone: (512)450-0987
Fax: (512)450-1649

- Certified Fireplace Hearth Specialist
- Certified Gas Appliance Hearth Specialist
- Certified Pellet Appliance Hearth Specialist
- Certified Woodstove Hearth Specialist

Horsemanship Safety Association (HSA)
Drawer 39
Fentress, TX 78622-0039
Toll Free: (800)798-8106

- Advanced Rider
- Beginning Rider
- Certified Rider Candidate
- Early Intermediate Rider
- Horse Safety Assistant Instructor (HSAI)
- Horse Safety Assistant Trail Guide (HSGA)
- Horse Safety Clinician (HSC)
- Horse Safety Instructor (HSI)
- Horse Safety Instructor/Trainer (HSI/T)
- Horse Safety Riding Instructor Basic (HSRIB)
- Horse Safety Trail Guide (HSG)
- Intermediate Rider

Hospitality Sales and Marketing Association International (HSMAI)
1300 L St., NW, Ste. 800
Washington, DC 20005
Phone: (202)789-0089
Fax: (202)789-1725

- Certified Hospitality Sales Executive (CHSE)

Human Resource Certification Institute (HRCI)
606 N. Washington St.
Alexandria, VA 22314
Phone: (703)548-3440
Fax: (703)836-0367

- Professional in Human Resources (PHR)
- Senior Professional in Human Resources (SPHR)

Humanist Society of Friends (HSA)
Seven Harwood Dr.
PO Box 1188
Amherst, NY 14226-7188
Phone: (716)839-5080
Toll Free: (800)743-6646

- Humanist Counselor
- Humanist Officiant

IBFI - The International Association
2111 Wilson Blvd., Ste. 350
Arlington, VA 22201-3042
Phone: (703)841-9191
Fax: (703)522-5750

- Certified Forms Press Operator

Independent Educational Consultants Association (IECA)
4085 Chain Bridge Rd.
Fairfax, VA 22030
Phone: (703)591-4850

- Certified Educational Planner

Independent Insurance Agents of America (IIAA)
127 S. Peyton St.
PO Box 1497
Alexandria, VA 22314
Phone: (703)683-4422
Fax: (703)688-7556
Toll Free: (800)221-7917

- Accredited Customer Service Representative (ACSR)

Information Systems Audit and Control Association
3701 Algonquin Rd., Ste. 1010
Rolling Meadows, IL 60008
Phone: (708)253-1545
Fax: (708)253-1443

- Certified Information Systems Auditor (CISA)

Institute of Business Appraisers (IBA)
PO Box 1447
Boynton Beach, FL 33425
Phone: (407)732-3202

- Certified Business Appraiser (CBA)

Institute for Certification of Computing Professionals (ICCP)
2200 E. Devon Ave., Ste. 268
Des Plaines, IL 60018-4503
Phone: (708)299-4227
Fax: (708)299-4280
E-mail: Compuserve 74040,3722

- Associate Computing Professional (ACP)
- Certified Computing Professional (CCP)

Institute for Certification of Tax Professionals (ICTP)
1832 Stratford Pl.
Pomona, CA 91628
Phone: (909)629-1460

- Certified Tax Consultant (CTC)

Institute for Certification of Tax Professionals (ICTP)
1832 Stratford Pl.
Pomona, CA 91768
Phone: (909)629-1460

- Certified Tax Accountant (CTA)

Institute for Certified Bankers (ICB)
1120 Connecticut Ave., NW, Ste. 600
Washington, DC 20036
Phone: (202)663-5380
Fax: (202)663-7543
Toll Free: (800)338-0626

- Certified Corporate Trust Specialist (CCTS)
- Certified Financial Services Security Professional (CFSSP)
- Certified Lender-Business Banking (CLBB)
- Certified Regulatory Compliance Manager (CRCM)
- Certified Trust and Financial Advisor (CTFA)
- Employee Benefit Certified Trust Professional (EBCTP)

Institute of Certified Business Counselors (ICBC)
PO Box 70326
Eugene, OR 97401
Phone: (503)345-8064
Fax: (503)726-2402

- Certified Business Counselor (CBC)

Institute of Certified Management Accountants (ICMA)
Ten Paragon Dr.
Montvale, NJ 07645-1759
Phone: (201)573-9000
Fax: (201)573-8438
Toll Free: (800)638-4427

- Certified Management Accountant (CMA)

Institute of Certified Professional Business Consultants (ICPBC)
330 S. Wells St., Ste. 1422
Chicago, IL 60606
Fax: (312)360-0388
Toll Free: (800)447-1684

- Certified Professional Business Consultant (CPBC)

Institute of Certified Professional Managers (ICPM)
James Madison Univ.
Harrisonburg, VA 22807
Phone: (703)568-3247
Fax: (703)568-3587
Toll Free: (800)568-4120

- Associate Certified Manager (ACM)
- Certified Manager (CM)

Institute of Certified Records Managers (ICRM)
PO Box 8188
Prairie Village, KS 66208
Toll Free: (800)825-4276

- Certified Records Manager (CRM)

Institute of Certified Travel Agents (ICTA)
148 Linden St.
PO Box 812059
Wellesley, MA 02181-0012
Phone: (617)237-0280
Fax: (617)237-3860
Toll Free: (800)542-4282

- Certified Travel Counselor (CTC)

Institute for Corporate Real Estate
440 Columbia Dr., Ste. 100
West Palm Beach, FL 33409
Phone: (407)683-8111
Fax: (407)697-4853

- Master of Corporate Real Estate (MCR)

Institute of Hazardous Materials Management (IHMM)
11900 Parklawn Dr., Ste. 450
Rockville, MD 20852
Phone: (301)984-8969

- Certified Hazardous Materials Manager (Master Level)
- Certified Hazardous Materials Manager (Senior Level)

Institute of Inspection, Cleaning, and Restoration Certification
2715 E. Mill Plain Blvd.
Vancouver, WA 98661
Phone: (206)693-5675
Fax: (206)693-4858

- Carpet Cleaning Technician
- Carpet Repair and Reinstallation Technician
- Color Repair Technician
- Fire and Smoke Restoration Technician
- Odor Control Technician
- Senior Carpet Inspector
- Upholstery and Fabric Cleaning Technician
- Water Damage Restoration Technician

Institute of Internal Auditors (IIA)
249 Maitland Ave.
Altamonte Springs, FL 32701-4201
Phone: (407)830-7600
Fax: (407)831-5171

- Certified Internal Auditor (CIA)

Institute of Management Consultants (IMC)
521 Fifth Ave., 35th Fl.
New York, NY 10175-3598
Phone: (212)697-8262
Fax: (212)949-6571

- Certified Management Consultant (CMC)

Institute of Packaging Professionals (IoPP)
481 Carlisle Dr.
Herndon, VA 22070
Phone: (703)318-8970
Fax: (703)318-0310

- Certified Packaging Professional (CPP)

Institute of Professional Environmental Practice (IPEP)
One Gateway Center, Third Fl.
Pittsburgh, PA 15222
Phone: (412)232-0901
Fax: (412)232-0181

- Qualified Environmental Professional (QEP)

Institute of Real Estate Management (IREM)
430 N. Michigan Ave.
PO Box 109025
Chicago, IL 60610-9025
Phone: (312)661-0004
Fax: (312)661-1936

- Accredited Residential Manager (ARM)
- Certified Property Manager (CPM)

Institute for Research in Hypnosis and Psychotherapy (IRHP)

1991 Broadway, Apt. 18B
New York, NY 10023
Phone: (212)874-5290
Fax: (914)238-1422

- Clinical Associate in Hypnotherapy

Institute of Tax Consultants (ITC)

7500 212th, SW, No. 205
Edmonds, WA 98026
Phone: (206)774-3521
Fax: (206)672-0461

- Certified Tax Preparer (CTP)
- Certified Tax Preparer Master (CTPM)
- Certified Tax Preparer Specialist (CTPS)

Institutional and Municipal Parking Congress (IMPC)

701 Kenmore Ave., Ste. 200
PO Box 7167
Fredericksburg, VA 22404-7167
Phone: (703)371-7535
Fax: (703)371-8022

- Certified Administrator of Public Parking

Insurance Data Management Association (IDMA)

85 John St.
New York, NY 10038
Phone: (212)669-0496
Fax: (212)669-0535

- Associate Insurance Data Manager (AIDM)
- Certified Insurance Data Manager (CIDM)

Insurance Institute of America (IIA)

720 Providence Rd.
PO Box 3016
Malvern, PA 19355-0716
Phone: (610)644-2100
Fax: (610)640-9576
Toll Free: (800)644-2101

- Accredited Adviser in Insurance (AAI)
- Associate in Automation Management (AAM)
- Associate in Claims (AIC)
- Associate in Fidelity and Surety Bonding (AFSB)
- Associate in Insurance Accounting and Finance Life and Health Insurance (AIAF)
- Associate in Insurance Accounting and Finance Property and Casualty (AIAF)
- Associate in Insurance Services (AIS)
- Associate in Loss Control Management (ALCM)
- Associate in Management (AIM)
- Associate in Marine Insurance Management (AMIM)
- Associate in Premium Auditing (APA)
- Associate in Reinsurance (ARe)
- Associate in Research and Planning (ARP)
- Associate in Research and Planning (Life Insurance Option) (ARP)
- Associate in Risk Management (ARM)
- Associate in Underwriting (AU)

Insurance Regulatory Examiners Society

130 N. Cherry, Ste. 202
Olathe, KS 66061
Phone: (913)768-4700
Fax: (913)768-4900

- Accredited Insurance Examiner (AIE)
- Certified Insurance Examiner (CIE)

International Association of Arson Investigators (IAAI)

300 S. Broadway, Ste. 100
St. Louis, MO 63102-2808
Phone: (314)621-1966
Fax: (314)621-5125

- Certified Fire Investigator (CFI)

International Association of Assessing Officers (IAAO)

130 E. Randolph St., Ste. 850
Chicago, IL 60601
Phone: (312)819-6104
Fax: (312)819-6149

- Assessment Administration Specialist (AAS)
- Cadastral Mapping Specialist (CMS)
- Certified Assessment Evaluator (CAE)
- Personal Property Specialist (PPS)
- Residential Evaluation Specialist (RES)

International Association of Business Communicators (IABC)

One Hallidie Plaza, Ste. 600
San Francisco, CA 94102
Phone: (415)433-3400
Fax: (415)362-8762

- Accredited Business Communicator (ABC)

International Association for Colon Hydrotherapy

2051 Hilltop Dr., Ste. A-11
Redding, CA 96002
Phone: (916)222-1498
Fax: (916)222-1497

- Certified Colon Hydrotherapist

International Association of Eating Disorders Professionals (IAEDP)

123 NW 13th St., Ste. 206
Boca Raton, FL 33432
Phone: (407)338-6494
Fax: (407)338-9913
Toll Free: (800)800-8126

- Certified Eating Disorders Associate (CEDA)
- Certified Eating Disorders Specialist (CEDS)

International Association of Equine Dental Technicians (IAEDT)

PO Box 6095
Wilmington, DE 19804
Phone: (302)892-9215
Toll Free: (800)334-6095

- Certified Member of the International Association of Equine Dental Technicians

International Association of Healthcare Central Service Material Management (IAHCSMM)

214 W. Institute Pl., Ste. 307
Chicago, IL 60610
Phone: (312)440-0078
Fax: (312)440-9474
Toll Free: (800)962-8274

- Certification in Central Service Management Concepts (CCSMC)
- Certified Registered Central Service Technician (CRCST)
- Fellowship in Central Service (FCS)

International Association of Hospitality Accountants (IAHA)

PO Box 203008
Austin, TX 78720-3008
Phone: (512)346-5680
Fax: (512)346-5760

- Certified Hospitality Accountant Executive (CHAE)

International Association of Knowledge Engineers (IAKE)

973D Russell Ave.
Gaithersburg, MD 20879-3276
Phone: (301)948-5390
Fax: (301)926-4243
Toll Free: (800)833-6464

- Certified Knowledge Engineer (CKE)

International Association of Lighting Management Companies (NALMCO)

34-C Washington Rd.
Princeton Junction, NJ 08550-1028
Phone: (609)799-5501

- Certified Lighting Management Consultant (CLMC)

International Association of Personnel in Employment Security (IAPES)
1801 Louisville Rd.
Frankfort, KY 40601
Phone: (502)223-4459
Fax: (502)223-4127
Toll Free: (800)662-2255

- Employment Services Specialist (ESS)
- Employment and Training Generalist (ETG)
- Employment and Training Master (ETM)
- Job Training Specialist (JTS)
- Labor Market Information Specialist (LMIS)
- Unemployment Insurance Specialist (UIS)

International Association of Plumbing and Mechanical Officials (IAPMO)
20001 Walnut Dr., S.
Walnut, CA 91789-2825
Phone: (909)595-8449
Fax: (909)594-1537

- Certified Plumbing Inspector

International Association of Professional Natural Hygienists (IAPNH)
204 Stambaugh Bldg.
Youngstown, OH 44503
Phone: (216)746-5000
Fax: (216)746-1836

- Certified Professional Natural Hygienist

International Association of Trichologists
1511 W. Florence St.
Los Angeles, CA 90047

- Certified Trichologist

International Board of Electrology Certification
106 Oak Ridge Rd.
Trumbull, CT 06611
Phone: (203)374-6667
Fax: (203)372-7134

- Certified Professional Electrologist (C.P.E.)

International Certification Commission (ICC)
3330 Washington Blvd., Ste. 400
Arlington, VA 22201
Phone: (703)525-4890
Fax: (703)276-0793
Toll Free: (800)332-2264

- Certified Biomedical Equipment Technician (CBET)
- Certified Laboratory Equipment Specialist (CLES)
- Certified Radiology Equipment Specialist (CRES)

International Claims Association (ICA)
2300 Windy Ridge Pkwy., Ste. 600
Atlanta, GA 30339-8443
Phone: (770)951-1770
Fax: (770)984-0441

- Associate, Life and Health Claims (ALHC)

International College of Real Estate Consulting Professionals
297 Dakota St.
Le Sueur, MN 56058
Phone: (612)665-6280
Fax: (612)665-6280

- Real Estate Consulting Professional (RECP)

International Conference of Building Officials (ICBO)
5360 Workman Mill Rd.
Whittier, CA 90601-2298
Phone: (310)699-0541
Fax: (310)692-3853

- ICBO Building Code Accessibility/Usability Specialist
- ICBO Building Contractor
- ICBO Building Inspector
- ICBO CABO One and Two Family Dwelling Inspector
- ICBO Combination Dwelling Inspector
- ICBO Combination Inspector
- ICBO Electrical Inspector
- ICBO Elevator Inspector
- ICBO General Contractor
- ICBO Light Commercial Combination Inspector
- ICBO Mechanical Inspector
- ICBO Plans Examiner
- ICBO Prestressed Concrete Special Inspector
- ICBO Reinforced Concrete Special Inspector
- ICBO Residential Contractor
- ICBO Spray-Applied Fireproofing Special Inspector
- ICBO Structural Masonry Special Inspector
- ICBO Structural Steel and Welding Special Inspector

International Council of Shopping Centers (ICSC)
665 Fifth Ave.
New York, NY 10022
Phone: (212)421-8181
Fax: (212)486-0849

- Certified Leasing Specialist (CLS)
- Certified Marketing Director (CMD)
- Certified Shopping Center Manager (CSM)
- Senior Certified Shopping Center Manager (SCSM)
- Senior Level Certified Marketing Director

International Electrical Testing Association (NETA)
106 Stone St.
PO Box 687
Morrison, CO 80465
Phone: (303)697-8441
Fax: (303)697-8431

- NETA Certified Test Technician

International Exhibitors Association (IEA)
5501 Backlick Rd., Ste. 105
Springfield, VA 22151
Phone: (703)941-3725
Fax: (703)941-8275

- Certified Manager of Exhibits (CME)

International Facility Management Association (IFMA)
One E. Greenway Plaza, Ste. 1100
Houston, TX 77046
Phone: (713)623-4363
Fax: (713)623-6124
Toll Free: (800)359-4362

- Certified Facility Manager (CFM)

International Fire Code Institute (IFCI)
5360 Workman Mill Rd.
Whittier, CA 90601-2298
Phone: (310)699-0541

- Company Fire Code Inspector
- Tank Tightness Testing Certification
- Underground Storage Tank Cathodic Certification
- Underground Storage Tank Decommissioning Certification
- Underground Storage Tank Installation/Retrofitting Certification
- Uniform Fire Code Inspector

International Food Service Executives Association (IFSEA)
1100 S. State Rd. 7, Ste. 103
Margate, FL 33068
Phone: (305)977-0767
Fax: (305)977-0874

- Certified Food Executive (CFE)
- Certified Food Manager (CFM)

International Foundation of Employee Benefit Plans
18700 W Bluemound Rd.
PO Box 1270
Brookfield, WI 53008-1270
Phone: (414)786-6700
Fax: (414)786-2990

- Certified Employee Benefits Specialist (CEBS)

International Foundation for Protection Officers (IFPO)

4200 Meridian, Ste. 200
Bellingham, WA 98226
Phone: (206)733-1571
Fax: (206)671-4329

- Certified Protection Officer (CPO)
- Certified Security Supervisor (CSS)

International Institute of Convention Management

9200 Bayard Pl.
Fairfax, VA 22032
Phone: (703)978-6287
Fax: (703)978-5524

- Certified International Convention Manager (CICM)

International Medical and Dental Hypnotherapy Association (IMDHA)

4110 Edgeland, Ste. 800
Royal Oak, MI 48073
Phone: (810)549-5594
Fax: (810)549-5421
Toll Free: (800)257-5467

- Certified Hypnotherapist (C.Ht.)

International Municipal Signal Association (IMSA)

165 E. Union St.
PO Box 539
Newark, NY 14513
Phone: (315)331-2182
Fax: (315)331-8205
Toll Free: (800)723-4672

- Apprentice Signs and Markings Specialist
- Associate Fire Alarm Technician
- Associate Interior Fire Alarm Technician
- Associate Signs and Markings Specialist
- Associate Traffic Signal Technician
- EMS Dispatcher
- Fire Alarm Engineering Technician
- Fire Service Dispatcher
- Flagging and Traffic Control Certification
- Law Enforcement Dispatcher
- Municipal Fire Alarm Technician
- Public Safety Dispatcher, Level I
- Public Safety Dispatcher, Level II
- Roadway Lighting Certification, Level I
- Roadway Lighting Certification, Level II
- Signs and Markings Specialist
- Traffic Signal Electrician
- Traffic Signal Technician
- Traffic Signal Technician, Level III
- Work Zone Traffic Safety Specialist

International Publishing Management Association (IPMA)

1205 W. College St.
Liberty, MO 64068-3733
Phone: (816)781-1111
Fax: (816)781-2790
E-mail: CompuServe 71674.1647

- Certified Graphics Communications Manager (CGCM)
- Certified Mail Manager (CMM)

International Real Estate Section, National Association of Realtors

430 N. Michigan Ave.
Chicago, IL 60611-4087
Phone: (312)329-3278
Fax: (312)329-8338
Toll Free: (800)874-6500

- Certified International Property Specialist (CIPS)

International Security and Detective Alliance (ISDA)

Box 6303
Corpus Christi, TX 78466-6303
Phone: (512)888-6164
Fax: (512)888-6164

- Certified Civil and Criminal Investigator (C.C.C.I.)
- Certified Civil Process Officer (C.C.P.O.)
- Certified Financial Fraud Investigator (C.F.F.I.)
- Certified Fire and Arson Investigator (C.F.A.I.)
- Certified Insurance Investigator (C.I.I.)
- Certified International Courier (C.I.C.)
- Certified International Investigator (C.I.I.)
- Certified Missing Persons Investigator (C.M.P.I.)
- Certified Professional Investigator (C.P.I.)
- Certified Protection Specialist (C.P.S.)
- Certified Security Consultant (C.S.C.)
- Certified Security Specialist (C.S.S.)
- Industrial Counter-Espionage Specialist (I.C.E.S.)

International Society of Appraisers (ISA)

Riverview Plaza Office Park, Ste. 320
16040 Christensen Rd.
Seattle, WA 98188
Phone: (206)241-0359
Fax: (206)241-0436

- Certified Appraiser of Personal Property (CAPP)
- Member, International Society of Appraisers

International Society of Arboriculture (ISA)

PO Box GG
Savoy, IL 61874-9902
Phone: (217)355-9411
Fax: (217)355-9516

- Certified Arborist

International Society of Certified Electronics Technicians (ISCET)

2708 W. Berry St.
Fort Worth, TX 76109
Phone: (817)921-9101
Fax: (817)921-3741

- Certified Appliance Technician (CAT)
- Certified Electronics Technician (Associate) (CET)
- Certified Electronics Technician (Journeyman) (CET)

International Society for Clinical Laboratory Technology (ISCLT)

818 Olive St., Ste. 918
St. Louis, MO 63101-1598
Phone: (314)241-1445
Fax: (314)241-1449

- Physician Office Laboratory Technician (POLT)
- Registered Laboratory Technician (RLT)
- Registered Medical Technologist (RMT)

International Veterinary Acupuncture Society (IVAS)

c/o Dr. Merideth L. Snader
2140 Conestoga Rd.
Chester Springs, PA 19425
Phone: (215)827-7245
Fax: (215)687-3605

- Certified Veterinary Acupuncturist

Intravenous Nurses Society (INS)

Two Brighton St.
Belmont, MA 02178
Phone: (617)489-5205
Fax: (617)489-0656
Toll Free: (800)434-INCC

- Certified Registered Nurse Intravenous (CRNI)

Investment Management Consultants Association (IMCA)

9101 E. Kenyon Ave., Ste. 300
Denver, CO 80237
Phone: (303)770-3377
Fax: (303)770-1812

- Certified Investment Management Analyst (CIMA)

Irrigation Association (IA)

8260 Wilow Oak Corp Dr.
Fairfax, VA 22031
Phone: (703)573-3551
Fax: (703)573-1913

- Certified Irrigation Contractor (CIC)
- Certified Irrigation Designer (CID)
- Certified Landscape Irrigation Auditor (CLIA)

ISA, The International Society for Measurement and Control

67 Alexander Dr.
PO Box 12277
Research Triangle Park, NC 27709
Phone: (919)549-8411
Fax: (919)549-8288
E-mail: INFO@ISA.ORG

- Certified Specialist in Analytical Technology (CSAT)
- Certified Specialist in Measurement Technology (CSMT)

Joint Commission on Allied Health Personnel in Ophthalmology (JCAHPO)

2025 Woodlane Dr.
St. Paul, MN 55125-2995
Phone: (612)731-2944
Fax: (612)731-0410
Toll Free: (800)284-3937

- Certified Ophthalmic Assistant (COA)
- Certified Ophthalmic Medical Technologist (COMT)
- Certified Ophthalmic Technician (COT)
- Ophthalmic Surgical Assisting (OSA)

Laubach Literacy Action (LLA)

1320 Jamesville Ave.
Box 131
Syracuse, NY 13210
Phone: (315)422-9121
Fax: (315)422-6369

- LLA Certified Trainer
- LLA Certified Supervising Trainer

Liaison Council on Certification for the Surgical Technologist (LCC-ST)

7108-C S. Alton Way
Englewood, CO 80112
Phone: (303)694-9264
Fax: (303)694-9169
Toll Free: (800)637-7433

- Certified Surgical Technologist (CST)
- Certified Surgical

Technologist/Certified First Assistant (CST/CFA)

Life Office Management Association (LOMA)

5770 Powers Ferry Rd.
Atlanta, GA 30327-4308
Phone: (404)951-1770
Fax: (404)984-0441

- Associate, Customer Service (ACS)
- Associate, Insurance Agency Administration (AIAA)
- Fellow, Life Management Institute (FLMI)

Life Underwriter Training Council (LUTC)

7625 Wisconsin Ave.
Bethesda, MD 20814
Phone: (301)913-5882
Fax: (301)913-0123

- Life Underwriter Training Council Fellow (LUTCF)

Lightning Protection Institute (LPI)

3365 N. Arlington Heights Rd., Ste. J
Arlington Heights, IL 60004
Phone: (708)255-3003
Fax: (708)577-7276
Toll Free: (800)488-6864

- LPI Certified Designer/Inspector
- LPI Certified Journeyman Installer
- LPI Certified Master Installer
- LPI Certified Master Installer/Designer

Mail Systems Management Association (MSMA)

J.A.F. Bldg.
Box 2155
New York, NY 10116
Phone: (607)746-7600
Toll Free: (800)955-MSMA

- Certified Mail and Distribution Systems Manager (CMDSM)

Manufacturers Representatives Educational Research Foundation (MRERF)

PO Box 247
Geneva, IL 60134
Phone: (708)208-1466
Fax: (708)208-1475
Toll Free: (800)346-7373

- Certified Professional Food Broker (CPFB)
- Certified Professional Manufacturers Representative (CPMR)

Manufacturing Engineering Certification Institute (MECI)

Society of Manufacturing Engineers
One SME Dr.
PO Box 930
Dearborn, MI 48121-0930
Phone: (313)271-1500
Fax: (313)271-2861
Toll Free: (800)733-4763

- Certified Manufacturing Engineer (CMfgE)
- Certified Manufacturing Technologist (CMfgT)

Materials Handling and Management Society (MHMS)

8720 Red Oak Blvd., Ste. 224
Charlotte, NC 28217-3990
Phone: (704)525-4667
Fax: (704)525-2880

- Professional Certified in Materials Handling (PCMH)
- Professional Certified in Materials Management (PCMM)

Medical-Dental-Hospital Bureaus of America (MDHBA)

1101 17th St., NW., Ste. 1200
Washington, DC 20036
Phone: (202)296-9200
Fax: (202)296-0023

- Certified Professional Bureau Executive (CPBE)

Microscopy Society of America (MSA)

PO Box MSA
Woods Hole, MA 02543
Phone: (508)540-7639
Fax: (508)548-9053
Toll Free: (800)538-3672
E-mail: bozzola@qm.c-chom.siu.edu

- Certified Electron Microscopy Technologist

Mortgage Bankers Association of America (MBA)

1125 15th St., NW
Washington, DC 20005
Phone: (202)861-6500

- Accredited Residential Underwriter (ARU)
- Certified Mortgage Banker (CMB)

MTM Association for Standards and Research (MTM)

1411 Peterson Ave.
Park Ridge, IL 60068
Phone: (708)823-7120
Fax: (708)823-2319

- Certification in Ergonomics
- Certification in MTM-1
- Certification in MTM-1(120)
- Certification in MTM-UAS-A
- Certification in MTM-UAS-B

Municipal Treasurers Association of the United States and Canada (MTA US&C)
1229 19th St., NW
Washington, DC 20036
Phone: (202)833-1017
Fax: (202)833-0375

- Certified Municipal Finance Administrator (CMFA)

NACE International
1440 S. Creek Dr.
PO Box 218340
Houston, TX 77218-8340
Phone: (713)492-0535
Fax: (713)492-8254

- Cathodic Protection Specialist
- Chemical Treatments Specialist
- Corrosion Specialist
- Corrosion Specialist, G
- Corrosion Specialist, P
- Corrosion Technician
- Corrosion Technologist
- Materials Selection/Design Specialist
- Protective Coatings Specialist
- Senior Corrosion Technologist

National Academy of Forensic Engineers
174 Brady Ave.
Hawthorne, NY 10532
Phone: (914)741-0633
Fax: (914)747-2988

- Fellow of the National Academy of Forensic Engineers (NAFE)
- Member, National Academy of Forensic Engineers (NAFE)
- Senior Member, National Academy of Forensic Engineers (NAFE)

National Apartment Association (NAA)
1111 Fourteenth St., NW, Ste. 900
Washington, DC 20005
Phone: (202)842-4050
Fax: (202)842-4056

- Certified Apartment Maintenance Technician (CAMT)
- Certified Apartment Manager (CAM)
- Certified Apartment Property Supervisor (CAPS)

National Association of Alcoholism and Drug Abuse Counselors Certification Commission (NCC)
3717 Columbia Pike, Ste. 300
Arlington, VA 22204-4254
Phone: (703)920-4644
Fax: (800)377-1136
Toll Free: (800)548-0497

- National Certified Addiction Counselor Level I (NCAC I)
- National Certified Addiction Counselor Level II (NCAC II)

National Association for Business and Educational Radio (NABER)
1501 Duke St.
Alexandria, VA 22314
Phone: (703)739-0300
Fax: (703)683-1608
Toll Free: (800)759-0300

- NABER Technician Certification

National Association of Catering Executives (NACE)
60 Revere Dr., Ste. 500
Northbrook, IL 60062
Phone: (708)480-9080
Fax: (708)480-9282

- Certified Professional Catering Executive (CPCE)

National Association of Catholic Chaplains (NACC)
3501 S. Lake Dr.
PO Box 07473
Milwaukee, WI 53207-0473
Phone: (414)483-4898
Fax: (414)483-6712

- Certified Chaplain

National Association of Certified Valuation Analysts (NACVA)
Brickyard Towers, Ste. 110
1245 E. Brickyard Rd.
Salt Lake City, UT 84106
Phone: (801)486-7500
Fax: (801)486-7500
Toll Free: (800)677-2009

- Certified Valuation Analyst (CVA)

National Association of Childbirth Assistants (NACA)
936-B Seventh St., No. 301
Novato, CA 94945
Toll Free: (800)868-NACA

- Childbirth Assistant (CA)
- Childbirth Educator (CE)
- Postpartum and Breastfeeding Assistant (PBA)

National Association of Church Food Service (NACFS)
76 Ivy Pkwy., NE
Atlanta, GA 30342-4241
Phone: (404)261-1794

- Certified Church Food Service Director

National Association of Claims Assistance Professionals (NACAP)
4724 Florence Ave.
Downers Grove, IL 60515
Phone: (708)963-3500
Fax: (708)803-6334
E-mail: Compuserve 70400.705

- Certified Claims Assistance Professional (CCAP)
- Certified Electronic Claims Professional (CECP)

National Association of College Stores (NACS)
500 E. Lorain St.
Oberlin, OH 44074
Phone: (216)775-7777
Fax: (216)775-4769
Toll Free: (800)622-7498
E-mail: mbecker@nacs.org

- Certified Store Professional (CSP)

National Association of Concessionaires (NAC)
35 E. Wacker Dr., Ste. 1545
Chicago, IL 60601
Phone: (312)236-3858
Fax: (312)236-7809

- Certified Concession Manager (CCM)

National Association of Counselors (NAC)
303 W. Cypress
Box 12528
San Antonio, TX 78212-0528
Phone: (210)225-2897
Fax: (210)225-8450
Toll Free: (800)531-5333

- Senior Real Estate Counselor (SRC)

National Association of County Recorders, Election Officials, and Clerks (NACRC)
PO Box 1270
Colorado Springs, CO 80901-1270
Phone: (719)520-6216
Fax: (719)520-6212

- Certified Public Official (CPO)

National Association of Credit Management (NACM)
8815 Centre Park Dr., Ste. 200
Columbia, MD 21045-2158
Phone: (410)740-5560
Fax: (410)740-5574

- Certified Credit Executive (CCE)
- Credit Business Associate (CBA)
- Credit Business Fellow (CBF)

National Association of Educational Office Professionals (NAEOP)
PO Box 12619
Wichita, KS 67277
Phone: (316)942-4822
Fax: (316)942-7100

- Certified Educational Office Employee (CEOE)

National Association of Entrepreneurs (NAE)
255 S. Orange Ave., Ste. 624
Orlando, FL 32802
Phone: (407)843-2032
Fax: (407)422-7425

- Certified Factoring Specialist
- Certified Mortgage Investor

National Association of Fire Investigators (NAFI)
PO Box 957257
Hoffman Estates, IL 60195
Phone: (312)427-6320

- Certified Fire and Explosion Investigator (CFEI)
- Certified Fire Investigation Instructor

National Association of Fleet Administrators (NAFA)
100 Wood Ave., S., Third Fl.
Iselin, NJ 08830-2709
Phone: (908)494-8100
Fax: (908)494-6789

- Certified Automotive Fleet Manager (CAFM)

National Association of Food Equipment Manufacturers (NAFEM)
401 N. Michigan Ave.
Chicago, IL 60611-4267
Phone: (312)644-6610
Fax: (312)245-1080

- Certified Foodservice Professional (CFSP)
- Certified Foodservice Professional Associate (CFSP Associate)

National Association of Health Underwriters (NAHU)
1000 Connecticut Ave., NW, Ste. 810
Washington, DC 20036
Phone: (202)223-5533
Fax: (202)785-2274

- Registered Employee Benefits Consultant (REBC)
- Registered Health Underwriter (RHU)

National Association of Health Unit Coordinators (NAHUC)
1311 Brentwood Terrace
Eau Claire, WI 54703
Phone: (715)834-8286

- Certified Health Unit Coordinator (CHUC)

National Association of Home Builders/Remodelers Council
1201 Fifteenth St., NW
Washington, DC 20005-2800
Phone: (202)822-0216
Fax: (202)822-0390
Toll Free: (800)368-5242

- Certified Graduate Remodeler (CGR)

National Association of Housing Cooperatives (NAHC)
1614 King St.
Alexandria, VA 22314
Phone: (703)549-5201
Fax: (703)549-5204

- Registered Cooperative Manager (RCM)

National Association of Housing and Redevelopment Officials (NAHRO)
1320 18th St., NW, 5th Fl.
Washington, DC 20036
Phone: (202)429-2960
Fax: (202)429-9684

- Certified Public Housing Managers (PHM)

National Association of Independent Fee Appraisers (NAIFA)
7501 Murdoch Ave.
St. Louis, MO 63119
Phone: (314)781-6688
Fax: (314)781-2872

- Independent Fee Appraiser (IFA)
- Independent Fee Appraiser/Agricultural (IFAA)
- Independent Fee Appraiser/Counselor (IFAC)
- Independent Fee Appraiser/Senior (IFAS)

National Association of Institutional Linen Management (NAILM)
2130 Lexington Rd., Ste. H
Richmond, KY 40475
Phone: (606)624-0177
Fax: (606)624-3580

- Certified Laundry/Linen Manager (CLLM)
- Registered Laundry/Linen Director (RLLD)

National Association of Insurance Women - International (NAIW)
1847 E. 15th
PO Box 4410
Tulsa, OK 74159
Phone: (918)744-5195
Fax: (918)743-1968
Toll Free: (800)766-6249

- Certified Professional Insurance Man (CPIM)
- Certified Professional Insurance Woman (CPIW)

National Association of Legal Assistants (NALA)
1516 S. Boston, Ste. 200
Tulsa, OK 74119
Phone: (918)587-6828
Fax: (918)582-6772

- Certified Legal Assistant (CLA)
- Certified Legal Assistant Specialist

National Association of Legal Investigators (NALI)
c/o Lynne K. Curtis, CLI
Posner and Houghton
1230 Market St., Ste. 420
San Francisco, CA 94102
Phone: (415)292-5513
Fax: (415)292-6052

- Certified Legal Investigator (CLI)

National Association of Legal Secretaries (International) (NALS)
2250 E. 73rd St., Ste. 550
Tulsa, OK 74136
Phone: (918)493-3540
Fax: (918)493-5784
Toll Free: (800)756-NALS

- Accredited Legal Secretary (ALS)
- Certified Professional Legal Secretary (PLS)

National Association of Marine Surveyors (NAMS)
PO Box 9306
Chesapeake, VA 23321-9306
Toll Free: (800)822-NAMS

- Certified Marine Surveyor (CMS)

National Association of Master Appraisers (NAMA)
303 W. Cypress St.
PO Box 12617
San Antonio, TX 78212-0617
Phone: (210)271-0781
Fax: (210)225-8450
Toll Free: (800)229-6262

- Master Farm and Land Appraiser (MFLA)
- Master Residential Appraiser (MRA)
- Master Senior Appraiser (MSA)

National Association Medical Staff Services (NAMSS)
PO Box 23350
Knoxville, TN 37933-1350
Phone: (615)531-3571
Fax: (615)531-9939

- Certified Medical Staff Coordinator (CMSC)

National Association of Mortgage Brokers (NAMB)
706 E. Bell Rd., Ste. 101
Phoenix, AZ 85022
Phone: (602)992-6181
Fax: (602)493-8711

- Certification in Residential Mortgage Lending (CRML)
- Certified Mortgage Consultant (CMC)
- Senior Mortgage Consultant (SMC)

National Association of Parliamentarians (NAP)
6601 Winchester Ave., Ste. 260
Kansas City, MO 64133
Phone: (816)356-5604

- Professional Registered Parliamentarians (PRP)
- Registered Parliamentarian (RP)

National Association of Personnel Services (NAPS)
3133 Mt. Vernon Ave.
Alexandria, VA 22305
Phone: (703)684-0180
Fax: (703)684-0071

- Certified Personnel Consultant (CPC)
- Certified Temporary-Staffing Specialist (CTS)

National Association of Plumbing-Heating-Cooling Contractors (NAPHCC)
180 S. Washington St.
PO Box 6808
Falls Church, VA 22046-1148
Phone: (703)237-8100
Fax: (703)237-7442
Toll Free: (800)533-7694

- CFC Technician Certification, Type I
- CFC Technician Certification, Type II
- CFC Technician Certification, Type III
- CFC Technician Certification, Universal

National Association for Poetry Therapy (NAPT)
PO Box 551
Port Washington, NY 11050
Phone: (516)944-9791
Fax: (516)944-5818

- Certified Poetry Therapist (CPT)
- Registered Poetry Therapist (RPT)

National Association of Printers and Lithographers (NAPL)
780 Palisade Ave.
Teaneck, NJ 07666
Phone: (201)342-0700
Fax: (201)692-0286
Toll Free: (800)642-NAPL

- Certified Business Planning Executive (CBPE)
- Certified Financial Management Executive (CFME)
- Certified Graphics Arts Executive (CGAE)
- Certified Production Management Executive (CPME)
- Certified Sales and Marketing Executive (CSME)

National Association of Property Inspectors (NAPI)
303 W. Cypress St.
PO Box 12528
San Antonio, TX 78212-0528
Phone: (210)225-2897
Fax: (210)225-8450
Toll Free: (800)486-3676

- Certified Real Property Inspector (CRPI)
- Certified Senior Inspector (CSI)

National Association of Public Insurance Adjusters (NAPIA)
1767 Business Center Dr., Ste. 302
Reston, VA 22090
Phone: (703)438-8254
Fax: (703)438-3113

- Certified Professional Public Adjuster (CPPA)
- Senior Professional Public Adjuster (SPPA)

National Association of Purchasing Management (NAPM)
2055 E. Centennial Cir.
PO Box 22160
Tempe, AZ 85285-2160
Phone: (602)752-6276
Fax: (602)752-7890
Toll Free: (800)888-6276

- Certified Purchasing Manager (C.P.M.)

National Association of Radio and Telecommunications Engineers (NARTE)
PO Box 678
Medway, MA 02053
Phone: (508)533-8333
Fax: (508)533-3815
Toll Free: (800)89N-ARTE

- Electromagnetic Compatibility Engineer
- Electromagnetic Compatibility Technicians
- Electrostatic Discharge Control Engineer
- Electrostatic Discharge Control Technician
- Radio and Telecommunications Engineer, Class I
- Radio and Telecommunications Engineer, Class II
- Radio and Telecommunications Engineer, Class III
- Radio and Telecommunications Technician, Class I
- Radio and Telecommunications Technician, Class II
- Radio and Telecommunications Technician, Class III
- Radio and Telecommunications Technician, Class IV

National Association of Real Estate Appraisers (NAREA)
8383 E. Evans Rd.
Scottsdale, AZ 85260
Phone: (602)948-8000
Fax: (602)998-8022
Toll Free: (800)537-2069

- Certified Commercial Real Estate Appraiser (CCRA)
- Certified Real Estate Appraiser (CREA)
- Registered Professional Member of the National Association of Real Estate Appraisers (RPM)

National Association of Realtors (NAR)
430 N. Michigan Ave.
Chicago, IL 60610-4087
Phone: (312)329-8200
Fax: (312)329-8391

- Realtor Association Certified Executive (RCE)

National Association of Review Appraisers and Mortgage Underwriters (NARA/MU)
8383 E. Evans Rd.
Scottsdale, AZ 85260
Phone: (602)998-3000
Fax: (602)998-8022

- Certified Review Appraiser (CRA)
- Certified Review Appraiser - Administrative (CRA-A)
- Registered Mortgage Underwriter (RMU)

National Association of RV Parks and Campgrounds (NARVC)
8605 Westwood Center Dr., Ste. 201
Vienna, VA 22182-2231
Phone: (703)734-3000
Fax: (703)734-3004

- Certified Park Operator (CPO)

National Association of School Nurses (NASN)
PO Box 130
Scarborough, ME 04070-1300
Phone: (207)883-2117
Fax: (207)883-2683

- Certified School Nurse (CSN)

National Association of School Psychologists (NASP)
8455 Colesville Rd., Ste. 1000
Silver Spring, MD 20910
Phone: (301)608-0500
Fax: (301)608-2514

- Nationally Certified School Psychologist (NCSP)

National Association of Service Managers (NASM)
1030 W. Higgins Rd., Ste. 109
Hoffman Estates, IL 60195
Phone: (708)310-9930
Fax: (708)310-9934

- Associate Service Executive (ASE)
- Certified Service Executive (CSE)
- Lifetime Certified Service Executive (LCSE)

National Association of Social Workers (NASW)
750 First St., NE, Ste. 700
Washington, DC 20002
Phone: (202)408-8600
Fax: (202)336-8327
Toll Free: (800)638-8799

- Diplomate in Clinical Social Work (DCSW)

National Association of Social Workers (NASW)
750 First St., NE, Ste. 700
Washington, DC 20002-4241
Phone: (202)336-8232
Fax: (202)336-8327
Toll Free: (800)638-8799

- School Social Work Specialist

National Association of Underwater Instructors (NAUI)
PO Box 14650
Montclair, CA 91763-1150
Phone: (909)621-5801
Fax: (909)621-6405
Toll Free: (800)553-6284

- Advanced Scuba Diver
- Master Scuba Diver
- NAUI Assistant Instructor
- NAUI Divemaster
- NAUI Diving Rescue Techniques Certification
- NAUI Instructor
- NAUI Skin Diving Leader
- Openwater I Scuba Diver
- Openwater II Scuba Diver
- Specialty Scuba Diver

National Athletic Trainers Association (NATA)
c/o Columbia Assessment Services
3725 National Dr., Ste. 213
Raleigh, NC 27612
Phone: (919)787-2721

- Athletic Trainer Certified (ATC)
- Certified Athletic Trainer (C.A.T.)

National Auctioneers Association (NAI)
8880 Ballentine
Overland Park, KS 66214
Phone: (913)541-8084
Fax: (913)894-5281

- Certified Auctioneer (CA)

National Automated Clearing House Association (NACHA)
607 Herndon Pkwy., Ste. 200
Herndon, VA 22070
Phone: (703)742-9190
Fax: (703)787-0996

- Accredited Automated Clearing House Professional (AAP)

National Automobile Dealers Association (NADA)
8400 Westpark Dr.
McLean, VA 22102
Phone: (703)821-7124
Fax: (703)821-7075
Toll Free: (800)252-6232

- NADA Certified

National Board for Certification in Dental Technology (NBC)
3801 Mt. Vernon Ave.
Alexandria, VA 22305
Phone: (703)683-5310
Fax: (703)549-4788
Toll Free: (800)950-1150

- Certified Dental Technician (CDT)

National Board for Certification in Hearing Instrument Sciences (NBCHIS)
20361 Middlebelt Rd.
Livonia, MI 48152
Phone: (810)478-5712
Fax: (810)478-4520
Toll Free: (800)521-5247

- Board Certified - Hearing Instrument Specialist (BC-HIS)
- Hearing Instrument Specialist

National Board for Certification of Hospice Nurses (NBCHN)
5512 Northumberland St.
Pittsburgh, PA 15217-1131
Phone: (412)687-3231
Fax: (412)687-9095

- Certified Registered Nurse Hospice (CRNH)

National Board for Certification of Orthopaedic Technologists (NBCOT)
3725 National Dr., Ste. 213
Raleigh, NC 27612
Phone: (919)787-2721
Fax: (919)781-3186

- Certified Orthopaedic Technologist

National Board for Certified Counselors (NBCC)
3-D Terrace Way
Greensboro, NC 27403
Phone: (910)547-0607
Fax: (910)547-0017
Toll Free: (800)398-5389

- Certified Clinical Mental Health Counselor (CCMHC)
- Master Addictions Counselor (MAC)
- National Certified Career Counselor (NCCC)
- National Certified Counselor (NCC)
- National Certified Gerontological Counselor (NCGC)
- National Certified School Counselor (NCSC)

National Board of Nutrition Support Certification (NBNSC)
8630 Fenton St., Ste. 412
Silver Spring, MD 20910-3805
Phone: (301)587-6315

- Certified Nutrition Support Dietician (CNSD)
- Certified Nutrition Support Nurse (CNSN)

National Board for Professional Teaching Standards (NBPTS)
300 River Pl., Ste. 3600
Detroit, MI 48207
Phone: (313)259-0830
Fax: (313)259-0973
Toll Free: (800)532-1813

- National Board Certified Teacher

National Board for Respiratory Care (NBRC)
8310 Nieman Rd.
Lenexa, KS 66214
Phone: (913)599-4200

- Certified Pulmonary Function Technologist (CPFT)
- Certified Respiratory Therapy Technician (CRTT)
- Perinatal/Pediatric Respiratory Care Specialist
- Registered Pulmonary Function Technologist (RPFT)
- Registered Respiratory Therapist (RRT)

National Board of Trial Advocacy (NBTA)

18 Tremont St., Fourth Fl., Ste. 403
Boston, MA 02108
Phone: (617)720-2032
Fax: (617)720-2038
E-mail: rhugus@word.std.com

- Civil Trial Advocate
- Criminal Trial Advocate

National Business Forms Association (NBFA)

433 E. Monroe Ave.
Alexandria, VA 22301-1693
Phone: (703)836-6232
Fax: (703)836-2241

- Certified Forms Consultant (CFC)

National Business Travel Association (NBTA)

1650 King St., Ste. 301
Alexandria, VA 22314
Phone: (703)684-0836
Fax: (703)684-0263

- Certified Corporate Travel Executive (CCTE)

National Cancer Registrars Association (NCRA)

505 E. Hawley St.
Mundelein, IL 60060
Phone: (708)566-0833
Fax: (708)566-7282

- Certified Tumor Registrar (CTR)

National Catholic Conference of Airport Chaplains (NCCAC)

Chicago O'Hare Airport
PO Box 66353
Chicago, IL 60666
Phone: (312)686-2636
Fax: (312)686-0130

- Certified Airport Chaplain (CAC)

National Center for Housing Management (NCHM)

1010 Massachusetts Ave., NW
Washington, DC 20001-5402
Phone: (202)872-1717
Toll Free: (800)368-5625

- Certified Financial Manager (CFM)
- Certified Manager of Housing (CMH)
- Certified Manager of Maintenance (CMM)
- Certified Occupancy Specialist (COS)

National Certification Agency for Medical Laboratory Personnel (NCA)

Dept. 5022
Washington, DC 20061-5022
Phone: (301)654-1622

- Clinical Laboratory Director (CLDir)
- Clinical Laboratory Phlebotomist (CLPlb)
- Clinical Laboratory Scientist (CLS)
- Clinical Laboratory Scientist in Clinical Chemistry (CLS(C))
- Clinical Laboratory Scientist in Hematology (CLS(H))
- Clinical Laboratory Scientist in Immunohematology (CLS(I))
- Clinical Laboratory Scientist in Microbiology (CLS(M))
- Clinical Laboratory Specialist in Cytogenetics (CLSp(CG))
- Clinical Laboratory Specialist in Hematology (CLSp(H))
- Clinical Laboratory Supervisor (CLSup)
- Clinical Laboratory Technician (CLT)

National Certification Board for Diabetes Educators (NCBDE)

444 N. Michigan Ave., Ste. 1240
Chicago, IL 60611-3901
Phone: (312)644-2233
Fax: (312)644-4411
Toll Free: (800)338-DMED

- Certified Diabetes Educator (CDE)

National Certification Board of Pediatric Nurse Practitioners and Nurses

416 Hungerford Dr., Ste. 222
Rockville, MD 20850-4127
Phone: (301)340-8213
Fax: (301)340-8604

- Certified Pediatric Nurse (CPN)
- Certified Pediatric Nurse Practitioner (CPNP)

National Certification Board: Perioperative Nursing

2170 S. Parker Rd., Ste. 295
Denver, CO 80231
Phone: (303)369-9566
Fax: (303)695-8464

- CNOR
- CRNFA

National Certification Board for Therapeutic Massage and Bodywork (NCBTMB)

1735 N. Lynn St., Ste. 950
Arlington, VA 22209
Phone: (703)524-9563
Toll Free: (800)296-0664

- Nationally Certified in Therapeutic Massage and Bodywork (NCTMB)

National Certification Commission (NCC)

PO Box 15282
Chevy Chase, MD 20825
Phone: (301)588-1212
Fax: (301)588-1212

- Approved Certification Administrator (ACA)

National Certification Commission in Chemistry and Chemical Engineering (NCCCCE)

American Institute of Chemists
7315 Wisconsin Ave., Ste. 502E
Bethesda, MD 20814-3209
Phone: (301)652-2447
Fax: (301)657-3549

- Certified Professional Chemical Engineer (CPChE)
- Certified Professional Chemist (CPC)

National Certification Corp. for the Obstetric, Gynecologic, and Neonatal Nursing Specialties (NCC)

645 N. Michigan Ave., Ste. 900
Chicago, IL 60611
Phone: (312)951-0207
Toll Free: (800)367-5613

- Ambulatory Women's Health Care Nurse
- High Risk Obstetric Nurse
- Inpatient Obstetric Nurse
- Low Risk Neonatal Nurse
- Maternal Newborn Nurse
- Neonatal Intensive Care Nurse
- Neonatal Nurse Practitioner
- Reproductive Endocrinology/Infertility Nurse
- Women's Health Care Nurse Practitioner

National Certification Council for Activity Professionals (NCCAP)

520 Stewart
Park Ridge, IL 60068
Phone: (708)698-4263
Fax: (708)698-9864

- Activity Assistant Certified (AAC)
- Activity Consultant Certified (ACC)
- Activity Director Certified (ADC)

National Certifying Board for Ophthalmic Registered Nurses (NCBORN)

PO Box 193030
San Francisco, CA 94119
Phone: (415)561-8513

- CRNO

National Commission for the Certification of Acupuncturists (NCCA)
1424 16th St., NW, Ste. 501
Washington, DC 20036
Phone: (202)232-1404
Fax: (202)462-6157

- Diplomate in Acupuncture
- Diplomate of Chinese Herbology

National Commission on Certification of Physician Assistants (NCCPA)
2845 Henderson Mill Rd., NE
Atlanta, GA 30341
Phone: (404)493-9100

- Physician Assistant - Certified (PA-C)

National Commission for Electrologist Certification (NCEC)
Six Abbott Rd. Annex
Wellesley Hills, MA 02181
Phone: (617)431-7263
Fax: (617)237-9039

- Certified Clinical Electrologist (C.C.E.)
- Certified Medical Electrologist (C.M.E.)

National Commission for Health Education Credentialing (NCHEC)
475 Riverside Dr., Ste. 470
New York, NY 10115
Phone: (212)870-2047
Fax: (212)870-3333

- Certified Health Education Specialist (CHES)

National Committee for Motor Fleet Supervisor Training (NCMFST)
2200 Mill Rd.
Alexandria, VA 22314-4677
Phone: (703)838-7952
Fax: (703)836-6070

- Certified Director of Equipment/Maintenance
- Certified Director of Pupil Transportation
- Certified Director of Safety
- Certified Maintenance Supervisor
- Certified Pupil Transportation Supervisor
- Certified Safety Supervisor
- Certified School Bus Driver Trainer
- Certified Shop Service Managers
- Certified Trainer of Commercial Drivers

National Consortium of Chemical Dependency Nurses (NCCDN)
1720 Willow Creek Cir., Ste. 519
Eugene, OR 97402
Phone: (503)485-4421
Fax: (503)485-7372
Toll Free: (800)87N-CCDN

- Certified Chemical Dependency Nurse (RN-CD)

National Contact Lens Examiners (NCLE)
10341 Democracy Ln.
Fairfax, VA 22030
Phone: (703)691-1061
Fax: (703)691-3929

- National Contact Lens Certified (NCLC)

National Contract Management Association (NCMA)
1912 Woodford Rd.
Vienna, VA 22182
Phone: (703)448-9231
Fax: (703)448-0939
Toll Free: (800)344-8096

- Certified Associate Contracts Manager (CACM)
- Certified Professional Contracts Manager (CPCM)

National Coordinating Council on Emergency Management (NCCEM)
7297 Lee Hwy., Ste. N
Falls Church, VA 22042
Phone: (703)533-7672
Fax: (703)241-5603

- Certified Emergency Manager (CEM)

National Council for Interior Design Qualification (NCIDQ)
50 Main St., 5th Fl.
White Plains, NY 10606
Phone: (914)948-9100
Fax: (914)948-9198

- Certified Interior Designer (NCIDQ Certified)

National Council of the Multifamily Housing Industry
1201 Fifteenth St., NW
Washington, DC 20005-2800
Phone: (202)822-0215
Fax: (202)861-2120
Toll Free: (800)368-5242

- Advanced Registered Apartment Manager
- Certified Leasing Professional (CLP)
- Registered Apartment Manager (RAM)

National Council on Seniors' Housing (NCOSH)
1201 Fifteenth St., NW
Washington, DC 20005-2800
Toll Free: (800)368-5242

- Senior Housing Management Specialist
- Senior Housing Marketing Specialist (SHMS)

National Council for Therapeutic Recreation Certification (NCTRC)
PO Box 479
Thiells, NY 10984-0479
Phone: (914)947-4346

- Certified Therapeutic Recreation Specialist (CTRS)

National Court Reporters Association (NCRA)
8224 Old Courthouse Rd.
Vienna, VA 22182
Phone: (703)556-6272
Fax: (703)556-6291
Toll Free: (800)272-6272

- Certified Legal Video Specialist (CLVS)
- Certified Manager of Reporting Services (CMRS)
- Certified Real time Reporter (CRR)
- Registered Professional Reporter (RPR)

National Dance-Exercise Instructor's Training Association (NDEITA)
1503 S. Washington Ave., Ste. 208
Minneapolis, MN 55454-1037
Phone: (612)340-1306
Fax: (612)340-1619
Toll Free: (800)237-6242

- Advanced Fitness Certification
- National Certified Aerobics Instructor
- National Certified Aerobics Instructor - Step

National Dog Groomers Association of America (NDGAA)
PO Box 101
Clark, PA 16113
Phone: (412)962-2711
Fax: (412)962-1919

- National Certified Groomer
- National Certified Master Groomer (NCMG)

National Employee Services and Recreation Association (NESRA)
2211 York Rd., Ste. 207
Oak Brook, IL 60521-2371
Phone: (708)368-1280
Fax: (708)368-1286

- Certified Employee Services and Recreation Administrator (CESRA)

National Environmental Health Association (NEHA)
720 S. Colorado Blvd, South Tower, 970
Denver, CO 80222-1925
Phone: (303)756-9090
Fax: (303)691-9490

- Certified Environmental Health Technician (CEHT)
- Registered Environmental Health Specialist/Registered Sanitarian (REHS/RS)
- Registered Hazardous Substances Professional (RHSP)
- Registered Hazardous Substances Specialist (RHSS)

National Environmental Training Association (NETA)
2930 E. Camelback Rd., Ste. 185
Phoenix, AZ 85016-4412
Phone: (602)956-6099
Fax: (602)956-6399

- Associate Environmental Trainer (AET)
- Certified Environmental Trainer (CET)

National Executive Housekeepers Association (NEHA)
1001 Eastwind Dr., Ste. 301
Westerville, OH 43081
Phone: (614)895-7166
Fax: (614)895-1248

- Registered Executive Housekeeper (REH)
- Certified Executive Housekeeper (CEH)

National Fire Protection Association International (NFPA)
One Batterymarch Park
PO Box 9101
Quincy, MA 02269-9101
Phone: (617)770-3000
Fax: (617)770-0700
Toll Free: (800)344-3555

- Certified Marine Chemist

National Foundation for Consumer Credit
8611 Second Ave., Ste. 100
Silver Spring, MD 20910
Phone: (301)589-5600
Fax: (301)495-5623

- Certified Consumer Credit Counselor (NFCC)

National Foundation for Non-Invasive Diagnostics (NFNID)
103 Carnegie Center, Ste. 311
Princeton, NJ 08540
Phone: (609)520-1300
Fax: (609)452-8544

- Certified Echocardiographic Technologist (CET)
- Professional Ultrasound Technologist

National Ground Water Association (NGWA)
6375 Riverside Dr.
PO Box 9050
Dublin, OH 43017-0950
Phone: (614)761-1711
Fax: (614)761-3446
Toll Free: (800)551-7379

- Certified Ground Water Professional (CGWP)
- Certified Pump Installer (CPI)
- Certified Well Driller (CWD)
- Certified Well Driller/Pump Installer (CWD/PI)
- Master Ground Water Contractor (MGWC)

National Handicapped Sports (NHS)
451 Hungerford Dr., Ste. 100
Rockville, MD 20850
Phone: (301)217-0960
Fax: (301)217-0968
Toll Free: (800)996-4NHS

- Adapted Group Exercise Leader

National Health Club Association (NHCA)
12596 W. Bayaud Ave.
Denver, CO 80228
Phone: (303)753-6422
Fax: (303)986-6813
Toll Free: (800)765-6422

- Professional Fitness Trainer

National High School Athletic Coaches Association
One Purlieu Pl., Ste. 128
Winter Park, FL 32792
Phone: (407)679-1414
Fax: (407)679-6621

- Certified Interscholastic Coach (CIC)

National Institute for Automotive Service Excellence (ASE)
13505 Dulles Technology Dr.
Herndon, VA 22071-3415
Phone: (703)713-3800
Fax: (703)713-0727

- ASE Certified Alternative Fuels Technician
- ASE Certified Automobile Technician
- ASE Certified Collision Repair and Refinish Technician
- ASE Certified Engine Machinist
- ASE Certified Master Autobody/Paint Technician
- ASE Certified Master Automobile Technician
- ASE Certified Master Engine Machinist
- ASE Certified Master Medium/Heavy Truck Technician
- ASE Certified Medium/Heavy Truck Technician
- ASE Certified Parts Specialist
- Automotive Advanced Engine Performance Specialist

National Institute for Certification in Engineering Technologies (NICET)
1420 King St.
Alexandria, VA 22314-2794
Phone: (703)684-2835

- Associate Engineering Technician (AET)
- Associate Engineering Technologist (ACT)
- Certified Engineering Technologist (CT)
- Engineering Technician (ET)
- Senior Engineering Technician (SET)
- Technician Trainee (TT)

National Institute for the Certification of Healthcare Sterile Processing and Distribution Personnel (NICHSPDP)
PO Box 558
Annandale, NJ 08801

- Certified Sterile Processing and Distribution Manager (CSPDM)
- Certified Sterile Processing and Distribution Supervisor (CSPDS)
- Certified Sterile Processing and Distribution Technician (CSPDT)

National Institute of Certified Moving Consultants (NICMC)
11150 Main St., Ste. 402
Fairfax, VA 22030
Phone: (703)934-9111
Fax: (703)934-9712
Toll Free: (800)538-6672

- Certified Moving Consultant (CMC)

National Institute of Fire Restoration (NIFR)
10830 Annapolis Junction Rd., Ste. 312
Annapolis Junction, MD 20701-1120
Phone: (301)604-4411
Fax: (301)604-4713

- Certified Restoration Technician

National Institute of Pension Administrators (NIPA)
145 W. First St., Ste. A
Tustin, CA 92680-3209
Phone: (714)731-3523
Fax: (714)731-1284

- Accredited Pension Administrator (APA)

National Interscholastic Athletic Administrators Association (NIAAA)
PO Box 20626
Kansas City, MO 64195-0626
Phone: (816)464-5400
Fax: (816)464-5571

- Certified Athletic Administrator (CAA)

National Intramural-Recreational Sports Association (NIRSA)
850 SW 15th St.
Corvallis, OR 97333
Phone: (503)737-2088
Fax: (503)737-2026

- Certified Recreational Sports Specialist (CRSS)

National Kitchen and Bath Association (NKBA)
687 Willow Grove St.
Hackettstown, NJ 07840
Phone: (908)852-0033
Fax: (908)852-1695
Toll Free: (800)843-6522

- Certified Bathroom Designer (CBD)
- Certified Kitchen Designer (CKD)

National Paraoptometric Registry
243 N. Lindbergh Blvd.
St. Louis, MO 63141-7881
Phone: (314)991-4100
Fax: (314)991-4104

- Registered Optometric Assistant (Opt. A., R.)
- Registered Optometric Technician (Opt. T., R.)

National Park and Recreation Association (NPRA)
2775 S. Quincy St., Ste. 300
Arlington, VA 22206
Phone: (703)578-5549
Fax: (703)671-6772

- Certified Playground Safety Inspector

National Parking Association (NPA)
1112 16th St., Ste. 300
Washington, DC 20036
Phone: (202)296-4336
Fax: (202)331-8523
Toll Free: (800)647-PARK

- Certified Parking Facility Manager (CPFM)

National PlasterCraft Association (NPCA)
c/o George L. Kirkpatrick
0465 North 300 East
Albion, IN 46701

- Advanced Painter
- Certified Painter
- Certified Teacher
- Master Certified Teacher
- Master Painter

National Private Truck Council (NPTC)
66 Canal Center Plaza, Ste. 600
Alexandria, VA 22314
Phone: (703)683-1300
Fax: (703)683-1217

- Certified Professional Fleet Manager (CPFM)

National Property Management Association (NPMA)
380 Main St., Ste. 290
Dunedin, FL 34698
Phone: (813)736-3788
Fax: (813)736-6707

- Certified Professional Property Administrator (CPPA)
- Certified Professional Property Manager (CPPM)
- Certified Professional Property Specialist (CPPS)
- Consulting Fellow of the National Property Management Association (CF)

National Recreation and Park Association (NRPA)
2775 S. Quincy St., Ste. 300
Arlington, VA 22206
Phone: (703)820-4940
Fax: (703)671-6772
Toll Free: (800)626-6772

- Certified Leisure Associate (CLA)
- Certified Leisure Professional (CLP)

National Register for Health Service Providers in Psychology
1120 G St., NW, Ste. 330
Washington, DC 20005
Phone: (202)783-7663
Fax: (202)347-0550

- Health Service Provider in Psychology

National Registry in Clinical Chemistry (NRCC)
1155 16th St., NW
Washington, DC 20036
Phone: (202)745-1698
Fax: (202)872-4615

- Clinical Chemist (CCT)
- Clinical Chemistry Technologist (CCT)
- Toxicological Chemist

National Registry of Emergency Medical Technicians (NREMT)
PO Box 29233
Columbus, OH 43229
Phone: (614)888-4484

- Registered EMT - Basic
- Registered EMT - Intermediate
- Registered EMT - Paramedic

National Registry of Environmental Professionals (NREP)
PO Box 2068
Glenview, IL 60025
Phone: (708)724-6631
Fax: (708)724-4223

- Associate Environmental Professional (AEP)
- Associate Environmental Property Assessor (AEPA)
- Certified Environmental Auditor (CEA)
- Registered Environmental Laboratory Technologist (RELT)
- Registered Environmental Manager (REM)
- Registered Environmental Professional (REP)
- Registered Environmental Property Assessor (REPA)
- Registered Environmental Scientist (RES)

National Residential Appraisers Institute (NRAI)
2001 Cooper Foster Park Rd.
Amherst, OH 44001
Phone: (216)282-7925
Fax: (216)282-8072
Toll Free: (800)331-2732

- Certified Market Data Analyst (CMDA)
- Graduate Senior Appraiser (GSA)
- Senior Certified Appraiser (SCA)
- Senior Licensed Appraiser (SLA)

National Restaurant Association Educational Foundation
250 S. Wacker Dr., Ste. 1400
Chicago, IL 60606-5834
Phone: (312)715-1010
Toll Free: (800)765-2122

- Foodservice Management Professional (FMP)

National Rural Electric Cooperative Association (NRECA)
1800 Massachusetts Ave., NW
Washington, DC 20036
Phone: (202)857-9513
Fax: (202)857-9791

- Certified Rural Electric Communicator (CREC)

National Sheriffs' Association (NSA)
1450 Duke St.
Alexandria, VA 22314-3490
Phone: (703)836-7827
Fax: (703)683-6541
Toll Free: (800)424-7827

- Certified Jail Technician

National Society of Environmental Consultants (NSEC)
PO Box 12528
303 W. Cypress
San Antonio, TX 78212
Phone: (210)225-2897
Fax: (210)225-8450
Toll Free: (800)486-3676

- Environmental Assessment Consultant (EAC)
- Environmental Screening Consultant (ESC)

National Society of Fund Raising Executives (NSFRE)
1101 King St., Ste. 700
Alexandria, VA 22314
Phone: (703)684-0410
Fax: (703)684-0540
Toll Free: (800)666-FUWD

- Advanced Certified Fund Raising Executive (ACFRE)
- Certified Fund Raising Executive (CFRE)

National Swimming Pool Foundation (NSPF)
10803 Gulfdale, Ste. 300
San Antonio, TX 78216
Phone: (210)525-1227
Fax: (210)344-3713

- Certified Instructor of the National Swimming Pool Foundation
- Certified Pool Spa Operator (CPO)

Nephrology Nursing Certification Board (NNCB)
East Holly Ave.
Box 56
Pitman, NJ 08071-0056
Phone: (609)256-2321
Fax: (609)589-7463

- Certified Nephrology Nurse (CNN)

Nine Lives Associates (NLA)
Executive Protection Institute
Arcadia Manor
Rte. 2, Box 3645
Berryville, VA 22611
Phone: (703)955-1128

- Personal Protection Specialist (PPS)

North American Lake Management Society (NALMS)
PO Box 5443
Madison, WI 53705-5443
Phone: (608)233-2836
Fax: (608)233-3186

- Certified Lake Manager (CLM)

North American Retail Dealers Association (NARDA)
Ten E. 22nd St.
Lombard, IL 60148
Phone: (708)953-8956
Fax: (708)953-9510
Toll Free: (800)394-TEST

- Refrigerant Recovery Certification

North American Riding for the Handicapped Association (NARHA)
PO Box 33150
Denver, CO 80233
Toll Free: (800)369-RIDE

- Certified Instructor
- Registered Instructor

Novell
122 East 1700 South
Provo, UT 84606-6194
Phone: (801)429-5508
Toll Free: (800)233-EDUC
- Certified NetWare 2 Administrator
- Certified NetWare 3 Administrator
- Certified NetWare 4 Administrator
- Certified NetWare Engineer (CNE)
- Certified NetWare Instructor (CNI)
- Certified UnixWare Administrator
- Enterprise Certified NetWare Engineer (CNE)

Nuclear Medicine Technology Certification Board (NMTCB)
2970 Clairmont Rd., Ste. 610
Atlanta, GA 30329
Phone: (404)315-1740
Fax: (404)315-6502
E-mail: REGJEG@GSUVM1.GSU.EDU

- Certified Nuclear Medicine Technologist (CNMT)

Office Automation Society International (OASI)
5170 Meadow Wood Blvd.
Lyndhurst, OH 44124
Phone: (216)461-4803
Fax: (216)461-4803
E-mail: JBDYKE@aol.com

- Certified Office Automation Professional (COAP)

Oncology Nursing Certification Corp. (ONCC)
501 Holiday Dr.
Pittsburgh, PA 15220-2749
Phone: (412)921-8597
Fax: (412)921-6565

- Advanced Oncology Certified Nurse (AOCN)
- Oncology Certified Nurse (OCN)

Ophthalmic Photographers' Society (OPS)
c/o Terrance L. Tomer, COPRA
Wills Eye Hospital
900 Walnut St.
Philadelphia, PA 19107
Phone: (215)928-3405
Fax: (215)928-3123

- Certified Ophthalmic Photographer and Retinal Angiographer (COPRA)
- Certified Retinal Angiographer (CRA)

OPSEC Professionals Society
7519 Ridge Rd.
Frederick, MD 21702-3519
Phone: (301)663-1418

- OPSEC Certified Professional (OCP)

Organization Development Institute
11234 Walnut Ridge Rd.
Chesterland, OH 44026
Phone: (216)461-4333
Fax: (216)729-9319

- Registered Organization Development Consultant (RODC)
- Registered Organization Development Professional (RODP)

Orthopaedic Nurses Certification Board (ONCB)
E. Holly Ave.
Box 56
Pitman, NJ 08071-0056
Phone: (609)256-2311
Fax: (609)589-7463

- Orthopaedic Nurse Certified (ONC)

Patience T'ai Chi Association (PTCA)
PO Box 350532
Brooklyn, NY 11235
Phone: (718)332-3477

- Assistant Instructor of Yang Short Form T'ai Chi
- Instructor of Yang Short Form T'ai Chi

Pet Industry Joint Advisory Council (PIJAC)
1220 19th St., NW, Ste. 400
Washington, DC 20036
Phone: (202)452-1525
Fax: (202)293-4377
Toll Free: (800)553-PETS

- Certified Avian Specialist (CAS)
- Certified Canine Specialist (CCS)
- Certified Freshwater Fish Specialist (CFFS)
- Certified Reptile Specialist (CRS)
- Certified Small Animal Specialist (CSAS)

Plastic Surgical Nursing Certification Board (PSNCB)
N. Woodbury Rd.
Box 56
Pitman, NJ 08071
Phone: (609)589-1490
Fax: (609)589-7463

- Certified Plastic Surgical Nurse (CPSN)

Portable Sanitation Association International (PSA)
7800 Metro Pkwy., Ste. 104
Bloomington, MN 55425
Phone: (612)854-8300
Fax: (612)854-7560
Toll Free: (800)822-3020

- Certified Health and Safety, Portable Sanitation Worker

Positive Pregnancy and Parenting Fitness (PPPF)
RR 1, Box 172
Glen View Rd.
Waitsfield, VT 05673
Phone: (802)496-5222
Fax: (802)496-5222
Toll Free: (800)433-5523

- Positive Pregnancy and Parenting Fitness Instructor

Professional Association of Health Care Office Managers (PAHCOM)
461 E. Ten Mile Rd.
Pensacola, FL 32534-9714
Phone: (904)474-9460
Fax: (904)474-6352
Toll Free: (800)451-9311

- Certified Medical Manager (CMM)

Professional Association of Resume Writers (PARW)
3637 4th St., N., Ste. 330
St. Petersburg, FL 33704-1336
Phone: (813)821-2274
Fax: (813)894-1277
Toll Free: (800)822-7279
E-mail: NNFP 40A.@Prodigy.com

- Certified Professional Resume Writer (CPRW)

Professional Certification Board (PCB)
303 W. Cypress
PO Box 12528
San Antonio, TX 78212-0528
Phone: (210)271-0781
Fax: (210)225-8450
Toll Free: (800)486-3676

- Board Certified in Business Valuation
- Board Certified in Manufactured Housing Valuation

Professional Grounds Management Society (PGMS)
120 Cockeysville Rd., Ste. 104
Hunt Valley, MD 21031
Phone: (410)584-9754
Fax: (410)584-9756
Toll Free: (800)609-7567

- Certified Grounds Manager (CGM)

Professional Lawn Care Association of America (PLCAA)
Principles of Turfgrass Mgmt. 23106
Community Learning Resources, Ste. 191
Georgia Center for Continuing Educ.
Univ. of Georgia
Athens, GA 30602-3603
Phone: (706)542-1756
Fax: (706)542-5990
Toll Free: (800)542-8097

- Certified Turfgrass Professional (CTP)

Professional Photographers of America (PP of A)
57 Forsythe St., Ste. 1600
Atlanta, GA 30303
Phone: (404)522-8600
Fax: (404)614-6405
Toll Free: (800)742-7468

- Certified Electronic Imager (CEI)
- Certified Professional Photographer (CPP)

Professional Picture Framers Association (PPFA)
4305 Sarellen Rd.
Richmond, VA 23231-4311
Phone: (804)226-0430
Fax: (804)222-2175

- Certified Picture Framer (CPF)

Professional Secretaries International (PSI)
10502 N.W. Ambassador Dr.
PO Box 20404
Kansas City, MO 64195-0404
Phone: (816)891-6600
Fax: (816)891-9118

- Certified Professional Secretary (CPS)

Professional Services Management Institute (PSMI)
4726 Park Rd., Ste. A
Charlotte, NC 28209
Phone: (704)521-8890
Fax: (704)521-8873

- Certified Professional Services Manager (CPM)

Professional Ski Instructors of America (PSIA)
133 S. Van Gordon, Ste. 101
Lakewood, CO 80228
Phone: (303)987-9390
Fax: (303)988-3005

- PSIA Certified Level I Instructor
- PSIA Certified Level II Instructor
- PSIA Certified Level III Instructor
- PSIA Registered Instructor

Project Management Institute (PMI)
130 S. State Rd.
Upper Darby, PA 19082
Phone: (610)734-3330
Fax: (610)734-3266

- Project Management Professional (PMP)

Public Relations Society of America (PRSA)
33 Irving Pl., 3rd Fl.
New York, NY 10003-2376
Phone: (212)995-2230
Fax: (212)995-0757

- Accredited in Public Relations (APR)

Radio Advertising Bureau (RAB)
1320 Greenway Dr., Ste. 500
Irving, TX 75038
Phone: (214)753-6750
Fax: (214)753-6727
Toll Free: (800)232-3131

- Certified Radio Marketing Consultant (CRMC)

Real Estate Brokerage Managers Council (RBMC)
430 N. Michigan Ave.
Chicago, IL 60611-4092
Phone: (312)670-3780
Fax: (312)329-8882
Toll Free: (800)621-8738

- Certified Real Estate Brokerage Manager (CRB)

Real Estate Educators Association (REEA)
11 S. LaSalle St., Ste. 1400
Chicago, IL 60603
Phone: (312)201-0101
Fax: (312)201-0214

- Designated Real Estate Instructor (DREI)

Real Estate Law Institute (RELI)
303 W. Cypress
PO Box 12528
San Antonio, TX 78212
Phone: (210)225-2897
Fax: (210)225-8450

- Board Certified in Business Appraisal (BCBA)
- Board Certified in Real Estate Litigation Management (RLM)

Realtors Land Institute (RLI)
430 N. Michigan Ave.
Chicago, IL 60611
Phone: (312)329-8440
Toll Free: (800)441-LAND

- Accredited Land Consultant (ALC)

Registered Financial Planners Institute (RFPI)
2001 Cooper Foster Park Rd.
Amherst, OH 44001
Phone: (216)282-7176

- Registered Financial Planner (RFP)

Registry of Interpreters for the Deaf (RID)
8630 Fenton St., Ste. 324
Silver Spring, MD 20910
Phone: (301)608-0050
Fax: (301)608-0508

- Certificate of Interpretation (CI)
- Certificate of Interpretation/Certificate of Transliteration (CI/CT)
- Certificate of Transliteration (CT)
- Certified Deaf Interpreter - Provisional (CDI-P)
- Conditional Legal Interpreting Permit (CLIP)
- Conditional Legal Interpreting Permit - Relay (CLIP-R)

Regulatory Affairs Professionals Society (RAPS)
PO Box 14953
Lenexa, KS 66285-4953
Phone: (913)541-1427
Fax: (913)541-0156

- Regulatory Affairs Certification

Rehabilitation Nursing Certification Board (RNCB)
5700 Old Orchard Rd., First Fl.
Skokie, IL 60077-1057
Phone: (708)966-3433
Fax: (708)966-9418

- Certified Rehabilitation Registered Nurse (CRRN)

Research Administrators Certification Council (RACC)
c/o Professional Testing Corp.
1211 Avenue of the Americas, 15th Fl.
New York, NY 10036
Phone: (212)852-0404

- Certified Research Administrator (CRA)

Residential Sales Council (RSC)
430 N. Michigan Ave.
Chicago, IL 60611-4092
Phone: (312)321-4448
Fax: (312)321-4520
Toll Free: (800)462-8841

- Certified Residential Specialist (CRS)

Rolf Institute
PO Box 1868
Boulder, CO 80306
Phone: (303)449-5903
Fax: (303)449-5978
Toll Free: (800)530-8875

- Certified Rolfer

Roof Consultants Institute (RCI)
7424 Chapel Hill Rd.
Raleigh, NC 27607
Phone: (919)859-0742
Fax: (919)859-1328
Toll Free: (800)828-1902

- Registered Roof Consultant (RRC)
- Registered Roof Observer (RRO)

Sales and Marketing Executives International (SMEI)
Statler Office Tower
Cleveland, OH 44115
Phone: (216)771-6650
Fax: (216)771-6652
Toll Free: (800)999-1414

- Certified Marketing Executive (CME)
- Certified Sales Executive (CSE)

School of Military Packaging Technology (SMPT)
U.S. Army Logistics Mgt. Coll.
Aberdeen Proving Grounds, MD 21005
Phone: (410)278-4770
Fax: (410)278-2176

- Military Packaging Professional (MPP)

Society of Actuaries (SoA)
475 N. Martingdale Rd., Ste. 800
Schaumburg, IL 60173-2226
Phone: (708)706-3500
Fax: (708)706-3599

- Associate of the Society of Actuaries (ASA)
- Fellow of the Society of Actuaries

Society of Broadcast Engineers (SBE)
8455 Keystone Crossing, Ste. 140
Indianapolis, IN 46240
Phone: (317)253-1640
Fax: (317)253-0418

- Certified Broadcast Radio Engineer (CBRE)
- Certified Broadcast Technologist (CBT)
- Certified Broadcast Television Engineer (CBTE)
- Certified Professional Broadcast Engineer (CPBE)
- Certified Radio Operator
- Certified Senior Radio Engineer (CSRE)
- Certified Senior Television Engineer (CSTE)

Society of Cable Television Engineers (SCTE)
669 Exton Commons
Exton, PA 19341
Phone: (215)363-6888
Fax: (215)363-5898
Toll Free: (800)542-5040
E-mail: MarvinSCTE@AOL.com

- Broadband Communications Engineer (BCE)
- Broadband Communications Technician (BCT)
- Installer Certification

Society of Certified Credit Executives (SCCE)
PO Box 419057
St. Louis, MO 63141-1757
Phone: (314)991-3030
Fax: (314)991-3029

- Associate Credit Executive (ACE)
- Certified Collection Agency Executive (CCAE)
- Certified Consumer Credit Executive (CCCE)
- Certified Credit Bureau Executive (CCBE)
- Certified Financial Counseling Executive (CFCE)
- Credit Associate (CA)

Society of Certified Insurance Counselors (CIC)
PO Box 27027
Austin, TX 78755-1027
Phone: (512)345-7932
Fax: (512)343-2167

- Certified Insurance Counselor (CIC)

Society of Certified Insurance Service Representatives
PO Box 27028
3630 North Hills Dr.
Austin, TX 78755-1028
Phone: (512)346-7358

- Certified Insurance Service Representative (CISR)

Society of Cost Estimating and Analysis (SCEA)
101 S. Whiting St., Ste. 201
Alexandria, VA 22303
Phone: (703)751-8069
Fax: (703)461-7328

- Certified Cost Estimator/Analyst (CCEA)

Society of Incentive Travel Executives (SITE)
21 W. 38th St., 10th Fl.
New York, NY 10018-5584
Phone: (212)575-0910
Fax: (212)575-1838

- Certified Incentive Travel Executive (CITE)

Society of Industrial and Office Realtors (SIOR)
777 Fourteenth St., NW, Ste. 400
Washington, DC 20005
Phone: (202)737-1150
Fax: (202)737-3142

- Specialist, Industrial/Office Real Estate (SIOR)
- Professional Real Estate Executive (PRE)

Society of Logistics Engineers (SOLE)
8100 Professional Pl., Ste. 211
New Carrollton, MD 20785
Phone: (301)459-8446
Fax: (301)459-1522

- Certified Professional Logistician (C.P.L.)

Society for Marketing Professional Services (SMPS)
99 Canal Center Plaza, Ste. 250
Alexandria, VA 22314
Phone: (703)549-6117
Fax: (703)549-2498
Toll Free: (800)292-7677

- Marketing Professional (MP)

Society of Photo Finishing Engineers (SPFE)
3000 Picture Pl.
Jackson, MI 49201
Phone: (517)788-8100
Fax: (517)788-8371

- Member, Society of Photo Finishing Engineers

Society of Photographic Counselors
3000 Picture Pl.
Jackson, MI 49201
Phone: (517)788-8100
Fax: (517)788-8371

- Certified Photographic Counselor (CPC)

Society for Range Management (SRM)
1839 York St.
Denver, CO 80206
Phone: (303)355-7070
Fax: (303)355-5059

- Certified Range Management Consultant (CRMC)

Society for Service Professionals in Printing
433 Monroe Ave.
Alexandria, VA 22301-1693
Phone: (703)684-0044
Fax: (703)548-9137

- Certified Printing Service Specialist

Society of State Filers (SSF)
3101 Broadway, Ste. 585
Kansas City, MO 64111
Phone: (816)931-4800
Fax: (816)561-7765

- Associate in State Filings (ASF)
- Certified State Filer (CSF)

Sociological Practice Association (SPA)
c/o Dr. Linda R. Webber
Dept. of Sociology and Anthropology
SUNY Institute of Technology
PO Box 3050
Utica, NY 13504-3050

- Certified Clinical Sociologist (CCS)

Soil and Water Conservation Society (SWCS)
7515 NE Ankeny Rd.
Ankeny, IA 50021-9764
Phone: (515)289-2331
Fax: (515)289-1227
Toll Free: (800)843-7645

- Certified Professional Soil Erosion and Sediment Control Specialist (CPESC)

Solid Waste Association of North America (SWANA)
PO Box 7219
Silver Spring, MD 20907-7219
Phone: (301)585-2898
Fax: (301)589-7068

- Certified Landfill Enforcement Officer
- Certified Manager of Landfill Operations

Statistical Process Control Society (SPCS)
PO Box 1203
Avon, CT 06001
Phone: (203)676-8890
Fax: (203)676-2238

- Certification in Statistical Process Control, Facilitator (CSPCF)
- Certification in Statistical Process Control, Operational (CSPCO)
- Certification in Statistical Process Control, Technical (CSPCT)

Survey Technician Certification Board (STCB)
c/o American Congress on Surveying and Mapping
5410 Grosvenor Ln.
Bethesda, MD 20814-2122
Phone: (301)493-0200
Fax: (301)493-8245

- Certified Survey Technician, Level I (CST)
- Certified Survey Technician, Level II (CST)
- Certified Survey Technician, Level III (CST)
- Certified Survey Technician, Level IV (CST)

Transportation Brokers Conference of America (TBCA)
5845 Richmond Hwy., Ste. 750
Alexandria, VA 22303-1865
Phone: (703)329-1894
Fax: (703)329-1898

- Certified Transportation Broker (CTB)

Treasury Management Association (TMA)
7315 Wisconsin Ave., Ste. 1250 W.
Bethesda, MD 20814
Phone: (301)907-2862
Fax: (301)907-2864

- Certified Cash Manager (CCM)

United Association of Journeymen and Apprentices of the Plumbing and Pipe Fitting Industry of the United States and Canada
PO Box 37800
Washington, DC 20013
Phone: (202)628-5823
Fax: (202)628-5024

- Certified Pipe Welder

United States Amateur Confederation of Roller Skating (USAC/RS)

4730 South St.
PO Box 6579
Lincoln, NE 68506
Phone: (402)483-7551
Fax: (402)483-1465

- Advanced Level Coach, United States Amateur Confederation of Roller Skating
- Certified Level Coach, United States Amateur Confederation of Roller Skating

United States Association of Independent Gymnastic Clubs (USAIGC)

235 Pinehurst Rd.
Wilmington, DE 19803
Phone: (302)656-3706

- Gymnastics Coach/Instructor

United States Judo Association

19 N. Union Blvd.
Colorado Springs, CO 80909
Phone: (309)647-1179

- Coach, United States Judo Association
- Examiner Certification, United States Judo Association
- Ju Jitsu Certification, United States Judo Association
- Kata Certification, United States Judo Association
- Kata Judge Certification, United States Judo Association
- Referee Certification, United States Judo Association

United States National Tennis Academy

1014 Ferris Ave., Ste. 1042-E
Waxahachie, TX 75165
Phone: (214)937-0311
Fax: (214)937-0450
Toll Free: (800)452-8519

- Certified Professional Tennis Instructor (CPTI)

United States Professional Racquetball Organization

1615 W. Uintah
Colorado Springs, CO 80904-2921
Phone: (719)635-5396

- Advanced Instructor, United States Professional Racquetball Organization
- Advanced Programmer, United States Professional Racquetball Organization
- High School/Collegiate Coach, United States Professional Racquetball Organization
- Instructor, United States Professional Racquetball Organization
- Master Professional, United States Professional Racquetball Organization
- National Team Coach, United States Professional Racquetball Organization
- Professional, United States Professional Racquetball Organization
- Programmer, United States Professional Racquetball Organization
- State/Individual Coach, United States Professional Racquetball Organization

United States Professional Tennis Registry (USPTR)

PO Box 4739
Hilton Head Island, SC 29938
Phone: (803)785-7244
Fax: (800)421-6289
Toll Free: (800)421-6289

- Associate Instructor, United States Professional Tennis Registry
- Instructor, United States Professional Tennis Registry
- Master Professional, United States Professional Tennis Registry
- Professional, United States Professional Tennis Registry

United States Tennis Court and Track Builders Association (U.S.T.C.T.B.A.)

720 Light St.
Baltimore, MD 21230-3816
Phone: (410)752-3500
Fax: (410)752-8295

- Certified Tennis Court Builder (CTCB)
- Certified Track Builder (CTB)

United States Water Fitness Association (USWFA)

PO Box 3279
Boynton Beach, FL 33424
Phone: (407)732-9908
Fax: (407)732-0950

- Coordinator of Water Fitness Programs
- Master Water Fitness Instructor
- Water Fitness Instructor

Universal Public Purchasing Certification Council

Reston International Center
11800 Sunrise Valley Dr., Ste. 1050
Reston, VA 22091
Phone: (703)715-9400
Fax: (703)715-9897
Toll Free: (800)FOR-NIGP

- Certified Professional Public Buyer (CPPB)
- Certified Public Purchasing Officer (CPPO)

Water Quality Association (WQA)

4151 Naperville Rd.
Lisle, IL 60532
Phone: (708)505-0160
Fax: (708)505-9637

- Certified Installer (CI)
- Certified Sales Representative (CSR)
- Certified Water Specialist, Level I (CWS I)
- Certified Water Specialist, Level II (CWS II)
- Certified Water Specialist, Level III (CWS III)
- Certified Water Specialist, Level IV (CWS IV)
- Certified Water Specialist, Level V (CWS V)

Wordperfect

c/o Novell
122 East 1700 South
Provo, UT 84606-6194
Phone: (801)429-5508
Fax: (801)429-5363
Toll Free: (800)233-EDUC

- Certified Professional Credential (CPC)
- Certified System Engineer (CSE)

World Safety Organization (WSO)

WSO World Mgmt. Center
305 E. Market St.
PO Box 518
Warrensburg, MO 64093
Phone: (816)747-3132
Fax: (816)747-2647

- Certified Hazardous Materials Executive (CHME)
- Certified Hazardous Materials Supervisor (CHMS)
- Certified Hazardous Materials Technician, Level I (CHMT I)
- Certified Hazardous Materials Technician, Level II (CHMT II)
- Certified Safety Executive (CSE)
- Certified Safety Manager (CSM)
- Certified Safety and Security Director (CSSD)
- Certified Safety Specialist (CSS)
- Certified Safety Technician (CST)

World Sidesaddle Federation

Box 1104
Bucyrus, OH 44820
Phone: (419)284-3176
Fax: (419)284-3176
E-mail: LBowlby@aol.com

- Certified Sidesaddle Instructor and Judge (CSI/J)

Wound Ostomy and Continence Nurses Society (WOCN)
2755 Bristol St., Ste. 110
Costa Mesa, CA 92626
Phone: (714)476-0268
Toll Free: (800)228-4238

- Certified Continence Care Nurse (CCCN)
- Certified Enterostomal Therapy Nurse (CETN)
- Certified Ostomy Care Nurse (COCN)
- Certified Wound Care Nurse (CWCN)

Xplor International
24238 Hawthorne Blvd.
Torrance, CA 90505-6505
Phone: (310)373-3633
Fax: (310)375-4240
Toll Free: (800)669-7567

- Electronic Document and Printing Professional (EDPP)

Appendix: Certification Acronyms

This appendix provides an alphabetical list of acronyms corresponding to the certifications covered in the *Certification Programs* section.

AAC Activity Assistant Certified

A.A.E. Accredited Airport Executive

AAEM Fellow of the Amer. Acad. of Environmental Medicine

AAI Accredited Adviser in Insurance

AALU Associate, Acad. of Life Underwriting

AAM Associate in Automation Management

AAP Accredited Automated Clearing House Professional

AAR Accredited in Appraisal Review

AAS Assessment Administration Specialist

ABC Accredited Business Communicator

ABPMR Diplomate of the Amer. Bd. of Physical Medicine and Rehabilitation

ACA Approved Certification Administrator

ACAS Associate, Casualty Actuarial Soc.

ACC Activity Consultant Certified

ACE Associate Credit Executive

ACFRE Advanced Certified Fund Raising Executive

ACM Associate Certified Manager

ACP Associate Computing Professional

ACS Associate, Customer Service

ACSR Accredited Customer Service Representative

ACT Associate Engineering Technologist

ADC Activity Director Certified

Adv. PFS Advanced Physical Fitness Specialist

AEP Associate Environmental Professional

AEPA Associate Environmental Property Assessor

AET Associate Engineering Technician

AET Associate Environmental Trainer

AFM Accredited Farm Manager

AFS Associate Fisheries Scientist

AFSB Associate in Fidelity and Surety Bonding

AIAA Associate, Insurance Agency Administration

AIAF Associate in Insurance Accounting and Finance Life and Health In surance

AIAF Associate in Insurance Accounting and Finance Property and Casualty

AIC Associate in Claims

AIDM Associate Insurance Data Manager

AIE Accredited Insurance Examiner

AIM Associate in Management

AIS Associate in Insurance Services

ALAT Assistant Laboratory Animal Technician

ALC Accredited Land Consultant

ALCM Associate in Loss Control Management

ALHC Associate, Life and Health Claims

ALS Accredited Legal Secretary

AM Accredited Member, Amer. Soc. of Appraisers

AMEA Accredited Machinery and Equipment Appraiser

AMIM Associate in Marine Insurance Management

AMS Assn. Management Specialist

ANP Adult Nurse Practitioner

AOCN Advanced Oncology Certified Nurse

APA Accredited Pension Administrator

APA Associate in Premium Auditing

APA Associate Professional Agronomist

APCS Associate Professional Crop Scientist

APCS Associate Professional Crop Specialist

APH Associate Professional in Horticulture

APM Associated Professional Member, Amer. Soc. of Pension Actuaries

APPP Associate Professional Plant Pathologist

APR Accredited in Public Relations

APSC Associate Professional Soil Classifier

APSS Associate Professional Soil Scientist

APSS Associate Professional Soil Specialist

APWS Associate Professional in Weed Science

ARA Accredited Rural Appraiser

ARe Associate in Reinsurance

ARM Accredited Residential Manager

ARM Associate in Risk Management

ARP Associate in Research and Planning

ARP Associate in Research and Planning (Life Insurance Option)

ART Accredited Record Technician

ARU Accredited Residential Underwriter

ASA Accredited Senior Appraiser

ASA Associate of the Soc. of Actuaries

ASE Associate Service Executive

ASF Associate in State Filings

ATC Athletic Trainer Certified

AU Associate in Underwriting

BB(ASCP) Technologist in Blood Banking

BC-HIS Bd. Certified - Hearing Instrument Specialist

BCBA Bd. Certified in Business Appraisal

BCE Bd. Certified Entomologist

BCE Broadband Communications Engineer

BCFE Bd. Certified Forensic Examiner

BCLD Bioanalyst Clinical Laboratory Director

BCNP Bd. Certified Nuclear Pharmacist

BCNSP Bd. Certified Nutrition Support Pharmacist

BCPS Bd. Certified Pharmacotherapy Specialist

BCT Broadband Communications Technician

BLM Bioanalyst Laboratory Manager

CA Certified Archivist

CA Certified Auctioneer

CA Childbirth Assistant

CA Credit Associate

CA-C Certified Appraiser Consultant

CA-FL Certified Appraiser Farm and Land

CA-R Certified Appraiser Residential

CA-S Certified Appraiser Senior

CAA Certified Athletic Administrator

CAC Certified Airport Chaplain

CACM Certified Associate Contracts Manager

CAE Certified Assessment Evaluator

CAE Certified Assn. Executive

CAFM Certified Automotive Fleet Manager

CAM Certified Apartment Manager

CAMT Certified Apartment Maintenance Technician

CAPA Certified Ambulatory Perianesthesia Nurse

CAPP Certified Appraiser of Personal Property

CAPS Certified Apartment Property Supervisor

CARN Certified Addictions Registered Nurse

CAS Certified Avian Specialist

C(ASCP) Technologist in Chemistry

CAT Certified Appliance Technician

C.A.T. Certified Athletic Trainer

CAWI Certified Associate Welding Inspector

CBA Certified Bank Auditor

CBA Certified Business Appraiser

CBA Credit Business Associate

CBC Certified Business Communicator

CBC Certified Business Counselor

CBCO Certified Bank Compliance Officer

CBD Certified Bathroom Designer

CBET Certified Biomedical Equipment Technician

CBF Credit Business Fellow

CBP Certified Benefits Professional

CBPE Certified Business Planning Executive

CBRE Certified Broadcast Radio Engineer

CBSE Certified Building Service Executives

CBT Certified Broadcast Technologist

CBTE Certified Broadcast Television Engineer

CC Certified Clockmaker

CC Certified Cook

CC Clinical Consultant

CCA Certified Crop Adviser

CCAE Certified Collection Agency Executive

CCAP Certified Claims Assistance Professional

CCBE Certified Credit Bur. Executive

CCC Certified Cost Consultant

CCCE Certified Consumer Credit Executive

C.C.C.I. Certified Civil and Criminal Investigator

CCCN Certified Continence Care Nurse

C.C.E. Certified Clinical Electrologist

CCE Certified Cost Engineer

CCE Certified Credit Executive

CCEA Certified Cost Estimator/Analyst

CCIM Certified Commercial Investment Member

CCLA Casualty Claim Law Associate

CCLA/FCLA Casualty-Fraud Claim Law Associate

CCLA/PCLA Casualty-Property Claim Law Associate

CCLA/WCLA Casualty-Workers' Compensation Claim Law Associate

CCLS Casualty Claim Law Specialist

CCM Certified Case Manager

CCM Certified Cash Manager

CCM Certified Club Manager

CCM Certified Concession Manager

CCM Certified Consulting Meteorologist

CCMHC Certified Clinical Mental Health Counselor

CCO Certified Confidentiality Officer

CCP Certified Claims Professional

CCP Certified Clinical Perfusionist

CCP Certified Cogeneration Professional

CCP Certified Compensation Professional

CCP Certified Computing Professional

C.C.P.O. Certified Civil Process Officer

CCRA Certified Commercial Real Estate Appraiser

CCS Certified Canine Specialist

CCS Certified Clinical Sociologist

CCS Certified Coding Specialist

CCSMC Certification in Central Service Management Concepts

CCSP Certified Chiropractic Sports Physician

CCT Certified Cardiovascular Technologist

CCT Clinical Chemist

CCT Clinical Chemistry Technologist

CCTE Certified Corporate Travel Executive

CCTS Certified Corporate Trust Specialist

CCUE Certified Credit Union Executive

CD Certified Drafter

CDA Certified Dental Assistant

CDA Child Development Associate

CDE Certified Data Educator

CDE Certified Diabetes Educator

CDE Certified Disability Examiner

CDI-P Certified Deaf Interpreter - Provisional

CDM Certified Dietary Manager

CDPMA Certified Dental Practice Management Assistant

CDSM Certified Demand-Side Management Professional

CDT Certified Dental Technician

CE Childbirth Educator

CEA Certified Environmental Auditor

CEAP Certified Employee Assistance Professional

CEBS Certified Employee Benefits Specialist

CECP Certified Electronic Claims Professional

CED Certified Economic Developer

CEDA Certified Eating Disorders Associate

CEDS Certified Eating Disorders Specialist

CEF Certified Electroplater-Finisher

CEF-SE Certified Electroplater Finisher - Specialist in Electronics

CEH Certified Executive Housekeeper

CEHT Certified Environmental Health Technician

CEI Certified Electronic Imager

CEM Certified Emergency Manager

CEM Certified Energy Manager

CEM Certified Expediting Manager

CEN Certified Emergency Nurse

CEOE Certified Educational Office Employee

CEOE Certified Engineering Operations Executive

CEP Certified Environmental Professional

CESRA Certified Employee Services and Recreation Administrator

CET Certified Echocardiographic Technologist

CET Certified Electronics Technician

CET Certified Electronics Technician (Associate)

CET Certified Electronics Technician (Journeyman)

CET Certified Environmental Trainer

CETN Certified Enterostomal Therapy Nurse

CF Consulting Fellow of the Natl. Property Management Assn.

CF-A Certified Form Appraiser

CFA Chartered Financial Analyst

C.F.A.I. Certified Fire and Arson Investigator

CFBE Certified Food and Beverage Executive

CFC Certified Forms Consultant

CFC Chartered Financial Consultant

CFCE Certified Financial Counseling Executive

CFE Certified Food Executive

CFE Certified Fraud Examiner

CFEI Certified Fire and Explosion Investigator

CFEP Certified Facilities Environmental Professional

C.F.F.I. Certified Financial Fraud Investigator

CFFS Certified Freshwater Fish Specialist

CFI Certified Fire Investigator

CFM Certified Facility Manager

CFM Certified Financial Manager

CFM Certified Food Manager

CFME Certified Financial Management Executive

CFP Certified Fence Professional

CFP Certified Financial Planner

CFPIM Certified Fellow in Production and Inventory Management

CFPS Certified Fire Protection Specialist

CFRE Certified Fund Raising Executive

CFRN Certified Flight Registered Nurse

CFS Certified Fisheries Scientist

CFSP Certified Foodservice Professional

CFSP Associate Certified Foodservice Professional Associate

CFSSP Certified Financial Services Security Professional

CG Certified Gemologist

CGA Certified Gastroenterology Associate

CGA Certified Gemologist Appraiser

CGAE Certified Graphics Arts Executive

CGASR Certified Graphic Arts Sales Representative

CGC Certified Genetic Counselor

CGCM Certified Graphics Communications Manager

CGCS Certified Golf Course Superintendent

CGM Certified Grounds Manager

CGN Certified Gastroenterology Licensed Vocational/Practical Nurse

CGR Certified Graduate Remodeler

CGRN Certified Gastroenterology Registered Nurse

CGT Certified Gastroenterology Technologist/Technician

CGWP Certified Ground Water Professional

CHA Certified Hotel Administrator

CHAE Certified Hospitality Accountant Executive

CHCM Certified Hazard Control Manager, Associate Level

CHCM Certified Hazard Control Manager, Master Level

CHCM Certified Hazard Control Manager, Senior Level

CHE Certified Home Economist

CHE Certified Hospitality Educator

CHES Certified Health Education Specialist

CHFP Certified Human Factors Professional

CHHE Certified Hospitality Housekeeping Executive

CHME Certified Hazardous Materials Executive

CHMS Certified Hazardous Materials Supervisor

CHMT I Certified Hazardous Materials Technician, Level I

CHMT II Certified Hazardous Materials Technician, Level II

CHN Certified Hemodialysis Nurse

CHN Certified Holistic Nurse

CHP Certified Health Physicist

CHRE Certified Human Resources Executive

CHS Certified Hospitality Supervisor

CHSE Certified Hospitality Sales Executive

CHSP Certified Healthcare Safety Professional, Associate Level

CHSP Certified Healthcare Safety Professional, Master Level

CHSP Certified Healthcare Safety Professional, Senior Level

CHSP Certified Hospitality Sales Professional

CHSP Certified Human Service Provider

CHT Certified Hemodialysis Technician

C.Ht. Certified Hypnotherapist

CHUC Certified Health Unit Coordinator

CI Certificate of Interpretation

CI Certified Installer

CI/CT Certificate of Interpretation/Certificate of Transliteration

CIA Certified Internal Auditor

CIAQP Certified Indoor Air Quality Professional

CIC Certification in Infection Control

CIC Certified Insurance Counselor

C.I.C. Certified Intl. Courier

CIC Certified Interscholastic Coach

CIC Certified Irrigation Contractor

CICM Certified Intl. Convention Manager

CID Certified Irrigation Designer

CIDM Certified Insurance Data Manager

CIE Certified Insurance Examiner

CIH Certified Industrial Hygienist

C.I.I. Certified Insurance Investigator

C.I.I. Certified Intl. Investigator

CIMA Certified Investment Management Analyst

CIP Certified Incentive Professional

CIPE Certified in Plumbing Engineering

CIPS Certified Intl. Property Specialist

CIRA Certified Insolvency and Reorganization Accountant

CIRM Certified in Integrated Resource Management

CIRS Certified Insurance Rehabilitation Specialist

CISA Certified Information Systems Auditor

CISR Certified Insurance Service Representative

CITE Certified Incentive Travel Executive

CKD Certified Kitchen Designer

CKE Certified Knowledge Engineer

CKO Certified Kennel Operator

CLA Certified Legal Assistant

CLA Certified Leisure Associate

CLBB Certified Lender-Business Banking

CLDir Clinical Laboratory Director

CLEP Certified Lighting Efficiency Professional

CLES Certified Laboratory Equipment Specialist

CLI Certified Legal Investigator

CLIA Certified Landscape Irrigation Auditor

CLIP Conditional Legal Interpreting Permit

CLIP-R Conditional Legal Interpreting Permit - Relay

CLLM Certified Laundry/Linen Manager

CLM Certified Lake Manager

CLMC Certified Lighting Management Consultant

CLMT Certified Landscape Management Technician

CLP Certified Landscape Professional

CLP Certified Leasing Professional

CLP Certified Leisure Professional

CLPlb Clinical Laboratory Phlebotomist

CLS Certified Leasing Specialist

CLS Clinical Laboratory Scientist

CLS(C) Clinical Laboratory Scientist in Clinical Chemistry

CLS(H) Clinical Laboratory Scientist in Hematology

CLS(I) Clinical Laboratory Scientist in Immunohematology

CLS(M) Clinical Laboratory Scientist in Microbiology

CLSp(CG) Clinical Laboratory Specialist in Cytogenetics

CLSp(H) Clinical Laboratory Specialist in Hematology

CLSup Clinical Laboratory Supervisor

CLT Certified Landscape Technician

CLT Clinical Laboratory Technician

CLU Chartered Life Underwriter

CLVS Certified Legal Video Specialist

CM Certified Manager

CMA Certified Management Accountant

CMA Certified Medical Assistant

CMB Certified Mortgage Banker

CMC Certified Management Consultant

CMC Certified Master Chef

CMC Certified Master Clockmaker

CMC Certified Mortgage Consultant

CMC Certified Moving Consultant

CMCE Certified Managed Care Executives

CMD Certified Marketing Director

CMDA Certified Market Data Analyst

CMDSM Certified Mail and Distribution Systems Manager

CME Certified Manager of Exhibits

CME Certified Marketing Executive

C.M.E. Certified Medical Electrologist

CMEA Certified Machinery and Equipment Appraiser

CMEW Certified Master Electronic Watchmaker

CMFA Certified Municipal Finance Administrator

CMfgE Certified Manufacturing Engineer

CMfgT Certified Manufacturing Technologist

CMH Certified Manager of Housing

CMI Certified Mechanical Inspector

CMM Certified Mail Manager

CMM Certified Manager of Maintenance

CMM Certified Medical Manager

CMP Certified Meeting Professional

CMPA Certified Manager of Patient Accounts

CMPC Certified Master Pastry Chef

C.M.P.I. Certified Missing Persons Investigator

CMR Certified Medical Representative

CMRS Certified Manager of Reporting Services

CMS Cadastral Mapping Specialist

CMS Certified Marine Surveyor

CMSC Certified Medical Staff Coordinator

CMT Certified Medical Transcriptionist

CMTSE Certified Machine Tool Sales Engineer

CMW Certified Master Watchmaker

CNC Certified Nutritional Consultant

CNE Certified NetWare Engineer

CNE Enterprise Certified NetWare Engineer

CNHA Certified Nursing Home Administrator

CNI Certified NetWare Instructor

CNM Certified Nurse-Midwife

CNMT Certified Nuclear Medicine Technologist

CNN Certified Nephrology Nurse

CNSD Certified Nutrition Support Dietician

CNSN Certified Nutrition Support Nurse

CO Certified Orthotist

COA Certified Ophthalmic Assistant

COA Certified Orthodontic Assistant

COAP Certified Office Automation Professional

COCN Certified Ostomy Care Nurse

COHN Certified Occupational Health Nurse

COMSA Certified Oral and Maxillofacial Surgery Assistant

COMT Certified Ophthalmic Medical Technologist

COPRA Certified Ophthalmic Photographer and Retinal Angiographer

COS Certified Occupancy Specialist

COT Certified Ophthalmic Technician

COTA Certified Occupational Therapy Assistant

CP Certified Parliamentarian

CP Certified Practitioner

CP Certified Prosthetist

CPA Certified Professional Agronomist

CPAN Certified Post Anesthesia Nurse

CPBC Certified Professional Business Consultant

CPBE Certified Professional Broadcast Engineer

CPBE Certified Professional Bur. Executive

CPC Certified Pastry Cook

CPC Certified Pension Consultant

CPC Certified Personnel Consultant

CPC Certified Photographic Counselor

CPC Certified Professional Chemist

CPC Certified Professional Coder

CPC Certified Professional Constructor

CPC Certified Professional Consultant

CPC Certified Professional Credential

CPC-H Certified Professional Coder - Hospital

CPCE Certified Professional Catering Executive

CPChE Certified Professional Chemical Engineer

CPCM Certified Professional Contracts Manager

CPCS Certified Professional Crop Scientist

CPCU Chartered Property Casualty Underwriter

CPDN Certified Peritoneal Dialysis Nurse

CPE Certified Plant Engineer

C.P.E. Certified Professional Electrologist

CPE Certified Professional Ergonomist

CPE Certified Professional Estimator

CPE Certified Purchasing Executive

C.Ped. Certified Pedorthist

CPESC Certified Professional Soil Erosion and Sediment Control Specialist

CPF Certified Picture Framer

CPFB Certified Professional Food Broker

CPFM Certified Parking Facility Manager

CPFM Certified Professional Fleet Manager

CPFT Certified Pulmonary Function Technologist

CPG Certified Professional Geologist

CPH Certified Professional Horticulturist

CPHM Certified Professional in Healthcare Materials Management

CPHQ Certified Professional in Healthcare Quality

C.P.I. Certified Professional Investigator

CPI Certified Pump Installer

CPIA Certified Professional Insurance Agent

CPIM Certified in Production and Inventory Management

CPIM Certified Professional Insurance Man

CPIW Certified Professional Insurance Woman

CPL Certified Professional Landman

C.P.L. Certified Professional Logistician

CPM Certified Professional Services Manager

CPM Certified Property Manager

C.P.M. Certified Purchasing Manager

CPME Certified Production Management Executive

CPMR Certified Professional Manufacturers Representative

CPN Certified Pediatric Nurse

CPNP Certified Pediatric Nurse Practitioner

CPO Certified Park Operator

CPO Certified Pool Spa Operator

CPO Certified Prosthetist/Orthotist

CPO Certified Protection Officer

CPO Certified Public Official

CPP Certified Packaging Professional

CPP Certified Payroll Professional

CPP Certified Professional Parliamentarian

CPP Certified Professional Photographer

CPP Certified Protection Professional

CPP Certified Purchasing Professional

CPPA Certified Professional Property Administrator

CPPA Certified Professional Public Adjuster

CPPB Certified Professional Public Buyer

CPPM Certified Professional Property Manager

CPPO Certified Public Purchasing Officer

CPPP Certified Professional Plant Pathologist

CPPS Certified Professional Property Specialist

CPRW Certified Professional Resume Writer

CPS Certified Professional Secretary

C.P.S. Certified Protection Specialist

CPSC Certified Professional Soil Classifier

CPSM Certified Product Safety Manager, Associate Level

CPSM Certified Product Safety Manager, Executive Level

CPSM Certified Product Safety Manager, Senior Level

CPSN Certified Plastic Surgical Nurse

CPSS Certified Professional Soil Scientist

CPSS Certified Professional Soil Specialist

CPT Certified Personal Trainer

CPT Certified Poetry Therapist

CPTI Certified Professional Tennis Instructor

CPWS Certified Professional in Weed Science

CQA Certified Quality Auditor

CQE Certified Quality Engineer

CQM Certified Quality Manager

CQT Certified Quality Technician

CQUAR Certified in Quality Assurance and Utilization Review

CRA Certified Research Administrator

CRA Certified Retinal Angiographer

CRA Certified Review Appraiser

CRA-A Certified Review Appraiser - Administrative

CRB Certified Real Estate Brokerage Manager

CRC Certified Rehabilitation Counselor

CRCM Certified Regulatory Compliance Manager

CRCST Certified Registered Central Service Technician

CRDE Certified Rooms Div. Executive

CRE Certified Reliability Engineer

CRE Counselor of Real Estate

CREA Certified Real Estate Appraiser

CREC Certified Rural Electric Communicator

CRES Certified Radiology Equipment Specialist

CRM Certified Records Manager

CRMC Certified Radio Marketing Consultant

CRMC Certified Range Management Consultant

CRML Certification in Residential Mortgage Lending

CRNA Certified Registered Nurse Anesthetist

CRNH Certified Registered Nurse Hospice

CRNI Certified Registered Nurse Intravenous

CRP Certified Relocation Professional

CRPI Certified Real Property Inspector

CRR Certified Real time Reporter

CRRN Certified Rehabilitation Registered Nurse

CRS Certified Reptile Specialist

CRS Certified Residential Specialist

CRSS Certified Recreational Sports Specialist

CRTT Certified Respiratory Therapy Technician

CSAS Certified Small Animal Specialist

CSAT Certified Specialist in Analytical Technology

C.S.C. Certified Security Consultant

CSCS Certified Strength and Conditioning Specialist

CSE Certified Safety Executive

CSE Certified Sales Executive

CSE Certified Service Executive

CSE Certified System Engineer

CSF Certified Service Facilitator

CSF Certified State Filer

CSI Certified Satellite Installer

CSI Certified Senior Inspector

CSI/J Certified Sidesaddle Instructor and Judge

CSM Certified Safety Manager

CSM Certified Shopping Center Manager

CSME Certified Sales and Marketing Executive

CSMT Certified Specialist in Measurement Technology

CSMT Certified Sports Medicine Trainer

CSN Certified School Nurse

CSP Certified Store Professional

CSPCF Certification in Statistical Process Control, Facilitator

CSPCO Certification in Statistical Process Control, Operational

CSPCT Certification in Statistical Process Control, Technical

CSPDM Certified Sterile Processing and Distribution Manager

CSPDS Certified Sterile Processing and Distribution Supervisor

CSPDT Certified Sterile Processing and Distribution Technician

CSR Certified Sales Representative

CSRE Certified Senior Radio Engineer

CSS Certified Customer Service Specialist

CSS Certified Safety Specialist

C.S.S. Certified Security Specialist

CSS Certified Security Supervisor

CSSD Certified Safety and Security Director

CSSP Certified Sanitary Supply Professional

CST Certified Safety Technician

CST Certified Security Trainer

CST Certified Surgical Technologist

CST Certified Survey Technician, Level I

CST Certified Survey Technician, Level II

CST Certified Survey Technician, Level III

CST Certified Survey Technician, Level IV

CST/CFA Certified Surgical Technologist/Certified First Assistant

CSTE Certified Senior Television Engineer

CT Certificate of Transliteration

CT Certified Engineering Technologist

CTA Certified Tax Accountant

CT(ASCP) Cytotechnologist

CTB Certified Track Builder

CTB Certified Transportation Broker

CTC Certified Tax Consultant

CTC Certified Travel Counselor

CTCB Certified Tennis Court Builder

CTFA Certified Trust and Financial Advisor

CTL Certification in Transportation and Logistics

CTP Certified Tax Preparer

CTP Certified Turfgrass Professional

CTPM Certified Tax Preparer Master

CTPS Certified Tax Preparer Specialist

CTR Certified Tumor Registrar

CTRS Certified Therapeutic Recreation Specialist

CTS Certified Temporary-Staffing Specialist

CVA Certified Valuation Analyst

CVA Certified in Volunteer Administration

CW Certified Watchmaker

CWCN Certified Wound Care Nurse

CWD Certified Well Driller

CWD/PI Certified Well Driller/Pump Installer

CWE Certified Welding Educator

CWI Certified Welding Inspector

CWS I Certified Water Specialist, Level I

CWS II Certified Water Specialist, Level II

CWS III Certified Water Specialist, Level III

CWS IV Certified Water Specialist, Level IV

CWS V Certified Water Specialist, Level V

DAAS Diplomate of the Amer. Acad. of Sanitarians

DABCC Diplomate of the Amer. Bd. of Clinical Chemistry

DABCI Diplomate of the Amer. Bd. of Chiropractic Internists

DABCO Diplomate of the Amer. Bd. of Chiropractic Orthopedics

DABFA Diplomate of the Amer. Bd. of Forensic Anthropology

DABNS Diplomate of the Amer. Bd. of Neurological Surgery

DACBN Diplomate of the Amer. Chiropractic Bd. of Nutrition

DACBOH Diplomate of the Amer. Chiropractic Bd. of Occupational Health

DACBR Diplomate of the Amer. Chiropractic Bd. of Radiology

DACBSP Diplomate of the Amer. Chiropractic Bd. of Sports Physicians

DACNB Diplomate of the Amer. Chiropractic Neurology Bd.

DACVN Diplomate of the Amer. Coll. of Veterinary Nutrition

DCSW Diplomate in Clinical Social Work

DLM(ASCP) Diplomate in Laboratory Management

DPHM Distinguished Professional in Healthcare Materials Management

DREI Designated Real Estate Instructor

EAC Environmental Assessment Consultant

EBCTP Employee Benefit Certified Trust Professional

EDPP Electronic Document and Printing Professional

ESC Electronics Specialist, Certified

ESC Environmental Screening Consultant

ESS Employment Services Specialist

ET Engineering Technician

ETG Employment and Training Generalist

ETM Employment and Training Master

FACACN Fellow of the Amer. Coun. of Applied Clinical Nutrition

FACCE Fellow of the Amer. Coll. of Childbirth Educators

FACHCA Fellow of the Amer. Coll. of Health Care Administrators

FACPE Distinguished Fellow of the Amer. Coll. of Physician Executives

FACPE Fellow of the Amer. Coll. of Physician Executives

FALU Fellow, Acad. of Life Underwriting

FASA Fellow of the Amer. Soc. of Appraisers

FCAS Fellow, Casualty Actuarial Soc.

FCLA Fraud Claim Law Associate

FCLS Fraud Claim Law Specialist

FCS Fellowship in Central Service

FHFMA Fellow, Healthcare Financial Management Assn.

FLA Forestland Appraiser

FLMI Fellow, Life Management Inst.

FMA Facilities Management Administrator

FMP Foodservice Management Professional

FNP Family Nurse Practitioner

FSPA Fellow, Soc. of Pension Actuaries

GEL Group Exercise Leadership

GS General Supervisor

GSA Graduate Senior Appraiser

H(ASCP) Technologist in Hematology

HCLD High-Complexity Clinical Laboratory Director

HIA Health Insurance Associate

HP(ASCP) Hemapheresis Practitioner

HSAI Horse Safety Assistant Instructor

HSC Horse Safety Clinician

HSG Horse Safety Trail Guide

HSGA Horse Safety Assistant Trail Guide

HSI Horse Safety Instructor

HSI/T Horse Safety Instructor/Trainer

HSRIB Horse Safety Riding Instructor Basic

HT(ASCP) Histologic Technician

HTL(ASCP) Histotechnologist

HTM Master Horticultural Therapist

HTR Horticultural Therapist Registered

HTR Horticultural Therapist Technician

I(ASCP) Technologist in Immunology

IBA Instructor of Beginner Through Advanced

IBCLC Intl. Bd. Certified Lactation Consultant

IBI Instructor of Beginner Through Intermediate

I.C.E.S. Industrial Counter-Espionage Specialist

IFA Independent Fee Appraiser

IFAA Independent Fee Appraiser/Agricultural

IFAC Independent Fee Appraiser/Counselor

IFAS Independent Fee Appraiser/Senior

IHIT Industrial Hygienist in Training

IT Instructor in Training

JTS Job Training Specialist

LAT Laboratory Animal Technician

LATG Laboratory Animal Technologist

LCSE Lifetime Certified Service Executive

LMIS Labor Market Information Specialist

LUTCF Life Underwriter Training Coun. Fellow

MAC Master Addictions Counselor

MAI Member, Appraisal Inst.

M(ASCP) Technologist in Microbiology

MASTER CET Master Certified Electronics Technician

MCLD Moderate-Complexity Clinical Laboratory Director

MCM Master Club Manager

MCR Master of Corporate Real Estate

MFLA Master Farm and Land Appraiser

MGA Master Gemologist Appraiser

MGA Master Governmental Appraiser

MGWC Master Ground Water Contractor

MHP Managed Healthcare Professional

MHS Master Hotel Supplier

MLT Medical Laboratory Technician

MLT(ASCP) Medical Laboratory Technician

MP Marketing Professional

MPP Military Packaging Professional

MRA Master Residential Appraiser

MSA Master Senior Appraiser

MSPA Member, Soc. of Pension Actuaries

MT Medical Technologist

MT-BC Music Therapist - Bd. Certified

MT(ASCP) Medical Technologist

NAFE Fellow of the Natl. Acad. of Forensic Engineers

NAFE Member, Natl. Acad. of Forensic Engineers

NAFE Senior Member, Natl. Acad. of Forensic Engineers

NCAC I Natl. Certified Addiction Counselor Level I

NCAC II Natl. Certified Addiction Counselor Level II

NCC Natl. Certified Counselor

NCCC Natl. Certified Career Counselor

NCGC Natl. Certified Gerontological Counselor

NCIDQ Certified Certified Interior Designer

NCLC Natl. Contact Lens Certified

NCMG Natl. Certified Master Groomer

NCPT1 Nationally Certified Psychiatric Technician, Level 1

NCPT2 Nationally Certified Psychiatric Technician, Level 2

NCPT3 Nationally Certified Psychiatric Technician, Level 3

NCPT4 Nationally Certified Psychiatric Technician, Level 4

NCSC Natl. Certified School Counselor

NCSP Nationally Certified School Psychologist

NCTMB Nationally Certified in Therapeutic Massage and Bodywork

NFCC Certified Consumer Credit Counselor

OCN Oncology Certified Nurse

OCP OPSEC Certified Professional

OHST Certified Occupational Health and Safety Technologist

ONC Orthopaedic Nurse Certified

Opt. A., R. Registered Optometric Assistant

Opt. T., R. Registered Optometric Technician

OSA Ophthalmic Surgical Assisting

OTR Occupational Therapist, Registered

PA-C Physician Assistant - Certified

PBA Postpartum and Breastfeeding Assistant

PBT(ASCP) Phlebotomy Technician

PCAM Professional Community Assn. Manager

PCLA Property Claim Law Associate

PCLA/FCLA Property-Fraud Claim Law Associate

PCLA/WCLA Property-Workers' Compensation Claim Law Associate

PCLS Property Claim Law Specialist

PCMH Professional Certified in Materials Handling

PCMM Professional Certified in Materials Management

PDS Program Director Specialist

PFS Personal Financial Specialist

PFS Physical Fitness Specialist
PH Professional Hydrologist
PH-GW Professional Hydrologist - Ground Water
PH-WQ Professional Hydrologist - Water Quality
PHG Professional Hydrogeologist
PHM Certified Public Housing Managers
PHR Professional in Human Resources
PLS Certified Professional Legal Secretary
PMP Project Management Professional
POE Petroleum Operations Engineer
POLT Physician Office Laboratory Technician
PPS Personal Property Specialist
PPS Personal Protection Specialist
PRE Professional Real Estate Executive
PRP Professional Registered Parliamentarians
PT, CCS Physical Therapist, Cardiopulmonary Certified Specialist
PT, CECS Physical Therapist, Clinical Electrophysiology Certified Specialist
PT, GCS Physical Therapist, Geriatrics Certified Specialist
PT, NCS Physical Therapist, Neurology Certified Specialist
PT, OCS Physical Therapist, Orthopaedics Certified Specialist
PT, PCS Physical Therapist, Pediatrics Certified Specialist
PT, SCS Physical Therapist, Sports Certified Specialist
QEP Qualified Environmental Professional
QPA Qualified Pension Administrator
RAM Registered Apartment Manager
RBP Registered Biological Photographer
RBSM Registered Building Service Manager
RCE Realtor Assn. Certified Executive
RCM Registered Cooperative Manager
RCVT Registered Cardiovascular Technologist
RD Registered Dietician
RDA Registered Dental Assistant
RDCS Registered Diagnostic Cardiac Sonographer
RDMS Registered Diagnostic Medical Sonographer
RDT Registered Dietetic Technician
REBC Registered Employee Benefits Consultant
RECP Real Estate Consulting Professional
REEGT Registered Electroencephalographic Technologist
REH Registered Executive Housekeeper
REHS/RS Registered Environmental Health Specialist/Registered Sanitarian
RELT Registered Environmental Laboratory Technologist

REM Registered Environmental Manager
REP Registered Environmental Professional
REPA Registered Environmental Property Assessor
REPT Registered Electroencephalographic Technologists
RES Registered Environmental Scientist
RES Residential Evaluation Specialist
RFP Registered Financial Planner
RHSP Registered Hazardous Substances Professional
RHSS Registered Hazardous Substances Specialist
RHU Registered Health Underwriter
RJ Registered Jeweler
RLLD Registered Laundry/Linen Director
RLM Bd. Certified in Real Estate Litigation Management
RLT Registered Laboratory Technician
RM Registered Microbiologist
R.M.A. Registered Medical Assistant
RMT Registered Medical Technologist
RMU Registered Mortgage Underwriter
RN-CD Certified Chemical Dependency Nurse
RODC Registered Org. Development Consultant
RODP Registered Org. Development Professional
ROF Registered Orthotic Fitter
RP Registered Parliamentarian
RPA Real Property Administrator
RPFT Registered Pulmonary Function Technologist
RPM Registered Professional Member of the Natl. Assn. of Real Estate Appraisers
RPR Registered Professional Reporter
RPRA Real Property Review Appraiser
RPSGT Registered Polysomnographic Technologist
RPT Registered Phlebotomy Technician
RPT Registered Poetry Therapist
RRA Registered Record Administrator
RRC Registered Roof Consultant
RRO Registered Roof Observer
RRT Registered Respiratory Therapist
RS Registered Supplier
R.T.(CV)(ARRT) Registered Technologist (Cardiovascular-Interventional Technology)
R.T.(M)(ARRT) Registered Technologist (Mammography)
R.T.(N)(ARRT) Registered Technologist (Nuclear Medicine Technology)
R.T.(R)(ARRT) Registered Technologist (Radiography)
R.T.(T)(ARRT) Registered Technologist (Radiation Therapy Technology)

RVT Registered Vascular Technologist
SAM Senior Asset Manager
SBB(ASCP) Specialist in Blood Banking
SCA Senior Certified Appraiser
SC(ASCP) Specialist in Chemistry
SCET Senior Certified Electronics Technician
SCLA Senior Claim Law Associate
SCRP Senior Certified Relocation Professional
SCSM Senior Certified Shopping Center Manager
SCT(ASCP) Specialist in Cytotechnology
SET Senior Engineering Technician
SH(ASCP) Specialist in Hematology
SHMS Senior Housing Marketing Specialist
SI(ASCP) Specialist in Immunology
SI(ASCP) Specialist in Microbiology
SIOR Specialist, Industrial/Office Real Estate
SLA Senior Licensed Appraiser
SM Specialist Microbiologist
SMA Systems Maintenance Administrator
SMC Senior Mortgage Consultant
SMT Systems Maintenance Technician
SPHR Senior Professional in Human Resources
SPPA Senior Professional Public Adjuster
SRA Specialist in Residential Appraisal
SRC Senior Real Estate Counselor
TC Technical Consultant
TEP Trainer, Educator, Practitioner
TS Technical Supervisor
TT Technician Trainee
UIS Unemployment Insurance Specialist
WCLA Workers' Compensation Claim Law Associate
WCLA/FCLA Workers' Compensation-Fraud Claim Law Associate
WCLS Workers' Compensation Claim Law Specialist

Master Index

This index contains citations to all certifications, accreditations, and sponsoring bodies covered in *CAPD*. Certification and accreditation program names are also listed alphabetically beneath corresponding job types and subject terms (in bold). Numbers refer to entry numbers, not page numbers.

Biology; Clinical Laboratory Scientist in Micro   1067

Biology; Comm. on Postdoctoral Educational Programs of the Amer. Acad. of Micro   1734

Biology; Diplomate, Amer. Bd. of Medical Micro   1125

Biology; Diplomate of the Amer. Bd. of Pathology with Special Qualification in Medical Micro   727

Biology; Specialist in Micro   1095

Biology; Technologist in Micro   1100

Biomedical Equipment Technician; Certified   1060

Birth Centers

Commn. for the Accreditation of Freestanding Birth Centers   1617

Birth Centers; Commn. for the Accreditation of Freestanding   1617

Birth Support Providers, Intl.   900

Blind and Visually Handicapped

Natl. Accreditation Coun. for Agencies Serving the Blind and Visually Handicapped   1618

Blind and Visually Handicapped; Natl. Accreditation Coun. for Agencies Serving the   1618

Blood Bank Schools; Comm. on Accreditation of Specialists in   1596

Blood Banking; Specialist in   1090

Blood Banking; Technologist in   1096

Blood Banking/Transfusion Medicine; Diplomate of the Amer. Bd. of Pathology with Special Qualification in   721

Blood Banks; Amer. Assn. of   1596

Bd. on Certification for Community Health Nursing Practice   985, 991, 1016

Bd. of Certification in Emergency Medicine   794

Bd. of Certification in Emergency Medicine; Diplomate of the   794

Bd. of Certification for Emergency Nursing   960, 962

Bd. of Certification in Family Practice   795

Bd. of Certification in Family Practice; Diplomate of the   795

Bd. for Certification of Genealogists   606, 607, 608, 609, 610, 611

Bd. on Certification for General Nursing Practice   995

Bd. of Certification in Geriatric Medicine   796

Bd. of Certification in Geriatric Medicine; Diplomate of the   796

Bd. on Certification for Gerontological Nursing Practice   986, 996, 997

Bd. on Certification for Informatics Nursing   1000

Bd. on Certification for Maternal-Child Nursing Practice   1010, 1011, 1012

Bd. on Certification for Medical-Surgical Nursing Practice   987, 1004

Bd. on Certification for Nursing Administration Practice   967, 968

Bd. on Certification for Nursing Continuing Education/Staff Development   1007

Bd. for Certification of Pedorthics   1142

Bd. on Certification for Primary Care in Adult and Family Nursing Practice   950, 994

Bd. of Certification in Professional Ergonomics   336, 337

Bd. on Certification for Psychiatric and Mental Health Nursing Practice   983, 984, 1013

Bd. of Certification in Surgery   797, 807, 837, 839

Bd. of Certification in Surgery; Diplomate of the   797

Bd. of Certification in Surgery; Diplomate in Critical Care Medicine of the   807

Bd. of Certification in Surgery; Diplomate in Ophthalmology of the   837

Bd. of Certification in Surgery; Diplomate in Otorhinolaryngology of the   839

Bd. Certified in Business Appraisal   1229

Bd. Certified in Business Valuation   1230

Bd. Certified Entomologist   362

Bd. Certified Forensic Examiner   1365

Bd. of Certified Healthcare Safety   133, 134, 135

Bd. Certified - Hearing Instrument Specialist   1024

Bd. Certified in Manufactured Housing Valuation   1231

Bd. Certified Nuclear Pharmacist   931

Bd. Certified Nutrition Support Pharmacist   932

Bd. Certified Pharmacotherapy Specialist   933

Bd. of Certified Product Safety Management   1414, 1415, 1416

Bd. Certified Psychiatric Pharmacist   934

Bd. Certified in Real Estate Litigation Management   1232

Bd. of Certified Safety Professionals   1413

Bd. Certified Thermographer   621

Bd. Eligible, Amer. Bd. of Anesthesiology   656

Bd. Eligible, Amer. Bd. of Chiropractic Orthopedics   622

Bd. Eligible, Amer. Bd. of Endodontics   637

Bd. Eligible, Amer. Bd. of Internal Medicine   657

Bd. Eligible, Amer. Bd. of Oral and Maxillofacial Surgery   638

Bd. Eligible, Amer. Bd. of Orthodontics   639

Bd. Eligible, Amer. Bd. of Pediatric Dentistry   640

Bd. Eligible, Amer. Bd. of Periodontology   641

Bd. Eligible, Amer. Bd. of Prosthodontics   642

Bd. Eligible, Amer. Chiropractic Bd. of Nutrition   623

Bd. Eligible, Amer. Chiropractic Bd. of Occupational Health   624

Bd. Eligible, Amer. Chiropractic Neurology Bd.   625

Bd. Eligible, Amer. Osteopathic Bd. of Anesthesiology   658

Bd. Eligible, Amer. Osteopathic Bd. of Dermatology   659

Bd. Eligible, Amer. Osteopathic Bd. of Emergency Medicine   660

Bd. Eligible, Amer. Osteopathic Bd. of Family Practice   661

Bd. Eligible, Amer. Osteopathic Bd. of Internal Medicine   662

Bd. Eligible, Amer. Osteopathic Bd. of Nuclear Medicine   663

Bd. Eligible, Amer. Osteopathic Bd. of Obstetrics and Gynecology   664

Bd. Eligible, Amer. Osteopathic Bd. of Ophthalmology and Otorhinolaryngology   665

Bd. Eligible, Amer. Osteopathic Bd. of Orthopaedic Surgery   666

Bd. Eligible, Amer. Osteopathic Bd. of Pathology   667

Bd. Eligible, Amer. Osteopathic Bd. of Pediatrics   668

Bd. Eligible, Amer. Osteopathic Bd. of Preventive Medicine   669

Bd. Eligible, Amer. Osteopathic Bd. of Proctology   670

Bd. Eligible, Amer. Osteopathic Bd. of Radiology   671

Bd. Eligible, Amer. Osteopathic Bd. of Rehabilitation Medicine   672

Bd. Eligible, Amer. Osteopathic Bd. of Surgery   673

Bd. of Hazard Control Management   1404, 1405, 1406, 1422

Bd. of Nephrology Examiners - Nursing and Technology   964, 974, 1443

Bd. for Orthotist Certification   1140, 1145, 1754

Bd. of Pharmaceutical Specialties   931, 932, 933, 934

Bd. Qualified, Amer. Bd. of Podiatric Orthopedics and Primary Medicine   861

Bd. Qualified, Amer. Bd. of Podiatric Surgery   862

Bd. of Review for Associate Degree Programs, Natl. League for Nursing   1744

Bd. of Review for Baccalaureate and Higher Degree Programs, Natl. League for Nursing   1745

Bd. of Review for Diploma Programs, Natl. League for Nursing   1746

Bd. of Review for Practical Nursing Programs, Natl. League for Nursing   1747

Boarding Kennel; Accredited   1688

Boarding Kennels Assn.; Amer.   1457, 1463, 1468, 1688

Correspondence Education
 Accrediting Commn. of the Distance
  Education and Training
  Coun. 1636
Corrosion Engineers and Technicians
 Cathodic Protection Specialist 273
 Chemical Treatments Specialist 274
 Corrosion Specialist 275
 Corrosion Specialist, G 276
 Corrosion Specialist, P 277
 Corrosion Technician 278
 Corrosion Technologist 279
 Materials Selection/Design
  Specialist 280
 Protective Coatings Specialist 281
 Senior Corrosion Technologist 282
Corrosion Specialist 275
Corrosion Specialist, G 276
Corrosion Specialist, P 277
Corrosion Technician 278
Corrosion Technologist 279
Corrosion Technologist; Senior 282
Cosmetology
 Natl. Accrediting Commn. of
  Cosmetology Arts and
  Sciences 1637
Cosmetology Arts and Sciences; Natl.
 Accrediting Commn. of 1637
Cost Consultant; Certified 72
Cost Engineer; Certified 73
Cost Estimating and Analysis; Soc.
 of 74
Cost Estimator/Analyst; Certified 74
Cost Estimators
 Certified Cost Consultant 72
 Certified Cost Engineer 73
 Certified Cost
  Estimator/Analyst 74
 Certified Professional Estimator 75
Coun. on Accreditation, Amer. Assn.
 for the Accreditation of Laboratory
 Animal Care 1693
Coun. for Accreditation of the Amer.
 Assn. of Family and Consumer
 Sciences 1657
Coun. for Accreditation of Counseling
 and Related Educational
 Programs 1639
Coun. on Accreditation, Natl.
 Recreation and Park Assn. 1769
Coun. on Accreditation of Nurse
 Anesthesia Educational
 Programs 1748
Coun. for Accreditation in Occupational
 Hearing Conservation 1025
Coun. on Accreditation of Services for
 Families and Children 1658
Coun. of Amer. Building Officials 59
Coun. on Certification of Nurse
 Anesthetists 977
Coun. on Chiropractic Education 1628
Coun. for Early Childhood Professional
 Recognition 895
Coun. on Education of Amer. Health
 Information Management
 Assn. 1597
Coun. on Education of the Amer.
 Veterinary Medical Assn. 1813

Coun. on Education for Public
 Health 1706
Coun. of Engineering Specialty
 Bds. 1648, 1649, 1650, 1651
Coun. on Hotel, Restaurant, and
 Institutional Education 1669
Coun. on Licensure, Enforcement, and
 Regulation 1300, 1301
Coun. on Naturopathic Medical
 Education 1741
Coun. on Naturopathic Medical
 Education; Commn. on
 Accreditation, 1741
Coun. on Optometric Education 1752
Coun. on Podiatric Medical
 Education 1764
Coun. on Postdoctoral Training of the
 Amer. Osteopathic Assn. 1758
Coun. for Qualifications of Residential
 Interior Designers 1039
Coun. on Rehabilitation
 Education 1791
Coun. on Rehabilitation Education;
 Commn. on Standards and
 Accreditation, 1791
Coun. on Social Work Education 1803
Counseling
 Community and Junior Coll.
  Counseling Services Bd. of
  Accreditation of the Intl. Assn. of
  Counseling Services 1638
 Coun. for Accreditation of
  Counseling and Related
  Educational Programs 1639
 Public and Private Counseling
  Services Bd. of Accreditation of
  the Intl. Assn. of Counseling
  Services 1640
 Univ. and Coll. Counseling Centers
  Bd. of Accreditation of the Intl.
  Assn. of Counseling
  Services 1641
Counseling; Amer. Bd. of Examiners in
 Pastoral 460, 461, 463
Counseling; Amer. Bd. of
 Genetic 1196, 1664
Counseling Assn.; Amer. 1639
Counseling Centers Bd. of Accreditation
 of the Intl. Assn. of Counseling
 Services; Univ. and Coll. 1641
Counseling; Counselor, Amer. Bd. of
 Examiners in Pastoral 460
Counseling; Diplomate, Amer. Bd. of
 Examiners in Pastoral 461
Counseling Executive; Certified
 Financial 88
Counseling; Fellow, Amer. Bd. of
 Examiners in Pastoral 463
Counseling Psychology; Amer. Bd.
 of 441
Counseling Psychology; Diplomate
 in 441
Counseling and Related Educational
 Programs; Coun. for Accreditation
 of 1639
Counseling Services Bd. of
 Accreditation of the Intl. Assn. of
 Counseling Services; Community and
 Junior Coll. 1638

Counseling Services Bd. of
 Accreditation of the Intl. Assn. of
 Counseling Services; Public and
 Private 1640
Counseling Services; Community and
 Junior Coll. Counseling Services Bd.
 of Accreditation of the Intl. Assn.
 of 1638
Counseling Services; Intl. Assn.
 of 1638, 1640, 1641
Counseling Services; Public and Private
 Counseling Services Bd. of
 Accreditation of the Intl. Assn.
 of 1640
Counseling Services; Univ. and Coll.
 Counseling Centers Bd. of
 Accreditation of the Intl. Assn.
 of 1641
Counselor, Amer. Bd. of Examiners in
 Pastoral Counseling 460
Counselor Certification; Commn. on
 Rehabilitation 459
Counselor; Certified Business 9
Counselor; Certified Clinical Mental
 Health 453
Counselor; Certified Consumer
 Credit 167
Counselor; Certified Genetic 1196
Counselor; Certified Insurance 1213
Counselor; Certified
 Photographic 1276
Counselor; Certified Rehabilitation 459
Counselor; Humanist 465
Counselor Level I; Natl. Certified
 Addiction 468
Counselor Level II; Natl. Certified
 Addiction 469
Counselor; Master Addictions 467
Counselor; Natl. Certified 471
Counselor; Natl. Certified Career 470
Counselor; Natl. Certified
 Gerontological 472
Counselor; Natl. Certified School 473
Counselor of Real Estate 1251
Counselors
 Certified Clinical Mental Health
  Counselor 453
 Certified Eating Disorders
  Associate 454
 Certified Eating Disorders
  Specialist 455
 Certified Educational Planner 456
 Certified Poetry Therapist 457
 Certified Practitioner 458
 Certified Rehabilitation
  Counselor 459
 Counselor, Amer. Bd. of Examiners
  in Pastoral Counseling 460
 Diplomate, Amer. Bd. of Examiners
  in Pastoral Counseling 461
 Diplomate of the Amer. Bd. of
  Vocational Experts 462
 Fellow, Amer. Bd. of Examiners in
  Pastoral Counseling 463
 Fellow of the Amer. Bd. of
  Vocational Experts 464
 Humanist Counselor 465
 Humanist Officiant 466

Dental Coll.; Diplomate of the Amer.
Veterinary 886
Dental Consultant; Certified 643
Dental Consultants; Amer. Assn.
of 643
Dental-Hospital Burs. of America;
Medical- 142
Dental Hypnotherapy Assn.; Intl.
Medical and 919
Dental Laboratories; Natl. Bd. for
Certification of 1690
Dental Laboratory; Certified 1690
Dental Laboratory Technicians
Certified Dental Technician 1440
Dental Practice Management Assistant;
Certified 1436
Dental Public Health; Amer. Bd.
of 644
Dental Public Health; Diplomate of the
Amer. Bd. of 644
Dental Technician; Certified 1440
Dental Technicians; Certified Member
of the Intl. Assn. of Equine 866
Dental Technicians; Intl. Assn. of
Equine 866
Dental Technology; Natl. Bd. for
Certification in 1440
Dentistry
Commn. on Dental
Accreditation 1644
Dentistry; Acad. of Laser 634, 635,
636
Dentistry; Bd. Eligible, Amer. Bd. of
Pediatric 640
Dentistry, Category I Certification;
Acad. of Laser 634
Dentistry, Category II Certification;
Acad. of Laser 635
Dentistry, Category III (Master Status)
Certification; Acad. of Laser 636
Dentistry; Diplomate of the Amer. Bd.
of Pediatric 649
Dentists
Acad. of Laser Dentistry, Category I
Certification 634
Acad. of Laser Dentistry, Category
II Certification 635
Acad. of Laser Dentistry, Category
III (Master Status)
Certification 636
Bd. Eligible, Amer. Bd. of
Endodontics 637
Bd. Eligible, Amer. Bd. of Oral and
Maxillofacial Surgery 638
Bd. Eligible, Amer. Bd. of
Orthodontics 639
Bd. Eligible, Amer. Bd. of Pediatric
Dentistry 640
Bd. Eligible, Amer. Bd. of
Periodontology 641
Bd. Eligible, Amer. Bd. of
Prosthodontics 642
Certified Dental Consultant 643
Diplomate of the Amer. Bd. of
Dental Public Health 644
Diplomate of the Amer. Bd. of
Endodontics 645
Diplomate of the Amer. Bd. of Oral
and Maxillofacial Surgery 646

Diplomate of the Amer. Bd. of Oral
Pathology 647
Diplomate of the Amer. Bd. of
Orthodontics 648
Diplomate of the Amer. Bd. of
Pediatric Dentistry 649
Diplomate of the Amer. Bd. of
Periodontology 650
Diplomate of the Amer. Bd. of
Prosthodontics 651
Dependency Nurse; Certified
Chemical 957
Dependency Nurses; Natl. Consortium
of Chemical 957
Dermatological Immunology; Diplomate
of the Amer. Bd. of Dermatology
with Special Qualification in Clinical
and Laboratory 698
Dermatology with Added Qualifications
in MOHS Micrographic Surgery;
Diplomate of the Amer. Osteopathic
Bd. of 757
Dermatology; Amer. Bd. of 697, 698,
699, 1711
Dermatology; Amer. Bd. of Certification
in 690
Dermatology; Amer. Coll. of
Veterinary 876
Dermatology; Amer. Osteopathic Bd.
of 659, 756, 757
Dermatology; Bd. Eligible, Amer.
Osteopathic Bd. of 659
Dermatology; Diplomate of the Amer.
Bd. of 697
Dermatology; Diplomate of the Amer.
Bd. of Certification in 690
Dermatology; Diplomate of the Amer.
Coll. of Veterinary 876
Dermatology; Diplomate of the Amer.
Osteopathic Bd. of 756
Dermatology; Residency Review Comm.
for 1711
Dermatology with Special Qualification
in Clinical and Laboratory
Dermatological Immunology;
Diplomate of the Amer. Bd. of 698
Dermatology with Special Qualification
in Dermatopathology; Diplomate of
the Amer. Bd. of 699
Dermatopathology; Diplomate of the
Amer. Bd. of Pathology with Special
Qualification in 723
Design; Commn. on Accreditation,
Natl. Assn. of Schools of Art
and 1615
Design Drafting Assn.; Amer. 1175
Design Education Research; Found. for
Interior 1686
Design; Natl. Assn. of Schools of Art
and 1615
Design Qualification; Natl. Coun. for
Interior 1037
Designated Real Estate
Instructor 1252
Designer; Certified Interior 1037
Designer; Registered/Certified
Residential Interior 1039
Designers; Coun. for Qualifications of
Residential Interior 1039

**Designers, Including Interior Designers
and Florists**
Certified Bathroom Designer 1036
Certified Interior Designer 1037
Certified Kitchen Designer 1038
Registered/Certified Residential
Interior Designer 1039
Detective Alliance; Intl. Security
and 1290, 1291, 1294, 1295, 1298,
1299, 1379, 1380, 1381, 1382, 1383,
1384, 1385
Diabetes Educator; Certified 904
Diabetes Educators; Natl. Certification
Bd. for 904
Diabetes, and Metabolism of the Amer.
Bd. of Internal Medicine; Diplomate
in Endocrinology, 812
Diagnostic Cardiac Sonographer;
Registered 1157
Diagnostic Medical Sonographer;
Registered 1158
Diagnostic Medical Sonographers;
Amer. Registry of 1157, 1158, 1159
Diagnostic Medical Sonography; Joint
Review Comm. on Education
in 1601
Diagnostic Radiology of the Amer. Bd.
of Radiology; Diplomate in 808
Diagnostic Radiology of the Amer.
Osteopathic Bd. of Radiology;
Diplomate in 809
Diagnostic Radiology with Special
Competence in Nuclear Radiology of
the Amer. Bd. of Radiology;
Diplomate in 810
Diagnostic Ultrasound; Diplomate of
the Amer. Osteopathic Bd. of
Radiology with Added Qualifications
in 785
Diagnostics; Natl. Found. for
Non-Invasive 1155, 1156
Dialysis Nurse; Certified
Peritoneal 974
Diamond Coun. of America 1569,
1571, 1573, 1578, 1579
Diamontologist; Certified 1571
Diaper Service Accreditation
Coun. 1645
Diaper Services
Diaper Service Accreditation
Coun. 1645
Dietary Manager; Certified 905
Dietary Managers; Certifying Bd.
for 905
Dietetic Assn.; Amer. 1646
Dietetic Registration; Commn. on 913,
914
Dietetic Technician; Registered 913
Dietetics
Commn. on Accreditation/Approval
for Dietetics Education 1646
Dietetics Education; Commn. on
Accreditation/Approval for 1646
Dietician; Certified Nutrition
Support 906
Dietician; Registered 914
Dietitians and Nutritionists
Certified Diabetes Educator 904

Foot and Ankle Surgery; Diplomate of the Amer. Bd. of Podiatric Surgery with Certification in   864

Foot Surgery; Diplomate of the Amer. Bd. of Podiatric Surgery with Certification in   865

Forensic Anthropology; Amer. Bd. of   1366

Forensic Anthropology; Diplomate of the Amer. Bd. of   1366

Forensic Document Examiners; Amer. Bd. of   1367

Forensic Document Examiners; Diplomate of the Amer. Bd. of   1367

Forensic Engineers; Fellow of the Natl. Acad. of   1369

Forensic Engineers; Member, Natl. Acad. of   1370

Forensic Engineers; Natl. Acad. of   1369, 1370, 1371

Forensic Engineers; Senior Member, Natl. Acad. of   1371

Forensic Examiner; Bd. Certified   1365

Forensic Examiners; Amer. Bd. of   1365, 1368

Forensic Examiners; Fellow, Amer. Bd. of   1368

Forensic Experts and Investigators

Bd. Certified Forensic Examiner   1365

Diplomate of the Amer. Bd. of Forensic Anthropology   1366

Diplomate of the Amer. Bd. of Forensic Document Examiners   1367

Fellow, Amer. Bd. of Forensic Examiners   1368

Fellow of the Natl. Acad. of Forensic Engineers   1369

Member, Natl. Acad. of Forensic Engineers   1370

Senior Member, Natl. Acad. of Forensic Engineers   1371

Forensic Pathology of the Amer. Osteopathic Bd. of Pathology; Diplomate in   814

Forensic Pathology; Diplomate of the Amer. Bd. of Pathology with Special Qualification in   724

Forensic Psychiatry; Diplomate in Psychiatry of the Amer. Bd. of Psychiatry and Neurology with Added Qualifications in   844

Forensic Psychology; Amer. Bd. of   443

Forensic Psychology; Diplomate in   443

Foresters of America; Assn. of Consulting   1253

Foresters; Comm. on Accreditation, Soc. of Amer.   1660

Foresters and Conservation Scientists and Workers

Certified Arborist   371

Certified Ground Water Professional   372

Certified Lake Manager   373

Certified Professional Soil Erosion and Sediment Control Specialist   374

Certified Range Management Consultant   375

Certified Water Specialist, Level I   376

Certified Water Specialist, Level II   377

Certified Water Specialist, Level III   378

Certified Water Specialist, Level IV   379

Certified Water Specialist, Level V   380

Professional Hydrogeologist   381

Professional Hydrologist   382

Professional Hydrologist - Ground Water   383

Professional Hydrologist - Water Quality   384

Forestland Appraiser   1253

Forestry

Academic Accreditation for Programs Leading to Degrees in Urban Forestry   1659

Comm. on Accreditation, Soc. of Amer. Foresters   1660

County Forestry Dept. Accreditation Program   1661

Municipal Forestry Dept. Accreditation Program   1662

Forestry; Academic Accreditation for Programs Leading to Degrees in Urban   1659

Forestry Dept. Accreditation Program; County   1661

Forestry Dept. Accreditation Program; Municipal   1662

Form Appraiser; Certified   1243

Forms Assn.; Natl. Business   21

Forms Consultant; Certified   21

Forms Press Operator; Certified   1545

Found. for Hospice and Homecare   1493

Found. for Interior Design Education Research   1686

Framer; Certified Picture   1547

Fraud Claim Law Associate   425

Fraud Claim Law Associate; Casualty-   422

Fraud Claim Law Associate; Property-   429

Fraud Claim Law Associate; Workers' Compensation-   434

Fraud Claim Law Specialist   426

Fraud Examiner; Certified   1296

Fraud Examiners; Assn. of Certified   1296

Fraud Investigator; Certified Financial   1294

Freestanding Birth Centers; Commn. for the Accreditation of   1617

Freshwater Fish Specialist; Certified   1461

Fuels Technician; ASE Certified Alternative   1500

Fund Raising Executive; Advanced Certified   96

Fund Raising Executive; Certified   109

Fund Raising Executives; Natl. Soc. of   96, 109

Funeral Service

Commn. on Accreditation, Amer. Bd. of Funeral Service Education   1663

Funeral Service Education; Amer. Bd. of   1663

Funeral Service Education; Commn. on Accreditation, Amer. Bd. of   1663

Gardeners, Horticulture Workers, and Groundskeepers

Certified Golf Course Superintendent   1485

Certified Grounds Manager   1486

Certified Landscape Management Technician   1487

Certified Landscape Professional   1488

Certified Landscape Technician   1489

Certified Turfgrass Professional   1490

Gas Appliance Hearth Specialist; Certified   1553

Gastroenterology of the Amer. Bd. of Internal Medicine; Diplomate in   815

Gastroenterology of the Amer. Osteopathic Bd. of Internal Medicine; Diplomate in   816

Gastroenterology Associate; Certified   1441

Gastroenterology; Diplomate of the Amer. Bd. of Pediatrics with Special Qualifications in Pediatric   737

Gastroenterology Licensed Vocational/Practical Nurse; Certified   945

Gastroenterology Nurses and Associates; Certifying Bd. of   945, 963, 1441, 1442

Gastroenterology Registered Nurse; Certified   963

Gastroenterology Technologist/Technician; Certified   1442

Gem Soc.; Amer.   1312, 1572, 1580, 1581

Gemologist Appraiser; Certified   1312

Gemologist Appraiser; Master   1316

Gemologist; Certified   1572

Gemologist; Guild   1578

Genealogical Instructor; Certified   608

Genealogical Lecturer; Certified   609

Genealogical Record Searcher; Certified   610

Genealogist; Certified   611

Genealogists

Certified Amer. Indian Lineage Specialist   606

Certified Amer. Lineage Specialist   607

Certified Genealogical Instructor   608

Certified Genealogical Lecturer   609

Certified Genealogical Record Searcher   610

Certified Genealogist   611

Genealogists; Bd. for Certification of   606, 607, 608, 609, 610, 611

Nurse Practitioner; Certified Pediatric 973
Nurse Practitioner; Family 994
Nurse Practitioner; Gerontological 997
Nurse Practitioner; Neonatal 1006
Nurse Practitioner; Pediatric 1011
Nurse Practitioner; School 1016
Nurse Practitioner; Women's Health Care 1018
Nurse Practitioners and Nurses; Natl. Certification Bd. of Pediatric 972, 973
Nurse; Psychiatric and Mental Health 1013
Nurse; Reproductive Endocrinology/ Infertility 1014
Nurse; School 1015
Nurse; Urology Registered 1017
Nurses; Amer. Assn. of Critical-Care 954
Nurses; Amer. Bd. for Occupational Health 970
Nurses and Associates; Certifying Bd. of Gastroenterology 945, 963, 1441, 1442
Nurses' Assn.; Amer. Holistic 965
Nurses Certification Bd.; Orthopaedic 1009
Nurses Credentialing Center; Amer. 953, 990, 999, 1015
Nurses; Natl. Assn. of School 981
Nurses; Natl. Bd. for Certification of Hospice 978
Nurses; Natl. Certification Bd. of Pediatric Nurse Practitioners and 972, 973
Nurses; Natl. Certifying Bd. for Ophthalmic Registered 993
Nurses; Natl. Consortium of Chemical Dependency 957
Nurses Soc.; Intravenous 979
Nurses Soc.; Wound Ostomy and Continence 959, 961, 971, 982, 1750
Nursing
　Amer. Bd. of Nursing Specialties 1743
　Bd. of Review for Associate Degree Programs, Natl. League for Nursing 1744
　Bd. of Review for Baccalaureate and Higher Degree Programs, Natl. League for Nursing 1745
　Bd. of Review for Diploma Programs, Natl. League for Nursing 1746
　Bd. of Review for Practical Nursing Programs, Natl. League for Nursing 1747
　Coun. on Accreditation of Nurse Anesthesia Educational Programs 1748
　Div. of Accreditation, Amer. Coll. of Nurse-Midwives 1749
　Wound Ostomy and Continence Nurses Soc. 1750
Nursing Administration, Advanced; Certified in 968
Nursing Administration; Certified in 967

Nursing Administration Practice; Bd. on Certification for 967, 968
Nursing Aides and Psychiatric Aides
　Nationally Certified Psychiatric Technician, Level 1 1453
　Nationally Certified Psychiatric Technician, Level 2 1454
　Nationally Certified Psychiatric Technician, Level 3 1455
　Nationally Certified Psychiatric Technician, Level 4 1456
Nursing; Amer. Bd. of Neuroscience 989
Nursing; Bd. of Certification for Emergency 960, 962
Nursing; Bd. on Certification for Informatics 1000
Nursing; Bd. of Review for Associate Degree Programs, Natl. League for 1744
Nursing; Bd. of Review for Baccalaureate and Higher Degree Programs, Natl. League for 1745
Nursing; Bd. of Review for Diploma Programs, Natl. League for 1746
Nursing; Bd. of Review for Practical Nursing Programs, Natl. League for 1747
Nursing Certification; Amer. Bd. of Post Anesthesia 956, 976
Nursing Certification Bd.; Addictions 955
Nursing Certification Bd.; Nephrology 966
Nursing Certification Bd.; Plastic Surgical 975
Nursing Certification Bd.; Rehabilitation 980
Nursing Certification Corp.; Oncology 951, 1008
Nursing; Clinical Specialist in Adult Psychiatric and Mental Health 983
Nursing; Clinical Specialist in Child and Adolescent Psychiatric and Mental Health 984
Nursing; Clinical Specialist in Community Health 985
Nursing; Clinical Specialist in Gerontological 986
Nursing; Clinical Specialist in Medical- Surgical 987
Nursing Continuing Education/Staff Development 1007
Nursing Continuing Education/Staff Development; Bd. on Certification for 1007
Nursing Home Administrator; Certified 141
Nursing; Natl. Certification Bd.: Perioperative 988, 992
Nursing; Natl. League for 1744, 1745, 1746, 1747
Nursing Practice; Bd. on Certification for Community Health 985, 991, 1016
Nursing Practice; Bd. on Certification for General 995
Nursing Practice; Bd. on Certification for Gerontological 986, 996, 997

Nursing Practice; Bd. on Certification for Maternal- Child 1010, 1011, 1012
Nursing Practice; Bd. on Certification for Medical- Surgical 987, 1004
Nursing Practice; Bd. on Certification for Primary Care in Adult and Family 950, 994
Nursing Practice; Bd. on Certification for Psychiatric and Mental Health 983, 984, 1013
Nursing Practice; General 995
Nursing Programs, Natl. League for Nursing; Bd. of Review for Practical 1747
Nursing Specialties; Amer. Bd. of 1743
Nursing Specialties; Natl. Certification Corp. for the Obstetric, Gynecologic, and Neonatal 952, 998, 1001, 1002, 1003, 1005, 1006, 1014, 1018
Nursing and Technology; Bd. of Nephrology Examiners - 964, 974, 1443
Nutrition; Amer. Bd. of 915, 916
Nutrition; Amer. Chiropractic Bd. of 623, 629
Nutrition; Amer. Coll. of Veterinary 880
Nutrition; Amer. Coun. of Applied Clinical 909
Nutrition; Bd. Eligible, Amer. Chiropractic Bd. of 623
Nutrition; Diplomate of the Amer. Chiropractic Bd. of 629
Nutrition; Diplomate of the Amer. Coll. of Veterinary 880
Nutrition; Fellow of the Amer. Coun. of Applied Clinical 909
Nutrition; Specialist in Clinical 915
Nutrition; Specialist in Human 916
Nutrition Support Certification; Natl. Bd. of 906, 969
Nutrition Support Dietician; Certified 906
Nutrition Support Nurse; Certified 969
Nutrition Support Pharmacist; Bd. Certified 932
Nutritional Consultant; Certified 907
Nutritional Consultants; Amer. Assn. of 907
Obstetric, Gynecologic, and Neonatal Nursing Specialties; Natl. Certification Corp. for the 952, 998, 1001, 1002, 1003, 1005, 1006, 1014, 1018
Obstetric Nurse; High Risk 998
Obstetric Nurse; Inpatient 1001
Obstetricians and Gynecologists for Osteopathic Specialists; Amer. Bd. of 712
Obstetricians and Gynecologists for Osteopathic Specialists; Diplomate of the Amer. Bd. of 712
Obstetrics; Amer. Soc. for Psychoprophylaxis in 893
Obstetrics and Gynecology with Added Qualification in Critical Care; Diplomate of the Amer. Bd. of 714

Bd. Eligible, Amer. Osteopathic Bd. of Radiology 671

Bd. Eligible, Amer. Osteopathic Bd. of Rehabilitation Medicine 672

Bd. Eligible, Amer. Osteopathic Bd. of Surgery 673

Certificate of Added Qualification in Clinical and Laboratory Immunology 674

Certificate of Added Qualifications in Surgical Critical Care 675

Certificate of Added Qualifications in Vascular and Interventional Radiology of the Amer. Bd. of Radiology 676

Certification of Added Qualifications in Occupational Medicine 677

Certification of Special Proficiency in Osteopathic Manipulative Medicine 678

Certification in Sports Medicine 679

Certified in Quality Assurance and Utilization Review 680

Diplomate in Aerospace Medicine of the Amer. Osteopathic Bd. of Preventive Medicine 681

Diplomate in Allergy and Immunology of the Amer. Osteopathic Bd. of Internal Medicine 682

Diplomate of the Amer. Bd. of Abdominal Surgery 683

Diplomate of the Amer. Bd. of Allergy and Immunology 684

Diplomate of the Amer. Bd. of Anesthesiology 685

Diplomate of the Amer. Bd. of Anesthesiology with Special Qualifications in Critical Care Medicine 686

Diplomate of the Amer. Bd. of Anesthesiology with Special Qualifications in Pain Management 687

Diplomate of the Amer. Bd. of Certification in Anesthesiology 688

Diplomate of Amer. Bd. of Certification in Anesthesiology with Added Qualifications in Pain Management 689

Diplomate of the Amer. Bd. of Certification in Dermatology 690

Diplomate of the Amer. Bd. of Certification in Internal Medicine 691

Diplomate of the Amer. Bd. of Certification in Neurology/Psychiatry 692

Diplomate of the Amer. Bd. of Certification in Orthopedic Surgery 693

Diplomate of the Amer. Bd. of Certification in Radiology 694

Diplomate of the Amer. Bd. of Chelation Therapy 695

Diplomate of the Amer. Bd. of Colon and Rectal Surgery 696

Diplomate of the Amer. Bd. of Dermatology 697

Diplomate of the Amer. Bd. of Dermatology with Special Qualification in Clinical and Laboratory Dermatological Immunology 698

Diplomate of the Amer. Bd. of Dermatology with Special Qualification in Dermatopathology 699

Diplomate of the Amer. Bd. of Emergency Medicine 700

Diplomate of the Amer. Bd. of Environmental Medicine 701

Diplomate of the Amer. Bd. of Family Practice 702

Diplomate of the Amer. Bd. of Internal Medicine 703

Diplomate of the Amer. Bd. of Internal Medicine with Added Qualifications in Adolescent Medicine 704

Diplomate of the Amer. Bd. of Internal Medicine with Added Qualifications in Clinical and Laboratory Immunology 705

Diplomate of the Amer. Bd. of Internal Medicine with Added Qualifications in Critical Care Medicine 706

Diplomate of the Amer. Bd. of Internal Medicine with Added Qualifications in Geriatric Medicine 707

Diplomate of the Amer. Bd. of Internal Medicine with Added Qualifications in Sports Medicine 708

Diplomate of the Amer. Bd. of Medical Management 709

Diplomate of the Amer. Bd. of Neurological Surgery 710

Diplomate of the Amer. Bd. of Nuclear Medicine 711

Diplomate of the Amer. Bd. of Obstetricians and Gynecologists for Osteopathic Specialists 712

Diplomate of the Amer. Bd. of Obstetrics and Gynecology 713

Diplomate of the Amer. Bd. of Obstetrics and Gynecology with Added Qualification in Critical Care 714

Diplomate of the Amer. Bd. of Ophthalmology 715

Diplomate of the Amer. Bd. of Orthopaedic Surgery 716

Diplomate of the Amer. Bd. of Orthopaedic Surgery with Added Qualifications in Surgery of the Hand 717

Diplomate of the Amer. Bd. of Otolaryngology 718

Diplomate of the Amer. Bd. of Pain Medicine 719

Diplomate of the Amer. Bd. of Pathology with Added Qualification in Cytopathology 720

Diplomate of the Amer. Bd. of Pathology with Special Qualification in Blood Banking/Transfusion Medicine 721

Diplomate of the Amer. Bd. of Pathology with Special Qualification in Chemical Pathology 722

Diplomate of the Amer. Bd. of Pathology with Special Qualification in Dermatopathology 723

Diplomate of the Amer. Bd. of Pathology with Special Qualification in Forensic Pathology 724

Diplomate of the Amer. Bd. of Pathology with Special Qualification in Hematology 725

Diplomate of the Amer. Bd. of Pathology with Special Qualification in Immunopathology 726

Diplomate of the Amer. Bd. of Pathology with Special Qualification in Medical Microbiology 727

Diplomate of the Amer. Bd. of Pathology with Special Qualification in Neuropathology 728

Diplomate of the Amer. Bd. of Pathology with Special Qualification in Pediatric Pathology 729

Diplomate of the Amer. Bd. of Pediatrics 730

Diplomate of the Amer. Bd. of Pediatrics with Special Qualifications in Adolescent Medicine 731

Diplomate of the Amer. Bd. of Pediatrics with Special Qualifications in Neonatal-Perinatal Medicine 732

Diplomate of the Amer. Bd. of Pediatrics with Special Qualifications in Pediatric Cardiology 733

Diplomate of the Amer. Bd. of Pediatrics with Special Qualifications in Pediatric Critical Care Medicine 734

Diplomate of the Amer. Bd. of Pediatrics with Special Qualifications in Pediatric Emergency Medicine 735

Diplomate of the Amer. Bd. of Pediatrics with Special Qualifications in Pediatric Endocrinology 736

Diplomate of the Amer. Bd. of Pediatrics with Special Qualifications in Pediatric Gastroenterology 737

Master Index

Social Workers; Acad. of Certified   489
Social Workers; Acad. of Certified
  Baccalaureate   488
Social Workers; Member of the Acad.
  of Certified   489
Social Workers; Member, Acad. of
  Certified Baccalaureate   488
Social Workers; Natl. Assn. of   487,
  490
Soc. of Actuaries   318, 322
Soc. of Actuaries; Associate of the   318
Soc. of Actuaries; Fellow of the   322
Soc. of Amer. Foresters; Comm. on
  Accreditation,   1660
Soc. of Broadcast Engineers   284, 285,
  291, 292, 293, 1165, 1166
Soc. of Cable Television
  Engineers   283, 1164, 1544
Soc. of Certified Credit Executives   82,
  84, 85, 87, 88, 1322
Soc. of Certified Insurance
  Counselors   1213
Soc. of Certified Insurance Service
  Representatives   1214
Soc. of Cost Estimating and
  Analysis   74
Soc. of Incentive Travel
  Executives   1282
Soc. of Industrial and Office
  Realtors   1265, 1274
Soc. of Logistics Engineers   301
Soc. for Marketing Professional
  Services   194
Soc. of Municipal Arborists   1659,
  1661, 1662
Soc. of Pension Actuaries; Fellow,   323
Soc. of Pension Actuaries;
  Member,   324
Soc. of Photo Finishing
  Engineers   1185
Soc. of Photo Finishing Engineers;
  Member,   1185
Soc. of Photographic Counselors   1276
Soc. for Range Management   375
Soc. for Service Professionals in
  Printing   190
Soc. of State Filers   1345, 1347
Sociological Practice Assn.   451
Sociologist; Certified Clinical   451
Sociologists
  Certified Clinical Sociologist   451
Sociometry, and Group Psychotherapy;
  Amer. Bd. of Examiners in
  Psychodrama,   458, 475
Soil Classifier; Associate
  Professional   348
Soil Classifier; Certified
  Professional   357
Soil Erosion and Sediment Control
  Specialist; Certified Professional   374
Soil Scientist; Associate
  Professional   349
Soil Scientist; Certified
  Professional   358
Soil Specialist; Associate
  Professional   350
Soil Specialist; Certified
  Professional   359

Soil and Water Conservation Soc.   374
Solid Waste Assn. of North
  America   162, 163
Sonographer; Registered Diagnostic
  Cardiac   1157
Sonographer; Registered Diagnostic
  Medical   1158
Sonographers
  Certified Echocardiographic
    Technologist   1155
  Professional Ultrasound
    Technologist   1156
  Registered Diagnostic Cardiac
    Sonographer   1157
  Registered Diagnostic Medical
    Sonographer   1158
  Registered Vascular
    Technologist   1159
Sonographers; Amer. Registry of
  Diagnostic Medical   1157, 1158,
  1159
Sonography; Joint Review Comm. on
  Education in Diagnostic
  Medical   1601
Southern Assn. of Colleges and
  Schools   1775, 1777, 1782, 1788
Southern Assn. of Colleges and Schools;
  Commn. on Colleges,   1775
Southern Assn. of Colleges and Schools;
  Commn. on Elementary
  Schools,   1777
Southern Assn. of Colleges and Schools;
  Commn. on Occupational Education
  Institutions,   1782
Southern Assn. of Colleges and Schools;
  Commn. on Secondary
  Schools,   1788
Southwest Assn. of Episcopal
  Schools   1800
Spa Operator; Certified Pool   237
Specialist in Blood Banking   1090
Specialist in Chemistry   1091
Specialist in Clinical Nutrition   915
Specialist in Cytotechnology   1092
Specialist in Hematology   1093
Specialist in Human Nutrition   916
Specialist in Immunology   1094
Specialist, Industrial/Office Real
  Estate   1274
Specialist Microbiologist   370
Specialist in Microbiology   1095
Specialist in Residential
  Appraisal   1275
Specialty Scuba Diver   601
Speech-Language-Hearing Assn.;
  Amer.   1804
Speech-Language-Hearing Assn.;
  Educational Standards Bd.,
  Amer.   1804
**Speech-Language Pathologists and
Audiologists**
  Bd. Certified - Hearing Instrument
    Specialist   1024
  Certified Occupational Hearing
    Conservationist   1025
  Hearing Instrument Specialist   1026
**Speech-Language Pathology and
Audiology**
  Educational Standards Bd., Amer.
    Speech-Language-Hearing
    Assn.   1804

Sports Assn.; Natl. Intramural-
  Recreational   572
Sports Certified Specialist; Physical
  Therapist,   942
Sports Medicine; Amer. Bd. of Family
  Practice Certificate of Added
  Qualification in   655
Sports Medicine; Amer. Coll. of   530,
  531, 532, 533, 534, 535
Sports Medicine Assn. Bd. of
  Certification; Amer.   523, 526, 527,
  528, 529
Sports Medicine; Certification in   679
Sports Medicine; Diplomate of the
  Amer. Bd. of Internal Medicine with
  Added Qualifications in   708
Sports Medicine; Diplomate of the
  Amer. Osteopathic Bd. of Family
  Practice with Added Qualifications
  in   762
Sports Medicine Trainer; Active   523
Sports Medicine Trainer; Certified   526
Sports Medicine Trainer;
  Pre-Active   528
Sports; Natl. Handicapped   536
Sports Physician; Certified
  Chiropractic   626
Sports Physicians; Amer. Chiropractic
  Bd. of   626, 632
Sports Physicians; Diplomate of the
  Amer. Chiropractic Bd. of   632
Sports Specialist; Certified
  Recreational   572
Spray-Applied Fireproofing Special
  Inspector; ICBO   48
Staff Coordinator; Certified
  Medical   139
Staff Development; Bd. on Certification
  for Nursing Continuing
  Education/   1007
Staff Development; Nursing Continuing
  Education/   1007
Staff Services; Natl. Assn. Medical   139
Staffing Specialist; Certified
  Temporary-   210
Standard First Aid Certification   1111
State Filer; Certified   1347
State Filers; Soc. of   1345, 1347
State Filings; Associate in   1345
State/Individual Coach, U.S.
  Professional Racquetball Org.   521
State Referee (Level I)   522
Stationary Engineers
  Certified Plant Engineer   304
Statistical Process Control, Facilitator;
  Certification in   340
Statistical Process Control, Operational;
  Certification in   341
Statistical Process Control Soc.   340,
  341, 342
Statistical Process Control, Technical;
  Certification in   342
Statisticians
  Certification in Statistical Process
    Control, Facilitator   340
  Certification in Statistical Process
    Control, Operational   341
  Certification in Statistical Process
    Control, Technical   342